The Qur'an

Translated by M.H. Shakir

Published by:
TAHRIKE TARSILE QUR'AN, INC.
P.O. Box 731115
Elmhurst, New York 11373-0115

INTRODUCTION

Tahrike Tarsile Qur'an, Inc., a non-profit religious organization, is devoted to the dissemination of authentic knowledge concerning Islam through the sale and free distribution of copies of Holy Qur'an and its translation. It also publishes other relevant material. This work is of genuine service to Islam in America and in other countries of the world.

We have not forgotten the need to educate our younger generation, and the young children in particular. We have published a set of board books recently, and are simultaneously working on another hundred books or more, for older children.

You will find most of our Qurans in many of the libraries. Still, it is our motto to see it in each and every library, and hotel room, throughout the world, so that everybody has an easy access to it. We are working very hard on achieving this goal, and any help from all our well-wishers is welcome, and highly appreciated. We have so far collected over 600 different translations of the Holy Quran in different languages. We are trying to acquire more, to establish a library, so that everybody can benefit.

This translation was originally published by Habib Esmail Benevolent Trust of Karachi, Pakistan; and later, was reprinted by the World Organization for Islamic Services of Tehran, Iran.

We have omitted the footnotes - with our sincere apologies to the soul of the late translator.

Tahrike Tarsile Qur'an, Inc

Published by

Tahrike Tarsile Qur'an, Inc.

Publishers and Distributors of Holy Qur'an

Seventh U.S. Edition 1999

ISBN: 0-940368-56-0 (paper rack size) Arabic & English

Murtaza Bandali

Tahrike Tarsile Qur'an Canada

P.O. Box 73088, White Shields Postal Outlet

2300 Lawrence Ave. E.

Scarborough, ON M1P 4Z5

Canada

Printed in England by Clays Ltd, St Ives plc

In the Name of Allah,
the Beneficent, the Merciful.
PREFACE

"... And Most surely it is a Mighty Book: Falsehood cannot come to it from before nor behind it: a revelation from the Wise, the Praised One." Ha Mim (41:41-42)

Praise is for God alone, our Creator and Sustainer. Peace and Blessings be upon His Beloved Prophet Muhammad and his pure family.

The book which is before you contains the final revelation from God Almighty to mankind. It is a Divine Book of Revelation given to the Prophet Muhammad Al-Mustafa, may the blessings of Allah be upon him and his family as a source of guidance, inspiration and guidance for himself and his adherents.

It is our belief as Muslims that Almighty Allah has continuously sent Prophets and Messengers to mankind throughout the course of human history. Some of these messengers and prophets received revelation while others continued with that which was received before them. The Qur'an has informed us that both Prophethood and Revelation has been terminated in the mission of our beloved Prophet Muhammad, may the Blessings of Allah be upon him and his family. This increases the significance of both the mission of the Prophet and the book which was revealed to him.

Although our Prophet was established in Arabia more than 1400 years, his mission was too great to be confined within the geographical, linguistic and cultural boundaries of Arabia. Allah, The Exalted, intended Islam to be a universal religion of mankind with guidance for every man of every language in every culture. The demographics of the Muslim peoples bears witness that Islam has traversed nearly every ethic, linguistic and cultural group on the earth, providing guidance for them as well as government.

Although many westerners view Islam as a departure from the teachings of the Prophets of the Torah and the Bible, in fact, Islam is a continuation of those Prophets teaching. The Qur'an came confirming the truths which had been taught by these great prophets and it also dispelled many of the falsehoods which had come to be associated with them. Thus, the Qur'an is sometimes referred to as "Al-Furqan" or the Criterion, it is the criterion by which other books, faiths and practices can be judged as to their accuracy and genuineness. It confirms that the prophets which have been mentioned in other Divine books were sent by only one God. Thus, the belief in one God and acceptance of these Divine prophets is a foundation of Islamic Faith.

I invite those who may be reading this Qur'an for the first time to look deeply and objectively into its meaning. The Muslims were promised by Allah that this book would always remain free from falsehood, alteration and misinterpretation. We are the only people following a Divine religion who can claim to have a book which is pure and unaltered, which had been given to the Prophet directly from God and written down in his lifetime and preserved unchanged thereafter.

Study it intensely as well as those books which assist in clarifying its meaning. In it are narrations of previous peoples in the history of mankind, the prophets and Holy men which God sent to them as a source of salvation. It has heavenly advices which therein, hold the keys to paradise. It has the laws of the religion of Islam and the sources of our religious obligations. Also within these pages are many scientific facts, many of which were not proven by science for some time after its revelation.

For those who have already read this book, I would advise myself and them as well, to delve deeper into its meaning and become its devotee. If you are reading it in English, then know that its full meaning is not conveyed in any other language except Arabic. Therefore we must devote ourselves to the study of this language to reach the aim of understanding it as it should be understood. To know it takes a lifetime of work and devotion, its rewards bring an eternity of wealth and blessings.

Those who are converts to Islam or contemplating this noble religion, I too am a convert. Place no other above this book, place no other philosophy before its philosophy and regard its laws and obligations with sanctity and sincerity. Know that Allah gave this Qur'an to our beloved Prophet for your sake, our beloved Prophet interpreted it to his followers for your sake. So take it and hold fast, it is the rope of Allah which leads to the path of salvation, it is the key to paradise and eternal peace.

Oh Allah! guide by this Glorious Qur'an. Increase our knowledge that we might know its meaning. Give us the strength and faith to practice what we find in it. Fix our feet firmly on the right path. Bless your beloved Prophet Muhammad Al-Mustafa and his pure family and all the righteous believers.

27 Ramadhan 1409
May 4, 1989

Ali Abdur Rasheed

EXTRACT FROM THE ORIGINAL PUBLICATION

The late Mr. Mahomedali Habib was well known throughout the country for having devoted his life to the cause of humanity. He with his brothers founded many educational and benevolent institutions, the most important being Masoomeen Hospital, Khoja Girls Orphanage, Masjid and Mahfil-e-Shah-e-Khorasan, Habib Public School, Habib Education Trust and other benevolent organisations.

This translation was his last work and was completed by him on the 14th of Shaban and the very next day 15th Shaban he suffered a severe heart attack and passed away on the 20th of Ramadan 1378 *i.e.* 30th March 1959.

CONTENTS

x

CONTENTS

CONTENTS

Chapter No.	SURAH		Page No.

CONTENTS

xi

NAMES

The following list shows the Arabic names and their English equivalents.

ARABIC NAMES:	ENGLISH EQUIVALENTS
Allah	God
Adam	Adam
Ayyub	Job
Dawood	David
Firon	Pharaoh
Habeel	Abel
Haroun	Aaron
Hasan	Shabur
Husain	Shabir
Ibrahim	Abraham
Ilyas	Elias
Imrān	Amran
Injeel	Gospel
Ishāq	Isaac
Ismail	Ishmael
Isa	Jesus
Jalut	Goliath
Jibreel	Gabriel
Qabeel	Cain
Lut	Lot
Majuj	Magog
Maryam	Mary
Masjid	Mosque
Mikaeel	Michael
Misr	Egypt
Musa	Moses
Nasrani	Christian
Nuh	Noah
Qarun	Korah
Saba	Sheba
Sulaiman	Solomon
Talut	Saul
Taurat	Torah
Uzair	Ezra
Yahudi	Jew
Yahya	John the Baptist
Yajuj	Gog
Yaqoub	Jacob
Yunus	Jonah
Yusuf	Joseph
Zakariya	Zacharias

NAMES

The following list shows the Arabic names and their English equivalents

ARABIC NAMES	ENGLISH EQUIVALENTS
Allah	God
Adam	Adam
Ayyub	Job
Dawood	David
Firon	Pharaoh
Habeel	Abel
Haroun	Aaron
Hasan	Shabar
Husain	Shabir
Ibrahim	Abraham
Ilyas	Elias
Imrân	Amran
Injeel	Gospel
Ishâq	Isaac
Ismail	Ishmael
Isa	Jesus
Jâlut	Goliath
Jibreel	Gabriel
Qabeel	Cain
Lut	Lot
Majuj	Magog
Maryam	Mary
Masjid	Mosque
Mikaeel	Michael
Misr	Egypt
Musa	Moses
Nasrani	Christian
Nuh	Noah
Qarun	Korah
Saba	Sheba
Sulaiman	Solomon
Tâlut	Saul
Taurat	Torah
Uzair	Ezra
Yahudi	Jew
Yahya	John the Baptist
Yajuj	Gog
Yaqub	Jacob
Yunus	Jonah
Yusuf	Joseph
Zakariya	Zacharias

اٰیٰتُهَا ۷ سُوْرَةُ الْفَاتِحَةِ مَکِّیَّةٌ رُوُعُهَا

THE OPENING
(FATEHAH)

1. **In the Name of Allah, the Beneficent. the Merciful.**

بِسْمِ اللهِ الرَّحْمٰنِ الرَّحِیْمِ ۝

2. All praise is due to Allah, the Lord of the Worlds.

اَلْحَمْدُ لِلّٰهِ رَبِّ الْعٰلَمِیْنَ ۝

3. The Beneficent, the Merciful.

الرَّحْمٰنِ الرَّحِیْمِ ۝

4. Master of the Day of Judgment.

مٰلِكِ یَوْمِ الدِّیْنِ ۝

5. Thee do we serve and Thee do we beseech for help.

اِیَّاكَ نَعْبُدُ وَاِیَّاكَ نَسْتَعِیْنُ ۝

6. Keep us on the right path.

اِهْدِنَا الصِّرَاطَ الْمُسْتَقِیْمَ ۝

7. The path of those upon whom Thou hast bestowed favors. Not (the path) of those upon whom Thy wrath is brought down, nor of those who go astray.

صِرَاطَ الَّذِیْنَ اَنْعَمْتَ عَلَیْهِمْ غَیْرِ الْمَغْضُوْبِ عَلَیْهِمْ وَلَا الضَّآلِّیْنَ ۝

THE COW
(BAQARAH)

**In the name of Allah,
the Beneficent, the Merciful.**

1. Alif Lam Mim.

2. This Book, there is no doubt in it, is a guide to those who guard (against evil).

3. Those who believe in the unseen and keep up prayer and spend out of what We have given them.

4. And who believe in that which has been revealed to you and that which was revealed before you and they are sure of the hereafter.

5. These are on a right course from their Lord and these it is that shall be successful.

6. Surely those who disbelieve, it being alike to them whether you warn them, or do not warn them, will not believe.

7. Allah has set a seal upon their hearts and upon their hearing and there is a covering over their eyes, and there is a great punishment for them.

8. And there are some people who say: We believe in Allah and the last day; and they are not at all believers.

9. They desire to deceive Allah and those who believe, and they deceive only themselves and they do not perceive.

10. There is a disease in their hearts, so Allah added to their disease and they shall have a painful chastisement because they lied.

11. And when it is said to them, Do not make mischief in the land, they say: We are but peace-makers.

12. Now surely they themselves are the mischief makers, but they do not perceive.

13. And when it is said to them: Believe as the people believe, they say: Shall we believe as the fools believe? Now surely they themselves are the fools, but they do not know.

14. And when they meet those who believe, they say: We believe; and when they are alone with their Shaitans, they say: Surely we are with you, we were only mocking.

15. Allah shall pay them back their mockery, and He leaves them alone in their inordinacy, blindly wandering on.

16. These are they who buy error for the right direction, so their bargain shall bring no gain, nor are they the followers of the right direction.

17. Their parable is like the parable of one who kindled a fire, but when it had illumined all around him, Allah took away their light, and left them in utter darkness— they do not see.

18. Deaf, dumb (and) blind, so they will not turn back.

19. Or like abundant rain from the cloud in which is utter darkness and thunder and lightning; they put their fingers into their ears because of the thunder peal, for fear of death, and Allah encompasses the unbelievers.

20. The lightning almost takes away their sight; whenever it shines on them they walk in it, and when it becomes dark to them they stand still; and if Allah had pleased He would certainly have taken away their hearing and their sight; surely Allah has power over all things.

وَاِذَا قِيْلَ لَهُمْ لَا تُفْسِدُوْا فِى الْاَرْضِ ۙ قَالُوْۤا اِنَّمَا نَحْنُ مُصْلِحُوْنَ ۝

اَلَاۤ اِنَّهُمْ هُمُ الْمُفْسِدُوْنَ وَلٰكِنْ لَّا يَشْعُرُوْنَ ۝

وَاِذَا قِيْلَ لَهُمْ اٰمِنُوْا كَمَاۤ اٰمَنَ النَّاسُ قَالُوْۤا اَنُؤْمِنُ كَمَاۤ اٰمَنَ السُّفَهَآءُ ۗ اَلَاۤ اِنَّهُمْ هُمُ السُّفَهَآءُ وَلٰكِنْ لَّا يَعْلَمُوْنَ ۝

وَاِذَا لَقُوا الَّذِيْنَ اٰمَنُوْا قَالُوْۤا اٰمَنَّا ۖ وَاِذَا خَلَوْا اِلٰى شَيٰطِيْنِهِمْ ۙ قَالُوْۤا اِنَّا مَعَكُمْ ۙ اِنَّمَا نَحْنُ مُسْتَهْزِءُوْنَ ۝

اَللّٰهُ يَسْتَهْزِئُ بِهِمْ وَيَمُدُّهُمْ فِىْ طُغْيَانِهِمْ يَعْمَهُوْنَ ۝

اُولٰٓئِكَ الَّذِيْنَ اشْتَرَوُا الضَّلٰلَةَ بِالْهُدٰى ۖ فَمَا رَبِحَتْ تِّجَارَتُهُمْ وَمَا كَانُوْا مُهْتَدِيْنَ ۝

مَثَلُهُمْ كَمَثَلِ الَّذِى اسْتَوْقَدَ نَارًا ۚ فَلَمَّاۤ اَضَآءَتْ مَا حَوْلَهٗ ذَهَبَ اللّٰهُ بِنُوْرِهِمْ وَتَرَكَهُمْ فِىْ ظُلُمٰتٍ لَّا يُبْصِرُوْنَ ۝

صُمٌّ بُكْمٌ عُمْىٌ فَهُمْ لَا يَرْجِعُوْنَ ۝

اَوْ كَصَيِّبٍ مِّنَ السَّمَآءِ فِيْهِ ظُلُمٰتٌ وَّرَعْدٌ وَّبَرْقٌ ۚ يَجْعَلُوْنَ اَصَابِعَهُمْ فِىْۤ اٰذَانِهِمْ مِّنَ الصَّوَاعِقِ حَذَرَ الْمَوْتِ ۗ وَاللّٰهُ مُحِيْطٌ بِالْكٰفِرِيْنَ ۝

يَكَادُ الْبَرْقُ يَخْطَفُ اَبْصَارَهُمْ ۗ كُلَّمَاۤ اَضَآءَ لَهُمْ مَّشَوْا فِيْهِ ۙ وَاِذَاۤ اَظْلَمَ عَلَيْهِمْ قَامُوْا ۗ وَلَوْ شَآءَ اللّٰهُ لَذَهَبَ بِسَمْعِهِمْ وَاَبْصَارِهِمْ ۗ اِنَّ اللّٰهَ عَلٰى كُلِّ شَىْءٍ قَدِيْرٌ ۝

3

21. O men! serve your Lord Who created you and those before you so that you may guard (against evil).

22. Who made the earth a resting place for you and the heaven a canopy and (Who) sends down rain from the cloud, then brings forth with it subsistence for you of the fruits; therefore do not set up rivals to Allah while you know.

23. And if you are in doubt as to that which We have revealed to Our servant, then produce a chapter like it and call on your witnesses besides Allah if you are truthful.

24. But if you do (it) not and never shall you do (it), then be on your guard against the fire of which men and stones are the fuel; it is prepared for the unbelievers.

25. And convey good news to those who believe and do good deeds, that they shall have gardens in which rivers flow; whenever they shall be given a portion of the fruit thereof, they shall say: This is what was given to us before; and they shall be given the like of it, and they shall have pure mates in them, and in them, they shall abide.

26. Surely Allah is not ashamed to set forth any parable—(that of) a gnat or any thing above that; then as for those who believe, they know that it is the truth from their Lord, and as for those who disbelieve, they say: What is it that Allah means by this parable: He causes many to err by it and many He leads aright by it! but He does not cause to err by it (any) except the transgressors,

27. Who break the covenant of Allah after its confirmation and cut asunder what Allah has ordered to be joined, and make mischief in the land; these it is that are the losers.

يَا أَيُّهَا النَّاسُ اعْبُدُوْا رَبَّكُمُ الَّذِيْ خَلَقَكُمْ وَالَّذِيْنَ مِنْ قَبْلِكُمْ لَعَلَّكُمْ تَتَّقُوْنَ ۞

الَّذِيْ جَعَلَ لَكُمُ الْأَرْضَ فِرَاشًا وَّالسَّمَاءَ بِنَآءً ۖ وَّأَنْزَلَ مِنَ السَّمَاءِ مَآءً فَأَخْرَجَ بِهٖ مِنَ الثَّمَرٰتِ رِزْقًا لَّكُمْ ۖ فَلَا تَجْعَلُوْا لِلّٰهِ أَنْدَادًا وَّأَنْتُمْ تَعْلَمُوْنَ ۞

وَإِنْ كُنْتُمْ فِيْ رَيْبٍ مِّمَّا نَزَّلْنَا عَلٰى عَبْدِنَا فَأْتُوْا بِسُوْرَةٍ مِّنْ مِّثْلِهٖ ۖ وَادْعُوْا شُهَدَآءَكُمْ مِّنْ دُوْنِ اللّٰهِ إِنْ كُنْتُمْ صٰدِقِيْنَ ۞

فَإِنْ لَّمْ تَفْعَلُوْا وَلَنْ تَفْعَلُوْا فَاتَّقُوا النَّارَ الَّتِيْ وَقُوْدُهَا النَّاسُ وَالْحِجَارَةُ ۖ أُعِدَّتْ لِلْكٰفِرِيْنَ ۞

وَبَشِّرِ الَّذِيْنَ اٰمَنُوْا وَعَمِلُوا الصّٰلِحٰتِ أَنَّ لَهُمْ جَنّٰتٍ تَجْرِيْ مِنْ تَحْتِهَا الْأَنْهٰرُ ۖ كُلَّمَا رُزِقُوْا مِنْهَا مِنْ ثَمَرَةٍ رِّزْقًا ۖ قَالُوْا هٰذَا الَّذِيْ رُزِقْنَا مِنْ قَبْلُ ۖ وَأُتُوْا بِهٖ مُتَشَابِهًا ۖ وَلَهُمْ فِيْهَا أَزْوَاجٌ مُّطَهَّرَةٌ ۖ وَّهُمْ فِيْهَا خٰلِدُوْنَ ۞

إِنَّ اللّٰهَ لَا يَسْتَحْيٖٓ أَنْ يَّضْرِبَ مَثَلًا مَّا بَعُوْضَةً فَمَا فَوْقَهَا ۖ فَأَمَّا الَّذِيْنَ اٰمَنُوْا فَيَعْلَمُوْنَ أَنَّهُ الْحَقُّ مِنْ رَّبِّهِمْ ۖ وَأَمَّا الَّذِيْنَ كَفَرُوْا فَيَقُوْلُوْنَ مَاذَا أَرَادَ اللّٰهُ بِهٰذَا مَثَلًا ۖ يُضِلُّ بِهٖ كَثِيْرًا وَّيَهْدِيْ بِهٖ كَثِيْرًا ۖ وَمَا يُضِلُّ بِهٖٓ إِلَّا الْفٰسِقِيْنَ ۞

الَّذِيْنَ يَنْقُضُوْنَ عَهْدَ اللّٰهِ مِنْ بَعْدِ مِيْثَاقِهٖ ۖ وَيَقْطَعُوْنَ مَآ أَمَرَ اللّٰهُ بِهٖٓ أَنْ يُّوْصَلَ وَيُفْسِدُوْنَ فِي الْأَرْضِ ۖ أُولٰٓئِكَ هُمُ الْخٰسِرُوْنَ ۞

28. How do you deny Allah and you were dead and He gave you life? Again He will cause you to die and again bring you to life; then you shall be brought back to Him.

29. He it is Who created for you all that is in the earth, and He directed Himself to the heaven, so He made them complete seven heavens, and He knows all things.

30. And when your Lord said to the angels, I am going to place in the earth a khalif, they said: What! wilt Thou place in it such as shall make mischief in it and shed blood, and we celebrate Thy praise and extol Thy holiness? He said: Surely I know what you do not know.

31. And He taught Adam all the names, then presented them to the angels; then He said: Tell me the names of those if you are right.

32. They said: Glory be to Thee! we have no knowledge but that which Thou hast taught us; surely Thou art the Knowing, the Wise.

33. He said: O Adam! inform them of their names. Then when he had informed them of their names, He said: Did I not say to you that I surely know what is ghaib in the heavens and the earth and (that) I know what you manifest and what you hide?

34. And when We said to the angels: Make obeisance to Adam they did obeisance, but Iblis (did it not). He refused and he was proud, and he was one of the unbelievers.

35. And We said: O Adam! dwell you and your wife in the garden and eat from it a plenteous (food) wherever you wish and do not approach this tree, for then you will be of the unjust.

36. But the Shaitan made them both fall from it, and caused them to depart from that (state) in which they were; and We said: Get forth, some of you being the enemies of others, and there is for you in the earth an abode and a provision for a time.

37. Then Adam received (some) words from his Lord, so He turned to him mercifully; surely He is Oft-returning (to mercy), the Merciful.

38. We said: Go forth from this (state) all; so surely there will come to you a guidance from Me, then whoever follows My guidance, no fear shall come upon them, nor shall they grieve.

39. And (as to) those who disbelieve in and reject My communications, they are the inmates of the fire, in it they shall abide.

40. O children of Israel! call to mind My favor which I bestowed on you and be faithful to (your) covenant with Me, I will fulfill (My) covenant with you; and of Me, Me alone, should you be afraid.

41. And believe in what I have revealed, verifying that which is with you, and be not the first to deny it, neither take a mean price in exchange for My communications; and Me, Me alone should you fear.

42. And do not mix up the truth with the falsehood, nor hide the truth while you know (it).

43. And keep up prayer and pay the poor-rate and bow down with those who bow down.

44. What! do you enjoin men to be good and neglect your own souls while you read the Book; have you then no sense?

45. And seek assistance through patience and prayer, and most surely it is a hard thing except for the humble ones,

46. Who know that they shall meet their Lord and that they shall return to Him.

فَأَزَلَّهُمَا الشَّيْطٰنُ عَنْهَا فَأَخْرَجَهُمَا مِمَّا كَانَا فِيْهِ ۖ وَقُلْنَا اهْبِطُوْا بَعْضُكُمْ لِبَعْضٍ عَدُوٌّ ۖ وَلَكُمْ فِى الْأَرْضِ مُسْتَقَرٌّ وَّمَتَاعٌ إِلٰى حِيْنٍ ۝

فَتَلَقّٰى اٰدَمُ مِنْ رَّبِّهٖ كَلِمٰتٍ فَتَابَ عَلَيْهِ ۚ إِنَّهٗ هُوَ التَّوَّابُ الرَّحِيْمُ ۝

قُلْنَا اهْبِطُوْا مِنْهَا جَمِيْعًا ۖ فَإِمَّا يَأْتِيَنَّكُمْ مِّنِّى هُدًى فَمَنْ تَبِعَ هُدَايَ فَلَا خَوْفٌ عَلَيْهِمْ وَلَا هُمْ يَحْزَنُوْنَ ۝ وَالَّذِيْنَ كَفَرُوْا وَكَذَّبُوْا بِاٰيٰتِنَا أُولٰئِكَ أَصْحٰبُ النَّارِ ۖ هُمْ فِيْهَا خٰلِدُوْنَ ۝

يٰبَنِىْ إِسْرَآءِيْلَ اذْكُرُوْا نِعْمَتِىَ الَّتِىْ أَنْعَمْتُ عَلَيْكُمْ وَأَوْفُوْا بِعَهْدِىْ أُوْفِ بِعَهْدِكُمْ وَإِيَّايَ فَارْهَبُوْنِ ۝ وَاٰمِنُوْا بِمَا أَنْزَلْتُ مُصَدِّقًا لِّمَا مَعَكُمْ وَلَا تَكُوْنُوْا أَوَّلَ كَافِرٍ بِهٖ ۖ وَلَا تَشْتَرُوْا بِاٰيٰتِىْ ثَمَنًا قَلِيْلًا ۖ وَّإِيَّايَ فَاتَّقُوْنِ ۝

وَلَا تَلْبِسُوا الْحَقَّ بِالْبَاطِلِ وَتَكْتُمُوا الْحَقَّ وَأَنْتُمْ تَعْلَمُوْنَ ۝

وَأَقِيْمُوا الصَّلٰوةَ وَاٰتُوا الزَّكٰوةَ وَارْكَعُوْا مَعَ الرّٰكِعِيْنَ ۝ أَتَأْمُرُوْنَ النَّاسَ بِالْبِرِّ وَتَنْسَوْنَ أَنْفُسَكُمْ وَأَنْتُمْ تَتْلُوْنَ الْكِتٰبَ ۚ أَفَلَا تَعْقِلُوْنَ ۝

وَاسْتَعِيْنُوْا بِالصَّبْرِ وَالصَّلٰوةِ ۚ وَإِنَّهَا لَكَبِيْرَةٌ إِلَّا عَلَى الْخٰشِعِيْنَ ۝

الَّذِيْنَ يَظُنُّوْنَ أَنَّهُمْ مُّلٰقُوْا رَبِّهِمْ وَأَنَّهُمْ إِلَيْهِ رٰجِعُوْنَ ۝

47. O children of Israel! call to mind My favor which I bestowed on you and that I made you excel the nations.

يٰبَنِىْۤ اِسْرَآءِيْلَ اذْكُرُوْا نِعْمَتِىَ الَّتِىْۤ اَنْعَمْتُ عَلَيْكُمْ وَاَنِّىْ فَضَّلْتُكُمْ عَلَى الْعٰلَمِيْنَ ۝

48. And be on your guard against a day when one soul shall not avail another in the least, neither shall intercession on its behalf be accepted, nor shall any compensation be taken from it, nor shall they be helped.

وَاتَّقُوْا يَوْمًا لَّا تَجْزِىْ نَفْسٌ عَنْ نَّفْسٍ شَيْئًا وَّلَا يُقْبَلُ مِنْهَا شَفَاعَةٌ وَّلَا يُؤْخَذُ مِنْهَا عَدْلٌ وَّلَا هُمْ يُنْصَرُوْنَ ۝

49. And when We delivered you from Firon's people, who subjected you to severe torment, killing your sons and sparing your women, and in this there was a great trial from your Lord.

وَاِذْ نَجَّيْنٰكُمْ مِّنْ اٰلِ فِرْعَوْنَ يَسُوْمُوْنَكُمْ سُوْءَ الْعَذَابِ يُذَبِّحُوْنَ اَبْنَآءَكُمْ وَيَسْتَحْيُوْنَ نِسَآءَكُمْ وَفِىْ ذٰلِكُمْ بَلَآءٌ مِّنْ رَّبِّكُمْ عَظِيْمٌ ۝

50. And when We parted the sea for you, so We saved you and drowned the followers of Firon and you watched by.

وَاِذْ فَرَقْنَا بِكُمُ الْبَحْرَ فَاَنْجَيْنٰكُمْ وَاَغْرَقْنَاۤ اٰلَ فِرْعَوْنَ وَاَنْتُمْ تَنْظُرُوْنَ ۝

51. And when We appointed a time of forty nights with Musa, then you took the calf (for a god) after him and you were unjust.

وَاِذْ وٰعَدْنَا مُوْسٰۤى اَرْبَعِيْنَ لَيْلَةً ثُمَّ اتَّخَذْتُمُ الْعِجْلَ مِنْ بَعْدِهٖ وَاَنْتُمْ ظٰلِمُوْنَ ۝

52. Then We pardoned you after that so that you might give thanks.

ثُمَّ عَفَوْنَا عَنْكُمْ مِّنْ بَعْدِ ذٰلِكَ لَعَلَّكُمْ تَشْكُرُوْنَ ۝

53. And when We gave Musa the Book and the distinction that you might walk aright.

وَاِذْ اٰتَيْنَا مُوْسَى الْكِتٰبَ وَالْفُرْقَانَ لَعَلَّكُمْ تَهْتَدُوْنَ ۝

54. And when Musa said to his people: O my people! you have surely been unjust to yourselves by taking the calf (for a god), therefore turn to your Creator (penitently), so kill your people, that is best for you with your Creator: so He turned to you (mercifully), for surely He is the Oft-returning (to mercy), the Merciful.

وَاِذْ قَالَ مُوْسٰى لِقَوْمِهٖ يٰقَوْمِ اِنَّكُمْ ظَلَمْتُمْ اَنْفُسَكُمْ بِاتِّخَاذِكُمُ الْعِجْلَ فَتُوْبُوْۤا اِلٰى بَارِئِكُمْ فَاقْتُلُوْۤا اَنْفُسَكُمْ ذٰلِكُمْ خَيْرٌ لَّكُمْ عِنْدَ بَارِئِكُمْ فَتَابَ عَلَيْكُمْ اِنَّهٗ هُوَ التَّوَّابُ الرَّحِيْمُ ۝

55. And when you said: O Musa! we will not believe in you until we see Allah manifestly, so the punishment overtook you while you looked on.

وَاِذْ قُلْتُمْ يٰمُوْسٰى لَنْ نُّؤْمِنَ لَكَ حَتّٰى نَرَى اللّٰهَ جَهْرَةً فَاَخَذَتْكُمُ الصّٰعِقَةُ وَاَنْتُمْ تَنْظُرُوْنَ ۝

56. Then We raised you up after your death that you may give thanks.

ثُمَّ بَعَثْنٰكُمْ مِّنْ بَعْدِ مَوْتِكُمْ لَعَلَّكُمْ تَشْكُرُوْنَ ۝

57. And We made the clouds to give shade over you and We sent to you manna and quails: Eat of the good things that We have given you; and they did not do Us any harm, but they made their own souls suffer the loss.

وَظَلَّلْنَا عَلَيْكُمُ الْغَمَامَ وَاَنْزَلْنَا عَلَيْكُمُ الْمَنَّ وَ السَّلْوٰى كُلُوْا مِنْ طَيِّبٰتِ مَا رَزَقْنٰكُمْ وَمَا ظَلَمُوْنَا وَ لٰكِنْ كَانُوْا اَنْفُسَهُمْ يَظْلِمُوْنَ ۝

58. And when We said: Enter this city, then eat from it a plenteous (food) wherever you wish, and enter the gate making obeisance, and say, forgiveness. We will forgive you your wrongs and give more to those who do good (to others).

وَاِذْ قُلْنَا ادْخُلُوْا هٰذِهِ الْقَرْيَةَ فَكُلُوْا مِنْهَا حَيْثُ شِئْتُمْ رَغَدًا وَّادْخُلُوا الْبَابَ سُجَّدًا وَّقُوْلُوْا حِطَّةٌ نَّغْفِرْ لَكُمْ خَطٰيٰكُمْ وَسَنَزِيْدُ الْمُحْسِنِيْنَ ۝

59. But those who were unjust changed it for a saying other than that which had been spoken to them, so We sent upon those who were unjust a pestilence from heaven, because they transgressed.

فَبَدَّلَ الَّذِيْنَ ظَلَمُوْا قَوْلًا غَيْرَ الَّذِيْ قِيْلَ لَهُمْ فَاَنْزَلْنَا عَلَى الَّذِيْنَ ظَلَمُوْا رِجْزًا مِّنَ السَّمَاءِ بِمَا كَانُوْا يَفْسُقُوْنَ ۝

60. And when Musa prayed for drink for his people, We said: Strike the rock with your staff. So there gushed from it twelve springs; each tribe knew its drinking place: Eat and drink of the provisions of Allah and do not act corruptly in the land, making mischief.

وَاِذِ اسْتَسْقٰى مُوْسٰى لِقَوْمِهٖ فَقُلْنَا اضْرِبْ بِّعَصَاكَ الْحَجَرَ فَانْفَجَرَتْ مِنْهُ اثْنَتَا عَشْرَةَ عَيْنًا قَدْ عَلِمَ كُلُّ اُنَاسٍ مَّشْرَبَهُمْ كُلُوْا وَاشْرَبُوْا مِنْ رِّزْقِ اللّٰهِ وَلَا تَعْثَوْا فِى الْاَرْضِ مُفْسِدِيْنَ ۝

61. And when you said: O Musa! we cannot bear with one food, therefore pray Lord on our behalf to bring forth for us out of what the earth grows, of its herbs and its cucumbers and its garlic and its lentils and its onions. He said: Will you exchange that which is better for that which is worse? Enter a city, so you will have what you ask for. And abasement and humiliation were brought down upon them, and they became deserving of Allah's wrath; this was so because they disbelieved in the communications of Allah and killed the prophets unjustly; this was so because they disobeyed and exceeded the limits.

وَاِذْ قُلْتُمْ يٰمُوْسٰى لَنْ نَّصْبِرَ عَلٰى طَعَامٍ وَّاحِدٍ فَادْعُ لَنَا رَبَّكَ يُخْرِجْ لَنَا مِمَّا تُنْبِتُ الْاَرْضُ مِنْ بَقْلِهَا وَ قِثَّائِهَا وَفُوْمِهَا وَعَدَسِهَا وَبَصَلِهَا قَالَ اَتَسْتَبْدِلُوْنَ الَّذِيْ هُوَ اَدْنٰى بِالَّذِيْ هُوَ خَيْرٌ اِهْبِطُوْا مِصْرًا فَاِنَّ لَكُمْ مَّا سَاَلْتُمْ وَضُرِبَتْ عَلَيْهِمُ الذِّلَّةُ وَالْمَسْكَنَةُ وَبَآؤُ بِغَضَبٍ مِّنَ اللّٰهِ ذٰلِكَ بِاَنَّهُمْ كَانُوْا يَكْفُرُوْنَ بِاٰيٰتِ اللّٰهِ وَيَقْتُلُوْنَ النَّبِيّٖنَ بِغَيْرِ الْحَقِّ ذٰلِكَ بِمَا عَصَوْا وَّكَانُوْا يَعْتَدُوْنَ ۝

62. Surely those who believe, and those who are Jews, and the Christians, and the Sabians, whoever believes in Allah and the Last day and does good, they shall have their reward from their Lord, and there is no fear for them, nor shall they grieve.

63. And when We took a promise from you and lifted the mountain over you: Take hold of the law (Tavrat) We have given you with firmness and bear in mind what is in it, so that you may guard (against evil).

64. Then you turned back after that; so were it not for the grace of Allah and His mercy on you, you would certainly have been among the losers.

65. And certainly you have known those among you who exceeded the limits of the Sabbath, so We said to them: Be (as) apes, despised and hated.

66. So We made them an example to those who witnessed it and those who came after it, and an admonition to those who guard (against evil).

67. And when Musa said to his people: Surely Allah commands you that you should sacrifice a cow; they said: Do you ridicule us? He said: I seek the protection of Allah from being one of the ignorant.

68. They said: Call on your Lord for our sake to make it plain to us what she is. Musa said: He says, Surely she is a cow neither advanced in age nor too young, of middle age between that (and this); do therefore what you are commanded.

69. They said: Call on your Lord for our sake to make it plain to us what her color is. Musa said: He says, Surely she is a yellow cow; her color is intensely yellow, giving delight to the beholders.

70. They said: Call on your Lord for our sake to make it plain to us what she is, for surely to us the cows are all alike, and if Allah please we shall surely be guided aright.

اِنَّ الَّذِيْنَ اٰمَنُوْا وَالَّذِيْنَ هَادُوْا وَالنَّصٰرٰى وَ الصّٰبِئِيْنَ مَنْ اٰمَنَ بِاللّٰهِ وَالْيَوْمِ الْاٰخِرِ وَعَمِلَ صَالِحًا فَلَهُمْ اَجْرُهُمْ عِنْدَ رَبِّهِمْ ۚ وَلَا خَوْفٌ عَلَيْهِمْ وَلَا هُمْ يَحْزَنُوْنَ ۝

وَاِذْ اَخَذْنَا مِيْثَاقَكُمْ وَرَفَعْنَا فَوْقَكُمُ الطُّوْرَ ؕ خُذُوْا مَآ اٰتَيْنٰكُمْ بِقُوَّةٍ وَّاذْكُرُوْا مَا فِيْهِ لَعَلَّكُمْ تَتَّقُوْنَ ۝

ثُمَّ تَوَلَّيْتُمْ مِّنْ بَعْدِ ذٰلِكَ ۚ فَلَوْلَا فَضْلُ اللّٰهِ عَلَيْكُمْ وَرَحْمَتُهُ لَكُنْتُمْ مِّنَ الْخٰسِرِيْنَ ۝

وَلَقَدْ عَلِمْتُمُ الَّذِيْنَ اعْتَدَوْا مِنْكُمْ فِي السَّبْتِ فَقُلْنَا لَهُمْ كُوْنُوْا قِرَدَةً خٰسِئِيْنَ ۝

فَجَعَلْنٰهَا نَكَالًا لِّمَا بَيْنَ يَدَيْهَا وَمَا خَلْفَهَا وَ مَوْعِظَةً لِّلْمُتَّقِيْنَ ۝

وَاِذْ قَالَ مُوْسٰى لِقَوْمِهٖ اِنَّ اللّٰهَ يَأْمُرُكُمْ اَنْ تَذْبَحُوْا بَقَرَةً ؕ قَالُوْا اَتَتَّخِذُنَا هُزُوًا ؕ قَالَ اَعُوْذُ بِاللّٰهِ اَنْ اَكُوْنَ مِنَ الْجٰهِلِيْنَ ۝

قَالُوا ادْعُ لَنَا رَبَّكَ يُبَيِّنْ لَّنَا مَا هِيَ ؕ قَالَ اِنَّهٗ يَقُوْلُ اِنَّهَا بَقَرَةٌ لَّا فَارِضٌ وَّلَا بِكْرٌ ؕ عَوَانٌ بَيْنَ ذٰلِكَ ؕ فَافْعَلُوْا مَا تُؤْمَرُوْنَ ۝

قَالُوا ادْعُ لَنَا رَبَّكَ يُبَيِّنْ لَّنَا مَا لَوْنُهَا ؕ قَالَ اِنَّهٗ يَقُوْلُ اِنَّهَا بَقَرَةٌ صَفْرَآءُ ۙ فَاقِعٌ لَّوْنُهَا تَسُرُّ النّٰظِرِيْنَ ۝

قَالُوا ادْعُ لَنَا رَبَّكَ يُبَيِّنْ لَّنَا مَا هِيَ ۙ اِنَّ الْبَقَرَ تَشَابَهَ عَلَيْنَا ؕ وَاِنَّآ اِنْ شَآءَ اللّٰهُ لَمُهْتَدُوْنَ ۝

71. Musa said: He says, Surely she is a cow not made submissive that she should plough the land, nor does she irrigate the tilth; sound, without a blemish in her. They said: Now you have brought the truth; so they sacrificed her, though they had not the mind to do (it).

قَالَ اِنَّهٗ يَقُوْلُ اِنَّهَا بَقَرَةٌ لَّا ذَلُوْلٌ تُثِيْرُ الْاَرْضَ وَلَا تَسْقِي الْحَرْثَ ۚ مُسَلَّمَةٌ لَّا شِيَةَ فِيْهَا ۚ قَالُوا الْـٰٔنَ جِئْتَ بِالْحَقِّ ۚ فَذَبَحُوْهَا وَمَا كَادُوْا يَفْعَلُوْنَ ۞

72. And when you killed a man, then you disagreed with respect to that, and Allah was to bring forth that which you were going to hide.

وَاِذْ قَتَلْتُمْ نَفْسًا فَادّٰرَءْتُمْ فِيْهَا ۚ وَاللّٰهُ مُخْرِجٌ مَّا كُنْتُمْ تَكْتُمُوْنَ ۞

73. So We said: Strike the (dead body) with part of the (sacrificed cow), thus Allah brings the dead to life, and He shows you His signs so that you may understand.

فَقُلْنَا اضْرِبُوْهُ بِبَعْضِهَا ۚ كَذٰلِكَ يُحْيِ اللّٰهُ الْمَوْتٰى ۚ وَ يُرِيْكُمْ اٰيٰتِهٖ لَعَلَّكُمْ تَعْقِلُوْنَ ۞

74. Then your hearts hardened after that, so that they were like rocks, rather worse in hardness; and surely there are some rocks from which streams burst forth, and surely there are some of them which split asunder so water issues out of them, and surely there are some of them which fall down for fear of Allah, and Allah is not at all heedless of what you do.

ثُمَّ قَسَتْ قُلُوْبُكُمْ مِّنْ بَعْدِ ذٰلِكَ فَهِيَ كَالْحِجَارَةِ اَوْ اَشَدُّ قَسْوَةً ۚ وَاِنَّ مِنَ الْحِجَارَةِ لَمَا يَتَفَجَّرُ مِنْهُ الْاَنْهٰرُ ۚ وَاِنَّ مِنْهَا لَمَا يَشَّقَّقُ فَيَخْرُجُ مِنْهُ الْمَاءُ ۚ وَاِنَّ مِنْهَا لَمَا يَهْبِطُ مِنْ خَشْيَةِ اللّٰهِ ۚ وَمَا اللّٰهُ بِغَافِلٍ عَمَّا تَعْمَلُوْنَ ۞

75. Do you then hope that they would believe in you, and a party from among them indeed used to hear the Word of Allah, then altered it after they had understood it, and they know (this).

اَفَتَطْمَعُوْنَ اَنْ يُّؤْمِنُوْا لَكُمْ وَقَدْ كَانَ فَرِيْقٌ مِّنْهُمْ يَسْمَعُوْنَ كَلٰمَ اللّٰهِ ثُمَّ يُحَرِّفُوْنَهٗ مِنْ بَعْدِ مَا عَقَلُوْهُ وَهُمْ يَعْلَمُوْنَ ۞

76. And when they meet those who believe they say: We believe, and when they are alone one with another they say: Do you talk to them of what Allah has disclosed to you that they may contend with you by this before your Lord? Do you not then understand?

وَاِذَا لَقُوا الَّذِيْنَ اٰمَنُوْا قَالُوْا اٰمَنَّا ۚ وَاِذَا خَلَا بَعْضُهُمْ اِلٰى بَعْضٍ قَالُوْا اَتُحَدِّثُوْنَهُمْ بِمَا فَتَحَ اللّٰهُ عَلَيْكُمْ لِيُحَاجُّوْكُمْ بِهٖ عِنْدَ رَبِّكُمْ ۚ اَفَلَا تَعْقِلُوْنَ ۞

77. Do they not know that Allah knows what they keep secret and what they make known?

اَوَلَا يَعْلَمُوْنَ اَنَّ اللّٰهَ يَعْلَمُ مَا يُسِرُّوْنَ وَمَا يُعْلِنُوْنَ ۞

78. And there are among them illiterates who know not the Book but only lies, and they do but conjecture.

وَمِنْهُمْ اُمِّيُّوْنَ لَا يَعْلَمُوْنَ الْكِتٰبَ اِلَّا اَمَانِيَّ وَاِنْ هُمْ اِلَّا يَظُنُّوْنَ ۞

79. Woe, then, to those who write the book with their hands and then say: This is from Allah, so that they may take for it a small price; therefore woe to them for what their hands have written and woe to them for what they earn.

فَوَيْلٌ لِّلَّذِيْنَ يَكْتُبُوْنَ الْكِتٰبَ بِاَيْدِيْهِمْ ثُمَّ يَقُوْلُوْنَ هٰذَا مِنْ عِنْدِ اللّٰهِ لِيَشْتَرُوْا بِهٖ ثَمَنًا قَلِيْلًا ۚ فَوَيْلٌ لَّهُمْ مِّمَّا كَتَبَتْ اَيْدِيْهِمْ وَوَيْلٌ لَّهُمْ مِّمَّا يَكْسِبُوْنَ ۞

80. And they say: Fire shall not touch us but for a few days. Say: Have you received a promise from Allah, then Allah will not fail to perform His promise, or do you speak against Allah what you do not know?

وَقَالُوا لَنْ تَمَسَّنَا النَّارُ اِلَّا اَيَّامًا مَّعْدُوْدَةً ۫ قُلْ اَتَّخَذْتُمْ عِنْدَ اللّٰهِ عَهْدًا فَلَنْ يُّخْلِفَ اللّٰهُ عَهْدَهٗۤ اَمْ تَقُوْلُوْنَ عَلَى اللّٰهِ مَا لَا تَعْلَمُوْنَ ۟

81. Yea! whoever earns evil and his sins beset him on every side, these are the inmates of the fire; in it they shall abide.

بَلٰى مَنْ كَسَبَ سَيِّئَةً وَّاَحَاطَتْ بِهٖ خَطِيْٓئَتُهٗ فَاُولٰٓئِكَ اَصْحٰبُ النَّارِ ۚ هُمْ فِيْهَا خٰلِدُوْنَ ۟

82. And (as for) those who believe and do good deeds, these are the dwellers of the garden; in it they shall abide.

وَالَّذِيْنَ اٰمَنُوْا وَعَمِلُوا الصّٰلِحٰتِ اُولٰٓئِكَ اَصْحٰبُ الْجَنَّةِ ۚ هُمْ فِيْهَا خٰلِدُوْنَ ۟

83. And when We made a covenant with the children of Israel: You shall not serve any but Allah and (you shall do) good to (your) parents, and to the near of kin and to the orphans and the needy, and you shall speak to men good words and keep up prayer and pay the poor-rate. Then you turned back except a few of you and (now too) you turn aside.

وَاِذْ اَخَذْنَا مِيْثَاقَ بَنِيْۤ اِسْرَآئِيْلَ لَا تَعْبُدُوْنَ اِلَّا اللّٰهَ ۟ وَبِالْوَالِدَيْنِ اِحْسَانًا وَّذِي الْقُرْبٰى وَالْيَتٰمٰى وَالْمَسٰكِيْنِ وَقُوْلُوْا لِلنَّاسِ حُسْنًا وَّاَقِيْمُوا الصَّلٰوةَ وَاٰتُوا الزَّكٰوةَ ۚ ثُمَّ تَوَلَّيْتُمْ اِلَّا قَلِيْلًا مِّنْكُمْ وَاَنْتُمْ مُّعْرِضُوْنَ ۟

84. And when We made a covenant with you: You shall not shed your blood and you shall not turn your people out of your cities; then you gave a promise while you witnessed.

وَاِذْ اَخَذْنَا مِيْثَاقَكُمْ لَا تَسْفِكُوْنَ دِمَآءَكُمْ وَلَا تُخْرِجُوْنَ اَنْفُسَكُمْ مِّنْ دِيَارِكُمْ ثُمَّ اَقْرَرْتُمْ وَاَنْتُمْ تَشْهَدُوْنَ ۟

85. Yet you it is who slay your people and turn a party from among you out of their homes, backing each other up against them unlawfully and exceeding the limits; and if they should come to you, as captives you would ransom them—while their very turning out was unlawful for you. Do you then believe in a part of the Book and disbelieve in the other? What then is the reward of such among you as do this but disgrace in the life of this world, and on the day of resurrection they shall be sent back to the most grievous chastisement, and Allah is not at all heedless of what you do.

ثُمَّ اَنْتُمْ هٰٓؤُلَآءِ تَقْتُلُوْنَ اَنْفُسَكُمْ وَتُخْرِجُوْنَ فَرِيْقًا مِّنْكُمْ مِّنْ دِيَارِهِمْ ۫ تَظٰهَرُوْنَ عَلَيْهِمْ بِالْاِثْمِ وَالْعُدْوَانِ ۫ وَاِنْ يَّأْتُوْكُمْ اُسٰرٰى تُفٰدُوْهُمْ وَهُوَ مُحَرَّمٌ عَلَيْكُمْ اِخْرَاجُهُمْ ۚ اَفَتُؤْمِنُوْنَ بِبَعْضِ الْكِتٰبِ وَتَكْفُرُوْنَ بِبَعْضٍ ۚ فَمَا جَزَآءُ مَنْ يَّفْعَلُ ذٰلِكَ مِنْكُمْ اِلَّا خِزْيٌ فِي الْحَيٰوةِ الدُّنْيَا ۚ وَيَوْمَ الْقِيٰمَةِ يُرَدُّوْنَ اِلٰٓى اَشَدِّ الْعَذَابِ ۚ وَمَا اللّٰهُ بِغَافِلٍ عَمَّا تَعْمَلُوْنَ ۟

86. These are they who buy the life of this world for the hereafter, so their chastisement shall not be lightened nor shall they be helped.

اُولٰٓئِكَ الَّذِيْنَ اشْتَرَوُا الْحَيٰوةَ الدُّنْيَا بِالْاٰخِرَةِ فَلَا يُخَفَّفُ عَنْهُمُ الْعَذَابُ وَلَا هُمْ يُنْصَرُوْنَ ۝

87. And most certainly We gave Musa the Book and We sent apostles after him one after another; and We gave Isa, the son of Marium, clear arguments and strengthened him with the holy spirit, What! whenever then an apostle came to you with that which your souls did not desire, you were insolent so you called some liars and some you slew.

وَلَقَدْ اٰتَيْنَا مُوْسَى الْكِتٰبَ وَقَفَّيْنَا مِنْۢ بَعْدِهٖ بِالرُّسُلِ ۖ وَاٰتَيْنَا عِيْسَى ابْنَ مَرْيَمَ الْبَيِّنٰتِ وَاَيَّدْنٰهُ بِرُوْحِ الْقُدُسِ ۗ اَفَكُلَّمَا جَآءَكُمْ رَسُوْلٌۢ بِمَا لَا تَهْوٰٓى اَنْفُسُكُمُ اسْتَكْبَرْتُمْ ۚ فَفَرِيْقًا كَذَّبْتُمْ وَفَرِيْقًا تَقْتُلُوْنَ ۝

88. And they say: Our hearts are covered. Nay, Allah has cursed them on account of their unbelief; so little it is that they believe.

وَقَالُوْا قُلُوْبُنَا غُلْفٌ ۚ بَلْ لَّعَنَهُمُ اللّٰهُ بِكُفْرِهِمْ فَقَلِيْلًا مَّا يُؤْمِنُوْنَ ۝

89. And when there came to them a Book from Allah verifying that which they have, and aforetime they used to pray for victory against those who disbelieve, but when there came to them (Prophet) that which they did not recognize, they disbelieved in him; so Allah's curse is on the unbelievers.

وَلَمَّا جَآءَهُمْ كِتٰبٌ مِّنْ عِنْدِ اللّٰهِ مُصَدِّقٌ لِّمَا مَعَهُمْ ۙ وَكَانُوْا مِنْ قَبْلُ يَسْتَفْتِحُوْنَ عَلَى الَّذِيْنَ كَفَرُوْا ۚ فَلَمَّا جَآءَهُمْ مَّا عَرَفُوْا كَفَرُوْا بِهٖ ۖ فَلَعْنَةُ اللّٰهِ عَلَى الْكٰفِرِيْنَ ۝

90. Evil is that for which they have sold their souls—that they should deny what Allah has revealed, out of envy that Allah should send down of His grace on whomsoever of His servants He pleases; so they have made themselves deserving of wrath upon wrath, and there is a disgraceful punishment for the unbelievers.

بِئْسَمَا اشْتَرَوْا بِهٖٓ اَنْفُسَهُمْ اَنْ يَّكْفُرُوْا بِمَآ اَنْزَلَ اللّٰهُ بَغْيًا اَنْ يُّنَزِّلَ اللّٰهُ مِنْ فَضْلِهٖ عَلٰى مَنْ يَّشَآءُ مِنْ عِبَادِهٖ ۚ فَبَآءُوْ بِغَضَبٍ عَلٰى غَضَبٍ ۚ وَلِلْكٰفِرِيْنَ عَذَابٌ مُّهِيْنٌ ۝

91. And when it is said to them, Believe in what Allah has revealed, they say: We believe in that which was revealed to us; and they deny what is besides that, while it is the truth verifying that which they have. Say: Why then did you kill Allah's Prophets before if you were indeed believers?

وَاِذَا قِيْلَ لَهُمْ اٰمِنُوْا بِمَآ اَنْزَلَ اللّٰهُ قَالُوْا نُؤْمِنُ بِمَآ اُنْزِلَ عَلَيْنَا وَيَكْفُرُوْنَ بِمَا وَرَآءَهٗ ۚ وَهُوَ الْحَقُّ مُصَدِّقًا لِّمَا مَعَهُمْ ۗ قُلْ فَلِمَ تَقْتُلُوْنَ اَنْبِيَآءَ اللّٰهِ مِنْ قَبْلُ اِنْ كُنْتُمْ مُّؤْمِنِيْنَ ۝

92. And most certainly Musa came to you with clear arguments, then you took the calf (for a god) in his absence and you were unjust.

وَلَقَدْ جَآءَكُمْ مُّوْسٰى بِالْبَيِّنٰتِ ثُمَّ اتَّخَذْتُمُ الْعِجْلَ مِنْۢ بَعْدِهٖ وَاَنْتُمْ ظٰلِمُوْنَ ۝

93. And when We made a covenant with you and raised the mountain over you: Take hold of what We have given you with firmness and be obedient. They said: We hear and disobey. And they were made to imbibe (the love of) the calf into their hearts on account of their unbelief. Say: Evil is that which your belief bids you if you are believers.

94. Say: If the future abode with Allah is specially for you to the exclusion of the people, then invoke death if you are truthful.

95. And they will never invoke it on account of what their hands have sent before, and Allah knows the unjust.

96. And you will most certainly find them the greediest of men for life (greedier) than even those who are polytheists; every one of them loves that he should be granted a life of a thousand years, and his being granted a long life will in no way remove him further off from the chastisement, and Allah sees what they do.

97. Say: Whoever is the enemy of Jibreel —for surely he revealed it to your heart by Allah's command, verifying that which is before it and guidance and good news for the believers.

98. Whoever is the enemy of Allah and His angels and His apostles and Jibreel and Meekaeel, so surely Allah is the enemy of the unbelievers.

99. And certainly We have revealed to you clear communications and none disbelieve in them except the transgressors.

100. What! whenever they make a covenant, a party of them cast it aside? Nay, most of them do not believe.

101. And when there came to them an Apostle from Allah verifying that which they have, a party of those who were given the Book threw the Book of Allah behind their backs as if they knew nothing.

وَلَمَّا جَآءَهُمْ رَسُوْلٌ مِّنْ عِنْدِ اللّٰهِ مُصَدِّقٌ لِّمَا مَعَهُمْ نَبَذَ فَرِيْقٌ مِّنَ الَّذِيْنَ اُوْتُوا الْكِتٰبَ كِتٰبَ اللّٰهِ وَرَآءَ ظُهُوْرِهِمْ كَاَنَّهُمْ لَا يَعْلَمُوْنَ ۟

102. And they followed what the Shaitans chanted of sorcery in the reign of Sulaiman, and Sulaiman was not an unbeliever, but the Shaitans disbelieved, they taught men sorcery and that was sent down to the two angels at Babel, Harut and Marut, yet these two taught no man until they had said, "Surely we are only a trial, therefore do not be a disbeliever." Even then men learned from these two, magic by which they might cause a separation between a man and his wife; and they cannot hurt with it any one except with Allah's permission, and they learned what harmed them and did not profit them, and certainly they know that he who bought it should have no share of good in the hereafter and evil was the price for which they sold their souls; had they but known this.

وَاتَّبَعُوْا مَا تَتْلُوا الشَّيٰطِيْنُ عَلٰى مُلْكِ سُلَيْمٰنَ ۚ وَ مَا كَفَرَ سُلَيْمٰنُ وَلٰكِنَّ الشَّيٰطِيْنَ كَفَرُوْا يُعَلِّمُوْنَ النَّاسَ السِّحْرَ ۗ وَمَا اُنْزِلَ عَلَى الْمَلَكَيْنِ بِبَابِلَ هَارُوْتَ وَمَارُوْتَ ۗ وَمَا يُعَلِّمٰنِ مِنْ اَحَدٍ حَتّٰى يَقُوْلَا اِنَّمَا نَحْنُ فِتْنَةٌ فَلَا تَكْفُرْ ۗ فَيَتَعَلَّمُوْنَ مِنْهُمَا مَا يُفَرِّقُوْنَ بِهٖ بَيْنَ الْمَرْءِ وَزَوْجِهٖ ۗ وَمَا هُمْ بِضَآرِّيْنَ بِهٖ مِنْ اَحَدٍ اِلَّا بِاِذْنِ اللّٰهِ ۗ وَيَتَعَلَّمُوْنَ مَا يَضُرُّهُمْ وَلَا يَنْفَعُهُمْ ۗ وَلَقَدْ عَلِمُوا لَمَنِ اشْتَرٰىهُ مَا لَهٗ فِي الْاٰخِرَةِ مِنْ خَلَاقٍ ۗ وَلَبِئْسَ مَا شَرَوْا بِهٖۤ اَنْفُسَهُمْ ۗ لَوْ كَانُوْا يَعْلَمُوْنَ ۟

103. And if they had believed and guarded themselves (against evil), reward from Allah would certainly have been better; had they but known (this).

وَلَوْ اَنَّهُمْ اٰمَنُوْا وَاتَّقَوْا لَمَثُوْبَةٌ مِّنْ عِنْدِ اللّٰهِ خَيْرٌ ۖ لَّوْ كَانُوْا يَعْلَمُوْنَ ۟

104. O you who believe! do not say Raina and say Unzurna and listen, and for the unbelievers there is a painful chastisement.

يٰۤاَيُّهَا الَّذِيْنَ اٰمَنُوْا لَا تَقُوْلُوْا رَاعِنَا وَقُوْلُوا انْظُرْنَا وَاسْمَعُوْا ۗ وَلِلْكٰفِرِيْنَ عَذَابٌ اَلِيْمٌ ۟

105. Those who disbelieve from among the followers of the Book do not like, nor do the polytheists, that the good should be sent down to you from your Lord, and Allah chooses especially whom He pleases for His mercy, and Allah is the Lord of mighty grace.

مَا يَوَدُّ الَّذِيْنَ كَفَرُوْا مِنْ اَهْلِ الْكِتٰبِ وَلَا الْمُشْرِكِيْنَ اَنْ يُّنَزَّلَ عَلَيْكُمْ مِّنْ خَيْرٍ مِّنْ رَّبِّكُمْ ۗ وَاللّٰهُ يَخْتَصُّ بِرَحْمَتِهٖ مَنْ يَّشَآءُ ۗ وَاللّٰهُ ذُو الْفَضْلِ الْعَظِيْمِ ۟

106. Whatever communications We abrogate or cause to be forgotten, We bring one better than it or like it. Do you not know that Allah has power over all things?

مَا نَنْسَخْ مِنْ اٰيَةٍ اَوْ نُنْسِهَا نَأْتِ بِخَيْرٍ مِّنْهَاۤ اَوْ مِثْلِهَا ۗ اَلَمْ تَعْلَمْ اَنَّ اللّٰهَ عَلٰى كُلِّ شَيْءٍ قَدِيْرٌ ۟

107. Do you not know that Allah's is the kingdom of the heavens and the earth, and that besides Allah you have no guardian or helper?

108. Rather you wish to put questions to your Apostle, as Musa was questioned before; and whoever adopts unbelief instead of faith, he indeed has lost the right direction of the way.

109. Many of the followers of the Book wish that they could turn you back into unbelievers after your faith, out of envy from themselves, (even) after the truth has become manifest to them; but pardon and forgive, so that Allah should bring about His command; surely Allah has power over all things.

110. And keep up prayer and pay the poor-rate and whatever good you send before for yourselves, you shall find it with Allah; surely Allah sees what you do.

111. And they say: None shall enter the garden (or paradise) except he who is a Jew or a Christian. These are their vain desires. Say: Bring your proof if you are truthful.

112. Yes! whoever submits himself entirely to Allah and he is the doer of good (to others) he has his reward from his Lord, and there is no fear for him nor shall he grieve.

113. And the Jews say: The Christians do not follow anything (good) and the Christians say: The Jews do not follow anything (good) while they recite the (same) Book. Even thus say those who have no knowledge, like to what they say; so Allah shall judge between them on the day of resurrection in what they differ.

اَلَمۡ تَعۡلَمۡ اَنَّ اللّٰهَ لَهٗ مُلۡكُ السَّمٰوٰتِ وَالۡاَرۡضِ ۫ وَمَا لَكُمۡ مِّنۡ دُوۡنِ اللّٰهِ مِنۡ وَّلِیٍّ وَّلَا نَصِیۡرٍ ۝

اَمۡ تُرِیۡدُوۡنَ اَنۡ تَسۡئَلُوۡا رَسُوۡلَكُمۡ كَمَا سُئِلَ مُوۡسٰی مِنۡ قَبۡلُ ۚ وَمَنۡ یَّتَبَدَّلِ الۡكُفۡرَ بِالۡاِیۡمَانِ فَقَدۡ ضَلَّ سَوَآءَ السَّبِیۡلِ ۝

وَدَّ كَثِیۡرٌ مِّنۡ اَهۡلِ الۡكِتٰبِ لَوۡ یَرُدُّوۡنَكُمۡ مِّنۡۢ بَعۡدِ اِیۡمَانِكُمۡ كُفَّارًا ۚ حَسَدًا مِّنۡ عِنۡدِ اَنۡفُسِهِمۡ مِّنۡۢ بَعۡدِ مَا تَبَیَّنَ لَهُمُ الۡحَقُّ ۚ فَاعۡفُوۡا وَاصۡفَحُوۡا حَتّٰی یَاۡتِیَ اللّٰهُ بِاَمۡرِهٖ ؕ اِنَّ اللّٰهَ عَلٰی كُلِّ شَیۡءٍ قَدِیۡرٌ ۝

وَاَقِیۡمُوا الصَّلٰوۃَ وَاٰتُوا الزَّكٰوۃَ ؕ وَمَا تُقَدِّمُوۡا لِاَنۡفُسِكُمۡ مِّنۡ خَیۡرٍ تَجِدُوۡهُ عِنۡدَ اللّٰهِ ؕ اِنَّ اللّٰهَ بِمَا تَعۡمَلُوۡنَ بَصِیۡرٌ ۝

وَقَالُوۡا لَنۡ یَّدۡخُلَ الۡجَنَّۃَ اِلَّا مَنۡ كَانَ هُوۡدًا اَوۡ نَصٰرٰی ؕ تِلۡكَ اَمَانِیُّهُمۡ ؕ قُلۡ هَاتُوۡا بُرۡهَانَكُمۡ اِنۡ كُنۡتُمۡ صٰدِقِیۡنَ ۝

بَلٰی مَنۡ اَسۡلَمَ وَجۡهَهٗ لِلّٰهِ وَهُوَ مُحۡسِنٌ فَلَهٗۤ اَجۡرُهٗ عِنۡدَ رَبِّهٖ ۪ وَلَا خَوۡفٌ عَلَیۡهِمۡ وَلَا هُمۡ یَحۡزَنُوۡنَ ۝

وَقَالَتِ الۡیَهُوۡدُ لَیۡسَتِ النَّصٰرٰی عَلٰی شَیۡءٍ ۙ وَّقَالَتِ النَّصٰرٰی لَیۡسَتِ الۡیَهُوۡدُ عَلٰی شَیۡءٍ ۙ وَّهُمۡ یَتۡلُوۡنَ الۡكِتٰبَ ؕ كَذٰلِكَ قَالَ الَّذِیۡنَ لَا یَعۡلَمُوۡنَ مِثۡلَ قَوۡلِهِمۡ ۚ فَاللّٰهُ یَحۡكُمُ بَیۡنَهُمۡ یَوۡمَ الۡقِیٰمَۃِ فِیۡمَا كَانُوۡا فِیۡهِ یَخۡتَلِفُوۡنَ ۝

114. And who is more unjust than he who prevents (men) from the masjids of Allah, that His name should be remembered in them, and strives to ruin them? (As for) these, it was not proper for them that they should have entered them except in fear; they shall meet with disgrace in this world, and they shall have great chastisement in the hereafter.

وَمَنْ أَظْلَمُ مِمَّنْ مَّنَعَ مَسَاجِدَ اللهِ أَنْ يُذْكَرَ فِيْهَا اسْمُهُ وَسَعَىٰ فِىْ خَرَابِهَا ۚ أُولٰٓئِكَ مَا كَانَ لَهُمْ أَنْ يَّدْخُلُوْهَآ إِلَّا خَآئِفِيْنَ ۚ لَهُمْ فِى الدُّنْيَا خِزْىٌ وَّ لَهُمْ فِى الْاٰخِرَةِ عَذَابٌ عَظِيْمٌ ۝

115. And Allah's is the East and the West, therefore, whither you turn, thither is Allah's purpose; surely Allah is Ample-giving, Knowing.

وَلِلّٰهِ الْمَشْرِقُ وَالْمَغْرِبُ ۚ فَأَيْنَمَا تُوَلُّوْا فَثَمَّ وَجْهُ اللهِ ۚ إِنَّ اللهَ وَاسِعٌ عَلِيْمٌ ۝

116. And they say: Allah has taken to himself a son. Glory be to Him; rather, whatever is in the heavens and the earth is His; all are obedient to Him.

وَقَالُوا اتَّخَذَ اللهُ وَلَدًا ۙ سُبْحٰنَهُ ۚ بَلْ لَّهُ مَا فِى السَّمٰوٰتِ وَالْأَرْضِ ۚ كُلٌّ لَّهُ قٰنِتُوْنَ ۝

117. Wonderful Originator of the heavens and the earth, and when He decrees an affair, He only says to it, Be, so there it is.

بَدِيْعُ السَّمٰوٰتِ وَالْأَرْضِ ۚ وَإِذَا قَضٰٓى أَمْرًا فَإِنَّمَا يَقُوْلُ لَهُ كُنْ فَيَكُوْنُ ۝

118. And those who have no knowledge say: Why does not Allah speak to us or a sign come to us? Even thus said those before them, the like of what they say; their hearts are all alike. Indeed We have made the communications clear for a people who are sure.

وَقَالَ الَّذِيْنَ لَا يَعْلَمُوْنَ لَوْلَا يُكَلِّمُنَا اللهُ أَوْ تَأْتِيْنَآ اٰيَةٌ ۗ كَذٰلِكَ قَالَ الَّذِيْنَ مِنْ قَبْلِهِمْ مِّثْلَ قَوْلِهِمْ ۘ تَشَابَهَتْ قُلُوْبُهُمْ ۗ قَدْ بَيَّنَّا الْاٰيٰتِ لِقَوْمٍ يُّوْقِنُوْنَ ۝

119. Surely We have sent you with the truth as a bearer of good news and as a warner, and you shall not be called upon to answer for the companions of the flaming fire.

إِنَّآ أَرْسَلْنٰكَ بِالْحَقِّ بَشِيْرًا وَّنَذِيْرًا ۙ وَّلَا تُسْئَلُ عَنْ أَصْحٰبِ الْجَحِيْمِ ۝

120. And the Jews will not be pleased with you, nor the Christians until you follow their religion. Say: Surely Allah's guidance, that is the (true) guidance. And if you follow their desires after the knowledge that has come to you, you shall have no guardian from Allah, nor any helper.

وَلَنْ تَرْضٰى عَنْكَ الْيَهُوْدُ وَلَا النَّصٰرٰى حَتّٰى تَتَّبِعَ مِلَّتَهُمْ ۗ قُلْ إِنَّ هُدَى اللهِ هُوَ الْهُدٰى ۗ وَلَئِنِ اتَّبَعْتَ أَهْوَآءَهُمْ بَعْدَ الَّذِىْ جَآءَكَ مِنَ الْعِلْمِ ۙ مَا لَكَ مِنَ اللهِ مِنْ وَّلِىٍّ وَّلَا نَصِيْرٍ ۝

121. Those to whom We have given the Book read it as it ought to be read. These believe in it; and whoever disbelieves in it, these it is that are the losers.

الَّذِيْنَ اٰتَيْنٰهُمُ الْكِتٰبَ يَتْلُوْنَهُ حَقَّ تِلَاوَتِهِ ۙ أُولٰٓئِكَ يُؤْمِنُوْنَ بِهِ ۗ وَمَنْ يَّكْفُرْ بِهِ فَأُولٰٓئِكَ هُمُ الْخٰسِرُوْنَ ۝

122. O children of Israel, call to mind My favor which I bestowed on you and that I made you excel the nations.

يٰبَنِىْ اِسْرَآءِيْلَ اذْكُرُوْا نِعْمَتِىَ الَّتِىْ اَنْعَمْتُ عَلَيْكُمْ وَاَنِّىْ فَضَّلْتُكُمْ عَلَى الْعٰلَمِيْنَ ۝

123. And be on your guard against a day when no soul shall avail another in the least neither shall any compensation be accepted from it, nor shall intercession profit it, nor shall they be helped.

وَاتَّقُوْا يَوْمًا لَّا تَجْزِىْ نَفْسٌ عَنْ نَّفْسٍ شَيْئًا وَّلَا يُقْبَلُ مِنْهَا عَدْلٌ وَّلَا تَنْفَعُهَا شَفَاعَةٌ وَّلَا هُمْ يُنْصَرُوْنَ ۝

124. And when his Lord tried Ibrahim with certain words, he fulfilled them. He said: Surely I will make you an Imam of men. Ibrahim said: And of my offspring? My covenant does not include the unjust, said He.

وَاِذِ ابْتَلٰى اِبْرٰهٖمَ رَبُّهٗ بِكَلِمٰتٍ فَاَتَمَّهُنَّ قَالَ اِنِّىْ جَاعِلُكَ لِلنَّاسِ اِمَامًا قَالَ وَمِنْ ذُرِّيَّتِىْ قَالَ لَا يَنَالُ عَهْدِى الظّٰلِمِيْنَ ۝

125. And when We made the House a pilgrimage for men and a (place of) security, and: Appoint for yourselves a place of prayer on the standing-place of Ibrahim. And We enjoined Ibrahim and Ismail saying: Purify My House for those who visit (it) and those who abide (in it) for devotion and those who bow down (and) those who prostrate themselves.

وَاِذْ جَعَلْنَا الْبَيْتَ مَثَابَةً لِّلنَّاسِ وَاَمْنًا وَّاتَّخِذُوْا مِنْ مَّقَامِ اِبْرٰهٖمَ مُصَلًّى وَّعَهِدْنَا اِلٰى اِبْرٰهٖمَ وَ اِسْمٰعِيْلَ اَنْ طَهِّرَا بَيْتِىَ لِلطَّآئِفِيْنَ وَالْعٰكِفِيْنَ وَالرُّكَّعِ السُّجُوْدِ ۝

126. And when Ibrahim said: My Lord, make it a secure town and provide its people with fruits, such of them as believe in Allah and the last day. He said: And whoever disbelieves, I will grant him enjoyment for a short while, then I will drive him to the chastisement of the fire; and it is an evil destination.

وَاِذْ قَالَ اِبْرٰهٖمُ رَبِّ اجْعَلْ هٰذَا بَلَدًا اٰمِنًا وَّارْزُقْ اَهْلَهٗ مِنَ الثَّمَرٰتِ مَنْ اٰمَنَ مِنْهُمْ بِاللّٰهِ وَالْيَوْمِ الْاٰخِرِ قَالَ وَمَنْ كَفَرَ فَاُمَتِّعُهٗ قَلِيْلًا ثُمَّ اَضْطَرُّهٗ اِلٰى عَذَابِ النَّارِ وَبِئْسَ الْمَصِيْرُ ۝

127. And when Ibrahim and Ismail raised the foundations of the House: Our Lord! accept from us; surely Thou art the Hearing, the Knowing:

وَاِذْ يَرْفَعُ اِبْرٰهٖمُ الْقَوَاعِدَ مِنَ الْبَيْتِ وَاِسْمٰعِيْلُ رَبَّنَا تَقَبَّلْ مِنَّا اِنَّكَ اَنْتَ السَّمِيْعُ الْعَلِيْمُ ۝

128. Our Lord! and make us both submissive to Thee and (raise) from our offspring a nation submitting to Thee, and show us our ways of devotion and turn to us (mercifully), surely Thou art the Oft-returning (to mercy), the Merciful.

رَبَّنَا وَاجْعَلْنَا مُسْلِمَيْنِ لَكَ وَمِنْ ذُرِّيَّتِنَا اُمَّةً مُّسْلِمَةً لَّكَ وَاَرِنَا مَنَاسِكَنَا وَتُبْ عَلَيْنَا اِنَّكَ اَنْتَ التَّوَّابُ الرَّحِيْمُ ۝

129. Our Lord! and raise up in them an Apostle from among them who shall recite to them Thy communications and teach them the Book and the wisdom, and purify them; surely Thou art the Mighty, the Wise.

رَبَّنَا وَابْعَثْ فِيْهِمْ رَسُوْلًا مِّنْهُمْ يَتْلُوْا عَلَيْهِمْ اٰيٰتِكَ وَيُعَلِّمُهُمُ الْكِتٰبَ وَالْحِكْمَةَ وَيُزَكِّيْهِمْ ؕ اِنَّكَ اَنْتَ الْعَزِيْزُ الْحَكِيْمُ ۞

130. And who forsakes the religion of Ibrahim but he who makes himself a fool, and most certainly We chose him in this world, and in the hereafter he is most surely among the righteous.

وَمَنْ يَّرْغَبُ عَنْ مِّلَّةِ اِبْرٰهٖمَ اِلَّا مَنْ سَفِهَ نَفْسَهٗ ؕ وَلَقَدِ اصْطَفَيْنٰهُ فِي الدُّنْيَا ۚ وَاِنَّهٗ فِي الْاٰخِرَةِ لَمِنَ الصّٰلِحِيْنَ ۞

131. When his Lord said to him, Be a Muslim, he said: I submit myself to the Lord of the worlds.

اِذْ قَالَ لَهٗ رَبُّهٗ اَسْلِمْ ۙ قَالَ اَسْلَمْتُ لِرَبِّ الْعٰلَمِيْنَ ۞

132. And the same did Ibrahim enjoin on his sons and (so did) Yaqoub. O my sons! surely Allah has chosen for you (this) faith, therefore die not unless you are Muslims.

وَوَصّٰى بِهَآ اِبْرٰهٖمُ بَنِيْهِ وَيَعْقُوْبُ ؕ يٰبَنِيَّ اِنَّ اللّٰهَ اصْطَفٰى لَكُمُ الدِّيْنَ فَلَا تَمُوْتُنَّ اِلَّا وَ اَنْتُمْ مُّسْلِمُوْنَ ۞

133. Nay! were you witnesses when death visited Yaqoub, when he said to his sons: What will you serve after me? They said: We will serve your God and the God of your fathers, Ibrahim and Ismail and Ishaq, one God only, and to Him do we submit.

اَمْ كُنْتُمْ شُهَدَآءَ اِذْ حَضَرَ يَعْقُوْبَ الْمَوْتُ ۙ اِذْ قَالَ لِبَنِيْهِ مَا تَعْبُدُوْنَ مِنْ بَعْدِيْ ؕ قَالُوْا نَعْبُدُ اِلٰهَكَ وَاِلٰهَ اٰبَآئِكَ اِبْرٰهٖمَ وَاِسْمٰعِيْلَ وَاِسْحٰقَ اِلٰهًا وَّاحِدًا ۚ وَّنَحْنُ لَهٗ مُسْلِمُوْنَ ۞

134. This is a people that have passed away; they shall have what they earned and you shall have what you earn, and you shall not be called upon to answer for what they did.

تِلْكَ اُمَّةٌ قَدْ خَلَتْ ۚ لَهَا مَا كَسَبَتْ وَلَكُمْ مَّا كَسَبْتُمْ ۚ وَلَا تُسْئَلُوْنَ عَمَّا كَانُوْا يَعْمَلُوْنَ ۞

135. And they say: Be Jews or Christians, you will be on the right course. Say: Nay! (we follow) the religion of Ibrahim, the Hanif, and he was not one of the polytheists.

وَقَالُوْا كُوْنُوْا هُوْدًا اَوْ نَصٰرٰى تَهْتَدُوْا ؕ قُلْ بَلْ مِلَّةَ اِبْرٰهٖمَ حَنِيْفًا ؕ وَمَا كَانَ مِنَ الْمُشْرِكِيْنَ ۞

136. Say: We believe in Allah and (in) that which had been revealed to us, and (in) that which was revealed to Ibrahim and Ismail and Ishaq and Yaqoub and the tribes, and (in) that which was given to Musa and Isa, and (in) that which was given to the prophets from their Lord, we do not make any distinction between any of them, and to Him do we submit.

قُوْلُوْا اٰمَنَّا بِاللّٰهِ وَمَا اُنْزِلَ اِلَيْنَا وَمَا اُنْزِلَ اِلٰى اِبْرٰهٖمَ وَاِسْمٰعِيْلَ وَاِسْحٰقَ وَيَعْقُوْبَ وَالْاَسْبَاطِ وَمَآ اُوْتِيَ مُوْسٰى وَعِيْسٰى وَمَآ اُوْتِيَ النَّبِيُّوْنَ مِنْ رَّبِّهِمْ ۚ لَا نُفَرِّقُ بَيْنَ اَحَدٍ مِّنْهُمْ ۖ وَنَحْنُ لَهٗ مُسْلِمُوْنَ ۞

137. If then they believe as you believe in Him, they are indeed on the right course, and if they turn back, then they are only in great opposition, so Allah will suffice you against them, and He is the Hearing, the Knowing.

138. (Receive) the baptism of Allah, and who is better than Allah in baptising? and Him do we serve.

139. Say: Do you dispute with us about Allah, and He is our Lord and your Lord, and we shall have our deeds and you shall have your deeds, and we are sincere to Him.

140. Nay! do you say that Ibrahim and Ismail and Yaqoub and the tribes were Jews or Christians? Say: Are you better knowing or Allah? And who is more unjust than he who conceals a testimony that he has from Allah? And Allah is not at all heedless of what you do.

141. This is a people that have passed away; they shall have what they earned and you shall have what you earn, and you shall not be called upon to answer for what they did.

142. The fools among the people will say: What has turned them from their qiblah which they had? Say: The East and the West belong only to Allah; He guides whom He likes to the right path.

143. And thus We have made you a medium (just) nation that you may be the bearers of witness to the people and (that) the Apostle may be a bearer of witness to you; and We did not make that which you would have to be the qiblah but that We might distinguish him who follows the Apostle from him who turns back upon his heels, and this was surely hard except for those whom Allah has guided aright; and Allah was not going to make your faith to be fruitless; most surely Allah is Affectionate, Merciful to the people.

144. Indeed We see the turning of your face to heaven, so We shall surely turn you to a qiblah which you shall like; turn then your face towards the Sacred Mosque, and wherever you are, turn your face towards it, and those who have been given the Book most surely know that it is the truth from their Lord; and Allah is not at all heedless of what they do.

145. And even if you bring to those who have been given the Book every sign they would not follow your qiblah, nor can you be a follower of their qiblah, neither are they the followers of each other's qiblah, and if you follow their desires after the knowledge that has come to you, then you shall most surely be among the unjust.

146. Those whom We have given the Book recognize him as they recognize their sons, and a party of them most surely conceal the truth while they know (it).

147. The truth is from your Lord, therefore you should not be of the doubters.

148. And every one has a direction to which he should turn, therefore hasten to (do) good works; wherever you are, Allah will bring you all together; surely Allah has power over all things.

149. And from whatsoever place you come forth, turn your face towards the Sacred Mosque; and surely it is the very truth from your Lord, and Allah is not at all heedless of what you do.

150. And from whatsoever place you come forth, turn your face towards the Sacred Mosque; and wherever you are turn your faces towards it, so that people shall have no accusation against you, except such of them as are unjust; so do not fear them, and fear Me, that I may complete My favor on you and that you may walk on the right course.

151. Even as We have sent among you an Apostle from among you who recites to you Our communications and purifies you and teaches you the Book and the wisdom and teaches you that which you did not know.

152. Therefore remember Me, I will remember you, and be thankful to Me, and do not be ungrateful to Me.

153. O you who believe! seek assistance through patience and prayer; surely Allah is with the patient.

154. And do not speak of those who are slain in Allah's way as dead; nay, (they are) alive, but you do not perceive.

155. And We will most certainly try you with somewhat of fear and hunger and loss of property and lives and fruits; and give good news to the patient,

156. Who, when a misfortune befalls them, say: Surely we are Allah's and to Him we shall surely return.

157. Those are they on whom are blessings and mercy from their Lord, and those are the followers of the right course.

158. Surely the Safa and the Marwa are among the signs appointed by Allah; so whoever makes a pilgrimage to the House or pays a visit (to it), there is no blame on him if he goes round them both; and whoever does good spontaneously, then surely Allah is Grateful, Knowing.

159. Surely those who conceal the clear proofs and the guidance that We revealed after We made it clear in the Book for men, these it is whom Allah shall curse, and those who curse shall curse them (too).

160. Except those who repent and amend and make manifest (the truth), these it is to whom I turn (mercifully); and I am the Oft-returning (to mercy), the Merciful.

161. Surely those who disbelieve and die while they are disbelievers, these it is on whom is the curse of Allah and the angels and men all;

اِنَّ الَّذِيْنَ كَفَرُوْا وَمَاتُوْا وَهُمْ كُفَّارٌ اُولٰٓئِكَ عَلَيْهِمْ لَعْنَةُ اللّٰهِ وَالْمَلٰٓئِكَةِ وَالنَّاسِ اَجْمَعِيْنَ ۞

162. Abiding in it; their chastisement shall not be lightened nor shall they be given respite.

خٰلِدِيْنَ فِيْهَا ۚ لَا يُخَفَّفُ عَنْهُمُ الْعَذَابُ وَلَا هُمْ يُنْظَرُوْنَ ۞

163. And your God is one God! there is no god but He; He is the Beneficent, the Merciful.

وَاِلٰهُكُمْ اِلٰهٌ وَّاحِدٌ ۚ لَاۤ اِلٰهَ اِلَّا هُوَ الرَّحْمٰنُ الرَّحِيْمُ ۞

164. Most surely in the creation of the heavens and the earth and the alternation of the night and the day, and the ships that run in the sea with that which profits men, and the water that Allah sends down from the cloud, then gives life with it to the earth after its death and spreads in it all (kinds of) animals, and the changing of the winds and the clouds made subservient between the heaven and the earth, there are signs for a people who understand.

اِنَّ فِيْ خَلْقِ السَّمٰوٰتِ وَالْاَرْضِ وَاخْتِلَافِ الَّيْلِ وَالنَّهَارِ وَالْفُلْكِ الَّتِيْ تَجْرِيْ فِى الْبَحْرِ بِمَا يَنْفَعُ النَّاسَ وَمَاۤ اَنْزَلَ اللّٰهُ مِنَ السَّمَاۤءِ مِنْ مَّاۤءٍ فَاَحْيَا بِهِ الْاَرْضَ بَعْدَ مَوْتِهَا وَبَثَّ فِيْهَا مِنْ كُلِّ دَاۤبَّةٍ ۚ وَتَصْرِيْفِ الرِّيٰحِ وَالسَّحَابِ الْمُسَخَّرِ بَيْنَ السَّمَاۤءِ وَالْاَرْضِ لَاٰيٰتٍ لِّقَوْمٍ يَّعْقِلُوْنَ ۞

165. And there are some among men who take for themselves objects of worship besides Allah, whom they love as they love Allah, and those who believe are stronger in love for Allah and O, that those who are unjust had seen, when they see the chastisement, that the power is wholly Allah's and that Allah is severe in requiting (evil).

وَمِنَ النَّاسِ مَنْ يَّتَّخِذُ مِنْ دُوْنِ اللّٰهِ اَنْدَادًا يُّحِبُّوْنَهُمْ كَحُبِّ اللّٰهِ ۚ وَالَّذِيْنَ اٰمَنُوْۤا اَشَدُّ حُبًّا لِّلّٰهِ ۗ وَلَوْ يَرَى الَّذِيْنَ ظَلَمُوْۤا اِذْ يَرَوْنَ الْعَذَابَ ۙ اَنَّ الْقُوَّةَ لِلّٰهِ جَمِيْعًا ۙ وَّاَنَّ اللّٰهَ شَدِيْدُ الْعَذَابِ ۞

166. When those who were followed shall renounce those who followed (them), and they see the chastisement and their ties are cut asunder.

اِذْ تَبَرَّاَ الَّذِيْنَ اتُّبِعُوْا مِنَ الَّذِيْنَ اتَّبَعُوْا وَرَاَوُا الْعَذَابَ وَتَقَطَّعَتْ بِهِمُ الْاَسْبَابُ ۞

167. And those who followed shall say: Had there been for us a return, then we would renounce them as they have renounced us. Thus will Allah show them their deeds to be intense regret to them, and they shall not come forth from the fire.

وَقَالَ الَّذِيْنَ اتَّبَعُوْا لَوْ اَنَّ لَنَا كَرَّةً فَنَتَبَرَّاَ مِنْهُمْ كَمَا تَبَرَّءُوْا مِنَّا ۗ كَذٰلِكَ يُرِيْهِمُ اللّٰهُ اَعْمَالَهُمْ حَسَرٰتٍ عَلَيْهِمْ ۗ وَمَا هُمْ بِخٰرِجِيْنَ مِنَ النَّارِ ۞

168. O men! eat the lawful and good things out of what is in the earth, and do not follow the footsteps of the Shaitan; surely he is your open enemy.

يٰۤاَيُّهَا النَّاسُ كُلُوْا مِمَّا فِى الْاَرْضِ حَلٰلًا طَيِّبًا ۖ وَّلَا تَتَّبِعُوْا خُطُوٰتِ الشَّيْطٰنِ ۗ اِنَّهُ لَكُمْ عَدُوٌّ مُّبِيْنٌ ۞

169. He only enjoins you evil and indecency, and that you may speak against Allah what you do not know.

اِنَّمَا يَاْمُرُكُمْ بِالسُّوْٓءِ وَالْفَحْشَآءِ وَاَنْ تَقُوْلُوْا عَلَى اللّٰهِ مَا لَا تَعْلَمُوْنَ ۞

170. And when it is said to them, Follow what Allah has revealed, they say: Nay! we follow what we found our fathers upon. What! and though their fathers had no sense at all, nor did they follow the right way.

وَاِذَا قِيْلَ لَهُمُ اتَّبِعُوْا مَا اَنْزَلَ اللّٰهُ قَالُوْا بَلْ نَتَّبِعُ مَا اَلْفَيْنَا عَلَيْهِ اٰبَآءَنَا ۗ اَوَلَوْ كَانَ اٰبَآؤُهُمْ لَا يَعْقِلُوْنَ شَيْئًا وَّلَا يَهْتَدُوْنَ ۞

171. And the parable of those who disbelieve is as the parable of one who calls out to that which hears no more than a call and a cry; deaf, dumb (and) blind, so they do not understand.

وَمَثَلُ الَّذِيْنَ كَفَرُوْا كَمَثَلِ الَّذِيْ يَنْعِقُ بِمَا لَا يَسْمَعُ اِلَّا دُعَآءً وَّنِدَآءً ۗ صُمٌّۢ بُكْمٌ عُمْيٌ فَهُمْ لَا يَعْقِلُوْنَ ۞

172. O you who believe! eat of the good things that We have provided you with, and give thanks to Allah if Him it is that you serve.

يٰٓاَيُّهَا الَّذِيْنَ اٰمَنُوْا كُلُوْا مِنْ طَيِّبٰتِ مَا رَزَقْنٰكُمْ وَاشْكُرُوْا لِلّٰهِ اِنْ كُنْتُمْ اِيَّاهُ تَعْبُدُوْنَ ۞

173. He has only forbidden you what dies of itself, and blood, and flesh of swine, and that over which any other (name) than (that of) Allah has been invoked; but whoever is driven to necessity, not desiring, nor exceeding the limit, no sin shall be upon him; surely Allah is Forgiving, Merciful.

اِنَّمَا حَرَّمَ عَلَيْكُمُ الْمَيْتَةَ وَالدَّمَ وَلَحْمَ الْخِنْزِيْرِ وَمَا اُهِلَّ بِهٖ لِغَيْرِ اللّٰهِ ۚ فَمَنِ اضْطُرَّ غَيْرَ بَاغٍ وَّلَا عَادٍ فَلَا اِثْمَ عَلَيْهِ ۗ اِنَّ اللّٰهَ غَفُوْرٌ رَّحِيْمٌ ۞

174. Surely those who conceal any part of the Book that Allah has revealed and take for it a small price, they eat nothing but fire into their bellies, and Allah will not speak to them on the day of resurrection, nor will He purify them, and they shall have a painful chastisement.

اِنَّ الَّذِيْنَ يَكْتُمُوْنَ مَا اَنْزَلَ اللّٰهُ مِنَ الْكِتٰبِ وَيَشْتَرُوْنَ بِهٖ ثَمَنًا قَلِيْلًا ۙ اُولٰٓئِكَ مَا يَاْكُلُوْنَ فِيْ بُطُوْنِهِمْ اِلَّا النَّارَ وَلَا يُكَلِّمُهُمُ اللّٰهُ يَوْمَ الْقِيٰمَةِ وَلَا يُزَكِّيْهِمْ ۖ وَلَهُمْ عَذَابٌ اَلِيْمٌ ۞

175. These are they who buy error for the right direction and chastisement for forgiveness; how bold they are to encounter fire.

اُولٰٓئِكَ الَّذِيْنَ اشْتَرَوُا الضَّلٰلَةَ بِالْهُدٰى وَالْعَذَابَ بِالْمَغْفِرَةِ ۚ فَمَا اَصْبَرَهُمْ عَلَى النَّارِ ۞

176. This is because Allah has revealed the Book with the truth; and surely those who go against the Book are in a great opposition.

ذٰلِكَ بِاَنَّ اللّٰهَ نَزَّلَ الْكِتٰبَ بِالْحَقِّ ۗ وَاِنَّ الَّذِيْنَ اخْتَلَفُوْا فِى الْكِتٰبِ لَفِيْ شِقَاقٍۭ بَعِيْدٍ ۞

177. It is not righteousness that you turn your faces towards the East and the West, but righteousness is this that one should believe in Allah and the last day and the angels and the Book and the prophets, and give away wealth out of love for Him to the near of kin and the orphans and the needy and the wayfarer and the beggars and for (the emancipation of) the captives, and keep up prayer and pay the poor-rate; and the performers of their promise when they make a promise, and the patient in distress and affliction and in time of conflicts— these are they who are true (to themselves) and these are they who guard (against evil).

178. O you who believe! retaliation is prescribed for you in the matter of the slain; the free for the free, and the slave for the slave, and the female for the female, but if any remission is made to any one by his (aggrieved) brother, then prosecution (for the bloodwit) should be made according to usage, and payment should be made to him in a good manner; this is an alleviation from your Lord and a mercy; so whoever exceeds the limit after this, he shall have a painful chastisement.

179. And there is life for you in (the law of) retaliation, O men of understanding, that you may guard yourselves.

180. Bequest is prescribed for you when death approaches one of you, if he leaves behind wealth for parents and near relatives, according to usage, a duty (incumbent) upon those who guard (against evil).

181. Whoever then alters it after he has heard it, the sin of it then is only upon those who alter it; surely Allah is Hearing, Knowing.

182. But he who fears an inclination to a wrong course or an act of disobedience on the part of the testator, and effects an agreement between the parties, there is no blame on him. Surely Allah is Forgiving, Merciful.

183. O you who believe! fasting is prescribed for you, as it was prescribed for those before you, so that you may guard (against evil).

لَيْسَ الْبِرَّ اَنْ تُوَلُّوْا وُجُوْهَكُمْ قِبَلَ الْمَشْرِقِ وَ الْمَغْرِبِ وَلٰكِنَّ الْبِرَّ مَنْ اٰمَنَ بِاللّٰهِ وَالْيَوْمِ الْاٰخِرِ وَالْمَلٰٓئِكَةِ وَالْكِتٰبِ وَالنَّبِيّٖنَ وَاٰتَى الْمَالَ عَلٰى حُبِّهٖ ذَوِى الْقُرْبٰى وَالْيَتٰمٰى وَالْمَسٰكِيْنَ وَابْنَ السَّبِيْلِ وَالسَّآئِلِيْنَ وَفِى الرِّقَابِ وَاَقَامَ الصَّلٰوةَ وَاٰتَى الزَّكٰوةَ وَالْمُوْفُوْنَ بِعَهْدِهِمْ اِذَا عَاهَدُوْا وَالصّٰبِرِيْنَ فِى الْبَأْسَآءِ وَالضَّرَّآءِ وَحِيْنَ الْبَأْسِ اُولٰٓئِكَ الَّذِيْنَ صَدَقُوْا وَاُولٰٓئِكَ هُمُ الْمُتَّقُوْنَ ۝

يٰٓاَيُّهَا الَّذِيْنَ اٰمَنُوْا كُتِبَ عَلَيْكُمُ الْقِصَاصُ فِى الْقَتْلٰى اَلْحُرُّ بِالْحُرِّ وَالْعَبْدُ بِالْعَبْدِ وَالْاُنْثٰى بِالْاُنْثٰى فَمَنْ عُفِيَ لَهٗ مِنْ اَخِيْهِ شَيْءٌ فَاتِّبَاعٌ بِالْمَعْرُوْفِ وَاَدَآءٌ اِلَيْهِ بِاِحْسَانٍ ذٰلِكَ تَخْفِيْفٌ مِّنْ رَّبِّكُمْ وَرَحْمَةٌ فَمَنِ اعْتَدٰى بَعْدَ ذٰلِكَ فَلَهٗ عَذَابٌ اَلِيْمٌ ۝

وَلَكُمْ فِى الْقِصَاصِ حَيٰوةٌ يّٰٓاُولِى الْاَلْبَابِ لَعَلَّكُمْ تَتَّقُوْنَ ۝ كُتِبَ عَلَيْكُمْ اِذَا حَضَرَ اَحَدَكُمُ الْمَوْتُ اِنْ تَرَكَ خَيْرًا ۙالْوَصِيَّةُ لِلْوَالِدَيْنِ وَالْاَقْرَبِيْنَ بِالْمَعْرُوْفِ حَقًّا عَلَى الْمُتَّقِيْنَ ۝

فَمَنْ بَدَّلَهٗ بَعْدَ مَا سَمِعَهٗ فَاِنَّمَآ اِثْمُهٗ عَلَى الَّذِيْنَ يُبَدِّلُوْنَهٗ اِنَّ اللّٰهَ سَمِيْعٌ عَلِيْمٌ ۝

فَمَنْ خَافَ مِنْ مُّوْصٍ جَنَفًا اَوْ اِثْمًا فَاَصْلَحَ بَيْنَهُمْ فَلَا اِثْمَ عَلَيْهِ اِنَّ اللّٰهَ غَفُوْرٌ رَّحِيْمٌ ۝

يٰٓاَيُّهَا الَّذِيْنَ اٰمَنُوْا كُتِبَ عَلَيْكُمُ الصِّيَامُ كَمَا كُتِبَ عَلَى الَّذِيْنَ مِنْ قَبْلِكُمْ لَعَلَّكُمْ تَتَّقُوْنَ ۝

184. For a certain number of days; but whoever among you is sick or on a journey, then (he shall fast) a (like) number of other days; and those who are not able to do it may effect a redemption by feeding a poor man; so whoever does good spontaneously it is better for him; and that you fast is better for you if you know.

185. The month of Ramazan is that in which the Quran was revealed, a guidance to men and clear proofs of the guidance and the distinction; therefore whoever of you is present in the month, he shall fast therein, and whoever is sick or upon a journey, then (he shall fast) a (like) number of other days; Allah desires ease for you, and He does not desire for you difficulty, and (He desires) that you should complete the number and that you should exalt the greatness of Allah for His having guided you and that you may give thanks.

186. And when My servants ask you concerning Me, then surely I am very near; I answer the prayer of the suppliant when he calls on Me, so they should answer My call and believe in Me that they may walk in the right way.

187. It is made lawful to you to go into your wives on the night of the fast; they are an apparel for you and you are an apparel for them; Allah knew that you acted unfaithfully to yourselves, so He has turned to you (mercifully) and removed from you (this burden); so now be in contact with them and seek what Allah has ordained for you, and eat and drink until the whiteness of the day becomes distinct from the blackness of the night at dawn, then complete the fast till night, and have not contact with them while you keep to the mosques; these are the limits of Allah, so do not go near them. Thus does Allah make clear His communications for men that they may guard (against evil).

أَيَّامًا مَّعْدُوْدٰتٍ ۚ فَمَنْ كَانَ مِنْكُمْ مَّرِيْضًا أَوْ عَلٰى سَفَرٍ فَعِدَّةٌ مِّنْ أَيَّامٍ أُخَرَ ۚ وَعَلَى الَّذِيْنَ يُطِيْقُوْنَهُ فِدْيَةٌ طَعَامُ مِسْكِيْنٍ ۚ فَمَنْ تَطَوَّعَ خَيْرًا فَهُوَ خَيْرٌ لَّهُ ۚ وَأَنْ تَصُوْمُوْا خَيْرٌ لَّكُمْ إِنْ كُنْتُمْ تَعْلَمُوْنَ ۝

شَهْرُ رَمَضَانَ الَّذِيْ أُنْزِلَ فِيْهِ الْقُرْاٰنُ هُدًى لِّلنَّاسِ وَبَيِّنٰتٍ مِّنَ الْهُدٰى وَالْفُرْقَانِ ۚ فَمَنْ شَهِدَ مِنْكُمُ الشَّهْرَ فَلْيَصُمْهُ ۚ وَمَنْ كَانَ مَرِيْضًا أَوْ عَلٰى سَفَرٍ فَعِدَّةٌ مِّنْ أَيَّامٍ أُخَرَ ۚ يُرِيْدُ اللّٰهُ بِكُمُ الْيُسْرَ وَلَا يُرِيْدُ بِكُمُ الْعُسْرَ ۚ وَلِتُكْمِلُوا الْعِدَّةَ وَلِتُكَبِّرُوا اللّٰهَ عَلٰى مَا هَدٰىكُمْ وَلَعَلَّكُمْ تَشْكُرُوْنَ ۝

وَإِذَا سَأَلَكَ عِبَادِيْ عَنِّيْ فَإِنِّيْ قَرِيْبٌ ۚ أُجِيْبُ دَعْوَةَ الدَّاعِ إِذَا دَعَانِ ۙ فَلْيَسْتَجِيْبُوْا لِيْ وَلْيُؤْمِنُوْا بِيْ لَعَلَّهُمْ يَرْشُدُوْنَ ۝

أُحِلَّ لَكُمْ لَيْلَةَ الصِّيَامِ الرَّفَثُ إِلٰى نِسَائِكُمْ ۚ هُنَّ لِبَاسٌ لَّكُمْ وَأَنْتُمْ لِبَاسٌ لَّهُنَّ ۗ عَلِمَ اللّٰهُ أَنَّكُمْ كُنْتُمْ تَخْتَانُوْنَ أَنْفُسَكُمْ فَتَابَ عَلَيْكُمْ وَعَفَا عَنْكُمْ ۖ فَالْاٰنَ بَاشِرُوْهُنَّ وَابْتَغُوْا مَا كَتَبَ اللّٰهُ لَكُمْ ۚ وَكُلُوْا وَاشْرَبُوْا حَتّٰى يَتَبَيَّنَ لَكُمُ الْخَيْطُ الْأَبْيَضُ مِنَ الْخَيْطِ الْأَسْوَدِ مِنَ الْفَجْرِ ۖ ثُمَّ أَتِمُّوا الصِّيَامَ إِلَى الَّيْلِ ۚ وَلَا تُبَاشِرُوْهُنَّ وَأَنْتُمْ عٰكِفُوْنَ فِي الْمَسٰجِدِ ۗ تِلْكَ حُدُوْدُ اللّٰهِ فَلَا تَقْرَبُوْهَا ۗ كَذٰلِكَ يُبَيِّنُ اللّٰهُ اٰيٰتِهِ لِلنَّاسِ لَعَلَّهُمْ يَتَّقُوْنَ ۝

25

188. And do not swallow up your property among yourselves by false means, neither seek to gain access thereby to the judges, so that you may swallow up a part of the property of men wrongfully while you know.

189. They ask you concerning the new moon. Say: They are times appointed for (the benefit of) men, and (for) the pilgrimage; and it is not righteousness that you should enter the houses at their backs, but righteousness is this that one should guard (against evil); and go into the houses by their doors and be careful (of your duty) to Allah, that you may be successful.

190. And fight in the way of Allah with those who fight with you, and do not exceed the limits, surely Allah does not love those who exceed the limits.

191. And kill them wherever you find them, and drive them out from whence they drove you out, and persecution is severer than slaughter, and do not fight with them at the Sacred Mosque until they fight with you in it, but if they do fight you, then slay them; such is the recompense of the unbelievers.

192. But if they desist, then surely Allah is Forgiving, Merciful.

193. And fight with them until there is no persecution, and religion should be only for Allah, but if they desist, then there should be no hostility except against the oppressors.

194. The Sacred month for the sacred month and all sacred things are (under the law of) retaliation; whoever then acts aggressively against you, inflict injury on him according to the injury he has inflicted on you and be careful (of your duty) to Allah and know that Allah is with those who guard (against evil).

195. And spend in the way of Allah and cast not yourselves to perdition with your own hands, and do good (to others); surely Allah loves the doers of good.

وَلَا تَأْكُلُوٓا اَمْوَالَكُمْ بَيْنَكُمْ بِالْبَاطِلِ وَتُدْلُوْا بِهَاۤ اِلَى الْحُكَّامِ لِتَأْكُلُوْا فَرِيْقًا مِّنْ اَمْوَالِ النَّاسِ بِالْاِثْمِ وَاَنْتُمْ تَعْلَمُوْنَ ۧ ۝

يَسْـَٔلُوْنَكَ عَنِ الْاَهِلَّةِ ۭ قُلْ هِيَ مَوَاقِيْتُ لِلنَّاسِ وَالْحَجِّ ۭ وَلَيْسَ الْبِرُّ بِاَنْ تَأْتُوا الْبُيُوْتَ مِنْ ظُهُوْرِهَا وَلٰكِنَّ الْبِرَّ مَنِ اتَّقٰى ۚ وَاْتُوا الْبُيُوْتَ مِنْ اَبْوَابِهَا ۚ وَاتَّقُوا اللّٰهَ لَعَلَّكُمْ تُفْلِحُوْنَ ۝

وَقَاتِلُوْا فِيْ سَبِيْلِ اللّٰهِ الَّذِيْنَ يُقَاتِلُوْنَكُمْ وَلَا تَعْتَدُوْا ۭ اِنَّ اللّٰهَ لَا يُحِبُّ الْمُعْتَدِيْنَ ۝

وَاقْتُلُوْهُمْ حَيْثُ ثَقِفْتُمُوْهُمْ وَاَخْرِجُوْهُمْ مِّنْ حَيْثُ اَخْرَجُوْكُمْ وَالْفِتْنَةُ اَشَدُّ مِنَ الْقَتْلِ ۚ وَ لَا تُقَاتِلُوْهُمْ عِنْدَ الْمَسْجِدِ الْحَرَامِ حَتّٰى يُقَاتِلُوْكُمْ فِيْهِ ۚ فَاِنْ قٰتَلُوْكُمْ فَاقْتُلُوْهُمْ ۭ كَذٰلِكَ جَزَاۤءُ الْكٰفِرِيْنَ ۝

فَاِنِ انْتَهَوْا فَاِنَّ اللّٰهَ غَفُوْرٌ رَّحِيْمٌ ۝

وَقٰتِلُوْهُمْ حَتّٰى لَا تَكُوْنَ فِتْنَةٌ وَّيَكُوْنَ الدِّيْنُ لِلّٰهِ ۭ فَاِنِ انْتَهَوْا فَلَا عُدْوَانَ اِلَّا عَلَى الظّٰلِمِيْنَ ۝

اَلشَّهْرُ الْحَرَامُ بِالشَّهْرِ الْحَرَامِ وَالْحُرُمٰتُ قِصَاصٌ ۭ فَمَنِ اعْتَدٰى عَلَيْكُمْ فَاعْتَدُوْا عَلَيْهِ بِمِثْلِ مَا اعْتَدٰى عَلَيْكُمْ ۪ وَاتَّقُوا اللّٰهَ وَاعْلَمُوْٓا اَنَّ اللّٰهَ مَعَ الْمُتَّقِيْنَ ۝

وَاَنْفِقُوْا فِيْ سَبِيْلِ اللّٰهِ وَلَا تُلْقُوْا بِاَيْدِيْكُمْ اِلَى التَّهْلُكَةِ ۛ ۚ وَاَحْسِنُوْا ۛ اِنَّ اللّٰهَ يُحِبُّ الْمُحْسِنِيْنَ ۝

196. And accomplish the pilgrimage and the visit for Allah, but if you are prevented, (send) whatever offering is easy to obtain, and do not shave your heads until the offering reaches its destination; but whoever among you is sick or has an ailment of the head, he (should effect) a compensation by fasting or alms or sacrificing; then when you are secure, whoever profits by combining the visit with the pilgrimage (should take) what offering is easy to obtain; but he who cannot find (any offering) should fast for three days during the pilgrimage and for seven days when you return; these (make) ten (days) complete; this is for him whose family is not present in the Sacred Mosque, and be careful (of your duty) to Allah, and know that Allah is severe in requiting (evil).

197. The pilgrimage is (performed in) the well-known months; so whoever determines the performance of the pilgrimage therein, there shall be no intercourse nor fornication nor quarrelling amongst one another; and whatever good you do, Allah knows it; and make provision, for surely the provision is the guarding of oneself, and be careful (of your duty) to Me, O men of understanding.

198. There is no blame on you in seeking bounty from your Lord, so when you hasten on from "Arafat", then remember Allah near the Holy Monument, and remember Him as He has guided you, though before that you were certainly of the erring ones.

199. Then hasten on from the Place from which the people hasten on and ask the forgiveness of Allah; surely Allah is Forgiving, Merciful.

200. So when you have performed your devotions, then laud Allah as you lauded your fathers, rather a greater lauding. But there are some people who say, Our Lord! give us in the world, and they shall have no resting place.

27

201. And there are some among them who say: Our Lord! grant us good in this world and good in the hereafter, and save us from the chastisement of the fire.

202. They shall have (their) portion of what they have earned, and Allah is swift in reckoning.

203. And laud Allah during the numbered days; then whoever hastens off in two days, there is no blame on him, and whoever remains behind, there is no blame on him, (this is) for him who guards (against evil), and be careful (of your duty) to Allah, and know that you shall be gathered together to Him.

204. And among men is he whose speech about the life of this world causes you to wonder, and he calls on Allah to witness as to what is in his heart, yet he is the most violent of adversaries.

205. And when he turns back, he runs along in the land that he may cause mischief in it and destroy the tilth and the stock, and Allah does not love mischief-making.

206. And when it is said to him, guard against (the punishment of) Allah; pride carries him off to sin; therefore hell is sufficient for him; and certainly it is an evil resting place.

207. And among men is he who sells himself to seek the pleasure of Allah; and Allah is Affectionate to the servants.

208. O you who believe! enter into submission one and all, and do not follow the footsteps of Shaitan; surely he is your open enemy.

209. But if you slip after clear arguments have come to you, then know that Allah is Mighty, Wise.

210. They do not wait aught but that Allah should come to them in the shadows of the clouds along with the angels, and the matter has (already) been decided; and (all) matters are returned to Allah.

وَمِنْهُمْ مَّنْ يَّقُوْلُ رَبَّنَآ اٰتِنَا فِى الدُّنْيَا حَسَنَةً وَّفِى الْاٰخِرَةِ حَسَنَةً وَّقِنَا عَذَابَ النَّارِ ۝

اُولٰٓئِكَ لَهُمْ نَصِيْبٌ مِّمَّا كَسَبُوْا ۚ وَاللّٰهُ سَرِيْعُ الْحِسَابِ ۝

وَاذْكُرُوا اللّٰهَ فِىْۤ اَيَّامٍ مَّعْدُوْدٰتٍ ۚ فَمَنْ تَعَجَّلَ فِىْ يَوْمَيْنِ فَلَاۤ اِثْمَ عَلَيْهِ ۚ وَمَنْ تَاَخَّرَ فَلَاۤ اِثْمَ عَلَيْهِ ۙ لِمَنِ اتَّقٰى ۗ وَاتَّقُوا اللّٰهَ وَاعْلَمُوْۤا اَنَّكُمْ اِلَيْهِ تُحْشَرُوْنَ ۝

وَمِنَ النَّاسِ مَنْ يُّعْجِبُكَ قَوْلُهٗ فِى الْحَيٰوةِ الدُّنْيَا وَيُشْهِدُ اللّٰهَ عَلٰى مَا فِىْ قَلْبِهٖ ۙ وَهُوَ اَلَدُّ الْخِصَامِ ۝

وَاِذَا تَوَلّٰى سَعٰى فِى الْاَرْضِ لِيُفْسِدَ فِيْهَا وَيُهْلِكَ الْحَرْثَ وَالنَّسْلَ ۗ وَاللّٰهُ لَا يُحِبُّ الْفَسَادَ ۝

وَاِذَا قِيْلَ لَهُ اتَّقِ اللّٰهَ اَخَذَتْهُ الْعِزَّةُ بِالْاِثْمِ فَحَسْبُهٗ جَهَنَّمُ ۗ وَلَبِئْسَ الْمِهَادُ ۝

وَمِنَ النَّاسِ مَنْ يَّشْرِىْ نَفْسَهُ ابْتِغَآءَ مَرْضَاتِ اللّٰهِ ۗ وَاللّٰهُ رَءُوْفٌۢ بِالْعِبَادِ ۝

يٰۤاَيُّهَا الَّذِيْنَ اٰمَنُوا ادْخُلُوْا فِى السِّلْمِ كَآفَّةً ۖ وَّلَا تَتَّبِعُوْا خُطُوٰتِ الشَّيْطٰنِ ۗ اِنَّهٗ لَكُمْ عَدُوٌّ مُّبِيْنٌ ۝

فَاِنْ زَلَلْتُمْ مِّنْۢ بَعْدِ مَا جَآءَتْكُمُ الْبَيِّنٰتُ فَاعْلَمُوْۤا اَنَّ اللّٰهَ عَزِيْزٌ حَكِيْمٌ ۝

هَلْ يَنْظُرُوْنَ اِلَّاۤ اَنْ يَّاْتِيَهُمُ اللّٰهُ فِىْ ظُلَلٍ مِّنَ الْغَمَامِ وَالْمَلٰٓئِكَةُ وَقُضِىَ الْاَمْرُ ۗ وَاِلَى اللّٰهِ تُرْجَعُ الْاُمُوْرُ ۞

211. Ask the Israelites how many a clear sign have We given them; and whoever changes the favor of Allah after it has come to him, then surely Allah is severe in requiting (evil).

سَلْ بَنِيْ اِسْرَآءِيْلَ كَمْ اٰتَيْنٰهُمْ مِّنْ اٰيَةٍ بَيِّنَةٍ ؕ وَمَنْ يُّبَدِّلْ نِعْمَةَ اللّٰهِ مِنْ بَعْدِ مَاجَآءَتْهُ فَاِنَّ اللّٰهَ شَدِيْدُ الْعِقَابِ ۞

212. The life of this world is made to seem fair to those who disbelieve, and they mock those who believe, and those who guard (against evil) shall be above them on the day of resurrection; and Allah gives means of subsistence to whom he pleases without measure.

زُيِّنَ لِلَّذِيْنَ كَفَرُوا الْحَيٰوةُ الدُّنْيَا وَيَسْخَرُوْنَ مِنَ الَّذِيْنَ اٰمَنُوْا ؕ وَالَّذِيْنَ اتَّقَوْا فَوْقَهُمْ يَوْمَ الْقِيٰمَةِ ؕ وَاللّٰهُ يَرْزُقُ مَنْ يَّشَآءُ بِغَيْرِ حِسَابٍ ۞

213. (All) people are a single nation; so Allah raised prophets as bearers of good news and as warners, and He revealed with them the Book with truth, that it might judge between people in that in which they differed; and none but the very people who were given it differed about it after clear arguments had come to them, revolting among themselves; so Allah has guided by His will those who believe to the truth about which they differed; and Allah guides whom He pleases to the right path.

كَانَ النَّاسُ اُمَّةً وَّاحِدَةً ۟ فَبَعَثَ اللّٰهُ النَّبِيّٖنَ مُبَشِّرِيْنَ وَمُنْذِرِيْنَ ۪ وَاَنْزَلَ مَعَهُمُ الْكِتٰبَ بِالْحَقِّ لِيَحْكُمَ بَيْنَ النَّاسِ فِيْمَا اخْتَلَفُوْا فِيْهِ ؕ وَمَا اخْتَلَفَ فِيْهِ اِلَّا الَّذِيْنَ اُوْتُوْهُ مِنْ بَعْدِ مَاجَآءَتْهُمُ الْبَيِّنٰتُ بَغْيًا بَيْنَهُمْ ۚ فَهَدَى اللّٰهُ الَّذِيْنَ اٰمَنُوْا لِمَا اخْتَلَفُوْا فِيْهِ مِنَ الْحَقِّ بِاِذْنِهٖ ؕ وَاللّٰهُ يَهْدِيْ مَنْ يَّشَآءُ اِلٰى صِرَاطٍ مُّسْتَقِيْمٍ ۞

214. Or do you think that you would enter the garden while yet the state of those who have passed away before you has not come upon you; distress and affliction befell them and they were shaken violently, so that the Apostle and those who believed with him said: When will the help of Allah come? Now surely the help of Allah is nigh!

اَمْ حَسِبْتُمْ اَنْ تَدْخُلُوا الْجَنَّةَ وَلَمَّا يَاْتِكُمْ مَّثَلُ الَّذِيْنَ خَلَوْا مِنْ قَبْلِكُمْ ؕ مَسَّتْهُمُ الْبَاْسَآءُ وَالضَّرَّآءُ وَزُلْزِلُوْا حَتّٰى يَقُوْلَ الرَّسُوْلُ وَالَّذِيْنَ اٰمَنُوْا مَعَهُ مَتٰى نَصْرُ اللّٰهِ ؕ اَلَاۤ اِنَّ نَصْرَ اللّٰهِ قَرِيْبٌ ۞

215. They ask you as to what they should spend. Say: Whatever wealth you spend, it is for the parents and the near of kin and the orphans and the needy and the wayfarer, and whatever good you do, Allah surely knows it.

يَسْـَٔلُوْنَكَ مَاذَا يُنْفِقُوْنَ ؕ قُلْ مَاۤ اَنْفَقْتُمْ مِّنْ خَيْرٍ فَلِلْوَالِدَيْنِ وَالْاَقْرَبِيْنَ وَالْيَتٰمٰى وَالْمَسٰكِيْنِ وَابْنِ السَّبِيْلِ ؕ وَمَا تَفْعَلُوْا مِنْ خَيْرٍ فَاِنَّ اللّٰهَ بِهٖ عَلِيْمٌ ۞

29

216. Fighting is enjoined on you, and it is an object of dislike to you; and it may be that you dislike a thing while it is good for you, and it may be that you love a thing while it is evil for you, and Allah knows, while you do not know.

كُتِبَ عَلَيْكُمُ الْقِتَالُ وَهُوَكُرْهٌ لَّكُمْ وَعَسَى أَنْ تَكْرَهُوْا شَيْئًا وَّهُوَ خَيْرٌ لَّكُمْ وَعَسَى أَنْ تُحِبُّوْا شَيْئًا وَّهُوَ شَرٌّ لَّكُمْ وَاللّٰهُ يَعْلَمُ وَأَنْتُمْ لَا تَعْلَمُوْنَ ۞

217. They ask you concerning the sacred month about fighting in it. Say: Fighting in it is a grave matter, and hindering (men) from Allah's way and denying Him, and (hindering men from) the Sacred Mosque and turning its people out of it, are still graver with Allah, and persecution is graver than slaughter; and they will not cease fighting with you until they turn you back from your religion, if they can; and whoever of you turns back from his religion, then he dies while an unbeliever— these it is whose works shall go for nothing in this world and the hereafter, and they are the inmates of the fire; therein they shall abide.

يَسْـَٔلُوْنَكَ عَنِ الشَّهْرِ الْحَرَامِ قِتَالٍ فِيْهِ قُلْ قِتَالٌ فِيْهِ كَبِيْرٌ وَصَدٌّ عَنْ سَبِيْلِ اللّٰهِ وَكُفْرٌ بِهٖ وَ الْمَسْجِدِ الْحَرَامِ وَإِخْرَاجُ أَهْلِهٖ مِنْهُ أَكْبَرُ عِنْدَ اللّٰهِ وَالْفِتْنَةُ أَكْبَرُ مِنَ الْقَتْلِ وَلَا يَزَالُوْنَ يُقَاتِلُوْنَكُمْ حَتّٰى يَرُدُّوْكُمْ عَنْ دِيْنِكُمْ إِنِ اسْتَطَاعُوْا وَمَنْ يَّرْتَدِدْ مِنْكُمْ عَنْ دِيْنِهٖ فَيَمُتْ وَهُوَ كَافِرٌ فَأُولٰٓئِكَ حَبِطَتْ أَعْمَالُهُمْ فِى الدُّنْيَا وَالْاٰخِرَةِ وَأُولٰٓئِكَ أَصْحَابُ النَّارِ هُمْ فِيْهَا خَالِدُوْنَ ۞

218. Surely those who believed and those who fled (their home) and strove hard in the way of Allah these hope for the mercy of Allah and Allah is Forgiving, Merciful.

إِنَّ الَّذِيْنَ اٰمَنُوْا وَالَّذِيْنَ هَاجَرُوْا وَجَاهَدُوْا فِىْ سَبِيْلِ اللّٰهِ أُولٰٓئِكَ يَرْجُوْنَ رَحْمَتَ اللّٰهِ وَاللّٰهُ غَفُوْرٌ رَّحِيْمٌ ۞

219. They ask you about intoxicants and games of chance. Say: In both of them there is a great sin and means of profit for men, and their sin is greater than their profit. And they ask you as to what they should spend. Say: What you can spare. Thus does Allah make clear to you the communications, that you may ponder,

يَسْـَٔلُوْنَكَ عَنِ الْخَمْرِ وَالْمَيْسِرِ قُلْ فِيْهِمَا إِثْمٌ كَبِيْرٌ وَّمَنَافِعُ لِلنَّاسِ وَإِثْمُهُمَا أَكْبَرُ مِنْ نَّفْعِهِمَا وَيَسْـَٔلُوْنَكَ مَاذَا يُنْفِقُوْنَ قُلِ الْعَفْوَ كَذٰلِكَ يُبَيِّنُ اللّٰهُ لَكُمُ الْاٰيٰتِ لَعَلَّكُمْ تَتَفَكَّرُوْنَ ۞

220. On this world and the hereafter. And they ask you concerning the orphans Say: To set right for them (their affairs) is good, and if you become co-partners with them, they are your brethren; and Allah knows the mischief-maker and the peace-maker; and if Allah had pleased, He would certainly have caused you to fall into a difficulty; surely Allah is Mighty, Wise.

فِى الدُّنْيَا وَالْاٰخِرَةِ وَيَسْـَٔلُوْنَكَ عَنِ الْيَتٰمٰى قُلْ إِصْلَاحٌ لَّهُمْ خَيْرٌ وَإِنْ تُخَالِطُوْهُمْ فَإِخْوَانُكُمْ وَاللّٰهُ يَعْلَمُ الْمُفْسِدَ مِنَ الْمُصْلِحِ وَلَوْ شَاءَ اللّٰهُ لَأَعْنَتَكُمْ إِنَّ اللّٰهَ عَزِيْزٌ حَكِيْمٌ ۞

221. And do not marry the idolatresses until they believe, and certainly a believing maid is better than an idolatress woman, even though she should please you; and do not give (believing women) in marriage to idolaters until they believe, and certainly a believing servant is better than an idolater, even though he should please you; these invite to the fire, and Allah invites to the garden and to forgiveness by His will, and makes clear His communications to men, that they may be mindful.

وَلَا تَنْكِحُوا الْمُشْرِكٰتِ حَتّٰى يُؤْمِنَّ وَلَأَمَةٌ مُؤْمِنَةٌ خَيْرٌ مِنْ مُشْرِكَةٍ وَّلَوْ اَعْجَبَتْكُمْ وَلَا تُنْكِحُوا الْمُشْرِكِيْنَ حَتّٰى يُؤْمِنُوْا وَلَعَبْدٌ مُؤْمِنٌ خَيْرٌ مِنْ مُشْرِكٍ وَّلَوْ اَعْجَبَكُمْ اُولٰئِكَ يَدْعُوْنَ اِلَى النَّارِ وَاللّٰهُ يَدْعُوْا اِلَى الْجَنَّةِ وَالْمَغْفِرَةِ بِاِذْنِهٖ وَيُبَيِّنُ اٰيٰتِهٖ لِلنَّاسِ لَعَلَّهُمْ يَتَذَكَّرُوْنَ ۝

222. And they ask you about menstruation. Say: It is a discomfort; therefore keep aloof from the women during the menstrual discharge and do not go near them until they have become clean; then when they have cleansed themselves, go in to them as Allah has commanded you; surely Allah loves those who turn much (to Him), and He loves those who purify themselves.

وَيَسْئَلُوْنَكَ عَنِ الْمَحِيْضِ قُلْ هُوَ اَذًى فَاعْتَزِلُوا النِّسَآءَ فِي الْمَحِيْضِ وَلَا تَقْرَبُوْهُنَّ حَتّٰى يَطْهُرْنَ فَاِذَا تَطَهَّرْنَ فَأْتُوْهُنَّ مِنْ حَيْثُ اَمَرَكُمُ اللّٰهُ اِنَّ اللّٰهَ يُحِبُّ التَّوَّابِيْنَ وَيُحِبُّ الْمُتَطَهِّرِيْنَ ۝

223. Your wives are a tilth for you, so go into your tilth when you like, and do good beforehand for yourselves; and be careful (of your duty) to Allah, and know that you will meet Him, and give good news to the believers.

نِسَآؤُكُمْ حَرْثٌ لَّكُمْ فَأْتُوْا حَرْثَكُمْ اَنّٰى شِئْتُمْ وَقَدِّمُوْا لِاَنْفُسِكُمْ وَاتَّقُوا اللّٰهَ وَاعْلَمُوْا اَنَّكُمْ مُّلٰقُوْهُ وَبَشِّرِ الْمُؤْمِنِيْنَ ۝

224. And make not Allah because of your swearing (by Him) an obstacle to your doing good and guarding (against evil) and making peace between men, and Allah is Hearing, Knowing.

وَلَا تَجْعَلُوا اللّٰهَ عُرْضَةً لِّاَيْمَانِكُمْ اَنْ تَبَرُّوْا وَتَتَّقُوْا وَتُصْلِحُوْا بَيْنَ النَّاسِ وَاللّٰهُ سَمِيْعٌ عَلِيْمٌ ۝

225. Allah does not call you to account for what is vain in your oaths, but He will call you to account for what your hearts have earned, and Allah is Forgiving, Forbearing.

لَا يُؤَاخِذُكُمُ اللّٰهُ بِاللَّغْوِ فِيْ اَيْمَانِكُمْ وَلٰكِنْ يُّؤَاخِذُكُمْ بِمَا كَسَبَتْ قُلُوْبُكُمْ وَاللّٰهُ غَفُوْرٌ حَلِيْمٌ ۝

226. Those who swear that they will not go in to their wives should wait four months; so if they go back, then Allah is surely Forgiving, Merciful.

لِلَّذِيْنَ يُؤْلُوْنَ مِنْ نِّسَآئِهِمْ تَرَبُّصُ اَرْبَعَةِ اَشْهُرٍ فَاِنْ فَآءُوْ فَاِنَّ اللّٰهَ غَفُوْرٌ رَّحِيْمٌ ۝

227. And if they have resolved on a divorce, then Allah is surely Hearing, Knowing.

وَاِنْ عَزَمُوا الطَّلَاقَ فَاِنَّ اللّٰهَ سَمِيْعٌ عَلِيْمٌ ۝

31

228. And the divorced women should keep themselves in waiting for three courses; and it is not lawful for them that they should conceal what Allah has created in their wombs, if they believe in Allah and the last day; and their husbands have a better right to take them back in the meanwhile if they wish for reconciliation; and they have rights similar to those against them in a just manner, and the men are a degree above them, and Allah is Mighty, Wise.

وَالْمُطَلَّقٰتُ يَتَرَبَّصْنَ بِأَنْفُسِهِنَّ ثَلٰثَةَ قُرُوْءٍ ۚ وَلَا يَحِلُّ لَهُنَّ أَنْ يَّكْتُمْنَ مَا خَلَقَ اللّٰهُ فِىْٓ أَرْحَامِهِنَّ اِنْ كُنَّ يُؤْمِنَّ بِاللّٰهِ وَالْيَوْمِ الْاٰخِرِ ۚ وَبُعُوْلَتُهُنَّ أَحَقُّ بِرَدِّهِنَّ فِىْ ذٰلِكَ اِنْ اَرَادُوْٓا اِصْلَاحًا ۚ وَلَهُنَّ مِثْلُ الَّذِىْ عَلَيْهِنَّ بِالْمَعْرُوْفِ ۖ وَلِلرِّجَالِ عَلَيْهِنَّ دَرَجَةٌ ۗ وَاللّٰهُ عَزِيْزٌ حَكِيْمٌ ۞

229. Divorce may be (pronounced) twice; then keep (them) in good fellowship or let (them) go with kindness; and it is not lawful for you to take any part of what you have given them, unless both fear that they cannot keep within the limits of Allah; then if you fear that they cannot keep within the limits of Allah, there is no blame on them for what she gives up to become free thereby. These are the limits of Allah, so do not exceed them, and whoever exceeds the limits of Allah these it is that are the unjust.

اَلطَّلَاقُ مَرَّتٰنِ ۖ فَاِمْسَاكٌ بِمَعْرُوْفٍ اَوْ تَسْرِيْحٌ بِاِحْسَانٍ ۗ وَلَا يَحِلُّ لَكُمْ اَنْ تَأْخُذُوْا مِمَّآ اٰتَيْتُمُوْهُنَّ شَيْئًا اِلَّآ اَنْ يَّخَافَآ اَلَّا يُقِيْمَا حُدُوْدَ اللّٰهِ ۚ فَاِنْ خِفْتُمْ اَلَّا يُقِيْمَا حُدُوْدَ اللّٰهِ ۙ فَلَا جُنَاحَ عَلَيْهِمَا فِيْمَا افْتَدَتْ بِهٖ ۗ تِلْكَ حُدُوْدُ اللّٰهِ فَلَا تَعْتَدُوْهَا ۚ وَمَنْ يَّتَعَدَّ حُدُوْدَ اللّٰهِ فَاُولٰٓئِكَ هُمُ الظّٰلِمُوْنَ ۞

230. So if he divorces her she shall not be lawful to him afterwards until she marries another husband; then if he divorces her there is no blame on them both if they return to each other (by marriage), if they think that they can keep within the limits of Allah, and these are the limits of Allah which He makes clear for a people who know.

فَاِنْ طَلَّقَهَا فَلَا تَحِلُّ لَهٗ مِنْ بَعْدُ حَتّٰى تَنْكِحَ زَوْجًا غَيْرَهٗ ۗ فَاِنْ طَلَّقَهَا فَلَا جُنَاحَ عَلَيْهِمَآ اَنْ يَّتَرَاجَعَآ اِنْ ظَنَّآ اَنْ يُّقِيْمَا حُدُوْدَ اللّٰهِ ۗ وَتِلْكَ حُدُوْدُ اللّٰهِ يُبَيِّنُهَا لِقَوْمٍ يَّعْلَمُوْنَ ۞

231. And when you divorce women and they reach their prescribed time, then either retain them in good fellowship or set them free with liberality, and do not retain them for injury, so that you exceed the limits, and whoever does this, he indeed is unjust to his own soul; and do not take Allah's communications for a mockery, and remember the favor of Allah upon you, and that which He has revealed to you of the Book and the Wisdom, admonishing you thereby; and be careful (of your duty to) Allah, and know that Allah is the Knower of all things.

وَاِذَا طَلَّقْتُمُ النِّسَاءَ فَبَلَغْنَ اَجَلَهُنَّ فَاَمْسِكُوْهُنَّ بِمَعْرُوْفٍ اَوْ سَرِّحُوْهُنَّ بِمَعْرُوْفٍ ۚ وَلَا تُمْسِكُوْهُنَّ ضِرَارًا لِّتَعْتَدُوْا ۚ وَمَنْ يَّفْعَلْ ذٰلِكَ فَقَدْ ظَلَمَ نَفْسَهٗ ۚ وَلَا تَتَّخِذُوْٓا اٰيٰتِ اللّٰهِ هُزُوًا ۖ وَّاذْكُرُوْا نِعْمَتَ اللّٰهِ عَلَيْكُمْ وَمَآ اَنْزَلَ عَلَيْكُمْ مِّنَ الْكِتٰبِ وَالْحِكْمَةِ يَعِظُكُمْ بِهٖ ۚ وَاتَّقُوا اللّٰهَ وَاعْلَمُوْٓا اَنَّ اللّٰهَ بِكُلِّ شَيْءٍ عَلِيْمٌ ۞

232. And when you have divorced women and they have ended their term (of waiting), then do not prevent them from marrying their husbands when they agree among themselves in a lawful manner; with this is admonished he among you who believes in Allah and the last day, this is more profitable and purer for you; and Allah knows while you do not know.

233. And the mothers should suckle their children for two whole years for him who desires to make complete the time of suckling; and their maintenance and their clothing must be borne by the father according to usage; no soul shall have imposed upon it a duty but to the extent of its capacity; neither shall a mother be made to suffer harm on account of her child, nor a father on account of his child, and a similar duty (devolves) on the (father's) heir; but if both desire weaning by mutual consent and counsel, there is no blame on them, and if you wish to engage a wet-nurse for your children, there is no blame on you so long as you pay what you promised for according to usage; and be careful of (your duty to) Allah and know that Allah sees what you do.

234. And (as for) those of you who die and leave wives behind, they should keep themselves in waiting for four months and ten days; then when they have fully attained their term, there is no blame on you for what they do for themselves in a lawful manner; and Allah is aware of what you do.

235. And there is no blame on you respecting that which you speak indirectly in the asking of (such) women in marriage or keep (the proposal) concealed within your minds; Allah knows that you will mention them, but do not give them a promise in secret unless you speak in a lawful manner, and do not confirm the marriage tie until the writing is fulfilled, and know that Allah knows what is in your minds, therefore beware of Him, and know that Allah is Forgiving, Forbearing.

33

236. There is no blame on you if you divorce women when you have not touched them or appointed for them a portion, and make provision for them, the wealthy according to his means and the straitened in circumstances according to his means, a provision according to usage; (this is) a duty on the doers of good (to others).

لَا جُنَاحَ عَلَيْكُمْ اِنْ طَلَّقْتُمُ النِّسَاۤءَ مَا لَمْ تَمَسُّوْهُنَّ اَوْ تَفْرِضُوْا لَهُنَّ فَرِيْضَةً ۖ وَّمَتِّعُوْهُنَّ ۚ عَلَى الْمُوْسِعِ قَدَرُهٗ وَعَلَى الْمُقْتِرِ قَدَرُهٗ ۚ مَتَاعًۢا بِالْمَعْرُوْفِ ۚ حَقًّا عَلَى الْمُحْسِنِيْنَ ۝

237. And if you divorce them before you have touched them and you have appointed for them a portion, then (pay to them) half of what you have appointed, unless they relinquish or he should relinquish in whose hand is the marriage tie; and it is nearer to righteousness that you should relinquish; and do not neglect the giving of free gifts between you; surely Allah sees what you do.

وَاِنْ طَلَّقْتُمُوْهُنَّ مِنْ قَبْلِ اَنْ تَمَسُّوْهُنَّ وَقَدْ فَرَضْتُمْ لَهُنَّ فَرِيْضَةً فَنِصْفُ مَا فَرَضْتُمْ اِلَّا اَنْ يَّعْفُوْنَ اَوْ يَعْفُوَا الَّذِيْ بِيَدِهٖ عُقْدَةُ النِّكَاحِ ۚ وَاَنْ تَعْفُوْا اَقْرَبُ لِلتَّقْوٰى ۚ وَلَا تَنْسَوُا الْفَضْلَ بَيْنَكُمْ ۚ اِنَّ اللّٰهَ بِمَا تَعْمَلُوْنَ بَصِيْرٌ ۝

238. Attend constantly to prayers and to the middle prayer and stand up truly obedient to Allah.

حَافِظُوْا عَلَى الصَّلَوٰتِ وَالصَّلٰوةِ الْوُسْطٰى ۖ وَقُوْمُوْا لِلّٰهِ قٰنِتِيْنَ ۝

239. But if you are in danger, then (say your prayers) on foot or on horseback; and when you are secure, then remember Allah, as He has taught you what you did not know.

فَاِنْ خِفْتُمْ فَرِجَالًا اَوْ رُكْبَانًا ۚ فَاِذَآ اَمِنْتُمْ فَاذْكُرُوا اللّٰهَ كَمَا عَلَّمَكُمْ مَّا لَمْ تَكُوْنُوْا تَعْلَمُوْنَ ۝

240. And those of you who die and leave wives behind, (make) a bequest in favor of their wives of maintenance for a year without turning (them) out, then if they themselves go away, there is no blame on you for what they do of lawful deeds by themselves, and Allah is Mighty, Wise.

وَالَّذِيْنَ يُتَوَفَّوْنَ مِنْكُمْ وَيَذَرُوْنَ اَزْوَاجًا ۖ وَّصِيَّةً لِّاَزْوَاجِهِمْ مَّتَاعًا اِلَى الْحَوْلِ غَيْرَ اِخْرَاجٍ ۚ فَاِنْ خَرَجْنَ فَلَا جُنَاحَ عَلَيْكُمْ فِيْ مَا فَعَلْنَ فِيْٓ اَنْفُسِهِنَّ مِنْ مَّعْرُوْفٍ ۗ وَاللّٰهُ عَزِيْزٌ حَكِيْمٌ ۝

241. And for the divorced women (too) provision (must be made) according to usage; (this is) a duty on those who guard (against evil).

وَلِلْمُطَلَّقٰتِ مَتَاعٌۢ بِالْمَعْرُوْفِ ۚ حَقًّا عَلَى الْمُتَّقِيْنَ ۝

242. Allah thus makes clear to you His communications that you may understand.

كَذٰلِكَ يُبَيِّنُ اللّٰهُ لَكُمْ اٰيٰتِهٖ لَعَلَّكُمْ تَعْقِلُوْنَ ۝

243. Have you not considered those who went forth from their homes, for fear of death, and they were thousands, then Allah said to them, Die; again He gave them life; most surely Allah is Gracious to people, but most people are not grateful.

الَمْ تَرَ اِلَى الَّذِيْنَ خَرَجُوْا مِنْ دِيَارِهِمْ وَهُمْ اُلُوْفٌ حَذَرَ الْمَوْتِ فَقَالَ لَهُمُ اللّٰهُ مُوْتُوْا ثُمَّ اَحْيَاهُمْ اِنَّ اللّٰهَ لَذُوْ فَضْلٍ عَلَى النَّاسِ وَلٰكِنَّ اَكْثَرَ النَّاسِ لَا يَشْكُرُوْنَ ۝

244. And fight in the way of Allah, and know that Allah is Hearing, Knowing.

وَقَاتِلُوْا فِيْ سَبِيْلِ اللّٰهِ وَاعْلَمُوْا اَنَّ اللّٰهَ سَمِيْعٌ عَلِيْمٌ ۝

245. Who is it that will offer to Allah a goodly gift, so He will multiply it to him manifold, and Allah straitens and amplifies, and you shall be returned to Him.

مَنْ ذَا الَّذِيْ يُقْرِضُ اللّٰهَ قَرْضًا حَسَنًا فَيُضٰعِفَهٗ لَهٗ اَضْعَافًا كَثِيْرَةً وَاللّٰهُ يَقْبِضُ وَيَبْصُطُ وَ اِلَيْهِ تُرْجَعُوْنَ ۝

246. Have you not considered the chiefs of the children of Israel after Musa, when they said to a prophet of theirs: Raise up for us a king, (that) we may fight in the way of Allah. He said: May it not be that you would not fight if fighting is ordained for you? They said: And what reason have we that we should not fight in the way of Allah, and we have indeed been compelled to abandon our homes and our children. But when fighting was ordained for them, they turned back, except a few of them, and Allah knows the unjust.

اَلَمْ تَرَ اِلَى الْمَلَاِ مِنْ بَنِيْ اِسْرَآءِيْلَ مِنْ بَعْدِ مُوْسٰى اِذْ قَالُوْا لِنَبِيٍّ لَّهُمُ ابْعَثْ لَنَا مَلِكًا نُّقَاتِلْ فِيْ سَبِيْلِ اللّٰهِ قَالَ هَلْ عَسَيْتُمْ اِنْ كُتِبَ عَلَيْكُمُ الْقِتَالُ اَلَّا تُقَاتِلُوْا قَالُوْا وَمَا لَنَا اَلَّا نُقَاتِلَ فِيْ سَبِيْلِ اللّٰهِ وَقَدْ اُخْرِجْنَا مِنْ دِيَارِنَا وَاَبْنَآئِنَا فَلَمَّا كُتِبَ عَلَيْهِمُ الْقِتَالُ تَوَلَّوْا اِلَّا قَلِيْلًا مِّنْهُمْ وَاللّٰهُ عَلِيْمٌ بِالظّٰلِمِيْنَ ۝

247. And their prophet said to them: Surely Allah has raised Talut to be a king over you. They said: How can he hold kingship over us while we have a greater right to kingship than he, and he has not been granted an abundance of wealth? He said: Surely Allah has chosen him in preference to you, and He has increased him abundantly in knowledge and physique, and Allah grants His kingdom to whom He pleases, and Allah is Ample-giving, Knowing.

وَقَالَ لَهُمْ نَبِيُّهُمْ اِنَّ اللّٰهَ قَدْ بَعَثَ لَكُمْ طَالُوْتَ مَلِكًا قَالُوْا اَنّٰى يَكُوْنُ لَهُ الْمُلْكُ عَلَيْنَا وَنَحْنُ اَحَقُّ بِالْمُلْكِ مِنْهُ وَلَمْ يُؤْتَ سَعَةً مِّنَ الْمَالِ قَالَ اِنَّ اللّٰهَ اصْطَفٰهُ عَلَيْكُمْ وَزَادَهٗ بَسْطَةً فِي الْعِلْمِ وَالْجِسْمِ وَاللّٰهُ يُؤْتِيْ مُلْكَهٗ مَنْ يَّشَآءُ وَاللّٰهُ وَاسِعٌ عَلِيْمٌ ۝

248. And the prophet said to them: Surely the sign of His kingdom is, that there shall come to you the chest in which there is tranquillity from your Lord and residue of the relics of what the children of Musa and the children of Haroun have left, the angels bearing it; most surely there is a sign in this for those who believe.

وَقَالَ لَهُمْ نَبِيُّهُمْ إِنَّ اٰيَةَ مُلْكِهٖۤ اَنْ يَّأْتِيَكُمُ التَّابُوْتُ فِيْهِ سَكِيْنَةٌ مِّنْ رَّبِّكُمْ وَ بَقِيَّةٌ مِّمَّا تَرَكَ اٰلُ مُوْسٰى وَاٰلُ هٰرُوْنَ تَحْمِلُهُ الْمَلٰٓئِكَةُ ؕ اِنَّ فِيْ ذٰلِكَ لَاٰيَةً لَّكُمْ اِنْ كُنْتُمْ مُّؤْمِنِيْنَ ۟ ﴾

249. So when Talut departed with the forces, he said: Surely Allah will try you with a river; whoever then drinks from it, he is not of me, and whoever does not taste of it, he is surely of me, except he who takes with his hand as much of it as fills the hand; but with the exception of a few of them they drank from it. So when he had crossed it, he and those who believed with him, they said: We have today no power against Jalut and his forces. Those who were sure that they would meet their Lord said: How often has a small party vanquished a numerous host by Allah's permission, and Allah is with the patient.

فَلَمَّا فَصَلَ طَالُوْتُ بِالْجُنُوْدِ ۙ قَالَ اِنَّ اللّٰهَ مُبْتَلِيْكُمْ بِنَهَرٍ ۚ فَمَنْ شَرِبَ مِنْهُ فَلَيْسَ مِنِّيْ ۚ وَ مَنْ لَّمْ يَطْعَمْهُ فَاِنَّهٗ مِنِّيْۤ اِلَّا مَنِ اغْتَرَفَ غُرْفَةً بِيَدِهٖ ۚ فَشَرِبُوْا مِنْهُ اِلَّا قَلِيْلًا مِّنْهُمْ ؕ فَلَمَّا جَاوَزَهٗ هُوَ وَالَّذِيْنَ اٰمَنُوْا مَعَهٗ ۙ قَالُوْا لَا طَاقَةَ لَنَا الْيَوْمَ بِجَالُوْتَ وَجُنُوْدِهٖ ؕ قَالَ الَّذِيْنَ يَظُنُّوْنَ اَنَّهُمْ مُّلٰقُوا اللّٰهِ ۙ كَمْ مِّنْ فِئَةٍ قَلِيْلَةٍ غَلَبَتْ فِئَةً كَثِيْرَةً بِاِذْنِ اللّٰهِ ؕ وَاللّٰهُ مَعَ الصّٰبِرِيْنَ ﴾

250. And when they went out against Jalut and his forces they said: Our Lord, pour down upon us patience, and make our steps firm and assist us against the unbelieving people.

وَلَمَّا بَرَزُوْا لِجَالُوْتَ وَجُنُوْدِهٖ قَالُوْا رَبَّنَاۤ اَفْرِغْ عَلَيْنَا صَبْرًا وَّثَبِّتْ اَقْدَامَنَا وَانْصُرْنَا عَلَى الْقَوْمِ الْكٰفِرِيْنَ ﴾

251. So they put them to flight by Allah's permission. And Dawood slew Jalut, and Allah gave him kingdom and wisdom, and taught him of what He pleased. And were it not for Allah's repelling some men with others, the earth would certainly be in a state of disorder; but Allah is Gracious to the creatures.

فَهَزَمُوْهُمْ بِاِذْنِ اللّٰهِ ۪ وَقَتَلَ دَاوٗدُ جَالُوْتَ وَ اٰتٰىهُ اللّٰهُ الْمُلْكَ وَالْحِكْمَةَ وَعَلَّمَهٗ مِمَّا يَشَآءُ ؕ وَلَوْ لَا دَفْعُ اللّٰهِ النَّاسَ بَعْضَهُمْ بِبَعْضٍ لَّفَسَدَتِ الْاَرْضُ ۙ وَلٰكِنَّ اللّٰهَ ذُوْ فَضْلٍ عَلَى الْعٰلَمِيْنَ ﴾

252. These are the communications of Allah: We recite them to you with truth; and most surely you are (one) of the apostles.

تِلْكَ اٰيٰتُ اللّٰهِ نَتْلُوْهَا عَلَيْكَ بِالْحَقِّ ؕ وَاِنَّكَ لَمِنَ الْمُرْسَلِيْنَ ﴾

253. We have made some of these apostles to excel the others; among them are they to whom Allah spoke, and some of them He exalted by (many degrees of) rank; and We gave clear miracles to Isa son of Marium, and strengthened him with the holy spirit. And if Allah had pleased, those after them would not have fought one with another after clear arguments had come to them, but they disagreed; so there were some of them who believed and others who denied; and if Allah had pleased they would not have fought one with another, but Allah brings about what He intends.

254. O you who believe! spend out of what We have given you before the day comes in which there is no bargaining, neither any friendship nor intercession, and the unbelievers—they are the unjust.

255. Allah is He besides Whom there is no god, the Everliving, the Self-subsisting by Whom all subsist; slumber does not overtake Him nor sleep; whatever is in the heavens and whatever is in the earth is His; who is he that can intercede with Him but by His permission? He knows what is before them and what is behind them, and they cannot comprehend anything out of His knowledge except what He pleases, His knowledge extends over the heavens and the earth, and the preservation of them both tires Him not, and He is the Most High, the Great.

256. There is no compulsion in religion; truly the right way has become clearly distinct from error; therefore, whoever disbelieves in the Shaitan and believes in Allah, he indeed has laid hold on the firmest handle, which shall not break off, and Allah is Hearing, Knowing.

257. Allah is the guardian of those who believe. He brings them out of the darkness into the light; and (as to) those who disbelieve, their guardians are Shaitans who take them out of the light into the darkness; they are the inmates of the fire, in it they shall abide.

258. Have you not considered him (Namrud) who disputed with Ibrahim about his Lord, because Allah had given him the kingdom? When Ibrahim said: My Lord is He who gives life and causes to die, he said: I give life and cause death. Ibrahim said: So surely Allah causes the sun to rise from the east, then make it rise from the west; thus he who disbelieved was confounded; and Allah does not guide aright the unjust people.

259. Or the like of him (Uzair) who passed by a town, and it had fallen down upon its roofs; he said: When will Allah give it life after its death? So Allah caused him to die for a hundred years, then raised him to life. He said: How long have you tarried? He said: I have tarried a day, or a part of a day. Said He: Nay! you have tarried a hundred years; then look at your food and drink—years have not passed over it; and look at your ass; and that We may make you a sign to men, and look at the bones, how We set them together, then clothed them with flesh; so when it became clear to him, he said: I know that Allah has power over all things.

260. And when Ibrahim said: My Lord! show me how Thou givest life to the dead, He said: What! and do you not believe? He said: Yes, but that my heart may be at ease. He said: Then take four of the birds, then train them to follow you, then place on every mountain a part of them, then call them, they will come to you flying; and know that Allah is Mighty, Wise.

261. The parable of those who spend their property in the way of Allah is as the parable of a grain growing seven ears (with) a hundred grains in every ear; and Allah multiplies for whom He pleases; and Allah is Ample-giving, Knowing.

262. (As for) those who spend their property in the way of Allah, then do not follow up what they have spent with reproach or injury, they shall have their reward from their Lord, and they shall have no fear nor shall they grieve.

263. Kind speech and forgiveness is better than charity followed by injury; and Allah is Self-sufficient, Forbearing.

264. O you who believe! do not make your charity worthless by reproach and injury, like him who spends his property to be seen of men and does not believe in Allah and the last day; so his parable is as the parable of a smooth rock with earth upon it, then a heavy rain falls upon it, so it leaves it bare; they shall not be able to gain anything of what they have earned; and Allah does not guide the unbelieving people.

265. And the parable of those who spend their property to seek the pleasure of Allah and for the certainty of their souls is as the parable of a garden on an elevated ground, upon which heavy rain falls so it brings forth its fruit twofold but if heavy rain does not fall upon it, then light rain (is sufficient); and Allah sees what you do.

266. Does one of you like that he should have a garden of palms and vines with streams flowing beneath it; he has in it all kinds of fruits; and old age has overtaken him and he has weak offspring, when, (lo!) a whirlwind with fire in it smites it so it becomes blasted; thus Allah makes the communications clear to you, that you may reflect.

39

267. O you who believe! spend (benevolently) of the good things that you earn and or what We have brought forth for you out of the earth, and do not aim at what is bad that you may spend (in alms) of it, while you would not take it yourselves unless you have its price lowered, and know that Allah is Self-sufficient, Praiseworthy.

يَا أَيُّهَا الَّذِينَ آمَنُوا أَنفِقُوا مِن طَيِّبَاتِ مَا كَسَبْتُمْ وَمِمَّا أَخْرَجْنَا لَكُم مِّنَ الْأَرْضِ وَلَا تَيَمَّمُوا الْخَبِيثَ مِنْهُ تُنفِقُونَ وَلَسْتُم بِآخِذِيهِ إِلَّا أَن تُغْمِضُوا فِيهِ وَاعْلَمُوا أَنَّ اللَّهَ غَنِيٌّ حَمِيدٌ ۝

268. Shaitan threatens you with poverty and enjoins you to be niggardly, and Allah promises you forgiveness from Himself and abundance; and Allah is Ample-giving, Knowing.

الشَّيْطَانُ يَعِدُكُمُ الْفَقْرَ وَيَأْمُرُكُم بِالْفَحْشَاءِ وَاللَّهُ يَعِدُكُم مَّغْفِرَةً مِّنْهُ وَفَضْلًا وَاللَّهُ وَاسِعٌ عَلِيمٌ ۝

269. He grants wisdom to whom He pleases, and whoever is granted wisdom, he indeed is given a great good and none but men of understanding mind.

يُؤْتِي الْحِكْمَةَ مَن يَشَاءُ وَمَن يُؤْتَ الْحِكْمَةَ فَقَدْ أُوتِيَ خَيْرًا كَثِيرًا وَمَا يَذَّكَّرُ إِلَّا أُولُو الْأَلْبَابِ ۝

270. And whatever alms you give or (whatever) vow you vow, surely Allah knows it; and the unjust shall have no helpers.

وَمَا أَنفَقْتُم مِّن نَّفَقَةٍ أَوْ نَذَرْتُم مِّن نَّذْرٍ فَإِنَّ اللَّهَ يَعْلَمُهُ وَمَا لِلظَّالِمِينَ مِنْ أَنصَارٍ ۝

271. If you give alms openly, it is well, and if you hide it and give it to the poor, it is better for you; and this will do away with some of your evil deeds; and Allah is aware of what you do.

إِن تُبْدُوا الصَّدَقَاتِ فَنِعِمَّا هِيَ وَإِن تُخْفُوهَا وَتُؤْتُوهَا الْفُقَرَاءَ فَهُوَ خَيْرٌ لَّكُمْ وَيُكَفِّرُ عَنكُم مِّن سَيِّئَاتِكُمْ وَاللَّهُ بِمَا تَعْمَلُونَ خَبِيرٌ ۝

272. To make them walk in the right way is not incumbent on you, but Allah guides aright whom He pleases; and whatever good thing you spend, it is to your own good; and you do not spend but to seek Allah's pleasure; and whatever good things you spend shall be paid back to you in full, and you shall not be wronged.

لَّيْسَ عَلَيْكَ هُدَاهُمْ وَلَٰكِنَّ اللَّهَ يَهْدِي مَن يَشَاءُ وَمَا تُنفِقُوا مِنْ خَيْرٍ فَلِأَنفُسِكُمْ وَمَا تُنفِقُونَ إِلَّا ابْتِغَاءَ وَجْهِ اللَّهِ وَمَا تُنفِقُوا مِنْ خَيْرٍ يُوَفَّ إِلَيْكُمْ وَأَنتُمْ لَا تُظْلَمُونَ ۝

273. (Alms are) for the poor who are confined in the way of Allah—they cannot go about in the land; the ignorant man thinks them to be rich on account of (their) abstaining (from begging); you can recognise them by their mark; they do not beg from men importunately; and whatever good thing you spend, surely Allah knows it.

لِلْفُقَرَاءِ الَّذِينَ أُحْصِرُوا فِي سَبِيلِ اللَّهِ لَا يَسْتَطِيعُونَ ضَرْبًا فِي الْأَرْضِ يَحْسَبُهُمُ الْجَاهِلُ أَغْنِيَاءَ مِنَ التَّعَفُّفِ تَعْرِفُهُم بِسِيمَاهُمْ لَا يَسْأَلُونَ النَّاسَ إِلْحَافًا وَمَا تُنفِقُوا مِنْ خَيْرٍ فَإِنَّ اللَّهَ بِهِ عَلِيمٌ ۝

274. (As for) those who spend their property by night and by day, secretly and openly, they shall have their reward from their Lord and they shall have no fear, nor shall they grieve.

275. Those who swallow down usury cannot arise except as one whom Shaitan has prostrated by (his) touch does rise. That is because they say, trading is only like usury; and Allah has allowed trading and forbidden usury. To whomsoever then the admonition has come from his Lord, then he desists, he shall have what has already passed, and his affair is in the hands of Allah; and whoever returns (to it)—these are the inmates of the fire; they shall abide in it.

276. Allah does not bless usury, and He causes charitable deeds to prosper, and Allah does not love any ungrateful sinner.

277. Surely they who believe and do good deeds and keep up prayer and pay the poor-rate they shall have their reward from their Lord, and they shall have no fear, nor shall they grieve.

278. O you who believe! Be careful of (your duty to) Allah and relinquish what remains (due) from usury, if you are believers.

279. But if you do (it) not, then be apprised of war from Allah and His Apostle; and if you repent, then you shall have your capital; neither shall you make (the debtor) suffer loss, nor shall you be made to suffer loss.

280. And if (the debtor) is in straitness, then let there be postponement until (he is in) ease; and that you remit (it) as alms is better for you, if you knew.

281. And guard yourselves against a day in which you shall be returned to Allah; then every soul shall be paid back in full what it has earned, and they shall not be dealt with unjustly.

282. O you who believe! when you deal with each other in contracting a debt for a fixed time, then write it down; and let a scribe write it down between you with fairness; and the scribe should not refuse to write as Allah has taught him, so he should write; and let him who owes the debt dictate, and he should be careful of (his duty to) Allah, his Lord, and not diminish anything from it; but if he who owes the debt is unsound in understanding, or weak, or (if) he is not able to dictate himself, let his guardian dictate with fairness; and call in to witness from among your men two witnesses; but if there are not two men, then one man and two women from among those whom you choose to be witnesses, so that if one of the two errs, the second of the two may remind the other; and the witnesses should not refuse when they are summoned; and be not averse to writing it (whether it is) small or large, with the time of its falling due; this is more equitable in the sight of Allah and assures greater accuracy in testimony, and the nearest (way) that you may not entertain doubts (afterwards), except when it is ready merchandise which you give and take among yourselves from hand to hand, then there is no blame on you in not writing it down; and have witnesses when you barter with one another, and let no harm be done to the scribe or to the witness; and if you do (it) then surely it will be a transgression in you, and be careful of (your duty to) Allah, Allah teaches you, and Allah knows all things.

283. And if you are upon a journey and you do not find a scribe, then (there may be) a security taken into possession; but if one of you trusts another, then he who is trusted should deliver his trust, and let him be careful (of his duty to) Allah, his Lord; and do not conceal testimony, and whoever conceals it, his heart is surely sinful; and Allah knows what you do.

يَا أَيُّهَا الَّذِينَ آمَنُوا إِذَا تَدَايَنتُم بِدَيْنٍ إِلَى أَجَلٍ مُّسَمًّى فَاكْتُبُوهُ ۚ وَلْيَكْتُب بَّيْنَكُمْ كَاتِبٌ بِالْعَدْلِ ۚ وَلَا يَأْبَ كَاتِبٌ أَن يَكْتُبَ كَمَا عَلَّمَهُ اللَّهُ ۚ فَلْيَكْتُبْ وَلْيُمْلِلِ الَّذِي عَلَيْهِ الْحَقُّ وَلْيَتَّقِ اللَّهَ رَبَّهُ وَلَا يَبْخَسْ مِنْهُ شَيْئًا ۚ فَإِن كَانَ الَّذِي عَلَيْهِ الْحَقُّ سَفِيهًا أَوْ ضَعِيفًا أَوْ لَا يَسْتَطِيعُ أَن يُمِلَّ هُوَ فَلْيُمْلِلْ وَلِيُّهُ بِالْعَدْلِ ۚ وَاسْتَشْهِدُوا شَهِيدَيْنِ مِن رِّجَالِكُمْ ۖ فَإِن لَّمْ يَكُونَا رَجُلَيْنِ فَرَجُلٌ وَامْرَأَتَانِ مِمَّن تَرْضَوْنَ مِنَ الشُّهَدَاءِ أَن تَضِلَّ إِحْدَاهُمَا فَتُذَكِّرَ إِحْدَاهُمَا الْأُخْرَىٰ ۚ وَلَا يَأْبَ الشُّهَدَاءُ إِذَا مَا دُعُوا ۚ وَلَا تَسْأَمُوا أَن تَكْتُبُوهُ صَغِيرًا أَوْ كَبِيرًا إِلَىٰ أَجَلِهِ ۚ ذَٰلِكُمْ أَقْسَطُ عِندَ اللَّهِ وَأَقْوَمُ لِلشَّهَادَةِ وَأَدْنَىٰ أَلَّا تَرْتَابُوا ۖ إِلَّا أَن تَكُونَ تِجَارَةً حَاضِرَةً تُدِيرُونَهَا بَيْنَكُمْ فَلَيْسَ عَلَيْكُمْ جُنَاحٌ أَلَّا تَكْتُبُوهَا ۗ وَأَشْهِدُوا إِذَا تَبَايَعْتُمْ ۚ وَلَا يُضَارَّ كَاتِبٌ وَلَا شَهِيدٌ ۚ وَإِن تَفْعَلُوا فَإِنَّهُ فُسُوقٌ بِكُمْ ۗ وَاتَّقُوا اللَّهَ ۖ وَيُعَلِّمُكُمُ اللَّهُ ۗ وَاللَّهُ بِكُلِّ شَيْءٍ عَلِيمٌ ۝

وَإِن كُنتُمْ عَلَىٰ سَفَرٍ وَلَمْ تَجِدُوا كَاتِبًا فَرِهَانٌ مَّقْبُوضَةٌ ۖ فَإِنْ أَمِنَ بَعْضُكُم بَعْضًا فَلْيُؤَدِّ الَّذِي اؤْتُمِنَ أَمَانَتَهُ وَلْيَتَّقِ اللَّهَ رَبَّهُ ۗ وَلَا تَكْتُمُوا الشَّهَادَةَ ۚ وَمَن يَكْتُمْهَا فَإِنَّهُ آثِمٌ قَلْبُهُ ۗ وَاللَّهُ بِمَا تَعْمَلُونَ عَلِيمٌ ۝

284. Whatever is in the heavens and whatever is in the earth is Allah's; and whether you manifest what is in your minds or hide it, Allah will call you to account according to it; then He will forgive whom He pleases and chastise whom He pleases, and Allah has power over all things.

لِلّٰهِ مَا فِي السَّمٰوٰتِ وَمَا فِي الْاَرْضِ ۚ وَاِنْ تُبْدُوْا مَا فِيْ اَنْفُسِكُمْ اَوْ تُخْفُوْهُ يُحَاسِبْكُمْ بِهِ اللّٰهُ ۚ فَيَغْفِرُ لِمَنْ يَّشَآءُ وَيُعَذِّبُ مَنْ يَّشَآءُ ۗ وَاللّٰهُ عَلٰى كُلِّ شَيْءٍ قَدِيْرٌ ۝

285. The apostle believes in what has been revealed to him from his Lord, and (so do) the believers; they all believe in Allah and His angels and His books and His apostles; We make no difference between any of His apostles; and they say: We hear and obey, our Lord! Thy forgiveness (do we crave), and to Thee is the eventual course.

اٰمَنَ الرَّسُوْلُ بِمَآ اُنْزِلَ اِلَيْهِ مِنْ رَّبِّهٖ وَالْمُؤْمِنُوْنَ ۚ كُلٌّ اٰمَنَ بِاللّٰهِ وَمَلٰٓئِكَتِهٖ وَكُتُبِهٖ وَرُسُلِهٖ ۚ لَا نُفَرِّقُ بَيْنَ اَحَدٍ مِّنْ رُّسُلِهٖ ۚ وَقَالُوْا سَمِعْنَا وَاَطَعْنَا ۖ غُفْرَانَكَ رَبَّنَا وَاِلَيْكَ الْمَصِيْرُ ۝

286. Allah does not impose upon any soul a duty but to the extent of its ability; for it is (the benefit of) what it has earned, and upon it (the evil of) what it has wrought: Our Lord! do not punish us if we forget or make a mistake; Our Lord! do not lay on us a burden as Thou didst lay on those before us; Our Lord! do not impose upon us that which we have not the strength to bear; and pardon us and grant us protection and have mercy on us, Thou art our Patron, so help us against the unbelieving people.

لَا يُكَلِّفُ اللّٰهُ نَفْسًا اِلَّا وُسْعَهَا ۚ لَهَا مَا كَسَبَتْ وَعَلَيْهَا مَا اكْتَسَبَتْ ۗ رَبَّنَا لَا تُؤَاخِذْنَآ اِنْ نَّسِيْنَآ اَوْ اَخْطَأْنَا ۚ رَبَّنَا وَلَا تَحْمِلْ عَلَيْنَآ اِصْرًا كَمَا حَمَلْتَهٗ عَلَى الَّذِيْنَ مِنْ قَبْلِنَا ۚ رَبَّنَا وَلَا تُحَمِّلْنَا مَا لَا طَاقَةَ لَنَا بِهٖ ۖ وَاعْفُ عَنَّا ۖ وَاغْفِرْ لَنَا ۖ وَارْحَمْنَا ۚ اَنْتَ مَوْلٰىنَا فَانْصُرْنَا عَلَى الْقَوْمِ الْكٰفِرِيْنَ ۝

43

THE FAMILY OF IMRAN
(A'LAY IMRAN)

بِسۡمِ اللهِ الرَّحۡمٰنِ الرَّحِيۡمِ ۞

**In the name of Allah,
the Beneficent, the Merciful.**

الٓمّٓ ۞

1. Alif Lam Mim.

اللهُ لَاۤ اِلٰهَ اِلَّا هُوَ ۙ الۡحَيُّ الۡقَيُّوۡمُ ۞

2. Allah, (there is) no god but He, the Everliving, the Self-subsisting by Whom all things subsist.

نَزَّلَ عَلَيۡكَ الۡكِتٰبَ بِالۡحَقِّ مُصَدِّقًا لِّمَا بَيۡنَ يَدَيۡهِ وَاَنۡزَلَ التَّوۡرٰىةَ وَالۡاِنۡجِيۡلَ ۞

3. He has revealed to you the Book with truth, verifying that which is before it, and He revealed the Tavrat and the Injeel aforetime, a guidance for the people, and He sent the Furqan.

مِنۡ قَبۡلُ هُدًى لِّلنَّاسِ وَاَنۡزَلَ الۡفُرۡقَانَ ۞ اِنَّ الَّذِيۡنَ كَفَرُوۡا بِاٰيٰتِ اللهِ لَهُمۡ عَذَابٌ شَدِيۡدٌ ؕ

4. Surely they who disbelieve in the communications of Allah—they shall have a severe chastisement; and Allah is Mighty, the Lord of retribution.

وَاللهُ عَزِيۡزٌ ذُو انۡتِقَامٍ ۞

5. Allah—surely nothing is hidden from Him in the earth or in the heaven.

اِنَّ اللهَ لَا يَخۡفٰى عَلَيۡهِ شَيۡءٌ فِى الۡاَرۡضِ وَلَا فِى السَّمَآءِ ؕ

6. He it is Who shapes you in the wombs as He likes; there is no god but He, the Mighty, the Wise.

هُوَ الَّذِىۡ يُصَوِّرُكُمۡ فِى الۡاَرۡحَامِ كَيۡفَ يَشَآءُ ؕ لَاۤ اِلٰهَ اِلَّا هُوَ الۡعَزِيۡزُ الۡحَكِيۡمُ ۞

7. He it is Who has revealed the Book to you; some of its verses are decisive, they are the basis of the Book, and others are allegorical; then as for those in whose hearts there is perversity, they follow the part of it which is allegorical, seeking to mislead, and seeking to give it (their own) interpretation, but none knows its interpretation except Allah, and those who are firmly rooted in knowledge say: We believe in it, it is all from our Lord; and none do mind except those having understanding.

هُوَ الَّذِىۡۤ اَنۡزَلَ عَلَيۡكَ الۡكِتٰبَ مِنۡهُ اٰيٰتٌ مُّحۡكَمٰتٌ هُنَّ اُمُّ الۡكِتٰبِ وَاُخَرُ مُتَشٰبِهٰتٌ ؕ فَاَمَّا الَّذِيۡنَ فِىۡ قُلُوۡبِهِمۡ زَيۡغٌ فَيَتَّبِعُوۡنَ مَا تَشَابَهَ مِنۡهُ ابۡتِغَآءَ الۡفِتۡنَةِ وَابۡتِغَآءَ تَاۡوِيۡلِهٖ ۚ وَمَا يَعۡلَمُ تَاۡوِيۡلَهٗۤ اِلَّا اللهُ ۘ وَالرّٰسِخُوۡنَ فِى الۡعِلۡمِ يَقُوۡلُوۡنَ اٰمَنَّا بِهٖ ۙ كُلٌّ مِّنۡ عِنۡدِ رَبِّنَا ۚ وَمَا يَذَّكَّرُ اِلَّاۤ اُولُوا الۡاَلۡبَابِ ۞

8. Our Lord! make not our hearts to deviate after Thou hast guided us aright, and grant us from Thee mercy; surely Thou art the most liberal Giver.

رَبَّنَا لَا تُزِغۡ قُلُوۡبَنَا بَعۡدَ اِذۡ هَدَيۡتَنَا وَهَبۡ لَنَا مِنۡ لَّدُنۡكَ رَحۡمَةً ۚ اِنَّكَ اَنۡتَ الۡوَهَّابُ ۞

9. Our Lord! surely Thou art the Gatherer of men on a day about which there is no doubt; surely Allah will not fail (His) promise.

رَبَّنَا اِنَّكَ جَامِعُ النَّاسِ لِيَوْمٍ لَّارَيْبَ فِيْهِ ﴿اِنَّ اللّٰهَ لَا يُخْلِفُ الْمِيْعَادَ ۞

10. (As for) those who disbelieve, surely neither their wealth nor their children shall avail them in the least against Allah, and these it is who are the fuel of the fire.

اِنَّ الَّذِيْنَ كَفَرُوْا لَنْ تُغْنِيَ عَنْهُمْ اَمْوَالُهُمْ وَلَا اَوْلَادُهُمْ مِّنَ اللّٰهِ شَيْئًا ۖ وَاُولٰٓئِكَ هُمْ وَقُوْدُ النَّارِ ۞

11. Like the striving of the people of Firon and those before them; they rejected Our communications, so Allah destroyed them on account of their faults; and Allah is severe in requiting (evil).

كَدَأْبِ اٰلِ فِرْعَوْنَ ۙ وَالَّذِيْنَ مِنْ قَبْلِهِمْ ۚ كَذَّبُوْا بِاٰيٰتِنَا ۚ فَاَخَذَهُمُ اللّٰهُ بِذُنُوْبِهِمْ ۗ وَاللّٰهُ شَدِيْدُ الْعِقَابِ ۞

12. Say to those who disbelieve: You shall be vanquished, and driven together to hell; and evil is the resting-place.

قُلْ لِّلَّذِيْنَ كَفَرُوْا سَتُغْلَبُوْنَ وَتُحْشَرُوْنَ اِلٰى جَهَنَّمَ ۚ وَبِئْسَ الْمِهَادُ ۞

13. Indeed there was a sign for you in the two hosts (which) met together in encounter; one party fighting in the way of Allah and the other unbelieving, whom they saw twice as many as themselves with the sight of the eye; and Allah strengthens with His aid whom He pleases; most surely there is a lesson in this for those who have sight.

قَدْ كَانَ لَكُمْ اٰيَةٌ فِيْ فِئَتَيْنِ الْتَقَتَا ۗ فِئَةٌ تُقَاتِلُ فِيْ سَبِيْلِ اللّٰهِ وَاُخْرٰى كَافِرَةٌ يَّرَوْنَهُمْ مِّثْلَيْهِمْ رَأْيَ الْعَيْنِ ۚ وَاللّٰهُ يُؤَيِّدُ بِنَصْرِهٖ مَنْ يَّشَاءُ ۗ اِنَّ فِيْ ذٰلِكَ لَعِبْرَةً لِّاُولِى الْاَبْصَارِ ۞

14. The love of desires, of women and sons and hoarded treasures of gold and silver and well bred horses and cattle and tilth, is made to seem fair to men; this is the provision of the life of this world; and Allah is He with Whom is the good goal (of life).

زُيِّنَ لِلنَّاسِ حُبُّ الشَّهَوٰتِ مِنَ النِّسَاءِ وَالْبَنِيْنَ وَالْقَنَاطِيْرِ الْمُقَنْطَرَةِ مِنَ الذَّهَبِ وَالْفِضَّةِ وَالْخَيْلِ الْمُسَوَّمَةِ وَالْاَنْعَامِ وَالْحَرْثِ ۗ ذٰلِكَ مَتَاعُ الْحَيٰوةِ الدُّنْيَا ۖ وَاللّٰهُ عِنْدَهٗ حُسْنُ الْمَاٰبِ ۞

15. Say: Shall I tell you of what is better than these? For those who guard (against evil) are gardens with their Lord, beneath which rivers flow, to abide in them, and pure mates and Allah's pleasure; and Allah sees the servants.

قُلْ اَؤُنَبِّئُكُمْ بِخَيْرٍ مِّنْ ذٰلِكُمْ ۚ لِلَّذِيْنَ اتَّقَوْا عِنْدَ رَبِّهِمْ جَنَّاتٌ تَجْرِيْ مِنْ تَحْتِهَا الْاَنْهَارُ خٰلِدِيْنَ فِيْهَا وَاَزْوَاجٌ مُّطَهَّرَةٌ وَّرِضْوَانٌ مِّنَ اللّٰهِ ۗ وَاللّٰهُ بَصِيْرٌ بِالْعِبَادِ ۞

16. Those who say: Our Lord! surely we believe, therefore forgive us our faults and save us from the chastisement of the fire.

الَّذِيْنَ يَقُوْلُوْنَ رَبَّنَآ اِنَّنَآ اٰمَنَّا فَاغْفِرْلَنَا ذُنُوْبَنَا وَقِنَا عَذَابَ النَّارِ ۞

17. The patient, and the truthful, and the obedient, and those who spend (benevolently) and those who ask forgiveness in the morning times.

الصّٰبِرِيْنَ وَالصّٰدِقِيْنَ وَالْقٰنِتِيْنَ وَالْمُنْفِقِيْنَ وَالْمُسْتَغْفِرِيْنَ بِالْاَسْحَارِ ۞

18. Allah bears witness that there is no god but He, and (so do) the angels and those possessed of knowledge, maintaining His creation with justice; there is no god but He, the Mighty, the Wise.

شَهِدَ اللهُ اَنَّهُ لَآ اِلٰهَ اِلَّا هُوَ ۙ وَالْمَلٰٓئِكَةُ وَاُولُوا الْعِلْمِ قَآئِمًۢا بِالْقِسْطِ ۚ لَآ اِلٰهَ اِلَّا هُوَ الْعَزِيْزُ الْحَكِيْمُ ۞

19. Surely the (true) religion with Allah is Islam, and those to whom the Book had been given did not show opposition but after knowledge had come to them, out of envy among themselves; and whoever disbelieves in the communications of Allah then surely Allah is quick in reckoning.

اِنَّ الدِّيْنَ عِنْدَ اللهِ الْاِسْلَامُ ۗ وَمَا اخْتَلَفَ الَّذِيْنَ اُوْتُوا الْكِتٰبَ اِلَّا مِنْۢ بَعْدِ مَا جَآءَهُمُ الْعِلْمُ بَغْيًاۢ بَيْنَهُمْ ۗ وَمَنْ يَّكْفُرْ بِاٰيٰتِ اللهِ فَاِنَّ اللهَ سَرِيْعُ الْحِسَابِ ۞

20. But if they dispute with you, say: I have submitted myself entirely to Allah and (so) every one who follows me; and say to those who have been given the Book and the unlearned people: Do you submit yourselves? So if they submit then indeed they follow the right way; and if they turn back, then upon you is only the delivery of the message and Allah sees the servants.

فَاِنْ حَآجُّوْكَ فَقُلْ اَسْلَمْتُ وَجْهِيَ لِلهِ وَمَنِ اتَّبَعَنِ ۗ وَقُلْ لِّلَّذِيْنَ اُوْتُوا الْكِتٰبَ وَالْاُمِّيّٖنَ ءَاَسْلَمْتُمْ ۗ فَاِنْ اَسْلَمُوْا فَقَدِ اهْتَدَوْا ۚ وَّاِنْ تَوَلَّوْا فَاِنَّمَا عَلَيْكَ الْبَلٰغُ ۗ وَاللهُ بَصِيْرٌۢ بِالْعِبَادِ ۞

21. Surely (as for) those who disbelieve in the communications of Allah and slay the prophets unjustly and slay those among men who enjoin justice, announce to them a painful chastisement.

اِنَّ الَّذِيْنَ يَكْفُرُوْنَ بِاٰيٰتِ اللهِ وَيَقْتُلُوْنَ النَّبِيّٖنَ بِغَيْرِ حَقٍّ ۙ وَّيَقْتُلُوْنَ الَّذِيْنَ يَاْمُرُوْنَ بِالْقِسْطِ مِنَ النَّاسِ ۙ فَبَشِّرْهُمْ بِعَذَابٍ اَلِيْمٍ ۞

22. Those are they whose works shall become null in this world as well as the hereafter, and they shall have no helpers.

اُولٰٓئِكَ الَّذِيْنَ حَبِطَتْ اَعْمَالُهُمْ فِي الدُّنْيَا وَالْاٰخِرَةِ ۖ وَمَا لَهُمْ مِّنْ نّٰصِرِيْنَ ۞

23. Have you not considered those (Jews) who are given a portion of the Book? They are invited to the Book of Allah that it might decide between them, then a part of them turn back and they withdraw.

اَلَمْ تَرَ اِلَى الَّذِيْنَ اُوْتُوْا نَصِيْبًا مِّنَ الْكِتٰبِ يُدْعَوْنَ اِلٰى كِتٰبِ اللهِ لِيَحْكُمَ بَيْنَهُمْ ثُمَّ يَتَوَلّٰى فَرِيْقٌ مِّنْهُمْ وَهُمْ مُّعْرِضُوْنَ ۞

24. This is because they say: The fire shall not touch us but for a few days; and what they have forged deceives them in the matter of their religion.

25. Then how will it be when We shall gather them together on a day about which there is no doubt, and every soul shall be fully paid what it has earned, and they shall not be dealt with unjustly?

26. Say: O Allah, Master of the Kingdom! Thou givest the kingdom to whomsoever Thou pleasest and takest away the kingdom from whomsoever Thou pleasest, and Thou exaltest whom Thou pleasest and abasest whom Thou pleasest; in Thine hand is the good; surely, Thou hast power over all things.

27. Thou makest the night to pass into the day and Thou makest the day to pass into the night, and Thou bringest forth the living from the dead and Thou bringest forth the dead from the living, and Thou givest sustenance to whom Thou pleasest without measure.

28. Let not the believers take the unbelievers for friends rather than believers; and whoever does this, he shall have nothing of (the guardianship of) Allah, but you should guard yourselves against them, guarding carefully; and Allah makes you cautious of (retribution from) Himself; and to Allah is the eventual coming.

29. Say: Whether you hide what is in your hearts or manifest it, Allah knows it, and He knows whatever is in the heavens and whatever is in the earth, and Allah has power over all things.

30. On the day that every soul shall find present what it has done of good and what it has done of evil, it shall wish that between it and that (evil) there were a long duration of time; and Allah makes you to be cautious of (retribution from) Himself; and Allah is Compassionate to the servants.

31. Say: If you love Allah, then follow me, Allah will love you and forgive you your faults, and Allah is Forgiving, Merciful.

47

32. Say: Obey Allah and the Apostle; but if they turn back, then surely Allah does not love the unbelievers.

قُلْ أَطِيعُوا اللّٰهَ وَالرَّسُوْلَ ۚ فَاِنْ تَوَلَّوْا فَاِنَّ اللّٰهَ لَا يُحِبُّ الْكٰفِرِيْنَ ۞

33. Surely Allah chose Adam and Nuh and the descendants of Ibrahim and the descendants of Imran above the nations.

اِنَّ اللّٰهَ اصْطَفٰۤى اٰدَمَ وَنُوْحًا وَّاٰلَ اِبْرٰهِيْمَ وَاٰلَ عِمْرٰنَ عَلَى الْعٰلَمِيْنَ ۞

34. Offspring, one of the other; and Allah is Hearing, Knowing.

ذُرِّيَّةً ۢبَعْضُهَا مِنْۢ بَعْضٍ ۗ وَاللّٰهُ سَمِيْعٌ عَلِيْمٌ ۞

35. When a woman of Imran said: My Lord! surely I vow to Thee what is in my womb, to be devoted (to Thy service); accept therefore from me, surely Thou art the Hearing, the Knowing.

اِذْ قَالَتِ امْرَاَتُ عِمْرٰنَ رَبِّ اِنِّيْ نَذَرْتُ لَكَ مَا فِيْ بَطْنِيْ مُحَرَّرًا فَتَقَبَّلْ مِنِّيْ ۚ اِنَّكَ اَنْتَ السَّمِيْعُ الْعَلِيْمُ ۞

36. So when she brought forth, she said: My Lord! Surely I have brought it forth a female—and Allah knew best what she brought forth—and the male is not like the female, and I have named it Marium, and I commend her and her offspring into Thy protection from the accursed Shaitan.

فَلَمَّا وَضَعَتْهَا قَالَتْ رَبِّ اِنِّيْ وَضَعْتُهَاۤ اُنْثٰى ۗ وَاللّٰهُ اَعْلَمُ بِمَا وَضَعَتْ ۚ وَلَيْسَ الذَّكَرُ كَالْاُنْثٰى ۚ وَاِنِّيْ سَمَّيْتُهَا مَرْيَمَ وَاِنِّيْ اُعِيْذُهَا بِكَ وَذُرِّيَّتَهَا مِنَ الشَّيْطٰنِ الرَّجِيْمِ ۞

37. So her Lord accepted her with a good acceptance and made her grow up a good growing, and gave her into the charge of Zakariya; whenever Zakariya entered the sanctuary to (see) her, he found with her food. He said: O Marium! whence comes this to you? She said: It is from Allah. Surely Allah gives to whom He pleases without measure.

فَتَقَبَّلَهَا رَبُّهَا بِقَبُوْلٍ حَسَنٍ وَّاَنْۢبَتَهَا نَبَاتًا حَسَنًا ۙ وَّكَفَّلَهَا زَكَرِيَّا ۚ كُلَّمَا دَخَلَ عَلَيْهَا زَكَرِيَّا الْمِحْرَابَ ۙ وَجَدَ عِنْدَهَا رِزْقًا ۚ قَالَ يٰمَرْيَمُ اَنّٰى لَكِ هٰذَا ۗ قَالَتْ هُوَ مِنْ عِنْدِ اللّٰهِ ۗ اِنَّ اللّٰهَ يَرْزُقُ مَنْ يَّشَاۤءُ بِغَيْرِ حِسَابٍ ۞

38. There did Zakariya pray to his Lord; he said: My Lord! grant me from Thee good offspring; surely Thou art the Hearer of prayer.

هُنَالِكَ دَعَا زَكَرِيَّا رَبَّهٗ ۚ قَالَ رَبِّ هَبْ لِيْ مِنْ لَّدُنْكَ ذُرِّيَّةً طَيِّبَةً ۚ اِنَّكَ سَمِيْعُ الدُّعَاۤءِ ۞

39. Then the angels called to him as he stood praying in the sanctuary: That Allah gives you the good news of Yahya verifying a Word from Allah, and honorable and chaste and a prophet from among the good ones.

فَنَادَتْهُ الْمَلٰۤئِكَةُ وَهُوَ قَاۤئِمٌ يُّصَلِّيْ فِى الْمِحْرَابِ ۙ اَنَّ اللّٰهَ يُبَشِّرُكَ بِيَحْيٰى مُصَدِّقًۢا بِكَلِمَةٍ مِّنَ اللّٰهِ وَسَيِّدًا وَّحَصُوْرًا وَّنَبِيًّا مِّنَ الصّٰلِحِيْنَ ۞

40. He said: My Lord! when shall there be a son (born) to me, and old age has already come upon me, and my wife is barren? He said: Even thus does Allah what He pleases.

قَالَ رَبِّ اَنّٰى يَكُوْنُ لِىْ غُلٰمٌ وَّقَدْ بَلَغَنِىَ الْكِبَرُ وَامْرَاَتِىْ عَاقِرٌ قَالَ كَذٰلِكَ اللّٰهُ يَفْعَلُ مَا يَشَآءُ ۴۰

41. He said: My Lord! appoint a sign for me. Said He: Your sign is that you should not speak to men for three days except by signs; and remember your Lord much and glorify Him in the evening and the morning.

قَالَ رَبِّ اجْعَلْ لِّىْٓ اٰيَةً قَالَ اٰيَتُكَ اَلَّا تُكَلِّمَ النَّاسَ ثَلٰثَةَ اَيَّامٍ اِلَّا رَمْزًا وَّاذْكُرْ رَّبَّكَ كَثِيْرًا وَّسَبِّحْ بِالْعَشِىِّ وَالْاِبْكَارِ ۴۱

42. And when the angels said: O Marium! surely Allah has chosen you and purified you and chosen you above the women of the world.

وَاِذْ قَالَتِ الْمَلٰٓئِكَةُ يٰمَرْيَمُ اِنَّ اللّٰهَ اصْطَفٰىكِ وَطَهَّرَكِ وَاصْطَفٰىكِ عَلٰى نِسَآءِ الْعٰلَمِيْنَ ۴۲

43. O Marium! keep to obedience to your Lord and humble yourself, and bow down with those who bow.

يٰمَرْيَمُ اقْنُتِىْ لِرَبِّكِ وَاسْجُدِىْ وَارْكَعِىْ مَعَ الرّٰكِعِيْنَ ۴۳

44. This is of the announcements relating to the unseen which We reveal to you; and you were not with them when they cast their pens (to decide) which of them should have Marium in his charge, and you were not with them when they contended one with another.

ذٰلِكَ مِنْ اَنْۢبَآءِ الْغَيْبِ نُوْحِيْهِ اِلَيْكَ وَمَا كُنْتَ لَدَيْهِمْ اِذْ يُلْقُوْنَ اَقْلَامَهُمْ اَيُّهُمْ يَكْفُلُ مَرْيَمَ وَمَا كُنْتَ لَدَيْهِمْ اِذْ يَخْتَصِمُوْنَ ۴۴

45. When the angels said: O Marium, surely Allah gives you good news with a Word from Him (of one) whose name is the Messiah, Isa son of Marium, worthy of regard in this world and the hereafter and of those who are made near (to Allah).

اِذْ قَالَتِ الْمَلٰٓئِكَةُ يٰمَرْيَمُ اِنَّ اللّٰهَ يُبَشِّرُكِ بِكَلِمَةٍ مِّنْهُ ١ اسْمُهُ الْمَسِيْحُ عِيْسَى ابْنُ مَرْيَمَ وَجِيْهًا فِى الدُّنْيَا وَالْاٰخِرَةِ وَمِنَ الْمُقَرَّبِيْنَ ۴۵

46. And he shall speak to the people when in the cradle and when of old age, and (he shall be) one of the good ones.

وَيُكَلِّمُ النَّاسَ فِى الْمَهْدِ وَكَهْلًا وَّمِنَ الصّٰلِحِيْنَ ۴۶

47. She said: My Lord! when shall there be a son (born) to me, and man has not touched me? He said: Even so, Allah creates what He pleases; when He has decreed a matter, He only says to it, Be, and it is.

قَالَتْ رَبِّ اَنّٰى يَكُوْنُ لِىْ وَلَدٌ وَّلَمْ يَمْسَسْنِىْ بَشَرٌ قَالَ كَذٰلِكِ اللّٰهُ يَخْلُقُ مَا يَشَآءُ اِذَا قَضٰٓى اَمْرًا فَاِنَّمَا يَقُوْلُ لَهُ كُنْ فَيَكُوْنُ ۴۷

48. And He will teach him the Book and the wisdom and the Tavrat and the Injeel.

وَيُعَلِّمُهُ الْكِتٰبَ وَالْحِكْمَةَ وَالتَّوْرٰىةَ وَالْاِنْجِيْلَ ۴۸

49. And (make him) an apostle to the children of Israel: That I have come to you with a sign from your Lord, that I determine for you out of dust like the form of a bird, then I breathe into it and it becomes a bird with Allah's permission and I heal the blind and the leprous, and bring the dead to life with Allah's permission and I inform you of what you should eat and what you should store in your houses; most surely there is a sign in this for you, if you are believers.

50. And a verifier of that which is before me of the Taurat, and that I may allow you part of that which has been forbidden you, and I have come to you with a sign from your Lord, therefore be careful of (your duty to) Allah and obey me.

51. Surely Allah is my Lord and your Lord, therefore serve Him; this is the right path.

52. But when Isa perceived unbelief on their part, he said: Who will be my helpers in Allah's way? The disciples said: We are helpers (in the way) of Allah: We believe in Allah and bear witness that we are submitting ones.

53. Our Lord! we believe in what Thou hast revealed and we follow the apostle, so write us down with those who bear witness.

54. And they planned and Allah (also) planned, and Allah is the best of planners.

55. And when Allah said: O Isa, I am going to terminate the period of your stay (on earth) and cause you to ascend unto Me and purify you of those who disbelieve and make those who follow you above those who disbelieve to the day of resurrection; then to Me shall be your return, so I will decide between you concerning that in which you differed.

56. Then as to those who disbelieve, I will chastise them with severe chastisement in this world and the hereafter, and they shall have no helpers.

وَرَسُوْلًا اِلٰى بَنِىْۤ اِسْرَآءِيْلَ ۙ۬ اَنِّىْ قَدْ جِئْتُكُمْ بِاٰيَةٍ مِّنْ رَّبِّكُمْ ۙ۬ اَنِّىْۤ اَخْلُقُ لَكُمْ مِّنَ الطِّيْنِ كَهَيْـَٔةِ الطَّيْرِ فَاَنْفُخُ فِيْهِ فَيَكُوْنُ طَيْرًۢا بِاِذْنِ اللّٰهِ ۚ وَاُبْرِئُ الْاَكْمَهَ وَالْاَبْرَصَ وَاُحْىِ الْمَوْتٰى بِاِذْنِ اللّٰهِ ۚ وَاُنَبِّئُكُمْ بِمَا تَاْكُلُوْنَ وَمَا تَدَّخِرُوْنَ ۙ۬ فِىْ بُيُوْتِكُمْ ؕ اِنَّ فِىْ ذٰلِكَ لَاٰيَةً لَّكُمْ اِنْ كُنْتُمْ مُّؤْمِنِيْنَ ۟۔

وَمُصَدِّقًا لِّمَا بَيْنَ يَدَىَّ مِنَ التَّوْرٰىةِ وَلِاُحِلَّ لَكُمْ بَعْضَ الَّذِىْ حُرِّمَ عَلَيْكُمْ وَجِئْتُكُمْ بِاٰيَةٍ مِّنْ رَّبِّكُمْ ۟ۙ فَاتَّقُوا اللّٰهَ وَاَطِيْعُوْنِ ۟

اِنَّ اللّٰهَ رَبِّىْ وَرَبُّكُمْ فَاعْبُدُوْهُ ؕ هٰذَا صِرَاطٌ مُّسْتَقِيْمٌ ۟

فَلَمَّاۤ اَحَسَّ عِيْسٰى مِنْهُمُ الْكُفْرَ قَالَ مَنْ اَنْصَارِىْۤ اِلَى اللّٰهِ ؕ قَالَ الْحَوَارِيُّوْنَ نَحْنُ اَنْصَارُ اللّٰهِ ۚ اٰمَنَّا بِاللّٰهِ ۚ وَاشْهَدْ بِاَنَّا مُسْلِمُوْنَ ۟

رَبَّنَاۤ اٰمَنَّا بِمَاۤ اَنْزَلْتَ وَاتَّبَعْنَا الرَّسُوْلَ فَاكْتُبْنَا مَعَ الشّٰهِدِيْنَ ۟

وَمَكَرُوْا وَمَكَرَ اللّٰهُ ؕ وَاللّٰهُ خَيْرُ الْمٰكِرِيْنَ ۟

اِذْ قَالَ اللّٰهُ يٰعِيْسٰۤى اِنِّىْ مُتَوَفِّيْكَ وَرَافِعُكَ اِلَىَّ وَمُطَهِّرُكَ مِنَ الَّذِيْنَ كَفَرُوْا وَجَاعِلُ الَّذِيْنَ اتَّبَعُوْكَ فَوْقَ الَّذِيْنَ كَفَرُوْۤا اِلٰى يَوْمِ الْقِيٰمَةِ ۚ ثُمَّ اِلَىَّ مَرْجِعُكُمْ فَاَحْكُمُ بَيْنَكُمْ فِيْمَا كُنْتُمْ فِيْهِ تَخْتَلِفُوْنَ ۟

فَاَمَّا الَّذِيْنَ كَفَرُوْا فَاُعَذِّبُهُمْ عَذَابًا شَدِيْدًا فِى الدُّنْيَا وَالْاٰخِرَةِ ۫ وَمَا لَهُمْ مِّنْ نّٰصِرِيْنَ ۟

57. And as to those who believe and do good deeds, He will pay them fully their rewards; and Allah does not love the unjust.

58. This We recite to you of the communications and the wise reminder.

59. Surely the likeness of Isa is with Allah as the likeness of Adam; He created him from dust, then said to him, Be, and he was.

60. (This is) the truth from your Lord, so be not of the disputers.

61. But whoever disputes with you in this matter after what has come to you of knowledge, then say: Come let us call our sons and your sons and our women and your women and our near people and your near people, then let us be earnest in prayer, and pray for the curse of Allah on the liars.

62. Most surely this is the true explanation, and there is no god but Allah; and most surely Allah—He is the Mighty, the Wise.

63. But if they turn back, then surely Allah knows the mischief-makers.

64. Say: O followers of the Book! come to an equitable proposition between us and you that we shall not serve any but Allah and (that) we shall not associate aught with Him, and (that) some of us shall not take others for lords besides Allah; but if they turn back, then say: Bear witness that we are Muslims.

65. O followers of the Book! why do you dispute about Ibrahim, when the Taurat and the Injeel were not revealed till after him; do you not then understand?

66. Behold! you are they who disputed about that of which you had knowledge; why then do you dispute about that of which you have no knowledge? And Allah knows while you do not know.

51

67. Ibrahim was not a Jew nor a Christian but he was (an) upright (man), a Muslim, and he was not one of the polytheists.

68. Most surely the nearest of people to Ibrahim are those who followed him and this Prophet and those who believe and Allah is the guardian of the believers.

69. A party of the followers of the Book desire that they should lead you astray, and they lead not astray but themselves, and they do not perceive.

70. O followers of the Book! Why do you disbelieve in the communications of Allah while you witness (them)?

71. O followers of the Book! Why do you confound the truth with the falsehood and hide the truth while you know?

72. And a party of the followers of the Book say: Avow belief in that which has been revealed to those who believe, in the first part of the day, and disbelieve at the end of it, perhaps they go back on their religion.

73. And do not believe but in him who follows your religion. Say: Surely the (true) guidance is the guidance of Allah—that one may be given (by Him) the like of what you were given; or they would contend with you by an argument before your Lord. Say: Surely grace is in the hand of Allah, He gives it to whom He pleases; and Allah is Ample-giving, Knowing.

74. He specially chooses for His mercy whom He pleases; and Allah is the Lord of mighty grace.

75. And among the followers of the Book there are some such that if you entrust one (of them) with a heap of wealth, he shall pay it back to you; and among them there are some such that if you entrust one (of them) with a dinar he shall not pay it back to you except so long as you remain firm in demanding it; this is because they say: There is not upon us in the matter of the unlearned people any way (to reproach); and they tell a lie against Allah while they know.

52

76. Yea, whoever fulfills his promise and guards (against evil)—then surely Allah loves those who guard (against evil).

77. (As for) those who take a small price for the covenant of Allah and their own oaths—surely they shall have no portion in the hereafter, and Allah will not speak to them, nor will He look upon them on the day of resurrection nor will He purify them, and they shall have a painful chastisement.

78. Most surely there is a party amongst those who distort the Book with their tongue that you may consider it to be (a part) of the Book, and they say, It is from Allah, while it is not from Allah; and they tell a lie against Allah whilst they know.

79. It is not meet for a mortal that Allah should give him the Book and the wisdom and prophethood, then he should say to men: Be my servants rather than Allah's; but rather (he would say): Be worshippers of the Lord because of your teaching the Book and your reading (it yourselves).

80. And neither would he enjoin you that you should take the angels and the prophets for lords; what! would he enjoin you with unbelief after you are Muslims?

81. And when Allah made a covenant through the prophets: Certainly what I have given you of Book and wisdom—then an apostle comes to you verifying that which is with you, you must believe in him, and you must aid him. He said: Do you affirm and accept My compact in this (matter)? They said: We do affirm. He said: Then bear witness, and I (too) am of the bearers of witness with you.

53

82. Whoever therefore turns back after this, these it is that are the transgressors.

فَمَنْ تَوَلَّى بَعْدَ ذٰلِكَ فَاُولٰٓئِكَ هُمُ الْفٰسِقُوْنَ ۝

83. Is it then other than Allah's religion that they seek (to follow), and to Him submits whoever is in the heavens and the earth, willingly or unwillingly, and to Him shall they be returned.

اَفَغَيْرَ دِيْنِ اللّٰهِ يَبْغُوْنَ وَلَهٗٓ اَسْلَمَ مَنْ فِى السَّمٰوٰتِ وَالْاَرْضِ طَوْعًا وَّكَرْهًا وَّاِلَيْهِ يُرْجَعُوْنَ ۝

84. Say: We believe in Allah and what has been revealed to us, and what was revealed to Ibrahim and Ismail and Ishaq and Yaqoub and the tribes, and what was given to Musa and Isa and to the prophets from their Lord; we do not make any distinction between any of them, and to Him do we submit.

قُلْ اٰمَنَّا بِاللّٰهِ وَمَآ اُنْزِلَ عَلَيْنَا وَمَآ اُنْزِلَ عَلٰٓى اِبْرٰهِيْمَ وَاِسْمٰعِيْلَ وَاِسْحٰقَ وَيَعْقُوْبَ وَالْاَسْبَاطِ وَمَآ اُوْتِيَ مُوْسٰى وَعِيْسٰى وَالنَّبِيُّوْنَ مِنْ رَّبِّهِمْ لَا نُفَرِّقُ بَيْنَ اَحَدٍ مِّنْهُمْ وَنَحْنُ لَهٗ مُسْلِمُوْنَ ۝

85. And whoever desires a religion other than Islam, it shall not be accepted from him, and in the hereafter he shall be one of the losers.

وَمَنْ يَّبْتَغِ غَيْرَ الْاِسْلَامِ دِيْنًا فَلَنْ يُّقْبَلَ مِنْهُ وَهُوَ فِى الْاٰخِرَةِ مِنَ الْخٰسِرِيْنَ ۝

86. How shall Allah guide a people who disbelieved after their believing and (after) they had borne witness that the Apostle was true and clear arguments had come to them; and Allah does not guide the unjust people.

كَيْفَ يَهْدِى اللّٰهُ قَوْمًا كَفَرُوْا بَعْدَ اِيْمَانِهِمْ وَشَهِدُوْا اَنَّ الرَّسُوْلَ حَقٌّ وَّجَآءَهُمُ الْبَيِّنٰتُ وَاللّٰهُ لَا يَهْدِى الْقَوْمَ الظّٰلِمِيْنَ ۝

87. (As for) these, their reward is that upon them is the curse of Allah and the angels and of men, all together.

اُولٰٓئِكَ جَزَآؤُهُمْ اَنَّ عَلَيْهِمْ لَعْنَةَ اللّٰهِ وَالْمَلٰٓئِكَةِ وَالنَّاسِ اَجْمَعِيْنَ ۝

88. Abiding in it; their chastisement shall not be lightened nor shall they be respited.

خٰلِدِيْنَ فِيْهَا لَا يُخَفَّفُ عَنْهُمُ الْعَذَابُ وَلَا هُمْ يُنْظَرُوْنَ ۝

89. Except those who repent after that and amend, then surely Allah is Forgiving, Merciful.

اِلَّا الَّذِيْنَ تَابُوْا مِنْ بَعْدِ ذٰلِكَ وَاَصْلَحُوْا فَاِنَّ اللّٰهَ غَفُوْرٌ رَّحِيْمٌ ۝

90. Surely, those who disbelieve after their believing, then increase in unbelief, their repentance shall not be accepted, and these are they that go astray.

اِنَّ الَّذِيْنَ كَفَرُوْا بَعْدَ اِيْمَانِهِمْ ثُمَّ ازْدَادُوْا كُفْرًا لَّنْ تُقْبَلَ تَوْبَتُهُمْ وَاُولٰٓئِكَ هُمُ الضَّآلُّوْنَ ۝

91. Surely, those who disbelieve and die while they are unbelievers, the earth full of gold shall not be accepted from one of them, though he should offer to ransom himself with it; these it is who shall have a painful chastisement, and they shall have no helpers.

92. By no means shall you attain to righteousness until you spend (benevolently) out of what you love; and whatever thing you spend, Allah surely knows it.

93. All food was lawful to the children of Israel except that which Israel had forbidden to himself, before the Taurat was revealed. Say: Bring then the Taurat and read it, if you are truthful.

94. Then whoever fabricates a lie against Allah after this, these it is that are the unjust.

95. Say: Allah has spoken the truth, therefore follow the religion of Ibrahim, the upright one; and he was not one of the polytheists.

96. Most surely the first house appointed for men is the one at Bekka, blessed and a guidance for the nations.

97. In it are clear signs, the standing place of Ibrahim, and whoever enters it shall be secure, and pilgrimage to the House is incumbent upon men for the sake of Allah, (upon) every one who is able to undertake the journey to it; and whoever disbelieves, then surely Allah is Self-sufficient, above any need of the worlds.

98. Say: O followers of the Book! why do you disbelieve in the communications of Allah? And Allah is a witness of what you do.

99. Say: O followers of the Book! why do you hinder him who believes from the way of Allah? You seek (to make) it crooked, while you are witnesses, and Allah is not heedless of what you do.

اِنَّ الَّذِيْنَ كَفَرُوْا وَمَاتُوْا وَهُمْ كُفَّارٌ فَلَنْ يُّقْبَلَ مِنْ اَحَدِهِمْ مِّلْءُ الْاَرْضِ ذَهَبًا وَّلَوِ افْتَدٰى بِهٖ ؕ اُولٰٓئِكَ لَهُمْ عَذَابٌ اَلِيْمٌ ۙ وَّمَا لَهُمْ مِّنْ نّٰصِرِيْنَ ۧ ۞

لَنْ تَنَالُوا الْبِرَّ حَتّٰى تُنْفِقُوْا مِمَّا تُحِبُّوْنَ ؕ وَمَا تُنْفِقُوْا مِنْ شَيْءٍ فَاِنَّ اللّٰهَ بِهٖ عَلِيْمٌ ۞

كُلُّ الطَّعَامِ كَانَ حِلًّا لِّبَنِيْۤ اِسْرَآءِيْلَ اِلَّا مَا حَرَّمَ اِسْرَآءِيْلُ عَلٰى نَفْسِهٖ مِنْ قَبْلِ اَنْ تُنَزَّلَ التَّوْرٰىةُ ؕ قُلْ فَأْتُوْا بِالتَّوْرٰىةِ فَاتْلُوْهَآ اِنْ كُنْتُمْ صٰدِقِيْنَ ۞

فَمَنِ افْتَرٰى عَلَى اللّٰهِ الْكَذِبَ مِنْ بَعْدِ ذٰلِكَ فَاُولٰٓئِكَ هُمُ الظّٰلِمُوْنَ ۞

قُلْ صَدَقَ اللّٰهُ ۟ فَاتَّبِعُوْا مِلَّةَ اِبْرٰهِيْمَ حَنِيْفًا ؕ وَمَا كَانَ مِنَ الْمُشْرِكِيْنَ ۞

اِنَّ اَوَّلَ بَيْتٍ وُّضِعَ لِلنَّاسِ لَلَّذِيْ بِبَكَّةَ مُبٰرَكًا وَّهُدًى لِّلْعٰلَمِيْنَ ۞

فِيْهِ اٰيٰتٌۢ بَيِّنٰتٌ مَّقَامُ اِبْرٰهِيْمَ ۟ وَمَنْ دَخَلَهٗ كَانَ اٰمِنًا ؕ وَلِلّٰهِ عَلَى النَّاسِ حِجُّ الْبَيْتِ مَنِ اسْتَطَاعَ اِلَيْهِ سَبِيْلًا ؕ وَمَنْ كَفَرَ فَاِنَّ اللّٰهَ غَنِيٌّ عَنِ الْعٰلَمِيْنَ ۞

قُلْ يٰۤاَهْلَ الْكِتٰبِ لِمَ تَكْفُرُوْنَ بِاٰيٰتِ اللّٰهِ ۖ وَاللّٰهُ شَهِيْدٌ عَلٰى مَا تَعْمَلُوْنَ ۞

قُلْ يٰۤاَهْلَ الْكِتٰبِ لِمَ تَصُدُّوْنَ عَنْ سَبِيْلِ اللّٰهِ مَنْ اٰمَنَ تَبْغُوْنَهَا عِوَجًا وَّاَنْتُمْ شُهَدَآءُ ؕ وَمَا اللّٰهُ بِغَافِلٍ عَمَّا تَعْمَلُوْنَ ۞

100. O you who believe! if you obey a party from among those who have been given the Book, they will turn you back as unbelievers after you have believed.

101. But how can you disbelieve while it is you to whom the communications of Allah are recited, and among you is His Apostle? And whoever holds fast to Allah, he indeed is guided to the right path.

102. O you who believe! be careful of (your duty to) Allah with the care which is due to Him, and do not die unless you are Muslims.

103. And hold fast by the covenant of Allah all together and be not disunited, and remember the favor of Allah on you when you were enemies, then He united your hearts so by His favor you became brethren; and you were on the brink of a pit of fire, then He saved you from it; thus does Allah make clear to you His communications that you may follow the right way.

104. And from among you there should be a party who invite to good and enjoin what is right and forbid the wrong, and these it is that shall be successful.

105. And be not like those who became divided and disagreed after clear arguments had come to them, and these it is that shall have a grievous chastisement.

106. On the day when (some) faces shall turn white and (some) faces shall turn black; then as to those whose faces turn black: Did you disbelieve after your believing? Taste therefore the chastisement because you disbelieved.

107. And as to those whose faces turn white, they shall be in Allah's mercy; in it they shall abide.

وَاَمَّاالَّذِيۡنَ ابۡيَضَّتۡ وُجُوۡهُهُمۡ فَفِىۡ رَحۡمَةِ اللهِ ۖ
هُمۡ فِيۡهَا خٰلِدُوۡنَ ۝

108. These are the communications of Allah which We recite to you with truth, and Allah does not desire any injustice to the creatures.

تِلۡكَ اٰيٰتُ اللهِ نَتۡلُوۡهَا عَلَيۡكَ بِالۡحَقِّ ۚ وَمَا اللهُ
يُرِيۡدُ ظُلۡمًا لِّلۡعٰلَمِيۡنَ ۝

109. And whatever is in the heavens and whatever is in the earth is Allah's; and to Allah all things return.

وَلِلّٰهِ مَا فِى السَّمٰوٰتِ وَمَا فِى الۡاَرۡضِ ۚ وَاِلَى اللهِ
تُرۡجَعُ الۡاُمُوۡرُ ۝

110. You are the best of the nations raised up for (the benefit of) men; you enjoin what is right and forbid the wrong and believe in Allah; and if the followers of the Book had believed it would have been better for them; of them (some) are believers and most of them are transgressors.

كُنۡتُمۡ خَيۡرَ اُمَّةٍ اُخۡرِجَتۡ لِلنَّاسِ تَاۡمُرُوۡنَ بِالۡمَعۡرُوۡفِ
وَتَنۡهَوۡنَ عَنِ الۡمُنۡكَرِ وَتُؤۡمِنُوۡنَ بِاللهِ ۗ وَلَوۡ اٰمَنَ
اَهۡلُ الۡكِتٰبِ لَكَانَ خَيۡرًا لَّهُمۡ ۚ مِّنۡهُمُ الۡمُؤۡمِنُوۡنَ
وَاَكۡثَرُهُمُ الۡفٰسِقُوۡنَ ۝

111. They shall by no means harm you but with a slight evil; and if they fight with you they shall turn (their) backs to you, then shall they not be helped.

لَنۡ يَّضُرُّوۡكُمۡ اِلَّآ اَذًى ۚ وَاِنۡ يُّقَاتِلُوۡكُمۡ يُوَلُّوۡكُمُ
الۡاَدۡبَارَ ۖ ثُمَّ لَا يُنۡصَرُوۡنَ ۝

112. Abasement is made to cleave to them wherever they are found, except under a covenant with Allah and a covenant with men, and they have become deserving of wrath from Allah, and humiliation is made to cleave to them; this is because they disbelieved in the communications of Allah and slew the prophets unjustly; this is because they disobeyed and exceeded the limits.

ضُرِبَتۡ عَلَيۡهِمُ الذِّلَّةُ اَيۡنَ مَا ثُقِفُوۡۤا اِلَّا بِحَبۡلٍ مِّنَ اللهِ وَ
حَبۡلٍ مِّنَ النَّاسِ وَبَآءُوۡ بِغَضَبٍ مِّنَ اللهِ وَضُرِبَتۡ عَلَيۡهِمُ
الۡمَسۡكَنَةُ ۚ ذٰلِكَ بِاَنَّهُمۡ كَانُوۡا يَكۡفُرُوۡنَ بِاٰيٰتِ اللهِ وَيَقۡتُلُوۡنَ
الۡاَنۡۢبِيَآءَ بِغَيۡرِ حَقٍّ ۚ ذٰلِكَ بِمَا عَصَوۡا وَّكَانُوۡا يَعۡتَدُوۡنَ ۝

113. They are not all alike; of the followers of the Book there is an upright party; they recite Allah's communications in the night time and they adore (Him).

لَيۡسُوۡا سَوَآءً ۗ مِّنۡ اَهۡلِ الۡكِتٰبِ اُمَّةٌ قَآئِمَةٌ يَّتۡلُوۡنَ
اٰيٰتِ اللهِ اٰنَآءَ الَّيۡلِ وَهُمۡ يَسۡجُدُوۡنَ ۝

114. They believe in Allah and the last day, and they enjoin what is right and forbid the wrong, and they strive with one another in hastening to good deeds, and those are among the good.

يُؤۡمِنُوۡنَ بِاللهِ وَالۡيَوۡمِ الۡاٰخِرِ وَيَاۡمُرُوۡنَ بِالۡمَعۡرُوۡفِ
وَيَنۡهَوۡنَ عَنِ الۡمُنۡكَرِ وَيُسَارِعُوۡنَ فِى الۡخَيۡرٰتِ ۗ وَ
اُولٰٓئِكَ مِنَ الصّٰلِحِيۡنَ ۝

115. And whatever good they do, they shall not be denied it, and Allah knows those who guard (against evil).

وَمَا يَفۡعَلُوۡا مِنۡ خَيۡرٍ فَلَنۡ يُّكۡفَرُوۡهُ ۗ وَاللهُ عَلِيۡمٌۢ بِالۡمُتَّقِيۡنَ ۝

116. (As for) those who disbelieve, surely neither their wealth nor their children shall avail them in the least against Allah; and these are the inmates of the fire; therein they shall abide.

اِنَّ الَّذِيْنَ كَفَرُوْا لَنْ تُغْنِيَ عَنْهُمْ اَمْوَالُهُمْ وَلَاۤ اَوْلَادُهُمْ مِّنَ اللّٰهِ شَيْئًا ؕ وَاُولٰٓئِكَ اَصْحٰبُ النَّارِ ۚ هُمْ فِيْهَا خٰلِدُوْنَ ۝

117. The likeness of what they spend in the life of this world is as the likeness of wind in which is intense cold (that) smites the seed produce of a people who have done injustice to their souls and destroys it; and Allah is not unjust to them, but they are unjust to themselves.

مَثَلُ مَا يُنْفِقُوْنَ فِيْ هٰذِهِ الْحَيٰوةِ الدُّنْيَا كَمَثَلِ رِيْحٍ فِيْهَا صِرٌّ اَصَابَتْ حَرْثَ قَوْمٍ ظَلَمُوْۤا اَنْفُسَهُمْ فَاَهْلَكَتْهُ ؕ وَمَا ظَلَمَهُمُ اللّٰهُ وَلٰكِنْ اَنْفُسَهُمْ يَظْلِمُوْنَ ۝

118. O you who believe! do not take for intimate friends from among others than your own people; they do not fall short of inflicting loss upon you; they love what distresses you; vehement hatred has already appeared from out of their mouths, and what their breasts conceal is greater still; indeed, We have made the communications clear to you, if you will understand.

يٰۤاَيُّهَا الَّذِيْنَ اٰمَنُوْا لَا تَتَّخِذُوْا بِطَانَةً مِّنْ دُوْنِكُمْ لَا يَاْلُوْنَكُمْ خَبَالًا ؕ وَدُّوْا مَا عَنِتُّمْ ۚ قَدْ بَدَتِ الْبَغْضَاۤءُ مِنْ اَفْوَاهِهِمْ ۖ وَمَا تُخْفِيْ صُدُوْرُهُمْ اَكْبَرُ ؕ قَدْ بَيَّنَّا لَكُمُ الْاٰيٰتِ اِنْ كُنْتُمْ تَعْقِلُوْنَ ۝

119. Lo! you are they who will love them while they do not love you, and you believe in the Book (in) the whole of it; and when they meet you they say: We believe, and when they are alone, they bite the ends of their fingers in rage against you. Say: Die in your rage; surely Allah knows what is in the breasts.

هٰۤاَنْتُمْ اُولَاۤءِ تُحِبُّوْنَهُمْ وَلَا يُحِبُّوْنَكُمْ وَتُؤْمِنُوْنَ بِالْكِتٰبِ كُلِّهٖ ۚ وَاِذَا لَقُوْكُمْ قَالُوْۤا اٰمَنَّا ۖ وَاِذَا خَلَوْا عَضُّوْا عَلَيْكُمُ الْاَنَامِلَ مِنَ الْغَيْظِ ؕ قُلْ مُوْتُوْا بِغَيْظِكُمْ ؕ اِنَّ اللّٰهَ عَلِيْمٌۢ بِذَاتِ الصُّدُوْرِ ۝

120. If good befalls you, it grieves them, and if an evil afflicts you, they rejoice at it; and if you are patient and guard yourselves, their scheme will not injure you in any way; surely Allah comprehends what they do.

اِنْ تَمْسَسْكُمْ حَسَنَةٌ تَسُؤْهُمْ ۖ وَاِنْ تُصِبْكُمْ سَيِّئَةٌ يَّفْرَحُوْا بِهَا ؕ وَاِنْ تَصْبِرُوْا وَتَتَّقُوْا لَا يَضُرُّكُمْ كَيْدُهُمْ شَيْئًا ؕ اِنَّ اللّٰهَ بِمَا يَعْمَلُوْنَ مُحِيْطٌ ۝

121. And when you did go forth early in the morning from your family to lodge the believers in encampments for war and Allah is Hearing, Knowing.

وَاِذْ غَدَوْتَ مِنْ اَهْلِكَ تُبَوِّئُ الْمُؤْمِنِيْنَ مَقَاعِدَ لِلْقِتَالِ ؕ وَاللّٰهُ سَمِيْعٌ عَلِيْمٌ ۝

122. When two parties from among you had determined that they should show cowardice, and Allah was the guardian of them both, and in Allah should the believers trust.

123. And Allah did certainly assist you at Badr when you were weak; be careful of (your duty to) Allah then, that you may give thanks.

124. When you said to the believers: Does it not suffice you that your Lord should assist you with three thousand of the angels sent down?

125. Yea! if you remain patient and are on your guard, and they come upon you in a headlong manner, your Lord will assist you with five thousand of the havoc-making angels.

126. And Allah did not make it but as good news for you, and that your hearts might be at ease thereby, and victory is only from Allah, the Mighty, the Wise.

127. That He may cut off a portion from among those who disbelieve, or abase them so that they should return disappointed of attaining what they desired.

128. You have no concern in the affair whether He turns to them (mercifully) or chastises them, for surely they are unjust.

129. And whatever is in the heavens and whatever is in the earth is Allah's; He forgives whom He pleases and chastises whom He pleases; and Allah is Forgiving, Merciful.

130. O you who believe! do not devour usury, making it double and redouble, and be careful of (your duty to) Allah, that you may be successful.

131. And guard yourselves against the fire which has been prepared for the unbelievers.

132. And obey Allah and the Apostle, that you may be shown mercy.

133. And hasten to forgiveness from your Lord; and a Garden, the extensiveness of which is (as) the heavens and the earth, it is prepared for those who guard (against evil).

134. Those who spend (benevolently) in ease as well as in straitness, and those who restrain (their) anger and pardon men; and Allah loves the doers of good (to others).

135. And those who when they commit an indecency or do injustice to their souls remember Allah and ask forgiveness for their faults—and who forgives the faults but Allah, and (who) do not knowingly persist in what they have done.

136. (As for) these—their reward is forgiveness from their Lord, and gardens beneath which rivers flow, to abide in them, and excellent is the reward of the laborers.

137. Indeed there have been examples before you; therefore travel in the earth and see what was the end of the rejecters.

138. This is a clear statement for men, and a guidance and an admonition to those who guard (against evil).

139. And be not infirm, and be not grieving, and you shall have the upper hand if you are believers.

140. If a wound has afflicted you (at Ohud), a wound like it has also afflicted the (unbelieving) people; and We bring these days to men by turns, and that Allah may know those who believe and take witnesses from among you; and Allah does not love the unjust.

141. And that He may purge those who believe and deprive the unbelievers of blessings.

142. Do you think that you will enter the garden while Allah has not yet known those who strive hard from among you, and (He has not) known the patient.

60

143. And certainly you desired death before you met it; so indeed you have seen it and you look (at it).

وَلَقَدْ كُنْتُمْ تَمَنَّوْنَ الْمَوْتَ مِنْ قَبْلِ اَنْ تَلْقَوْهُ فَقَدْ رَاَيْتُمُوْهُ وَاَنْتُمْ تَنْظُرُوْنَ ۝

144. And Muhammad is no more than an apostle; the apostles have already passed away before him; if then he dies or is killed, will you turn back upon your heels? And whoever turns back upon his heels, he will by no means do harm to Allah in the least; and Allah will reward the grateful.

وَمَا مُحَمَّدٌ اِلَّا رَسُوْلٌ ۚ قَدْ خَلَتْ مِنْ قَبْلِهِ الرُّسُلُ ۚ اَفَاِنْ مَّاتَ اَوْ قُتِلَ انْقَلَبْتُمْ عَلٰى اَعْقَابِكُمْ ۚ وَمَنْ يَّنْقَلِبْ عَلٰى عَقِبَيْهِ فَلَنْ يَّضُرَّ اللّٰهَ شَيْئًا ۚ وَسَيَجْزِى اللّٰهُ الشّٰكِرِيْنَ ۝

145. And a soul will not die but with the permission of Allah; the term is fixed; and whoever desires the reward of this world, I shall give him of it, and whoever desires the reward of the hereafter I shall give him of it; and I will reward the grateful.

وَمَا كَانَ لِنَفْسٍ اَنْ تَمُوْتَ اِلَّا بِاِذْنِ اللّٰهِ كِتٰبًا مُّؤَجَّلًا ۚ وَمَنْ يُّرِدْ ثَوَابَ الدُّنْيَا نُؤْتِهِ مِنْهَا ۚ وَمَنْ يُّرِدْ ثَوَابَ الْاٰخِرَةِ نُؤْتِهِ مِنْهَا ۚ وَسَنَجْزِى الشّٰكِرِيْنَ ۝

146. And how many a prophet has fought with whom were many worshippers of the Lord; so they did not become weak-hearted on account of what befell them in Allah's way, nor did they weaken, nor did they abase themselves; and Allah loves the patient.

وَكَاَيِّنْ مِّنْ نَّبِيٍّ قٰتَلَ ۙ مَعَهُ رِبِّيُّوْنَ كَثِيْرٌ ۚ فَمَا وَهَنُوْا لِمَا اَصَابَهُمْ فِيْ سَبِيْلِ اللّٰهِ وَمَا ضَعُفُوْا وَمَا اسْتَكَانُوْا ۚ وَاللّٰهُ يُحِبُّ الصّٰبِرِيْنَ ۝

147. And their saying was no other than that they said: Our Lord! forgive us our faults and our extravagance in our affair, and make firm our feet and help us against the unbelieving people.

وَمَا كَانَ قَوْلَهُمْ اِلَّا اَنْ قَالُوْا رَبَّنَا اغْفِرْ لَنَا ذُنُوْبَنَا وَاِسْرَافَنَا فِيْ اَمْرِنَا وَثَبِّتْ اَقْدَامَنَا وَانْصُرْنَا عَلَى الْقَوْمِ الْكٰفِرِيْنَ ۝

148. So Allah gave them the reward of this world and better reward of the hereafter and Allah loves those who do good (to others).

فَاٰتٰهُمُ اللّٰهُ ثَوَابَ الدُّنْيَا وَحُسْنَ ثَوَابِ الْاٰخِرَةِ ۚ وَاللّٰهُ يُحِبُّ الْمُحْسِنِيْنَ ۝

149. O you who believe! if you obey those who disbelieve, they will turn you back upon your heels, so you will turn back losers.

يٰٓاَيُّهَا الَّذِيْنَ اٰمَنُوْا اِنْ تُطِيْعُوا الَّذِيْنَ كَفَرُوْا يَرُدُّوْكُمْ عَلٰٓى اَعْقَابِكُمْ فَتَنْقَلِبُوْا خٰسِرِيْنَ ۝

150. Nay! Allah is your Patron and He is the best of the helpers.

بَلِ اللّٰهُ مَوْلٰكُمْ ۚ وَهُوَ خَيْرُ النّٰصِرِيْنَ ۝

151. We will cast terror into the hearts of those who disbelieve, because they set up with Allah that for which He has sent down no authority, and their abode is the fire; and evil is the abode of the unjust.

سَنُلْقِى فِى قُلُوبِ الَّذِيْنَ كَفَرُوا الرُّعْبَ بِمَا اَشْرَكُوْا بِاللّٰهِ مَا لَمْ يُنَزِّلْ بِهٖ سُلْطٰنًا ۚ وَمَأْوٰىهُمُ النَّارُ ۗ وَبِئْسَ مَثْوَى الظّٰلِمِيْنَ ۝

152. And certainly Allah made good to you His promise, when you slew them by His permission, until when you became weak-hearted and disputed about the affair and disobeyed after He had shown you that which you loved; of you were some who desired this world and of you were some who desired the hereafter; then He turned you away from them that He might try you; and He has certainly pardoned you, and Allah is Gracious to the believers.

وَلَقَدْ صَدَقَكُمُ اللّٰهُ وَعْدَهٗۤ اِذْ تَحُسُّوْنَهُمْ بِاِذْنِهٖ ۚ حَتّٰۤى اِذَا فَشِلْتُمْ وَتَنَازَعْتُمْ فِى الْاَمْرِ وَعَصَيْتُمْ مِّنْۢ بَعْدِ مَاۤ اَرٰىكُمْ مَّا تُحِبُّوْنَ ۗ مِنْكُمْ مَّنْ يُّرِيْدُ الدُّنْيَا وَمِنْكُمْ مَّنْ يُّرِيْدُ الْاٰخِرَةَ ۚ ثُمَّ صَرَفَكُمْ عَنْهُمْ لِيَبْتَلِيَكُمْ ۚ وَلَقَدْ عَفَا عَنْكُمْ ۗ وَاللّٰهُ ذُوْ فَضْلٍ عَلَى الْمُؤْمِنِيْنَ ۝

153. When you ran off precipitately and did not wait for any one, and the Apostle was calling you from your rear, so He gave you another sorrow instead of (your) sorrow, so that you might not grieve at what had escaped you, nor (at) what befell you; and Allah is aware of what you do.

اِذْ تُصْعِدُوْنَ وَلَا تَلْوٗنَ عَلٰۤى اَحَدٍ وَّالرَّسُوْلُ يَدْعُوْكُمْ فِىۡۤ اُخْرٰىكُمْ فَاَثَابَكُمْ غَمًّاۢ بِغَمٍّ لِّكَيْلَا تَحْزَنُوْا عَلٰى مَا فَاتَكُمْ وَلَا مَاۤ اَصَابَكُمْ ۗ وَاللّٰهُ خَبِيْرٌۢ بِمَا تَعْمَلُوْنَ ۝

154. Then after sorrow He sent down security upon you, a calm coming upon a party of you, and (there was) another party whom their own souls had rendered anxious; they entertained about Allah thoughts of ignorance quite unjustly, saying: We have no hand in the affair. Say: Surely the affair is wholly (in the hands) of Allah. They conceal within their souls what they would not reveal to you. They say: Had we any hand in the affair, we would not have been slain here. Say: Had you remained in your houses, those for whom slaughter was ordained would certainly have gone forth to the places where they would be slain, and that Allah might test what was in your breasts and that He might purge what was in your hearts; and Allah knows what is in the breasts.

ثُمَّ اَنْزَلَ عَلَيْكُمْ مِّنْۢ بَعْدِ الْغَمِّ اَمَنَةً نُّعَاسًا يَّغْشٰى طَآئِفَةً مِّنْكُمْ ۙ وَطَآئِفَةٌ قَدْ اَهَمَّتْهُمْ اَنْفُسُهُمْ يَظُنُّوْنَ بِاللّٰهِ غَيْرَ الْحَقِّ ظَنَّ الْجَاهِلِيَّةِ ۗ يَقُوْلُوْنَ هَلْ لَّنَا مِنَ الْاَمْرِ مِنْ شَىْءٍ ۗ قُلْ اِنَّ الْاَمْرَ كُلَّهٗ لِلّٰهِ ۗ يُخْفُوْنَ فِىْۤ اَنْفُسِهِمْ مَّا لَا يُبْدُوْنَ لَكَ ۗ يَقُوْلُوْنَ لَوْ كَانَ لَنَا مِنَ الْاَمْرِ شَىْءٌ مَّا قُتِلْنَا هٰهُنَا ۗ قُلْ لَّوْ كُنْتُمْ فِىْ بُيُوْتِكُمْ لَبَرَزَ الَّذِيْنَ كُتِبَ عَلَيْهِمُ الْقَتْلُ اِلٰى مَضَاجِعِهِمْ ۚ وَلِيَبْتَلِيَ اللّٰهُ مَا فِىْ صُدُوْرِكُمْ وَلِيُمَحِّصَ مَا فِىْ قُلُوْبِكُمْ ۗ وَاللّٰهُ عَلِيْمٌۢ بِذَاتِ الصُّدُوْرِ ۝

155. (As for) those of you who turned back on the day when the two armies met, only the Shaitan sought to cause them to make a slip on account of some deeds they had done, and certainly Allah has pardoned them; surely Allah is Forgiving, Forbearing.

اِنَّ الَّذِيْنَ تَوَلَّوْا مِنْكُمْ يَوْمَ الْتَقَى الْجَمْعٰنِ اِنَّمَا اسْتَزَلَّهُمُ الشَّيْطٰنُ بِبَعْضِ مَا كَسَبُوْا وَلَقَدْ عَفَا اللّٰهُ عَنْهُمْ اِنَّ اللّٰهَ غَفُوْرٌ حَلِيْمٌ ۠ ۝

156. O you who believe! be not like those who disbelieve and say of their brethren when they travel in the earth or engage in fighting: Had they been with us, they would not have died and they would not have been slain; so Allah makes this to be an intense regret in their hearts; and Allah gives life and causes death; and Allah sees what you do.

يٰۤاَيُّهَا الَّذِيْنَ اٰمَنُوْا لَا تَكُوْنُوْا كَالَّذِيْنَ كَفَرُوْا وَقَالُوْا لِاِخْوَانِهِمْ اِذَا ضَرَبُوْا فِى الْاَرْضِ اَوْ كَانُوْا غُزًّى لَّوْ كَانُوْا عِنْدَنَا مَا مَاتُوْا وَمَا قُتِلُوْا لِيَجْعَلَ اللّٰهُ ذٰلِكَ حَسْرَةً فِىْ قُلُوْبِهِمْ وَاللّٰهُ يُحْيٖ وَيُمِيْتُ وَ اللّٰهُ بِمَا تَعْمَلُوْنَ بَصِيْرٌ ۝

157. And if you are slain in the way of Allah or you die, certainly forgiveness from Allah and mercy is better than what they amass.

وَلَئِنْ قُتِلْتُمْ فِىْ سَبِيْلِ اللّٰهِ اَوْ مُتُّمْ لَمَغْفِرَةٌ مِّنَ اللّٰهِ وَرَحْمَةٌ خَيْرٌ مِّمَّا يَجْمَعُوْنَ ۝

158. And if indeed you die or you are slain, certainly to Allah shall you be gathered together.

وَلَئِنْ مُّتُّمْ اَوْ قُتِلْتُمْ لَاِلَى اللّٰهِ تُحْشَرُوْنَ ۝

159. Thus it is due to mercy from Allah that you deal with them gently, and had you been rough, hard hearted, they would certainly have dispersed from around you; pardon them therefore and ask pardon for them, and take counsel with them in the affair; so when you have decided, then place your trust in Allah; surely Allah loves those who trust.

فَبِمَا رَحْمَةٍ مِّنَ اللّٰهِ لِنْتَ لَهُمْ وَلَوْ كُنْتَ فَظًّا غَلِيْظَ الْقَلْبِ لَانْفَضُّوْا مِنْ حَوْلِكَ فَاعْفُ عَنْهُمْ وَاسْتَغْفِرْ لَهُمْ وَشَاوِرْهُمْ فِى الْاَمْرِ فَاِذَا عَزَمْتَ فَتَوَكَّلْ عَلَى اللّٰهِ اِنَّ اللّٰهَ يُحِبُّ الْمُتَوَكِّلِيْنَ ۝

160. If Allah assists you, then there is none that can overcome you, and if He forsakes you, who is there then that can assist you after Him? And on Allah should the believers rely.

اِنْ يَّنْصُرْكُمُ اللّٰهُ فَلَا غَالِبَ لَكُمْ وَاِنْ يَّخْذُلْكُمْ فَمَنْ ذَا الَّذِىْ يَنْصُرُكُمْ مِّنْ بَعْدِهٖ وَعَلَى اللّٰهِ فَلْيَتَوَكَّلِ الْمُؤْمِنُوْنَ ۝

161. And it is not attributable to a prophet that he should act unfaithfully; and he who acts unfaithfully shall bring that in respect of which he has acted unfaithfully on the day of resurrection; then shall every soul be paid back fully what it has earned, and they shall not be dealt with unjustly.

وَمَا كَانَ لِنَبِىٍّ اَنْ يَّغُلَّ وَمَنْ يَّغْلُلْ يَأْتِ بِمَا غَلَّ يَوْمَ الْقِيٰمَةِ ثُمَّ تُوَفّٰى كُلُّ نَفْسٍ مَّا كَسَبَتْ وَهُمْ لَا يُظْلَمُوْنَ ۝

162. Is then he who follows the pleasure of Allah like him who has made himself deserving of displeasure from Allah, and his abode is hell; and it is an evil destination.

اَفَمَنِ اتَّبَعَ رِضْوَانَ اللّٰهِ كَمَنْ بَآءَ بِسَخَطٍ مِّنَ اللّٰهِ وَمَأْوٰىهُ جَهَنَّمُ ۗ وَبِئْسَ الْمَصِيْرُ ۝

163. There are (varying) grades with Allah, and Allah sees what they do.

هُمْ دَرَجٰتٌ عِنْدَ اللّٰهِ ۗ وَاللّٰهُ بَصِيْرٌ ۢبِمَا يَعْمَلُوْنَ ۝

164. Certainly Allah conferred a benefit upon the believers when He raised among them an Apostle from among themselves, reciting to them His communications and purifying them, and teaching them the Book and the wisdom, although before that they were surely in manifest error.

لَقَدْ مَنَّ اللّٰهُ عَلَى الْمُؤْمِنِيْنَ اِذْ بَعَثَ فِيْهِمْ رَسُوْلًا مِّنْ اَنْفُسِهِمْ يَتْلُوْا عَلَيْهِمْ اٰيٰتِهٖ وَيُزَكِّيْهِمْ وَيُعَلِّمُهُمُ الْكِتٰبَ وَالْحِكْمَةَ ۚ وَاِنْ كَانُوْا مِنْ قَبْلُ لَفِيْ ضَلٰلٍ مُّبِيْنٍ ۝

165. What! when a misfortune befell you, and you had certainly afflicted (the unbelievers) with twice as much, you began to say: Whence is this? Say: It is from yourselves; surely Allah has power over all things.

اَوَلَمَّآ اَصَابَتْكُمْ مُّصِيْبَةٌ قَدْ اَصَبْتُمْ مِّثْلَيْهَا ۙ قُلْتُمْ اَنّٰى هٰذَا ۗ قُلْ هُوَ مِنْ عِنْدِ اَنْفُسِكُمْ ۗ اِنَّ اللّٰهَ عَلٰى كُلِّ شَيْءٍ قَدِيْرٌ ۝

166. And what befell you on the day when the two armies met (at Ohud) was with Allah's knowledge, and that He might know the believers.

وَمَآ اَصَابَكُمْ يَوْمَ الْتَقَى الْجَمْعٰنِ فَبِاِذْنِ اللّٰهِ وَلِيَعْلَمَ الْمُؤْمِنِيْنَ ۝

167. And that He might know the hypocrites; and it was said to them: Come, fight in Allah's way, or defend yourselves. They said: If we knew fighting, we would certainly have followed you. They were on that day much nearer to unbelief than to belief. They say with their mouths what is not in their hearts; and Allah best knows what they conceal.

وَلِيَعْلَمَ الَّذِيْنَ نَافَقُوْا ۚ وَقِيْلَ لَهُمْ تَعَالَوْا قَاتِلُوْا فِيْ سَبِيْلِ اللّٰهِ اَوِ ادْفَعُوْا ۗ قَالُوْا لَوْ نَعْلَمُ قِتَالًا لَّاتَّبَعْنٰكُمْ ۗ هُمْ لِلْكُفْرِ يَوْمَئِذٍ اَقْرَبُ مِنْهُمْ لِلْاِيْمَانِ ۚ يَقُوْلُوْنَ بِاَفْوَاهِهِمْ مَّا لَيْسَ فِيْ قُلُوْبِهِمْ ۗ وَاللّٰهُ اَعْلَمُ بِمَا يَكْتُمُوْنَ ۝

168. Those who said of their brethren whilst they (themselves) held back: Had they obeyed us, they would not have been killed. Say: Then avert death from yourselves if you speak the truth.

اَلَّذِيْنَ قَالُوْا لِاِخْوَانِهِمْ وَقَعَدُوْا لَوْ اَطَاعُوْنَا مَا قُتِلُوْا ۗ قُلْ فَادْرَءُوْا عَنْ اَنْفُسِكُمُ الْمَوْتَ اِنْ كُنْتُمْ صٰدِقِيْنَ ۝

169. And reckon not those who are killed in Allah's way as dead; nay, they are alive (and) are provided sustenance from their Lord;

وَلَا تَحْسَبَنَّ الَّذِيْنَ قُتِلُوْا فِيْ سَبِيْلِ اللّٰهِ اَمْوَاتًا ۗ بَلْ اَحْيَآءٌ عِنْدَ رَبِّهِمْ يُرْزَقُوْنَ ۝

170. Rejoicing in what Allah has given them out of His grace, and they rejoice for the sake of those who, (being left) behind them, have not yet joined them, that they shall have no fear, nor shall they grieve.

فَرِحِيْنَ بِمَا اٰتٰهُمُ اللّٰهُ مِنْ فَضْلِهٖ وَيَسْتَبْشِرُوْنَ بِالَّذِيْنَ لَمْ يَلْحَقُوْا بِهِمْ مِّنْ خَلْفِهِمْ ۙ اَلَّا خَوْفٌ عَلَيْهِمْ وَلَا هُمْ يَحْزَنُوْنَ ۝

171. They rejoice on account of favor from Allah and (His) grace, and that Allah will not waste the reward of the believers.

يَسْتَبْشِرُوْنَ بِنِعْمَةٍ مِّنَ اللّٰهِ وَفَضْلٍ ۙ وَّاَنَّ اللّٰهَ لَا يُضِيْعُ اَجْرَ الْمُؤْمِنِيْنَ ۝

172. (As for) those who responded (at Ohud) to the call of Allah and the Apostle after the wound had befallen them, those among them who do good (to others) and guard (against evil) shall have a great reward.

اَلَّذِيْنَ اسْتَجَابُوْا لِلّٰهِ وَالرَّسُوْلِ مِنْۢ بَعْدِ مَاۤ اَصَابَهُمُ الْقَرْحُ ۛ لِلَّذِيْنَ اَحْسَنُوْا مِنْهُمْ وَاتَّقَوْا اَجْرٌ عَظِيْمٌ ۝

173. Those to whom the people said: Surely men have gathered against you, therefore fear them, but this increased their faith, and they said: Allah is sufficient for us and most excellent is the Protector.

اَلَّذِيْنَ قَالَ لَهُمُ النَّاسُ اِنَّ النَّاسَ قَدْ جَمَعُوْا لَكُمْ فَاخْشَوْهُمْ فَزَادَهُمْ اِيْمَانًا ۖ وَّقَالُوْا حَسْبُنَا اللّٰهُ وَنِعْمَ الْوَكِيْلُ ۝

174. So they returned with favor from Allah and (His) grace; no evil touched them and they followed the pleasure of Allah; and Allah is the Lord of mighty grace.

فَانْقَلَبُوْا بِنِعْمَةٍ مِّنَ اللّٰهِ وَفَضْلٍ لَّمْ يَمْسَسْهُمْ سُوْٓءٌ ۙ وَّاتَّبَعُوْا رِضْوَانَ اللّٰهِ ۗ وَاللّٰهُ ذُوْ فَضْلٍ عَظِيْمٍ ۝

175. It is only the Shaitan that causes you to fear from his friends, but do not fear them, and fear Me if you are believers.

اِنَّمَا ذٰلِكُمُ الشَّيْطٰنُ يُخَوِّفُ اَوْلِيَآءَهٗ ۖ فَلَا تَخَافُوْهُمْ وَخَافُوْنِ اِنْ كُنْتُمْ مُّؤْمِنِيْنَ ۝

176. And let not those grieve you who fall into unbelief hastily; surely they can do no harm to Allah at all; Allah intends that He should not give them any portion in the hereafter, and they shall have a grievous chastisement.

وَلَا يَحْزُنْكَ الَّذِيْنَ يُسَارِعُوْنَ فِي الْكُفْرِ ۚ اِنَّهُمْ لَنْ يَّضُرُّوا اللّٰهَ شَيْئًا ۗ يُرِيْدُ اللّٰهُ اَلَّا يَجْعَلَ لَهُمْ حَظًّا فِي الْاٰخِرَةِ ۚ وَلَهُمْ عَذَابٌ عَظِيْمٌ ۝

177. Surely those who have bought unbelief at the price of faith shall do no harm at all to Allah, and they shall have a painful chastisement.

اِنَّ الَّذِيْنَ اشْتَرَوُا الْكُفْرَ بِالْاِيْمَانِ لَنْ يَّضُرُّوا اللّٰهَ شَيْئًا ۚ وَلَهُمْ عَذَابٌ اَلِيْمٌ ۝

178. And let not those who disbelieve think that Our granting them respite is better for their souls; We grant them respite only that they may add to their sins; and they shall have a disgraceful chastisement.

وَلَا يَحْسَبَنَّ الَّذِيْنَ كَفَرُوْۤا اَنَّمَا نُمْلِيْ لَهُمْ خَيْرٌ لِّاَنْفُسِهِمْ ۚ اِنَّمَا نُمْلِيْ لَهُمْ لِيَزْدَادُوْۤا اِثْمًا ۚ وَلَهُمْ عَذَابٌ مُّهِيْنٌ ۝

179. On no account will Allah leave the believers in the condition which you are in until He separates the evil from the good; nor is Allah going to make you acquainted with the unseen, but Allah chooses of His apostles whom He pleases; therefore believe in Allah and His apostles; and if you believe and guard (against evil), then you shall have a great reward.

180. And let not those deem, who are niggardly in giving away that which Allah has granted them out of His grace, that it is good for them; nay, it is worse for them; they shall have that whereof they were niggardly made to cleave to their necks on the resurrection day; and Allah's is the heritage of the heavens and the earth; and Allah is aware of what you do.

181. Allah has certainly heard the saying of those who said: Surely Allah is poor and we are rich. I will record what they say, and their killing the prophets unjustly, and I will say: Taste the chastisement of burning.

182. This is for what your own hands have sent before and because Allah is not in the least unjust to the servants.

183. (Those are they) who said: Surely Allah has enjoined us that we should not believe in any apostle until he brings us an offering which the fire consumes. Say: Indeed, there came to you apostles before me with clear arguments and with that which you demand; why then did you kill them if you are truthful?

184. But if they reject you, so indeed were rejected before you apostles who came with clear arguments and scriptures and the illuminating book.

185. Every soul shall taste of death, and you shall only be paid fully your reward on the resurrection day; then whoever is removed far away from the fire and is made to enter the garden, he indeed has attained the object; and the life of this world is nothing but a provision of vanities.

مَا كَانَ اللّٰهُ لِيَذَرَ الْمُؤْمِنِيْنَ عَلٰى مَاۤ اَنْتُمْ عَلَيْهِ حَتّٰى يَمِيْزَ الْخَبِيْثَ مِنَ الطَّيِّبِ ۗ وَمَا كَانَ اللّٰهُ لِيُطْلِعَكُمْ عَلَى الْغَيْبِ وَلٰكِنَّ اللّٰهَ يَجْتَبِيْ مِنْ رُّسُلِهٖ مَنْ يَّشَآءُ ۖ فَاٰمِنُوْا بِاللّٰهِ وَرُسُلِهٖ ۚ وَاِنْ تُؤْمِنُوْا وَتَتَّقُوْا فَلَكُمْ اَجْرٌ عَظِيْمٌ ١٧٩

وَلَا يَحْسَبَنَّ الَّذِيْنَ يَبْخَلُوْنَ بِمَاۤ اٰتٰىهُمُ اللّٰهُ مِنْ فَضْلِهٖ هُوَ خَيْرًا لَّهُمْ ۗ بَلْ هُوَ شَرٌّ لَّهُمْ ۗ سَيُطَوَّقُوْنَ مَا بَخِلُوْا بِهٖ يَوْمَ الْقِيٰمَةِ ۗ وَلِلّٰهِ مِيْرَاثُ السَّمٰوٰتِ وَ الْاَرْضِ ۗ وَاللّٰهُ بِمَا تَعْمَلُوْنَ خَبِيْرٌ ١٨٠

لَقَدْ سَمِعَ اللّٰهُ قَوْلَ الَّذِيْنَ قَالُوْۤا اِنَّ اللّٰهَ فَقِيْرٌ وَّ نَحْنُ اَغْنِيَآءُ ۘ سَنَكْتُبُ مَا قَالُوْا وَقَتْلَهُمُ الْاَنْبِيَآءَ بِغَيْرِ حَقٍّ ۙ وَّنَقُوْلُ ذُوْقُوْا عَذَابَ الْحَرِيْقِ ١٨١

ذٰلِكَ بِمَا قَدَّمَتْ اَيْدِيْكُمْ وَاَنَّ اللّٰهَ لَيْسَ بِظَلَّامٍ لِّلْعَبِيْدِ ١٨٢

الَّذِيْنَ قَالُوْۤا اِنَّ اللّٰهَ عَهِدَ اِلَيْنَاۤ اَلَّا نُؤْمِنَ لِرَسُوْلٍ حَتّٰى يَاْتِيَنَا بِقُرْبَانٍ تَاْكُلُهُ النَّارُ ۗ قُلْ قَدْ جَآءَكُمْ رُسُلٌ مِّنْ قَبْلِيْ بِالْبَيِّنٰتِ وَبِالَّذِيْ قُلْتُمْ فَلِمَ قَتَلْتُمُوْهُمْ اِنْ كُنْتُمْ صٰدِقِيْنَ ١٨٣

فَاِنْ كَذَّبُوْكَ فَقَدْ كُذِّبَ رُسُلٌ مِّنْ قَبْلِكَ جَآءُوْ بِالْبَيِّنٰتِ وَالزُّبُرِ وَالْكِتٰبِ الْمُنِيْرِ ١٨٤

كُلُّ نَفْسٍ ذَآئِقَةُ الْمَوْتِ ۗ وَاِنَّمَا تُوَفَّوْنَ اُجُوْرَكُمْ يَوْمَ الْقِيٰمَةِ ۖ فَمَنْ زُحْزِحَ عَنِ النَّارِ وَاُدْخِلَ الْجَنَّةَ فَقَدْ فَازَ ۗ وَمَا الْحَيٰوةُ الدُّنْيَاۤ اِلَّا مَتَاعُ الْغُرُوْرِ ١٨٥

186. You shall certainly be tried respecting your wealth and your souls, and you shall certainly hear from those who have been given the Book before you and from those who are polytheists much annoying talk; and if you are patient and guard (against evil), surely this is one of the affairs (which should be) determined upon.

187. And when Allah made a covenant with those who were given the Book: You shall certainly make it known to men and you shall not hide it; but they cast it behind their backs and took a small price for it; so evil is that which they buy.

188. Do not think those who rejoice for what they have done and love that they should be praised for what they have not done—so do by no means think them to be safe from the chastisement, and they shall have a painful chastisement.

189. And Allah's is the kingdom of the heavens and the earth, and Allah has power over all things.

190. Most surely in the creation of the heavens and the earth and the alternation of the night and the day there are signs for men who understand.

191. Those who remember Allah standing and sitting and lying on their sides and reflect on the creation of the heavens and the earth: Our Lord! Thou hast not created this in vain! Glory be to Thee; save us then from the chastisement of the fire:

192. Our Lord! surely whomsoever Thou makest enter the fire, him Thou hast indeed brought to disgrace, and there shall be no helpers for the unjust:

193. Our Lord! surely we have heard a preacher calling to the faith, saying: Believe in your Lord, so we did believe; Our Lord! forgive us therefore our faults, and cover our evil deeds and make us die with the righteous.

194. Our Lord! and grant us what Thou hast promised us by Thy apostles and disgrace us not on the day of resurrection; surely Thou dost not fail to perform the promise.

195. So their Lord accepted their prayer: That I will not waste the work of a worker among you, whether male or female, the one of you being from the other; they, therefore, who fled and were turned out of their homes and persecuted in My way and who fought and were slain, I will most certainly cover their evil deeds, and I will most certainly make them enter gardens beneath which rivers flow; a reward from Allah, and with Allah is yet better reward.

196. Let it not deceive you that those who disbelieve go to and fro in the cities fearlessly.

197. A brief enjoyment! then their abode is hell, and evil is the resting-place.

198. But as to those who are careful of (their duty to) their Lord, they shall have gardens beneath which rivers flow, abiding in them; an entertainment from their Lord, and that which is with Allah is best for the righteous.

199. And most surely of the followers of the Book there are those who believe in Allah and (in) that which has been revealed to you and (in) that which has been revealed to them, being lowly before Allah; they do not take a small price for the communications of Allah; these it is that have their reward with their Lord; surely Allah is quick in reckoning.

200. O you who believe! be patient and excel in patience and remain steadfast, and be careful of (your duty to) Allah, that you may be successful.

رَبَّنَا وَاٰتِنَا مَا وَعَدْتَّنَا عَلٰى رُسُلِكَ وَلَا تُخْزِنَا يَوْمَ الْقِيٰمَةِ ۗ اِنَّكَ لَا تُخْلِفُ الْمِيْعَادَ ۝

فَاسْتَجَابَ لَهُمْ رَبُّهُمْ اَنِّيْ لَاۤ اُضِيْعُ عَمَلَ عَامِلٍ مِّنْكُمْ مِّنْ ذَكَرٍ اَوْ اُنْثٰى ۚ بَعْضُكُمْ مِّنْ بَعْضٍ ۚ فَالَّذِيْنَ هَاجَرُوْا وَاُخْرِجُوْا مِنْ دِيَارِهِمْ وَاُوْذُوْا فِيْ سَبِيْلِيْ وَقٰتَلُوْا وَقُتِلُوْا لَاُكَفِّرَنَّ عَنْهُمْ سَيِّاٰتِهِمْ وَلَاُدْخِلَنَّهُمْ جَنّٰتٍ تَجْرِيْ مِنْ تَحْتِهَا الْاَنْهٰرُ ۚ ثَوَابًا مِّنْ عِنْدِ اللّٰهِ ۗ وَاللّٰهُ عِنْدَهٗ حُسْنُ الثَّوَابِ ۝

لَا يَغُرَّنَّكَ تَقَلُّبُ الَّذِيْنَ كَفَرُوْا فِي الْبِلَادِ ۝

مَتَاعٌ قَلِيْلٌ ۖ ثُمَّ مَأْوٰىهُمْ جَهَنَّمُ ۗ وَبِئْسَ الْمِهَادُ ۝

لٰكِنِ الَّذِيْنَ اتَّقَوْا رَبَّهُمْ لَهُمْ جَنّٰتٌ تَجْرِيْ مِنْ تَحْتِهَا الْاَنْهٰرُ خٰلِدِيْنَ فِيْهَا نُزُلًا مِّنْ عِنْدِ اللّٰهِ ۗ وَمَا عِنْدَ اللّٰهِ خَيْرٌ لِّلْاَبْرَارِ ۝

وَاِنَّ مِنْ اَهْلِ الْكِتٰبِ لَمَنْ يُّؤْمِنُ بِاللّٰهِ وَمَاۤ اُنْزِلَ اِلَيْكُمْ وَمَاۤ اُنْزِلَ اِلَيْهِمْ خٰشِعِيْنَ لِلّٰهِ ۙ لَا يَشْتَرُوْنَ بِاٰيٰتِ اللّٰهِ ثَمَنًا قَلِيْلًا ۗ اُولٰٓئِكَ لَهُمْ اَجْرُهُمْ عِنْدَ رَبِّهِمْ ۗ اِنَّ اللّٰهَ سَرِيْعُ الْحِسَابِ ۝

يٰۤاَيُّهَا الَّذِيْنَ اٰمَنُوا اصْبِرُوْا وَصَابِرُوْا وَرَابِطُوْا ۖ وَاتَّقُوا اللّٰهَ لَعَلَّكُمْ تُفْلِحُوْنَ ۝

68

WOMEN
(NISA)

بِسْمِ اللهِ الرَّحْمٰنِ الرَّحِيْمِ

**In the name of Allah,
the Beneficent, the Merciful.**

1. O people! be careful of (your duty to) your Lord, Who created you from a single being and created its mate of the same (kind) and spread from these two, many men and women; and be careful of (your duty to) Allah, by Whom you demand one of another (your rights), and (to) the ties of relationship; surely Allah ever watches over you.

2. And give to the orphans their property, and do not substitute worthless (things) for (their) good (ones), and do not devour their property (as an addition) to your own property; this is surely a great crime.

3. And if you fear that you cannot act equitably towards orphans, then marry such women as seem good to you, two and three and four; but if you fear that you will not do justice (between them), then (marry) only one or what your right hands possess; this is more proper, that you may not deviate from the right course.

4. And give women their dowries as a free gift, but if they of themselves be pleased to give up to you a portion of it, then eat it with enjoyment and with wholesome result.

5. And do not give away your property which Allah has made for you a (means of) support to the weak of understanding, and maintain them out of (the profits of) it, and clothe them and speak to them words of honest advice.

69

6. And test the orphans until they attain puberty; then if you find in them maturity of intellect, make over to them their property, and do not consume it extravagantly and hastily, lest they attain to full age; and whoever is rich, let him abstain altogether, and whoever is poor, let him eat reasonably; then when you make over to them their property, call witnesses in their presence; and Allah is enough as a Reckoner.

7. Men shall have a portion of what the parents and the near relatives leave, and women shall have a portion of what the parents and the near relatives leave, whether there is little or much of it; a stated portion.

8. And when there are present at the division the relatives and the orphans and the needy, give them (something) out of it and speak to them kind words.

9. And let those fear who, should they leave behind them weakly offspring, would fear on their account; so let them be careful of (their duty to) Allah, and let them speak right words.

10. (As for) those who swallow the property of the orphans unjustly, surely they only swallow fire into their bellies and they shall enter burning fire.

11. Allah enjoins you concerning your children: The male shall have the equal of the portion of two females; then if they are more than two females, they shall have two-thirds of what the deceased has left, and if there is one, she shall have the half; and as for his parents, each of them shall have the sixth of what he has left if he has a child, but if he has no child and (only) his two parents inherit him, then his mother shall have the third; but if he has brothers, then his mother shall have the sixth after (the payment of) a bequest he may have bequeathed or a debt; your parents and your children, you know not which of them is the nearer to you in usefulness; this is an ordinance from Allah: Surely Allah is Knowing, Wise.

70

12. And you shall have half of what your wives leave if they have no child, but if they have a child, then you shall have a fourth of what they leave after (payment of) any bequest they may have bequeathed or a debt; and they shall have the fourth of what you leave if you have no child, but if you have a child then they shall have the eighth of what you leave after (payment of) a bequest you may have bequeathed or a debt; and if a man or a woman leaves property to be inherited by neither parents nor offspring, and he (or she) has a brother or a sister, then each of them two shall have the sixth, but if they are more than that, they shall be sharers in the third after (payment of) any bequest that may have been bequeathed or a debt that does not harm (others); this is an ordinance from Allah: and Allah is Knowing, Forbearing.

ولكم نصف ما ترك ازواجكم ان لم يكن لهن ولد فان كان لهن ولد فلكم الربع مما تركن من بعد وصية يوصين بها او دين ولهن الربع مما تركتم ان لم يكن لكم ولد فان كان لكم ولد فلهن الثمن مما تركتم من بعد وصية توصون بها او دين وان كان رجل يورث كلالة او امراة وله اخ او اخت فلكل واحد منهما السدس فان كانوا اكثر من ذلك فهم شركآء في الثلث من بعد وصية يوصى بها او دين غير مضآر وصية من الله والله عليم حليم ۝

13. These are Allah's limits; and whoever obeys Allah and His Apostle, He will cause him to enter gardens beneath which rivers flow, to abide in them; and this is the great achievement.

تلك حدود الله ومن يطع الله ورسوله يدخله جنت تجري من تحتها الانهر خلدين فيها و ذلك الفوز العظيم ۝

14. And whoever disobeys Allah and His Apostle and goes beyond His limits, He will cause him to enter fire to abide in it, and he shall have an abasing chastisement.

ومن يعص الله ورسوله ويتعد حدوده يدخله نارا خالدا فيها وله عذاب مهين ۝

15. And as for those who are guilty of an indecency from among your women, call to witnesses against them four (witnesses) from among you; then if they bear witness confine them to the houses until death takes them away or Allah opens some way for them.

والتي يأتين الفاحشة من نسآئكم فاستشهدوا عليهن اربعة منكم فان شهدوا فامسكوهن في البيوت حتى يتوفهن الموت او يجعل الله لهن سبيلا ۝

16. And as for the two who are guilty of indecency from among you, give them both a punishment; then if they repent and amend, turn aside from them; surely Allah is Oft-returning (to mercy), the Merciful.

والذن يأتينها منكم فاذوهما فان تابا واصلحا فاعرضوا عنهما ان الله كان توابا رحيما ۝

17. Repentance with Allah is only for those who do evil in ignorance, then turn (to Allah) soon, so these it is to whom Allah turns (mercifully), and Allah is ever Knowing, Wise.

اِنَّمَا التَّوْبَةُ عَلَى اللهِ لِلَّذِيْنَ يَعْمَلُوْنَ السُّوْٓءَ بِجَهَالَةٍ ثُمَّ يَتُوْبُوْنَ مِنْ قَرِيْبٍ فَاُولٰٓئِكَ يَتُوْبُ اللهُ عَلَيْهِمْ ۗ وَكَانَ اللهُ عَلِيْمًا حَكِيْمًا ۝

18. And repentance is not for those who go on doing evil deeds, until when death comes to one of them, he says: Surely now I repent; nor (for) those who die while they are unbelievers. These are they for whom We have prepared a painful chastisement.

وَلَيْسَتِ التَّوْبَةُ لِلَّذِيْنَ يَعْمَلُوْنَ السَّيِّاٰتِ ۚ حَتّٰى اِذَا حَضَرَ اَحَدَهُمُ الْمَوْتُ قَالَ اِنِّيْ تُبْتُ الْـٰٔنَ وَلَا الَّذِيْنَ يَمُوْتُوْنَ وَهُمْ كُفَّارٌ ۚ اُولٰٓئِكَ اَعْتَدْنَا لَهُمْ عَذَابًا اَلِيْمًا ۝

19. O you who believe! it is not lawful for you that you should take women as heritage against (their) will, and do not straiten them in order that you may take part of what you have given them, unless they are guilty of manifest indecency, and treat them kindly; then if you hate them, it may be that you dislike a thing while Allah has placed abundant good in it.

يٰٓاَيُّهَا الَّذِيْنَ اٰمَنُوْا لَا يَحِلُّ لَكُمْ اَنْ تَرِثُوا النِّسَآءَ كَرْهًا ۗ وَلَا تَعْضُلُوْهُنَّ لِتَذْهَبُوْا بِبَعْضِ مَآ اٰتَيْتُمُوْهُنَّ اِلَّآ اَنْ يَّأْتِيْنَ بِفَاحِشَةٍ مُّبَيِّنَةٍ ۚ وَعَاشِرُوْهُنَّ بِالْمَعْرُوْفِ ۚ فَاِنْ كَرِهْتُمُوْهُنَّ فَعَسٰٓى اَنْ تَكْرَهُوْا شَيْئًا وَّيَجْعَلَ اللهُ فِيْهِ خَيْرًا كَثِيْرًا ۝

20. And if you wish to have (one) wife in place of another and you have given one of them a heap of gold, then take not from it anything; would you take it by slandering (her) and (doing her) manifest wrong?

وَاِنْ اَرَدْتُّمُ اسْتِبْدَالَ زَوْجٍ مَّكَانَ زَوْجٍ ۙ وَّاٰتَيْتُمْ اِحْدٰىهُنَّ قِنْطَارًا فَلَا تَأْخُذُوْا مِنْهُ شَيْئًا ۗ اَتَأْخُذُوْنَهٗ بُهْتَانًا وَّاِثْمًا مُّبِيْنًا ۝

21. And how can you take it when one of you has already gone in to the other and they have made with you a firm covenant?

وَكَيْفَ تَأْخُذُوْنَهٗ وَقَدْ اَفْضٰى بَعْضُكُمْ اِلٰى بَعْضٍ وَّاَخَذْنَ مِنْكُمْ مِّيْثَاقًا غَلِيْظًا ۝

22. And marry not woman whom your fathers married, except what has already passed; this surely is indecent and hateful, and it is an evil way.

وَلَا تَنْكِحُوْا مَا نَكَحَ اٰبَآؤُكُمْ مِّنَ النِّسَآءِ اِلَّا مَا قَدْ سَلَفَ ۗ اِنَّهٗ كَانَ فَاحِشَةً وَّمَقْتًا ۗ وَسَآءَ سَبِيْلًا ۝

23. Forbidden to you are your mothers and your daughters and your sisters and your paternal aunts and your maternal aunts and brothers' daughters and sisters' daughters and your mothers that have suckled you and your foster-sisters and mothers of your wives and your step-daughters who are in your guardianship, (born) of your wives to whom you have gone in; but if you have not gone in to them, there is no blame on you (in marrying them), and the wives of your sons who are of your own loins, and that you should have two sisters together, except what has already passed; surely Allah is Forgiving, Merciful.

24. And all married women except those whom your right hands possess (this is) Allah's ordinance to you; and lawful for you are (all women) besides those, provided that you seek (them) with your property, taking (them) in marriage not committing fornication. Then as to those whom you profit by, give them their dowries as appointed; and there is no blame on you about what you mutually agree after what is appointed; surely Allah is Knowing, Wise.

25. And whoever among you has not within his power ampleness of means to marry free believing women, then (he may marry) of those whom your right hands possess from among your believing maidens; and Allah knows best your faith: you are (sprung) the one from the other; so marry them with the permission of their masters, and give them their dowries justly, they being chaste, not fornicating, nor receiving paramours; and when they are taken in marriage, then if they are guilty of indecency, they shall suffer half the punishment which is (inflicted) upon free women. This is for him among you who fears falling into evil; and that you abstain is better for you, and Allah is Forgiving, Merciful.

حُرِّمَتْ عَلَيْكُمْ أُمَّهٰتُكُمْ وَبَنٰتُكُمْ وَأَخَوٰتُكُمْ وَعَمّٰتُكُمْ وَخٰلٰتُكُمْ وَبَنٰتُ الْأَخِ وَبَنٰتُ الْأُخْتِ وَأُمَّهٰتُكُمُ الّٰتِيْۤ أَرْضَعْنَكُمْ وَأَخَوٰتُكُمْ مِّنَ الرَّضَاعَةِ وَأُمَّهٰتُ نِسَآئِكُمْ وَرَبَآئِبُكُمُ الّٰتِيْ فِيْ حُجُوْرِكُمْ مِّنْ نِّسَآئِكُمُ الّٰتِيْ دَخَلْتُمْ بِهِنَّ فَإِنْ لَّمْ تَكُوْنُوْا دَخَلْتُمْ بِهِنَّ فَلَا جُنَاحَ عَلَيْكُمْ وَحَلَآئِلُ أَبْنَآئِكُمُ الَّذِيْنَ مِنْ أَصْلَابِكُمْ وَأَنْ تَجْمَعُوْا بَيْنَ الْأُخْتَيْنِ إِلَّا مَا قَدْ سَلَفَ إِنَّ اللّٰهَ كَانَ غَفُوْرًا رَّحِيْمًا ۝

وَّالْمُحْصَنٰتُ مِنَ النِّسَآءِ إِلَّا مَا مَلَكَتْ أَيْمَانُكُمْ كِتٰبَ اللّٰهِ عَلَيْكُمْ وَأُحِلَّ لَكُمْ مَّا وَرَآءَ ذٰلِكُمْ أَنْ تَبْتَغُوْا بِأَمْوَالِكُمْ مُّحْصِنِيْنَ غَيْرَ مُسٰفِحِيْنَ فَمَا اسْتَمْتَعْتُمْ بِهِ مِنْهُنَّ فَأٰتُوْهُنَّ أُجُوْرَهُنَّ فَرِيْضَةً وَلَا جُنَاحَ عَلَيْكُمْ فِيْمَا تَرَاضَيْتُمْ بِهِ مِنْ بَعْدِ الْفَرِيْضَةِ إِنَّ اللّٰهَ كَانَ عَلِيْمًا حَكِيْمًا ۝

وَمَنْ لَّمْ يَسْتَطِعْ مِنْكُمْ طَوْلًا أَنْ يَّنْكِحَ الْمُحْصَنٰتِ الْمُؤْمِنٰتِ فَمِنْ مَّا مَلَكَتْ أَيْمَانُكُمْ مِّنْ فَتَيٰتِكُمُ الْمُؤْمِنٰتِ وَاللّٰهُ أَعْلَمُ بِإِيْمَانِكُمْ بَعْضُكُمْ مِّنْ بَعْضٍ فَانْكِحُوْهُنَّ بِإِذْنِ أَهْلِهِنَّ وَأٰتُوْهُنَّ أُجُوْرَهُنَّ بِالْمَعْرُوْفِ مُحْصَنٰتٍ غَيْرَ مُسٰفِحٰتٍ وَّلَا مُتَّخِذٰتِ أَخْدَانٍ فَإِذَاۤ أُحْصِنَّ فَإِنْ أَتَيْنَ بِفَاحِشَةٍ فَعَلَيْهِنَّ نِصْفُ مَا عَلَى الْمُحْصَنٰتِ مِنَ الْعَذَابِ ذٰلِكَ لِمَنْ خَشِيَ الْعَنَتَ مِنْكُمْ وَأَنْ تَصْبِرُوْا خَيْرٌ لَّكُمْ وَاللّٰهُ غَفُوْرٌ رَّحِيْمٌ ۝

73

26. Allah desires to explain to you, and to guide you into the ways of those before you, and to turn to you (mercifully), and Allah is Knowing, Wise.

يُرِيْدُ اللّٰهُ لِيُبَيِّنَ لَكُمْ وَيَهْدِيَكُمْ سُنَنَ الَّذِيْنَ مِنْ قَبْلِكُمْ وَيَتُوْبَ عَلَيْكُمْ ۖ وَاللّٰهُ عَلِيْمٌ حَكِيْمٌ ۝

27. And Allah desires that He should turn to you (mercifully), and those who follow (their) lusts desire that you should deviate (with) a great deviation.

وَاللّٰهُ يُرِيْدُ اَنْ يَّتُوْبَ عَلَيْكُمْ ۖ وَيُرِيْدُ الَّذِيْنَ يَتَّبِعُوْنَ الشَّهَوٰتِ اَنْ تَمِيْلُوْا مَيْلًا عَظِيْمًا ۝

28. Allah desires that He should make light your burdens, and man is created weak.

يُرِيْدُ اللّٰهُ اَنْ يُّخَفِّفَ عَنْكُمْ ۚ وَخُلِقَ الْاِنْسَانُ ضَعِيْفًا ۝

29. O you who believe! do not devour your property among yourselves falsely, except that it be trading by your mutual consent; and do not kill your people; surely Allah is Merciful to you.

يٰٓاَيُّهَا الَّذِيْنَ اٰمَنُوْا لَا تَأْكُلُوْٓا اَمْوَالَكُمْ بَيْنَكُمْ بِالْبَاطِلِ اِلَّآ اَنْ تَكُوْنَ تِجَارَةً عَنْ تَرَاضٍ مِّنْكُمْ ۚ وَلَا تَقْتُلُوْٓا اَنْفُسَكُمْ ۚ اِنَّ اللّٰهَ كَانَ بِكُمْ رَحِيْمًا ۝

30. And whoever does this aggressively and unjustly, We will soon cast him into fire; and this is easy to Allah.

وَمَنْ يَّفْعَلْ ذٰلِكَ عُدْوَانًا وَّظُلْمًا فَسَوْفَ نُصْلِيْهِ نَارًا ۚ وَكَانَ ذٰلِكَ عَلَى اللّٰهِ يَسِيْرًا ۝

31. If you shun the great sins which you are forbidden, We will do away with your small sins and cause you to enter an honorable place of entering.

اِنْ تَجْتَنِبُوْا كَبَآئِرَ مَا تُنْهَوْنَ عَنْهُ نُكَفِّرْ عَنْكُمْ سَيِّاٰتِكُمْ وَنُدْخِلْكُمْ مُّدْخَلًا كَرِيْمًا ۝

32. And do not covet that by which Allah has made some of you excel others; men shall have the benefit of what they earn and women shall have the benefit of what they earn; and ask Allah of His grace; surely Allah knows all things.

وَلَا تَتَمَنَّوْا مَا فَضَّلَ اللّٰهُ بِهٖ بَعْضَكُمْ عَلٰى بَعْضٍ ۚ لِلرِّجَالِ نَصِيْبٌ مِّمَّا اكْتَسَبُوْا ۚ وَلِلنِّسَآءِ نَصِيْبٌ مِّمَّا اكْتَسَبْنَ ۚ وَسْئَلُوا اللّٰهَ مِنْ فَضْلِهٖ ۚ اِنَّ اللّٰهَ كَانَ بِكُلِّ شَيْءٍ عَلِيْمًا ۝

33. And to every one We have appointed heirs of what parents and near relatives leave; and as to those with whom your rights hands have ratified agreements, give them their portion; surely Allah is a witness over all things.

وَلِكُلٍّ جَعَلْنَا مَوَالِيَ مِمَّا تَرَكَ الْوَالِدٰنِ وَالْاَقْرَبُوْنَ ۚ وَالَّذِيْنَ عَقَدَتْ اَيْمَانُكُمْ فَاٰتُوْهُمْ نَصِيْبَهُمْ ۚ اِنَّ اللّٰهَ كَانَ عَلٰى كُلِّ شَيْءٍ شَهِيْدًا ۝

34. Men are the maintainers of women because Allah has made some of them to excel others and because they spend out of their property; the good women are therefore obedient, guarding the unseen as Allah has guarded; and (as to) those on whose part you fear desertion, admonish them, and leave them alone in the sleeping-places and beat them; then if they obey you, do not seek a way against them; surely Allah is High, Great.

الرِّجَالُ قَوَّامُوْنَ عَلَى النِّسَاءِ بِمَا فَضَّلَ اللّٰهُ بَعْضَهُمْ عَلٰى بَعْضٍ وَّبِمَآ اَنْفَقُوْا مِنْ اَمْوَالِهِمْ ۚ فَالصّٰلِحٰتُ قٰنِتٰتٌ حٰفِظٰتٌ لِّلْغَيْبِ بِمَا حَفِظَ اللّٰهُ ۚ وَالّٰتِيْ تَخَافُوْنَ نُشُوْزَهُنَّ فَعِظُوْهُنَّ وَاهْجُرُوْهُنَّ فِى الْمَضَاجِعِ وَاضْرِبُوْهُنَّ ۚ فَاِنْ اَطَعْنَكُمْ فَلَا تَبْغُوْا عَلَيْهِنَّ سَبِيْلًا ۗ اِنَّ اللّٰهَ كَانَ عَلِيًّا كَبِيْرًا ۞

35. And if you fear a breach between the two, then appoint a judge from his people and a judge from her people; if they both desire agreement, Allah will effect harmony between them; surely Allah is Knowing, Aware.

وَاِنْ خِفْتُمْ شِقَاقَ بَيْنِهِمَا فَابْعَثُوْا حَكَمًا مِّنْ اَهْلِهٖ وَحَكَمًا مِّنْ اَهْلِهَا ۚ اِنْ يُّرِيْدَآ اِصْلَاحًا يُّوَفِّقِ اللّٰهُ بَيْنَهُمَا ۗ اِنَّ اللّٰهَ كَانَ عَلِيْمًا خَبِيْرًا ۞

36. And serve Allah and do not associate any thing with Him, and be good to the parents and to the near of kin and the orphans and the needy and the neighbor of (your) kin and the alien neighbor, and the companion in a journey and the wayfarer and those whom your right hands possess; surely Allah does not love him who is proud, boastful;

وَاعْبُدُوا اللّٰهَ وَلَا تُشْرِكُوْا بِهٖ شَيْئًا وَّبِالْوَالِدَيْنِ اِحْسَانًا وَّبِذِى الْقُرْبٰى وَالْيَتٰمٰى وَالْمَسٰكِيْنِ وَالْجَارِ ذِى الْقُرْبٰى وَالْجَارِ الْجُنُبِ وَالصَّاحِبِ بِالْجَنْبِ وَ ابْنِ السَّبِيْلِ ۙ وَمَا مَلَكَتْ اَيْمَانُكُمْ ۗ اِنَّ اللّٰهَ لَا يُحِبُّ مَنْ كَانَ مُخْتَالًا فَخُوْرَا ۞

37. Those who are niggardly and bid people to be niggardly and hide what Allah has given them out of His grace; and We have prepared for the unbelievers a disgraceful chastisement.

الَّذِيْنَ يَبْخَلُوْنَ وَيَأْمُرُوْنَ النَّاسَ بِالْبُخْلِ وَيَكْتُمُوْنَ مَآ اٰتٰهُمُ اللّٰهُ مِنْ فَضْلِهٖ ۗ وَاَعْتَدْنَا لِلْكٰفِرِيْنَ عَذَابًا مُّهِيْنًا ۞

38. And those who spend their property (in alms) to be seen of the people and do not believe in Allah nor in the last day; and as for him whose associate is the Shaitan, an evil associate is he!

وَالَّذِيْنَ يُنْفِقُوْنَ اَمْوَالَهُمْ رِئَآءَ النَّاسِ وَلَا يُؤْمِنُوْنَ بِاللّٰهِ وَلَا بِالْيَوْمِ الْاٰخِرِ ۗ وَمَنْ يَّكُنِ الشَّيْطٰنُ لَهٗ قَرِيْنًا فَسَآءَ قَرِيْنًا ۞

39. And what (harm) would it have done them if they had believed in Allah and the last day and spent (benevolently) of what Allah had given them? And Allah knows them.

وَمَاذَا عَلَيْهِمْ لَوْ اٰمَنُوْا بِاللّٰهِ وَالْيَوْمِ الْاٰخِرِ وَاَنْفَقُوْا مِمَّا رَزَقَهُمُ اللّٰهُ ۗ وَكَانَ اللّٰهُ بِهِمْ عَلِيْمًا ۞

40. Surely Allah does not do injustice to the weight of an atom, and if it is a good deed He multiplies it and gives from Himself a great reward.

41. How will it be, then, when We bring from every people a witness and bring you as a witness against these?

42. On that day will those who disbelieve and disobey the Apostle desire that the earth were levelled with them, and they shall not hide any word from Allah.

43. O you who believe! do not go near prayer when you are intoxicated until you know (well) what you say, nor when you are under an obligation to perform a bath—unless (you are) travelling on the road—until you have washed yourselves; and if you are sick, or on a journey, or one of you come from the privy or you have touched the women, and you cannot find water, betake yourselves to pure earth, then wipe your faces and your hands; surely Allah is Pardoning, Forgiving.

44. Have you not considered those to whom a portion of the Book has been given? They buy error and desire that you should go astray from the way.

45. And Allah best knows your enemies; and Allah suffices as a Guardian, and Allah suffices as a Helper.

46. Of those who are Jews (there are those who) alter words from their places and say: We have heard and we disobey and: Hear, may you not be made to hear! and: Raina, distorting (the word) with their tongues and taunting about religion; and if they had said (instead): We have heard and we obey, and hearken, and unzurna it would have been better for them and more upright; but Allah has cursed them on account of their unbelief, so they do not believe but a little.

47. O you who have been given the Book! believe that which We have revealed, verifying what you have, before We alter faces then turn them on their backs, or curse them as We cursed the violaters of the Sabbath, and the command of Allah shall be executed.

48. Surely Allah does not forgive that anything should be associated with Him, and forgives what is besides that to whomsoever He pleases; and whoever associates anything with Allah, he devises indeed a great sin.

49. Have you not considered those who attribute purity to themselves? Nay, Allah purifies whom He pleases; and they shall not be wronged the husk of a date stone.

50. See how they forge the lie against Allah, and this is sufficient as a manifest sin.

51. Have you not seen those to whom a portion of the Book has been given? They believe in idols and false deities and say of those who disbelieve: These are better guided in the path than those who believe.

52. Those are they whom Allah has cursed, and whomever Allah curses you shall not find any helper for him.

53. Or have they a share in the kingdom? But then they would not give to people even the speck in the date stone.

54. Or do they envy the people for what Allah has given them of His grace? But indeed We have given to Ibrahim's children the Book and the wisdom, and We have given them a grand kingdom.

55. So of them is he who believes in him, and of them is he who turns away from him, and hell is sufficient to burn.

56. (As for) those who disbelieve in Our communications, We shall make them enter fire; so oft as their skins are thoroughly burned, We will change them for other skins, that they may taste the chastisement; surely Allah is Mighty, Wise.

اِنَّ الَّذِيْنَ كَفَرُوْا بِاٰيٰتِنَا سَوْفَ نُصْلِيْهِمْ نَارًا ۗ كُلَّمَا نَضِجَتْ جُلُوْدُهُمْ بَدَّلْنٰهُمْ جُلُوْدًا غَيْرَهَا لِيَذُوْقُوا الْعَذَابَ ؕ اِنَّ اللّٰهَ كَانَ عَزِيْزًا حَكِيْمًا ۝

57. And (as for) those who believe and do good deeds, We will make them enter gardens beneath which rivers flow, to abide in them for ever; they shall have therein pure mates, and We shall make them enter a dense shade.

وَالَّذِيْنَ اٰمَنُوْا وَعَمِلُوا الصّٰلِحٰتِ سَنُدْخِلُهُمْ جَنّٰتٍ تَجْرِيْ مِنْ تَحْتِهَا الْاَنْهٰرُ خٰلِدِيْنَ فِيْهَا اَبَدًا ؕ لَهُمْ فِيْهَآ اَزْوَاجٌ مُّطَهَّرَةٌ ۫ وَّنُدْخِلُهُمْ ظِلًّا ظَلِيْلًا ۝

58. Surely Allah commands you to make over trusts to their owners and that when you judge between people you judge with justice; surely Allah admonishes you with what is excellent; surely Allah is Seeing, Hearing.

اِنَّ اللّٰهَ يَأْمُرُكُمْ اَنْ تُؤَدُّوا الْاَمٰنٰتِ اِلٰٓى اَهْلِهَا ۙ وَاِذَا حَكَمْتُمْ بَيْنَ النَّاسِ اَنْ تَحْكُمُوْا بِالْعَدْلِ ؕ اِنَّ اللّٰهَ نِعِمَّا يَعِظُكُمْ بِهٖ ؕ اِنَّ اللّٰهَ كَانَ سَمِيْعًا بَصِيْرًا ۝

59. O you who believe! obey Allah and obey the Apostle and those in authority from among you; then if you quarrel about anything, refer it to Allah and the Apostle, if you believe in Allah and the last day; this is better and very good in the end.

يٰٓاَيُّهَا الَّذِيْنَ اٰمَنُوْٓا اَطِيْعُوا اللّٰهَ وَاَطِيْعُوا الرَّسُوْلَ وَاُولِى الْاَمْرِ مِنْكُمْ ۚ فَاِنْ تَنَازَعْتُمْ فِيْ شَيْءٍ فَرُدُّوْهُ اِلَى اللّٰهِ وَالرَّسُوْلِ اِنْ كُنْتُمْ تُؤْمِنُوْنَ بِاللّٰهِ وَالْيَوْمِ الْاٰخِرِ ؕ ذٰلِكَ خَيْرٌ وَّاَحْسَنُ تَأْوِيْلًا ۝

60. Have you not seen those who assert that they believe in what has been revealed to you and what was revealed before you? They desire to summon one another to the judgment of the Shaitan, though they were commanded to deny him, and the Shaitan desires to lead them astray into a remote error.

اَلَمْ تَرَ اِلَى الَّذِيْنَ يَزْعُمُوْنَ اَنَّهُمْ اٰمَنُوْا بِمَآ اُنْزِلَ اِلَيْكَ وَمَآ اُنْزِلَ مِنْ قَبْلِكَ يُرِيْدُوْنَ اَنْ يَّتَحَاكَمُوْٓا اِلَى الطَّاغُوْتِ وَقَدْ اُمِرُوْٓا اَنْ يَّكْفُرُوْا بِهٖ ؕ وَيُرِيْدُ الشَّيْطٰنُ اَنْ يُّضِلَّهُمْ ضَلٰلًا بَعِيْدًا ۝

61. And when it is said to them: Come to what Allah has revealed and to the Apostle, you will see the hypocrites turning away from you with (utter) aversion.

وَاِذَا قِيْلَ لَهُمْ تَعَالَوْا اِلٰى مَآ اَنْزَلَ اللّٰهُ وَاِلَى الرَّسُوْلِ رَاَيْتَ الْمُنٰفِقِيْنَ يَصُدُّوْنَ عَنْكَ صُدُوْدًا ۝

62. But how will it be when misfortune befalls them on account of what their hands have sent before? Then they will come to you swearing by Allah: We did not desire (anything) but good and concord.

فَكَيْفَ اِذَآ اَصَابَتْهُمْ مُّصِيْبَةٌ بِمَا قَدَّمَتْ اَيْدِيْهِمْ ثُمَّ جَآءُوْكَ يَحْلِفُوْنَ ۛ بِاللّٰهِ اِنْ اَرَدْنَآ اِلَّآ اِحْسَانًا وَّتَوْفِيْقًا ۝

63. These are they of whom Allah knows what is in their hearts; therefore turn aside from them and admonish them, and speak to them effectual words concerning themselves.

64. And We did not send any apostle but that he should be obeyed by Allah's permission; and had they, when they were unjust to themselves, come to you and asked forgiveness of Allah and the Apostle had (also) asked forgiveness for them, they would have found Allah Oft-returning (to mercy), Merciful.

65. But no! by your Lord! they do not believe (in reality) until they make you a judge of that which has become a matter of disagreement among them, and then do not find any straitness in their hearts as to what you have decided and submit with entire submission.

66. And if We had prescribed for them: Lay down your lives or go forth from your homes, they would not have done it except a few of them; and if they had done what they were admonished, it would have certainly been better for them and best in strengthening (them);

67. And then We would certainly have given them from Ourselves a great reward.

68. And We would certainly have guided them in the right path.

69. And whoever obeys Allah and the Apostle, these are with those upon whom Allah has bestowed favors from among the prophets and the truthful and the martyrs and the good, and a goodly company are they!

70. This is grace from Allah, and sufficient is Allah as the Knower.

71. O you who believe! take your precaution, then go forth in detachments or go forth in a body.

72. And surely among you is he who would certainly hang back! If then a misfortune befalls you he says: Surely Allah conferred a benefit on me that I was not present with them.

79

73. And if grace from Allah come to you, he would certainly cry out, as if there had not been any friendship between you and him: Would that I had been with them, then I should have attained a mighty good fortune.

وَلَئِنْ اَصَابَكُمْ فَضْلٌ مِّنَ اللّٰهِ لَيَقُوْلَنَّ كَاَنْ لَّمْ تَكُنْ بَيْنَكُمْ وَبَيْنَهٗ مَوَدَّةٌ يّٰلَيْتَنِيْ كُنْتُ مَعَهُمْ فَاَفُوْزَ فَوْزًا عَظِيْمًا ۞

74. Therefore let those fight in the way of Allah, who sell this world's life for the hereafter; and whoever fights in the way of Allah, then be he slain or be he victorious, We shall grant him a mighty reward.

فَلْيُقَاتِلْ فِيْ سَبِيْلِ اللّٰهِ الَّذِيْنَ يَشْرُوْنَ الْحَيٰوةَ الدُّنْيَا بِالْاٰخِرَةِ ۚ وَمَنْ يُّقَاتِلْ فِيْ سَبِيْلِ اللّٰهِ فَيُقْتَلْ اَوْ يَغْلِبْ فَسَوْفَ نُؤْتِيْهِ اَجْرًا عَظِيْمًا

75. And what reason have you that you should not fight in the way of Allah and of the weak among the men and the women and the children, (of) those who say: Our Lord! cause us to go forth from this town, whose people are oppressors, and give us from Thee a guardian and give us from Thee a helper.

وَمَا لَكُمْ لَا تُقَاتِلُوْنَ فِيْ سَبِيْلِ اللّٰهِ وَالْمُسْتَضْعَفِيْنَ مِنَ الرِّجَالِ وَالنِّسَآءِ وَالْوِلْدَانِ الَّذِيْنَ يَقُوْلُوْنَ رَبَّنَآ اَخْرِجْنَا مِنْ هٰذِهِ الْقَرْيَةِ الظَّالِمِ اَهْلُهَا ۚ وَاجْعَلْ لَّنَا مِنْ لَّدُنْكَ وَلِيًّا ۚ وَّاجْعَلْ لَّنَا مِنْ لَّدُنْكَ نَصِيْرًا ۞

76. Those who believe fight in the way of Allah, and those who disbelieve fight in the way of the Shaitan. Fight therefore against the friends of the Shaitan; surely the strategy of the Shaitan is weak.

اَلَّذِيْنَ اٰمَنُوْا يُقَاتِلُوْنَ فِيْ سَبِيْلِ اللّٰهِ ۚ وَالَّذِيْنَ كَفَرُوْا يُقَاتِلُوْنَ فِيْ سَبِيْلِ الطَّاغُوْتِ فَقَاتِلُوْا اَوْلِيَآءَ الشَّيْطٰنِ ۚ اِنَّ كَيْدَ الشَّيْطٰنِ كَانَ ضَعِيْفًا ع

77. Have you not seen those to whom it was said: Withhold your hands, and keep up prayer and pay the poor-rate; but when fighting is prescribed for them, lo! a party of them fear men as they ought to have feared Allah, or (even) with a greater fear, and say: Our Lord! why hast Thou ordained fighting for us? Wherefore didst Thou not grant us a delay to a near end? Say: The provision of this world is short, and the hereafter is better for him who guards (against evil); and you shall not be wronged the husk of a date stone.

اَلَمْ تَرَ اِلَى الَّذِيْنَ قِيْلَ لَهُمْ كُفُّوْا اَيْدِيَكُمْ وَاَقِيْمُوا الصَّلٰوةَ وَاٰتُوا الزَّكٰوةَ ۚ فَلَمَّا كُتِبَ عَلَيْهِمُ الْقِتَالُ اِذَا فَرِيْقٌ مِّنْهُمْ يَخْشَوْنَ النَّاسَ كَخَشْيَةِ اللّٰهِ اَوْ اَشَدَّ خَشْيَةً ۚ وَقَالُوْا رَبَّنَا لِمَ كَتَبْتَ عَلَيْنَا الْقِتَالَ ۚ لَوْ لَآ اَخَّرْتَنَآ اِلٰى اَجَلٍ قَرِيْبٍ ۚ قُلْ مَتَاعُ الدُّنْيَا قَلِيْلٌ ۚ وَالْاٰخِرَةُ خَيْرٌ لِّمَنِ اتَّقٰى ۚ وَلَا تُظْلَمُوْنَ فَتِيْلًا ۞

78. Wherever you are, death will overtake you, though you are in lofty towers, and if a benefit comes to them, they say: This is from Allah; and if a misfortune befalls them, they say: This is from you. Say: All is from Allah, but what is the matter with these people that they do not make approach to understanding what is told (them)?

اَیْنَ مَا تَکُوْنُوْا یُدْرِکْکُّمُ الْمَوْتُ وَلَوْ کُنْتُمْ فِیْ بُرُوْجٍ مُّشَیَّدَۃٍؕ وَاِنْ تُّصِبْهُمْ حَسَنَۃٌ یَّقُوْلُوْا هٰذِهٖ مِنْ عِنْدِ اللّٰهِۚ وَاِنْ تُّصِبْهُمْ سَیِّئَۃٌ یَّقُوْلُوْا هٰذِهٖ مِنْ عِنْدِکَؕ قُلْ کُلٌّ مِّنْ عِنْدِ اللّٰهِؕ فَمَالِ هٰٓؤُلَآءِ الْقَوْمِ لَا یَکَادُوْنَ یَفْقَهُوْنَ حَدِیْثًا ۟۷۸۠

79. Whatever benefit comes to you (O man!), it is from Allah, and whatever misfortune befalls you, it is from yourself; and We have sent you (O Prophet!), to mankind as an apostle; and Allah is sufficient as a witness.

مَآ اَصَابَکَ مِنْ حَسَنَۃٍ فَمِنَ اللّٰهِۖ وَمَآ اَصَابَکَ مِنْ سَیِّئَۃٍ فَمِنْ نَّفْسِکَؕ وَاَرْسَلْنٰکَ لِلنَّاسِ رَسُوْلًاؕ وَکَفٰی بِاللّٰهِ شَهِیْدًا ۟۷۹۠

80. Whoever obeys the Apostle, he indeed obeys Allah; and whoever turns back, so We have not sent you as a keeper over them.

مَنْ یُّطِعِ الرَّسُوْلَ فَقَدْ اَطَاعَ اللّٰهَۚ وَمَنْ تَوَلّٰی فَمَآ اَرْسَلْنٰکَ عَلَیْهِمْ حَفِیْظًا ۟۸۰۠

81. And they say: Obedience. But when they go out from your presence, a party of them decide by night upon doing otherwise than what you say; and Allah writes down what they decide by night, therefore turn aside from them and trust in Allah, and Allah is sufficient as a protector.

وَیَقُوْلُوْنَ طَاعَۃٌۖ فَاِذَا بَرَزُوْا مِنْ عِنْدِکَ بَیَّتَ طَآئِفَۃٌ مِّنْهُمْ غَیْرَ الَّذِیْ تَقُوْلُؕ وَاللّٰهُ یَکْتُبُ مَا یُبَیِّتُوْنَۚ فَاَعْرِضْ عَنْهُمْ وَتَوَکَّلْ عَلَی اللّٰهِؕ وَکَفٰی بِاللّٰهِ وَکِیْلًا ۟۸۱۠

82. Do they not then meditate on the Quran? And if it were from any other than Allah, they would have found in it many a discrepancy.

اَفَلَا یَتَدَبَّرُوْنَ الْقُرْاٰنَؕ وَلَوْ کَانَ مِنْ عِنْدِ غَیْرِ اللّٰهِ لَوَجَدُوْا فِیْهِ اخْتِلَافًا کَثِیْرًا ۟۸۲۠

83. And when there comes to them news of security or fear, they spread it abroad; and if they had referred it to the Apostle and to those in authority among them, those among them who can search out the knowledge of it would have known it, and were it not for the grace of Allah upon you and His mercy, you would have certainly followed the Shaitan save a few.

وَاِذَا جَآءَهُمْ اَمْرٌ مِّنَ الْاَمْنِ اَوِ الْخَوْفِ اَذَاعُوْا بِهٖؕ وَلَوْ رَدُّوْهُ اِلَی الرَّسُوْلِ وَاِلٰٓی اُولِی الْاَمْرِ مِنْهُمْ لَعَلِمَهُ الَّذِیْنَ یَسْتَنْۢبِطُوْنَهٗ مِنْهُمْؕ وَلَوْلَا فَضْلُ اللّٰهِ عَلَیْکُمْ وَرَحْمَتُهٗ لَاتَّبَعْتُمُ الشَّیْطٰنَ اِلَّا قَلِیْلًا ۟۸۳۠

84. Fight then in Allah's way; this is not imposed on you except in relation to yourself, and rouse the believers to ardor; maybe Allah will restrain the fighting of those who disbelieve, and Allah is strongest in prowess and strongest to give an exemplary punishment.

فَقَاتِلْ فِیْ سَبِیْلِ اللّٰهِۚ لَا تُکَلَّفُ اِلَّا نَفْسَکَ وَحَرِّضِ الْمُؤْمِنِیْنَۚ عَسَی اللّٰهُ اَنْ یَّکُفَّ بَاْسَ الَّذِیْنَ کَفَرُوْاؕ وَاللّٰهُ اَشَدُّ بَاْسًا وَّاَشَدُّ تَنْکِیْلًا ۟۸۴۠

85. Whoever joins himself (to another) in a good cause shall have a share of it, and whoever joins himself (to another) in an evil cause shall have the responsibility of it; and Allah controls all things.

86. And when you are greeted with a greeting, greet with a better (greeting) than it or return it; surely Allah takes account of all things.

87. Allah, there is no god but He—He will most certainly gather you together on the resurrection day, there is no doubt in it; and who is more true in word than Allah?

88. What is the matter with you, then, that you have become two parties about the hypocrites, while Allah has made them return (to unbelief) for what they have earned? Do you wish to guide him whom Allah has caused to err? And whomsoever Allah causes to err, you shall by no means find a way for him.

89. They desire that you should disbelieve as they have disbelieved, so that you might be (all) alike; therefore take not from among them friends until they fly (their homes) in Allah's way; but if they turn back, then seize them and kill them wherever you find them, and take not from among them a friend or a helper.

90. Except those who reach a people between whom and you there is an alliance, or who come to you, their hearts shrinking from fighting you or fighting their own people; and if Allah had pleased, He would have given them power over you, so that they should have certainly fought you; therefore if they withdraw from you and do not fight you and offer you peace, then Allah has not given you a way against them.

91. You will find others who desire that they should be safe from you and secure from their own people; as often as they are sent back to the mischief they get thrown into it headlong; therefore if they do not withdraw from you, and (do not) offer you peace and restrain their hands, then seize them and kill them wherever you find them; and against these We have given you a clear authority.

مَنْ يَشْفَعْ شَفَاعَةً حَسَنَةً يَكُنْ لَّهُ نَصِيْبٌ مِّنْهَا ۚ وَمَنْ يَشْفَعْ شَفَاعَةً سَيِّئَةً يَكُنْ لَّهُ كِفْلٌ مِّنْهَا ۗ وَكَانَ اللّٰهُ عَلٰى كُلِّ شَيْءٍ مُّقِيْتًا ۝

وَاِذَا حُيِّيْتُمْ بِتَحِيَّةٍ فَحَيُّوْا بِاَحْسَنَ مِنْهَآ اَوْ رُدُّوْهَا ۗ اِنَّ اللّٰهَ كَانَ عَلٰى كُلِّ شَيْءٍ حَسِيْبًا ۝

اَللّٰهُ لَآ اِلٰهَ اِلَّا هُوَ ۗ لَيَجْمَعَنَّكُمْ اِلٰى يَوْمِ الْقِيٰمَةِ لَا رَيْبَ فِيْهِ ۗ وَمَنْ اَصْدَقُ مِنَ اللّٰهِ حَدِيْثًا ۝

فَمَا لَكُمْ فِى الْمُنٰفِقِيْنَ فِئَتَيْنِ وَاللّٰهُ اَرْكَسَهُمْ بِمَا كَسَبُوْا ۚ اَتُرِيْدُوْنَ اَنْ تَهْدُوْا مَنْ اَضَلَّ اللّٰهُ ۗ وَمَنْ يُّضْلِلِ اللّٰهُ فَلَنْ تَجِدَ لَهُ سَبِيْلًا ۝

وَدُّوْا لَوْ تَكْفُرُوْنَ كَمَا كَفَرُوْا فَتَكُوْنُوْنَ سَوَآءً فَلَا تَتَّخِذُوْا مِنْهُمْ اَوْلِيَآءَ حَتّٰى يُهَاجِرُوْا فِىْ سَبِيْلِ اللّٰهِ ۚ فَاِنْ تَوَلَّوْا فَخُذُوْهُمْ وَاقْتُلُوْهُمْ حَيْثُ وَجَدْتُّمُوْهُمْ ۖ وَلَا تَتَّخِذُوْا مِنْهُمْ وَلِيًّا وَّلَا نَصِيْرًا ۙ۝

اِلَّا الَّذِيْنَ يَصِلُوْنَ اِلٰى قَوْمٍ بَيْنَكُمْ وَبَيْنَهُمْ مِّيْثَاقٌ اَوْ جَآءُوْكُمْ حَصِرَتْ صُدُوْرُهُمْ اَنْ يُّقَاتِلُوْكُمْ اَوْ يُقَاتِلُوْا قَوْمَهُمْ ۚ وَلَوْ شَآءَ اللّٰهُ لَسَلَّطَهُمْ عَلَيْكُمْ فَلَقَاتَلُوْكُمْ ۚ فَاِنِ اعْتَزَلُوْكُمْ فَلَمْ يُقَاتِلُوْكُمْ وَاَلْقَوْا اِلَيْكُمُ السَّلَمَ ۙ فَمَا جَعَلَ اللّٰهُ لَكُمْ عَلَيْهِمْ سَبِيْلًا ۝

سَتَجِدُوْنَ اٰخَرِيْنَ يُرِيْدُوْنَ اَنْ يَّأْمَنُوْكُمْ وَيَأْمَنُوْا قَوْمَهُمْ ۗ كُلَّ مَا رُدُّوْٓا اِلَى الْفِتْنَةِ اُرْكِسُوْا فِيْهَا ۚ فَاِنْ لَّمْ يَعْتَزِلُوْكُمْ وَيُلْقُوْٓا اِلَيْكُمُ السَّلَمَ وَيَكُفُّوْٓا اَيْدِيَهُمْ فَخُذُوْهُمْ وَاقْتُلُوْهُمْ حَيْثُ ثَقِفْتُمُوْهُمْ ۚ وَاُولٰٓئِكُمْ جَعَلْنَا لَكُمْ عَلَيْهِمْ سُلْطٰنًا مُّبِيْنًا ۝

82

92. And it does not behoove a believer to kill a believer except by mistake, and whoever kills a believer by mistake, he should free a believing slave, and blood-money should be paid to his people unless they remit it as alms; but if he be from a tribe hostile to you and he is a believer, the freeing of a believing slave (suffices), and if he is from a tribe between whom and you there is a convenant, the blood-money should be paid to his people along with the freeing of a believing slave; but he who cannot find (a slave) should fast for two months successively: a penance from Allah, and Allah is Knowing, Wise.

93. And whoever kills a believer intentionally, his punishment is hell; he shall abide in it, and Allah will send His wrath on him and curse him and prepare for him a painful chastisement.

94. O you who believe! when you go to war in Allah's way, make investigation, and do not say to any one who offers you peace: You are not a believer. Do you seek goods of this world's life! But with Allah there are abundant gains; you too were such before, then Allah conferred a benefit on you; therefore make investigation; surely Allah is aware of what you do.

95. The holders back from among the believers, not having any injury, and those who strive hard in Allah's way with their property and their persons are not equal; Allah has made the strivers with their property and their persons to excel the holders back a (high) degree, and to each (class) Allah has promised good; and Allah shall grant to the strivers above the holders back a mighty reward:

96. (High) degrees from Him and protection and mercy, and Allah is Forgiving, Merciful.

83

97. Surely (as for) those whom the angels cause to die while they are unjust to their souls, they shall say: In what state were you? They shall say: We were weak in the earth. They shall say: Was not Allah's earth spacious, so that you should have migrated therein? So these it is whose abode is hell, and it is an evil resort;

اِنَّ الَّذِيْنَ تَوَفّٰىهُمُ الْمَلٰٓئِكَةُ ظَالِمِيٓ اَنْفُسِهِمْ قَالُوْا فِيْمَ كُنْتُمْ قَالُوْا كُنَّا مُسْتَضْعَفِيْنَ فِى الْاَرْضِ قَالُوْٓا اَلَمْ تَكُنْ اَرْضُ اللّٰهِ وَاسِعَةً فَتُهَاجِرُوْا فِيْهَا فَاُولٰٓئِكَ مَأْوٰىهُمْ جَهَنَّمُ وَسَآءَتْ مَصِيْرًا ۞

98. Except the weak from among the men and the children who have not in their power the means nor can they find a way (to escape);

اِلَّا الْمُسْتَضْعَفِيْنَ مِنَ الرِّجَالِ وَالنِّسَآءِ وَالْوِلْدَانِ لَا يَسْتَطِيْعُوْنَ حِيْلَةً وَّلَا يَهْتَدُوْنَ سَبِيْلًا ۞

99. So these, it may be, Allah will pardon them, and Allah is Pardoning, Forgiving.

فَاُولٰٓئِكَ عَسَى اللّٰهُ اَنْ يَّعْفُوَ عَنْهُمْ وَكَانَ اللّٰهُ عَفُوًّا غَفُوْرًا ۞

100. And whoever flies in Allah's way, he will find in the earth many a place of refuge and abundant resources; and whoever goes forth from his house flying to Allah and His Apostle, and then death overtakes him, his reward is indeed with Allah and Allah is Forgiving, Merciful.

وَمَنْ يُّهَاجِرْ فِىْ سَبِيْلِ اللّٰهِ يَجِدْ فِى الْاَرْضِ مُرَاغَمًا كَثِيْرًا وَّسَعَةً وَمَنْ يَّخْرُجْ مِنْ بَيْتِهٖ مُهَاجِرًا اِلَى اللّٰهِ وَرَسُوْلِهٖ ثُمَّ يُدْرِكْهُ الْمَوْتُ فَقَدْ وَقَعَ اَجْرُهٗ عَلَى اللّٰهِ وَكَانَ اللّٰهُ غَفُوْرًا رَّحِيْمًا ۞

101. And when you journey in the earth, there is no blame on you if you shorten the prayer, if you fear that those who disbelieve will cause you distress; surely the unbelievers are your open enemy.

وَاِذَا ضَرَبْتُمْ فِى الْاَرْضِ فَلَيْسَ عَلَيْكُمْ جُنَاحٌ اَنْ تَقْصُرُوْا مِنَ الصَّلٰوةِ اِنْ خِفْتُمْ اَنْ يَّفْتِنَكُمُ الَّذِيْنَ كَفَرُوْا اِنَّ الْكٰفِرِيْنَ كَانُوْا لَكُمْ عَدُوًّا مُّبِيْنًا ۞

102. And when you are among them and keep up the prayer for them, let a party of them stand up with you, and let them take their arms; then when they have prostrated themselves let them go to your rear, and let another party who have not prayed come forward and pray with you, and let them take their precautions and their arms; (for) those who disbelieve desire that you may be careless of your arms and your luggage, so that they may then turn upon you with a sudden united attack; and there is no blame on you, if you are annoyed with rain or if you are sick, that you lay down your arms, and take your precautions; surely Allah has prepared a disgraceful chastisement for the unbelievers.

وَاِذَا كُنْتَ فِيْهِمْ فَاَقَمْتَ لَهُمُ الصَّلٰوةَ فَلْتَقُمْ طَآئِفَةٌ مِّنْهُمْ مَّعَكَ وَلْيَأْخُذُوْٓا اَسْلِحَتَهُمْ فَاِذَا سَجَدُوْا فَلْيَكُوْنُوْا مِنْ وَّرَآئِكُمْ وَلْتَأْتِ طَآئِفَةٌ اُخْرٰى لَمْ يُصَلُّوْا فَلْيُصَلُّوْا مَعَكَ وَلْيَأْخُذُوْا حِذْرَهُمْ وَاَسْلِحَتَهُمْ وَدَّ الَّذِيْنَ كَفَرُوْا لَوْ تَغْفُلُوْنَ عَنْ اَسْلِحَتِكُمْ وَاَمْتِعَتِكُمْ فَيَمِيْلُوْنَ عَلَيْكُمْ مَّيْلَةً وَّاحِدَةً وَلَا جُنَاحَ عَلَيْكُمْ اِنْ كَانَ بِكُمْ اَذًى مِّنْ مَّطَرٍ اَوْ كُنْتُمْ مَّرْضٰٓى اَنْ تَضَعُوْٓا اَسْلِحَتَكُمْ وَخُذُوْا حِذْرَكُمْ اِنَّ اللّٰهَ اَعَدَّ لِلْكٰفِرِيْنَ عَذَابًا مُّهِيْنًا ۞

103. Then when you have finished the prayer, remember Allah standing and sitting and reclining; but when you are secure (from danger) keep up prayer; surely prayer is a timed ordinance for the believers.

فَإِذَا قَضَيْتُمُ الصَّلٰوةَ فَاذْكُرُوا اللّٰهَ قِيٰمًا وَّقُعُوْدًا وَّعَلٰى جُنُوْبِكُمْ ۚ فَإِذَا اطْمَأْنَنْتُمْ فَأَقِيْمُوا الصَّلٰوةَ ۚ اِنَّ الصَّلٰوةَ كَانَتْ عَلَى الْمُؤْمِنِيْنَ كِتٰبًا مَّوْقُوْتًا ۝

104. And be not weak hearted in pursuit of the enemy; if you suffer pain, then surely they (too) suffer pain as you suffer pain, and you hope from Allah what they do not hope; and Allah is Knowing, Wise.

وَلَا تَهِنُوْا فِى ابْتِغَاءِ الْقَوْمِ ۚ اِنْ تَكُوْنُوْا تَأْلَمُوْنَ فَإِنَّهُمْ يَأْلَمُوْنَ كَمَا تَأْلَمُوْنَ وَتَرْجُوْنَ مِنَ اللّٰهِ مَا لَا يَرْجُوْنَ ۚ وَكَانَ اللّٰهُ عَلِيْمًا حَكِيْمًا ۝

105. Surely We have revealed the Book to you with the truth that you may judge between people by means of that which Allah has taught you; and be not an advocate on behalf of the treacherous.

اِنَّا اَنْزَلْنَا اِلَيْكَ الْكِتٰبَ بِالْحَقِّ لِتَحْكُمَ بَيْنَ النَّاسِ بِمَا اَرٰىكَ اللّٰهُ ۚ وَلَا تَكُنْ لِّلْخَائِنِيْنَ خَصِيْمًا ۝

106. And ask forgiveness of Allah; surely Allah is Forgiving, Merciful.

وَّاسْتَغْفِرِ اللّٰهَ ۗ اِنَّ اللّٰهَ كَانَ غَفُوْرًا رَّحِيْمًا ۝

107. And do not plead on behalf of those who act unfaithfully to their souls; surely Allah does not love him who is treacherous, sinful;

وَلَا تُجَادِلْ عَنِ الَّذِيْنَ يَخْتَانُوْنَ اَنْفُسَهُمْ ۚ اِنَّ اللّٰهَ لَا يُحِبُّ مَنْ كَانَ خَوَّانًا اَثِيْمًا ۝

108. They hide themselves from men and do not hide themselves from Allah, and He is with them when they meditate by night words which please Him not, and Allah encompasses what they do.

يَّسْتَخْفُوْنَ مِنَ النَّاسِ وَلَا يَسْتَخْفُوْنَ مِنَ اللّٰهِ وَهُوَ مَعَهُمْ اِذْ يُبَيِّتُوْنَ مَا لَا يَرْضٰى مِنَ الْقَوْلِ ۚ وَكَانَ اللّٰهُ بِمَا يَعْمَلُوْنَ مُحِيْطًا ۝

109. Behold! you are they who (may) plead for them in this world's life, but who will plead for them with Allah on the resurrection day, or who shall be their protector?

هٰاَنْتُمْ هٰؤُلَاءِ جٰدَلْتُمْ عَنْهُمْ فِى الْحَيٰوةِ الدُّنْيَا ۚ فَمَنْ يُّجَادِلُ اللّٰهَ عَنْهُمْ يَوْمَ الْقِيٰمَةِ اَمْ مَّنْ يَّكُوْنُ عَلَيْهِمْ وَكِيْلًا ۝

110. And whoever does evil or acts unjustly to his soul, then asks forgiveness of Allah, he shall find Allah Forgiving, Merciful.

وَمَنْ يَّعْمَلْ سُوْءًا اَوْ يَظْلِمْ نَفْسَهُ ثُمَّ يَسْتَغْفِرِ اللّٰهَ يَجِدِ اللّٰهَ غَفُوْرًا رَّحِيْمًا ۝

111. And whoever commits a sin, he only commits it against his own soul; and Allah is Knowing, Wise.

وَمَنْ يَّكْسِبْ اِثْمًا فَإِنَّمَا يَكْسِبُهُ عَلٰى نَفْسِهِ ۚ وَكَانَ اللّٰهُ عَلِيْمًا حَكِيْمًا ۝

112. And whoever commits a fault or a sin, then accuses of it one innocent, he indeed takes upon himself the burden of a calumny and a manifest sin.

113. And were it not for Allah's grace upon you and His mercy, a party of them had certainly designed to bring you to perdition, and they do not bring (aught) to perdition but their own souls, and they shall not harm you in any way, and Allah has revealed to you the Book and the wisdom, and He has taught you what you did not know, and Allah's grace on you is very great.

114. There is no good in most of their secret counsels except (in his) who enjoins charity or goodness or reconciliation between people; and whoever does this seeking Allah's pleasure, We will give him a mighty reward.

115. And whoever acts hostilely to the Apostle after that guidance has become manifest to him, and follows other than the way of the believers, We will turn him to that to which he has (himself) turned and make him enter hell; and it is an evil resort.

116. Surely Allah does not forgive that anything should be associated with Him, and He forgives what is besides this to whom He pleases; and whoever associates anything with Allah, he indeed strays off into a remote error.

117. They do not call besides Him on anything but idols, and they do not call on anything but a rebellious Shaitan.

118. Allah has cursed him; and he said: Most certainly I will take of Thy servants an appointed portion:

86

119. And most certainly I will lead them astray and excite in them vain desires, and bid them so that they shall slit the ears of the cattle, and most certainly I will bid them so that they shall alter Allah's creation; and whoever takes the Shaitan for a guardian rather than Allah he indeed shall suffer a manifest loss.

ولاُضِلَّنَّهُمْ وَلاُمَنِّيَنَّهُمْ وَلاٰمُرَنَّهُمْ فَلَيُبَتِّكُنَّ اٰذَانَ الْاَنْعَامِ وَلاٰمُرَنَّهُمْ فَلَيُغَيِّرُنَّ خَلْقَ اللّٰهِ ۚ وَمَنْ يَّتَّخِذِ الشَّيْطٰنَ وَلِيًّا مِّنْ دُوْنِ اللّٰهِ فَقَدْ خَسِرَ خُسْرَانًا مُّبِيْنًا ۰

120. He gives them promises and excites vain desires in them; and the Shaitan does not promise them but to deceive.

يَعِدُهُمْ وَيُمَنِّيْهِمْ ۚ وَمَا يَعِدُهُمُ الشَّيْطٰنُ اِلَّا غُرُوْرًا ۰

121. These are they whose abode is hell, and they shall not find any refuge from it.

اُولٰٓئِكَ مَاْوٰىهُمْ جَهَنَّمُ ۚ وَلَا يَجِدُوْنَ عَنْهَا مَحِيْصًا ۰

122. And (as for) those who believe and do good, We will make them enter into gardens beneath which rivers flow, to abide therein for ever; (it is) a promise of Allah, true (indeed); and who is truer of word than Allah?

وَالَّذِيْنَ اٰمَنُوْا وَعَمِلُوا الصّٰلِحٰتِ سَنُدْخِلُهُمْ جَنّٰتٍ تَجْرِيْ مِنْ تَحْتِهَا الْاَنْهٰرُ خٰلِدِيْنَ فِيْهَا اَبَدًا ۚ وَعْدَ اللّٰهِ حَقًّا ۚ وَمَنْ اَصْدَقُ مِنَ اللّٰهِ قِيْلًا ۰

123. (This) shall not be in accordance with your vain desires nor in accordance with the vain desires of the followers of the Book; whoever does evil, he shall be requited with it, and besides Allah he will find for himself neither a guardian nor a helper.

لَيْسَ بِاَمَانِيِّكُمْ وَلَآ اَمَانِيِّ اَهْلِ الْكِتٰبِ ۚ مَنْ يَّعْمَلْ سُوْٓءًا يُّجْزَ بِهٖ ۚ وَلَا يَجِدْ لَهٗ مِنْ دُوْنِ اللّٰهِ وَلِيًّا وَّلَا نَصِيْرًا ۰

124. And whoever does good deeds whether male or female and he (or she) is a believer—these shall enter the garden, and they shall not be dealt with a jot unjustly.

وَمَنْ يَّعْمَلْ مِنَ الصّٰلِحٰتِ مِنْ ذَكَرٍ اَوْ اُنْثٰى وَهُوَ مُؤْمِنٌ فَاُولٰٓئِكَ يَدْخُلُوْنَ الْجَنَّةَ وَلَا يُظْلَمُوْنَ نَقِيْرًا ۰

125. And who has a better religion than he who submits himself entirely to Allah? And he is the doer of good (to others) and follows the faith of Ibrahim, the upright one, and Allah took Ibrahim as a friend.

وَمَنْ اَحْسَنُ دِيْنًا مِّمَّنْ اَسْلَمَ وَجْهَهٗ لِلّٰهِ وَهُوَ مُحْسِنٌ وَّاتَّبَعَ مِلَّةَ اِبْرٰهِيْمَ حَنِيْفًا ۚ وَاتَّخَذَ اللّٰهُ اِبْرٰهِيْمَ خَلِيْلًا ۰

126. And whatever is in the heavens and whatever is in the earth is Allah's; and Allah encompasses all things.

وَلِلّٰهِ مَا فِى السَّمٰوٰتِ وَمَا فِى الْاَرْضِ ۚ وَكَانَ اللّٰهُ بِكُلِّ شَيْءٍ مُّحِيْطًا ۰

127. And they ask you a decision about women. Say: Allah makes known to you His decision concerning them, and that which is recited to you in the Book concerning female orphans whom you do not give what is appointed for them while you desire to marry them, and concerning the weak among children, and that you should deal towards orphans with equity; and whatever good you do, Allah surely knows it.

128. And if a woman fears ill usage or desertion on the part of her husband, there is no blame on them, if they effect a reconciliation between them, and reconciliation is better, and avarice has been made to be present in the (people's) minds; and if you do good (to others) and guard (against evil), then surely Allah is aware of what you do.

129. And you have it not in your power to do justice between wives, even though you may wish (it), but be not disinclined (from one) with total disinclination, so that you leave her as it were in suspense; and if you effect a reconciliation and guard (against evil), then surely Allah is Forgiving, Merciful.

130. And if they separate, Allah will render them both free from want out of His ampleness, and Allah is Ample-giving, Wise.

131. And whatever is in the heavens and whatever is in the earth is Allah's and certainly We enjoined those who were given the Book before you and (We enjoin) you too that you should be careful of (your duty to) Allah; and if you disbelieve, then surely whatever is in the heavens and whatever is in the earth is Allah's and Allah is Self-sufficient, Praise-worthy.

132. And whatever is in the heavens and whatever is in the earth is Allah's, and Allah is sufficient as a Protector.

133. If He please, He can make you pass away, O people! and bring others; and Allah has the power to do this.

وَيَسْتَفْتُوْنَكَ فِي النِّسَآءِ ۚ قُلِ اللهُ يُفْتِيْكُمْ فِيْهِنَّ ۙ وَ مَا يُتْلٰى عَلَيْكُمْ فِي الْكِتٰبِ فِيْ يَتٰمَى النِّسَآءِ الّٰتِيْ لَا تُؤْتُوْنَهُنَّ مَا كُتِبَ لَهُنَّ وَتَرْغَبُوْنَ اَنْ تَنْكِحُوْهُنَّ وَالْمُسْتَضْعَفِيْنَ مِنَ الْوِلْدَانِ ۙ وَاَنْ تَقُوْمُوْا لِلْيَتٰمٰى بِالْقِسْطِ ۗ وَمَا تَفْعَلُوْا مِنْ خَيْرٍ فَاِنَّ اللهَ كَانَ بِهٖ عَلِيْمًا ۝

وَاِنِ امْرَاَةٌ خَافَتْ مِنْۢ بَعْلِهَا نُشُوْزًا اَوْ اِعْرَاضًا فَلَا جُنَاحَ عَلَيْهِمَآ اَنْ يُّصْلِحَا بَيْنَهُمَا صُلْحًا ۗ وَالصُّلْحُ خَيْرٌ ۗ وَاُحْضِرَتِ الْاَنْفُسُ الشُّحَّ ۗ وَاِنْ تُحْسِنُوْا وَ تَتَّقُوْا فَاِنَّ اللهَ كَانَ بِمَا تَعْمَلُوْنَ خَبِيْرًا ۝

وَلَنْ تَسْتَطِيْعُوْا اَنْ تَعْدِلُوْا بَيْنَ النِّسَآءِ وَلَوْ حَرَصْتُمْ فَلَا تَمِيْلُوْا كُلَّ الْمَيْلِ فَتَذَرُوْهَا كَالْمُعَلَّقَةِ ۗ وَاِنْ تُصْلِحُوْا وَتَتَّقُوْا فَاِنَّ اللهَ كَانَ غَفُوْرًا رَّحِيْمًا ۝

وَاِنْ يَّتَفَرَّقَا يُغْنِ اللهُ كُلًّا مِّنْ سَعَتِهٖ ۗ وَكَانَ اللهُ وَاسِعًا حَكِيْمًا ۝

وَلِلّٰهِ مَا فِي السَّمٰوٰتِ وَمَا فِي الْاَرْضِ ۗ وَلَقَدْ وَصَّيْنَا الَّذِيْنَ اُوْتُوا الْكِتٰبَ مِنْ قَبْلِكُمْ وَاِيَّاكُمْ اَنِ اتَّقُوا اللهَ ۗ وَاِنْ تَكْفُرُوْا فَاِنَّ لِلّٰهِ مَا فِي السَّمٰوٰتِ وَمَا فِي الْاَرْضِ ۗ وَكَانَ اللهُ غَنِيًّا حَمِيْدًا ۝

وَلِلّٰهِ مَا فِي السَّمٰوٰتِ وَمَا فِي الْاَرْضِ ۗ وَكَفٰى بِاللهِ وَكِيْلًا ۝

اِنْ يَّشَأْ يُذْهِبْكُمْ اَيُّهَا النَّاسُ وَيَأْتِ بِاٰخَرِيْنَ ۗ وَكَانَ اللهُ عَلٰى ذٰلِكَ قَدِيْرًا ۝

134. Whoever desires the reward of this world, then with Allah is the reward of this world and the hereafter; and Allah is Hearing, Seeing.

مَنْ كَانَ يُرِيْدُ ثَوَابَ الدُّنْيَا فَعِنْدَ اللهِ ثَوَابُ الدُّنْيَا وَالْاٰخِرَةِ ۗ وَكَانَ اللهُ سَمِيْعًا بَصِيْرًا ۝

135. O you who believe! be maintainers of justice, bearers of witness of Allah's sake, though it may be against your own selves or (your) parents or near relatives; if he be rich or poor, Allah is nearer to them both in compassion; therefore do not follow (your) low desires, lest you deviate; and if you swerve or turn aside, then surely Allah is aware of what you do.

يٰٓاَيُّهَا الَّذِيْنَ اٰمَنُوْا كُوْنُوْا قَوّٰمِيْنَ بِالْقِسْطِ شُهَدَآءَ لِلّٰهِ وَلَوْ عَلٰٓى اَنْفُسِكُمْ اَوِ الْوَالِدَيْنِ وَالْاَقْرَبِيْنَ ۚ اِنْ يَّكُنْ غَنِيًّا اَوْ فَقِيْرًا فَاللهُ اَوْلٰى بِهِمَا ۖ فَلَا تَتَّبِعُوا الْهَوٰٓى اَنْ تَعْدِلُوْا ۚ وَاِنْ تَلْوٗٓا اَوْ تُعْرِضُوْا فَاِنَّ اللهَ كَانَ بِمَا تَعْمَلُوْنَ خَبِيْرًا ۝

136. O you who believe! believe in Allah and His Apostle and the Book which He has revealed to His Apostle and the Book which He revealed before; and whoever disbelieves in Allah and His angels and His apostles and the last day, he indeed strays off into a remote error.

يٰٓاَيُّهَا الَّذِيْنَ اٰمَنُوْٓا اٰمِنُوْا بِاللهِ وَرَسُوْلِهٖ وَالْكِتٰبِ الَّذِيْ نَزَّلَ عَلٰى رَسُوْلِهٖ وَالْكِتٰبِ الَّذِيْٓ اَنْزَلَ مِنْ قَبْلُ ۚ وَمَنْ يَّكْفُرْ بِاللهِ وَمَلٰٓئِكَتِهٖ وَكُتُبِهٖ وَرُسُلِهٖ وَالْيَوْمِ الْاٰخِرِ فَقَدْ ضَلَّ ضَلٰلًا بَعِيْدًا ۝

137. Surely (as for) those who believe then disbelieve, again believe and again disbelieve, then increase in disbelief, Allah will not forgive them nor guide them in the (right) path.

اِنَّ الَّذِيْنَ اٰمَنُوْا ثُمَّ كَفَرُوْا ثُمَّ اٰمَنُوْا ثُمَّ كَفَرُوْا ثُمَّ ازْدَادُوْا كُفْرًا لَّمْ يَكُنِ اللهُ لِيَغْفِرَ لَهُمْ وَلَا لِيَهْدِيَهُمْ سَبِيْلًا ۝

138. Announce to the hypocrites that they shall have a painful chastisement:

بَشِّرِ الْمُنٰفِقِيْنَ بِاَنَّ لَهُمْ عَذَابًا اَلِيْمًا ۝

139. Those who take the unbelievers for guardians rather than believers. Do they seek honor from them? Then surely all honor is for Allah.

اِلَّذِيْنَ يَتَّخِذُوْنَ الْكٰفِرِيْنَ اَوْلِيَآءَ مِنْ دُوْنِ الْمُؤْمِنِيْنَ ۚ اَيَبْتَغُوْنَ عِنْدَهُمُ الْعِزَّةَ فَاِنَّ الْعِزَّةَ لِلّٰهِ جَمِيْعًا ۝

140. And indeed He has revealed to you in the Book that when you hear Allah's communications disbelieved in and mocked at, do not sit with them until they enter into some other discourse; surely then you would be like them; surely Allah will gather together the hypocrites and the unbelievers all in hell.

وَقَدْ نَزَّلَ عَلَيْكُمْ فِي الْكِتٰبِ اَنْ اِذَا سَمِعْتُمْ اٰيٰتِ اللهِ يُكْفَرُ بِهَا وَيُسْتَهْزَاُ بِهَا فَلَا تَقْعُدُوْا مَعَهُمْ حَتّٰى يَخُوْضُوْا فِيْ حَدِيْثٍ غَيْرِهٖٓ ۖ اِنَّكُمْ اِذًا مِّثْلُهُمْ ۗ اِنَّ اللهَ جَامِعُ الْمُنٰفِقِيْنَ وَالْكٰفِرِيْنَ فِيْ جَهَنَّمَ جَمِيْعًا ۝

141. Those who wait for (some misfortune to befall) you; then if you have a victory from Allah they say: Were we not with you? And if there is a chance for the unbelievers, they say: Did we not acquire the mastery over you and defend you from the believers? So Allah shall judge between you on the day of resurrection; and Allah will by no means give the unbelievers a way against the believers.

الَّذِينَ يَتَرَبَّصُونَ بِكُمْ فَإِنْ كَانَ لَكُمْ فَتْحٌ مِّنَ اللّٰهِ قَالُوۤا اَلَمْ نَكُنْ مَّعَكُمْ وَاِنْ كَانَ لِلْكٰفِرِينَ نَصِيْبٌ قَالُوۤا اَلَمْ نَسْتَحْوِذْ عَلَيْكُمْ وَنَمْنَعْكُمْ مِّنَ الْمُؤْمِنِيْنَ فَاللّٰهُ يَحْكُمُ بَيْنَكُمْ يَوْمَ الْقِيٰمَةِ وَلَنْ يَّجْعَلَ اللّٰهُ لِلْكٰفِرِينَ عَلَى الْمُؤْمِنِيْنَ سَبِيْلاً ۞

142. Surely the hypocrites strive to deceive Allah, and He shall requite their deceit to them, and when they stand up to prayer, they stand up sluggishly; they do it only to be seen of men and do not remember Allah save a little.

اِنَّ الْمُنٰفِقِيْنَ يُخٰدِعُوْنَ اللّٰهَ وَهُوَ خَادِعُهُمْ وَاِذَا قَامُوۤا اِلَى الصَّلٰوةِ قَامُوْا كُسَالٰى يُرَآءُوْنَ النَّاسَ وَلَا يَذْكُرُوْنَ اللّٰهَ اِلَّا قَلِيْلاً ۞

143. Wavering between that (and this), (belonging) neither to these nor to those; and whomsoever Allah causes to err, you shall not find a way for him.

مُّذَبْذَبِيْنَ بَيْنَ ذٰلِكَ لَاۤ اِلٰى هٰۤؤُلَاۤءِ وَلَاۤ اِلٰى هٰۤؤُلَاۤءِ وَمَنْ يُّضْلِلِ اللّٰهُ فَلَنْ تَجِدَ لَهُ سَبِيْلاً ۞

144. O you who believe! do not take the unbelievers for friends rather than the believers; do you desire that you should give to Allah a manifest proof against yourselves?

يٰۤاَيُّهَا الَّذِيْنَ اٰمَنُوْا لَا تَتَّخِذُوا الْكٰفِرِيْنَ اَوْلِيَاۤءَ مِنْ دُوْنِ الْمُؤْمِنِيْنَ اَتُرِيْدُوْنَ اَنْ تَجْعَلُوْا لِلّٰهِ عَلَيْكُمْ سُلْطٰنًا مُّبِيْنًا ۞

145. Surely the hypocrites are in the lowest stage of the fire, and you shall not find a helper for them.

اِنَّ الْمُنٰفِقِيْنَ فِى الدَّرْكِ الْاَسْفَلِ مِنَ النَّارِ وَلَنْ تَجِدَ لَهُمْ نَصِيْرًا ۞

146. Except those who repent and amend and hold fast to Allah and are sincere in their religion to Allah; these are with the believers, and Allah will grant the believers a mighty reward.

اِلَّا الَّذِيْنَ تَابُوْا وَاَصْلَحُوْا وَاعْتَصَمُوْا بِاللّٰهِ وَاَخْلَصُوْا دِيْنَهُمْ لِلّٰهِ فَاُولٰۤئِكَ مَعَ الْمُؤْمِنِيْنَ وَسَوْفَ يُؤْتِ اللّٰهُ الْمُؤْمِنِيْنَ اَجْرًا عَظِيْمًا ۞

147. Why should Allah chastise you if you are grateful and believe? And Allah is the Multiplier of rewards, Knowing.

مَا يَفْعَلُ اللّٰهُ بِعَذَابِكُمْ اِنْ شَكَرْتُمْ وَاٰمَنْتُمْ وَكَانَ اللّٰهُ شَاكِرًا عَلِيْمًا ۞

148. Allah does not love the public utterance of hurtful speech, unless (it be) by one to whom injustice has been done; and Allah is Hearing, Knowing.

لَا يُحِبُّ اللّٰهُ الْجَهْرَ بِالسُّوۤءِ مِنَ الْقَوْلِ اِلَّا مَنْ ظُلِمَ وَكَانَ اللّٰهُ سَمِيْعًا عَلِيْمًا ۞

149. If you do good openly or do it in secret or pardon an evil, then surely Allah is Pardoning, Powerful.

اِنْ تُبْدُوْا خَيْرًا اَوْ تُخْفُوْهُ اَوْتَعْفُوْا عَنْ سُوْٓءٍ فَاِنَّ اللهَ كَانَ عَفُوًّا قَدِيْرًا ۝

150. Surely those who disbelieve in Allah and His apostles and (those who) desire to make a distinction between Allah and His apostles and say: We believe in some and disbelieve in others; and desire to take a course between (this and) that.

اِنَّ الَّذِيْنَ يَكْفُرُوْنَ بِاللهِ وَرُسُلِهٖ وَيُرِيْدُوْنَ اَنْ يُّفَرِّقُوْا بَيْنَ اللهِ وَرُسُلِهٖ وَيَقُوْلُوْنَ نُؤْمِنُ بِبَعْضٍ وَّنَكْفُرُ بِبَعْضٍ وَّيُرِيْدُوْنَ اَنْ يَّتَّخِذُوْا بَيْنَ ذٰلِكَ سَبِيْلًا ۝

151. These it is that are truly unbelievers, and We have prepared for the unbelievers a disgraceful chastisement.

اُولٰٓئِكَ هُمُ الْكٰفِرُوْنَ حَقًّا وَاَعْتَدْنَا لِلْكٰفِرِيْنَ عَذَابًا مُّهِيْنًا ۝

152. And those who believe in Allah and His apostles and do not make a distinction between any of them—Allah will grant them their rewards; and Allah is Forgiving, Merciful.

وَالَّذِيْنَ اٰمَنُوْا بِاللهِ وَرُسُلِهٖ وَلَمْ يُفَرِّقُوْا بَيْنَ اَحَدٍ مِّنْهُمْ اُولٰٓئِكَ سَوْفَ يُؤْتِيْهِمْ اُجُوْرَهُمْ وَكَانَ اللهُ غَفُوْرًا رَّحِيْمًا ۝

153. The followers of the Book ask you to bring down to them a book from heaven; so indeed they demanded of Musa a greater thing than that, for they said: Show us Allah manifestly; so the lightning overtook them on account of their injustice. Then they took the calf (for a god), after clear signs had come to them, but We pardoned this; and We gave to Musa clear authority.

يَسْئَلُكَ اَهْلُ الْكِتٰبِ اَنْ تُنَزِّلَ عَلَيْهِمْ كِتٰبًا مِّنَ السَّمَاءِ فَقَدْ سَاَلُوْا مُوْسٰٓى اَكْبَرَ مِنْ ذٰلِكَ فَقَالُوْٓا اَرِنَا اللهَ جَهْرَةً فَاَخَذَتْهُمُ الصّٰعِقَةُ بِظُلْمِهِمْ ثُمَّ اتَّخَذُوا الْعِجْلَ مِنْ بَعْدِ مَا جَاءَتْهُمُ الْبَيِّنٰتُ فَعَفَوْنَا عَنْ ذٰلِكَ وَاٰتَيْنَا مُوْسٰى سُلْطٰنًا مُّبِيْنًا ۝

154. And We lifted the mountain (Sinai) over them at (the taking of the covenant) and We said to them: Enter the door making obeisance; and We said to them: Do not exceed the limits of the Sabbath; and We made with them a firm covenant.

وَرَفَعْنَا فَوْقَهُمُ الطُّوْرَ بِمِيْثَاقِهِمْ وَقُلْنَا لَهُمُ ادْخُلُوا الْبَابَ سُجَّدًا وَّقُلْنَا لَهُمْ لَا تَعْدُوْا فِى السَّبْتِ وَاَخَذْنَا مِنْهُمْ مِّيْثَاقًا غَلِيْظًا ۝

155. Therefore, for their breaking their covenant and their disbelief in the communications of Allah and their killing the prophets wrongfully and their saying: Our hearts are covered; nay! Allah set a seal upon them owing to their unbelief, so they shall not believe except a few.

فَبِمَا نَقْضِهِمْ مِّيْثَاقَهُمْ وَكُفْرِهِمْ بِاٰيٰتِ اللهِ وَقَتْلِهِمُ الْاَنْبِيَاءَ بِغَيْرِ حَقٍّ وَّقَوْلِهِمْ قُلُوْبُنَا غُلْفٌ بَلْ طَبَعَ اللهُ عَلَيْهَا بِكُفْرِهِمْ فَلَا يُؤْمِنُوْنَ اِلَّا قَلِيْلًا ۝

156. And for their unbelief and for their having uttered against Marium a grievous calumny.

وَّبِكُفْرِهِمْ وَقَوْلِهِمْ عَلٰى مَرْيَمَ بُهْتَانًا عَظِيْمًا ۝

157. And their saying: Surely we have killed the Messiah, Isa son of Marium, the apostle of Allah; and they did not kill him nor did they crucify him, but it appeared to them so (like Isa) and most surely those who differ therein are only in a doubt about it; they have no knowledge respecting it, but only follow a conjecture, and they killed him not for sure.

وَّقَوْلِهِمْ اِنَّا قَتَلْنَا الْمَسِيْحَ عِيْسَى ابْنَ مَرْيَمَ رَسُوْلَ اللّٰهِ ۚ وَمَا قَتَلُوْهُ وَمَا صَلَبُوْهُ وَلٰكِنْ شُبِّهَ لَهُمْ ۚ وَاِنَّ الَّذِيْنَ اخْتَلَفُوْا فِيْهِ لَفِيْ شَكٍّ مِّنْهُ ۚ مَا لَهُمْ بِهٖ مِنْ عِلْمٍ اِلَّا اتِّبَاعَ الظَّنِّ ۚ وَمَا قَتَلُوْهُ يَقِيْنًا ۝

158. Nay! Allah took him up to Himself; and Allah is Mighty, Wise.

بَلْ رَّفَعَهُ اللّٰهُ اِلَيْهِ ۚ وَكَانَ اللّٰهُ عَزِيْزًا حَكِيْمًا ۝

159. And there is not one of the followers of the Book but most certainly believes in this before his death, and on the day of resurrection he (Isa) shall be a witness against them.

وَاِنْ مِّنْ اَهْلِ الْكِتٰبِ اِلَّا لَيُؤْمِنَنَّ بِهٖ قَبْلَ مَوْتِهٖ ۚ وَيَوْمَ الْقِيٰمَةِ يَكُوْنُ عَلَيْهِمْ شَهِيْدًا ۝

160. Wherefore for the iniquity of those who are Jews did We disallow to them the good things which had been made lawful for them, and for their hindering many (people) from Allah's way.

فَبِظُلْمٍ مِّنَ الَّذِيْنَ هَادُوْا حَرَّمْنَا عَلَيْهِمْ طَيِّبٰتٍ اُحِلَّتْ لَهُمْ وَبِصَدِّهِمْ عَنْ سَبِيْلِ اللّٰهِ كَثِيْرًا ۝

161. And their taking usury though indeed they were forbidden it and their devouring the property of people falsely; and We have prepared for the unbelievers from among them a painful chastisement.

وَّاَخْذِهِمُ الرِّبٰوا وَقَدْ نُهُوْا عَنْهُ وَاَكْلِهِمْ اَمْوَالَ النَّاسِ بِالْبَاطِلِ ۚ وَاَعْتَدْنَا لِلْكٰفِرِيْنَ مِنْهُمْ عَذَابًا اَلِيْمًا ۝

162. But the firm in knowledge among them and the believers believe in what has been revealed to you and what was revealed before you, and those who keep up prayers and those who give the poor-rate and the believers in Allah and the last day, these it is whom We will give a mighty reward.

لٰكِنِ الرّٰسِخُوْنَ فِى الْعِلْمِ مِنْهُمْ وَالْمُؤْمِنُوْنَ يُؤْمِنُوْنَ بِمَا اُنْزِلَ اِلَيْكَ وَمَا اُنْزِلَ مِنْ قَبْلِكَ وَالْمُقِيْمِيْنَ الصَّلٰوةَ وَالْمُؤْتُوْنَ الزَّكٰوةَ وَالْمُؤْمِنُوْنَ بِاللّٰهِ وَ الْيَوْمِ الْاٰخِرِ ۚ اُولٰٓئِكَ سَنُؤْتِيْهِمْ اَجْرًا عَظِيْمًا ۝

163. Surely We have revealed to you as We revealed to Nuh, and the prophets after him, and We revealed to Ibrahim and Ismail and Ishaq and Yaqoob and the tribes, and Isa and Ayub and Yunus and Haroun and Sulaiman and We gave to Dawood Psalms.

اِنَّا اَوْحَيْنَا اِلَيْكَ كَمَا اَوْحَيْنَا اِلٰى نُوْحٍ وَّالنَّبِيّٖنَ مِنْ بَعْدِهٖ ۚ وَاَوْحَيْنَا اِلٰى اِبْرٰهِيْمَ وَاِسْمٰعِيْلَ وَ اِسْحٰقَ وَيَعْقُوْبَ وَالْاَسْبَاطِ وَعِيْسٰى وَاَيُّوْبَ وَ يُوْنُسَ وَهٰرُوْنَ وَسُلَيْمٰنَ ۚ وَاٰتَيْنَا دَاوٗدَ زَبُوْرًا ۝

164. And (We sent) apostles We have mentioned to you before and apostles we have not mentioned to you; and to Musa, Allah addressed His Word, speaking (to him):

وَرُسُلًا قَدْ قَصَصْنٰهُمْ عَلَيْكَ مِنْ قَبْلُ وَرُسُلًا لَّمْ نَقْصُصْهُمْ عَلَيْكَ ۚ وَكَلَّمَ اللّٰهُ مُوْسٰى تَكْلِيْمًا ۝

165. (We sent) apostles as the givers of good news and as warners, so that people should not have a plea against Allah after the (coming of) apostles; and Allah is Mighty, Wise.

رُسُلًا مُّبَشِّرِيْنَ وَمُنْذِرِيْنَ لِئَلَّا يَكُوْنَ لِلنَّاسِ عَلَى اللّٰهِ حُجَّةٌ بَعْدَ الرُّسُلِ ۚ وَكَانَ اللّٰهُ عَزِيْزًا حَكِيْمًا ۝

166. But Allah bears witness by what He has revealed to you that He has revealed it with His knowledge, and the angels bear witness (also); and Allah is sufficient as a witness.

لٰكِنِ اللّٰهُ يَشْهَدُ بِمَا أَنْزَلَ إِلَيْكَ أَنْزَلَهُ بِعِلْمِهٖ ۚ وَالْمَلٰئِكَةُ يَشْهَدُوْنَ ۚ وَكَفٰى بِاللّٰهِ شَهِيْدًا ۝

167. Surely (as for) those who disbelieve and hinder (men) from Allah's way, they indeed have strayed off into a remote error.

إِنَّ الَّذِيْنَ كَفَرُوْا وَصَدُّوْا عَنْ سَبِيْلِ اللّٰهِ قَدْ ضَلُّوْا ضَلٰلًا بَعِيْدًا ۝

168. Surely (as for) those who disbelieve and act unjustly, Allah will not forgive them nor guide them to a path,

إِنَّ الَّذِيْنَ كَفَرُوْا وَظَلَمُوْا لَمْ يَكُنِ اللّٰهُ لِيَغْفِرَ لَهُمْ وَلَا لِيَهْدِيَهُمْ طَرِيْقًا ۝

169. Except the path of hell, to abide in it for ever, and this is easy to Allah.

إِلَّا طَرِيْقَ جَهَنَّمَ خٰلِدِيْنَ فِيْهَا أَبَدًا ۚ وَكَانَ ذٰلِكَ عَلَى اللّٰهِ يَسِيْرًا ۝

170. O people! surely the Apostle has come to you with the truth from your Lord, therefore believe, (it shall be) good for you; and if you disbelieve, then surely whatever is in the heavens and the earth is Allah's; and Allah is Knowing, Wise.

يٰٓأَيُّهَا النَّاسُ قَدْ جَآءَكُمُ الرَّسُوْلُ بِالْحَقِّ مِنْ رَّبِّكُمْ فَاٰمِنُوْا خَيْرًا لَّكُمْ ۚ وَإِنْ تَكْفُرُوْا فَإِنَّ لِلّٰهِ مَا فِى السَّمٰوٰتِ وَالْأَرْضِ ۚ وَكَانَ اللّٰهُ عَلِيْمًا حَكِيْمًا ۝

171. O followers of the Book! do not exceed the limits in your religion, and do not speak (lies) against Allah, but (speak) the truth; the Messiah, Isa son of Marium is only an apostle of Allah and His Word which He communicated to Marium and a spirit from Him; believe therefore in Allah and His apostles, and say not, Three. Desist, it is better for you; Allah is only one God: far be it from His glory that He should have a son; whatever is in the heavens and whatever is in the earth is His; and Allah is sufficient for a Protector.

يٰٓأَهْلَ الْكِتٰبِ لَا تَغْلُوْا فِىْ دِيْنِكُمْ وَلَا تَقُوْلُوْا عَلَى اللّٰهِ إِلَّا الْحَقَّ ۚ إِنَّمَا الْمَسِيْحُ عِيْسَى ابْنُ مَرْيَمَ رَسُوْلُ اللّٰهِ وَكَلِمَتُهٗ ۚ أَلْقٰهَا إِلٰى مَرْيَمَ وَرُوْحٌ مِّنْهُ ۖ فَاٰمِنُوْا بِاللّٰهِ وَرُسُلِهٖ ۚ وَلَا تَقُوْلُوْا ثَلٰثَةٌ ۚ اِنْتَهُوْا خَيْرًا لَّكُمْ ۚ إِنَّمَا اللّٰهُ إِلٰهٌ وَّاحِدٌ ۚ سُبْحٰنَهٗ أَنْ يَّكُوْنَ لَهٗ وَلَدٌ ۘ لَهٗ مَا فِى السَّمٰوٰتِ وَمَا فِى الْأَرْضِ ۚ وَكَفٰى بِاللّٰهِ وَكِيْلًا ۝

172. The Messiah does by no means disdain that he should be a servant of Allah, nor do the angels who are near to Him, and whoever disdains His service and is proud, He will gather them all together to Himself.

لَنْ يَّسْتَنْكِفَ الْمَسِيْحُ اَنْ يَّكُوْنَ عَبْدًا لِلّٰهِ وَلَا الْمَلٰٓئِكَةُ الْمُقَرَّبُوْنَ وَمَنْ يَّسْتَنْكِفْ عَنْ عِبَادَتِهٖ وَيَسْتَكْبِرْ فَسَيَحْشُرُهُمْ اِلَيْهِ جَمِيْعًا ۝

173. Then as for those who believe and do good, He will pay them fully their rewards and give them more out of His grace; and as for those who disdain and are proud, He will chastise them with a painful chastisement. And they shall not find for themselves besides Allah a guardian or a helper.

فَاَمَّا الَّذِيْنَ اٰمَنُوْا وَعَمِلُوا الصّٰلِحٰتِ فَيُوَفِّيْهِمْ اُجُوْرَهُمْ وَيَزِيْدُهُمْ مِّنْ فَضْلِهٖ وَاَمَّا الَّذِيْنَ اسْتَنْكَفُوْا وَاسْتَكْبَرُوْا فَيُعَذِّبُهُمْ عَذَابًا اَلِيْمًا وَّلَا يَجِدُوْنَ لَهُمْ مِّنْ دُوْنِ اللّٰهِ وَلِيًّا وَّلَا نَصِيْرًا ۝

174. O people! Surely there has come to you manifest proof from your Lord and We have sent to you clear light.

يٰٓاَيُّهَا النَّاسُ قَدْ جَآءَكُمْ بُرْهَانٌ مِّنْ رَّبِّكُمْ وَاَنْزَلْنَآ اِلَيْكُمْ نُوْرًا مُّبِيْنًا ۝

175. Then as for those who believe in Allah and hold fast by Him, He will cause them to enter into His mercy and grace and guide them to Himself on a right path.

فَاَمَّا الَّذِيْنَ اٰمَنُوْا بِاللّٰهِ وَاعْتَصَمُوْا بِهٖ فَسَيُدْخِلُهُمْ فِيْ رَحْمَةٍ مِّنْهُ وَفَضْلٍ وَّيَهْدِيْهِمْ اِلَيْهِ صِرَاطًا مُّسْتَقِيْمًا ۝

176. They ask you for a decision of the law. Say: Allah gives you a decision concerning the person who has neither parents nor offspring; if a man dies (and) he has no son and he has a sister, she shall have half of what he leaves, and he shall be her heir if she has no son; but if there be two (sisters), they shall have two-thirds of what he leaves; and if there are brethren, men and women, then the male shall have the like of the portion of two females; Allah makes clear to you, lest you err; and Allah knows all things.

يَسْتَفْتُوْنَكَ قُلِ اللّٰهُ يُفْتِيْكُمْ فِى الْكَلٰلَةِ اِنِ امْرُؤٌا هَلَكَ لَيْسَ لَهٗ وَلَدٌ وَّلَهٗٓ اُخْتٌ فَلَهَا نِصْفُ مَا تَرَكَ وَهُوَ يَرِثُهَآ اِنْ لَّمْ يَكُنْ لَّهَا وَلَدٌ فَاِنْ كَانَتَا اثْنَتَيْنِ فَلَهُمَا الثُّلُثٰنِ مِمَّا تَرَكَ وَاِنْ كَانُوْٓا اِخْوَةً رِّجَالًا وَّنِسَآءً فَلِلذَّكَرِ مِثْلُ حَظِّ الْاُنْثَيَيْنِ يُبَيِّنُ اللّٰهُ لَكُمْ اَنْ تَضِلُّوْا وَاللّٰهُ بِكُلِّ شَيْءٍ عَلِيْمٌ ۝

THE FOOD
(MAIDAH)

In the name of Allah,
the Beneficent, the Merciful.

1. O you who believe! fulfill the obligations. The cattle quadrupeds are allowed to you except that which is recited to you, not violating the prohibition against game when you are entering upon the performance of the pilgrimage; surely Allah orders what He desires.

2. O you who believe! do not violate the signs appointed by Allah nor the sacred month, nor (interfere with) the offerings, nor the sacrificial animals with garlands, nor those going to the sacred house seeking the grace and pleasure of their Lord; and when you are free from the obligations of the pilgrimage, then hunt, and let not hatred of a people—because they hindered you from the Sacred Masjid—incite you to exceed the limits, and help one another in goodness and piety, and do not help one another in sin and aggression; and be careful of (your duty to) Allah; surely Allah is severe in requiting (evil).

3. Forbidden to you is that which dies of itself, and blood, and flesh of swine, and that on which any other name than that of Allah has been invoked, and the strangled (animal) and that beaten to death, and that killed by a fall and that killed by being smitten with the horn, and that which wild beasts have eaten, except what you slaughter, and what is sacrificed on stones set up (for idols) and that you divide by the arrows; that is a transgression. This day have those who disbelieve despaired of your religion, so fear them not, and fear Me. This day have I perfected for you your religion and completed My favor on you and chosen for you Islam as a religion; but whoever is compelled by hunger, not inclining willfully to sin, then surely Allah is Forgiving, Merciful.

4. They ask you as to what is allowed to them. Say: The good things are allowed to you, and what you have taught the beasts and birds of prey, training them to hunt— you teach them of what Allah has taught you—so eat of that which they catch for you and mention the name of Allah over it; and be careful of (your duty to) Allah; surely Allah is swift in reckoning.

5. This day (all) the good things are allowed to you; and the food of those who have been given the Book is lawful for you and your food is lawful for them; and the chaste from among the believing women and the chaste from among those who have been given the Book before you (are lawful for you); when you have given them their dowries, taking (them) in marriage, not fornicating nor taking them for paramours in secret; and whoever denies faith, his work indeed is of no account, and in the hereafter he shall be one of the losers.

6. O you who believe! when you rise up to prayer, wash your faces and your hands as far as the elbows, and wipe your heads and your feet to the ankles; and if you are under an obligation to perform a total ablution, then wash (yourselves) and if you are sick or on a journey, or one of you come from the privy, or you have touched the women, and you cannot find water, betake yourselves to pure earth and wipe your faces and your hands therewith, Allah does not desire to put on you any difficulty, but He wishes to purify you and that He may complete His favor on you, so that you may be grateful.

7. And remember the favor of Allah on you and His covenant with which He bound you firmly, when you said: We have heard and we obey, and be careful of (your duty to) Allah, surely Allah knows what is in the breasts.

8. O you who believe! Be upright for Allah, bearers of witness with justice, and let not hatred of a people incite you not to act equitably; act equitably, that is nearer to piety, and be careful of (your duty to) Allah; surely Allah is Aware of what you do.

9. Allah has promised to those who believe and do good deeds (that) they shall have forgiveness and a mighty reward.

10. And (as for) those who disbelieve and reject our communications, these are the companions of the flame.

11. O you who believe! remember Allah's favor on you when a people had determined to stretch forth their hands towards you, but He withheld their hands from you, and be careful of (your duty to) Allah; and on Allah let the believers rely.

12. And certainly Allah made a covenant with the children of Israel, and We raised up among them twelve chieftains; and Allah said: Surely I am with you; if you keep up prayer and pay the poor-rate and believe in My apostles and assist them and offer to Allah a goodly gift, I will most certainly cover your evil deeds, and I will most certainly cause you to enter into gardens beneath which rivers flow, but whoever disbelieves from among you after that, he indeed shall lose the right way.

13. But on account of their breaking their covenant We cursed them and made their hearts hard; they altered the words from their places and they neglected a portion of what they were reminded of; and you shall always discover treachery in them excepting a few of them; so pardon them and turn away; surely Allah loves those who do good (to others).

٩٧

14. And with those who say, We are Christians, We made a covenant, but they neglected a portion of what they were reminded of, therefore We excited among them enmity and hatred to the day of resurrection; and Allah will inform them of what they did.

15. O followers of the Book! indeed Our Apostle has come to you making clear to you much of what you concealed of the Book and passing over much; indeed, there has come to you light and a clear Book from Allah;

16. With it Allah guides him who will follow His pleasure into the ways of safety and brings them out of utter darkness into light by His will and guides them to the right path.

17. Certainly they disbelieve who say: Surely, Allah—He is the Messiah, son of Marium. Say: Who then could control anything as against Allah when He wished to destroy the Messiah son of Marium and his mother and all those on the earth? And Allah's is the kingdom of the heavens and the earth and what is between them; He creates what He pleases; and Allah has power over all things.

18. And the Jews and the Christians say: We are the sons of Allah and His beloved ones. Say: Why does He then chastise you for your faults? Nay, you are mortals from among those whom He has created; He forgives whom He pleases and chastises whom He pleases; and Allah's is the kingdom of the heavens and the earth and what is between them, and to Him is the eventual coming.

19. O followers of the Book! indeed Our Apostle has come to you explaining to you after a cessation of the (mission of the) apostles, lest you say: There came not to us a giver of good news or a warner, so indeed there has come to you a giver of good news and a warner; and Allah has power over all things.

98

20. And when Musa said to his people: O my people! remember the favor of Allah upon you when He raised prophets among you and made you kings and gave you what He had not given to any other among the nations.

21. O my people! enter the holy land which Allah has prescribed for you and turn not on your backs for then you will turn back losers.

22. They said: O Musa! surely there is a strong race in it, and we will on no account enter it until they go out from it, so if they go out from it, then surely we will enter.

23. Two men of those who feared, upon both of whom Allah had bestowed a favor, said: Enter upon them by the gate, for when you have entered it you shall surely be victorious, and on Allah should you rely if you are believers.

24. They said: O Musa! we shall never enter it so long as they are in it; go therefore you and your Lord, then fight you both, surely we will here sit down.

25. He said: My Lord! Surely I have no control (upon any) but my own self and my brother; therefore make a separation between us and the nation of transgressors.

26. He said: So it shall surely be forbidden to them for forty years, they shall wander about in the land, therefore do not grieve for the nation of transgressors.

27. And relate to them the story of the two sons of Adam with truth when they both offered an offering, but it was accepted from one of them and was not accepted from the other. He said: I will most certainly slay you. (The other) said: Allah only accepts from those who guard (against evil).

28. If you will stretch forth your hand towards me to slay me, I am not one to stretch forth my hand towards you to slay you; surely I fear Allah, the Lord of the worlds:

29. Surely I wish that you should bear the sin committed against me and your own sin, and so you would be of the inmates of the fire, and this is the recompense of the unjust.

30. Then his mind facilitated to him the slaying of his brother, so he slew him; then he became one of the losers.

31. Then Allah sent a crow digging up the earth so that he might show him how he should cover the dead body of his brother. He said: Woe me! do I lack the strength that I should be like this crow and cover the dead body of my brother? So he became of those who regret.

32. For this reason did We prescribe to the children of Israel that whoever slays a soul, unless it be for manslaughter or for mischief in the land, it is as though he slew all men; and whoever keeps it alive, it is as though he kept alive all men; and certainly Our apostles came to them with clear arguments, but even after that many of them certainly act extravagantly in the land.

33. The punishment of those who wage war against Allah and His apostle and strive to make mischief in the land is only this, that they should be murdered or crucified or their hands and their feet should be cut off on opposite sides or they should be imprisoned; this shall be as a disgrace for them in this world, and in the hereafter they shall have a grievous chastisement,

34. Except those who repent before you have them in your power; so know that Allah is Forgiving, Merciful.

35. O you who believe! be careful of (your duty to) Allah and seek means of nearness to Him and strive hard in His way that you may be successful.

36. Surely (as for) those who disbelieve, even if they had what is in the earth, all of it, and the like of it with it, that they might ransom themselves with it from the punishment of the day of resurrection, it shall not be accepted from them, and they shall have a painful punishment.

37. They would desire to go forth from the fire, and they shall not go forth from it, and they shall have a lasting punishment.

38. And (as for) the man who steals and the woman who steals, cut off their hands as a punishment for what they have earned, an exemplary punishment from Allah; and Allah is Mighty, Wise.

39. But whoever repents after his iniquity and reforms (himself), then surely Allah will turn to him (mercifully); surely Allah is Forgiving, Merciful.

40. Do you not know that Allah—His is the kingdom of the heavens and the earth; He chastises whom He pleases; and forgives whom He pleases and Allah has power over all things.

41. O Apostle! let not those grieve you who strive together in hastening to unbelief from among those who say with their mouths: We believe, and their hearts do not believe, and from among those who are Jews; they are listeners for the sake of a lie, listeners for another people who have not come to you; they alter the words from their places, saying: If you are given this, take it, and if you are not given this, be cautious; and as for him whose temptation Allah desires, you cannot control anything for him with Allah. Those are they for whom Allah does not desire that He should purify their hearts; they shall have disgrace in this world, and they shall have a grievous chastisement in the hereafter.

42. (They are) listeners of a lie, devourers of what is forbidden; therefore if they come to you, judge between them or turn aside from them, and if you turn aside from them, they shall not harm you in any way; and if you judge, judge between them with equity; surely Allah loves those who judge equitably.

سَمّٰعُوْنَ لِلْكَذِبِ اَكّٰلُوْنَ لِلسُّحْتِ فَاِنْ جَآءُوْكَ فَاحْكُمْ بَيْنَهُمْ اَوْ اَعْرِضْ عَنْهُمْ وَاِنْ تُعْرِضْ عَنْهُمْ فَلَنْ يَّضُرُّوْكَ شَيْئًا وَاِنْ حَكَمْتَ فَاحْكُمْ بَيْنَهُمْ بِالْقِسْطِ اِنَّ اللّٰهَ يُحِبُّ الْمُقْسِطِيْنَ ۝

43. And how do they make you a judge and they have the Taurat wherein is Allah's judgment? Yet they turn back after that, and these are not the believers.

وَكَيْفَ يُحَكِّمُوْنَكَ وَعِنْدَهُمُ التَّوْرٰىةُ فِيْهَا حُكْمُ اللّٰهِ ثُمَّ يَتَوَلَّوْنَ مِنْ بَعْدِ ذٰلِكَ وَمَآ اُولٰٓئِكَ بِالْمُؤْمِنِيْنَ ۝

44. Surely We revealed the Taurat in which was guidance and light; with it the prophets who submitted themselves (to Allah) judged (matters) for those who were Jews, and the masters of Divine knowledge and the doctors, because they were required to guard (part) of the Book of Allah, and they were witnesses thereof; therefore fear not the people and fear Me, and do not take a small price for My communications; and whoever did not judge by what Allah revealed, those are they that are the unbelievers.

اِنَّآ اَنْزَلْنَا التَّوْرٰىةَ فِيْهَا هُدًى وَّنُوْرٌ يَّحْكُمُ بِهَا النَّبِيُّوْنَ الَّذِيْنَ اَسْلَمُوْا لِلَّذِيْنَ هَادُوْا وَالرَّبَّانِيُّوْنَ وَالْاَحْبَارُ بِمَا اسْتُحْفِظُوْا مِنْ كِتٰبِ اللّٰهِ وَكَانُوْا عَلَيْهِ شُهَدَآءَ فَلَا تَخْشَوُا النَّاسَ وَاخْشَوْنِ وَلَا تَشْتَرُوْا بِاٰيٰتِيْ ثَمَنًا قَلِيْلًا وَمَنْ لَّمْ يَحْكُمْ بِمَآ اَنْزَلَ اللّٰهُ فَاُولٰٓئِكَ هُمُ الْكٰفِرُوْنَ ۝

45. And We prescribed to them in it that life is for life, and eye for eye, and nose for nose, and ear for ear, and tooth for tooth, and (that there is) reprisal in wounds; but he who foregoes it, it shall be an expiation for him; and whoever did not judge by what Allah revealed, those are they that are the unjust.

وَكَتَبْنَا عَلَيْهِمْ فِيْهَآ اَنَّ النَّفْسَ بِالنَّفْسِ وَالْعَيْنَ بِالْعَيْنِ وَالْاَنْفَ بِالْاَنْفِ وَالْاُذُنَ بِالْاُذُنِ وَالسِّنَّ بِالسِّنِّ وَالْجُرُوْحَ قِصَاصٌ فَمَنْ تَصَدَّقَ بِهِ فَهُوَ كَفَّارَةٌ لَّهُ وَمَنْ لَّمْ يَحْكُمْ بِمَآ اَنْزَلَ اللّٰهُ فَاُولٰٓئِكَ هُمُ الظّٰلِمُوْنَ ۝

46. And We sent after them in their footsteps Isa, son of Marium, verifying what was before him of the Taurat and We gave him the Injeel in which was guidance and light, and verifying what was before it of Taurat and a guidance and an admonition for those who guard (against evil).

وَقَفَّيْنَا عَلٰٓى اٰثَارِهِمْ بِعِيْسَى ابْنِ مَرْيَمَ مُصَدِّقًا لِّمَا بَيْنَ يَدَيْهِ مِنَ التَّوْرٰىةِ وَاٰتَيْنٰهُ الْاِنْجِيْلَ فِيْهِ هُدًى وَّنُوْرٌ وَّمُصَدِّقًا لِّمَا بَيْنَ يَدَيْهِ مِنَ التَّوْرٰىةِ وَهُدًى وَّمَوْعِظَةً لِّلْمُتَّقِيْنَ ۝

47. And the followers of the Injeel should have judged by what Allah revealed in it; and whoever did not judge by what Allah revealed, those are they that are the transgressors.

48. And We have revealed to you the Book with the truth, verifying what is before it of the Book and a guardian over it, therefore judge between them by what Allah has revealed, and do not follow their low desires (to turn away) from the truth that has come to you; for every one of you did We appoint a law and a way, and if Allah had pleased He would have made you (all) a single people, but that He might try you in what He gave you, therefore strive with one another to hasten to virtuous deeds; to Allah is your return, of all (of you), so He will let you know that in which you differed;

49. And that you should judge between them by what Allah has revealed, and do not follow their low desires, and be cautious of them, lest they seduce you from part of what Allah has revealed to you; but if they turn back, then know that Allah desires to afflict them on account of some of their faults; and most surely many of the people are transgressors.

50. Is it then the judgment of (the times of) ignorance that they desire? And who is better than Allah to judge for a people who are sure?

51. O you who believe! do not take the Jews and the Christians for friends; they are friends of each other; and whoever amongst you takes them for a friend, then surely he is one of them; surely Allah does not guide the unjust people.

52. But you will see those in whose hearts is a disease, hastening towards them, saying: We fear lest a calamity should befall us; but it may be that Allah will bring the victory or a punishment from Himself, so that they shall be regretting on account of what they hid in their souls.

103

53. And those who believe will say: Are these they who swore by Allah with the most forcible of their oaths that they were most surely with you? Their deeds shall go for nothing, so they shall become losers.

54. O you who believe! whoever from among you turns back from his religion, then Allah will bring a people, He shall love them and they shall love Him, lowly before the believers, mighty against the unbelievers, they shall strive hard in Allah's way and shall not fear the censure of any censurer; this is Allah's grace, He gives it to whom He pleases, and Allah is Ample-giving, Knowing.

55. Only Allah is your Vali and His Apostle and those who believe, those who keep up prayers and pay the poor-rate while they bow.

56. And whoever takes Allah and His Apostle and those who believe for a guardian, then surely the party of Allah are they that shall be triumphant.

57. O you who believe! do not take for guardians those who take your religion for a mockery and a joke, from among those who were given the Book before you and the unbelievers; and be careful of (your duty to) Allah if you are believers.

58. And when you call to prayer they make it a mockery and a joke; this is because they are a people who do not understand.

59. Say: O followers of the Book! do you find fault with us (for aught) except that we believe in Allah and in what has been revealed to us and what was revealed before, and that most of you are transgressors?

60. Say: Shall I inform you of (him who is) worse than this in retribution from Allah? (Worse is he) whom Allah has cursed and brought His wrath upon, and of whom He made apes and swine, and he who served the Shaitan; these are worse in place and more erring from the straight path.

104

لايحب الله ٦ المائدة ٥

61. And when they come to you, they say: We believe; and indeed they come in with unbelief and indeed they go forth with it; and Allah knows best what they concealed.

وَاِذَا جَآءُوْكُمْ قَالُوْۤا اٰمَنَّا وَقَدْ دَّخَلُوْا بِالْكُفْرِ وَهُمْ قَدْ خَرَجُوْا بِهٖ ۗ وَاللّٰهُ اَعْلَمُ بِمَا كَانُوْا يَكْتُمُوْنَ ۝

62. And you will see many of them striving with one another to hasten in sin and exceeding the limits, and their eating of what is unlawfully acquired; certainly evil is that which they do.

وَتَرٰى كَثِيْرًا مِّنْهُمْ يُسَارِعُوْنَ فِى الْاِثْمِ وَالْعُدْوَانِ وَاَكْلِهِمُ السُّحْتَ ۗ لَبِئْسَ مَا كَانُوْا يَعْمَلُوْنَ ۝

63. Why do not the learned men and the doctors of law prohibit them from their speaking of what is sinful and their eating of what is unlawfully acquired? Certainly evil is that which they work.

لَوْلَا يَنْهٰىهُمُ الرَّبَّانِيُّوْنَ وَالْاَحْبَارُ عَنْ قَوْلِهِمُ الْاِثْمَ وَاَكْلِهِمُ السُّحْتَ ۗ لَبِئْسَ مَا كَانُوْا يَصْنَعُوْنَ ۝

64. And the Jews say: The hand of Allah is tied up! Their hands shall be shackled and they shall be cursed for what they say. Nay, both His hands are spread out, He expends as He pleases; and what has been revealed to you from your Lord will certainly make many of them increase in inordinacy and unbelief; and We have put enmity and hatred among them till the day of resurrection; whenever they kindle a fire for war Allah puts it out, and they strive to make mischief in the land; and Allah does not love the mischief makers.

وَقَالَتِ الْيَهُوْدُ يَدُ اللّٰهِ مَغْلُوْلَةٌ ۗ غُلَّتْ اَيْدِيْهِمْ وَلُعِنُوْا بِمَا قَالُوْا ۘ بَلْ يَدَاهُ مَبْسُوْطَتٰنِ ۙ يُنْفِقُ كَيْفَ يَشَآءُ ۗ وَلَيَزِيْدَنَّ كَثِيْرًا مِّنْهُمْ مَّاۤ اُنْزِلَ اِلَيْكَ مِنْ رَّبِّكَ طُغْيَانًا وَّكُفْرًا ۗ وَاَلْقَيْنَا بَيْنَهُمُ الْعَدَاوَةَ وَالْبَغْضَآءَ اِلٰى يَوْمِ الْقِيٰمَةِ ۗ كُلَّمَاۤ اَوْقَدُوْا نَارًا لِّلْحَرْبِ اَطْفَاَهَا اللّٰهُ ۙ وَيَسْعَوْنَ فِى الْاَرْضِ فَسَادًا ۗ وَاللّٰهُ لَا يُحِبُّ الْمُفْسِدِيْنَ ۝

65. And if the followers of the Book had believed and guarded (against evil) We would certainly have covered their evil deeds and We would certainly have made them enter gardens of bliss,

وَلَوْ اَنَّ اَهْلَ الْكِتٰبِ اٰمَنُوْا وَاتَّقَوْا لَكَفَّرْنَا عَنْهُمْ سَيِّاٰتِهِمْ وَلَاَدْخَلْنٰهُمْ جَنّٰتِ النَّعِيْمِ ۝

66. And if they had kept up the Taurat and the Injeel and that which was revealed to them from their Lord, they would certainly have eaten from above them and from beneath their feet; there is a party of them keeping to the moderate course, and (as for) most of them, evil is that which they do.

وَلَوْ اَنَّهُمْ اَقَامُوا التَّوْرٰىةَ وَالْاِنْجِيْلَ وَمَاۤ اُنْزِلَ اِلَيْهِمْ مِّنْ رَّبِّهِمْ لَاَكَلُوْا مِنْ فَوْقِهِمْ وَمِنْ تَحْتِ اَرْجُلِهِمْ ۗ مِنْهُمْ اُمَّةٌ مُّقْتَصِدَةٌ ۗ وَكَثِيْرٌ مِّنْهُمْ سَآءَ مَا يَعْمَلُوْنَ ۝

67. O Apostle! deliver what has been revealed to you from your Lord; and if you do it not, then you have not delivered His message, and Allah will protect you from the people; surely Allah will not guide the unbelieving people.

يٰۤاَيُّهَا الرَّسُوْلُ بَلِّغْ مَاۤ اُنْزِلَ اِلَيْكَ مِنْ رَّبِّكَ ۗ وَاِنْ لَّمْ تَفْعَلْ فَمَا بَلَّغْتَ رِسَالَتَهٗ ۗ وَاللّٰهُ يَعْصِمُكَ مِنَ النَّاسِ ۗ اِنَّ اللّٰهَ لَا يَهْدِى الْقَوْمَ الْكٰفِرِيْنَ ۝

68. Say: O followers of the Book! you follow no good till you keep up the Taurat and the Injeel and that which is revealed to you from your Lord; and surely that which has been revealed to you from your Lord shall make many of them increase in inordinacy and unbelief; grieve not therefore for the unbelieving people.

قُلْ يَا أَهْلَ الْكِتٰبِ لَسْتُمْ عَلٰى شَيْءٍ حَتّٰى تُقِيْمُوا التَّوْرٰىةَ وَالْإِنْجِيْلَ وَمَا أُنْزِلَ إِلَيْكُمْ مِّنْ رَّبِّكُمْ وَلَيَزِيْدَنَّ كَثِيْرًا مِّنْهُمْ مَّا أُنْزِلَ إِلَيْكَ مِنْ رَّبِّكَ طُغْيَانًا وَّكُفْرًا فَلَا تَأْسَ عَلَى الْقَوْمِ الْكٰفِرِيْنَ ۝

69. Surely those who believe and those who are Jews and the Sebeans and the Christians whoever believes in Allah and the last day and does good—they shall have no fear nor shall they grieve.

إِنَّ الَّذِيْنَ اٰمَنُوْا وَالَّذِيْنَ هَادُوْا وَالصّٰبِئُوْنَ وَالنَّصٰرٰى مَنْ اٰمَنَ بِاللّٰهِ وَالْيَوْمِ الْاٰخِرِ وَعَمِلَ صَالِحًا فَلَا خَوْفٌ عَلَيْهِمْ وَلَاهُمْ يَحْزَنُوْنَ ۝

70. Certainly We made a covenant with the children of Israel and We sent to them apostles; whenever there came to them an apostle with what that their souls did not desire, some (of them) did they call liars and some they slew.

لَقَدْ أَخَذْنَا مِيْثَاقَ بَنِيْ إِسْرَاءِيْلَ وَأَرْسَلْنَا إِلَيْهِمْ رُسُلًا كُلَّمَا جَاءَهُمْ رَسُوْلٌ بِمَا لَا تَهْوٰى أَنْفُسُهُمْ فَرِيْقًا كَذَّبُوْا وَفَرِيْقًا يَّقْتُلُوْنَ ۝

71. And they thought that there would be no affliction, so they became blind and deaf; then Allah turned to them mercifully, but many of them became blind and deaf; and Allah is well seeing what they do.

وَحَسِبُوْا أَلَّا تَكُوْنَ فِتْنَةٌ فَعَمُوْا وَصَمُّوْا ثُمَّ تَابَ اللّٰهُ عَلَيْهِمْ ثُمَّ عَمُوْا وَصَمُّوْا كَثِيْرٌ مِّنْهُمْ وَاللّٰهُ بَصِيْرٌ بِمَا يَعْمَلُوْنَ ۝

72. Certainly they disbelieve who say: Surely Allah, He is the Messiah, son of Marium; and the Messiah said: O Children of Israel! serve Allah, my Lord and your Lord. Surely whoever associates (others) with Allah, then Allah has forbidden to him the garden, and his abode is the fire; and there shall be no helpers for the unjust.

لَقَدْ كَفَرَ الَّذِيْنَ قَالُوْا إِنَّ اللّٰهَ هُوَ الْمَسِيْحُ ابْنُ مَرْيَمَ وَقَالَ الْمَسِيْحُ يٰبَنِيْ إِسْرَاءِيْلَ اعْبُدُوا اللّٰهَ رَبِّيْ وَرَبَّكُمْ إِنَّهُ مَنْ يُّشْرِكْ بِاللّٰهِ فَقَدْ حَرَّمَ اللّٰهُ عَلَيْهِ الْجَنَّةَ وَمَأْوَاهُ النَّارُ وَمَا لِلظّٰلِمِيْنَ مِنْ أَنْصَارٍ ۝

73. Certainly they disbelieve who say: Surely Allah is the third (person) of the three; and there is no god but the one God, and if they desist not from what they say, a painful chastisement shall befall those among them who disbelieve.

لَقَدْ كَفَرَ الَّذِيْنَ قَالُوْا إِنَّ اللّٰهَ ثَالِثُ ثَلٰثَةٍ وَمَا مِنْ إِلٰهٍ إِلَّا إِلٰهٌ وَّاحِدٌ وَإِنْ لَّمْ يَنْتَهُوْا عَمَّا يَقُوْلُوْنَ لَيَمَسَّنَّ الَّذِيْنَ كَفَرُوْا مِنْهُمْ عَذَابٌ أَلِيْمٌ ۝

74. Will they not then turn to Allah and ask His forgiveness? And Allah is Forgiving, Merciful.

أَفَلَا يَتُوْبُوْنَ إِلَى اللّٰهِ وَيَسْتَغْفِرُوْنَهُ وَاللّٰهُ غَفُوْرٌ رَّحِيْمٌ ۝

75. The Messiah, son of Marium is but an apostle; apostles before him have indeed passed away; and his mother was a truthful woman; they both used to eat food. See how We make the communications clear to them, then behold, how they are turned away.

76. Say: Do you serve besides Allah that which does not control for you any harm, or any profit? And Allah—He is the Hearing, the Knowing.

77. Say: O followers of the Book! be not unduly immoderate in your religion, and do not follow the low desires of people who went astray before and led many astray and went astray from the right path.

78. Those who disbelieved from among the children of Israel were cursed by the tongue of Dawood and Isa, son of Marium; this was because they disobeyed and used to exceed the limit.

79. They used not to forbid each other the hateful things (which) they did; certainly evil was that which they did.

80. You will see many of them befriending those who disbelieve; certainly evil is that which their souls have sent before for them, that Allah became displeased with them and in chastisement shall they abide.

81. And had they believed in Allah and the prophet and what was revealed to him, they would not have taken them for friends, but most of them are transgressors.

82. Certainly you will find the most violent of people in enmity for those who believe (to be) the Jews and those who are polytheists, and you will certainly find the nearest in friendship to those who believe (to be) those who say: We are Christians; this is because there are priests and monks among them and because they do not behave proudly.

مَا الْمَسِيْحُ ابْنُ مَرْيَمَ اِلَّا رَسُوْلٌ قَدْ خَلَتْ مِنْ قَبْلِهِ الرُّسُلُ وَأُمُّهُ صِدِّيْقَةٌ كَانَا يَأْكُلَانِ الطَّعَامَ اُنْظُرْ كَيْفَ نُبَيِّنُ لَهُمُ الْاٰيٰتِ ثُمَّ انْظُرْ اَنّٰى يُؤْفَكُوْنَ ۞

قُلْ اَتَعْبُدُوْنَ مِنْ دُوْنِ اللّٰهِ مَا لَا يَمْلِكُ لَكُمْ ضَرًّا وَّلَا نَفْعًا وَاللّٰهُ هُوَ السَّمِيْعُ الْعَلِيْمُ ۞

قُلْ يٰٓاَهْلَ الْكِتٰبِ لَا تَغْلُوْا فِيْ دِيْنِكُمْ غَيْرَ الْحَقِّ وَلَا تَتَّبِعُوْا اَهْوَآءَ قَوْمٍ قَدْ ضَلُّوْا مِنْ قَبْلُ وَاَضَلُّوْا كَثِيْرًا وَّضَلُّوْا عَنْ سَوَآءِ السَّبِيْلِ ۞

لُعِنَ الَّذِيْنَ كَفَرُوْا مِنْ بَنِيْٓ اِسْرَآءِيْلَ عَلٰى لِسَانِ دَاوٗدَ وَعِيْسَى ابْنِ مَرْيَمَ ذٰلِكَ بِمَا عَصَوْا وَّكَانُوْا يَعْتَدُوْنَ ۞

كَانُوْا لَا يَتَنَاهَوْنَ عَنْ مُّنْكَرٍ فَعَلُوْهُ لَبِئْسَ مَا كَانُوْا يَفْعَلُوْنَ ۞

تَرٰى كَثِيْرًا مِّنْهُمْ يَتَوَلَّوْنَ الَّذِيْنَ كَفَرُوْا لَبِئْسَ مَا قَدَّمَتْ لَهُمْ اَنْفُسُهُمْ اَنْ سَخِطَ اللّٰهُ عَلَيْهِمْ وَ فِي الْعَذَابِ هُمْ خٰلِدُوْنَ ۞

وَلَوْ كَانُوْا يُؤْمِنُوْنَ بِاللّٰهِ وَالنَّبِيِّ وَمَآ اُنْزِلَ اِلَيْهِ مَا اتَّخَذُوْهُمْ اَوْلِيَآءَ وَلٰكِنَّ كَثِيْرًا مِّنْهُمْ فٰسِقُوْنَ ۞

لَتَجِدَنَّ اَشَدَّ النَّاسِ عَدَاوَةً لِّلَّذِيْنَ اٰمَنُوا الْيَهُوْدَ وَالَّذِيْنَ اَشْرَكُوْا وَلَتَجِدَنَّ اَقْرَبَهُمْ مَّوَدَّةً لِّلَّذِيْنَ اٰمَنُوا الَّذِيْنَ قَالُوْٓا اِنَّا نَصٰرٰى ذٰلِكَ بِاَنَّ مِنْهُمْ قِسِّيْسِيْنَ وَرُهْبَانًا وَّاَنَّهُمْ لَا يَسْتَكْبِرُوْنَ ۞

83. And when they hear what has been revealed to the apostle, you will see their eyes overflowing with tears on account of the truth that they recognize; they say: Our Lord! we believe, so write us down with the witnesses (of truth).

وَإِذَا سَمِعُوْا مَآ اُنْزِلَ اِلَى الرَّسُوْلِ تَرٰى اَعْيُنَهُمْ تَفِيْضُ مِنَ الدَّمْعِ مِمَّا عَرَفُوْا مِنَ الْحَقِّ يَقُوْلُوْنَ رَبَّنَآ اٰمَنَّا فَاكْتُبْنَا مَعَ الشّٰهِدِيْنَ ۞

84. And what (reason) have we that we should not believe in Allah and in the truth that has come to us, while we earnestly desire that our Lord should cause us to enter with the good people?

وَمَا لَنَا لَا نُؤْمِنُ بِاللّٰهِ وَمَا جَآءَنَا مِنَ الْحَقِّ وَنَطْمَعُ اَنْ يُّدْخِلَنَا رَبُّنَا مَعَ الْقَوْمِ الصّٰلِحِيْنَ ۞

85. Therefore Allah rewarded them on account of what they said, with gardens in which rivers flow to abide in them; and this is the reward of those who do good (to others).

فَاَثَابَهُمُ اللّٰهُ بِمَا قَالُوْا جَنّٰتٍ تَجْرِيْ مِنْ تَحْتِهَا الْاَنْهٰرُ خٰلِدِيْنَ فِيْهَا وَذٰلِكَ جَزَآءُ الْمُحْسِنِيْنَ ۞

86. And (as for) those who disbelieve and reject Our communications, these are the companions of the flame.

وَالَّذِيْنَ كَفَرُوْا وَكَذَّبُوْا بِاٰيٰتِنَآ اُولٰٓئِكَ اَصْحٰبُ الْجَحِيْمِ ۞

87. O you who believe! do not forbid (yourselves) the good things which Allah has made lawful for you and do not exceed the limits; surely Allah does not love those who exceed the limits.

يٰٓاَيُّهَا الَّذِيْنَ اٰمَنُوْا لَا تُحَرِّمُوْا طَيِّبٰتِ مَآ اَحَلَّ اللّٰهُ لَكُمْ وَلَا تَعْتَدُوْا اِنَّ اللّٰهَ لَا يُحِبُّ الْمُعْتَدِيْنَ ۞

88. And eat of the lawful and good (things) that Allah has given you, and be careful of (your duty to) Allah, in Whom you believe.

وَكُلُوْا مِمَّا رَزَقَكُمُ اللّٰهُ حَلٰلًا طَيِّبًا وَّاتَّقُوا اللّٰهَ الَّذِيْٓ اَنْتُمْ بِهٖ مُؤْمِنُوْنَ ۞

89. Allah does not call you to account for what is vain in your oaths, but He calls you to account for the making of deliberate oaths; so its expiation is the feeding of ten poor men out of the middling (food) you feed your families with, or their clothing, or the freeing of a neck; but whosoever cannot find (means) then fasting for three days; this is the expiation of your oaths when you swear; and guard your oaths. Thus does Allah make clear to you His communications, that you may be grateful.

لَا يُؤَاخِذُكُمُ اللّٰهُ بِاللَّغْوِ فِيْٓ اَيْمَانِكُمْ وَلٰكِنْ يُّؤَاخِذُكُمْ بِمَا عَقَّدْتُّمُ الْاَيْمَانَ فَكَفَّارَتُهٗٓ اِطْعَامُ عَشَرَةِ مَسٰكِيْنَ مِنْ اَوْسَطِ مَا تُطْعِمُوْنَ اَهْلِيْكُمْ اَوْ كِسْوَتُهُمْ اَوْ تَحْرِيْرُ رَقَبَةٍ فَمَنْ لَّمْ يَجِدْ فَصِيَامُ ثَلٰثَةِ اَيَّامٍ ذٰلِكَ كَفَّارَةُ اَيْمَانِكُمْ اِذَا حَلَفْتُمْ وَاحْفَظُوْٓا اَيْمَانَكُمْ كَذٰلِكَ يُبَيِّنُ اللّٰهُ لَكُمْ اٰيٰتِهٖ لَعَلَّكُمْ تَشْكُرُوْنَ ۞

90. O you who believe! intoxicants and games of chance and (sacrificing to) stones set up and (dividing by) arrows are only an uncleanness, the Shaitan's work; shun it therefore that you may be successful.

يٰٓاَيُّهَا الَّذِيْنَ اٰمَنُوْٓا اِنَّمَا الْخَمْرُ وَالْمَيْسِرُ وَالْاَنْصَابُ وَالْاَزْلَامُ رِجْسٌ مِّنْ عَمَلِ الشَّيْطٰنِ فَاجْتَنِبُوْهُ لَعَلَّكُمْ تُفْلِحُوْنَ ۞

91. The Shaitan only desires to cause enmity and hatred to spring in your midst by means of intoxicants and games of chance, and to keep you off from the remembrance of Allah and from prayer. Will you then desist?

92. And obey Allah and obey the apostle and be cautious; but if you turn back, then know that only a clear deliverance of the message is (incumbent) on Our apostle.

93. On those who believe and do good there is no blame for what they eat, when they are careful (of their duty) and believe and do good deeds, then they are careful (of their duty) and believe, then they are careful (of their duty) and do good (to others), and Allah loves those who do good (to others).

94. O you who believe! Allah will certainly try you in respect of some game which your hands and your lances can reach, that Allah might know who fears Him in secret; but whoever exceeds the limit after this, he shall have a painful punishment.

95. O you who believe! do not kill game while you are on pilgrimage, and whoever among you shall kill it intentionally, the compensation (of it) is the like of what he killed, from the cattle, as two just persons among you shall judge, as an offering to be brought to the Kaaba or the expiation (of it) is the feeding of the poor or the equivalent of it in fasting, that he may taste the unwholesome result of his deed; Allah has pardoned what is gone by; and whoever returns (to it), Allah will inflict retribution on him; and Allah is Mighty, Lord of Retribution.

96. Lawful to you is the game of the sea and its food, a provision for you and for the travellers, and the game of the land is forbidden to you so long as you are on pilgrimage, and be careful of (your duty to) Allah, to Whom you shall be gathered.

97. Allah has made the Kaaba, the sacred house, a maintenance for the people, and the sacred month and the offerings and the sacrificial animals with garlands; this is that you may know that Allah knows whatever is in the heavens and whatever is in the earth, and that Allah is the Knower of all things.

98. Know that Allah is severe in requiting (evil) and that Allah is Forgiving, Merciful.

99. Nothing is (incumbent) on the Apostle but to deliver (the message), and Allah knows what you do openly and what you hide.

100. Say: The bad and the good are not equal, though the abundance of the bad may please you; so be careful of (your duty to) Allah, O men of understanding, that you may be successful.

101. O you who believe! do not put questions about things which if declared to you may trouble you, and if you question about them when the Quran is being revealed, they shall be declared to you; Allah pardons this, and Allah is Forgiving, Forbearing.

102. A people before you indeed asked such questions, and then became disbelievers on account of them.

103. Allah has not ordained (the making of) a bahirah or a saibah or a wasilah or a hami but those who disbelieve fabricate a lie against Allah, and most of them do not understand.

104. And when it is said to them, Come to what Allah has revealed and to the Apostle, they say: That on which we found our fathers is sufficient for us. What! even though their fathers knew nothing and did not follow the right way.

جَعَلَ اللّٰهُ الْكَعْبَةَ الْبَيْتَ الْحَرَامَ قِيٰمًا لِّلنَّاسِ وَالشَّهْرَ الْحَرَامَ وَالْهَدْيَ وَالْقَلَائِدَ ۚ ذٰلِكَ لِتَعْلَمُوْا اَنَّ اللّٰهَ يَعْلَمُ مَا فِي السَّمٰوٰتِ وَمَا فِي الْاَرْضِ وَ اَنَّ اللّٰهَ بِكُلِّ شَيْءٍ عَلِيْمٌ ۝

اِعْلَمُوْا اَنَّ اللّٰهَ شَدِيْدُ الْعِقَابِ وَاَنَّ اللّٰهَ غَفُوْرٌ رَّحِيْمٌ ۝

مَا عَلَى الرَّسُوْلِ اِلَّا الْبَلٰغُ ۚ وَاللّٰهُ يَعْلَمُ مَا تُبْدُوْنَ وَمَا تَكْتُمُوْنَ ۝

قُلْ لَّا يَسْتَوِى الْخَبِيْثُ وَالطَّيِّبُ وَلَوْ اَعْجَبَكَ كَثْرَةُ الْخَبِيْثِ ۚ فَاتَّقُوا اللّٰهَ يٰۤاُولِي الْاَلْبَابِ لَعَلَّكُمْ تُفْلِحُوْنَ ۝

يٰۤاَيُّهَا الَّذِيْنَ اٰمَنُوْا لَا تَسْئَلُوْا عَنْ اَشْيَآءَ اِنْ تُبْدَ لَكُمْ تَسُؤْكُمْ ۚ وَاِنْ تَسْئَلُوْا عَنْهَا حِيْنَ يُنَزَّلُ الْقُرْاٰنُ تُبْدَ لَكُمْ ۚ عَفَا اللّٰهُ عَنْهَا ۚ وَاللّٰهُ غَفُوْرٌ حَلِيْمٌ ۝

قَدْ سَاَلَهَا قَوْمٌ مِّنْ قَبْلِكُمْ ثُمَّ اَصْبَحُوْا بِهَا كٰفِرِيْنَ ۝

مَا جَعَلَ اللّٰهُ مِنْ بَحِيْرَةٍ وَّلَا سَآئِبَةٍ وَّلَا وَصِيْلَةٍ وَّلَا حَامٍ ۙ وَّلٰكِنَّ الَّذِيْنَ كَفَرُوْا يَفْتَرُوْنَ عَلَى اللّٰهِ الْكَذِبَ ۚ وَاَكْثَرُهُمْ لَا يَعْقِلُوْنَ ۝

وَاِذَا قِيْلَ لَهُمْ تَعَالَوْا اِلٰى مَا اَنْزَلَ اللّٰهُ وَاِلَى الرَّسُوْلِ قَالُوْا حَسْبُنَا مَا وَجَدْنَا عَلَيْهِ اٰبَآءَنَا ۚ اَوَلَوْ كَانَ اٰبَآؤُهُمْ لَا يَعْلَمُوْنَ شَيْئًا وَّلَا يَهْتَدُوْنَ ۝

105. O you who believe! take care of your souls; he who errs cannot hurt you when you are on the right way; to Allah is your return, of all (of you), so He will inform you of what you did.

يٰۤاَيُّهَا الَّذِيْنَ اٰمَنُوْا عَلَيْكُمْ اَنْفُسَكُمْ ۚ لَا يَضُرُّكُمْ مَّنْ ضَلَّ اِذَا اهْتَدَيْتُمْ ۚ اِلَى اللّٰهِ مَرْجِعُكُمْ جَمِيْعًا فَيُنَبِّئُكُمْ بِمَا كُنْتُمْ تَعْمَلُوْنَ ۝

106. O you who believe! call to witness between you when death draws nigh to one of you, at the time of making the will, two just persons from among you, or two others from among others than you, if you are travelling in the land and the calamity of death befalls you; the two (witnesses) you should detain after the prayer; then if you doubt (them), they shall both swear by Allah, (saying): We will not take for it a price, though there be a relative, and we will not hide the testimony of Allah for then certainly we should be among the sinners.

يٰۤاَيُّهَا الَّذِيْنَ اٰمَنُوْا شَهَادَةُ بَيْنِكُمْ اِذَا حَضَرَ اَحَدَكُمُ الْمَوْتُ حِيْنَ الْوَصِيَّةِ اثْنٰنِ ذَوَا عَدْلٍ مِّنْكُمْ اَوْ اٰخَرٰنِ مِنْ غَيْرِكُمْ اِنْ اَنْتُمْ ضَرَبْتُمْ فِي الْاَرْضِ فَاَصَابَتْكُمْ مُّصِيْبَةُ الْمَوْتِ تَحْبِسُوْنَهُمَا مِنْ بَعْدِ الصَّلٰوةِ فَيُقْسِمٰنِ بِاللّٰهِ اِنِ ارْتَبْتُمْ لَا نَشْتَرِيْ بِهٖ ثَمَنًا وَّلَوْ كَانَ ذَا قُرْبٰى ۙ وَلَا نَكْتُمُ شَهَادَةَ اللّٰهِ اِنَّا اِذًا لَّمِنَ الْاٰثِمِيْنَ ۝

107. Then if it becomes known that they both have been guilty of a sin, two others shall stand up in their place from among those who have a claim against them, the two nearest in kin; so they two should swear by Allah: Certainly our testimony is truer than the testimony of those two, and we have not exceeded the limit, for then most surely we should be of the unjust.

فَاِنْ عُثِرَ عَلٰۤى اَنَّهُمَا اسْتَحَقَّآ اِثْمًا فَاٰخَرٰنِ يَقُوْمٰنِ مَقَامَهُمَا مِنَ الَّذِيْنَ اسْتَحَقَّ عَلَيْهِمُ الْاَوْلَيٰنِ فَيُقْسِمٰنِ بِاللّٰهِ لَشَهَادَتُنَآ اَحَقُّ مِنْ شَهَادَتِهِمَا وَمَا اعْتَدَيْنَآ ۖ اِنَّآ اِذًا لَّمِنَ الظّٰلِمِيْنَ ۝

108. This is more proper in order that they should give testimony truly or fear that other oaths be given after their oaths; and be careful of (your duty to) Allah, and hear; and Allah does not guide the transgressing people.

ذٰلِكَ اَدْنٰۤى اَنْ يَّاْتُوْا بِالشَّهَادَةِ عَلٰى وَجْهِهَآ اَوْ يَخَافُوْۤا اَنْ تُرَدَّ اَيْمَانٌۢ بَعْدَ اَيْمَانِهِمْ ۖ وَاتَّقُوا اللّٰهَ وَاسْمَعُوْا ۚ وَاللّٰهُ لَا يَهْدِي الْقَوْمَ الْفٰسِقِيْنَ ۝

109. On the day when Allah will assemble the apostles, then say: What answer were you given? They shall say: We have no knowledge, surely Thou art the great Knower of the unseen things.

يَوْمَ يَجْمَعُ اللّٰهُ الرُّسُلَ فَيَقُوْلُ مَاذَآ اُجِبْتُمْ ۖ قَالُوْا لَا عِلْمَ لَنَا ۚ اِنَّكَ اَنْتَ عَلَّامُ الْغُيُوْبِ ۝

110. When Allah will say: O Isa son of Marium! Remember My favor on you and on your mother, when I strengthened you with the holy Spirit, you spoke to the people in the cradle and when of old age, and when I taught you the Book and the wisdom and the Taurat and the Injeel; and when you determined out of clay a thing like the form of a bird by My permission, then you breathed into it and it became a bird by My permission, and you healed the blind and the leprous by My permission; and when you brought forth the dead by My permission; and when I withheld the children of Israel from you when you came to them with clear arguments, but those who disbelieved among them said: This is nothing but clear enchantment.

111. And when I revealed to the disciples, saying, Believe in Me and My apostle, they said: We believe and bear witness that we submit (ourselves).

112. When the disciples said: O Isa son of Marium! will your Lord consent to send down to us food from heaven? He said: Be careful of (your duty to) Allah if you are believers.

113. They said: We desire that we should eat of it and that our hearts should be at rest, and that we may know that you have indeed spoken the truth to us and that we may be of the witnesses to it.

114. Isa the son of Marium said: O Allah, our Lord! send down to us food from heaven which should be to us an ever-recurring happiness, to the first of us and to the last of us, and a sign from Thee, and grant us means of subsistence, and Thou art the best of the Providers.

115. Allah said: Surely I will send it down to you, but whoever shall disbelieve afterwards from among you, surely I will chastise him with a chastisement with which I will not chastise anyone among the nations.

116. And when Allah will say: O Isa son of Marium! did you say to men, Take me and my mother for two gods besides Allah, he will say: Glory be to Thee, it did not befit me that I should say what I had no right to (say); if I had said it, Thou wouldst indeed have known it; Thou knowest what is in my mind, and I do not know what is in Thy mind, surely Thou art the great Knower of the unseen things.

117. I did not say to them aught save what Thou didst enjoin me with: That serve Allah, my Lord and your Lord, and I was a witness of them so long as I was among them, but when Thou didst cause me to die, Thou wert the watcher over them, and Thou art witness of all things.

118. If Thou shouldst chastise them, then surely they are Thy servants; and if Thou shouldst forgive them, then surely Thou art the Mighty, the Wise.

119. Allah will say: This is the day when their truth shall benefit the truthful ones; they shall have gardens beneath which rivers flow to abide in them for ever: Allah is well pleased with them and they are well pleased with Allah; this is the mighty achievement.

120. Allah's is the kingdom of the heavens and the earth and what is in them; and He has power over all things.

THE CATTLE
(ANAM)

**In the name of Allah,
the Beneficent, the Merciful.**

1. All praise is due to Allah, Who created the heavens and the earth and made the darkness and the light; yet those who disbelieve set up equals with their Lord.

2. He it is Who created you from clay, then He decreed a term; and there is a term named with Him; still you doubt.

3. And He is Allah in the heavens and in the earth; He knows your secret (thoughts) and your open (words), and He knows what you earn.

4. And there does not come to them any communication of the communications of their Lord but they turn aside from it.

5. So they have indeed rejected the truth when it came to them; therefore the truth of what they mocked at will shine upon them.

6. Do they not consider how many a generation We have destroyed before them, whom We had established in the earth as We have not established you, and We sent the clouds pouring rain on them in abundance, and We made the rivers to flow beneath them, then We destroyed them on account of their faults and raised up after them another generation.

7. And if We had sent to you a writing on a paper, then they had touched it with their hands, certainly those who disbelieve would have said: This is nothing but clear enchantment.

8. And they say: Why has not an angel been sent down to him? And had We sent down an angel, the matter would have certainly been decided and then they would not have been respited.

114

9. And if We had made him angel, We would certainly have made him a man, and We would certainly have made confused to them what they make confused.

دَرَوْجَعَلْنَٰهُ مَلَكًا لَّجَعَلْنَٰهُ رَجُلًا وَّلَلَبَسْنَا عَلَيْهِمْ مَّا يَلْبِسُوْنَ ۞

10. And certainly apostles before you were mocked at, but that which they mocked at encompassed the scoffers among them.

وَلَقَدِ اسْتُهْزِئَ بِرُسُلٍ مِّنْ قَبْلِكَ فَحَاقَ بِالَّذِيْنَ سَخِرُوْا مِنْهُمْ مَّا كَانُوْا بِهٖ يَسْتَهْزِءُوْنَ ۞

11. Say: Travel in the land, then see what was the end of the rejecters.

قُلْ سِيْرُوْا فِى الْاَرْضِ ثُمَّ انْظُرُوْا كَيْفَ كَانَ عَاقِبَةُ الْمُكَذِّبِيْنَ ۞

12. Say: To whom belongs what is in the heavens and the earth? Say: To Allah; He has ordained mercy on Himself; most certainly He will gather you on the resurrection day—there is no doubt about it. (As for) those who have lost their souls, they will not believe.

قُلْ لِّمَنْ مَّا فِى السَّمٰوٰتِ وَالْاَرْضِ قُلْ لِّلّٰهِ كَتَبَ عَلٰى نَفْسِهِ الرَّحْمَةَ لَيَجْمَعَنَّكُمْ اِلٰى يَوْمِ الْقِيٰمَةِ لَا رَيْبَ فِيْهِ اَلَّذِيْنَ خَسِرُوْا اَنْفُسَهُمْ فَهُمْ لَا يُؤْمِنُوْنَ ۞

13. And to Him belongs whatever dwells in the night and the day; and He is the Hearing, the Knowing.

وَلَهٗ مَا سَكَنَ فِى الَّيْلِ وَالنَّهَارِ وَهُوَ السَّمِيْعُ الْعَلِيْمُ ۞

14. Say: Shall I take a guardian besides Allah, the Originator of the heavens and the earth, and He feeds (others) and is not (Himself) fed. Say: I am commanded to be the first who submits himself, and you should not be of the polytheists.

قُلْ اَغَيْرَ اللّٰهِ اَتَّخِذُ وَلِيًّا فَاطِرِ السَّمٰوٰتِ وَالْاَرْضِ وَهُوَ يُطْعِمُ وَلَا يُطْعَمُ قُلْ اِنِّيْ اُمِرْتُ اَنْ اَكُوْنَ اَوَّلَ مَنْ اَسْلَمَ وَلَا تَكُوْنَنَّ مِنَ الْمُشْرِكِيْنَ ۞

15. Say: Surely I fear, if I disobey my Lord, the chastisement of a grievous day.

قُلْ اِنِّيْ اَخَافُ اِنْ عَصَيْتُ رَبِّيْ عَذَابَ يَوْمٍ عَظِيْمٍ ۞

16. He from whom it is averted on that day, Allah indeed has shown mercy to him; and this is a manifest achievement.

مَنْ يُّصْرَفْ عَنْهُ يَوْمَئِذٍ فَقَدْ رَحِمَهٗ وَذٰلِكَ الْفَوْزُ الْمُبِيْنُ ۞

17. And if Allah touch you with affliction, there is none to take it off but He; and if He visit you with good, then He has power over all things.

وَاِنْ يَّمْسَسْكَ اللّٰهُ بِضُرٍّ فَلَا كَاشِفَ لَهٗ اِلَّا هُوَ وَاِنْ يَّمْسَسْكَ بِخَيْرٍ فَهُوَ عَلٰى كُلِّ شَيْءٍ قَدِيْرٌ ۞

18. And He is the Supreme, above His servants; and He is the Wise, the Aware.

وَهُوَ الْقَاهِرُ فَوْقَ عِبَادِهٖ وَهُوَ الْحَكِيْمُ الْخَبِيْرُ ۞

19. Say: What thing is the weightiest in testimony? Say: Allah is witness between you and me; and this Quran has been revealed to me that with it I may warn you and whomsoever it reaches. Do you really bear witness that there are other gods with Allah? Say: I do not bear witness. Say: He is only one God, and surely I am clear of that which you set up (with Him).

20. Those whom We have given the Book recognize him as they recognize their sons; (as for) those who have lost their souls, they will not believe.

21. And who is more unjust than he who forges a lie against Allah or (he who) gives the lie to His communications; surely the unjust will not be successful.

22. And on the day when We shall gather them all together, then shall We say to those who associated others (with Allah): Where are your associates whom you asserted?

23. Then their excuse would be nothing but that they would say: By Allah, our Lord, we were not polytheists.

24. See how they lie against their own souls, and that which they forged has passed away from them.

25. And of them is he who hearkens to you, and We have cast veils over their hearts lest they understand it and a heaviness into their ears; and even if they see every sign they will not believe in it; so much so that when they come to you they only dispute with you; those who disbelieve say: This is naught but the stories of the ancients.

26. And they prohibit (others) from it and go far away from it, and they only bring destruction upon their own souls while they do not perceive.

27. And could you see when they are made to stand before the fire, then they shall say: Would that we were sent back, and we would not reject the communications of our Lord and we would be of the believers.

28. Nay, what they concealed before shall become manifest to them; and if they were sent back, they would certainly go back to that which they are forbidden, and most surely they are liars.

29. And they say: There is nothing but our life of this world, and we shall not be raised.

30. And could you see when they are made to stand before their Lord. He will say: Is not this the truth? They will say: Yea! by our Lord. He will say: Taste then the chastisement because you disbelieved.

31. They are losers indeed who reject the meeting of Allah; until when the hour comes upon them all of a sudden they shall say: O our grief for our neglecting it! and they shall bear their burdens on their backs; now surely evil is that which they bear.

32. And this world's life is naught but a play and an idle sport; and certainly the abode of the hereafter is better for those who guard (against evil); do you not then understand?

33. We know indeed that what they say certainly grieves you, but surely they do not call you a liar; but the unjust deny the communications of Allah.

34. And certainly apostles before you were rejected, but they were patient on being rejected and persecuted until Our help came to them; and there is none to change the words of Allah, and certainly there has come to you some information about the messengers.

35. And if their turning away is hard on you, then if you can seek an opening (to go down) into the earth or a ladder (to ascend up) to heaven so that you should bring them a sign and if Allah had pleased He would certainly have gathered them all on guidance, therefore be not of the ignorant.

بَلْ بَدَا لَهُمْ مَا كَانُوا يُخْفُونَ مِنْ قَبْلُ وَلَوْ رُدُّوا لَعَادُوا لِمَا نُهُوا عَنْهُ وَإِنَّهُمْ لَكَاذِبُونَ ۝

وَقَالُوا إِنْ هِيَ إِلَّا حَيَاتُنَا الدُّنْيَا وَمَا نَحْنُ بِمَبْعُوثِينَ ۝

وَلَوْ تَرَى إِذْ وُقِفُوا عَلَى رَبِّهِمْ قَالَ أَلَيْسَ هَذَا بِالْحَقِّ قَالُوا بَلَى وَرَبِّنَا قَالَ فَذُوقُوا الْعَذَابَ بِمَا كُنْتُمْ تَكْفُرُونَ ۝

قَدْ خَسِرَ الَّذِينَ كَذَّبُوا بِلِقَاءِ اللّٰهِ حَتَّى إِذَا جَاءَتْهُمُ السَّاعَةُ بَغْتَةً قَالُوا يَا حَسْرَتَنَا عَلَى مَا فَرَّطْنَا فِيهَا وَهُمْ يَحْمِلُونَ أَوْزَارَهُمْ عَلَى ظُهُورِهِمْ أَلَا سَاءَ مَا يَزِرُونَ ۝

وَمَا الْحَيَاةُ الدُّنْيَا إِلَّا لَعِبٌ وَلَهْوٌ وَلَلدَّارُ الْآخِرَةُ خَيْرٌ لِلَّذِينَ يَتَّقُونَ أَفَلَا تَعْقِلُونَ ۝

قَدْ نَعْلَمُ إِنَّهُ لَيَحْزُنُكَ الَّذِي يَقُولُونَ فَإِنَّهُمْ لَا يُكَذِّبُونَكَ وَلَكِنَّ الظَّالِمِينَ بِآيَاتِ اللّٰهِ يَجْحَدُونَ ۝

وَلَقَدْ كُذِّبَتْ رُسُلٌ مِنْ قَبْلِكَ فَصَبَرُوا عَلَى مَا كُذِّبُوا وَأُوذُوا حَتَّى أَتَاهُمْ نَصْرُنَا وَلَا مُبَدِّلَ لِكَلِمَاتِ اللّٰهِ وَلَقَدْ جَاءَكَ مِنْ نَبَإِ الْمُرْسَلِينَ ۝

وَإِنْ كَانَ كَبُرَ عَلَيْكَ إِعْرَاضُهُمْ فَإِنِ اسْتَطَعْتَ أَنْ تَبْتَغِيَ نَفَقًا فِي الْأَرْضِ أَوْ سُلَّمًا فِي السَّمَاءِ فَتَأْتِيَهُمْ بِآيَةٍ وَلَوْ شَاءَ اللّٰهُ لَجَمَعَهُمْ عَلَى الْهُدَى فَلَا تَكُونَنَّ مِنَ الْجَاهِلِينَ ۝

36. Only those accept who listen; and (as to) the dead, Allah will raise them, then to Him they shall be returned.

اِنَّمَا يَسْتَجِيبُ الَّذِيْنَ يَسْمَعُوْنَ وَالْمَوْتٰى يَبْعَثُهُمُ اللّٰهُ ثُمَّ اِلَيْهِ يُرْجَعُوْنَ ۝

37. And they say: Why has not a sign been sent down to him from his Lord? Say: Surely Allah is able to send down a sign, but most of them do not know.

وَقَالُوْا لَوْلَا نُزِّلَ عَلَيْهِ اٰيَةٌ مِّنْ رَّبِّهٖ ۚ قُلْ اِنَّ اللّٰهَ قَادِرٌ عَلٰى اَنْ يُّنَزِّلَ اٰيَةً وَّلٰكِنَّ اَكْثَرَهُمْ لَا يَعْلَمُوْنَ ۝

38. And there is no animal that walks upon the earth nor a bird that flies with its two wings but (they are) genera like yourselves; We have not neglected anything in the Book, then to their Lord shall they be gathered.

وَمَا مِنْ دَآبَّةٍ فِى الْاَرْضِ وَلَا طٰٓئِرٍ يَّطِيْرُ بِجَنَاحَيْهِ اِلَّا اُمَمٌ اَمْثَالُكُمْ ۚ مَا فَرَّطْنَا فِى الْكِتٰبِ مِنْ شَيْءٍ ثُمَّ اِلٰى رَبِّهِمْ يُحْشَرُوْنَ ۝

39. And they who reject Our communications are deaf and dumb, in utter darkness; whom Allah pleases He causes to err, and whom He pleases He puts on the right way.

وَالَّذِيْنَ كَذَّبُوْا بِاٰيٰتِنَا صُمٌّ وَّبُكْمٌ فِى الظُّلُمٰتِ ۗ مَنْ يَّشَاِ اللّٰهُ يُضْلِلْهُ ۗ وَمَنْ يَّشَاْ يَجْعَلْهُ عَلٰى صِرَاطٍ مُّسْتَقِيْمٍ ۝

40. Say: Tell me if the chastisement of Allah should overtake you or the hour should come upon you, will you call (on others) besides Allah, if you are truthful?

قُلْ اَرَءَيْتَكُمْ اِنْ اَتٰىكُمْ عَذَابُ اللّٰهِ اَوْ اَتَتْكُمُ السَّاعَةُ اَغَيْرَ اللّٰهِ تَدْعُوْنَ ۚ اِنْ كُنْتُمْ صٰدِقِيْنَ ۝

41. Nay, Him you call upon, so He clears away that for which you pray if He pleases and you forget what you set up (with Him).

بَلْ اِيَّاهُ تَدْعُوْنَ فَيَكْشِفُ مَا تَدْعُوْنَ اِلَيْهِ اِنْ شَآءَ وَتَنْسَوْنَ مَا تُشْرِكُوْنَ ۝

42. And certainly We sent (apostles) to nations before you, then We seized them with distress and affliction in order that they might humble themselves.

وَلَقَدْ اَرْسَلْنَآ اِلٰٓى اُمَمٍ مِّنْ قَبْلِكَ فَاَخَذْنٰهُمْ بِالْبَأْسَآءِ وَالضَّرَّآءِ لَعَلَّهُمْ يَتَضَرَّعُوْنَ ۝

43. Yet why did they not, when Our punishment came to them, humble themselves? But their hearts hardened and the Shaitan made what they did fair-seeming to them.

فَلَوْلَا اِذْ جَآءَهُمْ بَأْسُنَا تَضَرَّعُوْا وَلٰكِنْ قَسَتْ قُلُوْبُهُمْ وَزَيَّنَ لَهُمُ الشَّيْطٰنُ مَا كَانُوْا يَعْمَلُوْنَ ۝

44. But when they neglected that with which they had been admonished, We opened for them the doors of all things, until when they rejoiced in what they were given We seized them suddenly; then lo! they were in utter despair.

فَلَمَّا نَسُوْا مَا ذُكِّرُوْا بِهٖ فَتَحْنَا عَلَيْهِمْ اَبْوَابَ كُلِّ شَيْءٍ ۚ حَتّٰٓى اِذَا فَرِحُوْا بِمَآ اُوْتُوْٓا اَخَذْنٰهُمْ بَغْتَةً فَاِذَا هُمْ مُّبْلِسُوْنَ ۝

45. So the roots of the people who were unjust were cut off; and all praise is due to Allah, the Lord of the worlds.

فَقُطِعَ دَابِرُ الْقَوْمِ الَّذِيْنَ ظَلَمُوْا وَالْحَمْدُ لِلّٰهِ رَبِّ الْعٰلَمِيْنَ ۟

46. Say: Have you considered that if Allah takes away your hearing and your sight and sets a seal on your hearts, who is the god besides Allah that can bring it to you? See how We repeat the communications, yet they turn away.

قُلْ اَرَءَيْتُمْ اِنْ اَخَذَ اللّٰهُ سَمْعَكُمْ وَاَبْصَارَكُمْ وَ خَتَمَ عَلٰى قُلُوْبِكُمْ مَّنْ اِلٰهٌ غَيْرُ اللّٰهِ يَاْتِيْكُمْ بِهٖ اُنْظُرْ كَيْفَ نُصَرِّفُ الْاٰيٰتِ ثُمَّ هُمْ يَصْدِفُوْنَ ۟

47. Say: Have you considered if the chastisement of Allah should overtake you suddenly or openly, will any be destroyed but the unjust people?

قُلْ اَرَءَيْتَكُمْ اِنْ اَتٰىكُمْ عَذَابُ اللّٰهِ بَغْتَةً اَوْ جَهْرَةً هَلْ يُهْلَكُ اِلَّا الْقَوْمُ الظّٰلِمُوْنَ ۟

48. And We send not messengers but as announcers of good news and givers of warning; then whoever believes and acts aright, they shall have no fear, nor shall they grieve.

وَمَا نُرْسِلُ الْمُرْسَلِيْنَ اِلَّا مُبَشِّرِيْنَ وَمُنْذِرِيْنَ فَمَنْ اٰمَنَ وَاَصْلَحَ فَلَا خَوْفٌ عَلَيْهِمْ وَلَاهُمْ يَحْزَنُوْنَ ۟

49. And (as for) those who reject Our communications, chastisement shall afflict them because they transgressed.

وَالَّذِيْنَ كَذَّبُوْا بِاٰيٰتِنَا يَمَسُّهُمُ الْعَذَابُ بِمَا كَانُوْا يَفْسُقُوْنَ ۟

50. Say: I do not say to you, I have with me the treasures of Allah, nor do I know the unseen, nor do I say to you that I am an angel; I do not follow aught save that which is revealed to me. Say: Are the blind and the seeing one alike? Do you not then reflect?

قُلْ لَّا اَقُوْلُ لَكُمْ عِنْدِيْ خَزَائِنُ اللّٰهِ وَلَا اَعْلَمُ الْغَيْبَ وَلَا اَقُوْلُ لَكُمْ اِنِّيْ مَلَكٌ اِنْ اَتَّبِعُ اِلَّا مَا يُوْحٰى اِلَيَّ قُلْ هَلْ يَسْتَوِى الْاَعْمٰى وَ الْبَصِيْرُ اَفَلَا تَتَفَكَّرُوْنَ ۟

51. And warn with it those who fear that they shall be gathered to their Lord—there is no guardian for them, nor any intercessor besides Him—that they may guard (against evil).

وَاَنْذِرْ بِهِ الَّذِيْنَ يَخَافُوْنَ اَنْ يُّحْشَرُوْا اِلٰى رَبِّهِمْ لَيْسَ لَهُمْ مِّنْ دُوْنِهٖ وَلِيٌّ وَّلَا شَفِيْعٌ لَّعَلَّهُمْ يَتَّقُوْنَ ۟

52. And do not drive away those who call upon their Lord in the morning and the evening, they desire only His favor; neither are you answerable for any reckoning of theirs, nor are they answerable for any reckoning of yours, so that you should drive them away and thus be of the unjust.

وَلَا تَطْرُدِ الَّذِيْنَ يَدْعُوْنَ رَبَّهُمْ بِالْغَدٰوةِ وَالْعَشِيِّ يُرِيْدُوْنَ وَجْهَهٗ مَا عَلَيْكَ مِنْ حِسَابِهِمْ مِّنْ شَيْءٍ وَّمَا مِنْ حِسَابِكَ عَلَيْهِمْ مِّنْ شَيْءٍ فَتَطْرُدَهُمْ فَتَكُوْنَ مِنَ الظّٰلِمِيْنَ ۟

53. And thus do We try some of them by others so that they say: Are these they upon whom Allah has conferred benefit from among us? Does not Allah best know the grateful?

وَكَذٰلِكَ فَتَنَّا بَعْضَهُمْ بِبَعْضٍ لِّيَقُوْلُوْا اَهٰؤُلَاءِ مَنَّ اللّٰهُ عَلَيْهِمْ مِّنْ بَيْنِنَا ؕ اَلَيْسَ اللّٰهُ بِاَعْلَمَ بِالشّٰكِرِيْنَ ۝

54. And when those who believe in Our communications come to you, say: Peace be on you, your Lord has ordained mercy on Himself, (so) that if any one of you does evil in ignorance, then turns after that and acts aright, then He is Forgiving, Merciful.

وَاِذَا جَآءَكَ الَّذِيْنَ يُؤْمِنُوْنَ بِاٰيٰتِنَا فَقُلْ سَلٰمٌ عَلَيْكُمْ كَتَبَ رَبُّكُمْ عَلٰى نَفْسِهِ الرَّحْمَةَ ۙ اَنَّهٗ مَنْ عَمِلَ مِنْكُمْ سُوْٓءًۢا بِجَهَالَةٍ ثُمَّ تَابَ مِنْۢ بَعْدِهٖ وَاَصْلَحَ فَاَنَّهٗ غَفُوْرٌ رَّحِيْمٌ ۝

55. And thus do We make distinct the communications and so that the way of the guilty may become clear.

وَكَذٰلِكَ نُفَصِّلُ الْاٰيٰتِ وَلِتَسْتَبِيْنَ سَبِيْلُ الْمُجْرِمِيْنَ ۝

56. Say: I am forbidden to serve those whom you call upon besides Allah. Say: I do not follow your low desires, for then indeed I should have gone astray and I should not be of those who go aright.

قُلْ اِنِّيْ نُهِيْتُ اَنْ اَعْبُدَ الَّذِيْنَ تَدْعُوْنَ مِنْ دُوْنِ اللّٰهِ ؕ قُلْ لَّاۤ اَتَّبِعُ اَهْوَآءَكُمْ ۙ قَدْ ضَلَلْتُ اِذًا وَّمَاۤ اَنَا مِنَ الْمُهْتَدِيْنَ ۝

57. Say: Surely I have manifest proof from my Lord and you call it a lie; I have not with me that which you would hasten; the judgment is only Allah's; He relates the truth and He is the best of deciders.

قُلْ اِنِّيْ عَلٰى بَيِّنَةٍ مِّنْ رَّبِّيْ وَكَذَّبْتُمْ بِهٖ ؕ مَا عِنْدِيْ مَا تَسْتَعْجِلُوْنَ بِهٖ ؕ اِنِ الْحُكْمُ اِلَّا لِلّٰهِ ؕ يَقُصُّ الْحَقَّ وَهُوَ خَيْرُ الْفٰصِلِيْنَ ۝

58. Say: If that which you desire to hasten were with me, the matter would have certainly been decided between you and me; and Allah best knows the unjust.

قُلْ لَّوْ اَنَّ عِنْدِيْ مَا تَسْتَعْجِلُوْنَ بِهٖ لَقُضِيَ الْاَمْرُ بَيْنِيْ وَبَيْنَكُمْ ؕ وَاللّٰهُ اَعْلَمُ بِالظّٰلِمِيْنَ ۝

59. And with Him are the keys of the unseen treasures—none knows them but He; and He knows what is in the land and the sea; and there falls not a leaf but He knows it, nor a grain in the darkness of the earth, nor anything green nor dry but (it is all) in a clear book.

وَعِنْدَهٗ مَفَاتِحُ الْغَيْبِ لَا يَعْلَمُهَاۤ اِلَّا هُوَ ؕ وَيَعْلَمُ مَا فِي الْبَرِّ وَالْبَحْرِ ؕ وَمَا تَسْقُطُ مِنْ وَّرَقَةٍ اِلَّا يَعْلَمُهَا وَلَا حَبَّةٍ فِيْ ظُلُمٰتِ الْاَرْضِ وَلَا رَطْبٍ وَّلَا يَابِسٍ اِلَّا فِيْ كِتٰبٍ مُّبِيْنٍ ۝

60. And He it is Who takes your souls at night (in sleep), and He knows what you acquire in the day, then He raises you up therein that an appointed term may be fulfilled; then to Him is your return, then He will inform you of what you were doing.

وَهُوَ الَّذِيْ يَتَوَفّٰىكُمْ بِالَّيْلِ وَيَعْلَمُ مَا جَرَحْتُمْ بِالنَّهَارِ ثُمَّ يَبْعَثُكُمْ فِيْهِ لِيُقْضٰۤى اَجَلٌ مُّسَمًّى ۚ ثُمَّ اِلَيْهِ مَرْجِعُكُمْ ثُمَّ يُنَبِّئُكُمْ بِمَا كُنْتُمْ تَعْمَلُوْنَ ۝

61. And He is the Supreme, above His servants, and He sends keepers over you; until when death comes to one of you, Our messengers cause him to die, and they are not remiss.

وَهُوَ الْقَاهِرُ فَوْقَ عِبَادِهٖ وَيُرْسِلُ عَلَيْكُمْ حَفَظَةً ۗ حَتّٰى اِذَا جَآءَ اَحَدَكُمُ الْمَوْتُ تَوَفَّتْهُ رُسُلُنَا وَهُمْ لَا يُفَرِّطُوْنَ ۝

62. Then are they sent back to Allah, their Master, the True one; now surely His is the judgment and He is swiftest in taking account.

ثُمَّ رُدُّوْۤا اِلَى اللّٰهِ مَوْلٰىهُمُ الْحَقِّ ۗ اَلَا لَهُ الْحُكْمُ ۫ وَهُوَ اَسْرَعُ الْحٰسِبِيْنَ ۝

63. Say: Who is it that delivers you from the dangers of the land and the sea (when) you call upon Him (openly) humiliating yourselves, and in secret: If He delivers us from this, we should certainly be of the grateful ones.

قُلْ مَنْ يُّنَجِّيْكُمْ مِّنْ ظُلُمٰتِ الْبَرِّ وَالْبَحْرِ تَدْعُوْنَهٗ تَضَرُّعًا وَّخُفْيَةً ۚ لَئِنْ اَنْجٰنَا مِنْ هٰذِهٖ لَنَكُوْنَنَّ مِنَ الشّٰكِرِيْنَ ۝

64. Say: Allah delivers you from them and from every distress, but again you set up others (with Him).

قُلِ اللّٰهُ يُنَجِّيْكُمْ مِّنْهَا وَمِنْ كُلِّ كَرْبٍ ثُمَّ اَنْتُمْ تُشْرِكُوْنَ ۝

65. Say: He has the power that He should send on you a chastisement from above you or from beneath your feet, or that He should throw you into confusion, (making you) of different parties; and make some of you taste the fighting of others. See how We repeat the communications that they may understand.

قُلْ هُوَ الْقَادِرُ عَلٰۤى اَنْ يَّبْعَثَ عَلَيْكُمْ عَذَابًا مِّنْ فَوْقِكُمْ اَوْ مِنْ تَحْتِ اَرْجُلِكُمْ اَوْ يَلْبِسَكُمْ شِيَعًا وَّيُذِيْقَ بَعْضَكُمْ بَأْسَ بَعْضٍ ۗ اُنْظُرْ كَيْفَ نُصَرِّفُ الْاٰيٰتِ لَعَلَّهُمْ يَفْقَهُوْنَ ۝

66. And your people call it a lie and it is the very truth. Say: I am not placed in charge of you.

وَكَذَّبَ بِهٖ قَوْمُكَ وَهُوَ الْحَقُّ ۗ قُلْ لَّسْتُ عَلَيْكُمْ بِوَكِيْلٍ ۝

67. For every prophecy is a term, and you will come to know (it).

لِكُلِّ نَبَإٍ مُّسْتَقَرٌّ ۫ وَّسَوْفَ تَعْلَمُوْنَ ۝

68. And when you see those who enter into false discourses about Our communications, withdraw from them until they enter into some other discourse, and if the Shaitan causes you to forget, then do not sit after recollection with the unjust people.

وَاِذَا رَاَيْتَ الَّذِيْنَ يَخُوْضُوْنَ فِيْۤ اٰيٰتِنَا فَاَعْرِضْ عَنْهُمْ حَتّٰى يَخُوْضُوْا فِيْ حَدِيْثٍ غَيْرِهٖ ۗ وَاِمَّا يُنْسِيَنَّكَ الشَّيْطٰنُ فَلَا تَقْعُدْ بَعْدَ الذِّكْرٰى مَعَ الْقَوْمِ الظّٰلِمِيْنَ ۝

69. And nought of the reckoning of their (deeds) shall be against those who guard (against evil), but (theirs) is only to remind, haply they may guard.

وَمَا عَلَى الَّذِيْنَ يَتَّقُوْنَ مِنْ حِسَابِهِمْ مِّنْ شَيْءٍ وَّلٰكِنْ ذِكْرٰى لَعَلَّهُمْ يَتَّقُوْنَ ۝

70. And leave those who have taken their religion for a play and an idle sport, and whom this world's life has deceived, and remind (them) thereby lest a soul should be given up to destruction for what it has earned; it shall not have besides Allah any guardian nor an intercessor, and if it should seek to give every compensation, it shall not be accepted from it; these are they who shall be given up to destruction for what they earned; they shall have a drink of boiling water and a painful chastisement because they disbelieved.

وَذَرِ الَّذِيْنَ اتَّخَذُوْا دِيْنَهُمْ لَعِبًا وَّلَهْوًا وَّغَرَّتْهُمُ الْحَيٰوةُ الدُّنْيَا وَذَكِّرْ بِهٖۤ اَنْ تُبْسَلَ نَفْسٌۢ بِمَا كَسَبَتْ ۖ لَيْسَ لَهَا مِنْ دُوْنِ اللّٰهِ وَلِيٌّ وَّلَا شَفِيْعٌ ۚ وَاِنْ تَعْدِلْ كُلَّ عَدْلٍ لَّا يُؤْخَذْ مِنْهَا ۗ اُولٰٓئِكَ الَّذِيْنَ اُبْسِلُوْا بِمَا كَسَبُوْا ۚ لَهُمْ شَرَابٌ مِّنْ حَمِيْمٍ وَّعَذَابٌ اَلِيْمٌۢ بِمَا كَانُوْا يَكْفُرُوْنَ ۞

71. Say: Shall we call on that besides Allah, which does not benefit us nor harm us, and shall we be returned back on our heels after Allah has guided us, like him whom the Shaitans have made to fall down perplexed in the earth? He has companions who call him to the right way, (saying): Come to us. Say: Surely the guidance of Allah, that is the (true) guidance, and we are commanded that we should submit to the Lord of the worlds.

قُلْ اَنَدْعُوْا مِنْ دُوْنِ اللّٰهِ مَا لَا يَنْفَعُنَا وَلَا يَضُرُّنَا وَنُرَدُّ عَلٰٓى اَعْقَابِنَا بَعْدَ اِذْ هَدٰىنَا اللّٰهُ كَالَّذِى اسْتَهْوَتْهُ الشَّيٰطِيْنُ فِى الْاَرْضِ حَيْرَانَ ۙ لَهٗۤ اَصْحٰبٌ يَّدْعُوْنَهٗۤ اِلَى الْهُدَى ائْتِنَا ۗ قُلْ اِنَّ هُدَى اللّٰهِ هُوَ الْهُدٰى ۗ وَاُمِرْنَا لِنُسْلِمَ لِرَبِّ الْعٰلَمِيْنَ ۞

72. And that you should keep up prayer and be careful of (your duty to) Him; and He it is to Whom you shall be gathered.

وَاَنْ اَقِيْمُوا الصَّلٰوةَ وَاتَّقُوْهُ ۗ وَهُوَ الَّذِىْۤ اِلَيْهِ تُحْشَرُوْنَ ۞

73. And He it is Who has created the heavens and the earth with truth; and on the day He says: Be, it is. His word is the truth, and His is the kingdom on the day when the trumpet shall be blown; the Knower of the unseen and the seen; and He is the Wise, the Aware.

وَهُوَ الَّذِىْ خَلَقَ السَّمٰوٰتِ وَالْاَرْضَ بِالْحَقِّ ۗ وَيَوْمَ يَقُوْلُ كُنْ فَيَكُوْنُ ۗ قَوْلُهُ الْحَقُّ ۗ وَلَهُ الْمُلْكُ يَوْمَ يُنْفَخُ فِى الصُّوْرِ ۗ عٰلِمُ الْغَيْبِ وَالشَّهَادَةِ ۗ وَهُوَ الْحَكِيْمُ الْخَبِيْرُ ۞

74. And when Ibrahim said to his sire, Azar: Do you take idols for gods? Surely I see you and your people in manifest error.

وَاِذْ قَالَ اِبْرٰهِيْمُ لِاَبِيْهِ اٰزَرَ اَتَتَّخِذُ اَصْنَامًا اٰلِهَةً ۚ اِنِّىْۤ اَرٰىكَ وَقَوْمَكَ فِىْ ضَلٰلٍ مُّبِيْنٍ ۞

75. And thus did We show Ibrahim the kingdom of the heavens and the earth and that he might be of those who are sure.

وَكَذٰلِكَ نُرِىْۤ اِبْرٰهِيْمَ مَلَكُوْتَ السَّمٰوٰتِ وَالْاَرْضِ وَلِيَكُوْنَ مِنَ الْمُوْقِنِيْنَ ۞

76. So when the night overshadowed him, he saw a star; said he: Is this my Lord? So when it set, he said: I do not love the setting ones.

فَلَمَّا جَنَّ عَلَيْهِ الَّيْلُ رَاٰ كَوْكَبًا ۚ قَالَ هٰذَا رَبِّيْ ۚ فَلَمَّاۤ اَفَلَ قَالَ لَاۤ اُحِبُّ الْاٰفِلِيْنَ ۝

77. Then when he saw the moon rising, he said: Is this my Lord? So when it set, he said: If my Lord had not guided me I should certainly be of the erring people.

فَلَمَّا رَاَ الْقَمَرَ بَازِغًا قَالَ هٰذَا رَبِّيْ ۚ فَلَمَّاۤ اَفَلَ قَالَ لَئِنْ لَّمْ يَهْدِنِيْ رَبِّيْ لَاَكُوْنَنَّ مِنَ الْقَوْمِ الضَّآلِّيْنَ ۝

78. Then when he saw the sun rising, he said: Is this my Lord? Is this the greatest? So when it set, he said: O my people! surely I am clear of what you set up (with Allah).

فَلَمَّا رَاَ الشَّمْسَ بَازِغَةً قَالَ هٰذَا رَبِّيْ هٰذَاۤ اَكْبَرُ ۚ فَلَمَّاۤ اَفَلَتْ قَالَ يٰقَوْمِ اِنِّيْ بَرِيْٓءٌ مِّمَّا تُشْرِكُوْنَ ۝

79. Surely I have turned myself, being upright, wholly to Him Who originated the heavens and the earth, and I am not of the polytheists.

اِنِّيْ وَجَّهْتُ وَجْهِيَ لِلَّذِيْ فَطَرَ السَّمٰوٰتِ وَالْاَرْضَ حَنِيْفًا وَّمَاۤ اَنَا مِنَ الْمُشْرِكِيْنَ ۝

80. And his people disputed with him. He said: Do you dispute with me respecting Allah? And He has guided me indeed; and I do not fear in any way those that you set up with Him, unless my Lord pleases; my Lord comprehends all things in His knowledge; will you not then mind?

وَحَآجَّهٗ قَوْمُهٗ ۚ قَالَ اَتُحَآجُّوْٓنِّيْ فِي اللّٰهِ وَقَدْ هَدٰنِ ۚ وَلَاۤ اَخَافُ مَا تُشْرِكُوْنَ بِهٖۤ اِلَّاۤ اَنْ يَّشَآءَ رَبِّيْ شَيْئًا ۚ وَسِعَ رَبِّيْ كُلَّ شَيْءٍ عِلْمًا ۚ اَفَلَا تَتَذَكَّرُوْنَ ۝

81. And how should I fear what you have set up (with Him), while you do not fear that you have set up with Allah that for which He has not sent down to you any authority; which then of the two parties is surer of security, if you know?

وَكَيْفَ اَخَافُ مَاۤ اَشْرَكْتُمْ وَلَا تَخَافُوْنَ اَنَّكُمْ اَشْرَكْتُمْ بِاللّٰهِ مَا لَمْ يُنَزِّلْ بِهٖ عَلَيْكُمْ سُلْطٰنًا ۚ فَاَيُّ الْفَرِيْقَيْنِ اَحَقُّ بِالْاَمْنِ ۚ اِنْ كُنْتُمْ تَعْلَمُوْنَ ۝

82. Those who believe and do not mix up their faith with iniquity, those are they who shall have the security and they are those who go aright.

اَلَّذِيْنَ اٰمَنُوْا وَلَمْ يَلْبِسُوْٓا اِيْمَانَهُمْ بِظُلْمٍ اُولٰٓئِكَ لَهُمُ الْاَمْنُ وَهُمْ مُّهْتَدُوْنَ ۝

83. And this was Our argument which we gave to Ibrahim against his people; We exalt in dignity whom We please; surely your Lord is Wise, Knowing.

وَتِلْكَ حُجَّتُنَاۤ اٰتَيْنٰهَاۤ اِبْرٰهِيْمَ عَلٰى قَوْمِهٖ ۚ نَرْفَعُ دَرَجٰتٍ مَّنْ نَّشَآءُ ۚ اِنَّ رَبَّكَ حَكِيْمٌ عَلِيْمٌ ۝

84. And We gave to him Ishaq and Yaqoob; each did We guide, and Nuh did We guide before, and of his descendants, Dawood and Sulaiman and Ayub and Yusuf and Haroon; and thus do We reward those who do good (to others).

وَوَهَبْنَا لَهٗۤ اِسْحٰقَ وَيَعْقُوْبَ ۚ كُلًّا هَدَيْنَا ۚ وَنُوْحًا هَدَيْنَا مِنْ قَبْلُ وَمِنْ ذُرِّيَّتِهٖ دَاوٗدَ وَسُلَيْمٰنَ وَاَيُّوْبَ وَيُوْسُفَ وَمُوْسٰى وَهٰرُوْنَ ۚ وَكَذٰلِكَ نَجْزِي الْمُحْسِنِيْنَ ۝

85. And Zakariya and Yahya and Isa and Ilyas; every one was of the good;

وَزَكَرِيَّا وَيَحْيٰى وَعِيْسٰى وَاِلْيَاسَ كُلٌّ مِّنَ الصّٰلِحِيْنَ ۙ

86. And Ismail and Al-Yasha and Yunus and Lut; and every one We made to excel (in) the worlds:

وَاِسْمٰعِيْلَ وَالْيَسَعَ وَيُوْنُسَ وَلُوْطًا ۗ وَكُلًّا فَضَّلْنَا عَلَى الْعٰلَمِيْنَ ۙ

87. And from among their fathers and their descendants and their brethren, and We chose them and guided them into the right way.

وَمِنْ اٰبَآئِهِمْ وَذُرِّيّٰتِهِمْ وَاِخْوَانِهِمْ ۚ وَاجْتَبَيْنٰهُمْ وَهَدَيْنٰهُمْ اِلٰى صِرَاطٍ مُّسْتَقِيْمٍ ٨٧

88. This is Allah's guidance, He guides thereby whom He pleases of His servants; and if they had set up others (with Him), certainly what they did would have become ineffectual for them.

ذٰلِكَ هُدَى اللهِ يَهْدِيْ بِهٖ مَنْ يَّشَآءُ مِنْ عِبَادِهٖ ۗ وَلَوْ اَشْرَكُوْا لَحَبِطَ عَنْهُمْ مَّا كَانُوْا يَعْمَلُوْنَ ٨٨

89. These are they to whom We gave the book and the wisdom and the prophecy; therefore if these disbelieve in it We have already entrusted with it a people who are not disbelievers in it.

اُولٰٓئِكَ الَّذِيْنَ اٰتَيْنٰهُمُ الْكِتٰبَ وَالْحُكْمَ وَالنُّبُوَّةَ ۚ فَاِنْ يَّكْفُرْ بِهَا هٰٓؤُلَآءِ فَقَدْ وَكَّلْنَا بِهَا قَوْمًا لَّيْسُوْا بِهَا بِكٰفِرِيْنَ ٨٩

90. These are they whom Allah guided, therefore follow their guidance. Say: I do not ask you for any reward for it; it is nothing but a reminder to the nations.

اُولٰٓئِكَ الَّذِيْنَ هَدَى اللهُ فَبِهُدٰىهُمُ اقْتَدِهْ ۗ قُلْ لَّا اَسْئَلُكُمْ عَلَيْهِ اَجْرًا ۗ اِنْ هُوَ اِلَّا ذِكْرٰى لِلْعٰلَمِيْنَ ٩٠

91. And they do not assign to Allah the attributes due to Him when they say: Allah has not revealed anything to a mortal. Say: Who revealed the Book which Musa brought, a light and a guidance to men, which you make into scattered writings which you show while you conceal much? And you were taught what you did not know, (neither) you nor your fathers. Say: Allah; then leave them sporting in their vain discourses.

وَمَا قَدَرُوا اللهَ حَقَّ قَدْرِهٖ اِذْ قَالُوْا مَا اَنْزَلَ اللهُ عَلٰى بَشَرٍ مِّنْ شَيْءٍ ۗ قُلْ مَنْ اَنْزَلَ الْكِتٰبَ الَّذِيْ جَآءَ بِهٖ مُوْسٰى نُوْرًا وَّهُدًى لِّلنَّاسِ تَجْعَلُوْنَهٗ قَرَاطِيْسَ تُبْدُوْنَهَا وَتُخْفُوْنَ كَثِيْرًا ۚ وَعُلِّمْتُمْ مَّا لَمْ تَعْلَمُوْا اَنْتُمْ وَلَا اٰبَآؤُكُمْ ۗ قُلِ اللهُ ۙ ثُمَّ ذَرْهُمْ فِيْ خَوْضِهِمْ يَلْعَبُوْنَ ٩١

92. And this is a Book We have revealed, blessed, verifying that which is before it, and that you may warn the metropolis and those around her; and those who believe in the hereafter believe in it, and they attend to their prayers constantly.

وَهٰذَا كِتٰبٌ اَنْزَلْنٰهُ مُبٰرَكٌ مُّصَدِّقُ الَّذِيْ بَيْنَ يَدَيْهِ وَلِتُنْذِرَ اُمَّ الْقُرٰى وَمَنْ حَوْلَهَا ۗ وَالَّذِيْنَ يُؤْمِنُوْنَ بِالْاٰخِرَةِ يُؤْمِنُوْنَ بِهٖ وَهُمْ عَلٰى صَلَاتِهِمْ يُحَافِظُوْنَ ٩٢

93. And who is more unjust than he who forges a lie against Allah, or says: It has been revealed to me; while nothing has been revealed to him, and he who says: I can reveal the like of what Allah has revealed? and if you had seen when the unjust shall be in the agonies of death and the angels shall spread forth their hands: Give up your souls; today shall you be recompensed with an ignominious chastisement because you spoke against Allah other than the truth and (because) you showed pride against His communications.

وَمَنْ أَظْلَمُ مِمَّنِ افْتَرٰى عَلَى اللّٰهِ كَذِبًا أَوْ قَالَ أُوْحِيَ إِلَيَّ وَلَمْ يُوحَ إِلَيْهِ شَيْءٌ وَّمَنْ قَالَ سَأُنْزِلُ مِثْلَ مَاۤ أَنْزَلَ اللّٰهُ وَلَوْ تَرٰۤى إِذِ الظّٰلِمُوْنَ فِيْ غَمَرٰتِ الْمَوْتِ وَالْمَلٰٓئِكَةُ بَاسِطُوْۤا أَيْدِيْهِمْ أَخْرِجُوْۤا أَنْفُسَكُمُ اَلْيَوْمَ تُجْزَوْنَ عَذَابَ الْهُوْنِ بِمَا كُنْتُمْ تَقُوْلُوْنَ عَلَى اللّٰهِ غَيْرَ الْحَقِّ وَكُنْتُمْ عَنْ اٰيٰتِهِ تَسْتَكْبِرُوْنَ ۝

94. And certainly you have come to Us alone as We created you at first, and you have left behind your backs the things which We gave you, and We do not see with you your intercessors about whom you asserted that they were (Allah's) associates in respect to you; certainly the ties between you are now cut off and what you asserted is gone from you.

وَلَقَدْ جِئْتُمُوْنَا فُرَادٰى كَمَا خَلَقْنٰكُمْ أَوَّلَ مَرَّةٍ وَّتَرَكْتُمْ مَّا خَوَّلْنٰكُمْ وَرَآءَ ظُهُوْرِكُمْ وَمَا نَرٰى مَعَكُمْ شُفَعَآءَكُمُ الَّذِيْنَ زَعَمْتُمْ أَنَّهُمْ فِيْكُمْ شُرَكٰٓؤُا لَقَدْ تَّقَطَّعَ بَيْنَكُمْ وَضَلَّ عَنْكُمْ مَّا كُنْتُمْ تَزْعُمُوْنَ ۝

95. Surely Allah causes the grain and the stone to germinate; He brings forth the living from the dead and He is the bringer forth of the dead from the living; that is Allah! how are you then turned away?

إِنَّ اللّٰهَ فَالِقُ الْحَبِّ وَالنَّوٰى يُخْرِجُ الْحَيَّ مِنَ الْمَيِّتِ وَمُخْرِجُ الْمَيِّتِ مِنَ الْحَيِّ ذٰلِكُمُ اللّٰهُ فَأَنّٰى تُؤْفَكُوْنَ ۝

96. He causes the dawn to break; and He has made the night for rest, and the sun and the moon for reckoning; this is an arrangement of the Mighty, the Knowing.

فَالِقُ الْإِصْبَاحِ وَجَعَلَ الَّيْلَ سَكَنًا وَّالشَّمْسَ وَالْقَمَرَ حُسْبَانًا ذٰلِكَ تَقْدِيْرُ الْعَزِيْزِ الْعَلِيْمِ ۝

97. And He it is Who has made the stars for you that you might follow the right way thereby in the darkness of the land and the sea; truly We have made plain the communications for a people who know.

وَهُوَ الَّذِيْ جَعَلَ لَكُمُ النُّجُوْمَ لِتَهْتَدُوْا بِهَا فِيْ ظُلُمٰتِ الْبَرِّ وَالْبَحْرِ قَدْ فَصَّلْنَا الْاٰيٰتِ لِقَوْمٍ يَّعْلَمُوْنَ ۝

98. And He it is Who has brought you into being from a single soul, then there is (for you) a resting-place and a depository; indeed We have made plain the communications for a people who understand.

وَهُوَ الَّذِيْ أَنْشَأَكُمْ مِّنْ نَّفْسٍ وَّاحِدَةٍ فَمُسْتَقَرٌّ وَّمُسْتَوْدَعٌ قَدْ فَصَّلْنَا الْاٰيٰتِ لِقَوْمٍ يَّفْقَهُوْنَ ۝

99. And He it is Who sends down water from the cloud, then We bring forth with it buds of all (plants), then We bring forth from it green (foliage) from which We produce grain piled up (in the ear); and of the palm-tree, of the sheaths of it, come forth clusters (of dates) within reach, and gardens of grapes and olives and pomegranates, alike and unlike; behold the fruit of it when it yields the fruit and the ripening of it; most surely there are signs in this for a people who believe.

وَهُوَ الَّذِىٓ اَنۡزَلَ مِنَ السَّمَآءِ مَآءً ۚ فَاَخۡرَجۡنَا بِهٖ
نَبَاتَ كُلِّ شَىۡءٍ فَاَخۡرَجۡنَا مِنۡهُ خَضِرًا نُّخۡرِجُ مِنۡهُ
حَبًّا مُّتَرَاكِبًا ۚ وَمِنَ النَّخۡلِ مِنۡ طَلۡعِهَا قِنۡوَانٌ دَانِيَةٌ
وَّجَنّٰتٍ مِّنۡ اَعۡنَابٍ وَّالزَّيۡتُوۡنَ وَالرُّمَّانَ مُشۡتَبِهًا
وَّغَيۡرَ مُتَشَابِهٍ ۗ اُنۡظُرُوۡٓا اِلٰى ثَمَرِهٖٓ اِذَآ اَثۡمَرَ وَيَنۡعِهٖ ۚ
اِنَّ فِىۡ ذٰلِكُمۡ لَاٰيٰتٍ لِّقَوۡمٍ يُّؤۡمِنُوۡنَ ۞

100. And they make the jinn associates with Allah, while He created them, and they falsely attributed to Him sons and daughters without knowledge; glory be to Him, and highly exalted is He above what they ascribe (to Him).

وَجَعَلُوۡا لِلّٰهِ شُرَكَآءَ الۡجِنَّ وَخَلَقَهُمۡ وَخَرَقُوۡا لَهٗ
بَنِيۡنَ وَبَنٰتٍۢ بِغَيۡرِ عِلۡمٍ ۚ سُبۡحٰنَهٗ وَتَعٰلٰى عَمَّا
يَصِفُوۡنَ ۞

101. Wonderful Originator of the heavens and the earth! How could He have a son when He has no consort, and He (Himself) created everything, and He is the Knower of all things.

بَدِيۡعُ السَّمٰوٰتِ وَالۡاَرۡضِ ۚ اَنّٰى يَكُوۡنُ لَهٗ وَلَدٌ وَّ
لَمۡ تَكُنۡ لَّهٗ صَاحِبَةٌ ۚ وَخَلَقَ كُلَّ شَىۡءٍ ۚ وَهُوَ بِكُلِّ
شَىۡءٍ عَلِيۡمٌ ۞

102. That is Allah, your Lord, there is no god but He; the Creator of all things, therefore serve Him, and He has charge of all things.

ذٰلِكُمُ اللّٰهُ رَبُّكُمۡ ۚ لَآ اِلٰهَ اِلَّا هُوَ ۚ خَالِقُ كُلِّ شَىۡءٍ
فَاعۡبُدُوۡهُ ۚ وَهُوَ عَلٰى كُلِّ شَىۡءٍ وَّكِيۡلٌ ۞

103. Vision comprehends Him not, and He comprehends (all) vision; and He is the Knower of subtleties, the Aware.

لَا تُدۡرِكُهُ الۡاَبۡصَارُ ۖ وَهُوَ يُدۡرِكُ الۡاَبۡصَارَ ۚ وَهُوَ
اللَّطِيۡفُ الۡخَبِيۡرُ ۞

104. Indeed there have come to you clear proofs from your Lord; whoever will therefore see, it is for his own soul and whoever will be blind, it shall be against himself and I am not a keeper over you.

قَدۡ جَآءَكُمۡ بَصَآئِرُ مِنۡ رَّبِّكُمۡ ۚ فَمَنۡ اَبۡصَرَ فَلِنَفۡسِهٖ ۚ وَ
مَنۡ عَمِىَ فَعَلَيۡهَا ۚ وَمَآ اَنَا عَلَيۡكُمۡ بِحَفِيۡظٍ ۞

105. And thus do We repeat the communications and that they may say: You have read; and that We may make it clear to a people who know.

وَكَذٰلِكَ نُصَرِّفُ الۡاٰيٰتِ وَلِيَقُوۡلُوۡا دَرَسۡتَ وَلِنُبَيِّنَهٗ
لِقَوۡمٍ يَّعۡلَمُوۡنَ ۞

106. Follow what is revealed to you from your Lord; there is no god but He; and withdraw from the polytheists.

اِتَّبِعۡ مَآ اُوۡحِىَ اِلَيۡكَ مِنۡ رَّبِّكَ ۚ لَآ اِلٰهَ اِلَّا هُوَ ۚ وَ
اَعۡرِضۡ عَنِ الۡمُشۡرِكِيۡنَ ۞

107. And if Allah had pleased, they would not have set up others (with Him) and We have not appointed you a keeper over them, and you are not placed in charge of them.

108. And do not abuse those whom they call upon besides Allah, lest exceeding the limits they should abuse Allah out of ignorance. Thus have We made fair seeming to every people their deeds; then to their Lords shall be their return, so He will inform them of what they did.

109. And they swear by Allah with the strongest of their oaths, that if a sign came to them they would most certainly believe in it. Say: Signs are only with Allah; and what should make you know that when it comes they will not believe?

110. And We will turn their hearts and their sights, even as they did not believe in it the first time, and We will leave them in their inordinacy, blindly wandering on.

111. And even if We had sent down to them the angels and the dead had spoken to them and We had brought together all things before them, they would not believe unless Allah pleases, but most of them are ignorant.

112. And thus did We make for every prophet an enemy, the Shaitans from among men and jinn, some of them suggesting to others varnished falsehood to deceive (them), and had your Lord pleased they would not have done it, therefore leave them and that which they forge.

113. And that the hearts of those who do not believe in the hereafter may incline to it and that they may be well pleased with it and that they may earn what they are going to earn (of evil).

114. Shall I then seek a judge other than Allah? And He it is Who has revealed to you the Book (which is) made plain; and those whom We have given the Book know that it is revealed by your Lord with truth, therefore you should not be of the disputers.

127

115. And the word of your Lord has been accomplished truly and justly; there is none who can change His words, and He is the Hearing, the Knowing.

وَتَمَّتْ كَلِمَتُ رَبِّكَ صِدْقًا وَّعَدْلًا لَا مُبَدِّلَ لِكَلِمَاتِهٖ وَهُوَ السَّمِيْعُ الْعَلِيْمُ ۝

116. And if you obey most of those in the earth, they will lead you astray from Allah's way; they follow but conjecture and they only lie.

وَاِنْ تُطِعْ اَكْثَرَ مَنْ فِى الْاَرْضِ يُضِلُّوْكَ عَنْ سَبِيْلِ اللّٰهِ اِنْ يَّتَّبِعُوْنَ اِلَّا الظَّنَّ وَاِنْ هُمْ اِلَّا يَخْرُصُوْنَ ۝

117. Surely your Lord—He best knows who goes astray from His way, and He best knows those who follow the right course.

اِنَّ رَبَّكَ هُوَ اَعْلَمُ مَنْ يَّضِلُّ عَنْ سَبِيْلِهٖ وَهُوَ اَعْلَمُ بِالْمُهْتَدِيْنَ ۝

118. Therefore eat of that on which Allah's name has been mentioned if you are believers in His communications.

فَكُلُوْا مِمَّا ذُكِرَ اسْمُ اللّٰهِ عَلَيْهِ اِنْ كُنْتُمْ بِاٰيٰتِهٖ مُؤْمِنِيْنَ ۝

119. And what reason have you that you should not eat of that on which Allah's name has been mentioned, and He has already made plain to you what He has forbidden to you—excepting what you are compelled to; and most surely many would lead (people) astray by their low desires out of ignorance; surely your Lord—He best knows those who exceed the limits.

وَمَا لَكُمْ اَلَّا تَأْكُلُوْا مِمَّا ذُكِرَ اسْمُ اللّٰهِ عَلَيْهِ وَقَدْ فَصَّلَ لَكُمْ مَّا حَرَّمَ عَلَيْكُمْ اِلَّا مَا اضْطُرِرْتُمْ اِلَيْهِ وَاِنَّ كَثِيْرًا لَّيُضِلُّوْنَ بِاَهْوَآئِهِمْ بِغَيْرِ عِلْمٍ اِنَّ رَبَّكَ هُوَ اَعْلَمُ بِالْمُعْتَدِيْنَ ۝

120. And abandon open and secret sin; surely they who earn sin shall be recompensed with what they earned.

وَذَرُوْا ظَاهِرَ الْاِثْمِ وَبَاطِنَهٗ اِنَّ الَّذِيْنَ يَكْسِبُوْنَ الْاِثْمَ سَيُجْزَوْنَ بِمَا كَانُوْا يَقْتَرِفُوْنَ ۝

121. And do not eat of that on which Allah's name has not been mentioned, and that is most surely a transgression; and most surely the Shaitans suggest to their friends that they should contend with you; and if you obey them, you shall most surely be polytheists.

وَلَا تَأْكُلُوْا مِمَّا لَمْ يُذْكَرِ اسْمُ اللّٰهِ عَلَيْهِ وَاِنَّهٗ لَفِسْقٌ وَاِنَّ الشَّيٰطِيْنَ لَيُوْحُوْنَ اِلٰى اَوْلِيٰئِهِمْ لِيُجَادِلُوْكُمْ وَاِنْ اَطَعْتُمُوْهُمْ اِنَّكُمْ لَمُشْرِكُوْنَ ۝

122. Is he who was dead then We raised him to life and made for him a light by which he walks among the people, like him whose likeness is that of one in utter darkness whence he cannot come forth? Thus what they did was made fair seeming to the unbelievers.

اَوَمَنْ كَانَ مَيْتًا فَاَحْيَيْنٰهُ وَجَعَلْنَا لَهٗ نُوْرًا يَّمْشِيْ بِهٖ فِى النَّاسِ كَمَنْ مَّثَلُهٗ فِى الظُّلُمٰتِ لَيْسَ بِخَارِجٍ مِّنْهَا كَذٰلِكَ زُيِّنَ لِلْكٰفِرِيْنَ مَا كَانُوْا يَعْمَلُوْنَ ۝

123. And thus have We made in every town the great ones to be its guilty ones, that they may plan therein; and they do not plan but against their own souls, and they do not perceive.

124. And when a communication comes to them they say: We will not believe till we are given the like of what Allah's apostles are given. Allah best knows where He places His message. There shall befall those who are guilty humiliation from Allah and severe chastisement because of what they planned.

125. Therefore (for) whomsoever Allah intends that He would guide him aright, He expands his breast for Islam, and (for) whomsoever He intends that He should cause him to err, He makes his breast strait and narrow as though he were ascending upwards; thus does Allah lay uncleanness on those who do not believe.

126. And this is the path of your Lord, (a) right (path); indeed We have made the communications clear for a people who mind.

127. They shall have the abode of peace with their Lord, and He is their guardian because of what they did.

128. And on the day when He shall gather them all together: O assembly of jinn! you took away a great part of mankind. And their friends from among the men shall say: Our Lord! some of us profited by others and we have reached our appointed term which Thou didst appoint for us. He shall say: The fire is your abode, to abide in it, except as Allah is pleased; surely your Lord is Wise, Knowing.

129. And thus do We make some of the iniquitous to befriend others on account of what they earned.

130. O assembly of jinn and men! did there not come to you apostles from among you, relating to you My communications and warning you of the meeting of this day of yours? They shall say: We bear witness against ourselves; and this world's life deceived them, and they shall bear witness against their own souls that they were unbelievers.

يٰمَعْشَرَ الْجِنِّ وَالْاِنْسِ اَلَمْ يَاْتِكُمْ رُسُلٌ مِّنْكُمْ يَقُصُّوْنَ عَلَيْكُمْ اٰيٰتِيْ وَيُنْذِرُوْنَكُمْ لِقَآءَ يَوْمِكُمْ هٰذَا ۚ قَالُوْا شَهِدْنَا عَلٰۤى اَنْفُسِنَا وَغَرَّتْهُمُ الْحَيٰوةُ الدُّنْيَا وَشَهِدُوْا عَلٰۤى اَنْفُسِهِمْ اَنَّهُمْ كَانُوْا كٰفِرِيْنَ ۞

131. This is because your Lord would not destroy towns unjustly while their people were negligent.

ذٰلِكَ اَنْ لَّمْ يَكُنْ رَّبُّكَ مُهْلِكَ الْقُرٰى بِظُلْمٍ وَّاَهْلُهَا غٰفِلُوْنَ ۞

132. And all have degrees according to what they do; and your Lord is not heedless of what they do.

وَلِكُلٍّ دَرَجٰتٌ مِّمَّا عَمِلُوْا ۚ وَمَا رَبُّكَ بِغَافِلٍ عَمَّا يَعْمَلُوْنَ ۞

133. And your Lord is the Self-sufficient one, the Lord of mercy; if He pleases, He may take you off, and make whom He pleases successors after you, even as He raised you up from the seed of another people.

وَرَبُّكَ الْغَنِيُّ ذُو الرَّحْمَةِ ۚ اِنْ يَّشَاْ يُذْهِبْكُمْ وَيَسْتَخْلِفْ مِنْ بَعْدِكُمْ مَّا يَشَآءُ كَمَاۤ اَنْشَاَكُمْ مِّنْ ذُرِّيَّةِ قَوْمٍ اٰخَرِيْنَ ۞

134. Surely what you are threatened with must come to pass and you cannot escape (it).

اِنَّ مَا تُوْعَدُوْنَ لَاٰتٍ ۙ وَّمَاۤ اَنْتُمْ بِمُعْجِزِيْنَ ۞

135. Say: O my people! act according to your ability; I too am acting; so you will soon come to know, for whom (of us) will be the (good) end of the abode; surely the unjust shall not be successful.

قُلْ يٰقَوْمِ اعْمَلُوْا عَلٰى مَكَانَتِكُمْ اِنِّيْ عَامِلٌ ۚ فَسَوْفَ تَعْلَمُوْنَ ۙ مَنْ تَكُوْنُ لَهٗ عَاقِبَةُ الدَّارِ ۚ اِنَّهٗ لَا يُفْلِحُ الظّٰلِمُوْنَ ۞

136. And they set apart a portion for Allah out of what He has created of tilth and cattle, and say: This is for Allah—so they assert—and this for our associates; then what is for their associates, it reaches not to Allah, and whatever is (set apart) for Allah, it reaches to their associates; evil is that which they judge.

وَجَعَلُوْا لِلّٰهِ مِمَّا ذَرَاَ مِنَ الْحَرْثِ وَالْاَنْعَامِ نَصِيْبًا فَقَالُوْا هٰذَا لِلّٰهِ بِزَعْمِهِمْ وَهٰذَا لِشُرَكَآئِنَا ۚ فَمَا كَانَ لِشُرَكَآئِهِمْ فَلَا يَصِلُ اِلَى اللّٰهِ ۚ وَمَا كَانَ لِلّٰهِ فَهُوَ يَصِلُ اِلٰى شُرَكَآئِهِمْ ۚ سَآءَ مَا يَحْكُمُوْنَ ۞

137. And thus their associates have made fair seeming to most of the polytheists the killing of their children, that they may cause them to perish and obscure for them their religion; and if Allah had pleased, they would not have done it, therefore leave them and that which they forge.

وَكَذٰلِكَ زَيَّنَ لِكَثِيْرٍ مِّنَ الْمُشْرِكِيْنَ قَتْلَ اَوْلَادِهِمْ شُرَكَآؤُهُمْ لِيُرْدُوْهُمْ وَلِيَلْبِسُوْا عَلَيْهِمْ دِيْنَهُمْ ۚ وَلَوْ شَآءَ اللّٰهُ مَا فَعَلُوْهُ فَذَرْهُمْ وَمَا يَفْتَرُوْنَ ۞

138. And they say: These are cattle and tilth prohibited; none shall eat them except such as We please—so they assert—and cattle whose backs are forbidden, and cattle on which they would not mention Allah's name—forging a lie against Him; He shall requite them for what they forged.

وَقَالُوْا هٰذِهٖۤ اَنْعَامٌ وَّحَرْثٌ حِجْرٌ لَّا يَطْعَمُهَاۤ اِلَّا مَنْ نَّشَآءُ بِزَعْمِهِمْ وَاَنْعَامٌ حُرِّمَتْ ظُهُوْرُهَا وَاَنْعَامٌ لَّا يَذْكُرُوْنَ اسْمَ اللّٰهِ عَلَيْهَا افْتِرَآءً عَلَيْهِ سَيَجْزِيْهِمْ بِمَا كَانُوْا يَفْتَرُوْنَ ۝

139. And they say: What is in the wombs of these cattle is specially for our males, and forbidden to our wives, and if it be still-born, then they are all partners in it; He will reward them for their attributing (false-hood to Allah); surely He is Wise, Knowing.

وَقَالُوْا مَا فِيْ بُطُوْنِ هٰذِهِ الْاَنْعَامِ خَالِصَةٌ لِّذُكُوْرِنَا وَمُحَرَّمٌ عَلٰۤى اَزْوَاجِنَا وَاِنْ يَّكُنْ مَّيْتَةً فَهُمْ فِيْهِ شُرَكَآءُ سَيَجْزِيْهِمْ وَصْفَهُمْ اِنَّهٗ حَكِيْمٌ عَلِيْمٌ ۝

140. They are lost indeed who kill their children foolishly without knowledge, and forbid what Allah has given to them, forging a lie against Allah; they have indeed gone astray, and they are not the followers of the right course.

قَدْ خَسِرَ الَّذِيْنَ قَتَلُوْۤا اَوْلَادَهُمْ سَفَهًا بِغَيْرِ عِلْمٍ وَّحَرَّمُوْا مَا رَزَقَهُمُ اللّٰهُ افْتِرَآءً عَلَى اللّٰهِ قَدْ ضَلُّوْا وَمَا كَانُوْا مُهْتَدِيْنَ ۩

141. And He it is Who produces gardens (of vine), trellised and untrellised, and palms and seed-produce of which the fruits are of various sorts, and olives and pome-granates, like and unlike; eat of its fruit when it bears fruit, and pay the due of it on the day of its reaping, and do not act extravagantly; surely He does not love the extravagant.

وَهُوَ الَّذِيْۤ اَنْشَاَ جَنّٰتٍ مَّعْرُوْشٰتٍ وَّغَيْرَ مَعْرُوْشٰتٍ وَّالنَّخْلَ وَالزَّرْعَ مُخْتَلِفًا اُكُلُهٗ وَالزَّيْتُوْنَ وَالرُّمَّانَ مُتَشَابِهًا وَّغَيْرَ مُتَشَابِهٍ كُلُوْا مِنْ ثَمَرِهٖۤ اِذَاۤ اَثْمَرَ وَاٰتُوْا حَقَّهٗ يَوْمَ حَصَادِهٖ وَلَا تُسْرِفُوْا اِنَّهٗ لَا يُحِبُّ الْمُسْرِفِيْنَ ۝

142. And of cattle (He created) beasts of burden and those which are fit for slaughter only; eat of what Allah has given you and do not follow the footsteps of the Shaitan; surely he is your open enemy.

وَمِنَ الْاَنْعَامِ حَمُوْلَةً وَّفَرْشًا كُلُوْا مِمَّا رَزَقَكُمُ اللّٰهُ وَلَا تَتَّبِعُوْا خُطُوٰتِ الشَّيْطٰنِ اِنَّهٗ لَكُمْ عَدُوٌّ مُّبِيْنٌ ۝

143. Eight in pairs—two of sheep and two of goats. Say: Has He forbidden the two males or the two females or that which the wombs of the two females contain? Inform me with knowledge if you are truthful.

ثَمٰنِيَةَ اَزْوَاجٍ مِّنَ الضَّأْنِ اثْنَيْنِ وَمِنَ الْمَعْزِ اثْنَيْنِ قُلْ ءَآلذَّكَرَيْنِ حَرَّمَ اَمِ الْاُنْثَيَيْنِ اَمَّا اشْتَمَلَتْ عَلَيْهِ اَرْحَامُ الْاُنْثَيَيْنِ نَبِّئُوْنِيْ بِعِلْمٍ اِنْ كُنْتُمْ صٰدِقِيْنَ ۝

144. And two of camels and two of cows. Say: Has He forbidden the two males or the two females or that which the wombs of the two females contain? Or were you witnesses when Allah enjoined you this? Who, then, is more unjust than he who forges a lie against Allah that he should lead astray men without knowledge? Surely Allah does not guide the unjust people.

وَمِنَ الْاِبِلِ اثْنَيْنِ وَمِنَ الْبَقَرِ اثْنَيْنِ ۗ قُلْ ءَآلذَّكَرَيْنِ حَرَّمَ اَمِ الْاُنْثَيَيْنِ اَمَّا اشْتَمَلَتْ عَلَيْهِ اَرْحَامُ الْاُنْثَيَيْنِ ۗ اَمْ كُنْتُمْ شُهَدَآءَ اِذْ وَصّٰىكُمُ اللّٰهُ بِهٰذَا ۚ فَمَنْ اَظْلَمُ مِمَّنِ افْتَرٰى عَلَى اللّٰهِ كَذِبًا لِّيُضِلَّ النَّاسَ بِغَيْرِ عِلْمٍ ۗ اِنَّ اللّٰهَ لَا يَهْدِي الْقَوْمَ الظّٰلِمِيْنَ ۝

145. Say: I do not find in that which has been revealed to me anything forbidden for an eater to eat of except that it be what has died of itself, or blood poured forth, or flesh of swine—for that surely is unclean—or that which is a transgression, other than (the name of) Allah having been invoked on it; but whoever is driven to necessity, not desiring nor exceeding the limit, then surely your Lord is Forgiving, Merciful.

قُلْ لَّا اَجِدُ فِيْ مَا اُوْحِيَ اِلَيَّ مُحَرَّمًا عَلٰى طَاعِمٍ يَّطْعَمُهٗۤ اِلَّا اَنْ يَّكُوْنَ مَيْتَةً اَوْ دَمًا مَّسْفُوْحًا اَوْ لَحْمَ خِنْزِيْرٍ فَاِنَّهٗ رِجْسٌ اَوْ فِسْقًا اُهِلَّ لِغَيْرِ اللّٰهِ بِهٖ ۚ فَمَنِ اضْطُرَّ غَيْرَ بَاغٍ وَّلَا عَادٍ فَاِنَّ رَبَّكَ غَفُوْرٌ رَّحِيْمٌ ۝

146. And to those who were Jews We made unlawful every animal having claws, and of oxen and sheep We made unlawful to them the fat of both, except such as was on their backs or the entrails or what was mixed with bones: this was a punishment We gave them on account of their rebellion, and We are surely Truthful.

وَعَلَى الَّذِيْنَ هَادُوْا حَرَّمْنَا كُلَّ ذِيْ ظُفُرٍ ۚ وَمِنَ الْبَقَرِ وَالْغَنَمِ حَرَّمْنَا عَلَيْهِمْ شُحُوْمَهُمَآ اِلَّا مَا حَمَلَتْ ظُهُوْرُهُمَآ اَوِ الْحَوَايَآ اَوْ مَا اخْتَلَطَ بِعَظْمٍ ۗ ذٰلِكَ جَزَيْنٰهُمْ بِبَغْيِهِمْ ۖ وَاِنَّا لَصٰدِقُوْنَ ۝

147. But if they give you the lie, then say: Your Lord is the Lord of All-encompassing mercy; and His punishment cannot be averted from the guilty people.

فَاِنْ كَذَّبُوْكَ فَقُلْ رَّبُّكُمْ ذُوْ رَحْمَةٍ وَّاسِعَةٍ ۚ وَلَا يُرَدُّ بَأْسُهٗ عَنِ الْقَوْمِ الْمُجْرِمِيْنَ ۝

148. Those who are polytheists will say: If Allah had pleased we would not have associated (aught with Him) nor our fathers, nor would we have forbidden (to ourselves) anything; even so did those before them reject until they tasted Our punishment. Say: Have you any knowledge with you so you should bring it forth to us? You only follow a conjecture and you only tell lies.

سَيَقُوْلُ الَّذِيْنَ اَشْرَكُوْا لَوْ شَآءَ اللّٰهُ مَآ اَشْرَكْنَا وَلَا اٰبَآؤُنَا وَلَا حَرَّمْنَا مِنْ شَيْءٍ ۗ كَذٰلِكَ كَذَّبَ الَّذِيْنَ مِنْ قَبْلِهِمْ حَتّٰى ذَاقُوْا بَأْسَنَا ۗ قُلْ هَلْ عِنْدَكُمْ مِّنْ عِلْمٍ فَتُخْرِجُوْهُ لَنَا ۗ اِنْ تَتَّبِعُوْنَ اِلَّا الظَّنَّ وَاِنْ اَنْتُمْ اِلَّا تَخْرُصُوْنَ ۝

149. Say: Then Allah's is the conclusive argument; so if He please, He would certainly guide you all.

قُلْ فَلِلّٰهِ الْحُجَّةُ الْبَالِغَةُ ۚ فَلَوْ شَآءَ لَهَدٰىكُمْ اَجْمَعِيْنَ ۝

150. Say: Bring your witnesses who should bear witness that Allah has forbidden this, then if they bear witness, do not bear witness with them; and follow not the low desires of those who reject Our communications and of those who do not believe in the hereafter, and they make (others) equal to their Lord.

قُلْ هَلُمَّ شُهَدَاءَكُمُ الَّذِيْنَ يَشْهَدُوْنَ اَنَّ اللّٰهَ حَرَّمَ هٰذَا ۚ فَاِنْ شَهِدُوْا فَلَا تَشْهَدْ مَعَهُمْ ۚ وَلَا تَتَّبِعْ اَهْوَاءَ الَّذِيْنَ كَذَّبُوْا بِاٰيٰتِنَا وَالَّذِيْنَ لَا يُؤْمِنُوْنَ بِالْاٰخِرَةِ وَهُمْ بِرَبِّهِمْ يَعْدِلُوْنَ ۞

151. Say: Come I will recite what your Lord has forbidden to you—(remember) that you do not associate anything with Him and show kindness to your parents, and do not slay your children for (fear of) poverty—We provide for you and for them—and do not draw nigh to indecencies, those of them which are apparent and those which are concealed, and do not kill the soul which Allah has forbidden except for the requirements of justice; this He has enjoined you with that you may understand.

قُلْ تَعَالَوْا اَتْلُ مَا حَرَّمَ رَبُّكُمْ عَلَيْكُمْ اَلَّا تُشْرِكُوْا بِهٖ شَيْئًا وَّبِالْوَالِدَيْنِ اِحْسَانًا ۚ وَلَا تَقْتُلُوْا اَوْلَادَكُمْ مِّنْ اِمْلَاقٍ ۚ نَحْنُ نَرْزُقُكُمْ وَاِيَّاهُمْ ۚ وَلَا تَقْرَبُوا الْفَوَاحِشَ مَا ظَهَرَ مِنْهَا وَمَا بَطَنَ ۚ وَلَا تَقْتُلُوا النَّفْسَ الَّتِيْ حَرَّمَ اللّٰهُ اِلَّا بِالْحَقِّ ۚ ذٰلِكُمْ وَصّٰكُمْ بِهٖ لَعَلَّكُمْ تَعْقِلُوْنَ ۞

152. And do not approach the property of the orphan except in the best manner until he attains his maturity; and give full measure and weight with justice—We do not impose on any soul a duty except to the extent of its ability; and when you speak, then be just though it be (against) a relative, and fulfill Allah's covenant; this He has enjoined you with that you may be mindful;

وَلَا تَقْرَبُوْا مَالَ الْيَتِيْمِ اِلَّا بِالَّتِيْ هِيَ اَحْسَنُ حَتّٰى يَبْلُغَ اَشُدَّهٗ ۚ وَاَوْفُوا الْكَيْلَ وَالْمِيْزَانَ بِالْقِسْطِ ۚ لَا نُكَلِّفُ نَفْسًا اِلَّا وُسْعَهَا ۚ وَاِذَا قُلْتُمْ فَاعْدِلُوْا وَلَوْ كَانَ ذَا قُرْبٰى ۚ وَبِعَهْدِ اللّٰهِ اَوْفُوْا ۚ ذٰلِكُمْ وَصّٰكُمْ بِهٖ لَعَلَّكُمْ تَذَكَّرُوْنَ ۞

153. And (know) that this is My path, the right one, therefore follow it, and follow not (other) ways, for they will lead you away from His way; this He has enjoined you with that you may guard (against evil).

وَاَنَّ هٰذَا صِرَاطِيْ مُسْتَقِيْمًا فَاتَّبِعُوْهُ ۚ وَلَا تَتَّبِعُوا السُّبُلَ فَتَفَرَّقَ بِكُمْ عَنْ سَبِيْلِهٖ ۚ ذٰلِكُمْ وَصّٰكُمْ بِهٖ لَعَلَّكُمْ تَتَّقُوْنَ ۞

154. Again, We gave the Book to Musa to complete (Our blessings) on him who would do good (to others), and making plain all things and a guidance and a mercy, so that they should believe in the meeting of their Lord.

ثُمَّ اٰتَيْنَا مُوْسَى الْكِتٰبَ تَمَامًا عَلَى الَّذِيْ اَحْسَنَ وَتَفْصِيْلًا لِّكُلِّ شَيْءٍ وَّهُدًى وَّرَحْمَةً لَّعَلَّهُمْ بِلِقَاءِ رَبِّهِمْ يُؤْمِنُوْنَ ۞

133

155. And this is a Book We have revealed, blessed; therefore follow it and guard (against evil) that mercy may be shown to you.

وَهٰذَا كِتٰبٌ اَنْزَلْنٰهُ مُبٰرَكٌ فَاتَّبِعُوْهُ وَاتَّقُوْا لَعَلَّكُمْ تُرْحَمُوْنَ ۞

156. Lest you say that the Book was only revealed to two parties before us and We were truly unaware of what they read.

اَنْ تَقُوْلُوْٓا اِنَّمَآ اُنْزِلَ الْكِتٰبُ عَلٰى طَآئِفَتَيْنِ مِنْ قَبْلِنَا وَاِنْ كُنَّا عَنْ دِرَاسَتِهِمْ لَغٰفِلِيْنَ ۞

157. Or lest you should say: If the Book had been revealed to us, we would certainly have been better guided than they; so indeed there has come to you clear proof from your Lord, and guidance and mercy. Who then is more unjust than he who rejects Allah's communications and turns away from them? We will reward those who turn away from Our communications with an evil chastisement because they turned away.

اَوْ تَقُوْلُوْا لَوْ اَنَّآ اُنْزِلَ عَلَيْنَا الْكِتٰبُ لَكُنَّآ اَهْدٰى مِنْهُمْ فَقَدْ جَآءَكُمْ بَيِّنَةٌ مِّنْ رَّبِّكُمْ وَهُدًى وَّرَحْمَةٌ فَمَنْ اَظْلَمُ مِمَّنْ كَذَّبَ بِاٰيٰتِ اللّٰهِ وَصَدَفَ عَنْهَا سَنَجْزِى الَّذِيْنَ يَصْدِفُوْنَ عَنْ اٰيٰتِنَا سُوْٓءَ الْعَذَابِ بِمَا كَانُوْا يَصْدِفُوْنَ ۞

158. They do not wait aught but that the angels should come to them, or that your Lord should come, or that some of the signs of your Lord should come. On the day when some of the signs of your Lord shall come, its faith shall not profit a soul which did not believe before, or earn good through its faith. Say: Wait; we too are waiting.

هَلْ يَنْظُرُوْنَ اِلَّآ اَنْ تَأْتِيَهُمُ الْمَلٰٓئِكَةُ اَوْ يَأْتِيَ رَبُّكَ اَوْ يَأْتِيَ بَعْضُ اٰيٰتِ رَبِّكَ يَوْمَ يَأْتِيْ بَعْضُ اٰيٰتِ رَبِّكَ لَا يَنْفَعُ نَفْسًا اِيْمَانُهَا لَمْ تَكُنْ اٰمَنَتْ مِنْ قَبْلُ اَوْ كَسَبَتْ فِيْٓ اِيْمَانِهَا خَيْرًا قُلِ انْتَظِرُوْٓا اِنَّا مُنْتَظِرُوْنَ ۞

159. Surely they who divided their religion into parts and became sects, you have no concern with them; their affair is only with Allah, then He will inform them of what they did.

اِنَّ الَّذِيْنَ فَرَّقُوْا دِيْنَهُمْ وَكَانُوْا شِيَعًا لَّسْتَ مِنْهُمْ فِيْ شَيْءٍ اِنَّمَآ اَمْرُهُمْ اِلَى اللّٰهِ ثُمَّ يُنَبِّئُهُمْ بِمَا كَانُوْا يَفْعَلُوْنَ ۞

160. Whoever brings a good deed, he shall have ten like it, and whoever brings an evil deed, he shall be recompensed only with the like of it, and they shall not be dealt with unjustly.

مَنْ جَآءَ بِالْحَسَنَةِ فَلَهُ عَشْرُ اَمْثَالِهَا وَمَنْ جَآءَ بِالسَّيِّئَةِ فَلَا يُجْزٰٓى اِلَّا مِثْلَهَا وَهُمْ لَا يُظْلَمُوْنَ ۞

161. Say: Surely, (as for) me, my Lord has guided me to the right path; (to) a most right religion, the faith of Ibrahim the upright one, and he was not of the polytheists.

قُلْ اِنَّنِيْ هَدٰنِيْ رَبِّيْ اِلٰى صِرَاطٍ مُّسْتَقِيْمٍ دِيْنًا قِيَمًا مِّلَّةَ اِبْرٰهِيْمَ حَنِيْفًا وَمَا كَانَ مِنَ الْمُشْرِكِيْنَ ۞

162. Say: Surely my prayer and my sacrifice and my life and my death are (all) for Allah, the Lord of the worlds;

163. No associate has He; and this am I commanded, and I am the first of those who submit.

164. Say: What! shall I seek a Lord other than Allah? And He is the Lord of all things; and no soul earns (evil) but against itself, and no bearer of burden shall bear the burden of another; then to your Lord is your return, so He will inform you of that in which you differed.

165. And He it is Who has made you successors in the land and raised some of you above others by (various) grades, that He might try you by what He has given you; surely your Lord is quick to requite (evil), and He is most surely the Forgiving, the Merciful.

قُلْ اِنَّ صَلَاتِيْ وَنُسُكِيْ وَمَحْيَايَ وَمَمَاتِيْ لِلّٰهِ رَبِّ الْعٰلَمِيْنَ ۝

لَا شَرِيْكَ لَهُ ۚ وَبِذٰلِكَ اُمِرْتُ وَاَنَا اَوَّلُ الْمُسْلِمِيْنَ ۝

قُلْ اَغَيْرَ اللّٰهِ اَبْغِيْ رَبًّا وَّهُوَ رَبُّ كُلِّ شَيْءٍ ۚ وَلَا تَكْسِبُ كُلُّ نَفْسٍ اِلَّا عَلَيْهَا ۚ وَلَا تَزِرُ وَازِرَةٌ وِّزْرَ اُخْرٰى ۚ ثُمَّ اِلٰى رَبِّكُمْ مَّرْجِعُكُمْ فَيُنَبِّئُكُمْ بِمَا كُنْتُمْ فِيْهِ تَخْتَلِفُوْنَ ۝

وَهُوَ الَّذِيْ جَعَلَكُمْ خَلٰٓئِفَ الْاَرْضِ وَرَفَعَ بَعْضَكُمْ فَوْقَ بَعْضٍ دَرَجٰتٍ لِّيَبْلُوَكُمْ فِيْ مَا اٰتٰىكُمْ ۚ اِنَّ رَبَّكَ سَرِيْعُ الْعِقَابِ ۚ وَاِنَّهُ لَغَفُوْرٌ رَّحِيْمٌ ۝

135

THE ELEVATED PLACES
(ARAF)

بِسْمِ اللهِ الرَّحْمٰنِ الرَّحِيْمِ

In the name of Allah,
the Beneficent, the Merciful.

1. Alif Lam Mim Suad.

2. A Book revealed to you—so let there
be no straitness in your breast on account
of it—that you may warn thereby, and a
reminder close to the believers.

3. Follow what has been revealed to you
from your Lord and do not follow guardians besides Him, how little do you mind.

4. And how many a town that We
destroyed, so Our punishment came to it by
night or while they slept at midday.

5. Yet their cry, when Our punishment
came to them, was nothing but that they
said: Surely we were unjust.

6. Most certainly then We will question
those to whom (the apostles) were sent, and
most certainly We will also question the
apostles;

7. Then most certainly We will relate to
them with knowledge, and We were not
absent.

8. And the measuring out on that day
will be just; then as for him whose measure
(of good deeds) is heavy, those are they
who shall be successful;

9. And as for him whose measure (of
good deeds) is light, those are they who
have made their souls suffer loss because
they disbelieved in Our communications.

10. And certainly We have established
you in the earth and made in it means of
livelihood for you; little it is that you give
thanks.

11. And certainly We created you, then
We fashioned you, then We said to the
angels: Make obeisance to Adam. So they
did obeisance except Iblis; he was not of
those who did obeisance.

136

12. He said: What hindered you so that you did not make obeisance when I commanded you? He said: I am better than he: Thou hast created me of fire, while him Thou didst create of dust.

قَالَ مَا مَنَعَكَ اَلَّا تَسْجُدَ اِذْ اَمَرْتُكَ قَالَ اَنَا خَيْرٌ مِّنْهُ خَلَقْتَنِيْ مِنْ نَّارٍ وَّخَلَقْتَهُ مِنْ طِيْنٍ ۝

13. He said: Then get forth from this (state), for it does not befit you to behave proudly therein. Go forth, therefore, surely you are of the abject ones.

قَالَ فَاهْبِطْ مِنْهَا فَمَا يَكُوْنُ لَكَ اَنْ تَتَكَبَّرَ فِيْهَا فَاخْرُجْ اِنَّكَ مِنَ الصَّغِرِيْنَ ۝

14. He said: Respite me until the day when they are raised up.

قَالَ اَنْظِرْنِيْ اِلٰى يَوْمِ يُبْعَثُوْنَ ۝

15. He said: Surely you are of the respited ones.

قَالَ اِنَّكَ مِنَ الْمُنْظَرِيْنَ ۝

16. He said: As Thou hast caused me to remain disappointed I will certainly lie in wait for them in Thy straight path.

قَالَ فَبِمَا اَغْوَيْتَنِيْ لَاَقْعُدَنَّ لَهُمْ صِرَاطَكَ الْمُسْتَقِيْمَ ۝

17. Then I will certainly come to them from before them and from behind them, and from their right-hand side and from their left-hand side; and Thou shalt not find most of them thankful.

ثُمَّ لَاٰتِيَنَّهُمْ مِّنْ بَيْنِ اَيْدِيْهِمْ وَمِنْ خَلْفِهِمْ وَعَنْ اَيْمَانِهِمْ وَعَنْ شَمَآئِلِهِمْ وَلَا تَجِدُ اَكْثَرَهُمْ شٰكِرِيْنَ ۝

18. He said: Get out of this (state), despised, driven away; whoever of them will follow you, I will certainly fill hell with you all.

قَالَ اخْرُجْ مِنْهَا مَذْءُوْمًا مَّدْحُوْرًا لَمَنْ تَبِعَكَ مِنْهُمْ لَاَمْلَئَنَّ جَهَنَّمَ مِنْكُمْ اَجْمَعِيْنَ ۝

19. And (We said): O Adam! Dwell you and your wife in the garden; so eat from where you desire, but do not go near this tree, for then you will be of the unjust.

وَيٰاٰدَمُ اسْكُنْ اَنْتَ وَزَوْجُكَ الْجَنَّةَ فَكُلَا مِنْ حَيْثُ شِئْتُمَا وَلَا تَقْرَبَا هٰذِهِ الشَّجَرَةَ فَتَكُوْنَا مِنَ الظّٰلِمِيْنَ ۝

20. But the Shaitan made an evil suggestion to them that he might make manifest to them what had been hidden from them of their evil inclinations, and he said: Your Lord has not forbidden you this tree except that you may not both become two angels or that you may (not) become of the immortals.

فَوَسْوَسَ لَهُمَا الشَّيْطٰنُ لِيُبْدِيَ لَهُمَا مَا وُرِيَ عَنْهُمَا مِنْ سَوْاٰتِهِمَا وَقَالَ مَا نَهٰكُمَا رَبُّكُمَا عَنْ هٰذِهِ الشَّجَرَةِ اِلَّا اَنْ تَكُوْنَا مَلَكَيْنِ اَوْ تَكُوْنَا مِنَ الْخٰلِدِيْنَ ۝

21. And he swore to them both: Most surely I am a sincere adviser to you.

وَقَاسَمَهُمَا اِنِّيْ لَكُمَا لَمِنَ النّٰصِحِيْنَ ۝

137

22. Then he caused them to fall by deceit; so when they tasted of the tree, their evil inclinations became manifest to them, and they both began to cover themselves with the leaves of the garden; and their Lord called out to them: Did I not forbid you both from that tree and say to you that the Shaitan is your open enemy?

فَدَلَّهُمَا بِغُرُورٍ فَلَمَّا ذَاقَا الشَّجَرَةَ بَدَتْ لَهُمَا سَوْآتُهُمَا وَطَفِقَا يَخْصِفَانِ عَلَيْهِمَا مِنْ وَّرَقِ الْجَنَّةِ وَنَادَاهُمَا رَبُّهُمَا أَلَمْ أَنْهَكُمَا عَنْ تِلْكُمَا الشَّجَرَةِ وَأَقُلْ لَّكُمَا إِنَّ الشَّيْطَانَ لَكُمَا عَدُوٌّ مُّبِينٌ ۩

23. They said: Our Lord! We have been unjust to ourselves, and if Thou forgive us not, and have (not) mercy on us, we shall certainly be of the losers.

قَالَا رَبَّنَا ظَلَمْنَا أَنْفُسَنَا وَإِنْ لَّمْ تَغْفِرْ لَنَا وَتَرْحَمْنَا لَنَكُونَنَّ مِنَ الْخَاسِرِينَ ۩

24. He said: Get forth, some of you, the enemies of others, and there is for you in the earth an abode and a provision for a time.

قَالَ اهْبِطُوا بَعْضُكُمْ لِبَعْضٍ عَدُوٌّ وَلَكُمْ فِي الْأَرْضِ مُسْتَقَرٌّ وَمَتَاعٌ إِلَى حِينٍ ۩

25. He (also) said: Therein shall you live, and therein shall you die, and from it shall you be raised.

قَالَ فِيهَا تَحْيَوْنَ وَفِيهَا تَمُوتُونَ وَمِنْهَا تُخْرَجُونَ ۩

26. O children of Adam! We have indeed sent down to you clothing to cover your shame, and (clothing) for beauty and clothing that guards (against evil); that is the best. This is of the communications of Allah that they may be mindful.

يَا بَنِي آدَمَ قَدْ أَنْزَلْنَا عَلَيْكُمْ لِبَاسًا يُوَارِي سَوْآتِكُمْ وَرِيشًا وَلِبَاسُ التَّقْوَى ذَلِكَ خَيْرٌ ذَلِكَ مِنْ آيَاتِ اللهِ لَعَلَّهُمْ يَذَّكَّرُونَ ۩

27. O children of Adam! let not the Shaitan cause you to fall into affliction as he expelled your parents from the garden, pulling off from them both their clothing that he might show them their evil inclinations, he surely sees you, he as well as his host, from whence you cannot see them; surely We have made the Shaitans to be the guardians of those who do not believe.

يَا بَنِي آدَمَ لَا يَفْتِنَنَّكُمُ الشَّيْطَانُ كَمَا أَخْرَجَ أَبَوَيْكُمْ مِنَ الْجَنَّةِ يَنْزِعُ عَنْهُمَا لِبَاسَهُمَا لِيُرِيَهُمَا سَوْآتِهِمَا إِنَّهُ يَرَاكُمْ هُوَ وَقَبِيلُهُ مِنْ حَيْثُ لَا تَرَوْنَهُمْ إِنَّا جَعَلْنَا الشَّيَاطِينَ أَوْلِيَاءَ لِلَّذِينَ لَا يُؤْمِنُونَ ۩

28. And when they commit an indecency they say: We found our fathers doing this, and Allah has enjoined it on us. Say: Surely Allah does not enjoin indecency; do you say against Allah what you do not know?

وَإِذَا فَعَلُوا فَاحِشَةً قَالُوا وَجَدْنَا عَلَيْهَا آبَاءَنَا وَاللهُ أَمَرَنَا بِهَا قُلْ إِنَّ اللهَ لَا يَأْمُرُ بِالْفَحْشَاءِ أَتَقُولُونَ عَلَى اللهِ مَا لَا تَعْلَمُونَ ۩

29. Say: My Lord has enjoined justice, and set upright your faces at every time of prayer and call on Him, being sincere to Him in obedience; as He brought you forth in the beginning, so shall you also return.

30. A part has He guided aright and (as for another) part, error is justly their due, surely they took the Shaitans for guardians beside Allah, and they think that they are followers of the right way.

31. O children of Adam! attend to your embellishments at every time of prayer, and eat and drink and be not extravagant; surely He does not love the extravagant.*

32. Say: Who has prohibited the embellishment of Allah which He has brought forth for His servants and the good provisions? Say: These are for the believers in the life of this world, purely (theirs) on the resurrection day; thus do We make the communications clear for a people who know.

33. Say: My Lord has only prohibited indecencies, those of them that are apparent as well as those that are concealed, and sin and rebellion without justice, and that you associate with Allah that for which He has not sent down any authority, and that you say against Allah what you do not know.

34. And for every nation there is a doom, so when their doom is come they shall not remain behind the least while, nor shall they go before.

35. O children of Adam! if there come to you apostles from among you relating to you My communications, then whoever shall guard (against evil) and act aright— they shall have no fear, nor shall they grieve.

36. And (as for) those who reject Our communications and turn away from them haughtily—these are the inmates of the fire; they shall abide in it.

37. Who is then more unjust than he who forges a lie against Allah or rejects His communications? (As for) those, their portion of the Book shall reach them, until when Our messengers come to them causing them to die, they shall say: Where is that which you used to call upon besides Allah? They would say: They are gone away from us; and they shall bear witness against themselves that they were unbelievers.

فَمَنْ أَظْلَمُ مِمَّنِ افْتَرٰى عَلَى اللّٰهِ كَذِبًا أَوْ كَذَّبَ بِاٰيٰتِهِ ۚ أُولٰٓئِكَ يَنَالُهُمْ نَصِيبُهُمْ مِّنَ الْكِتٰبِ ۚ حَتّٰى إِذَا جَآءَتْهُمْ رُسُلُنَا يَتَوَفَّوْنَهُمْ ۙ قَالُوٓا أَيْنَ مَا كُنْتُمْ تَدْعُوْنَ مِنْ دُوْنِ اللّٰهِ ۚ قَالُوا ضَلُّوْا عَنَّا وَشَهِدُوْا عَلٰٓى أَنْفُسِهِمْ أَنَّهُمْ كَانُوْا كٰفِرِيْنَ ۝

38. He will say: Enter into fire among the nations that have passed away before you from among jinn and men; whenever a nation shall enter, it shall curse its sister, until when they have all come up with one another into it; the last of them shall say with regard to the foremost of them: Our Lord! these led us astray, therefore give them a double chastisement of the fire. He will say: Every one shall have double but you do not know.

قَالَ ادْخُلُوْا فِيْٓ أُمَمٍ قَدْ خَلَتْ مِنْ قَبْلِكُمْ مِّنَ الْجِنِّ وَالْإِنْسِ فِي النَّارِ ۚ كُلَّمَا دَخَلَتْ أُمَّةٌ لَّعَنَتْ أُخْتَهَا ۚ حَتّٰٓى إِذَا ادَّارَكُوْا فِيْهَا جَمِيْعًا ۙ قَالَتْ أُخْرٰىهُمْ لِأُوْلٰىهُمْ رَبَّنَا هٰٓؤُلَآءِ أَضَلُّوْنَا فَآتِهِمْ عَذَابًا ضِعْفًا مِّنَ النَّارِ ۚ قَالَ لِكُلٍّ ضِعْفٌ وَّلٰكِنْ لَّا تَعْلَمُوْنَ ۝

39. And the foremost of them will say to the last of them: So you have no preference over us; therefore taste the chastisement for what you earned.

وَقَالَتْ أُوْلٰىهُمْ لِأُخْرٰىهُمْ فَمَا كَانَ لَكُمْ عَلَيْنَا مِنْ فَضْلٍ فَذُوْقُوا الْعَذَابَ بِمَا كُنْتُمْ تَكْسِبُوْنَ ۝

40. Surely (as for) those who reject Our communications and turn away from them haughtily, the doors of heaven shall not be opened for them, nor shall they enter the garden until the camel pass through the eye of the needle; and thus do We reward the guilty.

إِنَّ الَّذِيْنَ كَذَّبُوْا بِاٰيٰتِنَا وَاسْتَكْبَرُوْا عَنْهَا لَا تُفَتَّحُ لَهُمْ أَبْوَابُ السَّمَآءِ وَلَا يَدْخُلُوْنَ الْجَنَّةَ حَتّٰى يَلِجَ الْجَمَلُ فِيْ سَمِّ الْخِيَاطِ ۚ وَكَذٰلِكَ نَجْزِي الْمُجْرِمِيْنَ ۝

41. They shall have a bed of hell-fire and from above them coverings (of it); and thus do We reward the unjust.

لَهُمْ مِّنْ جَهَنَّمَ مِهَادٌ وَّمِنْ فَوْقِهِمْ غَوَاشٍ ۚ وَكَذٰلِكَ نَجْزِي الظّٰلِمِيْنَ ۝

42. And (as for) those who believe and do good—We do not impose on any soul a duty except to the extent of its ability—they are the dwellers of the garden; in it they shall abide.

وَالَّذِيْنَ اٰمَنُوْا وَعَمِلُوا الصّٰلِحٰتِ لَا نُكَلِّفُ نَفْسًا إِلَّا وُسْعَهَآ ۙ أُولٰٓئِكَ أَصْحٰبُ الْجَنَّةِ ۚ هُمْ فِيْهَا خٰلِدُوْنَ ۝

43. And We will remove whatever of ill-feeling is in their breasts; the rivers shall flow beneath them and they shall say: All praise is due to Allah Who guided us to this, and we would not have found the way had it not been that Allah had guided us; certainly the apostles of our Lord brought the truth; and it shall be cried out to them that this is the garden of which you are made heirs for what you did.

44. And the dwellers of the garden will call out to the inmates of the fire: Surely we have found what our Lord promised us to be true; have you too found what your Lord promised to be true? They will say: Yes. Then a crier will cry out among them that the curse of Allah is on the unjust.

45. Who hinder (people) from Allah's way and seek to make it crooked, and they are disbelievers in the hereafter.

46. And between the two there shall be a veil, and on the most elevated places there shall be men who know all by their marks, and they shall call out to the dwellers of the garden: Peace be on you; they shall not have yet entered it, though they hope.

47. And when their eyes shall be turned towards the inmates of the fire, they shall say: Our Lord! place us not with the unjust people.

48. And the dwellers of the most elevated places shall call out to men whom they will recognize by their marks saying: Of no avail were to you your amassings and your behaving haughtily:

49. Are these they about whom you swore that Allah will not bestow mercy on them? Enter the garden; you shall have no fear, nor shall you grieve.

50. And the inmates of the fire shall call out to the dwellers of the garden, saying: Pour on us some water or of that which Allah has given you. They shall say: Surely Allah has prohibited them both to the unbelievers.

51. Who take their religion for an idle sport and a play and this life's world deceives them; so today We forsake them, as they neglected the meeting of this day of theirs and as they denied Our communications.

52. And certainly We have brought them a Book which We have made clear with knowledge, a guidance and a mercy for a people who believe.

53. Do they wait for aught but its final sequel? On the day when its final sequel comes about, those who neglected it before will say: Indeed the apostles of our Lord brought the truth; are there for us then any intercessors so that they should intercede on our behalf? Or could we be sent back so that we should do (deeds) other than those which we did? Indeed they have lost their souls, and that which they forged has gone away from them.

54. Surely your Lord is Allah, Who created the heavens and the earth in six periods of time, and He is firm in power; He throws the veil of night over the day, which it pursues incessantly; and (He created) the sun and the moon and the stars, made subservient by His command; surely His is the creation and the command; blessed is Allah, the Lord of the worlds.

55. Call on your Lord humbly and secretly; surely He does not love those who exceed the limits.

56. And do not make mischief in the earth after its reformation, and call on Him fearing and hoping; surely the mercy of Allah is nigh to those who do good (to others).

57. And He it is Who sends forth the winds bearing good news before His mercy, until, when they bring up a laden cloud, We drive it to a dead land, then We send down water on it, then bring forth with it of fruits of all kinds; thus shall We bring forth the dead that you may be mindful.

الَّذِيْنَ اتَّخَذُوْا دِيْنَهُمْ لَهْوًا وَّلَعِبًا وَّغَرَّتْهُمُ الْحَيٰوةُ الدُّنْيَا ۚ فَالْيَوْمَ نَنْسٰىهُمْ كَمَا نَسُوْا لِقَآءَ يَوْمِهِمْ هٰذَا ۙ وَمَا كَانُوْا بِاٰيٰتِنَا يَجْحَدُوْنَ ۞

وَلَقَدْ جِئْنٰهُمْ بِكِتٰبٍ فَصَّلْنٰهُ عَلٰى عِلْمٍ هُدًى وَّرَحْمَةً لِّقَوْمٍ يُّؤْمِنُوْنَ ۞

هَلْ يَنْظُرُوْنَ اِلَّا تَأْوِيْلَهٗ ۚ يَوْمَ يَأْتِيْ تَأْوِيْلُهٗ يَقُوْلُ الَّذِيْنَ نَسُوْهُ مِنْ قَبْلُ قَدْ جَآءَتْ رُسُلُ رَبِّنَا بِالْحَقِّ ۚ فَهَلْ لَّنَا مِنْ شُفَعَآءَ فَيَشْفَعُوْا لَنَآ اَوْ نُرَدُّ فَنَعْمَلَ غَيْرَ الَّذِيْ كُنَّا نَعْمَلُ ۚ قَدْ خَسِرُوْۤا اَنْفُسَهُمْ وَضَلَّ عَنْهُمْ مَّا كَانُوْا يَفْتَرُوْنَ ۞

اِنَّ رَبَّكُمُ اللّٰهُ الَّذِيْ خَلَقَ السَّمٰوٰتِ وَالْاَرْضَ فِيْ سِتَّةِ اَيَّامٍ ثُمَّ اسْتَوٰى عَلَى الْعَرْشِ ۚ يُغْشِى الَّيْلَ النَّهَارَ يَطْلُبُهٗ حَثِيْثًا ۙ وَّالشَّمْسَ وَالْقَمَرَ وَالنُّجُوْمَ مُسَخَّرٰتٍ بِاَمْرِهٖ ۗ اَلَا لَهُ الْخَلْقُ وَالْاَمْرُ ۗ تَبٰرَكَ اللّٰهُ رَبُّ الْعٰلَمِيْنَ ۞

اُدْعُوْا رَبَّكُمْ تَضَرُّعًا وَّخُفْيَةً ۗ اِنَّهٗ لَا يُحِبُّ الْمُعْتَدِيْنَ ۞

وَلَا تُفْسِدُوْا فِى الْاَرْضِ بَعْدَ اِصْلَاحِهَا وَادْعُوْهُ خَوْفًا وَّطَمَعًا ۚ اِنَّ رَحْمَتَ اللّٰهِ قَرِيْبٌ مِّنَ الْمُحْسِنِيْنَ ۞

وَهُوَ الَّذِيْ يُرْسِلُ الرِّيٰحَ بُشْرًۢا بَيْنَ يَدَيْ رَحْمَتِهٖ ۚ حَتّٰۤى اِذَاۤ اَقَلَّتْ سَحَابًا ثِقَالًا سُقْنٰهُ لِبَلَدٍ مَّيِّتٍ فَاَنْزَلْنَا بِهِ الْمَآءَ فَاَخْرَجْنَا بِهٖ مِنْ كُلِّ الثَّمَرٰتِ ۚ كَذٰلِكَ نُخْرِجُ الْمَوْتٰى لَعَلَّكُمْ تَذَكَّرُوْنَ ۞

58. And as for the good land, its vegetation springs forth (abundantly) by the permission of its Lord, and (as for) that which is inferior (its herbage) comes forth but scantily; thus do We repeat the communications for a people who give thanks.

وَالْبَلَدُ الطَّيِّبُ يَخْرُجُ نَبَاتُهُ بِاِذْنِ رَبِّهِ وَالَّذِىْ خَبُثَ لَا يَخْرُجُ اِلَّا نَكِدًا ۚ كَذٰلِكَ نُصَرِّفُ الْاٰيٰتِ لِقَوْمٍ يَّشْكُرُوْنَ ۞

59. Certainly We sent Nuh to his people, so he said: O my people! serve Allah, you have no god other than Him; surely I fear for you the chastisement of a grievous day.

لَقَدْ اَرْسَلْنَا نُوْحًا اِلٰى قَوْمِهٖ فَقَالَ يٰقَوْمِ اعْبُدُوا اللّٰهَ مَا لَكُمْ مِّنْ اِلٰهٍ غَيْرُهٗ ۚ اِنِّىْ اَخَافُ عَلَيْكُمْ عَذَابَ يَوْمٍ عَظِيْمٍ ۞

60. The chiefs of his people said: Most surely we see you in clear error.

قَالَ الْمَلَاُ مِنْ قَوْمِهٖ اِنَّا لَنَرٰىكَ فِىْ ضَلٰلٍ مُّبِيْنٍ ۞

61. He said: O my people! there is no error in me, but I am an apostle from the Lord of the worlds.

قَالَ يٰقَوْمِ لَيْسَ بِىْ ضَلٰلَةٌ وَّلٰكِنِّىْ رَسُوْلٌ مِّنْ رَّبِّ الْعٰلَمِيْنَ ۞

62. I deliver to you the messages of my Lord, and I offer you good advice and I know from Allah what you do not know.

اُبَلِّغُكُمْ رِسٰلٰتِ رَبِّىْ وَاَنْصَحُ لَكُمْ وَاَعْلَمُ مِنَ اللّٰهِ مَا لَا تَعْلَمُوْنَ ۞

63. What! do you wonder that a reminder has come to you from your Lord through a man from among you, that he might warn you and that you might guard (against evil) and so that mercy may be shown to you?

اَوَعَجِبْتُمْ اَنْ جَآءَكُمْ ذِكْرٌ مِّنْ رَّبِّكُمْ عَلٰى رَجُلٍ مِّنْكُمْ لِيُنْذِرَكُمْ وَلِتَتَّقُوْا وَلَعَلَّكُمْ تُرْحَمُوْنَ ۞

64. But they called him a liar, so We delivered him and those with him in the ark, and We drowned those who rejected Our communications; surely they were a blind people.

فَكَذَّبُوْهُ فَاَنْجَيْنٰهُ وَالَّذِيْنَ مَعَهٗ فِى الْفُلْكِ وَاَغْرَقْنَا الَّذِيْنَ كَذَّبُوْا بِاٰيٰتِنَا ۚ اِنَّهُمْ كَانُوْا قَوْمًا عَمِيْنَ ۞

65. And to Ad (We sent) their brother Hud. He said: O my people! serve Allah, you have no god other than Him; will you not then guard (against evil)?

وَاِلٰى عَادٍ اَخَاهُمْ هُوْدًا ۚ قَالَ يٰقَوْمِ اعْبُدُوا اللّٰهَ مَا لَكُمْ مِّنْ اِلٰهٍ غَيْرُهٗ ۚ اَفَلَا تَتَّقُوْنَ ۞

66. The chiefs of those who disbelieved from among his people said: Most surely we see you in folly, and most surely we think you to be of the liars.

قَالَ الْمَلَاُ الَّذِيْنَ كَفَرُوْا مِنْ قَوْمِهٖ اِنَّا لَنَرٰىكَ فِىْ سَفَاهَةٍ وَّاِنَّا لَنَظُنُّكَ مِنَ الْكٰذِبِيْنَ ۞

67. He said: O my people! there is no folly in me, but I am an apostle of the Lord of the worlds.

قَالَ يٰقَوْمِ لَيْسَ بِىْ سَفَاهَةٌ وَّلٰكِنِّىْ رَسُوْلٌ مِّنْ رَّبِّ الْعٰلَمِيْنَ ۞

68. I deliver to you the messages of my Lord and I am a faithful adviser to you:

اُبَلِّغُكُمْ رِسٰلٰتِ رَبِّىْ وَاَنَا لَكُمْ نَاصِحٌ اَمِيْنٌ ۞

69. What! do you wonder that a reminder has come to you from your Lord through a man from among you that he might warn you? And remember when He made you successors after Nuh's people and increased you in excellence in respect of make; therefore remember the benefits of Allah, that you may be successful.

70. They said: Have you come to us that we may serve Allah alone and give up what our fathers used to serve? Then bring to us what you threaten us with, if you are of the truthful ones.

71. He said: Indeed uncleanness and wrath from your Lord have lighted upon you; what! do you dispute with me about names which you and your fathers have given? Allah has not sent any authority for them; wait then, I too with you will be of those who wait.

72. So We delivered him and those with him by mercy from Us, and We cut off the last of those who rejected Our communications and were not believers.

73. And to Samood (We sent) their brother Salih. He said: O my people! serve Allah, you have no god other than Him; clear proof indeed has come to you from your Lord; this is (as) Allah's she-camel for you—a sign, therefore leave her alone to pasture on Allah's earth, and do not touch her with any harm, otherwise painful chastisement will overtake you.

74. And remember when He made you successors after Ad and settled you in the land—you make mansions on its plains and hew out houses in the mountains—remember therefore Allah's benefits and do not act corruptly in the land, making mischief.

144

75. The chief of those who behaved proudly among his people said to those who were considered weak, to those who believed from among them: Do you know that Salih is sent by his Lord? They said: Surely we are believers in what he has been sent with.

76. Those who were haughty said: Surely we are deniers of what you believe in.

77. So they slew the she-camel and revolted against their Lord's commandment, and they said: O Salih! bring us what you threatened us with, if you are one of the apostles.

78. Then the earthquake overtook them, so they became motionless bodies in their abode.

79. Then he turned away from them and said: O my people, I did certainly deliver to you the message of my Lord, and I gave you good advice, but you do not love those who give good advice.

80. And (We sent) Lut when he said to his people: What! do you commit an indecency which any one in the world has not done before you?

81. Most surely you come to males in lust besides females; nay, you are an extravagant people.

82. And the answer of his people was no other than that they said: Turn them out of your town, surely they are a people who seek to purify (themselves).

83. So We delivered him and his followers, except his wife; she was of those who remained behind.

84. And We rained upon them a rain; consider then what was the end of the guilty.

85. And to Madyan (We sent) their brother Shu'aib. He said: O my people! serve Allah, you have no god other than Him; clear proof indeed has come to you from your Lord, therefore give full measure and weight and do not diminish to men their things, and do not make mischief in the land after its reform; this is better for you if you are believers:

86. And do not lie in wait in every path, threatening and turning away from Allah's way him who believes in Him and seeking to make it crooked; and remember when you were few, then He multiplied you, and consider what was the end of the mischief-makers.

87. And if there is a party of you who believe in that with which I am sent, and another party who do not believe, then wait patiently until Allah judges between us; and He is the best of the Judges.

88. The chiefs, those who were proud from among his people, said: We will most certainly turn you out, O Shu'aib, and (also) those who believe with you, from our town, or you shall come back to our faith. He said: What! though we dislike (it)?

89. Indeed we shall have forged a lie against Allah if we go back to your religion after Allah has delivered us from it, and it befits us not that we should go back to it, except if Allah our Lord please: Our Lord comprehends all things in His knowledge; in Allah do we trust: Our Lord! decide between us and our people with truth; and Thou art the best of deciders.

90. And the chiefs of those who disbelieved from among his people said: If you follow Shu'aib, you shall then most surely be losers.

91. Then the earthquake overtook them, so they became motionless bodies in their abode.

92. Those who called Shu'aib a liar were as though they had never dwelt therein; those who called Shu'aib a liar, they were the losers.

93. So he turned away from them and said: O my people! certainly I delivered to you the messages of my Lord and I gave you good advice; how shall I then be sorry for an unbelieving people?

146

94. And We did not send a prophet in a town but We overtook its people with distress and affliction in order that they might humble themselves.

وَمَاۤ اَرۡسَلۡنَا فِيۡ قَرۡيَةٍ مِّنۡ نَّبِيٍّ اِلَّاۤ اَخَذۡنَاۤ اَهۡلَهَا بِالۡبَاۡسَاۤءِ وَالضَّرَّاۤءِ لَعَلَّهُمۡ يَضَّرَّعُوۡنَ ٩٤

95. Then We gave them good in the place of evil until they became many and said: Distress and happiness did indeed befall our fathers. Then We took them by surprise while they did not perceive.

ثُمَّ بَدَّلۡنَا مَكَانَ السَّيِّئَةِ الۡحَسَنَةَ حَتّٰى عَفَوۡا وَّقَالُوۡا قَدۡ مَسَّ اٰبَاۤءَنَا الضَّرَّاۤءُ وَالسَّرَّاۤءُ فَاَخَذۡنٰهُمۡ بَغۡتَةً وَّ هُمۡ لَا يَشۡعُرُوۡنَ ٩٥

96. And if the people of the towns had believed and guarded (against evil) We would certainly have opened up for them blessings from the heaven and the earth, but they rejected, so We overtook them for what they had earned.

وَلَوۡ اَنَّ اَهۡلَ الۡقُرٰۤى اٰمَنُوۡا وَاتَّقَوۡا لَفَتَحۡنَا عَلَيۡهِمۡ بَرَكٰتٍ مِّنَ السَّمَاۤءِ وَالۡاَرۡضِ وَلٰكِنۡ كَذَّبُوۡا فَاَخَذۡنٰهُمۡ بِمَا كَانُوۡا يَكۡسِبُوۡنَ ٩٦

97. What! do the people of the towns then feel secure from Our punishment coming to them by night while they sleep?

اَفَاَمِنَ اَهۡلُ الۡقُرٰۤى اَنۡ يَّاۡتِيَهُمۡ بَاۡسُنَا بَيَاتًا وَّهُمۡ نَاۤئِمُوۡنَ ٩٧

98. What! do the people of the towns feel secure from Our punishment coming to them in the morning while they play?

اَوَ اَمِنَ اَهۡلُ الۡقُرٰۤى اَنۡ يَّاۡتِيَهُمۡ بَاۡسُنَا ضُحًى وَّ هُمۡ يَلۡعَبُوۡنَ ٩٨

99. What! do they then feel secure from Allah's plan? But none feels secure from Allah's plan except the people who shall perish.

اَفَاَمِنُوۡا مَكۡرَ اللّٰهِ فَلَا يَاۡمَنُ مَكۡرَ اللّٰهِ اِلَّا الۡقَوۡمُ الۡخٰسِرُوۡنَ ٩٩

100. Is it not clear to those who inherit the earth after its (former) residents that if We please We would afflict them on account of their faults and set a seal on their hearts so they would not hear.

اَوَ لَمۡ يَهۡدِ لِلَّذِيۡنَ يَرِثُوۡنَ الۡاَرۡضَ مِنۡ بَعۡدِ اَهۡلِهَاۤ اَنۡ لَّوۡ نَشَاۤءُ اَصَبۡنٰهُمۡ بِذُنُوۡبِهِمۡ وَنَطۡبَعُ عَلٰى قُلُوۡبِهِمۡ فَهُمۡ لَا يَسۡمَعُوۡنَ ١٠٠

101. These towns—We relate to you some of their stories, and certainly their apostles came to them with clear arguments, but they would not believe in what they rejected at first; thus does Allah set a seal over the hearts of the unbelievers.

تِلۡكَ الۡقُرٰى نَقُصُّ عَلَيۡكَ مِنۡ اَنۡبَاۤئِهَا وَلَقَدۡ جَاۤءَتۡهُمۡ رُسُلُهُمۡ بِالۡبَيِّنٰتِ فَمَا كَانُوۡا لِيُؤۡمِنُوۡا بِمَا كَذَّبُوۡا مِنۡ قَبۡلُ كَذٰلِكَ يَطۡبَعُ اللّٰهُ عَلٰى قُلُوۡبِ الۡكٰفِرِيۡنَ ١٠١

102. And We did not find in most of them any (faithfulness to) covenant, and We found most of them to be certainly transgressors.

وَمَا وَجَدۡنَا لِاَكۡثَرِهِمۡ مِّنۡ عَهۡدٍ وَاِنۡ وَّجَدۡنَاۤ اَكۡثَرَهُمۡ لَفٰسِقِيۡنَ ١٠٢

103. Then we raised after them Musa with Our communications to Firon and his chiefs, but they disbelieved in them; consider then what was the end of the mischief makers.

ثُمَّ بَعَثۡنَا مِنۡۢ بَعۡدِهِمۡ مُّوۡسٰى بِاٰيٰتِنَاۤ اِلٰى فِرۡعَوۡنَ وَمَلَا۟ئِهِ فَظَلَمُوۡا بِهَا فَانۡظُرۡ كَيۡفَ كَانَ عَاقِبَةُ الۡمُفۡسِدِيۡنَ ١٠٣

104. And Musa said: O Firon! surely I am an apostle from the Lord of the worlds:

وَقَالَ مُوْسٰى يٰفِرْعَوْنُ اِنِّىْ رَسُوْلٌ مِّنْ رَّبِّ الْعٰلَمِيْنَ ۙ ۝

105. (I am) worthy of not saying anything about Allah except the truth: I have come to you indeed with clear proof from your Lord, therefore send with me the children of Israel.

حَقِيْقٌ عَلٰى اَنْ لَّآ اَقُوْلَ عَلَى اللّٰهِ اِلَّا الْحَقَّ ۗ قَدْ جِئْتُكُمْ بِبَيِّنَةٍ مِّنْ رَّبِّكُمْ فَاَرْسِلْ مَعِىَ بَنِىْٓ اِسْرَآءِيْلَ ۝

106. He said: If you have come with a sign, then bring it, if you are of the truthful ones.

قَالَ اِنْ كُنْتَ جِئْتَ بِاٰيَةٍ فَاْتِ بِهَآ اِنْ كُنْتَ مِنَ الصّٰدِقِيْنَ ۝

107. So he threw his rod, then lo! it was a clear serpent.

فَاَلْقٰى عَصَاهُ فَاِذَا هِىَ ثُعْبَانٌ مُّبِيْنٌ ۙ ۝

108. And he drew forth his hand, and lo! it was white to the beholders.

وَّنَزَعَ يَدَهُ فَاِذَا هِىَ بَيْضَآءُ لِلنّٰظِرِيْنَ ۝

109. The chiefs of Firon's people said: most surely this is an enchanter possessed of knowledge:

قَالَ الْمَلَاُ مِنْ قَوْمِ فِرْعَوْنَ اِنَّ هٰذَا لَسٰحِرٌ عَلِيْمٌ ۙ ۝

110. He intends to turn you out of your land. What counsel do you then give?

يُّرِيْدُ اَنْ يُّخْرِجَكُمْ مِّنْ اَرْضِكُمْ ۚ فَمَاذَا تَاْمُرُوْنَ ۝

111. They said: Put him off and his brother, and send collectors into the cities:

قَالُوْٓا اَرْجِهْ وَاَخَاهُ وَاَرْسِلْ فِى الْمَدَآئِنِ حٰشِرِيْنَ ۙ ۝

112. That they may bring to you every enchanter possessed of knowledge.

يَاْتُوْكَ بِكُلِّ سٰحِرٍ عَلِيْمٍ ۝

113. And the enchanters came to Firon (and) said: We must surely have a reward if we are the prevailing ones.

وَجَآءَ السَّحَرَةُ فِرْعَوْنَ قَالُوْٓا اِنَّ لَنَا لَاَجْرًا اِنْ كُنَّا نَحْنُ الْغٰلِبِيْنَ ۝

114. He said: Yes, and you shall certainly be of those who are near (to me).

قَالَ نَعَمْ وَاِنَّكُمْ لَمِنَ الْمُقَرَّبِيْنَ ۝

115. They said: O Musa! will you cast, or shall we be the first to cast?

قَالُوْا يٰمُوْسٰٓى اِمَّآ اَنْ تُلْقِىَ وَاِمَّآ اَنْ نَّكُوْنَ نَحْنُ الْمُلْقِيْنَ ۝

116. He said: Cast. So when they cast, they deceived the people's eyes and frightened them, and they produced a mighty enchantment.

قَالَ اَلْقُوْا ۚ فَلَمَّآ اَلْقَوْا سَحَرُوْٓا اَعْيُنَ النَّاسِ وَاسْتَرْهَبُوْهُمْ وَجَآءُوْ بِسِحْرٍ عَظِيْمٍ ۝

117. And We revealed to Musa, saying: Cast your rod; then lo! it devoured the lies they told.

وَاَوْحَيْنَآ اِلٰى مُوْسٰٓى اَنْ اَلْقِ عَصَاكَ ۚ فَاِذَا هِىَ تَلْقَفُ مَا يَاْفِكُوْنَ ۝

118. So the truth was established, and what they did became null.

فَوَقَعَ الْحَقُّ وَبَطَلَ مَا كَانُوْا يَعْمَلُوْنَ ۝

119. Thus they were vanquished there, and they went back abased.

فَغُلِبُوْا هُنَالِكَ وَانْقَلَبُوْا صٰغِرِيْنَ ۝

120. And the enchanters were thrown down, prostrating (themselves).

وَاُلْقِىَ السَّحَرَةُ سٰجِدِيْنَ ۝

121. They said: We believe in the Lord of the worlds,

قَالُوْٓا اٰمَنَّا بِرَبِّ الْعٰلَمِيْنَ ۝

122. The Lord of Musa and Haroun.

رَبِّ مُوْسٰى وَهٰرُوْنَ ۝

123. Firon said: Do you believe in Him before I have given you permission? Surely this is a plot which you have secretly devised in this city, that you may turn out of it its people, but you shall know:

قَالَ فِرْعَوْنُ اٰمَنْتُمْ بِهٖ قَبْلَ اَنْ اٰذَنَ لَكُمْ ۚ اِنَّ هٰذَا لَمَكْرٌ مَّكَرْتُمُوْهُ فِى الْمَدِيْنَةِ لِتُخْرِجُوْا مِنْهَآ اَهْلَهَا ۚ فَسَوْفَ تَعْلَمُوْنَ ۝

124. I will certainly cut off your hands and your feet on opposite sides, then will I crucify you all together.

لَاُقَطِّعَنَّ اَيْدِيَكُمْ وَاَرْجُلَكُمْ مِّنْ خِلَافٍ ثُمَّ لَاُصَلِّبَنَّكُمْ اَجْمَعِيْنَ ۝

125. They said: Surely to our Lord shall we go back:

قَالُوْٓا اِنَّآ اِلٰى رَبِّنَا مُنْقَلِبُوْنَ ۝

126. And you do not take revenge on us except because we have believed in the communications of our Lord when they came to us! Our Lord: Pour out upon us patience and cause us to die in submission.

وَمَا تَنْقِمُ مِنَّآ اِلَّآ اَنْ اٰمَنَّا بِاٰيٰتِ رَبِّنَا لَمَّا جَآءَتْنَا ۗ رَبَّنَآ اَفْرِغْ عَلَيْنَا صَبْرًا وَّتَوَفَّنَا مُسْلِمِيْنَ ۝

127. And the chiefs of Firon's people said: Do you leave Musa and his people to make mischief in the land and to forsake you and your gods? He said: We will slay their sons and spare their women, and surely we are masters over them.

وَقَالَ الْمَلَاُ مِنْ قَوْمِ فِرْعَوْنَ اَتَذَرُ مُوْسٰى وَقَوْمَهٗ لِيُفْسِدُوْا فِى الْاَرْضِ وَيَذَرَكَ وَاٰلِهَتَكَ ۗ قَالَ سَنُقَتِّلُ اَبْنَآءَهُمْ وَنَسْتَحْيٖ نِسَآءَهُمْ ۚ وَاِنَّا فَوْقَهُمْ قٰهِرُوْنَ ۝

128. Musa said to his people: Ask help from Allah and be patient; surely the land is Allah's; He causes such of His servants to inherit it as He pleases, and the end is for those who guard (against evil).

قَالَ مُوْسٰى لِقَوْمِهِ اسْتَعِيْنُوْا بِاللّٰهِ وَاصْبِرُوْا ۚ اِنَّ الْاَرْضَ لِلّٰهِ ۣ يُوْرِثُهَا مَنْ يَّشَآءُ مِنْ عِبَادِهٖ ۗ وَالْعَاقِبَةُ لِلْمُتَّقِيْنَ ۝

129. They said: We have been persecuted before you came to us and since you have come to us. He said: It may be that your Lord will destroy your enemy and make you rulers in the land, then He will see how you act.

قَالُوْٓا اُوْذِيْنَا مِنْ قَبْلِ اَنْ تَأْتِيَنَا وَمِنْۢ بَعْدِ مَا جِئْتَنَا ۗ قَالَ عَسٰى رَبُّكُمْ اَنْ يُّهْلِكَ عَدُوَّكُمْ وَيَسْتَخْلِفَكُمْ فِى الْاَرْضِ فَيَنْظُرَ كَيْفَ تَعْمَلُوْنَ ۝

130. And certainly We overtook Firon's people with droughts and diminution of fruits that they may be mindful.

وَلَقَدْ اَخَذْنَآ اٰلَ فِرْعَوْنَ بِالسِّنِيْنَ وَنَقْصٍ مِّنَ الثَّمَرٰتِ لَعَلَّهُمْ يَذَّكَّرُوْنَ ۝

131. But when good befell them they said: This is due to us; and when evil afflicted them, they attributed it to the ill-luck of Musa and those with him; surely their evil fortune is only from Allah, but most of them do not know.

فَاِذَا جَآءَتْهُمُ الْحَسَنَةُ قَالُوْا لَنَا هٰذِهٖ ۚ وَاِنْ تُصِبْهُمْ سَيِّئَةٌ يَّطَّيَّرُوْا بِمُوْسٰى وَمَنْ مَّعَهٗ ۗ اَلَا اِنَّمَا طٰۤئِرُهُمْ عِنْدَ اللّٰهِ وَلٰكِنَّ اَكْثَرَهُمْ لَا يَعْلَمُوْنَ ۝

132. And they said: Whatever sign you may bring to us to charm us with it—we will not believe in you.

وَقَالُوْا مَهْمَا تَأْتِنَا بِهٖ مِنْ اٰيَةٍ لِّتَسْحَرَنَا بِهَا ۙ فَمَا نَحْنُ لَكَ بِمُؤْمِنِيْنَ ۝

133. Therefore We sent upon them widespread death, and the locusts and the lice and the frog and the blood, clear signs; but they behaved haughtily and they were a guilty people.

فَاَرْسَلْنَا عَلَيْهِمُ الطُّوْفَانَ وَالْجَرَادَ وَالْقُمَّلَ وَ الضَّفَادِعَ وَالدَّمَ اٰيٰتٍ مُّفَصَّلٰتٍ ۗ فَاسْتَكْبَرُوْا وَ كَانُوْا قَوْمًا مُّجْرِمِيْنَ ۝

134. And when the plague fell upon them, they said: O Musa! pray for us to your Lord as He has promised with you, if you remove the plague from us, we will certainly believe in you and we will certainly send away with you the children of Israel.

وَلَمَّا وَقَعَ عَلَيْهِمُ الرِّجْزُ قَالُوْا يٰمُوْسَى ادْعُ لَنَا رَبَّكَ بِمَا عَهِدَ عِنْدَكَ ۚ لَئِنْ كَشَفْتَ عَنَّا الرِّجْزَ لَنُؤْمِنَنَّ لَكَ وَلَنُرْسِلَنَّ مَعَكَ بَنِيْ اِسْرَآءِيْلَ ۝

135. But when We removed the plague from them till a term which they should attain, lo! they broke (the promise).

فَلَمَّا كَشَفْنَا عَنْهُمُ الرِّجْزَ اِلٰۤى اَجَلٍ هُمْ بٰلِغُوْهُ اِذَا هُمْ يَنْكُثُوْنَ ۝

136. Therefore We inflicted retribution on them and drowned them in the sea because they rejected Our signs and were heedless of them.

فَانْتَقَمْنَا مِنْهُمْ فَاَغْرَقْنٰهُمْ فِى الْيَمِّ بِاَنَّهُمْ كَذَّبُوْا بِاٰيٰتِنَا وَكَانُوْا عَنْهَا غٰفِلِيْنَ ۝

137. And We made the people who were deemed weak to inherit the eastern lands and the western ones which We had blessed; and the good word of your Lord was fulfilled in the children of Israel because they bore up (sufferings) patiently; and We utterly destroyed what Firon and his people had wrought and what they built.

وَاَوْرَثْنَا الْقَوْمَ الَّذِيْنَ كَانُوْا يُسْتَضْعَفُوْنَ مَشَارِقَ الْاَرْضِ وَمَغَارِبَهَا الَّتِيْ بٰرَكْنَا فِيْهَا ۗ وَتَمَّتْ كَلِمَتُ رَبِّكَ الْحُسْنٰى عَلٰى بَنِيْ اِسْرَآءِيْلَ ۙ بِمَا صَبَرُوْا ۗ وَ دَمَّرْنَا مَا كَانَ يَصْنَعُ فِرْعَوْنُ وَقَوْمُهٗ وَمَا كَانُوْا يَعْرِشُوْنَ ۝

138. And We made the children of Israel to pass the sea; then they came upon a people who kept to the worship of their idols. They said: O Musa! make for us a god as they have (their) gods. He said: Surely you are a people acting ignorantly:

وَجَاوَزْنَا بِبَنِيٓ اِسۡرَآءِيۡلَ الۡبَحۡرَ فَاَتَوۡا عَلٰى قَوۡمٍ يَّعۡكُفُوۡنَ عَلٰٓى اَصۡنَامٍ لَّهُمۡ قَالُوۡا يٰمُوۡسَى اجۡعَلۡ لَّنَاۤ اِلٰهًا كَمَا لَهُمۡ اٰلِهَةٌ قَالَ اِنَّكُمۡ قَوۡمٌ تَجۡهَلُوۡنَ ۝

139. (As to) these, surely that about which they are shall be brought to naught and that which they do is vain.

اِنَّ هٰٓؤُلَآءِ مُتَبَّرٌ مَّا هُمۡ فِيۡهِ وَبٰطِلٌ مَّا كَانُوۡا يَعۡمَلُوۡنَ ۝

140. He said: What! shall I seek for you a god other than Allah while He has made you excel (all) created things?

قَالَ اَغَيۡرَ اللّٰهِ اَبۡغِيۡكُمۡ اِلٰهًا وَّهُوَ فَضَّلَكُمۡ عَلَى الۡعٰلَمِيۡنَ ۝

141. And when We delivered you from Firon's people who subjected you to severe torment, killing your sons and sparing your women, and in this there was a great trial from your Lord.

وَاِذۡ اَنۡجَيۡنٰكُمۡ مِّنۡ اٰلِ فِرۡعَوۡنَ يَسُوۡمُوۡنَكُمۡ سُوۡٓءَ الۡعَذَابِ يُقَتِّلُوۡنَ اَبۡنَآءَكُمۡ وَيَسۡتَحۡيُوۡنَ نِسَآءَكُمۡ وَفِىۡ ذٰلِكُمۡ بَلَآءٌ مِّنۡ رَّبِّكُمۡ عَظِيۡمٌ ۝

142. And We appointed with Musa a time of thirty nights and completed them with ten (more), so the appointed time of his Lord was complete forty nights, and Musa said to his brother Haroun: Take my place among my people, and act well and do not follow the way of the mischief-makers.

وَوٰعَدۡنَا مُوۡسٰى ثَلٰثِيۡنَ لَيۡلَةً وَّاَتۡمَمۡنٰهَا بِعَشۡرٍ فَتَمَّ مِيۡقَاتُ رَبِّهٖۤ اَرۡبَعِيۡنَ لَيۡلَةً وَقَالَ مُوۡسٰى لِاَخِيۡهِ هٰرُوۡنَ اخۡلُفۡنِىۡ فِىۡ قَوۡمِىۡ وَاَصۡلِحۡ وَلَا تَتَّبِعۡ سَبِيۡلَ الۡمُفۡسِدِيۡنَ ۝

143. And when Musa came at Our appointed time and his Lord spoke to him, he said: My Lord! show me (Thyself), so that I may look upon Thee. He said: You cannot (bear to) see Me, but look at the mountain, if it remains firm in its place, then will you see Me; but when his Lord manifested His glory to the mountain He made it crumble and Musa fell down in a swoon; then when he recovered, he said: Glory be to Thee, I turn to Thee, and I am the first of the believers.

وَلَمَّا جَآءَ مُوۡسٰى لِمِيۡقَاتِنَا وَكَلَّمَهٗ رَبُّهٗ قَالَ رَبِّ اَرِنِىۡ اَنۡظُرۡ اِلَيۡكَ قَالَ لَنۡ تَرٰىنِىۡ وَلٰكِنِ انۡظُرۡ اِلَى الۡجَبَلِ فَاِنِ اسۡتَقَرَّ مَكَانَهٗ فَسَوۡفَ تَرٰىنِىۡ فَلَمَّا تَجَلّٰى رَبُّهٗ لِلۡجَبَلِ جَعَلَهٗ دَكًّا وَّخَرَّ مُوۡسٰى صَعِقًا فَلَمَّاۤ اَفَاقَ قَالَ سُبۡحٰنَكَ تُبۡتُ اِلَيۡكَ وَاَنَا اَوَّلُ الۡمُؤۡمِنِيۡنَ ۝

144. He said: O Musa! surely I have chosen you above the people with My messages and with My words, therefore take hold of what I give to you and be of the grateful ones.

قَالَ يٰمُوۡسٰٓى اِنِّى اصۡطَفَيۡتُكَ عَلَى النَّاسِ بِرِسٰلٰتِىۡ وَبِكَلَامِىۡ فَخُذۡ مَاۤ اٰتَيۡتُكَ وَكُنۡ مِّنَ الشّٰكِرِيۡنَ ۝

145. And We ordained for him in the tablets admonition of every kind and clear explanation of all things; so take hold of them with firmness and enjoin your people to take hold of what is best thereof; I will show you the abode of the transgressors.

وَكَتَبْنَا لَهُ فِي الْأَلْوَاحِ مِنْ كُلِّ شَيْءٍ مَّوْعِظَةً وَّتَفْصِيْلًا لِّكُلِّ شَيْءٍ ۚ فَخُذْهَا بِقُوَّةٍ وَّأْمُرْ قَوْمَكَ يَأْخُذُوْا بِأَحْسَنِهَا ۚ سَأُوْرِيْكُمْ دَارَ الْفٰسِقِيْنَ ۞

146. I will turn away from My communications those who are unjustly proud in the earth; and if they see every sign they will not believe in it; and if they see the way of rectitude they do not take it for a way, and if they see the way of error, they take it for a way; this is because they rejected Our communications and were heedless of them.

سَأَصْرِفُ عَنْ اٰيٰتِيَ الَّذِيْنَ يَتَكَبَّرُوْنَ فِي الْأَرْضِ بِغَيْرِ الْحَقِّ ۚ وَإِنْ يَّرَوْا كُلَّ اٰيَةٍ لَّا يُؤْمِنُوْا بِهَا ۚ وَإِنْ يَّرَوْا سَبِيْلَ الرُّشْدِ لَا يَتَّخِذُوْهُ سَبِيْلًا ۚ وَإِنْ يَّرَوْا سَبِيْلَ الْغَيِّ يَتَّخِذُوْهُ سَبِيْلًا ۚ ذٰلِكَ بِأَنَّهُمْ كَذَّبُوْا بِاٰيٰتِنَا وَكَانُوْا عَنْهَا غٰفِلِيْنَ ۞

147. And (as to) those who reject Our communications and the meeting of the hereafter, their deeds are null. Shall they be rewarded except for what they have done?

وَالَّذِيْنَ كَذَّبُوْا بِاٰيٰتِنَا وَلِقَاءِ الْاٰخِرَةِ حَبِطَتْ أَعْمَالُهُمْ ۚ هَلْ يُجْزَوْنَ إِلَّا مَا كَانُوْا يَعْمَلُوْنَ ۞

148. And Musa's people made of their ornaments a calf after him, a (mere) body, which gave a mooing sound. What! could they not see that it did not speak to them nor guide them in the way? They took it (for worship) and they were unjust.

وَاتَّخَذَ قَوْمُ مُوْسٰى مِنْ بَعْدِهِ مِنْ حُلِيِّهِمْ عِجْلًا جَسَدًا لَّهُ خُوَارٌ ۚ أَلَمْ يَرَوْا أَنَّهُ لَا يُكَلِّمُهُمْ وَلَا يَهْدِيْهِمْ سَبِيْلًا ۘ اتَّخَذُوْهُ وَكَانُوْا ظٰلِمِيْنَ ۞

149. And when they repented and saw that they had gone astray, they said: If our Lord show not mercy to us and forgive us, we shall certainly be of the losers.

وَلَمَّا سُقِطَ فِيْ أَيْدِيْهِمْ وَرَأَوْا أَنَّهُمْ قَدْ ضَلُّوْا ۙ قَالُوْا لَئِنْ لَّمْ يَرْحَمْنَا رَبُّنَا وَيَغْفِرْ لَنَا لَنَكُوْنَنَّ مِنَ الْخٰسِرِيْنَ ۞

150. And when Musa returned to his people, wrathful (and) in violent grief, he said: Evil is it that you have done after me; did you turn away from the bidding of your Lord? And he threw down the tablets and seized his brother by the head, dragging him towards him. He said: Son of my mother! surely the people reckoned me weak and had well-nigh slain me, therefore make not the enemies to rejoice over me and count me not among the unjust people.

وَلَمَّا رَجَعَ مُوْسٰى إِلٰى قَوْمِهِ غَضْبَانَ أَسِفًا ۙ قَالَ بِئْسَمَا خَلَفْتُمُوْنِيْ مِنْ بَعْدِيْ ۚ أَعَجِلْتُمْ أَمْرَ رَبِّكُمْ ۚ وَأَلْقَى الْأَلْوَاحَ وَأَخَذَ بِرَأْسِ أَخِيْهِ يَجُرُّهُ إِلَيْهِ ۚ قَالَ ابْنَ أُمَّ إِنَّ الْقَوْمَ اسْتَضْعَفُوْنِيْ وَكَادُوْا يَقْتُلُوْنَنِيْ ۖ فَلَا تُشْمِتْ بِيَ الْأَعْدَاءَ وَلَا تَجْعَلْنِيْ مَعَ الْقَوْمِ الظّٰلِمِيْنَ ۞

151. He said: My Lord! forgive me and my brother and cause us to enter into Thy mercy, and Thou art the most Merciful of the merciful ones.

قَالَ رَبِّ اغۡفِرۡ لِيۡ وَلِاَخِيۡ وَاَدۡخِلۡنَا فِيۡ رَحۡمَتِكَ وَاَنۡتَ اَرۡحَمُ الرّٰحِمِيۡنَ ۝

152. (As for) those who took the calf (for a god), surely wrath from their Lord and disgrace in this world's life shall overtake them, and thus do We recompense the devisers of lies.

اِنَّ الَّذِيۡنَ اتَّخَذُوا الۡعِجۡلَ سَيَنَالُهُمۡ غَضَبٌ مِّنۡ رَّبِّهِمۡ وَذِلَّةٌ فِي الۡحَيٰوةِ الدُّنۡيَا ؕ وَكَذٰلِكَ نَجۡزِى الۡمُفۡتَرِيۡنَ ۝

153. And (as to) those who do evil deeds, then repent after that and believe, your Lord after that is most surely Forgiving, Merciful.

وَالَّذِيۡنَ عَمِلُوا السَّيِّاٰتِ ثُمَّ تَابُوۡا مِنۡۢ بَعۡدِهَا وَاٰمَنُوۡۤا ۡ اِنَّ رَبَّكَ مِنۡۢ بَعۡدِهَا لَغَفُوۡرٌ رَّحِيۡمٌ ۝

154. And when Musa's anger calmed down he took up the tablets, and in the writing thereof was guidance and mercy for those who fear for the sake of their Lord.

وَلَمَّا سَكَتَ عَنۡ مُّوۡسَى الۡغَضَبُ اَخَذَ الۡاَلۡوَاحَ ۚ وَفِيۡ نُسۡخَتِهَا هُدًى وَّرَحۡمَةٌ لِّلَّذِيۡنَ هُمۡ لِرَبِّهِمۡ يَرۡهَبُوۡنَ ۝

155. And Musa chose out of his people seventy men for Our appointment; so when the earthquake overtook them, he said: My Lord! if Thou hadst pleased, Thou hadst destroyed them before and myself (too); wilt Thou destroy us for what the fools among us have done? It is naught but Thy trial, Thou makest err with it whom Thou pleasest and guidest whom Thou pleasest: Thou art our Guardian, therefore forgive us and have mercy on us, and Thou art the best of the forgivers.

وَاخۡتَارَ مُوۡسٰى قَوۡمَهٗ سَبۡعِيۡنَ رَجُلًا لِّمِيۡقَاتِنَا ۚ فَلَمَّآ اَخَذَتۡهُمُ الرَّجۡفَةُ قَالَ رَبِّ لَوۡ شِئۡتَ اَهۡلَكۡتَهُمۡ مِّنۡ قَبۡلُ وَاِيَّايَ ؕ اَتُهۡلِكُنَا بِمَا فَعَلَ السُّفَهَآءُ مِنَّا ۚ اِنۡ هِيَ اِلَّا فِتۡنَتُكَ ؕ تُضِلُّ بِهَا مَنۡ تَشَآءُ وَتَهۡدِيۡ مَنۡ تَشَآءُ ؕ اَنۡتَ وَلِيُّنَا فَاغۡفِرۡ لَنَا وَارۡحَمۡنَا وَاَنۡتَ خَيۡرُ الۡغَافِرِيۡنَ ۝

156. And ordain for us good in this world's life and in the hereafter, for surely we turn to Thee. He said: (As for) My chastisement, I will afflict with it whom I please, and My mercy encompasses all things; so I will ordain it (specially) for those who guard (against evil) and pay the poor-rate, and those who believe in Our communications.

وَاكۡتُبۡ لَنَا فِيۡ هٰذِهِ الدُّنۡيَا حَسَنَةً وَّفِي الۡاٰخِرَةِ اِنَّا هُدۡنَآ اِلَيۡكَ ؕ قَالَ عَذَابِيۡۤ اُصِيۡبُ بِهٖ مَنۡ اَشَآءُ ۚ وَرَحۡمَتِيۡ وَسِعَتۡ كُلَّ شَيۡءٍ ؕ فَسَاَكۡتُبُهَا لِلَّذِيۡنَ يَتَّقُوۡنَ وَيُؤۡتُوۡنَ الزَّكٰوةَ وَالَّذِيۡنَ هُمۡ بِاٰيٰتِنَا يُؤۡمِنُوۡنَ ۝

157. Those who follow the Apostle-Prophet, the Ummi, whom they find written down with them in the Taurat and the Injeel, (who) enjoins them good and forbids them evil, and makes lawful to them the good things and makes unlawful to them impure things, and removes from them their burden and the shackles which were upon them; so (as for) those who believe in him and honor him and help him, and follow the light which has been sent down with him, these it is that are the successful.

158. Say: O people! surely I am the Apostle of Allah to you all, of Him Whose is the kingdom of the heavens and the earth, there is no god but He; He brings to life and causes to die, therefore believe in Allah and His apostle, the Ummi Prophet who believes in Allah and His words, and follow him so that you may walk in the right way.

159. And of Musa's people was a party who guided (people) with the truth, and thereby did they do justice.

160. And We divided them into twelve tribes, as nations; and We revealed to Musa when his people asked him for water: Strike the rock with your staff, so out-flowed from it twelve springs; each tribe knew its drinking place; and We made the clouds to give shade over them and We sent to them manna and quails: Eat of the good things We have given you. And they did not do Us any harm, but they did injustice to their own souls.

161. And when it was said to them: Reside in this town and eat from it wherever you wish, and say: Put down from us our heavy burdens; and enter the gate making obeisance, We will forgive you your wrongs: We will give more to those who do good (to others).

154

162. But those who were unjust among them changed it for a saying other than that which had been spoken to them; so We sent upon them a pestilence from heaven because they were unjust.

فَبَدَّلَ الَّذِيْنَ ظَلَمُوْا مِنْهُمْ قَوْلًا غَيْرَ الَّذِيْ قِيْلَ لَهُمْ فَاَرْسَلْنَا عَلَيْهِمْ رِجْزًا مِّنَ السَّمَآءِ بِمَا كَانُوْا يَظْلِمُوْنَ ۝

163. And ask them about the town which stood by the sea; when they exceeded the limits of the Sabbath, when their fish came to them on the day of their Sabbath, appearing on the surface of the water, and on the day on which they did not keep the Sabbath they did not come to them; thus did We try them because they transgressed.

وَسْئَلْهُمْ عَنِ الْقَرْيَةِ الَّتِيْ كَانَتْ حَاضِرَةَ الْبَحْرِ اِذْ يَعْدُوْنَ فِى السَّبْتِ اِذْ تَأْتِيْهِمْ حِيْتَانُهُمْ يَوْمَ سَبْتِهِمْ شُرَّعًا وَّيَوْمَ لَا يَسْبِتُوْنَ لَا تَأْتِيْهِمْ ۚ كَذَٰلِكَ نَبْلُوْهُمْ بِمَا كَانُوْا يَفْسُقُوْنَ ۝

164. And when a party of them said: Why do you admonish a people whom Allah would destroy or whom He would chastise with a severe chastisement? They said: To be free from blame before your Lord, and that haply they may guard (against evil).

وَاِذْ قَالَتْ اُمَّةٌ مِّنْهُمْ لِمَ تَعِظُوْنَ قَوْمَا ۙ اللّٰهُ مُهْلِكُهُمْ اَوْ مُعَذِّبُهُمْ عَذَابًا شَدِيْدًا ۚ قَالُوْا مَعْذِرَةً اِلٰى رَبِّكُمْ وَلَعَلَّهُمْ يَتَّقُوْنَ ۝

165. So when they neglected what they had been reminded of, We delivered those who forbade evil and We overtook those who were unjust with an evil chastisement because they transgressed.

فَلَمَّا نَسُوْا مَا ذُكِّرُوْا بِهٖٓ اَنْجَيْنَا الَّذِيْنَ يَنْهَوْنَ عَنِ السُّوْٓءِ وَاَخَذْنَا الَّذِيْنَ ظَلَمُوْا بِعَذَابٍ بَئِيْسٍ بِمَا كَانُوْا يَفْسُقُوْنَ ۝

166. Therefore when they revoltingly persisted in what they had been forbidden, We said to them: Be (as) apes, despised and hated.

فَلَمَّا عَتَوْا عَنْ مَّا نُهُوْا عَنْهُ قُلْنَا لَهُمْ كُوْنُوْا قِرَدَةً خَاسِئِيْنَ ۝

167. And when your Lord announced that He would certainly send against them to the day of resurrection those who would subject them to severe torment; most surely your Lord is quick to requite (evil) and most surely He is Forgiving, Merciful.

وَاِذْ تَأَذَّنَ رَبُّكَ لَيَبْعَثَنَّ عَلَيْهِمْ اِلٰى يَوْمِ الْقِيٰمَةِ مَنْ يَّسُوْمُهُمْ سُوْٓءَ الْعَذَابِ ۗ اِنَّ رَبَّكَ لَسَرِيْعُ الْعِقَابِ ۖ وَاِنَّهٗ لَغَفُوْرٌ رَّحِيْمٌ ۝

168. And We cut them up on the earth into parties, (some) of them being righteous and (others) of them falling short of that, and We tried them with blessings and misfortunes that they might turn.

وَقَطَّعْنٰهُمْ فِى الْاَرْضِ اُمَمًا ۚ مِنْهُمُ الصّٰلِحُوْنَ وَمِنْهُمْ دُوْنَ ذٰلِكَ ۖ وَبَلَوْنٰهُمْ بِالْحَسَنٰتِ وَالسَّيِّاٰتِ لَعَلَّهُمْ يَرْجِعُوْنَ ۝

155

169. Then there came after them an evil posterity who inherited the Book, taking only the frail good of this low life and saying: It will be forgiven us. And if the like good came to them, they would take it (too). Was not a promise taken from them in the Book that they would not speak anything about Allah but the truth, and they have read what is in it; and the abode of the hereafter is better for those who guard (against evil). Do you not then understand?

فَخَلَفَ مِنْ بَعْدِهِمْ خَلْفٌ وَرِثُوا الْكِتَابَ يَأْخُذُوْنَ عَرَضَ هٰذَا الْأَدْنٰى وَيَقُوْلُوْنَ سَيُغْفَرُ لَنَا ۚ وَإِنْ يَّأْتِهِمْ عَرَضٌ مِّثْلُهٗ يَأْخُذُوْهُ ۚ أَلَمْ يُؤْخَذْ عَلَيْهِمْ مِّيْثَاقُ الْكِتَابِ أَنْ لَّا يَقُوْلُوْا عَلَى اللّٰهِ إِلَّا الْحَقَّ وَدَرَسُوْا مَا فِيْهِ ۗ وَالدَّارُ الْاٰخِرَةُ خَيْرٌ لِّلَّذِيْنَ يَتَّقُوْنَ ۗ أَفَلَا تَعْقِلُوْنَ ۝

170. And (as for) those who hold fast by the Book and keep up prayer, surely We do not waste the reward of the right doers.

وَالَّذِيْنَ يُمَسِّكُوْنَ بِالْكِتَابِ وَأَقَامُوا الصَّلٰوةَ ۗ إِنَّا لَا نُضِيْعُ أَجْرَ الْمُصْلِحِيْنَ ۝

171. And when We shook the mountain over them as if it were a covering overhead, and they thought that it was going to fall down upon them: Take hold of what We have given you with firmness, and be mindful of what is in it, so that you may guard (against evil).

وَإِذْ نَتَقْنَا الْجَبَلَ فَوْقَهُمْ كَأَنَّهٗ ظُلَّةٌ وَّظَنُّوْا أَنَّهٗ وَاقِعٌ بِهِمْ ۚ خُذُوْا مَآ اٰتَيْنٰكُمْ بِقُوَّةٍ وَّاذْكُرُوْا مَا فِيْهِ لَعَلَّكُمْ تَتَّقُوْنَ ۝

172. And when your Lord brought forth from the children of Adam, from their backs, their descendants, and made them bear witness against their own souls: Am I not your Lord? They said: Yes! we bear witness. Lest you should say on the day of resurrection: Surely we were heedless of this.

وَإِذْ أَخَذَ رَبُّكَ مِنْ بَنِيْ اٰدَمَ مِنْ ظُهُوْرِهِمْ ذُرِّيَّتَهُمْ وَأَشْهَدَهُمْ عَلٰى أَنْفُسِهِمْ ۚ أَلَسْتُ بِرَبِّكُمْ ۗ قَالُوْا بَلٰى ۛ شَهِدْنَا ۛ أَنْ تَقُوْلُوْا يَوْمَ الْقِيٰمَةِ إِنَّا كُنَّا عَنْ هٰذَا غٰفِلِيْنَ ۝

173. Or you should say: Only our fathers associated others (with Allah) before, and we were an offspring after them: Wilt Thou then destroy us for what the vain doers did?

أَوْ تَقُوْلُوْا إِنَّمَآ أَشْرَكَ اٰبَاؤُنَا مِنْ قَبْلُ وَكُنَّا ذُرِّيَّةً مِّنْ بَعْدِهِمْ ۚ أَفَتُهْلِكُنَا بِمَا فَعَلَ الْمُبْطِلُوْنَ ۝

174. And thus do We make clear the communications, and that haply they might return.

وَكَذٰلِكَ نُفَصِّلُ الْاٰيٰتِ وَلَعَلَّهُمْ يَرْجِعُوْنَ ۝

175. And recite to them the narrative of him to whom We give Our communications, but he withdraws himself from them, so the Shaitan overtakes him, so he is of those who go astray.

وَاتْلُ عَلَيْهِمْ نَبَأَ الَّذِيْ اٰتَيْنٰهُ اٰيٰتِنَا فَانْسَلَخَ مِنْهَا فَأَتْبَعَهُ الشَّيْطٰنُ فَكَانَ مِنَ الْغٰوِيْنَ ۝

176. And if We had pleased, We would certainly have exalted him thereby; but he clung to the earth and followed his low desire, so his parable is as the parable of the dog; if you attack him he lolls out his tongue; and if you leave him alone he lolls out his tongue; this is the parable of the people who reject Our communications; therefore relate the narrative that they may reflect.

وَلَوْ شِئْنَا لَرَفَعْنٰهُ بِهَا وَلٰكِنَّهٗ أَخْلَدَ إِلَى الْأَرْضِ وَاتَّبَعَ هَوٰىهُ ۚ فَمَثَلُهٗ كَمَثَلِ الْكَلْبِ ۚ إِنْ تَحْمِلْ عَلَيْهِ يَلْهَثْ أَوْ تَتْرُكْهُ يَلْهَثْ ۚ ذٰلِكَ مَثَلُ الْقَوْمِ الَّذِيْنَ كَذَّبُوْا بِاٰيٰتِنَا ۚ فَاقْصُصِ الْقَصَصَ لَعَلَّهُمْ يَتَفَكَّرُوْنَ ۝

177. Evil is the likeness of the people who reject Our communications and are unjust to their own souls.

سَاۤءَ مَثَلَاۨ الْقَوْمُ الَّذِيْنَ كَذَّبُوْا بِاٰيٰتِنَا وَاَنْفُسَهُمْ كَانُوْا يَظْلِمُوْنَ ۝

178. Whomsoever Allah guides, he is the one who follows the right way; and whomsoever He causes to err, these are the losers.

مَنْ يَّهْدِ اللّٰهُ فَهُوَ الْمُهْتَدِيْ وَمَنْ يُّضْلِلْ فَاُولٰۤئِكَ هُمُ الْخٰسِرُوْنَ ۝

179. And certainly We have created for hell many of the jinn and the men; they have hearts with which they do not understand, and they have eyes with which they do not see, and they have ears with which they do not hear; they are as cattle, nay, they are in worse errors; these are the heedless ones.

وَلَقَدْ ذَرَأْنَا لِجَهَنَّمَ كَثِيْرًا مِّنَ الْجِنِّ وَالْاِنْسِ لَهُمْ قُلُوْبٌ لَّا يَفْقَهُوْنَ بِهَا وَلَهُمْ اَعْيُنٌ لَّا يُبْصِرُوْنَ بِهَا وَلَهُمْ اٰذَانٌ لَّا يَسْمَعُوْنَ بِهَا اُولٰۤئِكَ كَالْاَنْعَامِ بَلْ هُمْ اَضَلُّ اُولٰۤئِكَ هُمُ الْغٰفِلُوْنَ ۝

180. And Allah's are the best names, therefore call on Him thereby, and leave alone those who violate the sanctity of His names; they shall be recompensed for what they did.

وَلِلّٰهِ الْاَسْمَاۤءُ الْحُسْنٰى فَادْعُوْهُ بِهَا وَذَرُوا الَّذِيْنَ يُلْحِدُوْنَ فِيْۤ اَسْمَائِهٖ سَيُجْزَوْنَ مَا كَانُوْا يَعْمَلُوْنَ ۝

181. And of those whom We have created are a people who guide with the truth and thereby they do justice.

وَمِمَّنْ خَلَقْنَاۤ اُمَّةٌ يَّهْدُوْنَ بِالْحَقِّ وَبِهٖ يَعْدِلُوْنَ ۝

182. And (as to) those who reject Our communications, We draw them near (to destruction) by degrees from whence they know not.

وَالَّذِيْنَ كَذَّبُوْا بِاٰيٰتِنَا سَنَسْتَدْرِجُهُمْ مِّنْ حَيْثُ لَا يَعْلَمُوْنَ ۝

183. And I grant them respite; surely My scheme is effective.

وَاُمْلِيْ لَهُمْ اِنَّ كَيْدِيْ مَتِيْنٌ ۝

184. Do they not reflect that their companion has not unsoundness in mind; he is only a plain warner.

اَوَلَمْ يَتَفَكَّرُوْا مَا بِصَاحِبِهِمْ مِّنْ جِنَّةٍ اِنْ هُوَ اِلَّا نَذِيْرٌ مُّبِيْنٌ ۝

185. Do they not consider the kingdom of the heavens and the earth and whatever things Allah has created, and that may be their doom shall have drawn nigh; what announcement would they then believe in after this?

اَوَلَمْ يَنْظُرُوْا فِيْ مَلَكُوْتِ السَّمٰوٰتِ وَالْاَرْضِ وَمَا خَلَقَ اللّٰهُ مِنْ شَيْءٍ وَّاَنْ عَسٰۤى اَنْ يَّكُوْنَ قَدِ اقْتَرَبَ اَجَلُهُمْ فَبِاَيِّ حَدِيْثٍ بَعْدَهٗ يُؤْمِنُوْنَ ۝

186. Whomsoever Allah causes to err, there is no guide for him; and He leaves them alone in their inordinacy, blindly wandering on.

مَنْ يُّضْلِلِ اللّٰهُ فَلَا هَادِيَ لَهٗ وَيَذَرُهُمْ فِيْ طُغْيَانِهِمْ يَعْمَهُوْنَ ۝

187. They ask you about the hour, when will be its taking place? Say: The knowledge of it is only with my Lord; none but He shall manifest it at its time; it will be momentous in the heavens and the earth; it will not come on you but of a sudden. They ask you as if you were solicitous about it. Say: Its knowledge is only with Allah, but most people do not know.

188. Say: I do not control any benefit or harm for my own soul except as Allah please; and had I known the unseen I would have had much of good and no evil would have touched me; I am nothing but a warner and the giver of good news to a people who believe.

189. He it is Who created you from a single being, and of the same (kind) did He make his mate, that he might incline to her; so when he covers her she bears a light burden, then moves about with it; but when it grows heavy, they both call upon Allah, their Lord: If Thou givest us a good one, we shall certainly be of the grateful ones.

190. But when He gives them a good one, they set up with Him associates in what He has given them; but high is Allah above what they associate (with Him).

191. What! they associate (with Him) that which does not create any thing, while they are themselves created!

192. And they have no power to give them help, nor can they help themselves.

193. And if you invite them to guidance, they will not follow you; it is the same to you whether you invite them or you are silent.

194. Surely those whom you call on besides Allah are in a state of subjugation like yourselves; therefore call on them, then let them answer you if you are truthful.

195. Have they feet with which they walk, or have they hands with which they hold, or have they eyes with which they see, or have they ears with which they hear? Say: Call your associates, then make a struggle (to prevail) against me and give me no respite.

196. Surely my guardian is Allah, Who revealed the Book, and He befriends the good.

197. And those whom you call upon besides Him are not able to help you, nor can they help themselves.

198. And if you invite them to guidance, they do not hear; and you see them looking towards you, yet they do not see.

199. Take to forgiveness and enjoin good and turn aside from the ignorant.

200. And if a false imputation from the Shaitan afflict you, seek refuge in Allah; surely He is Hearing, Knowing.

201. Surely those who guard (against evil), when a visitation from the Shaitan afflicts them they become mindful, then lo! they see.

202. And their brethren increase them in error, then they cease not.

203. And when you bring them not a revelation they say: Why do you not forge it? Say: I only follow what is revealed to me from my Lord; these are clear proofs from your Lord and a guidance and a mercy for a people who believe.

204. And when the Quran is recited, then listen to it and remain silent, that mercy may be shown to you.

205. And remember your Lord within yourself humbly and fearing and in a voice not loud in the morning and the evening, and be not of the heedless ones.

206. Surely those who are with your Lord are not too proud to serve Him, and they declare His glory and throw themselves down in humility before Him.

159

THE SPOILS OF WAR
(ANFAL)

بِسْمِ اللهِ الرَّحْمٰنِ الرَّحِيْمِ

**In the name of Allah,
the Beneficent, the Merciful.**

1. They ask you about the windfalls. Say: The windfalls are for Allah and the Apostle. So be careful of (your duty to) Allah and set aright matters of your difference, and obey Allah and His Apostle if you are believers.

2. Those only are believers whose hearts become full of fear when Allah is mentioned, and when His communications are recited to them they increase them in faith, and in their Lord do they trust.

3. Those who keep up prayer and spend (benevolently) out of what We have given them.

4. These are the believers in truth; they shall have from their Lord exalted grades and forgiveness and an honorable sustenance.

5. Even as your Lord caused you to go forth from your house with the truth, though a party of the believers were surely averse;

6. They disputed with you about the truth after it had become clear, (and they went forth) as if they were being driven to death while they saw (it).

7. And when Allah promised you one of the two parties that it shall be yours and you loved that the one not armed should be yours, and Allah desired to manifest the truth of what was true by His words and to cut off the root of the unbelievers.

8. That He may manifest the truth of what was true and show the falsehood of what was false, though the guilty disliked.

ايَاتُهَا ٨) سُوْرَةُ الْاَنْفَالِ مَدَنِيَّةٌ رُكُوْعَاتُهَا

يَسْئَلُوْنَكَ عَنِ الْاَنْفَالِ قُلِ الْاَنْفَالُ لِلهِ وَالرَّسُوْلِ فَاتَّقُوا اللهَ وَاَصْلِحُوْا ذَاتَ بَيْنِكُمْ وَاَطِيْعُوا اللهَ وَرَسُوْلَهٗ اِنْ كُنْتُمْ مُّؤْمِنِيْنَ ۞

اِنَّمَا الْمُؤْمِنُوْنَ الَّذِيْنَ اِذَا ذُكِرَ اللهُ وَجِلَتْ قُلُوْبُهُمْ وَاِذَا تُلِيَتْ عَلَيْهِمْ اٰيٰتُهٗ زَادَتْهُمْ اِيْمَانًا وَّعَلٰى رَبِّهِمْ يَتَوَكَّلُوْنَ ۞

الَّذِيْنَ يُقِيْمُوْنَ الصَّلٰوةَ وَمِمَّا رَزَقْنٰهُمْ يُنْفِقُوْنَ ۞

اُولٰٓئِكَ هُمُ الْمُؤْمِنُوْنَ حَقًّا لَّهُمْ دَرَجٰتٌ عِنْدَ رَبِّهِمْ وَمَغْفِرَةٌ وَّرِزْقٌ كَرِيْمٌ ۞

كَمَا اَخْرَجَكَ رَبُّكَ مِنْ بَيْتِكَ بِالْحَقِّ وَاِنَّ فَرِيْقًا مِّنَ الْمُؤْمِنِيْنَ لَكٰرِهُوْنَ ۞

يُجَادِلُوْنَكَ فِى الْحَقِّ بَعْدَ مَا تَبَيَّنَ كَاَنَّمَا يُسَاقُوْنَ اِلَى الْمَوْتِ وَهُمْ يَنْظُرُوْنَ ۞

وَاِذْ يَعِدُكُمُ اللهُ اِحْدَى الطَّائِفَتَيْنِ اَنَّهَا لَكُمْ وَتَوَدُّوْنَ اَنَّ غَيْرَ ذَاتِ الشَّوْكَةِ تَكُوْنُ لَكُمْ وَيُرِيْدُ اللهُ اَنْ يُّحِقَّ الْحَقَّ بِكَلِمٰتِهٖ وَيَقْطَعَ دَابِرَ الْكٰفِرِيْنَ ۞

لِيُحِقَّ الْحَقَّ وَيُبْطِلَ الْبَاطِلَ وَلَوْ كَرِهَ الْمُجْرِمُوْنَ ۞

9. When you sought aid from your Lord, so He answered you: I will assist you with a thousand of the angels following one another.

اِذْ تَسْتَغِيْثُوْنَ رَبَّكُمْ فَاسْتَجَابَ لَكُمْ اَنِّيْ مُمِدُّكُمْ بِاَلْفٍ مِّنَ الْمَلٰٓئِكَةِ مُرْدِفِيْنَ ۝

10. And Allah only gave it as a good news and that your hearts might be at ease thereby; and victory is only from Allah; surely Allah is Mighty, Wise.

وَمَا جَعَلَهُ اللّٰهُ اِلَّا بُشْرٰى وَلِتَطْمَئِنَّ بِهٖ قُلُوْبُكُمْ وَمَا النَّصْرُ اِلَّا مِنْ عِنْدِ اللّٰهِ اِنَّ اللّٰهَ عَزِيْزٌ حَكِيْمٌ ۝

11. When He caused calm to fall on you as a security from Him and sent down upon you water from the cloud that He might thereby purify you, and take away from you the uncleanness of the Shaitan, and that He might fortify your hearts and steady (your) footsteps thereby.

اِذْ يُغَشِّيْكُمُ النُّعَاسَ اَمَنَةً مِّنْهُ وَيُنَزِّلُ عَلَيْكُمْ مِّنَ السَّمَآءِ مَآءً لِّيُطَهِّرَكُمْ بِهٖ وَيُذْهِبَ عَنْكُمْ رِجْزَ الشَّيْطٰنِ وَلِيَرْبِطَ عَلٰى قُلُوْبِكُمْ وَيُثَبِّتَ بِهِ الْاَقْدَامَ ۝

12. When your Lord revealed to the angels: I am with you, therefore make firm those who believe. I will cast terror into the hearts of those who disbelieve. Therefore strike off their heads and strike off every fingertip of them.

اِذْ يُوْحِيْ رَبُّكَ اِلَى الْمَلٰٓئِكَةِ اَنِّيْ مَعَكُمْ فَثَبِّتُوا الَّذِيْنَ اٰمَنُوْا سَاُلْقِيْ فِيْ قُلُوْبِ الَّذِيْنَ كَفَرُوا الرُّعْبَ فَاضْرِبُوْا فَوْقَ الْاَعْنَاقِ وَاضْرِبُوْا مِنْهُمْ كُلَّ بَنَانٍ ۝

13. This is because they acted adversely to Allah and His Apostle; and whoever acts adversely to Allah and His Apostle—then surely Allah is severe in requiting (evil).

ذٰلِكَ بِاَنَّهُمْ شَآقُّوا اللّٰهَ وَرَسُوْلَهٗ وَمَنْ يُّشَاقِقِ اللّٰهَ وَرَسُوْلَهٗ فَاِنَّ اللّٰهَ شَدِيْدُ الْعِقَابِ ۝

14. This—taste it, and (know) that for the unbelievers is the chastisement of fire.

ذٰلِكُمْ فَذُوْقُوْهُ وَاَنَّ لِلْكٰفِرِيْنَ عَذَابَ النَّارِ ۝

15. O you who believe! when you meet those who disbelieve marching for war, then turn not your backs to them.

يٰٓاَيُّهَا الَّذِيْنَ اٰمَنُوْا اِذَا لَقِيْتُمُ الَّذِيْنَ كَفَرُوْا زَحْفًا فَلَا تُوَلُّوْهُمُ الْاَدْبَارَ ۝

16. And whoever shall turn his back to them on that day—unless he turn aside for the sake of fighting or withdraws to a company—then he, indeed, becomes deserving of Allah's wrath, and his abode is hell; and an evil destination shall it be.

وَمَنْ يُّوَلِّهِمْ يَوْمَئِذٍ دُبُرَهٗ اِلَّا مُتَحَرِّفًا لِّقِتَالٍ اَوْ مُتَحَيِّزًا اِلٰى فِئَةٍ فَقَدْ بَآءَ بِغَضَبٍ مِّنَ اللّٰهِ وَمَأْوٰىهُ جَهَنَّمُ وَبِئْسَ الْمَصِيْرُ ۝

17. So you did not slay them, but it was Allah Who slew them, and you did not smite when you smote (the enemy), but it was Allah Who smote, and that He might confer upon the believers a good gift from Himself; surely Allah is Hearing, Knowing.

فَلَمْ تَقْتُلُوْهُمْ وَلٰكِنَّ اللّٰهَ قَتَلَهُمْ وَمَا رَمَيْتَ اِذْ رَمَيْتَ وَلٰكِنَّ اللّٰهَ رَمٰى وَلِيُبْلِيَ الْمُؤْمِنِيْنَ مِنْهُ بَلَآءً حَسَنًا اِنَّ اللّٰهَ سَمِيْعٌ عَلِيْمٌ ۝

18. This, and that Allah is the weakener of the struggle of the unbelievers.

ذٰلِكُمْ وَاَنَّ اللّٰهَ مُوْهِنُ كَيْدِ الْكٰفِرِيْنَ ۝

19. If you demanded a judgment, the judgment has then indeed come to you; and if you desist, it will be better for you; and if you turn back (to fight), We (too) shall turn back, and your forces shall avail you nothing, though they may be many, and (know) that Allah is with the believers.

اِنْ تَسْتَفْتِحُوْا فَقَدْ جَآءَكُمُ الْفَتْحُ وَاِنْ تَنْتَهُوْا فَهُوَ خَيْرٌ لَّكُمْ وَاِنْ تَعُوْدُوْا نَعُدْ وَلَنْ تُغْنِيَ عَنْكُمْ فِئَتُكُمْ شَيْئًا وَّلَوْ كَثُرَتْ وَاَنَّ اللّٰهَ مَعَ الْمُؤْمِنِيْنَ ۟

20. O you who believe! obey Allah and His Apostle and do not turn back from Him while you hear.

يٰۤاَيُّهَا الَّذِيْنَ اٰمَنُوْۤا اَطِيْعُوا اللّٰهَ وَرَسُوْلَهٗ وَلَا تَوَلَّوْا عَنْهُ وَاَنْتُمْ تَسْمَعُوْنَ ۟

21. And be not like those who said, We hear, and they did not obey.

وَلَا تَكُوْنُوْا كَالَّذِيْنَ قَالُوْا سَمِعْنَا وَهُمْ لَا يَسْمَعُوْنَ ۟

22. Surely the vilest of animals, in Allah's sight, are the deaf, the dumb, who do not understand.

اِنَّ شَرَّ الدَّوَآبِّ عِنْدَ اللّٰهِ الصُّمُّ الْبُكْمُ الَّذِيْنَ لَا يَعْقِلُوْنَ ۟

23. And if Allah had known any good in them He would have made them hear, and if He makes them hear they would turn back while they withdraw.

وَلَوْ عَلِمَ اللّٰهُ فِيْهِمْ خَيْرًا لَّاَسْمَعَهُمْ وَلَوْ اَسْمَعَهُمْ لَتَوَلَّوْا وَّهُمْ مُّعْرِضُوْنَ ۟

24. O you who believe! answer (the call of) Allah and His Apostle when he calls you to that which gives you life; and know that Allah intervenes between man and his heart, and that to Him you shall be gathered.

يٰۤاَيُّهَا الَّذِيْنَ اٰمَنُوا اسْتَجِيْبُوْا لِلّٰهِ وَلِلرَّسُوْلِ اِذَا دَعَاكُمْ لِمَا يُحْيِيْكُمْ وَاعْلَمُوْۤا اَنَّ اللّٰهَ يَحُوْلُ بَيْنَ الْمَرْءِ وَقَلْبِهٖ وَاَنَّهٗۤ اِلَيْهِ تُحْشَرُوْنَ ۟

25. And fear an affliction which may not smite those of you in particular who are unjust; and know that Allah is severe in requiting (evil).

وَاتَّقُوْا فِتْنَةً لَّا تُصِيْبَنَّ الَّذِيْنَ ظَلَمُوْا مِنْكُمْ خَآصَّةً وَاعْلَمُوْۤا اَنَّ اللّٰهَ شَدِيْدُ الْعِقَابِ ۟

26. And remember when you were few, deemed weak in the land, fearing lest people might carry you off by force, but He sheltered you and strengthened you with His aid and gave you of the good things that you may give thanks.

وَاذْكُرُوْۤا اِذْ اَنْتُمْ قَلِيْلٌ مُّسْتَضْعَفُوْنَ فِى الْاَرْضِ تَخَافُوْنَ اَنْ يَّتَخَطَّفَكُمُ النَّاسُ فَاٰوٰىكُمْ وَاَيَّدَكُمْ بِنَصْرِهٖ وَرَزَقَكُمْ مِّنَ الطَّيِّبٰتِ لَعَلَّكُمْ تَشْكُرُوْنَ ۟

27. O you who believe! be not unfaithful to Allah and the Apostle, nor be unfaithful to your trusts while you know.

يٰۤاَيُّهَا الَّذِيْنَ اٰمَنُوْا لَا تَخُوْنُوا اللّٰهَ وَالرَّسُوْلَ وَتَخُوْنُوْۤا اَمٰنٰتِكُمْ وَاَنْتُمْ تَعْلَمُوْنَ ۟

28. And know that your property and your children are a temptation, and that Allah is He with Whom there is a mighty reward.

وَاعْلَمُوْۤا اَنَّمَاۤ اَمْوَالُكُمْ وَاَوْلَادُكُمْ فِتْنَةٌ وَّاَنَّ اللّٰهَ عِنْدَهٗۤ اَجْرٌ عَظِيْمٌ ۟

29. O you who believe! If you are careful of (your duty to) Allah, He will grant you a distinction and do away with your evils and forgive you; and Allah is the Lord of mighty grace.

يٰۤاَيُّهَا الَّذِيۡنَ اٰمَنُوۡۤا اِنۡ تَتَّقُوا اللّٰهَ يَجۡعَلۡ لَّكُمۡ فُرۡقَانًا وَّيُكَفِّرۡ عَنۡكُمۡ سَيِّاٰتِكُمۡ وَيَغۡفِرۡ لَكُمۡ وَاللّٰهُ ذُو الۡفَضۡلِ الۡعَظِيۡمِ ۝

30. And when those who disbelieved devised plans against you that they might confine you or slay you or drive you away; and they devised plans and Allah too had arranged a plan; and Allah is the best of planners.

وَاِذۡ يَمۡكُرُ بِكَ الَّذِيۡنَ كَفَرُوۡا لِيُثۡبِتُوۡكَ اَوۡ يَقۡتُلُوۡكَ اَوۡ يُخۡرِجُوۡكَ وَيَمۡكُرُوۡنَ وَيَمۡكُرُ اللّٰهُ وَاللّٰهُ خَيۡرُ الۡمٰكِرِيۡنَ ۝

31. And when Our communications are recited to them, they say: We have heard indeed; if we pleased we could say the like of it; this is nothing but the stories of the ancients.

وَاِذَا تُتۡلٰى عَلَيۡهِمۡ اٰيٰتُنَا قَالُوۡا قَدۡ سَمِعۡنَا لَوۡ نَشَآءُ لَقُلۡنَا مِثۡلَ هٰذَاۤ اِنۡ هٰذَاۤ اِلَّاۤ اَسَاطِيۡرُ الۡاَوَّلِيۡنَ ۝

32. And when they said: O Allah! if this is the truth from Thee, then rain upon us stones from heaven or inflict on us a painful punishment.

وَاِذۡ قَالُوا اللّٰهُمَّ اِنۡ كَانَ هٰذَا هُوَ الۡحَقَّ مِنۡ عِنۡدِكَ فَاَمۡطِرۡ عَلَيۡنَا حِجَارَةً مِّنَ السَّمَآءِ اَوِ ائۡتِنَا بِعَذَابٍ اَلِيۡمٍ ۝

33. But Allah was not going to chastise them while you were among them, nor is Allah going to chastise them while yet they ask for forgiveness.

وَمَا كَانَ اللّٰهُ لِيُعَذِّبَهُمۡ وَاَنۡتَ فِيۡهِمۡ وَمَا كَانَ اللّٰهُ مُعَذِّبَهُمۡ وَهُمۡ يَسۡتَغۡفِرُوۡنَ ۝

34. And what (excuse) have they that Allah should not chastise them while they hinder (men) from the Sacred Mosque and they are not (fit to be) guardians of it; its guardians are only those who guard (against evil), but most of them do not know.

وَمَا لَهُمۡ اَلَّا يُعَذِّبَهُمُ اللّٰهُ وَهُمۡ يَصُدُّوۡنَ عَنِ الۡمَسۡجِدِ الۡحَرَامِ وَمَا كَانُوۡۤا اَوۡلِيَآءَهٗ اِنۡ اَوۡلِيَآؤُهٗۤ اِلَّا الۡمُتَّقُوۡنَ وَلٰكِنَّ اَكۡثَرَهُمۡ لَا يَعۡلَمُوۡنَ ۝

35. And their prayer before the House is nothing but whistling and clapping of hands; taste then the chastisement, for you disbelieved.

وَمَا كَانَ صَلَاتُهُمۡ عِنۡدَ الۡبَيۡتِ اِلَّا مُكَآءً وَّتَصۡدِيَةً فَذُوۡقُوا الۡعَذَابَ بِمَا كُنۡتُمۡ تَكۡفُرُوۡنَ ۝

36. Surely those who disbelieve spend their wealth to hinder (people) from the way of Allah; so they shall spend it, then it shall be to them an intense regret, then they shall be overcome; and those who disbelieve shall be driven together to hell.

اِنَّ الَّذِيۡنَ كَفَرُوۡا يُنۡفِقُوۡنَ اَمۡوَالَهُمۡ لِيَصُدُّوۡا عَنۡ سَبِيۡلِ اللّٰهِ فَسَيُنۡفِقُوۡنَهَا ثُمَّ تَكُوۡنُ عَلَيۡهِمۡ حَسۡرَةً ثُمَّ يُغۡلَبُوۡنَ وَالَّذِيۡنَ كَفَرُوۡۤا اِلٰى جَهَنَّمَ يُحۡشَرُوۡنَ لَ

37. That Allah might separate the impure from the good, and put the impure, some of it upon the other, and pile it up together, then cast it into hell; these it is that are the losers.

لِيَمِيْزَ اللّٰهُ الْخَبِيْثَ مِنَ الطَّيِّبِ وَيَجْعَلَ الْخَبِيْثَ بَعْضَهٗ عَلٰى بَعْضٍ فَيَرْكُمَهٗ جَمِيْعًا فَيَجْعَلَهٗ فِيْ جَهَنَّمَ ۚ اُولٰٓئِكَ هُمُ الْخٰسِرُوْنَ ۞

38. Say to those who disbelieve, if they desist, that which is past shall be forgiven to them; and if they return, then what happened to the ancients has already passed.

قُلْ لِّلَّذِيْنَ كَفَرُوْٓا اِنْ يَّنْتَهُوْا يُغْفَرْ لَهُمْ مَّا قَدْ سَلَفَ ۚ وَاِنْ يَّعُوْدُوْا فَقَدْ مَضَتْ سُنَّتُ الْاَوَّلِيْنَ ۞

39. And fight with them until there is no more persecution and religion should be only for Allah; but if they desist, then surely Allah sees what they do.

وَقَاتِلُوْهُمْ حَتّٰى لَا تَكُوْنَ فِتْنَةٌ وَّيَكُوْنَ الدِّيْنُ كُلُّهٗ لِلّٰهِ ۚ فَاِنِ انْتَهَوْا فَاِنَّ اللّٰهَ بِمَا يَعْمَلُوْنَ بَصِيْرٌ۞

40. And if they turn back, then know that Allah is your Patron; most excellent is the Patron and most excellent is the Helper.

وَاِنْ تَوَلَّوْا فَاعْلَمُوْٓا اَنَّ اللّٰهَ مَوْلٰىكُمْ ۚ نِعْمَ الْمَوْلٰى وَ نِعْمَ النَّصِيْرُ۞

41. And know that whatever thing you gain, a fifth of it is for Allah and for the Apostle and for the near of kin and the orphans and the needy and the wayfarer, if you believe in Allah and in that which We revealed to Our servant, on the day of distinction, the day on which the two parties met; and Allah has power over all things.

وَاعْلَمُوْٓا اَنَّمَا غَنِمْتُمْ مِّنْ شَيْءٍ فَاَنَّ لِلّٰهِ خُمُسَهٗ وَلِلرَّسُوْلِ وَلِذِى الْقُرْبٰى وَالْيَتٰمٰى وَالْمَسٰكِيْنِ وَ ابْنِ السَّبِيْلِ ۚ اِنْ كُنْتُمْ اٰمَنْتُمْ بِاللّٰهِ وَمَآ اَنْزَلْنَا عَلٰى عَبْدِنَا يَوْمَ الْفُرْقَانِ يَوْمَ الْتَقَى الْجَمْعٰنِ ۚ وَاللّٰهُ عَلٰى كُلِّ شَيْءٍ قَدِيْرٌ۞

42. When you were on the nearer side (of the valley) and they were on the farthest side, while the caravan was in a lower place than you; and if you had mutually made an appointment, you would certainly have broken away from the appointment, but—in order that Allah might bring about a matter which was to be done, that he who would perish might perish by clear proof, and he who would live might live by clear proof; and most surely Allah is Hearing, Knowing;

اِذْ اَنْتُمْ بِالْعُدْوَةِ الدُّنْيَا وَهُمْ بِالْعُدْوَةِ الْقُصْوٰى وَالرَّكْبُ اَسْفَلَ مِنْكُمْ ۚ وَلَوْ تَوَاعَدْتُّمْ لَاخْتَلَفْتُمْ فِى الْمِيْعٰدِ ۙ وَلٰكِنْ لِّيَقْضِيَ اللّٰهُ اَمْرًا كَانَ مَفْعُوْلًا ۙ لِّيَهْلِكَ مَنْ هَلَكَ عَنْ بَيِّنَةٍ وَّيَحْيٰى مَنْ حَيَّ عَنْ بَيِّنَةٍ ۚ وَاِنَّ اللّٰهَ لَسَمِيْعٌ عَلِيْمٌ۞

43. When Allah showed them to you in your dream as few; and if He had shown them to you as many you would certainly have become weak-hearted and you would have disputed about the matter, but Allah saved (you); surely He is the Knower of what is in the breasts.

اِذْ يُرِيْكَهُمُ اللّٰهُ فِيْ مَنَامِكَ قَلِيْلًا ۚ وَلَوْ اَرٰىكَهُمْ كَثِيْرًا لَّفَشِلْتُمْ وَلَتَنَازَعْتُمْ فِى الْاَمْرِ وَلٰكِنَّ اللّٰهَ سَلَّمَ ۚ اِنَّهٗ عَلِيْمٌ بِذَاتِ الصُّدُوْرِ۞

44. And when He showed them to you, when you met, as few in your eyes and He made you to appear little in their eyes, in order that Allah might bring about a matter which was to be done, and to Allah are all affairs returned.

وَإِذْ يُرِيْكُمُوْهُمْ اِذِ الْتَقَيْتُمْ فِيْ اَعْيُنِكُمْ قَلِيْلًا وَّيُقَلِّلُكُمْ فِيْ اَعْيُنِهِمْ لِيَقْضِيَ اللهُ اَمْرًا كَانَ مَفْعُوْلًا ۗ وَاِلَى اللهِ تُرْجَعُ الْاُمُوْرُ ۟

45. O you who believe! when you meet a party, then be firm, and remember Allah much, that you may be successful.

يٰۤاَيُّهَا الَّذِيْنَ اٰمَنُوْۤا اِذَا لَقِيْتُمْ فِئَةً فَاثْبُتُوْا وَاذْكُرُوا اللهَ كَثِيْرًا لَّعَلَّكُمْ تُفْلِحُوْنَ ۟

46. And obey Allah and His Apostle and do not quarrel for then you will be weak in hearts and your power will depart, and be patient; surely Allah is with the patient.

وَاَطِيْعُوا اللهَ وَرَسُوْلَهٗ وَلَا تَنَازَعُوْا فَتَفْشَلُوْا وَتَذْهَبَ رِيْحُكُمْ وَاصْبِرُوْا ۗ اِنَّ اللهَ مَعَ الصّٰبِرِيْنَ ۟

47. And be not like those who came forth from their homes in great exultation and to be seen of men, and (who) turn away from the way of Allah, and Allah comprehends what they do.

وَلَا تَكُوْنُوْا كَالَّذِيْنَ خَرَجُوْا مِنْ دِيَارِهِمْ بَطَرًا وَّرِئَآءَ النَّاسِ وَيَصُدُّوْنَ عَنْ سَبِيْلِ اللهِ ۗ وَاللهُ بِمَا يَعْمَلُوْنَ مُحِيْطٌ ۟

48. And when the Shaitan made their works fair seeming to them, and said: No one can overcome you this day, and surely I am your protector: but when the two parties came in sight of each other he turned upon his heels, and said: Surely I am clear of you, surely I see what you do not see, surely I fear Allah; and Allah is severe in requiting (evil).

وَاِذْ زَيَّنَ لَهُمُ الشَّيْطٰنُ اَعْمَالَهُمْ وَقَالَ لَا غَالِبَ لَكُمُ الْيَوْمَ مِنَ النَّاسِ وَاِنِّيْ جَارٌ لَّكُمْ ۚ فَلَمَّا تَرَآءَتِ الْفِئَتٰنِ نَكَصَ عَلٰى عَقِبَيْهِ وَقَالَ اِنِّيْ بَرِيْٓءٌ مِّنْكُمْ اِنِّيْٓ اَرٰى مَا لَا تَرَوْنَ اِنِّيْٓ اَخَافُ اللهَ ۚ وَاللهُ شَدِيْدُ الْعِقَابِ ۟

49. When the hypocrites and those in whose hearts was disease said: Their religion has deceived them; and whoever trusts in Allah, then surely Allah is Mighty, Wise.

اِذْ يَقُوْلُ الْمُنٰفِقُوْنَ وَالَّذِيْنَ فِيْ قُلُوْبِهِمْ مَّرَضٌ غَرَّ هٰٓؤُلَآءِ دِيْنُهُمْ ۗ وَمَنْ يَّتَوَكَّلْ عَلَى اللهِ فَاِنَّ اللهَ عَزِيْزٌ حَكِيْمٌ ۟

50. And had you seen when the angels will cause to die those who disbelieve, smiting their faces and their backs, and (saying): Taste the punishment of burning.

وَلَوْ تَرٰۤى اِذْ يَتَوَفَّى الَّذِيْنَ كَفَرُوا الْمَلٰٓئِكَةُ يَضْرِبُوْنَ وُجُوْهَهُمْ وَاَدْبَارَهُمْ ۚ وَذُوْقُوْا عَذَابَ الْحَرِيْقِ ۟

51. This is for what your own hands have sent on before, and because Allah is not in the least unjust to the servants;

ذٰلِكَ بِمَا قَدَّمَتْ اَيْدِيْكُمْ وَاَنَّ اللهَ لَيْسَ بِظَلَّامٍ لِّلْعَبِيْدِ ۟

52. In the manner of the people of Firon and those before them; they disbelieved in Allah's communications, therefore Allah destroyed them on account of their faults; surely Allah is strong, severe in requiting (evil).

53. This is because Allah has never changed a favor which He has conferred upon a people until they change their own condition; and because Allah is Hearing, Knowing;

54. In the manner of the people of Firon and those before them; they rejected the communications of their Lord, therefore We destroyed them on account of their faults and We drowned Firon's people, and they were all unjust.

55. Surely the vilest of animals in Allah's sight are those who disbelieve, then they would not believe.

56. Those with whom you make an agreement, then they break their agreement every time and they do not guard (against punishment).

57. Therefore if you overtake them in fighting, then scatter by (making an example of) them those who are in their rear, that they may be mindful.

58. And if you fear treachery on the part of a people, then throw back to them on terms of equality; surely Allah does not love the treacherous.

59. And let not those who disbelieve think that they shall come in first; surely they will not escape.

60. And prepare against them what force you can and horses tied at the frontier, to frighten thereby the enemy of Allah and your enemy and others besides them, whom you do not know (but) Allah knows them; and whatever thing you will spend in Allah's way, it will be paid back to you fully and you shall not be dealt with unjustly.

كَدَأْبِ اٰلِ فِرْعَوْنَ وَالَّذِيْنَ مِنْ قَبْلِهِمْ كَفَرُوْا بِاٰيٰتِ اللّٰهِ فَاَخَذَهُمُ اللّٰهُ بِذُنُوْبِهِمْ ۚ اِنَّ اللّٰهَ قَوِيٌّ شَدِيْدُ الْعِقَابِ ۞

ذٰلِكَ بِاَنَّ اللّٰهَ لَمْ يَكُ مُغَيِّرًا نِّعْمَةً اَنْعَمَهَا عَلٰى قَوْمٍ حَتّٰى يُغَيِّرُوْا مَا بِاَنْفُسِهِمْ ۙ وَاَنَّ اللّٰهَ سَمِيْعٌ عَلِيْمٌ ۞

كَدَأْبِ اٰلِ فِرْعَوْنَ وَالَّذِيْنَ مِنْ قَبْلِهِمْ كَذَّبُوْا بِاٰيٰتِ رَبِّهِمْ فَاَهْلَكْنٰهُمْ بِذُنُوْبِهِمْ وَاَغْرَقْنَا اٰلَ فِرْعَوْنَ ۚ وَكُلٌّ كَانُوْا ظٰلِمِيْنَ ۞

اِنَّ شَرَّ الدَّوَآبِّ عِنْدَ اللّٰهِ الَّذِيْنَ كَفَرُوْا فَهُمْ لَا يُؤْمِنُوْنَ ۞

اَلَّذِيْنَ عَاهَدْتَّ مِنْهُمْ ثُمَّ يَنْقُضُوْنَ عَهْدَهُمْ فِيْ كُلِّ مَرَّةٍ وَّهُمْ لَا يَتَّقُوْنَ ۞

فَاِمَّا تَثْقَفَنَّهُمْ فِي الْحَرْبِ فَشَرِّدْ بِهِمْ مَّنْ خَلْفَهُمْ لَعَلَّهُمْ يَذَّكَّرُوْنَ ۞

وَاِمَّا تَخَافَنَّ مِنْ قَوْمٍ خِيَانَةً فَانْبِذْ اِلَيْهِمْ عَلٰى سَوَآءٍ ۚ اِنَّ اللّٰهَ لَا يُحِبُّ الْخَآئِنِيْنَ ۞

وَلَا يَحْسَبَنَّ الَّذِيْنَ كَفَرُوْا سَبَقُوْا ۚ اِنَّهُمْ لَا يُعْجِزُوْنَ ۞

وَاَعِدُّوْا لَهُمْ مَّا اسْتَطَعْتُمْ مِّنْ قُوَّةٍ وَّمِنْ رِّبَاطِ الْخَيْلِ تُرْهِبُوْنَ بِهٖ عَدُوَّ اللّٰهِ وَعَدُوَّكُمْ وَاٰخَرِيْنَ مِنْ دُوْنِهِمْ ۚ لَا تَعْلَمُوْنَهُمْ ۚ اَللّٰهُ يَعْلَمُهُمْ ۗ وَمَا تُنْفِقُوْا مِنْ شَيْءٍ فِيْ سَبِيْلِ اللّٰهِ يُوَفَّ اِلَيْكُمْ وَاَنْتُمْ لَا تُظْلَمُوْنَ ۞

61. And if they incline to peace, then incline to it and trust in Allah; surely He is the Hearing, the Knowing.

62. And if they intend to deceive you— then surely Allah is sufficient for you; He it is Who strengthened you with His help and with the believers,

63. And united their hearts; had you spent all that is in the earth, you could not have united their hearts, but Allah united them; surely He is Mighty, Wise.

64. O Prophet! Allah is sufficient for you and (for) such of the believers as follow you.

65. O Prophet! urge the believers to war; if there are twenty patient ones of you they shall overcome two hundred, and if there are a hundred of you they shall overcome a thousand of those who disbelieve, because they are a people who do not understand.

66. For the present Allah has made light your burden, and He knows that there is weakness in you; so if there are a hundred patient ones of you they shall overcome two hundred, and if there are a thousand they shall overcome two thousand by Allah's permission; and Allah is with the patient.

67. It is not fit for a prophet that he should take captives unless he has fought and triumphed in the land; you desire the frail goods of the world, while Allah desires (for you) the hereafter; and Allah is Mighty, Wise.

68. Were it not for an ordinance from Allah that had already gone forth, surely there would have befallen you a great chastisement for what you had taken to.

69. Eat then of the lawful and good (things) which you have acquired in war, and be careful of (your duty to) Allah; surely Allah is Forgiving, Merciful.

70. O Prophet! say to those of the captives who are in your hands: If Allah knows anything good in your hearts, He will give to you better than that which has been taken away from you and will forgive you, and Allah is Forgiving, Merciful.

يٰۤاَيُّهَا النَّبِيُّ قُلْ لِّمَنْ فِيْۤ اَيْدِيْكُمْ مِّنَ الْاَسْرٰىۤ اِنْ يَّعْلَمِ اللّٰهُ فِيْ قُلُوْبِكُمْ خَيْرًا يُّؤْتِكُمْ خَيْرًا مِّمَّاۤ اُخِذَ مِنْكُمْ وَيَغْفِرْ لَكُمْ وَاللّٰهُ غَفُوْرٌ رَّحِيْمٌ ۝

71. And if they intend to act unfaithfully towards you, so indeed they acted unfaithfully towards Allah before, but He gave (you) mastery over them; and Allah is Knowing, Wise.

وَاِنْ يُّرِيْدُوْا خِيَانَتَكَ فَقَدْ خَانُوا اللّٰهَ مِنْ قَبْلُ فَاَمْكَنَ مِنْهُمْ وَاللّٰهُ عَلِيْمٌ حَكِيْمٌ ۝

72. Surely those who believed and fled (their homes) and struggled hard in Allah's way with their property and their souls, and those who gave shelter and helped— these are guardians of each other; and (as for) those who believed and did not fly, not yours is their guardianship until they fly; and if they seek aid from you in the matter of religion, aid is incumbent on you except against a people between whom and you there is a treaty, and Allah sees what you do.

اِنَّ الَّذِيْنَ اٰمَنُوْا وَهَاجَرُوْا وَجَاهَدُوْا بِاَمْوَالِهِمْ وَاَنْفُسِهِمْ فِيْ سَبِيْلِ اللّٰهِ وَالَّذِيْنَ اٰوَوْا وَّنَصَرُوْۤا اُولٰٓئِكَ بَعْضُهُمْ اَوْلِيَآءُ بَعْضٍ وَالَّذِيْنَ اٰمَنُوْا وَلَمْ يُهَاجِرُوْا مَا لَكُمْ مِّنْ وَّلَايَتِهِمْ مِّنْ شَيْءٍ حَتّٰى يُهَاجِرُوْا وَاِنِ اسْتَنْصَرُوْكُمْ فِى الدِّيْنِ فَعَلَيْكُمُ النَّصْرُ اِلَّا عَلٰى قَوْمٍ بَيْنَكُمْ وَبَيْنَهُمْ مِّيْثَاقٌ وَاللّٰهُ بِمَا تَعْمَلُوْنَ بَصِيْرٌ ۝

73. And (as for) those who disbelieve, some of them are the guardians of others; if you will not do it, there will be in the land persecution and great mischief.

وَالَّذِيْنَ كَفَرُوْا بَعْضُهُمْ اَوْلِيَآءُ بَعْضٍ اِلَّا تَفْعَلُوْهُ تَكُنْ فِتْنَةٌ فِى الْاَرْضِ وَفَسَادٌ كَبِيْرٌ ۝

74. And (as for) those who believed and fled and struggled hard in Allah's way, and those who gave shelter and helped, these are the believers truly; they shall have forgiveness and honorable provision.

وَالَّذِيْنَ اٰمَنُوْا وَهَاجَرُوْا وَجَاهَدُوْا فِيْ سَبِيْلِ اللّٰهِ وَالَّذِيْنَ اٰوَوْا وَّنَصَرُوْۤا اُولٰٓئِكَ هُمُ الْمُؤْمِنُوْنَ حَقًّا لَّهُمْ مَّغْفِرَةٌ وَّرِزْقٌ كَرِيْمٌ ۝

75. And (as for) those who believed afterwards and fled and struggled hard along with you, they are of you; and the possessors of relationships are nearer to each other in the ordinance of Allah; surely Allah knows all things.

وَالَّذِيْنَ اٰمَنُوْا مِنْ بَعْدُ وَهَاجَرُوْا وَجَاهَدُوْا مَعَكُمْ فَاُولٰٓئِكَ مِنْكُمْ وَاُولُوا الْاَرْحَامِ بَعْضُهُمْ اَوْلٰى بِبَعْضٍ فِيْ كِتٰبِ اللّٰهِ اِنَّ اللّٰهَ بِكُلِّ شَيْءٍ عَلِيْمٌ ۝

REPENTANCE
(BARAAT)

1. (This is a declaration of) immunity by Allah and His Apostle towards those of the idolaters with whom you made an agreement.

2. So go about in the land for four months and know that you cannot weaken Allah and that Allah will bring disgrace to the unbelievers.

3. And an announcement from Allah and His Apostle to the people on the day of the greater pilgrimage that Allah and His Apostle are free from liability to the idolaters; therefore if you repent, it will be better for you, and if you turn back, then know that you will not weaken Allah; and announce painful punishment to those who disbelieve.

4. Except those of the idolaters with whom you made an agreement, then they have not failed you in anything and have not backed up any one against you, so fulfill their agreement to the end of their term; surely Allah loves those who are careful (of their duty).

5. So when the sacred months have passed away, then slay the idolaters wherever you find them, and take them captives and besiege them and lie in wait for them in every ambush, then if they repent and keep up prayer and pay the poor-rate, leave their way free to them; surely Allah is Forgiving, Merciful.

6. And if one of the idolaters seek protection from you, grant him protection till he hears the word of Allah, then make him attain his place of safety; this is because they are a people who do not know.

169

7. How can there be an agreement for the idolaters with Allah and with His Apostle; except those with whom you made an agreement at the Sacred Mosque? So as long as they are true to you, be true to them; surely Allah loves those who are careful (of their duty).

كَيْفَ يَكُوْنُ لِلْمُشْرِكِيْنَ عَهْدٌ عِنْدَ اللّٰهِ وَعِنْدَ رَسُوْلِهٖ اِلَّا الَّذِيْنَ عٰهَدْتُّمْ عِنْدَ الْمَسْجِدِ الْحَرَامِ ۚ فَمَا اسْتَقَامُوْا لَكُمْ فَاسْتَقِيْمُوْا لَهُمْ ۚ اِنَّ اللّٰهَ يُحِبُّ الْمُتَّقِيْنَ ۝

8. How (can it be)! while if they prevail against you, they would not pay regard in your case to ties of relationship, nor those of covenant; they please you with their mouths while their hearts do not consent; and most of them are transgressors.

كَيْفَ وَاِنْ يَّظْهَرُوْا عَلَيْكُمْ لَا يَرْقُبُوْا فِيْكُمْ اِلًّا وَّلَا ذِمَّةً ۚ يُرْضُوْنَكُمْ بِاَفْوَاهِهِمْ وَتَأْبٰى قُلُوْبُهُمْ ۚ وَاَكْثَرُهُمْ فٰسِقُوْنَ ۝

9. They have taken a small price for the communications of Allah, so they turn away from His way; surely evil is it that they do.

اِشْتَرَوْا بِاٰيٰتِ اللّٰهِ ثَمَنًا قَلِيْلًا فَصَدُّوْا عَنْ سَبِيْلِهٖ ۚ اِنَّهُمْ سَاءَ مَا كَانُوْا يَعْمَلُوْنَ ۝

10. They do not pay regard to ties of relationship nor those of covenant in the case of a believer; and these are they who go beyond the limits.

لَا يَرْقُبُوْنَ فِيْ مُؤْمِنٍ اِلًّا وَّلَا ذِمَّةً ۚ وَاُولٰٓئِكَ هُمُ الْمُعْتَدُوْنَ ۝

11. But if they repent and keep up prayer and pay the poor-rate, they are your brethren in faith; and We make the communications clear for a people who know.

فَاِنْ تَابُوْا وَاَقَامُوا الصَّلٰوةَ وَاٰتَوُا الزَّكٰوةَ فَاِخْوَانُكُمْ فِي الدِّيْنِ ۚ وَنُفَصِّلُ الْاٰيٰتِ لِقَوْمٍ يَّعْلَمُوْنَ ۝

وَاِنْ نَّكَثُوْۤا اَيْمَانَهُمْ مِّنْ بَعْدِ عَهْدِهِمْ وَطَعَنُوْا فِيْ

12. And if they break their oaths after their agreement and (openly) revile your religion, then fight the leaders of unbelief—surely their oaths are nothing—so that they may desist.

دِيْنِكُمْ فَقَاتِلُوْۤا اَئِمَّةَ الْكُفْرِ ۙ اِنَّهُمْ لَاۤ اَيْمَانَ لَهُمْ لَعَلَّهُمْ يَنْتَهُوْنَ ۝

13. What! will you not fight a people who broke their oaths and aimed at the expulsion of the Apostle, and they attacked you first; do you fear them? But Allah is most deserving that you should fear Him, if you are believers.

اَلَا تُقَاتِلُوْنَ قَوْمًا نَّكَثُوْۤا اَيْمَانَهُمْ وَهَمُّوْا بِاِخْرَاجِ الرَّسُوْلِ وَهُمْ بَدَءُوْكُمْ اَوَّلَ مَرَّةٍ ۚ اَتَخْشَوْنَهُمْ ۚ فَاللّٰهُ اَحَقُّ اَنْ تَخْشَوْهُ اِنْ كُنْتُمْ مُّؤْمِنِيْنَ ۝

14. Fight them; Allah will punish them by your hands and bring them to disgrace, and assist you against them and heal the hearts of a believing people.

قَاتِلُوْهُمْ يُعَذِّبْهُمُ اللّٰهُ بِاَيْدِيْكُمْ وَيُخْزِهِمْ وَيَنْصُرْكُمْ عَلَيْهِمْ وَيَشْفِ صُدُوْرَ قَوْمٍ مُّؤْمِنِيْنَ ۝

15. And remove the rage of their hearts; and Allah turns (mercifully) to whom He pleases, and Allah is Knowing, Wise.

وَيُذْهِبْ غَيْظَ قُلُوْبِهِمْ ۚ وَيَتُوْبُ اللّٰهُ عَلٰى مَنْ يَّشَاءُ ۚ وَاللّٰهُ عَلِيْمٌ حَكِيْمٌ ۝

16. What! do you think that you will be left alone while Allah has not yet known those of you who have struggled hard and have not taken any one as an adherent besides Allah and His Apostle and the believers; and Allah is aware of what you do.

17. The idolaters have no right to visit the mosques of Allah while bearing witness to unbelief against themselves; these it is whose doings are null, and in the fire shall they abide.

18. Only he shall visit the mosques of Allah who believes in Allah and the latter day, and keeps up prayer and pays the poor-rate and fears none but Allah; so (as for) these, it may be that they are of the followers of the right course.

19. What! do you make (one who undertakes) the giving of drink to the pilgrims and the guarding of the Sacred Mosque like him who believes in Allah and the latter day and strives hard in Allah's way? They are not equal with Allah; and Allah does not guide the unjust people.

20. Those who believed and fled (their homes), and strove hard in Allah's way with their property and their souls, are much higher in rank with Allah; and those are they who are the achievers (of their objects).

21. Their Lord gives them good news of mercy from Himself and (His) good pleasure and gardens, wherein lasting blessings shall be theirs;

22. Abiding therein for ever; surely Allah has a Mighty reward with Him.

23. O you who believe! do not take your fathers and your brothers for guardians if they love unbelief more than belief; and whoever of you takes them for a guardian, these it is that are the unjust.

أَمْ حَسِبْتُمْ أَنْ تُتْرَكُوْا وَلَمَّا يَعْلَمِ اللّٰهُ الَّذِيْنَ جَهَدُوْا مِنْكُمْ وَلَمْ يَتَّخِذُوْا مِنْ دُوْنِ اللّٰهِ وَلَا رَسُوْلِهِ وَلَا الْمُؤْمِنِيْنَ وَلِيْجَةً ۖ وَاللّٰهُ خَبِيْرٌ بِمَا تَعْمَلُوْنَ ۞

مَا كَانَ لِلْمُشْرِكِيْنَ أَنْ يَّعْمُرُوْا مَسَاجِدَ اللّٰهِ شٰهِدِيْنَ عَلٰى أَنْفُسِهِمْ بِالْكُفْرِ ۚ أُولٰٓئِكَ حَبِطَتْ أَعْمَالُهُمْ ۖ وَفِي النَّارِ هُمْ خٰلِدُوْنَ ۞

إِنَّمَا يَعْمُرُ مَسٰجِدَ اللّٰهِ مَنْ اٰمَنَ بِاللّٰهِ وَالْيَوْمِ الْاٰخِرِ وَأَقَامَ الصَّلٰوةَ وَاٰتَى الزَّكٰوةَ وَلَمْ يَخْشَ إِلَّا اللّٰهَ ۖ فَعَسٰٓى أُولٰٓئِكَ أَنْ يَّكُوْنُوْا مِنَ الْمُهْتَدِيْنَ ۞

أَجَعَلْتُمْ سِقَايَةَ الْحَاجِّ وَعِمَارَةَ الْمَسْجِدِ الْحَرَامِ كَمَنْ اٰمَنَ بِاللّٰهِ وَالْيَوْمِ الْاٰخِرِ وَجَاهَدَ فِيْ سَبِيْلِ اللّٰهِ ۚ لَا يَسْتَوُوْنَ عِنْدَ اللّٰهِ ۖ وَاللّٰهُ لَا يَهْدِي الْقَوْمَ الظّٰلِمِيْنَ ۞

الَّذِيْنَ اٰمَنُوْا وَهَاجَرُوْا وَجَاهَدُوْا فِيْ سَبِيْلِ اللّٰهِ بِأَمْوَالِهِمْ وَأَنْفُسِهِمْ أَعْظَمُ دَرَجَةً عِنْدَ اللّٰهِ ۚ وَأُولٰٓئِكَ هُمُ الْفَائِزُوْنَ ۞

يُبَشِّرُهُمْ رَبُّهُمْ بِرَحْمَةٍ مِّنْهُ وَرِضْوَانٍ وَّجَنّٰتٍ لَّهُمْ فِيْهَا نَعِيْمٌ مُّقِيْمٌ ۞

خٰلِدِيْنَ فِيْهَا أَبَدًا ۚ إِنَّ اللّٰهَ عِنْدَهُ أَجْرٌ عَظِيْمٌ ۞

يَا أَيُّهَا الَّذِيْنَ اٰمَنُوْا لَا تَتَّخِذُوْا اٰبَاءَكُمْ وَإِخْوَانَكُمْ أَوْلِيَاءَ إِنِ اسْتَحَبُّوا الْكُفْرَ عَلَى الْإِيْمَانِ ۚ وَمَنْ يَّتَوَلَّهُمْ مِّنْكُمْ فَأُولٰٓئِكَ هُمُ الظّٰلِمُوْنَ ۞

24. Say: If your fathers and your sons and your brethren and your mates and your kinsfolk and property which you have acquired, and the slackness of trade which you fear and dwellings which you like, are dearer to you than Allah and His Apostle and striving in His way, then wait till Allah brings about His command; and Allah does not guide the transgressing people.

قُلْ اِنْ كَانَ اٰبَآؤُكُمْ وَاَبْنَآؤُكُمْ وَاِخْوَانُكُمْ وَاَزْوَاجُكُمْ وَعَشِيْرَتُكُمْ وَاَمْوَالُ ۨاقْتَرَفْتُمُوْهَا وَتِجَارَةٌ تَخْشَوْنَ كَسَادَهَا وَمَسٰكِنُ تَرْضَوْنَهَآ اَحَبَّ اِلَيْكُمْ مِّنَ اللّٰهِ وَرَسُوْلِهٖ وَجِهَادٍ فِيْ سَبِيْلِهٖ فَتَرَبَّصُوْا حَتّٰى يَاْتِيَ اللّٰهُ بِاَمْرِهٖ ۗ وَاللّٰهُ لَا يَهْدِى الْقَوْمَ الْفٰسِقِيْنَ ۝

25. Certainly Allah helped you in many battlefields and on the day of Hunain, when your great numbers made you vain, but they availed you nothing and the earth became strait to you notwithstanding its spaciousness, then you turned back retreating.

لَقَدْ نَصَرَكُمُ اللّٰهُ فِيْ مَوَاطِنَ كَثِيْرَةٍ ۙ وَّيَوْمَ حُنَيْنٍ ۙ اِذْ اَعْجَبَتْكُمْ كَثْرَتُكُمْ فَلَمْ تُغْنِ عَنْكُمْ شَيْئًا وَّضَاقَتْ عَلَيْكُمُ الْاَرْضُ بِمَا رَحُبَتْ ثُمَّ وَلَّيْتُمْ مُّدْبِرِيْنَ ۝

26. Then Allah sent down His tranquillity upon His Apostle and upon the believers, and sent down hosts which you did not see, and chastised those who disbelieved, and that is the reward of the unbelievers.

ثُمَّ اَنْزَلَ اللّٰهُ سَكِيْنَتَهٗ عَلٰى رَسُوْلِهٖ وَعَلَى الْمُؤْمِنِيْنَ وَاَنْزَلَ جُنُوْدًا لَّمْ تَرَوْهَا وَعَذَّبَ الَّذِيْنَ كَفَرُوْا ۗ وَذٰلِكَ جَزَآءُ الْكٰفِرِيْنَ ۝

27. Then will Allah after this turn (mercifully) to whom He pleases, and Allah is Forgiving, Merciful.

ثُمَّ يَتُوْبُ اللّٰهُ مِنْۢ بَعْدِ ذٰلِكَ عَلٰى مَنْ يَّشَآءُ ۗ وَاللّٰهُ غَفُوْرٌ رَّحِيْمٌ ۝

28. O you who believe! the idolaters are nothing but unclean, so they shall not approach the Sacred Mosque after this year; and if you fear poverty then Allah will enrich you out of His grace if He please; surely Allah is Knowing, Wise.

يٰٓاَيُّهَا الَّذِيْنَ اٰمَنُوْٓا اِنَّمَا الْمُشْرِكُوْنَ نَجَسٌ فَلَا يَقْرَبُوا الْمَسْجِدَ الْحَرَامَ بَعْدَ عَامِهِمْ هٰذَا ۚ وَاِنْ خِفْتُمْ عَيْلَةً فَسَوْفَ يُغْنِيْكُمُ اللّٰهُ مِنْ فَضْلِهٖٓ اِنْ شَآءَ ۗ اِنَّ اللّٰهَ عَلِيْمٌ حَكِيْمٌ ۝

29. Fight those who do not believe in Allah, nor in the latter day, nor do they prohibit what Allah and His Apostle have prohibited, nor follow the religion of truth, out of those who have been given the Book, until they pay the tax in acknowledgment of superiority and they are in a state of subjection.

قَاتِلُوا الَّذِيْنَ لَا يُؤْمِنُوْنَ بِاللّٰهِ وَلَا بِالْيَوْمِ الْاٰخِرِ وَلَا يُحَرِّمُوْنَ مَا حَرَّمَ اللّٰهُ وَرَسُوْلُهٗ وَلَا يَدِيْنُوْنَ دِيْنَ الْحَقِّ مِنَ الَّذِيْنَ اُوْتُوا الْكِتٰبَ حَتّٰى يُعْطُوا الْجِزْيَةَ عَنْ يَّدٍ وَّهُمْ صٰغِرُوْنَ ۝

30. And the Jews say: Uzair is the son of Allah; and the Christians say: The Messiah is the son of Allah; these are the words of their mouths; they imitate the saying of those who disbelieved before; may Allah destroy them; how they are turned away!

31. They have taken their doctors of law and their monks for lords besides Allah, and (also) the Messiah son of Marium and they were enjoined that they should serve one God only, there is no god but He; far from His glory be what they set up (with Him).

32. They desire to put out the light of Allah with their mouths, and Allah will not consent save to perfect His light, though the unbelievers are averse.

33. He it is Who sent His Apostle with guidance and the religion of truth, that He might cause it to prevail over all religions, though the polytheists may be averse.

34. O you who believe! most surely many of the doctors of law and the monks eat away the property of men falsely, and turn (them) from Allah's way; and (as for) those who hoard up gold and silver and do not spend it in Allah's way, announce to them a painful chastisement,

35. On the day when it shall be heated in the fire of hell, then their foreheads and their sides and their backs shall be branded with it; this is what you hoarded up for yourselves, therefore taste what you hoarded.

36. Surely the number of months with Allah is twelve months in Allah's ordinance since the day when He created the heavens and the earth, of these four being sacred; that is the right reckoning; therefore be not unjust to yourselves regarding them, and fight the polytheists all together as they fight you all together; and know that Allah is with those who guard (against evil).

37. Postponing (of the sacred month) is only an addition in unbelief, wherewith those who disbelieve are led astray, violating it one year and keeping it sacred another, that they may agree in the number (of months) that Allah has made sacred, and thus violate what Allah has made sacred; the evil of their doings is made fairseeming to them; and Allah does not guide the unbelieving people.

38. O you who believe! What (excuse) have you that when it is said to you: Go forth in Allah's way, you should incline heavily to earth; are you contented with this world's life instead of the hereafter? But the provision of this world's life compared with the hereafter is but little.

39. If you do not go forth, He will chastise you with a painful chastisement and bring in your place a people other than you, and you will do Him no harm; and Allah has power over all things.

40. If you will not aid him, Allah certainly aided him when those who disbelieved expelled him, he being the second of the two, when they were both in the cave, when he said to his companion: Grieve not, surely Allah is with us. So Allah sent down His tranquillity upon him and strengthened him with hosts which you did not see, and made lowest the word of those who disbelieved; and the word of Allah, that is the highest; and Allah is Mighty, Wise.

41. Go forth light and heavy, and strive hard in Allah's way with your property and your persons; this is better for you, if you know.

42. Had it been a near advantage and a short journey, they would certainly have followed you, but the tedious journey was too long for them; and they swear by Allah: If we had been able, we would certainly have gone forth with you; they cause their own souls to perish, and Allah knows that they are most surely liars.

اِنَّمَا النَّسِيْٓءُ زِيَادَةٌ فِي الْكُفْرِ يُضَلُّ بِهِ الَّذِيْنَ كَفَرُوْا

يُحِلُّوْنَهٗ عَامًا وَّيُحَرِّمُوْنَهٗ عَامًا لِّيُوَاطِئُوْا عِدَّةَ مَا حَرَّمَ

اللّٰهُ فَيُحِلُّوْا مَا حَرَّمَ اللّٰهُ ۚ زُيِّنَ لَهُمْ سُوْٓءُ اَعْمَالِهِمْ ۗ

وَاللّٰهُ لَا يَهْدِي الْقَوْمَ الْكٰفِرِيْنَ ۝

يٰٓاَيُّهَا الَّذِيْنَ اٰمَنُوْا مَا لَكُمْ اِذَا قِيْلَ لَكُمُ انْفِرُوْا فِيْ

سَبِيْلِ اللّٰهِ اثَّاقَلْتُمْ اِلَى الْاَرْضِ ۗ اَرَضِيْتُمْ بِالْحَيٰوةِ

الدُّنْيَا مِنَ الْاٰخِرَةِ ۚ فَمَا مَتَاعُ الْحَيٰوةِ الدُّنْيَا فِي

الْاٰخِرَةِ اِلَّا قَلِيْلٌ ۝

اِلَّا تَنْفِرُوْا يُعَذِّبْكُمْ عَذَابًا اَلِيْمًا ۙ وَّيَسْتَبْدِلْ قَوْمًا

غَيْرَكُمْ وَلَا تَضُرُّوْهُ شَيْئًا ۗ وَاللّٰهُ عَلٰى كُلِّ شَيْءٍ قَدِيْرٌ ۝

اِلَّا تَنْصُرُوْهُ فَقَدْ نَصَرَهُ اللّٰهُ اِذْ اَخْرَجَهُ الَّذِيْنَ

كَفَرُوْا ثَانِيَ اثْنَيْنِ اِذْ هُمَا فِي الْغَارِ اِذْ يَقُوْلُ لِصَاحِبِهٖ

لَا تَحْزَنْ اِنَّ اللّٰهَ مَعَنَا ۚ فَاَنْزَلَ اللّٰهُ سَكِيْنَتَهٗ عَلَيْهِ

وَاَيَّدَهٗ بِجُنُوْدٍ لَّمْ تَرَوْهَا وَجَعَلَ كَلِمَةَ الَّذِيْنَ

كَفَرُوا السُّفْلٰى ۗ وَكَلِمَةُ اللّٰهِ هِيَ الْعُلْيَا ۗ وَاللّٰهُ عَزِيْزٌ

حَكِيْمٌ ۝

اِنْفِرُوْا خِفَافًا وَّثِقَالًا وَّجَاهِدُوْا بِاَمْوَالِكُمْ وَاَنْفُسِكُمْ

فِيْ سَبِيْلِ اللّٰهِ ۚ ذٰلِكُمْ خَيْرٌ لَّكُمْ اِنْ كُنْتُمْ تَعْلَمُوْنَ ۝

لَوْ كَانَ عَرَضًا قَرِيْبًا وَّسَفَرًا قَاصِدًا لَّاتَّبَعُوْكَ وَ

لٰكِنْ بَعُدَتْ عَلَيْهِمُ الشُّقَّةُ ۚ وَسَيَحْلِفُوْنَ بِاللّٰهِ

لَوِ اسْتَطَعْنَا لَخَرَجْنَا مَعَكُمْ ۚ يُهْلِكُوْنَ اَنْفُسَهُمْ ۚ

وَاللّٰهُ يَعْلَمُ اِنَّهُمْ لَكٰذِبُوْنَ ۝

43. Allah pardon you! Why did you give them leave until those who spoke the truth had become manifest to you and you had known the liars?

عَفَا اللّٰهُ عَنْكَ لِمَ اَذِنْتَ لَهُمْ حَتّٰى يَتَبَيَّنَ لَكَ الَّذِيْنَ صَدَقُوْا وَتَعْلَمَ الْكٰذِبِيْنَ ۞

44. They do not ask leave of you who believe in Allah and the latter day (to stay away) from striving hard with their property and their persons, and Allah knows those who guard (against evil).

لَا يَسْتَأْذِنُكَ الَّذِيْنَ يُؤْمِنُوْنَ بِاللّٰهِ وَالْيَوْمِ الْاٰخِرِ اَنْ يُّجَاهِدُوْا بِاَمْوَالِهِمْ وَاَنْفُسِهِمْ وَاللّٰهُ عَلِيْمٌ بِالْمُتَّقِيْنَ ۞

45. They only ask leave of you who do not believe in Allah and the latter day and their hearts are in doubt, so in their doubt do they waver.

اِنَّمَا يَسْتَأْذِنُكَ الَّذِيْنَ لَا يُؤْمِنُوْنَ بِاللّٰهِ وَالْيَوْمِ الْاٰخِرِ وَارْتَابَتْ قُلُوْبُهُمْ فَهُمْ فِيْ رَيْبِهِمْ يَتَرَدَّدُوْنَ ۞

46. And if they had intended to go forth, they would certainly have provided equipment for it, but Allah did not like their going forth, so He withheld them, and it was said (to them): Hold back with those who hold back.

وَلَوْ اَرَادُوا الْخُرُوْجَ لَاَعَدُّوْا لَهُ عُدَّةً وَّلٰكِنْ كَرِهَ اللّٰهُ انْبِعَاثَهُمْ فَثَبَّطَهُمْ وَقِيْلَ اقْعُدُوْا مَعَ الْقٰعِدِيْنَ ۞

47. Had they gone forth with you, they would not have added to you aught save corruption, and they would certainly have hurried about among you seeking (to sow) dissension among you, and among you there are those who hearken for their sake; and Allah knows the unjust.

لَوْ خَرَجُوْا فِيْكُمْ مَّا زَادُوْكُمْ اِلَّا خَبَالًا وَّلَاَ اَوْضَعُوْا خِلَالَكُمْ يَبْغُوْنَكُمُ الْفِتْنَةَ وَفِيْكُمْ سَمّٰعُوْنَ لَهُمْ وَاللّٰهُ عَلِيْمٌ بِالظّٰلِمِيْنَ ۞

48. Certainly they sought (to sow) dissension before, and they meditated plots against you until the truth came, and Allah's commandment prevailed although they were averse (from it).

لَقَدِ ابْتَغَوُا الْفِتْنَةَ مِنْ قَبْلُ وَقَلَّبُوْا لَكَ الْاُمُوْرَ حَتّٰى جَآءَ الْحَقُّ وَظَهَرَ اَمْرُ اللّٰهِ وَهُمْ كٰرِهُوْنَ ۞

49. And among them there is he who says: Allow me and do not try me. Surely into trial have they already tumbled down, and most surely hell encompasses the unbelievers.

وَمِنْهُمْ مَّنْ يَّقُوْلُ ائْذَنْ لِّيْ وَلَا تَفْتِنِّيْ اَلَا فِي الْفِتْنَةِ سَقَطُوْا وَاِنَّ جَهَنَّمَ لَمُحِيْطَةٌ بِالْكٰفِرِيْنَ ۞

50. If good befalls you, it grieves them, and if hardship afflicts you, they say: Indeed we had taken care of our affair before; and they turn back and are glad.

اِنْ تُصِبْكَ حَسَنَةٌ تَسُؤْهُمْ وَاِنْ تُصِبْكَ مُصِيْبَةٌ يَّقُوْلُوْا قَدْ اَخَذْنَا اَمْرَنَا مِنْ قَبْلُ وَيَتَوَلَّوْا وَّهُمْ فَرِحُوْنَ ۞

51. Say: Nothing will afflict us save what Allah has ordained for us; He is our Patron; and on Allah let the believers rely.

قُلْ لَّنْ يُّصِيْبَنَا اِلَّا مَا كَتَبَ اللّٰهُ لَنَا هُوَ مَوْلٰىنَا وَعَلَى اللّٰهِ فَلْيَتَوَكَّلِ الْمُؤْمِنُوْنَ ۞

52. Say: Do you await for us but one of two most excellent things? And we await for you that Allah will afflict you with punishment from Himself or by our hands. So wait; we too will wait with you.

قُلْ هَلْ تَرَبَّصُوْنَ بِنَآ اِلَّآ اِحْدَى الْحُسْنَيَيْنِ وَنَحْنُ نَتَرَبَّصُ بِكُمْ اَنْ يُّصِيْبَكُمُ اللّٰهُ بِعَذَابٍ مِّنْ عِنْدِهٖۤ اَوْ بِاَيْدِيْنَا ۖ فَتَرَبَّصُوْۤا اِنَّا مَعَكُمْ مُّتَرَبِّصُوْنَ ۞

53. Say: Spend willingly or unwillingly, it shall not be accepted from you; surely you are a transgressing people.

قُلْ اَنْفِقُوْا طَوْعًا اَوْ كَرْهًا لَّنْ يُّتَقَبَّلَ مِنْكُمْ ۖ اِنَّكُمْ كُنْتُمْ قَوْمًا فٰسِقِيْنَ ۞

54. And nothing hinders their spendings being accepted from them, except that they disbelieve in Allah and in His Apostle and they do not come to prayer but while they are sluggish, and they do not spend but while they are unwilling.

وَمَا مَنَعَهُمْ اَنْ تُقْبَلَ مِنْهُمْ نَفَقٰتُهُمْ اِلَّآ اَنَّهُمْ كَفَرُوْا بِاللّٰهِ وَبِرَسُوْلِهٖ وَلَا يَاْتُوْنَ الصَّلٰوةَ اِلَّا وَهُمْ كُسَالٰى وَلَا يُنْفِقُوْنَ اِلَّا وَهُمْ كٰرِهُوْنَ ۞

55. Let not then their property and their children excite your admiration; Allah only wishes to chastise them with these in this world's life and (that) their souls may depart while they are unbelievers.

فَلَا تُعْجِبْكَ اَمْوَالُهُمْ وَلَآ اَوْلَادُهُمْ ۚ اِنَّمَا يُرِيْدُ اللّٰهُ لِيُعَذِّبَهُمْ بِهَا فِى الْحَيٰوةِ الدُّنْيَا وَتَزْهَقَ اَنْفُسُهُمْ وَهُمْ كٰفِرُوْنَ ۞

56. And they swear by Allah that they are most surely of you, and they are not of you, but they are a people who are afraid (of you).

وَيَحْلِفُوْنَ بِاللّٰهِ اِنَّهُمْ لَمِنْكُمْ ۚ وَمَا هُمْ مِّنْكُمْ وَلٰكِنَّهُمْ قَوْمٌ يَّفْرَقُوْنَ ۞

57. If they could find a refuge or cave or a place to enter into, they would certainly have turned thereto, running away in all haste.

لَوْ يَجِدُوْنَ مَلْجَأً اَوْ مَغٰرٰتٍ اَوْ مُدَّخَلًا لَّوَلَّوْا اِلَيْهِ وَهُمْ يَجْمَحُوْنَ ۞

58. And of them there are those who blame you with respect to the alms; so if they are given from it they are pleased, and if they are not given from it, lo! they are full of rage.

وَمِنْهُمْ مَّنْ يَّلْمِزُكَ فِى الصَّدَقٰتِ ۚ فَاِنْ اُعْطُوْا مِنْهَا رَضُوْا وَاِنْ لَّمْ يُعْطَوْا مِنْهَآ اِذَا هُمْ يَسْخَطُوْنَ ۞

59. And if they were content with what Allah and His Apostle gave them, and had said: Allah is sufficient for us; Allah will soon give us (more) out of His grace and His Apostle too; surely to Allah do we make our petition.

وَلَوْ اَنَّهُمْ رَضُوْا مَآ اٰتٰىهُمُ اللّٰهُ وَرَسُوْلُهٗ ۙ وَقَالُوْا حَسْبُنَا اللّٰهُ سَيُؤْتِيْنَا اللّٰهُ مِنْ فَضْلِهٖ وَرَسُوْلُهٗ ۤ اِنَّآ اِلَى اللّٰهِ رٰغِبُوْنَ ۞

60. Alms are only for the poor and the needy, and the officials (appointed) over them, and those whose hearts are made to incline (to truth) and the (ransoming of) captives and those in debts and in the way of Allah and the wayfarer; an ordinance from Allah; and Allah is knowing, Wise.

اِنَّمَا الصَّدَقٰتُ لِلْفُقَرَآءِ وَالْمَسٰكِيْنِ وَالْعٰمِلِيْنَ عَلَيْهَا وَالْمُؤَلَّفَةِ قُلُوْبُهُمْ وَفِى الرِّقَابِ وَالْغٰرِمِيْنَ وَفِىْ سَبِيْلِ اللهِ وَابْنِ السَّبِيْلِ فَرِيْضَةً مِّنَ اللهِ وَاللهُ عَلِيْمٌ حَكِيْمٌ ۝

61. And there are some of them who molest the Prophet and say: He is one who believes every thing that he hears; say: A hearer of good for you (who) believes in Allah and believes the faithful and a mercy for those of you who believe; and (as for) those who molest the Apostle of Allah, they shall have a painful punishment.

وَمِنْهُمُ الَّذِيْنَ يُؤْذُوْنَ النَّبِيَّ وَيَقُوْلُوْنَ هُوَ اُذُنٌ قُلْ اُذُنُ خَيْرٍ لَّكُمْ يُؤْمِنُ بِاللهِ وَيُؤْمِنُ لِلْمُؤْمِنِيْنَ وَرَحْمَةٌ لِّلَّذِيْنَ اٰمَنُوْا مِنْكُمْ وَالَّذِيْنَ يُؤْذُوْنَ رَسُوْلَ اللهِ لَهُمْ عَذَابٌ اَلِيْمٌ ۝

62. They swear to you by Allah that they might please you, and Allah, as well as His Apostle, has a greater right that they should please Him, if they are believers.

يَحْلِفُوْنَ بِاللهِ لَكُمْ لِيُرْضُوْكُمْ وَاللهُ وَرَسُوْلُهُ اَحَقُّ اَنْ يُّرْضُوْهُ اِنْ كَانُوْا مُؤْمِنِيْنَ ۝

63. Do they not know that whoever acts in opposition to Allah and His Apostle, he shall surely have the fire of hell to abide in it? That is the grievous abasement.

اَلَمْ يَعْلَمُوْٓا اَنَّهُ مَنْ يُّحَادِدِ اللهَ وَرَسُوْلَهُ فَاَنَّ لَهُ نَارَ جَهَنَّمَ خَالِدًا فِيْهَا ذٰلِكَ الْخِزْيُ الْعَظِيْمُ ۝

64. The hypocrites fear lest a chapter should be sent down to them telling them plainly of what is in their hearts. Say: Go on mocking, surely Allah will bring forth what you fear.

يَحْذَرُ الْمُنٰفِقُوْنَ اَنْ تُنَزَّلَ عَلَيْهِمْ سُوْرَةٌ تُنَبِّئُهُمْ بِمَا فِىْ قُلُوْبِهِمْ قُلِ اسْتَهْزِءُوْا اِنَّ اللهَ مُخْرِجٌ مَّا تَحْذَرُوْنَ ۝

65. And if you should question them, they would certainly say: We were only idly discoursing and sporting. Say: Was it at Allah and His communications and His Apostle that you mocked?

وَلَئِنْ سَاَلْتَهُمْ لَيَقُوْلُنَّ اِنَّمَا كُنَّا نَخُوْضُ وَنَلْعَبُ قُلْ اَبِاللهِ وَاٰيٰتِهِ وَرَسُوْلِهِ كُنْتُمْ تَسْتَهْزِءُوْنَ ۝

66. Do not make excuses; you have denied indeed after you had believed; if We pardon a party of you, We will chastise (another) party because they are guilty.

لَا تَعْتَذِرُوْا قَدْ كَفَرْتُمْ بَعْدَ اِيْمَانِكُمْ اِنْ نَّعْفُ عَنْ طَآئِفَةٍ مِّنْكُمْ نُعَذِّبْ طَآئِفَةً بِاَنَّهُمْ كَانُوْا مُجْرِمِيْنَ ۝

67. The hypocritical men and the hypocritical women are all alike; they enjoin evil and forbid good and withhold their hands; they have forsaken Allah, so He has forsaken them; surely the hypocrites are the transgressors.

اَلْمُنٰفِقُوْنَ وَالْمُنٰفِقٰتُ بَعْضُهُمْ مِّنْ بَعْضٍ يَاْمُرُوْنَ بِالْمُنْكَرِ وَيَنْهَوْنَ عَنِ الْمَعْرُوْفِ وَيَقْبِضُوْنَ اَيْدِيَهُمْ نَسُوا اللهَ فَنَسِيَهُمْ اِنَّ الْمُنٰفِقِيْنَ هُمُ الْفٰسِقُوْنَ ۝

177

68. Allah has promised the hypocritical men and the hypocritical women and the unbelievers the fire of hell to abide therein; it is enough for them; and Allah has cursed them and they shall have lasting punishment.

وَعَدَ اللهُ الْمُنٰفِقِيْنَ وَالْمُنٰفِقٰتِ وَالْكُفَّارَ نَارَ جَهَنَّمَ خٰلِدِيْنَ فِيْهَا ۖ هِيَ حَسْبُهُمْ ۚ وَلَعَنَهُمُ اللهُ ۚ وَلَهُمْ عَذَابٌ مُّقِيْمٌ ۙ ٦٨

69. Like those before you; they were stronger than you in power and more abundant in wealth and children, so they enjoyed their portion; thus have you enjoyed your portion as those before you enjoyed their portion; and you entered into vain discourses like the vain discourses in which entered those before you. These are they whose works are null in this world and the hereafter; and these are they who are the losers.

كَالَّذِيْنَ مِنْ قَبْلِكُمْ كَانُوْۤا أَشَدَّ مِنْكُمْ قُوَّةً وَّأَكْثَرَ أَمْوَالًا وَّأَوْلَادًا ۖ فَاسْتَمْتَعُوْا بِخَلَاقِهِمْ فَاسْتَمْتَعْتُمْ بِخَلَاقِكُمْ كَمَا اسْتَمْتَعَ الَّذِيْنَ مِنْ قَبْلِكُمْ بِخَلَاقِهِمْ وَخُضْتُمْ كَالَّذِيْ خَاضُوْا ۚ أُولٰئِكَ حَبِطَتْ أَعْمَالُهُمْ فِي الدُّنْيَا وَالْآخِرَةِ ۚ وَأُولٰئِكَ هُمُ الْخَاسِرُوْنَ ٦٩

70. Has not the news of those before them come to them; of the people of Nuh and Ad and Samood, and the people of Ibrahim and the dwellers of Madyan and the overthrown cities; their apostles came to them with clear arguments; so it was not Allah Who should do them injustice, but they were unjust to themselves.

أَلَمْ يَأْتِهِمْ نَبَأُ الَّذِيْنَ مِنْ قَبْلِهِمْ قَوْمِ نُوْحٍ وَّعَادٍ وَّثَمُوْدَ ۙ وَقَوْمِ إِبْرَاهِيْمَ وَأَصْحٰبِ مَدْيَنَ وَالْمُؤْتَفِكٰتِ ۚ أَتَتْهُمْ رُسُلُهُمْ بِالْبَيِّنٰتِ ۖ فَمَا كَانَ اللهُ لِيَظْلِمَهُمْ وَلٰكِنْ كَانُوْۤا أَنْفُسَهُمْ يَظْلِمُوْنَ ٧٠

71. And (as for) the believing men and the believing women, they are guardians of each other; they enjoin good and forbid evil and keep up prayer and pay the poor-rate, and obey Allah and His Apostle; (as for) these, Allah will show mercy to them; surely Allah is Mighty, Wise.

وَالْمُؤْمِنُوْنَ وَالْمُؤْمِنٰتُ بَعْضُهُمْ أَوْلِيَآءُ بَعْضٍ ۚ يَأْمُرُوْنَ بِالْمَعْرُوْفِ وَيَنْهَوْنَ عَنِ الْمُنْكَرِ وَيُقِيْمُوْنَ الصَّلٰوةَ وَيُؤْتُوْنَ الزَّكٰوةَ وَيُطِيْعُوْنَ اللهَ وَرَسُوْلَهُ ۚ أُولٰئِكَ سَيَرْحَمُهُمُ اللهُ ۗ إِنَّ اللهَ عَزِيْزٌ حَكِيْمٌ ٧١

72. Allah has promised to the believing men and the believing women gardens, beneath which rivers flow, to abide in them, and goodly dwellings in gardens of perpetual abode; and best of all is Allah's goodly pleasure that is the grand achievement.

وَعَدَ اللهُ الْمُؤْمِنِيْنَ وَالْمُؤْمِنٰتِ جَنّٰتٍ تَجْرِيْ مِنْ تَحْتِهَا الْأَنْهٰرُ خٰلِدِيْنَ فِيْهَا وَمَسٰكِنَ طَيِّبَةً فِيْ جَنّٰتِ عَدْنٍ ۚ وَرِضْوَانٌ مِّنَ اللهِ أَكْبَرُ ۚ ذٰلِكَ هُوَ الْفَوْزُ الْعَظِيْمُ ۙ ٧٢

73. O Prophet! strive hard against the unbelievers and the hypocrites and be unyielding to them; and their abode is hell, and evil is the destination.

يَا۟يُّهَا النَّبِيُّ جَاهِدِ الْكُفَّارَ وَالْمُنَافِقِيْنَ وَاغْلُظْ عَلَيْهِمْ ۗ وَمَأْوٰىهُمْ جَهَنَّمُ ۗ وَبِئْسَ الْمَصِيْرُ ۞

74. They swear by Allah that they did not speak, and certainly they did speak, the word of unbelief, and disbelieved after their Islam, and they had determined upon what they have not been able to effect, and they did not find fault except because Allah and His Apostle enriched them out of His grace; therefore if they repent, it will be good for them; and if they turn back, Allah will chastise them with a painful chastisement in this world and the hereafter, and they shall not have in the land any guardian or a helper.

يَحْلِفُوْنَ بِاللهِ مَا قَالُوْا ۗ وَلَقَدْ قَالُوْا كَلِمَةَ الْكُفْرِ وَكَفَرُوْا بَعْدَ اِسْلَامِهِمْ وَهَمُّوْا بِمَا لَمْ يَنَالُوْا ۚ وَمَا نَقَمُوْا اِلَّا اَنْ اَغْنٰىهُمُ اللهُ وَرَسُوْلُهٗ مِنْ فَضْلِهٖ ۚ فَاِنْ يَّتُوْبُوْا يَكُ خَيْرًا لَّهُمْ ۚ وَاِنْ يَّتَوَلَّوْا يُعَذِّبْهُمُ اللهُ عَذَابًا اَلِيْمًا فِى الدُّنْيَا وَالْاٰخِرَةِ ۚ وَمَا لَهُمْ فِى الْاَرْضِ مِنْ وَّلِيٍّ وَّلَا نَصِيْرٍ ۞

75. And there are those of them who made a covenant with Allah: If He give us out of His grace, we will certainly give alms and we will certainly be of the good.

وَمِنْهُمْ مَّنْ عَاهَدَ اللهَ لَئِنْ اٰتٰىنَا مِنْ فَضْلِهٖ لَنَصَّدَّقَنَّ وَلَنَكُوْنَنَّ مِنَ الصّٰلِحِيْنَ ۞

76. But when He gave them out of His grace, they became niggardly of it and they turned back and they withdrew.

فَلَمَّا اٰتٰىهُمْ مِّنْ فَضْلِهٖ بَخِلُوْا بِهٖ وَتَوَلَّوْا وَّهُمْ مُّعْرِضُوْنَ ۞

77. So He made hypocrisy to follow as a consequence into their hearts till the day when they shall meet Him because they failed to perform towards Allah what they had promised with Him and because they told lies.

فَاَعْقَبَهُمْ نِفَاقًا فِيْ قُلُوْبِهِمْ اِلٰى يَوْمِ يَلْقَوْنَهٗ بِمَا اَخْلَفُوا اللهَ مَا وَعَدُوْهُ وَبِمَا كَانُوْا يَكْذِبُوْنَ ۞

78. Do they not know that Allah knows their hidden thoughts and their secret counsels, and that Allah is the great Knower of the unseen things?

اَلَمْ يَعْلَمُوْا اَنَّ اللهَ يَعْلَمُ سِرَّهُمْ وَنَجْوٰىهُمْ وَاَنَّ اللهَ عَلَّامُ الْغُيُوْبِ ۞

79. They who taunt those of the faithful who give their alms freely, and those who give to the extent of their earnings, and scoff at them; Allah will pay them back their scoffing, and they shall have a painful chastisement.

اَلَّذِيْنَ يَلْمِزُوْنَ الْمُطَّوِّعِيْنَ مِنَ الْمُؤْمِنِيْنَ فِى الصَّدَقٰتِ وَالَّذِيْنَ لَا يَجِدُوْنَ اِلَّا جُهْدَهُمْ فَيَسْخَرُوْنَ مِنْهُمْ ۙ سَخِرَ اللهُ مِنْهُمْ ۖ وَلَهُمْ عَذَابٌ اَلِيْمٌ ۞

80. Ask forgiveness for them or do not ask forgiveness for them; even if you ask forgiveness for them seventy times, Allah will not forgive them; this is because they disbelieve in Allah and His Apostle, and Allah does not guide the transgressing people.

اِسْتَغْفِرْ لَهُمْ اَوْ لَا تَسْتَغْفِرْ لَهُمْ ۗ اِنْ تَسْتَغْفِرْ لَهُمْ سَبْعِيْنَ مَرَّةً فَلَنْ يَّغْفِرَ اللهُ لَهُمْ ۚ ذٰلِكَ بِاَنَّهُمْ كَفَرُوْا بِاللهِ وَرَسُوْلِهٖ ۗ وَاللهُ لَا يَهْدِى الْقَوْمَ الْفٰسِقِيْنَ ۞

81. Those who were left behind were glad on account of their sitting behind Allah's Apostle and they were averse from striving in Allah's way with their property and their persons, and said: Do not go forth in the heat. Say: The fire of hell is much severe in heat. Would that they understood (it).

فَرِحَ الْمُخَلَّفُوْنَ بِمَقْعَدِهِمْ خِلْفَ رَسُوْلِ اللهِ وَكَرِهُوْا اَنْ يُّجَاهِدُوْا بِاَمْوَالِهِمْ وَاَنْفُسِهِمْ فِيْ سَبِيْلِ اللهِ وَقَالُوْا لَا تَنْفِرُوْا فِى الْحَرِّ ۖ قُلْ نَارُ جَهَنَّمَ اَشَدُّ حَرًّا ۚ لَوْ كَانُوْا يَفْقَهُوْنَ ۝

82. Therefore they shall laugh little and weep much as a recompense for what they earned.

فَلْيَضْحَكُوْا قَلِيْلًا وَّلْيَبْكُوْا كَثِيْرًا ۚ جَزَاءًۢ بِمَا كَانُوْا يَكْسِبُوْنَ ۝

83. Therefore if Allah brings you back to a party of them, and then they ask your permission to go forth, say: By no means shall you ever go forth with me and by no means shall you fight an enemy with me; surely you chose to sit the first time, therefore sit (now) with those who remain behind.

فَاِنْ رَّجَعَكَ اللهُ اِلٰى طَآئِفَةٍ مِّنْهُمْ فَاسْتَأْذَنُوْكَ لِلْخُرُوْجِ فَقُلْ لَّنْ تَخْرُجُوْا مَعِيَ اَبَدًا وَّلَنْ تُقَاتِلُوْا مَعِيَ عَدُوًّا ۚ اِنَّكُمْ رَضِيْتُمْ بِالْقُعُوْدِ اَوَّلَ مَرَّةٍ فَاقْعُدُوْا مَعَ الْخٰلِفِيْنَ ۝

84. And never offer prayer for any one of them who dies and do not stand by his grave; surely they disbelieve in Allah and His Apostle and they shall die in transgression.

وَلَا تُصَلِّ عَلٰٓى اَحَدٍ مِّنْهُمْ مَّاتَ اَبَدًا وَّلَا تَقُمْ عَلٰى قَبْرِهٖ ۚ اِنَّهُمْ كَفَرُوْا بِاللهِ وَرَسُوْلِهٖ وَمَاتُوْا وَهُمْ فٰسِقُوْنَ ۝

85. And let not their property and their children excite your admiration; Allah only wishes to chastise them with these in this world and (that) their souls may depart while they are unbelievers

وَلَا تُعْجِبْكَ اَمْوَالُهُمْ وَاَوْلَادُهُمْ ۚ اِنَّمَا يُرِيْدُ اللهُ اَنْ يُّعَذِّبَهُمْ بِهَا فِى الدُّنْيَا وَتَزْهَقَ اَنْفُسُهُمْ وَهُمْ كٰفِرُوْنَ ۝

86. And whenever a chapter is revealed, saying: Believe in Allah and strive hard along with His Apostle, those having ampleness of means ask permission of you and say: Leave us (behind), that we may be with those who sit.

وَاِذَآ اُنْزِلَتْ سُوْرَةٌ اَنْ اٰمِنُوْا بِاللهِ وَجَاهِدُوْا مَعَ رَسُوْلِهِ اسْتَأْذَنَكَ اُولُوا الطَّوْلِ مِنْهُمْ وَقَالُوْا ذَرْنَا نَكُنْ مَّعَ الْقٰعِدِيْنَ ۝

87. They preferred to be with those who remained behind, and a seal is set on their hearts so they do not understand.

رَضُوْا بِاَنْ يَّكُوْنُوْا مَعَ الْخَوَالِفِ وَطُبِعَ عَلٰى قُلُوْبِهِمْ فَهُمْ لَا يَفْقَهُوْنَ ۝

88. But the Apostle and those who believe with him strive hard with their property and their persons; and these it is who shall have the good things and these it is who shall be successful.

لكِنِ الرَّسُوْلُ وَالَّذِيْنَ اٰمَنُوْا مَعَهٗ جٰهَدُوْا بِاَمْوَالِهِمْ وَاَنْفُسِهِمْ وَاُولٰٓئِكَ لَهُمُ الْخَيْرٰتُ وَاُولٰٓئِكَ هُمُ الْمُفْلِحُوْنَ ۝

89. Allah has prepared for them gardens beneath which rivers flow, to abide in them; that is the great achievement.

اَعَدَّ اللّٰهُ لَهُمْ جَنّٰتٍ تَجْرِيْ مِنْ تَحْتِهَا الْاَنْهٰرُ خٰلِدِيْنَ فِيْهَا ذٰلِكَ الْفَوْزُ الْعَظِيْمُ ۝

90. And the defaulters from among the dwellers of the desert came that permission may be given to them and they sat (at home) who lied to Allah and His Apostle; a painful chastisement shall afflict those of them who disbelieved.

وَجَآءَ الْمُعَذِّرُوْنَ مِنَ الْاَعْرَابِ لِيُؤْذَنَ لَهُمْ وَقَعَدَ الَّذِيْنَ كَذَبُوا اللّٰهَ وَرَسُوْلَهٗ سَيُصِيْبُ الَّذِيْنَ كَفَرُوْا مِنْهُمْ عَذَابٌ اَلِيْمٌ ۝

91. It shall be no crime in the weak, nor in the sick, nor in those who do not find what they should spend (to stay behind), so long as they are sincere to Allah and His Apostle; there is no way (to blame) against the doers of good; and Allah is Forgiving, Merciful;

لَيْسَ عَلَى الضُّعَفَآءِ وَلَا عَلَى الْمَرْضٰى وَلَا عَلَى الَّذِيْنَ لَا يَجِدُوْنَ مَا يُنْفِقُوْنَ حَرَجٌ اِذَا نَصَحُوْا لِلّٰهِ وَرَسُوْلِهٖ مَا عَلَى الْمُحْسِنِيْنَ مِنْ سَبِيْلٍ وَ اللّٰهُ غَفُوْرٌ رَّحِيْمٌ ۝

92. Nor in those who when they came to you that you might carry them, you said: I cannot find that on which to carry you; they went back while their eyes overflowed with tears on account of grief for not finding that which they should spend.

وَّلَا عَلَى الَّذِيْنَ اِذَا مَا اَتَوْكَ لِتَحْمِلَهُمْ قُلْتَ لَا اَجِدُ مَا اَحْمِلُكُمْ عَلَيْهِ تَوَلَّوْا وَّاَعْيُنُهُمْ تَفِيْضُ مِنَ الدَّمْعِ حَزَنًا اَلَّا يَجِدُوْا مَا يُنْفِقُوْنَ ۝

93. The way (to blame) is only against those who ask permission of you though they are rich; they have chosen to be with those who remained behind, and Allah has set a seal upon their hearts so they do not know.

اِنَّمَا السَّبِيْلُ عَلَى الَّذِيْنَ يَسْتَأْذِنُوْنَكَ وَهُمْ اَغْنِيَآءُ رَضُوْا بِاَنْ يَّكُوْنُوْا مَعَ الْخَوَالِفِ وَطَبَعَ اللّٰهُ عَلٰى قُلُوْبِهِمْ فَهُمْ لَا يَعْلَمُوْنَ ۝

94. They will excuse themselves to you when you go back to them. Say: Urge no excuse, by no means will we believe you; indeed Allah has informed us of matters relating to you; and now Allah and His Apostle will see your doings, then you shall be brought back to the Knower of the unseen and the seen, then He will inform you of what you did.

يَعْتَذِرُوْنَ اِلَيْكُمْ اِذَا رَجَعْتُمْ اِلَيْهِمْ قُلْ لَّا تَعْتَذِرُوْا لَنْ نُّؤْمِنَ لَكُمْ قَدْ نَبَّاَنَا اللّٰهُ مِنْ اَخْبَارِكُمْ وَسَيَرَى اللّٰهُ عَمَلَكُمْ وَرَسُوْلُهٗ ثُمَّ تُرَدُّوْنَ اِلٰى عٰلِمِ الْغَيْبِ وَالشَّهَادَةِ فَيُنَبِّئُكُمْ بِمَا كُنْتُمْ تَعْمَلُوْنَ ۝

95. They will swear to you by Allah when you return to them so that you may turn aside from them; so do turn aside from them; surely they are unclean and their abode is hell; a recompense for what they earned.

سَيَحْلِفُوْنَ بِاللّٰهِ لَكُمْ اِذَا انْقَلَبْتُمْ اِلَيْهِمْ لِتُعْرِضُوْا عَنْهُمْ فَاَعْرِضُوْا عَنْهُمْ اِنَّهُمْ رِجْسٌ وَّمَاْوٰىهُمْ جَهَنَّمُ جَزَاۤءًۢ بِمَا كَانُوْا يَكْسِبُوْنَ ۟

96. They will swear to you that you may be pleased with them; but if you are pleased with them, yet surely Allah is not pleased with the transgressing people.

يَحْلِفُوْنَ لَكُمْ لِتَرْضَوْا عَنْهُمْ فَاِنْ تَرْضَوْا عَنْهُمْ فَاِنَّ اللّٰهَ لَا يَرْضٰى عَنِ الْقَوْمِ الْفٰسِقِيْنَ ۟

97. The dwellers of the desert are very hard in unbelief and hypocrisy, and more disposed not to know the limits of what Allah has revealed to His Apostle; and Allah is Knowing, Wise.

اَلْاَعْرَابُ اَشَدُّ كُفْرًا وَّنِفَاقًا وَّاَجْدَرُ اَلَّا يَعْلَمُوْا حُدُوْدَ مَاۤ اَنْزَلَ اللّٰهُ عَلٰى رَسُوْلِهٖ وَاللّٰهُ عَلِيْمٌ حَكِيْمٌ ۟

98. And of the dwellers of the desert are those who take what they spend to be a fine, and they wait (the befalling of) calamities to you; on them (will be) the evil calamity; and Allah is Hearing, Knowing.

وَمِنَ الْاَعْرَابِ مَنْ يَّتَّخِذُ مَا يُنْفِقُ مَغْرَمًا وَّيَتَرَبَّصُ بِكُمُ الدَّوَاۤئِرَ عَلَيْهِمْ دَاۤئِرَةُ السَّوْءِ وَاللّٰهُ سَمِيْعٌ عَلِيْمٌ ۟

99. And of the dwellers of the desert are those who believe in Allah and the latter day and take what they spend to be (means of) the nearness of Allah and the Apostle's prayers; surely it shall be means of nearness for them; Allah will make them enter into His mercy; surely Allah is Forgiving, Merciful.

وَمِنَ الْاَعْرَابِ مَنْ يُّؤْمِنُ بِاللّٰهِ وَالْيَوْمِ الْاٰخِرِ وَيَتَّخِذُ مَا يُنْفِقُ قُرُبٰتٍ عِنْدَ اللّٰهِ وَصَلَوٰتِ الرَّسُوْلِ اَلَاۤ اِنَّهَا قُرْبَةٌ لَّهُمْ سَيُدْخِلُهُمُ اللّٰهُ فِيْ رَحْمَتِهٖ اِنَّ اللّٰهَ غَفُوْرٌ رَّحِيْمٌ ۟

100. And (as for) the foremost, the first of the Muhajirs and the Ansars, and those who followed them in goodness, Allah is well pleased with them and they are well pleased with Him, and He has prepared for them gardens beneath which rivers flow, to abide in them for ever; that is the mighty achievement.

وَالسّٰبِقُوْنَ الْاَوَّلُوْنَ مِنَ الْمُهٰجِرِيْنَ وَالْاَنْصَارِ وَالَّذِيْنَ اتَّبَعُوْهُمْ بِاِحْسَانٍ رَّضِيَ اللّٰهُ عَنْهُمْ وَرَضُوْا عَنْهُ وَاَعَدَّ لَهُمْ جَنّٰتٍ تَجْرِيْ تَحْتَهَا الْاَنْهٰرُ خٰلِدِيْنَ فِيْهَاۤ اَبَدًا ذٰلِكَ الْفَوْزُ الْعَظِيْمُ ۟

101. And from among those who are round about you of the dwellers of the desert there are hypocrites, and from among the people of Medina (also); they are stubborn in hypocrisy; you do not know them; We know them; We will chastise them twice, then shall they be turned back to a grievous chastisement.

وَمِمَّنْ حَوْلَكُمْ مِّنَ الْاَعْرَابِ مُنٰفِقُوْنَ وَمِنْ اَهْلِ الْمَدِيْنَةِ مَرَدُوْا عَلَى النِّفَاقِ لَا تَعْلَمُهُمْ نَحْنُ نَعْلَمُهُمْ سَنُعَذِّبُهُمْ مَّرَّتَيْنِ ثُمَّ يُرَدُّوْنَ اِلٰى عَذَابٍ عَظِيْمٍ ۟

182

102. And others have confessed their faults, they have mingled a good deed and an evil one; may be Allah will turn to them (mercifully); surely Allah is Forgiving, Merciful.

103. Take alms out of their property, you would cleanse them and purify them thereby, and pray for them; surely your prayer is a relief to them; and Allah is Hearing, Knowing.

104. Do they not know that Allah accepts repentance from His servants and takes the alms, and that Allah is the Oft-returning (to mercy), the Merciful?

105. And say: Work; so Allah will see your work and (so will) His Apostle and the believers; and you shall be brought back to the Knower of the unseen and the seen, then He will inform you of what you did.

106. And others are made to await Allah's command, whether He chastise them or whether He turn to them (mercifully); and Allah is Knowing, Wise.

107. And those who built a masjid to cause harm and for unbelief and to cause disunion among the believers and an ambush to him who made war against Allah and His Apostle before; and they will certainly swear: We did not desire aught but good; and Allah bears witness that they are most surely liars.

108. Never stand in it; certainly a masjid founded on piety from the very first day is more deserving that you should stand in it; in it are men who love that they should be purified; and Allah loves those who purify themselves.

109. Is he, therefore, better who lays his foundation on fear of Allah and (His) good pleasure, or he who lays his foundation on the edge of a cracking hollowed bank, so it broke down with him into the fire of hell; and Allah does not guide the unjust people.

وَاٰخَرُوۡنَ اعۡتَرَفُوۡا بِذُنُوۡبِهِمۡ خَلَطُوۡا عَمَلًا صَالِحًا وَّاٰخَرَ سَيِّئًا ؕ عَسَى اللّٰهُ اَنۡ يَّتُوۡبَ عَلَيۡهِمۡ ؕ اِنَّ اللّٰهَ غَفُوۡرٌ رَّحِيۡمٌ ۞

خُذۡ مِنۡ اَمۡوَالِهِمۡ صَدَقَةً تُطَهِّرُهُمۡ وَتُزَكِّيۡهِمۡ بِهَا وَصَلِّ عَلَيۡهِمۡ ؕ اِنَّ صَلٰوتَكَ سَكَنٌ لَّهُمۡ ؕ وَاللّٰهُ سَمِيۡعٌ عَلِيۡمٌ ۞

اَلَمۡ يَعۡلَمُوۡۤا اَنَّ اللّٰهَ هُوَ يَقۡبَلُ التَّوۡبَةَ عَنۡ عِبَادِهٖ وَيَاۡخُذُ الصَّدَقٰتِ وَاَنَّ اللّٰهَ هُوَ التَّوَّابُ الرَّحِيۡمُ ۞

وَقُلِ اعۡمَلُوۡا فَسَيَرَى اللّٰهُ عَمَلَكُمۡ وَرَسُوۡلُهٗ وَالۡمُؤۡمِنُوۡنَ ؕ وَسَتُرَدُّوۡنَ اِلٰى عٰلِمِ الۡغَيۡبِ وَالشَّهَادَةِ فَيُنَبِّئُكُمۡ بِمَا كُنۡتُمۡ تَعۡمَلُوۡنَ ۞

وَاٰخَرُوۡنَ مُرۡجَوۡنَ لِاَمۡرِ اللّٰهِ اِمَّا يُعَذِّبُهُمۡ وَاِمَّا يَتُوۡبُ عَلَيۡهِمۡ ؕ وَاللّٰهُ عَلِيۡمٌ حَكِيۡمٌ ۞

وَالَّذِيۡنَ اتَّخَذُوۡا مَسۡجِدًا ضِرَارًا وَّكُفۡرًا وَّتَفۡرِيۡقًا بَيۡنَ الۡمُؤۡمِنِيۡنَ وَاِرۡصَادًا لِّمَنۡ حَارَبَ اللّٰهَ وَرَسُوۡلَهٗ مِنۡ قَبۡلُ ؕ وَلَيَحۡلِفُنَّ اِنۡ اَرَدۡنَاۤ اِلَّا الۡحُسۡنٰى ؕ وَاللّٰهُ يَشۡهَدُ اِنَّهُمۡ لَكٰذِبُوۡنَ ۞

لَا تَقُمۡ فِيۡهِ اَبَدًا ؕ لَمَسۡجِدٌ اُسِّسَ عَلَى التَّقۡوٰى مِنۡ اَوَّلِ يَوۡمٍ اَحَقُّ اَنۡ تَقُوۡمَ فِيۡهِ ؕ فِيۡهِ رِجَالٌ يُّحِبُّوۡنَ اَنۡ يَّتَطَهَّرُوۡا ؕ وَاللّٰهُ يُحِبُّ الۡمُطَّهِّرِيۡنَ ۞

اَفَمَنۡ اَسَّسَ بُنۡيَانَهٗ عَلٰى تَقۡوٰى مِنَ اللّٰهِ وَرِضۡوَانٍ خَيۡرٌ اَمۡ مَّنۡ اَسَّسَ بُنۡيَانَهٗ عَلٰى شَفَا جُرُفٍ هَارٍ فَانۡهَارَ بِهٖ فِيۡ نَارِ جَهَنَّمَ ؕ وَاللّٰهُ لَا يَهۡدِى الۡقَوۡمَ الظّٰلِمِيۡنَ ۞

110. The building which they have built will ever continue to be a source of disquiet in their hearts, except that their hearts get cut into pieces; and Allah is Knowing, Wise.

لَا يَزَالُ بُنْيَانُهُمُ الَّذِى بَنَوْا رِيبَةً فِى قُلُوبِهِمْ اِلَّا اَنْ تَقَطَّعَ قُلُوبُهُمْ وَاللهُ عَلِيْمٌ حَكِيْمٌ ۝

111. Surely Allah has bought of the believers their persons and their property for this, that they shall have the garden; they fight in Allah's way, so they slay and are slain; a promise which is binding on Him in the Taurat and the Injeel and the Quran; and who is more faithful to his covenant than Allah? Rejoice therefore in the pledge which you have made; and that is the mighty achievement.

اِنَّ اللهَ اشْتَرٰى مِنَ الْمُؤْمِنِيْنَ اَنْفُسَهُمْ وَاَمْوَالَهُمْ بِاَنَّ لَهُمُ الْجَنَّةَ يُقَاتِلُوْنَ فِى سَبِيْلِ اللهِ فَيَقْتُلُوْنَ وَيُقْتَلُوْنَ وَعْدًا عَلَيْهِ حَقًّا فِى التَّوْرٰىةِ وَالْاِنْجِيْلِ وَالْقُرْاٰنِ وَمَنْ اَوْفٰى بِعَهْدِهٖ مِنَ اللهِ فَاسْتَبْشِرُوْا بِبَيْعِكُمُ الَّذِى بَايَعْتُمْ بِهٖ وَذٰلِكَ هُوَ الْفَوْزُ الْعَظِيْمُ ۝

112. They who turn (to Allah), who serve (Him), who praise (Him), who fast, who bow down, who prostrate themselves, who enjoin what is good and forbid what is evil, and who keep the limits of Allah; and give good news to the believers.

اَلتَّائِبُوْنَ الْعَابِدُوْنَ الْحَامِدُوْنَ السَّائِحُوْنَ الرَّاكِعُوْنَ السَّاجِدُوْنَ الْاٰمِرُوْنَ بِالْمَعْرُوْفِ وَالنَّاهُوْنَ عَنِ الْمُنْكَرِ وَالْحٰفِظُوْنَ لِحُدُوْدِ اللهِ وَبَشِّرِ الْمُؤْمِنِيْنَ ۝

113. It is not (fit) for the Prophet and those who believe that they should ask forgiveness for the polytheists, even though they should be near relatives, after it has become clear to them that they are inmates of the flaming fire.

مَا كَانَ لِلنَّبِىِّ وَالَّذِيْنَ اٰمَنُوْا اَنْ يَّسْتَغْفِرُوْا لِلْمُشْرِكِيْنَ وَلَوْ كَانُوْا اُولِى قُرْبٰى مِنْ بَعْدِ مَا تَبَيَّنَ لَهُمْ اَنَّهُمْ اَصْحٰبُ الْجَحِيْمِ ۝

114. And Ibrahim asking forgiveness for his sire was only owing to a promise which he had made to him; but when it became clear to him that he was an enemy of Allah, he declared himself to be clear of him; most surely Ibrahim was very tender-hearted, forbearing.

وَمَا كَانَ اسْتِغْفَارُ اِبْرٰهِيْمَ لِاَبِيْهِ اِلَّا عَنْ مَّوْعِدَةٍ وَّعَدَهَا اِيَّاهُ فَلَمَّا تَبَيَّنَ لَهٗ اَنَّهٗ عَدُوٌّ لِّلّٰهِ تَبَرَّاَ مِنْهُ اِنَّ اِبْرٰهِيْمَ لَاَوَّاهٌ حَلِيْمٌ ۝

115. It is not (attributable to) Allah that He should lead a people astray after He has guided them; He even makes clear to them what they should guard against; surely Allah knows all things.

وَمَا كَانَ اللهُ لِيُضِلَّ قَوْمًا بَعْدَ اِذْ هَدٰىهُمْ حَتّٰى يُبَيِّنَ لَهُمْ مَا يَتَّقُوْنَ اِنَّ اللهَ بِكُلِّ شَىْءٍ عَلِيْمٌ ۝

116. Surely Allah's is the kingdom of the heavens and the earth; He brings to life and causes to die; and there is not for you besides Allah any Guardian or Helper.

اِنَّ اللهَ لَهٗ مُلْكُ السَّمٰوٰتِ وَالْاَرْضِ يُحْيٖ وَيُمِيْتُ وَمَا لَكُمْ مِّنْ دُوْنِ اللهِ مِنْ وَّلِىٍّ وَّلَا نَصِيْرٍ ۝

117. Certainly Allah has turned (mercifully) to the Prophet and those who fled (their homes) and the helpers who followed him in the hour of straitness after the hearts of a part of them were about to deviate, then He turned to them (mercifully); surely to them He is Compassionate, Merciful.

118. And to the three who were left behind, until the earth became strait to them notwithstanding its spaciousness and their souls were also straitened to them; and they knew it for certain that there was no refuge from Allah but in Him; then He turned to them (mercifully) that they might turn (to Him); surely Allah is the Oft-returning (to mercy), the Merciful.

119. O you who believe! be careful of (your duty to) Allah and be with the true ones.

120. It did not beseem the people of Medina and those round about them of the dwellers of the desert to remain behind the Apostle of Allah, nor should they desire (anything) for themselves in preference to him; this is because there afflicts them not thirst or fatigue or hunger in Allah's way, nor do they tread a path which enrages the unbelievers, nor do they attain from the enemy what they attain, but a good work is written down to them on account of it; surely Allah does not waste the reward of the doers of good;

121. Nor do they spend anything that may be spent, small or great, nor do they traverse a valley, but it is written down to their credit, that Allah may reward them with the best of what they have done.

122. And it does not beseem the believers that they should go forth all together; why should not then a company from every party from among them go forth that they may apply themselves to obtain understanding in religion, and that they may warn their people when they come back to them that they may be cautious?

185

123. O you who believe! fight those of the unbelievers who are near to you and let them find in you hardness; and know that Allah is with those who guard (against evil).

يَاۤ اَيُّهَا الَّذِيْنَ اٰمَنُوْا قَاتِلُوا الَّذِيْنَ يَلُوْنَكُمْ مِّنَ الْكُفَّارِ وَلْيَجِدُوْا فِيْكُمْ غِلْظَةً ۚ وَاعْلَمُوْۤا اَنَّ اللّٰهَ مَعَ الْمُتَّقِيْنَ ۝

124. And whenever a chapter is revealed, there are some of them who say: Which of you has it strengthened in faith? Then as for those who believe, it strengthens them in faith and they rejoice.

وَاِذَا مَاۤ اُنْزِلَتْ سُوْرَةٌ فَمِنْهُمْ مَّنْ يَّقُوْلُ اَيُّكُمْ زَادَتْهُ هٰذِهٖۤ اِيْمَانًا ۚ فَاَمَّا الَّذِيْنَ اٰمَنُوْا فَزَادَتْهُمْ اِيْمَانًا وَّهُمْ يَسْتَبْشِرُوْنَ ۝

125. And as for those in whose hearts is a disease, it adds uncleanness to their uncleanness and they die while they are unbelievers.

وَاَمَّا الَّذِيْنَ فِيْ قُلُوْبِهِمْ مَّرَضٌ فَزَادَتْهُمْ رِجْسًا اِلٰى رِجْسِهِمْ وَمَاتُوْا وَهُمْ كٰفِرُوْنَ ۝

126. Do they not see that they are tried once or twice in every year, yet they do not turn (to Allah) nor do they mind.

اَوَلَا يَرَوْنَ اَنَّهُمْ يُفْتَنُوْنَ فِيْ كُلِّ عَامٍ مَّرَّةً اَوْ مَرَّتَيْنِ ثُمَّ لَا يَتُوْبُوْنَ وَلَا هُمْ يَذَّكَّرُوْنَ ۝

127. And whenever a chapter is revealed, they cast glances at one another: Does any one see you? Then they turn away: Allah has turned away their hearts because they are a people who do not understand.

وَاِذَا مَاۤ اُنْزِلَتْ سُوْرَةٌ نَّظَرَ بَعْضُهُمْ اِلٰى بَعْضٍ ۚ هَلْ يَرٰىكُمْ مِّنْ اَحَدٍ ثُمَّ انْصَرَفُوْا ۚ صَرَفَ اللّٰهُ قُلُوْبَهُمْ بِاَنَّهُمْ قَوْمٌ لَّا يَفْقَهُوْنَ ۝

128. Certainly an Apostle has come to you from among yourselves; grievous to him is your falling into distress, excessively solicitous respecting you; to the believers (he is) compassionate, merciful.

لَقَدْ جَآءَكُمْ رَسُوْلٌ مِّنْ اَنْفُسِكُمْ عَزِيْزٌ عَلَيْهِ مَا عَنِتُّمْ حَرِيْصٌ عَلَيْكُمْ بِالْمُؤْمِنِيْنَ رَءُوْفٌ رَّحِيْمٌ ۝

129. But if they turn back, say: Allah is sufficient for me, there is no god but He; on Him do I rely, and He is the Lord of mighty power.

فَاِنْ تَوَلَّوْا فَقُلْ حَسْبِيَ اللّٰهُ ۖ لَاۤ اِلٰهَ اِلَّا هُوَ ۖ عَلَيْهِ تَوَكَّلْتُ وَهُوَ رَبُّ الْعَرْشِ الْعَظِيْمِ ۝

YUNUS

**In the name of Allah,
the Beneficent, the Merciful.**

1. Alif Lam Ra. These are the verses of the wise Book.

2. What! is it a wonder to the people that We revealed to a man from among themselves, saying: Warn the people and give good news to those who believe that theirs is a footing of firmness with their Lord. The unbelievers say: This is most surely a manifest enchanter.

3. Surely your Lord is Allah, Who created the heavens and the earth in six periods, and He is firm in power, regulating the affair; there is no intercessor except after His permission; this is Allah, your Lord, therefore serve Him; will you not then mind?

4. To Him is your return, of all (of you); the promise of Allah (made) in truth; surely He begins the creation in the first instance, then He reproduces it, that He may with justice recompense those who believe and do good; and (as for) those who disbelieve, they shall have a drink of hot water and painful punishment because they disbelieved.

5. He it is Who made the sun a shining brightness and the moon a light, and ordained for it mansions that you might know the computation of years and the reckoning. Allah did not create it but with truth; He makes the signs manifest for a people who know.

6. Most surely in the variation of the night and the day, and what Allah has created in the heavens and the earth, there are signs for a people who guard (against evil).

بِسْمِ اللّٰهِ الرَّحْمٰنِ الرَّحِيْمِ ۝

الٓرٰ ۣ تِلْكَ اٰيٰتُ الْكِتٰبِ الْحَكِيْمِ ۝

اَكَانَ لِلنَّاسِ عَجَبًا اَنْ اَوْحَيْنَآ اِلٰى رَجُلٍ مِّنْهُمْ اَنْ اَنْذِرِ النَّاسَ وَبَشِّرِ الَّذِيْنَ اٰمَنُوْٓا اَنَّ لَهُمْ قَدَمَ صِدْقٍ عِنْدَ رَبِّهِمْ ۣ قَالَ الْكٰفِرُوْنَ اِنَّ هٰذَا لَسٰحِرٌ مُّبِيْنٌ ۝

اِنَّ رَبَّكُمُ اللّٰهُ الَّذِيْ خَلَقَ السَّمٰوٰتِ وَالْاَرْضَ فِيْ سِتَّةِ اَيَّامٍ ثُمَّ اسْتَوٰى عَلَى الْعَرْشِ يُدَبِّرُ الْاَمْرَ ۣ مَا مِنْ شَفِيْعٍ اِلَّا مِنْ بَعْدِ اِذْنِهٖ ۣ ذٰلِكُمُ اللّٰهُ رَبُّكُمْ فَاعْبُدُوْهُ ۣ اَفَلَا تَذَكَّرُوْنَ ۝

اِلَيْهِ مَرْجِعُكُمْ جَمِيْعًا ۣ وَعْدَ اللّٰهِ حَقًّا ۣ اِنَّهٗ يَبْدَؤُا الْخَلْقَ ثُمَّ يُعِيْدُهٗ لِيَجْزِيَ الَّذِيْنَ اٰمَنُوْا وَعَمِلُوا الصّٰلِحٰتِ بِالْقِسْطِ ۣ وَالَّذِيْنَ كَفَرُوْا لَهُمْ شَرَابٌ مِّنْ حَمِيْمٍ وَّعَذَابٌ اَلِيْمٌ ۣ بِمَا كَانُوْا يَكْفُرُوْنَ ۝

هُوَ الَّذِيْ جَعَلَ الشَّمْسَ ضِيَآءً وَّالْقَمَرَ نُوْرًا وَّقَدَّرَهٗ مَنَازِلَ لِتَعْلَمُوْا عَدَدَ السِّنِيْنَ وَالْحِسَابَ ۣ مَا خَلَقَ اللّٰهُ ذٰلِكَ اِلَّا بِالْحَقِّ ۣ يُفَصِّلُ الْاٰيٰتِ لِقَوْمٍ يَّعْلَمُوْنَ ۝

اِنَّ فِيْ اخْتِلَافِ الَّيْلِ وَالنَّهَارِ وَمَا خَلَقَ اللّٰهُ فِي السَّمٰوٰتِ وَالْاَرْضِ لَاٰيٰتٍ لِّقَوْمٍ يَّتَّقُوْنَ ۝

187

7. Surely those who do not hope in Our meeting and are pleased with this world's life and are content with it, and those who are heedless of Our communications:

8. (As for) those, their abode is the fire because of what they earned.

9. Surely (as for) those who believe and do good, their Lord will guide them by their faith; there shall flow from beneath them rivers in gardens of bliss.

10. Their cry in it shall be: Glory to Thee, O Allah! and their greeting in it shall be: Peace; and the last of their cry shall be: Praise be to Allah, the Lord of the worlds.

11. And if Allah should hasten the evil to men as they desire the hastening on of good, their doom should certainly have been decreed for them; but We leave those alone who hope not for Our meeting in their inordinacy, blindly wandering on.

12. And when affliction touches a man, he calls on Us, whether lying on his side or sitting or standing; but when We remove his affliction from him, he passes on as though he had never called on Us on account of an affliction that touched him; thus that which they do is made fair-seeming to the extravagant.

13. And certainly We did destroy generations before you when they were unjust, and their apostles had come to them with clear arguments, and they would not believe; thus do We recompense the guilty people.

14. Then We made you successors in the land after them so that We may see how you act.

15. And when Our clear communications are recited to them, those who hope not for Our meeting say: Bring a Quran other than this or change it. Say: It does not beseem me that I should change it of myself; I follow naught but what is revealed to me; surely I fear, if I disobey my Lord, the punishment of a mighty day.

16. Say: If Allah had desired (otherwise) I would not have recited it to you, nor would He have taught it to you; indeed I have lived a lifetime among you before it; do you not then understand?

قُلْ لَّوْ شَاءَ اللّٰهُ مَا تَلَوْتُهُ عَلَيْكُمْ وَلَاۤ اَدْرٰىكُمْ بِهٖ فَقَدْ لَبِثْتُ فِيْكُمْ عُمُرًا مِّنْ قَبْلِهٖ اَفَلَا تَعْقِلُوْنَ ۝

17. Who is then more unjust than who forges a lie against Allah or (who) gives the lie to His communications? Surely the guilty shall not be successful.

فَمَنْ اَظْلَمُ مِمَّنِ افْتَرٰى عَلَى اللّٰهِ كَذِبًا اَوْ كَذَّبَ بِاٰيٰتِهٖ اِنَّهٗ لَا يُفْلِحُ الْمُجْرِمُوْنَ ۝

18. And they serve beside Allah what can neither harm them nor profit them, and they say: These are our intercessors with Allah. Say: Do you (presume to) inform Allah of what He knows not in the heavens and the earth? Glory be to Him, and supremely exalted is He above what they set up (with Him).

وَيَعْبُدُوْنَ مِنْ دُوْنِ اللّٰهِ مَا لَا يَضُرُّهُمْ وَلَا يَنْفَعُهُمْ وَيَقُوْلُوْنَ هٰۤؤُلَاۤءِ شُفَعَاۤؤُنَا عِنْدَ اللّٰهِ قُلْ اَتُنَبِّئُوْنَ اللّٰهَ بِمَا لَا يَعْلَمُ فِى السَّمٰوٰتِ وَلَا فِى الْاَرْضِ سُبْحٰنَهٗ وَتَعٰلٰى عَمَّا يُشْرِكُوْنَ ۝

19. And people are naught but a single nation, so they disagree; and had not a word already gone forth from your Lord, the matter would have certainly been decided between them in respect of that concerning which they disagree.

وَمَا كَانَ النَّاسُ اِلَّاۤ اُمَّةً وَّاحِدَةً فَاخْتَلَفُوْا وَلَوْلَا كَلِمَةٌ سَبَقَتْ مِنْ رَّبِّكَ لَقُضِيَ بَيْنَهُمْ فِيْمَا فِيْهِ يَخْتَلِفُوْنَ ۝

20. And they say: Why is not a sign sent to him from his Lord? Say: The unseen is only for Allah; therefore wait—surely I too, with you am of those who wait.

وَيَقُوْلُوْنَ لَوْلَاۤ اُنْزِلَ عَلَيْهِ اٰيَةٌ مِّنْ رَّبِّهٖ فَقُلْ اِنَّمَا الْغَيْبُ لِلّٰهِ فَانْتَظِرُوْا اِنِّيْ مَعَكُمْ مِّنَ الْمُنْتَظِرِيْنَ ۝

21. And when We make people taste of mercy after an affliction touches them, lo! they devise plans against Our communication. Say: Allah is quicker to plan; surely Our messengers write down what you plan.

وَاِذَاۤ اَذَقْنَا النَّاسَ رَحْمَةً مِّنْ بَعْدِ ضَرَّاۤءَ مَسَّتْهُمْ اِذَا لَهُمْ مَّكْرٌ فِيْۤ اٰيَاتِنَا قُلِ اللّٰهُ اَسْرَعُ مَكْرًا اِنَّ رُسُلَنَا يَكْتُبُوْنَ مَا تَمْكُرُوْنَ ۝

22. He it is Who makes you travel by land and sea; until when you are in the ships, and they sail on with them in a pleasant breeze, and they rejoice, a violent wind overtakes them and the billows surge in on them from all sides, and they become certain that they are encompassed about, they pray to Allah, being sincere to Him in obedience: If Thou dost deliver us from this, we will most certainly be of the grateful ones.

هُوَ الَّذِيْ يُسَيِّرُكُمْ فِى الْبَرِّ وَالْبَحْرِ حَتّٰۤى اِذَا كُنْتُمْ فِى الْفُلْكِ وَجَرَيْنَ بِهِمْ بِرِيْحٍ طَيِّبَةٍ وَّفَرِحُوْا بِهَا جَاۤءَتْهَا رِيْحٌ عَاصِفٌ وَّجَاۤءَهُمُ الْمَوْجُ مِنْ كُلِّ مَكَانٍ وَّظَنُّوْۤا اَنَّهُمْ اُحِيْطَ بِهِمْ دَعَوُا اللّٰهَ مُخْلِصِيْنَ لَهُ الدِّيْنَ لَئِنْ اَنْجَيْتَنَا مِنْ هٰذِهٖ لَنَكُوْنَنَّ مِنَ الشّٰكِرِيْنَ ۝

189

23. But when He delivers them, lo! they are unjustly rebellious in the earth. O men! your rebellion is against your own souls—provision (only) of this world's life—then to Us shall be your return, so We will inform you of what you did.

فَلَمَّا أَنْجَاهُمْ إِذَا هُمْ يَبْغُوْنَ فِي الْأَرْضِ بِغَيْرِ الْحَقِّ يَا أَيُّهَا النَّاسُ إِنَّمَا بَغْيُكُمْ عَلَى أَنْفُسِكُمْ مَتَاعَ الْحَيٰوةِ الدُّنْيَا ثُمَّ إِلَيْنَا مَرْجِعُكُمْ فَنُنَبِّئُكُمْ بِمَا كُنْتُمْ تَعْمَلُوْنَ ۞

24. The likeness of this world's life is only as water which We send down from the cloud, then the herbage of the earth of which men and cattle eat grows luxuriantly thereby; until when the earth puts on its golden raiment and it becomes garnished, and its people think that they have power over it, Our command comes to it, by night or by day, so We render it as reaped seed-produce, as though it had not been in existence yesterday; thus do We make clear the communications for a people who reflect.

إِنَّمَا مَثَلُ الْحَيٰوةِ الدُّنْيَا كَمَاءٍ أَنْزَلْنٰهُ مِنَ السَّمَاءِ فَاخْتَلَطَ بِهِ نَبَاتُ الْأَرْضِ مِمَّا يَأْكُلُ النَّاسُ وَ الْأَنْعَامُ حَتّٰى إِذَا أَخَذَتِ الْأَرْضُ زُخْرُفَهَا وَ ازَّيَّنَتْ وَظَنَّ أَهْلُهَا أَنَّهُمْ قٰدِرُوْنَ عَلَيْهَا أَتٰهَا أَمْرُنَا لَيْلًا أَوْ نَهَارًا فَجَعَلْنٰهَا حَصِيْدًا كَأَنْ لَمْ تَغْنَ بِالْأَمْسِ كَذٰلِكَ نُفَصِّلُ الْأٰيٰتِ لِقَوْمٍ يَتَفَكَّرُوْنَ ۞

25. And Allah invites to the abode of peace and guides whom He pleases into the right path.

وَاللّٰهُ يَدْعُوْا إِلٰى دَارِ السَّلٰمِ وَيَهْدِيْ مَنْ يَّشَاءُ إِلٰى صِرَاطٍ مُّسْتَقِيْمٍ ۞

26. For those who do good is good (reward) and more (than this); and blackness or ignominy shall not cover their faces; these are the dwellers of the garden; in it they shall abide.

لِلَّذِيْنَ أَحْسَنُوا الْحُسْنٰى وَزِيَادَةٌ وَلَا يَرْهَقُ وُجُوْهَهُمْ قَتَرٌ وَلَا ذِلَّةٌ أُولٰئِكَ أَصْحٰبُ الْجَنَّةِ هُمْ فِيْهَا خٰلِدُوْنَ ۞

27. And (as for) those who have earned evil, the punishment of an evil is the like of it, and abasement shall come upon them—they shall have none to protect them from Allah—as if their faces had been covered with slices of the dense darkness of night; these are the inmates of the fire; in it they shall abide.

وَالَّذِيْنَ كَسَبُوا السَّيِّئَاتِ جَزَاءُ سَيِّئَةٍ بِمِثْلِهَا وَ تَرْهَقُهُمْ ذِلَّةٌ مَّا لَهُمْ مِّنَ اللّٰهِ مِنْ عَاصِمٍ كَأَنَّمَا أُغْشِيَتْ وُجُوْهُهُمْ قِطَعًا مِّنَ الَّيْلِ مُظْلِمًا أُولٰئِكَ أَصْحٰبُ النَّارِ هُمْ فِيْهَا خٰلِدُوْنَ ۞

28. And on the day when We will gather them all together, then We will say to those who associated others (with Allah): Keep where you are, you and your associates; then We shall separate them widely one from another and their associates would say: It was not us that you served:

وَيَوْمَ نَحْشُرُهُمْ جَمِيْعًا ثُمَّ نَقُوْلُ لِلَّذِيْنَ أَشْرَكُوْا مَكَانَكُمْ أَنْتُمْ وَشُرَكَاؤُكُمْ فَزَيَّلْنَا بَيْنَهُمْ وَقَالَ شُرَكَاؤُهُمْ مَّا كُنْتُمْ إِيَّانَا تَعْبُدُوْنَ ۞

29. Therefore Allah is sufficient as a witness between us and you that we were quite unaware of your serving (us).

فَكَفٰى بِاللّٰهِ شَهِيْدًا بَيْنَنَا وَبَيْنَكُمْ اِنْ كُنَّا عَنْ عِبَادَتِكُمْ لَغٰفِلِيْنَ ۟

30. There shall every soul become acquainted with what it sent before, and they shall be brought back to Allah, their true Patron, and what they devised shall escape from them.

هُنَالِكَ تَبْلُوْا كُلُّ نَفْسٍ مَّا اَسْلَفَتْ وَرُدُّوْۤا اِلَى اللّٰهِ مَوْلٰىهُمُ الْحَقِّ وَضَلَّ عَنْهُمْ مَّا كَانُوْا يَفْتَرُوْنَ ۟

31. Say: Who gives you sustenance from the heaven and the earth? Or Who controls the hearing and the sight? And Who brings forth the living from the dead, and brings forth the dead from the living? And Who regulates the affairs? Then they will say: Allah. Say then: Will you not then guard (against evil)?

قُلْ مَنْ يَّرْزُقُكُمْ مِّنَ السَّمَآءِ وَالْاَرْضِ اَمَّنْ يَّمْلِكُ السَّمْعَ وَالْاَبْصَارَ وَمَنْ يُّخْرِجُ الْحَيَّ مِنَ الْمَيِّتِ وَيُخْرِجُ الْمَيِّتَ مِنَ الْحَيِّ وَمَنْ يُّدَبِّرُ الْاَمْرَ فَسَيَقُوْلُوْنَ اللّٰهُ فَقُلْ اَفَلَا تَتَّقُوْنَ ۟

32. This then is Allah, your true Lord; and what is there after the truth but error; how are you then turned back?

فَذٰلِكُمُ اللّٰهُ رَبُّكُمُ الْحَقُّ فَمَاذَا بَعْدَ الْحَقِّ اِلَّا الضَّلٰلُ فَاَنّٰى تُصْرَفُوْنَ ۟

33. Thus does the word of your Lord prove true against those who transgress that they do not believe.

كَذٰلِكَ حَقَّتْ كَلِمَتُ رَبِّكَ عَلَى الَّذِيْنَ فَسَقُوْۤا اَنَّهُمْ لَا يُؤْمِنُوْنَ ۟

34. Say: Is there any one among your associates who can bring into existence the creation in the first instance, then reproduce it? Say: Allah brings the creation into existence, then He reproduces it; how are you then turned away?

قُلْ هَلْ مِنْ شُرَكَآئِكُمْ مَّنْ يَّبْدَؤُا الْخَلْقَ ثُمَّ يُعِيْدُهُ قُلِ اللّٰهُ يَبْدَؤُا الْخَلْقَ ثُمَّ يُعِيْدُهُ فَاَنّٰى تُؤْفَكُوْنَ ۟

35. Say: Is there any of your associates who guides to the truth? Say: Allah guides to the truth. Is He then Who guides to the truth more worthy to be followed, or he who himself does not go aright unless he is guided? What then is the matter with you; how do you judge?

قُلْ هَلْ مِنْ شُرَكَآئِكُمْ مَّنْ يَّهْدِىْۤ اِلَى الْحَقِّ قُلِ اللّٰهُ يَهْدِىْ لِلْحَقِّ اَفَمَنْ يَّهْدِىْۤ اِلَى الْحَقِّ اَحَقُّ اَنْ يُّتَّبَعَ اَمَّنْ لَّا يَهِدِّىْۤ اِلَّاۤ اَنْ يُّهْدٰى فَمَا لَكُمْ كَيْفَ تَحْكُمُوْنَ ۟

36. And most of them do not follow (anything) but conjecture; surely conjecture will not avail aught against the truth; surely Allah is cognizant of what they do.

وَمَا يَتَّبِعُ اَكْثَرُهُمْ اِلَّا ظَنًّا اِنَّ الظَّنَّ لَا يُغْنِىْ مِنَ الْحَقِّ شَيْئًا اِنَّ اللّٰهَ عَلِيْمٌ بِمَا يَفْعَلُوْنَ ۟

37. And this Quran is not such as could be forged by those besides Allah, but it is a verification of that which is before it and a clear explanation of the book, there is no doubt in it, from the Lord of the worlds.

وَمَا كَانَ هٰذَا الْقُرْاٰنُ اَنْ يُّفْتَرٰى مِنْ دُوْنِ اللّٰهِ وَلٰكِنْ تَصْدِيْقَ الَّذِيْ بَيْنَ يَدَيْهِ وَتَفْصِيْلَ الْكِتٰبِ لَا رَيْبَ فِيْهِ مِنْ رَّبِّ الْعٰلَمِيْنَ ۝

38. Or do they say: He has forged it? Say: Then bring a chapter like this and invite whom you can besides Allah, if you are truthful.

اَمْ يَقُوْلُوْنَ افْتَرٰىهُ قُلْ فَأْتُوْا بِسُوْرَةٍ مِّثْلِهٖ وَادْعُوْا مَنِ اسْتَطَعْتُمْ مِّنْ دُوْنِ اللّٰهِ اِنْ كُنْتُمْ صٰدِقِيْنَ ۝

39. Nay, they reject that of which they have no comprehensive knowledge, and the final sequel of it has not yet come to them; even thus did those before them reject (the truth); see then what was the end of the unjust.

بَلْ كَذَّبُوْا بِمَا لَمْ يُحِيْطُوْا بِعِلْمِهٖ وَلَمَّا يَأْتِهِمْ تَأْوِيْلُهٗ كَذٰلِكَ كَذَّبَ الَّذِيْنَ مِنْ قَبْلِهِمْ فَانْظُرْ كَيْفَ كَانَ عَاقِبَةُ الظّٰلِمِيْنَ ۝

40. And of them is he who believes in it, and of them is he who does not believe in it, and your Lord best knows the mischief-makers.

وَمِنْهُمْ مَّنْ يُّؤْمِنُ بِهٖ وَمِنْهُمْ مَّنْ لَّا يُؤْمِنُ بِهٖ وَرَبُّكَ اَعْلَمُ بِالْمُفْسِدِيْنَ ۝

41. And if they call you a liar, say: My work is for me and your work for you; you are clear of what I do and I am clear of what you do.

وَاِنْ كَذَّبُوْكَ فَقُلْ لِّيْ عَمَلِيْ وَلَكُمْ عَمَلُكُمْ اَنْتُمْ بَرِيْٓـُٔوْنَ مِمَّآ اَعْمَلُ وَاَنَا بَرِيْٓءٌ مِّمَّا تَعْمَلُوْنَ ۝

42. And there are those of them who hear you, but can you make the deaf to hear though they will not understand?

وَمِنْهُمْ مَّنْ يَّسْتَمِعُوْنَ اِلَيْكَ اَفَاَنْتَ تُسْمِعُ الصُّمَّ وَلَوْ كَانُوْا لَا يَعْقِلُوْنَ ۝

43. And there are those of them who look at you, but can you show the way to the blind though they will not see?

وَمِنْهُمْ مَّنْ يَّنْظُرُ اِلَيْكَ اَفَاَنْتَ تَهْدِى الْعُمْىَ وَلَوْ كَانُوْا لَا يُبْصِرُوْنَ ۝

44. Surely Allah does not do any injustice to men, but men are unjust to themselves.

اِنَّ اللّٰهَ لَا يَظْلِمُ النَّاسَ شَيْئًا وَّلٰكِنَّ النَّاسَ اَنْفُسَهُمْ يَظْلِمُوْنَ ۝

45. And on the day when He will gather them as though they had not stayed but an hour of the day, they will know each other. They will perish indeed who called the meeting with Allah to be a lie, and they are not followers of the right direction.

وَيَوْمَ يَحْشُرُهُمْ كَاَنْ لَّمْ يَلْبَثُوْٓا اِلَّا سَاعَةً مِّنَ النَّهَارِ يَتَعَارَفُوْنَ بَيْنَهُمْ قَدْ خَسِرَ الَّذِيْنَ كَذَّبُوْا بِلِقَاءِ اللّٰهِ وَمَا كَانُوْا مُهْتَدِيْنَ ۝

46. And if We show you something of what We threaten them with, or cause you to die, yet to Us is their return, and Allah is the bearer of witness to what they do.

وَإِمَّا نُرِيَنَّكَ بَعْضَ الَّذِي نَعِدُهُمْ أَوْ نَتَوَفَّيَنَّكَ فَإِلَيْنَا مَرْجِعُهُمْ ثُمَّ اللّٰهُ شَهِيدٌ عَلٰى مَا يَفْعَلُوْنَ ﴿٤٦﴾

47. And every nation had an apostle; so when their apostle came, the matter was decided between them with justice and they shall not be dealt with unjustly.

وَلِكُلِّ أُمَّةٍ رَسُوْلٌ ۚ فَإِذَا جَاءَ رَسُوْلُهُمْ قُضِيَ بَيْنَهُمْ بِالْقِسْطِ وَهُمْ لَا يُظْلَمُوْنَ ﴿٤٧﴾

48. And they say: When will this threat come about, if you are truthful?

وَيَقُوْلُوْنَ مَتٰى هٰذَا الْوَعْدُ إِنْ كُنْتُمْ صٰدِقِيْنَ ﴿٤٨﴾

49. Say: I do not control for myself any harm, or any benefit except what Allah pleases; every nation has a term; when their term comes, they shall not then remain behind for an hour, nor can they go before (their time).

قُلْ لَّا أَمْلِكُ لِنَفْسِيْ ضَرًّا وَّلَا نَفْعًا إِلَّا مَا شَاءَ اللّٰهُ لِكُلِّ أُمَّةٍ أَجَلٌ ۚ إِذَا جَاءَ أَجَلُهُمْ فَلَا يَسْتَأْخِرُوْنَ سَاعَةً وَّلَا يَسْتَقْدِمُوْنَ ﴿٤٩﴾

50. Say: Tell me if His punishment overtakes you by night or by day! what then is there of it that the guilty would hasten on?

قُلْ أَرَأَيْتُمْ إِنْ أَتٰىكُمْ عَذَابُهُ بَيَاتًا أَوْ نَهَارًا مَّاذَا يَسْتَعْجِلُ مِنْهُ الْمُجْرِمُوْنَ ﴿٥٠﴾

51. And when it comes to pass, will you believe in it? What! now (you believe), and already you wished to have it hastened on.

أَثُمَّ إِذَا مَا وَقَعَ آمَنْتُمْ بِهِ ۚ آلْآنَ وَقَدْ كُنْتُمْ بِهِ تَسْتَعْجِلُوْنَ ﴿٥١﴾

52. Then it shall be said to those who were unjust: Taste abiding chastisement; you are not requited except for what you earned.

ثُمَّ قِيْلَ لِلَّذِيْنَ ظَلَمُوْا ذُوْقُوْا عَذَابَ الْخُلْدِ ۚ هَلْ تُجْزَوْنَ إِلَّا بِمَا كُنْتُمْ تَكْسِبُوْنَ ﴿٥٢﴾

53. And they ask you: Is that true? Say: Aye! by my Lord! it is most surely the truth, and you will not escape.

وَيَسْتَنْبِئُوْنَكَ أَحَقٌّ هُوَ ۚ قُلْ إِيْ وَرَبِّيْ إِنَّهُ لَحَقٌّ ۚ وَمَا أَنْتُمْ بِمُعْجِزِيْنَ ﴿٥٣﴾

54. And if every soul that has done injustice had all that is in the earth, it would offer it for ransom, and they will manifest regret when they see the chastisement and the matter shall be decided between them with justice and they shall not be dealt with unjustly.

وَلَوْ أَنَّ لِكُلِّ نَفْسٍ ظَلَمَتْ مَا فِي الْأَرْضِ لَافْتَدَتْ بِهِ ۚ وَأَسَرُّوا النَّدَامَةَ لَمَّا رَأَوُا الْعَذَابَ ۚ وَقُضِيَ بَيْنَهُمْ بِالْقِسْطِ وَهُمْ لَا يُظْلَمُوْنَ ﴿٥٤﴾

55. Now surely Allah's is what is in the heavens and the earth; now surely Allah's promise is true, but most of them do not know.

أَلَا إِنَّ لِلّٰهِ مَا فِي السَّمٰوٰتِ وَالْأَرْضِ ۚ أَلَا إِنَّ وَعْدَ اللّٰهِ حَقٌّ وَّلٰكِنَّ أَكْثَرَهُمْ لَا يَعْلَمُوْنَ ﴿٥٥﴾

56. He gives life and causes death, and to Him you shall be brought back.

هُوَ يُحْيِ وَيُمِيْتُ وَإِلَيْهِ تُرْجَعُوْنَ ﴿٥٦﴾

57. O men! there has come to you indeed an admonition from your Lord and a healing for what is in the breasts and a guidance and a mercy for the believers.

يَاۤيُّهَا النَّاسُ قَدْ جَآءَتْكُمْ مَّوْعِظَةٌ مِّنْ رَّبِّكُمْ وَ شِفَآءٌ لِّمَا فِى الصُّدُوْرِ ۙ وَهُدًى وَّرَحْمَةٌ لِّلْمُؤْمِنِيْنَ ۝

58. Say: In the grace of Allah and in His mercy—in that they should rejoice; it is better than that which they gather.

قُلْ بِفَضْلِ اللّٰهِ وَبِرَحْمَتِهٖ فَبِذٰلِكَ فَلْيَفْرَحُوْا ؕ هُوَ خَيْرٌ مِّمَّا يَجْمَعُوْنَ ۝

59. Say: Tell me what Allah has sent down for you of sustenance, then you make (a part) of it unlawful and (a part) lawful. Say: Has Allah commanded you, or do you forge a lie against Allah?

قُلْ اَرَءَيْتُمْ مَّاۤ اَنْزَلَ اللّٰهُ لَكُمْ مِّنْ رِّزْقٍ فَجَعَلْتُمْ مِّنْهُ حَرَامًا وَّحَلَالًا ؕ قُلْ آٰللّٰهُ اَذِنَ لَكُمْ اَمْ عَلَى اللّٰهِ تَفْتَرُوْنَ ۝

60. And what will be the thought of those who forge lies against Allah on the day of resurrection? Most surely Allah is the Lord of grace towards men, but most of them do not give thanks.

وَمَا ظَنُّ الَّذِيْنَ يَفْتَرُوْنَ عَلَى اللّٰهِ الْكَذِبَ يَوْمَ الْقِيٰمَةِ ؕ اِنَّ اللّٰهَ لَذُوْ فَضْلٍ عَلَى النَّاسِ وَلٰكِنَّ اَكْثَرَهُمْ لَا يَشْكُرُوْنَ ۞

61. And you are not (engaged) in any affair, nor do you recite concerning it any portion of the Quran, nor do you do any work but We are witnesses over you when you enter into it, and there does not lie concealed from your Lord the weight of an atom in the earth or in the heaven, nor any thing less than that nor greater, but it is in a clear book.

وَمَا تَكُوْنُ فِيْ شَأْنٍ وَّمَا تَتْلُوْا مِنْهُ مِنْ قُرْآنٍ وَّ لَا تَعْمَلُوْنَ مِنْ عَمَلٍ اِلَّا كُنَّا عَلَيْكُمْ شُهُوْدًا اِذْ تُفِيْضُوْنَ فِيْهِ ؕ وَمَا يَعْزُبُ عَنْ رَّبِّكَ مِنْ مِّثْقَالِ ذَرَّةٍ فِى الْاَرْضِ وَلَا فِى السَّمَآءِ وَلَاۤ اَصْغَرَ مِنْ ذٰلِكَ وَلَاۤ اَكْبَرَ اِلَّا فِيْ كِتٰبٍ مُّبِيْنٍ ۝

62. Now surely the friends of Allah—they shall have no fear nor shall they grieve.

اَلَاۤ اِنَّ اَوْلِيَآءَ اللّٰهِ لَا خَوْفٌ عَلَيْهِمْ وَلَا هُمْ يَحْزَنُوْنَ ۞

63. Those who believe and guarded (against evil):

الَّذِيْنَ اٰمَنُوْا وَكَانُوْا يَتَّقُوْنَ ۝

64. They shall have good news in this world's life and in the hereafter; there is no changing the words of Allah; that is the mighty achievement.

لَهُمُ الْبُشْرٰى فِى الْحَيٰوةِ الدُّنْيَا وَفِى الْاٰخِرَةِ ؕ لَا تَبْدِيْلَ لِكَلِمٰتِ اللّٰهِ ؕ ذٰلِكَ هُوَ الْفَوْزُ الْعَظِيْمُ ۝

65. And let not their speech grieve you; surely might is wholly Allah's; He is the Hearing, the Knowing.

وَلَا يَحْزُنْكَ قَوْلُهُمْ ۘ اِنَّ الْعِزَّةَ لِلّٰهِ جَمِيْعًا ؕ هُوَ السَّمِيْعُ الْعَلِيْمُ ۝

66. Now, surely, whatever is in the heavens and whatever is in the earth is Allah's; and they do not (really) follow any associates, who call on others besides Allah; they do not follow (anything) but conjectures, and they only lie.

اَلَآ اِنَّ لِلّٰهِ مَنْ فِى السَّمٰوٰتِ وَمَنْ فِى الْاَرْضِ وَ مَا يَتَّبِعُ الَّذِيْنَ يَدْعُوْنَ مِنْ دُوْنِ اللّٰهِ شُرَكَآءَ اِنْ يَّتَّبِعُوْنَ اِلَّا الظَّنَّ وَاِنْ هُمْ اِلَّا يَخْرُصُوْنَ ٦٦

67. He it is Who made for you the night that you might rest in it, and the day giving light; most surely there are signs in it for a people who would hear.

هُوَ الَّذِيْ جَعَلَ لَكُمُ الَّيْلَ لِتَسْكُنُوْا فِيْهِ وَالنَّهَارَ مُبْصِرًا اِنَّ فِىْ ذٰلِكَ لَاٰيٰتٍ لِّقَوْمٍ يَّسْمَعُوْنَ ٦٧

68. They say: Allah has taken a son (to Himself)! Glory be to Him; He is the Self-sufficient; His is what is in the heavens and what is in the earth; you have no authority for this; do you say against Allah what you do not know?

قَالُوا اتَّخَذَ اللّٰهُ وَلَدًا سُبْحٰنَهُ هُوَ الْغَنِيُّ لَهُ مَا فِى السَّمٰوٰتِ وَمَا فِى الْاَرْضِ اِنْ عِنْدَكُمْ مِّنْ سُلْطٰنٍ بِهٰذَا اَتَقُوْلُوْنَ عَلَى اللّٰهِ مَا لَا تَعْلَمُوْنَ ٦٨

69. Say: Those who forge a lie against Allah shall not be successful.

قُلْ اِنَّ الَّذِيْنَ يَفْتَرُوْنَ عَلَى اللّٰهِ الْكَذِبَ لَا يُفْلِحُوْنَ ٦٩

70. (It is only) a provision in this world, then to Us shall be their return; then We shall make them taste severe punishment because they disbelieved.

مَتَاعٌ فِى الدُّنْيَا ثُمَّ اِلَيْنَا مَرْجِعُهُمْ ثُمَّ نُذِيْقُهُمُ الْعَذَابَ الشَّدِيْدَ بِمَا كَانُوْا يَكْفُرُوْنَ ٧٠

71. And recite to them the story of Nuh when he said to his people: O my people! if my stay and my reminding (you) by the communications of Allah is hard on you— yet on Allah do I rely—then resolve upon your affair and (gather) your associates, then let not your affair remain dubious to you, then have it executed against me and give me no respite:

وَاتْلُ عَلَيْهِمْ نَبَاَ نُوْحٍ اِذْ قَالَ لِقَوْمِهٖ يٰقَوْمِ اِنْ كَانَ كَبُرَ عَلَيْكُمْ مَّقَامِيْ وَتَذْكِيْرِيْ بِاٰيٰتِ اللّٰهِ فَعَلَى اللّٰهِ تَوَكَّلْتُ فَاَجْمِعُوْا اَمْرَكُمْ وَشُرَكَآءَكُمْ ثُمَّ لَا يَكُنْ اَمْرُكُمْ عَلَيْكُمْ غُمَّةً ثُمَّ اقْضُوْا اِلَيَّ وَ لَا تُنْظِرُوْنِ ٧١

72. But if you turn back, I did not ask for any reward from you; my reward is only with Allah, and I am commanded that I should be of those who submit.

فَاِنْ تَوَلَّيْتُمْ فَمَا سَاَلْتُكُمْ مِّنْ اَجْرٍ اِنْ اَجْرِيَ اِلَّا عَلَى اللّٰهِ وَاُمِرْتُ اَنْ اَكُوْنَ مِنَ الْمُسْلِمِيْنَ ٧٢

73. But they rejected him, so We delivered him and those with him in the ark, and We made them rulers and drowned those who rejected Our communications; see then what was the end of the (people) warned.

فَكَذَّبُوْهُ فَنَجَّيْنٰهُ وَمَنْ مَّعَهٗ فِى الْفُلْكِ وَجَعَلْنٰهُمْ خَلٰٓئِفَ وَاَغْرَقْنَا الَّذِيْنَ كَذَّبُوْا بِاٰيٰتِنَا فَانْظُرْ كَيْفَ كَانَ عَاقِبَةُ الْمُنْذَرِيْنَ ٧٣

74. Then did We raise up after him apostles to their people, so they came to them with clear arguments, but they would not believe in what they had rejected before; thus it is that We set seals upon the hearts of those who exceed the limits.

75. Then did We send up after them Musa and Haroun to Firon and his chiefs with Our signs, but they showed pride and they were a guilty people.

76. So when the truth came to them from Us they said: This is most surely clear enchantment!

77. Musa said: Do you say (this) of the truth when it has come to you? Is it magic? And the magicians are not successful.

78. They said: Have you come to us to turn us away from what we found our fathers upon, and (that) greatness in the land should be for you two? And we are not going to believe in you.

79. And Firon said: Bring to me every skillful magician.

80. And when the magicians came, Musa said to them: Cast down what you have to cast.

81. So when they cast down, Musa said to them: What you have brought is deception; surely Allah will make it naught; surely Allah does not make the work of mischief-makers to thrive.

82. And Allah will show the truth to be the truth by His words, though the guilty may be averse (to it).

83. But none believed in Musa except the offspring of his people, on account of the fear of Firon and their chiefs, lest he should persecute them; and most surely Firon was lofty in the land; and most surely he was of the extravagant.

84. And Musa said: O my people! if you believe in Allah, then rely on Him (alone) if you submit (to Allah).

ثُمَّ بَعَثْنَا مِنْ بَعْدِهِ رُسُلًا إِلَى قَوْمِهِمْ فَجَآءُوهُمْ بِالْبَيِّنَاتِ فَمَا كَانُوا لِيُؤْمِنُوا بِمَا كَذَّبُوا بِهِ مِنْ قَبْلُ كَذٰلِكَ نَطْبَعُ عَلَى قُلُوبِ الْمُعْتَدِينَ ۞

ثُمَّ بَعَثْنَا مِنْ بَعْدِهِمْ مُّوسَى وَهَارُونَ إِلَى فِرْعَوْنَ وَمَلَأِهِ بِآيَاتِنَا فَاسْتَكْبَرُوا وَكَانُوا قَوْمًا مُّجْرِمِينَ ۞

فَلَمَّا جَآءَهُمُ الْحَقُّ مِنْ عِنْدِنَا قَالُوا إِنَّ هٰذَا لَسِحْرٌ مُّبِينٌ ۞

قَالَ مُوسَى أَتَقُولُونَ لِلْحَقِّ لَمَّا جَآءَكُمْ أَسِحْرٌ هٰذَا وَلَا يُفْلِحُ السَّاحِرُونَ ۞

قَالُوا أَجِئْتَنَا لِتَلْفِتَنَا عَمَّا وَجَدْنَا عَلَيْهِ آبَآءَنَا وَتَكُونَ لَكُمَا الْكِبْرِيَاءُ فِي الْأَرْضِ وَمَا نَحْنُ لَكُمَا بِمُؤْمِنِينَ ۞

وَقَالَ فِرْعَوْنُ ائْتُونِي بِكُلِّ سَاحِرٍ عَلِيمٍ ۞

فَلَمَّا جَآءَ السَّحَرَةُ قَالَ لَهُمْ مُّوسَى أَلْقُوا مَا أَنْتُمْ مُلْقُونَ ۞

فَلَمَّا أَلْقَوْا قَالَ مُوسَى مَا جِئْتُمْ بِهِ السِّحْرُ إِنَّ اللّٰهَ سَيُبْطِلُهُ إِنَّ اللّٰهَ لَا يُصْلِحُ عَمَلَ الْمُفْسِدِينَ ۞

وَيُحِقُّ اللّٰهُ الْحَقَّ بِكَلِمَاتِهِ وَلَوْ كَرِهَ الْمُجْرِمُونَ ۞

فَمَا آمَنَ لِمُوسَى إِلَّا ذُرِّيَّةٌ مِّنْ قَوْمِهِ عَلَى خَوْفٍ مِّنْ فِرْعَوْنَ وَمَلَأِهِمْ أَنْ يَفْتِنَهُمْ وَإِنَّ فِرْعَوْنَ لَعَالٍ فِي الْأَرْضِ وَإِنَّهُ لَمِنَ الْمُسْرِفِينَ ۞

وَقَالَ مُوسَى يَا قَوْمِ إِنْ كُنْتُمْ آمَنْتُمْ بِاللّٰهِ فَعَلَيْهِ تَوَكَّلُوا إِنْ كُنْتُمْ مُسْلِمِينَ ۞

85. So they said: On Allah we rely: O our Lord! make us not subject to the persecution of the unjust people:

فَقَالُوْا عَلَى اللّٰهِ تَوَكَّلْنَا ۚ رَبَّنَا لَا تَجْعَلْنَا فِتْنَةً لِّلْقَوْمِ الظّٰلِمِيْنَ ۞

86. And do Thou deliver us by Thy mercy from the unbelieving people.

وَنَجِّنَا بِرَحْمَتِكَ مِنَ الْقَوْمِ الْكٰفِرِيْنَ ۞

87. And We revealed to Musa and his brother, saying: Take for your people houses to abide in Egypt and make your houses places of worship and keep up prayer and give good news to the believers.

وَأَوْحَيْنَا إِلٰى مُوْسٰى وَأَخِيْهِ أَنْ تَبَوَّآ لِقَوْمِكُمَا بِمِصْرَ بُيُوْتًا وَّاجْعَلُوْا بُيُوْتَكُمْ قِبْلَةً وَّأَقِيْمُوا الصَّلٰوةَ ۗ وَبَشِّرِ الْمُؤْمِنِيْنَ ۞

88. And Musa said: Our Lord! surely Thou hast given to Firon and his chiefs finery and riches in this world's life, to this end, our Lord, that they lead (people) astray from Thy way: Our Lord! destroy their riches and harden their hearts so that they believe not until they see the painful punishment.

وَقَالَ مُوْسٰى رَبَّنَا إِنَّكَ اٰتَيْتَ فِرْعَوْنَ وَمَلَأَهٗ زِيْنَةً وَّأَمْوَالًا فِي الْحَيٰوةِ الدُّنْيَا ۙ رَبَّنَا لِيُضِلُّوْا عَنْ سَبِيْلِكَ ۚ رَبَّنَا اطْمِسْ عَلٰى أَمْوَالِهِمْ وَاشْدُدْ عَلٰى قُلُوْبِهِمْ فَلَا يُؤْمِنُوْا حَتّٰى يَرَوُا الْعَذَابَ الْأَلِيْمَ ۞

89. He said: The prayer of you both has indeed been accepted, therefore continue in the right way and do not follow the path of those who do not know.

قَالَ قَدْ أُجِيْبَتْ دَّعْوَتُكُمَا فَاسْتَقِيْمَا وَلَا تَتَّبِعٰنِّ سَبِيْلَ الَّذِيْنَ لَا يَعْلَمُوْنَ ۞

90. And We made the children of Israel to pass through the sea, then Firon and his hosts followed them for oppression and tyranny; until when drowning overtook him, he said: I believe that there is no god but He in Whom the children of Israel believe and I am of those who submit.

وَجٰوَزْنَا بِبَنِيْ إِسْرَآءِيْلَ الْبَحْرَ فَأَتْبَعَهُمْ فِرْعَوْنُ وَجُنُوْدُهٗ بَغْيًا وَّعَدْوًا ۗ حَتّٰى إِذَآ أَدْرَكَهُ الْغَرَقُ قَالَ اٰمَنْتُ أَنَّهٗ لَا إِلٰهَ إِلَّا الَّذِيْ اٰمَنَتْ بِهٖ بَنُوْا إِسْرَآءِيْلَ وَأَنَا مِنَ الْمُسْلِمِيْنَ ۞

91. What! now? and indeed you disobeyed before and you were of the mischiefmakers.

اٰلْٰٔنَ وَقَدْ عَصَيْتَ قَبْلُ وَكُنْتَ مِنَ الْمُفْسِدِيْنَ ۞

92. But We will this day deliver you with your body that you may be a sign to those after you, and most surely the majority of the people are heedless to Our communications.

فَالْيَوْمَ نُنَجِّيْكَ بِبَدَنِكَ لِتَكُوْنَ لِمَنْ خَلْفَكَ اٰيَةً ۚ وَإِنَّ كَثِيْرًا مِّنَ النَّاسِ عَنْ اٰيٰتِنَا لَغٰفِلُوْنَ ۞

93. And certainly We lodged the children of Israel in a goodly abode and We provided them with good things; but they did not disagree until the knowledge had come to them; surely your Lord will judge between them on the resurrection day concerning that in which they disagreed.

وَلَقَدْ بَوَّأْنَا بَنِيْ إِسْرَآءِيْلَ مُبَوَّأَ صِدْقٍ وَّرَزَقْنٰهُمْ مِّنَ الطَّيِّبٰتِ ۚ فَمَا اخْتَلَفُوْا حَتّٰى جَآءَهُمُ الْعِلْمُ ۚ إِنَّ رَبَّكَ يَقْضِيْ بَيْنَهُمْ يَوْمَ الْقِيٰمَةِ فِيْمَا كَانُوْا فِيْهِ يَخْتَلِفُوْنَ ۞

94. But if you are in doubt as to what We have revealed to you, ask those who read the Book before you; certainly the truth has come to you from your Lord, therefore you should not be of the disputers.

95. And you should not be of those who reject the communications of Allah, (for) then you should be one of the losers.

96. Surely those against whom the word of your Lord has proved true will not believe,

97. Though every sign should come to them, until they witness the painful chastisement.

98. And wherefore was there not a town which should believe so that their belief should have profited them but the people of Yunus? When they believed, We removed from them the chastisement of disgrace in this world's life and We gave them provision till a time.

99. And if your Lord had pleased, surely all those who are in the earth would have believed, all of them; will you then force men till they become believers?

100. And it is not for a soul to believe except by Allah's permission; and He casts uncleanness on those who will not understand.

101. Say: Consider what is it that is in the heavens and the earth; and signs and warners do not avail a people who would not believe.

102. What do they wait for then but the like of the days of those who passed away before them? Say: Wait then; surely I too am with you of those who wait.

103. Then We deliver Our apostles and those who believe—even so (now), it is binding on Us (that) We deliver the believers.

فَإِنْ كُنْتَ فِيْ شَكٍّ مِّمَّا اَنْزَلْنَآ اِلَيْكَ فَسْئَلِ الَّذِيْنَ يَقْرَءُوْنَ الْكِتٰبَ مِنْ قَبْلِكَ لَقَدْ جَآءَكَ الْحَقُّ مِنْ رَّبِّكَ فَلَا تَكُوْنَنَّ مِنَ الْمُمْتَرِيْنَ ۙ ۝

وَلَا تَكُوْنَنَّ مِنَ الَّذِيْنَ كَذَّبُوْا بِاٰيٰتِ اللّٰهِ فَتَكُوْنَ مِنَ الْخٰسِرِيْنَ ۝

اِنَّ الَّذِيْنَ حَقَّتْ عَلَيْهِمْ كَلِمَتُ رَبِّكَ لَا يُؤْمِنُوْنَ ۝

وَلَوْ جَآءَتْهُمْ كُلُّ اٰيَةٍ حَتّٰى يَرَوُا الْعَذَابَ الْاَلِيْمَ ۝

فَلَوْلَا كَانَتْ قَرْيَةٌ اٰمَنَتْ فَنَفَعَهَآ اِيْمَانُهَآ اِلَّا قَوْمَ يُوْنُسَ لَمَّآ اٰمَنُوْا كَشَفْنَا عَنْهُمْ عَذَابَ الْخِزْيِ فِى الْحَيٰوةِ الدُّنْيَا وَمَتَّعْنٰهُمْ اِلٰى حِيْنٍ ۝

وَلَوْ شَآءَ رَبُّكَ لَاٰمَنَ مَنْ فِى الْاَرْضِ كُلُّهُمْ جَمِيْعًا اَفَاَنْتَ تُكْرِهُ النَّاسَ حَتّٰى يَكُوْنُوْا مُؤْمِنِيْنَ ۝

وَمَا كَانَ لِنَفْسٍ اَنْ تُؤْمِنَ اِلَّا بِاِذْنِ اللّٰهِ وَيَجْعَلُ الرِّجْسَ عَلَى الَّذِيْنَ لَا يَعْقِلُوْنَ ۝

قُلِ انْظُرُوْا مَاذَا فِى السَّمٰوٰتِ وَالْاَرْضِ وَمَا تُغْنِى الْاٰيٰتُ وَالنُّذُرُ عَنْ قَوْمٍ لَّا يُؤْمِنُوْنَ ۝

فَهَلْ يَنْتَظِرُوْنَ اِلَّا مِثْلَ اَيَّامِ الَّذِيْنَ خَلَوْا مِنْ قَبْلِهِمْ قُلْ فَانْتَظِرُوْا اِنِّيْ مَعَكُمْ مِّنَ الْمُنْتَظِرِيْنَ ۝

ثُمَّ نُنَجِّيْ رُسُلَنَا وَالَّذِيْنَ اٰمَنُوْا كَذٰلِكَ حَقًّا عَلَيْنَا نُنْجِ الْمُؤْمِنِيْنَ ۞

104. Say: O people! if you are in doubt as to my religion, then (know that) I do not serve those whom you serve besides Allah, but I do serve Allah, Who will cause you to die, and I am commanded that I should be of the believers.

قُلْ يَا أَيُّهَا النَّاسُ إِنْ كُنْتُمْ فِي شَكٍّ مِّنْ دِينِي فَلَا أَعْبُدُ الَّذِينَ تَعْبُدُونَ مِنْ دُونِ اللّٰهِ وَلٰكِنْ أَعْبُدُ اللّٰهَ الَّذِي يَتَوَفّٰىكُمْ ۖ وَأُمِرْتُ أَنْ أَكُونَ مِنَ الْمُؤْمِنِينَ ۝

105. And that you should keep your course towards the religion uprightly; and you should not be of the polytheists.

وَأَنْ أَقِمْ وَجْهَكَ لِلدِّينِ حَنِيفًا ۖ وَلَا تَكُونَنَّ مِنَ الْمُشْرِكِينَ ۝

106. And do not call besides Allah on that which can neither benefit you nor harm you, for if you do then surely you will in that case be of the unjust.

وَلَا تَدْعُ مِنْ دُونِ اللّٰهِ مَا لَا يَنْفَعُكَ وَلَا يَضُرُّكَ ۖ فَإِنْ فَعَلْتَ فَإِنَّكَ إِذًا مِنَ الظَّالِمِينَ ۝

107. And if Allah should afflict you with harm, then there is none to remove it but He; and if He intends good to you there is none to repel His grace; He brings it to whom He pleases of His servants; and He is the Forgiving, the Merciful.

وَإِنْ يَمْسَسْكَ اللّٰهُ بِضُرٍّ فَلَا كَاشِفَ لَهُ إِلَّا هُوَ ۖ وَإِنْ يُرِدْكَ بِخَيْرٍ فَلَا رَادَّ لِفَضْلِهِ ۚ يُصِيبُ بِهِ مَنْ يَشَاءُ مِنْ عِبَادِهِ ۚ وَهُوَ الْغَفُورُ الرَّحِيمُ ۝

108. Say: O people! indeed there has come to you the truth from your Lord, therefore whoever goes aright, he goes aright only for the good of his own soul, and whoever goes astray, he goes astray only to the detriment of it, and I am not a custodian over you.

قُلْ يَا أَيُّهَا النَّاسُ قَدْ جَاءَكُمُ الْحَقُّ مِنْ رَبِّكُمْ ۖ فَمَنِ اهْتَدَى فَإِنَّمَا يَهْتَدِي لِنَفْسِهِ ۚ وَمَنْ ضَلَّ فَإِنَّمَا يَضِلُّ عَلَيْهَا ۖ وَمَا أَنَا عَلَيْكُمْ بِوَكِيلٍ ۝

109. And follow what is revealed to you and be patient till Allah should give judgment, and He is the best of the judges.

وَاتَّبِعْ مَا يُوحَى إِلَيْكَ وَاصْبِرْ حَتّٰى يَحْكُمَ اللّٰهُ ۚ وَهُوَ خَيْرُ الْحَاكِمِينَ ۝

HUD

اياتها (۱۱) سُوْرَةُ هُوْدٍ مَكِّيَّةٌ نُزُوْلِهَا

**In the name of Allah,
the Beneficent, the Merciful.**

بِسْمِ اللهِ الرَّحْمٰنِ الرَّحِيْمِ۞

1. Alif Lam Ra (This is) a Book, whose verses are made decisive, then are they made plain, from the Wise, All-aware:

الٓرٰ كِتٰبٌ اُحْكِمَتْ اٰيٰتُهٗ ثُمَّ فُصِّلَتْ مِنْ لَّدُنْ حَكِيْمٍ خَبِيْرٍۙ۞

2. That you shall not serve (any) but Allah; surely I am a warner for you from Him and a giver of good news,

اَلَّا تَعْبُدُوْٓا اِلَّا اللهَ اِنَّنِيْ لَكُمْ مِّنْهُ نَذِيْرٌ وَّبَشِيْرٌۙ۞

3. And you that ask forgiveness of your Lord, then turn to Him; He will provide you with a goodly provision to an appointed term and bestow His grace on every one endowed with grace, and if you turn back, then surely I fear for you the chastisement of a great day.

وَّاَنِ اسْتَغْفِرُوْا رَبَّكُمْ ثُمَّ تُوْبُوْٓا اِلَيْهِ يُمَتِّعْكُمْ مَّتَاعًا حَسَنًا اِلٰٓى اَجَلٍ مُّسَمًّى وَّيُؤْتِ كُلَّ ذِيْ فَضْلٍ فَضْلَهٗ وَاِنْ تَوَلَّوْا فَاِنِّيْٓ اَخَافُ عَلَيْكُمْ عَذَابَ يَوْمٍ كَبِيْرٍ۞

4. To Allah is your return, and He has power over all things.

اِلَى اللهِ مَرْجِعُكُمْ وَهُوَ عَلٰى كُلِّ شَيْءٍ قَدِيْرٌ۞

5. Now surely they fold up their breasts that they may conceal (their enmity) from Him; now surely, when they use their garments as a covering, He knows what they conceal and what they make public; surely He knows what is in the breasts.

اَلَآ اِنَّهُمْ يَثْنُوْنَ صُدُوْرَهُمْ لِيَسْتَخْفُوْا مِنْهُ اَلَا حِيْنَ يَسْتَغْشُوْنَ ثِيَابَهُمْ يَعْلَمُ مَا يُسِرُّوْنَ وَمَا يُعْلِنُوْنَ اِنَّهٗ عَلِيْمٌ بِذَاتِ الصُّدُوْرِ۞

6. And there is no animal in the earth but on Allah is the sustenance of it, and He knows its resting place and its depository; all (things) are in a manifest book.

وَمَا مِنْ دَآبَّةٍ فِى الْاَرْضِ اِلَّا عَلَى اللهِ رِزْقُهَا وَيَعْلَمُ مُسْتَقَرَّهَا وَمُسْتَوْدَعَهَا كُلٌّ فِيْ كِتٰبٍ مُّبِيْنٍ۞

7. And He it is Who created the heavens and the earth in six periods—and His dominion (extends) on the water—that He might manifest to you, which of you is best in action, and if you say, surely you shall be raised up after death, those who disbelieve would certainly say: This is nothing but clear magic.

وَهُوَ الَّذِيْ خَلَقَ السَّمٰوٰتِ وَالْاَرْضَ فِيْ سِتَّةِ اَيَّامٍ وَّكَانَ عَرْشُهٗ عَلَى الْمَآءِ لِيَبْلُوَكُمْ اَيُّكُمْ اَحْسَنُ عَمَلًا وَلَئِنْ قُلْتَ اِنَّكُمْ مَّبْعُوْثُوْنَ مِنْ بَعْدِ الْمَوْتِ لَيَقُوْلَنَّ الَّذِيْنَ كَفَرُوْٓا اِنْ هٰذَآ اِلَّا سِحْرٌ مُّبِيْنٌ۞

8. And if We hold back from them the punishment until a stated period of time, they will certainly say: What prevents it? Now surely on the day when it will come to them, it shall not be averted from them and that which they scoffed at shall beset them.

9. And if We make man taste mercy from Us, then take it off from him, most surely he is despairing, ungrateful.

10. And if We make him taste a favor after distress has afflicted him, he will certainly say: The evils are gone away from me. Most surely he is exulting, boasting;

11. Except those who are patient and do good; they shall have forgiveness and a great reward.

12. Then, it may be that you will give up part of what is revealed to you and your breast will become straitened by it because they say: Why has not a treasure been sent down upon him or an angel come with him? You are only a warner; and Allah is custodian over all things.

13. Or, do they say: He has forged it. Say: Then bring ten forged chapters like it and call upon whom you can besides Allah, if you are truthful.

14. But if they do not answer you, then know that it is revealed by Allah's knowledge and that there is no god but He; will you then submit?

15. Whoever desires this world's life and its finery, We will pay them in full their deeds therein, and they shall not be made to suffer loss in respect of them.

16. These are they for whom there is nothing but fire in the hereafter, and what they wrought in it shall go for nothing, and vain is what they do.

17. Is he then who has with him clear proof from his Lord, and a witness from Him recites it and before it (is) the Book of Musa, a guide and a mercy? These believe in it; and whoever of the (different) parties disbelieves in it, surely it is the truth from your Lord, but most men do not believe.

أَفَمَنْ كَانَ عَلَى بَيِّنَةٍ مِّنْ رَّبِّهٖ وَيَتْلُوْهُ شَاهِدٌ مِّنْهُ

وَمِنْ قَبْلِهٖ كِتٰبُ مُوْسٰى اِمَامًا وَّرَحْمَةً ۚ اُولٰٓئِكَ

يُؤْمِنُوْنَ بِهٖ ۚ وَمَنْ يَّكْفُرْ بِهٖ مِنَ الْاَحْزَابِ فَالنَّارُ

مَوْعِدُهٗ ۚ فَلَا تَكُ فِيْ مِرْيَةٍ مِّنْهُ ۚ اِنَّهُ الْحَقُّ مِنْ رَّبِّكَ

وَلٰكِنَّ اَكْثَرَ النَّاسِ لَا يُؤْمِنُوْنَ ۝

18. And who is more unjust than he who forges a lie against Allah? These shall be brought before their Lord, and the witnesses shall say: These are they who lied against their Lord. Now surely the curse of Allah is on the unjust.

وَمَنْ اَظْلَمُ مِمَّنِ افْتَرٰى عَلَى اللّٰهِ كَذِبًا ۚ اُولٰٓئِكَ

يُعْرَضُوْنَ عَلٰى رَبِّهِمْ وَيَقُوْلُ الْاَشْهَادُ هٰٓؤُلَاءِ

الَّذِيْنَ كَذَبُوْا عَلٰى رَبِّهِمْ ۚ اَلَا لَعْنَةُ اللّٰهِ عَلَى

الظّٰلِمِيْنَ ۝

19. Who turn away from the path of Allah and desire to make it crooked; and they are disbelievers in the hereafter.

الَّذِيْنَ يَصُدُّوْنَ عَنْ سَبِيْلِ اللّٰهِ وَيَبْغُوْنَهَا عِوَجًا ۚ

وَهُمْ بِالْاٰخِرَةِ هُمْ كٰفِرُوْنَ ۝

20. These shall not escape in the earth, nor shall they have any guardians besides Allah; the punishment shall be doubled for them; they could not bear to hear and they did not see.

اُولٰٓئِكَ لَمْ يَكُوْنُوْا مُعْجِزِيْنَ فِي الْاَرْضِ وَمَا كَانَ

لَهُمْ مِّنْ دُوْنِ اللّٰهِ مِنْ اَوْلِيَاءَ ۘ يُضٰعَفُ لَهُمُ

الْعَذَابُ ۚ مَا كَانُوْا يَسْتَطِيْعُوْنَ السَّمْعَ وَمَا كَانُوْا

يُبْصِرُوْنَ ۝

21. These are they who have lost their souls, and what they forged is gone from them.

اُولٰٓئِكَ الَّذِيْنَ خَسِرُوْا اَنْفُسَهُمْ وَضَلَّ عَنْهُمْ مَّا

كَانُوْا يَفْتَرُوْنَ ۝

22. Truly in the hereafter they are the greatest losers.

لَا جَرَمَ اَنَّهُمْ فِي الْاٰخِرَةِ هُمُ الْاَخْسَرُوْنَ ۝

23. Surely (as to) those who believe and do good and humble themselves to their Lord, these are the dwellers of the garden, in it they will abide.

اِنَّ الَّذِيْنَ اٰمَنُوْا وَعَمِلُوا الصّٰلِحٰتِ وَاَخْبَتُوْا اِلٰى

رَبِّهِمْ اُولٰٓئِكَ اَصْحٰبُ الْجَنَّةِ ۚ هُمْ فِيْهَا خٰلِدُوْنَ ۝

24. The likeness of the two parties is as the blind and the deaf, and the seeing and the hearing: are they equal in condition? Will you not then mind?

مَثَلُ الْفَرِيْقَيْنِ كَالْاَعْمٰى وَالْاَصَمِّ وَالْبَصِيْرِ وَ

السَّمِيْعِ ۚ هَلْ يَسْتَوِيٰنِ مَثَلًا ۚ اَفَلَا تَذَكَّرُوْنَ ۝

25. And certainly We sent Nuh to his people: Surely I am a plain warner for you:

26. That you shall not serve any but Allah, surely I fear for you the punishment of a painful day.

27. But the chiefs of those who disbelieved from among his people said: We do not consider you but a mortal like ourselves, and we do not see any have followed you but those who are the meanest of us at first thought and we do not see in you any excellence over us; nay, we deem you liars.

28. He said: O my people! tell me if I have with me clear proof from my Lord, and He has granted me mercy from Himself and it has been made obscure to you; shall we constrain you to (accept) it while you are averse from it?

29. And, O my people! I ask you not for wealth in return for it; my reward is only with Allah and I am not going to drive away those who believe; surely they shall meet their Lord, but I consider you a people who are ignorant:

30. And, O my people! who will help me against Allah if I drive them away? Will you not then mind?

31. And I do not say to you that I have the treasures of Allah; and I do not know the unseen, nor do I say that I am an angel; nor do I say about those whom your eyes hold in mean estimation (that) Allah will never grant them (any) good—Allah knows best what is in their souls—for then most surely I should be of the unjust.

32. They said: O Nuh! indeed you have disputed with us and lengthened dispute with us, therefore bring to us what you threaten us with, if you are of the truthful ones.

وَلَقَدْ اَرْسَلْنَا نُوْحًا اِلٰى قَوْمِهٖ اِنِّىْ لَكُمْ نَذِيْرٌ مُّبِيْنٌ ۞

اَنْ لَّا تَعْبُدُوْٓا اِلَّا اللّٰهَ اِنِّىْٓ اَخَافُ عَلَيْكُمْ عَذَابَ يَوْمٍ اَلِيْمٍ ۞

فَقَالَ الْمَلَاُ الَّذِيْنَ كَفَرُوْا مِنْ قَوْمِهٖ مَا نَرٰىكَ اِلَّا بَشَرًا مِّثْلَنَا وَمَا نَرٰىكَ اتَّبَعَكَ اِلَّا الَّذِيْنَ هُمْ اَرَاذِلُنَا بَادِىَ الرَّاْىِ وَمَا نَرٰى لَكُمْ عَلَيْنَا مِنْ فَضْلٍ بَلْ نَظُنُّكُمْ كٰذِبِيْنَ ۞

قَالَ يٰقَوْمِ اَرَءَيْتُمْ اِنْ كُنْتُ عَلٰى بَيِّنَةٍ مِّنْ رَّبِّىْ وَاٰتٰىنِىْ رَحْمَةً مِّنْ عِنْدِهٖ فَعُمِّيَتْ عَلَيْكُمْ اَنُلْزِمُكُمُوْهَا وَاَنْتُمْ لَهَا كٰرِهُوْنَ ۞

وَيٰقَوْمِ لَا اَسْئَلُكُمْ عَلَيْهِ مَالًا اِنْ اَجْرِىَ اِلَّا عَلَى اللّٰهِ وَمَآ اَنَا بِطَارِدِ الَّذِيْنَ اٰمَنُوْا اِنَّهُمْ مُّلٰقُوْا رَبِّهِمْ وَلٰكِنِّىْٓ اَرٰىكُمْ قَوْمًا تَجْهَلُوْنَ ۞

وَيٰقَوْمِ مَنْ يَّنْصُرُنِىْ مِنَ اللّٰهِ اِنْ طَرَدْتُّهُمْ اَفَلَا تَذَكَّرُوْنَ ۞

وَلَآ اَقُوْلُ لَكُمْ عِنْدِىْ خَزَآئِنُ اللّٰهِ وَلَآ اَعْلَمُ الْغَيْبَ وَلَآ اَقُوْلُ اِنِّىْ مَلَكٌ وَّلَآ اَقُوْلُ لِلَّذِيْنَ تَزْدَرِىْٓ اَعْيُنُكُمْ لَنْ يُّؤْتِيَهُمُ اللّٰهُ خَيْرًا اَللّٰهُ اَعْلَمُ بِمَا فِىْٓ اَنْفُسِهِمْ اِنِّىْٓ اِذًا لَّمِنَ الظّٰلِمِيْنَ ۞

قَالُوْا يٰنُوْحُ قَدْ جَادَلْتَنَا فَاَكْثَرْتَ جِدَالَنَا فَاْتِنَا بِمَا تَعِدُنَآ اِنْ كُنْتَ مِنَ الصّٰدِقِيْنَ ۞

33. He said: Allah only will bring it to you if He please, and you will not escape:

قَالَ اِنَّمَا يَأْتِيْكُمْ بِهِ اللّٰهُ اِنْ شَآءَ وَمَآ اَنْتُمْ بِمُعْجِزِيْنَ ۞

34. And if I intend to give you good advice, my advice will not profit you if Allah intended that He should leave you to go astray; He is your Lord, and to Him shall you be returned.

وَلَا يَنْفَعُكُمْ نُصْحِيْٓ اِنْ اَرَدْتُّ اَنْ اَنْصَحَ لَكُمْ اِنْ كَانَ اللّٰهُ يُرِيْدُ اَنْ يُّغْوِيَكُمْ ۖ هُوَ رَبُّكُمْ ۚ وَاِلَيْهِ تُرْجَعُوْنَ ۞

35. Or do they say: He has forged it? Say: If I have forged it, on me is my guilt, and I am clear of that of which you are guilty.

اَمْ يَقُوْلُوْنَ افْتَرٰىهُ ۚ قُلْ اِنِ افْتَرَيْتُهٗ فَعَلَيَّ اِجْرَامِيْ وَاَنَا بَرِيْٓءٌ مِّمَّا تُجْرِمُوْنَ ۞

36. And it was revealed to Nuh: That none of your people will believe except those who have already believed, therefore do not grieve at what they do:

وَاُوْحِيَ اِلٰى نُوْحٍ اَنَّهٗ لَنْ يُّؤْمِنَ مِنْ قَوْمِكَ اِلَّا مَنْ قَدْ اٰمَنَ فَلَا تَبْتَئِسْ بِمَا كَانُوْا يَفْعَلُوْنَ ۞

37. And make the ark before Our eyes and (according to) Our revelation, and do not speak to Me in respect of those who are unjust; surely they shall be drowned.

وَاصْنَعِ الْفُلْكَ بِاَعْيُنِنَا وَوَحْيِنَا وَلَا تُخَاطِبْنِيْ فِى الَّذِيْنَ ظَلَمُوْا ۚ اِنَّهُمْ مُّغْرَقُوْنَ ۞

38. And he began to make the ark; and whenever the chiefs from among his people passed by him they laughed at him. He said: If you laugh at us, surely we too laugh at you as you laugh (at us).

وَيَصْنَعُ الْفُلْكَ ۥ وَكُلَّمَا مَرَّ عَلَيْهِ مَلَاٌ مِّنْ قَوْمِهٖ سَخِرُوْا مِنْهُ ۚ قَالَ اِنْ تَسْخَرُوْا مِنَّا فَاِنَّا نَسْخَرُ مِنْكُمْ كَمَا تَسْخَرُوْنَ ۞

39. So shall you know who it is on whom will come a chastisement which will disgrace him, and on whom will lasting chastisement come down.

فَسَوْفَ تَعْلَمُوْنَ ۙ مَنْ يَّأْتِيْهِ عَذَابٌ يُّخْزِيْهِ وَيَحِلُّ عَلَيْهِ عَذَابٌ مُّقِيْمٌ ۞

40. Until when Our command came and water came forth from the valley, We said: Carry in it two of all things, a pair, and your own family—except those against whom the word has already gone forth, and those who believe. And there believed not with him but a few.

حَتّٰىٓ اِذَا جَآءَ اَمْرُنَا وَفَارَ التَّنُّوْرُ ۙ قُلْنَا احْمِلْ فِيْهَا مِنْ كُلٍّ زَوْجَيْنِ اثْنَيْنِ وَاَهْلَكَ اِلَّا مَنْ سَبَقَ عَلَيْهِ الْقَوْلُ وَمَنْ اٰمَنَ ۚ وَمَآ اٰمَنَ مَعَهٗٓ اِلَّا قَلِيْلٌ ۞

41. And he said: Embark in it, in the name of Allah be its sailing and its anchoring; most surely my Lord is Forgiving, Merciful.

وَقَالَ ارْكَبُوْا فِيْهَا بِسْمِ اللّٰهِ مَجْرٰىهَا وَمُرْسٰىهَا ۚ اِنَّ رَبِّيْ لَغَفُوْرٌ رَّحِيْمٌ ۞

42. And it moved on with them amid waves like mountains; and Nuh called out to his son, and he was aloof: O my son! embark with us and be not with the unbelievers.

43. He said: I will betake myself for refuge to a mountain that shall protect me from the water. Nuh said: There is no protector today from Allah's punishment but He Who has mercy; and a wave intervened between them, so he was of the drowned.

44. And it was said: O earth, swallow down your water, and O cloud, clear away; and the water was made to abate and the affair was decided, and the ark rested on the Judi, and it was said: Away with the unjust people.

45. And Nuh cried out to his Lord and said: My Lord! surely my son is of my family, and Thy promise is surely true, and Thou art the most just of the judges.

46. He said: O Nuh! surely he is not of your family; surely he is (the doer of) other than good deeds, therefore ask not of Me that of which you have no knowledge; surely I admonish you lest you may be of the ignorant.

47. He said: My Lord! I seek refuge in Thee from asking Thee that of which I have no knowledge; and if Thou shouldst not forgive me and have mercy on me, I should be of the losers.

48. It was said: O Nuh! descend with peace from Us and blessings on you and on the people from among those who are with you, and there shall be nations whom We will afford provisions, then a painful punishment from Us shall afflict them.

49. These are announcements relating to the unseen which We reveal to you, you did not know them—(neither) you nor your people—before this; therefore be patient; surely the end is for those who guard (against evil).

وَهِيَ تَجْرِيْ بِهِمْ فِيْ مَوْجٍ كَالْجِبَالِ ۖ وَنَادٰى نُوْحُ ابْنَهٗ وَكَانَ فِيْ مَعْزِلٍ يّٰبُنَيَّ ارْكَبْ مَّعَنَا وَلَا تَكُنْ مَّعَ الْكٰفِرِيْنَ ۝

قَالَ سَاٰوِيْۤ اِلٰى جَبَلٍ يَّعْصِمُنِيْ مِنَ الْمَآءِ ۚ قَالَ لَا عَاصِمَ الْيَوْمَ مِنْ اَمْرِ اللّٰهِ اِلَّا مَنْ رَّحِمَ ۚ وَحَالَ بَيْنَهُمَا الْمَوْجُ فَكَانَ مِنَ الْمُغْرَقِيْنَ ۝

وَقِيْلَ يٰۤاَرْضُ ابْلَعِيْ مَآءَكِ وَيٰسَمَآءُ اَقْلِعِيْ وَ غِيْضَ الْمَآءُ وَقُضِيَ الْاَمْرُ وَاسْتَوَتْ عَلَى الْجُوْدِيِّ وَقِيْلَ بُعْدًا لِّلْقَوْمِ الظّٰلِمِيْنَ ۝

وَنَادٰى نُوْحٌ رَّبَّهٗ فَقَالَ رَبِّ اِنَّ ابْنِيْ مِنْ اَهْلِيْ وَاِنَّ وَعْدَكَ الْحَقُّ وَاَنْتَ اَحْكَمُ الْحٰكِمِيْنَ ۝

قَالَ يٰنُوْحُ اِنَّهٗ لَيْسَ مِنْ اَهْلِكَ ۚ اِنَّهٗ عَمَلٌ غَيْرُ صَالِحٍ ۖ فَلَا تَسْـَٔلْنِ مَا لَيْسَ لَكَ بِهٖ عِلْمٌ ۖ اِنِّيْۤ اَعِظُكَ اَنْ تَكُوْنَ مِنَ الْجٰهِلِيْنَ ۝

قَالَ رَبِّ اِنِّيْۤ اَعُوْذُ بِكَ اَنْ اَسْـَٔلَكَ مَا لَيْسَ لِيْ بِهٖ عِلْمٌ ۚ وَاِلَّا تَغْفِرْ لِيْ وَتَرْحَمْنِيْۤ اَكُنْ مِّنَ الْخٰسِرِيْنَ ۝

قِيْلَ يٰنُوْحُ اهْبِطْ بِسَلٰمٍ مِّنَّا وَبَرَكٰتٍ عَلَيْكَ وَعَلٰۤى اُمَمٍ مِّمَّنْ مَّعَكَ ۚ وَاُمَمٌ سَنُمَتِّعُهُمْ ثُمَّ يَمَسُّهُمْ مِّنَّا عَذَابٌ اَلِيْمٌ ۝

تِلْكَ مِنْ اَنْبَآءِ الْغَيْبِ نُوْحِيْهَاۤ اِلَيْكَ ۚ مَا كُنْتَ تَعْلَمُهَاۤ اَنْتَ وَلَا قَوْمُكَ مِنْ قَبْلِ هٰذَا ۖ فَاصْبِرْ ۚ اِنَّ الْعَاقِبَةَ لِلْمُتَّقِيْنَ ۝

50. And to Ad (We sent) their brother Hud. He said: O my people! serve Allah, you have no god other than He; you are nothing but forgers (of lies).

51. O my people! I do not ask of you any reward for it; my reward is only with Him Who created me; do you not then understand?

52. And, O my people! ask forgiveness of your Lord, then turn to Him, He will send on you clouds pouring down abundance of rain and add strength to your strength, and do not turn back guilty.

53. They said: O Hud! you have not brought to us any clear argument and we are not going to desert our gods for your word, and we are not believers in you:

54. We cannot say aught but that some of our gods have smitten you with evil. He said: Surely I call Allah to witness, and do you bear witness too, that I am clear of what you associate (with Allah),

55. Besides Him, therefore scheme against me all together; then give me no respite:

56. Surely I rely on Allah, my Lord and your Lord; there is no living creature but He holds it by its forelock; surely my Lord is on the right path.

57. But if you turn back, then indeed I have delivered to you the message with which I have been sent to you, and my Lord will bring another people in your place, and you cannot do Him any harm; surely my Lord is the Preserver of all things.

58. And when Our decree came to pass, We delivered Hud and those who believed with him with mercy from Us, and We delivered them from a hard chastisement.

59. And this was Ad; they denied the communications of their Lord, and disobeyed His apostles and followed the bidding of every insolent opposer (of truth).

وَاِلٰى عَادٍ اَخَاهُمْ هُوْدًا ۘ قَالَ يٰقَوْمِ اعْبُدُوا اللّٰهَ مَا لَكُمْ مِّنْ اِلٰهٍ غَيْرُهٗ ۘ اِنْ اَنْتُمْ اِلَّا مُفْتَرُوْنَ ۝

يٰقَوْمِ لَاۤ اَسْئَلُكُمْ عَلَيْهِ اَجْرًا ۘ اِنْ اَجْرِيَ اِلَّا عَلَى الَّذِيْ فَطَرَنِيْ ۘ اَفَلَا تَعْقِلُوْنَ ۝

وَيٰقَوْمِ اسْتَغْفِرُوْا رَبَّكُمْ ثُمَّ تُوْبُوْۤا اِلَيْهِ يُرْسِلِ السَّمَآءَ عَلَيْكُمْ مِّدْرَارًا وَّيَزِدْكُمْ قُوَّةً اِلٰى قُوَّتِكُمْ وَلَا تَتَوَلَّوْا مُجْرِمِيْنَ ۝

قَالُوْا يٰهُوْدُ مَا جِئْتَنَا بِبَيِّنَةٍ وَّمَا نَحْنُ بِتَارِكِيْۤ اٰلِهَتِنَا عَنْ قَوْلِكَ وَمَا نَحْنُ لَكَ بِمُؤْمِنِيْنَ ۝

اِنْ نَّقُوْلُ اِلَّا اعْتَرٰىكَ بَعْضُ اٰلِهَتِنَا بِسُوْٓءٍ ۘ قَالَ اِنِّيْۤ اُشْهِدُ اللّٰهَ وَاشْهَدُوْۤا اَنِّيْ بَرِيْٓءٌ مِّمَّا تُشْرِكُوْنَ ۝

مِنْ دُوْنِهٖ فَكِيْدُوْنِيْ جَمِيْعًا ثُمَّ لَا تُنْظِرُوْنِ ۝

اِنِّيْ تَوَكَّلْتُ عَلَى اللّٰهِ رَبِّيْ وَرَبِّكُمْ ۘ مَا مِنْ دَآبَّةٍ اِلَّا هُوَ اٰخِذٌۢ بِنَاصِيَتِهَا ۘ اِنَّ رَبِّيْ عَلٰى صِرَاطٍ مُّسْتَقِيْمٍ ۝

فَاِنْ تَوَلَّوْا فَقَدْ اَبْلَغْتُكُمْ مَّاۤ اُرْسِلْتُ بِهٖۤ اِلَيْكُمْ ۘ وَيَسْتَخْلِفُ رَبِّيْ قَوْمًا غَيْرَكُمْ ۘ وَلَا تَضُرُّوْنَهٗ شَيْئًا ۘ اِنَّ رَبِّيْ عَلٰى كُلِّ شَيْءٍ حَفِيْظٌ ۝

وَلَمَّا جَآءَ اَمْرُنَا نَجَّيْنَا هُوْدًا وَّالَّذِيْنَ اٰمَنُوْا مَعَهٗ بِرَحْمَةٍ مِّنَّا ۘ وَنَجَّيْنٰهُمْ مِّنْ عَذَابٍ غَلِيْظٍ ۝

وَتِلْكَ عَادٌ ۙ جَحَدُوْا بِاٰيٰتِ رَبِّهِمْ وَعَصَوْا رُسُلَهٗ وَاتَّبَعُوْۤا اَمْرَ كُلِّ جَبَّارٍ عَنِيْدٍ ۝

60. And they were overtaken by curse in this world and on the resurrection day; now surely Ad disbelieved in their Lord; now surely, away with Ad, the people of Hud.

61. And to Samood (We sent) their brother Salih. He said: O my people! serve Allah, you have no god other than He; He brought you into being from the earth, and made you dwell in it, therefore ask forgiveness of Him, then turn to Him; surely my Lord is Nigh, Answering.

62. They said: O Salih! surely you were one amongst us in whom great expectations were placed before this; do you (now) forbid us from worshipping what our fathers worshipped? And as to that which you call us to, most surely we are in disquieting doubt.

63. He said: O my people! tell me if I have clear proof from my Lord and He has granted to me mercy from Himself—who will then help me against Allah if I disobey Him? Therefore you do not add to me other than loss:

64. And, O my people! this will be (as) Allah's she-camel for you, a sign; therefore leave her to pasture on Allah's earth and do not touch her with evil, for then a near chastisement will overtake you.

65. But they slew her, so he said: Enjoy yourselves in your abode for three days, that is a promise not to be belied.

66. So when Our decree came to pass, We delivered Salih and those who believed with him by mercy from Us, and (We saved them) from the disgrace of that day; surely your Lord is the Strong, the Mighty.

67. And the rumbling overtook those who were unjust, so they became motionless bodies in their abodes,

وَأُتْبِعُوْا فِىْ هٰذِهِ الدُّنْيَا لَعْنَةً وَّيَوْمَ الْقِيٰمَةِ ۗ اَلَا اِنَّ عَادًا كَفَرُوْا رَبَّهُمْ ۗ اَلَا بُعْدًا لِّعَادٍ قَوْمِ هُوْدٍ ۟ ٦٠

وَاِلٰى ثَمُوْدَ اَخَاهُمْ صٰلِحًا ۘ قَالَ يٰقَوْمِ اعْبُدُوا اللّٰهَ مَا لَكُمْ مِّنْ اِلٰهٍ غَيْرُهٗ ۗ هُوَ اَنْشَاَكُمْ مِّنَ الْاَرْضِ وَاسْتَعْمَرَكُمْ فِيْهَا فَاسْتَغْفِرُوْهُ ثُمَّ تُوْبُوْٓا اِلَيْهِ ۗ اِنَّ رَبِّيْ قَرِيْبٌ مُّجِيْبٌ ٦١

قَالُوْا يٰصٰلِحُ قَدْ كُنْتَ فِيْنَا مَرْجُوًّا قَبْلَ هٰذَآ اَتَنْهٰنَآ اَنْ نَّعْبُدَ مَا يَعْبُدُ اٰبَاؤُنَا وَاِنَّنَا لَفِيْ شَكٍّ مِّمَّا تَدْعُوْنَآ اِلَيْهِ مُرِيْبٍ ٦٢

قَالَ يٰقَوْمِ اَرَءَيْتُمْ اِنْ كُنْتُ عَلٰى بَيِّنَةٍ مِّنْ رَّبِّيْ وَاٰتٰنِيْ مِنْهُ رَحْمَةً فَمَنْ يَّنْصُرُنِيْ مِنَ اللّٰهِ اِنْ عَصَيْتُهٗ ۖ فَمَا تَزِيْدُوْنَنِيْ غَيْرَ تَخْسِيْرٍ ٦٣

وَيٰقَوْمِ هٰذِهٖ نَاقَةُ اللّٰهِ لَكُمْ اٰيَةً فَذَرُوْهَا تَأْكُلْ فِيْٓ اَرْضِ اللّٰهِ وَلَا تَمَسُّوْهَا بِسُوْۤءٍ فَيَأْخُذَكُمْ عَذَابٌ قَرِيْبٌ ٦٤

فَعَقَرُوْهَا فَقَالَ تَمَتَّعُوْا فِيْ دَارِكُمْ ثَلٰثَةَ اَيَّامٍ ۗ ذٰلِكَ وَعْدٌ غَيْرُ مَكْذُوْبٍ ٦٥

فَلَمَّا جَاۤءَ اَمْرُنَا نَجَّيْنَا صٰلِحًا وَّالَّذِيْنَ اٰمَنُوْا مَعَهٗ بِرَحْمَةٍ مِّنَّا وَمِنْ خِزْيِ يَوْمِئِذٍ ۗ اِنَّ رَبَّكَ هُوَ الْقَوِيُّ الْعَزِيْزُ ٦٦

وَاَخَذَ الَّذِيْنَ ظَلَمُوا الصَّيْحَةُ فَاَصْبَحُوْا فِيْ دِيَارِهِمْ جٰثِمِيْنَ ۙ ٦٧

68. As though they had never dwelt in them; now surely did Samood disbelieve in their Lord; now surely, away with Samood.

كَأَنْ لَّمْ يَغْنَوْا فِيهَا ۗ أَلَا إِنَّ ثَمُوْدَا۟ كَفَرُوْا رَبَّهُمْ ۗ أَلَا بُعْدًا لِّثَمُوْدَ ۞

69. And certainly Our messengers came to Ibrahim with good news. They said: Peace. Peace, said he, and he made no delay in bringing a roasted calf.

وَلَقَدْ جَآءَتْ رُسُلُنَآ اِبْرٰهِيْمَ بِالْبُشْرٰى قَالُوْا سَلٰمًا ۖ قَالَ سَلٰمٌ ۖ فَمَا لَبِثَ اَنْ جَآءَ بِعِجْلٍ حَنِيْذٍ ۞

70. But when he saw that their hands were not extended towards it, he deemed them strange and conceived fear of them. They said: Fear not, surely we are sent to Lut's people.

فَلَمَّا رَاٰ اَيْدِيَهُمْ لَا تَصِلُ اِلَيْهِ نَكِرَهُمْ وَاَوْجَسَ مِنْهُمْ خِيْفَةً ۗ قَالُوْا لَا تَخَفْ اِنَّآ اُرْسِلْنَآ اِلٰى قَوْمِ لُوْطٍ ۞

71. And his wife was standing (by), so she laughed, then We gave her the good news of Ishaq and after Ishaq of (a son's son) Yaqoub.

وَامْرَاَتُهٗ قَآئِمَةٌ فَضَحِكَتْ فَبَشَّرْنٰهَا بِاِسْحٰقَ ۙ وَمِنْ وَّرَآءِ اِسْحٰقَ يَعْقُوْبَ ۞

72. She said: O wonder! shall I bear a son when I am an extremely old woman and this my husband an extremely old man? Most surely this is a wonderful thing.

قَالَتْ يٰوَيْلَتٰىٓ ءَاَلِدُ وَاَنَا عَجُوْزٌ وَّهٰذَا بَعْلِيْ شَيْخًا ۗ اِنَّ هٰذَا لَشَيْءٌ عَجِيْبٌ ۞

73. They said: Do you wonder at Allah's bidding? The mercy of Allah and His blessings are on you, O people of the house, surely He is Praised, Glorious.

قَالُوْٓا اَتَعْجَبِيْنَ مِنْ اَمْرِ اللّٰهِ رَحْمَتُ اللّٰهِ وَبَرَكٰتُهٗ عَلَيْكُمْ اَهْلَ الْبَيْتِ ۗ اِنَّهٗ حَمِيْدٌ مَّجِيْدٌ ۞

74. So when fear had gone away from Ibrahim and good news came to him, he began to plead with Us for Lut's people.

فَلَمَّا ذَهَبَ عَنْ اِبْرٰهِيْمَ الرَّوْعُ وَجَآءَتْهُ الْبُشْرٰى يُجَادِلُنَا فِيْ قَوْمِ لُوْطٍ ۞

75. Most surely Ibrahim was forbearing, tender-hearted, oft-returning (to Allah):

اِنَّ اِبْرٰهِيْمَ لَحَلِيْمٌ اَوَّاهٌ مُّنِيْبٌ ۞

76. O Ibrahim! leave off this, surely the decree of your Lord has come to pass, and surely there must come to them a chastisement that cannot be averted.

يٰٓاِبْرٰهِيْمُ اَعْرِضْ عَنْ هٰذَا ۚ اِنَّهٗ قَدْ جَآءَ اَمْرُ رَبِّكَ ۚ وَاِنَّهُمْ اٰتِيْهِمْ عَذَابٌ غَيْرُ مَرْدُوْدٍ ۞

77. And when Our messengers came to Lut, he was grieved for them, and he lacked strength to protect them, and said: This is a hard day.

وَلَمَّا جَآءَتْ رُسُلُنَا لُوْطًا سِيْٓءَ بِهِمْ وَضَاقَ بِهِمْ ذَرْعًا وَّقَالَ هٰذَا يَوْمٌ عَصِيْبٌ ۞

208

78. And his people came to him, (as if) rushed on towards him, and already they did evil deeds. He said: O my people! these are my daughters—they are purer for you, so guard against (the punishment of) Allah and do not disgrace me with regard to my guests; is there not among you one right-minded man?

وَجَاءَهُ قَوْمُهُ يُهْرَعُوْنَ اِلَيْهِ وَمِنْ قَبْلُ كَانُوْا يَعْمَلُوْنَ السَّيِّاٰتِ قَالَ يٰقَوْمِ هٰٓؤُلَاءِ بَنَاتِيْ هُنَّ اَطْهَرُ لَكُمْ فَاتَّقُوا اللّٰهَ وَلَا تُخْزُوْنِ فِيْ ضَيْفِيْ اَلَيْسَ مِنْكُمْ رَجُلٌ رَّشِيْدٌ ۝

79. They said: Certainly you know that we have no claim on your daughters, and most surely you know what we desire.

قَالُوْا لَقَدْ عَلِمْتَ مَا لَنَا فِيْ بَنٰتِكَ مِنْ حَقٍّ وَاِنَّكَ لَتَعْلَمُ مَا نُرِيْدُ ۝

80. He said: Ah! that I had power to suppress you, rather I shall have recourse to a strong support.

قَالَ لَوْ اَنَّ لِيْ بِكُمْ قُوَّةً اَوْ اٰوِيْٓ اِلٰى رُكْنٍ شَدِيْدٍ ۝

81. They said: O Lut! we are the messengers of your Lord; they shall by no means reach you; so remove your followers in a part of the night—and let none of you turn back—except your wife, for surely whatsoever befalls them shall befall her; surely their appointed time is the morning; is not the morning nigh?

قَالُوْا يٰلُوْطُ اِنَّا رُسُلُ رَبِّكَ لَنْ يَّصِلُوْٓا اِلَيْكَ فَاَسْرِ بِاَهْلِكَ بِقِطْعٍ مِّنَ الَّيْلِ وَلَا يَلْتَفِتْ مِنْكُمْ اَحَدٌ اِلَّا امْرَاَتَكَ اِنَّهُ مُصِيْبُهَا مَا اَصَابَهُمْ اِنَّ مَوْعِدَهُمُ الصُّبْحُ اَلَيْسَ الصُّبْحُ بِقَرِيْبٍ ۝

82. So when Our decree came to pass, We turned them upside down and rained down upon them stones, of what had been decreed, one after another.

فَلَمَّا جَاءَ اَمْرُنَا جَعَلْنَا عَالِيَهَا سَافِلَهَا وَاَمْطَرْنَا عَلَيْهَا حِجَارَةً مِّنْ سِجِّيْلٍ مَّنْضُوْدٍ ۝

83. Marked (for punishment) with your Lord and it is not far off from the unjust.

مُّسَوَّمَةً عِنْدَ رَبِّكَ وَمَا هِيَ مِنَ الظّٰلِمِيْنَ بِبَعِيْدٍ ۝

84. And to Madyan (We sent) their brother Shu'aib. He said: O my people! serve Allah, you have no god other than He, and do not give short measure and weight: surely I see you in prosperity and surely I fear for you the punishment of an all-encompassing day.

وَاِلٰى مَدْيَنَ اَخَاهُمْ شُعَيْبًا قَالَ يٰقَوْمِ اعْبُدُوا اللّٰهَ مَا لَكُمْ مِّنْ اِلٰهٍ غَيْرُهُ وَلَا تَنْقُصُوا الْمِكْيَالَ وَالْمِيْزَانَ اِنِّيْٓ اَرٰىكُمْ بِخَيْرٍ وَّاِنِّيْٓ اَخَافُ عَلَيْكُمْ عَذَابَ يَوْمٍ مُّحِيْطٍ ۝

85. And, O my people! give full measure and weight fairly, and defraud not men their things, and do not act corruptly in the land, making mischief:

وَيٰقَوْمِ اَوْفُوا الْمِكْيَالَ وَالْمِيْزَانَ بِالْقِسْطِ وَلَا تَبْخَسُوا النَّاسَ اَشْيَاءَهُمْ وَلَا تَعْثَوْا فِي الْاَرْضِ مُفْسِدِيْنَ ۝

86. What remains with Allah is better for you if you are believers, and I am not a keeper over you.

بَقِيَّتُ اللّٰهِ خَيْرٌ لَّكُمْ اِنْ كُنْتُمْ مُّؤْمِنِيْنَ ۚ۬ وَمَاۤ اَنَا عَلَيْكُمْ بِحَفِيْظٍ ۝

87. They said: O Shu'aib! does your prayer enjoin you that we should forsake what our fathers worshipped or that we should not do what we please with regard to our property? Forsooth you are the forbearing, the right-directing one.

قَالُوْا يٰشُعَيْبُ اَصَلٰوتُكَ تَأْمُرُكَ اَنْ نَّتْرُكَ مَا يَعْبُدُ اٰبَآؤُنَاۤ اَوْ اَنْ نَّفْعَلَ فِيْۤ اَمْوَالِنَا مَا نَشٰٓؤُا ۚ اِنَّكَ لَاَنْتَ الْحَلِيْمُ الرَّشِيْدُ ۝

88. He said: O my people! have you considered if I have a clear proof from my Lord and He has given me a goodly sustenance from Himself; and I do not desire that in opposition to you I should betake myself to that which I forbid you: I desire nothing but reform so far as I am able, and with none but Allah is the direction of my affair to a right issue; on Him do I rely and to Him do I turn:

قَالَ يٰقَوْمِ اَرَءَيْتُمْ اِنْ كُنْتُ عَلٰى بَيِّنَةٍ مِّنْ رَّبِّيْ وَ رَزَقَنِيْ مِنْهُ رِزْقًا حَسَنًا ۚ وَمَاۤ اُرِيْدُ اَنْ اُخَالِفَكُمْ اِلٰى مَاۤ اَنْهٰىكُمْ عَنْهُ ۚ اِنْ اُرِيْدُ اِلَّا الْاِصْلَاحَ مَا اسْتَطَعْتُ ۚ وَمَا تَوْفِيْقِيْۤ اِلَّا بِاللّٰهِ ۚ عَلَيْهِ تَوَكَّلْتُ وَاِلَيْهِ اُنِيْبُ ۝

89. And, O my people! let not opposition to me make you guilty so that there may befall you the like of what befell the people of Nuh, or the people of Hud, or the people of Salih, nor are the people of Lut far off from you;

وَيٰقَوْمِ لَا يَجْرِمَنَّكُمْ شِقَاقِيْۤ اَنْ يُّصِيْبَكُمْ مِّثْلُ مَاۤ اَصَابَ قَوْمَ نُوْحٍ اَوْ قَوْمَ هُوْدٍ اَوْ قَوْمَ صٰلِحٍ ۚ وَمَا قَوْمُ لُوْطٍ مِّنْكُمْ بِبَعِيْدٍ ۝

90. And ask forgiveness of your Lord, then turn to Him; surely my Lord is Merciful, Loving-kind.

وَاسْتَغْفِرُوْا رَبَّكُمْ ثُمَّ تُوْبُوْۤا اِلَيْهِ ۚ اِنَّ رَبِّيْ رَحِيْمٌ وَّدُوْدٌ ۝

91. They said: O Shu'aib! we do not understand much of what you say and most surely we see you to be weak among us, and were it not for your family we would surely stone you, and you are not mighty against us.

قَالُوْا يٰشُعَيْبُ مَا نَفْقَهُ كَثِيْرًا مِّمَّا تَقُوْلُ وَاِنَّا لَنَرٰىكَ فِيْنَا ضَعِيْفًا ۚ وَلَوْلَا رَهْطُكَ لَرَجَمْنٰكَ ۖ وَمَاۤ اَنْتَ عَلَيْنَا بِعَزِيْزٍ ۝

92. He said: O my people! is my family more esteemed by you than Allah? And you neglect Him as a thing cast behind your back; surely my Lord encompasses what you do:

قَالَ يٰقَوْمِ اَرَهْطِيْۤ اَعَزُّ عَلَيْكُمْ مِّنَ اللّٰهِ ۚ وَاتَّخَذْتُمُوْهُ وَرَآءَكُمْ ظِهْرِيًّا ۚ اِنَّ رَبِّيْ بِمَا تَعْمَلُوْنَ مُحِيْطٌ ۝

93. And, O my people! act according to your ability, I too am acting; you will come to know soon who it is on whom will light the punishment that will disgrace him and who it is that is a liar, and watch, surely I too am watching with you.

وَيٰقَوْمِ اعْمَلُوْا عَلٰى مَكَانَتِكُمْ اِنِّيْ عَامِلٌ ۚ سَوْفَ تَعْلَمُوْنَ ۙ مَنْ يَّأْتِيْهِ عَذَابٌ يُّخْزِيْهِ وَمَنْ هُوَ كَاذِبٌ ۚ وَارْتَقِبُوْۤا اِنِّيْ مَعَكُمْ رَقِيْبٌ ۝

94. And when Our decree came to pass We delivered Shu'aib, and those who believed with him by mercy from Us, and the rumbling overtook those who were unjust so they became motionless bodies in their abodes,

95. As though they had never dwelt in them; now surely perdition overtook Madyan as had perished Samood.

96. And certainly We sent Musa with Our communications and a clear authority,

97. To Firon and his chiefs, but they followed the bidding of Firon, and Firon's bidding was not right-directing.

98. He shall lead his people on the resurrection day, and bring them down to the fire; and evil the place to which they are brought.

99. And they are overtaken by curse in this (world), and on the resurrection day; evil the gift which shall be given.

100. This is an account of (the fate of) the towns which We relate to you; of them are some that stand and (others) mown down.

101. And We did not do them injustice, but they were unjust to themselves, so their gods whom they called upon besides Allah did not avail them aught when the decree of your Lord came to pass; and they added but to their ruin.

102. And such is the punishment of your Lord when He punishes the towns while they are unjust; surely His punishment is painful, severe.

103. Most surely there is a sign in this for him who fears the chastisement of the hereafter; this is a day on which the people shall be gathered together and this is a day that shall be witnessed.

104. And We do not delay it but to an appointed term.

وَلَمَّا جَآءَ اَمْرُنَا نَجَّيْنَا شُعَيْبًا وَّالَّذِيْنَ اٰمَنُوْا مَعَهٗ بِرَحْمَةٍ مِّنَّا وَاَخَذَتِ الَّذِيْنَ ظَلَمُوا الصَّيْحَةُ فَاَصْبَحُوْا فِيْ دِيَارِهِمْ جٰثِمِيْنَ ۙ ۝

كَاَنْ لَّمْ يَغْنَوْا فِيْهَا ۗ اَلَا بُعْدًا لِّمَدْيَنَ كَمَا بَعِدَتْ ثَمُوْدُ ۝

وَلَقَدْ اَرْسَلْنَا مُوْسٰى بِاٰيٰتِنَا وَسُلْطٰنٍ مُّبِيْنٍ ۙ ۝

اِلٰى فِرْعَوْنَ وَمَلَاۡئِهٖ فَاتَّبَعُوْۤا اَمْرَ فِرْعَوْنَ ۚ وَمَاۤ اَمْرُ فِرْعَوْنَ بِرَشِيْدٍ ۝

يَقْدُمُ قَوْمَهٗ يَوْمَ الْقِيٰمَةِ فَاَوْرَدَهُمُ النَّارَ ۚ وَبِئْسَ الْوِرْدُ الْمَوْرُوْدُ ۝

وَاُتْبِعُوْا فِيْ هٰذِهٖ لَعْنَةً وَّيَوْمَ الْقِيٰمَةِ ۚ بِئْسَ الرِّفْدُ الْمَرْفُوْدُ ۝

ذٰلِكَ مِنْ اَنْبَآءِ الْقُرٰى نَقُصُّهٗ عَلَيْكَ مِنْهَا قَآئِمٌ وَّحَصِيْدٌ ۝

وَمَا ظَلَمْنٰهُمْ وَلٰكِنْ ظَلَمُوْۤا اَنْفُسَهُمْ فَمَاۤ اَغْنَتْ عَنْهُمْ اٰلِهَتُهُمُ الَّتِيْ يَدْعُوْنَ مِنْ دُوْنِ اللّٰهِ مِنْ شَيْءٍ لَّمَّا جَآءَ اَمْرُ رَبِّكَ ۚ وَمَا زَادُوْهُمْ غَيْرَ تَتْبِيْبٍ ۝

وَكَذٰلِكَ اَخْذُ رَبِّكَ اِذَاۤ اَخَذَ الْقُرٰى وَهِيَ ظَالِمَةٌ ۚ اِنَّ اَخْذَهٗۤ اَلِيْمٌ شَدِيْدٌ ۝

اِنَّ فِيْ ذٰلِكَ لَاٰيَةً لِّمَنْ خَافَ عَذَابَ الْاٰخِرَةِ ۚ ذٰلِكَ يَوْمٌ مَّجْمُوْعٌ لَّهُ النَّاسُ وَذٰلِكَ يَوْمٌ مَّشْهُوْدٌ ۝

وَمَا نُؤَخِّرُهٗۤ اِلَّا لِاَجَلٍ مَّعْدُوْدٍ ۝

105. On the day when it shall come, no soul shall speak except with His permission, then (some) of them shall be unhappy and (others) happy.

يَوْمَ يَأْتِ لَا تَكَلَّمُ نَفْسٌ اِلَّا بِاِذْنِهٖ فَمِنْهُمْ شَقِيٌّ وَّسَعِيْدٌ ۝

106. So as to those who are unhappy, they shall be in the fire; for them shall be sighing and groaning in it:

فَاَمَّا الَّذِيْنَ شَقُوْا فَفِى النَّارِ لَهُمْ فِيْهَا زَفِيْرٌ وَّشَهِيْقٌ ۝

107. Abiding therein so long as the heavens and the earth endure, except as your Lord please; surely your Lord is the mighty doer of what He intends.

خٰلِدِيْنَ فِيْهَا مَا دَامَتِ السَّمٰوٰتُ وَالْاَرْضُ اِلَّا مَا شَاۤءَ رَبُّكَ اِنَّ رَبَّكَ فَعَّالٌ لِّمَا يُرِيْدُ ۝

108. And as to those who are made happy, they shall be in the garden, abiding in it as long as the heavens and the earth endure, except as your Lord please; a gift which shall never be cut off.

وَاَمَّا الَّذِيْنَ سُعِدُوْا فَفِى الْجَنَّةِ خٰلِدِيْنَ فِيْهَا مَا دَامَتِ السَّمٰوٰتُ وَالْاَرْضُ اِلَّا مَا شَاۤءَ رَبُّكَ عَطَاۤءً غَيْرَ مَجْذُوْذٍ ۝

109. Therefore be not in doubt as to what these worship; they do not worship but as their fathers worshipped before; and most surely We will pay them back in full their portion undiminished.

فَلَا تَكُ فِيْ مِرْيَةٍ مِّمَّا يَعْبُدُ هٰؤُلَاۤءِ مَا يَعْبُدُوْنَ اِلَّا كَمَا يَعْبُدُ اٰبَاۤؤُهُمْ مِّنْ قَبْلُ وَاِنَّا لَمُوَفُّوْهُمْ نَصِيْبَهُمْ غَيْرَ مَنْقُوْصٍ ۝

110. And certainly We gave the book to Musa, but it was gone against; and had not a word gone forth from your Lord, the matter would surely have been decided between them; and surely they are in a disquieting doubt about it.

وَلَقَدْ اٰتَيْنَا مُوْسَى الْكِتٰبَ فَاخْتُلِفَ فِيْهِ وَلَوْلَا كَلِمَةٌ سَبَقَتْ مِنْ رَّبِّكَ لَقُضِيَ بَيْنَهُمْ وَاِنَّهُمْ لَفِيْ شَكٍّ مِّنْهُ مُرِيْبٍ ۝

111. And your Lord will most surely pay back to all their deeds in full; surely He is aware of what they do.

وَاِنَّ كُلًّا لَّمَّا لَيُوَفِّيَنَّهُمْ رَبُّكَ اَعْمَالَهُمْ اِنَّهٗ بِمَا يَعْمَلُوْنَ خَبِيْرٌ ۝

112. Continue then in the right way as you are commanded, as also he who has turned (to Allah) with you, and be not inordinate (O men!), surely He sees what you do.

فَاسْتَقِمْ كَمَا اُمِرْتَ وَمَنْ تَابَ مَعَكَ وَلَا تَطْغَوْا اِنَّهٗ بِمَا تَعْمَلُوْنَ بَصِيْرٌ ۝

113. And do not incline to those who are unjust, lest the fire touch you, and you have no guardians besides Allah, then you shall not be helped.

وَلَا تَرْكَنُوْا اِلَى الَّذِيْنَ ظَلَمُوْا فَتَمَسَّكُمُ النَّارُ وَمَا لَكُمْ مِّنْ دُوْنِ اللّٰهِ مِنْ اَوْلِيَاۤءَ ثُمَّ لَا تُنْصَرُوْنَ ۝

114. And keep up prayer in the two parts of the day and in the first hours of the night; surely good deeds take away evil deeds; this is a reminder to the mindful.

وَاَقِمِ الصَّلٰوةَ طَرَفَيِ النَّهَارِ وَزُلَفًا مِّنَ الَّيْلِ ۗ اِنَّ الْحَسَنٰتِ يُذْهِبْنَ السَّيِّاٰتِ ۗ ذٰلِكَ ذِكْرٰى لِلذّٰكِرِيْنَ ۝

115. And be patient, for surely Allah does not waste the reward of the good doers.

وَاصْبِرْ فَاِنَّ اللّٰهَ لَا يُضِيْعُ اَجْرَ الْمُحْسِنِيْنَ ۝

116. But why were there not among the generations before you those possessing understanding, who should have forbidden the making of mischief in the earth, except a few of those whom We delivered from among them? And those who were unjust went after what they are made to enjoy of plenty, and they were guilty.

فَلَوْلَا كَانَ مِنَ الْقُرُوْنِ مِنْ قَبْلِكُمْ اُولُوْا بَقِيَّةٍ يَّنْهَوْنَ عَنِ الْفَسَادِ فِى الْاَرْضِ اِلَّا قَلِيْلًا مِّمَّنْ اَنْجَيْنَا مِنْهُمْ ۚ وَاتَّبَعَ الَّذِيْنَ ظَلَمُوْا مَا اُتْرِفُوْا فِيْهِ وَكَانُوْا مُجْرِمِيْنَ ۝

117. And it did not beseem your Lord to have destroyed the towns tyrannously, while their people acted well.

وَمَا كَانَ رَبُّكَ لِيُهْلِكَ الْقُرٰى بِظُلْمٍ وَّاَهْلُهَا مُصْلِحُوْنَ ۝

118. And if your Lord had pleased He would certainly have made people a single nation, and they shall continue to differ.

وَلَوْ شَآءَ رَبُّكَ لَجَعَلَ النَّاسَ اُمَّةً وَّاحِدَةً وَّلَا يَزَالُوْنَ مُخْتَلِفِيْنَ ۝

119. Except those on whom your Lord has mercy; and for this did He create them; and the word of your Lord is fulfilled: Certainly I will fill hell with the jinn and the men, all together.

اِلَّا مَنْ رَّحِمَ رَبُّكَ ۗ وَلِذٰلِكَ خَلَقَهُمْ ۗ وَتَمَّتْ كَلِمَةُ رَبِّكَ لَاَمْلَئَنَّ جَهَنَّمَ مِنَ الْجِنَّةِ وَالنَّاسِ اَجْمَعِيْنَ ۝

120. And all we relate to you of the accounts of the apostles is to strengthen your heart therewith; and in this has come to you the truth and an admonition, and a reminder to the believers.

وَكُلًّا نَّقُصُّ عَلَيْكَ مِنْ اَنْبَآءِ الرُّسُلِ مَا نُثَبِّتُ بِهِ فُؤَادَكَ ۚ وَجَآءَكَ فِى هٰذِهِ الْحَقُّ وَمَوْعِظَةٌ وَّذِكْرٰى لِلْمُؤْمِنِيْنَ ۝

121. And say to those who do not believe: Act according to your state; surely we too are acting.

وَقُلْ لِّلَّذِيْنَ لَا يُؤْمِنُوْنَ اعْمَلُوْا عَلٰى مَكَانَتِكُمْ ۗ اِنَّا عٰمِلُوْنَ ۝

122. And wait; surely we are waiting also.

وَانْتَظِرُوْا ۚ اِنَّا مُنْتَظِرُوْنَ ۝

123. And Allah's is the unseen in the heavens and the earth, and to Him is returned the whole of the affair; therefore serve Him and rely on Him, and your Lord is not heedless of what you do.

وَلِلّٰهِ غَيْبُ السَّمٰوٰتِ وَالْاَرْضِ وَاِلَيْهِ يُرْجَعُ الْاَمْرُ كُلُّهُ فَاعْبُدْهُ وَتَوَكَّلْ عَلَيْهِ ۚ وَمَا رَبُّكَ بِغَافِلٍ عَمَّا تَعْمَلُوْنَ ۝

YUSUF

بِسۡمِ اللهِ الرَّحۡمٰنِ الرَّحِيۡمِ

In the name of Allah,
the Beneficent, the Merciful.

1. Alif Lam Ra. These are the verses of the Book that makes (things) manifest.

الٓرٰ ۣ تِلۡكَ اٰيٰتُ الۡكِتٰبِ الۡمُبِيۡنِ ۞

2. Surely We have revealed it—an Arabic Quran—that you may understand.

اِنَّاۤ اَنۡزَلۡنٰهُ قُرۡءٰنًا عَرَبِيًّا لَّعَلَّكُمۡ تَعۡقِلُوۡنَ ۞

3. We narrate to you the best of narratives, by Our revealing to you this Quran, though before this you were certainly one of those who did not know.

نَحۡنُ نَقُصُّ عَلَيۡكَ اَحۡسَنَ الۡقَصَصِ بِمَاۤ اَوۡحَيۡنَاۤ اِلَيۡكَ هٰذَا الۡقُرۡاٰنَ ۖ وَاِنۡ كُنۡتَ مِنۡ قَبۡلِهٖ لَمِنَ الۡغٰفِلِيۡنَ ۞

4. When Yusuf said to his father: O my father! surely I saw eleven stars and the sun and the moon—I saw them making obeisance to me.

اِذۡ قَالَ يُوۡسُفُ لِاَبِيۡهِ يٰۤاَبَتِ اِنِّيۡ رَاَيۡتُ اَحَدَ عَشَرَ كَوۡكَبًا وَّالشَّمۡسَ وَالۡقَمَرَ رَاَيۡتُهُمۡ لِيۡ سٰجِدِيۡنَ ۞

5. He said: O my son! do not relate your vision to your brothers, lest they devise a plan against you; surely the Shaitan is an open enemy to man.

قَالَ يٰبُنَيَّ لَا تَقۡصُصۡ رُءۡيَاكَ عَلٰۤى اِخۡوَتِكَ فَيَكِيۡدُوۡا لَكَ كَيۡدًا ۭ اِنَّ الشَّيۡطٰنَ لِلۡاِنۡسَانِ عَدُوٌّ مُّبِيۡنٌ ۞

6. And thus will your Lord choose you and teach you the interpretation of sayings and make His favor complete to you and to the children of Yaqoub, as He made it complete before to your fathers, Ibrahim and Ishaq; surely your Lord is Knowing, Wise.

وَكَذٰلِكَ يَجۡتَبِيۡكَ رَبُّكَ وَيُعَلِّمُكَ مِنۡ تَاۡوِيۡلِ الۡاَحَادِيۡثِ وَيُتِمُّ نِعۡمَتَهٗ عَلَيۡكَ وَعَلٰۤى اٰلِ يَعۡقُوۡبَ كَمَاۤ اَتَمَّهَا عَلٰۤى اَبَوَيۡكَ مِنۡ قَبۡلُ اِبۡرٰهِيۡمَ وَاِسۡحٰقَ ۭ اِنَّ رَبَّكَ عَلِيۡمٌ حَكِيۡمٌ ۞

7. Certainly in Yusuf and his brothers there are signs for the inquirers.

لَقَدۡ كَانَ فِيۡ يُوۡسُفَ وَاِخۡوَتِهٖۤ اٰيٰتٌ لِّلسَّآئِلِيۡنَ ۞

8. When they said: Certainly Yusuf and his brother are dearer to our father than we, though we are a (stronger) company; most surely our father is in manifest error:

اِذۡ قَالُوۡا لَيُوۡسُفُ وَاَخُوۡهُ اَحَبُّ اِلٰۤى اَبِيۡنَا مِنَّا وَنَحۡنُ عُصۡبَةٌ ۭ اِنَّ اَبَانَا لَفِيۡ ضَلٰلٍ مُّبِيۡنِ ۞

9. Slay Yusuf or cast him (forth) into some land, so that your father's regard may be exclusively for you, and after that you may be a righteous people.

اقۡتُلُوۡا يُوۡسُفَ اَوِ اطۡرَحُوۡهُ اَرۡضًا يَّخۡلُ لَكُمۡ وَجۡهُ اَبِيۡكُمۡ وَتَكُوۡنُوۡا مِنۢ بَعۡدِهٖ قَوۡمًا صٰلِحِيۡنَ ۞

10. A speaker from among them said: Do not slay Yusuf, and cast him down into the bottom of the pit if you must do (it), (so that) some of the travellers may pick him up.

11. They said: O our father! what reason have you that you do not trust in us with respect to Yusuf? And most surely we are his sincere well-wishers:

12. Send him with us tomorrow that he may enjoy himself and sport, and surely we will guard him well.

13. He said: Surely it grieves me that you should take him off, and I fear lest the wolf devour him while you are heedless of him.

14. They said: Surely if the wolf should devour him notwithstanding that we are a (strong) company, we should then certainly be losers.

15. So when they had gone off with him and agreed that they should put him down at the bottom of the pit, and We revealed to him: You will most certainly inform them of this their affair while they do not perceive.

16. And they came to their father at nightfall, weeping.

17. They said: O our father! surely we went off racing and left Yusuf by our goods, so the wolf devoured him, and you will not believe us though we are truthful.

18. And they brought his shirt with false blood upon it. He said: Nay, your souls have made the matter light for you, but patience is good and Allah is He Whose help is sought for against what you describe.

19. And there came travellers and they sent their water-drawer and he let down his bucket. He said: O good news! this is a youth; and they concealed him as an article of merchandise, and Allah knew what they did.

قَالَ قَآئِلٌ مِّنْهُمْ لَا تَقْتُلُوا يُوْسُفَ وَاَلْقُوْهُ فِيْ غَيٰبَتِ الْجُبِّ يَلْتَقِطْهُ بَعْضُ السَّيَّارَةِ اِنْ كُنْتُمْ فٰعِلِيْنَ ۝

قَالُوْا يٰٓاَبَانَا مَا لَكَ لَا تَأْمَنَّا عَلٰى يُوْسُفَ وَاِنَّا لَهٗ لَنٰصِحُوْنَ ۝

اَرْسِلْهُ مَعَنَا غَدًا يَّرْتَعْ وَيَلْعَبْ وَاِنَّا لَهٗ لَحٰفِظُوْنَ ۝

قَالَ اِنِّيْ لَيَحْزُنُنِيْ اَنْ تَذْهَبُوْا بِهٖ وَاَخَافُ اَنْ يَّأْكُلَهُ الذِّئْبُ وَاَنْتُمْ عَنْهُ غٰفِلُوْنَ ۝

قَالُوْا لَئِنْ اَكَلَهُ الذِّئْبُ وَنَحْنُ عُصْبَةٌ اِنَّآ اِذًا لَّخٰسِرُوْنَ ۝ فَلَمَّا ذَهَبُوْا بِهٖ وَاَجْمَعُوْا اَنْ يَّجْعَلُوْهُ فِيْ غَيٰبَتِ الْجُبِّ وَاَوْحَيْنَآ اِلَيْهِ لَتُنَبِّئَنَّهُمْ بِاَمْرِهِمْ هٰذَا وَهُمْ لَا يَشْعُرُوْنَ ۝

وَجَآءُوْ اَبَاهُمْ عِشَآءً يَّبْكُوْنَ ۝

قَالُوْا يٰٓاَبَانَآ اِنَّا ذَهَبْنَا نَسْتَبِقُ وَتَرَكْنَا يُوْسُفَ عِنْدَ مَتَاعِنَا فَاَكَلَهُ الذِّئْبُ وَمَآ اَنْتَ بِمُؤْمِنٍ لَّنَا وَلَوْ كُنَّا صٰدِقِيْنَ ۝

وَجَآءُوْ عَلٰى قَمِيْصِهٖ بِدَمٍ كَذِبٍ قَالَ بَلْ سَوَّلَتْ لَكُمْ اَنْفُسُكُمْ اَمْرًا فَصَبْرٌ جَمِيْلٌ وَاللّٰهُ الْمُسْتَعَانُ عَلٰى مَا تَصِفُوْنَ ۝

وَجَآءَتْ سَيَّارَةٌ فَاَرْسَلُوْا وَارِدَهُمْ فَاَدْلٰى دَلْوَهٗ قَالَ يٰبُشْرٰى هٰذَا غُلٰمٌ وَاَسَرُّوْهُ بِضَاعَةً وَاللّٰهُ عَلِيْمٌ بِمَا يَعْمَلُوْنَ ۝

20. And they sold him for a small price, a few pieces of silver, and they showed no desire for him.

وَشَرَوْهُ بِثَمَنٍ بَخْسٍ دَرَاهِمَ مَعْدُوْدَةٍ وَكَانُوْا فِيْهِ مِنَ الزَّاهِدِيْنَ ۞

21. And the Egyptian who bought him said to his wife: Give him an honorable abode, maybe he will be useful to us, or we may adopt him as a son. And thus did We establish Yusuf in the land and that We might teach him the interpretation of sayings; and Allah is the master of His affair, but most people do not know.

وَقَالَ الَّذِى اشْتَرٰىهُ مِنْ مِّصْرَ لِامْرَاَتِهٖ اَكْرِمِىْ مَثْوٰىهُ عَسٰى اَنْ يَّنْفَعَنَا اَوْ نَتَّخِذَهٗ وَلَدًا ۗ وَكَذٰلِكَ مَكَّنَّا لِيُوْسُفَ فِى الْاَرْضِ ۖ وَلِنُعَلِّمَهٗ مِنْ تَأْوِيْلِ الْاَحَادِيْثِ ۚ وَاللّٰهُ غَالِبٌ عَلٰى اَمْرِهٖ وَلٰكِنَّ اَكْثَرَ النَّاسِ لَا يَعْلَمُوْنَ ۞

22. And when he had attained his maturity, We gave him wisdom and knowledge: and thus do We reward those who do good.

وَلَمَّا بَلَغَ اَشُدَّهٗٓ اٰتَيْنٰهُ حُكْمًا وَّعِلْمًا ۗ وَكَذٰلِكَ نَجْزِى الْمُحْسِنِيْنَ ۞

23. And she in whose house he was sought to make himself yield (to her), and she made fast the doors and said: Come forward. He said: I seek Allah's refuge, surely my Lord made good my abode: Surely the unjust do not prosper.

وَرَاوَدَتْهُ الَّتِى هُوَ فِى بَيْتِهَا عَنْ نَّفْسِهٖ وَغَلَّقَتِ الْاَبْوَابَ وَقَالَتْ هَيْتَ لَكَ ۗ قَالَ مَعَاذَ اللّٰهِ اِنَّهٗ رَبِّىْٓ اَحْسَنَ مَثْوَاىَ ۗ اِنَّهٗ لَا يُفْلِحُ الظّٰلِمُوْنَ ۞

24. And certainly she made for him, and he would have made for her, were it not that he had seen the manifest evidence of his Lord; thus (it was) that We might turn away from him evil and indecency, surely he was one of Our sincere servants.

وَلَقَدْ هَمَّتْ بِهٖ ۚ وَهَمَّ بِهَا لَوْلَاۤ اَنْ رَّاٰ بُرْهَانَ رَبِّهٖ ۚ كَذٰلِكَ لِنَصْرِفَ عَنْهُ السُّوْٓءَ وَالْفَحْشَاۤءَ ۗ اِنَّهٗ مِنْ عِبَادِنَا الْمُخْلَصِيْنَ ۞

25. And they both hastened to the door, and she rent his shirt from behind and they met her husband at the door. She said: What is the punishment of him who intends evil to your wife except imprisonment or a painful chastisement?

وَاسْتَبَقَا الْبَابَ وَقَدَّتْ قَمِيْصَهٗ مِنْ دُبُرٍ وَّاَلْفَيَا سَيِّدَهَا لَدَا الْبَابِ ۗ قَالَتْ مَا جَزَاۤءُ مَنْ اَرَادَ بِاَهْلِكَ سُوْٓءًا اِلَّآ اَنْ يُّسْجَنَ اَوْ عَذَابٌ اَلِيْمٌ ۞

26. He said: She sought to make me yield (to her); and a witness of her own family bore witness: If his shirt is rent from front, she speaks the truth and he is one of the liars:

قَالَ هِىَ رَاوَدَتْنِىْ عَنْ نَّفْسِىْ وَشَهِدَ شَاهِدٌ مِّنْ اَهْلِهَا ۚ اِنْ كَانَ قَمِيْصُهٗ قُدَّ مِنْ قُبُلٍ فَصَدَقَتْ وَهُوَ مِنَ الْكٰذِبِيْنَ ۞

27. And if his shirt is rent from behind, she tells a lie and he is one of the truthful.

وَإِنْ كَانَ قَمِيصُهُ قُدَّ مِنْ دُبُرٍ فَكَذَبَتْ وَهُوَ مِنَ الصّٰدِقِينَ ۞

28. So when he saw his shirt rent from behind, he said: Surely it is a guile of you women; surely your guile is great:

فَلَمَّا رَأَ قَمِيصَهُ قُدَّ مِنْ دُبُرٍ قَالَ إِنَّهُ مِنْ كَيْدِكُنَّ إِنَّ كَيْدَكُنَّ عَظِيمٌ ۞

29. O Yusuf! turn aside from this; and (O my wife)! ask forgiveness for your fault, surely you are one of the wrong-doers.

يُوسُفُ أَعْرِضْ عَنْ هٰذَا وَاسْتَغْفِرِي لِذَنْبِكِ إِنَّكِ كُنْتِ مِنَ الْخٰطِئِينَ ۞

30. And women in the city said: The chief's wife seeks her slave to yield himself (to her), surely he has affected her deeply with (his) love; most surely we see her in manifest error.

وَقَالَ نِسْوَةٌ فِي الْمَدِينَةِ امْرَأَتُ الْعَزِيزِ تُرَاوِدُ فَتٰهَا عَنْ نَفْسِهِ قَدْ شَغَفَهَا حُبًّا إِنَّا لَنَرٰهَا فِي ضَلٰلٍ مُبِينٍ ۞

31. So when she heard of their sly talk she sent for them and prepared for them a repast, and gave each of them a knife, and said (to Yusuf): Come forth to them. So when they saw him, they deemed him great, and cut their hands (in amazement), and said: Remote is Allah (from imperfection); this is not a mortal; this is but a noble angel.

فَلَمَّا سَمِعَتْ بِمَكْرِهِنَّ أَرْسَلَتْ إِلَيْهِنَّ وَأَعْتَدَتْ لَهُنَّ مُتَّكَأً وَآتَتْ كُلَّ وَاحِدَةٍ مِنْهُنَّ سِكِّينًا وَقَالَتِ اخْرُجْ عَلَيْهِنَّ فَلَمَّا رَأَيْنَهُ أَكْبَرْنَهُ وَقَطَّعْنَ أَيْدِيَهُنَّ وَقُلْنَ حَاشَ لِلّٰهِ مَا هٰذَا بَشَرًا إِنْ هٰذَا إِلَّا مَلَكٌ كَرِيمٌ ۞

32. She said: This is he with respect to whom you blamed me, and certainly I sought his yielding himself (to me), but he abstained, and if he does not do what I bid him, he shall certainly be imprisoned, and he shall certainly be of those who are in a state of ignominy.

قَالَتْ فَذٰلِكُنَّ الَّذِي لُمْتُنَّنِي فِيهِ وَلَقَدْ رَاوَدْتُّهُ عَنْ نَفْسِهِ فَاسْتَعْصَمَ وَلَئِنْ لَمْ يَفْعَلْ مَا آمُرُهُ لَيُسْجَنَنَّ وَلَيَكُونًا مِنَ الصّٰغِرِينَ ۞

33. He said: My Lord! the prison house is dearer to me than that to which they invite me; and if Thou turn not away their device from me, I will yearn towards them and become (one) of the ignorant.

قَالَ رَبِّ السِّجْنُ أَحَبُّ إِلَيَّ مِمَّا يَدْعُونَنِي إِلَيْهِ وَإِلَّا تَصْرِفْ عَنِّي كَيْدَهُنَّ أَصْبُ إِلَيْهِنَّ وَأَكُنْ مِنَ الْجٰهِلِينَ ۞

34. Thereupon his Lord accepted his prayer and turned away their guile from him; surely He is the Hearing, the Knowing.

فَاسْتَجَابَ لَهُ رَبُّهُ فَصَرَفَ عَنْهُ كَيْدَهُنَّ إِنَّهُ هُوَ السَّمِيعُ الْعَلِيمُ ۞

35. Then it occurred to them after they had seen the signs that they should imprison him till a time.

ثُمَّ بَدَا لَهُمْ مِّنْ بَعْدِ مَا رَاَوُا الْاٰیٰتِ لَیَسْجُنُنَّهٗ حَتّٰى حِیْنٍ ۟ ۠

36. And two youths entered the prison with him. One of them said: I saw myself pressing wine. And the other said: I saw myself carrying bread on my head, of which birds ate. Inform us of its interpretation; surely we see you to be of the doers of good.

وَدَخَلَ مَعَهُ السِّجْنَ فَتَیٰنِ ؕ قَالَ اَحَدُهُمَاۤ اِنِّیْۤ اَرٰىنِیْۤ اَعْصِرُ خَمْرًا ۚ وَقَالَ الْاٰخَرُ اِنِّیْۤ اَرٰىنِیْۤ اَحْمِلُ فَوْقَ رَاْسِیْ خُبْزًا تَاْكُلُ الطَّیْرُ مِنْهُ ؕ نَبِّئْنَا بِتَاْوِیْلِهٖ ۚ اِنَّا نَرٰىكَ مِنَ الْمُحْسِنِیْنَ ۟

37. He said: There shall not come to you the food with which you are fed, but I will inform you both of its interpretation before it comes to you; this is of what my Lord has taught me; surely I have forsaken the religion of a people who do not believe in Allah, and they are deniers of the hereafter:

قَالَ لَا یَاْتِیْكُمَا طَعَامٌ تُرْزَقٰنِهٖۤ اِلَّا نَبَّاْتُكُمَا بِتَاْوِیْلِهٖ قَبْلَ اَنْ یَّاْتِیَكُمَا ؕ ذٰلِكُمَا مِمَّا عَلَّمَنِیْ رَبِّیْ ؕ اِنِّیْ تَرَكْتُ مِلَّةَ قَوْمٍ لَّا یُؤْمِنُوْنَ بِاللّٰهِ وَهُمْ بِالْاٰخِرَةِ هُمْ كٰفِرُوْنَ ۟

38. And I follow the religion of my fathers, Ibrahim and Ishaq and Yaqoub; it beseems us not that we should associate aught with Allah; this is by Allah's grace upon us and on mankind, but most people do not give thanks:

وَاتَّبَعْتُ مِلَّةَ اٰبَآءِیْۤ اِبْرٰهِیْمَ وَاِسْحٰقَ وَیَعْقُوْبَ ؕ مَا كَانَ لَنَاۤ اَنْ نُّشْرِكَ بِاللّٰهِ مِنْ شَیْءٍ ؕ ذٰلِكَ مِنْ فَضْلِ اللّٰهِ عَلَیْنَا وَعَلَى النَّاسِ وَلٰكِنَّ اَكْثَرَ النَّاسِ لَا یَشْكُرُوْنَ ۟

39. O my two mates of the prison! are sundry lords better or Allah the One, the Supreme?

یٰصَاحِبَیِ السِّجْنِ ءَاَرْبَابٌ مُّتَفَرِّقُوْنَ خَیْرٌ اَمِ اللّٰهُ الْوَاحِدُ الْقَهَّارُ ؕ

40. You do not serve besides Him but names which you have named, you and your fathers; Allah has not sent down any authority for them; judgment is only Allah's; He has commanded that you shall not serve aught but Him; this is the right religion but most people do not know:

مَا تَعْبُدُوْنَ مِنْ دُوْنِهٖۤ اِلَّاۤ اَسْمَآءً سَمَّیْتُمُوْهَاۤ اَنْتُمْ وَاٰبَآؤُكُمْ مَّاۤ اَنْزَلَ اللّٰهُ بِهَا مِنْ سُلْطٰنٍ ؕ اِنِ الْحُكْمُ اِلَّا لِلّٰهِ ؕ اَمَرَ اَلَّا تَعْبُدُوْۤا اِلَّاۤ اِیَّاهُ ؕ ذٰلِكَ الدِّیْنُ الْقَیِّمُ وَلٰكِنَّ اَكْثَرَ النَّاسِ لَا یَعْلَمُوْنَ ۟

41. O my two mates of the prison! as for one of you, he shall give his lord to drink wine; and as for the other, he shall be crucified, so that the birds shall eat from his head; the matter is decreed concerning which you inquired.

یٰصَاحِبَیِ السِّجْنِ اَمَّاۤ اَحَدُكُمَا فَیَسْقِیْ رَبَّهٗ خَمْرًا ۚ وَاَمَّا الْاٰخَرُ فَیُصْلَبُ فَتَاْكُلُ الطَّیْرُ مِنْ رَّاْسِهٖ ؕ قُضِیَ الْاَمْرُ الَّذِیْ فِیْهِ تَسْتَفْتِیٰنِ ۟

42. And he said to him whom he knew would be delivered of the two: Remember me with your lord; but the Shaitan caused him to forget mentioning (it) to his lord, so he remained in the prison a few years.

وَقَالَ لِلَّذِىْ ظَنَّ اَنَّهٗ نَاجٍ مِّنْهُمَا اذْكُرْنِىْ عِنْدَ رَبِّكَ ۖ فَاَنْسٰىهُ الشَّيْطٰنُ ذِكْرَ رَبِّهٖ فَلَبِثَ فِى السِّجْنِ بِضْعَ سِنِيْنَ ۚ ۽

43. And the king said: Surely I see seven fat kine which seven lean ones devoured; and seven green ears and (seven) others dry; O chiefs! explain to me my dream, if you can interpret the dream.

وَقَالَ الْمَلِكُ اِنِّىْ اَرٰى سَبْعَ بَقَرٰتٍ سِمَانٍ يَّاْكُلُهُنَّ سَبْعٌ عِجَافٌ وَّسَبْعَ سُنْبُلٰتٍ خُضْرٍ وَّاُخَرَ يٰبِسٰتٍ ۖ يٰٓاَيُّهَا الْمَلَاُ اَفْتُوْنِىْ فِىْ رُءْيَاىَ اِنْ كُنْتُمْ لِلرُّءْيَا تَعْبُرُوْنَ ۝

44. They said: Confused dreams, and we do not know the interpretation of dreams.

قَالُوْٓا اَضْغَاثُ اَحْلَامٍ ۚ وَّمَا نَحْنُ بِتَاْوِيْلِ الْاَحْلَامِ بِعٰلِمِيْنَ ۝

45. And of the two (prisoners) he who had found deliverance and remembered after a long time said: I will inform you of its interpretation, so let me go:

وَقَالَ الَّذِىْ نَجَا مِنْهُمَا وَادَّكَرَ بَعْدَ اُمَّةٍ اَنَا اُنَبِّئُكُمْ بِتَاْوِيْلِهٖ فَاَرْسِلُوْنِ ۝

46. Yusuf! O truthful one! explain to us seven fat kine which seven lean ones devoured, and seven green ears and (seven) others dry, that I may go back to the people so that they may know.

يُوْسُفُ اَيُّهَا الصِّدِّيْقُ اَفْتِنَا فِىْ سَبْعِ بَقَرٰتٍ سِمَانٍ يَّاْكُلُهُنَّ سَبْعٌ عِجَافٌ وَّسَبْعِ سُنْبُلٰتٍ خُضْرٍ وَّاُخَرَ يٰبِسٰتٍ ۙ لَّعَلِّىْٓ اَرْجِعُ اِلَى النَّاسِ لَعَلَّهُمْ يَعْلَمُوْنَ ۝

47. He said: You shall sow for seven years continuously, then what you reap leave it in its ear except a little of which you eat.

قَالَ تَزْرَعُوْنَ سَبْعَ سِنِيْنَ دَاَبًا ۚ فَمَا حَصَدْتُّمْ فَذَرُوْهُ فِىْ سُنْبُلِهٖٓ اِلَّا قَلِيْلًا مِّمَّا تَاْكُلُوْنَ ۝

48. Then there shall come after that seven years of hardship which shall eat away all that you have beforehand laid up in store for them, except a little of what you shall have preserved:

ثُمَّ يَاْتِىْ مِنْ بَعْدِ ذٰلِكَ سَبْعٌ شِدَادٌ يَّاْكُلْنَ مَا قَدَّمْتُمْ لَهُنَّ اِلَّا قَلِيْلًا مِّمَّا تُحْصِنُوْنَ ۝

49. Then there will come after that a year in which people shall have rain and in which they shall press (grapes).

ثُمَّ يَاْتِىْ مِنْ بَعْدِ ذٰلِكَ عَامٌ فِيْهِ يُغَاثُ النَّاسُ وَفِيْهِ يَعْصِرُوْنَ ۝

50. And the king said: Bring him to me. So when the messenger came to him, he said: Go back to your lord and ask him, what is the case of the women who cut their hands; surely my Lord knows their guile.

وَقَالَ الْمَلِكُ ائْتُوْنِىْ بِهٖ ۚ فَلَمَّا جَآءَهُ الرَّسُوْلُ قَالَ ارْجِعْ اِلٰى رَبِّكَ فَسْـَٔلْهُ مَا بَالُ النِّسْوَةِ الّٰتِىْ قَطَّعْنَ اَيْدِيَهُنَّ ۗ اِنَّ رَبِّىْ بِكَيْدِهِنَّ عَلِيْمٌ ۝

51. He said: How was your affair when you sought Yusuf to yield himself (to you)? They said: Remote is Allah (from imperfection), we knew of no evil on his part. The chief's wife said: Now has the truth become established: I sought him to yield himself (to me), and he is most surely of the truthful ones.

قَالَ مَا خَطْبُكُنَّ اِذْ رَاوَدْتُّنَّ يُوْسُفَ عَنْ نَّفْسِهٖ ؕ قُلْنَ حَاشَ لِلّٰهِ مَا عَلِمْنَا عَلَيْهِ مِنْ سُوْٓءٍ ؕ قَالَتِ امْرَاَتُ الْعَزِيْزِ الْـٰٔنَ حَصْحَصَ الْحَقُّ ۫ اَنَا رَاوَدْتُّهٗ عَنْ نَّفْسِهٖ وَاِنَّهٗ لَمِنَ الصّٰدِقِيْنَ ۞

52. This is that he might know that I have not been unfaithful to him in secret and that Allah does not guide the device of the unfaithful.

ذٰلِكَ لِيَعْلَمَ اَنِّيْ لَمْ اَخُنْهُ بِالْغَيْبِ وَاَنَّ اللّٰهَ لَا يَهْدِيْ كَيْدَ الْخَآئِنِيْنَ ۞

53. And I do not declare myself free, most surely (man's) self is wont to command (him to do) evil, except such as my Lord has had mercy on, surely my Lord is Forgiving, Merciful.

وَمَاۤ اُبَرِّئُ نَفْسِيْ ۚ اِنَّ النَّفْسَ لَاَمَّارَةٌۢ بِالسُّوْٓءِ اِلَّا مَا رَحِمَ رَبِّيْ ؕ اِنَّ رَبِّيْ غَفُوْرٌ رَّحِيْمٌ ۞

54. And the king said: Bring him to me, I will choose him for myself. So when he had spoken with him, he said: Surely you are in our presence today an honorable, a faithful one.

وَقَالَ الْمَلِكُ ائْتُوْنِيْ بِهٖۤ اَسْتَخْلِصْهُ لِنَفْسِيْ ۚ فَلَمَّا كَلَّمَهٗ قَالَ اِنَّكَ الْيَوْمَ لَدَيْنَا مَكِيْنٌ اَمِيْنٌ ۞

55. He said: Place me (in authority) over the treasures of the land, surely I am a good keeper, knowing well.

قَالَ اجْعَلْنِيْ عَلٰى خَزَآئِنِ الْاَرْضِ ۚ اِنِّيْ حَفِيْظٌ عَلِيْمٌ ۞

56. And thus did We give to Yusuf power in the land—he had mastery in it wherever he liked; We send down Our mercy on whom We please, and We do not waste the reward of those who do good.

وَكَذٰلِكَ مَكَّنَّا لِيُوْسُفَ فِى الْاَرْضِ ۚ يَتَبَوَّاُ مِنْهَا حَيْثُ يَشَآءُ ؕ نُصِيْبُ بِرَحْمَتِنَا مَنْ نَّشَآءُ وَلَا نُضِيْعُ اَجْرَ الْمُحْسِنِيْنَ ۞

57. And certainly the reward of the hereafter is much better for those who believe and guard (against evil).

وَلَاَجْرُ الْاٰخِرَةِ خَيْرٌ لِّلَّذِيْنَ اٰمَنُوْا وَكَانُوْا يَتَّقُوْنَ ۞

58. And Yusuf's brothers came and went in to him, and he knew them, while they did not recognize him.

وَجَآءَ اِخْوَةُ يُوْسُفَ فَدَخَلُوْا عَلَيْهِ فَعَرَفَهُمْ وَهُمْ لَهٗ مُنْكِرُوْنَ ۞

59. And when he furnished them with their provision, he said: Bring to me a brother of yours from your father; do you not see that I give full measure and that I am the best of hosts?

وَلَمَّا جَهَّزَهُمْ بِجَهَازِهِمْ قَالَ ائْتُوْنِيْ بِاَخٍ لَّكُمْ مِّنْ اَبِيْكُمْ ۚ اَلَا تَرَوْنَ اَنِّيْۤ اُوْفِى الْكَيْلَ وَاَنَا خَيْرُ الْمُنْزِلِيْنَ ۞

60. But if you do not bring him to me, you shall have no measure (of corn) from me, nor shall you come near me.

فَاِنْ لَّمْ تَأْتُوْنِيْ بِهٖ فَلَا كَيْلَ لَكُمْ عِنْدِيْ وَلَا تَقْرَبُوْنِ ۞

61. They said: We will strive to make his father yield in respect of him, and we are sure to do (it).

62. And he said to his servants: Put their money into their bags that they may recognize it when they go back to their family, so that they may come back.

63. So when they returned to their father, they said: O our father, the measure is withheld from us, therefore send with us our brother, (so that) we may get the measure, and we will most surely guard him.

64. He said: I cannot trust in you with respect to him, except as I trusted in you with respect to his brother before; but Allah is the best Keeper, and He is the most Merciful of the merciful ones.

65. And when they opened their goods, they found their money returned to them. They said: O our father! what (more) can we desire? This is our property returned to us, and we will bring corn for our family and guard our brother, and will have in addition the measure of a camel-(load); this is an easy measure.

66. He said: I will by no means send him with you until you give me a firm covenant in Allah's name that you will most certainly bring him back to me, unless you are completely surrounded. And when they gave him their covenant, he said: Allah is the One in Whom trust is placed as regards what we say.

67. And he said: O my sons! do not (all) enter by one gate and enter by different gates and I cannot avail you aught against Allah; judgment is only Allah's; on Him do I rely, and on Him let those who are reliant rely.

68. And when they had entered as their father had bidden them, it did not avail them aught against Allah, but (it was only) a desire in the soul of Yaqoub which he satisfied; and surely he was possessed of knowledge because We had given him knowledge, but most people do not know.

قَالُوْا سَنُرَاوِدُ عَنْهُ اَبَاهُ وَاِنَّا لَفٰعِلُوْنَ ۞

وَقَالَ لِفِتْيٰنِهِ اجْعَلُوْا بِضَاعَتَهُمْ فِيْ رِحَالِهِمْ لَعَلَّهُمْ يَعْرِفُوْنَهَاۤ اِذَا انْقَلَبُوْۤا اِلٰۤى اَهْلِهِمْ لَعَلَّهُمْ يَرْجِعُوْنَ ۞

فَلَمَّا رَجَعُوْۤا اِلٰۤى اَبِيْهِمْ قَالُوْا يٰۤاَبَانَا مُنِعَ مِنَّا الْكَيْلُ فَاَرْسِلْ مَعَنَاۤ اَخَانَا نَكْتَلْ وَاِنَّا لَهٗ لَحٰفِظُوْنَ ۞

قَالَ هَلْ اٰمَنُكُمْ عَلَيْهِ اِلَّا كَمَاۤ اَمِنْتُكُمْ عَلٰۤى اَخِيْهِ مِنْ قَبْلُ ۖ فَاللّٰهُ خَيْرٌ حٰفِظًا ۖ وَّهُوَ اَرْحَمُ الرّٰحِمِيْنَ ۞

وَلَمَّا فَتَحُوْا مَتَاعَهُمْ وَجَدُوْا بِضَاعَتَهُمْ رُدَّتْ اِلَيْهِمْ ۖ قَالُوْا يٰۤاَبَانَا مَا نَبْغِيْ ۚ هٰذِهٖ بِضَاعَتُنَا رُدَّتْ اِلَيْنَا ۚ وَنَمِيْرُ اَهْلَنَا وَنَحْفَظُ اَخَانَا وَنَزْدَادُ كَيْلَ بَعِيْرٍ ۖ ذٰلِكَ كَيْلٌ يَّسِيْرٌ ۞

قَالَ لَنْ اُرْسِلَهٗ مَعَكُمْ حَتّٰى تُؤْتُوْنِ مَوْثِقًا مِّنَ اللّٰهِ لَتَأْتُنَّنِيْ بِهٖۤ اِلَّاۤ اَنْ يُّحَاطَ بِكُمْ ۚ فَلَمَّاۤ اٰتَوْهُ مَوْثِقَهُمْ قَالَ اللّٰهُ عَلٰى مَا نَقُوْلُ وَكِيْلٌ ۞

وَقَالَ يٰبَنِيَّ لَا تَدْخُلُوْا مِنْۢ بَابٍ وَّاحِدٍ وَّادْخُلُوْا مِنْ اَبْوَابٍ مُّتَفَرِّقَةٍ ۖ وَمَاۤ اُغْنِيْ عَنْكُمْ مِّنَ اللّٰهِ مِنْ شَيْءٍ ۖ اِنِ الْحُكْمُ اِلَّا لِلّٰهِ ۖ عَلَيْهِ تَوَكَّلْتُ ۚ وَعَلَيْهِ فَلْيَتَوَكَّلِ الْمُتَوَكِّلُوْنَ ۞

وَلَمَّا دَخَلُوْا مِنْ حَيْثُ اَمَرَهُمْ اَبُوْهُمْ ۖ مَا كَانَ يُغْنِيْ عَنْهُمْ مِّنَ اللّٰهِ مِنْ شَيْءٍ اِلَّا حَاجَةً فِيْ نَفْسِ يَعْقُوْبَ قَضٰهَا ۚ وَاِنَّهٗ لَذُوْ عِلْمٍ لِّمَا عَلَّمْنٰهُ وَلٰكِنَّ اَكْثَرَ النَّاسِ لَا يَعْلَمُوْنَ ۞

69. And when they went in to Yusuf, he lodged his brother with himself, saying: I am your brother, therefore grieve not at what they do.

70. So when he furnished them with their provisions, (someone) placed the drinking cup in his brother's bag. Then a crier cried out: O caravan! you are most surely thieves.

71. They said while they were facing them: What is it that you miss?

72. They said: We miss the king's drinking cup, and he who shall bring it shall have a camel-load and I am responsible for it.

73. They said: By Allah! you know for certain that we have not come to make mischief in the land, and we are not thieves.

74. They said: But what shall be the requital of this, if you are liars?

75. They said: The requital of this is that the person in whose bag it is found shall himself be (held for) the satisfaction thereof; thus do we punish the wrongdoers.

76. So he began with their sacks before the sack of his brother, then he brought it out from his brother's sack. Thus did We plan for the sake of Yusuf; it was not (lawful) that he should take his brother under the king's law unless Allah pleased; We raise the degrees of whomsoever We please, and above every one possessed of knowledge is the All-knowing one.

77. They said: If he steal, a brother of his did indeed steal before; but Yusuf kept it secret in his heart and did not disclose it to them. He said: You are in an evil condition and Allah knows best what you state.

78. They said: O chief! he has a father, a very old man, therefore retain one of us in his stead; surely we see you to be of the doers of good.

وَلَمَّا دَخَلُوْا عَلٰى يُوْسُفَ اٰوٰى اِلَيْهِ اَخَاهُ قَالَ اِنِّىْ اَنَا اَخُوْكَ فَلَا تَبْتَئِسْ بِمَا كَانُوْا يَعْمَلُوْنَ ۝

فَلَمَّا جَهَّزَهُمْ بِجَهَازِهِمْ جَعَلَ السِّقَايَةَ فِىْ رَحْلِ اَخِيْهِ ثُمَّ اَذَّنَ مُؤَذِّنٌ اَيَّتُهَا الْعِيْرُ اِنَّكُمْ لَسَارِقُوْنَ ۝

قَالُوْا وَاَقْبَلُوْا عَلَيْهِمْ مَّاذَا تَفْقِدُوْنَ ۝

قَالُوْا نَفْقِدُ صُوَاعَ الْمَلِكِ وَلِمَنْ جَآءَ بِهٖ حِمْلُ بَعِيْرٍ وَّاَنَا بِهٖ زَعِيْمٌ ۝

قَالُوْا تَاللّٰهِ لَقَدْ عَلِمْتُمْ مَّا جِئْنَا لِنُفْسِدَ فِى الْاَرْضِ وَمَا كُنَّا سَارِقِيْنَ ۝

قَالُوْا فَمَا جَزَآؤُهٗ اِنْ كُنْتُمْ كٰذِبِيْنَ ۝

قَالُوْا جَزَآؤُهٗ مَنْ وُّجِدَ فِىْ رَحْلِهٖ فَهُوَ جَزَآؤُهٗ ۚ كَذٰلِكَ نَجْزِى الظّٰلِمِيْنَ ۝

فَبَدَاَ بِاَوْعِيَتِهِمْ قَبْلَ وِعَآءِ اَخِيْهِ ثُمَّ اسْتَخْرَجَهَا مِنْ وِّعَآءِ اَخِيْهِ ۚ كَذٰلِكَ كِدْنَا لِيُوْسُفَ ۚ مَا كَانَ لِيَاْخُذَ اَخَاهُ فِىْ دِيْنِ الْمَلِكِ اِلَّا اَنْ يَّشَآءَ اللّٰهُ ۚ نَرْفَعُ دَرَجٰتٍ مَّنْ نَّشَآءُ ۚ وَفَوْقَ كُلِّ ذِىْ عِلْمٍ عَلِيْمٌ ۝

قَالُوْا اِنْ يَّسْرِقْ فَقَدْ سَرَقَ اَخٌ لَّهٗ مِنْ قَبْلُ ۚ فَاَسَرَّهَا يُوْسُفُ فِىْ نَفْسِهٖ وَلَمْ يُبْدِهَا لَهُمْ ۚ قَالَ اَنْتُمْ شَرٌّ مَّكَانًا ۚ وَاللّٰهُ اَعْلَمُ بِمَا تَصِفُوْنَ ۝

قَالُوْا يٰاَيُّهَا الْعَزِيْزُ اِنَّ لَهٗ اَبًا شَيْخًا كَبِيْرًا فَخُذْ اَحَدَنَا مَكَانَهٗ ۚ اِنَّا نَرٰىكَ مِنَ الْمُحْسِنِيْنَ ۝

222

79. He said: Allah protect us that we should seize other than him with whom we found our property, for then most surely we would be unjust.

80. Then when they despaired of him, they retired, conferring privately together. The eldest of them said: Do you not know that your father took from you a covenant in Allah's name, and how you fell short of your duty with respect to Yusuf before? Therefore I will by no means depart from this land until my father permits me or Allah decides for me, and He is the best of the judges:

81. Go back to your father and say: O our father! surely your son committed theft, and we do not bear witness except to what we have known, and we could not keep watch over the unseen:

82. And inquire in the town in which we were and the caravan with which we proceeded, and most surely we are truthful.

83. He (Yaqoub) said: Nay, your souls have made a matter light for you, so patience is good; maybe Allah will bring them all together to me; surely He is the Knowing, the Wise.

84. And he turned away from them, and said: O my sorrow for Yusuf! and his eyes became white on account of the grief, and he was a repressor (of grief).

85. They said: By Allah! you will not cease to remember Yusuf until you are a prey to constant disease or (until) you are of those who perish.

86. He said: I only complain of my grief and sorrow to Allah, and I know from Allah what you do not know.

87. O my sons! Go and inquire respecting Yusuf and his brother, and despair not of Allah's mercy; surely none despairs of Allah's mercy except the unbelieving people.

قَالَ مَعَاذَ اللهِ أَنْ نَّأْخُذَ إِلَّا مَنْ وَّجَدْنَا مَتَاعَنَا عِنْدَهُ إِنَّا إِذًا لَّظَالِمُوْنَ ۝

فَلَمَّا اسْتَيْـَٔسُوْا مِنْهُ خَلَصُوْا نَجِيًّا ۚ قَالَ كَبِيْرُهُمْ اَلَمْ تَعْلَمُوْا اَنَّ اَبَاكُمْ قَدْ اَخَذَ عَلَيْكُمْ مَّوْثِقًا مِّنَ اللهِ وَمِنْ قَبْلُ مَا فَرَّطْتُّمْ فِيْ يُوْسُفَ ۚ فَلَنْ اَبْرَحَ الْاَرْضَ حَتّٰى يَأْذَنَ لِيْ اَبِيْ اَوْ يَحْكُمَ اللهُ لِيْ ۚ وَهُوَ خَيْرُ الْحٰكِمِيْنَ ۝

اِرْجِعُوْا اِلٰى اَبِيْكُمْ فَقُوْلُوْا يٰاَبَانَا اِنَّ ابْنَكَ سَرَقَ ۚ وَمَا شَهِدْنَا اِلَّا بِمَا عَلِمْنَا وَمَا كُنَّا لِلْغَيْبِ حٰفِظِيْنَ ۝

وَسْـَٔلِ الْقَرْيَةَ الَّتِيْ كُنَّا فِيْهَا وَالْعِيْرَ الَّتِيْ اَقْبَلْنَا فِيْهَا ۚ وَاِنَّا لَصٰدِقُوْنَ ۝

قَالَ بَلْ سَوَّلَتْ لَكُمْ اَنْفُسُكُمْ اَمْرًا ۚ فَصَبْرٌ جَمِيْلٌ ۖ عَسَى اللهُ اَنْ يَّأْتِيَنِيْ بِهِمْ جَمِيْعًا ۗ اِنَّهُ هُوَ الْعَلِيْمُ الْحَكِيْمُ ۝

وَتَوَلّٰى عَنْهُمْ وَقَالَ يٰاَسَفٰى عَلٰى يُوْسُفَ وَابْيَضَّتْ عَيْنٰهُ مِنَ الْحُزْنِ فَهُوَ كَظِيْمٌ ۝

قَالُوْا تَاللهِ تَفْتَؤُا تَذْكُرُ يُوْسُفَ حَتّٰى تَكُوْنَ حَرَضًا اَوْ تَكُوْنَ مِنَ الْهٰلِكِيْنَ ۝

قَالَ اِنَّمَا اَشْكُوْا بَثِّيْ وَحُزْنِيْ اِلَى اللهِ وَاَعْلَمُ مِنَ اللهِ مَا لَا تَعْلَمُوْنَ ۝

يٰبَنِيَّ اذْهَبُوْا فَتَحَسَّسُوْا مِنْ يُّوْسُفَ وَاَخِيْهِ وَلَا تَايْـَٔسُوْا مِنْ رَّوْحِ اللهِ ۚ اِنَّهُ لَا يَايْـَٔسُ مِنْ رَّوْحِ اللهِ اِلَّا الْقَوْمُ الْكٰفِرُوْنَ ۝

88. So when they came in to him, they said: O chief! distress has afflicted us and our family and we have brought scanty money, so give us full measure and be charitable to us; surely Allah rewards the charitable.

89. He said: Do you know how you treated Yusuf and his brother when you were ignorant?

90. They said: Are you indeed Yusuf? He said: I am Yusuf and this is my brother; Allah has indeed been gracious to us; surely he who guards (against evil) and is patient (is rewarded) for surely Allah does not waste the reward of those who do good.

91. They said: By Allah! now has Allah certainly chosen you over us, and we were certainly sinners.

92. He said: (There shall be) no reproof against you this day; Allah may forgive you, and He is the most Merciful of the merciful.

93. Take this my shirt and cast it on my father's face; he will (again) be able to see, and come to me with all your families.

94. And when the caravan had departed, their father said: Most surely I perceive the greatness of Yusuf, unless you pronounce me to be weak in judgment.

95. They said: By Allah, you are most surely in your old error.

96. So when the bearer of good news came he cast it on his face, so forthwith he regained his sight. He said: Did I not say to you that I know from Allah what you do not know?

97. They said: O our father! ask forgiveness of our faults for us, surely we were sinners.

فَلَمَّا دَخَلُوْا عَلَيْهِ قَالُوْا يٰٓاَيُّهَا الْعَزِيْزُ مَسَّنَا وَاَهْلَنَا الضُّرُّ وَجِئْنَا بِبِضَاعَةٍ مُّزْجٰىةٍ فَاَوْفِ لَنَا الْكَيْلَ وَتَصَدَّقْ عَلَيْنَا ؕ اِنَّ اللّٰهَ يَجْزِى الْمُتَصَدِّقِيْنَ ۸۸

قَالَ هَلْ عَلِمْتُمْ مَّا فَعَلْتُمْ بِيُوْسُفَ وَاَخِيْهِ اِذْ اَنْتُمْ جٰهِلُوْنَ ۸۹

قَالُوْٓا ءَاِنَّكَ لَاَنْتَ يُوْسُفُ ؕ قَالَ اَنَا يُوْسُفُ وَهٰذَآ اَخِيْ ۫ قَدْ مَنَّ اللّٰهُ عَلَيْنَا ؕ اِنَّهٗ مَنْ يَّتَّقِ وَيَصْبِرْ فَاِنَّ اللّٰهَ لَا يُضِيْعُ اَجْرَ الْمُحْسِنِيْنَ ۹۰

قَالُوْا تَاللّٰهِ لَقَدْ اٰثَرَكَ اللّٰهُ عَلَيْنَا وَاِنْ كُنَّا لَخٰطِئِيْنَ ۹۱

قَالَ لَا تَثْرِيْبَ عَلَيْكُمُ الْيَوْمَ ؕ يَغْفِرُ اللّٰهُ لَكُمْ ۫ وَهُوَ اَرْحَمُ الرّٰحِمِيْنَ ۹۲

اِذْهَبُوْا بِقَمِيْصِيْ هٰذَا فَاَلْقُوْهُ عَلٰى وَجْهِ اَبِيْ يَاْتِ بَصِيْرًا ۚ وَاْتُوْنِيْ بِاَهْلِكُمْ اَجْمَعِيْنَ ۹۳

وَلَمَّا فَصَلَتِ الْعِيْرُ قَالَ اَبُوْهُمْ اِنِّيْ لَاَجِدُ رِيْحَ يُوْسُفَ لَوْلَآ اَنْ تُفَنِّدُوْنِ ۹۴

قَالُوْا تَاللّٰهِ اِنَّكَ لَفِيْ ضَلٰلِكَ الْقَدِيْمِ ۹۵

فَلَمَّآ اَنْ جَآءَ الْبَشِيْرُ اَلْقٰىهُ عَلٰى وَجْهِهٖ فَارْتَدَّ بَصِيْرًا ۚ قَالَ اَلَمْ اَقُلْ لَّكُمْ ۙ اِنِّيْٓ اَعْلَمُ مِنَ اللّٰهِ مَا لَا تَعْلَمُوْنَ ۹۶

قَالُوْا يٰٓاَبَانَا اسْتَغْفِرْ لَنَا ذُنُوْبَنَآ اِنَّا كُنَّا خٰطِئِيْنَ ۹۷

98. He said: I will ask for you forgiveness from my Lord; surely He is the Forgiving, the Merciful.

قَالَ سَوْفَ اَسْتَغْفِرُ لَكُمْ رَبِّىْ اِنَّهُ هُوَ الْغَفُوْرُ الرَّحِيْمُ ۝

99. Then when they came in to Yusuf, he took his parents to lodge with him and said: Enter safe into Egypt, if Allah please.

فَلَمَّا دَخَلُوْا عَلٰى يُوْسُفَ اٰوٰٓى اِلَيْهِ اَبَوَيْهِ وَقَالَ ادْخُلُوْا مِصْرَ اِنْ شَاۤءَ اللّٰهُ اٰمِنِيْنَ ۝

100. And he raised his parents upon the throne and they fell down in prostration before him, and he said: O my father! this is the significance of my vision of old; my Lord has indeed made it to be true; and He was indeed kind to me when He brought me forth from the prison and brought you from the desert after the Shaitan had sown dissensions between me and my brothers, surely my Lord is benignant to whom He pleases; surely He is the Knowing, the Wise.

وَرَفَعَ اَبَوَيْهِ عَلَى الْعَرْشِ وَخَرُّوْا لَهٗ سُجَّدًا ۚ وَ قَالَ يٰٓاَبَتِ هٰذَا تَأْوِيْلُ رُءْيَايَ مِنْ قَبْلُ ۖ قَدْ جَعَلَهَا رَبِّىْ حَقًّا ۗ وَقَدْ اَحْسَنَ بِىْ اِذْ اَخْرَجَنِىْ مِنَ السِّجْنِ وَجَاۤءَ بِكُمْ مِّنَ الْبَدْوِ مِنْ بَعْدِ اَنْ نَّزَغَ الشَّيْطٰنُ بَيْنِىْ وَبَيْنَ اِخْوَتِىْ ۗ اِنَّ رَبِّىْ لَطِيْفٌ لِّمَا يَشَاۤءُ ۗ اِنَّهٗ هُوَ الْعَلِيْمُ الْحَكِيْمُ ۝

101. My Lord! Thou hast given me of the kingdom and taught me of the interpretation of sayings: Originator of the heavens and the earth! Thou art my guardian in this world and the hereafter; make me die a muslim and join me with the good.

رَبِّ قَدْ اٰتَيْتَنِىْ مِنَ الْمُلْكِ وَعَلَّمْتَنِىْ مِنْ تَأْوِيْلِ الْاَحَادِيْثِ ۚ فَاطِرَ السَّمٰوٰتِ وَالْاَرْضِ ۖ اَنْتَ وَلِيِّىْ فِى الدُّنْيَا وَالْاٰخِرَةِ ۚ تَوَفَّنِىْ مُسْلِمًا وَّ اَلْحِقْنِىْ بِالصّٰلِحِيْنَ ۝

102. This is of the announcements relating to the unseen (which) We reveal to you, and you were not with them when they resolved upon their affair, and they were devising plans.

ذٰلِكَ مِنْ اَنْبَاۤءِ الْغَيْبِ نُوْحِيْهِ اِلَيْكَ ۚ وَمَا كُنْتَ لَدَيْهِمْ اِذْ اَجْمَعُوْٓا اَمْرَهُمْ وَهُمْ يَمْكُرُوْنَ ۝

103. And most men will not believe though you desire it eagerly.

وَمَاۤ اَكْثَرُ النَّاسِ وَلَوْ حَرَصْتَ بِمُؤْمِنِيْنَ ۝

104. And you do not ask them for a reward for this; it is nothing but a reminder for all mankind.

وَمَا تَسْـَٔلُهُمْ عَلَيْهِ مِنْ اَجْرٍ ۚ اِنْ هُوَ اِلَّا ذِكْرٌ لِّلْعٰلَمِيْنَ ۝

105. And how many a sign in the heavens and the earth which they pass by, yet they turn aside from it.

وَكَاَيِّنْ مِّنْ اٰيَةٍ فِى السَّمٰوٰتِ وَالْاَرْضِ يَمُرُّوْنَ عَلَيْهَا وَهُمْ عَنْهَا مُعْرِضُوْنَ ۝

106. And most of them do not believe in Allah without associating others (with Him).

وَمَا يُؤْمِنُ اَكْثَرُهُمْ بِاللّٰهِ اِلَّا وَهُمْ مُّشْرِكُوْنَ ۝

107. Do they then feel secure that there may come to them an extensive chastisement from Allah or (that) the hour may come to them suddenly while they do not perceive?

108. Say: This is my way: I call to Allah, I and those who follow me being certain, and glory be to Allah, and I am not one of the polytheists.

109. And We have not sent before you but men from (among) the people of the towns, to whom We sent revelations. Have they not then travelled in the land and seen what was the end of those before them? And certainly the abode of the hereafter is best for those who guard (against evil); do you not then understand?

110. Until when the apostles despaired and the people became sure that they were indeed told a lie, Our help came to them and whom We pleased was delivered; and Our punishment is not averted from the guilty people.

111. In their histories there is certainly a lesson for men of understanding. It is not a narrative which could be forged, but a verification of what is before it and a distinct explanation of all things and a guide and a mercy to a people who believe.

أَفَأَمِنُوا أَن تَأْتِيَهُمْ غَاشِيَةٌ مِّنْ عَذَابِ اللَّهِ أَوْ تَأْتِيَهُمُ السَّاعَةُ بَغْتَةً وَّهُمْ لَا يَشْعُرُونَ ۱۰۷

قُلْ هَٰذِهِ سَبِيلِي أَدْعُوا إِلَى اللَّهِ عَلَىٰ بَصِيرَةٍ أَنَا وَمَنِ اتَّبَعَنِي وَسُبْحَانَ اللَّهِ وَمَا أَنَا مِنَ الْمُشْرِكِينَ ۱۰۸

وَمَا أَرْسَلْنَا مِن قَبْلِكَ إِلَّا رِجَالًا نُّوحِي إِلَيْهِم مِّنْ أَهْلِ الْقُرَىٰ أَفَلَمْ يَسِيرُوا فِي الْأَرْضِ فَيَنظُرُوا كَيْفَ كَانَ عَاقِبَةُ الَّذِينَ مِن قَبْلِهِمْ وَلَدَارُ الْآخِرَةِ خَيْرٌ لِّلَّذِينَ اتَّقَوْا أَفَلَا تَعْقِلُونَ ۱۰۹

حَتَّىٰ إِذَا اسْتَيْأَسَ الرُّسُلُ وَظَنُّوا أَنَّهُمْ قَدْ كُذِبُوا جَاءَهُمْ نَصْرُنَا فَنُجِّيَ مَن نَّشَاءُ وَلَا يُرَدُّ بَأْسُنَا عَنِ الْقَوْمِ الْمُجْرِمِينَ ۱۱۰

لَقَدْ كَانَ فِي قَصَصِهِمْ عِبْرَةٌ لِّأُولِي الْأَلْبَابِ مَا كَانَ حَدِيثًا يُفْتَرَىٰ وَلَٰكِن تَصْدِيقَ الَّذِي بَيْنَ يَدَيْهِ وَتَفْصِيلَ كُلِّ شَيْءٍ وَهُدًى وَرَحْمَةً لِّقَوْمٍ يُؤْمِنُونَ ۱۱۱

THE THUNDER
(RA'D)

**In the name of Allah,
the Beneficent, the Merciful.**

1. Alif Lam Mim Ra. These are the verses of the Book; and that which is revealed to you from your Lord is the truth, but most people do not believe.

2. Allah is He Who raised the heavens without any pillars that you see, and He is firm in power and He made the sun and the moon subservient (to you); each one pursues its course to an appointed time; He regulates the affair, making clear the signs that you may be certain of meeting your Lord.

3. And He it is Who spread the earth and made in it firm mountains and rivers, and of all fruits He has made in it two kinds; He makes the night cover the day; most surely there are signs in this for a people who reflect.

4. And in the earth there are tracts side by side and gardens of grapes and corn and palm trees having one root and (others) having distinct roots—they are watered with one water, and We make some of them excel others in fruit; most surely there are signs in this for a people who understand.

5. And if you would wonder, then wondrous is their saying: What! when we are dust, shall we then certainly be in a new creation? These are they who disbelieve in their Lord, and these have chains on their necks, and they are the inmates of the fire; in it they shall abide.

6. And they ask you to hasten on the evil before the good, and indeed there have been exemplary punishments before them; and most surely your Lord is the Lord of forgiveness to people, notwithstanding their injustice; and most surely your Lord is severe in requiting (evil).

227

7. And those who disbelieve say: Why has not a sign been sent down upon him from his Lord? You are only a warner and (there is) a guide for every people.

8. Allah knows what every female bears, and that of which the wombs fall short of completion and that in which they increase; and there is a measure with Him of everything.

9. The knower of the unseen and the seen, the Great, the Most High.

10. Alike (to Him) among you is he who conceals (his) words and he who speaks them openly, and he who hides himself by night and (who) goes forth by day.

11. For his sake there are angels following one another, before him and behind him, who guard him by Allah's commandment; surely Allah does not change the condition of a people until they change their own condition; and when Allah intends evil to a people, there is no averting it, and besides Him they have no protector.

12. He it is Who shows you the lightning causing fear and hope and (Who) brings up the heavy cloud.

13. And the thunder declares His glory with His praise, and the angels too for awe of Him; and He sends the thunderbolts and smites with them whom He pleases, yet they dispute concerning Allah, and He is mighty in prowess.

14. To Him is due the true prayer; and those whom they pray to besides Allah give them no answer, but (they are) like one who stretches forth his two hands towards water that it may reach his mouth, but it will not reach it; and the prayer of the unbelievers is only in error.

15. And whoever is in the heavens and the earth makes obeisance to Allah only, willingly and unwillingly, and their shadows too at morn and eve.

وَيَقُوْلُ الَّذِيْنَ كَفَرُوْا لَوْلَاۤ اُنْزِلَ عَلَيْهِ اٰيَةٌ مِّنْ رَّبِّهٖ ؕ اِنَّمَاۤ اَنْتَ مُنْذِرٌ وَّلِكُلِّ قَوْمٍ هَادٍ ۟

اَللّٰهُ يَعْلَمُ مَا تَحْمِلُ كُلُّ اُنْثٰى وَمَا تَغِيْضُ الْاَرْحَامُ وَمَا تَزْدَادُ ؕ وَكُلُّ شَيْءٍ عِنْدَهٗ بِمِقْدَارٍ ۟۸

عٰلِمُ الْغَيْبِ وَالشَّهَادَةِ الْكَبِيْرُ الْمُتَعَالِ ۟۹

سَوَآءٌ مِّنْكُمْ مَّنْ اَسَرَّ الْقَوْلَ وَمَنْ جَهَرَ بِهٖ وَمَنْ هُوَ مُسْتَخْفٍ بِالَّيْلِ وَسَارِبٌۢ بِالنَّهَارِ ۟۱۰

لَهٗ مُعَقِّبٰتٌ مِّنْۢ بَيْنِ يَدَيْهِ وَمِنْ خَلْفِهٖ يَحْفَظُوْنَهٗ مِنْ اَمْرِ اللّٰهِ ؕ اِنَّ اللّٰهَ لَا يُغَيِّرُ مَا بِقَوْمٍ حَتّٰى يُغَيِّرُوْا مَا بِاَنْفُسِهِمْ ؕ وَاِذَاۤ اَرَادَ اللّٰهُ بِقَوْمٍ سُوْۤءًا فَلَا مَرَدَّ لَهٗ ۚ وَمَا لَهُمْ مِّنْ دُوْنِهٖ مِنْ وَّالٍ ۟۱۱

هُوَ الَّذِيْ يُرِيْكُمُ الْبَرْقَ خَوْفًا وَّطَمَعًا وَّيُنْشِئُ السَّحَابَ الثِّقَالَ ۟۱۲

وَيُسَبِّحُ الرَّعْدُ بِحَمْدِهٖ وَالْمَلٰٓئِكَةُ مِنْ خِيْفَتِهٖ ۚ وَيُرْسِلُ الصَّوَاعِقَ فَيُصِيْبُ بِهَا مَنْ يَّشَآءُ وَهُمْ يُجَادِلُوْنَ فِى اللّٰهِ ۚ وَهُوَ شَدِيْدُ الْمِحَالِ ۟۱۳

لَهٗ دَعْوَةُ الْحَقِّ ؕ وَالَّذِيْنَ يَدْعُوْنَ مِنْ دُوْنِهٖ لَا يَسْتَجِيْبُوْنَ لَهُمْ بِشَيْءٍ اِلَّا كَبَاسِطِ كَفَّيْهِ اِلَى الْمَآءِ لِيَبْلُغَ فَاهُ وَمَا هُوَ بِبَالِغِهٖ ؕ وَمَا دُعَآءُ الْكٰفِرِيْنَ اِلَّا فِيْ ضَلٰلٍ ۟۱۴

وَلِلّٰهِ يَسْجُدُ مَنْ فِى السَّمٰوٰتِ وَالْاَرْضِ طَوْعًا وَّكَرْهًا وَّظِلٰلُهُمْ بِالْغُدُوِّ وَالْاٰصَالِ ۩ ۟۱۵

228

16. Say: Who is the Lord of the heavens and the earth?—Say: Allah. Say: Do you take then besides Him guardians who do not control any profit or harm for themselves? Say: Are the blind and the seeing alike? Or can the darkness and the light be equal? Or have they set up with Allah associates who have created creation like His, so that what is created became confused to them? Say: Allah is the Creator of all things, and He is the One, the Supreme.

17. He sends down water from the cloud, then watercourses flow (with water) according to their measure, and the torrent bears along the swelling foam, and from what they melt in the fire for the sake of making ornaments or apparatus arises a scum like it; thus does Allah compare truth and falsehood; then as for the scum, it passes away as a worthless thing; and as for that which profits the people, it tarries in the earth; thus does Allah set forth parables.

18. For those who respond to their Lord is good; and (as for) those who do not respond to Him, had they all that is in the earth and the like thereof with it they would certainly offer it for a ransom. (As for) those, an evil reckoning shall be theirs and their abode is hell, and evil is the resting-place.

19. Is he then who knows that what has been revealed to you from your Lord is the truth like him who is blind? Only those possessed of understanding will mind,

20. Those who fulfil the promise of Allah and do not break the covenant,

21. And those who join that which Allah has bidden to be joined and have awe of their Lord and fear the evil reckoning.

229

22. And those who are constant, seeking the pleasure of their Lord, and keep up prayer and spend (benevolently) out of what We have given them secretly and openly and repel evil with good, as for those, they shall have the (happy) issue of the abode,

23. The gardens of perpetual abode which they will enter along with those who do good from among their parents and their spouses and their offspring; and the angels will enter in upon them from every gate:

24. Peace be on you because you were constant, how excellent, is then, the issue of the abode.

25. And those who break the covenant of Allah after its confirmation and cut asunder that which Allah has ordered to be joined and make mischief in the land; (as for) those, upon them shall be curse and they shall have the evil (issue) of the abode.

26. Allah amplifies and straitens the means of subsistence for whom He pleases; and they rejoice in this world's life, and this world's life is nothing compared with the hereafter but a temporary enjoyment.

27. And those who disbelieve say: Why is not a sign sent down upon him by his Lord? Say: Surely Allah makes him who will go astray, and guides to Himself those who turn (to Him).

28. Those who believe and whose hearts are set at rest by the remembrance of Allah; now surely by Allah's remembrance are the hearts set at rest.

29. (As for) those who believe and do good, a good final state shall be theirs and a goodly return.

وَالَّذِيْنَ صَبَرُوا ابْتِغَآءَ وَجْهِ رَبِّهِمْ وَاَقَامُوا الصَّلٰوةَ وَاَنْفَقُوْا مِمَّا رَزَقْنٰهُمْ سِرًّا وَّعَلَانِيَةً وَّ يَدْرَءُوْنَ بِالْحَسَنَةِ السَّيِّئَةَ اُولٰٓئِكَ لَهُمْ عُقْبَى الدَّارِ ۙ ٢٢

جَنّٰتُ عَدْنٍ يَّدْخُلُوْنَهَا وَمَنْ صَلَحَ مِنْ اٰبَآئِهِمْ وَاَزْوَاجِهِمْ وَذُرِّيّٰتِهِمْ وَالْمَلٰٓئِكَةُ يَدْخُلُوْنَ عَلَيْهِمْ مِّنْ كُلِّ بَابٍ ۚ ٢٣

سَلٰمٌ عَلَيْكُمْ بِمَا صَبَرْتُمْ فَنِعْمَ عُقْبَى الدَّارِ ۗ ٢٤

وَالَّذِيْنَ يَنْقُضُوْنَ عَهْدَ اللّٰهِ مِنْ بَعْدِ مِيْثَاقِهٖ وَ يَقْطَعُوْنَ مَآ اَمَرَ اللّٰهُ بِهٖٓ اَنْ يُّوْصَلَ وَيُفْسِدُوْنَ فِى الْاَرْضِ ۙ اُولٰٓئِكَ لَهُمُ اللَّعْنَةُ وَلَهُمْ سُوْٓءُ الدَّارِ ٢٥

اَللّٰهُ يَبْسُطُ الرِّزْقَ لِمَنْ يَّشَآءُ وَيَقْدِرُ ۚ وَفَرِحُوْا بِالْحَيٰوةِ الدُّنْيَا ۗ وَمَا الْحَيٰوةُ الدُّنْيَا فِى الْاٰخِرَةِ اِلَّا مَتَاعٌ ﻉ ٢٦

وَيَقُوْلُ الَّذِيْنَ كَفَرُوْا لَوْلَآ اُنْزِلَ عَلَيْهِ اٰيَةٌ مِّنْ رَّبِّهٖ ۗ قُلْ اِنَّ اللّٰهَ يُضِلُّ مَنْ يَّشَآءُ وَيَهْدِيْٓ اِلَيْهِ مَنْ اَنَابَ ۖ ٢٧

اَلَّذِيْنَ اٰمَنُوْا وَتَطْمَئِنُّ قُلُوْبُهُمْ بِذِكْرِ اللّٰهِ ۗ اَلَا بِذِكْرِ اللّٰهِ تَطْمَئِنُّ الْقُلُوْبُ ٢٨

اَلَّذِيْنَ اٰمَنُوْا وَعَمِلُوا الصّٰلِحٰتِ طُوْبٰى لَهُمْ وَ حُسْنُ مَاٰبٍ ٢٩

30. And thus We have sent you among a nation before which other nations have passed away, that you might recite to them what We have revealed to you and (still) they deny the Beneficent God. Say: He is my Lord, there is no god but He; on Him do I rely and to Him is my return.

31. And even if there were a Quran with which the mountains were made to pass away, or the earth were travelled over with it, or the dead were made to speak thereby; nay! the commandment is wholly Allah's. Have not yet those who believe known that if Allah please He would certainly guide all the people? And (as for) those who disbelieve, there will not cease to afflict them because of what they do a repelling calamity, or it will alight close by their abodes, until the promise of Allah comes about; surely Allah will not fail in (His) promise.

32. And apostles before you were certainly mocked at, but I gave respite to those who disbelieved, then I destroyed them; how then was My requital (of evil)?

33. Is He then Who watches every soul as to what it earns? And yet they give associates to Allah! Say: Give them a name; nay, do you mean to inform Him of what He does not know in the earth, or (do you affirm this) by an outward saying? Rather, their plans are made to appear fair-seeming to those who disbelieve, and they are kept back from the path; and whom Allah makes err, he shall have no guide.

34. They shall have chastisement in this world's life, and the chastisement of the hereafter is certainly more grievous, and they shall have no protector against Allah.

35. A likeness of the garden which the righteous are promised; there flow beneath it rivers, its food and shades are perpetual; this is the requital of those who guarded (against evil), and the requital of the unbelievers is the fire.

كَذٰلِكَ اَرْسَلْنٰكَ فِيْۤ اُمَّةٍ قَدْ خَلَتْ مِنْ قَبْلِهَاۤ اُمَمٌ لِّتَتْلُوَا۟ عَلَيْهِمُ الَّذِيْۤ اَوْحَيْنَاۤ اِلَيْكَ وَهُمْ يَكْفُرُوْنَ بِالرَّحْمٰنِ ۚ قُلْ هُوَ رَبِّيْ لَاۤ اِلٰهَ اِلَّا هُوَ ۚ عَلَيْهِ تَوَكَّلْتُ وَاِلَيْهِ مَتَابِ ۝

وَلَوْ اَنَّ قُرْاٰنًا سُيِّرَتْ بِهِ الْجِبَالُ اَوْ قُطِّعَتْ بِهِ الْاَرْضُ اَوْ كُلِّمَ بِهِ الْمَوْتٰى ۚ بَلْ لِّلّٰهِ الْاَمْرُ جَمِيْعًا ۗ اَفَلَمْ يَايْـَٔسِ الَّذِيْنَ اٰمَنُوْۤا اَنْ لَّوْ يَشَاۤءُ اللّٰهُ لَهَدَى النَّاسَ جَمِيْعًا ۗ وَلَا يَزَالُ الَّذِيْنَ كَفَرُوْا تُصِيْبُهُمْ بِمَا صَنَعُوْا قَارِعَةٌ اَوْ تَحُلُّ قَرِيْبًا مِّنْ دَارِهِمْ حَتّٰى يَاْتِيَ وَعْدُ اللّٰهِ ۚ اِنَّ اللّٰهَ لَا يُخْلِفُ الْمِيْعَادَ ۝

وَلَقَدِ اسْتُهْزِئَ بِرُسُلٍ مِّنْ قَبْلِكَ فَاَمْلَيْتُ لِلَّذِيْنَ كَفَرُوْا ثُمَّ اَخَذْتُهُمْ ۖ فَكَيْفَ كَانَ عِقَابِ ۝ اَفَمَنْ هُوَ قَآئِمٌ عَلٰى كُلِّ نَفْسٍۭ بِمَا كَسَبَتْ ۚ وَجَعَلُوْا لِلّٰهِ شُرَكَآءَ ۗ قُلْ سَمُّوْهُمْ ۗ اَمْ تُنَبِّئُوْنَهٗ بِمَا لَا يَعْلَمُ فِى الْاَرْضِ اَمْ بِظَاهِرٍ مِّنَ الْقَوْلِ ۗ بَلْ زُيِّنَ لِلَّذِيْنَ كَفَرُوْا مَكْرُهُمْ وَصُدُّوْا عَنِ السَّبِيْلِ ۗ وَمَنْ يُّضْلِلِ اللّٰهُ فَمَا لَهٗ مِنْ هَادٍ ۝

لَهُمْ عَذَابٌ فِى الْحَيٰوةِ الدُّنْيَا وَلَعَذَابُ الْاٰخِرَةِ اَشَقُّ ۚ وَمَا لَهُمْ مِّنَ اللّٰهِ مِنْ وَّاقٍ ۝ مَثَلُ الْجَنَّةِ الَّتِيْ وُعِدَ الْمُتَّقُوْنَ ۖ تَجْرِيْ مِنْ تَحْتِهَا الْاَنْهٰرُ ۚ اُكُلُهَا دَآئِمٌ وَّظِلُّهَا ۚ تِلْكَ عُقْبَى الَّذِيْنَ اتَّقَوْا ۖ وَّعُقْبَى الْكٰفِرِيْنَ النَّارُ ۝

36. And those to whom We have given the Book rejoice in that which has been revealed to you, and of the confederates are some who deny a part of it. Say: I am only commanded that I should serve Allah and not associate anything with Him, to Him do I invite (you) and to Him is my return.

37. And thus have We revealed it, a true judgment in Arabic, and if you follow their low desires after what has come to you of knowledge, you shall not have against Allah any guardian or a protector.

38. And certainly We sent apostles before you and gave them wives and children, and it is not in (the power of) an apostle to bring a sign except by Allah's permission; for every term there is an appointment.

39. Allah makes to pass away and establishes what He pleases, and with Him is the basis of the Book.

40. And We will either let you see part of what We threaten them with or cause you to die, for only the delivery of the message is (incumbent) on you, while calling (them) to account is Our (business).

41. Do they not see that We are bringing destruction upon the land by curtailing it of its sides? And Allah pronounces a doom—there is no repeller of His decree, and He is swift to take account.

42. And those before them did indeed make plans, but all planning is Allah's; He knows what every soul earns, and the unbelievers shall come to know for whom is the (better) issue of the abode.

43. And those who disbelieve say: You are not a messenger. Say: Allah is sufficient as a witness between me and you and whoever has knowledge of the Book.

وَالَّذِيْنَ اٰتَيْنٰهُمُ الْكِتٰبَ يَفْرَحُوْنَ بِمَا اُنْزِلَ اِلَيْكَ وَمِنَ الْاَحْزَابِ مَنْ يُّنْكِرُ بَعْضَهٗ ۗ قُلْ اِنَّمَا اُمِرْتُ اَنْ اَعْبُدَ اللّٰهَ وَلَاۤ اُشْرِكَ بِهٖ ۗ اِلَيْهِ اَدْعُوْا وَاِلَيْهِ مَاٰبِ ۝

وَكَذٰلِكَ اَنْزَلْنٰهُ حُكْمًا عَرَبِيًّا ۗ وَلَئِنِ اتَّبَعْتَ اَهْوَآءَهُمْ بَعْدَمَا جَآءَكَ مِنَ الْعِلْمِ ۙ مَا لَكَ مِنَ اللّٰهِ مِنْ وَّلِيٍّ وَّلَا وَاقٍ ۝

وَلَقَدْ اَرْسَلْنَا رُسُلًا مِّنْ قَبْلِكَ وَجَعَلْنَا لَهُمْ اَزْوَاجًا وَّذُرِّيَّةً ۗ وَمَا كَانَ لِرَسُوْلٍ اَنْ يَّاْتِيَ بِاٰيَةٍ اِلَّا بِاِذْنِ اللّٰهِ ۗ لِكُلِّ اَجَلٍ كِتَابٌ ۝

يَمْحُوا اللّٰهُ مَا يَشَآءُ وَيُثْبِتُ ۖ وَعِنْدَهٗۤ اُمُّ الْكِتٰبِ ۝ وَاِنْ مَّا نُرِيَنَّكَ بَعْضَ الَّذِيْ نَعِدُهُمْ اَوْ نَتَوَفَّيَنَّكَ فَاِنَّمَا عَلَيْكَ الْبَلٰغُ وَعَلَيْنَا الْحِسَابُ ۝

اَوَلَمْ يَرَوْا اَنَّا نَاْتِي الْاَرْضَ نَنْقُصُهَا مِنْ اَطْرَافِهَا ۗ وَاللّٰهُ يَحْكُمُ لَا مُعَقِّبَ لِحُكْمِهٖ ۗ وَهُوَ سَرِيْعُ الْحِسَابِ ۝ وَقَدْ مَكَرَ الَّذِيْنَ مِنْ قَبْلِهِمْ فَلِلّٰهِ الْمَكْرُ جَمِيْعًا ۗ يَعْلَمُ مَا تَكْسِبُ كُلُّ نَفْسٍ ۗ وَسَيَعْلَمُ الْكُفّٰرُ لِمَنْ عُقْبَى الدَّارِ ۝

وَيَقُوْلُ الَّذِيْنَ كَفَرُوْا لَسْتَ مُرْسَلًا ۗ قُلْ كَفٰى بِاللّٰهِ شَهِيْدًا بَيْنِيْ وَبَيْنَكُمْ ۙ وَمَنْ عِنْدَهٗ عِلْمُ الْكِتٰبِ ۝

IBRAHIM

اَیَاتِهَا (۱٤) سُوْرَةُ اِبْرٰهِیْمَ مَکِّیَّةٌ رُکُوْعَاتُهَا

In the name of Allah,
the Beneficent, the Merciful.

بِسْمِ اللهِ الرَّحْمٰنِ الرَّحِیْمِ ۟

1. Alif Lam Ra. (This is) a Book which We have revealed to you that you may bring forth men, by their Lord's permission from utter darkness into light—to the way of the Mighty, the Praised One,

الٓرٰ ۟ کِتٰبٌ اَنْزَلْنٰهُ اِلَیْکَ لِتُخْرِجَ النَّاسَ مِنَ الظُّلُمٰتِ اِلَی النُّوْرِ ۙ۬ بِاِذْنِ رَبِّهِمْ اِلٰی صِرَاطِ الْعَزِیْزِ الْحَمِیْدِ ۟

2. (Of) Allah, Whose is whatever is in the heavens and whatever is in the earth; and woe to the unbelievers on account of the severe chastisement,

اللهِ الَّذِیْ لَهٗ مَا فِی السَّمٰوٰتِ وَمَا فِی الْاَرْضِ ؕ وَوَیْلٌ لِّلْکٰفِرِیْنَ مِنْ عَذَابٍ شَدِیْدِ ۟ۙ

3. (To) those who love this world's life more than the hereafter, and turn away from Allah's path and desire to make it crooked; these are in a great error.

الَّذِیْنَ یَسْتَحِبُّوْنَ الْحَیٰوةَ الدُّنْیَا عَلَی الْاٰخِرَةِ وَ یَصُدُّوْنَ عَنْ سَبِیْلِ اللهِ وَیَبْغُوْنَهَا عِوَجًا ؕ اُولٰٓئِکَ فِیْ ضَلٰلٍ بَعِیْدٍ ۟

4. And We did not send any apostle but with the language of his people, so that he might explain to them clearly; then Allah makes whom He pleases err and He guides whom He pleases, and He is the Mighty, the Wise.

وَمَا اَرْسَلْنَا مِنْ رَّسُوْلٍ اِلَّا بِلِسَانِ قَوْمِهٖ لِیُبَیِّنَ لَهُمْ ؕ فَیُضِلُّ اللهُ مَنْ یَّشَآءُ وَیَهْدِیْ مَنْ یَّشَآءُ ؕ وَهُوَ الْعَزِیْزُ الْحَکِیْمُ ۟

5. And certainly We sent Musa with Our communications, saying: Bring forth your people from utter darkness into light and remind them of the days of Allah; most surely there are signs in this for every patient, grateful one.

وَلَقَدْ اَرْسَلْنَا مُوْسٰی بِاٰیٰتِنَا ٓ اَنْ اَخْرِجْ قَوْمَکَ مِنَ الظُّلُمٰتِ اِلَی النُّوْرِ ۙ۬ وَذَکِّرْهُمْ بِاَیّٰمِ اللهِ ؕ اِنَّ فِیْ ذٰلِکَ لَاٰیٰتٍ لِّکُلِّ صَبَّارٍ شَکُوْرٍ ۟

6. And when Musa said to his people: Call to mind Allah's favor to you when He delivered you from Firon's people, who subjected you to severe torment, and slew your sons and spared your women; and in this there was a great trial from your Lord.

وَاِذْ قَالَ مُوْسٰی لِقَوْمِهِ اذْکُرُوْا نِعْمَةَ اللهِ عَلَیْکُمْ اِذْ اَنْجٰکُمْ مِّنْ اٰلِ فِرْعَوْنَ یَسُوْمُوْنَکُمْ سُوْٓءَ الْعَذَابِ وَیُذَبِّحُوْنَ اَبْنَآءَکُمْ وَ یَسْتَحْیُوْنَ نِسَآءَکُمْ ؕ وَفِیْ ذٰلِکُمْ بَلَآءٌ مِّنْ رَّبِّکُمْ عَظِیْمٌ ۟

7. And when your Lord made it known: If you are grateful, I would certainly give to you more, and if you are ungrateful, My chastisement is truly severe.

8. And Musa said: If you are ungrateful, you and those on earth all together, most surely Allah is Self-sufficient, Praised;

9. Has not the account reached you of those before you, of the people of Nuh and Ad and Samood, and those after them? None knows them but Allah. Their apostles come to them with clear arguments, but they thrust their hands into their mouths and said: Surely we deny that with which you are sent, and most surely we are in serious doubt as to that to which you invite us.

10. Their apostles said: Is there doubt about Allah, the Maker of the heavens and the earth? He invites you to forgive you your faults and to respite you till an appointed term. They said: You are nothing but mortals like us; you wish to turn us away from what our fathers used to worship; bring us therefore some clear authority.

11. Their apostles said to them: We are nothing but mortals like yourselves, but Allah bestows (His) favors on whom He pleases of His servants, and it is not for us that we should bring you an authority except by Allah's permission; and on Allah should the believers rely.

12. And what reason have we that we should not rely on Allah? And He has indeed guided us in our ways; and certainly we would bear with patience your persecution of us; and on Allah should the reliant rely.

وَإِذْ تَأَذَّنَ رَبُّكُمْ لَئِنْ شَكَرْتُمْ لَأَزِيدَنَّكُمْ وَلَئِنْ كَفَرْتُمْ إِنَّ عَذَابِي لَشَدِيدٌ ۝

وَقَالَ مُوسَى إِنْ تَكْفُرُوا أَنْتُمْ وَمَنْ فِي الْأَرْضِ جَمِيعًا فَإِنَّ اللّٰهَ لَغَنِيٌّ حَمِيدٌ ۝

أَلَمْ يَأْتِكُمْ نَبَؤُا الَّذِينَ مِنْ قَبْلِكُمْ قَوْمِ نُوحٍ وَعَادٍ وَثَمُودَ وَالَّذِينَ مِنْ بَعْدِهِمْ لَا يَعْلَمُهُمْ إِلَّا اللّٰهُ جَاءَتْهُمْ رُسُلُهُمْ بِالْبَيِّنَاتِ فَرَدُّوا أَيْدِيَهُمْ فِي أَفْوَاهِهِمْ وَقَالُوا إِنَّا كَفَرْنَا بِمَا أُرْسِلْتُمْ بِهِ وَإِنَّا لَفِي شَكٍّ مِمَّا تَدْعُونَنَا إِلَيْهِ مُرِيبٍ ۝

قَالَتْ رُسُلُهُمْ أَفِي اللّٰهِ شَكٌّ فَاطِرِ السَّمَوَاتِ وَالْأَرْضِ يَدْعُوكُمْ لِيَغْفِرَ لَكُمْ مِنْ ذُنُوبِكُمْ وَيُؤَخِّرَكُمْ إِلَى أَجَلٍ مُسَمًّى قَالُوا إِنْ أَنْتُمْ إِلَّا بَشَرٌ مِثْلُنَا تُرِيدُونَ أَنْ تَصُدُّونَا عَمَّا كَانَ يَعْبُدُ آبَاؤُنَا فَأْتُونَا بِسُلْطَانٍ مُبِينٍ ۝

قَالَتْ لَهُمْ رُسُلُهُمْ إِنْ نَحْنُ إِلَّا بَشَرٌ مِثْلُكُمْ وَلَكِنَّ اللّٰهَ يَمُنُّ عَلَى مَنْ يَشَاءُ مِنْ عِبَادِهِ وَمَا كَانَ لَنَا أَنْ نَأْتِيَكُمْ بِسُلْطَانٍ إِلَّا بِإِذْنِ اللّٰهِ وَعَلَى اللّٰهِ فَلْيَتَوَكَّلِ الْمُؤْمِنُونَ ۝

وَمَا لَنَا أَلَّا نَتَوَكَّلَ عَلَى اللّٰهِ وَقَدْ هَدَانَا سُبُلَنَا وَلَنَصْبِرَنَّ عَلَى مَا آذَيْتُمُونَا وَعَلَى اللّٰهِ فَلْيَتَوَكَّلِ الْمُتَوَكِّلُونَ ۝

13. And those who disbelieved said to their apostles: We will most certainly drive you forth from our land, or else you shall come back into our religion. So their Lord revealed to them: Most certainly We will destroy the unjust.

14. And most certainly We will settle you in the land after them; this is for him who fears standing in My presence and who fears My threat.

15. And they asked for judgment and every insolent opposer was disappointed:

16. Hell is before him and he shall be given to drink of festering water:

17. He will drink it little by little and will not be able to swallow it agreeably, and death will come to him from every quarter, but he shall not die; and there shall be vehement chastisement before him.

18. The parable of those who disbelieve in their Lord: their actions are like ashes on which the wind blows hard on a stormy day; they shall not have power over any thing out of what they have earned; this is the great error.

19. Do you not see that Allah created the heavens and the earth with truth? If He please He will take you off and bring a new creation,

20. And this is not difficult for Allah.

21. And they shall all come forth before Allah, then the weak shall say to those who were proud: Surely we were your followers, can you therefore avert from us any part of the chastisement of Allah? They would say: If Allah had guided us, we too would have guided you; it is the same to us whether we are impatient (now) or patient, there is no place for us to fly to.

235

22. And the Shaitan shall say after the affair is decided: Surely Allah promised you the promise of truth, and I gave you promises, then failed to keep them to you, and I had no authority over you, except that I called you and you obeyed me, therefore do not blame me but blame yourselves: I cannot be your aider (now) nor can you be my aiders; surely I disbelieved in your associating me with Allah before; surely it is the unjust that shall have the painful punishment.

23. And those who believe and do good are made to enter gardens, beneath which rivers flow, to abide in them by their Lord's permission; their greeting therein is, Peace.

24. Have you not considered how Allah sets forth a parable of a good word (being) like a good tree, whose root is firm and whose branches are in heaven,

25. Yielding its fruit in every season by the permission of its Lord? And Allah sets forth parables for men that they may be mindful.

26. And the parable of an evil word is as an evil tree pulled up from the earth's surface; it has no stability.

27. Allah confirms those who believe with the sure word in this world's life and in the hereafter, and Allah causes the unjust to go astray, and Allah does what He pleases.

28. Have you not seen those who have changed Allah's favor for ungratefulness and made their people to alight into the abode of perdition;

29. (Into) hell? They shall enter into it and an evil place it is to settle in.

30. And they set up equals with Allah that they may lead (people) astray from His path. Say: Enjoy yourselves, for surely your return is to the fire.

31. Say to My servants who believe that they should keep up prayer and spend out of what We have given them secretly and openly before the coming of the day in which there shall be no bartering nor mutual befriending.

32. Allah is He Who created the heavens and the earth and sent down water from the clouds, then brought forth with it fruits as a sustenance for you, and He has made the ships subservient to you, that they might run their course in the sea by His command, and He has made the rivers subservient to you.

33. And He has made subservient to you the sun and the moon pursuing their courses, and He has made subservient to you the night and the day.

34. And He gives you of all that you ask Him; and if you count Allah's favors, you will not be able to number them; most surely man is very unjust, very ungrateful.

35. And when Ibrahim said: My Lord! make this city secure, and save me and my sons from worshipping idols:

36. My Lord! surely they have led many men astray; then whoever follows me, he is surely of me, and whoever disobeys me, Thou surely art Forgiving, Merciful:

37. O our Lord! surely I have settled a part of my offspring in a valley unproductive of fruit near Thy Sacred House, our Lord! that they may keep up prayer; therefore make the hearts of some people yearn towards them and provide them with fruits; haply they may be grateful:

وَجَعَلُوْا لِلّٰهِ اَنْدَادًا لِّيُضِلُّوْا عَنْ سَبِيْلِهٖ ۗ قُلْ تَمَتَّعُوْا فَاِنَّ مَصِيْرَكُمْ اِلَى النَّارِ ۝

قُلْ لِّعِبَادِيَ الَّذِيْنَ اٰمَنُوْا يُقِيْمُوا الصَّلٰوةَ وَيُنْفِقُوْا مِمَّا رَزَقْنٰهُمْ سِرًّا وَّعَلَانِيَةً مِّنْ قَبْلِ اَنْ يَّأْتِيَ يَوْمٌ لَّا بَيْعٌ فِيْهِ وَلَا خِلٰلٌ ۝

اَللّٰهُ الَّذِيْ خَلَقَ السَّمٰوٰتِ وَالْاَرْضَ وَاَنْزَلَ مِنَ السَّمَآءِ مَآءً فَاَخْرَجَ بِهٖ مِنَ الثَّمَرٰتِ رِزْقًا لَّكُمْ ۚ وَسَخَّرَ لَكُمُ الْفُلْكَ لِتَجْرِيَ فِى الْبَحْرِ بِاَمْرِهٖ ۚ وَسَخَّرَ لَكُمُ الْاَنْهٰرَ ۝

وَسَخَّرَ لَكُمُ الشَّمْسَ وَالْقَمَرَ دَآئِبَيْنِ ۚ وَسَخَّرَ لَكُمُ الَّيْلَ وَالنَّهَارَ ۝

وَاٰتٰكُمْ مِّنْ كُلِّ مَا سَاَلْتُمُوْهُ ۗ وَاِنْ تَعُدُّوْا نِعْمَتَ اللّٰهِ لَا تُحْصُوْهَا ۗ اِنَّ الْاِنْسَانَ لَظَلُوْمٌ كَفَّارٌ ۝

وَاِذْ قَالَ اِبْرٰهِيْمُ رَبِّ اجْعَلْ هٰذَا الْبَلَدَ اٰمِنًا وَّاجْنُبْنِيْ وَبَنِيَّ اَنْ نَّعْبُدَ الْاَصْنَامَ ۝

رَبِّ اِنَّهُنَّ اَضْلَلْنَ كَثِيْرًا مِّنَ النَّاسِ ۚ فَمَنْ تَبِعَنِيْ فَاِنَّهٗ مِنِّيْ ۚ وَمَنْ عَصَانِيْ فَاِنَّكَ غَفُوْرٌ رَّحِيْمٌ ۝

رَبَّنَا اِنِّيْ اَسْكَنْتُ مِنْ ذُرِّيَّتِيْ بِوَادٍ غَيْرِ ذِيْ زَرْعٍ عِنْدَ بَيْتِكَ الْمُحَرَّمِ ۙ رَبَّنَا لِيُقِيْمُوا الصَّلٰوةَ فَاجْعَلْ اَفْئِدَةً مِّنَ النَّاسِ تَهْوِيْ اِلَيْهِمْ وَارْزُقْهُمْ مِّنَ الثَّمَرٰتِ لَعَلَّهُمْ يَشْكُرُوْنَ ۝

38. O our Lord! Surely Thou knowest what we hide and what we make public, and nothing in the earth nor any thing in heaven is hidden from Allah:

رَبَّنَآ اِنَّكَ تَعْلَمُ مَا نُخْفِىْ وَمَا نُعْلِنُ وَمَا يَخْفٰى عَلَى اللّٰهِ مِنْ شَىْءٍ فِى الْاَرْضِ وَلَا فِى السَّمَآءِ ۞

39. Praise be to Allah, Who has given me in old age Ismail and Ishaq; most surely my Lord is the Hearer of prayer:

اَلْحَمْدُ لِلّٰهِ الَّذِىْ وَهَبَ لِىْ عَلَى الْكِبَرِ اِسْمٰعِیْلَ وَاِسْحٰقَ اِنَّ رَبِّىْ لَسَمِیْعُ الدُّعَآءِ ۞

40. My Lord! make me keep up prayer and from my offspring (too), O our Lord, and accept my prayer:

رَبِّ اجْعَلْنِىْ مُقِیْمَ الصَّلٰوةِ وَمِنْ ذُرِّیَّتِىْ ۚ رَبَّنَا وَتَقَبَّلْ دُعَآءِ ۞

41. O our Lord! grant me protection and my parents and the believers on the day when the reckoning shall come to pass!

رَبَّنَا اغْفِرْ لِىْ وَلِوَالِدَىَّ وَلِلْمُؤْمِنِیْنَ یَوْمَ یَقُوْمُ الْحِسَابُ ۞

42. And do not think Allah to be heedless of what the unjust do; He only respites them to a day on which the eyes shall be fixedly open,

وَلَا تَحْسَبَنَّ اللّٰهَ غَافِلًا عَمَّا یَعْمَلُ الظّٰلِمُوْنَ ۙ اِنَّمَا یُؤَخِّرُهُمْ لِیَوْمٍ تَشْخَصُ فِیْهِ الْاَبْصَارُ ۞

43. Hastening forward, their heads upraised, their eyes not reverting to them and their hearts vacant.

مُهْطِعِیْنَ مُقْنِعِىْ رُءُوْسِهِمْ لَا یَرْتَدُّ اِلَیْهِمْ طَرْفُهُمْ ۚ وَاَفْئِدَتُهُمْ هَوَآءٌ ۞

44. And warn people of the day when the chastisement shall come to them, then those who were unjust will say: O our Lord! respite us to a near term, (so) we shall respond to Thy call and follow the apostles. What! did you not swear before (that) there will be no passing away for you!

وَاَنْذِرِ النَّاسَ یَوْمَ یَأْتِیْهِمُ الْعَذَابُ فَیَقُوْلُ الَّذِیْنَ ظَلَمُوْا رَبَّنَآ اَخِّرْنَآ اِلٰى اَجَلٍ قَرِیْبٍ ۙ نُّجِبْ دَعْوَتَكَ وَنَتَّبِعِ الرُّسُلَ ۗ اَوَلَمْ تَكُوْنُوْآ اَقْسَمْتُمْ مِّنْ قَبْلُ مَا لَكُمْ مِّنْ زَوَالٍ ۞

45. And you dwell in the abodes of those who were unjust to themselves, and it is clear to you how We dealt with them and We have made (them) examples to you.

وَّسَكَنْتُمْ فِىْ مَسٰكِنِ الَّذِیْنَ ظَلَمُوْآ اَنْفُسَهُمْ وَتَبَیَّنَ لَكُمْ كَیْفَ فَعَلْنَا بِهِمْ وَضَرَبْنَا لَكُمُ الْاَمْثَالَ ۞

46. And they have indeed planned their plan, but their plan is with Allah, though their plan was such that the mountains should pass away thereby.

وَقَدْ مَكَرُوْا مَكْرَهُمْ وَعِنْدَ اللّٰهِ مَكْرُهُمْ ۗ وَاِنْ كَانَ مَكْرُهُمْ لِتَزُوْلَ مِنْهُ الْجِبَالُ ۞

47. Therefore do not think Allah (to be one) failing in His promise to His apostles; surely Allah is Mighty, the Lord of Retribution.

فَلَا تَحْسَبَنَّ اللّٰهَ مُخْلِفَ وَعْدِهٖ رُسُلَهٗ ۗ اِنَّ اللّٰهَ عَزِیْزٌ ذُو انْتِقَامٍ ۞

48. On the day when the earth shall be changed into a different earth, and the heavens (as well), and they shall come forth before Allah, the One, the Supreme.

49. And you will see the guilty on that day linked together in chains.

50. Their shirts made of pitch and the fire covering their faces,

51. That Allah may requite each soul (according to) what it has earned; surely Allah is swift in reckoning.

52. This is a sufficient exposition for the people and that they may be warned thereby, and that they may know that He is One God and that those possessed of understanding may mind.

يَوْمَ تُبَدَّلُ الْأَرْضُ غَيْرَ الْأَرْضِ وَالسَّمٰوٰتُ وَبَرَزُوْا لِلّٰهِ الْوَاحِدِ الْقَهَّارِ ۝

وَتَرَى الْمُجْرِمِيْنَ يَوْمَئِذٍ مُّقَرَّنِيْنَ فِي الْأَصْفَادِ ۝

سَرَابِيْلُهُمْ مِّنْ قَطِرَانٍ وَّتَغْشٰى وُجُوْهَهُمُ النَّارُ ۝

لِيَجْزِيَ اللّٰهُ كُلَّ نَفْسٍ مَّا كَسَبَتْ إِنَّ اللّٰهَ سَرِيْعُ الْحِسَابِ ۝

هٰذَا بَلٰغٌ لِّلنَّاسِ وَلِيُنْذَرُوْا بِهِ وَلِيَعْلَمُوْا أَنَّمَا هُوَ إِلٰهٌ وَّاحِدٌ وَّلِيَذَّكَّرَ أُولُوا الْأَلْبَابِ ۝

THE ROCK
(HIJR)

**In the name of Allah,
the Beneficent, the Merciful.**

1. Alif Lam Ra. These are the verses of the Book and (of) a Quran that makes (things) clear.

2. Often will those who disbelieve wish that they had been Muslims.

3. Leave them that they may eat and enjoy themselves and (that) hope may beguile them, for they will soon know.

4. And never did We destroy a town but it had a term made known.

5. No people can hasten on their doom nor can they postpone (it).

6. And they say: O you to whom the Reminder has been revealed! you are most surely insane:

7. Why do you not bring to us the angels if you are of the truthful ones?

8. We do not send the angels but with truth, and then they would not be respited.

9. Surely We have revealed the Reminder and We will most surely be its guardian.

10. And certainly We sent (apostles) before you among the nations of yore.

11. And there never came an apostle to them but they mocked him.

12. Thus do We make it to enter into the hearts of the guilty;

13. They do not believe in it, and indeed the example of the former people has already passed.

14. And even if We open to them a gateway of heaven, so that they ascend into it all the while,

15. They would certainly say: Only our eyes have been covered over, rather we are an enchanted people.

16. And certainly We have made strongholds in heaven and We have made it fair seeming to the beholders.

17. And We guard it against every accursed Shaitan,

اياتها (١٥) سُوْرَةُ الْحِجْرِ مَكِّيَةٌ رُكُوعاتها

بِسْمِ اللهِ الرَّحْمٰنِ الرَّحِيْمِ ۝

الۤرٰ تِلْكَ اٰيٰتُ الْكِتٰبِ وَقُرْاٰنٍ مُبِيْنٍ ۝

رُبَمَا يَوَدُّ الَّذِيْنَ كَفَرُوْا لَوْ كَانُوْا مُسْلِمِيْنَ ۝

ذَرْهُمْ يَأْكُلُوْا وَيَتَمَتَّعُوْا وَيُلْهِهِمُ الْاَمَلُ فَسَوْفَ يَعْلَمُوْنَ ۝

وَمَا اَهْلَكْنَا مِنْ قَرْيَةٍ اِلَّا وَلَهَا كِتَابٌ مَعْلُوْمٌ ۝

مَا تَسْبِقُ مِنْ اُمَّةٍ اَجَلَهَا وَمَا يَسْتَأْخِرُوْنَ ۝

وَقَالُوْا يٰاَيُّهَا الَّذِيْ نُزِّلَ عَلَيْهِ الذِّكْرُ اِنَّكَ لَمَجْنُوْنٌ ۝

لَوْ مَا تَأْتِيْنَا بِالْمَلٰئِكَةِ اِنْ كُنْتَ مِنَ الصّٰدِقِيْنَ ۝

مَا نُنَزِّلُ الْمَلٰئِكَةَ اِلَّا بِالْحَقِّ وَمَا كَانُوْا اِذًا مُنْظَرِيْنَ ۝

اِنَّا نَحْنُ نَزَّلْنَا الذِّكْرَ وَاِنَّا لَهٗ لَحٰفِظُوْنَ ۝

وَلَقَدْ اَرْسَلْنَا مِنْ قَبْلِكَ فِيْ شِيَعِ الْاَوَّلِيْنَ ۝

وَمَا يَأْتِيْهِمْ مِنْ رَسُوْلٍ اِلَّا كَانُوْا بِهٖ يَسْتَهْزِئُوْنَ ۝

كَذٰلِكَ نَسْلُكُهٗ فِيْ قُلُوْبِ الْمُجْرِمِيْنَ ۝

لَا يُؤْمِنُوْنَ بِهٖ وَقَدْ خَلَتْ سُنَّةُ الْاَوَّلِيْنَ ۝

وَلَوْ فَتَحْنَا عَلَيْهِمْ بَابًا مِنَ السَّمَاءِ فَظَلُّوْا فِيْهِ يَعْرُجُوْنَ ۝

لَقَالُوْا اِنَّمَا سُكِّرَتْ اَبْصَارُنَا بَلْ نَحْنُ قَوْمٌ مَسْحُوْرُوْنَ ۝

وَلَقَدْ جَعَلْنَا فِي السَّمَاءِ بُرُوْجًا وَزَيَّنّٰهَا لِلنّٰظِرِيْنَ ۝

وَحَفِظْنٰهَا مِنْ كُلِّ شَيْطٰنٍ رَجِيْمٍ ۝

18. But he who steals a hearing, so there follows him a visible flame.

اِلَّا مَنِ اسْتَرَقَ السَّمْعَ فَاَتْبَعَهُ شِهَابٌ مُّبِيْنٌ ۝

19. And the earth—We have spread it forth and made in it firm mountains and caused to grow in it of every suitable thing.

وَالْاَرْضَ مَدَدْنٰهَا وَاَلْقَيْنَا فِيْهَا رَوَاسِيَ وَاَنْبَتْنَا فِيْهَا مِنْ كُلِّ شَيْءٍ مَّوْزُوْنٍ ۝

20. And We have made in it means of subsistence for you and for him for whom you are not the suppliers.

وَجَعَلْنَا لَكُمْ فِيْهَا مَعَايِشَ وَمَنْ لَّسْتُمْ لَهٗ بِرٰزِقِيْنَ ۝

21. And there is not a thing but with Us are the treasures of it, and We do not send it down but in a known measure.

وَاِنْ مِّنْ شَيْءٍ اِلَّا عِنْدَنَا خَزَائِنُهٗ وَمَا نُنَزِّلُهٗ اِلَّا بِقَدَرٍ مَّعْلُوْمٍ ۝

22. And We send the winds fertilizing, then send down water from the cloud so We give it to you to drink of, nor is it you who store it up.

وَاَرْسَلْنَا الرِّيٰحَ لَوَاقِحَ فَاَنْزَلْنَا مِنَ السَّمَاءِ مَاءً فَاَسْقَيْنٰكُمُوْهُ وَمَا اَنْتُمْ لَهٗ بِخٰزِنِيْنَ ۝

23. And most surely We bring to life and cause to die and We are the heirs.

وَاِنَّا لَنَحْنُ نُحْيٖ وَنُمِيْتُ وَنَحْنُ الْوٰرِثُوْنَ ۝

24. And certainly We know those of you who have gone before and We certainly know those who shall come later.

وَلَقَدْ عَلِمْنَا الْمُسْتَقْدِمِيْنَ مِنْكُمْ وَلَقَدْ عَلِمْنَا الْمُسْتَاْخِرِيْنَ ۝

25. And surely your Lord will gather them together; surely He is Wise, Knowing.

وَاِنَّ رَبَّكَ هُوَ يَحْشُرُهُمْ اِنَّهٗ حَكِيْمٌ عَلِيْمٌ ۝

26. And certainly We created man of clay that gives forth sound, of black mud fashioned in shape.

وَلَقَدْ خَلَقْنَا الْاِنْسَانَ مِنْ صَلْصَالٍ مِّنْ حَمَاٍ مَّسْنُوْنٍ ۝

27. And the jinn We created before, of intensely hot fire.

وَالْجَانَّ خَلَقْنٰهُ مِنْ قَبْلُ مِنْ نَّارِ السَّمُوْمِ ۝

28. And when your Lord said to the angels: Surely I am going to create a mortal of the essence of black mud fashioned in shape.

وَاِذْ قَالَ رَبُّكَ لِلْمَلٰئِكَةِ اِنِّيْ خَالِقٌ بَشَرًا مِّنْ صَلْصَالٍ مِّنْ حَمَاٍ مَّسْنُوْنٍ ۝

29. So when I have made him complete and breathed into him of My spirit, fall down making obeisance to him.

فَاِذَا سَوَّيْتُهٗ وَنَفَخْتُ فِيْهِ مِنْ رُّوْحِيْ فَقَعُوْا لَهٗ سٰجِدِيْنَ ۝

30. So the angels made obeisance, all of them together,

فَسَجَدَ الْمَلٰئِكَةُ كُلُّهُمْ اَجْمَعُوْنَ ۝

31. But Iblis (did it not); he refused to be with those who made obeisance.

اِلَّا اِبْلِيْسَ اَبٰى اَنْ يَّكُوْنَ مَعَ السّٰجِدِيْنَ ۝

32. He said: O Iblis! what excuse have you that you are not with those who make obeisance?

33. He said: I am not such that I should make obeisance to a mortal whom Thou hast created of the essence of black mud fashioned in shape.

34. He said: Then get out of it, for surely you are driven away:

35. And surely on you is curse until the day of judgment.

36. He said: My Lord! then respite me till the time when they are raised.

37. He said: So surely you are of the respited ones,

38. Till the period of the time made known.

39. He said: My Lord! because Thou hast made life evil to me, I will certainly make (evil) fair-seeming to them on earth, and I will certainly cause them all to deviate,

40. Except Thy servants from among them, the devoted ones.

41. He said: This is a right way with Me:

42. Surely, as regards My servants, you have no authority over them except those who follow you of the deviators.

43. And surely Hell is the promised place of them all:

44. It has seven gates; for every gate there shall be a separate party of them.

45. Surely those who guard (against evil) shall be in the midst of gardens and fountains:

46. Enter them in peace, secure.

47. And We will root out whatever of rancor is in their breasts—(they shall be) as brethren, on raised couches, face to face.

48. Toil shall not afflict them in it, nor shall they be ever ejected from it.

49. Inform My servants that I am the Forgiving, the Merciful,

قَالَ يَا إِبْلِيسُ مَا لَكَ أَلَّا تَكُونَ مَعَ السَّاجِدِينَ ۝

قَالَ لَمْ أَكُنْ لِّأَسْجُدَ لِبَشَرٍ خَلَقْتَهُ مِنْ صَلْصَالٍ مِّنْ حَمَإٍ مَّسْنُونٍ ۝

قَالَ فَاخْرُجْ مِنْهَا فَإِنَّكَ رَجِيمٌ ۝

وَّإِنَّ عَلَيْكَ اللَّعْنَةَ إِلَى يَوْمِ الدِّينِ ۝

قَالَ رَبِّ فَأَنْظِرْنِي إِلَى يَوْمِ يُبْعَثُونَ ۝

قَالَ فَإِنَّكَ مِنَ الْمُنْظَرِينَ ۝

إِلَى يَوْمِ الْوَقْتِ الْمَعْلُومِ ۝

قَالَ رَبِّ بِمَا أَغْوَيْتَنِي لَأُزَيِّنَنَّ لَهُمْ فِي الْأَرْضِ وَلَأُغْوِيَنَّهُمْ أَجْمَعِينَ ۝

إِلَّا عِبَادَكَ مِنْهُمُ الْمُخْلَصِينَ ۝

قَالَ هَذَا صِرَاطٌ عَلَيَّ مُسْتَقِيمٌ ۝

إِنَّ عِبَادِي لَيْسَ لَكَ عَلَيْهِمْ سُلْطَانٌ إِلَّا مَنِ اتَّبَعَكَ مِنَ الْغَاوِينَ ۝

وَإِنَّ جَهَنَّمَ لَمَوْعِدُهُمْ أَجْمَعِينَ ۝

لَهَا سَبْعَةُ أَبْوَابٍ لِّكُلِّ بَابٍ مِّنْهُمْ جُزْءٌ مَّقْسُومٌ ۝

إِنَّ الْمُتَّقِينَ فِي جَنَّاتٍ وَعُيُونٍ ۝

ادْخُلُوهَا بِسَلَامٍ آمِنِينَ ۝

وَنَزَعْنَا مَا فِي صُدُورِهِمْ مِّنْ غِلٍّ إِخْوَانًا عَلَى سُرُرٍ مُّتَقَابِلِينَ ۝

لَا يَمَسُّهُمْ فِيهَا نَصَبٌ وَّمَا هُمْ مِّنْهَا بِمُخْرَجِينَ ۝

نَبِّئْ عِبَادِي أَنِّي أَنَا الْغَفُورُ الرَّحِيمُ ۝

242

50. And that My punishment—that is the painful punishment.

51. And inform them of the guests of Ibrahim:

52. When they entered upon him, they said, Peace. He said: Surely we are afraid of you.

53. They said: Be not afraid, surely we give you the good news of a boy, possessing knowledge.

54. He said: Do you give me good news (of a son) when old age has come upon me?—Of what then do you give me good news!

55. They said: We give you good news with truth, therefore be not of the despairing.

56. He said: And who despairs of the mercy of his Lord but the erring ones?

57. He said: What is your business then, O messengers?

58. They said: Surely we are sent towards a guilty people,

59. Except Lut's followers: We will most surely deliver them all,

60. Except his wife; We ordained that she shall surely be of those who remain behind.

61. So when the messengers came to Lut's followers,

62. He said: Surely you are an unknown people.

63. They said: Nay, we have come to you with that about which they disputed.

64. And we have come to you with the truth, and we are most surely truthful.

65. Therefore go forth with your followers in a part of the night and yourself follow their rear, and let not any one of you turn round, and go forth whither you are commanded.

66. And We revealed to him this decree, that the roots of these shall be cut off in the morning.

67. And the people of the town came rejoicing.

68. He said: Surely these are my guests, therefore do not disgrace me,

69. And guard against (the punishment of) Allah and do not put me to shame.

70. They said: Have we not forbidden you from (other) people?

قَالُوٓا اَوَلَمْ نَنْهَكَ عَنِ الْعٰلَمِيْنَ ۝

71. He said: These are my daughters, if you will do (aught).

قَالَ هٰٓؤُلَاۤءِ بَنٰتِيْٓ اِنْ كُنْتُمْ فٰعِلِيْنَ ۝

72. By your life! they were blindly wandering on in their intoxication.

لَعَمْرُكَ اِنَّهُمْ لَفِيْ سَكْرَتِهِمْ يَعْمَهُوْنَ ۝

73. So the rumbling overtook them (while) entering upon the time of sunrise;

فَاَخَذَتْهُمُ الصَّيْحَةُ مُشْرِقِيْنَ ۝

74. Thus did We turn it upside down, and rained down upon them stones of what had been decreed.

فَجَعَلْنَا عَالِيَهَا سَافِلَهَا وَاَمْطَرْنَا عَلَيْهِمْ حِجَارَةً مِّنْ سِجِّيْلٍ ۝

75. Surely in this are signs for those who examine.

اِنَّ فِيْ ذٰلِكَ لَاٰيٰتٍ لِّلْمُتَوَسِّمِيْنَ ۝

76. And surely it is on a road that still abides.

وَاِنَّهَا لَبِسَبِيْلٍ مُّقِيْمٍ ۝

77. Most surely there is a sign in this for the believers.

اِنَّ فِيْ ذٰلِكَ لَاٰيَةً لِّلْمُؤْمِنِيْنَ ۝

78. And the dwellers of the thicket also were most surely unjust.

وَاِنْ كَانَ اَصْحٰبُ الْاَيْكَةِ لَظٰلِمِيْنَ ۝

79. So We inflicted retribution on them, and they are both, indeed, on an open road (still) pursued.

فَانْتَقَمْنَا مِنْهُمْ وَاِنَّهُمَا لَبِاِمَامٍ مُّبِيْنٍ ۝

80. And the dwellers of the Rock certainly rejected the messengers;

وَلَقَدْ كَذَّبَ اَصْحٰبُ الْحِجْرِ الْمُرْسَلِيْنَ ۝

81. And We gave them Our communications, but they turned aside from them;

وَاٰتَيْنٰهُمْ اٰيٰتِنَا فَكَانُوْا عَنْهَا مُعْرِضِيْنَ ۝

82. And they hewed houses in the mountains in security.

وَكَانُوْا يَنْحِتُوْنَ مِنَ الْجِبَالِ بُيُوْتًا اٰمِنِيْنَ ۝

83. So the rumbling overtook them in the morning;

فَاَخَذَتْهُمُ الصَّيْحَةُ مُصْبِحِيْنَ ۝

84. And what they earned did not avail them.

فَمَآ اَغْنٰى عَنْهُمْ مَّا كَانُوْا يَكْسِبُوْنَ ۝

85. And We did not create the heavens and the earth and what is between them two but in truth; and the hour is most surely coming, so turn away with kindly forgiveness.

وَمَا خَلَقْنَا السَّمٰوٰتِ وَالْاَرْضَ وَمَا بَيْنَهُمَآ اِلَّا بِالْحَقِّ ۚ وَاِنَّ السَّاعَةَ لَاٰتِيَةٌ فَاصْفَحِ الصَّفْحَ الْجَمِيْلَ ۝

86. Surely your Lord is the Creator of all things, the Knowing.

اِنَّ رَبَّكَ هُوَ الْخَلّٰقُ الْعَلِيْمُ ۝

87. And certainly We have given you seven of the oft-repeated (verses) and the grand Quran.

وَلَقَدْ اٰتَيْنٰكَ سَبْعًا مِّنَ الْمَثَانِيْ وَالْقُرْاٰنَ الْعَظِيْمَ ۝

88. Do not strain your eyes after what We have given certain classes of them to enjoy, and do not grieve for them, and make yourself gentle to the believers.

89. And say: Surely I am the plain warner.

90. Like as We sent down on the dividers,

91. Those who made the Quran into shreds.

92. So, by your Lord, We would most certainly question them all,

93. As to what they did.

94. Therefore declare openly what you are bidden and turn aside from the polytheists.

95. Surely We will suffice you against the scoffers,

96. Those who set up another god with Allah; so they shall soon know.

97. And surely We know that your breast straitens at what they say;

98. Therefore celebrate the praise of your Lord, and be of those who make obeisance.

99. And serve your Lord until there comes to you that which is certain.

لَا تَمُدَّنَّ عَيْنَيْكَ إِلَى مَا مَتَّعْنَا بِهٖ أَزْوَاجًا مِّنْهُمْ وَلَا تَحْزَنْ عَلَيْهِمْ وَاخْفِضْ جَنَاحَكَ لِلْمُؤْمِنِيْنَ ۝

وَقُلْ إِنِّيْ أَنَا النَّذِيْرُ الْمُبِيْنُ ۝

كَمَا أَنْزَلْنَا عَلَى الْمُقْتَسِمِيْنَ ۝

الَّذِيْنَ جَعَلُوا الْقُرْآنَ عِضِيْنَ ۝

فَوَرَبِّكَ لَنَسْئَلَنَّهُمْ أَجْمَعِيْنَ ۝

عَمَّا كَانُوْا يَعْمَلُوْنَ ۝

فَاصْدَعْ بِمَا تُؤْمَرُ وَأَعْرِضْ عَنِ الْمُشْرِكِيْنَ ۝

إِنَّا كَفَيْنَاكَ الْمُسْتَهْزِئِيْنَ ۝

الَّذِيْنَ يَجْعَلُوْنَ مَعَ اللّٰهِ إِلٰهًا آخَرَ فَسَوْفَ يَعْلَمُوْنَ ۝

وَلَقَدْ نَعْلَمُ أَنَّكَ يَضِيْقُ صَدْرُكَ بِمَا يَقُوْلُوْنَ ۝

فَسَبِّحْ بِحَمْدِ رَبِّكَ وَكُنْ مِّنَ السّٰجِدِيْنَ ۝

وَاعْبُدْ رَبَّكَ حَتّٰى يَأْتِيَكَ الْيَقِيْنُ ۝

THE BEE (NAHL)

ايأتها (١٦) سُوْرَةُ النَّحْلِ مَكِّيَّةٌ رُكُوْعَاتُهَا

**In the name of Allah,
the Beneficent, the Merciful.**

بِسْمِ اللّٰهِ الرَّحْمٰنِ الرَّحِيْمِۚ

1. Allah's commandment has come, therefore do not desire to hasten it; glory be to Him, and highly exalted be He above what they associate (with Him).

اَتٰۤى اَمْرُ اللّٰهِ فَلَا تَسْتَعْجِلُوْهُ ؕ سُبْحٰنَهٗ وَتَعٰلٰى عَمَّا يُشْرِكُوْنَ ۞

2. He sends down the angels with the inspiration by His commandment on whom He pleases of His servants, saying: Give the warning that there is no god but Me, therefore be careful (of your duty) to Me.

يُنَزِّلُ الْمَلٰٓئِكَةَ بِالرُّوْحِ مِنْ اَمْرِهٖ عَلٰى مَنْ يَّشَآءُ مِنْ عِبَادِهٖۤ اَنْ اَنْذِرُوْۤا اَنَّهٗ لَاۤ اِلٰهَ اِلَّاۤ اَنَا فَاتَّقُوْنِ ۞

3. He created the heavens and the earth with the truth, highly exalted be He above what they associate (with Him).

خَلَقَ السَّمٰوٰتِ وَالْاَرْضَ بِالْحَقِّ ؕ تَعٰلٰى عَمَّا يُشْرِكُوْنَ ۞

4. He created man from a small seed, and lo! he is an open contender.

خَلَقَ الْاِنْسَانَ مِنْ نُّطْفَةٍ فَاِذَا هُوَ خَصِيْمٌ مُّبِيْنٌ ۞

5. And He created the cattle for you; you have in them warm clothing and (many) advantages, and of them do you eat.

وَالْاَنْعَامَ خَلَقَهَا ۚ لَكُمْ فِيْهَا دِفْءٌ وَّمَنَافِعُ وَمِنْهَا تَأْكُلُوْنَ ۞

6. And there is beauty in them for you when you drive them back (to home), and when you send them forth (to pasture).

وَلَكُمْ فِيْهَا جَمَالٌ حِيْنَ تُرِيْحُوْنَ وَحِيْنَ تَسْرَحُوْنَ ۞

7. And they carry your heavy loads to regions which you could not reach but with distress of the souls; most surely your Lord is Compassionate, Merciful.

وَتَحْمِلُ اَثْقَالَكُمْ اِلٰى بَلَدٍ لَّمْ تَكُوْنُوْا بٰلِغِيْهِ اِلَّا بِشِقِّ الْاَنْفُسِ ؕ اِنَّ رَبَّكُمْ لَرَءُوْفٌ رَّحِيْمٌۙ ۞

8. And (He made) horses and mules and asses that you might ride upon them and as an ornament; and He creates what you do not know.

وَّالْخَيْلَ وَالْبِغَالَ وَالْحَمِيْرَ لِتَرْكَبُوْهَا وَزِيْنَةً ؕ وَيَخْلُقُ مَا لَا تَعْلَمُوْنَ ۞

9. And upon Allah it rests to show the right way, and there are some deviating (ways); and if He please He would certainly guide you all aright.

وَعَلَى اللّٰهِ قَصْدُ السَّبِيْلِ وَمِنْهَا جَآئِرٌ ؕ وَلَوْ شَآءَ لَهَدٰىكُمْ اَجْمَعِيْنَ ۞

10. He it is Who sends down water from the cloud for you; it gives drink, and by it (grow) the trees upon which you pasture.

هُوَ الَّذِيْۤ اَنْزَلَ مِنَ السَّمَآءِ مَآءً لَّكُمْ مِّنْهُ شَرَابٌ وَّمِنْهُ شَجَرٌ فِيْهِ تُسِيْمُوْنَ ۞

11. He causes to grow for you thereby herbage, and the olives, and the palm trees, and the grapes, and of all the fruits; most surely there is a sign in this for a people who reflect.

يُنْۢبِتُ لَكُمْ بِهِ الزَّرْعَ وَالزَّيْتُوْنَ وَالنَّخِيْلَ وَالْاَعْنَابَ وَمِنْ كُلِّ الثَّمَرٰتِ ۚ اِنَّ فِيْ ذٰلِكَ لَاٰيَةً لِّقَوْمٍ يَّتَفَكَّرُوْنَ ۝

12. And He has made subservient for you the night and the day and the sun and the moon, and the stars are made subservient by His commandment; most surely there are signs in this for a people who ponder;

وَسَخَّرَ لَكُمُ الَّيْلَ وَالنَّهَارَ ۙ وَالشَّمْسَ وَالْقَمَرَ ۚ وَالنُّجُوْمُ مُسَخَّرٰتٌۢ بِاَمْرِهٖ ۚ اِنَّ فِيْ ذٰلِكَ لَاٰيٰتٍ لِّقَوْمٍ يَّعْقِلُوْنَ ۝

13. And what He has created in the earth of varied hues; most surely there is a sign in this for a people who are mindful.

وَمَا ذَرَاَ لَكُمْ فِى الْاَرْضِ مُخْتَلِفًا اَلْوَانُهٗ ۚ اِنَّ فِيْ ذٰلِكَ لَاٰيَةً لِّقَوْمٍ يَّذَّكَّرُوْنَ ۝

14. And He it is Who has made the sea subservient that you may eat fresh flesh from it and bring forth from it ornaments which you wear, and you see the ships cleaving through it, and that you might seek of His bounty and that you may give thanks.

وَهُوَ الَّذِيْ سَخَّرَ الْبَحْرَ لِتَاْكُلُوْا مِنْهُ لَحْمًا طَرِيًّا وَّتَسْتَخْرِجُوْا مِنْهُ حِلْيَةً تَلْبَسُوْنَهَا ۚ وَتَرَى الْفُلْكَ مَوَاخِرَ فِيْهِ وَلِتَبْتَغُوْا مِنْ فَضْلِهٖ وَلَعَلَّكُمْ تَشْكُرُوْنَ ۝

15. And He has cast great mountains in the earth lest it might be convulsed with you, and rivers and roads that you may go aright,

وَاَلْقٰى فِى الْاَرْضِ رَوَاسِيَ اَنْ تَمِيْدَ بِكُمْ وَاَنْهٰرًا وَّسُبُلًا لَّعَلَّكُمْ تَهْتَدُوْنَ ۝

16. And landmarks; and by the stars they find the right way.

وَعَلٰمٰتٍ ۚ وَبِالنَّجْمِ هُمْ يَهْتَدُوْنَ ۝

17. Is He then Who creates like him who does not create? Do you not then mind?

اَفَمَنْ يَّخْلُقُ كَمَنْ لَّا يَخْلُقُ ۚ اَفَلَا تَذَكَّرُوْنَ ۝

18. And if you would count Allah's favors, you will not be able to number them; most surely Allah is Forgiving, Merciful.

وَاِنْ تَعُدُّوْا نِعْمَةَ اللّٰهِ لَا تُحْصُوْهَا ۚ اِنَّ اللّٰهَ لَغَفُوْرٌ رَّحِيْمٌ ۝

19. And Allah knows what you conceal and what you do openly.

وَاللّٰهُ يَعْلَمُ مَا تُسِرُّوْنَ وَمَا تُعْلِنُوْنَ ۝

20. And those whom they call on besides Allah have not created anything while they are themselves created;

وَالَّذِيْنَ يَدْعُوْنَ مِنْ دُوْنِ اللّٰهِ لَا يَخْلُقُوْنَ شَيْئًا وَّهُمْ يُخْلَقُوْنَ ۝

21. Dead (are they), not living, and they know not when they shall be raised.

اَمْوَاتٌ غَيْرُ اَحْيَاءٍ ۚ وَمَا يَشْعُرُوْنَ ۙ اَيَّانَ يُبْعَثُوْنَ ۝

22. Your God is one God; so (as for) those who do not believe in the hereafter, their hearts are ignorant and they are proud.

23. Truly Allah knows what they hide and what they manifest; surely He does not love the proud.

24. And when it is said to them, what is it that your Lord has revealed? They say: Stories of the ancients;

25. That they may bear their burdens entirely on the day of resurrection and also of the burdens of those whom they lead astray without knowledge; now surely evil is what they bear.

26. Those before them did indeed devise plans, but Allah demolished their building from the foundations, so the roof fell down on them from above them, and the punishment came to them from whence they did not perceive.

27. Then on the resurrection day He will bring them to disgrace and say: Where are the associates you gave Me, for whose sake you became hostile? Those who are given the knowledge will say: Surely the disgrace and the evil are this day upon the unbelievers:

28. Those whom the angels cause to die while they are unjust to themselves. Then would they offer submission: We used not to do any evil. Aye! surely Allah knows what you did.

29. Therefore enter the gates of hell, to abide therein; so certainly evil is the dwelling place of the proud.

30. And it is said to those who guard (against evil): What is it that your Lord has revealed? They say, Good. For those who do good in this world is good, and certainly the abode of the hereafter is better; and certainly most excellent is the abode of those who guard (against evil);

وَقِيلَ اِلهُكُمْ اِلهٌ وَّاحِدٌ ۚ فَالَّذِيْنَ لَا يُؤْمِنُوْنَ بِالْاٰخِرَةِ قُلُوْبُهُمْ مُّنْكِرَةٌ وَّهُمْ مُّسْتَكْبِرُوْنَ ۝

لَا جَرَمَ اَنَّ اللّٰهَ يَعْلَمُ مَا يُسِرُّوْنَ وَمَا يُعْلِنُوْنَ ۚ اِنَّهٗ لَا يُحِبُّ الْمُسْتَكْبِرِيْنَ ۝

وَاِذَا قِيْلَ لَهُمْ مَّاذَآ اَنْزَلَ رَبُّكُمْ ۙ قَالُوْٓا اَسَاطِيْرُ الْاَوَّلِيْنَ ۝

لِيَحْمِلُوْٓا اَوْزَارَهُمْ كَامِلَةً يَّوْمَ الْقِيٰمَةِ ۙ وَمِنْ اَوْزَارِ الَّذِيْنَ يُضِلُّوْنَهُمْ بِغَيْرِ عِلْمٍ ۗ اَلَا سَآءَ مَا يَزِرُوْنَ ۝

قَدْ مَكَرَ الَّذِيْنَ مِنْ قَبْلِهِمْ فَاَتَى اللّٰهُ بُنْيَانَهُمْ مِّنَ الْقَوَاعِدِ فَخَرَّ عَلَيْهِمُ السَّقْفُ مِنْ فَوْقِهِمْ وَاَتٰىهُمُ الْعَذَابُ مِنْ حَيْثُ لَا يَشْعُرُوْنَ ۝

ثُمَّ يَوْمَ الْقِيٰمَةِ يُخْزِيْهِمْ وَيَقُوْلُ اَيْنَ شُرَكَآءِيَ الَّذِيْنَ كُنْتُمْ تُشَآقُّوْنَ فِيْهِمْ ۗ قَالَ الَّذِيْنَ اُوْتُوا الْعِلْمَ اِنَّ الْخِزْيَ الْيَوْمَ وَالسُّوْٓءَ عَلَى الْكٰفِرِيْنَ ۝

الَّذِيْنَ تَتَوَفّٰىهُمُ الْمَلٰٓئِكَةُ ظَالِمِيْٓ اَنْفُسِهِمْ ۖ فَاَلْقَوُا السَّلَمَ مَا كُنَّا نَعْمَلُ مِنْ سُوْٓءٍ ۚ بَلٰٓى اِنَّ اللّٰهَ عَلِيْمٌ بِمَا كُنْتُمْ تَعْمَلُوْنَ ۝

فَادْخُلُوْٓا اَبْوَابَ جَهَنَّمَ خٰلِدِيْنَ فِيْهَا ۚ فَلَبِئْسَ مَثْوَى الْمُتَكَبِّرِيْنَ ۝

وَقِيْلَ لِلَّذِيْنَ اتَّقَوْا مَاذَآ اَنْزَلَ رَبُّكُمْ ۗ قَالُوْا خَيْرًا ۚ لِلَّذِيْنَ اَحْسَنُوْا فِيْ هٰذِهِ الدُّنْيَا حَسَنَةٌ ۗ وَلَدَارُ الْاٰخِرَةِ خَيْرٌ ۚ وَلَنِعْمَ دَارُ الْمُتَّقِيْنَ ۝

248

31. The gardens of perpetuity, they shall enter them, rivers flowing beneath them; they shall have in them what they please. Thus does Allah reward those who guard (against evil),

جَنَّتُ عَدْنٍ يَّدْخُلُوْنَهَا تَجْرِيْ مِنْ تَحْتِهَا الْاَنْهٰرُ لَهُمْ فِيْهَا مَا يَشَآءُوْنَ كَذٰلِكَ يَجْزِى اللّٰهُ الْمُتَّقِيْنَ ۟ۙ

32. Those whom the angels cause to die in a good state, saying: Peace be on you: enter the garden for what you did.

الَّذِيْنَ تَتَوَفّٰهُمُ الْمَلٰٓئِكَةُ طَيِّبِيْنَ يَقُوْلُوْنَ سَلٰمٌ عَلَيْكُمُ ادْخُلُوا الْجَنَّةَ بِمَا كُنْتُمْ تَعْمَلُوْنَ ۟

33. They do not wait aught but that the angels should come to them or that the commandment of your Lord should come to pass. Thus did those before them; and Allah was not unjust to them, but they were unjust to themselves.

هَلْ يَنْظُرُوْنَ اِلَّآ اَنْ تَاْتِيَهُمُ الْمَلٰٓئِكَةُ اَوْ يَاْتِيَ اَمْرُ رَبِّكَ كَذٰلِكَ فَعَلَ الَّذِيْنَ مِنْ قَبْلِهِمْ وَ مَا ظَلَمَهُمُ اللّٰهُ وَ لٰكِنْ كَانُوْۤا اَنْفُسَهُمْ يَظْلِمُوْنَ ۟

34. So the evil (consequences) of what they did shall afflict them and that which they mocked shall encompass them.

فَاَصَابَهُمْ سَيِّاٰتُ مَا عَمِلُوْا وَ حَاقَ بِهِمْ مَّا كَانُوْا بِهٖ يَسْتَهْزِءُوْنَ ۟ۙ

35. And they who give associates (to Allah) say: If Allah had pleased, we would not have served anything besides Allah, (neither) we nor our fathers, nor would we have prohibited anything without (order from) Him. Thus did those before them; is then aught incumbent upon the apostles except a plain delivery (of the message)?

وَ قَالَ الَّذِيْنَ اَشْرَكُوْا لَوْ شَآءَ اللّٰهُ مَا عَبَدْنَا مِنْ دُوْنِهٖ مِنْ شَيْءٍ نَّحْنُ وَ لَاۤ اٰبَآؤُنَا وَ لَا حَرَّمْنَا مِنْ دُوْنِهٖ مِنْ شَيْءٍ كَذٰلِكَ فَعَلَ الَّذِيْنَ مِنْ قَبْلِهِمْ فَهَلْ عَلَى الرُّسُلِ اِلَّا الْبَلٰغُ الْمُبِيْنُ ۟

36. And certainly We raised in every nation an apostle saying: Serve Allah and shun the Shaitan. So there were some of them whom Allah guided and there were others against whom error was due; therefore travel in the land, then see what was the end of the rejecters.

وَ لَقَدْ بَعَثْنَا فِيْ كُلِّ اُمَّةٍ رَّسُوْلًا اَنِ اعْبُدُوا اللّٰهَ وَ اجْتَنِبُوا الطَّاغُوْتَ فَمِنْهُمْ مَّنْ هَدَى اللّٰهُ وَ مِنْهُمْ مَّنْ حَقَّتْ عَلَيْهِ الضَّلٰلَةُ فَسِيْرُوْا فِى الْاَرْضِ فَانْظُرُوْا كَيْفَ كَانَ عَاقِبَةُ الْمُكَذِّبِيْنَ ۟

37. If you desire for their guidance, yet surely Allah does not guide him who leads astray, nor shall they have any helpers.

اِنْ تَحْرِصْ عَلٰى هُدٰىهُمْ فَاِنَّ اللّٰهَ لَا يَهْدِيْ مَنْ يُّضِلُّ وَ مَا لَهُمْ مِّنْ نّٰصِرِيْنَ ۟

38. And they swear by Allah with the most energetic of their oaths: Allah will not raise up him who dies. Yea! it is a promise binding on Him, quite true, but most people do not know;

وَ اَقْسَمُوْا بِاللّٰهِ جَهْدَ اَيْمَانِهِمْ لَا يَبْعَثُ اللّٰهُ مَنْ يَّمُوْتُ بَلٰى وَعْدًا عَلَيْهِ حَقًّا وَّ لٰكِنَّ اَكْثَرَ النَّاسِ لَا يَعْلَمُوْنَ ۟ۙ

39. So that He might make manifest to them that about which they differ, and that those who disbelieve might know that they were liars.

40. Our word for a thing when We intend it, is only that We say to it, Be, and it is.

41. And those who fly for Allah's sake after they are oppressed, We will most certainly give them a good abode in the world, and the reward of the hereafter is certainly much greater, did they but know;

42. Those who are patient and on their Lord do they rely.

43. And We did not send before you any but men to whom We sent revelation—so ask the followers of the Reminder if you do not know—

44. With clear arguments and scriptures; and We have revealed to you the Reminder that you may make clear to men what has been revealed to them, and that haply they may reflect.

45. Do they then who plan evil (deeds) feel secure (of this) that Allah will not cause the earth to swallow them or that punishment may not overtake them from whence they do not perceive?

46. Or that He may not seize them in the course of their journeys, then shall they not escape;

47. Or that He may not seize them by causing them to suffer gradual loss, for your Lord is most surely Compassionate, Merciful.

48. Do they not consider everything that Allah has created? Its (very) shadows return from right and left, making obeisance to Allah while they are in utter abasement.

49. And whatever creature that is in the heavens and that is in the earth makes obeisance to Allah (only), and the angels (too) and they do not show pride.

50. They fear their Lord above them and do what they are commanded.

51. And Allah has said: Take not two gods, He is only one God; so of Me alone should you be afraid.

وَقَالَ اللّٰهُ لَا تَتَّخِذُوْا اِلٰهَيْنِ اثْنَيْنِ ۚ اِنَّمَا هُوَ اِلٰهٌ وَّاحِدٌ ۚ فَاِيَّايَ فَارْهَبُوْنِ ۝

52. And whatever is in the heavens and the earth is His, and to Him should obedience be (rendered) constantly; will you then guard against other than (the punishment of) Allah?

وَلَهُ مَا فِى السَّمٰوٰتِ وَالْاَرْضِ وَلَهُ الدِّيْنُ وَاصِبًا ۚ اَفَغَيْرَ اللّٰهِ تَتَّقُوْنَ ۝

53. And whatever favor is (bestowed) on you it is from Allah; then when evil afflicts you, to Him do you cry for aid.

وَمَا بِكُمْ مِّنْ نِّعْمَةٍ فَمِنَ اللّٰهِ ثُمَّ اِذَا مَسَّكُمُ الضُّرُّ فَاِلَيْهِ تَجْأَرُوْنَ ۝

54. Yet when He removes the evil from you, lo! a party of you associate others with their Lord;

ثُمَّ اِذَا كَشَفَ الضُّرَّ عَنْكُمْ اِذَا فَرِيْقٌ مِّنْكُمْ بِرَبِّهِمْ يُشْرِكُوْنَ ۝

55. So that they be ungrateful for what We have given them; then enjoy yourselves; for soon will you know.

لِيَكْفُرُوْا بِمَا اٰتَيْنٰهُمْ ۚ فَتَمَتَّعُوْا ۚ فَسَوْفَ تَعْلَمُوْنَ ۝

56. And they set apart for what they do not know a portion of what We have given them. By Allah, you shall most certainly be questioned about that which you forged.

وَيَجْعَلُوْنَ لِمَا لَا يَعْلَمُوْنَ نَصِيْبًا مِّمَّا رَزَقْنٰهُمْ ۚ تَاللّٰهِ لَتُسْـَٔلُنَّ عَمَّا كُنْتُمْ تَفْتَرُوْنَ ۝

57. And they ascribe daughters to Allah, glory be to Him; and for themselves (they would have) what they desire.

وَيَجْعَلُوْنَ لِلّٰهِ الْبَنٰتِ سُبْحٰنَهُ ۙ وَلَهُمْ مَّا يَشْتَهُوْنَ ۝

58. And when a daughter is announced to one of them his face becomes black and he is full of wrath.

وَاِذَا بُشِّرَ اَحَدُهُمْ بِالْاُنْثٰى ظَلَّ وَجْهُهُ مُسْوَدًّا وَّهُوَ كَظِيْمٌ ۝

59. He hides himself from the people because of the evil of that which is announced to him. Shall he keep it with disgrace or bury it (alive) in the dust? Now surely evil is what they judge.

يَتَوَارٰى مِنَ الْقَوْمِ مِنْ سُوْٓءِ مَا بُشِّرَ بِهٖ ۚ اَيُمْسِكُهُ عَلٰى هُوْنٍ اَمْ يَدُسُّهُ فِى التُّرَابِ ۗ اَلَا سَآءَ مَا يَحْكُمُوْنَ ۝

60. For those who do not believe in the hereafter is an evil attribute, and Allah's is the loftiest attribute; and He is the Mighty, the Wise.

لِلَّذِيْنَ لَا يُؤْمِنُوْنَ بِالْاٰخِرَةِ مَثَلُ السَّوْءِ ۚ وَلِلّٰهِ الْمَثَلُ الْاَعْلٰى ۚ وَهُوَ الْعَزِيْزُ الْحَكِيْمُ ۝

61. And if Allah had destroyed men for their iniquity, He would not leave on the earth a single creature, but He respites them till an appointed time; so when their doom will come they shall not be able to delay (it) an hour nor can they bring (it) on (before its time).

وَلَوْ يُؤَاخِذُ اللّٰهُ النَّاسَ بِظُلْمِهِمْ مَّا تَرَكَ عَلَيْهَا مِنْ دَآبَّةٍ وَّلٰكِنْ يُّؤَخِّرُهُمْ اِلٰٓى اَجَلٍ مُّسَمًّى ۚ فَاِذَا جَآءَ اَجَلُهُمْ لَا يَسْتَأْخِرُوْنَ سَاعَةً وَّلَا يَسْتَقْدِمُوْنَ ۝

251

62. And they ascribe to Allah what they (themselves) hate and their tongues relate the lie that they shall have the good; there is no avoiding it that for them is the fire and that they shall be sent before.

وَيَجْعَلُوْنَ لِلّٰهِ مَا يَكْرَهُوْنَ وَتَصِفُ اَلْسِنَتُهُمُ الْكَذِبَ اَنَّ لَهُمُ الْحُسْنٰى لَاجَرَمَ اَنَّ لَهُمُ النَّارَ وَاَنَّهُمْ مُفْرَطُوْنَ ۝

63. By Allah, most certainly We sent (apostles) to nations before you, but the Shaitan made their deeds fair-seeming to them, so he is their guardian today, and they shall have a painful punishment.

تَاللّٰهِ لَقَدْ اَرْسَلْنَا اِلٰى اُمَمٍ مِّنْ قَبْلِكَ فَزَيَّنَ لَهُمُ الشَّيْطٰنُ اَعْمَالَهُمْ فَهُوَ وَلِيُّهُمُ الْيَوْمَ وَ لَهُمْ عَذَابٌ اَلِيْمٌ ۝

64. And We have not revealed to you the Book except that you may make clear to them that about which they differ, and (as) a guidance and a mercy for a people who believe.

وَمَا اَنْزَلْنَا عَلَيْكَ الْكِتٰبَ اِلَّا لِتُبَيِّنَ لَهُمُ الَّذِى اخْتَلَفُوْا فِيْهِ وَهُدًى وَّرَحْمَةً لِّقَوْمٍ يُّؤْمِنُوْنَ ۝

65. And Allah has sent down water from the cloud and therewith given life to the earth after its death; most surely there is a sign in this for a people who would listen.

وَاللّٰهُ اَنْزَلَ مِنَ السَّمَاءِ مَاءً فَاَحْيَا بِهِ الْاَرْضَ بَعْدَ مَوْتِهَا اِنَّ فِىْ ذٰلِكَ لَاٰيَةً لِّقَوْمٍ يَّسْمَعُوْنَ ۝

66. And most surely there is a lesson for you in the cattle; We give you to drink of what is in their bellies—from betwixt the feces and the blood—pure milk, easy and agreeable to swallow for those who drink.

وَاِنَّ لَكُمْ فِى الْاَنْعَامِ لَعِبْرَةً نُّسْقِيْكُمْ مِّمَّا فِىْ بُطُوْنِهٖ مِنْ بَيْنِ فَرْثٍ وَّدَمٍ لَّبَنًا خَالِصًا سَائِغًا لِّلشّٰرِبِيْنَ ۝

67. And of the fruits of the palms and the grapes—you obtain from them intoxication and goodly provision; most surely there is a sign in this for a people who ponder.

وَمِنْ ثَمَرٰتِ النَّخِيْلِ وَالْاَعْنَابِ تَتَّخِذُوْنَ مِنْهُ سَكَرًا وَّرِزْقًا حَسَنًا اِنَّ فِىْ ذٰلِكَ لَاٰيَةً لِّقَوْمٍ يَّعْقِلُوْنَ ۝

68. And your Lord revealed to the bee saying: Make hives in the mountains and in the trees and in what they build:

وَاَوْحٰى رَبُّكَ اِلَى النَّحْلِ اَنِ اتَّخِذِىْ مِنَ الْجِبَالِ بُيُوْتًا وَّمِنَ الشَّجَرِ وَمِمَّا يَعْرِشُوْنَ ۝

69. Then eat of all the fruits and walk in the ways of your Lord submissively. There comes forth from within it a beverage of many colors, in which there is healing for men; most surely there is a sign in this for a people who reflect.

ثُمَّ كُلِىْ مِنْ كُلِّ الثَّمَرٰتِ فَاسْلُكِىْ سُبُلَ رَبِّكِ ذُلُلًا يَخْرُجُ مِنْ بُطُوْنِهَا شَرَابٌ مُّخْتَلِفٌ اَلْوَانُهٗ فِيْهِ شِفَاءٌ لِّلنَّاسِ اِنَّ فِىْ ذٰلِكَ لَاٰيَةً لِّقَوْمٍ يَّتَفَكَّرُوْنَ ۝

70. And Allah has created you, then He causes you to die, and of you is he who is brought back to the worst part of life, so that after having knowledge he does not know anything; surely Allah is Knowing, Powerful.

وَاللّٰهُ خَلَقَكُمْ ثُمَّ يَتَوَفّٰىكُمْ وَمِنْكُمْ مَّنْ يُّرَدُّ اِلٰى اَرْذَلِ الْعُمُرِ لِكَىْ لَا يَعْلَمَ بَعْدَ عِلْمٍ شَيْئًا اِنَّ اللّٰهَ عَلِيْمٌ قَدِيْرٌ ۝

71. And Allah has made some of you excel others in the means of subsistence, so those who are made to excel do not give away their sustenance to those whom their right hands possess, so that they should be equal therein; is it then the favor of Allah which they deny?

72. And Allah has made wives for you from among yourselves, and has given you sons and grandchildren from your wives, and has given you of the good things; is it then in the falsehood that they believe while it is in the favor of Allah that they disbelieve?

73. And they serve besides Allah that which does not control for them any sustenance at all from the heavens and the earth, nor have they any power.

74. Therefore do not give likenesses to Allah; surely Allah knows and you do not know.

75. Allah sets forth a parable: (consider) a slave, the property of another, (who) has no power over anything, and one whom We have granted from Ourselves a goodly sustenance so he spends from it secretly and openly; are the two alike? (All) praise is due to Allah! Nay, most of them do not know.

76. And Allah sets forth a parable of two men; one of them is dumb, not able to do anything, and he is a burden to his master; wherever he sends him, he brings no good; can he be held equal with him who enjoins what is just, and he (himself) is on the right path?

77. And Allah's is the unseen of the heavens and the earth; and the matter of the hour is but as the twinkling of an eye or it is higher still; surely Allah has power over all things.

وَاللّٰهُ فَضَّلَ بَعْضَكُمْ عَلٰى بَعْضٍ فِى الرِّزْقِ ۚ فَمَا الَّذِيْنَ فُضِّلُوْا بِرَآدِّيْ رِزْقِهِمْ عَلٰى مَا مَلَكَتْ اَيْمَانُهُمْ فَهُمْ فِيْهِ سَوَآءٌ ۚ اَفَبِنِعْمَةِ اللّٰهِ يَجْحَدُوْنَ ۝

وَاللّٰهُ جَعَلَ لَكُمْ مِّنْ اَنْفُسِكُمْ اَزْوَاجًا وَّجَعَلَ لَكُمْ مِّنْ اَزْوَاجِكُمْ بَنِيْنَ وَحَفَدَةً وَّرَزَقَكُمْ مِّنَ الطَّيِّبٰتِ ۚ اَفَبِالْبَاطِلِ يُؤْمِنُوْنَ وَبِنِعْمَتِ اللّٰهِ هُمْ يَكْفُرُوْنَ ۝

وَيَعْبُدُوْنَ مِنْ دُوْنِ اللّٰهِ مَا لَا يَمْلِكُ لَهُمْ رِزْقًا مِّنَ السَّمٰوٰتِ وَالْاَرْضِ شَيْئًا وَّلَا يَسْتَطِيْعُوْنَ ۝

فَلَا تَضْرِبُوْا لِلّٰهِ الْاَمْثَالَ ۚ اِنَّ اللّٰهَ يَعْلَمُ وَاَنْتُمْ لَا تَعْلَمُوْنَ ۝

ضَرَبَ اللّٰهُ مَثَلًا عَبْدًا مَّمْلُوْكًا لَّا يَقْدِرُ عَلٰى شَىْءٍ وَّمَنْ رَّزَقْنٰهُ مِنَّا رِزْقًا حَسَنًا فَهُوَ يُنْفِقُ مِنْهُ سِرًّا وَّجَهْرًا ۚ هَلْ يَسْتَوٗنَ ۚ اَلْحَمْدُ لِلّٰهِ ۚ بَلْ اَكْثَرُهُمْ لَا يَعْلَمُوْنَ ۝

وَضَرَبَ اللّٰهُ مَثَلًا رَّجُلَيْنِ اَحَدُهُمَآ اَبْكَمُ لَا يَقْدِرُ عَلٰى شَىْءٍ وَّهُوَ كَلٌّ عَلٰى مَوْلٰىهُ ۙ اَيْنَمَا يُوَجِّهْهُّ لَا يَأْتِ بِخَيْرٍ ۚ هَلْ يَسْتَوِيْ هُوَ وَمَنْ يَّأْمُرُ بِالْعَدْلِ ۙ وَهُوَ عَلٰى صِرَاطٍ مُّسْتَقِيْمٍ ۝

وَلِلّٰهِ غَيْبُ السَّمٰوٰتِ وَالْاَرْضِ ۚ وَمَآ اَمْرُ السَّاعَةِ اِلَّا كَلَمْحِ الْبَصَرِ اَوْ هُوَ اَقْرَبُ ۚ اِنَّ اللّٰهَ عَلٰى كُلِّ شَىْءٍ قَدِيْرٌ ۝

78. And Allah has brought you forth from the wombs of your mothers—you did not know anything—and He gave you hearing and sight and hearts that you may give thanks.

79. Do they not see the birds, constrained in the middle of the sky? None withholds them but Allah; most surely there are signs in this for a people who believe.

80. And Allah has given you a place to abide in your houses, and He has given you tents of the skins of cattle which you find light to carry on the day of your march and on the day of your halting, and of their wool and their fur and their hair (He has given you) household stuff and a provision for a time.

81. And Allah has made for you of what He has created shelters, and He has given you in the mountains places of retreat, and He has given you garments to preserve you from the heat and coats of mail to preserve you in your fighting; even thus does He complete His favor upon you, that haply you may submit.

82. But if they turn back, then on you devolves only the clear deliverance (of the message).

83. They recognize the favor of Allah, yet they deny it, and most of them are ungrateful.

84. And on the day when We will raise up a witness out of every nation, then shall no permission be given to those who disbelieve, nor shall they be made to solicit favor.

85. And when those who are unjust shall see the chastisement, it shall not be lightened for them, nor shall they be respited.

86. And when those who associate (others with Allah) shall see their associate-gods, they shall say: Our Lord, these are our associate-gods on whom we called besides Thee. But they will give them back the reply: Most surely you are liars.

وَاللّٰهُ أَخْرَجَكُمْ مِّنْ بُطُوْنِ أُمَّهٰتِكُمْ لَا تَعْلَمُوْنَ شَيْئًا ۙ وَّجَعَلَ لَكُمُ السَّمْعَ وَالْأَبْصَارَ وَالْأَفْئِدَةَ ۙ لَعَلَّكُمْ تَشْكُرُوْنَ ۝

أَلَمْ يَرَوْا إِلَى الطَّيْرِ مُسَخَّرٰتٍ فِيْ جَوِّ السَّمَاءِ ۗ مَا يُمْسِكُهُنَّ إِلَّا اللّٰهُ ۗ إِنَّ فِيْ ذٰلِكَ لَأَيٰتٍ لِّقَوْمٍ يُّؤْمِنُوْنَ ۝

وَاللّٰهُ جَعَلَ لَكُمْ مِّنْ بُيُوْتِكُمْ سَكَنًا وَّجَعَلَ لَكُمْ مِّنْ جُلُوْدِ الْأَنْعَامِ بُيُوْتًا تَسْتَخِفُّوْنَهَا يَوْمَ ظَعْنِكُمْ وَيَوْمَ إِقَامَتِكُمْ ۙ وَمِنْ أَصْوَافِهَا وَأَوْبَارِهَا وَأَشْعَارِهَا أَثَاثًا وَّمَتَاعًا إِلٰى حِيْنٍ ۝

وَاللّٰهُ جَعَلَ لَكُمْ مِّمَّا خَلَقَ ظِلٰلًا وَّجَعَلَ لَكُمْ مِّنَ الْجِبَالِ أَكْنَانًا وَّجَعَلَ لَكُمْ سَرَابِيْلَ تَقِيْكُمُ الْحَرَّ وَسَرَابِيْلَ تَقِيْكُمْ بَأْسَكُمْ ۗ كَذٰلِكَ يُتِمُّ نِعْمَتَهٗ عَلَيْكُمْ لَعَلَّكُمْ تُسْلِمُوْنَ ۝

فَإِنْ تَوَلَّوْا فَإِنَّمَا عَلَيْكَ الْبَلٰغُ الْمُبِيْنُ ۝

يَعْرِفُوْنَ نِعْمَتَ اللّٰهِ ثُمَّ يُنْكِرُوْنَهَا وَأَكْثَرُهُمُ الْكٰفِرُوْنَ ۝

وَيَوْمَ نَبْعَثُ مِنْ كُلِّ أُمَّةٍ شَهِيْدًا ثُمَّ لَا يُؤْذَنُ لِلَّذِيْنَ كَفَرُوْا وَلَا هُمْ يُسْتَعْتَبُوْنَ ۝

وَإِذَا رَأَ الَّذِيْنَ ظَلَمُوا الْعَذَابَ فَلَا يُخَفَّفُ عَنْهُمْ وَلَا هُمْ يُنْظَرُوْنَ ۝

وَإِذَا رَأَ الَّذِيْنَ أَشْرَكُوْا شُرَكَاءَهُمْ قَالُوْا رَبَّنَا هٰؤُلَاءِ شُرَكَاؤُنَا الَّذِيْنَ كُنَّا نَدْعُوْا مِنْ دُوْنِكَ ۖ فَأَلْقَوْا إِلَيْهِمُ الْقَوْلَ إِنَّكُمْ لَكٰذِبُوْنَ ۝

87. And they shall tender submission to Allah on that day; and what they used to forge shall depart from them.

وَأَلْقَوْا إِلَى اللّٰهِ يَوْمَئِذِ السَّلَمَ وَضَلَّ عَنْهُمْ مَّا كَانُوْا يَفْتَرُوْنَ ۝

88. (As for) those who disbelieve and turn away from Allah's way, We will add chastisement to their chastisement because they made mischief.

اَلَّذِيْنَ كَفَرُوْا وَصَدُّوْا عَنْ سَبِيْلِ اللّٰهِ زِدْنٰهُمْ عَذَابًا فَوْقَ الْعَذَابِ بِمَا كَانُوْا يُفْسِدُوْنَ ۝

89. And on the day when We will raise up in every people a witness against them from among themselves, and bring you as a witness against these—and We have revealed the Book to you explaining clearly everything, and a guidance and mercy and good news for those who submit.

وَيَوْمَ نَبْعَثُ فِيْ كُلِّ أُمَّةٍ شَهِيْدًا عَلَيْهِمْ مِّنْ أَنْفُسِهِمْ وَجِئْنَا بِكَ شَهِيْدًا عَلٰى هٰؤُلَاءِ وَنَزَّلْنَا عَلَيْكَ الْكِتٰبَ تِبْيَانًا لِّكُلِّ شَيْءٍ وَّهُدًى وَّرَحْمَةً وَّبُشْرٰى لِلْمُسْلِمِيْنَ ۝

90. Surely Allah enjoins the doing of justice and the doing of good (to others) and the giving to the kindred, and He forbids indecency and evil and rebellion; He admonishes you that you may be mindful.

إِنَّ اللّٰهَ يَأْمُرُ بِالْعَدْلِ وَالْإِحْسَانِ وَإِيْتَاءِ ذِى الْقُرْبٰى وَيَنْهٰى عَنِ الْفَحْشَاءِ وَالْمُنْكَرِ وَالْبَغْيِ يَعِظُكُمْ لَعَلَّكُمْ تَذَكَّرُوْنَ ۝

91. And fulfill the covenant of Allah when you have made a covenant, and do not break the oaths after making them fast, and you have indeed made Allah a surety for you; surely Allah knows what you do.

وَأَوْفُوْا بِعَهْدِ اللّٰهِ إِذَا عَاهَدْتُّمْ وَلَا تَنْقُضُوا الْأَيْمَانَ بَعْدَ تَوْكِيْدِهَا وَقَدْ جَعَلْتُمُ اللّٰهَ عَلَيْكُمْ كَفِيْلًا إِنَّ اللّٰهَ يَعْلَمُ مَا تَفْعَلُوْنَ ۝

92. And be not like her who unravels her yarn, disintegrating it into pieces after she has spun it strongly. You make your oaths to be means of deceit between you because (one) nation is more numerous than (another) nation. Allah only tries you by this; and He will most certainly make clear to you on the resurrection day that about which you differed.

وَلَا تَكُوْنُوْا كَالَّتِيْ نَقَضَتْ غَزْلَهَا مِنْ بَعْدِ قُوَّةٍ أَنْكَاثًا تَتَّخِذُوْنَ أَيْمَانَكُمْ دَخَلًا بَيْنَكُمْ أَنْ تَكُوْنَ أُمَّةٌ هِيَ أَرْبٰى مِنْ أُمَّةٍ إِنَّمَا يَبْلُوْكُمُ اللّٰهُ بِهِ وَلَيُبَيِّنَنَّ لَكُمْ يَوْمَ الْقِيٰمَةِ مَا كُنْتُمْ فِيْهِ تَخْتَلِفُوْنَ ۝

93. And if Allah please He would certainly make you a single nation, but He causes to err whom He pleases and guides whom He pleases; and most certainly you will be questioned as to what you did.

وَلَوْ شَاءَ اللّٰهُ لَجَعَلَكُمْ أُمَّةً وَّاحِدَةً وَّلٰكِنْ يُضِلُّ مَنْ يَشَاءُ وَيَهْدِيْ مَنْ يَشَاءُ وَلَتُسْأَلُنَّ عَمَّا كُنْتُمْ تَعْمَلُوْنَ ۝

94. And do not make your oaths a means of deceit between you, lest a foot should slip after its stability and you should taste evil because you turned away from Allah's way and grievous punishment be your (lot).

وَلَا تَتَّخِذُوْا اَيْمَانَكُمْ دَخَلًا بَيْنَكُمْ فَتَزِلَّ قَدَمٌ بَعْدَ ثُبُوْتِهَا وَتَذُوْقُوا السُّوْٓءَ بِمَا صَدَدْتُّمْ عَنْ سَبِيْلِ اللّٰهِ ۚ وَلَكُمْ عَذَابٌ عَظِيْمٌ ۞

95. And do not take a small price in exchange for Allah's covenant; surely what is with Allah is better for you, did you but know.

وَلَا تَشْتَرُوْا بِعَهْدِ اللّٰهِ ثَمَنًا قَلِيْلًا ۚ اِنَّمَا عِنْدَ اللّٰهِ هُوَ خَيْرٌ لَّكُمْ اِنْ كُنْتُمْ تَعْلَمُوْنَ ۞

96. What is with you passes away and what is with Allah is enduring; and We will most certainly give to those who are patient their reward for the best of what they did.

مَا عِنْدَكُمْ يَنْفَدُ وَمَا عِنْدَ اللّٰهِ بَاقٍ ۗ وَلَنَجْزِيَنَّ الَّذِيْنَ صَبَرُوْٓا اَجْرَهُمْ بِاَحْسَنِ مَا كَانُوْا يَعْمَلُوْنَ ۞

97. Whoever does good whether male or female and he is a believer, We will most certainly make him live a happy life, and We will most certainly give them their reward for the best of what they did.

مَنْ عَمِلَ صَالِحًا مِّنْ ذَكَرٍ اَوْ اُنْثٰى وَهُوَ مُؤْمِنٌ فَلَنُحْيِيَنَّهٗ حَيٰوةً طَيِّبَةً ۚ وَلَنَجْزِيَنَّهُمْ اَجْرَهُمْ بِاَحْسَنِ مَا كَانُوْا يَعْمَلُوْنَ ۞

98. So when you recite the Quran, seek refuge with Allah from the accursed Shaitan,

فَاِذَا قَرَأْتَ الْقُرْاٰنَ فَاسْتَعِذْ بِاللّٰهِ مِنَ الشَّيْطٰنِ الرَّجِيْمِ ۞

99. Surely he has no authority over those who believe and rely on their Lord.

اِنَّهٗ لَيْسَ لَهٗ سُلْطٰنٌ عَلَى الَّذِيْنَ اٰمَنُوْا وَعَلٰى رَبِّهِمْ يَتَوَكَّلُوْنَ ۞

100. His authority is only over those who befriend him and those who associate others with Him.

اِنَّمَا سُلْطٰنُهٗ عَلَى الَّذِيْنَ يَتَوَلَّوْنَهٗ وَالَّذِيْنَ هُمْ بِهٖ مُشْرِكُوْنَ ۞

101. And when We change (one) communication for (another) communication, and Allah knows best what He reveals, they say: You are only a forger. Nay, most of them do not know.

وَاِذَا بَدَّلْنَا اٰيَةً مَّكَانَ اٰيَةٍ ۙ وَّاللّٰهُ اَعْلَمُ بِمَا يُنَزِّلُ قَالُوْٓا اِنَّمَا اَنْتَ مُفْتَرٍ ۗ بَلْ اَكْثَرُهُمْ لَا يَعْلَمُوْنَ ۞

102. Say: The Holy Spirit has revealed it from your Lord with the truth, that it may establish those who believe and as a guidance and good news for those who submit.

قُلْ نَزَّلَهٗ رُوْحُ الْقُدُسِ مِنْ رَّبِّكَ بِالْحَقِّ لِيُثَبِّتَ الَّذِيْنَ اٰمَنُوْا وَهُدًى وَّبُشْرٰى لِلْمُسْلِمِيْنَ ۞

103. And certainly We know that they say: Only a mortal teaches him. The tongue of him whom they reproach is barbarous, and this is clear Arabic tongue.

وَلَقَدْ نَعْلَمُ اَنَّهُمْ يَقُوْلُوْنَ اِنَّمَا يُعَلِّمُهُ بَشَرٌ لِسَانُ الَّذِيْ يُلْحِدُوْنَ اِلَيْهِ اَعْجَمِيٌّ وَّهٰذَا لِسَانٌ عَرَبِيٌّ مُّبِيْنٌ ۝

104. (As for) those who do not believe in Allah's communications, surely Allah will not guide them, and they shall have a painful punishment.

اِنَّ الَّذِيْنَ لَا يُؤْمِنُوْنَ بِاٰيٰتِ اللّٰهِ لَا يَهْدِيْهِمُ اللّٰهُ وَلَهُمْ عَذَابٌ اَلِيْمٌ ۝

105. Only they forge the lie who do not believe in Allah's communications, and these are the liars.

اِنَّمَا يَفْتَرِى الْكَذِبَ الَّذِيْنَ لَا يُؤْمِنُوْنَ بِاٰيٰتِ اللّٰهِ وَاُولٰٓئِكَ هُمُ الْكٰذِبُوْنَ ۝

106. He who disbelieves in Allah after his having believed, not he who is compelled while his heart is at rest on account of faith, but he who opens (his) breast to disbelief—on these is the wrath of Allah, and they shall have a grievous chastisement.

مَنْ كَفَرَ بِاللّٰهِ مِنْ بَعْدِ اِيْمَانِهٖ اِلَّا مَنْ اُكْرِهَ وَقَلْبُهٗ مُطْمَئِنٌّ بِالْاِيْمَانِ وَلٰكِنْ مَّنْ شَرَحَ بِالْكُفْرِ صَدْرًا فَعَلَيْهِمْ غَضَبٌ مِّنَ اللّٰهِ وَلَهُمْ عَذَابٌ عَظِيْمٌ ۝

107. This is because they love this world's life more than the hereafter, and because Allah does not guide the unbelieving people.

ذٰلِكَ بِاَنَّهُمُ اسْتَحَبُّوا الْحَيٰوةَ الدُّنْيَا عَلَى الْاٰخِرَةِ وَاَنَّ اللّٰهَ لَا يَهْدِى الْقَوْمَ الْكٰفِرِيْنَ ۝

108. These are they on whose hearts and their hearing and their eyes Allah has set a seal, and these are the heedless ones.

اُولٰٓئِكَ الَّذِيْنَ طَبَعَ اللّٰهُ عَلٰى قُلُوْبِهِمْ وَسَمْعِهِمْ وَاَبْصَارِهِمْ وَاُولٰٓئِكَ هُمُ الْغٰفِلُوْنَ ۝

109. No doubt that in the hereafter they will be the losers.

لَا جَرَمَ اَنَّهُمْ فِى الْاٰخِرَةِ هُمُ الْخٰسِرُوْنَ ۝

110. Yet surely your Lord, with respect to those who fly after they are persecuted, then they struggle hard and are patient, most surely your Lord after that is Forgiving, Merciful.

ثُمَّ اِنَّ رَبَّكَ لِلَّذِيْنَ هَاجَرُوْا مِنْ بَعْدِ مَا فُتِنُوْا ثُمَّ جَاهَدُوْا وَصَبَرُوْا اِنَّ رَبَّكَ مِنْ بَعْدِهَا لَغَفُوْرٌ رَّحِيْمٌ ۝

111. (Remember) the day when every soul shall come, pleading for itself and every soul shall be paid in full what it has done, and they shall not be dealt with unjustly.

يَوْمَ تَأْتِىْ كُلُّ نَفْسٍ تُجَادِلُ عَنْ نَّفْسِهَا وَتُوَفّٰى كُلُّ نَفْسٍ مَّا عَمِلَتْ وَهُمْ لَا يُظْلَمُوْنَ ۝

112. And Allah sets forth a parable:
(Consider) a town safe and secure to which
its means of subsistence come in abundance
from every quarter; but it became ungrateful for Allah's favors, therefore Allah made
it to taste the utmost degree of hunger and
fear because of what they wrought.

وَضَرَبَ اللّٰهُ مَثَلًا قَرْيَةً كَانَتْ اٰمِنَةً مُّطْمَئِنَّةً يَّأْتِيْهَا
رِزْقُهَا رَغَدًا مِّنْ كُلِّ مَكَانٍ فَكَفَرَتْ بِأَنْعُمِ اللّٰهِ فَأَذَاقَهَا
اللّٰهُ لِبَاسَ الْجُوْعِ وَالْخَوْفِ بِمَا كَانُوْا يَصْنَعُوْنَ ١١٢

113. And certainly there came to them
an Apostle from among them, but they
rejected him, so the punishment overtook
them while they were unjust.

وَلَقَدْ جَآءَهُمْ رَسُوْلٌ مِّنْهُمْ فَكَذَّبُوْهُ فَأَخَذَهُمُ
الْعَذَابُ وَهُمْ ظٰلِمُوْنَ ١١٣

114. Therefore eat of what Allah has
given you, lawful and good (things), and
give thanks for Allah's favor if Him do
you serve.

فَكُلُوْا مِمَّا رَزَقَكُمُ اللّٰهُ حَلٰلًا طَيِّبًا وَّاشْكُرُوْا نِعْمَتَ
اللّٰهِ اِنْ كُنْتُمْ اِيَّاهُ تَعْبُدُوْنَ ١١٤

115. He has only forbidden you what
dies of itself and blood and flesh of swine
and that over which any other name than
that of Allah has been invoked, but
whoever is driven to necessity, not desiring
nor exceeding the limit, then surely Allah is
Forgiving, Merciful.

اِنَّمَا حَرَّمَ عَلَيْكُمُ الْمَيْتَةَ وَالدَّمَ وَلَحْمَ الْخِنْزِيْرِ وَمَا
اُهِلَّ لِغَيْرِ اللّٰهِ بِهٖ فَمَنِ اضْطُرَّ غَيْرَ بَاغٍ وَّلَا عَادٍ
فَاِنَّ اللّٰهَ غَفُوْرٌ رَّحِيْمٌ ١١٥

116. And, for what your tongues describe, do not utter the lie, (saying) This is
lawful and this is unlawful, in order to
forge a lie against Allah; surely those who
forge the lie against Allah shall not prosper.

وَلَا تَقُوْلُوْا لِمَا تَصِفُ اَلْسِنَتُكُمُ الْكَذِبَ هٰذَا حَلٰلٌ
وَّهٰذَا حَرَامٌ لِّتَفْتَرُوْا عَلَى اللّٰهِ الْكَذِبَ اِنَّ الَّذِيْنَ
يَفْتَرُوْنَ عَلَى اللّٰهِ الْكَذِبَ لَا يُفْلِحُوْنَ ١١٦

117. A little enjoyment and they shall
have a painful punishment.

مَتَاعٌ قَلِيْلٌ وَّلَهُمْ عَذَابٌ اَلِيْمٌ ١١٧

118. And for those who were Jews We
prohibited what We have related to you
already, and We did them no injustice, but
they were unjust to themselves.

وَعَلَى الَّذِيْنَ هَادُوْا حَرَّمْنَا مَا قَصَصْنَا عَلَيْكَ
مِنْ قَبْلُ وَمَا ظَلَمْنٰهُمْ وَلٰكِنْ كَانُوْا اَنْفُسَهُمْ
يَظْلِمُوْنَ ١١٨

119. Yet surely your Lord, with respect
to those who do an evil in ignorance, then
turn after that and make amends, most
surely your Lord after that is Forgiving,
Merciful.

ثُمَّ اِنَّ رَبَّكَ لِلَّذِيْنَ عَمِلُوا السُّوْٓءَ بِجَهَالَةٍ ثُمَّ
تَابُوْا مِنْ بَعْدِ ذٰلِكَ وَاَصْلَحُوْٓا اِنَّ رَبَّكَ مِنْ
بَعْدِهَا لَغَفُوْرٌ رَّحِيْمٌ ١١٩

120. Surely Ibrahim was an exemplar,
obedient to Allah, upright, and he was not
of the polytheists.

اِنَّ اِبْرٰهِيْمَ كَانَ اُمَّةً قَانِتًا لِّلّٰهِ حَنِيْفًا وَلَمْ يَكُ
مِنَ الْمُشْرِكِيْنَ ١٢٠

121. Grateful for His favors; He chose him and guided him on the right path.

شَاكِرًا لِّاَنْعُمِهِ ۙ اِجْتَبٰهُ وَهَدٰىهُ اِلٰى صِرَاطٍ مُّسْتَقِيْمٍ ۞

122. And We gave him good in this world, and in the next he will most surely be among the good.

وَاٰتَيْنٰهُ فِى الدُّنْيَا حَسَنَةً ۗ وَاِنَّهٗ فِى الْاٰخِرَةِ لَمِنَ الصّٰلِحِيْنَ ۞

123. Then We revealed to you: Follow the faith of Ibrahim, the upright one, and he was not of the polytheists.

ثُمَّ اَوْحَيْنَا اِلَيْكَ اَنِ اتَّبِعْ مِلَّةَ اِبْرٰهِيْمَ حَنِيْفًا ۗ وَمَا كَانَ مِنَ الْمُشْرِكِيْنَ ۞

124. The Sabbath was ordained only for those who differed about it, and most surely your Lord will judge between them on the resurrection day concerning that about which they differed.

اِنَّمَا جُعِلَ السَّبْتُ عَلَى الَّذِيْنَ اخْتَلَفُوْا فِيْهِ ۗ وَاِنَّ رَبَّكَ لَيَحْكُمُ بَيْنَهُمْ يَوْمَ الْقِيٰمَةِ فِيْمَا كَانُوْا فِيْهِ يَخْتَلِفُوْنَ ۞

125. Call to the way of your Lord with wisdom and goodly exhortation, and have disputations with them in the best manner; surely your Lord best knows those who go astray from His path, and He knows best those who follow the right way.

اُدْعُ اِلٰى سَبِيْلِ رَبِّكَ بِالْحِكْمَةِ وَالْمَوْعِظَةِ الْحَسَنَةِ وَجَادِلْهُمْ بِالَّتِيْ هِيَ اَحْسَنُ ۗ اِنَّ رَبَّكَ هُوَ اَعْلَمُ بِمَنْ ضَلَّ عَنْ سَبِيْلِهٖ وَهُوَ اَعْلَمُ بِالْمُهْتَدِيْنَ ۞

126. And if you take your turn, then retaliate with the like of that with which you were afflicted; but if you are patient, it will certainly be best for those who are patient.

وَاِنْ عَاقَبْتُمْ فَعَاقِبُوْا بِمِثْلِ مَا عُوْقِبْتُمْ بِهٖ ۗ وَلَئِنْ صَبَرْتُمْ لَهُوَ خَيْرٌ لِّلصّٰبِرِيْنَ ۞

127. And be patient and your patience is not but by (the assistance of) Allah, and grieve not for them, and do not distress yourself at what they plan.

وَاصْبِرْ وَمَا صَبْرُكَ اِلَّا بِاللّٰهِ وَلَا تَحْزَنْ عَلَيْهِمْ وَلَا تَكُ فِيْ ضَيْقٍ مِّمَّا يَمْكُرُوْنَ ۞

128. Surely Allah is with those who guard (against evil) and those who do good (to others).

اِنَّ اللّٰهَ مَعَ الَّذِيْنَ اتَّقَوْا وَّالَّذِيْنَ هُمْ مُّحْسِنُوْنَ ۞

THE ISRAELITES
(BANI-ISRAEL)

In the name of Allah,
the Beneficent, the Merciful.

1. Glory be to Him Who made His servant to go on a night from the Sacred Mosque to the remote mosque of which We have blessed the precincts, so that We may show to him some of Our signs; surely He is the Hearing, the Seeing.

2. And We gave Musa the Book and made it a guidance to the children of Israel, saying: Do not take a protector besides Me;

3. The offspring of those whom We bore with Nuh; surely he was a grateful servant.

4. And We had made known to the children of Israel in the Book: Most certainly you will make mischief in the land twice, and most certainly you will behave insolently with great insolence.

5. So when the promise for the first of the two came, We sent over you Our servants, of mighty prowess, so they went to and fro among the houses, and it was a promise to be accomplished.

6. Then We gave you back the turn to prevail against them, and aided you with wealth and children and made you a numerous band.

7. If you do good, you will do good for your own souls, and if you do evil, it shall be for them. So when the second promise came (We raised another people) that they may bring you to grief and that they may enter the mosque as they entered it the first time, and that they might destroy whatever they gained ascendancy over with utter destruction.

8. It may be that your Lord will have mercy on you, and if you again return (to disobedience) We too will return (to punishment), and We have made hell a prison for the unbelievers.

بِسْمِ اللهِ الرَّحْمٰنِ الرَّحِيْمِ ۞

سُبْحٰنَ الَّذِيْۤ اَسْرٰى بِعَبْدِهٖ لَيْلًا مِّنَ الْمَسْجِدِ الْحَرَامِ اِلَى الْمَسْجِدِ الْاَقْصَا الَّذِيْ بٰرَكْنَا حَوْلَهٗ لِنُرِيَهٗ مِنْ اٰيٰتِنَا ؕ اِنَّهٗ هُوَ السَّمِيْعُ الْبَصِيْرُ ۞

وَاٰتَيْنَا مُوْسَى الْكِتٰبَ وَجَعَلْنٰهُ هُدًى لِّبَنِيْۤ اِسْرَآءِيْلَ اَلَّا تَتَّخِذُوْا مِنْ دُوْنِيْ وَكِيْلًا ۞

ذُرِّيَّةَ مَنْ حَمَلْنَا مَعَ نُوْحٍ ؕ اِنَّهٗ كَانَ عَبْدًا شَكُوْرًا ۞

وَقَضَيْنَاۤ اِلٰى بَنِيْۤ اِسْرَآءِيْلَ فِى الْكِتٰبِ لَتُفْسِدُنَّ فِى الْاَرْضِ مَرَّتَيْنِ وَلَتَعْلُنَّ عُلُوًّا كَبِيْرًا ۞

فَاِذَا جَآءَ وَعْدُ اُوْلٰىهُمَا بَعَثْنَا عَلَيْكُمْ عِبَادًا لَّنَاۤ اُولِيْ بَأْسٍ شَدِيْدٍ فَجَاسُوْا خِلٰلَ الدِّيَارِ ؕ وَكَانَ وَعْدًا مَّفْعُوْلًا ۞

ثُمَّ رَدَدْنَا لَكُمُ الْكَرَّةَ عَلَيْهِمْ وَاَمْدَدْنٰكُمْ بِاَمْوَالٍ وَّبَنِيْنَ وَجَعَلْنٰكُمْ اَكْثَرَ نَفِيْرًا ۞

اِنْ اَحْسَنْتُمْ اَحْسَنْتُمْ لِاَنْفُسِكُمْ ؕ وَاِنْ اَسَأْتُمْ فَلَهَا ؕ فَاِذَا جَآءَ وَعْدُ الْاٰخِرَةِ لِيَسُوْٓءُوْا وُجُوْهَكُمْ وَلِيَدْخُلُوا الْمَسْجِدَ كَمَا دَخَلُوْهُ اَوَّلَ مَرَّةٍ وَّلِيُتَبِّرُوْا مَا عَلَوْا تَتْبِيْرًا ۞

عَسٰى رَبُّكُمْ اَنْ يَّرْحَمَكُمْ ۚ وَاِنْ عُدْتُّمْ عُدْنَا ۘ وَجَعَلْنَا جَهَنَّمَ لِلْكٰفِرِيْنَ حَصِيْرًا ۞

9. Surely this Quran guides to that which is most upright and gives good news to the believers who do good that they shall have a great reward.

10. And that (as for) those who do not believe in the hereafter, We have prepared for them a painful chastisement.

11. And man prays for evil as he ought to pray for good, and man is ever hasty.

12. And We have made the night and the day two signs, then We have made the sign of the night to pass away and We have made the sign of the day manifest, so that you may seek grace from your Lord, and that you might know the numbering of years and the reckoning; and We have explained everything with distinctness.

13. And We have made every man's actions to cling to his neck, and We will bring forth to him on the resurrection day a book which he will find wide open:

14. Read your book; your own self is sufficient as a reckoner against you this day.

15. Whoever goes aright, for his own soul does he go aright; and whoever goes astray, to its detriment only does he go astray; nor can the bearer of a burden bear the burden of another, nor do We chastise until We raise an apostle.

16. And when We wish to destroy a town, We send Our commandment to the people of it who lead easy lives, but they transgress therein; thus the word proves true against it, so We destroy it with utter destruction.

17. And how many of the generations did We destroy after Nuh! and your Lord is sufficient as Knowing and Seeing with regard to His servants' faults.

261

18. Whoever desires this present life, We hasten to him therein what We please for whomsoever We desire, then We assign to him the hell; he shall enter it despised, driven away.

مَنْ كَانَ يُرِيْدُ الْعَاجِلَةَ عَجَّلْنَا لَهُ فِيْهَا مَا نَشَاءُ لِمَنْ نُّرِيْدُ ثُمَّ جَعَلْنَا لَهُ جَهَنَّمَ يَصْلٰهَا مَذْمُوْمًا مَّدْحُوْرًا ۝

19. And whoever desires the hereafter and strives for it as he ought to strive and he is a believer; (as for) these, their striving shall surely be accepted.

وَمَنْ أَرَادَ الْاٰخِرَةَ وَسَعٰى لَهَا سَعْيَهَا وَهُوَ مُؤْمِنٌ فَأُولٰٓئِكَ كَانَ سَعْيُهُمْ مَّشْكُوْرًا ۝

20. All do We aid—these as well as those—out of the bounty of your Lord, and the bounty of your Lord is not confined.

كُلًّا نُّمِدُّ هٰٓؤُلَاءِ وَهٰٓؤُلَاءِ مِنْ عَطَاءِ رَبِّكَ وَمَا كَانَ عَطَاءُ رَبِّكَ مَحْظُوْرًا ۝

21. See how We have made some of them to excel others, and certainly the hereafter is much superior in respect of excellence.

أُنْظُرْ كَيْفَ فَضَّلْنَا بَعْضَهُمْ عَلٰى بَعْضٍ وَلَلْاٰخِرَةُ أَكْبَرُ دَرَجٰتٍ وَّأَكْبَرُ تَفْضِيْلًا ۝

22. Do not associate with Allah any other god, lest you sit down despised, neglected.

لَا تَجْعَلْ مَعَ اللّٰهِ إِلٰهًا اٰخَرَ فَتَقْعُدَ مَذْمُوْمًا مَّخْذُوْلًا ۝

23. And your Lord has commanded that you shall not serve (any) but Him, and goodness to your parents. If either or both of them reach old age with you, say not to them (so much as) "Ugh" nor chide them, and speak to them a generous word.

وَقَضٰى رَبُّكَ أَلَّا تَعْبُدُوْا إِلَّا إِيَّاهُ وَبِالْوَالِدَيْنِ إِحْسَانًا إِمَّا يَبْلُغَنَّ عِنْدَكَ الْكِبَرَ أَحَدُهُمَا أَوْ كِلٰهُمَا فَلَا تَقُلْ لَّهُمَا أُفٍّ وَّلَا تَنْهَرْهُمَا وَقُلْ لَّهُمَا قَوْلًا كَرِيْمًا ۝

24. And make yourself submissively gentle to them with compassion, and say: O my Lord! have compassion on them, as they brought me up (when I was) little.

وَاخْفِضْ لَهُمَا جَنَاحَ الذُّلِّ مِنَ الرَّحْمَةِ وَقُلْ رَّبِّ ارْحَمْهُمَا كَمَا رَبَّيٰنِيْ صَغِيْرًا ۝

25. Your Lord knows best what is in your minds; if you are good, then He is surely Forgiving to those who turn (to Him) frequently.

رَبُّكُمْ أَعْلَمُ بِمَا فِيْ نُفُوْسِكُمْ إِنْ تَكُوْنُوْا صَالِحِيْنَ فَإِنَّهُ كَانَ لِلْأَوَّابِيْنَ غَفُوْرًا ۝

26. And give to the near of kin his due and (to) the needy and the wayfarer, and do not squander wastefully.

وَاٰتِ ذَا الْقُرْبٰى حَقَّهُ وَالْمِسْكِيْنَ وَابْنَ السَّبِيْلِ وَلَا تُبَذِّرْ تَبْذِيْرًا ۝

27. Surely the squanderers are the fellows of the Shaitans and the Shaitan is ever ungrateful to his Lord.

إِنَّ الْمُبَذِّرِيْنَ كَانُوْا إِخْوَانَ الشَّيٰطِيْنِ وَكَانَ الشَّيْطٰنُ لِرَبِّهِ كَفُوْرًا ۝

28. And if you turn away from them to seek mercy from your Lord, which you hope for, speak to them a gentle word.

وَإِمَّا تُعْرِضَنَّ عَنْهُمُ ابْتِغَآءَ رَحْمَةٍ مِّنْ رَّبِّكَ تَرْجُوْهَا فَقُلْ لَّهُمْ قَوْلًا مَّيْسُوْرًا ۝

29. And do not make your hand to be shackled to your neck nor stretch it forth to the utmost (limit) of its stretching forth, lest you should (afterwards) sit down blamed, stripped off.

وَلَا تَجْعَلْ يَدَكَ مَغْلُوْلَةً إِلٰى عُنُقِكَ وَلَا تَبْسُطْهَا كُلَّ الْبَسْطِ فَتَقْعُدَ مَلُوْمًا مَّحْسُوْرًا ۝

30. Surely your Lord makes plentiful the means of subsistence for whom He pleases and He straitens (them); surely He is ever Aware of, Seeing, His servants.

إِنَّ رَبَّكَ يَبْسُطُ الرِّزْقَ لِمَنْ يَّشَآءُ وَيَقْدِرُ ۗ إِنَّهُ كَانَ بِعِبَادِهٖ خَبِيْرًۢا بَصِيْرًا ۝

31. And do not kill your children for fear of poverty; We give them sustenance and yourselves (too); surely to kill them is a great wrong.

وَلَا تَقْتُلُوْا أَوْلَادَكُمْ خَشْيَةَ إِمْلَاقٍ ۗ نَحْنُ نَرْزُقُهُمْ وَإِيَّاكُمْ ۚ إِنَّ قَتْلَهُمْ كَانَ خِطْأً كَبِيْرًا ۝

32. And go not nigh to fornication; surely it is an indecency and an evil way.

وَلَا تَقْرَبُوا الزِّنٰى إِنَّهُ كَانَ فَاحِشَةً ۗ وَسَآءَ سَبِيْلًا ۝

33. And do not kill any one whom Allah has forbidden, except for a just cause, and whoever is slain unjustly, We have indeed given to his heir authority, so let him not exceed the just limits in slaying; surely he is aided.

وَلَا تَقْتُلُوا النَّفْسَ الَّتِيْ حَرَّمَ اللّٰهُ إِلَّا بِالْحَقِّ ۗ وَمَنْ قُتِلَ مَظْلُوْمًا فَقَدْ جَعَلْنَا لِوَلِيِّهٖ سُلْطٰنًا فَلَا يُسْرِفْ فِّى الْقَتْلِ ۗ إِنَّهُ كَانَ مَنْصُوْرًا ۝

34. And draw not near to the property of the orphan except in a goodly way till he attains his maturity and fulfill the promise; surely (every) promise shall be questioned about.

وَلَا تَقْرَبُوْا مَالَ الْيَتِيْمِ إِلَّا بِالَّتِيْ هِيَ أَحْسَنُ حَتّٰى يَبْلُغَ أَشُدَّهٗ ۖ وَأَوْفُوْا بِالْعَهْدِ ۖ إِنَّ الْعَهْدَ كَانَ مَسْئُوْلًا ۝

35. And give full measure when you measure out, and weigh with a true balance; this is fair and better in the end.

وَأَوْفُوا الْكَيْلَ إِذَا كِلْتُمْ وَزِنُوْا بِالْقِسْطَاسِ الْمُسْتَقِيْمِ ۚ ذٰلِكَ خَيْرٌ وَّأَحْسَنُ تَأْوِيْلًا ۝

36. And follow not that of which you have not the knowledge; surely the hearing and the sight and the heart, all of these, shall be questioned about that.

وَلَا تَقْفُ مَا لَيْسَ لَكَ بِهٖ عِلْمٌ ۗ إِنَّ السَّمْعَ وَالْبَصَرَ وَالْفُؤَادَ كُلُّ أُولٰٓئِكَ كَانَ عَنْهُ مَسْئُوْلًا ۝

37. And do not go about in the land exultingly, for you cannot cut through the earth nor reach the mountains in height.

وَلَا تَمْشِ فِى الْأَرْضِ مَرَحًا ۖ إِنَّكَ لَنْ تَخْرِقَ الْأَرْضَ وَلَنْ تَبْلُغَ الْجِبَالَ طُوْلًا ۝

38. All this—the evil of it—is hateful in the sight of your Lord.

كُلُّ ذٰلِكَ كَانَ سَيِّئُهٗ عِنْدَ رَبِّكَ مَكْرُوْهًا ۝

39. This is of what your Lord has revealed to you of wisdom, and do not associate any other god with Allah lest you should be thrown into hell, blamed, cast away.

ذٰلِكَ مِمَّا اَوْحٰى اِلَيْكَ رَبُّكَ مِنَ الْحِكْمَةِ وَلَا تَجْعَلْ مَعَ اللّٰهِ اِلٰهًا اٰخَرَ فَتُلْقٰى فِيْ جَهَنَّمَ مَلُوْمًا مَّدْحُوْرًا ۝

40. What! has then your Lord preferred to give you sons, and (for Himself) taken daughters from among the angels? Most surely you utter a grievous saying.

اَفَاَصْفٰكُمْ رَبُّكُمْ بِالْبَنِيْنَ وَاتَّخَذَ مِنَ الْمَلٰٓئِكَةِ اِنَاثًا اِنَّكُمْ لَتَقُوْلُوْنَ قَوْلًا عَظِيْمًا ۝

41. And certainly We have repeated (warnings) in this Quran that they may be mindful, but it does not add save to their aversion.

وَلَقَدْ صَرَّفْنَا فِيْ هٰذَا الْقُرْاٰنِ لِيَذَّكَّرُوْا ۖ وَمَا يَزِيْدُهُمْ اِلَّا نُفُوْرًا

42. Say: If there were with Him gods as they say, then certainly they would have been able to seek a way to the Lord of power.

قُلْ لَّوْ كَانَ مَعَهٗٓ اٰلِهَةٌ كَمَا يَقُوْلُوْنَ اِذًا لَّابْتَغَوْا اِلٰى ذِى الْعَرْشِ سَبِيْلًا ۝

43. Glory be to Him and exalted be He in high exaltation above what they say.

سُبْحٰنَهٗ وَتَعٰلٰى عَمَّا يَقُوْلُوْنَ عُلُوًّا كَبِيْرًا ۝

44. The seven heavens declare His glory and the earth (too), and those who are in them; and there is not a single thing but glorifies Him with His praise, but you do not understand their glorification; surely He is Forbearing, Forgiving.

تُسَبِّحُ لَهُ السَّمٰوٰتُ السَّبْعُ وَالْاَرْضُ وَمَنْ فِيْهِنَّ ۖ وَاِنْ مِّنْ شَيْءٍ اِلَّا يُسَبِّحُ بِحَمْدِهٖ وَلٰكِنْ لَّا تَفْقَهُوْنَ تَسْبِيْحَهُمْ ۗ اِنَّهٗ كَانَ حَلِيْمًا غَفُوْرًا ۝

45. And when you recite the Quran, We place between you and those who do not believe in the hereafter a hidden barrier;

وَاِذَا قَرَاْتَ الْقُرْاٰنَ جَعَلْنَا بَيْنَكَ وَبَيْنَ الَّذِيْنَ لَا يُؤْمِنُوْنَ بِالْاٰخِرَةِ حِجَابًا مَّسْتُوْرًا ۝

46. And We have placed coverings on their hearts and a heaviness in their ears lest they understand it, and when you mention your Lord alone in the Quran they turn their backs in aversion.

وَّجَعَلْنَا عَلٰى قُلُوْبِهِمْ اَكِنَّةً اَنْ يَّفْقَهُوْهُ وَفِيْٓ اٰذَانِهِمْ وَقْرًا ۗ وَاِذَا ذَكَرْتَ رَبَّكَ فِى الْقُرْاٰنِ وَحْدَهٗ وَلَّوْا عَلٰٓى اَدْبَارِهِمْ نُفُوْرًا ۝

47. We know best what they listen to when they listen to you, and when they take counsel secretly, when the unjust say: You follow only a man deprived of reason.

نَحْنُ اَعْلَمُ بِمَا يَسْتَمِعُوْنَ بِهٖٓ اِذْ يَسْتَمِعُوْنَ اِلَيْكَ وَاِذْ هُمْ نَجْوٰٓى اِذْ يَقُوْلُ الظّٰلِمُوْنَ اِنْ تَتَّبِعُوْنَ اِلَّا رَجُلًا مَّسْحُوْرًا ۝

48. See what they liken you to! So they have gone astray and cannot find the way.

اُنْظُرْ كَيْفَ ضَرَبُوْا لَكَ الْاَمْثَالَ فَضَلُّوْا فَلَا يَسْتَطِيْعُوْنَ سَبِيْلًا ۝

49. And they say: What! when we shall have become bones and decayed particles, shall we then certainly be raised up, being a new creation?

وَقَالُوْٓا ءَاِذَا كُنَّا عِظَامًا وَّرُفَاتًا ءَاِنَّا لَمَبْعُوْثُوْنَ خَلْقًا جَدِيْدًا ۟

50. Say: Become stones or iron,

قُلْ كُوْنُوْا حِجَارَةً اَوْ حَدِيْدًا ۟

51. Or some other creature of those which are too hard (to receive life) in your minds! But they will say: Who will return us? Say: Who created you at first. Still they will shake their heads at you and say: When will it be? Say: Maybe it has drawn nigh.

اَوْ خَلْقًا مِّمَّا يَكْبُرُ فِىْ صُدُوْرِكُمْ ۚ فَسَيَقُوْلُوْنَ مَنْ يُّعِيْدُنَا ۚ قُلِ الَّذِىْ فَطَرَكُمْ اَوَّلَ مَرَّةٍ ۚ فَسَيُنْغِضُوْنَ اِلَيْكَ رُءُوْسَهُمْ وَيَقُوْلُوْنَ مَتٰى هُوَ ۚ قُلْ عَسٰٓى اَنْ يَّكُوْنَ قَرِيْبًا ۟

52. On the day when He will call you forth, then shall you obey Him, giving Him praise, and you will think that you tarried but a little (while).

يَوْمَ يَدْعُوْكُمْ فَتَسْتَجِيْبُوْنَ بِحَمْدِهٖ وَتَظُنُّوْنَ اِنْ لَّبِثْتُمْ اِلَّا قَلِيْلًا ۟

53. And say to My servants (that) they speak that which is best; surely the Shaitan sows dissensions among them; surely the Shaitan is an open enemy to man.

وَقُلْ لِّعِبَادِىْ يَقُوْلُوا الَّتِىْ هِىَ اَحْسَنُ ۚ اِنَّ الشَّيْطٰنَ يَنْزَغُ بَيْنَهُمْ ۚ اِنَّ الشَّيْطٰنَ كَانَ لِلْاِنْسَانِ عَدُوًّا مُّبِيْنًا ۟

54. Your Lord knows you best; He will have mercy on you if He pleases, or He will chastise you if He pleases; and We have not sent you as being in charge of them.

رَبُّكُمْ اَعْلَمُ بِكُمْ ۚ اِنْ يَّشَأْ يَرْحَمْكُمْ اَوْ اِنْ يَّشَأْ يُعَذِّبْكُمْ ۚ وَمَآ اَرْسَلْنٰكَ عَلَيْهِمْ وَكِيْلًا ۟

55. And your Lord best knows those who are in the heavens and the earth; and certainly We have made some of the prophets to excel others, and to Dawood We gave a scripture.

وَرَبُّكَ اَعْلَمُ بِمَنْ فِى السَّمٰوٰتِ وَالْاَرْضِ ۚ وَلَقَدْ فَضَّلْنَا بَعْضَ النَّبِيِّيْنَ عَلٰى بَعْضٍ وَّاٰتَيْنَا دَاوٗدَ زَبُوْرًا ۟

56. Say: Call on those whom you assert besides Him, so they shall not control the removal of distress from you nor (its) transference.

قُلِ ادْعُوا الَّذِيْنَ زَعَمْتُمْ مِّنْ دُوْنِهٖ فَلَا يَمْلِكُوْنَ كَشْفَ الضُّرِّ عَنْكُمْ وَلَا تَحْوِيْلًا ۟

57. Those whom they call upon, themselves seek the means of access to their Lord—whoever of them is nearest—and they hope for His mercy and fear His chastisement; surely the chastisement of your Lord is a thing to be cautious of.

اُولٰٓئِكَ الَّذِيْنَ يَدْعُوْنَ يَبْتَغُوْنَ اِلٰى رَبِّهِمُ الْوَسِيْلَةَ اَيُّهُمْ اَقْرَبُ وَيَرْجُوْنَ رَحْمَتَهٗ وَيَخَافُوْنَ عَذَابَهٗ ۚ اِنَّ عَذَابَ رَبِّكَ كَانَ مَحْذُوْرًا ۟

58. And there is not a town but We will destroy it before the day of resurrection or chastise it with a severe chastisement; this is written in the Divine ordinance.

وَاِنْ مِّنْ قَرْيَةٍ اِلَّا نَحْنُ مُهْلِكُوْهَا قَبْلَ يَوْمِ الْقِيٰمَةِ اَوْ مُعَذِّبُوْهَا عَذَابًا شَدِيْدًا ۤ كَانَ ذٰلِكَ فِى الْكِتٰبِ مَسْطُوْرًا ۝

59. And nothing could have hindered Us that We should send signs except that the ancients rejected them; and We gave to Samood the she-camel—a manifest sign—but on her account they did injustice, and We do not send signs but to make (men) fear.

وَمَا مَنَعَنَا اَنْ نُّرْسِلَ بِالْاٰيٰتِ اِلَّا اَنْ كَذَّبَ بِهَا الْاَوَّلُوْنَ ۚ وَاٰتَيْنَا ثَمُوْدَ النَّاقَةَ مُبْصِرَةً فَظَلَمُوْا بِهَا ۚ وَمَا نُرْسِلُ بِالْاٰيٰتِ اِلَّا تَخْوِيْفًا ۝

60. And when We said to you: Surely your Lord encompasses men; and We did not make the vision which We showed you but a trial for men and the cursed tree in the Quran as well; and We cause them to fear, but it only adds to their great inordinacy.

وَاِذْ قُلْنَا لَكَ اِنَّ رَبَّكَ اَحَاطَ بِالنَّاسِ ۚ وَمَا جَعَلْنَا الرُّءْيَا الَّتِيْ اَرَيْنٰكَ اِلَّا فِتْنَةً لِّلنَّاسِ وَالشَّجَرَةَ الْمَلْعُوْنَةَ فِى الْقُرْاٰنِ ۚ وَنُخَوِّفُهُمْ ۙ فَمَا يَزِيْدُهُمْ اِلَّا طُغْيَانًا كَبِيْرًا ۝

61. And when We said to the angels: Make obeisance to Adam; they made obeisance, but Iblis (did it not). He said: Shall I make obeisance to him whom Thou hast created of dust?

وَاِذْ قُلْنَا لِلْمَلٰٓئِكَةِ اسْجُدُوْا لِاٰدَمَ فَسَجَدُوْا اِلَّا اِبْلِيْسَ ۚ قَالَ ءَاَسْجُدُ لِمَنْ خَلَقْتَ طِيْنًا ۝

62. He said: Tell me, is this he whom Thou hast honored above me? If Thou shouldst respite me to the day of resurrection, I will most certainly cause his progeny to perish except a few.

قَالَ اَرَءَيْتَكَ هٰذَا الَّذِيْ كَرَّمْتَ عَلَيَّ ۚ لَئِنْ اَخَّرْتَنِ اِلٰى يَوْمِ الْقِيٰمَةِ لَاَحْتَنِكَنَّ ذُرِّيَّتَهٗٓ اِلَّا قَلِيْلًا ۝

63. He said: Be gone! for whoever of them will follow you, then surely hell is your recompense, a full recompense:

قَالَ اذْهَبْ فَمَنْ تَبِعَكَ مِنْهُمْ فَاِنَّ جَهَنَّمَ جَزَآؤُكُمْ جَزَآءً مَّوْفُوْرًا ۝

64. And beguile whomsoever of them you can with your voice, and collect against them your forces riding and on foot, and share with them in wealth and children, and hold out promises to them; and the Shaitan makes not promises to them but to deceive:

وَاسْتَفْزِزْ مَنِ اسْتَطَعْتَ مِنْهُمْ بِصَوْتِكَ وَاَجْلِبْ عَلَيْهِمْ بِخَيْلِكَ وَرَجِلِكَ وَشَارِكْهُمْ فِى الْاَمْوَالِ وَالْاَوْلَادِ وَعِدْهُمْ ۚ وَمَا يَعِدُهُمُ الشَّيْطٰنُ اِلَّا غُرُوْرًا ۝

65. Surely (as for) My servants, you have no authority over them; and your Lord is sufficient as a Protector.

اِنَّ عِبَادِيْ لَيْسَ لَكَ عَلَيْهِمْ سُلْطٰنٌ ۚ وَكَفٰى بِرَبِّكَ وَكِيْلًا ۝

66. Your Lord is He Who speeds the ships for you in the sea that you may seek of His grace; surely He is ever Merciful to you.

رَبُّكُمُ الَّذِيْ يُزْجِيْ لَكُمُ الْفُلْكَ فِى الْبَحْرِ لِتَبْتَغُوْا مِنْ فَضْلِهٖ ۚ اِنَّهٗ كَانَ بِكُمْ رَحِيْمًا ۝

67. And when distress afflicts you in the sea, away go those whom you call on except He; but when He brings you safe to the land, you turn aside; and man is ever ungrateful.

68. What! do you then feel secure that He will not cause a tract of land to engulf you, or send on you a tornado? Then you shall not find a protector for yourselves.

69. Or, do you feel secure that He will (not) take you back into it another time, then send on you a fierce gale and thus drown you on account of your ungratefulness? Then you shall not find any aider against Us in the matter.

70. And surely We have honored the children of Adam, and We carry them in the land and the sea, and We have given them of the good things, and We have made them to excel by an appropriate excellence over most of those whom We have created.

71. (Remember) the day when We will call every people with their Imam; then whoever is given his book in his right hand, these shall read their book; and they shall not be dealt with a whit unjustly.

72. And whoever is blind in this, he shall (also) be blind in the hereafter; and more erring from the way.

73. And surely they had purposed to turn you away from that which We have revealed to you, that you should forge against Us other than that, and then they would certainly have taken you for a friend.

74. And had it not been that We had already established you, you would certainly have been near to incline to them a little;

75. In that case We would certainly have made you to taste a double (punishment) in this life and a double (punishment) after death, then you would not have found any helper against Us.

وَإِذَا مَسَّكُمُ الضُّرُّ فِي الْبَحْرِ ضَلَّ مَنْ تَدْعُوْنَ اِلَّا اِيَّاهُ ۚ فَلَمَّا نَجّٰىكُمْ اِلَى الْبَرِّ اَعْرَضْتُمْ ۚ وَكَانَ الْاِنْسَانُ كَفُوْرًا ۝

اَفَاَمِنْتُمْ اَنْ يَّخْسِفَ بِكُمْ جَانِبَ الْبَرِّ اَوْ يُرْسِلَ عَلَيْكُمْ حَاصِبًا ثُمَّ لَا تَجِدُوْا لَكُمْ وَكِيْلًا ۝

اَمْ اَمِنْتُمْ اَنْ يُّعِيْدَكُمْ فِيْهِ تَارَةً اُخْرٰى فَيُرْسِلَ عَلَيْكُمْ قَاصِفًا مِّنَ الرِّيْحِ فَيُغْرِقَكُمْ بِمَا كَفَرْتُمْ ۙ ثُمَّ لَا تَجِدُوْا لَكُمْ عَلَيْنَا بِهٖ تَبِيْعًا ۝

وَلَقَدْ كَرَّمْنَا بَنِيْٓ اٰدَمَ وَحَمَلْنٰهُمْ فِي الْبَرِّ وَالْبَحْرِ وَرَزَقْنٰهُمْ مِّنَ الطَّيِّبٰتِ وَفَضَّلْنٰهُمْ عَلٰى كَثِيْرٍ مِّمَّنْ خَلَقْنَا تَفْضِيْلًا ۝

يَوْمَ نَدْعُوْا كُلَّ اُنَاسٍۭ بِاِمَامِهِمْ ۚ فَمَنْ اُوْتِيَ كِتٰبَهٗ بِيَمِيْنِهٖ فَاُولٰٓئِكَ يَقْرَءُوْنَ كِتٰبَهُمْ وَلَا يُظْلَمُوْنَ فَتِيْلًا ۝

وَمَنْ كَانَ فِيْ هٰذِهٖٓ اَعْمٰى فَهُوَ فِي الْاٰخِرَةِ اَعْمٰى وَاَضَلُّ سَبِيْلًا ۝

وَاِنْ كَادُوْا لَيَفْتِنُوْنَكَ عَنِ الَّذِيْٓ اَوْحَيْنَآ اِلَيْكَ لِتَفْتَرِيَ عَلَيْنَا غَيْرَهٗ ۖ وَاِذًا لَّاتَّخَذُوْكَ خَلِيْلًا ۝

وَلَوْلَا اَنْ ثَبَّتْنٰكَ لَقَدْ كِدْتَّ تَرْكَنُ اِلَيْهِمْ شَيْئًا قَلِيْلًا ۝

اِذًا لَّاَذَقْنٰكَ ضِعْفَ الْحَيٰوةِ وَضِعْفَ الْمَمَاتِ ثُمَّ لَا تَجِدُ لَكَ عَلَيْنَا نَصِيْرًا ۝

267

76. And surely they purposed to unsettle you from the land that they might expel you from it, and in that case they will not tarry behind you but a little.

وَإِنْ كَادُوْا لَيَسْتَفِزُّوْنَكَ مِنَ الْأَرْضِ لِيُخْرِجُوْكَ مِنْهَا وَاِذًا لَّا يَلْبَثُوْنَ خِلْفَكَ اِلَّا قَلِيْلًا ۞

77. (This is Our) course with regard to those of Our apostles whom We sent before you, and you shall not find a change in Our course.

سُنَّةَ مَنْ قَدْ اَرْسَلْنَا قَبْلَكَ مِنْ رُّسُلِنَا وَلَا تَجِدُ لِسُنَّتِنَا تَحْوِيْلًا ۞

78. Keep up prayer from the declining of the sun till the darkness of the night and the morning recitation; surely the morning recitation is witnessed.

اَقِمِ الصَّلٰوةَ لِدُلُوْكِ الشَّمْسِ اِلٰى غَسَقِ الَّيْلِ وَقُرْاٰنَ الْفَجْرِ اِنَّ قُرْاٰنَ الْفَجْرِ كَانَ مَشْهُوْدًا ۞

79. And during a part of the night, pray Tahajjud beyond what is incumbent on you; maybe your Lord will raise you to a position of great glory.

وَمِنَ الَّيْلِ فَتَهَجَّدْ بِهٖ نَافِلَةً لَّكَ عَسٰى اَنْ يَّبْعَثَكَ رَبُّكَ مَقَامًا مَّحْمُوْدًا ۞

80. And say: My Lord! make me to enter a goodly entering, and cause me to go forth a goodly going forth, and grant me from near Thee power to assist (me).

وَقُلْ رَّبِّ اَدْخِلْنِيْ مُدْخَلَ صِدْقٍ وَّاَخْرِجْنِيْ مُخْرَجَ صِدْقٍ وَّاجْعَلْ لِّيْ مِنْ لَّدُنْكَ سُلْطَانًا نَّصِيْرًا ۞

81. And say: The truth has come and the falsehood has vanished; surely falsehood is a vanishing (thing).

وَقُلْ جَآءَ الْحَقُّ وَزَهَقَ الْبَاطِلُ اِنَّ الْبَاطِلَ كَانَ زَهُوْقًا ۞

82. And We reveal of the Quran that which is a healing and a mercy to the believers, and it adds only to the perdition of the unjust.

وَنُنَزِّلُ مِنَ الْقُرْاٰنِ مَا هُوَ شِفَآءٌ وَّرَحْمَةٌ لِّلْمُؤْمِنِيْنَ وَلَا يَزِيْدُ الظّٰلِمِيْنَ اِلَّا خَسَارًا ۞

83. And when We bestow favor on man, he turns aside and behaves proudly, and when evil afflicts him, he is despairing.

وَاِذَآ اَنْعَمْنَا عَلَى الْاِنْسَانِ اَعْرَضَ وَنَاٰ بِجَانِبِهٖ وَاِذَا مَسَّهُ الشَّرُّ كَانَ يَؤُوْسًا ۞

84. Say: Every one acts according to his manner; but your Lord best knows who is best guided in the path.

قُلْ كُلٌّ يَّعْمَلُ عَلٰى شَاكِلَتِهٖ فَرَبُّكُمْ اَعْلَمُ بِمَنْ هُوَ اَهْدٰى سَبِيْلًا ۞

85. And they ask you about the soul. Say: The soul is one of the commands of my Lord, and you are not given aught of knowledge but a little.

وَيَسْئَلُوْنَكَ عَنِ الرُّوْحِ قُلِ الرُّوْحُ مِنْ اَمْرِ رَبِّيْ وَمَآ اُوْتِيْتُمْ مِّنَ الْعِلْمِ اِلَّا قَلِيْلًا ۞

86. And if We please, We should certainly take away that which We have revealed to you, then you would not find for it any protector against Us.

وَلَئِنْ شِئْنَا لَنَذْهَبَنَّ بِالَّذِيْ اَوْحَيْنَا اِلَيْكَ ثُمَّ لَا تَجِدُ لَكَ بِهٖ عَلَيْنَا وَكِيْلًا ۞

87. But on account of mercy from your Lord—surely His grace to you is abundant.

اِلَّا رَحْمَةً مِّنْ رَّبِّكَ اِنَّ فَضْلَهٗ كَانَ عَلَيْكَ كَبِيْرًا ۞

88. Say: If men and jinn should combine together to bring the like of this Quran, they could not bring the like of it, though some of them were aiders of others.

قُلْ لَّئِنِ اجْتَمَعَتِ الْاِنْسُ وَالْجِنُّ عَلٰى اَنْ يَّأْتُوْا بِمِثْلِ هٰذَا الْقُرْاٰنِ لَا يَأْتُوْنَ بِمِثْلِهٖ وَلَوْ كَانَ بَعْضُهُمْ لِبَعْضٍ ظَهِيْرًا ۞

89. And certainly We have explained for men in this Quran every kind of similitude, but most men do not consent to aught but denying.

وَلَقَدْ صَرَّفْنَا لِلنَّاسِ فِيْ هٰذَا الْقُرْاٰنِ مِنْ كُلِّ مَثَلٍ فَاَبٰٓى اَكْثَرُ النَّاسِ اِلَّا كُفُوْرًا ۞

90. And they say: We will by no means believe in you until you cause a fountain to gush forth from the earth for us.

وَقَالُوْا لَنْ نُّؤْمِنَ لَكَ حَتّٰى تَفْجُرَ لَنَا مِنَ الْاَرْضِ يَنْبُوْعًا ۞

91. Or you should have a garden of palms and grapes in the midst of which you should cause rivers to flow forth, gushing out.

اَوْ تَكُوْنَ لَكَ جَنَّةٌ مِّنْ نَّخِيْلٍ وَّعِنَبٍ فَتُفَجِّرَ الْاَنْهٰرَ خِلٰلَهَا تَفْجِيْرًا ۞

92. Or you should cause the heaven to come down upon us in pieces as you think, or bring Allah and the angels face to face (with us).

اَوْ تُسْقِطَ السَّمَآءَ كَمَا زَعَمْتَ عَلَيْنَا كِسَفًا اَوْ تَأْتِيَ بِاللّٰهِ وَالْمَلٰٓئِكَةِ قَبِيْلًا ۞

93. Or you should have a house of gold, or you should ascend into heaven, and we will not believe in your ascending until you bring down to us a book which we may read. Say: Glory be to my Lord; am I aught but a mortal apostle?

اَوْ يَكُوْنَ لَكَ بَيْتٌ مِّنْ زُخْرُفٍ اَوْ تَرْقٰى فِى السَّمَآءِ وَلَنْ نُّؤْمِنَ لِرُقِيِّكَ حَتّٰى تُنَزِّلَ عَلَيْنَا كِتٰبًا نَّقْرَؤُهٗ قُلْ سُبْحَانَ رَبِّيْ هَلْ كُنْتُ اِلَّا بَشَرًا رَّسُوْلًا ۞

94. And nothing prevented people from believing when the guidance came to them except that they said: What! has Allah raised up a mortal to be an apostle?

وَمَا مَنَعَ النَّاسَ اَنْ يُّؤْمِنُوْا اِذْ جَآءَهُمُ الْهُدٰٓى اِلَّا اَنْ قَالُوْا اَبَعَثَ اللّٰهُ بَشَرًا رَّسُوْلًا ۞

95. Say: Had there been in the earth angels walking about as settlers, We would certainly have sent down to them from the heaven an angel as an apostle.

قُلْ لَّوْ كَانَ فِى الْاَرْضِ مَلٰٓئِكَةٌ يَّمْشُوْنَ مُطْمَئِنِّيْنَ لَنَزَّلْنَا عَلَيْهِمْ مِّنَ السَّمَآءِ مَلَكًا رَّسُوْلًا ۞

96. Say: Allah suffices as a witness between me and you; surely He is Aware of His servants, Seeing.

قُلْ كَفٰى بِاللّٰهِ شَهِيْدًا بَيْنِيْ وَبَيْنَكُمْ اِنَّهٗ كَانَ بِعِبَادِهٖ خَبِيْرًا بَصِيْرًا ۞

269

97. And whomsoever Allah guides, he is the follower of the right way, and whomsoever He causes to err, you shall not find for him guardians besides Him; and We will gather them together on the day of resurrection on their faces, blind and dumb and deaf; their abode is hell; whenever it becomes allayed We will add to their burning.

ومن يهد الله فهو المهتد ومن يضلل فلن تجد لهم اولياء من دونه ونحشرهم يوم القيمة على وجوههم عميا وبكما وصما مأواهم جهنم كلما خبت زدنهم سعيرا ٩

98. This is their retribution because they disbelieved in Our communications and said: What! when we shall have become bones and decayed particles, shall we then indeed be raised up into a new creation?

ذلك جزاؤهم بانهم كفروا بايتنا وقالوا ءاذا كنا عظاما ورفاتا ءانا لمبعوثون خلقا جديدا ٩

99. Do they not consider that Allah, Who created the heavens and the earth, is able to create their like, and He has appointed for them a doom about which there is no doubt? But the unjust do not consent to aught but denying.

اولم يروا ان الله الذى خلق السموت والارض قادر على ان يخلق مثلهم وجعل لهم اجلا لا ريب فيه فابى الظلمون الا كفورا ٩

100. Say: If you control the treasures of the mercy of my Lord, then you would withhold (them) from fear of spending, and man is niggardly.

قل لو انتم تملكون خزآئن رحمة ربى اذا لامسكتم خشية الانفاق وكان الانسان قتورا ٩

101. And certainly We gave Musa nine clear signs; so ask the children if Israel. When he came to them, Firon said to him: Most surely I deem you, O Musa, to be a man deprived of reason.

ولقد اتينا موسى تسع ايت بينت فسئل بنى اسرآءيل اذ جآءهم فقال له فرعون انى لاظنك يموسى مسحورا ٩

102. He said: Truly you know that none but the Lord of the heavens and the earth has sent down these as clear proof, and most surely I believe you, O Firon, to be given over to perdition.

قال لقد علمت مآ انزل هؤلاء الا رب السموت والارض بصآئر وانى لاظنك يفرعون مثبورا ٩

103. So he desired to destroy them out of the earth, but We drowned him and those with him all together;

فاراد ان يستفزهم من الارض فاغرقنه ومن معه جميعا ٩

104. And We said to the Israelites after him: Dwell in the land: and when the promise of the next life shall come to pass, we will bring you both together in judgment.

وقلنا من بعده لبنى اسرآءيل اسكنوا الارض فاذا جآء وعد الاخرة جئنا بكم لفيفا ٩

105. And with truth have We revealed it, and with truth did it come; and We have not sent you but as the giver of good news and as a warner.

وبالحق انزلنه وبالحق نزل ومآ ارسلنك الا مبشرا ونذيرا ٩

106. And it is a Quran which We have revealed in portions so that you may read it to the people by slow degrees, and We have revealed it, revealing in portions.

107. Say: Believe in it or believe not; surely those who are given the knowledge before it fall down on their faces, making obeisance when it is recited to them.

108. And they say: Glory be to our Lord! most surely the promise of our Lord was to be fulfilled.

109. And they fall down on their faces weeping, and it adds to their humility.

110. Say: Call upon Allah or call upon, the Beneficent God; whichever you call upon, He has the best names; and do not utter your prayer with a very raised voice nor be silent with regard to it, and seek a way between these.

111. And say: (All) praise is due to Allah, Who has not taken a son and Who has not a partner in the kingdom, and Who has not a helper to save Him from disgrace; and proclaim His greatness magnifying (Him).

وَقُرْاٰنًا فَرَقْنٰهُ لِتَقْرَاَهٗ عَلَى النَّاسِ عَلٰى مُكْثٍ وَّ نَزَّلْنٰهُ تَنْزِيْلًا ۝

قُلْ اٰمِنُوْا بِهٖۤ اَوْ لَا تُؤْمِنُوْا ۚ اِنَّ الَّذِيْنَ اُوْتُوا الْعِلْمَ مِنْ قَبْلِهٖۤ اِذَا يُتْلٰى عَلَيْهِمْ يَخِرُّوْنَ لِلْاَذْقَانِ سُجَّدًا ۝

وَّيَقُوْلُوْنَ سُبْحٰنَ رَبِّنَاۤ اِنْ كَانَ وَعْدُ رَبِّنَا لَمَفْعُوْلًا ۝

وَيَخِرُّوْنَ لِلْاَذْقَانِ يَبْكُوْنَ وَيَزِيْدُهُمْ خُشُوْعًا ۝

قُلِ ادْعُوا اللّٰهَ اَوِ ادْعُوا الرَّحْمٰنَ ۚ اَيًّا مَّا تَدْعُوْا فَلَهُ الْاَسْمَآءُ الْحُسْنٰى ۚ وَلَا تَجْهَرْ بِصَلَاتِكَ وَلَا تُخَافِتْ بِهَا وَابْتَغِ بَيْنَ ذٰلِكَ سَبِيْلًا ۝

وَقُلِ الْحَمْدُ لِلّٰهِ الَّذِيْ لَمْ يَتَّخِذْ وَلَدًا وَّلَمْ يَكُنْ لَّهٗ شَرِيْكٌ فِى الْمُلْكِ وَلَمْ يَكُنْ لَّهٗ وَلِيٌّ مِّنَ الذُّلِّ وَكَبِّرْهُ تَكْبِيْرًا ۝

THE CAVE
(KAHF)

أيانها (١٨) سُوْرَةُ الْكَهْفِ مَكِّيَّةٌ رُوْعَانِها

**In the name of Allah,
the Beneficent, the Merciful.**

بِسْمِ اللهِ الرَّحْمٰنِ الرَّحِيْمِ ۝

1. (All) praise is due to Allah, Who revealed the Book to His servant and did not make in it any crookedness.

الْحَمْدُ لِلّٰهِ الَّذِيْٓ اَنْزَلَ عَلٰى عَبْدِهِ الْكِتٰبَ وَلَمْ يَجْعَلْ لَّهٗ عِوَجًا ۜ ۝

2. Rightly directing, that he might give warning of severe punishment from Him and give good news to the believers who do good that they shall have a goodly reward,

قَيِّمًا لِّيُنْذِرَ بَأْسًا شَدِيْدًا مِّنْ لَّدُنْهُ وَيُبَشِّرَ الْمُؤْمِنِيْنَ الَّذِيْنَ يَعْمَلُوْنَ الصّٰلِحٰتِ اَنَّ لَهُمْ اَجْرًا حَسَنًا ۝

3. Staying in it for ever;

مَّاكِثِيْنَ فِيْهِ اَبَدًا ۝

4. And warn those who say: Allah has taken a son.

وَّيُنْذِرَ الَّذِيْنَ قَالُوا اتَّخَذَ اللهُ وَلَدًا ۝

5. They have no knowledge of it, nor had their fathers; a grievous word it is that comes out of their mouths; they speak nothing but a lie.

مَالَهُمْ بِهٖ مِنْ عِلْمٍ وَّلَا لِاٰبَآئِهِمْ كَبُرَتْ كَلِمَةً تَخْرُجُ مِنْ اَفْوَاهِهِمْ اِنْ يَّقُوْلُوْنَ اِلَّا كَذِبًا ۝

6. Then maybe you will kill yourself with grief, sorrowing after them, if they do not believe in this announcement.

فَلَعَلَّكَ بَاخِعٌ نَّفْسَكَ عَلٰٓى اٰثَارِهِمْ اِنْ لَّمْ يُؤْمِنُوْا بِهٰذَا الْحَدِيْثِ اَسَفًا ۝

7. Surely We have made whatever is on the earth an embellishment for it, so that We may try them (as to) which of them is best in works.

اِنَّا جَعَلْنَا مَا عَلَى الْاَرْضِ زِيْنَةً لَّهَا لِنَبْلُوَهُمْ اَيُّهُمْ اَحْسَنُ عَمَلًا ۝

8. And most surely We will make what is on it bare ground without herbage.

وَاِنَّا لَجَاعِلُوْنَ مَا عَلَيْهَا صَعِيْدًا جُرُزًا ۝

9. Or, do you think that the Fellows of the Cave and the Inscription were of Our wonderful signs?

اَمْ حَسِبْتَ اَنَّ اَصْحٰبَ الْكَهْفِ وَالرَّقِيْمِ كَانُوْا مِنْ اٰيٰتِنَا عَجَبًا ۝

10. When the youths sought refuge in the cave, they said: Our Lord! grant us mercy from Thee, and provide for us a right course in our affair.

اِذْ اَوَى الْفِتْيَةُ اِلَى الْكَهْفِ فَقَالُوْا رَبَّنَآ اٰتِنَا مِنْ لَّدُنْكَ رَحْمَةً وَّهَيِّئْ لَنَا مِنْ اَمْرِنَا رَشَدًا ۝

11. So We prevented them from hearing in the cave for a number of years.

12. Then We raised them up that We might know which of the two parties was best able to compute the time for which they remained.

13. We relate to you their story with the truth; surely they were youths who believed in their Lord and We increased them in guidance.

14. And We strengthened their hearts with patience, when they stood up and said: Our Lord is the Lord of the heavens and the earth; we will by no means call upon any god besides Him, for then indeed we should have said an extravagant thing.

15. These our people have taken gods besides Him; why do they not produce any clear authority in their support? Who is then more unjust than he who forges a lie against Allah?

16. And when you forsake them and what they worship save Allah, betake yourselves for refuge to the cave; your Lord will extend to you largely of His mercy and provide for you a profitable course in your affair.

17. And you might see the sun when it rose, decline from their cave towards the right hand, and when it set, leave them behind on the left while they were in a wide space thereof. This is of the signs of Allah; whomsoever Allah guides, he is the rightly guided one, and whomsoever He causes to err, you shall not find for him any friend to lead (him) aright.

18. And you might think them awake while they were asleep, and We turned them about to the right and to the left, while their dog (lay) outstretching its paws at the entrance; if you looked at them you would certainly turn back from them in flight, and you would certainly be filled with awe because of them.

فَضَرَبْنَا عَلَىٰٓ اٰذَانِهِمْ فِى الْكَهْفِ سِنِيْنَ عَدَدًا ۞

ثُمَّ بَعَثْنٰهُمْ لِنَعْلَمَ اَىُّ الْحِزْبَيْنِ اَحْصٰى لِمَا لَبِثُوْٓا اَمَدًا ۞

نَحْنُ نَقُصُّ عَلَيْكَ نَبَاَهُمْ بِالْحَقِّ ؕ اِنَّهُمْ فِتْيَةٌ اٰمَنُوْا بِرَبِّهِمْ وَزِدْنٰهُمْ هُدًى ۞

وَّرَبَطْنَا عَلٰى قُلُوْبِهِمْ اِذْ قَامُوْا فَقَالُوْا رَبُّنَا رَبُّ السَّمٰوٰتِ وَالْاَرْضِ لَنْ نَّدْعُوَا۟ مِنْ دُوْنِهٖٓ اِلٰهًا لَّقَدْ قُلْنَآ اِذًا شَطَطًا ۞

هٰٓؤُلَآءِ قَوْمُنَا اتَّخَذُوْا مِنْ دُوْنِهٖٓ اٰلِهَةً ؕ لَوْلَا يَاْتُوْنَ عَلَيْهِمْ بِسُلْطٰنٍ بَيِّنٍ ؕ فَمَنْ اَظْلَمُ مِمَّنِ افْتَرٰى عَلَى اللّٰهِ كَذِبًا ۞

وَاِذِ اعْتَزَلْتُمُوْهُمْ وَمَا يَعْبُدُوْنَ اِلَّا اللّٰهَ فَاْوٗٓا اِلَى الْكَهْفِ يَنْشُرْ لَكُمْ رَبُّكُمْ مِنْ رَّحْمَتِهٖ وَيُهَيِّئْ لَكُمْ مِنْ اَمْرِكُمْ مِّرْفَقًا ۞

وَتَرَى الشَّمْسَ اِذَا طَلَعَتْ تَّزٰوَرُ عَنْ كَهْفِهِمْ ذَاتَ الْيَمِيْنِ وَاِذَا غَرَبَتْ تَّقْرِضُهُمْ ذَاتَ الشِّمَالِ وَهُمْ فِيْ فَجْوَةٍ مِّنْهُ ؕ ذٰلِكَ مِنْ اٰيٰتِ اللّٰهِ ؕ مَنْ يَّهْدِ اللّٰهُ فَهُوَ الْمُهْتَدِ ۚ وَمَنْ يُّضْلِلْ فَلَنْ تَجِدَ لَهٗ وَلِيًّا مُّرْشِدًا ۞

وَتَحْسَبُهُمْ اَيْقَاظًا وَّهُمْ رُقُوْدٌ ۖ وَّنُقَلِّبُهُمْ ذَاتَ الْيَمِيْنِ وَذَاتَ الشِّمَالِ ۖ وَكَلْبُهُمْ بَاسِطٌ ذِرَاعَيْهِ بِالْوَصِيْدِ ؕ لَوِ اطَّلَعْتَ عَلَيْهِمْ لَوَلَّيْتَ مِنْهُمْ فِرَارًا وَّلَمُلِئْتَ مِنْهُمْ رُعْبًا ۞

19. And thus did We rouse them that they might question each other. A speaker among them said: How long have you tarried? They said: We have tarried for a day or a part of a day. (Others) said: Your Lord knows best how long you have tarried. Now send one of you with this silver (coin) of yours to the city, then let him see which of them has purest food, so let him bring you provision from it, and let him behave with gentleness, and by no means make your case known to any one:

وَكَذٰلِكَ بَعَثْنٰهُمْ لِيَتَسَاءَلُوْا بَيْنَهُمْ قَالَ قَآئِلٌ مِّنْهُمْ
كَمْ لَبِثْتُمْ قَالُوْا لَبِثْنَا يَوْمًا اَوْ بَعْضَ يَوْمٍ قَالُوْا
رَبُّكُمْ اَعْلَمُ بِمَا لَبِثْتُمْ فَابْعَثُوْا اَحَدَكُمْ بِوَرِقِكُمْ
هٰذِهٖ اِلَى الْمَدِيْنَةِ فَلْيَنْظُرْ اَيُّهَا اَزْكٰى طَعَامًا
فَلْيَأْتِكُمْ بِرِزْقٍ مِّنْهُ وَلْيَتَلَطَّفْ وَلَا يُشْعِرَنَّ
بِكُمْ اَحَدًا ۝

20. For surely if they prevail against you they would stone you to death or force you back to their religion, and then you will never succeed.

اِنَّهُمْ اِنْ يَّظْهَرُوْا عَلَيْكُمْ يَرْجُمُوْكُمْ اَوْ يُعِيْدُوْكُمْ
فِيْ مِلَّتِهِمْ وَلَنْ تُفْلِحُوْا اِذًا اَبَدًا ۝

21. And thus did We make (men) to get knowledge of them, that they might know that Allah's promise is true and that as for the hour there is no doubt about it. When they disputed among themselves about their affair and said: Erect an edifice over them—their Lord best knows them. Those who prevailed in their affair said: We will certainly raise a masjid over them.

وَكَذٰلِكَ اَعْثَرْنَا عَلَيْهِمْ لِيَعْلَمُوْا اَنَّ وَعْدَ اللّٰهِ
حَقٌّ وَّاَنَّ السَّاعَةَ لَا رَيْبَ فِيْهَا اِذْ يَتَنَازَعُوْنَ
بَيْنَهُمْ اَمْرَهُمْ فَقَالُوا ابْنُوْا عَلَيْهِمْ بُنْيَانًا رَبُّهُمْ
اَعْلَمُ بِهِمْ قَالَ الَّذِيْنَ غَلَبُوْا عَلٰى اَمْرِهِمْ لَنَتَّخِذَنَّ
عَلَيْهِمْ مَّسْجِدًا ۝

22. (Some) say: (They are) three, the fourth of them being their dog; and (others) say: Five, the sixth of them being their dog, making conjectures at what is unknown; and (others yet) say: Seven, and the eighth of them is their dog. Say: My Lord best knows their number, none knows them but a few; therefore contend not in the matter of them but with an outward contention, and do not question concerning them any of them.

سَيَقُوْلُوْنَ ثَلٰثَةٌ رَّابِعُهُمْ كَلْبُهُمْ وَيَقُوْلُوْنَ خَمْسَةٌ
سَادِسُهُمْ كَلْبُهُمْ رَجْمًا بِالْغَيْبِ وَيَقُوْلُوْنَ
سَبْعَةٌ وَّثَامِنُهُمْ كَلْبُهُمْ قُلْ رَّبِّيْ اَعْلَمُ
بِعِدَّتِهِمْ مَّا يَعْلَمُهُمْ اِلَّا قَلِيْلٌ فَلَا تُمَارِ
فِيْهِمْ اِلَّا مِرَاءً ظَاهِرًا وَّلَا تَسْتَفْتِ فِيْهِمْ
مِّنْهُمْ اَحَدًا ۝

23. And do not say of anything: Surely I will do it tomorrow,

وَلَا تَقُوْلَنَّ لِشَايْءٍ اِنِّيْ فَاعِلٌ ذٰلِكَ غَدًا ۝

24. Unless Allah pleases; and remember your Lord when you forget and say: Maybe my Lord will guide me to a nearer course to the right than this.

اِلَّا اَنْ يَّشَاءَ اللّٰهُ وَاذْكُرْ رَّبَّكَ اِذَا نَسِيْتَ وَقُلْ
عَسٰى اَنْ يَّهْدِيَنِ رَبِّيْ لِاَقْرَبَ مِنْ هٰذَا رَشَدًا ۝

25. And they remained in their cave three hundred years and (some) add (another) nine.

26. Say: Allah knows best how long they remained; to Him are (known) the unseen things of the heavens and the earth; how clear His sight and how clear His hearing! There is none to be a guardian for them besides Him, and He does not make any one His associate in His Judgment.

27. And recite what has been revealed to you of the Book of your Lord; there is none who can alter His words; and you shall not find any refuge besides Him.

28. And withhold yourself with those who call on their Lord morning and evening desiring His goodwill, and let not your eyes pass from them, desiring the beauties of this world's life; and do not follow him whose heart We have made unmindful to Our remembrance, and he follows his low desires and his case is one in which due bounds are exceeded.

29. And say: The truth is from your Lord, so let him who please believe, and let him who please disbelieve; surely We have prepared for the iniquitous a fire, the curtains of which shall encompass them about; and if they cry for water, they shall be given water like molten brass which will scald their faces; evil the drink and ill the resting place.

30. Surely (as for) those who believe and do good, We do not waste the reward of him who does a good work.

31. These it is for whom are gardens of perpetuity beneath which rivers flow; ornaments shall be given to them therein of bracelets of gold, and they shall wear green robes of fine silk and thick silk brocade interwoven with gold, reclining therein on raised couches; excellent the recompense and goodly the resting place.

32. And set forth to them a parable of two men; for one of them We made two gardens of grape vines, and We surrounded them both with palms, and in the midst of them We made cornfields.

واضْرِبْ لَهُمْ مَثَلاً رَّجُلَيْنِ جَعَلْنَا لِاَحَدِهِمَا جَنَّتَيْنِ مِنْ اَعْنَابٍ وَّحَفَفْنٰهُمَا بِنَخْلٍ وَّجَعَلْنَا بَيْنَهُمَا زَرْعًا ۞

33. Both these gardens yielded their fruits, and failed not aught thereof, and We caused a river to gush forth in their midst,

كِلْتَا الْجَنَّتَيْنِ اٰتَتْ اُكُلَهَا وَلَمْ تَظْلِمْ مِّنْهُ شَيْئًا ۙ وَّفَجَّرْنَا خِلٰلَهُمَا نَهَرًا ۞

34. And he possessed much wealth; so he said to his companion, while he disputed with him: I have greater wealth than you, and am mightier in followers.

وَّكَانَ لَهٗ ثَمَرٌ ۚ فَقَالَ لِصَاحِبِهٖ وَهُوَ يُحَاوِرُهٗ اَنَا اَكْثَرُ مِنْكَ مَالاً وَّاَعَزُّ نَفَرًا ۞

35. And he entered his garden while he was unjust to himself. He said: I do not think that this will ever perish,

وَدَخَلَ جَنَّتَهٗ وَهُوَ ظَالِمٌ لِّنَفْسِهٖ ۚ قَالَ مَآ اَظُنُّ اَنْ تَبِيْدَ هٰذِهٖ اَبَدًا ۞

36. And I do not think the hour will come, and even if I am returned to my Lord I will most certainly find a returning place better than this.

وَّمَآ اَظُنُّ السَّاعَةَ قَآئِمَةً ۙ وَّلَئِنْ رُّدِدْتُّ اِلٰى رَبِّيْ لَاَجِدَنَّ خَيْرًا مِّنْهَا مُنْقَلَبًا ۞

37. His companion said to him while disputing with him: Do you disbelieve in Him Who created you from dust, then from a small seed, then He made you a perfect man?

قَالَ لَهٗ صَاحِبُهٗ وَهُوَ يُحَاوِرُهٗۤ اَكَفَرْتَ بِالَّذِيْ خَلَقَكَ مِنْ تُرَابٍ ثُمَّ مِنْ نُّطْفَةٍ ثُمَّ سَوّٰىكَ رَجُلاً ۞

38. But as for me, He, Allah, is my Lord, and I do not associate anyone with my Lord.

لٰكِنَّا هُوَ اللهُ رَبِّيْ وَلَاۤ اُشْرِكُ بِرَبِّيْۤ اَحَدًا ۞

39. And wherefore did you not say when you entered your garden: It is as Allah has pleased, there is no power save in Allah? If you consider me to be inferior to you in wealth and children,

وَلَوْلَاۤ اِذْ دَخَلْتَ جَنَّتَكَ قُلْتَ مَا شَآءَ اللهُ ۙ لَا قُوَّةَ اِلَّا بِاللهِ ۚ اِنْ تَرَنِ اَنَا اَقَلَّ مِنْكَ مَالاً وَّوَلَدًا ۞

40. Then maybe my Lord will give me what is better than your garden, and send of it a thunderbolt from heaven so that it shall become even ground without plant,

فَعَسٰى رَبِّيْۤ اَنْ يُّؤْتِيَنِ خَيْرًا مِّنْ جَنَّتِكَ وَيُرْسِلَ عَلَيْهَا حُسْبَانًا مِّنَ السَّمَآءِ فَتُصْبِحَ صَعِيْدًا زَلَقًا ۞

41. Or its waters should sink down into the ground so that you are unable to find it.

أَوۡ يُصۡبِحَ مَآؤُهَا غَوۡرًا فَلَنۡ تَسۡتَطِيعَ لَهُ طَلَبًا ۝

42. And his wealth was destroyed; so he began to wring his hands for what he had spent on it, while it lay, having fallen down upon its roofs, and he said: Ah me! would that I had not associated anyone with my Lord.

وَأُحِيطَ بِثَمَرِهِ فَأَصۡبَحَ يُقَلِّبُ كَفَّيۡهِ عَلَىٰ مَا أَنۡفَقَ فِيهَا وَهِيَ خَاوِيَةٌ عَلَىٰ عُرُوشِهَا وَيَقُولُ يٰلَيۡتَنِي لَمۡ أُشۡرِكۡ بِرَبِّي أَحَدًا ۝

43. And he had no host to help him besides Allah nor could he defend himself.

وَلَمۡ تَكُنۡ لَهُ فِئَةٌ يَنۡصُرُونَهُ مِنۡ دُونِ اللهِ وَمَا كَانَ مُنۡتَصِرًا ۝

44. Here is protection only Allah's, the True One; He is best in (the giving of) reward and best in requiting.

هُنَالِكَ الۡوَلَايَةُ لِلّٰهِ الۡحَقِّ هُوَ خَيۡرٌ ثَوَابًا وَخَيۡرٌ عُقۡبًا ۝

45. And set forth to them parable of the life of this world: like water which We send down from the cloud so the herbage of the earth becomes tangled on account of it, then it becomes dry, broken into pieces which the winds scatter; and Allah is the holder of power over all things.

وَاضۡرِبۡ لَهُمۡ مَثَلَ الۡحَيٰوةِ الدُّنۡيَا كَمَآءٍ أَنۡزَلۡنٰهُ مِنَ السَّمَآءِ فَاخۡتَلَطَ بِهِ نَبَاتُ الۡأَرۡضِ فَأَصۡبَحَ هَشِيمًا تَذۡرُوهُ الرِّيَاحُ وَكَانَ اللهُ عَلَىٰ كُلِّ شَيۡءٍ مُقۡتَدِرًا ۝

46. Wealth and children are an adornment of the life of this world; and the ever-abiding, the good works, are better with your Lord in reward and better in expectation.

الۡمَالُ وَالۡبَنُونَ زِينَةُ الۡحَيٰوةِ الدُّنۡيَا وَالۡبَاقِيٰتُ الصّٰلِحٰتُ خَيۡرٌ عِنۡدَ رَبِّكَ ثَوَابًا وَخَيۡرٌ أَمَلًا ۝

47. And the day on which We will cause the mountains to pass away and you will see the earth a levelled plain and We will gather them and leave not any one of them behind.

وَيَوۡمَ نُسَيِّرُ الۡجِبَالَ وَتَرَى الۡأَرۡضَ بَارِزَةً وَحَشَرۡنٰهُمۡ فَلَمۡ نُغَادِرۡ مِنۡهُمۡ أَحَدًا ۝

48. And they shall be brought before your Lord, standing in ranks: Now certainly you have come to Us as We created you at first. Nay, you thought that We had not appointed to you a time of the fulfillment of the promise.

وَعُرِضُوا عَلَىٰ رَبِّكَ صَفًّا لَقَدۡ جِئۡتُمُونَا كَمَا خَلَقۡنٰكُمۡ أَوَّلَ مَرَّةٍ بَلۡ زَعَمۡتُمۡ أَلَّنۡ نَجۡعَلَ لَكُمۡ مَوۡعِدًا ۝

49. And the Book shall be placed, then you will see the guilty fearing from what is in it, and they will say: Ah! woe to us! what a book is this! it does not omit a small one nor a great one, but numbers them (all); and what they had done they shall find present (there); and your Lord does not deal unjustly with anyone.

وَوُضِعَ الۡكِتٰبُ فَتَرَى الۡمُجۡرِمِينَ مُشۡفِقِينَ مِمَّا فِيهِ وَيَقُولُونَ يٰوَيۡلَتَنَا مَالِ هٰذَا الۡكِتٰبِ لَا يُغَادِرُ صَغِيرَةً وَلَا كَبِيرَةً إِلَّا أَحۡصٰهَا وَوَجَدُوا مَا عَمِلُوا حَاضِرًا وَلَا يَظۡلِمُ رَبُّكَ أَحَدًا ۝

50. And when We said to the angels: Make obeisance to Adam; they made obeisance but Iblis (did it not). He was of the jinn, so he transgressed the commandment of his Lord. What! would you then take him and his offspring for friends rather than Me, and they are your enemies? Evil is (this) change for the unjust.

51. I did not make them witnesses of the creation of the heavens and the earth, nor of the creation of their own souls; nor could I take those who lead (others) astray for aiders.

52. And on the day when He shall say: Call on those whom you considered to be My associates. So they shall call on them, but they shall not answer them, and We will cause a separation between them.

53. And the guilty shall see the fire, then they shall know that they are going to fall into it, and they shall not find a place to which to turn away from it.

54. And certainly We have explained in this Quran every kind of example; and man is most of all given to contention.

55. And nothing prevents men from believing when the guidance comes to them, and from asking forgiveness of their Lord, except that what happened to the ancients should overtake them, or that the chastisement should come face to face with them.

56. And We do not send apostles but as givers of good news and warning, and those who disbelieve make a false contention that they may render null thereby the truth, and they take My communications and that with which they are warned for a mockery.

57. And who is more unjust than he who is reminded of the communications of his Lord, then he turns away from them and forgets what his two hands have sent before? Surely We have placed veils over their hearts lest they should understand it and a heaviness in their ears; and if you call them to the guidance, they will not ever follow the right course in that case.

58. And your Lord is Forgiving, the Lord of Mercy; were He to punish them for what they earn, He would certainly have hastened the chastisement for them; but for them there is an appointed time from which they shall not find a refuge.

وَرَبُّكَ الْغَفُوْرُ ذُو الرَّحْمَةِ لَوْ يُؤَاخِذُهُمْ بِمَا كَسَبُوْا لَعَجَّلَ لَهُمُ الْعَذَابَ بَلْ لَّهُمْ مَّوْعِدٌ لَّنْ يَّجِدُوْا مِنْ دُوْنِهِ مَوْئِلًا ۝

59. And (as for) these towns, We destroyed them when they acted unjustly, and We have appointed a time for their destruction.

وَتِلْكَ الْقُرٰٓى اَهْلَكْنٰهُمْ لَمَّا ظَلَمُوْا وَجَعَلْنَا لِمَهْلِكِهِمْ مَّوْعِدًا ۝

60. And when Musa said to his servant: I will not cease until I reach the junction of the two rivers or I will go on for years.

وَاِذْ قَالَ مُوْسٰى لِفَتٰىهُ لَاۤ اَبْرَحُ حَتّٰٓى اَبْلُغَ مَجْمَعَ الْبَحْرَيْنِ اَوْ اَمْضِيَ حُقُبًا ۝

61. So when they had reached the junction of the two (rivers), they forgot their fish, and it took its way into the sea, going away.

فَلَمَّا بَلَغَا مَجْمَعَ بَيْنِهِمَا نَسِيَا حُوْتَهُمَا فَاتَّخَذَ سَبِيْلَهُ فِى الْبَحْرِ سَرَبًا ۝

62. But when they had gone farther, he said to his servant: Bring to us our morning meal, certainly we have met with fatigue from this our journey.

فَلَمَّا جَاوَزَا قَالَ لِفَتٰىهُ اٰتِنَا غَدَآءَنَا ۙ لَقَدْ لَقِيْنَا مِنْ سَفَرِنَا هٰذَا نَصَبًا ۝

63. He said: Did you see when we took refuge on the rock, then I forgot the fish, and nothing made me forget to speak of it but the Shaitan, and it took its way into the river; what a wonder!

قَالَ اَرَءَيْتَ اِذْ اَوَيْنَاۤ اِلَى الصَّخْرَةِ فَاِنِّىْ نَسِيْتُ الْحُوْتَ ۫ وَمَاۤ اَنْسٰنِيْهُ اِلَّا الشَّيْطٰنُ اَنْ اَذْكُرَهُ ۚ وَاتَّخَذَ سَبِيْلَهُ فِى الْبَحْرِ ۖ عَجَبًا ۝

64. He said: This is what we sought for; so they returned retracing their footsteps.

قَالَ ذٰلِكَ مَا كُنَّا نَبْغِ ۫ فَارْتَدَّا عَلٰۤى اٰثَارِهِمَا قَصَصًا ۝

65. Then they found one from among Our servants whom We had granted mercy from Us and whom We had taught knowledge from Ourselves.

فَوَجَدَا عَبْدًا مِّنْ عِبَادِنَاۤ اٰتَيْنٰهُ رَحْمَةً مِّنْ عِنْدِنَا وَعَلَّمْنٰهُ مِنْ لَّدُنَّا عِلْمًا ۝

66. Musa said to him: Shall I follow you on condition that you should teach me right knowledge of what you have been taught?

قَالَ لَهُ مُوْسٰى هَلْ اَتَّبِعُكَ عَلٰۤى اَنْ تُعَلِّمَنِ مِمَّا عُلِّمْتَ رُشْدًا ۝

67. He said: Surely you cannot have patience with me:

قَالَ اِنَّكَ لَنْ تَسْتَطِيْعَ مَعِىَ صَبْرًا ۝

68. And how can you have patience in that of which you have not got a comprehensive knowledge?

وَكَيْفَ تَصْبِرُ عَلٰى مَا لَمْ تُحِطْ بِهٖ خُبْرًا ۝

69. He said: If Allah pleases, you will find me patient and I shall not disobey you in any matter.

70. He said: If you would follow me, then do not question me about any thing until I myself speak to you about it.

71. So they went (their way) until when they embarked in the boat he made a hole in it. (Musa said): Have you made a hole in it to drown its inmates? Certainly you have done a grievous thing.

72. He said: Did I not say that you will not be able to have patience with me?

73. He said: Blame me not for what I forgot, and do not constrain me to a difficult thing in my affair.

74. So they went on until, when they met a boy, he slew him. (Musa said): Have you slain an innocent person otherwise than for manslaughter? Certainly you have done an evil thing.

75. He said: Did I not say to you that you will not be able to have patience with me?

76. He said: If I ask you about anything after this, keep me not in your company; indeed you shall have (then) found an excuse in my case.

77. So they went on until when they came to the people of a town, they asked them for food, but they refused to entertain them as guests. Then they found in it a wall which was on the point of falling, so he put it into a right state. (Musa said): If you had pleased, you might certainly have taken a recompense for it.

78. He said: This shall be separation between me and you; now I will inform you of the significance of that with which you could not have patience.

قَالَ سَتَجِدُنِيْۤ اِنْ شَآءَ اللّٰهُ صَابِرًا وَّلَاۤ اَعْصِیْ لَكَ اَمْرًا ۞

قَالَ فَاِنِ اتَّبَعْتَنِیْ فَلَا تَسْـَٔلْنِیْ عَنْ شَیْءٍ حَتّٰۤی اُحْدِثَ لَكَ مِنْهُ ذِكْرًا ۞

فَانْطَلَقَا ٮحَتّٰۤی اِذَا رَكِبَا فِی السَّفِیْنَةِ خَرَقَهَا ۖ قَالَ اَخَرَقْتَهَا لِتُغْرِقَ اَهْلَهَا ۚ لَقَدْ جِئْتَ شَیْئًا اِمْرًا ۞

قَالَ اَلَمْ اَقُلْ اِنَّكَ لَنْ تَسْتَطِیْعَ مَعِیَ صَبْرًا ۞

قَالَ لَا تُؤَاخِذْنِیْ بِمَا نَسِیْتُ وَلَا تُرْهِقْنِیْ مِنْ اَمْرِیْ عُسْرًا ۞

فَانْطَلَقَا ٮحَتّٰۤی اِذَا لَقِیَا غُلٰمًا فَقَتَلَهٗ ۙ قَالَ اَقَتَلْتَ نَفْسًا زَكِیَّةً ۢ بِغَیْرِ نَفْسٍ ؕ لَقَدْ جِئْتَ شَیْئًا نُّكْرًا ۞

قَالَ اَلَمْ اَقُلْ لَّكَ اِنَّكَ لَنْ تَسْتَطِیْعَ مَعِیَ صَبْرًا ۞

قَالَ اِنْ سَاَلْتُكَ عَنْ شَیْءٍ ۢ بَعْدَهَا فَلَا تُصٰحِبْنِیْ ۚ قَدْ بَلَغْتَ مِنْ لَّدُنِّیْ عُذْرًا ۞

فَانْطَلَقَا ٮحَتّٰۤی اِذَاۤ اَتَیَاۤ اَهْلَ قَرْیَةِ ۨ اسْتَطْعَمَاۤ اَهْلَهَا فَاَبَوْا اَنْ یُّضَیِّفُوْهُمَا فَوَجَدَا فِیْهَا جِدَارًا یُّرِیْدُ اَنْ یَّنْقَضَّ فَاَقَامَهٗ ؕ قَالَ لَوْ شِئْتَ لَتَّخَذْتَ عَلَیْهِ اَجْرًا ۞

قَالَ هٰذَا فِرَاقُ بَیْنِیْ وَبَیْنِكَ ۚ سَاُنَبِّئُكَ بِتَاْوِیْلِ مَا لَمْ تَسْتَطِعْ عَّلَیْهِ صَبْرًا ۞

79. As for the boat, it belonged to (some) poor men who worked on the river and I wished that I should damage it, and there was behind them a king who seized every boat by force.

اَمَّا السَّفِيْنَةُ فَكَانَتْ لِمَسٰكِيْنَ يَعْمَلُوْنَ فِى الْبَحْرِ فَاَرَدْتُّ اَنْ اَعِيْبَهَا وَكَانَ وَرَآءَهُمْ مَّلِكٌ يَّاْخُذُ كُلَّ سَفِيْنَةٍ غَصْبًا ۝

80. And as for the boy, his parents were believers and we feared lest he should make disobedience and ingratitude to come upon them:

وَاَمَّا الْغُلٰمُ فَكَانَ اَبَوٰهُ مُؤْمِنَيْنِ فَخَشِيْنَاۤ اَنْ يُّرْهِقَهُمَا طُغْيَانًا وَّكُفْرًا ۝

81. So we desired that their Lord might give them in his place one better than him in purity and nearer to having compassion.

فَاَرَدْنَاۤ اَنْ يُّبْدِلَهُمَا رَبُّهُمَا خَيْرًا مِّنْهُ زَكٰوةً وَّاَقْرَبَ رُحْمًا ۝

82. And as for the wall, it belonged to two orphan boys in the city, and there was beneath it a treasure belonging to them, and their father was a righteous man; so your Lord desired that they should attain their maturity and take out their treasure, a mercy from your Lord, and I did not do it of my own accord. This is the significance of that with which you could not have patience.

وَاَمَّا الْجِدَارُ فَكَانَ لِغُلٰمَيْنِ يَتِيْمَيْنِ فِى الْمَدِيْنَةِ وَكَانَ تَحْتَهُ كَنْزٌ لَّهُمَا وَكَانَ اَبُوْهُمَا صَالِحًا ۚ فَاَرَادَ رَبُّكَ اَنْ يَّبْلُغَاۤ اَشُدَّهُمَا وَيَسْتَخْرِجَا كَنْزَهُمَا ۖ رَحْمَةً مِّنْ رَّبِّكَ ۚ وَمَا فَعَلْتُهُ عَنْ اَمْرِيْ ۚ ذٰلِكَ تَأْوِيْلُ مَا لَمْ تَسْطِعْ عَّلَيْهِ صَبْرًا ۝

83. And they ask you about Zulqarnain, Say: I will recite to you an account of him.

وَيَسْئَلُوْنَكَ عَنْ ذِى الْقَرْنَيْنِ ۚ قُلْ سَاَتْلُوْا عَلَيْكُمْ مِّنْهُ ذِكْرًا ۝

84. Surely We established him in the land and granted him means of access to every thing,

اِنَّا مَكَّنَّا لَهُ فِى الْاَرْضِ وَاٰتَيْنٰهُ مِنْ كُلِّ شَيْءٍ سَبَبًا ۝

85. So he followed a course.

فَاَتْبَعَ سَبَبًا ۝

86. Until when he reached the place where the sun set, he found it going down into a black sea, and found by it a people. We said: O Zulqarnain! either give them a chastisement or do them a benefit.

حَتّٰۤى اِذَا بَلَغَ مَغْرِبَ الشَّمْسِ وَجَدَهَا تَغْرُبُ فِىْ عَيْنٍ حَمِئَةٍ وَّوَجَدَ عِنْدَهَا قَوْمًا ۚ قُلْنَا يٰذَا الْقَرْنَيْنِ اِمَّاۤ اَنْ تُعَذِّبَ وَاِمَّاۤ اَنْ تَتَّخِذَ فِيْهِمْ حُسْنًا ۝

281

87. He said: As to him who is injust, we will chastise him, then shall he be returned to his Lord, and He will chastise him with an exemplary chastisement:

88. And as for him who believes and does good, he shall have goodly reward, and We will speak to him an easy word of Our command.

89. Then he followed (another) course.

90. Until when he reached the land of the rising of the sun, he found it rising on a people to whom We had given no shelter from it;

91. Even so! and We had a full knowledge of what he had.

92. Then he followed (another) course.

93. Until when he reached (a place) between the two mountains, he found on that side of them a people who could hardly understand a word.

94. They said: O Zulqarnain! surely Gog and Magog make mischief in the land. Shall we then pay you a tribute on condition that you should raise a barrier between us and them.

95. He said: That in which my Lord has established me is better, therefore you only help me with workers, I will make a fortified barrier between you and them;

96. Bring me blocks of iron; until when he had filled up the space between the two mountain sides, he said: Blow; until when he had made it (as) fire, he said: Bring me molten brass which I may pour over it.

97. So they were not able to scale it nor could they make a hole in it.

قَالَ اَمَّا مَنْ ظَلَمَ فَسَوْفَ نُعَذِّبُهٗ ثُمَّ يُرَدُّ اِلٰى رَبِّهٖ فَيُعَذِّبُهٗ عَذَابًا نُّكْرًا ۞

وَاَمَّا مَنْ اٰمَنَ وَعَمِلَ صَالِحًا فَلَهٗ جَزَآءَ ۨالْحُسْنٰى ۚ وَسَنَقُوْلُ لَهٗ مِنْ اَمْرِنَا يُسْرًا ۞

ثُمَّ اَتْبَعَ سَبَبًا ۞

حَتّٰى اِذَا بَلَغَ مَطْلِعَ الشَّمْسِ وَجَدَهَا تَطْلُعُ عَلٰى قَوْمٍ لَّمْ نَجْعَلْ لَّهُمْ مِّنْ دُوْنِهَا سِتْرًا ۞

كَذٰلِكَ ۚ وَقَدْ اَحَطْنَا بِمَا لَدَيْهِ خُبْرًا ۞

ثُمَّ اَتْبَعَ سَبَبًا ۞

حَتّٰى اِذَا بَلَغَ بَيْنَ السَّدَّيْنِ وَجَدَ مِنْ دُوْنِهِمَا قَوْمًا لَّا يَكَادُوْنَ يَفْقَهُوْنَ قَوْلًا ۞

قَالُوْا يٰذَا الْقَرْنَيْنِ اِنَّ يَأْجُوْجَ وَمَأْجُوْجَ مُفْسِدُوْنَ فِى الْاَرْضِ فَهَلْ نَجْعَلُ لَكَ خَرْجًا عَلٰى اَنْ تَجْعَلَ بَيْنَنَا وَبَيْنَهُمْ سَدًّا ۞

قَالَ مَا مَكَّنِّيْ فِيْهِ رَبِّيْ خَيْرٌ فَاَعِيْنُوْنِيْ بِقُوَّةٍ اَجْعَلْ بَيْنَكُمْ وَبَيْنَهُمْ رَدْمًا ۞

اٰتُوْنِيْ زُبَرَ الْحَدِيْدِ ۚ حَتّٰى اِذَا سَاوٰى بَيْنَ الصَّدَفَيْنِ قَالَ انْفُخُوْا ۚ حَتّٰى اِذَا جَعَلَهٗ نَارًا ۙ قَالَ اٰتُوْنِيْ اُفْرِغْ عَلَيْهِ قِطْرًا ۞

فَمَا اسْطَاعُوْا اَنْ يَّظْهَرُوْهُ وَمَا اسْتَطَاعُوْا لَهٗ نَقْبًا ۞

98. He said: This is a mercy from my Lord, but when the promise of my Lord comes to pass He will make it level with the ground, and the promise of my Lord is ever true.

قَالَ هٰذَا رَحْمَةٌ مِّنْ رَّبِّيْ ۚ فَاِذَا جَآءَ وَعْدُ رَبِّيْ جَعَلَهٗ دَكَّآءَ ۚ وَكَانَ وَعْدُ رَبِّيْ حَقًّا ۝

99. And on that day We will leave a part of them in conflict with another part, and the trumpet will be blown, so We will gather them all together;

وَتَرَكْنَا بَعْضَهُمْ يَوْمَئِذٍ يَّمُوْجُ فِيْ بَعْضٍ وَّنُفِخَ فِي الصُّوْرِ فَجَمَعْنٰهُمْ جَمْعًا ۝

100. And We will bring forth hell, exposed to view, on that day before the unbelievers.

وَّعَرَضْنَا جَهَنَّمَ يَوْمَئِذٍ لِّلْكٰفِرِيْنَ عَرْضًا ۝

101. They whose eyes were under a cover from My reminder, and they could not even hear.

اِلَّذِيْنَ كَانَتْ اَعْيُنُهُمْ فِيْ غِطَآءٍ عَنْ ذِكْرِيْ وَكَانُوْا لَا يَسْتَطِيْعُوْنَ سَمْعًا ۝

102. What! do then those who disbelieve think that they can take My servants to be guardians besides Me? Surely We have prepared hell for the entertainment of the unbelievers.

اَفَحَسِبَ الَّذِيْنَ كَفَرُوْا اَنْ يَّتَّخِذُوْا عِبَادِيْ مِنْ دُوْنِيْ اَوْلِيَآءَ ۚ اِنَّا اَعْتَدْنَا جَهَنَّمَ لِلْكٰفِرِيْنَ نُزُلًا ۝

103. Say: Shall We inform you of the greatest losers in (their) deeds?

قُلْ هَلْ نُنَبِّئُكُمْ بِالْاَخْسَرِيْنَ اَعْمَالًا ۝

104. (These are) they whose labor is lost in this world's life and they think that they are well versed in skill of the work of hands.

اَلَّذِيْنَ ضَلَّ سَعْيُهُمْ فِي الْحَيٰوةِ الدُّنْيَا وَهُمْ يَحْسَبُوْنَ اَنَّهُمْ يُحْسِنُوْنَ صُنْعًا ۝

105. These are they who disbelieve in the communications of their Lord and His meeting, so their deeds become null, and therefore We will not set up a balance for them on the day of resurrection.

اُولٰٓئِكَ الَّذِيْنَ كَفَرُوْا بِاٰيٰتِ رَبِّهِمْ وَلِقَآئِهٖ فَحَبِطَتْ اَعْمَالُهُمْ فَلَا نُقِيْمُ لَهُمْ يَوْمَ الْقِيٰمَةِ وَزْنًا ۝

106. Thus it is that their recompense is hell, because they disbelieved and held My communications and My apostles in mockery.

ذٰلِكَ جَزَآؤُهُمْ جَهَنَّمُ بِمَا كَفَرُوْا وَاتَّخَذُوْا اٰيٰتِيْ وَرُسُلِيْ هُزُوًا ۝

107. Surely (as for) those who believe and do good deeds, their place of entertainment shall be the gardens of paradise,

اِنَّ الَّذِيْنَ اٰمَنُوْا وَعَمِلُوا الصّٰلِحٰتِ كَانَتْ لَهُمْ جَنّٰتُ الْفِرْدَوْسِ نُزُلًا ۝

108. Abiding therein; they shall not desire removal from them.

خٰلِدِيْنَ فِيْهَا لَا يَبْغُوْنَ عَنْهَا حِوَلًا ۝

109. Say: If the sea were ink for the words of my Lord, the sea would surely be consumed before the words of my Lord are exhausted, though We were to bring the like of that (sea) to add thereto.

قُلْ لَّوْ كَانَ الْبَحْرُ مِدَادًا لِّكَلِمَاتِ رَبِّيْ لَنَفِدَ الْبَحْرُ قَبْلَ اَنْ تَنْفَدَ كَلِمَاتُ رَبِّيْ وَلَوْ جِئْنَا بِمِثْلِهٖ مَدَدًا ۝

110. Say: I am only a mortal like you; it is revealed to me that your god is one God, therefore whoever hopes to meet his Lord, he should do good deeds, and not join any one in the service of his Lord.

قُلْ اِنَّمَاۤ اَنَا بَشَرٌ مِّثْلُكُمْ يُوْحٰۤى اِلَيَّ اَنَّمَاۤ اِلٰهُكُمْ اِلٰهٌ وَّاحِدٌ ۚ فَمَنْ كَانَ يَرْجُوْا لِقَآءَ رَبِّهٖ فَلْيَعْمَلْ عَمَلًا صَالِحًا وَّلَا يُشْرِكْ بِعِبَادَةِ رَبِّهٖۤ اَحَدًا ۝

MARIUM

ايّاتها ۷۸ (١٩) سُوْرَةُ مَرْيَمَ مَكِّيَّةٌ رُكُوْعَاتُهَا

**In the name of Allah,
the Beneficent, the Merciful.**

بِسْمِ اللّٰهِ الرَّحْمٰنِ الرَّحِيْمِ ۟

1. Kaf Ha Ya Ain Suad.

كٓهٰيٰعٓصٓ ۟

2. A mention of the mercy of your Lord to His servant Zakariya.

ذِكْرُ رَحْمَتِ رَبِّكَ عَبْدَهٗ زَكَرِيَّا ۟

3. When he called upon his Lord in a low voice,

اِذْ نَادٰى رَبَّهٗ نِدَآءً خَفِيًّا ۟

4. He said: My Lord! surely my bones are weakened and my head flares with hoariness, and, my Lord! I have never been unsuccessful in my prayer to Thee:

قَالَ رَبِّ اِنِّيْ وَهَنَ الْعَظْمُ مِنِّيْ وَاشْتَعَلَ الرَّاْسُ شَيْبًا وَّلَمْ اَكُنْ بِدُعَآئِكَ رَبِّ شَقِيًّا ۟

5. And surely I fear my cousins after me, and my wife is barren, therefore grant me from Thyself an heir,

وَاِنِّيْ خِفْتُ الْمَوَالِيَ مِنْ وَّرَآءِيْ وَكَانَتِ امْرَاَتِيْ عَاقِرًا فَهَبْ لِيْ مِنْ لَّدُنْكَ وَلِيًّا ۟

6. Who should inherit me and inherit from the children of Yaqoub, and make him, my Lord, one in whom Thou art well pleased.

يَّرِثُنِيْ وَيَرِثُ مِنْ اٰلِ يَعْقُوْبَ وَاجْعَلْهُ رَبِّ رَضِيًّا ۟

7. O Zakariya! surely We give you good news of a boy whose name shall be Yahya: We have not made before anyone his equal.

يٰزَكَرِيَّا اِنَّا نُبَشِّرُكَ بِغُلٰمِ اسْمُهٗ يَحْيٰى لَمْ نَجْعَلْ لَّهٗ مِنْ قَبْلُ سَمِيًّا ۟

8. He said: O my Lord! when shall I have a son, and my wife is barren, and I myself have reached indeed the extreme degree of old age?

قَالَ رَبِّ اَنّٰى يَكُوْنُ لِيْ غُلٰمٌ وَّكَانَتِ امْرَاَتِيْ عَاقِرًا وَّقَدْ بَلَغْتُ مِنَ الْكِبَرِ عِتِيًّا ۟

9. He said: So shall it be; your Lord says: It is easy to Me, and indeed I created you before, when you were nothing.

قَالَ كَذٰلِكَ قَالَ رَبُّكَ هُوَ عَلَيَّ هَيِّنٌ وَّقَدْ خَلَقْتُكَ مِنْ قَبْلُ وَلَمْ تَكُ شَيْئًا ۟

10. He said: My Lord! give me a sign. He said: Your sign is that you will not be able to speak to the people three nights while in sound health.

قَالَ رَبِّ اجْعَلْ لِّيْ اٰيَةً قَالَ اٰيَتُكَ اَلَّا تُكَلِّمَ النَّاسَ ثَلٰثَ لَيَالٍ سَوِيًّا ۟

11. So he went forth to his people from his place of worship, then he made known to them that they should glorify (Allah) morning and evening.

فَخَرَجَ عَلٰى قَوْمِهٖ مِنَ الْمِحْرَابِ فَاَوْحٰى اِلَيْهِمْ اَنْ سَبِّحُوْا بُكْرَةً وَّعَشِيًّا ۟

12. O Yahya! take hold of the Book with strength, and We granted him wisdom while yet a child,

يَا يَحْيٰى خُذِ الْكِتٰبَ بِقُوَّةٍ ۖ وَاٰتَيْنٰهُ الْحُكْمَ صَبِيًّا ۙ

13. And tenderness from Us and purity, and he was one who guarded (against evil),

وَّحَنَانًا مِّنْ لَّدُنَّا وَزَكٰوةً ۚ وَكَانَ تَقِيًّا ۙ

14. And dutiful to his parents, and he was not insolent, disobedient.

وَّبَرًّۢا بِوَالِدَيْهِ وَلَمْ يَكُنْ جَبَّارًا عَصِيًّا

15. And peace on him on the day he was born, and on the day he dies, and on the day he is raised to life.

وَسَلٰمٌ عَلَيْهِ يَوْمَ وُلِدَ وَيَوْمَ يَمُوْتُ وَيَوْمَ يُبْعَثُ حَيًّا ۟ع

16. And mention Marium in the Book when she drew aside from her family to an eastern place;

وَاذْكُرْ فِي الْكِتٰبِ مَرْيَمَ ۘ اِذِ انْتَبَذَتْ مِنْ اَهْلِهَا مَكَانًا شَرْقِيًّا ۙ

17. So she took a veil (to screen herself) from them; then We sent to her Our spirit, and there appeared to her a well-made man.

فَاتَّخَذَتْ مِنْ دُوْنِهِمْ حِجَابًا ۖ فَاَرْسَلْنَآ اِلَيْهَا رُوْحَنَا فَتَمَثَّلَ لَهَا بَشَرًا سَوِيًّا

18. She said: Surely I fly for refuge from you to the Beneficent God, if you are one guarding (against evil).

قَالَتْ اِنِّيْٓ اَعُوْذُ بِالرَّحْمٰنِ مِنْكَ اِنْ كُنْتَ تَقِيًّا

19. He said: I am only a messenger of your Lord: That I will give you a pure boy.

قَالَ اِنَّمَآ اَنَا۠ رَسُوْلُ رَبِّكِ ۖ لِاَهَبَ لَكِ غُلٰمًا زَكِيًّا

20. She said: When shall I have a boy and no mortal has yet touched me, nor have I been unchaste?

قَالَتْ اَنّٰى يَكُوْنُ لِيْ غُلٰمٌ وَّلَمْ يَمْسَسْنِيْ بَشَرٌ وَّلَمْ اَكُ بَغِيًّا

21. He said: Even so; your Lord says: It is easy to Me: and that We may make him a sign to men and a mercy from Us; and it is a matter which has been decreed.

قَالَ كَذٰلِكِ ۚ قَالَ رَبُّكِ هُوَ عَلَيَّ هَيِّنٌ ۚ وَلِنَجْعَلَهٗٓ اٰيَةً لِّلنَّاسِ وَرَحْمَةً مِّنَّا ۚ وَكَانَ اَمْرًا مَّقْضِيًّا

22. So she conceived him; then withdrew herself with him to a remote place.

فَحَمَلَتْهُ فَانْتَبَذَتْ بِهٖ مَكَانًا قَصِيًّا

23. And the throes (of childbirth) compelled her to betake herself to the trunk of a palm tree. She said: Oh, would that I had died before this, and had been a thing quite forgotten!

فَاَجَآءَهَا الْمَخَاضُ اِلٰى جِذْعِ النَّخْلَةِ ۚ قَالَتْ يٰلَيْتَنِيْ مِتُّ قَبْلَ هٰذَا وَكُنْتُ نَسْيًا مَّنْسِيًّا

24. Then (the child) called out to her from beneath her: Grieve not, surely your Lord has made a stream to flow beneath you;

فَنَادٰىهَا مِنْ تَحْتِهَآ اَلَّا تَحْزَنِيْ قَدْ جَعَلَ رَبُّكِ تَحْتَكِ سَرِيًّا

25. And shake towards you the trunk of the palmtree, it will drop on you fresh ripe dates:

وَهُزِّيٓ اِلَيۡكِ بِجِذۡعِ النَّخۡلَةِ تُسٰقِطۡ عَلَيۡكِ رُطَبًا جَنِيًّا ۞

26. So eat and drink and refresh the eye. Then if you see any mortal, say: Surely I have vowed a fast to the Beneficent God, so I shall not speak to any man today.

فَكُلِيۡ وَاشۡرَبِيۡ وَقَرِّيۡ عَيۡنًا ۚ فَاِمَّا تَرَيِنَّ مِنَ الۡبَشَرِ اَحَدًا ۙ فَقُوۡلِيۡٓ اِنِّيۡ نَذَرۡتُ لِلرَّحۡمٰنِ صَوۡمًا فَلَنۡ اُكَلِّمَ الۡيَوۡمَ اِنۡسِيًّا ۞

27. And she came to her people with him, carrying him (with her). They said: O Marium! surely you have done a strange thing.

فَاَتَتۡ بِهٖ قَوۡمَهَا تَحۡمِلُهٗ ۚ قَالُوۡا يٰمَرۡيَمُ لَقَدۡ جِئۡتِ شَيۡئًا فَرِيًّا ۞

28. O sister of Haroun! your father was not a bad man, nor was your mother an unchaste woman.

يٰٓاُخۡتَ هٰرُوۡنَ مَا كَانَ اَبُوۡكِ امۡرَاَ سَوۡءٍ وَّمَا كَانَتۡ اُمُّكِ بَغِيًّا ۞

29. But she pointed to him. They said: How should we speak to one who was a child in the cradle?

فَاَشَارَتۡ اِلَيۡهِ ۚ قَالُوۡا كَيۡفَ نُكَلِّمُ مَنۡ كَانَ فِي الۡمَهۡدِ صَبِيًّا ۞

30. He said: Surely I am a servant of Allah; He has given me the Book and made me a prophet;

قَالَ اِنِّيۡ عَبۡدُ اللّٰهِ ۟ اٰتٰىنِيَ الۡكِتٰبَ وَجَعَلَنِيۡ نَبِيًّا ۞

31. And He has made me blessed wherever I may be, and He has enjoined on me prayer and poor-rate so long as I live;

وَّجَعَلَنِيۡ مُبٰرَكًا اَيۡنَ مَا كُنۡتُ ۖ وَاَوۡصٰنِيۡ بِالصَّلٰوةِ وَالزَّكٰوةِ مَا دُمۡتُ حَيًّا ۞

32. And dutiful to my mother, and He has not made me insolent, unblessed;

وَّبَرًّۢا بِوَالِدَتِيۡ ۖ وَلَمۡ يَجۡعَلۡنِيۡ جَبَّارًا شَقِيًّا ۞

33. And peace on me on the day I was born, and on the day I die, and on the day I am raised to life.

وَالسَّلٰمُ عَلَيَّ يَوۡمَ وُلِدۡتُّ وَيَوۡمَ اَمُوۡتُ وَيَوۡمَ اُبۡعَثُ حَيًّا ۞

34. Such is Isa, son of Marium; (this is) the saying of truth about which they dispute.

ذٰلِكَ عِيۡسَى ابۡنُ مَرۡيَمَ ۚ قَوۡلَ الۡحَقِّ الَّذِيۡ فِيۡهِ يَمۡتَرُوۡنَ ۞

35. It beseems not Allah that He should take to Himself a son, glory be to Him; when He has decreed a matter He only says to it "Be," and it is.

مَا كَانَ لِلّٰهِ اَنۡ يَّتَّخِذَ مِنۡ وَّلَدٍ ۙ سُبۡحٰنَهٗ ۚ اِذَا قَضٰٓى اَمۡرًا فَاِنَّمَا يَقُوۡلُ لَهٗ كُنۡ فَيَكُوۡنُ ۞

287

36. And surely Allah is my Lord and your Lord, therefore serve Him; this is the right path.

وَاِنَّ اللّٰهَ رَبِّیْ وَرَبُّکُمْ فَاعْبُدُوْهُ ٰهذَا صِرَاطٌ مُّسْتَقِیْمٌ ۞

37. But parties from among them disagreed with each other, so woe to those who disbelieve, because of presence on a great day.

فَاخْتَلَفَ الْاَحْزَابُ مِنْۢ بَیْنِہِمْ فَوَیْلٌ لِّلَّذِیْنَ کَفَرُوْا مِنْ مَّشْہَدِ یَوْمٍ عَظِیْمٍ ۞

38. How clearly shall they hear and how clearly shall they see on the day when they come to Us; but the unjust this day are in manifest error.

اَسْمِعْ بِہِمْ وَاَبْصِرْ یَوْمَ یَاْتُوْنَنَا لٰکِنِ الظّٰلِمُوْنَ الْیَوْمَ فِیْ ضَلٰلٍ مُّبِیْنٍ ۞

39. And warn them of the day of intense regret, when the matter shall have been decided; and they are (now) in negligence and they do not believe.

وَاَنْذِرْهُمْ یَوْمَ الْحَسْرَةِ اِذْ قُضِیَ الْاَمْرُ وَهُمْ فِیْ غَفْلَةٍ وَّهُمْ لَا یُؤْمِنُوْنَ ۞

40. Surely We inherit the earth and all those who are on it, and to Us they shall be returned.

اِنَّا نَحْنُ نَرِثُ الْاَرْضَ وَمَنْ عَلَیْہَا وَاِلَیْنَا یُرْجَعُوْنَ ۞

41. And mention Ibrahim in the Book; surely he was a truthful man, a prophet.

وَاذْکُرْ فِی الْکِتٰبِ اِبْرٰهِیْمَ ٝ اِنَّہٗ کَانَ صِدِّیْقًا نَّبِیًّا ۞

42. When he said to his father; O my father! why do you worship what neither hears nor sees, nor does it avail you in the least:

اِذْ قَالَ لِاَبِیْہِ یٰٓاَبَتِ لِمَ تَعْبُدُ مَا لَا یَسْمَعُ وَلَا یُبْصِرُ وَلَا یُغْنِیْ عَنْکَ شَیْئًا ۞

43. O my father! truly the knowledge has come to me which has not come to you, therefore follow me, I will guide you on a right path:

یٰٓاَبَتِ اِنِّیْ قَدْ جَآءَنِیْ مِنَ الْعِلْمِ مَا لَمْ یَاْتِکَ فَاتَّبِعْنِیْ اَهْدِکَ صِرَاطًا سَوِیًّا ۞

44. O my father! serve not the Shaitan, surely the Shaitan is disobedient to the Beneficent God:

یٰٓاَبَتِ لَا تَعْبُدِ الشَّیْطٰنَ ٝ اِنَّ الشَّیْطٰنَ کَانَ لِلرَّحْمٰنِ عَصِیًّا ۞

45. O my father! surely I fear that a punishment from the Beneficent God should afflict you so that you should be a friend of the Shaitan.

یٰٓاَبَتِ اِنِّیْ اَخَافُ اَنْ یَّمَسَّکَ عَذَابٌ مِّنَ الرَّحْمٰنِ فَتَکُوْنَ لِلشَّیْطٰنِ وَلِیًّا ۞

46. He said: Do you dislike my gods, O Ibrahim? If you do not desist I will certainly revile you, and leave me for a time.

قَالَ اَرَاغِبٌ اَنْتَ عَنْ اٰلِہَتِیْ یٰٓاِبْرٰهِیْمُ ٝ لَئِنْ لَّمْ تَنْتَهِ لَاَرْجُمَنَّکَ وَاهْجُرْنِیْ مَلِیًّا ۞

47. He said: Peace be on you, I will pray to my Lord to forgive you; surely He is ever Affectionate to me:

قَالَ سَلَامٌ عَلَيْكَ سَاَسْتَغْفِرُ لَكَ رَبِّيْ اِنَّهٗ كَانَ بِيْ حَفِيًّا ۞

48. And I will withdraw from you and what you call on besides Allah, and I will call upon my Lord; may be I shall not remain unblessed in calling upon my Lord.

وَاَعْتَزِلُكُمْ وَمَا تَدْعُوْنَ مِنْ دُوْنِ اللّٰهِ وَاَدْعُوْا رَبِّيْ عَسٰۤى اَلَّاۤ اَكُوْنَ بِدُعَآءِ رَبِّيْ شَقِيًّا ۞

49. So when he withdrew from them and what they worshipped besides Allah, We gave to him Ishaq and Yaqoub, and each one of them We made a prophet.

فَلَمَّا اعْتَزَلَهُمْ وَمَا يَعْبُدُوْنَ مِنْ دُوْنِ اللّٰهِ وَهَبْنَا لَهٗۤ اِسْحٰقَ وَيَعْقُوْبَ ۖ وَكُلًّا جَعَلْنَا نَبِيًّا ۞

50. And We granted to them of Our mercy, and We left (behind them) a truthful mention of eminence for them.

وَوَهَبْنَا لَهُمْ مِّنْ رَّحْمَتِنَا وَجَعَلْنَا لَهُمْ لِسَانَ صِدْقٍ عَلِيًّا ۞

51. And mention Musa in the Book; surely he was one purified, and he was an apostle, a prophet.

وَاذْكُرْ فِى الْكِتٰبِ مُوْسٰۤى ۖ اِنَّهٗ كَانَ مُخْلَصًا وَّكَانَ رَسُوْلًا نَّبِيًّا ۞

52. And We called to him from the blessed side of the mountain, and We made him draw nigh, holding communion (with Us).

وَنَادَيْنٰهُ مِنْ جَانِبِ الطُّوْرِ الْاَيْمَنِ وَقَرَّبْنٰهُ نَجِيًّا ۞

53. And We gave to him out of Our mercy his brother Haroun a prophet.

وَوَهَبْنَا لَهٗ مِنْ رَّحْمَتِنَاۤ اَخَاهُ هٰرُوْنَ نَبِيًّا ۞

54. And mention Ismail in the Book; surely he was truthful in (his) promise, and he was an apostle, a prophet.

وَاذْكُرْ فِى الْكِتٰبِ اِسْمٰعِيْلَ ۖ اِنَّهٗ كَانَ صَادِقَ الْوَعْدِ وَكَانَ رَسُوْلًا نَّبِيًّا ۞

55. And he enjoined on his family prayer and almsgiving, and was one in whom his Lord was well pleased.

وَكَانَ يَأْمُرُ اَهْلَهٗ بِالصَّلٰوةِ وَالزَّكٰوةِ ۖ وَكَانَ عِنْدَ رَبِّهٖ مَرْضِيًّا ۞

56. And mention Idris in the Book; surely he was a truthful man, a prophet,

وَاذْكُرْ فِى الْكِتٰبِ اِدْرِيْسَ ۖ اِنَّهٗ كَانَ صِدِّيْقًا نَّبِيًّا ۞

57. And We raised him high in Heaven.

وَرَفَعْنٰهُ مَكَانًا عَلِيًّا ۞

58. These are they on whom Allah bestowed favors, from among the prophets of the seed of Adam, and of those whom We carried with Nuh, and of the seed of Ibrahim and Israel, and of those whom We guided and chose; when the communications of the Beneficent God were recited to them, they fell down making obeisance and weeping.

59. But there came after them an evil generation, who neglected prayers and followed the sensual desires, so they will meet perdition,

60. Except such as repent and believe and do good, these shall enter the garden, and they shall not be dealt with unjustly in any way:

61. The gardens of perpetuity which the Beneficent God has promised to His servants while unseen; surely His promise shall come to pass.

62. They shall not hear therein any vain discourse, but only: Peace, and they shall have their sustenance therein morning and evening.

63. This is the garden which We cause those of Our servants to inherit who guard (against evil).

64. And we do not descend but by the command of your Lord; to Him belongs whatever is before us and whatever is behind us and whatever is between these, and your Lord is not forgetful.

65. The Lord of the heavens and the earth and what is between them, so serve Him and be patient in His service. Do you know any one equal to Him?

66. And says man: What! when I am dead shall I truly be brought forth alive?

67. Does not man remember that We created him before, when he was nothing?

أُولَـٰئِكَ الَّذِينَ أَنْعَمَ اللهُ عَلَيْهِمْ مِّنَ النَّبِيِّنَ مِنْ ذُرِّيَّةِ اٰدَمَ وَمِمَّنْ حَمَلْنَا مَعَ نُوحٍ وَّمِنْ ذُرِّيَّةِ إِبْرٰهِيْمَ وَإِسْرَآءِيْلَ وَمِمَّنْ هَدَيْنَا وَاجْتَبَيْنَا إِذَا تُتْلٰى عَلَيْهِمْ اٰيٰتُ الرَّحْمٰنِ خَرُّوا سُجَّدًا وَّبُكِيًّا ۩

فَخَلَفَ مِنْ بَعْدِهِمْ خَلْفٌ أَضَاعُوا الصَّلٰوةَ وَاتَّبَعُوا الشَّهَوٰتِ فَسَوْفَ يَلْقَوْنَ غَيًّا ۙ

إِلَّا مَنْ تَابَ وَاٰمَنَ وَعَمِلَ صَالِحًا فَأُولَـٰئِكَ يَدْخُلُوْنَ الْجَنَّةَ وَلَا يُظْلَمُوْنَ شَيْئًا ۙ

جَنّٰتِ عَدْنِ الَّتِي وَعَدَ الرَّحْمٰنُ عِبَادَهُ بِالْغَيْبِ ۚ إِنَّهُ كَانَ وَعْدُهُ مَأْتِيًّا ۝

لَا يَسْمَعُوْنَ فِيْهَا لَغْوًا إِلَّا سَلٰمًا ۚ وَلَهُمْ رِزْقُهُمْ فِيْهَا بُكْرَةً وَّعَشِيًّا ۝

تِلْكَ الْجَنَّةُ الَّتِي نُوْرِثُ مِنْ عِبَادِنَا مَنْ كَانَ تَقِيًّا ۝

وَمَا نَتَنَزَّلُ إِلَّا بِأَمْرِ رَبِّكَ ۚ لَهُ مَا بَيْنَ أَيْدِيْنَا وَمَا خَلْفَنَا وَمَا بَيْنَ ذٰلِكَ ۚ وَمَا كَانَ رَبُّكَ نَسِيًّا ۝

رَبُّ السَّمٰوٰتِ وَالْأَرْضِ وَمَا بَيْنَهُمَا فَاعْبُدْهُ وَاصْطَبِرْ لِعِبَادَتِهِ ۚ هَلْ تَعْلَمُ لَهُ سَمِيًّا ۝

وَيَقُوْلُ الْإِنْسَانُ ءَاِذَا مَا مِتُّ لَسَوْفَ أُخْرَجُ حَيًّا ۝

أَوَلَا يَذْكُرُ الْإِنْسَانُ أَنَّا خَلَقْنٰهُ مِنْ قَبْلُ وَلَمْ يَكُ شَيْئًا ۝

68. So by your Lord! We will most certainly gather them together and the Shaitans, then shall We certainly cause them to be present round hell on their knees.

69. Then We will most certainly draw forth from every sect of them him who is most exorbitantly rebellious against the Beneficent God.

70. Again We do certainly know best those who deserve most to be burned therein.

71. And there is not one of you but shall come to it; this is an unavoidable decree of your Lord.

72. And We will deliver those who guarded (against evil), and We will leave the unjust therein on their knees.

73. And when Our clear communications are recited to them, those who disbelieve say to those who believe: Which of the two parties is best in abiding and best in assembly?

74. And how many of the generations have We destroyed before them who were better in respect of goods and outward appearance!

75. Say: As for him who remains in error, the Beneficent God will surely prolong his length of days, until they see what they were threatened with, either the punishment or the hour; then they shall know who is in more evil plight and weaker in forces.

76. And Allah increases in guidance those who go aright; and ever-abiding good works are with your Lord best in recompense and best in yielding fruit.

77. Have you, then, seen him who disbelieves in Our communications and says: I shall certainly be given wealth and children?

فَوَرَبِّكَ لَنَحْشُرَنَّهُمْ وَالشَّيَاطِيْنَ ثُمَّ لَنُحْضِرَنَّهُمْ حَوْلَ جَهَنَّمَ جِثِيًّا ۞

ثُمَّ لَنَنْزِعَنَّ مِنْ كُلِّ شِيْعَةٍ اَيُّهُمْ اَشَدُّ عَلَى الرَّحْمٰنِ عِتِيًّا ۞

ثُمَّ لَنَحْنُ اَعْلَمُ بِالَّذِيْنَ هُمْ اَوْلٰى بِهَا صِلِيًّا ۞

وَاِنْ مِّنْكُمْ اِلَّا وَارِدُهَا ۚ كَانَ عَلٰى رَبِّكَ حَتْمًا مَّقْضِيًّا ۞

ثُمَّ نُنَجِّي الَّذِيْنَ اتَّقَوْا وَّنَذَرُ الظّٰلِمِيْنَ فِيْهَا جِثِيًّا ۞

وَاِذَا تُتْلٰى عَلَيْهِمْ اٰيٰتُنَا بَيِّنٰتٍ قَالَ الَّذِيْنَ كَفَرُوْا لِلَّذِيْنَ اٰمَنُوْا ۙ اَيُّ الْفَرِيْقَيْنِ خَيْرٌ مَّقَامًا وَّاَحْسَنُ نَدِيًّا ۞

وَكَمْ اَهْلَكْنَا قَبْلَهُمْ مِّنْ قَرْنٍ هُمْ اَحْسَنُ اَثَاثًا وَّرِئْيًا ۞

قُلْ مَنْ كَانَ فِى الضَّلٰلَةِ فَلْيَمْدُدْ لَهُ الرَّحْمٰنُ مَدًّا ۚ حَتّٰى اِذَا رَاَوْا مَا يُوْعَدُوْنَ اِمَّا الْعَذَابَ وَاِمَّا السَّاعَةَ ۚ فَسَيَعْلَمُوْنَ مَنْ هُوَ شَرٌّ مَّكَانًا وَّاَضْعَفُ جُنْدًا ۞

وَيَزِيْدُ اللّٰهُ الَّذِيْنَ اهْتَدَوْا هُدًى ۗ وَالْبٰقِيٰتُ الصّٰلِحٰتُ خَيْرٌ عِنْدَ رَبِّكَ ثَوَابًا وَّخَيْرٌ مَّرَدًّا ۞

اَفَرَاَيْتَ الَّذِيْ كَفَرَ بِاٰيٰتِنَا وَقَالَ لَاُوْتَيَنَّ مَالًا وَّوَلَدًا ۞

78. Has he gained knowledge of the unseen, or made a covenant with the Beneficent God?

79. By no means! We write down what he says, and We will lengthen to him the length of the chastisement,

80. And We will inherit of him what he says, and he shall come to Us alone.

81. And they have taken gods besides Allah, that they should be to them a source of strength;

82. By no means! They shall soon deny their worshipping them, and they shall be adversaries to them.

83. Do you not see that We have sent the Shaitans against the unbelievers, inciting them by incitement?

84. Therefore be not in haste against them, We only number out to them a number (of days).

85. The day on which We will gather those who guard (against evil) to the Beneficent God to receive honors,

86. And We will drive the guilty to hell thirsty.

87. They shall not control intercession, save he who has made a covenant with the Beneficent God.

88. And they say: The Beneficent God has taken (to Himself) a son.

89. Certainly you have made an abominable assertion:

90. The heavens may almost be rent thereat, and the earth cleave asunder, and the mountains fall down in pieces,

91. That they ascribe a son to the Beneficent God.

92. And it is not worthy of the Beneficent God that He should take (to Himself) a son.

93. There is no one in the heavens and the earth but will come to the Beneficent God as a servant.

اَطَّلَعَ الْغَيْبَ اَمِ اتَّخَذَ عِنْدَ الرَّحْمٰنِ عَهْدًا ۞

كَلَّا سَنَكْتُبُ مَا يَقُوْلُ وَنَمُدُّ لَهٗ مِنَ الْعَذَابِ مَدًّا ۞

وَّنَرِثُهٗ مَا يَقُوْلُ وَ يَأْتِيْنَا فَرْدًا ۞

وَاتَّخَذُوْا مِنْ دُوْنِ اللّٰهِ اٰلِهَةً لِّيَكُوْنُوْا لَهُمْ عِزًّا ۞

كَلَّا سَيَكْفُرُوْنَ بِعِبَادَتِهِمْ وَيَكُوْنُوْنَ عَلَيْهِمْ ضِدًّا ۞

اَلَمْ تَرَ اَنَّا اَرْسَلْنَا الشَّيٰطِيْنَ عَلَى الْكٰفِرِيْنَ تَؤُزُّهُمْ اَزًّا ۞

فَلَا تَعْجَلْ عَلَيْهِمْ اِنَّمَا نَعُدُّ لَهُمْ عَدًّا ۞

يَوْمَ نَحْشُرُ الْمُتَّقِيْنَ اِلَى الرَّحْمٰنِ وَفْدًا ۞

وَّنَسُوْقُ الْمُجْرِمِيْنَ اِلٰى جَهَنَّمَ وِرْدًا ۞

لَا يَمْلِكُوْنَ الشَّفَاعَةَ اِلَّا مَنِ اتَّخَذَ عِنْدَ الرَّحْمٰنِ عَهْدًا ۞

وَقَالُوا اتَّخَذَ الرَّحْمٰنُ وَلَدًا ۞

لَقَدْ جِئْتُمْ شَيْئًا اِدًّا ۞

تَكَادُ السَّمٰوٰتُ يَتَفَطَّرْنَ مِنْهُ وَتَنْشَقُّ الْاَرْضُ وَ تَخِرُّ الْجِبَالُ هَدًّا ۞

اَنْ دَعَوْا لِلرَّحْمٰنِ وَلَدًا ۞

وَمَا يَنْبَغِيْ لِلرَّحْمٰنِ اَنْ يَّتَّخِذَ وَلَدًا ۞

اِنْ كُلُّ مَنْ فِى السَّمٰوٰتِ وَالْاَرْضِ اِلَّا اٰتِى الرَّحْمٰنِ عَبْدًا ۞

94. Certainly He has a comprehensive knowledge of them, and He has numbered them a (comprehensive) numbering.

95. And every one of them will come to Him on the day of resurrection alone.

96. Surely (as for) those who believe and do good deeds for them will Allah bring about love.

97. So We have only made it easy in your tongue that you may give good news thereby to those who guard (against evil) and warn thereby a vehemently contentious people.

98. And how many a generation have We destroyed before them! Do you see any one of them or hear a sound of them?

‏لَقَدْ اَحْصٰهُمْ وَعَدَّهُمْ عَدًّا ۝‏

‏وَكُلُّهُمْ اٰتِيْهِ يَوْمَ الْقِيٰمَةِ فَرْدًا ۝‏

‏اِنَّ الَّذِيْنَ اٰمَنُوْا وَعَمِلُوا الصّٰلِحٰتِ سَيَجْعَلُ لَهُمُ الرَّحْمٰنُ وُدًّا ۝‏

‏فَاِنَّمَا يَسَّرْنٰهُ بِلِسَانِكَ لِتُبَشِّرَ بِهِ الْمُتَّقِيْنَ وَتُنْذِرَ بِهٖ قَوْمًا لُّدًّا ۝‏

‏وَكَمْ اَهْلَكْنَا قَبْلَهُمْ مِّنْ قَرْنٍ ۖ هَلْ تُحِسُّ مِنْهُمْ مِّنْ اَحَدٍ اَوْ تَسْمَعُ لَهُمْ رِكْزًا ۝‏

TA HA

**In the name of Allah,
the Beneficent, the Merciful.**

1. Ta Ha.

2. We have not revealed the Quran to you that you may be unsuccessful.

3. Nay, it is a reminder to him who fears:

4. A revelation from Him Who created the earth and the high heavens.

5. The Beneficent God is firm in power.

6. His is what is in the heavens and what is in the earth and what is between them two and what is beneath the ground.

7. And if you utter the saying aloud, then surely He knows the secret, and what is yet more hidden.

8. Allah—there is no god but He; His are the very best names.

9. And has the story of Musa come to you?

10. When he saw fire, he said to his family: Stop, for surely I see a fire, haply I may bring to you therefrom a live coal or find a guidance at the fire.

11. So when he came to it, a voice was uttered: O Musa:

12. Surely I am your Lord, therefore put off your shoes; surely you are in the sacred valley, Tuwa,

13. And I have chosen you, so listen to what is revealed:

14. Surely I am Allah, there is no god but I, therefore serve Me and keep up prayer for My remembrance:

اياتها ١٣٤ (٢٠) سُوْرَةُ طٰهٰ مَكِّيَّةٌ رُكُوْعَاتُهَا

بِسْمِ اللهِ الرَّحْمٰنِ الرَّحِيْمِ ۞

طٰهٰ ۞

مَاۤ اَنْزَلْنَا عَلَيْكَ الْقُرْاٰنَ لِتَشْقٰى ۞

اِلَّا تَذْكِرَةً لِّمَنْ يَّخْشٰى ۞

تَنْزِيْلًا مِّمَّنْ خَلَقَ الْاَرْضَ وَالسَّمٰوٰتِ الْعُلٰى ۞

اَلرَّحْمٰنُ عَلَى الْعَرْشِ اسْتَوٰى ۞

لَهٗ مَا فِى السَّمٰوٰتِ وَمَا فِى الْاَرْضِ وَمَا بَيْنَهُمَا وَمَا تَحْتَ الثَّرٰى ۞

وَاِنْ تَجْهَرْ بِالْقَوْلِ فَاِنَّهٗ يَعْلَمُ السِّرَّ وَاَخْفٰى ۞

اَللهُ لَاۤ اِلٰهَ اِلَّا هُوَ لَهُ الْاَسْمَاۤءُ الْحُسْنٰى ۞

وَهَلْ اَتٰىكَ حَدِيْثُ مُوْسٰى ۞

اِذْ رَاٰ نَارًا فَقَالَ لِاَهْلِهِ امْكُثُوْۤا اِنِّيْ اٰنَسْتُ نَارًا لَّعَلِّيْۤ اٰتِيْكُمْ مِّنْهَا بِقَبَسٍ اَوْ اَجِدُ عَلَى النَّارِ هُدًى ۞

فَلَمَّاۤ اَتٰىهَا نُوْدِيَ يٰمُوْسٰى ۞

اِنِّيْۤ اَنَا رَبُّكَ فَاخْلَعْ نَعْلَيْكَ اِنَّكَ بِالْوَادِ الْمُقَدَّسِ طُوًى ۞

وَاَنَا اخْتَرْتُكَ فَاسْتَمِعْ لِمَا يُوْحٰى ۞

اِنَّنِيْۤ اَنَا اللهُ لَاۤ اِلٰهَ اِلَّاۤ اَنَا فَاعْبُدْنِيْ وَاَقِمِ الصَّلٰوةَ لِذِكْرِيْ ۞

15. Surely the hour is coming—I am about to make it manifest—so that every soul may be rewarded as it strives:

اِنَّ السَّاعَةَ اٰتِيَةٌ اَكَادُ اُخْفِيْهَا لِتُجْزٰى كُلُّ نَفْسٍ بِمَا تَسْعٰى ۝

16. Therefore let not him who believes not in it and follows his low desires turn you away from it so that you should perish;

فَلَا يَصُدَّنَّكَ عَنْهَا مَنْ لَّا يُؤْمِنُ بِهَا وَاتَّبَعَ هَوٰىهُ فَتَرْدٰى ۝

17. And what is this in your right hand, O Musa!

وَمَا تِلْكَ بِيَمِيْنِكَ يٰمُوْسٰى ۝

18. He said: This is my staff: I recline on it and I beat the leaves with it to make them fall upon my sheep, and I have other uses for it.

قَالَ هِيَ عَصَايَ ۚ اَتَوَكَّؤُا عَلَيْهَا وَاَهُشُّ بِهَا عَلٰى غَنَمِيْ وَلِيَ فِيْهَا مَاٰرِبُ اُخْرٰى ۝

19. He said: Cast it down, O Musa!

قَالَ اَلْقِهَا يٰمُوْسٰى ۝

20. So he cast it down; and lo! it was a serpent running.

فَاَلْقٰىهَا فَاِذَا هِيَ حَيَّةٌ تَسْعٰى ۝

21. He said: Take hold of it and fear not; We will restore it to its former state:

قَالَ خُذْهَا وَلَا تَخَفْ ۖ سَنُعِيْدُهَا سِيْرَتَهَا الْاُوْلٰى ۝

22. And press your hand to your side, it shall come out white without evil: another sign:

وَاضْمُمْ يَدَكَ اِلٰى جَنَاحِكَ تَخْرُجْ بَيْضَاءَ مِنْ غَيْرِ سُوْءٍ اٰيَةً اُخْرٰى ۝

23. That We may show you of Our greater signs:

لِنُرِيَكَ مِنْ اٰيٰتِنَا الْكُبْرٰى ۝

24. Go to Firon, surely he has exceeded all limits.

اِذْهَبْ اِلٰى فِرْعَوْنَ اِنَّهُ طَغٰى ۝

25. He said: O my Lord! Expand my breast for me,

قَالَ رَبِّ اشْرَحْ لِيْ صَدْرِيْ ۝

26. And make my affair easy to me,

وَيَسِّرْ لِيْ اَمْرِيْ ۝

27. And loose the knot from my tongue,

وَاحْلُلْ عُقْدَةً مِّنْ لِّسَانِيْ ۝

28. (That) they may understand my word;

يَفْقَهُوْا قَوْلِيْ ۝

29. And give to me an aider from my family:

وَاجْعَلْ لِّيْ وَزِيْرًا مِّنْ اَهْلِيْ ۝

30. Haroun, my brother,

هٰرُوْنَ اَخِيْ ۝

31. Strengthen my back by him,

اشْدُدْ بِهٖ اَزْرِيْ ۝

32. And associate him (with me) in my affair,

33. So that we should glorify Thee much,

34. And remember Thee oft.

35. Surely, Thou art seeing us.

36. He said: You are indeed granted your petition, O Musa;

37. And certainly We bestowed on you a favor at another time;

38. When We revealed to your mother what was revealed;

39. Saying: Put him into a chest, then cast it down into the river, then the river shall throw him on the shore; there shall take him up one who is an enemy to Me and enemy to him; and I cast down upon you love from Me, and that you might be brought up before My eyes.

40. When your sister went and said: Shall I direct you to one who will take charge of him? So We brought you back to your mother, that her eye might be cooled and she should not grieve; and you killed a man, then We delivered you from the grief, and We tried you with (a severe) trying. Then you stayed for years among the people of Madyan; then you came hither as ordained, O Musa.

41. And I have chosen you for Myself:

42. Go you and your brother with My communications and be not remiss in remembering Me;

43. Go both to Firon, surely he has become inordinate;

44. Then speak to him a gentle word; haply he may mind or fear.

45. Both said: O our Lord! surely we fear that he may hasten to do evil to us or that he may become inordinate.

46. He said: Fear not, surely I am with you both: I do hear and see.

296

47. So go you both to him and say: Surely we are two apostles of your Lord; therefore send the children of Israel with us and do not torment them! Indeed we have brought to you a communication from your Lord, and peace is on him who follows the guidance;

48. Surely it has been revealed to us that the chastisement will surely come upon him who rejects and turns back.

49. (Firon) said: And who is your Lord, O Musa?

50. He said: Our Lord is He Who gave to everything its creation, then guided it (to its goal).

51. He said: Then what is the state of the former generations?

52. He said: The knowledge thereof is with my Lord in a book; my Lord errs not, nor does He forget;

53. Who made the earth for you an expanse and made for you therein paths and sent down water from the cloud; then thereby We have brought forth many species of various herbs.

54. Eat and pasture your cattle; most surely there are signs in this for those endowed with understanding.

55. From it We created you and into it We shall send you back and from it will We raise you a second time.

56. And truly We showed him Our signs, all of them, but he rejected and refused.

57. Said he: Have you come to us that you should turn us out of our land by your magic, O Musa?

58. So we too will produce before you magic like it, therefore make between us and you an appointment, which we should not break, (neither) we nor you, (in) a central place.

59. (Musa) said: Your appointment is the day of the Festival and let the people be gathered together in the early forenoon.

فَأْتِيٰهُ فَقُوْلَاۤ اِنَّا رَسُوْلَا رَبِّكَ فَاَرْسِلْ مَعَنَا بَنِيْۤ
اِسْرَآءِيْلَ ۙ وَلَا تُعَذِّبْهُمْ ۭ قَدْ جِئْنٰكَ بِاٰيَةٍ مِّنْ
رَّبِّكَ ۭ وَالسَّلٰمُ عَلٰى مَنِ اتَّبَعَ الْهُدٰى ۞

اِنَّا قَدْ اُوْحِيَ اِلَيْنَاۤ اَنَّ الْعَذَابَ عَلٰى مَنْ كَذَّبَ
وَتَوَلّٰى ۞

قَالَ فَمَنْ رَّبُّكُمَا يٰمُوْسٰى ۞

قَالَ رَبُّنَا الَّذِيْۤ اَعْطٰى كُلَّ شَيْءٍ خَلْقَهٗ ثُمَّ هَدٰى ۞

قَالَ فَمَا بَالُ الْقُرُوْنِ الْاُوْلٰى ۞

قَالَ عِلْمُهَا عِنْدَ رَبِّيْ فِيْ كِتٰبٍ ۚ لَا يَضِلُّ رَبِّيْ وَ
لَا يَنْسَى ۞

الَّذِيْ جَعَلَ لَكُمُ الْاَرْضَ مَهْدًا وَّسَلَكَ لَكُمْ
فِيْهَا سُبُلًا وَّاَنْزَلَ مِنَ السَّمَآءِ مَآءً ۭ فَاَخْرَجْنَا
بِهٖۤ اَزْوَاجًا مِّنْ نَّبَاتٍ شَتّٰى ۞

كُلُوْا وَارْعَوْا اَنْعَامَكُمْ ۭ اِنَّ فِيْ ذٰلِكَ لَاٰيٰتٍ لِّاُولِي
النُّهٰى ۞

مِنْهَا خَلَقْنٰكُمْ وَفِيْهَا نُعِيْدُكُمْ وَمِنْهَا نُخْرِجُكُمْ
تَارَةً اُخْرٰى ۞

وَلَقَدْ اَرَيْنٰهُ اٰيٰتِنَا كُلَّهَا فَكَذَّبَ وَاَبٰى ۞

قَالَ اَجِئْتَنَا لِتُخْرِجَنَا مِنْ اَرْضِنَا بِسِحْرِكَ يٰمُوْسٰى ۞

فَلَنَأْتِيَنَّكَ بِسِحْرٍ مِّثْلِهٖ فَاجْعَلْ بَيْنَنَا وَبَيْنَكَ
مَوْعِدًا لَّا نُخْلِفُهٗ نَحْنُ وَلَاۤ اَنْتَ مَكَانًا سُوًى ۞

قَالَ مَوْعِدُكُمْ يَوْمُ الزِّيْنَةِ وَاَنْ يُّحْشَرَ النَّاسُ ضُحًى ۞

60. So Firon turned his back and settled his plan, then came.

61. Musa said to them: Woe to you! do not forge a lie against Allah, lest He destroy you by a punishment, and he who forges (a lie) indeed fails to attain (his desire).

62. So they disputed with one another about their affair and kept the discourse secret.

63. They said: These are most surely two magicians who wish to turn you out from your land by their magic and to take away your best traditions.

64. Therefore settle your plan, then come standing in ranks, and he will prosper indeed this day who overcomes.

65. They said: O Musa! will you cast, or shall we be the first who cast down?

66. He said: Nay! cast down. then lo! their cords and their rods—it was imaged to him on account of their magic as if they were running.

67. So Musa conceived in his mind a fear.

68. We said: Fear not, surely you shall be the uppermost,

69. And cast down what is in your right hand; it shall devour what they have wrought; they have wrought only the plan of a magician, and the magician shall not be successful wheresoever he may come from.

70. And the magicians were cast down making obeisance; they said: We believe in the Lord of Haroun and Musa.

71. (Firon) said: You believe in him before I give you leave; most surely he is the chief of you who taught you enchantment, therefore I will certainly cut off your hands and your feet on opposite sides, and I will certainly crucify you on the trunks of the palm trees, and certainly you will come to know which of us is the more severe and the more abiding in chastising.

تَوَلّٰى فِرْعَوْنُ فَجَمَعَ كَيْدَهٗ ثُمَّ اَتٰى ۝

قَالَ لَهُمْ مُّوْسٰى وَيْلَكُمْ لَا تَفْتَرُوْا عَلَى اللّٰهِ كَذِبًا فَيُسْحِتَكُمْ بِعَذَابٍ ۚ وَقَدْ خَابَ مَنِ افْتَرٰى ۝

فَتَنَازَعُوْا اَمْرَهُمْ بَيْنَهُمْ وَاَسَرُّوا النَّجْوٰى ۝

قَالُوْا اِنْ هٰذٰنِ لَسٰحِرٰنِ يُرِيْدٰنِ اَنْ يُّخْرِجٰكُمْ مِّنْ اَرْضِكُمْ بِسِحْرِهِمَا وَيَذْهَبَا بِطَرِيْقَتِكُمُ الْمُثْلٰى ۝

فَاَجْمِعُوْا كَيْدَكُمْ ثُمَّ ائْتُوْا صَفًّا ۚ وَقَدْ اَفْلَحَ الْيَوْمَ مَنِ اسْتَعْلٰى ۝

قَالُوْا يٰمُوْسٰى اِمَّا اَنْ تُلْقِيَ وَاِمَّا اَنْ نَّكُوْنَ اَوَّلَ مَنْ اَلْقٰى ۝

قَالَ بَلْ اَلْقُوْا ۚ فَاِذَا حِبَالُهُمْ وَعِصِيُّهُمْ يُخَيَّلُ اِلَيْهِ مِنْ سِحْرِهِمْ اَنَّهَا تَسْعٰى ۝

فَاَوْجَسَ فِيْ نَفْسِهٖ خِيْفَةً مُّوْسٰى ۝

قُلْنَا لَا تَخَفْ اِنَّكَ اَنْتَ الْاَعْلٰى ۝

وَاَلْقِ مَا فِيْ يَمِيْنِكَ تَلْقَفْ مَا صَنَعُوْا ۚ اِنَّمَا صَنَعُوْا كَيْدُ سٰحِرٍ ۚ وَلَا يُفْلِحُ السَّاحِرُ حَيْثُ اَتٰى ۝

فَاُلْقِيَ السَّحَرَةُ سُجَّدًا قَالُوْا اٰمَنَّا بِرَبِّ هٰرُوْنَ وَمُوْسٰى ۝

قَالَ اٰمَنْتُمْ لَهٗ قَبْلَ اَنْ اٰذَنَ لَكُمْ ۚ اِنَّهٗ لَكَبِيْرُكُمُ الَّذِيْ عَلَّمَكُمُ السِّحْرَ ۚ فَلَاُقَطِّعَنَّ اَيْدِيَكُمْ وَاَرْجُلَكُمْ مِّنْ خِلَافٍ وَّلَاُصَلِّبَنَّكُمْ فِيْ جُذُوْعِ النَّخْلِ ۚ وَلَتَعْلَمُنَّ اَيُّنَا اَشَدُّ عَذَابًا وَّاَبْقٰى ۝

72. They said: We do not prefer you to what has come to us of clear arguments and to He Who made us, therefore decide what you are going to decide; you can only decide about this world's life.

73. Surely we believe in our Lord that He may forgive us our sins and the magic to which you compelled us; and Allah is better and more abiding.

74. Whoever comes to his Lord (being) guilty, for him is surely hell; he shall not die therein, nor shall he live.

75. And whoever comes to Him a believer (and) he has done good deeds indeed, these it is who shall have the high ranks,

76. The gardens of perpetuity, beneath which rivers flow, to abide therein; and this is the reward of him who has purified himself.

77. And certainly We revealed to Musa, saying: Travel by night with My servants, then make for them a dry path in the sea, not fearing to be overtaken, nor being afraid.

78. And Firon followed them with his armies, so there came upon them of the sea that which came upon them.

79. And Firon led astray his people and he did not guide (them) aright.

80. O children of Israel! indeed We delivered you from your enemy, and We made a covenant with you on the blessed side of the mountain, and We sent to you the manna and the quails.

81. Eat of the good things We have given you for sustenance, and be not inordinate with respect to them, lest My wrath should be due to you, and to whomsoever My wrath is due he shall perish indeed.

قَالُوْا لَنْ نُّؤْثِرَكَ عَلٰى مَا جَآءَنَا مِنَ الْبَيِّنٰتِ وَالَّذِيْ فَطَرَنَا فَاقْضِ مَآ اَنْتَ قَاضٍ اِنَّمَا تَقْضِيْ هٰذِهِ الْحَيٰوةَ الدُّنْيَا ۗ ٧٢

اِنَّا اٰمَنَّا بِرَبِّنَا لِيَغْفِرَ لَنَا خَطٰيٰنَا وَمَآ اَكْرَهْتَنَا عَلَيْهِ مِنَ السِّحْرِ ۗ وَاللّٰهُ خَيْرٌ وَّاَبْقٰى ٧٣

اِنَّهٗ مَنْ يَّأْتِ رَبَّهٗ مُجْرِمًا فَاِنَّ لَهٗ جَهَنَّمَ ۚ لَا يَمُوْتُ فِيْهَا وَلَا يَحْيٰى ٧٤

وَمَنْ يَّأْتِهٖ مُؤْمِنًا قَدْ عَمِلَ الصّٰلِحٰتِ فَاُولٰٓئِكَ لَهُمُ الدَّرَجٰتُ الْعُلٰى ۙ ٧٥

جَنّٰتُ عَدْنٍ تَجْرِيْ مِنْ تَحْتِهَا الْاَنْهٰرُ خٰلِدِيْنَ فِيْهَا ۗ وَذٰلِكَ جَزٰٓؤُا مَنْ تَزَكّٰى ٧٦

وَلَقَدْ اَوْحَيْنَآ اِلٰى مُوْسٰٓى اَنْ اَسْرِ بِعِبَادِيْ فَاضْرِبْ لَهُمْ طَرِيْقًا فِى الْبَحْرِ يَبَسًا ۙ لَّا تَخٰفُ دَرَكًا وَّلَا تَخْشٰى ٧٧

فَاَتْبَعَهُمْ فِرْعَوْنُ بِجُنُوْدِهٖ فَغَشِيَهُمْ مِّنَ الْيَمِّ مَا غَشِيَهُمْ ۗ ٧٨

وَاَضَلَّ فِرْعَوْنُ قَوْمَهٗ وَمَا هَدٰى ٧٩

يٰبَنِيْ اِسْرَآءِيْلَ قَدْ اَنْجَيْنٰكُمْ مِّنْ عَدُوِّكُمْ وَوٰعَدْنٰكُمْ جَانِبَ الطُّوْرِ الْاَيْمَنَ وَنَزَّلْنَا عَلَيْكُمُ الْمَنَّ وَالسَّلْوٰى ٨٠

كُلُوْا مِنْ طَيِّبٰتِ مَا رَزَقْنٰكُمْ وَلَا تَطْغَوْا فِيْهِ فَيَحِلَّ عَلَيْكُمْ غَضَبِيْ ۚ وَمَنْ يَّحْلِلْ عَلَيْهِ غَضَبِيْ فَقَدْ هَوٰى ٨١

82. And most surely I am most Forgiving to him who repents and believes and does good, then continues to follow the right direction.

وَإِنِّي لَغَفَّارٌ لِّمَنْ تَابَ وَاٰمَنَ وَعَمِلَ صَالِحًا ثُمَّ اهْتَدٰى ۝

83. And what caused you to hasten from your people, O Musa?

وَمَآ أَعْجَلَكَ عَنْ قَوْمِكَ يٰمُوسٰى ۝

84. He said: They are here on my track and I hastened on to Thee, my Lord, that Thou mightest be pleased.

قَالَ هُمْ أُولَاءِ عَلٰى أَثَرِي وَعَجِلْتُ إِلَيْكَ رَبِّ لِتَرْضٰى ۝

85. He said: So surely We have tried your people after you, and the Samiri has led them astray.

قَالَ فَإِنَّا قَدْ فَتَنَّا قَوْمَكَ مِنْ بَعْدِكَ وَأَضَلَّهُمُ السَّامِرِيُّ ۝

86. So Musa returned to his people wrathful, sorrowing. Said he: O my people! did not your Lord promise you a goodly promise: did then the time seem long to you, or did you wish that displeasure from your Lord should be due to you, so that you broke (your) promise to me?

فَرَجَعَ مُوسٰى إِلٰى قَوْمِهِ غَضْبَانَ أَسِفًا قَالَ يٰقَوْمِ أَلَمْ يَعِدْكُمْ رَبُّكُمْ وَعْدًا حَسَنًا أَفَطَالَ عَلَيْكُمُ الْعَهْدُ أَمْ أَرَدْتُّمْ أَنْ يَّحِلَّ عَلَيْكُمْ غَضَبٌ مِّنْ رَّبِّكُمْ فَأَخْلَفْتُمْ مَّوْعِدِي ۝

87. They said: We did not break (our) promise to you of our own accord, but we were made to bear the burdens of the ornaments of the people, then we made a casting of them, and thus did the Samiri suggest.

قَالُوا مَآ أَخْلَفْنَا مَوْعِدَكَ بِمَلْكِنَا وَلٰكِنَّا حُمِّلْنَآ أَوْزَارًا مِّنْ زِينَةِ الْقَوْمِ فَقَذَفْنٰهَا فَكَذٰلِكَ أَلْقَى السَّامِرِيُّ ۝

88. So he brought forth for them a calf, a (mere) body, which had a mooing sound, so they said: This is your god and the god of Musa, but he forgot.

فَأَخْرَجَ لَهُمْ عِجْلًا جَسَدًا لَّهُ خُوَارٌ فَقَالُوا هٰذَآ إِلٰهُكُمْ وَإِلٰهُ مُوسٰى ه فَنَسِيَ ۝

89. What! could they not see that it did not return to them a reply, and (that) it did not control any harm or benefit for them?

أَفَلَا يَرَوْنَ أَلَّا يَرْجِعُ إِلَيْهِمْ قَوْلًا وَلَا يَمْلِكُ لَهُمْ ضَرًّا وَّلَا نَفْعًا ۝

90. And certainly Haroun had said to them before: O my people! you are only tried by it, and surely your Lord is the Beneficent God, therefore follow me and obey my order.

وَلَقَدْ قَالَ لَهُمْ هٰرُونُ مِنْ قَبْلُ يٰقَوْمِ إِنَّمَا فُتِنْتُمْ بِهِ وَإِنَّ رَبَّكُمُ الرَّحْمٰنُ فَاتَّبِعُونِي وَأَطِيعُوا أَمْرِي ۝

91. They said: We will by no means cease to keep to its worship until Musa returns to us.

قَالُوا لَنْ نَّبْرَحَ عَلَيْهِ عَاكِفِينَ حَتّٰى يَرْجِعَ إِلَيْنَا مُوسٰى ۝

92. (Musa) said: O Haroun! what prevented you, when you saw them going astray,

93. So that you did not follow me? Did you then disobey my order?

94. He said: O son of my mother! seize me not by my beard nor by my head; surely I was afraid lest you should say: You have caused a division among the children of Israel and not waited for my word.

95. He said: What was then your object, O Samiri?

96. He said: I saw (Jibreel) what they did not see, so I took a handful (of the dust) from the footsteps of the messenger, then I threw it in the casting; thus did my soul commend to me.

97. He said: Begone then, surely for you it will be in this life to say, Touch (me) not; and surely there is a threat for you, which shall not be made to fail to you, and look at your god to whose worship you kept (so long); we will certainly burn it, then we will certainly scatter it a (wide) scattering in the sea.

98. Your God is only Allah, there is no god but He; He comprehends all things in (His) knowledge.

99. Thus do We relate to you (some) of the news of what has gone before; and indeed We have given to you a Reminder from Ourselves.

100. Whoever turns aside from it, he shall surely bear a burden on the day of resurrection,

101. Abiding in this (state), and evil will it be for them to bear on the day of resurrection;

102. On the day when the trumpet shall be blown, and We will gather the guilty, blue-eyed, on that day;

103. They shall consult together secretly: You did tarry but ten (centuries).

104. We know best what they say, when the fairest of them in course would say: You tarried but a day.

105. And they ask you about the mountains. Say: My Lord will carry them away from the roots.

106. Then leave it a plain, smooth level;

107. You shall not see therein any crookedness or unevenness.

108. On that day they shall follow the inviter, there is no crookedness in him, and the voices shall be low before the Beneficent God so that you shall not hear aught but a soft sound.

109. On that day shall no intercession avail except of him whom the Beneficent God allows and whose word He is pleased with.

110. He knows what is before them and what is behind them, while they do not comprehend it in knowledge.

111. And the faces shall be humbled before the Living, the Self-subsistent God, and he who bears iniquity is indeed a failure.

112. And whoever does good works and he is a believer, he shall have no fear of injustice nor of the withholding of his due.

113. And thus have We sent it down an Arabic Quran, and have distinctly set forth therein of threats that they may guard (against evil) or that it may produce a reminder for them.

114. Supremely exalted is therefore Allah, the King, the Truth; and do not make haste with the Quran before its revelation is made complete to you and say: O my Lord! increase me in knowledge.

115. And certainly We gave a commandment to Adam before, but he forgot; and We did not find in him any determination.

116. And when We said to the angels: Make obeisance to Adam, they made obeisance, but Iblis (did it not); he refused.

117. So We said: O Adam! This is an enemy to you and to your wife; therefore let him not drive you both forth from the garden so that you should be unhappy;

118. Surely it is (ordained) for you that you shall not be hungry therein nor bare of clothing;

119. And that you shall not be thirsty therein nor shall you feel the heat of the sun.

120. But the Shaitan made an evil suggestion to him; he said: O Adam! Shall I guide you to the tree of immortality and a kingdom which decays not?

121. Then they both ate of it, so their evil inclinations became manifest to them, and they both began to cover themselves with leaves of the garden, and Adam disobeyed his Lord, so his life became evil (to him).

122. Then his Lord chose him, so He turned to him and guided (him).

123. He said: Get forth you two there-from, all (of you), one of you (is) enemy to another. So there will surely come to you guidance from Me, then whoever follows My guidance, he shall not go astray nor be unhappy;

124. And whoever turns away from My reminder, his shall surely be a straitened life, and We will raise him on the day of resurrection, blind.

125. He shall say: My Lord! why hast Thou raised me blind, and I was a seeing one indeed?

126. He will say: Even so, Our com-munications came to you, but you neglected them; even thus shall you be forsaken this day.

127. And thus do We recompense him who is extravagant and does not believe in the communications of his Lord; and certainly the chastisement of the hereafter is severer and more lasting.

وَاِذْ قُلْنَا لِلْمَلٰٓئِكَةِ اسْجُدُوْا لِاٰدَمَ فَسَجَدُوْٓا اِلَّآ اِبْلِيْسَ ؕ اَبٰى ۝

فَقُلْنَا يٰٓاٰدَمُ اِنَّ هٰذَا عَدُوٌّ لَّكَ وَلِزَوْجِكَ فَلَا يُخْرِجَنَّكُمَا مِنَ الْجَنَّةِ فَتَشْقٰى ۝

اِنَّ لَكَ اَلَّا تَجُوْعَ فِيْهَا وَلَا تَعْرٰى ۙ۝

وَاَنَّكَ لَا تَظْمَؤُا فِيْهَا وَلَا تَضْحٰى ۝

فَوَسْوَسَ اِلَيْهِ الشَّيْطٰنُ قَالَ يٰٓاٰدَمُ هَلْ اَدُلُّكَ عَلٰى شَجَرَةِ الْخُلْدِ وَمُلْكٍ لَّا يَبْلٰى ۝

فَاَكَلَا مِنْهَا فَبَدَتْ لَهُمَا سَوْاٰتُهُمَا وَطَفِقَا يَخْصِفٰنِ عَلَيْهِمَا مِنْ وَّرَقِ الْجَنَّةِ ؗ وَعَصٰٓى اٰدَمُ رَبَّهٗ فَغَوٰى ۝

ثُمَّ اجْتَبٰهُ رَبُّهٗ فَتَابَ عَلَيْهِ وَهَدٰى ۝

قَالَ اهْبِطَا مِنْهَا جَمِيْعًۢا بَعْضُكُمْ لِبَعْضٍ عَدُوٌّ ۚ فَاِمَّا يَاْتِيَنَّكُمْ مِّنِّيْ هُدًى ۙ۬ فَمَنِ اتَّبَعَ هُدَايَ فَلَا يَضِلُّ وَلَا يَشْقٰى ۝

وَمَنْ اَعْرَضَ عَنْ ذِكْرِيْ فَاِنَّ لَهٗ مَعِيْشَةً ضَنْكًا وَّنَحْشُرُهٗ يَوْمَ الْقِيٰمَةِ اَعْمٰى ۝

قَالَ رَبِّ لِمَ حَشَرْتَنِيْٓ اَعْمٰى وَقَدْ كُنْتُ بَصِيْرًا ۝

قَالَ كَذٰلِكَ اَتَتْكَ اٰيٰتُنَا فَنَسِيْتَهَا ؕ وَكَذٰلِكَ الْيَوْمَ تُنْسٰى ۝

وَكَذٰلِكَ نَجْزِيْ مَنْ اَسْرَفَ وَلَمْ يُؤْمِنْۢ بِاٰيٰتِ رَبِّهٖ ؕ وَلَعَذَابُ الْاٰخِرَةِ اَشَدُّ وَاَبْقٰى ۝

128. Does it not then direct them aright how many of the generations in whose dwelling-places they go about We destroyed before them? Most surely there are signs in this for those endowed with understanding.

129. And had there not been a word (that had) already gone forth from your Lord and an appointed term, it would surely have been made to cleave (to them).

130. Bear then patiently what they say, and glorify your Lord by the praising of Him before the rising of the sun and before its setting, and during hours of the night do also glorify (Him) and during parts of the day, that you may be well pleased.

131. And do not stretch your eyes after that with which We have provided different classes of them, (of) the splendor of this world's life, that We may thereby try them; and the sustenance (given) by your Lord is better and more abiding.

132. And enjoin prayer on your followers, and steadily adhere to it; We do not ask you for subsistence; We do give you subsistence, and the (good) end is for guarding (against evil).

133. And they say: Why does he not bring to us a sign from his Lord? Has not there come to them a clear evidence of what is in the previous books?

134. And had We destroyed them with chastisement before this, they would certainly have said: O our Lord! why didst Thou not send to us an apostle, for then we should have followed Thy communications before that we met disgrace and shame.

135. Say: Every one (of us) is awaiting, therefore do await: So you will come to know who is the follower of the even path and who goes aright.

أَفَلَمْ يَهْدِ لَهُمْ كَمْ اَهْلَكْنَا قَبْلَهُمْ مِّنَ الْقُرُوْنِ يَمْشُوْنَ فِيْ مَسٰكِنِهِمْ ۚ اِنَّ فِيْ ذٰلِكَ لَاٰيٰتٍ لِّاُولِي النُّهٰى ۝

وَلَوْلَا كَلِمَةٌ سَبَقَتْ مِنْ رَّبِّكَ لَكَانَ لِزَامًا وَّاَجَلٌ مُّسَمًّى ۝

فَاصْبِرْ عَلٰى مَا يَقُوْلُوْنَ وَسَبِّحْ بِحَمْدِ رَبِّكَ قَبْلَ طُلُوْعِ الشَّمْسِ وَقَبْلَ غُرُوْبِهَا ۚ وَمِنْ اٰنَآئِ الَّيْلِ فَسَبِّحْ وَاَطْرَافَ النَّهَارِ لَعَلَّكَ تَرْضٰى ۝

وَلَا تَمُدَّنَّ عَيْنَيْكَ اِلٰى مَا مَتَّعْنَا بِهٖۤ اَزْوَاجًا مِّنْهُمْ زَهْرَةَ الْحَيٰوةِ الدُّنْيَا ۙ لِنَفْتِنَهُمْ فِيْهِ ۚ وَرِزْقُ رَبِّكَ خَيْرٌ وَّاَبْقٰى ۝

وَأْمُرْ اَهْلَكَ بِالصَّلٰوةِ وَاصْطَبِرْ عَلَيْهَا ۚ لَا نَسْـَٔلُكَ رِزْقًا ۚ نَحْنُ نَرْزُقُكَ ۚ وَالْعَاقِبَةُ لِلتَّقْوٰى ۝

وَقَالُوْا لَوْلَا يَأْتِيْنَا بِاٰيَةٍ مِّنْ رَّبِّهٖ ۚ اَوَلَمْ تَأْتِهِمْ بَيِّنَةُ مَا فِي الصُّحُفِ الْاُوْلٰى ۝

وَلَوْ اَنَّا اَهْلَكْنٰهُمْ بِعَذَابٍ مِّنْ قَبْلِهٖ لَقَالُوْا رَبَّنَا لَوْلَا اَرْسَلْتَ اِلَيْنَا رَسُوْلًا فَنَتَّبِعَ اٰيٰتِكَ مِنْ قَبْلِ اَنْ نَّذِلَّ وَنَخْزٰى ۝

قُلْ كُلٌّ مُّتَرَبِّصٌ فَتَرَبَّصُوْا ۚ فَسَتَعْلَمُوْنَ مَنْ اَصْحٰبُ الصِّرَاطِ السَّوِيِّ وَمَنِ اهْتَدٰى ۝

THE PROPHETS
(ANBIYA)

**In the name of Allah,
the Beneficent, the Merciful.**

بِسْمِ اللهِ الرَّحْمٰنِ الرَّحِيْمِ ۞

1. Their reckoning has drawn near to men, and in heedlessness are they turning aside.

2. There comes not to them a new reminder from their Lord but they hear it while they sport,

3. Their hearts trifling; and those who are unjust counsel together in secret: He is nothing but a mortal like yourselves; what! will you then yield to enchantment while you see?

4. He said: My Lord knows what is spoken in the heaven and the earth, and He is the Hearing, the Knowing.

5. Nay! say they: Medleys of dreams; nay! he has forged it; nay! he is a poet; so let him bring to us a sign as the former (prophets) were sent (with).

6. There did not believe before them any town which We destroyed; will they then believe?

7. And We did not send before you any but men to whom We sent revelation, so ask the followers of the reminder if you do not know.

8. And We did not make them bodies not eating the food, and they were not to abide (forever).

9. Then We made Our promise good to them, so We delivered them and those whom We pleased, and We destroyed the extravagant.

10. Certainly We have revealed to you a Book in which is your good remembrance; what! do you not then understand?

اِقْتَرَبَ لِلنَّاسِ حِسَابُهُمْ وَهُمْ فِيْ غَفْلَةٍ مُّعْرِضُوْنَ ۞

مَا يَأْتِيْهِمْ مِّنْ ذِكْرٍ مِّنْ رَّبِّهِمْ مُّحْدَثٍ اِلَّا اسْتَمَعُوْهُ وَهُمْ يَلْعَبُوْنَ ۞

لَاهِيَةً قُلُوْبُهُمْ وَاَسَرُّوا النَّجْوَى الَّذِيْنَ ظَلَمُوْا هَلْ هٰذَا اِلَّا بَشَرٌ مِّثْلُكُمْ اَفَتَأْتُوْنَ السِّحْرَ وَاَنْتُمْ تُبْصِرُوْنَ ۞

قٰلَ رَبِّيْ يَعْلَمُ الْقَوْلَ فِي السَّمَآءِ وَالْاَرْضِ وَهُوَ السَّمِيْعُ الْعَلِيْمُ ۞

بَلْ قَالُوْا اَضْغَاثُ اَحْلَامٍ بَلِ افْتَرَاهُ بَلْ هُوَ شَاعِرٌ فَلْيَأْتِنَا بِاٰيَةٍ كَمَا اُرْسِلَ الْاَوَّلُوْنَ ۞

مَا اٰمَنَتْ قَبْلَهُمْ مِّنْ قَرْيَةٍ اَهْلَكْنَاهَا اَفَهُمْ يُؤْمِنُوْنَ ۞

وَمَا اَرْسَلْنَا قَبْلَكَ اِلَّا رِجَالًا نُّوْحِيْ اِلَيْهِمْ فَسْـئَلُوْا اَهْلَ الذِّكْرِ اِنْ كُنْتُمْ لَا تَعْلَمُوْنَ ۞

وَمَا جَعَلْنَاهُمْ جَسَدًا لَّا يَأْكُلُوْنَ الطَّعَامَ وَمَا كَانُوْا خٰلِدِيْنَ ۞

ثُمَّ صَدَقْنَاهُمُ الْوَعْدَ فَاَنْجَيْنَاهُمْ وَمَنْ نَّشَآءُ وَاَهْلَكْنَا الْمُسْرِفِيْنَ ۞

لَقَدْ اَنْزَلْنَا اِلَيْكُمْ كِتٰبًا فِيْهِ ذِكْرُكُمْ اَفَلَا تَعْقِلُوْنَ ۞

11. And how many a town which was iniquitous did We demolish, and We raised up after it another people!

وَكَمْ قَصَمْنَا مِنْ قَرْيَةٍ كَانَتْ ظَالِمَةً وَّاَنْشَأْنَا بَعْدَهَا قَوْمًا اٰخَرِيْنَ ۞

12. So when they felt Our punishment, lo! they began to fly from it.

فَلَمَّآ اَحَسُّوْا بَأْسَنَآ اِذَا هُمْ مِّنْهَا يَرْكُضُوْنَ ۞

13. Do not fly (now) and come back to what you were made to lead easy lives in and to your dwellings, haply you will be questioned.

لَا تَرْكُضُوْا وَارْجِعُوْٓا اِلٰى مَآ اُتْرِفْتُمْ فِيْهِ وَمَسٰكِنِكُمْ لَعَلَّكُمْ تُسْـَٔلُوْنَ ۞

14. They said: O woe to us! surely we were unjust.

قَالُوْا يٰوَيْلَنَآ اِنَّا كُنَّا ظٰلِمِيْنَ ۞

15. And this ceased not to be their cry till We made them cut off, extinct.

فَمَا زَالَتْ تِّلْكَ دَعْوٰىهُمْ حَتّٰى جَعَلْنٰهُمْ حَصِيْدًا خٰمِدِيْنَ ۞

16. And We did not create the heaven and the earth and what is between them for sport.

وَمَا خَلَقْنَا السَّمَآءَ وَالْاَرْضَ وَمَا بَيْنَهُمَا لٰعِبِيْنَ ۞

17. Had We wished to make a diversion, We would have made it from before Ourselves: by no means would We do (it).

لَوْ اَرَدْنَآ اَنْ نَّتَّخِذَ لَهْوًا لَّاتَّخَذْنٰهُ مِنْ لَّدُنَّآ ۖ اِنْ كُنَّا فٰعِلِيْنَ ۞

18. Nay! We cast the truth against the falsehood, so that it breaks its head, and lo! it vanishes; and woe to you for what you describe;

بَلْ نَقْذِفُ بِالْحَقِّ عَلَى الْبَاطِلِ فَيَدْمَغُهٗ فَاِذَا هُوَ زَاهِقٌ ۚ وَلَكُمُ الْوَيْلُ مِمَّا تَصِفُوْنَ ۞

19. And whoever is in the heavens and the earth is His; and those who are with Him are not proud to serve Him, nor do they grow weary.

وَلَهٗ مَنْ فِى السَّمٰوٰتِ وَالْاَرْضِ ۚ وَمَنْ عِنْدَهٗ لَا يَسْتَكْبِرُوْنَ عَنْ عِبَادَتِهٖ وَلَا يَسْتَحْسِرُوْنَ ۞

20. They glorify (Him) by night and day; they are never languid.

يُسَبِّحُوْنَ الَّيْلَ وَالنَّهَارَ لَا يَفْتُرُوْنَ ۞

21. Or have they taken gods from the earth who raise (the dead).

اَمِ اتَّخَذُوْٓا اٰلِهَةً مِّنَ الْاَرْضِ هُمْ يُنْشِرُوْنَ ۞

22. If there had been in them any gods except Allah, they would both have certainly been in a state of disorder; therefore glory be to Allah, the Lord of the dominion, above what they attribute (to Him).

لَوْ كَانَ فِيْهِمَآ اٰلِهَةٌ اِلَّا اللّٰهُ لَفَسَدَتَا ۚ فَسُبْحٰنَ اللّٰهِ رَبِّ الْعَرْشِ عَمَّا يَصِفُوْنَ ۞

23. He cannot be questioned concerning what He does and they shall be questioned.

لَا يُسْـَٔلُ عَمَّا يَفْعَلُ وَهُمْ يُسْـَٔلُوْنَ ۞

24. Or, have they taken gods besides Him? Say: Bring your proof; this is the reminder of those with me and the reminder of those before me. Nay! most of them do not know the truth, so they turn aside.

اَمِ اتَّخَذُوْا مِنْ دُوْنِهٖٓ اٰلِهَةً ۚ قُلْ هَاتُوْا بُرْهَانَكُمْ ۚ هٰذَا ذِكْرُ مَنْ مَّعِيَ وَذِكْرُ مَنْ قَبْلِيْ ۗ بَلْ اَكْثَرُهُمْ لَا يَعْلَمُوْنَ الْحَقَّ فَهُمْ مُّعْرِضُوْنَ ۞

25. And We did not send before you any apostle but We revealed to him that there is no god but Me, therefore serve Me.

وَمَا أَرْسَلْنَا مِنْ قَبْلِكَ مِنْ رَّسُوْلٍ اِلَّا نُوْحِىْٓ اِلَيْهِ اَنَّهٗ لَا اِلٰهَ اِلَّا اَنَا فَاعْبُدُوْنِ ۝

26. And they say: The Beneficent God has taken to Himself a son. Glory be to Him. Nay! they are honored servants;

وَقَالُوا اتَّخَذَ الرَّحْمٰنُ وَلَدًا سُبْحٰنَهٗ بَلْ عِبَادٌ مُّكْرَمُوْنَ ۝

27. They do not precede Him in speech and (only) according to His commandment do they act.

لَا يَسْبِقُوْنَهٗ بِالْقَوْلِ وَهُمْ بِاَمْرِهٖ يَعْمَلُوْنَ ۝

28. He knows what is before them and what is behind them, and they do not intercede except for him whom He approves, and for fear of Him they tremble.

يَعْلَمُ مَا بَيْنَ اَيْدِيْهِمْ وَمَا خَلْفَهُمْ وَلَا يَشْفَعُوْنَ اِلَّا لِمَنِ ارْتَضٰى وَهُمْ مِّنْ خَشْيَتِهٖ مُشْفِقُوْنَ ۝

29. And whoever of them should say: Surely I am a god besides Him, such a one do We recompense with hell; thus do We recompense the unjust.

وَمَنْ يَّقُلْ مِنْهُمْ اِنِّيْٓ اِلٰهٌ مِّنْ دُوْنِهٖ فَذٰلِكَ نَجْزِيْهِ جَهَنَّمَ كَذٰلِكَ نَجْزِى الظّٰلِمِيْنَ ۝

30. Do not those who disbelieve see that the heavens and the earth were closed up, but We have opened them; and We have made of water everything living, will they not then believe?

اَوَلَمْ يَرَ الَّذِيْنَ كَفَرُوْٓا اَنَّ السَّمٰوٰتِ وَالْاَرْضَ كَانَتَا رَتْقًا فَفَتَقْنٰهُمَا وَجَعَلْنَا مِنَ الْمَاءِ كُلَّ شَيْءٍ حَيٍّ اَفَلَا يُؤْمِنُوْنَ ۝

31. And We have made great mountains in the earth lest it might be convulsed with them, and We have made in it wide ways that they may follow a right direction.

وَجَعَلْنَا فِى الْاَرْضِ رَوَاسِىَ اَنْ تَمِيْدَ بِهِمْ وَجَعَلْنَا فِيْهَا فِجَاجًا سُبُلًا لَّعَلَّهُمْ يَهْتَدُوْنَ ۝

32. And We have made the heaven a guarded canopy and (yet) they turn aside from its signs.

وَجَعَلْنَا السَّمَاءَ سَقْفًا مَّحْفُوْظًا وَهُمْ عَنْ اٰيٰتِهَا مُعْرِضُوْنَ ۝

33. And He it is Who created the night and the day and the sun and the moon; all (orbs) travel along swiftly in their celestial spheres.

وَهُوَ الَّذِىْ خَلَقَ الَّيْلَ وَالنَّهَارَ وَالشَّمْسَ وَالْقَمَرَ كُلٌّ فِىْ فَلَكٍ يَّسْبَحُوْنَ ۝

34. And We did not ordain abiding for any mortal before you. What! then if you die, will they abide?

وَمَا جَعَلْنَا لِبَشَرٍ مِّنْ قَبْلِكَ الْخُلْدَ اَفَاِنْ مِّتَّ فَهُمُ الْخٰلِدُوْنَ ۝

35. Every soul must taste of death and We try you by evil and good by way of probation; and to Us you shall be brought back.

كُلُّ نَفْسٍ ذَائِقَةُ الْمَوْتِ وَنَبْلُوْكُمْ بِالشَّرِّ وَالْخَيْرِ فِتْنَةً وَاِلَيْنَا تُرْجَعُوْنَ ۝

36. And when those who disbelieve see you, they do not take you but for one to be scoffed at: Is this he who speaks of your gods? And they are deniers at the mention of the Beneficent God.

37. Man is created of haste; now will I show to you My signs, therefore do not ask Me to hasten (them) on.

38. And they say: When will this threat come to pass if you are truthful?

39. Had those who disbelieve but known (of the time) when they shall not be able to ward off the fire from their faces nor from their backs, nor shall they be helped.

40. Nay, it shall come on them all of a sudden and cause them to become confounded, so they shall not have the power to avert it, nor shall they be respited.

41. And certainly apostles before you were scoffed at, then there befell those of them who scoffed that at which they had scoffed.

42. Say: Who guards you by night and by day from the Beneficent God? Nay, they turn aside at the mention of their Lord.

43. Or, have they gods who can defend them against Us? They shall not be able to assist themselves, nor shall they be defended from Us.

44. Nay, We gave provision to these and their fathers until life was prolonged to them. Do they not then see that We are visiting the land, curtailing it of its sides? Shall they then prevail?

45. Say: I warn you only by revelation; and the deaf do not hear the call whenever they are warned.

308

46. And if a blast of the chastisement of your Lord were to touch them, they will certainly say: O woe to us! surely we were unjust.

47. And We will set up a just balance on the day of resurrection, so no soul shall be dealt with unjustly in the least; and though there be the weight of a grain of mustard seed, (yet) will We bring it, and sufficient are We to take account.

48. And certainly We gave to Musa and Haroun the Furqan and a light and a reminder for those who would guard (against evil).

49. (For) those who fear their Lord in secret and they are fearful of the hour.

50. And this is a blessed Reminder which We have revealed; will you then deny it?

51. And certainly We gave to Ibrahim his rectitude before, and We knew him fully well.

52. When he said to his father and his people: What are these images to whose worship you cleave?

53. They said: We found our fathers worshipping them.

54. He said: Certainly you have been, (both) you and your fathers, in manifest error.

55. They said: Have you brought to us the truth, or are you one of the triflers?

56. He said: Nay! your Lord is the Lord of the heavens and the earth, Who brought them into existence, and I am of those who bear witness to this:

57. And, by Allah! I will certainly do something against your idols after you go away, turning back.

وَلَئِنْ مَّسَّتْهُمْ نَفْحَةٌ مِّنْ عَذَابِ رَبِّكَ لَيَقُوْلُنَّ يٰوَيْلَنَا ٓ اِنَّا كُنَّا ظٰلِمِيْنَ ۞

وَنَضَعُ الْمَوَازِيْنَ الْقِسْطَ لِيَوْمِ الْقِيٰمَةِ فَلَا تُظْلَمُ نَفْسٌ شَيْئًا ۗ وَاِنْ كَانَ مِثْقَالَ حَبَّةٍ مِّنْ خَرْدَلٍ اَتَيْنَا بِهَا ۗ وَكَفٰى بِنَا حٰسِبِيْنَ ۞

وَلَقَدْ اٰتَيْنَا مُوْسٰى وَهٰرُوْنَ الْفُرْقَانَ وَضِيَآءً وَّذِكْرًا لِّلْمُتَّقِيْنَ ۞

الَّذِيْنَ يَخْشَوْنَ رَبَّهُمْ بِالْغَيْبِ وَهُمْ مِّنَ السَّاعَةِ مُشْفِقُوْنَ ۞

وَهٰذَا ذِكْرٌ مُّبٰرَكٌ اَنْزَلْنٰهُ ۚ اَفَاَنْتُمْ لَهٗ مُنْكِرُوْنَ ۞

وَلَقَدْ اٰتَيْنَا اِبْرٰهِيْمَ رُشْدَهٗ مِنْ قَبْلُ وَكُنَّا بِهٖ عٰلِمِيْنَ ۞

اِذْ قَالَ لِاَبِيْهِ وَقَوْمِهٖ مَا هٰذِهِ التَّمَاثِيْلُ الَّتِيْ اَنْتُمْ لَهَا عٰكِفُوْنَ ۞

قَالُوْا وَجَدْنَا ٓ اٰبَآءَنَا لَهَا عٰبِدِيْنَ ۞

قَالَ لَقَدْ كُنْتُمْ اَنْتُمْ وَاٰبَآؤُكُمْ فِيْ ضَلٰلٍ مُّبِيْنٍ ۞

قَالُوْا اَجِئْتَنَا بِالْحَقِّ اَمْ اَنْتَ مِنَ اللّٰعِبِيْنَ ۞

قَالَ بَلْ رَّبُّكُمْ رَبُّ السَّمٰوٰتِ وَالْاَرْضِ الَّذِيْ فَطَرَهُنَّ ۖ وَاَنَا عَلٰى ذٰلِكُمْ مِّنَ الشّٰهِدِيْنَ ۞

وَتَاللّٰهِ لَاَكِيْدَنَّ اَصْنَامَكُمْ بَعْدَ اَنْ تُوَلُّوْا مُدْبِرِيْنَ ۞

309

58. So he broke them into pieces, except the chief of them, that haply they may return to it.

فَجَعَلَهُمْ جُذٰذًا اِلَّا كَبِيْرًا لَّهُمْ لَعَلَّهُمْ اِلَيْهِ يَرْجِعُوْنَ ۝

59. They said: Who has done this to our gods? Most surely he is one of the unjust.

قَالُوْا مَنْ فَعَلَ هٰذَا بِاٰلِهَتِنَآ اِنَّهٗ لَمِنَ الظّٰلِمِيْنَ

60. They said: We heard a youth called Ibrahim speak of them.

قَالُوْا سَمِعْنَا فَتًى يَّذْكُرُهُمْ يُقَالُ لَهٗٓ اِبْرٰهِيْمُ ۝

61. Said they: Then bring him before the eyes of the people, perhaps they may bear witness.

قَالُوْا فَأْتُوْا بِهٖ عَلٰٓى اَعْيُنِ النَّاسِ لَعَلَّهُمْ يَشْهَدُوْنَ ۝

62. They said: Have you done this to our gods, O Ibrahim?

قَالُوْٓا ءَاَنْتَ فَعَلْتَ هٰذَا بِاٰلِهَتِنَا يَاۤاِبْرٰهِيْمُ ۝

63. He said: Surely (some doer) has done it; the chief of them is this, therefore ask them, if they can speak.

قَالَ بَلْ فَعَلَهٗ ۖ كَبِيْرُهُمْ هٰذَا فَاسْـَٔلُوْهُمْ اِنْ كَانُوْا يَنْطِقُوْنَ ۝

64. Then they turned to themselves and said: Surely you yourselves are the unjust;

فَرَجَعُوْٓا اِلٰٓى اَنْفُسِهِمْ فَقَالُوْٓا اِنَّكُمْ اَنْتُمُ الظّٰلِمُوْنَ ۝

65. Then they were made to hang down their heads: Certainly you know that they do not speak.

ثُمَّ نُكِسُوْا عَلٰى رُءُوْسِهِمْ ۚ لَقَدْ عَلِمْتَ مَا هٰٓؤُلَاۤءِ يَنْطِقُوْنَ ۝

66. He said: What! do you then serve besides Allah what brings you not any benefit at all, nor does it harm you?

قَالَ اَفَتَعْبُدُوْنَ مِنْ دُوْنِ اللّٰهِ مَا لَا يَنْفَعُكُمْ شَيْـًٔا وَّلَا يَضُرُّكُمْ ۝

67. Fie on you and on what you serve besides Allah; what! do you not then understand?

اُفٍّ لَّكُمْ وَلِمَا تَعْبُدُوْنَ مِنْ دُوْنِ اللّٰهِ ۚ اَفَلَا تَعْقِلُوْنَ ۝

68. They said: Burn him and help your gods, if you are going to do (anything).

قَالُوْا حَرِّقُوْهُ وَانْصُرُوْٓا اٰلِهَتَكُمْ اِنْ كُنْتُمْ فٰعِلِيْنَ ۝

69. We said: O fire! be a comfort and peace to Ibrahim;

قُلْنَا يَا نَارُ كُوْنِيْ بَرْدًا وَّسَلٰمًا عَلٰٓى اِبْرٰهِيْمَ ۝

70. And they desired a war on him, but We made them the greatest losers.

وَاَرَادُوْا بِهٖ كَيْدًا فَجَعَلْنٰهُمُ الْاَخْسَرِيْنَ ۝

71. And We delivered him as well as Lut (removing them) to the land which We had blessed for all people.

وَنَجَّيْنٰهُ وَلُوْطًا اِلَى الْاَرْضِ الَّتِيْ بٰرَكْنَا فِيْهَا لِلْعٰلَمِيْنَ ۝

72. And We gave him Ishaq and Yaqoub, a son's son, and We made (them) all good.

وَوَهَبْنَا لَهٗٓ اِسْحٰقَ ۚ وَيَعْقُوْبَ نَافِلَةً ۚ وَكُلًّا جَعَلْنَا صٰلِحِيْنَ ۝

73. And We made them Imams who guided (people) by Our command, and We revealed to them the doing of good and the keeping up of prayer and the giving of the alms, and Us (alone) did they serve;

وَجَعَلْنٰهُمْ اَئِمَّةً يَّهْدُوْنَ بِاَمْرِنَا وَاَوْحَيْنَآ اِلَيْهِمْ فِعْلَ الْخَيْرٰتِ وَاِقَامَ الصَّلٰوةِ وَاِيْتَآءَ الزَّكٰوةِ ۚ وَكَانُوْا لَنَا عٰبِدِيْنَ ۟ۙ

74. And (as for) Lut, We gave him wisdom and knowledge, and We delivered him from the town which wrought abominations; surely they were an evil people, transgressors;

وَلُوْطًا اٰتَيْنٰهُ حُكْمًا وَّعِلْمًا وَّنَجَّيْنٰهُ مِنَ الْقَرْيَةِ الَّتِيْ كَانَتْ تَّعْمَلُ الْخَبٰٓئِثَ ۗ اِنَّهُمْ كَانُوْا قَوْمَ سَوْءٍ فٰسِقِيْنَ ۟ۙ

75. And We took him into Our mercy; surely he was of the good.

وَاَدْخَلْنٰهُ فِيْ رَحْمَتِنَا ۗ اِنَّهُ مِنَ الصّٰلِحِيْنَ ۟

76. And Nuh, when he cried aforetime, so We answered him, and delivered him and his followers from the great calamity.

وَنُوْحًا اِذْ نَادٰى مِنْ قَبْلُ فَاسْتَجَبْنَا لَهُ فَنَجَّيْنٰهُ وَاَهْلَهُ مِنَ الْكَرْبِ الْعَظِيْمِ ۟ۙ

77. And We helped him against the people who rejected Our communications; surely they were an evil people, so We drowned them all.

وَنَصَرْنٰهُ مِنَ الْقَوْمِ الَّذِيْنَ كَذَّبُوْا بِاٰيٰتِنَا ۗ اِنَّهُمْ كَانُوْا قَوْمَ سَوْءٍ فَاَغْرَقْنٰهُمْ اَجْمَعِيْنَ ۟

78. And Dawood and Sulaiman when they gave judgment concerning the field when the people's sheep pastured therein by night, and We were bearers of witness to their judgment.

وَدَاوٗدَ وَسُلَيْمٰنَ اِذْ يَحْكُمٰنِ فِى الْحَرْثِ اِذْ نَفَشَتْ فِيْهِ غَنَمُ الْقَوْمِ ۚ وَكُنَّا لِحُكْمِهِمْ شٰهِدِيْنَ ۟ۙ

79. So We made Sulaiman to understand it; and to each one We gave wisdom and knowledge; and We made the mountains, and the birds to celebrate Our praise with Dawood; and We were the doers.

فَفَهَّمْنٰهَا سُلَيْمٰنَ ۚ وَكُلًّا اٰتَيْنَا حُكْمًا وَّعِلْمًا ۙ وَّسَخَّرْنَا مَعَ دَاوٗدَ الْجِبَالَ يُسَبِّحْنَ وَالطَّيْرَ ۗ وَكُنَّا فٰعِلِيْنَ ۟

80. And We taught him the making of coats of mail for you, that they might protect you in your wars; will you then be grateful?

وَعَلَّمْنٰهُ صَنْعَةَ لَبُوْسٍ لَّكُمْ لِتُحْصِنَكُمْ مِّنْ بَأْسِكُمْ ۚ فَهَلْ اَنْتُمْ شٰكِرُوْنَ ۟

81. And (We made subservient) to Sulaiman the wind blowing violent, pursuing its course by his command to the land which We had blessed, and We are knower of all things.

وَلِسُلَيْمٰنَ الرِّيْحَ عَاصِفَةً تَجْرِيْ بِاَمْرِهِ اِلَى الْاَرْضِ الَّتِيْ بٰرَكْنَا فِيْهَا ۗ وَكُنَّا بِكُلِّ شَيْءٍ عٰلِمِيْنَ ۟

82. And of the rebellious people there were those who dived for him and did other work besides that, and We kept guard over them;

وَمِنَ الشَّيٰطِيْنِ مَنْ يَّغُوْصُوْنَ لَهُ وَيَعْمَلُوْنَ عَمَلًا دُوْنَ ذٰلِكَ ۚ وَكُنَّا لَهُمْ حٰفِظِيْنَ ۟ۙ

83. And Ayub, when he cried to his Lord, (saying): Harm has afflicted me, and Thou art the most Merciful of the merciful.

وَأَيُّوْبَ اِذْ نَادٰى رَبَّهٗٓ اَنِّيْ مَسَّنِيَ الضُّرُّ وَاَنْتَ اَرْحَمُ الرّٰحِمِيْنَ ۞

84. Therefore We responded to him and took off what harm he had, and We gave him his family and the like of them with them: a mercy from Us and a reminder to the worshippers.

فَاسْتَجَبْنَا لَهٗ فَكَشَفْنَا مَا بِهٖ مِنْ ضُرٍّ وَّاٰتَيْنٰهُ اَهْلَهٗ وَمِثْلَهُمْ مَّعَهُمْ رَحْمَةً مِّنْ عِنْدِنَا وَ ذِكْرٰى لِلْعٰبِدِيْنَ ۞

85. And Ismail and Idris and Zulkifl; all were of the patient ones;

وَاِسْمٰعِيْلَ وَاِدْرِيْسَ وَذَا الْكِفْلِ كُلٌّ مِّنَ الصّٰبِرِيْنَ ۞

86. And We caused them to enter into Our mercy; surely they were of the good ones.

وَاَدْخَلْنٰهُمْ فِيْ رَحْمَتِنَا اِنَّهُمْ مِّنَ الصّٰلِحِيْنَ ۞

87. And Yunus, when he went away in wrath, so he thought that We would not straiten him, so he called out among afflictions: There is no god but Thou, glory be to Thee; surely I am of those who make themselves to suffer loss.

وَذَا النُّوْنِ اِذْ ذَّهَبَ مُغَاضِبًا فَظَنَّ اَنْ لَّنْ نَّقْدِرَ عَلَيْهِ فَنَادٰى فِي الظُّلُمٰتِ اَنْ لَّآ اِلٰهَ اِلَّآ اَنْتَ سُبْحٰنَكَ اِنِّيْ كُنْتُ مِنَ الظّٰلِمِيْنَ ۞

88. So We responded to him and delivered him from the grief, and thus do We deliver the believers.

فَاسْتَجَبْنَا لَهٗ وَنَجَّيْنٰهُ مِنَ الْغَمِّ وَكَذٰلِكَ نُنْجِي الْمُؤْمِنِيْنَ ۞

89. And Zakariya, when he cried to his Lord: O my Lord! leave me not alone; and Thou art the best of inheritors.

وَزَكَرِيَّآ اِذْ نَادٰى رَبَّهٗ رَبِّ لَا تَذَرْنِيْ فَرْدًا وَّ اَنْتَ خَيْرُ الْوٰرِثِيْنَ ۞

90. So We responded to him and gave him Yahya and made his wife fit for him; surely they used to hasten, one with another, in deeds of goodness and to call upon Us, hoping and fearing; and they were humble before Us.

فَاسْتَجَبْنَا لَهٗ وَوَهَبْنَا لَهٗ يَحْيٰى وَاَصْلَحْنَا لَهٗ زَوْجَهٗ اِنَّهُمْ كَانُوْا يُسٰرِعُوْنَ فِي الْخَيْرٰتِ وَ يَدْعُوْنَنَا رَغَبًا وَّرَهَبًا وَكَانُوْا لَنَا خٰشِعِيْنَ ۞

91. And she who guarded her chastity, so We breathed into her of Our inspiration and made her and her son a sign for the nations.

وَالَّتِيْٓ اَحْصَنَتْ فَرْجَهَا فَنَفَخْنَا فِيْهَا مِنْ رُّوْحِنَا وَجَعَلْنٰهَا وَابْنَهَآ اٰيَةً لِّلْعٰلَمِيْنَ ۞

92. Surely this Islam is your religion, one religion (only), and I am your Lord, therefore serve Me.

اِنَّ هٰذِهٖٓ اُمَّتُكُمْ اُمَّةً وَّاحِدَةً وَّاَنَا رَبُّكُمْ فَاعْبُدُوْنِ ۞

93. And they broke their religion (into sects) between them: to Us shall all come back.

وَتَقَطَّعُوا اَمْرَهُمْ بَيْنَهُمْ كُلٌّ اِلَيْنَا رٰجِعُوْنَ ۝

94. Therefore whoever shall do of good deeds and he is a believer, there shall be no denying of his exertion, and surely We will write (it) down for him.

فَمَنْ يَّعْمَلْ مِنَ الصّٰلِحٰتِ وَهُوَ مُؤْمِنٌ فَلَا كُفْرَانَ لِسَعْيِهٖ ۚ وَاِنَّا لَهٗ كٰتِبُوْنَ ۝

95. And it is binding on a town which We destroy that they shall not return.

وَحَرٰمٌ عَلٰى قَرْيَةٍ اَهْلَكْنٰهَآ اَنَّهُمْ لَا يَرْجِعُوْنَ ۝

96. Even when Gog and Magog are let loose and they shall break forth from every elevated place.

حَتّٰى اِذَا فُتِحَتْ يَاْجُوْجُ وَمَاْجُوْجُ وَهُمْ مِّنْ كُلِّ حَدَبٍ يَّنْسِلُوْنَ ۝

97. And the true promise shall draw nigh, then lo! the eyes of those who disbelieved shall be fixedly open: O woe to us! surely we were in a state of heedlessness as to this; nay, we were unjust.

وَاقْتَرَبَ الْوَعْدُ الْحَقُّ فَاِذَا هِيَ شَاخِصَةٌ اَبْصَارُ الَّذِيْنَ كَفَرُوْا ۚ يٰوَيْلَنَا قَدْ كُنَّا فِيْ غَفْلَةٍ مِّنْ هٰذَا بَلْ كُنَّا ظٰلِمِيْنَ ۝

98. Surely you and what you worship besides Allah are the firewood of hell; to it you shall come.

اِنَّكُمْ وَمَا تَعْبُدُوْنَ مِنْ دُوْنِ اللّٰهِ حَصَبُ جَهَنَّمَ ۖ اَنْتُمْ لَهَا وَارِدُوْنَ ۝

99. Had these been gods, they would not have come to it and all shall abide therein.

لَوْ كَانَ هٰٓؤُلَاۤءِ اٰلِهَةً مَّا وَرَدُوْهَا ۚ وَكُلٌّ فِيْهَا خٰلِدُوْنَ ۝

100. For them therein shall be groaning and therein they shall not hear.

لَهُمْ فِيْهَا زَفِيْرٌ وَّهُمْ فِيْهَا لَا يَسْمَعُوْنَ ۝

101. Surely (as for) those for whom the good has already gone forth from Us, they shall be kept far off from it;

اِنَّ الَّذِيْنَ سَبَقَتْ لَهُمْ مِّنَّا الْحُسْنٰٓى اُولٰٓئِكَ عَنْهَا مُبْعَدُوْنَ ۝

102. They will not hear its faintest sound, and they shall abide in that which their souls long for.

لَا يَسْمَعُوْنَ حَسِيْسَهَا ۚ وَهُمْ فِيْ مَا اشْتَهَتْ اَنْفُسُهُمْ خٰلِدُوْنَ ۝

103. The great fearful event shall not grieve them, and the angels shall meet them: This is your day which you were promised.

لَا يَحْزُنُهُمُ الْفَزَعُ الْاَكْبَرُ وَتَتَلَقّٰهُمُ الْمَلٰٓئِكَةُ ۚ هٰذَا يَوْمُكُمُ الَّذِيْ كُنْتُمْ تُوْعَدُوْنَ ۝

104. On the day when We will roll up heaven like the rolling up of the scroll for writings; as We originated the first creation, (so) We shall reproduce it; a promise (binding on Us); surely We will bring it about.

يَوْمَ نَطْوِى السَّمَاۤءَ كَطَيِّ السِّجِلِّ لِلْكُتُبِ ۚ كَمَا بَدَأْنَآ اَوَّلَ خَلْقٍ نُّعِيْدُهٗ ۚ وَعْدًا عَلَيْنَا ۚ اِنَّا كُنَّا فٰعِلِيْنَ ۝

105. And certainly We wrote in the Book after the reminder that (as for) the land, My righteous servants shall inherit it.

106. Most surely in this is a message to a people who serve (Us).

107. And We have not sent you but as a mercy to the worlds.

108. Say: It is only revealed to me that your God is one God; will you then submit?

109. But if they turn back, say: I have given you warning in fairness and I do not know whether what you are threatened with is near or far:

110. Surely He knows what is spoken openly and He knows what you hide:

111. And I do not know if this may be a trial for you and a provision till a time.

112. He said: O my Lord! judge Thou with truth; and our Lord is the Beneficent God, Whose help is sought against what you ascribe (to Him).

وَلَقَدْ كَتَبْنَا فِى الزَّبُورِ مِنْ بَعْدِ الذِّكْرِ أَنَّ الْأَرْضَ يَرِثُهَا عِبَادِىَ الصَّالِحُوْنَ ۞

اِنَّ فِىْ هٰذَا لَبَلٰغًا لِّقَوْمٍ عٰبِدِيْنَ ۞

وَمَآ اَرْسَلْنٰكَ اِلَّا رَحْمَةً لِّلْعٰلَمِيْنَ ۞

قُلْ اِنَّمَا يُوْحٰى اِلَىَّ اَنَّمَآ اِلٰهُكُمْ اِلٰهٌ وَّاحِدٌ فَهَلْ اَنْتُمْ مُّسْلِمُوْنَ ۞

فَاِنْ تَوَلَّوْا فَقُلْ اٰذَنْتُكُمْ عَلٰى سَوَآءٍ وَاِنْ اَدْرِىْٓ اَقَرِيْبٌ اَمْ بَعِيْدٌ مَّا تُوْعَدُوْنَ ۞

اِنَّهٗ يَعْلَمُ الْجَهْرَ مِنَ الْقَوْلِ وَيَعْلَمُ مَا تَكْتُمُوْنَ ۞

وَاِنْ اَدْرِىْ لَعَلَّهٗ فِتْنَةٌ لَّكُمْ وَمَتَاعٌ اِلٰى حِيْنٍ ۞

قُلْ رَبِّ احْكُمْ بِالْحَقِّ وَرَبُّنَا الرَّحْمٰنُ الْمُسْتَعَانُ عَلٰى مَا تَصِفُوْنَ ۞

314

THE PILGRIMAGE
(HAJ)

**In the name of Allah,
the Beneficent, the Merciful.**

1. O people! guard against (the punishment from) your Lord; surely the violence of the hour is a grievous thing.

2. On the day when you shall see it, every woman giving suck shall quit in confusion what she suckled, and every pregnant woman shall lay down her burden, and you shall see men intoxicated, and they shall not be intoxicated but the chastisement of Allah will be severe.

3. And among men there is he who disputes about Allah without knowledge and follows every rebellious Shaitan;

4. Against him it is written down that whoever takes him for a friend, he shall lead him astray and conduct him to the chastisement of the burning fire.

5. O people! if you are in doubt about the raising, then surely We created you from dust, then from a small seed, then from a clot, then from a lump of flesh, complete in make and incomplete, that We may make clear to you; and We cause what We please to stay in the wombs till an appointed time, then We bring you forth as babies, then that you may attain your maturity; and of you is he who is caused to die, and of you is he who is brought back to the worst part of life, so that after having knowledge he does not know anything; and you see the earth sterile land, but when We send down on it the water, it stirs and swells and brings forth of every kind a beautiful herbage.

315

6. This is because Allah is the Truth and because He gives life to the dead and because He has power over all things,

ذٰلِكَ بِاَنَّ اللهَ هُوَ الْحَقُّ وَاَنَّهُ يُحْيِ الْمَوْتٰى وَ اَنَّهُ عَلٰى كُلِّ شَىْءٍ قَدِيْرٌ ۙ ٦

7. And because the hour is coming, there is no doubt about it; and because Allah shall raise up those who are in the graves.

وَّاَنَّ السَّاعَةَ اٰتِيَةٌ لَّا رَيْبَ فِيْهَا ۙ وَاَنَّ اللهَ يَبْعَثُ مَنْ فِى الْقُبُوْرِ ٧

8. And among men there is he who disputes about Allah without knowledge and without guidance and without an illuminating book,

وَمِنَ النَّاسِ مَنْ يُّجَادِلُ فِى اللهِ بِغَيْرِ عِلْمٍ وَّلَا هُدًى وَّلَا كِتٰبٍ مُّنِيْرٍ ۙ ٨

9. Turning away haughtily that he may lead (others) astray from the way of Allah; for him is disgrace in this world, and on the day of resurrection We will make him taste the punishment of burning:

ثَانِىَ عِطْفِهٖ لِيُضِلَّ عَنْ سَبِيْلِ اللهِ ۙ لَهُ فِى الدُّنْيَا خِزْىٌ وَّنُذِيْقُهُ يَوْمَ الْقِيٰمَةِ عَذَابَ الْحَرِيْقِ ٩

10. This is due to what your two hands have sent before, and because Allah is not in the least unjust to the servants.

ذٰلِكَ بِمَا قَدَّمَتْ يَدٰكَ وَاَنَّ اللهَ لَيْسَ بِظَلَّامٍ لِّلْعَبِيْدِ ۙ ١٠

11. And among men is he who serves Allah (standing) on the verge, so that if good befalls him he is satisfied therewith, but if a trial afflict him he turns back headlong; he loses this world as well as the hereafter; that is a manifest loss.

وَمِنَ النَّاسِ مَنْ يَّعْبُدُ اللهَ عَلٰى حَرْفٍ ۚ فَاِنْ اَصَابَهُ خَيْرٌ اطْمَاَنَّ بِهٖ ۚ وَاِنْ اَصَابَتْهُ فِتْنَةٌ ۨ انْقَلَبَ عَلٰى وَجْهِهٖ ۟ خَسِرَ الدُّنْيَا وَالْاٰخِرَةَ ۚ ذٰلِكَ هُوَ الْخُسْرَانُ الْمُبِيْنُ ١١

12. He calls besides Allah upon that which does not harm him and that which does not profit him; that is the great straying.

يَدْعُوْا مِنْ دُوْنِ اللهِ مَا لَا يَضُرُّهُ وَمَا لَا يَنْفَعُهُ ۚ ذٰلِكَ هُوَ الضَّلٰلُ الْبَعِيْدُ ۚ ١٢

13. He calls upon him whose harm is nearer than his profit; evil certainly is the guardian and evil certainly is the associate.

يَدْعُوْا لَمَنْ ضَرُّهُ اَقْرَبُ مِنْ نَّفْعِهٖ ۚ لَبِئْسَ الْمَوْلٰى وَلَبِئْسَ الْعَشِيْرُ ١٣

14. Surely Allah will cause those who believe and do good deeds to enter gardens beneath which rivers flow; surely Allah does what He pleases.

اِنَّ اللهَ يُدْخِلُ الَّذِيْنَ اٰمَنُوْا وَعَمِلُوا الصّٰلِحٰتِ جَنّٰتٍ تَجْرِيْ مِنْ تَحْتِهَا الْاَنْهٰرُ ۗ اِنَّ اللهَ يَفْعَلُ مَا يُرِيْدُ ١٤

15. Whoever thinks that Allah will not assist him in this life and the hereafter, let him stretch a rope to the ceiling, then let him cut (it) off, then let him see if his struggle will take away that at which he is enraged.

مَنْ كَانَ يَظُنُّ اَنْ لَّنْ يَّنْصُرَهُ اللّٰهُ فِى الدُّنْيَا وَالْاٰخِرَةِ فَلْيَمْدُدْ بِسَبَبٍ اِلَى السَّمَآءِ ثُمَّ لِيَقْطَعْ فَلْيَنْظُرْ هَلْ يُذْهِبَنَّ كَيْدُهٗ مَا يَغِيْظُ ۝

16. And thus have We revealed it, being clear arguments, and because Allah guides whom He intends.

وَكَذٰلِكَ اَنْزَلْنٰهُ اٰيٰتٍۭ بَيِّنٰتٍ ۙ وَّاَنَّ اللّٰهَ يَهْدِيْ مَنْ يُّرِيْدُ ۝

17. Surely those who believe and those who are Jews and the Sabeans and the Christians and the Magians and those who associate (others with Allah)—surely Allah will decide between them on the day of resurrection; surely Allah is a witness over all things.

اِنَّ الَّذِيْنَ اٰمَنُوْا وَالَّذِيْنَ هَادُوْا وَالصّٰبِئِيْنَ وَالنَّصٰرٰى وَالْمَجُوْسَ وَالَّذِيْنَ اَشْرَكُوْٓا ۖ اِنَّ اللّٰهَ يَفْصِلُ بَيْنَهُمْ يَوْمَ الْقِيٰمَةِ ۗ اِنَّ اللّٰهَ عَلٰى كُلِّ شَيْءٍ شَهِيْدٌ ۝

18. Do you not see that Allah is He, Whom obeys whoever is in the heavens and whoever is in the earth, and the sun and the moon and the stars, and the mountains and the trees, and the animals and many of the people; and many there are against whom chastisement has become necessary; and whomsoever Allah abases, there is none who can make him honorable; surely Allah does what He pleases.

اَلَمْ تَرَ اَنَّ اللّٰهَ يَسْجُدُ لَهٗ مَنْ فِى السَّمٰوٰتِ وَمَنْ فِى الْاَرْضِ وَالشَّمْسُ وَالْقَمَرُ وَالنُّجُوْمُ وَالْجِبَالُ وَالشَّجَرُ وَالدَّوَآبُّ وَكَثِيْرٌ مِّنَ النَّاسِ ۗ وَكَثِيْرٌ حَقَّ عَلَيْهِ الْعَذَابُ ۗ وَمَنْ يُّهِنِ اللّٰهُ فَمَا لَهٗ مِنْ مُّكْرِمٍ ۗ اِنَّ اللّٰهَ يَفْعَلُ مَا يَشَآءُ ۩ ۝

19. These are two adversaries who dispute about their Lord; then (as to) those who disbelieve, for them are cut out garments of fire; boiling water shall be poured over their heads.

هٰذٰنِ خَصْمٰنِ اخْتَصَمُوْا فِيْ رَبِّهِمْ ۫ فَالَّذِيْنَ كَفَرُوْا قُطِّعَتْ لَهُمْ ثِيَابٌ مِّنْ نَّارٍ ۗ يُصَبُّ مِنْ فَوْقِ رُءُوْسِهِمُ الْحَمِيْمُ ۝

20. With it shall be melted what is in their bellies and (their) skins as well.

يُصْهَرُ بِهٖ مَا فِيْ بُطُوْنِهِمْ وَالْجُلُوْدُ ۝

21. And for them are whips of iron.

وَلَهُمْ مَّقَامِعُ مِنْ حَدِيْدٍ ۝

22. Whenever they will desire to go forth from it, from grief, they shall be turned back into it, and taste the chastisement of burning.

كُلَّمَآ اَرَادُوْٓا اَنْ يَّخْرُجُوْا مِنْهَا مِنْ غَمٍّ اُعِيْدُوْا فِيْهَا وَذُوْقُوْا عَذَابَ الْحَرِيْقِ ۝

23. Surely Allah will make those who believe and do good deeds enter gardens beneath which rivers flow; they shall be adorned therein with bracelets of gold and (with) pearls, and their garments therein shall be of silk.

24. And they are guided to goodly words and they are guided into the path of the Praised One.

25. Surely (as for) those who disbelieve, and hinder (men) from Allah's way and from the Sacred Mosque which We have made equally for all men, (for) the dweller therein and (for) the visitor, and whoever shall incline therein to wrong unjustly, We will make him taste of a painful chastisement.

26. And when We assigned to Ibrahim the place of the House, saying: Do not associate with Me aught, and purify My House for those who make the circuit and stand to pray and bow and prostrate themselves.

27. And proclaim among men the Pilgrimage: they will come to you on foot and on every lean camel, coming from every remote path,

28. That they may witness advantages for them and mention the name of Allah during stated days over what He has given them of the cattle quadrupeds, then eat of them and feed the distressed one, the needy.

29. Then let them accomplish their needful acts of shaving and cleansing, and let them fulfil their vows and let them go round the Ancient House.

30. That (shall be so); and whoever respects the sacred ordinances of Allah, it is better for him with his Lord; and the cattle are made lawful for you, except that which is recited to you, therefore avoid the uncleanness of the idols and avoid false words,

إِنَّ اللّٰهَ يُدْخِلُ الَّذِيْنَ اٰمَنُوْا وَعَمِلُوا الصّٰلِحٰتِ جَنّٰتٍ تَجْرِىْ مِنْ تَحْتِهَا الْاَنْهٰرُ يُحَلَّوْنَ فِيْهَا مِنْ اَسَاوِرَ مِنْ ذَهَبٍ وَّلُؤْلُؤًا وَلِبَاسُهُمْ فِيْهَا حَرِيْرٌ ۝

وَهُدُوْا اِلَى الطَّيِّبِ مِنَ الْقَوْلِ وَهُدُوْا اِلٰى صِرَاطِ الْحَمِيْدِ ۝

إِنَّ الَّذِيْنَ كَفَرُوْا وَيَصُدُّوْنَ عَنْ سَبِيْلِ اللّٰهِ وَالْمَسْجِدِ الْحَرَامِ الَّذِيْ جَعَلْنٰهُ لِلنَّاسِ سَوَاءً الْعَاكِفُ فِيْهِ وَالْبَادِ وَمَنْ يُّرِدْ فِيْهِ بِاِلْحَادٍ بِظُلْمٍ نُّذِقْهُ مِنْ عَذَابٍ اَلِيْمٍ ۝

وَاِذْ بَوَّأْنَا لِاِبْرٰهِيْمَ مَكَانَ الْبَيْتِ اَنْ لَّا تُشْرِكْ بِيْ شَيْئًا وَّطَهِّرْ بَيْتِيَ لِلطَّآئِفِيْنَ وَالْقَآئِمِيْنَ وَالرُّكَّعِ السُّجُوْدِ ۝

وَاَذِّنْ فِى النَّاسِ بِالْحَجِّ يَأْتُوْكَ رِجَالًا وَّعَلٰى كُلِّ ضَامِرٍ يَّأْتِيْنَ مِنْ كُلِّ فَجٍّ عَمِيْقٍ ۝

لِّيَشْهَدُوْا مَنَافِعَ لَهُمْ وَيَذْكُرُوا اسْمَ اللّٰهِ فِيْ اَيَّامٍ مَّعْلُوْمٰتٍ عَلٰى مَا رَزَقَهُمْ مِّنْ بَهِيْمَةِ الْاَنْعَامِ فَكُلُوْا مِنْهَا وَاَطْعِمُوا الْبَائِسَ الْفَقِيْرَ ۝

ثُمَّ لِيَقْضُوْا تَفَثَهُمْ وَلْيُوْفُوْا نُذُوْرَهُمْ وَلْيَطَّوَّفُوْا بِالْبَيْتِ الْعَتِيْقِ ۝

ذٰلِكَ وَمَنْ يُّعَظِّمْ حُرُمٰتِ اللّٰهِ فَهُوَ خَيْرٌ لَّهُ عِنْدَ رَبِّهٖ وَاُحِلَّتْ لَكُمُ الْاَنْعَامُ اِلَّا مَا يُتْلٰى عَلَيْكُمْ فَاجْتَنِبُوا الرِّجْسَ مِنَ الْاَوْثَانِ وَاجْتَنِبُوْا قَوْلَ الزُّوْرِ ۝

31. Being upright for Allah, not associating aught with Him and whoever associates (others) with Allah, it is as though he had fallen from on high, then the birds snatch him away or the wind carries him off to a far-distant place.

32. That (shall be so); and whoever respects the signs of Allah, this surely is (the outcome) of the piety of hearts.

33. You have advantages in them till a fixed time, then their place of sacrifice is the Ancient House.

34. And to every nation We appointed acts of devotion that they may mention the name of Allah on what He has given them of the cattle quadrupeds; so your God is One God, therefore to Him should you submit, and give good news to the humble,

35. (To) those whose hearts tremble when Allah is mentioned, and those who are patient under that which afflicts them, and those who keep up prayer, and spend (benevolently) out of what We have given them.

36. And (as for) the camels, We have made them of the signs of the religion of Allah for you; for you therein is much good; therefore mention the name of Allah on them as they stand in a row, then when they fall down eat of them and feed the poor man who is contented and the beggar; thus have We made them subservient to you, that you may be grateful.

37. There does not reach Allah their flesh nor their blood, but to Him is acceptable the guarding (against evil) on your part; thus has He made them subservient to you, that you may magnify Allah because He has guided you aright; and give good news to those who do good (to others).

38. Surely Allah will defend those who believe; surely Allah does not love any one who is unfaithful, ungrateful.

319

39. Permission (to fight) is given to those upon whom war is made because they are oppressed, and most surely Allah is well able to assist them;

40. Those who have been expelled from their homes without a just cause except that they say: Our Lord is Allah. And had there not been Allah's repelling some people by others, certainly there would have been pulled down cloisters and churches and synagogues and mosques in which Allah's name is much remembered; and surely Allah will help him who helps His cause; most surely Allah is Strong, Mighty.

41. Those who, should We establish them in the land, will keep up prayer and pay the poor-rate and enjoin good and forbid evil; and Allah's is the end of affairs.

42. And if they reject you, then already before you did the people of Nuh and Ad and Samood reject (prophets).

43. And the people of Ibrahim and the people of Lut,

44. As well as those of Madyan and Musa (too) was rejected, but I gave respite to the unbelievers, then did I overtake them, so how (severe) was My disapproval.

45. So how many a town did We destroy while it was unjust, so it was fallen down upon its roofs, and (how many a) deserted well and palace raised high.

46. Have they not travelled in the land so that they should have hearts with which to understand, or ears with which to hear? For surely it is not the eyes that are blind, but blind are the hearts which are in the breasts.

47. And they ask you to hasten on the punishment, and Allah will by no means fail in His promise, and surely a day with your Lord is as a thousand years of what you number.

48. And how many a town to which I gave respite while it was unjust, then I overtook it, and to Me is the return.

49. Say: O people! I am only a plain warner to you.

50. Then (as for) those who believe and do good, they shall have forgiveness and an honorable sustenance.

51. And (as for) those who strive to oppose Our communications, they shall be the inmates of the flaming fire.

52. And We did not send before you any apostle or prophet, but when he desired, the Shaitan made a suggestion respecting his desire; but Allah annuls that which the Shaitan casts, then does Allah establish His communications, and Allah is Knowing, Wise,

53. So that He may make what the Shaitan casts a trial for those in whose hearts is disease and those whose hearts are hard; and most surely the unjust are in a great opposition,

54. And that those who have been given the knowledge may know that it is the truth from your Lord, so they may believe in it and their hearts may be lowly before it; and most surely Allah is the Guide of those who believe into a right path.

55. And those who disbelieve shall not cease to be in doubt concerning it until the hour overtakes them suddenly, or there comes on them the chastisement of a destructive day.

321

56. The kingdom on that day shall be Allah's; He will judge between them; so those who believe and do good will be in gardens of bliss.

الْمُلْكُ يَوْمَئِذٍ لِلّٰهِ يَحْكُمُ بَيْنَهُمْ فَالَّذِيْنَ اٰمَنُوْا وَعَمِلُوا الصّٰلِحٰتِ فِيْ جَنّٰتِ النَّعِيْمِ ۝

57. And (as for) those who disbelieve in and reject Our communications, these it is who shall have a disgraceful chastisement.

وَالَّذِيْنَ كَفَرُوْا وَكَذَّبُوْا بِاٰيٰتِنَا فَأُولٰٓئِكَ لَهُمْ عَذَابٌ مُّهِيْنٌ ۝

58. And (as for) those who fly in Allah's way and are then slain or die, Allah will most certainly grant them a goodly sustenance, and most surely Allah is the best Giver of sustenance.

وَالَّذِيْنَ هَاجَرُوْا فِيْ سَبِيْلِ اللّٰهِ ثُمَّ قُتِلُوْا أَوْ مَاتُوْا لَيَرْزُقَنَّهُمُ اللّٰهُ رِزْقًا حَسَنًا وَإِنَّ اللّٰهَ لَهُوَ خَيْرُ الرّٰزِقِيْنَ ۝

59. He will certainly cause them to enter a place of entrance which they shall be well pleased with; and most surely Allah is Knowing, Forbearing.

لَيُدْخِلَنَّهُمْ مُّدْخَلًا يَّرْضَوْنَهُ وَإِنَّ اللّٰهَ لَعَلِيْمٌ حَلِيْمٌ ۝

60. That (shall be so); and he who retaliates with the like of that with which he has been afflicted and he has been oppressed, Allah will most certainly aid him; most surely Allah is Pardoning, Forgiving.

ذٰلِكَ وَمَنْ عَاقَبَ بِمِثْلِ مَا عُوْقِبَ بِهِ ثُمَّ بُغِيَ عَلَيْهِ لَيَنْصُرَنَّهُ اللّٰهُ إِنَّ اللّٰهَ لَعَفُوٌّ غَفُوْرٌ ۝

61. That is because Allah causes the night to enter into the day and causes the day to enter into the night, and because Allah is Hearing, Seeing.

ذٰلِكَ بِأَنَّ اللّٰهَ يُوْلِجُ الَّيْلَ فِي النَّهَارِ وَيُوْلِجُ النَّهَارَ فِي الَّيْلِ وَأَنَّ اللّٰهَ سَمِيْعٌ بَصِيْرٌ ۝

62. That is because Allah is the Truth, and that what they call upon besides Him—that is the falsehood, and because Allah is the High, the Great.

ذٰلِكَ بِأَنَّ اللّٰهَ هُوَ الْحَقُّ وَأَنَّ مَا يَدْعُوْنَ مِنْ دُوْنِهِ هُوَ الْبَاطِلُ وَأَنَّ اللّٰهَ هُوَ الْعَلِيُّ الْكَبِيْرُ ۝

63. Do you not see that Allah sends down water from the cloud so the earth becomes green? Surely Allah is Benignant, Aware.

أَلَمْ تَرَ أَنَّ اللّٰهَ أَنْزَلَ مِنَ السَّمَآءِ مَآءً فَتُصْبِحُ الْأَرْضُ مُخْضَرَّةً إِنَّ اللّٰهَ لَطِيْفٌ خَبِيْرٌ ۝

64. His is whatsoever is in the heavens and whatsoever is in the earth; and most surely Allah is the Self-sufficient, the Praised.

لَهُ مَا فِي السَّمٰوٰتِ وَمَا فِي الْأَرْضِ وَإِنَّ اللّٰهَ لَهُوَ الْغَنِيُّ الْحَمِيْدُ ۝

65. Do you not see that Allah has made subservient to you whatsoever is in the earth and the ships running in the sea by His command? And He withholds the heaven from falling on the earth except with His permission; most surely Allah is Compassionate, Merciful to men.

66. And He it is Who has brought you to life, then He will cause you to die, then bring you to life (again); most surely man is ungrateful.

67. To every nation We appointed acts of devotion which they observe, therefore they should not dispute with you about the matter and call to your Lord; most surely you are on a right way.

68. And if they contend with you, say: Allah best knows what you do.

69. Allah will judge between you on the day of resurrection respecting that in which you differ.

70. Do you not know that Allah knows what is in the heaven and the earth? Surely this is in a book; surely this is easy to Allah.

71. And they serve besides Allah that for which He has not sent any authority, and that of which they have no knowledge; and for the unjust there shall be no helper.

72. And when Our clear communications are recited to them, you will find denial on the faces of those who disbelieve; they almost spring upon those who recite to them Our communications. Say: Shall I inform you of what is worse than this? The fire; Allah has promised it to those who disbelieve; and how evil the resort!

أَلَمْ تَرَ أَنَّ اللّٰهَ سَخَّرَ لَكُمْ مَّا فِى الْأَرْضِ وَالْفُلْكَ تَجْرِى فِى الْبَحْرِ بِأَمْرِهٖ ۖ وَيُمْسِكُ السَّمَآءَ أَنْ تَقَعَ عَلَى الْأَرْضِ إِلَّا بِإِذْنِهٖ ۗ إِنَّ اللّٰهَ بِالنَّاسِ لَرَءُوْفٌ رَّحِيْمٌ ۝

وَهُوَ الَّذِىْ أَحْيَاكُمْ ثُمَّ يُمِيْتُكُمْ ثُمَّ يُحْيِيْكُمْ ۗ إِنَّ الْإِنْسَانَ لَكَفُوْرٌ ۝

لِكُلِّ أُمَّةٍ جَعَلْنَا مَنْسَكًا هُمْ نَاسِكُوْهُ فَلَا يُنَازِعُنَّكَ فِى الْأَمْرِ وَادْعُ إِلٰى رَبِّكَ ۗ إِنَّكَ لَعَلٰى هُدًى مُّسْتَقِيْمٍ ۝

وَإِنْ جَادَلُوْكَ فَقُلِ اللّٰهُ أَعْلَمُ بِمَا تَعْمَلُوْنَ ۝

اللّٰهُ يَحْكُمُ بَيْنَكُمْ يَوْمَ الْقِيٰمَةِ فِيْمَا كُنْتُمْ فِيْهِ تَخْتَلِفُوْنَ ۝

أَلَمْ تَعْلَمْ أَنَّ اللّٰهَ يَعْلَمُ مَا فِى السَّمَآءِ وَالْأَرْضِ ۗ إِنَّ ذٰلِكَ فِىْ كِتٰبٍ ۗ إِنَّ ذٰلِكَ عَلَى اللّٰهِ يَسِيْرٌ ۝

وَيَعْبُدُوْنَ مِنْ دُوْنِ اللّٰهِ مَا لَمْ يُنَزِّلْ بِهٖ سُلْطٰنًا وَّمَا لَيْسَ لَهُمْ بِهٖ عِلْمٌ ۗ وَمَا لِلظّٰلِمِيْنَ مِنْ نَّصِيْرٍ ۝

وَإِذَا تُتْلٰى عَلَيْهِمْ اٰيٰتُنَا بَيِّنٰتٍ تَعْرِفُ فِىْ وُجُوْهِ الَّذِيْنَ كَفَرُوا الْمُنْكَرَ ۗ يَكَادُوْنَ يَسْطُوْنَ بِالَّذِيْنَ يَتْلُوْنَ عَلَيْهِمْ اٰيٰتِنَا ۗ قُلْ أَفَأُنَبِّئُكُمْ بِشَرٍّ مِّنْ ذٰلِكُمْ ۗ النَّارُ ۗ وَعَدَهَا اللّٰهُ الَّذِيْنَ كَفَرُوا ۗ وَبِئْسَ الْمَصِيْرُ ۝

323

73. O people! a parable is set forth, therefore listen to it; surely those whom you call upon besides Allah cannot create a fly, though they should all gather for it, and should the fly snatch away anything from them, they could not take it back from it; weak are the invoker and the invoked.

يٰۤاَيُّهَا النَّاسُ ضُرِبَ مَثَلٌ فَاسْتَمِعُوْا لَهٗ ؕ اِنَّ الَّذِيْنَ تَدْعُوْنَ مِنْ دُوْنِ اللّٰهِ لَنْ يَّخْلُقُوْا ذُبَابًا وَّلَوِ اجْتَمَعُوْا لَهٗ ؕ وَاِنْ يَّسْلُبْهُمُ الذُّبَابُ شَيْئًا لَّا يَسْتَنْقِذُوْهُ مِنْهُ ؕ ضَعُفَ الطَّالِبُ وَ الْمَطْلُوْبُ ۝

74. They have not estimated Allah with the estimation that is due to Him; most surely Allah is Strong, Mighty.

مَا قَدَرُوا اللّٰهَ حَقَّ قَدْرِهٖ ؕ اِنَّ اللّٰهَ لَقَوِيٌّ عَزِيْزٌ ۝

75. Allah chooses messengers from among the angels and from among the men; surely Allah is Hearing, Seeing.

اَللّٰهُ يَصْطَفِيْ مِنَ الْمَلٰٓئِكَةِ رُسُلًا وَّمِنَ النَّاسِ ؕ اِنَّ اللّٰهَ سَمِيْعٌ بَصِيْرٌ ۝

76. He knows what is before them and what is behind them, and to Allah are all affairs turned back.

يَعْلَمُ مَا بَيْنَ اَيْدِيْهِمْ وَمَا خَلْفَهُمْ ؕ وَاِلَى اللّٰهِ تُرْجَعُ الْاُمُوْرُ ۝

77. O you who believe! bow down and prostrate yourselves and serve your Lord, and do good that you may succeed.

يٰۤاَيُّهَا الَّذِيْنَ اٰمَنُوا ارْكَعُوْا وَاسْجُدُوْا وَاعْبُدُوْا رَبَّكُمْ وَافْعَلُوا الْخَيْرَ لَعَلَّكُمْ تُفْلِحُوْنَ ۩۝

78. And strive hard in (the way of) Allah, (such) a striving as is due to Him; He has chosen you and has not laid upon you any hardship in religion; the faith of your father Ibrahim; He named you Muslims before and in this, that the Apostle may be a bearer of witness to you, and you may be bearers of witness to the people; therefore keep up prayer and pay the poor-rate and hold fast by Allah; He is your Guardian; how excellent the Guardian and how excellent the Helper!

وَجَاهِدُوْا فِى اللّٰهِ حَقَّ جِهَادِهٖ ؕ هُوَ اجْتَبٰىكُمْ وَمَا جَعَلَ عَلَيْكُمْ فِى الدِّيْنِ مِنْ حَرَجٍ ؕ مِلَّةَ اَبِيْكُمْ اِبْرٰهِيْمَ ؕ هُوَ سَمّٰىكُمُ الْمُسْلِمِيْنَ ۙ مِنْ قَبْلُ وَفِيْ هٰذَا لِيَكُوْنَ الرَّسُوْلُ شَهِيْدًا عَلَيْكُمْ وَتَكُوْنُوْا شُهَدَآءَ عَلَى النَّاسِ ۚ فَاَقِيْمُوا الصَّلٰوةَ وَاٰتُوا الزَّكٰوةَ وَاعْتَصِمُوْا بِاللّٰهِ ؕ هُوَ مَوْلٰىكُمْ ۚ فَنِعْمَ الْمَوْلٰى وَنِعْمَ النَّصِيْرُ ۝

THE BELIEVERS
(MOAMINUN)

**In the name of Allah,
the Beneficent, the Merciful.**

1. Successful indeed are the believers,

2. Who are humble in their prayers,

3. And who keep aloof from what is vain,

4. And who are givers of poor-rate,

5. And who guard their private parts,

6. Except before their mates or those whom their right hands possess, for they surely are not blameable,

7. But whoever seeks to go beyond that, these are they that exceed the limits;

8. And those who are keepers of their trusts and their covenant,

9. And those who keep a guard on their prayers;

10. These are they who are the heirs,

11. Who shall inherit the Paradise; they shall abide therein.

12. And certainly We created man of an extract of clay,

13. Then We made him a small seed in a firm resting-place,

14. Then We made the seed a clot, then We made the clot a lump of flesh, then We made (in) the lump of flesh bones, then We clothed the bones with flesh, then We caused it to grow into another creation, so blessed be Allah, the best of the creators.

15. Then after that you will most surely die.

16. Then surely on the day of resurrection you shall be raised.

325

17. And certainly We made above you seven heavens; and never are We heedless of creation.

18. And We send down water from the cloud according to a measure, then We cause it to settle in the earth, and most surely We are able to carry it away.

19. Then We cause to grow thereby gardens of palm trees and grapes for you; you have in them many fruits and from them do you eat;

20. And a tree that grows out of Mount Sinai which produces oil and a condiment for those who eat.

21. And most surely there is a lesson for you in the cattle: We make you to drink of what is in their bellies, and you have in them many advantages and of them you eat,

22. And on them and on the ships you are borne.

23. And certainly We sent Nuh to his people, and he said: O my people! serve Allah, you have no god other than Him; will you not then guard (against evil)?

24. And the chiefs of those who disbelieved from among his people said: He is nothing but a mortal like yourselves who desires that he may have superiority over you, and if Allah had pleased, He could certainly have sent down angels. We have not heard of this among our fathers of yore:

25. He is only a madman, so bear with him for a time.

26. He said: O my Lord! help me against their calling me a liar.

27. So We revealed to him, saying: Make the ark before Our eyes and (according to) Our revelation; and when Our command is given and the valley overflows, take into it of every kind a pair, two, and your followers, except those among them against whom the word has gone forth, and do not speak to Me in respect of those who are unjust; surely they shall be drowned.

وَلَقَدْ خَلَقْنَا فَوْقَكُمْ سَبْعَ طَرَائِقَ ۖ وَمَا كُنَّا عَنِ الْخَلْقِ غَافِلِينَ ۝

وَأَنْزَلْنَا مِنَ السَّمَاءِ مَاءً بِقَدَرٍ فَأَسْكَنَّاهُ فِي الْأَرْضِ ۖ وَإِنَّا عَلَى ذَهَابٍ بِهِ لَقَادِرُونَ ۝

فَأَنْشَأْنَا لَكُمْ بِهِ جَنَّاتٍ مِّنْ نَّخِيلٍ وَأَعْنَابٍ ۘ لَّكُمْ فِيهَا فَوَاكِهُ كَثِيرَةٌ وَّمِنْهَا تَأْكُلُونَ ۝

وَشَجَرَةً تَخْرُجُ مِنْ طُورِ سَيْنَاءَ تَنْبُتُ بِالدُّهْنِ وَصِبْغٍ لِّلْآكِلِينَ ۝

وَإِنَّ لَكُمْ فِي الْأَنْعَامِ لَعِبْرَةً ۖ نُّسْقِيكُمْ مِّمَّا فِي بُطُونِهَا وَلَكُمْ فِيهَا مَنَافِعُ كَثِيرَةٌ وَّمِنْهَا تَأْكُلُونَ ۝

وَعَلَيْهَا وَعَلَى الْفُلْكِ تُحْمَلُونَ ۝

وَلَقَدْ أَرْسَلْنَا نُوحًا إِلَى قَوْمِهِ فَقَالَ يَا قَوْمِ اعْبُدُوا اللَّهَ مَا لَكُمْ مِّنْ إِلَهٍ غَيْرُهُ ۖ أَفَلَا تَتَّقُونَ ۝

فَقَالَ الْمَلَأُ الَّذِينَ كَفَرُوا مِنْ قَوْمِهِ مَا هَذَا إِلَّا بَشَرٌ مِّثْلُكُمْ ۙ يُرِيدُ أَنْ يَتَفَضَّلَ عَلَيْكُمْ ۖ وَلَوْ شَاءَ اللَّهُ لَأَنْزَلَ مَلَائِكَةً ۖ مَّا سَمِعْنَا بِهَذَا فِي آبَائِنَا الْأَوَّلِينَ ۝

إِنْ هُوَ إِلَّا رَجُلٌ بِهِ جِنَّةٌ فَتَرَبَّصُوا بِهِ حَتَّى حِينٍ ۝

قَالَ رَبِّ انْصُرْنِي بِمَا كَذَّبُونِ ۝

فَأَوْحَيْنَا إِلَيْهِ أَنِ اصْنَعِ الْفُلْكَ بِأَعْيُنِنَا وَوَحْيِنَا فَإِذَا جَاءَ أَمْرُنَا وَفَارَ التَّنُّورُ ۙ فَاسْلُكْ فِيهَا مِنْ كُلٍّ زَوْجَيْنِ اثْنَيْنِ وَأَهْلَكَ إِلَّا مَنْ سَبَقَ عَلَيْهِ الْقَوْلُ مِنْهُمْ ۖ وَلَا تُخَاطِبْنِي فِي الَّذِينَ ظَلَمُوا ۚ إِنَّهُمْ مُّغْرَقُونَ ۝

28. And when you are firmly seated, you and those with you, in the ark, say: All praise is due to Allah who delivered us from the unjust people:

29. And say: O my Lord! cause me to disembark a blessed alighting, and Thou art the best to cause to alight.

30. Most surely there are signs in this, and most surely We are ever trying (men).

31. Then We raised up after them another generation.

32. So We sent among them an apostle from among them, saying: Serve Allah, you have no god other than Him; will you not then guard (against evil)?

33. And the chiefs of his people who disbelieved and called the meeting of the hereafter a lie, and whom We had given plenty to enjoy in this world's life, said: This is nothing but a mortal like yourselves, eating of what you eat from and drinking of what you drink.

34. And if you obey a mortal like yourselves, then most surely you will be losers:

35. What! does he threaten you that when you are dead and become dust and bones that you shall then be brought forth?

36. Far, far is that which you are threatened with.

37. There is naught but our life in this world; we die and we live and we shall not be raised again.

38. He is naught but a man who has forged a lie against Allah, and we are not going to believe in him.

39. He said: O my Lord! help me against their calling me a liar.

40. He said: In a little while they will most certainly be repenting.

41. So the punishment overtook them in justice, and We made them as rubbish; so away with the unjust people.

فَأَخَذَتْهُمُ الصَّيْحَةُ بِالْحَقِّ فَجَعَلْنَاهُمْ غُثَآءً ۚ فَبُعْدًا لِّلْقَوْمِ الظَّالِمِينَ ۝

42. Then We raised after them other generations.

ثُمَّ أَنْشَأْنَا مِنْ بَعْدِهِمْ قُرُونًا آخَرِينَ ۝

43. No people can hasten on their doom nor can they postpone (it).

مَا تَسْبِقُ مِنْ أُمَّةٍ أَجَلَهَا وَمَا يَسْتَأْخِرُونَ ۝

44. Then We sent Our apostles one after another; whenever there came to a people their apostle, they called him a liar, so We made some of them follow others and We made them stories; so away with a people who do not believe!

ثُمَّ أَرْسَلْنَا رُسُلَنَا تَتْرَا ۖ كُلَّمَا جَآءَ أُمَّةً رَّسُولُهَا كَذَّبُوهُ فَأَتْبَعْنَا بَعْضَهُمْ بَعْضًا وَجَعَلْنَاهُمْ أَحَادِيثَ ۚ فَبُعْدًا لِّقَوْمٍ لَّا يُؤْمِنُونَ ۝

45. Then We sent Musa and his brother Haroun, with Our communications and a clear authority,

ثُمَّ أَرْسَلْنَا مُوسَى وَأَخَاهُ هَارُونَ ۙ بِآيَاتِنَا وَسُلْطَانٍ مُّبِينٍ ۝

46. To Firon and his chiefs, but they behaved haughtily and they were an insolent people.

إِلَى فِرْعَوْنَ وَمَلَئِهِ فَاسْتَكْبَرُوا وَكَانُوا قَوْمًا عَالِينَ ۝

47. And they said: What! shall we believe in two mortals like ourselves while their people serve us?

فَقَالُوا أَنُؤْمِنُ لِبَشَرَيْنِ مِثْلِنَا وَقَوْمُهُمَا لَنَا عَابِدُونَ ۝

48. So they rejected them and became of those who were destroyed.

فَكَذَّبُوهُمَا فَكَانُوا مِنَ الْمُهْلَكِينَ ۝

49. And certainly We gave Musa the Book that they may follow a right direction.

وَلَقَدْ آتَيْنَا مُوسَى الْكِتَابَ لَعَلَّهُمْ يَهْتَدُونَ ۝

50. And We made the son of Marium and his mother a sign, and We gave them a shelter on a lofty ground having meadows and springs.

وَجَعَلْنَا ابْنَ مَرْيَمَ وَأُمَّهُ آيَةً وَآوَيْنَاهُمَا إِلَى رَبْوَةٍ ذَاتِ قَرَارٍ وَمَعِينٍ ۝

51. O apostles! eat of the good things and do good; surely I know what you do.

يَا أَيُّهَا الرُّسُلُ كُلُوا مِنَ الطَّيِّبَاتِ وَاعْمَلُوا صَالِحًا ۖ إِنِّي بِمَا تَعْمَلُونَ عَلِيمٌ ۝

52. And surely this your religion is one religion and I am your Lord, therefore be careful (of your duty) to Me.

وَإِنَّ هَذِهِ أُمَّتُكُمْ أُمَّةً وَاحِدَةً وَأَنَا رَبُّكُمْ فَاتَّقُونِ ۝

53. But they cut off their religion among themselves into sects, each part rejoicing in that which is with them.

فَتَقَطَّعُوا أَمْرَهُمْ بَيْنَهُمْ زُبُرًا ۖ كُلُّ حِزْبٍ بِمَا لَدَيْهِمْ فَرِحُونَ ۝

54. Therefore leave them in their overwhelming ignorance till a time.

55. Do they think that by what We aid them with of wealth and children,

56. We are hastening to them of good things? Nay, they do not perceive.

57. Surely they who from fear of their Lord are cautious,

58. And those who believe in the communications of their Lord,

59. And those who do not associate (aught) with their Lord,

60. And those who give what they give (in alms) while their hearts are full of fear that to their Lord they must return,

61. These hasten to good things and they are foremost in (attaining) them.

62. And We do not lay on any soul a burden except to the extent of its ability, and with Us is a book which speaks the truth, and they shall not be dealt with unjustly.

63. Nay, their hearts are in overwhelming ignorance with respect to it and they have besides this other deeds which they do.

64. Until when We overtake those who lead easy lives among them with punishment, lo! they cry for succor.

65. Cry not for succor this day; surely you shall not be given help from Us.

66. My communications were indeed recited to you, but you used to turn back on your heels,

67. In arrogance; talking nonsense about the Quran, and left him like one telling fables by night.

68. Is it then that they do not ponder over what is said, or is it that there has come to them that which did not come to their fathers of old?

فَذَرْهُمْ فِيْ غَمْرَتِهِمْ حَتّٰى حِيْنٍ ۞

اَيَحْسَبُوْنَ اَنَّمَا نُمِدُّهُمْ بِهٖ مِنْ مَّالٍ وَّبَنِيْنَ ۞

نُسَارِعُ لَهُمْ فِي الْخَيْرٰتِ ؕ بَلْ لَّا يَشْعُرُوْنَ ۞

اِنَّ الَّذِيْنَ هُمْ مِّنْ خَشْيَةِ رَبِّهِمْ مُّشْفِقُوْنَ ۞

وَالَّذِيْنَ هُمْ بِاٰيٰتِ رَبِّهِمْ يُؤْمِنُوْنَ ۞

وَالَّذِيْنَ هُمْ بِرَبِّهِمْ لَا يُشْرِكُوْنَ ۞

وَالَّذِيْنَ يُؤْتُوْنَ مَا اٰتَوْا وَّقُلُوْبُهُمْ وَجِلَةٌ اَنَّهُمْ اِلٰى رَبِّهِمْ رٰجِعُوْنَ ۞

اُولٰٓئِكَ يُسٰرِعُوْنَ فِي الْخَيْرٰتِ وَهُمْ لَهَا سٰبِقُوْنَ ۞

وَلَا نُكَلِّفُ نَفْسًا اِلَّا وُسْعَهَا وَلَدَيْنَا كِتٰبٌ يَّنْطِقُ بِالْحَقِّ وَهُمْ لَا يُظْلَمُوْنَ ۞

بَلْ قُلُوْبُهُمْ فِيْ غَمْرَةٍ مِّنْ هٰذَا وَلَهُمْ اَعْمَالٌ مِّنْ دُوْنِ ذٰلِكَ هُمْ لَهَا عٰمِلُوْنَ ۞

حَتّٰى اِذَا اَخَذْنَا مُتْرَفِيْهِمْ بِالْعَذَابِ اِذَا هُمْ يَجْـَٔرُوْنَ ۞

لَا تَجْـَٔرُوا الْيَوْمَ ؕ اِنَّكُمْ مِّنَّا لَا تُنْصَرُوْنَ ۞

قَدْ كَانَتْ اٰيٰتِيْ تُتْلٰى عَلَيْكُمْ فَكُنْتُمْ عَلٰى اَعْقَابِكُمْ تَنْكِصُوْنَ ۞

مُسْتَكْبِرِيْنَ ۖ بِهٖ سٰمِرًا تَهْجُرُوْنَ ۞

اَفَلَمْ يَدَّبَّرُوا الْقَوْلَ اَمْ جَآءَهُمْ مَّا لَمْ يَاْتِ اٰبَآءَهُمُ الْاَوَّلِيْنَ ۞

69. Or is it that they have not recognized their Apostle, so that they deny him?

أَمْ لَمْ يَعْرِفُوْا رَسُوْلَهُمْ فَهُمْ لَهُ مُنْكِرُوْنَ ۞

70. Or do they say: There is madness in him? Nay! he has brought them the truth, and most of them are averse from the truth.

أَمْ يَقُوْلُوْنَ بِهِ جِنَّةٌ ۗ بَلْ جَآءَهُمْ بِالْحَقِّ وَ اَكْثَرُهُمْ لِلْحَقِّ كَارِهُوْنَ ۞

71. And should the truth follow their low desires, surely the heavens and the earth and all those who are therein would have perished. Nay! We have brought to them their reminder, but from their reminder they turn aside.

وَلَوِ اتَّبَعَ الْحَقُّ اَهْوَآءَهُمْ لَفَسَدَتِ السَّمٰوٰتُ وَ الْاَرْضُ وَمَنْ فِيْهِنَّ ۗ بَلْ اَتَيْنٰهُمْ بِذِكْرِهِمْ فَهُمْ عَنْ ذِكْرِهِمْ مُّعْرِضُوْنَ ۞

72. Or is it that you ask them a recompense? But the recompense of your Lord is best, and He is the best of those who provide sustenance.

أَمْ تَسْـَٔلُهُمْ خَرْجًا فَخَرَاجُ رَبِّكَ خَيْرٌ ۗ وَّهُوَ خَيْرُ الرّٰزِقِيْنَ ۞

73. And most surely you invite them to a right way.

وَاِنَّكَ لَتَدْعُوْهُمْ اِلٰى صِرَاطٍ مُّسْتَقِيْمٍ ۞

74. And most surely those who do not believe in the hereafter are deviating from the way.

وَاِنَّ الَّذِيْنَ لَا يُؤْمِنُوْنَ بِالْاٰخِرَةِ عَنِ الصِّرَاطِ لَنٰكِبُوْنَ ۞

75. And if We show mercy to them and remove the distress they have, they would persist in their inordinacy, blindly wandering on.

وَلَوْ رَحِمْنٰهُمْ وَكَشَفْنَا مَا بِهِمْ مِّنْ ضُرٍّ لَّلَجُّوْا فِيْ طُغْيَانِهِمْ يَعْمَهُوْنَ ۞

76. And already We overtook them with chastisement, but they were not submissive to their Lord, nor do they humble themselves.

وَلَقَدْ اَخَذْنٰهُمْ بِالْعَذَابِ فَمَا اسْتَكَانُوْا لِرَبِّهِمْ وَمَا يَتَضَرَّعُوْنَ ۞

77. Until when We open upon them a door of severe chastisement, lo! they are in despair at it.

حَتّٰى اِذَا فَتَحْنَا عَلَيْهِمْ بَابًا ذَا عَذَابٍ شَدِيْدٍ اِذَا هُمْ فِيْهِ مُبْلِسُوْنَ ۞

78. And He it is Who made for you the ears and the eyes and the hearts; little is it that you give thanks.

وَهُوَ الَّذِيْٓ اَنْشَاَ لَكُمُ السَّمْعَ وَالْاَبْصَارَ وَالْاَفْئِدَةَ ۗ قَلِيْلًا مَّا تَشْكُرُوْنَ ۞

79. And He it is Who multiplied you in the earth, and to Him you shall be gathered.

وَهُوَ الَّذِيْ ذَرَاَكُمْ فِى الْاَرْضِ وَاِلَيْهِ تُحْشَرُوْنَ ۞

80. And He it is Who gives life and causes death, and (in) His (control) is the alternation of the night and the day; do you not then understand?

وَهُوَ الَّذِيْ يُحْيٖ وَيُمِيْتُ وَلَهُ اخْتِلَافُ الَّيْلِ وَ النَّهَارِ ۗ اَفَلَا تَعْقِلُوْنَ ۞

81. Nay, they say the like of what the ancients said:

بَلْ قَالُوْا مِثْلَ مَا قَالَ الْأَوَّلُوْنَ ۝

82. They say: What! When we are dead and become dust and bones, shall we then be raised?

قَالُوْا ءَاِذَا مِتْنَا وَكُنَّا تُرَابًا وَّعِظَامًا ءَاِنَّا لَمَبْعُوْثُوْنَ ۝

83. Certainly we are promised this, and (so were) our fathers aforetime; this is naught but stories of those of old.

لَقَدْ وُعِدْنَا نَحْنُ وَ اٰبَآؤُنَا هٰذَا مِنْ قَبْلُ اِنْ هٰذَا اِلَّا اَسَاطِيْرُ الْاَوَّلِيْنَ ۝

84. Say: Whose is the earth, and whoever is therein, if you know?

قُلْ لِّمَنِ الْاَرْضُ وَمَنْ فِيْهَا اِنْ كُنْتُمْ تَعْلَمُوْنَ ۝

85. They will say: Allah's. Say: Will you not then mind?

سَيَقُوْلُوْنَ لِلّٰهِ قُلْ اَفَلَا تَذَكَّرُوْنَ ۝

86. Say: Who is the Lord of the seven heavens and the Lord of the mighty dominion?

قُلْ مَنْ رَّبُّ السَّمٰوٰتِ السَّبْعِ وَرَبُّ الْعَرْشِ الْعَظِيْمِ ۝

87. They will say: (This is) Allah's. Say: Will you not then guard (against evil)?

سَيَقُوْلُوْنَ لِلّٰهِ قُلْ اَفَلَا تَتَّقُوْنَ ۝

88. Say: Who is it in Whose hand is the kingdom of all things and Who gives succor, but against Him Succor is not given, if you do but know?

قُلْ مَنْ بِيَدِهٖ مَلَكُوْتُ كُلِّ شَيْءٍ وَّهُوَ يُجِيْرُ وَلَا يُجَارُ عَلَيْهِ اِنْ كُنْتُمْ تَعْلَمُوْنَ ۝

89. They will say: (This is) Allah's. Say: From whence are you then deceived?

سَيَقُوْلُوْنَ لِلّٰهِ قُلْ فَاَنّٰى تُسْحَرُوْنَ ۝

90. Nay! We have brought to them the truth, and most surely they are liars.

بَلْ اَتَيْنٰهُمْ بِالْحَقِّ وَاِنَّهُمْ لَكٰذِبُوْنَ ۝

91. Never did Allah take to Himself a son, and never was there with him any (other) god—in that case would each god have certainly taken away what he created, and some of them would certainly have overpowered others; glory be to Allah above what they describe!

مَا اتَّخَذَ اللّٰهُ مِنْ وَّلَدٍ وَّمَا كَانَ مَعَهٗ مِنْ اِلٰهٍ اِذًا لَّذَهَبَ كُلُّ اِلٰهٍ بِمَا خَلَقَ وَلَعَلَا بَعْضُهُمْ عَلٰى بَعْضٍ سُبْحٰنَ اللّٰهِ عَمَّا يَصِفُوْنَ ۝

92. The Knower of the unseen and the seen, so may He be exalted above what they associate (with Him).

عٰلِمِ الْغَيْبِ وَالشَّهَادَةِ فَتَعٰلٰى عَمَّا يُشْرِكُوْنَ ۝

93. Say: O my Lord! if Thou shouldst make me see what they are threatened with:

قُلْ رَّبِّ اِمَّا تُرِيَنِّيْ مَا يُوْعَدُوْنَ ۝

94. My Lord! then place me not with the unjust.

رَبِّ فَلَا تَجْعَلْنِيْ فِى الْقَوْمِ الظّٰلِمِيْنَ ۝

95. And most surely We are well able to make you see what We threaten them with.

وَاِنَّا عَلٰى اَنْ نُّرِيَكَ مَا نَعِدُهُمْ لَقٰدِرُوْنَ ۝

96. Repel evil by what is best; We know best what they describe.

اِدْفَعْ بِالَّتِيْ هِيَ اَحْسَنُ السَّيِّئَةَ نَحْنُ اَعْلَمُ بِمَا يَصِفُوْنَ ۝

97. And say: O my Lord! I seek refuge in Thee from the evil suggestions of the Shaitans;

وَقُلْ رَّبِّ اَعُوْذُ بِكَ مِنْ هَمَزٰتِ الشَّيٰطِيْنِ ۝

98. And I seek refuge in Thee! O my Lord! from their presence.

وَاَعُوْذُ بِكَ رَبِّ اَنْ يَّحْضُرُوْنِ ۝

99. Until when death overtakes one of them, he says: Send me back, my Lord, send me back;

حَتّٰى اِذَا جَآءَ اَحَدَهُمُ الْمَوْتُ قَالَ رَبِّ ارْجِعُوْنِ ۝

100. Haply I may do good in that which I have left. By no means! it is a (mere) word that he speaks; and before them is a barrier until the day they are raised.

لَعَلِّيْ اَعْمَلُ صَالِحًا فِيْمَا تَرَكْتُ كَلَّا اِنَّهَا كَلِمَةٌ هُوَ قَآئِلُهَا وَمِنْ وَّرَآئِهِمْ بَرْزَخٌ اِلٰى يَوْمِ يُبْعَثُوْنَ ۝

101. So when the trumpet is blown, there shall be no ties of relationship between them on that day, nor shall they ask of each other.

فَاِذَا نُفِخَ فِى الصُّوْرِ فَلَاۤ اَنْسَابَ بَيْنَهُمْ يَوْمَئِذٍ وَّلَا يَتَسَآءَلُوْنَ ۝

102. Then as for him whose good deeds are preponderant, these are the successful.

فَمَنْ ثَقُلَتْ مَوَازِيْنُهُ فَاُولٰٓئِكَ هُمُ الْمُفْلِحُوْنَ ۝

103. And as for him whose good deeds are light, these are they who shall have lost their souls, abiding in hell.

وَمَنْ خَفَّتْ مَوَازِيْنُهُ فَاُولٰٓئِكَ الَّذِيْنَ خَسِرُوْاۤ اَنْفُسَهُمْ فِيْ جَهَنَّمَ خٰلِدُوْنَ ۝

104. The fire shall scorch their faces, and they therein shall be in severe affliction.

تَلْفَحُ وُجُوْهَهُمُ النَّارُ وَهُمْ فِيْهَا كٰلِحُوْنَ ۝

105. Were not My communications recited to you? But you used to reject them.

اَلَمْ تَكُنْ اٰيٰتِيْ تُتْلٰى عَلَيْكُمْ فَكُنْتُمْ بِهَا تُكَذِّبُوْنَ ۝

106. They shall say: O our Lord! our adversity overcame us and we were an erring people:

قَالُوْا رَبَّنَا غَلَبَتْ عَلَيْنَا شِقْوَتُنَا وَكُنَّا قَوْمًا ضَآلِّيْنَ ۝

107. O our Lord! Take us out of it; then if we return (to evil) surely we shall be unjust.

رَبَّنَاۤ اَخْرِجْنَا مِنْهَا فَاِنْ عُدْنَا فَاِنَّا ظٰلِمُوْنَ ۝

108. He shall say: Go away into it and speak not to Me;

قَالَ اخْسَئُوْا فِيْهَا وَلَا تُكَلِّمُوْنِ ۝

109. Surely there was a party of My servants who said: O our Lord! we believe, so do Thou forgive us and have mercy on us, and Thou art the best of the Merciful ones.

اِنَّهُ كَانَ فَرِيْقٌ مِّنْ عِبَادِيْ يَقُوْلُوْنَ رَبَّنَاۤ اٰمَنَّا فَاغْفِرْ لَنَا وَارْحَمْنَا وَاَنْتَ خَيْرُ الرّٰحِمِيْنَ ۝

110. But you took them for a mockery until they made you forget My remembrance and you used to laugh at them.

فَاتَّخَذْتُمُوهُمْ سِخْرِيًّا حَتّٰى اَنْسَوْكُمْ ذِكْرِيْ وَكُنْتُمْ مِّنْهُمْ تَضْحَكُوْنَ ۞

111. Surely I have rewarded them this day because they were patient, that they are the achievers.

اِنِّىْ جَزَيْتُهُمُ الْيَوْمَ بِمَا صَبَرُوْا اَنَّهُمْ هُمُ الْفَآئِزُوْنَ ۞

112. He will say: How many years did you tarry in the earth?

قٰلَ كَمْ لَبِثْتُمْ فِى الْاَرْضِ عَدَدَ سِنِيْنَ ۞

113. They will say: We tarried a day or part of a day, but ask those who keep account.

قَالُوْا لَبِثْنَا يَوْمًا اَوْ بَعْضَ يَوْمٍ فَسْئَلِ الْعَآدِّيْنَ ۞

114. He will say: You did tarry but a little—had you but known (it):

قٰلَ اِنْ لَّبِثْتُمْ اِلَّا قَلِيْلًا لَّوْ اَنَّكُمْ كُنْتُمْ تَعْلَمُوْنَ ۞

115. What! did you then think that We had created you in vain and that you shall not be returned to Us?

اَفَحَسِبْتُمْ اَنَّمَا خَلَقْنٰكُمْ عَبَثًا وَّاَنَّكُمْ اِلَيْنَا لَا تُرْجَعُوْنَ ۞

116. So exalted be Allah, the True King; no god is there but He, the Lord of the honorable dominion.

فَتَعٰلَى اللهُ الْمَلِكُ الْحَقُّ لَا اِلٰهَ اِلَّا هُوَ رَبُّ الْعَرْشِ الْكَرِيْمِ ۞

117. And whoever invokes with Allah another god—he has no proof of this—his reckoning is only with his Lord; surely the unbelievers shall not be successful.

وَمَنْ يَّدْعُ مَعَ اللهِ اِلٰهًا اٰخَرَ لَا بُرْهَانَ لَهٗ بِهٖ فَاِنَّمَا حِسَابُهٗ عِنْدَ رَبِّهٖ اِنَّهٗ لَا يُفْلِحُ الْكٰفِرُوْنَ ۞

118. And say: O my Lord! forgive and have mercy, and Thou art the best of the Merciful ones.

وَقُلْ رَّبِّ اغْفِرْ وَارْحَمْ وَاَنْتَ خَيْرُ الرّٰحِمِيْنَ ۞

THE LIGHT
(NUR)

**In the name of Allah,
the Beneficent, the Merciful.**

1. (This is) a chapter which We have revealed and made obligatory and in which We have revealed clear communications that you may be mindful.

2. (As for) the fornicatress and the fornicator, flog each of them, (giving) a hundred stripes, and let not pity for them detain you in the matter of obedience to Allah, if you believe in Allah and the last day, and let a party of believers witness their chastisement.

3. The fornicator shall not marry any but a fornicatress or idolatress, and (as for) the fornicatress, none shall marry her but a fornicator or an idolater; and it is forbidden to the believers.

4. And those who accuse free women then do not bring four witnesses, flog them, (giving) eighty stripes, and do not admit any evidence from them ever; and these it is that are the transgressors,

5. Except those who repent after this and act aright, for surely Allah is Forgiving, Merciful.

6. And (as for) those who accuse their wives and have no witnesses except themselves, the evidence of one of these (should be taken) four times, bearing Allah to witness that he is most surely of the truthful ones.

بِسْمِ اللهِ الرَّحْمٰنِ الرَّحِيْمِ ۟

سُوْرَةٌ اَنْزَلْنٰهَا وَفَرَضْنٰهَا وَاَنْزَلْنَا فِيْهَآ اٰيٰتٍۭ بَيِّنٰتٍ لَّعَلَّكُمْ تَذَكَّرُوْنَ ۟

اَلزَّانِيَةُ وَالزَّانِيْ فَاجْلِدُوْا كُلَّ وَاحِدٍ مِّنْهُمَا مِائَةَ جَلْدَةٍ ۠ وَّلَا تَأْخُذْكُمْ بِهِمَا رَأْفَةٌ فِيْ دِيْنِ اللهِ اِنْ كُنْتُمْ تُؤْمِنُوْنَ بِاللهِ وَالْيَوْمِ الْاٰخِرِ ۚ وَلْيَشْهَدْ عَذَابَهُمَا طَآئِفَةٌ مِّنَ الْمُؤْمِنِيْنَ ۟

اَلزَّانِيْ لَا يَنْكِحُ اِلَّا زَانِيَةً اَوْ مُشْرِكَةً ۫ وَّالزَّانِيَةُ لَا يَنْكِحُهَآ اِلَّا زَانٍ اَوْ مُشْرِكٌ ۚ وَحُرِّمَ ذٰلِكَ عَلَى الْمُؤْمِنِيْنَ ۟

وَالَّذِيْنَ يَرْمُوْنَ الْمُحْصَنٰتِ ثُمَّ لَمْ يَأْتُوْا بِاَرْبَعَةِ شُهَدَآءَ فَاجْلِدُوْهُمْ ثَمٰنِيْنَ جَلْدَةً وَّلَا تَقْبَلُوْا لَهُمْ شَهَادَةً اَبَدًا ۚ وَاُولٰٓئِكَ هُمُ الْفٰسِقُوْنَ ۟

اِلَّا الَّذِيْنَ تَابُوْا مِنْۢ بَعْدِ ذٰلِكَ وَاَصْلَحُوْا ۚ فَاِنَّ اللهَ غَفُوْرٌ رَّحِيْمٌ ۟

وَالَّذِيْنَ يَرْمُوْنَ اَزْوَاجَهُمْ وَلَمْ يَكُنْ لَّهُمْ شُهَدَآءُ اِلَّآ اَنْفُسُهُمْ فَشَهَادَةُ اَحَدِهِمْ اَرْبَعُ شَهٰدٰتٍۢ بِاللهِ ۙ اِنَّهٗ لَمِنَ الصّٰدِقِيْنَ ۟

7. And the fifth (time) that the curse of Allah be on him if he is one of the liars.

وَالْخَامِسَةُ اَنَّ لَعْنَتَ اللّٰهِ عَلَيْهِ اِنْ كَانَ مِنَ الْكٰذِبِيْنَ ۟

8. And it shall avert the chastisement from her if she testify four times, bearing Allah to witness that he is most surely one of the liars;

وَيَدْرَؤُا عَنْهَا الْعَذَابَ اَنْ تَشْهَدَ اَرْبَعَ شَهٰدٰتٍ بِاللّٰهِ اِنَّهُ لَمِنَ الْكٰذِبِيْنَ ۟

9. And the fifth (time) that the wrath of Allah be on her if he is one of the truthful.

وَالْخَامِسَةَ اَنَّ غَضَبَ اللّٰهِ عَلَيْهَا اِنْ كَانَ مِنَ الصّٰدِقِيْنَ ۟

10. And were it not for Allah's grace upon you and His mercy—and that Allah is Oft-returning (to mercy), Wise!

وَلَوْلَا فَضْلُ اللّٰهِ عَلَيْكُمْ وَرَحْمَتُهُ وَاَنَّ اللّٰهَ تَوَّابٌ حَكِيْمٌ ۟

11. Surely they who concocted the lie are a party from among you. Do not regard it an evil to you; nay, it is good for you. Every man of them shall have what he has earned of sin; and (as for) him who took upon himself the main part thereof, he shall have a grievous chastisement.

اِنَّ الَّذِيْنَ جَآءُوْ بِالْاِفْكِ عُصْبَةٌ مِّنْكُمْ لَا تَحْسَبُوْهُ شَرًّا لَّكُمْ بَلْ هُوَ خَيْرٌ لَّكُمْ لِكُلِّ امْرِئٍ مِّنْهُمْ مَّا اكْتَسَبَ مِنَ الْاِثْمِ وَالَّذِيْ تَوَلّٰى كِبْرَهُ مِنْهُمْ لَهُ عَذَابٌ عَظِيْمٌ ۟

12. Why did not the believing men and the believing women, when you heard it, think well of their own people, and say: This is an evident falsehood?

لَوْلَا اِذْ سَمِعْتُمُوْهُ ظَنَّ الْمُؤْمِنُوْنَ وَالْمُؤْمِنٰتُ بِاَنْفُسِهِمْ خَيْرًا وَّقَالُوْا هٰذَا اِفْكٌ مُّبِيْنٌ ۟

13. Why did they not bring four witnesses of it? But as they have not brought witnesses they are liars before Allah.

لَوْلَا جَآءُوْ عَلَيْهِ بِاَرْبَعَةِ شُهَدَآءَ فَاِذْ لَمْ يَأْتُوْا بِالشُّهَدَآءِ فَاُولٰٓئِكَ عِنْدَ اللّٰهِ هُمُ الْكٰذِبُوْنَ ۟

14. And were it not for Allah's grace upon you and His mercy in this world and the hereafter, a grievous chastisement would certainly have touched you on account of the discourse which you entered into.

وَلَوْلَا فَضْلُ اللّٰهِ عَلَيْكُمْ وَرَحْمَتُهُ فِي الدُّنْيَا وَالْاٰخِرَةِ لَمَسَّكُمْ فِيْ مَآ اَفَضْتُمْ فِيْهِ عَذَابٌ عَظِيْمٌ ۟

15. When you received it with your tongues and spoke with your mouths what you had no knowledge of, and you deemed it an easy matter while with Allah it was grievous.

اِذْ تَلَقَّوْنَهُ بِاَلْسِنَتِكُمْ وَتَقُوْلُوْنَ بِاَفْوَاهِكُمْ مَّا لَيْسَ لَكُمْ بِهِ عِلْمٌ وَّتَحْسَبُوْنَهُ هَيِّنًا وَّهُوَ عِنْدَ اللّٰهِ عَظِيْمٌ ۟

16. And why did you not, when you heard it, say: It does not beseem us that we should talk of it; glory be to Thee! this is a great calumny?

دَوَلَوْلَا اِذْ سَمِعْتُمُوْهُ قُلْتُمْ مَّا يَكُوْنُ لَنَاۤ اَنْ نَّتَكَلَّمَ بِهٰذَاۚ سُبْحٰنَكَ هٰذَا بُهْتَانٌ عَظِيْمٌ ۝

17. Allah admonishes you that you should not return to the like of it ever again if you are believers.

يَعِظُكُمُ اللّٰهُ اَنْ تَعُوْدُوْا لِمِثْلِهٖۤ اَبَدًا اِنْ كُنْتُمْ مُّؤْمِنِيْنَ ۝

18. And Allah makes clear to you the communications; and Allah is Knowing, Wise.

وَيُبَيِّنُ اللّٰهُ لَكُمُ الْاٰيٰتِ وَاللّٰهُ عَلِيْمٌ حَكِيْمٌ ۝

19. Surely (as for) those who love that scandal should circulate respecting those who believe, they shall have a grievous chastisement in this world and the hereafter; and Allah knows, while you do not know.

اِنَّ الَّذِيْنَ يُحِبُّوْنَ اَنْ تَشِيْعَ الْفَاحِشَةُ فِى الَّذِيْنَ اٰمَنُوْا لَهُمْ عَذَابٌ اَلِيْمٌ فِى الدُّنْيَا وَالْاٰخِرَةِ وَاللّٰهُ يَعْلَمُ وَاَنْتُمْ لَا تَعْلَمُوْنَ ۝

20. And were it not for Allah's grace on you and His mercy, and that Allah is Compassionate, Merciful.

وَلَوْلَا فَضْلُ اللّٰهِ عَلَيْكُمْ وَرَحْمَتُهٗ وَاَنَّ اللّٰهَ رَءُوْفٌ رَّحِيْمٌ ۝

21. O you who believe! do not follow the footsteps of the Shaitan; and whoever follows the footsteps of the Shaitan, then surely he bids the doing of indecency and evil; and were it not for Allah's grace upon you and His mercy, not one of you would have ever been pure, but Allah purifies whom He pleases; and Allah is Hearing, Knowing.

يٰۤاَيُّهَا الَّذِيْنَ اٰمَنُوْا لَا تَتَّبِعُوْا خُطُوٰتِ الشَّيْطٰنِ وَمَنْ يَّتَّبِعْ خُطُوٰتِ الشَّيْطٰنِ فَاِنَّهٗ يَاْمُرُ بِالْفَحْشَآءِ وَالْمُنْكَرِ وَلَوْلَا فَضْلُ اللّٰهِ عَلَيْكُمْ وَرَحْمَتُهٗ مَا زَكٰى مِنْكُمْ مِّنْ اَحَدٍ اَبَدًا وَّلٰكِنَّ اللّٰهَ يُزَكِّيْ مَنْ يَّشَآءُ وَاللّٰهُ سَمِيْعٌ عَلِيْمٌ ۝

22. And let not those of you who possess grace and abundance swear against giving to the near of kin and the poor and those who have fled in Allah's way, and they should pardon and turn away. Do you not love that Allah should forgive you? And Allah is Forgiving, Merciful.

وَلَا يَاْتَلِ اُولُوا الْفَضْلِ مِنْكُمْ وَالسَّعَةِ اَنْ يُّؤْتُوْۤا اُولِى الْقُرْبٰى وَالْمَسٰكِيْنَ وَالْمُهٰجِرِيْنَ فِى سَبِيْلِ اللّٰهِ وَلْيَعْفُوْا وَلْيَصْفَحُوْا اَلَا تُحِبُّوْنَ اَنْ يَّغْفِرَ اللّٰهُ لَكُمْ وَاللّٰهُ غَفُوْرٌ رَّحِيْمٌ ۝

23. Surely those who accuse chaste believing women, unaware (of the evil), are cursed in this world and the hereafter, and they shall have a grievous chastisement.

اِنَّ الَّذِيْنَ يَرْمُوْنَ الْمُحْصَنٰتِ الْغٰفِلٰتِ الْمُؤْمِنٰتِ لُعِنُوْا فِى الدُّنْيَا وَالْاٰخِرَةِ وَلَهُمْ عَذَابٌ عَظِيْمٌ ۝

24. On the day when their tongues and their hands and their feet shall bear witness against them as to what they did.

يَوْمَ تَشْهَدُ عَلَيْهِمْ اَلْسِنَتُهُمْ وَاَيْدِيْهِمْ وَاَرْجُلُهُمْ بِمَا كَانُوْا يَعْمَلُوْنَ ۞

25. On that day Allah will pay back to them in full their just reward, and they shall know that Allah is the evident Truth.

يَوْمَئِذٍ يُّوَفِّيْهِمُ اللهُ دِيْنَهُمُ الْحَقَّ وَيَعْلَمُوْنَ اَنَّ اللهَ هُوَ الْحَقُّ الْمُبِيْنُ ۞

26. Unclean things are for unclean ones and unclean ones are for unclean things, and the good things are for good ones and the good ones are for good things; these are free from what they say; they shall have forgiveness and an honorable sustenance.

اَلْخَبِيْثٰتُ لِلْخَبِيْثِيْنَ وَالْخَبِيْثُوْنَ لِلْخَبِيْثٰتِ ۚ وَالطَّيِّبٰتُ لِلطَّيِّبِيْنَ وَالطَّيِّبُوْنَ لِلطَّيِّبٰتِ ۚ اُولٰٓئِكَ مُبَرَّءُوْنَ مِمَّا يَقُوْلُوْنَ ۚ لَهُمْ مَّغْفِرَةٌ وَّرِزْقٌ كَرِيْمٌ ۞

27. O you who believe! Do not enter houses other than your own houses until you have asked permission and saluted their inmates; this is better for you, that you may be mindful.

يٰٓاَيُّهَا الَّذِيْنَ اٰمَنُوْا لَا تَدْخُلُوْا بُيُوْتًا غَيْرَ بُيُوْتِكُمْ حَتّٰى تَسْتَأْنِسُوْا وَتُسَلِّمُوْا عَلٰٓى اَهْلِهَا ۚ ذٰلِكُمْ خَيْرٌ لَّكُمْ لَعَلَّكُمْ تَذَكَّرُوْنَ ۞

28. But if you do not find any one therein, then do not enter them until permission is given to you; and if it is said to you: Go back, then go back; this is purer for you; and Allah is Cognizant of what you do.

فَاِنْ لَّمْ تَجِدُوْا فِيْهَآ اَحَدًا فَلَا تَدْخُلُوْهَا حَتّٰى يُؤْذَنَ لَكُمْ ۚ وَاِنْ قِيْلَ لَكُمُ ارْجِعُوْا فَارْجِعُوْا هُوَ اَزْكٰى لَكُمْ ۚ وَاللهُ بِمَا تَعْمَلُوْنَ عَلِيْمٌ ۞

29. It is no sin in you that you enter uninhabited houses wherein you have your necessaries; and Allah knows what you do openly and what you hide.

لَيْسَ عَلَيْكُمْ جُنَاحٌ اَنْ تَدْخُلُوْا بُيُوْتًا غَيْرَ مَسْكُوْنَةٍ فِيْهَا مَتَاعٌ لَّكُمْ ۚ وَاللهُ يَعْلَمُ مَا تُبْدُوْنَ وَمَا تَكْتُمُوْنَ ۞

30. Say to the believing men that they cast down their looks and guard their private parts; that is purer for them; surely Allah is Aware of what they do.

قُلْ لِّلْمُؤْمِنِيْنَ يَغُضُّوْا مِنْ اَبْصَارِهِمْ وَيَحْفَظُوْا فُرُوْجَهُمْ ۚ ذٰلِكَ اَزْكٰى لَهُمْ ۚ اِنَّ اللهَ خَبِيْرٌ بِمَا يَصْنَعُوْنَ ۞

31. And say to the believing women that they cast down their looks and guard their private parts and do not display their ornaments except what appears thereof, and let them wear their head-coverings over their bosoms, and not display their ornaments except to their husbands or their fathers, or the fathers of their husbands, or their sons, or the sons of their husbands, or their brothers, or their brothers' sons, or their sisters' sons, or their women, or those whom their right hands possess, or the male servants not having need (of women), or the children who have not attained knowledge of what is hidden of women; and let them not strike their feet so that what they hide of their ornaments may be known; and turn to Allah all of you, O believers! so that you may be successful.

32. And marry those among you who are single and those who are fit among your male slaves and your female slaves; if they are needy, Allah will make them free from want out of His grace; and Allah is Ample-giving, Knowing.

33. And let those who do not find the means to marry keep chaste until Allah makes them free from want out of His grace. And (as for) those who ask for a writing from among those whom your right hands possess, give them the writing if you know any good in them, and give them of the wealth of Allah which He has given you; and do not compel your slave girls to prostitution, when they desire to keep chaste, in order to seek the frail good of this world's life; and whoever compels them, then surely after their compulsion Allah is Forgiving, Merciful.

34. And certainly We have sent to you clear communications and a description of those who have passed away before you, and an admonition to those who guard (against evil).

وَقُلْ لِّلْمُؤْمِنٰتِ يَغْضُضْنَ مِنْ اَبْصَارِهِنَّ وَيَحْفَظْنَ فُرُوجَهُنَّ وَلَا يُبْدِيْنَ زِيْنَتَهُنَّ اِلَّا مَا ظَهَرَ مِنْهَا وَلْيَضْرِبْنَ بِخُمُرِهِنَّ عَلٰى جُيُوْبِهِنَّ وَلَا يُبْدِيْنَ زِيْنَتَهُنَّ اِلَّا لِبُعُوْلَتِهِنَّ اَوْ اٰبَآئِهِنَّ اَوْ اٰبَآءِ بُعُوْلَتِهِنَّ اَوْ اَبْنَآئِهِنَّ اَوْ اَبْنَآءِ بُعُوْلَتِهِنَّ اَوْ اِخْوَانِهِنَّ اَوْ بَنِىْ اِخْوَانِهِنَّ اَوْ بَنِىْ اَخَوٰتِهِنَّ اَوْ نِسَآئِهِنَّ اَوْ مَا مَلَكَتْ اَيْمَانُهُنَّ اَوِ التّٰبِعِيْنَ غَيْرِ اُولِى الْاِرْبَةِ مِنَ الرِّجَالِ اَوِ الطِّفْلِ الَّذِيْنَ لَمْ يَظْهَرُوْا عَلٰى عَوْرٰتِ النِّسَآءِ ۖ وَلَا يَضْرِبْنَ بِاَرْجُلِهِنَّ لِيُعْلَمَ مَا يُخْفِيْنَ مِنْ زِيْنَتِهِنَّ وَ تُوْبُوْا اِلَى اللهِ جَمِيْعًا اَيُّهَ الْمُؤْمِنُوْنَ لَعَلَّكُمْ تُفْلِحُوْنَ ۞

وَاَنْكِحُوا الْاَيَامٰى مِنْكُمْ وَالصّٰلِحِيْنَ مِنْ عِبَادِكُمْ وَاِمَآئِكُمْ ۚ اِنْ يَّكُوْنُوْا فُقَرَآءَ يُغْنِهِمُ اللهُ مِنْ فَضْلِهٖ ۗ وَاللهُ وَاسِعٌ عَلِيْمٌ ۞

وَلْيَسْتَعْفِفِ الَّذِيْنَ لَا يَجِدُوْنَ نِكَاحًا حَتّٰى يُغْنِيَهُمُ اللهُ مِنْ فَضْلِهٖ ۗ وَالَّذِيْنَ يَبْتَغُوْنَ الْكِتٰبَ مِمَّا مَلَكَتْ اَيْمَانُكُمْ فَكَاتِبُوْهُمْ اِنْ عَلِمْتُمْ فِيْهِمْ خَيْرًا ۖ وَّ اٰتُوْهُمْ مِّنْ مَّالِ اللهِ الَّذِيْ اٰتٰىكُمْ ۗ وَلَا تُكْرِهُوْا فَتَيٰتِكُمْ عَلَى الْبِغَآءِ اِنْ اَرَدْنَ تَحَصُّنًا لِّتَبْتَغُوْا عَرَضَ الْحَيٰوةِ الدُّنْيَا ۗ وَمَنْ يُّكْرِهْهُّنَّ فَاِنَّ اللهَ مِنْ بَعْدِ اِكْرَاهِهِنَّ غَفُوْرٌ رَّحِيْمٌ ۞

وَلَقَدْ اَنْزَلْنَا اِلَيْكُمْ اٰيٰتٍ مُّبَيِّنٰتٍ وَّمَثَلًا مِّنَ الَّذِيْنَ خَلَوْا مِنْ قَبْلِكُمْ وَمَوْعِظَةً لِّلْمُتَّقِيْنَ ۞

338

35. Allah is the light of the heavens and the earth; a likeness of His light is as a niche in which is a lamp, the lamp is in a glass, (and) the glass is as it were a brightly shining star, lit from a blessed olive-tree, neither eastern nor western, the oil whereof almost gives light though fire touch it not—light upon light—Allah guides to His light whom He pleases, and Allah sets forth parables for men, and Allah is Cognizant of all things.

اَللّٰهُ نُوْرُ السَّمٰوٰتِ وَالْاَرْضِ مَثَلُ نُوْرِهٖ كَمِشْكٰوةٍ فِيْهَا مِصْبَاحٌ اَلْمِصْبَاحُ فِيْ زُجَاجَةٍ اَلزُّجَاجَةُ كَاَنَّهَا كَوْكَبٌ دُرِّيٌّ يُّوْقَدُ مِنْ شَجَرَةٍ مُّبٰرَكَةٍ زَيْتُوْنَةٍ لَّا شَرْقِيَّةٍ وَّلَا غَرْبِيَّةٍ يَّكَادُ زَيْتُهَا يُضِيْٓءُ وَلَوْ لَمْ تَمْسَسْهُ نَارٌ نُوْرٌ عَلٰى نُوْرٍ يَهْدِي اللّٰهُ لِنُوْرِهٖ مَنْ يَّشَآءُ وَيَضْرِبُ اللّٰهُ الْاَمْثَالَ لِلنَّاسِ وَاللّٰهُ بِكُلِّ شَيْءٍ عَلِيْمٌ ۙ ٣٥

36. In houses which Allah has permitted to be exalted and that His name may be remembered in them; there glorify Him therein in the mornings and the evenings,

فِيْ بُيُوْتٍ اَذِنَ اللّٰهُ اَنْ تُرْفَعَ وَيُذْكَرَ فِيْهَا اسْمُهٗ يُسَبِّحُ لَهٗ فِيْهَا بِالْغُدُوِّ وَالْاٰصَالِ ۙ ٣٦

37. Men whom neither merchandise nor selling diverts from the remembrance of Allah and the keeping up of prayer and the giving of poor-rate; they fear a day in which the hearts and eyes shall turn about;

رِجَالٌ لَّا تُلْهِيْهِمْ تِجَارَةٌ وَّلَا بَيْعٌ عَنْ ذِكْرِ اللّٰهِ وَاِقَامِ الصَّلٰوةِ وَاِيْتَآءِ الزَّكٰوةِ يَخَافُوْنَ يَوْمًا تَتَقَلَّبُ فِيْهِ الْقُلُوْبُ وَالْاَبْصَارُ ۙ ٣٧

38. That Allah may give them the best reward of what they have done, and give them more out of His grace; and Allah gives sustenance to whom He pleases without measure.

لِيَجْزِيَهُمُ اللّٰهُ اَحْسَنَ مَا عَمِلُوْا وَيَزِيْدَهُمْ مِّنْ فَضْلِهٖ وَاللّٰهُ يَرْزُقُ مَنْ يَّشَآءُ بِغَيْرِ حِسَابٍ ٣٨

39. And (as for) those who disbelieve, their deeds are like the mirage in a desert, which the thirsty man deems to be water; until when he comes to it he finds it to be naught, and there he finds Allah, so He pays back to him his reckoning in full; and Allah is quick in reckoning;

وَالَّذِيْنَ كَفَرُوْٓا اَعْمَالُهُمْ كَسَرَابٍ بِقِيْعَةٍ يَّحْسَبُهُ الظَّمْاٰنُ مَآءً حَتّٰى اِذَا جَآءَهٗ لَمْ يَجِدْهُ شَيْئًا وَّوَجَدَ اللّٰهَ عِنْدَهٗ فَوَفّٰهُ حِسَابَهٗ وَاللّٰهُ سَرِيْعُ الْحِسَابِ ۙ ٣٩

40. Or like utter darkness in the deep sea: there covers it a wave above which is another wave, above which is a cloud, (layers of) utter darkness one above another; when he holds out his hand, he is almost unable to see it; and to whomsoever Allah does not give light, he has no light.

اَوْ كَظُلُمٰتٍ فِيْ بَحْرٍ لُّجِّيٍّ يَّغْشٰهُ مَوْجٌ مِّنْ فَوْقِهٖ مَوْجٌ مِّنْ فَوْقِهٖ سَحَابٌ ظُلُمٰتٌ بَعْضُهَا فَوْقَ بَعْضٍ اِذَآ اَخْرَجَ يَدَهٗ لَمْ يَكَدْ يَرٰهَا وَمَنْ لَّمْ يَجْعَلِ اللّٰهُ لَهٗ نُوْرًا فَمَا لَهٗ مِنْ نُوْرٍ ع

41. Do you not see that Allah is He Whom do glorify all those who are in the heavens and the earth, and the (very) birds with expanded wings? He knows the prayer of each one and its glorification, and Allah is Cognizant of what they do.

42. And Allah's is the kingdom of the heavens and the earth, and to Allah is the eventual coming.

43. Do you not see that Allah drives along the clouds, then gathers them together, then piles them up, so that you see the rain coming forth from their midst? And He sends down of the clouds that are (like) mountains wherein is hail, afflicting therewith whom He pleases and turning it away from whom He pleases; the flash of His lightning almost takes away the sight.

44. Allah turns over the night and the day; most surely there is a lesson in this for those who have sight.

45. And Allah has created from water every living creature: so of them is that which walks upon its belly, and of them is that which walks upon two feet, and of them is that which walks upon four; Allah creates what He pleases; surely Allah has power over all things.

46. Certainly We have revealed clear communications, and Allah guides whom He pleases to the right way.

47. And they say: We believe in Allah and in the apostle and we obey; then a party of them turn back after this, and these are not believers.

48. And when they are called to Allah and His Apostle that he may judge between them, lo! a party of them turn aside.

49. And if the truth be on their side, they come to him quickly, obedient.

340

50. Is there in their hearts a disease, or are they in doubt, or do they fear that Allah and His Apostle will act wrongfully towards them? Nay! they themselves are the unjust.

اَفِىْ قُلُوْبِهِمْ مَّرَضٌ اَمِ ارْتَابُوْٓا اَمْ يَخَافُوْنَ اَنْ يَّحِيْفَ اللّٰهُ عَلَيْهِمْ وَرَسُوْلُهٗ ۭ بَلْ اُولٰٓئِكَ هُمُ الظّٰلِمُوْنَ ۟

51. The response of the believers, when they are invited to Allah and His Apostle that he may judge between them, is only to say: We hear and we obey; and these it is that are the successful.

اِنَّمَا كَانَ قَوْلَ الْمُؤْمِنِيْنَ اِذَا دُعُوْٓا اِلَى اللّٰهِ وَرَسُوْلِهٖ لِيَحْكُمَ بَيْنَهُمْ اَنْ يَّقُوْلُوْا سَمِعْنَا وَاَطَعْنَا ۭ وَاُولٰٓئِكَ هُمُ الْمُفْلِحُوْنَ ۟

52. And he who obeys Allah and His Apostle, and fears Allah, and is careful of (his duty to) Him, these it is that are the achievers.

وَمَنْ يُّطِعِ اللّٰهَ وَرَسُوْلَهٗ وَيَخْشَ اللّٰهَ وَيَتَّقْهِ فَاُولٰٓئِكَ هُمُ الْفَائِزُوْنَ ۟

53. And they swear by Allah with the most energetic of their oaths that if you command them they would certainly go forth. Say: Swear not; reasonable obedience (is desired); surely Allah is aware of what you do.

وَاَقْسَمُوْا بِاللّٰهِ جَهْدَ اَيْمَانِهِمْ لَئِنْ اَمَرْتَهُمْ لَيَخْرُجُنَّ ۭ قُلْ لَّا تُقْسِمُوْا ۚ طَاعَةٌ مَّعْرُوْفَةٌ ۭ اِنَّ اللّٰهَ خَبِيْرٌۢ بِمَا تَعْمَلُوْنَ ۟

54. Say: Obey Allah and obey the Apostle; but if you turn back, then on him rests that which is imposed on him and on you rests that which is imposed on you; and if you obey him, you are on the right way; and nothing rests on the Apostle but clear delivering (of the message).

قُلْ اَطِيْعُوا اللّٰهَ وَاَطِيْعُوا الرَّسُوْلَ ۚ فَاِنْ تَوَلَّوْا فَاِنَّمَا عَلَيْهِ مَا حُمِّلَ وَعَلَيْكُمْ مَّا حُمِّلْتُمْ ۭ وَاِنْ تُطِيْعُوْهُ تَهْتَدُوْا ۭ وَمَا عَلَى الرَّسُوْلِ اِلَّا الْبَلٰغُ الْمُبِيْنُ ۟

55. Allah has promised to those of you who believe and do good that He will most certainly make them rulers in the earth as He made rulers those before them, and that He will most certainly establish for them their religion which He has chosen for them, and that He will most certainly, after their fear, give them security in exchange; they shall serve Me, not associating aught with Me; and whoever is ungrateful after this, these it is who are the transgressors.

وَعَدَ اللّٰهُ الَّذِيْنَ اٰمَنُوْا مِنْكُمْ وَعَمِلُوا الصّٰلِحٰتِ لَيَسْتَخْلِفَنَّهُمْ فِى الْاَرْضِ كَمَا اسْتَخْلَفَ الَّذِيْنَ مِنْ قَبْلِهِمْ ۠ وَلَيُمَكِّنَنَّ لَهُمْ دِيْنَهُمُ الَّذِى ارْتَضٰى لَهُمْ وَلَيُبَدِّلَنَّهُمْ مِّنْۢ بَعْدِ خَوْفِهِمْ اَمْنًا ۭ يَعْبُدُوْنَنِىْ لَا يُشْرِكُوْنَ بِىْ شَيْئًا ۭ وَمَنْ كَفَرَ بَعْدَ ذٰلِكَ فَاُولٰٓئِكَ هُمُ الْفٰسِقُوْنَ ۟

56. And keep up prayer and pay the poor-rate and obey the Apostle, so that mercy may be shown to you.

وَاَقِيْمُوا الصَّلٰوةَ وَاٰتُوا الزَّكٰوةَ وَاَطِيْعُوا الرَّسُوْلَ لَعَلَّكُمْ تُرْحَمُوْنَ ۟

57. Think not that those who disbelieve shall escape in the earth, and their abode is the fire; and certainly evil is the resort!

لَا تَحْسَبَنَّ الَّذِيْنَ كَفَرُوْا مُعْجِزِيْنَ فِى الْاَرْضِ ۚ وَمَأْوٰىهُمُ النَّارُ ۭ وَلَبِئْسَ الْمَصِيْرُ ۟

58. O you who believe! let those whom your right hands possess and those of you who have not attained to puberty ask permission of you three times; before the morning prayer, and when you put off your clothes at midday in summer, and after the prayer of the nightfall; these are three times of privacy for you; neither is it a sin for you nor for them besides these, some of you must go round about (waiting) upon others; thus does Allah make clear to you the communications, and Allah is Knowing, Wise.

59. And when the children among you have attained to puberty, let them seek permission as those before them sought permission; thus does Allah make clear to you His communications, and Allah is knowing, Wise.

60. And (as for) women advanced in years who do not hope for a marriage, it is no sin for them if they put off their clothes without displaying their ornaments; and if they restrain themselves it is better for them; and Allah is Hearing, Knowing.

61. There is no blame on the blind man, nor is there blame on the lame, nor is there blame on the sick, nor on yourselves that you eat from your houses, or your fathers' houses or your mothers' houses, or your brothers' houses, or your sisters' houses, or your paternal uncles' houses, or your paternal aunts' houses, or your maternal uncles' houses, or your maternal aunts' houses, or what you possess the keys of, or your friends' (houses). It is no sin in you that you eat together or separately. So when you enter houses, greet your people with a salutation from Allah, blessed (and) goodly; thus does Allah make clear to you the communications that you may understand.

62. Only those are believers who believe in Allah and His Apostle, and when they are with him on a momentous affair they go not away until they have asked his permission; surely they who ask your permission are they who believe in Allah and His Apostle; so when they ask your permission for some affair of theirs, give permission to whom you please of them and ask forgiveness for them from Allah; surely Allah is Forgiving, Merciful.

63. Do not hold the Apostle's calling (you) among you to be like your calling one to the other; Allah indeed knows those who steal away from among you, concealing themselves; therefore let those beware who go against his order lest a trial afflict them or there befall them a painful chastisement.

64. Now surely Allah's is whatever is in the heavens and the earth; He knows indeed that to which you are conforming yourselves; and on the day on which they are returned to Him, He will inform them of what they did; and Allah is Cognizant of all things.

إِنَّمَا الْمُؤْمِنُونَ الَّذِينَ اٰمَنُوْا بِاللّٰهِ وَرَسُوْلِهٖ وَاِذَا كَانُوْا مَعَهٗ عَلٰۤى اَمْرٍ جَامِعٍ لَّمْ يَذْهَبُوْا حَتّٰى يَسْتَأْذِنُوْهُ اِنَّ الَّذِيْنَ يَسْتَأْذِنُوْنَكَ اُولٰٓئِكَ الَّذِيْنَ يُؤْمِنُوْنَ بِاللّٰهِ وَرَسُوْلِهٖ فَاِذَا اسْتَأْذَنُوْكَ لِبَعْضِ شَأْنِهِمْ فَأْذَنْ لِّمَنْ شِئْتَ مِنْهُمْ وَاسْتَغْفِرْ لَهُمُ اللّٰهَ اِنَّ اللّٰهَ غَفُوْرٌ رَّحِيْمٌ ۝

لَا تَجْعَلُوْا دُعَآءَ الرَّسُوْلِ بَيْنَكُمْ كَدُعَآءِ بَعْضِكُمْ بَعْضًا قَدْ يَعْلَمُ اللّٰهُ الَّذِيْنَ يَتَسَلَّلُوْنَ مِنْكُمْ لِوَاذًا فَلْيَحْذَرِ الَّذِيْنَ يُخَالِفُوْنَ عَنْ اَمْرِهٖۤ اَنْ تُصِيْبَهُمْ فِتْنَةٌ اَوْ يُصِيْبَهُمْ عَذَابٌ اَلِيْمٌ ۝

اَلَاۤ اِنَّ لِلّٰهِ مَا فِى السَّمٰوٰتِ وَالْاَرْضِ قَدْ يَعْلَمُ مَاۤ اَنْتُمْ عَلَيْهِ وَيَوْمَ يُرْجَعُوْنَ اِلَيْهِ فَيُنَبِّئُهُمْ بِمَا عَمِلُوْا وَاللّٰهُ بِكُلِّ شَيْءٍ عَلِيْمٌ ۝

THE CRITERION
(FURQAN)

In the name of Allah, the Beneficent, the Merciful.

1. Blessed is He Who sent down the Furqan upon His servant that he may be a warner to the nations;

2. He, Whose is the kingdom of the heavens and the earth, and Who did not take to Himself a son, and Who has no associate in the kingdom, and Who created everything, then ordained for it a measure.

3. And they have taken besides Him gods, who do not create anything while they are themselves created, and they control not for themselves any harm or profit, and they control not death, nor life, nor raising (the dead) to life.

4. And those who disbelieve say: This is nothing but a lie which he has forged, and other people have helped him at it; so indeed they have done injustice and (uttered) a falsehood.

5. And they say: The stories of the ancients—he has got them written—so these are read out to him morning and evening.

6. Say: He has revealed it Who knows the secret in the heavens and the earth; surely He is ever Forgiving, Merciful.

7. And they say: What is the matter with this Apostle that he eats food and goes about in the markets; why has not an angel been sent down to him, so that he should have been a warner with him?

8. Or (why is not) a treasure sent down to him, or he is made to have a garden from which he should eat? And the unjust say: You do not follow any but a man deprived of reason.

اَوْ يُلْقٰى اِلَيْهِ كَنْزٌ اَوْ تَكُوْنُ لَهٗ جَنَّةٌ يَّاْكُلُ مِنْهَا ۚ وَقَالَ الظّٰلِمُوْنَ اِنْ تَتَّبِعُوْنَ اِلَّا رَجُلًا مَّسْحُوْرًا ۝

9. See what likenesses do they apply to you, so they have gone astray, therefore they shall not be able to find a way.

اُنْظُرْ كَيْفَ ضَرَبُوْا لَكَ الْاَمْثَالَ فَضَلُّوْا فَلَا يَسْتَطِيْعُوْنَ سَبِيْلًا ۝

10. Blessed is He Who, if He please, will give you what is better than this, gardens beneath which rivers flow, and He will give you palaces.

تَبٰرَكَ الَّذِيْٓ اِنْ شَآءَ جَعَلَ لَكَ خَيْرًا مِّنْ ذٰلِكَ جَنّٰتٍ تَجْرِيْ مِنْ تَحْتِهَا الْاَنْهٰرُ ۙ وَيَجْعَلْ لَّكَ قُصُوْرًا ۝

11. But they reject the hour, and We have prepared a burning fire for him who rejects the hour.

بَلْ كَذَّبُوْا بِالسَّاعَةِ ۫ وَاَعْتَدْنَا لِمَنْ كَذَّبَ بِالسَّاعَةِ سَعِيْرًا ۝

12. When it shall come into their sight from a distant place, they shall hear its vehement raging and roaring.

اِذَا رَاَتْهُمْ مِّنْ مَّكَانٍ بَعِيْدٍ سَمِعُوْا لَهَا تَغَيُّظًا وَّزَفِيْرًا ۝

13. And when they are cast into a narrow place in it, bound, they shall there call out for destruction.

وَاِذَآ اُلْقُوْا مِنْهَا مَكَانًا ضَيِّقًا مُّقَرَّنِيْنَ دَعَوْا هُنَالِكَ ثُبُوْرًا ۝

14. Call not this day for one destruction, but call for destructions many.

لَا تَدْعُوا الْيَوْمَ ثُبُوْرًا وَّاحِدًا وَّادْعُوْا ثُبُوْرًا كَثِيْرًا ۝

15. Say: Is this better or the abiding garden which those who guard (against evil) are promised? That shall be a reward and a resort for them.

قُلْ اَذٰلِكَ خَيْرٌ اَمْ جَنَّةُ الْخُلْدِ الَّتِيْ وُعِدَ الْمُتَّقُوْنَ ۚ كَانَتْ لَهُمْ جَزَآءً وَّمَصِيْرًا ۝

16. They shall have therein what they desire abiding (in it); it is a promise which it is proper to be prayed for from your Lord.

لَهُمْ فِيْهَا مَا يَشَآءُوْنَ خٰلِدِيْنَ ۚ كَانَ عَلٰى رَبِّكَ وَعْدًا مَّسْئُوْلًا ۝

17. And on the day when He shall gather them, and whatever they served besides Allah, He shall say: Was it you who led astray these My servants, or did they themselves go astray from the path?

وَيَوْمَ يَحْشُرُهُمْ وَمَا يَعْبُدُوْنَ مِنْ دُوْنِ اللّٰهِ فَيَقُوْلُ ءَاَنْتُمْ اَضْلَلْتُمْ عِبَادِيْ هٰٓؤُلَآءِ اَمْ هُمْ ضَلُّوا السَّبِيْلَ ۝

18. They shall say: Glory be to Thee; it was not beseeming for us that we should take any guardians besides Thee, but Thou didst make them and their fathers to enjoy until they forsook the reminder, and they were a people in perdition,

قَالُوْا سُبْحٰنَكَ مَا كَانَ يَنْبَغِيْ لَنَاۤ اَنْ نَّتَّخِذَ مِنْ دُوْنِكَ مِنْ اَوْلِيَآءَ وَلٰكِنْ مَّتَّعْتَهُمْ وَاٰبَآءَهُمْ حَتّٰى نَسُوا الذِّكْرَ ۚ وَكَانُوْا قَوْمًاۢ بُوْرًا ۝

19. So they shall indeed give you the lie in what you say, then you shall not be able to ward off or help, and whoever among you is unjust, We will make him taste a great chastisement.

فَقَدْ كَذَّبُوْكُمْ بِمَا تَقُوْلُوْنَ ۙ فَمَا تَسْتَطِيْعُوْنَ صَرْفًا وَّلَا نَصْرًا ۚ وَمَنْ يَّظْلِمْ مِّنْكُمْ نُذِقْهُ عَذَابًا كَبِيْرًا ۝

20. And We have not sent before you any messengers but they most surely ate food and went about in the markets; and We have made some of you a trial for others; will you bear patiently? And your Lord is ever Seeing.

وَمَاۤ اَرْسَلْنَا قَبْلَكَ مِنَ الْمُرْسَلِيْنَ اِلَّاۤ اِنَّهُمْ لَيَأْكُلُوْنَ الطَّعَامَ وَيَمْشُوْنَ فِى الْاَسْوَاقِ ۗ وَجَعَلْنَا بَعْضَكُمْ لِبَعْضٍ فِتْنَةً ۗ اَتَصْبِرُوْنَ ۚ وَكَانَ رَبُّكَ بَصِيْرًا ۝

21. And those who do not hope for Our meeting, say: Why have not angels been sent down upon us, or (why) do we not see our Lord? Now certainly they are too proud of themselves and have revolted in great revolt.

وَقَالَ الَّذِيْنَ لَا يَرْجُوْنَ لِقَآءَنَا لَوْلَاۤ اُنْزِلَ عَلَيْنَا الْمَلٰٓئِكَةُ اَوْ نَرٰى رَبَّنَا ۗ لَقَدِ اسْتَكْبَرُوْا فِيْۤ اَنْفُسِهِمْ وَعَتَوْ عُتُوًّا كَبِيْرًا ۝

22. On the day when they shall see the angels, there shall be no joy on that day for the guilty, and they shall say: It is a forbidden thing totally prohibited.

يَوْمَ يَرَوْنَ الْمَلٰٓئِكَةَ لَا بُشْرٰى يَوْمَئِذٍ لِّلْمُجْرِمِيْنَ وَيَقُوْلُوْنَ حِجْرًا مَّحْجُوْرًا ۝

23. And We will proceed to what they have done of deeds, so We shall render them as scattered floating dust.

وَقَدِمْنَاۤ اِلٰى مَا عَمِلُوْا مِنْ عَمَلٍ فَجَعَلْنٰهُ هَبَآءً مَّنْثُوْرًا ۝

24. The dwellers of the garden shall on that day be in a better abiding-place and a better resting-place.

اَصْحٰبُ الْجَنَّةِ يَوْمَئِذٍ خَيْرٌ مُّسْتَقَرًّا وَّاَحْسَنُ مَقِيْلًا ۝

25. And on the day when the heaven shall burst asunder with the clouds, and the angels shall be sent down descending (in ranks).

وَيَوْمَ تَشَقَّقُ السَّمَآءُ بِالْغَمَامِ وَنُزِّلَ الْمَلٰٓئِكَةُ تَنْزِيْلًا ۝

26. The kingdom on that day shall rightly belong to the Beneficent God, and a hard day shall it be for the unbelievers.

اَلْمُلْكُ يَوْمَئِذٍ الْحَقُّ لِلرَّحْمٰنِ ۗ وَكَانَ يَوْمًا عَلَى الْكٰفِرِيْنَ عَسِيْرًا ۝

27. And the day when the unjust one shall bite his hands, saying: O! would that I had taken a way with the Apostle;

وَيَوْمَ يَعَضُّ الظَّالِمُ عَلَى يَدَيْهِ يَقُوْلُ يَلَيْتَنِى اتَّخَذْتُ مَعَ الرَّسُوْلِ سَبِيْلًا ۞

28. O woe is me! would that I had not taken such a one for a friend!

يٰوَيْلَتٰى لَيْتَنِى لَمْ اتَّخِذْ فُلَانًا خَلِيْلًا ۞

29. Certainly he led me astray from the reminder after it had come to me; and the Shaitan fails to aid man.

لَقَدْ اَضَلَّنِى عَنِ الذِّكْرِ بَعْدَ اِذْ جَآءَنِى ۚ وَكَانَ الشَّيْطٰنُ لِلْاِنْسَانِ خَذُوْلًا ۞

30. And the Apostle cried out: O my Lord! surely my people have treated this Quran as a forsaken thing.

وَقَالَ الرَّسُوْلُ يٰرَبِّ اِنَّ قَوْمِى اتَّخَذُوْا هٰذَا الْقُرْاٰنَ مَهْجُوْرًا ۞

31. And thus have We made for every prophet an enemy from among the sinners and sufficient is your Lord as a Guide and a Helper.

وَكَذٰلِكَ جَعَلْنَا لِكُلِّ نَبِيٍّ عَدُوًّا مِّنَ الْمُجْرِمِيْنَ ۗ وَكَفٰى بِرَبِّكَ هَادِيًا وَّنَصِيْرًا ۞

32. And those who disbelieve say: Why has not the Quran been revealed to him all at once? Thus, that We may strengthen your heart by it and We have arranged it well in arranging.

وَقَالَ الَّذِيْنَ كَفَرُوْا لَوْلَا نُزِّلَ عَلَيْهِ الْقُرْاٰنُ جُمْلَةً وَّاحِدَةً ۚ كَذٰلِكَ ۛ لِنُثَبِّتَ بِهٖ فُؤَادَكَ وَرَتَّلْنٰهُ تَرْتِيْلًا ۞

33. And they shall not bring to you any argument, but We have brought to you (one) with truth and best in signficance.

وَلَا يَأْتُوْنَكَ بِمَثَلٍ اِلَّا جِئْنٰكَ بِالْحَقِّ وَاَحْسَنَ تَفْسِيْرًا ۞

34. (As for) those who shall be gathered upon their faces to hell, they are in a worse plight and straying farther away from the path.

اَلَّذِيْنَ يُحْشَرُوْنَ عَلٰى وُجُوْهِهِمْ اِلٰى جَهَنَّمَ ۙ اُولٰٓئِكَ شَرٌّ مَّكَانًا وَّاَضَلُّ سَبِيْلًا ۞

35. And certainly We gave Musa the Book and We appointed with him his brother Haroun an aider.

وَلَقَدْ اٰتَيْنَا مُوْسَى الْكِتٰبَ وَجَعَلْنَا مَعَهٗٓ اَخَاهُ هٰرُوْنَ وَزِيْرًا ۞

36. Then We said: Go you both to the people who rejected Our communications; so We destroyed them with utter destruction.

فَقُلْنَا اذْهَبَا اِلَى الْقَوْمِ الَّذِيْنَ كَذَّبُوْا بِاٰيٰتِنَا ۗ فَدَمَّرْنٰهُمْ تَدْمِيْرًا ۞

37. And the people of Nuh, when they rejected the apostles, We drowned them, and made them a sign for men, and We have prepared a painful punishment for the unjust;

وَقَوْمَ نُوْحٍ لَّمَّا كَذَّبُوا الرُّسُلَ اَغْرَقْنٰهُمْ وَجَعَلْنٰهُمْ لِلنَّاسِ اٰيَةً ۖ وَاَعْتَدْنَا لِلظّٰلِمِيْنَ عَذَابًا اَلِيْمًا ۞

38. And Ad and Samood and the dwellers of the Rass and many generations between them.

وَعَادًا وَّثَمُوْدَا۟ وَاَصْحٰبَ الرَّسِّ وَقُرُوْنًۢا بَيْنَ ذٰلِكَ كَثِيْرًا۟

39. And to every one We gave examples and every one did We destroy with utter destruction.

وَكُلًّا ضَرَبْنَا لَهُ الْاَمْثَالَ ۖ وَكُلًّا تَبَّرْنَا تَتْبِيْرًا۟

40. And certainly they have (often) passed by the town on which was rained an evil rain; did they not then see it? Nay! they did not hope to be raised again.

وَلَقَدْ اَتَوْا عَلَى الْقَرْيَةِ الَّتِيْٓ اُمْطِرَتْ مَطَرَ السَّوْءِ ۖ اَفَلَمْ يَكُوْنُوْا يَرَوْنَهَا ۚ بَلْ كَانُوْا لَا يَرْجُوْنَ نُشُوْرًا۟

41. And when they see you, they do not take you for aught but a mockery: Is this he whom Allah has raised to be an apostle?

وَاِذَا رَاَوْكَ اِنْ يَّتَّخِذُوْنَكَ اِلَّا هُزُوًا ۚ اَهٰذَا الَّذِيْ بَعَثَ اللّٰهُ رَسُوْلًا۟

42. He had well-nigh led us astray from our gods had we not adhered to them patiently! And they will know, when they see the punishment, who is straying farther off from the path.

اِنْ كَادَ لَيُضِلُّنَا عَنْ اٰلِهَتِنَا لَوْلَآ اَنْ صَبَرْنَا عَلَيْهَا ۚ وَسَوْفَ يَعْلَمُوْنَ حِيْنَ يَرَوْنَ الْعَذَابَ مَنْ اَضَلُّ سَبِيْلًا۟

43. Have you seen him who takes his low desires for his god? Will you then be a protector over him?

اَرَءَيْتَ مَنِ اتَّخَذَ اِلٰهَهٗ هَوٰىهُ ۚ اَفَاَنْتَ تَكُوْنُ عَلَيْهِ وَكِيْلًا۟

44. Or do you think that most of them do hear or understand? They are nothing but as cattle; nay, they are straying farther off from the path.

اَمْ تَحْسَبُ اَنَّ اَكْثَرَهُمْ يَسْمَعُوْنَ اَوْ يَعْقِلُوْنَ ۚ اِنْ هُمْ اِلَّا كَالْاَنْعَامِ بَلْ هُمْ اَضَلُّ سَبِيْلًا۟

45. Have you not considered (the work of) your Lord, how He extends the shade? And if He had pleased He would certainly have made it stationary; then We have made the sun an indication of it;

اَلَمْ تَرَ اِلٰى رَبِّكَ كَيْفَ مَدَّ الظِّلَّ ۚ وَلَوْ شَآءَ لَجَعَلَهٗ سَاكِنًا ۚ ثُمَّ جَعَلْنَا الشَّمْسَ عَلَيْهِ دَلِيْلًا۟

46. Then We take it to Ourselves, taking little by little.

ثُمَّ قَبَضْنٰهُ اِلَيْنَا قَبْضًا يَّسِيْرًا۟

47. And He it is Who made the night a covering for you, and the sleep a rest, and He made the day to rise up again.

وَهُوَ الَّذِيْ جَعَلَ لَكُمُ الَّيْلَ لِبَاسًا وَّالنَّوْمَ سُبَاتًا وَّجَعَلَ النَّهَارَ نُشُوْرًا۟

48. And He it is Who sends the winds as good news before His mercy; and We send down pure water from the cloud,

وَهُوَ الَّذِيْٓ اَرْسَلَ الرِّيٰحَ بُشْرًاۢ بَيْنَ يَدَيْ رَحْمَتِهٖ ۚ وَاَنْزَلْنَا مِنَ السَّمَآءِ مَآءً طَهُوْرًا۟

348

49. That We may give life thereby to a dead land and give it for drink, out of what We have created, to cattle and many people.

لِّنُحْيِ بِهٖ بَلْدَةً مَّيْتًا وَّنُسْقِيَهٗ مِمَّا خَلَقْنَاۤ اَنْعَامًا وَّاَنَاسِيَّ كَثِيْرًا ۝

50. And certainly We have repeated this to them that they may be mindful, but the greater number of men do not consent to aught except denying.

وَلَقَدْ صَرَّفْنٰهُ بَيْنَهُمْ لِيَذَّكَّرُوْا ۖ فَاَبٰۤى اَكْثَرُ النَّاسِ اِلَّا كُفُوْرًا ۝

51. And if We had pleased We would certainly have raised a warner in every town.

وَلَوْ شِئْنَا لَبَعَثْنَا فِيْ كُلِّ قَرْيَةٍ نَّذِيْرًا ۝

52. So do not follow the unbelievers, and strive against them a mighty striving with it.

فَلَا تُطِعِ الْكٰفِرِيْنَ وَجَاهِدْهُمْ بِهٖ جِهَادًا كَبِيْرًا ۝

53. And He it is Who has made two seas to flow freely, the one sweet that subdues thirst by its sweetness, and the other salt that burns by its saltness; and between the two He has made a barrier and inviolable obstruction.

وَهُوَ الَّذِيْ مَرَجَ الْبَحْرَيْنِ هٰذَا عَذْبٌ فُرَاتٌ وَّهٰذَا مِلْحٌ اُجَاجٌ وَّجَعَلَ بَيْنَهُمَا بَرْزَخًا وَّحِجْرًا مَّحْجُوْرًا ۝

54. And He it is Who has created man from the water, then He has made for him blood relationship and marriage relationship, and your Lord is powerful.

وَهُوَ الَّذِيْ خَلَقَ مِنَ الْمَآءِ بَشَرًا فَجَعَلَهٗ نَسَبًا وَّصِهْرًا ۖ وَكَانَ رَبُّكَ قَدِيْرًا ۝

55. And they serve besides Allah that which neither profits them nor causes them harm; and the unbeliever is a partisan against his Lord.

وَيَعْبُدُوْنَ مِنْ دُوْنِ اللّٰهِ مَا لَا يَنْفَعُهُمْ وَلَا يَضُرُّهُمْ ۖ وَكَانَ الْكَافِرُ عَلٰى رَبِّهٖ ظَهِيْرًا ۝

56. And We have not sent you but as a giver of good news and as a warner.

وَمَاۤ اَرْسَلْنٰكَ اِلَّا مُبَشِّرًا وَّنَذِيْرًا ۝

57. Say: I do not ask you aught in return except that he who will, may take the way to his Lord.

قُلْ مَاۤ اَسْـَٔلُكُمْ عَلَيْهِ مِنْ اَجْرٍ اِلَّا مَنْ شَآءَ اَنْ يَّتَّخِذَ اِلٰى رَبِّهٖ سَبِيْلًا ۝

58. And rely on the Ever-living Who dies not, and celebrate His praise; and Sufficient is He as being aware of the faults of His servants,

وَتَوَكَّلْ عَلَى الْحَيِّ الَّذِيْ لَا يَمُوْتُ وَسَبِّحْ بِحَمْدِهٖ ۚ وَكَفٰى بِهٖ بِذُنُوْبِ عِبَادِهٖ خَبِيْرًا ۝

59. Who created the heavens and the earth and what is between them in six periods, and He is firmly established on the throne of authority; the Beneficent God, so ask respecting it one aware.

اَلَّذِيْ خَلَقَ السَّمٰوٰتِ وَالْاَرْضَ وَمَا بَيْنَهُمَا فِيْ سِتَّةِ اَيَّامٍ ثُمَّ اسْتَوٰى عَلَى الْعَرْشِ الرَّحْمٰنُ فَسْـَٔلْ بِهٖ خَبِيْرًا ۝

60. And when it is said to them: Make obeisance to the Beneficent God, they say: And what is the God of beneficence? Shall we make obeisance to what you bid us? And it adds to their aversion.

وَاِذَا قِيْلَ لَهُمُ اسْجُدُوْا لِلرَّحْمٰنِ قَالُوْا وَمَا الرَّحْمٰنُ اَنَسْجُدُ لِمَا تَأْمُرُنَا وَزَادَهُمْ نُفُوْرًا ۝

61. Blessed is He Who made the constellations in the heavens and made therein a lamp and a shining moon.

تَبَارَكَ الَّذِىْ جَعَلَ فِى السَّمَآءِ بُرُوْجًا وَّجَعَلَ فِيْهَا سِرَاجًا وَّقَمَرًا مُّنِيْرًا ۞

62. And He it is Who made the night and the day to follow each other for him who desires to be mindful or desires to be thankful.

وَهُوَ الَّذِىْ جَعَلَ الَّيْلَ وَالنَّهَارَ خِلْفَةً لِّمَنْ اَرَادَ اَنْ يَّذَّكَّرَ اَوْ اَرَادَ شُكُوْرًا ۞

63. And the servants of the Beneficent God are they who walk on the earth in humbleness, and when the ignorant address them, they say: Peace.

وَعِبَادُ الرَّحْمٰنِ الَّذِيْنَ يَمْشُوْنَ عَلَى الْاَرْضِ هَوْنًا وَّاِذَا خَاطَبَهُمُ الْجٰهِلُوْنَ قَالُوْا سَلٰمًا ۞

64. And they who pass the night prostrating themselves before their Lord and standing.

وَالَّذِيْنَ يَبِيْتُوْنَ لِرَبِّهِمْ سُجَّدًا وَّقِيَامًا ۞

65. And they who say: O our Lord! turn away from us the punishment of hell, surely the punishment thereof is a lasting evil.

وَالَّذِيْنَ يَقُوْلُوْنَ رَبَّنَا اصْرِفْ عَنَّا عَذَابَ جَهَنَّمَ اِنَّ عَذَابَهَا كَانَ غَرَامًا ۞

66. Surely it is an evil abode and (evil) place to stay.

اِنَّهَا سَآءَتْ مُسْتَقَرًّا وَّمُقَامًا ۞

67. And they who when they spend, are neither extravagant nor parsimonious, and (keep) between these the just mean.

وَالَّذِيْنَ اِذَآ اَنْفَقُوْا لَمْ يُسْرِفُوْا وَلَمْ يَقْتُرُوْا وَكَانَ بَيْنَ ذٰلِكَ قَوَامًا ۞

68. And they who do not call upon another god with Allah and do not slay the soul, which Allah has forbidden except in the requirements of justice, and (who) do not commit fornication and he who does this shall find a requital of sin;

وَالَّذِيْنَ لَا يَدْعُوْنَ مَعَ اللهِ اِلٰهًا اٰخَرَ وَلَا يَقْتُلُوْنَ النَّفْسَ الَّتِىْ حَرَّمَ اللهُ اِلَّا بِالْحَقِّ وَلَا يَزْنُوْنَ وَمَنْ يَّفْعَلْ ذٰلِكَ يَلْقَ اَثَامًا ۞

69. The punishment shall be doubled to him on the day of resurrection, and he shall abide therein in abasement;

يُّضٰعَفْ لَهُ الْعَذَابُ يَوْمَ الْقِيٰمَةِ وَيَخْلُدْ فِيْهِ مُهَانًا ۞

70. Except him who repents and believes and does a good deed; so these are they of whom Allah changes the evil deeds to good ones; and Allah is Forgiving, Merciful.

اِلَّا مَنْ تَابَ وَاٰمَنَ وَعَمِلَ عَمَلًا صَالِحًا فَاُولٰٓئِكَ يُبَدِّلُ اللهُ سَيِّاٰتِهِمْ حَسَنٰتٍ وَكَانَ اللهُ غَفُوْرًا رَّحِيْمًا ۞

71. And whoever repents and does good, he surely turns to Allah a (goodly) turning.

وَمَنْ تَابَ وَعَمِلَ صَالِحًا فَاِنَّهٗ يَتُوْبُ اِلَى اللهِ مَتَابًا ۞

72. And they who do not bear witness to what is false, and when they pass by what is vain, they pass by nobly.

وَالَّذِيْنَ لَا يَشْهَدُوْنَ الزُّوْرَ وَإِذَا مَرُّوْا بِاللَّغْوِ مَرُّوْا كِرَامًا ۞

73. And they who, when reminded of the communications of their Lord, do not fall down thereat deaf and blind.

وَالَّذِيْنَ إِذَا ذُكِّرُوْا بِاٰيٰتِ رَبِّهِمْ لَمْ يَخِرُّوْا عَلَيْهَا صُمًّا وَّعُمْيَانًا ۞

74. And they who say: O our Lord! grant us in our wives and our offspring the joy of our eyes, and make us guides to those who guard (against evil).

وَالَّذِيْنَ يَقُوْلُوْنَ رَبَّنَا هَبْ لَنَا مِنْ أَزْوَاجِنَا وَذُرِّيّٰتِنَا قُرَّةَ أَعْيُنٍ وَّاجْعَلْنَا لِلْمُتَّقِيْنَ إِمَامًا ۞

75. These shall be rewarded with high places because they were patient, and shall be met therein with greetings and salutations.

أُولٰٓئِكَ يُجْزَوْنَ الْغُرْفَةَ بِمَا صَبَرُوْا وَيُلَقَّوْنَ فِيْهَا تَحِيَّةً وَّسَلٰمًا ۞

76. Abiding therein; goodly the abode and the resting-place.

خٰلِدِيْنَ فِيْهَا ۚ حَسُنَتْ مُسْتَقَرًّا وَّمُقَامًا ۞

77. Say: My Lord would not care for you were it not for your prayer; but you have indeed rejected (the truth), so that which shall cleave shall come.

قُلْ مَا يَعْبَؤُا بِكُمْ رَبِّيْ لَوْلَا دُعَآؤُكُمْ ۚ فَقَدْ كَذَّبْتُمْ فَسَوْفَ يَكُوْنُ لِزَامًا ۞

بِسْمِ اللهِ الرَّحْمٰنِ الرَّحِيْمِ

THE POETS
(SHUARA)

In the name of Allah,
the Beneficent, the Merciful.

1. Ta Sin Mim.

2. These are the verses of the Book that makes (things) clear.

3. Perhaps you will kill yourself with grief because they do not believe.

4. If We please, We should send down upon them a sign from the heaven so that their necks should stoop to it.

5. And there does not come to them a new reminder from the Beneficent God but they turn aside from it.

6. So they have indeed rejected (the truth), therefore the news of that which they mock shall soon come to them.

7. Do they not see the earth, how many of every noble kind We have caused to grow in it?

8. Most surely there is a sign in that, but most of them will not believe.

9. And most surely your Lord is the Mighty, the Merciful.

10. And when your Lord called out to Musa, saying: Go to the unjust people,

11. The people of Firon: Will they not guard (against evil)?

12. He said: O my Lord! surely I fear that they will reject me;

13. And my breast straitens, and my tongue is not eloquent, therefore send Thou to Haroun (to help me);

14. And they have a crime against me, therefore I fear that they may slay me.

15. He said: By no means, so go you both with Our signs; surely We are with you, hearing;

اٰیَاتُهَا ٢٦ ، ٢٧ سُوْرَةُ الشُّعَرَاءِ مَكِّیَّةٌ رُکُوْعَاتُهَا

بِسْمِ اللهِ الرَّحْمٰنِ الرَّحِيْمِ ۞

طٰسٓمّٓ ۞

تِلْكَ اٰیٰتُ الْکِتٰبِ الْمُبِیْنِ ۞

لَعَلَّکَ بَاخِعٌ نَّفْسَکَ اَلَّا یَکُوْنُوْا مُؤْمِنِیْنَ ۞

اِنْ نَّشَاْ نُنَزِّلْ عَلَیْهِمْ مِّنَ السَّمَآءِ اٰیَةً فَظَلَّتْ اَعْنَاقُهُمْ لَهَا خٰضِعِیْنَ ۞

وَمَا یَاْتِیْهِمْ مِّنْ ذِکْرٍ مِّنَ الرَّحْمٰنِ مُحْدَثٍ اِلَّا کَانُوْا عَنْهُ مُعْرِضِیْنَ ۞

فَقَدْ کَذَّبُوْا فَسَیَاْتِیْهِمْ اَنْۢبٰٓؤُا مَا کَانُوْا بِهٖ یَسْتَهْزِءُوْنَ ۞

اَوَلَمْ یَرَوْا اِلَی الْاَرْضِ کَمْ اَنْۢبَتْنَا فِیْهَا مِنْ کُلِّ زَوْجٍ کَرِیْمٍ ۞

اِنَّ فِیْ ذٰلِکَ لَاٰیَةً ۭ وَمَا کَانَ اَکْثَرُهُمْ مُّؤْمِنِیْنَ ۞

وَاِنَّ رَبَّکَ لَهُوَ الْعَزِیْزُ الرَّحِیْمُ ۞

وَاِذْ نَادٰی رَبُّکَ مُوْسٰٓی اَنِ ائْتِ الْقَوْمَ الظّٰلِمِیْنَ ۞

قَوْمَ فِرْعَوْنَ ۭ اَلَا یَتَّقُوْنَ ۞

قَالَ رَبِّ اِنِّیْۤ اَخَافُ اَنْ یُّکَذِّبُوْنِ ۞

وَیَضِیْقُ صَدْرِیْ وَلَا یَنْطَلِقُ لِسَانِیْ فَاَرْسِلْ اِلٰی هٰرُوْنَ ۞

وَلَهُمْ عَلَیَّ ذَنْۢبٌ فَاَخَافُ اَنْ یَّقْتُلُوْنِ ۞

قَالَ کَلَّا ۚ فَاذْهَبَا بِاٰیٰتِنَاۤ اِنَّا مَعَکُمْ مُّسْتَمِعُوْنَ ۞

16. Then come to Firon and say: Surely we are the messengers of the Lord of the worlds:

17. Then send with us the children of Israel.

18. (Firon) said: Did we not bring you up as a child among us, and you tarried among us for (many) years of your life?

19. And you did (that) deed of yours which you did, and you are one of the ungrateful.

20. He said: I did it then while I was of those unable to see the right course;

21. So I fled from you when I feared you, then my Lord granted me wisdom and made me of the apostles;

22. And is it a favor of which you remind me that you have enslaved the children of Israel?

23. Firon said: And what is the Lord of the worlds?

24. He said: The Lord of the heavens and the earth and what is between them, if you would be sure.

25. (Firon) said to those around him: Do you not hear?

26. He said: Your Lord and the Lord of your fathers of old.

27. Said he: Most surely your Apostle who is sent to you is mad.

28. He said: The Lord of the east and the west and what is between them, if you understand.

29. Said he: If you will take a god besides me, I will most certainly make you one of the imprisoned.

30. He said: What! even if I bring to you something manifest?

31. Said he: Bring it then, if you are of the truthful ones.

32. So he cast down his rod, and lo! it was an obvious serpent,

فَأْتِيَا فِرْعَوْنَ فَقُوْلَاۤ اِنَّا رَسُوْلُ رَبِّ الْعٰلَمِيْنَ ۙ ١٦

اَنْ اَرْسِلْ مَعَنَا بَنِيْۤ اِسْرَآءِيْلَ ؕ ١٧

قَالَ اَلَمْ نُرَبِّكَ فِيْنَا وَلِيْدًا وَّلَبِثْتَ فِيْنَا مِنْ عُمُرِكَ سِنِيْنَ ۙ ١٨

وَفَعَلْتَ فَعْلَتَكَ الَّتِيْ فَعَلْتَ وَاَنْتَ مِنَ الْكٰفِرِيْنَ ١٩

قَالَ فَعَلْتُهَاۤ اِذًا وَّاَنَا مِنَ الضَّآلِّيْنَ ۙ ٢٠

فَفَرَرْتُ مِنْكُمْ لَمَّا خِفْتُكُمْ فَوَهَبَ لِيْ رَبِّيْ حُكْمًا وَّجَعَلَنِيْ مِنَ الْمُرْسَلِيْنَ ٢١

وَتِلْكَ نِعْمَةٌ تَمُنُّهَا عَلَيَّ اَنْ عَبَّدْتَّ بَنِيْۤ اِسْرَآءِيْلَ ؕ ٢٢

قَالَ فِرْعَوْنُ وَمَا رَبُّ الْعٰلَمِيْنَ ٢٣

قَالَ رَبُّ السَّمٰوٰتِ وَالْاَرْضِ وَمَا بَيْنَهُمَا ؕ اِنْ كُنْتُمْ مُّوْقِنِيْنَ ٢٤

قَالَ لِمَنْ حَوْلَهٗۤ اَلَا تَسْتَمِعُوْنَ ٢٥

قَالَ رَبُّكُمْ وَرَبُّ اٰبَآئِكُمُ الْاَوَّلِيْنَ ٢٦

قَالَ اِنَّ رَسُوْلَكُمُ الَّذِيْۤ اُرْسِلَ اِلَيْكُمْ لَمَجْنُوْنٌ ٢٧

قَالَ رَبُّ الْمَشْرِقِ وَالْمَغْرِبِ وَمَا بَيْنَهُمَا ؕ اِنْ كُنْتُمْ تَعْقِلُوْنَ ٢٨

قَالَ لَئِنِ اتَّخَذْتَ اِلٰهًا غَيْرِيْ لَاَجْعَلَنَّكَ مِنَ الْمَسْجُوْنِيْنَ ٢٩

قَالَ اَوَلَوْ جِئْتُكَ بِشَيْءٍ مُّبِيْنٍ ۙ ٣٠

قَالَ فَأْتِ بِهٖۤ اِنْ كُنْتَ مِنَ الصّٰدِقِيْنَ ٣١

فَاَلْقٰى عَصَاهُ فَاِذَا هِيَ ثُعْبَانٌ مُّبِيْنٌ ۚۖ ٣٢

33. And he drew forth his hand, and lo! it appeared white to the onlookers.

وَنَزَعَ يَدَهُ فَإِذَا هِىَ بَيْضَآءُ لِّلنّٰظِرِيْنَ ۝

34. (Firon) said to the chiefs around him: Most surely this is a skillful magician,

قَالَ لِلْمَلَاِ حَوْلَهُ إِنَّ هٰذَا لَسٰحِرٌ عَلِيْمٌ ۝

35. Who desires to turn you out of your land with his magic; what is it then that you advise?

يُّرِيْدُ أَنْ يُّخْرِجَكُمْ مِّنْ أَرْضِكُمْ بِسِحْرِهٖ ۖ فَمَاذَا تَأْمُرُوْنَ ۝

36. They said: Give him and his brother respite and send heralds into the cities;

قَالُوْۤا أَرْجِهْ وَأَخَاهُ وَابْعَثْ فِى الْمَدَآئِنِ حٰشِرِيْنَ ۝

37. That they should bring to you every skillful magician.

يَأْتُوْكَ بِكُلِّ سَحَّارٍ عَلِيْمٍ ۝

38. So the magicians were gathered together at the appointed time on the fixed day,

فَجُمِعَ السَّحَرَةُ لِمِيْقَاتِ يَوْمٍ مَّعْلُوْمٍ ۝

39. And it was said to the people: Will you gather together?

وَّقِيْلَ لِلنَّاسِ هَلْ أَنْتُمْ مُّجْتَمِعُوْنَ ۝

40. Haply we may follow the magicians, if they are the vanquishers.

لَعَلَّنَا نَتَّبِعُ السَّحَرَةَ إِنْ كَانُوْا هُمُ الْغٰلِبِيْنَ ۝

41. And when the magicians came, they said to Firon: Shall we get a reward if we are the vanquishers?

فَلَمَّا جَآءَ السَّحَرَةُ قَالُوْا لِفِرْعَوْنَ أَئِنَّ لَنَا لَأَجْرًا إِنْ كُنَّا نَحْنُ الْغٰلِبِيْنَ ۝

42. He said: Yes, and surely you will then be of those who are made near.

قَالَ نَعَمْ وَإِنَّكُمْ إِذًا لَّمِنَ الْمُقَرَّبِيْنَ ۝

43. Musa said to them: Cast what you are going to cast.

قَالَ لَهُمْ مُّوْسٰۤى أَلْقُوْا مَاۤ أَنْتُمْ مُّلْقُوْنَ ۝

44. So they cast down their cords and their rods and said: By Firon's power, we shall most surely be victorious.

فَأَلْقَوْا حِبَالَهُمْ وَعِصِيَّهُمْ وَقَالُوْا بِعِزَّةِ فِرْعَوْنَ إِنَّا لَنَحْنُ الْغٰلِبُوْنَ ۝

45. Then Musa cast down his staff and lo! it swallowed up the lies they told.

فَأَلْقٰى مُوْسٰى عَصَاهُ فَإِذَا هِىَ تَلْقَفُ مَا يَأْفِكُوْنَ ۝

46. And the magicians were thrown down prostrate;

فَأُلْقِىَ السَّحَرَةُ سٰجِدِيْنَ ۝

47. They said: We believe in the Lord of the worlds:

قَالُوْۤا آمَنَّا بِرَبِّ الْعٰلَمِيْنَ ۝

48. The Lord of Musa and Haroun.

رَبِّ مُوْسٰى وَهٰرُوْنَ ۝

49. Said he: You believe in him before I give you permission; most surely he is the chief of you who taught you the magic, so you shall know: certainly I will cut off your hands and your feet on opposite sides, and certainly I will crucify you all.

قَالَ آمَنْتُمْ لَهُ قَبْلَ أَنْ آذَنَ لَكُمْ ۖ إِنَّهُ لَكَبِيْرُكُمُ الَّذِيْ عَلَّمَكُمُ السِّحْرَ ۖ فَلَسَوْفَ تَعْلَمُوْنَ ۚ لَأُقَطِّعَنَّ أَيْدِيَكُمْ وَأَرْجُلَكُمْ مِّنْ خِلَافٍ وَّلَأُصَلِّبَنَّكُمْ أَجْمَعِيْنَ ۝

50. They said: No harm; surely to our Lord we go back;

قَالُوْا لَا ضَيْرَ اِنَّا اِلٰى رَبِّنَا مُنْقَلِبُوْنَ ۞

51. Surely we hope that our Lord will forgive us our wrongs because we are the first of the believers.

اِنَّا نَطْمَعُ اَنْ يَّغْفِرَ لَنَا رَبُّنَا خَطٰيٰنَا اَنْ كُنَّا اَوَّلَ الْمُؤْمِنِيْنَ ۞

52. And We revealed to Musa, saying: Go away with My servants travelling by night, surely you will be pursued.

وَاَوْحَيْنَا اِلٰى مُوْسٰى اَنْ اَسْرِ بِعِبَادِيْ اِنَّكُمْ مُّتَّبَعُوْنَ ۞

53. So Firon sent heralds into the cities;

فَاَرْسَلَ فِرْعَوْنُ فِى الْمَدَآئِنِ حٰشِرِيْنَ ۞

54. Most surely these are a small company;

اِنَّ هٰٓؤُلَآءِ لَشِرْذِمَةٌ قَلِيْلُوْنَ ۞

55. And most surely they have enraged us;

وَاِنَّهُمْ لَنَا لَغَآئِظُوْنَ ۞

56. And most surely we are a vigilant multitude.

وَاِنَّا لَجَمِيْعٌ حٰذِرُوْنَ ۞

57. So We turned them out of gardens and springs,

فَاَخْرَجْنٰهُمْ مِّنْ جَنّٰتٍ وَّعُيُوْنٍ ۞

58. And treasures and goodly dwellings,

وَّكُنُوْزٍ وَّمَقَامٍ كَرِيْمٍ ۞

59. Even so. And We gave them as a heritage to the children of Israel.

كَذٰلِكَ وَاَوْرَثْنٰهَا بَنِيْ اِسْرَآءِيْلَ ۞

60. Then they pursued them at sunrise.

فَاَتْبَعُوْهُمْ مُّشْرِقِيْنَ ۞

61. So when the two hosts saw each other, the companions of Musa cried out: Most surely we are being overtaken.

فَلَمَّا تَرَآءَ الْجَمْعٰنِ قَالَ اَصْحٰبُ مُوْسٰى اِنَّا لَمُدْرَكُوْنَ ۞

62. He said: By no means; surely my Lord is with me: He will show me a way out.

قَالَ كَلَّا اِنَّ مَعِيَ رَبِّيْ سَيَهْدِيْنِ ۞

63. Then We revealed to Musa: Strike the sea with your staff. So it had cloven asunder, and each part was like a huge mound.

فَاَوْحَيْنَا اِلٰى مُوْسٰى اَنِ اضْرِبْ بِّعَصَاكَ الْبَحْرَ فَانْفَلَقَ فَكَانَ كُلُّ فِرْقٍ كَالطَّوْدِ الْعَظِيْمِ ۞

64. And We brought near, there, the others.

وَاَزْلَفْنَا ثَمَّ الْاٰخَرِيْنَ ۞

65. And We saved Musa and those with him, all of them.

وَاَنْجَيْنَا مُوْسٰى وَمَنْ مَّعَهٗٓ اَجْمَعِيْنَ ۞

66. Then We drowned the others.

ثُمَّ اَغْرَقْنَا الْاٰخَرِيْنَ ۞

67. Most surely there is a sign in this, but most of them do not believe.

اِنَّ فِيْ ذٰلِكَ لَاٰيَةً ۚ وَمَا كَانَ اَكْثَرُهُمْ مُّؤْمِنِيْنَ ۞

68. And most surely your Lord is the Mighty, the Merciful.

وَاِنَّ رَبَّكَ لَهُوَ الْعَزِيْزُ الرَّحِيْمُ ۞

69. And recite to them the story of Ibrahim.

70. When he said to his father and his people: What do you worship?

71. They said: We worship idols, so we shall be their votaries.

72. He said: Do they hear you when you call?

73. Or do they profit you or cause you harm?

74. They said: Nay, we found our fathers doing so.

75. He said: Have you then considered what you have been worshipping:

76. You and your ancient sires.

77. Surely they are enemies to me, but not (so) the Lord of the worlds;

78. Who created me, then He has shown me the way:

79. And He Who gives me to eat and gives me to drink:

80. And when I am sick, then He restores me to health;

81. And He Who will cause me to die, then give me life;

82. And Who, I hope, will forgive me my mistakes on the day of judgment.

83. My Lord: Grant me wisdom, and join me with the good;

84. And ordain for me a goodly mention among posterity;

85. And make me of the heirs of the garden of bliss;

86. And forgive my father, for surely he is of those who have gone astray;

87. And disgrace me not on the day when they are raised,

88. The day on which property will not avail, nor sons,

89. Except him who comes to Allah with a heart free (from evil).

90. And the garden shall be brought near for those who guard (against evil),

وَاتْلُ عَلَيْهِمْ نَبَاَ اِبْرٰهِيْمَ ۞

اِذْ قَالَ لِاَبِيْهِ وَقَوْمِهٖ مَا تَعْبُدُوْنَ ۞

قَالُوْا نَعْبُدُ اَصْنَامًا فَنَظَلُّ لَهَا عٰكِفِيْنَ ۞

قَالَ هَلْ يَسْمَعُوْنَكُمْ اِذْ تَدْعُوْنَ ۞

اَوْ يَنْفَعُوْنَكُمْ اَوْ يَضُرُّوْنَ ۞

قَالُوْا بَلْ وَجَدْنَا اٰبَآءَنَا كَذٰلِكَ يَفْعَلُوْنَ ۞

قَالَ اَفَرَءَيْتُمْ مَّا كُنْتُمْ تَعْبُدُوْنَ ۞

اَنْتُمْ وَاٰبَآؤُكُمُ الْاَقْدَمُوْنَ ۞

فَاِنَّهُمْ عَدُوٌّ لِّيْ اِلَّا رَبَّ الْعٰلَمِيْنَ ۞

الَّذِيْ خَلَقَنِيْ فَهُوَ يَهْدِيْنِ ۞

وَالَّذِيْ هُوَ يُطْعِمُنِيْ وَيَسْقِيْنِ ۞

وَاِذَا مَرِضْتُ فَهُوَ يَشْفِيْنِ ۞

وَالَّذِيْ يُمِيْتُنِيْ ثُمَّ يُحْيِيْنِ ۞

وَالَّذِيْ اَطْمَعُ اَنْ يَّغْفِرَ لِيْ خَطِيْٓئَتِيْ يَوْمَ الدِّيْنِ ۞

رَبِّ هَبْ لِيْ حُكْمًا وَّاَلْحِقْنِيْ بِالصّٰلِحِيْنَ ۞

وَاجْعَلْ لِّيْ لِسَانَ صِدْقٍ فِي الْاٰخِرِيْنَ ۞

وَاجْعَلْنِيْ مِنْ وَّرَثَةِ جَنَّةِ النَّعِيْمِ ۞

وَاغْفِرْ لِاَبِيْٓ اِنَّهٗ كَانَ مِنَ الضَّآلِّيْنَ ۞

وَلَا تُخْزِنِيْ يَوْمَ يُبْعَثُوْنَ ۞

يَوْمَ لَا يَنْفَعُ مَالٌ وَّلَا بَنُوْنَ ۞

اِلَّا مَنْ اَتَى اللّٰهَ بِقَلْبٍ سَلِيْمٍ ۞

وَاُزْلِفَتِ الْجَنَّةُ لِلْمُتَّقِيْنَ ۞

91. And the hell shall be made manifest to the erring ones,

وَبُرِّزَتِ الْجَحِيْمُ لِلْغٰوِيْنَ ۞

92. And it shall be said to them: Where are those that you used to worship;

وَقِيْلَ لَهُمْ اَيْنَ مَا كُنْتُمْ تَعْبُدُوْنَ ۞

93. Besides Allah? Can they help you or yet help themselves?

مِنْ دُوْنِ اللّٰهِ هَلْ يَنْصُرُوْنَكُمْ اَوْ يَنْتَصِرُوْنَ ۞

94. So they shall be thrown down into it, they and the erring ones,

فَكُبْكِبُوْا فِيْهَا هُمْ وَالْغَاوٗنَ ۞

95. And the hosts of the Shaitan, all.

وَجُنُوْدُ اِبْلِيْسَ اَجْمَعُوْنَ ۞

96. They shall say while they contend therein:

قَالُوْا وَهُمْ فِيْهَا يَخْتَصِمُوْنَ ۞

97. By Allah! we were certainly in manifest error,

تَاللّٰهِ اِنْ كُنَّا لَفِيْ ضَلٰلٍ مُبِيْنٍ ۞

98. When we made you equal to the Lord of the worlds;

اِذْ نُسَوِّيْكُمْ بِرَبِّ الْعٰلَمِيْنَ ۞

99. And none but the guilty led us astray;

وَمَا اَضَلَّنَا اِلَّا الْمُجْرِمُوْنَ ۞

100. So we have no intercessors,

فَمَا لَنَا مِنْ شَافِعِيْنَ ۞

101. Nor a true friend;

وَلَا صَدِيْقٍ حَمِيْمٍ ۞

102. But if we could but once return, we would be of the believers.

فَلَوْ اَنَّ لَنَا كَرَّةً فَنَكُوْنَ مِنَ الْمُؤْمِنِيْنَ ۞

103. Most surely there is a sign in this, but most of them do not believe.

اِنَّ فِيْ ذٰلِكَ لَاٰيَةً وَمَا كَانَ اَكْثَرُهُمْ مُؤْمِنِيْنَ ۞

104. And most surely your Lord is the Mighty, the Merciful.

وَاِنَّ رَبَّكَ لَهُوَ الْعَزِيْزُ الرَّحِيْمُ ۞

105. The people of Nuh rejected the apostles.

كَذَّبَتْ قَوْمُ نُوْحِ الْمُرْسَلِيْنَ ۞

106. When their brother Nuh said to them: Will you not guard (against evil)?

اِذْ قَالَ لَهُمْ اَخُوْهُمْ نُوْحٌ اَلَا تَتَّقُوْنَ ۞

107. Surely I am a faithful apostle to you;

اِنِّيْ لَكُمْ رَسُوْلٌ اَمِيْنٌ ۞

108. Therefore guard against (the punishment of) Allah and obey me;

فَاتَّقُوا اللّٰهَ وَاَطِيْعُوْنِ ۞

109. And I do not ask you any reward for it; my reward is only with the Lord of the worlds:

وَمَا اَسْئَلُكُمْ عَلَيْهِ مِنْ اَجْرٍ اِنْ اَجْرِيَ اِلَّا عَلٰى رَبِّ الْعٰلَمِيْنَ ۞

110. So guard against (the punishment of) Allah and obey me.

فَاتَّقُوا اللّٰهَ وَاَطِيْعُوْنِ ۞

111. They said: Shall we believe in you while the meanest follow you?

قَالُوْا اَنُؤْمِنُ لَكَ وَاتَّبَعَكَ الْاَرْذَلُوْنَ ۞

112. He said: And what knowledge have I of what they do?

قَالَ وَمَا عِلْمِيْ بِمَا كَانُوْا يَعْمَلُوْنَ ۞

113. Their account is only with my Lord, if you could perceive;

اِنْ حِسَابُهُمْ اِلَّا عَلٰى رَبِّيْ لَوْ تَشْعُرُوْنَ ۞

114. And I am not going to drive away the believers;

وَمَا أَنَا بِطَارِدِ الْمُؤْمِنِيْنَ ۞

115. I am naught but a plain warner.

اِنْ أَنَا اِلَّا نَذِيْرٌ مُّبِيْنٌ ۞

116. They said: If you desist not, O Nuh, you shall most certainly be of those stoned to death.

قَالُوْا لَئِنْ لَّمْ تَنْتَهِ يٰنُوْحُ لَتَكُوْنَنَّ مِنَ الْمَرْجُوْمِيْنَ ۞

117. He said: My Lord! Surely my people give me the lie!

قَالَ رَبِّ اِنَّ قَوْمِيْ كَذَّبُوْنِ ۞

118. Therefore judge Thou between me and them with a (just) judgment, and deliver me and those who are with me of the believers.

فَافْتَحْ بَيْنِيْ وَبَيْنَهُمْ فَتْحًا وَّنَجِّنِيْ وَمَنْ مَّعِيَ مِنَ الْمُؤْمِنِيْنَ ۞

119. So We delivered him and those with him in the laden ark.

فَأَنْجَيْنٰهُ وَمَنْ مَّعَهُ فِي الْفُلْكِ الْمَشْحُوْنِ ۞

120. Then We drowned the rest afterwards.

ثُمَّ أَغْرَقْنَا بَعْدُ الْبٰقِيْنَ ۞

121. Most surely there is a sign in this, but most of them do not believe.

اِنَّ فِيْ ذٰلِكَ لَأٰيَةً وَمَا كَانَ أَكْثَرُهُمْ مُّؤْمِنِيْنَ ۞

122. And most surely your Lord is the Mighty, the Merciful.

وَاِنَّ رَبَّكَ لَهُوَ الْعَزِيْزُ الرَّحِيْمُ ۞

123. Ad gave the lie to the apostles.

كَذَّبَتْ عَادُ الْمُرْسَلِيْنَ ۞

124. When their brother Hud said to them: Will you not guard (against evil)?

اِذْ قَالَ لَهُمْ أَخُوْهُمْ هُوْدٌ أَلَا تَتَّقُوْنَ ۞

125. Surely I am a faithful apostle to you;

اِنِّيْ لَكُمْ رَسُوْلٌ أَمِيْنٌ ۞

126. Therefore guard against (the punishment of) Allah and obey me:

فَاتَّقُوا اللّٰهَ وَأَطِيْعُوْنِ ۞

127. And I do not ask you any reward for it; surely my reward is only with the Lord of the worlds;

وَمَا أَسْأَلُكُمْ عَلَيْهِ مِنْ أَجْرٍ اِنْ أَجْرِيَ اِلَّا عَلٰى رَبِّ الْعٰلَمِيْنَ ۞

128. Do you build on every height a monument? Vain is it that you do:

أَتَبْنُوْنَ بِكُلِّ رِيْعٍ أٰيَةً تَعْبَثُوْنَ ۞

129. And you make strong fortresses that perhaps you may abide;

وَتَتَّخِذُوْنَ مَصَانِعَ لَعَلَّكُمْ تَخْلُدُوْنَ ۞

130. And when you lay hands (on men) you lay hands (like) tyrants;

وَاِذَا بَطَشْتُمْ بَطَشْتُمْ جَبَّارِيْنَ ۞

131. So guard against (the punishment of) Allah and obey me;

فَاتَّقُوا اللّٰهَ وَأَطِيْعُوْنِ ۞

132. And be careful of (your duty to) Him Who has given you abundance of what you know.

وَاتَّقُوا الَّذِىٓ اَمَدَّكُمۡ بِمَا تَعۡلَمُوۡنَ ۚ۞

133. He has given you abundance of cattle and children,

اَمَدَّكُمۡ بِاَنۡعَامٍ وَّبَنِيۡنَ ۙ۞

134. And gardens and fountains;

وَجَنّٰتٍ وَّعُيُوۡنٍ ۚ۞

135. Surely I fear for you the chastisement of a grievous day.

اِنِّىٓ اَخَافُ عَلَيۡكُمۡ عَذَابَ يَوۡمٍ عَظِيۡمٍ ۗ۞

136. They said: It is the same to us whether you admonish or are not one of the admonishers;

قَالُوۡا سَوَآءٌ عَلَيۡنَآ اَوَعَظۡتَ اَمۡ لَمۡ تَكُنۡ مِّنَ الۡوٰعِظِيۡنَ ۙ۞

137. This is naught but a custom of the ancients;

اِنۡ هٰذَآ اِلَّا خُلُقُ الۡاَوَّلِيۡنَ ۙ۞

138. And we are not going to be punished.

وَمَا نَحۡنُ بِمُعَذَّبِيۡنَ ۚ۞

139. So they gave him the lie, then We destroyed them. Most surely there is a sign in this, but most of them do not believe.

فَكَذَّبُوۡهُ فَاَهۡلَكۡنٰهُمۡ ۗ اِنَّ فِىۡ ذٰلِكَ لَاٰيَةً ۗ وَمَا كَانَ اَكۡثَرُهُمۡ مُّؤۡمِنِيۡنَ ۞

140. And most surely your Lord is the Mighty, the Merciful.

وَاِنَّ رَبَّكَ لَهُوَ الۡعَزِيۡزُ الرَّحِيۡمُ ۞

141. Samood gave the lie to the apostles.

كَذَّبَتۡ ثَمُوۡدُ الۡمُرۡسَلِيۡنَ ۞

142. When their brother Salih said to them: Will you not guard (against evil)?

اِذۡ قَالَ لَهُمۡ اَخُوۡهُمۡ صٰلِحٌ اَلَا تَتَّقُوۡنَ ۞

143. Surely I am a faithful apostle to you;

اِنِّىۡ لَكُمۡ رَسُوۡلٌ اَمِيۡنٌ ۙ۞

144. Therefore guard against (the punishment of) Allah and obey me:

فَاتَّقُوا اللّٰهَ وَاَطِيۡعُوۡنِ ۚ۞

145. And I do not ask you any reward for it; my reward is only with the Lord of the worlds:

وَمَآ اَسۡـَٔلُكُمۡ عَلَيۡهِ مِنۡ اَجۡرٍ ۚ اِنۡ اَجۡرِىَ اِلَّا عَلٰى رَبِّ الۡعٰلَمِيۡنَ ۙ۞

146. Will you be left secure in what is here;

اَتُتۡرَكُوۡنَ فِىۡ مَا هٰهُنَآ اٰمِنِيۡنَ ۙ۞

147. In gardens and fountains,

فِىۡ جَنّٰتٍ وَّعُيُوۡنٍ ۙ۞

148. And cornfields and palm-trees having fine spadices?

وَّزُرُوۡعٍ وَّنَخۡلٍ طَلۡعُهَا هَضِيۡمٌ ۚ۞

149. And you hew houses out of the mountains exultingly;

وَتَنۡحِتُوۡنَ مِنَ الۡجِبَالِ بُيُوۡتًا فٰرِهِيۡنَ ۚ۞

150. Therefore guard against (the punishment of) Allah and obey me;

فَاتَّقُوا اللّٰهَ وَاَطِيۡعُوۡنِ ۚ۞

151. And do not obey the bidding of the extravagant,

وَلَا تُطِيۡعُوۡٓا اَمۡرَ الۡمُسۡرِفِيۡنَ ۙ۞

152. Who make mischief in the land and do not act aright.

153. They said: You are only of the deluded ones;

154. You are naught but a mortal like ourselves; so bring a sign if you are one of the truthful.

155. He said: This is a she-camel; she shall have her portion of water, and you have your portion of water on an appointed time;

156. And do not touch her with evil, lest the punishment of a grievous day should overtake you.

157. But they hamstrung her, then regretted;

158. So the punishment overtook them. Most surely there is a sign in this, but most of them do not believe.

159. And most surely your Lord is the Mighty, the Merciful.

160. The people of Lut gave the lie to the apostles.

161. When their brother Lut said to them: Will you not guard (against evil)?

162. Surely I am a faithful apostle to you;

163. Therefore guard against (the punishment of) Allah and obey me:

164. And I do not ask you any reward for it; my reward is only with the Lord of the worlds;

165. What! do you come to the males from among the creatures,

166. And leave what your Lord has created for you of your wives? Nay, you are a people exceeding limits.

167. They said: If you desist not, O Lut! you shall surely be of those who are expelled.

168. He said: Surely I am of those who utterly abhor your doing;

اَلَّذِيْنَ يُفْسِدُوْنَ فِى الْاَرْضِ وَلَا يُصْلِحُوْنَ ۝

قَالُوْۤا اِنَّمَاۤ اَنْتَ مِنَ الْمُسَحَّرِيْنَ ۝

مَاۤ اَنْتَ اِلَّا بَشَرٌ مِّثْلُنَا ۖ فَاْتِ بِاٰيَةٍ اِنْ كُنْتَ مِنَ الصّٰدِقِيْنَ ۝

قَالَ هٰذِهٖ نَاقَةٌ لَّهَا شِرْبٌ وَّلَكُمْ شِرْبُ يَوْمٍ مَّعْلُوْمٍ ۝

وَلَا تَمَسُّوْهَا بِسُوْۤءٍ فَيَاْخُذَكُمْ عَذَابُ يَوْمٍ عَظِيْمٍ ۝

فَعَقَرُوْهَا فَاَصْبَحُوْا نٰدِمِيْنَ ۝

فَاَخَذَهُمُ الْعَذَابُ ۗ اِنَّ فِىْ ذٰلِكَ لَاٰيَةً ۖ وَمَا كَانَ اَكْثَرُهُمْ مُّؤْمِنِيْنَ ۝

وَاِنَّ رَبَّكَ لَهُوَ الْعَزِيْزُ الرَّحِيْمُ ۝

كَذَّبَتْ قَوْمُ لُوْطٍ الْمُرْسَلِيْنَ ۝

اِذْ قَالَ لَهُمْ اَخُوْهُمْ لُوْطٌ اَلَا تَتَّقُوْنَ ۝

اِنِّىْ لَكُمْ رَسُوْلٌ اَمِيْنٌ ۝

فَاتَّقُوا اللّٰهَ وَاَطِيْعُوْنِ ۝

وَمَاۤ اَسْـَٔلُكُمْ عَلَيْهِ مِنْ اَجْرٍ ۖ اِنْ اَجْرِىَ اِلَّا عَلٰى رَبِّ الْعٰلَمِيْنَ ۝

اَتَاْتُوْنَ الذُّكْرَانَ مِنَ الْعٰلَمِيْنَ ۝

وَتَذَرُوْنَ مَا خَلَقَ لَكُمْ رَبُّكُمْ مِّنْ اَزْوَاجِكُمْ ۚ بَلْ اَنْتُمْ قَوْمٌ عٰدُوْنَ ۝

قَالُوْا لَئِنْ لَّمْ تَنْتَهِ يٰلُوْطُ لَتَكُوْنَنَّ مِنَ الْمُخْرَجِيْنَ ۝

قَالَ اِنِّىْ لِعَمَلِكُمْ مِّنَ الْقَالِيْنَ ۝

169. My Lord! deliver me and my followers from what they do.

رَبِّ نَجِّنِيْ وَاَهْلِيْ مِمَّا يَعْمَلُوْنَ ۞

170. So We delivered him and his followers all,

فَنَجَّيْنٰهُ وَاَهْلَهٗ اَجْمَعِيْنَ ۙ

171. Except an old woman, among those who remained behind.

اِلَّا عَجُوْزًا فِى الْغٰبِرِيْنَ ۚ

172. Then We utterly destroyed the others.

ثُمَّ دَمَّرْنَا الْاٰخَرِيْنَ ۚ

173. And We rained down upon them a rain, and evil was the rain on those warned.

وَاَمْطَرْنَا عَلَيْهِمْ مَّطَرًا ۚ فَسَآءَ مَطَرُ الْمُنْذَرِيْنَ ۞

174. Most surely there is a sign in this, but most of them do not believe.

اِنَّ فِيْ ذٰلِكَ لَاٰيَةً ۚ وَمَا كَانَ اَكْثَرُهُمْ مُّؤْمِنِيْنَ ۞

175. And most surely your Lord is the Mighty, the Merciful.

وَاِنَّ رَبَّكَ لَهُوَ الْعَزِيْزُ الرَّحِيْمُ ۞

176. The dwellers of the thicket gave the lie to the apostles.

كَذَّبَ اَصْحٰبُ لْـَٔيْكَةِ الْمُرْسَلِيْنَ ۚ

177. When Shu'aib said to them: Will you not guard (against evil)?

اِذْ قَالَ لَهُمْ شُعَيْبٌ اَلَا تَتَّقُوْنَ ۙ

178. Surely I am a faithful apostle to you;

اِنِّيْ لَكُمْ رَسُوْلٌ اَمِيْنٌ ۙ

179. Therefore guard against (the punishment of) Allah and obey me:

فَاتَّقُوا اللّٰهَ وَاَطِيْعُوْنِ ۚ

180. And I do not ask you any reward for it; my reward is only with the Lord of the worlds;

وَمَا اَسْـَٔلُكُمْ عَلَيْهِ مِنْ اَجْرٍ ۚ اِنْ اَجْرِيَ اِلَّا عَلٰى رَبِّ الْعٰلَمِيْنَ ۚ

181. Give a full measure and be not of those who diminish;

اَوْفُوا الْكَيْلَ وَلَا تَكُوْنُوْا مِنَ الْمُخْسِرِيْنَ ۚ

182. And weigh (things) with a right balance,

وَزِنُوْا بِالْقِسْطَاسِ الْمُسْتَقِيْمِ ۚ

183. And do not wrong men of their things, and do not act corruptly in the earth, making mischief.

وَلَا تَبْخَسُوا النَّاسَ اَشْيَآءَهُمْ وَلَا تَعْثَوْا فِى الْاَرْضِ مُفْسِدِيْنَ ۚ

184. And guard against (the punishment of) Him who created you and the former nations.

وَاتَّقُوا الَّذِيْ خَلَقَكُمْ وَالْجِبِلَّةَ الْاَوَّلِيْنَ ۚ

185. They said: You are only of those deluded;

قَالُوْا اِنَّمَا اَنْتَ مِنَ الْمُسَحَّرِيْنَ ۚ

186. And you are naught but a mortal like ourselves, and we know you to be certainly of the liars.

وَمَا اَنْتَ اِلَّا بَشَرٌ مِّثْلُنَا وَاِنْ نَّظُنُّكَ لَمِنَ الْكٰذِبِيْنَ ۚ

187. Therefore cause a portion of the heaven to come down upon us, if you are one of the truthful.

فَاَسْقِطْ عَلَيْنَا كِسَفًا مِّنَ السَّمَآءِ اِنْ كُنْتَ مِنَ الصّٰدِقِيْنَ ۞

188. He said: My Lord knows best what you do.

قَالَ رَبِّىْ اَعْلَمُ بِمَا تَعْمَلُوْنَ ۝

189. But they called him a liar, so the punishment of the day of covering overtook them; surely it was the punishment of a grievous day.

فَكَذَّبُوْهُ فَاَخَذَهُمْ عَذَابُ يَوْمِ الظُّلَّةِ ؕ اِنَّهٗ كَانَ عَذَابَ يَوْمٍ عَظِيْمٍ ۝

190. Most surely there is a sign in this, but most of them do not believe.

اِنَّ فِىْ ذٰلِكَ لَاٰيَةً ؕ وَمَا كَانَ اَكْثَرُهُمْ مُّؤْمِنِيْنَ ۝

191. And most surely your Lord is Mighty, the Merciful.

وَاِنَّ رَبَّكَ لَهُوَ الْعَزِيْزُ الرَّحِيْمُ ۝

192. And most surely this is a revelation from the Lord of the worlds.

وَاِنَّهٗ لَتَنْزِيْلُ رَبِّ الْعٰلَمِيْنَ ۝

193. The Faithful Spirit has descended with it,

نَزَلَ بِهِ الرُّوْحُ الْاَمِيْنُ ۝

194. Upon your heart that you may be of the warners,

عَلٰى قَلْبِكَ لِتَكُوْنَ مِنَ الْمُنْذِرِيْنَ ۝

195. In plain Arabic language.

بِلِسَانٍ عَرَبِىٍّ مُّبِيْنٍ ۝

196. And most surely the same is in the scriptures of the ancients.

وَاِنَّهٗ لَفِىْ زُبُرِ الْاَوَّلِيْنَ ۝

197. Is it not a sign to them that the learned men of the Israelites know it?

اَوَلَمْ يَكُنْ لَّهُمْ اٰيَةً اَنْ يَّعْلَمَهٗ عُلَمٰٓؤُا بَنِىْٓ اِسْرَآءِيْلَ ۝

198. And if We had revealed it to any of the foreigners,

وَلَوْ نَزَّلْنٰهُ عَلٰى بَعْضِ الْاَعْجَمِيْنَ ۝

199. So that he should have recited it to them, they would not have believed therein.

فَقَرَاَهٗ عَلَيْهِمْ مَّا كَانُوْا بِهٖ مُؤْمِنِيْنَ ۝

200. Thus have We caused it to enter into the hearts of the guilty.

كَذٰلِكَ سَلَكْنٰهُ فِىْ قُلُوْبِ الْمُجْرِمِيْنَ ۝

201. They will not believe in it until they see the painful punishment.

لَا يُؤْمِنُوْنَ بِهٖ حَتّٰى يَرَوُا الْعَذَابَ الْاَلِيْمَ ۝

202. And it shall come to them all of a sudden, while they shall not perceive;

فَيَاْتِيَهُمْ بَغْتَةً وَّهُمْ لَا يَشْعُرُوْنَ ۝

203. Then they will say: Shall we be respited?

فَيَقُوْلُوْا هَلْ نَحْنُ مُنْظَرُوْنَ ۝

204. What! do they still seek to hasten on Our punishment?

اَفَبِعَذَابِنَا يَسْتَعْجِلُوْنَ ۝

205. Have you then considered if We let them enjoy themselves for years,

اَفَرَءَيْتَ اِنْ مَّتَّعْنٰهُمْ سِنِيْنَ ۝

206. Then there comes to them that with which they are threatened,

ثُمَّ جَآءَهُمْ مَّا كَانُوْا يُوْعَدُوْنَ ۝

207. That which they were made to enjoy shall not avail them?

مَآ اَغْنٰى عَنْهُمْ مَّا كَانُوْا يَسْتَمْتِعُوْنَ ۝

208. And We did not destroy any town but it had (its) warners,

وَمَآ اَهْلَكْنَا مِنْ قَرْيَةٍ اِلَّا لَهَا مُنْذِرُوْنَ ۞

209. To remind, and We are never unjust.

مَعْ ذِكْرٰى ڗ وَمَا كُنَّا ظٰلِمِيْنَ ۞

210. And the Shaitans have not come down with it.

وَمَا تَنَزَّلَتْ بِهِ الشَّيٰطِيْنُ ۞

211. And it behoves them not, and they have not the power to do (it).

وَمَا يَنْبَغِيْ لَهُمْ وَمَا يَسْتَطِيْعُوْنَ ۞

212. Most surely they are far removed from the hearing of it.

اِنَّهُمْ عَنِ السَّمْعِ لَمَعْزُوْلُوْنَ ۞

213. So call not upon another god with Allah, lest you be of those who are punished.

فَلَا تَدْعُ مَعَ اللّٰهِ اِلٰهًا اٰخَرَ فَتَكُوْنَ مِنَ الْمُعَذَّبِيْنَ ۞

214. And warn your nearest relations,

وَاَنْذِرْ عَشِيْرَتَكَ الْاَقْرَبِيْنَ ۞

215. And be kind to him who follows you of the believers.

وَاخْفِضْ جَنَاحَكَ لِمَنِ اتَّبَعَكَ مِنَ الْمُؤْمِنِيْنَ ۞

216. But if they disobey you, then say: Surely I am clear of what you do.

فَاِنْ عَصَوْكَ فَقُلْ اِنِّيْ بَرِيْءٌ مِّمَّا تَعْمَلُوْنَ ۞

217. And rely on the Mighty, the Merciful,

وَتَوَكَّلْ عَلَى الْعَزِيْزِ الرَّحِيْمِ ۞

218. Who sees you when you stand up.

الَّذِيْ يَرٰىكَ حِيْنَ تَقُوْمُ ۞

219. And your turning over and over among those who prostrate themselves before Allah.

وَتَقَلُّبَكَ فِى السَّاجِدِيْنَ ۞

220. Surely He is the Hearing, the Knowing.

اِنَّهُ هُوَ السَّمِيْعُ الْعَلِيْمُ ۞

221. Shall I inform you (of him) upon whom the Shaitans descend?

هَلْ اُنَبِّئُكُمْ عَلٰى مَنْ تَنَزَّلُ الشَّيٰطِيْنُ ۞

222. They descend upon every lying, sinful one,

تَنَزَّلُ عَلٰى كُلِّ اَفَّاكٍ اَثِيْمٍ ۞

223. They incline their ears, and most of them are liars.

يُلْقُوْنَ السَّمْعَ وَاَكْثَرُهُمْ كٰذِبُوْنَ ۞

224. And as to the poets, those who go astray follow them.

وَالشُّعَرَآءُ يَتَّبِعُهُمُ الْغَاوٗنَ ۞

225. Do you not see that they wander about bewildered in every valley?

اَلَمْ تَرَ اَنَّهُمْ فِيْ كُلِّ وَادٍ يَهِيْمُوْنَ ۞

226. And that they say that which they do not do,

وَاَنَّهُمْ يَقُوْلُوْنَ مَا لَا يَفْعَلُوْنَ ۞

227. Except those who believe and do good and remember Allah much, and defend themselves after they are oppressed; and they who act unjustly shall know to what final place of turning they shall turn back.

اِلَّا الَّذِيْنَ اٰمَنُوْا وَعَمِلُوا الصّٰلِحٰتِ وَذَكَرُوا اللّٰهَ كَثِيْرًا وَّانْتَصَرُوْا مِنْ بَعْدِ مَا ظُلِمُوْا وَسَيَعْلَمُ الَّذِيْنَ ظَلَمُوْۤا اَيَّ مُنْقَلَبٍ يَّنْقَلِبُوْنَ ۞

THE ANT
(NAML)

**In the name of Allah,
the Beneficent, the Merciful.**

1. Ta Sin! These are the verses of the Quran and the Book that makes (things) clear,

2. A guidance and good news for the believers,

3. Who keep up prayer and pay the poor-rate, and of the hereafter, they are sure.

4. As to those who do not believe in the hereafter, We have surely made their deeds fair-seeming to them, but they blindly wander on.

5. These are they who shall have an evil punishment, and in the hereafter they shall be the greatest losers.

6. And most surely you are made to receive the Quran from the Wise, the Knowing God.

7. When Musa said to his family: Surely I see fire; I will bring to you from it some news, or I will bring to you therefrom a burning firebrand so that you may warm yourselves.

8. So when he came to it a voice was uttered saying: Blessed is Whoever is in the fire and whatever is about it; and glory be to Allah, the Lord of the worlds;

9. O Musa! surely I am Allah, the Mighty, the Wise;

10. And cast down your staff. So when he saw it in motion as if it were a serpent, he turned back retreating and did not return: O Musa! fear not; surely the apostles shall not fear in My presence;

11. Neither he who has been unjust, then he does good instead after evil, for surely I am the Forgiving, the Merciful:

آیاتها ۹۳ (۲۷) سُوْرَةُ النَّمْلِ مَكِّیَّةٌ رُكُوْعَاتُهَا ٧

بِسْمِ اللهِ الرَّحْمٰنِ الرَّحِيْمِ ۞

طٰسٓ ۟ تِلْكَ اٰیٰتُ الْقُرْاٰنِ وَكِتَابٍ مُّبِيْنٍ ۞

هُدًى وَّبُشْرٰى لِلْمُؤْمِنِيْنَ ۞

الَّذِیْنَ یُقِیْمُوْنَ الصَّلٰوةَ وَیُؤْتُوْنَ الزَّكٰوةَ وَهُمْ بِالْاٰخِرَةِ هُمْ یُوْقِنُوْنَ ۞

اِنَّ الَّذِیْنَ لَا یُؤْمِنُوْنَ بِالْاٰخِرَةِ زَیَّنَّا لَهُمْ اَعْمَالَهُمْ فَهُمْ یَعْمَهُوْنَ ۞

اُولٰٓئِكَ الَّذِیْنَ لَهُمْ سُوْٓءُ الْعَذَابِ وَهُمْ فِی الْاٰخِرَةِ هُمُ الْاَخْسَرُوْنَ ۞

وَاِنَّكَ لَتُلَقَّی الْقُرْاٰنَ مِنْ لَّدُنْ حَكِیْمٍ عَلِیْمٍ ۞

اِذْ قَالَ مُوْسٰى لِاَهْلِهٖۤ اِنِّیْۤ اٰنَسْتُ نَارًا ۖ سَاٰتِیْكُمْ مِّنْهَا بِخَبَرٍ اَوْ اٰتِیْكُمْ بِشِهَابٍ قَبَسٍ لَّعَلَّكُمْ تَصْطَلُوْنَ ۞

فَلَمَّا جَآءَهَا نُوْدِیَ اَنْۢ بُوْرِكَ مَنْ فِی النَّارِ وَمَنْ حَوْلَهَا ۚ وَسُبْحٰنَ اللهِ رَبِّ الْعٰلَمِيْنَ ۞

یٰمُوْسٰۤى اِنَّهٗۤ اَنَا اللهُ الْعَزِیْزُ الْحَكِیْمُ ۞

وَاَلْقِ عَصَاكَ ۚ فَلَمَّا رَاٰهَا تَهْتَزُّ كَاَنَّهَا جَآنٌّ وَّلّٰى مُدْبِرًا وَّلَمْ یُعَقِّبْ ۚ یٰمُوْسٰى لَا تَخَفْ ۖ اِنِّیْ لَا یَخَافُ لَدَیَّ الْمُرْسَلُوْنَ ۞

اِلَّا مَنْ ظَلَمَ ثُمَّ بَدَّلَ حُسْنًۢا بَعْدَ سُوْٓءٍ فَاِنِّیْ غَفُوْرٌ رَّحِیْمٌ ۞

12. And enter your hand into the opening of your bosom, it shall come forth white without evil; among nine signs to Firon and his people, surely they are a transgressing people.

وَاَدْخِلْ يَدَكَ فِيْ جَيْبِكَ تَخْرُجْ بَيْضَآءَ مِنْ غَيْرِ سُوْٓءٍ ۖ فِيْ تِسْعِ اٰيٰتٍ اِلٰى فِرْعَوْنَ وَقَوْمِهٖ ۚ اِنَّهُمْ كَانُوْا قَوْمًا فٰسِقِيْنَ ۝

13. So when Our clear signs came to them, they said: This is clear enchantment.

فَلَمَّا جَآءَتْهُمْ اٰيٰتُنَا مُبْصِرَةً قَالُوْا هٰذَا سِحْرٌ مُّبِيْنٌ ۝

14. And they denied them unjustly and proudly while their soul had been convinced of them; consider, then how was the end of the mischief-makers.

وَجَحَدُوْا بِهَا وَاسْتَيْقَنَتْهَآ اَنْفُسُهُمْ ظُلْمًا وَّعُلُوًّا ۚ فَانْظُرْ كَيْفَ كَانَ عَاقِبَةُ الْمُفْسِدِيْنَ ۝

15. And certainly We gave knowledge to Dawood and Sulaiman, and they both said: Praise be to Allah, Who has made us to excel many of His believing servants.

وَلَقَدْ اٰتَيْنَا دَاوٗدَ وَسُلَيْمٰنَ عِلْمًا ۚ وَقَالَا الْحَمْدُ لِلّٰهِ الَّذِيْ فَضَّلَنَا عَلٰى كَثِيْرٍ مِّنْ عِبَادِهِ الْمُؤْمِنِيْنَ ۝

16. And Sulaiman was Dawood's heir, and he said: O men! we have been taught the language of birds, and we have been given all things; most surely this is manifest grace.

وَوَرِثَ سُلَيْمٰنُ دَاوٗدَ وَقَالَ يٰٓاَيُّهَا النَّاسُ عُلِّمْنَا مَنْطِقَ الطَّيْرِ وَاُوْتِيْنَا مِنْ كُلِّ شَيْءٍ ۚ اِنَّ هٰذَا لَهُوَ الْفَضْلُ الْمُبِيْنُ ۝

17. And his hosts of the jinn and the men and the birds were gathered to him, and they were formed into groups.

وَحُشِرَ لِسُلَيْمٰنَ جُنُوْدُهٗ مِنَ الْجِنِّ وَالْاِنْسِ وَ الطَّيْرِ فَهُمْ يُوْزَعُوْنَ ۝

18. Until when they came to the valley of the Naml, a Namlite said: O Naml! enter your houses, (that) Sulaiman and his hosts may not crush you while they do not know.

حَتّٰى اِذَآ اَتَوْا عَلٰى وَادِ النَّمْلِ ۙ قَالَتْ نَمْلَةٌ يٰٓاَيُّهَا النَّمْلُ ادْخُلُوْا مَسٰكِنَكُمْ ۚ لَا يَحْطِمَنَّكُمْ سُلَيْمٰنُ وَجُنُوْدُهٗ ۙ وَهُمْ لَا يَشْعُرُوْنَ ۝

19. So he smiled, wondering at her word, and said: My Lord! grant me that I should be grateful for Thy favor which Thou hast bestowed on me and on my parents, and that I should do good such as Thou art pleased with, and make me enter, by Thy mercy, into Thy servants, the good ones.

فَتَبَسَّمَ ضَاحِكًا مِّنْ قَوْلِهَا وَقَالَ رَبِّ اَوْزِعْنِيْ اَنْ اَشْكُرَ نِعْمَتَكَ الَّتِيْٓ اَنْعَمْتَ عَلَيَّ وَعَلٰى وَالِدَيَّ وَاَنْ اَعْمَلَ صَالِحًا تَرْضٰهُ وَاَدْخِلْنِيْ بِرَحْمَتِكَ فِيْ عِبَادِكَ الصّٰلِحِيْنَ ۝

20. And he reviewed the birds, then said: How is it I see not the hoopoe or is it that he is of the absentees?

21. I will most certainly punish him with a severe punishment, or kill him, or he shall bring to me a clear plea.

22. And he tarried not long, then said: I comprehend that which you do not comprehend and I have brought to you a sure information from Sheba.

23. Surely I found a woman ruling over them, and she has been given abundance and she has a mighty throne:

24. I found her and her people adoring the sun instead of Allah, and the Shaitan has made their deeds fair-seeming to them and thus turned them from the way, so they do not go aright;

25. That they do not make obeisance to Allah, Who brings forth what is hidden in the heavens and the earth and knows what you hide and what you make manifest:

26. Allah, there is no god but He: He is the Lord of mighty power.

27. He said: We will see whether you have told the truth or whether you are of the liars:

28. Take this my letter and hand it over to them, then turn away from them and see what (answer) they return.

29. She said: O chief! surely an honorable letter has been delivered to me;

30. Surely it is from Sulaiman, and surely it is in the name of Allah, the Beneficent, the Merciful;

31. Saying: exalt not yourselves against me and come to me in submission.

32. She said: O chiefs! give me advice respecting my affair: I never decide an affair until you are in my presence.

366

33. They said: We are possessors of strength and possessors of mighty prowess, and the command is yours, therefore see what you will command.

قَالُوْا نَحْنُ اُولُوْا قُوَّةٍ وَّاُولُوْا بَأْسٍ شَدِيْدٍ ۚ وَّ الْاَمْرُ اِلَيْكِ فَانْظُرِيْ مَاذَا تَأْمُرِيْنَ ۝

34. She said: Surely the kings, when they enter a town, ruin it and make the noblest of its people to be low, and thus they (always) do;

قَالَتْ اِنَّ الْمُلُوْكَ اِذَا دَخَلُوْا قَرْيَةً اَفْسَدُوْهَا وَ جَعَلُوْا اَعِزَّةَ اَهْلِهَا اَذِلَّةً ۚ وَكَذٰلِكَ يَفْعَلُوْنَ ۝

35. And surely I am going to send a present to them, and shall wait to see what (answer) do the messengers bring back.

وَاِنِّيْ مُرْسِلَةٌ اِلَيْهِمْ بِهَدِيَّةٍ فَنٰظِرَةٌۢ بِمَ يَرْجِعُ الْمُرْسَلُوْنَ ۝

36. So when he came to Sulaiman, he said: What! will you help me with wealth? But what Allah has given me is better than what He has given you. Nay, you are exultant because of your present;

فَلَمَّا جَآءَ سُلَيْمٰنَ قَالَ اَتُمِدُّوْنَنِ بِمَالٍ ۚ فَمَآ اٰتٰىنِۦ اللّٰهُ خَيْرٌ مِّمَّآ اٰتٰىكُمْ ۚ بَلْ اَنْتُمْ بِهَدِيَّتِكُمْ تَفْرَحُوْنَ ۝

37. Go back to them, so we will most certainly come to them with hosts which they shall have no power to oppose, and we will most certainly expel them therefrom in abasement, and they shall be in a state of ignominy.

اِرْجِعْ اِلَيْهِمْ فَلَنَأْتِيَنَّهُمْ بِجُنُوْدٍ لَّا قِبَلَ لَهُمْ بِهَا وَلَنُخْرِجَنَّهُمْ مِّنْهَآ اَذِلَّةً وَّهُمْ صٰغِرُوْنَ ۝

38. He said: O chiefs! which of you can bring to me her throne before they come to me in submission?

قَالَ يٰٓاَيُّهَا الْمَلَؤُا اَيُّكُمْ يَأْتِيْنِيْ بِعَرْشِهَا قَبْلَ اَنْ يَّأْتُوْنِيْ مُسْلِمِيْنَ ۝

39. One audacious among the jinn said: I will bring it to you before you rise up from your place; and most surely I am strong (and) trusty for it.

قَالَ عِفْرِيْتٌ مِّنَ الْجِنِّ اَنَا اٰتِيْكَ بِهٖ قَبْلَ اَنْ تَقُوْمَ مِنْ مَّقَامِكَ ۚ وَاِنِّيْ عَلَيْهِ لَقَوِيٌّ اَمِيْنٌ ۝

40. One who had the knowledge of the Book said: I will bring it to you in the twinkling of an eye. Then when he saw it settled beside him, he said: This is of the grace of my Lord that He may try me whether I am grateful or ungrateful; and whoever is grateful, he is grateful only for his own soul, and whoever is ungrateful, then surely my Lord is Self-sufficient, Honored.

قَالَ الَّذِيْ عِنْدَهٗ عِلْمٌ مِّنَ الْكِتٰبِ اَنَا اٰتِيْكَ بِهٖ قَبْلَ اَنْ يَّرْتَدَّ اِلَيْكَ طَرْفُكَ ۚ فَلَمَّا رَاٰهُ مُسْتَقِرًّا عِنْدَهٗ قَالَ هٰذَا مِنْ فَضْلِ رَبِّيْ ۚ لِيَبْلُوَنِيْٓ ءَاَشْكُرُ اَمْ اَكْفُرُ ۚ وَمَنْ شَكَرَ فَاِنَّمَا يَشْكُرُ لِنَفْسِهٖ ۚ وَمَنْ كَفَرَ فَاِنَّ رَبِّيْ غَنِيٌّ كَرِيْمٌ ۝

41. He said: Alter her throne for her; we will see whether she follows the right way or is of those who do not go aright.

قَالَ نَكِّرُوْا لَهَا عَرْشَهَا نَنْظُرْ اَتَهْتَدِيْٓ اَمْ تَكُوْنُ مِنَ الَّذِيْنَ لَا يَهْتَدُوْنَ ۝

42. So when she came, it was said: Is your throne like this? She said: It is as it were the same, and we were given the knowledge before it, and we were submissive.

43. And what she worshipped besides Allah prevented her, surely she was of an unbelieving people.

44. It was said to her: Enter the palace; but when she saw it she deemed it to be a great expanse of water, and bared her legs. He said: Surely it is a palace made smooth with glass. She said: My Lord! surely I have been unjust to myself, and I submit with Sulaiman to Allah, the Lord of the worlds.

45. And certainly We sent to Samood their brother Salih, saying: Serve Allah; and lo! they became two sects quarrelling with each other.

46. He said: O my people! why do you seek to hasten on the evil before the good? Why do you not ask forgiveness of Allah so that you may be dealt with mercifully?

47. They said: We have met with ill luck on account of you and on account of those with you. He said: The cause of your evil fortune is with Allah; nay, you are a people who are tried.

48. And there were in the city nine persons who made mischief in the land and did not act aright.

49. They said: Swear to each other by Allah that we will certainly make a sudden attack on him and his family by night, then we will say to his heir: We did not witness the destruction of his family, and we are most surely truthful.

50. And they planned a plan, and We planned a plan while they perceived not.

51. See, then, how was the end of their plan that We destroyed them and their people, all (of them).

368

52. So those are their houses fallen down because they were unjust; most surely there is a sign in this for a people who know.

فَتِلْكَ بُيُوْتُهُمْ خَاوِيَةً بِمَا ظَلَمُوْا ۚ اِنَّ فِيْ ذٰلِكَ لَاٰيَةً لِّقَوْمٍ يَّعْلَمُوْنَ ۝

53. And We delivered those who believed and who guarded (against evil).

وَاَنْجَيْنَا الَّذِيْنَ اٰمَنُوْا وَكَانُوْا يَتَّقُوْنَ ۝

54. And (We sent) Lut, when he said to his people: What! do you commit indecency while you see?

وَلُوْطًا اِذْ قَالَ لِقَوْمِهٖۤ اَتَاْتُوْنَ الْفَاحِشَةَ وَاَنْتُمْ تُبْصِرُوْنَ ۝

55. What! do you indeed approach men lustfully rather than women? Nay, you are a people who act ignorantly.

اَئِنَّكُمْ لَتَاْتُوْنَ الرِّجَالَ شَهْوَةً مِّنْ دُوْنِ النِّسَآءِ ۚ بَلْ اَنْتُمْ قَوْمٌ تَجْهَلُوْنَ ۝

56. But the answer of his people was no other except that they said: Turn out Lut's followers from your town; surely they are a people who would keep pure!

فَمَا كَانَ جَوَابَ قَوْمِهٖۤ اِلَّاۤ اَنْ قَالُوْۤا اَخْرِجُوْۤا اٰلَ لُوْطٍ مِّنْ قَرْيَتِكُمْ ۚ اِنَّهُمْ اُنَاسٌ يَّتَطَهَّرُوْنَ ۝

57. But We delivered him and his followers except his wife; We ordained her to be of those who remained behind.

فَاَنْجَيْنٰهُ وَاَهْلَهٗۤ اِلَّا امْرَاَتَهٗ ۖ قَدَّرْنٰهَا مِنَ الْغٰبِرِيْنَ ۝

58. And We rained on them a rain, and evil was the rain of those who had been warned.

وَاَمْطَرْنَا عَلَيْهِمْ مَّطَرًا ۚ فَسَآءَ مَطَرُ الْمُنْذَرِيْنَ ۝

59. Say: Praise be to Allah and peace on His servants whom He has chosen: is Allah better, or what they associate (with Him)?

قُلِ الْحَمْدُ لِلّٰهِ وَسَلٰمٌ عَلٰى عِبَادِهِ الَّذِيْنَ اصْطَفٰى ۗ ءَآللّٰهُ خَيْرٌ اَمَّا يُشْرِكُوْنَ ۝

60. Nay, He Who created the heavens and the earth, and sent down for you water from the cloud; then We cause to grow thereby beautiful gardens; it is not possible for you that you should make the trees thereof to grow. Is there a god with Allah? Nay! they are a people who deviate.

اَمَّنْ خَلَقَ السَّمٰوٰتِ وَالْاَرْضَ وَاَنْزَلَ لَكُمْ مِّنَ السَّمَآءِ مَآءً ۚ فَاَنْبَتْنَا بِهٖ حَدَآئِقَ ذَاتَ بَهْجَةٍ ۚ مَا كَانَ لَكُمْ اَنْ تُنْبِتُوْا شَجَرَهَا ۗ ءَاِلٰهٌ مَّعَ اللّٰهِ ۚ بَلْ هُمْ قَوْمٌ يَّعْدِلُوْنَ ۝

61. Or, Who made the earth a resting-place, and made in it rivers, and raised on it mountains, and placed between the two seas a barrier. Is there a god with Allah? Nay! most of them do not know!

اَمَّنْ جَعَلَ الْاَرْضَ قَرَارًا وَّجَعَلَ خِلٰلَهَاۤ اَنْهٰرًا وَّجَعَلَ لَهَا رَوَاسِيَ وَجَعَلَ بَيْنَ الْبَحْرَيْنِ حَاجِزًا ۚ ءَاِلٰهٌ مَّعَ اللّٰهِ ۚ بَلْ اَكْثَرُهُمْ لَا يَعْلَمُوْنَ ۝

62. Or, Who answers the distressed one when he calls upon Him and removes the evil, and He will make you successors in the earth. Is there a god with Allah? Little is it that you mind!

اَمَّنْ يُّجِيْبُ الْمُضْطَرَّ اِذَا دَعَاهُ وَيَكْشِفُ السُّوْٓءَ وَيَجْعَلُكُمْ خُلَفَاۤءَ الْاَرْضِ ءَاِلٰهٌ مَّعَ اللّٰهِ قَلِيْلًا مَّا تَذَكَّرُوْنَۗ ۝

63. Or, Who guides you in utter darkness of the land and the sea, and Who sends the winds as good news before His mercy. Is there a god with Allah? Exalted be Allah above what they associate (with Him).

اَمَّنْ يَّهْدِيْكُمْ فِيْ ظُلُمٰتِ الْبَرِّ وَالْبَحْرِ وَمَنْ يُّرْسِلُ الرِّيٰحَ بُشْرًا بَيْنَ يَدَيْ رَحْمَتِهٖ ءَاِلٰهٌ مَّعَ اللّٰهِ تَعٰلَى اللّٰهُ عَمَّا يُشْرِكُوْنَ ۝

64. Or, Who originates the creation, then reproduces it, and Who gives you sustenance from the heaven and the earth. Is there a god with Allah? Say: Bring your proof if you are truthful.

اَمَّنْ يَّبْدَؤُا الْخَلْقَ ثُمَّ يُعِيْدُهٗ وَمَنْ يَّرْزُقُكُمْ مِّنَ السَّمَاۤءِ وَالْاَرْضِ ءَاِلٰهٌ مَّعَ اللّٰهِ قُلْ هَاتُوْا بُرْهَانَكُمْ اِنْ كُنْتُمْ صٰدِقِيْنَ ۝

65. Say: No one in the heavens and the earth knows the unseen but Allah; and they do not know when they shall be raised.

قُلْ لَّا يَعْلَمُ مَنْ فِى السَّمٰوٰتِ وَالْاَرْضِ الْغَيْبَ اِلَّا اللّٰهُ وَمَا يَشْعُرُوْنَ اَيَّانَ يُبْعَثُوْنَ ۝

66. Nay, their knowledge respecting the hereafter is slight and hasty; nay, they are in doubt about it; nay, they are quite blind to it.

بَلِ ادّٰرَكَ عِلْمُهُمْ فِى الْاٰخِرَةِ بَلْ هُمْ فِيْ شَكٍّ مِّنْهَا بَلْ هُمْ مِّنْهَا عَمُوْنَ ۝

67. And those who disbelieve say: What! when we have become dust and our fathers (too), shall we certainly be brought forth?

وَقَالَ الَّذِيْنَ كَفَرُوْٓا ءَاِذَا كُنَّا تُرٰبًا وَّاٰبَاۤؤُنَآ اَئِنَّا لَمُخْرَجُوْنَ ۝

68. We have certainly been promised this, we and our fathers before; these are naught but stories of the ancients.

لَقَدْ وُعِدْنَا هٰذَا نَحْنُ وَاٰبَاۤؤُنَا مِنْ قَبْلُ اِنْ هٰذَآ اِلَّا اَسَاطِيْرُ الْاَوَّلِيْنَ ۝

69. Say: Travel in the earth, then see how was the end of the guilty.

قُلْ سِيْرُوْا فِى الْاَرْضِ فَانْظُرُوْا كَيْفَ كَانَ عَاقِبَةُ الْمُجْرِمِيْنَ ۝

70. And grieve not for them and be not distressed because of what they plan.

وَلَا تَحْزَنْ عَلَيْهِمْ وَلَا تَكُنْ فِيْ ضَيْقٍ مِّمَّا يَمْكُرُوْنَ ۝

71. And they say: When will this threat come to pass, if you are truthful?

وَيَقُوْلُوْنَ مَتٰى هٰذَا الْوَعْدُ اِنْ كُنْتُمْ صٰدِقِيْنَ ۝

72. Say: Maybe there may have drawn near to you somewhat of that which you seek to hasten on.

قُلْ عَسٰۤى اَنْ يَّكُوْنَ رَدِفَ لَكُمْ بَعْضُ الَّذِيْ تَسْتَعْجِلُوْنَ ۝

73. And surely your Lord is the Lord of grace to men, but most of them are not grateful.

وَلَنَّ رَبَّكَ لَذُوْ فَضْلٍ عَلَى النَّاسِ وَلٰكِنَّ اَكْثَرَهُمْ لَا يَشْكُرُوْنَ ۞

74. And most surely your Lord knows what their breasts conceal and what they manifest.

وَإِنَّ رَبَّكَ لَيَعْلَمُ مَا تُكِنُّ صُدُوْرُهُمْ وَمَا يُعْلِنُوْنَ ۞

75. And there is nothing concealed in the heaven and the earth but it is in a clear book.

وَمَا مِنْ غَآئِبَةٍ فِي السَّمَآءِ وَالْاَرْضِ اِلَّا فِيْ كِتٰبٍ مُّبِيْنٍ ۞

76. Surely this Quran declares to the children of Israel most of what they differ in.

اِنَّ هٰذَا الْقُرْاٰنَ يَقُصُّ عَلٰى بَنِيْۤ اِسْرَآءِيْلَ اَكْثَرَ الَّذِيْ هُمْ فِيْهِ يَخْتَلِفُوْنَ ۞

77. And most surely it is a guidance and a mercy for the believers.

وَإِنَّهٗ لَهُدًى وَّرَحْمَةٌ لِّلْمُؤْمِنِيْنَ ۞

78. Surely your Lord will judge between them by His judgment, and He is the Mighty, the Knowing.

اِنَّ رَبَّكَ يَقْضِيْ بَيْنَهُمْ بِحُكْمِهٖ ۚ وَهُوَ الْعَزِيْزُ الْعَلِيْمُ ۞

79. Therefore rely on Allah; surely you are on the clear truth.

فَتَوَكَّلْ عَلَى اللّٰهِ ۗ اِنَّكَ عَلَى الْحَقِّ الْمُبِيْنِ ۞

80. Surely you do not make the dead to hear, and you do not make the deaf to hear the call when they go back retreating.

اِنَّكَ لَا تُسْمِعُ الْمَوْتٰى وَلَا تُسْمِعُ الصُّمَّ الدُّعَآءَ اِذَا وَلَّوْا مُدْبِرِيْنَ ۞

81. Nor can you be a guide to the blind out of their error; you cannot make to hear (any one) except those who believe in Our communications, so they submit.

وَمَآ اَنْتَ بِهٰدِي الْعُمْيِ عَنْ ضَلٰلَتِهِمْ ۗ اِنْ تُسْمِعُ اِلَّا مَنْ يُّؤْمِنُ بِاٰيٰتِنَا فَهُمْ مُّسْلِمُوْنَ ۞

82. And when the word shall come to pass against them, We shall bring forth for them a creature from the earth that shall wound them, because people did not believe in Our communications.

وَإِذَا وَقَعَ الْقَوْلُ عَلَيْهِمْ اَخْرَجْنَا لَهُمْ دَآبَّةً مِّنَ الْاَرْضِ تُكَلِّمُهُمْ ۙ اَنَّ النَّاسَ كَانُوْا بِاٰيٰتِنَا لَا يُوْقِنُوْنَ ۞

83. And on the day when We will gather from every nation a party from among those who rejected Our communications, then they shall be formed into groups.

وَيَوْمَ نَحْشُرُ مِنْ كُلِّ اُمَّةٍ فَوْجًا مِّمَّنْ يُّكَذِّبُ بِاٰيٰتِنَا فَهُمْ يُوْزَعُوْنَ ۞

84. Until when they come, He will say: Did you reject My communications while you had no comprehensive knowledge of them? Or what was it that you did?

حَتّٰۤى اِذَا جَآءُوْ قَالَ اَكَذَّبْتُمْ بِاٰيٰتِيْ وَلَمْ تُحِيْطُوْا بِهَا عِلْمًا اَمَّا ذَا كُنْتُمْ تَعْمَلُوْنَ ۞

85. And the word shall come to pass against them because they were unjust, so they shall not speak.

وَوَقَعَ الْقَوْلُ عَلَيْهِمْ بِمَا ظَلَمُوْا فَهُمْ لَا يَنْطِقُوْنَ ۝

86. Do they not consider that We have made the night that they may rest therein, and the day to give light? Most surely there are signs in this for a people who believe.

اَلَمْ يَرَوْا اَنَّا جَعَلْنَا الَّيْلَ لِيَسْكُنُوْا فِيْهِ وَالنَّهَارَ مُبْصِرًا ۚ اِنَّ فِيْ ذٰلِكَ لَاٰيٰتٍ لِّقَوْمٍ يُّؤْمِنُوْنَ ۝

87. And on the day when the trumpet shall be blown, then those who are in the heavens and those who are in the earth shall be terrified except such as Allah please, and all shall come to Him abased.

وَيَوْمَ يُنْفَخُ فِى الصُّوْرِ فَفَزِعَ مَنْ فِى السَّمٰوٰتِ وَمَنْ فِى الْاَرْضِ اِلَّا مَنْ شَاءَ اللّٰهُ ۚ وَكُلٌّ اَتَوْهُ دٰخِرِيْنَ ۝

88. And you see the mountains, you think them to be solid, and they shall pass away as the passing away of the cloud—the handiwork of Allah Who has made every thing thoroughly; surely He is Aware of what you do.

وَتَرَى الْجِبَالَ تَحْسَبُهَا جَامِدَةً وَّهِىَ تَمُرُّ مَرَّ السَّحَابِ ۚ صُنْعَ اللّٰهِ الَّذِيْ اَتْقَنَ كُلَّ شَىْءٍ ۚ اِنَّهٗ خَبِيْرٌ بِمَا تَفْعَلُوْنَ ۝

89. Whoever brings good, he shall have better than it; and they shall be secure from terror on that day.

مَنْ جَاءَ بِالْحَسَنَةِ فَلَهٗ خَيْرٌ مِّنْهَا ۚ وَهُمْ مِّنْ فَزَعٍ يَّوْمَئِذٍ اٰمِنُوْنَ ۝

90. And whoever brings evil, these shall be thrown down on their faces into the fire; shall you be rewarded (for) aught except what you did?

وَمَنْ جَاءَ بِالسَّيِّئَةِ فَكُبَّتْ وُجُوْهُهُمْ فِى النَّارِ ۚ هَلْ تُجْزَوْنَ اِلَّا مَا كُنْتُمْ تَعْمَلُوْنَ ۝

91. I am commanded only that I should serve the Lord of this city, Who has made it sacred, and His are all things; and I am commanded that I should be of those who submit;

اِنَّمَا اُمِرْتُ اَنْ اَعْبُدَ رَبَّ هٰذِهِ الْبَلْدَةِ الَّذِيْ حَرَّمَهَا وَلَهٗ كُلُّ شَىْءٍ ۚ وَاُمِرْتُ اَنْ اَكُوْنَ مِنَ الْمُسْلِمِيْنَ ۝

92. And that I should recite the Quran. Therefore whoever goes aright, he goes aright for his own soul, and whoever goes astray, then say: I am only one of the warners.

وَاَنْ اَتْلُوَا الْقُرْاٰنَ ۚ فَمَنِ اهْتَدٰى فَاِنَّمَا يَهْتَدِيْ لِنَفْسِهٖ ۚ وَمَنْ ضَلَّ فَقُلْ اِنَّمَا اَنَا مِنَ الْمُنْذِرِيْنَ ۝

93. And say: Praise be to Allah, He will show you His signs so that you shall recognize them; nor is your Lord heedless of what you do.

وَقُلِ الْحَمْدُ لِلّٰهِ سَيُرِيْكُمْ اٰيٰتِهٖ فَتَعْرِفُوْنَهَا ۚ وَمَا رَبُّكَ بِغَافِلٍ عَمَّا تَعْمَلُوْنَ ۝

THE NARRATIVE
(QASAS)

**In the name of Allah,
the Beneficent, the Merciful.**

1. Ta sin Mim.

2. These are the verses of the Book that makes (things) clear.

3. We recite to you from the account of Musa and Firon with truth for people who believe.

4. Surely Firon exalted himself in the land and made its people into parties, weakening one party from among them; he slaughtered their sons and let their women live; surely he was one of the mischief-makers.

5. And We desired to bestow a favor upon those who were deemed weak in the land, and to make them the Imams, and to make them the heirs,

6. And to grant them power in the land, and to make Firon and Haman and their hosts see from them what they feared.

7. And We revealed to Musa's mother, saying: Give him suck, then when you fear for him, cast him into the river and do not fear nor grieve; surely We will bring him back to you and make him one of the apostles.

8. And Firon's family took him up that he might be an enemy and a grief for them; surely Firon and Haman and their hosts were wrongdoers.

9. And Firon's wife said: A refreshment of the eye to me and to you; do not slay him; maybe he will be useful to us, or we may take him for a son; and they did not perceive.

بِسْمِ اللهِ الرَّحْمٰنِ الرَّحِيْمِ ۟

طٰسٓمّٓ ۟

تِلْكَ اٰيٰتُ الْكِتٰبِ الْمُبِيْنِ ۟

نَتْلُوْا عَلَيْكَ مِنْ نَّبَاِ مُوْسٰى وَفِرْعَوْنَ بِالْحَقِّ لِقَوْمٍ يُّؤْمِنُوْنَ ۟

اِنَّ فِرْعَوْنَ عَلَا فِى الْاَرْضِ وَجَعَلَ اَهْلَهَا شِيَعًا يَّسْتَضْعِفُ طَآئِفَةً مِّنْهُمْ يُذَبِّحُ اَبْنَآءَهُمْ وَيَسْتَحْىٖ نِسَآءَهُمْ ۖ اِنَّهٗ كَانَ مِنَ الْمُفْسِدِيْنَ ۟

وَنُرِيْدُ اَنْ نَّمُنَّ عَلَى الَّذِيْنَ اسْتُضْعِفُوْا فِى الْاَرْضِ وَنَجْعَلَهُمْ اَئِمَّةً وَّنَجْعَلَهُمُ الْوٰرِثِيْنَ ۟ۙ

وَنُمَكِّنَ لَهُمْ فِى الْاَرْضِ وَنُرِيَ فِرْعَوْنَ وَهَامٰنَ وَجُنُوْدَهُمَا مِنْهُمْ مَّا كَانُوْا يَحْذَرُوْنَ ۟

وَاَوْحَيْنَآ اِلٰٓى اُمِّ مُوْسٰٓى اَنْ اَرْضِعِيْهِ ۖ فَاِذَا خِفْتِ عَلَيْهِ فَاَلْقِيْهِ فِى الْيَمِّ وَلَا تَخَافِىْ وَلَا تَحْزَنِىْ ۖ اِنَّا رَآدُّوْهُ اِلَيْكِ وَجَاعِلُوْهُ مِنَ الْمُرْسَلِيْنَ ۟

فَالْتَقَطَهٗٓ اٰلُ فِرْعَوْنَ لِيَكُوْنَ لَهُمْ عَدُوًّا وَّحَزَنًا ۗ اِنَّ فِرْعَوْنَ وَهَامٰنَ وَجُنُوْدَهُمَا كَانُوْا خٰطِئِيْنَ ۟

وَقَالَتِ امْرَاَتُ فِرْعَوْنَ قُرَّتُ عَيْنٍ لِّىْ وَلَكَ ۗ لَا تَقْتُلُوْهُ ۖ عَسٰٓى اَنْ يَّنْفَعَنَآ اَوْ نَتَّخِذَهٗ وَلَدًا وَّهُمْ لَا يَشْعُرُوْنَ ۟

10. And the heart of Musa's mother was free (from anxiety); she would have almost disclosed it had We not strengthened her heart so that she might be of the believers.

وَأَصْبَحَ فُؤَادُ أُمِّ مُوْسٰى فٰرِغًا إِنْ كَادَتْ لَتُبْدِيْ بِهٖ لَوْلَا أَنْ رَّبَطْنَا عَلٰى قَلْبِهَا لِتَكُوْنَ مِنَ الْمُؤْمِنِيْنَ ۝

11. And she said to his sister: Follow him up. So she watched him from a distance while they did not perceive,

وَقَالَتْ لِأُخْتِهٖ قُصِّيْهِ فَبَصُرَتْ بِهٖ عَنْ جُنُبٍ وَّهُمْ لَا يَشْعُرُوْنَ ۝

12. And We ordained that he refuse to suck any foster mother before, so she said: Shall I point out to you the people of a house who will take care of him for you, and they will be benevolent to him?

وَحَرَّمْنَا عَلَيْهِ الْمَرَاضِعَ مِنْ قَبْلُ فَقَالَتْ هَلْ أَدُلُّكُمْ عَلٰى أَهْلِ بَيْتٍ يَّكْفُلُوْنَهٗ لَكُمْ وَهُمْ لَهٗ نٰصِحُوْنَ ۝

13. So We gave him back to his mother that her eye might be refreshed, and that she might not grieve, and that she might know that the promise of Allah is true, but most of them do not know.

فَرَدَدْنٰهُ إِلٰى أُمِّهٖ كَيْ تَقَرَّ عَيْنُهَا وَلَا تَحْزَنَ وَلِتَعْلَمَ أَنَّ وَعْدَ اللّٰهِ حَقٌّ وَّلٰكِنَّ أَكْثَرَهُمْ لَا يَعْلَمُوْنَ ۝

14. And when he attained his maturity and became full grown, We granted him wisdom and knowledge; and thus do We reward those who do good (to others).

وَلَمَّا بَلَغَ أَشُدَّهٗ وَاسْتَوٰى اٰتَيْنٰهُ حُكْمًا وَّعِلْمًا وَكَذٰلِكَ نَجْزِي الْمُحْسِنِيْنَ ۝

15. And he went into the city at a time of unvigilance on the part of its people, so he found therein two men fighting, one being of his party and the other of his foes, and he who was of his party cried out to him for help against him who was of his enemies, so Musa struck him with his fist and killed him. He said: This is on account of the Shaitan's doing; surely he is an enemy, openly leading astray.

وَدَخَلَ الْمَدِيْنَةَ عَلٰى حِيْنِ غَفْلَةٍ مِّنْ أَهْلِهَا فَوَجَدَ فِيْهَا رَجُلَيْنِ يَقْتَتِلٰنِ هٰذَا مِنْ شِيْعَتِهٖ وَهٰذَا مِنْ عَدُوِّهٖ فَاسْتَغَاثَهُ الَّذِيْ مِنْ شِيْعَتِهٖ عَلَى الَّذِيْ مِنْ عَدُوِّهٖ فَوَكَزَهٗ مُوْسٰى فَقَضٰى عَلَيْهِ قَالَ هٰذَا مِنْ عَمَلِ الشَّيْطٰنِ إِنَّهٗ عَدُوٌّ مُّضِلٌّ مُّبِيْنٌ ۝

16. He said: My Lord! surely I have done harm to myself, so do Thou protect me. So He protected him; surely He is the Forgiving, the Merciful.

قَالَ رَبِّ إِنِّيْ ظَلَمْتُ نَفْسِيْ فَاغْفِرْ لِيْ فَغَفَرَ لَهٗ إِنَّهٗ هُوَ الْغَفُوْرُ الرَّحِيْمُ ۝

17. He said: My Lord! because Thou hast bestowed a favor on me, I shall never be a backer of the guilty.

قَالَ رَبِّ بِمَا أَنْعَمْتَ عَلَيَّ فَلَنْ أَكُوْنَ ظَهِيْرًا لِّلْمُجْرِمِيْنَ ۝

18. And he was in the city, fearing, awaiting, when lo! he who had asked his assistance the day before was crying out to him for aid. Musa said to him: You are most surely one erring manifestly.

فَأَصْبَحَ فِي الْمَدِيْنَةِ خَائِفًا يَّتَرَقَّبُ فَإِذَا الَّذِي اسْتَنْصَرَهٗ بِالْأَمْسِ يَسْتَصْرِخُهٗ قَالَ لَهٗ مُوْسٰى إِنَّكَ لَغَوِيٌّ مُّبِيْنٌ ۝

19. So when he desired to seize him who was an enemy to them both, he said: O Musa! do you intend to kill me as you killed a person yesterday? You desire nothing but that you should be a tyrant in the land, and you do not desire to be of those who act aright.

فَلَمَّاۤ اَنْ اَرَادَ اَنْ يَّبْطِشَ بِالَّذِيْ هُوَ عَدُوٌّ لَّهُمَا ۙ قَالَ يٰمُوْسٰۤى اَتُرِيْدُ اَنْ تَقْتُلَنِيْ كَمَا قَتَلْتَ نَفْسًۢا بِالْاَمْسِ ۖ اِنْ تُرِيْدُ اِلَّاۤ اَنْ تَكُوْنَ جَبَّارًا فِى الْاَرْضِ وَمَا تُرِيْدُ اَنْ تَكُوْنَ مِنَ الْمُصْلِحِيْنَ ۝

20. And a man came running from the remotest part of the city. He said: O Musa! surely the chiefs are consulting together to slay you, therefore depart (at once); surely I am of those who wish well to you.

وَجَآءَ رَجُلٌ مِّنْ اَقْصَا الْمَدِيْنَةِ يَسْعٰى ۙ قَالَ يٰمُوْسٰۤى اِنَّ الْمَلَاَ يَاْتَمِرُوْنَ بِكَ لِيَقْتُلُوْكَ فَاخْرُجْ اِنِّيْ لَكَ مِنَ النّٰصِحِيْنَ ۝

21. So he went forth therefrom, fearing, awaiting, (and) he said: My Lord! deliver me from the unjust people.

فَخَرَجَ مِنْهَا خَآئِفًا يَّتَرَقَّبُ ۖ قَالَ رَبِّ نَجِّنِيْ مِنَ الْقَوْمِ الظّٰلِمِيْنَ ۝

22. And when he turned his face towards Madyan, he said: Maybe my Lord will guide me in the right path.

وَلَمَّا تَوَجَّهَ تِلْقَآءَ مَدْيَنَ قَالَ عَسٰى رَبِّيْۤ اَنْ يَّهْدِيَنِيْ سَوَآءَ السَّبِيْلِ ۝

23. And when he came to the water of Madyan, he found on it a group of men watering, and he found besides them two women keeping back (their flocks). He said: What is the matter with you? They said: We cannot water until the shepherds take away (their sheep) from the water, and our father is a very old man.

وَلَمَّا وَرَدَ مَآءَ مَدْيَنَ وَجَدَ عَلَيْهِ اُمَّةً مِّنَ النَّاسِ يَسْقُوْنَ ۖ وَوَجَدَ مِنْ دُوْنِهِمُ امْرَاَتَيْنِ تَذُوْدٰنِ ۖ قَالَ مَا خَطْبُكُمَا ۖ قَالَتَا لَا نَسْقِيْ حَتّٰى يُصْدِرَ الرِّعَآءُ ۖ وَاَبُوْنَا شَيْخٌ كَبِيْرٌ ۝

24. So he watered (their sheep) for them, then went back to the shade and said: My Lord! surely I stand in need of whatever good Thou mayest send down to me.

فَسَقٰى لَهُمَا ثُمَّ تَوَلّٰۤى اِلَى الظِّلِّ فَقَالَ رَبِّ اِنِّيْ لِمَاۤ اَنْزَلْتَ اِلَيَّ مِنْ خَيْرٍ فَقِيْرٌ ۝

25. Then one of the two women came to him walking bashfully. She said: My father invites you that he may give you the reward of your having watered for us. So when he came to him and gave to him the account, he said: Fear not, you are secure from the unjust people.

فَجَآءَتْهُ اِحْدٰىهُمَا تَمْشِيْ عَلَى اسْتِحْيَآءٍ ۖ قَالَتْ اِنَّ اَبِيْ يَدْعُوْكَ لِيَجْزِيَكَ اَجْرَ مَا سَقَيْتَ لَنَا ۖ فَلَمَّا جَآءَهٗ وَقَصَّ عَلَيْهِ الْقَصَصَ ۙ قَالَ لَا تَخَفْ ۖ نَجَوْتَ مِنَ الْقَوْمِ الظّٰلِمِيْنَ ۝

26. Said one of them: O my father! employ him, surely the best of those that you can employ is the strong man, the faithful one.

27. He said: I desire to marry one of these two daughters of mine to you on condition that you should serve me for eight years; but if you complete ten, it will be of your own free will, and I do not wish to be hard to you; if Allah please, you will find me one of the good.

28. He said: This shall be (an agreement) between me and you; whichever of the two terms I fulfil, there shall be no wrongdoing to me; and Allah is a witness of what we say.

29. So when Musa had fulfilled the term, and he journeyed with his family, he perceived on this side of the mountain a fire. He said to his family: Wait, I have seen a fire, maybe I will bring to you from it some news or a brand of fire, so that you may warm yourselves.

30. And when he came to it, a voice was uttered from the right side of the valley in the blessed spot of the bush, saying: O Musa! surely I am Allah, the Lord of the worlds.

31. And saying: Cast down your staff. So when he saw it in motion as if it were a serpent, he turned back retreating, and did not return. O Musa! come forward and fear not; surely you are of those who are secure;

32. Enter your hand into the opening of your bosom, it will come forth white without evil, and draw your hand to yourself to ward off fear: so these two shall be two arguments from your Lord to Firon and his chiefs, surely they are a transgressing people.

قَالَتْ اِحْدٰىهُمَا يٰٓاَبَتِ اسْتَاْجِرْهُ اِنَّ خَيْرَ مَنِ اسْتَاْجَرْتَ الْقَوِيُّ الْاَمِيْنُ ۝

قَالَ اِنِّيْٓ اُرِيْدُ اَنْ اُنْكِحَكَ اِحْدَى ابْنَتَيَّ هٰتَيْنِ عَلٰٓى اَنْ تَاْجُرَنِيْ ثَمٰنِيَ حِجَجٍ ۚ فَاِنْ اَتْمَمْتَ عَشْرًا فَمِنْ عِنْدِكَ ۚ وَمَآ اُرِيْدُ اَنْ اَشُقَّ عَلَيْكَ ۚ سَتَجِدُنِيْٓ اِنْ شَآءَ اللّٰهُ مِنَ الصّٰلِحِيْنَ ۝

قَالَ ذٰلِكَ بَيْنِيْ وَبَيْنَكَ ۚ اَيَّمَا الْاَجَلَيْنِ قَضَيْتُ فَلَا عُدْوَانَ عَلَيَّ ۚ وَاللّٰهُ عَلٰى مَا نَقُوْلُ وَكِيْلٌ ۝

فَلَمَّا قَضٰى مُوْسَى الْاَجَلَ وَسَارَ بِاَهْلِهٖٓ اٰنَسَ مِنْ جَانِبِ الطُّوْرِ نَارًا ۚ قَالَ لِاَهْلِهِ امْكُثُوْٓا اِنِّيْٓ اٰنَسْتُ نَارًا لَّعَلِّيْٓ اٰتِيْكُمْ مِّنْهَا بِخَبَرٍ اَوْ جَذْوَةٍ مِّنَ النَّارِ لَعَلَّكُمْ تَصْطَلُوْنَ ۝

فَلَمَّآ اَتٰىهَا نُوْدِيَ مِنْ شَاطِئِ الْوَادِ الْاَيْمَنِ فِى الْبُقْعَةِ الْمُبٰرَكَةِ مِنَ الشَّجَرَةِ اَنْ يّٰمُوْسٰٓى اِنِّيْٓ اَنَا اللّٰهُ رَبُّ الْعٰلَمِيْنَ ۝

وَاَنْ اَلْقِ عَصَاكَ ۚ فَلَمَّا رَاٰهَا تَهْتَزُّ كَاَنَّهَا جَآنٌّ وَّلّٰى مُدْبِرًا وَّلَمْ يُعَقِّبْ ۚ يٰمُوْسٰٓى اَقْبِلْ وَلَا تَخَفْ ۖ اِنَّكَ مِنَ الْاٰمِنِيْنَ ۝

اُسْلُكْ يَدَكَ فِيْ جَيْبِكَ تَخْرُجْ بَيْضَآءَ مِنْ غَيْرِ سُوْٓءٍ ۖ وَّاضْمُمْ اِلَيْكَ جَنَاحَكَ مِنَ الرَّهْبِ فَذٰنِكَ بُرْهَانَانِ مِنْ رَّبِّكَ اِلٰى فِرْعَوْنَ وَمَلَئِهٖ ۚ اِنَّهُمْ كَانُوْا قَوْمًا فٰسِقِيْنَ ۝

33. He said: My Lord! surely I killed one of them, so I fear lest they should slay me;

قَالَ رَبِّ اِنِّى قَتَلْتُ مِنْهُمْ نَفْسًا فَاَخَافُ اَنْ يَّقْتُلُوْنِ ۞

34. And my brother, Haroun, he is more eloquent of tongue than I, therefore send him with me as an aider, verifying me: surely I fear that they would reject me.

وَاَخِىْ هٰرُوْنُ هُوَ اَفْصَحُ مِنِّىْ لِسَانًا فَاَرْسِلْهُ مَعِىَ رِدْاً يُّصَدِّقُنِىْٓ اِنِّىْٓ اَخَافُ اَنْ يُّكَذِّبُوْنِ ۞

35. He said: We will strengthen your arm with your brother, and We will give you both an authority, so that they shall not reach you; (go) with Our signs; you two and those who follow you shall be uppermost.

قَالَ سَنَشُدُّ عَضُدَكَ بِاَخِيْكَ وَنَجْعَلُ لَكُمَا سُلْطٰنًا فَلَا يَصِلُوْنَ اِلَيْكُمَا بِاٰيٰتِنَآ اَنْتُمَا وَمَنِ اتَّبَعَكُمَا الْغٰلِبُوْنَ ۞

36. So when Musa came to them with Our clear signs, they said: This is nothing but forged enchantment, and we never heard of it amongst our fathers of old.

فَلَمَّا جَآءَهُمْ مُّوْسٰى بِاٰيٰتِنَا بَيِّنٰتٍ قَالُوْا مَا هٰذَآ اِلَّا سِحْرٌ مُّفْتَرًى وَّمَا سَمِعْنَا بِهٰذَا فِىْٓ اٰبَآئِنَا الْاَوَّلِيْنَ ۞

37. And Musa said: My Lord knows best who comes with guidance from Him, and whose shall be the good end of the abode; surely the unjust shall not be successful.

وَقَالَ مُوْسٰى رَبِّىْٓ اَعْلَمُ بِمَنْ جَآءَ بِالْهُدٰى مِنْ عِنْدِهٖ وَمَنْ تَكُوْنُ لَهٗ عَاقِبَةُ الدَّارِ اِنَّهٗ لَا يُفْلِحُ الظّٰلِمُوْنَ ۞

38. And Firon said: O chiefs! I do not know of any god for you besides myself; therefore kindle a fire for me, O Haman, for brick, then prepare for me a lofty building so that I may obtain knowledge of Musa's God, and most surely I think him to be one of the liars.

وَقَالَ فِرْعَوْنُ يٰٓاَيُّهَا الْمَلَاُ مَا عَلِمْتُ لَكُمْ مِّنْ اِلٰهٍ غَيْرِىْ فَاَوْقِدْ لِىْ يٰهَامٰنُ عَلَى الطِّيْنِ فَاجْعَلْ لِّىْ صَرْحًا لَّعَلِّىْٓ اَطَّلِعُ اِلٰٓى اِلٰهِ مُوْسٰى وَاِنِّىْ لَاَظُنُّهٗ مِنَ الْكٰذِبِيْنَ ۞

39. And he was unjustly proud in the land, he and his hosts, and they deemed that they would not be brought back to Us.

وَاسْتَكْبَرَ هُوَ وَجُنُوْدُهٗ فِى الْاَرْضِ بِغَيْرِ الْحَقِّ وَظَنُّوْٓا اَنَّهُمْ اِلَيْنَا لَا يُرْجَعُوْنَ ۞

40. So We caught hold of him and his hosts, then We cast them into the sea, and see how was the end of the unjust.

فَاَخَذْنٰهُ وَجُنُوْدَهٗ فَنَبَذْنٰهُمْ فِى الْيَمِّ فَانْظُرْ كَيْفَ كَانَ عَاقِبَةُ الظّٰلِمِيْنَ ۞

41. And We made them Imams who call to the fire, and on the day of resurrection they shall not be assisted.

وَجَعَلْنٰهُمْ اَئِمَّةً يَّدْعُوْنَ اِلَى النَّارِ وَيَوْمَ الْقِيٰمَةِ لَا يُنْصَرُوْنَ ۞

377

42. And We caused a curse to follow them in this world, and on the day of resurrection they shall be of those made to appear hideous.

وَاَتْبَعْنٰهُمْ فِيْ هٰذِهِ الدُّنْيَا لَعْنَةً ۚ وَيَوْمَ الْقِيٰمَةِ هُمْ مِّنَ الْمَقْبُوْحِيْنَ ۟

43. And certainly We gave Musa the Book after We had destroyed the former generations, clear arguments for men and a guidance and a mercy, that they may be mindful.

وَلَقَدْ اٰتَيْنَا مُوْسَى الْكِتٰبَ مِنْ بَعْدِ مَاۤ اَهْلَكْنَا الْقُرُوْنَ الْاُوْلٰى بَصَآئِرَ لِلنَّاسِ وَهُدًى وَّرَحْمَةً لَّعَلَّهُمْ يَتَذَكَّرُوْنَ ۟

44. And you were not on the western side when We revealed to Musa the commandment, and you were not among the witnesses;

وَمَا كُنْتَ بِجَانِبِ الْغَرْبِيِّ اِذْ قَضَيْنَاۤ اِلٰى مُوْسَى الْاَمْرَ وَمَا كُنْتَ مِنَ الشّٰهِدِيْنَ ۙ

45. But We raised up generations, then life became prolonged to them; and you were not dwelling among the people of Madyan, reciting to them Our communications, but We were the senders.

وَلٰكِنَّاۤ اَنْشَأْنَا قُرُوْنًا فَتَطَاوَلَ عَلَيْهِمُ الْعُمُرُ ۚ وَمَا كُنْتَ ثَاوِيًا فِيْۤ اَهْلِ مَدْيَنَ تَتْلُوْا عَلَيْهِمْ اٰيٰتِنَا ۙ وَلٰكِنَّا كُنَّا مُرْسِلِيْنَ ۟

46. And you were not on this side of the mountain when We called, but a mercy from your Lord that you may warn a people to whom no warner came before you, that they may be mindful.

وَمَا كُنْتَ بِجَانِبِ الطُّوْرِ اِذْ نَادَيْنَا وَلٰكِنْ رَّحْمَةً مِّنْ رَّبِّكَ لِتُنْذِرَ قَوْمًا مَّاۤ اَتٰىهُمْ مِّنْ نَّذِيْرٍ مِّنْ قَبْلِكَ لَعَلَّهُمْ يَتَذَكَّرُوْنَ ۟

47. And were it not that there should befall them a disaster for what their hands have sent before, then they should say: Our Lord! why didst Thou not send to us an apostle so that we should have followed Thy communications and been of the believers!

وَلَوْلَاۤ اَنْ تُصِيْبَهُمْ مُّصِيْبَةٌ بِمَا قَدَّمَتْ اَيْدِيْهِمْ فَيَقُوْلُوْا رَبَّنَا لَوْلَاۤ اَرْسَلْتَ اِلَيْنَا رَسُوْلًا فَنَتَّبِعَ اٰيٰتِكَ وَنَكُوْنَ مِنَ الْمُؤْمِنِيْنَ ۟

48. But (now) when the truth has come to them from Us, they say: Why is he not given the like of what was given to Musa? What! did they not disbelieve in what Musa was given before? They say: Two magicians backing up each other; and they say: Surely we are unbelievers in all.

فَلَمَّا جَآءَهُمُ الْحَقُّ مِنْ عِنْدِنَا قَالُوْا لَوْلَاۤ اُوْتِيَ مِثْلَ مَاۤ اُوْتِيَ مُوْسٰى ؕ اَوَلَمْ يَكْفُرُوْا بِمَاۤ اُوْتِيَ مُوْسٰى مِنْ قَبْلُ ۚ قَالُوْا سِحْرٰنِ تَظَاهَرَا ۟ وَقَالُوْاۤ اِنَّا بِكُلٍّ كٰفِرُوْنَ ۟

49. Say: Then bring some (other) book from Allah which is a better guide than both of them, (that) I may follow it, if you are truthful.

قُلْ فَأْتُوْا بِكِتٰبٍ مِّنْ عِنْدِ اللّٰهِ هُوَ اَهْدٰى مِنْهُمَاۤ اَتَّبِعْهُ اِنْ كُنْتُمْ صٰدِقِيْنَ ۟

50. But if they do not answer you, then know that they only follow their low desires; and who is more erring than he who follows his low desires without any guidance from Allah? Surely Allah does not guide the unjust people.

فَإِنْ لَّمْ يَسْتَجِيبُوْا لَكَ فَاعْلَمْ اَنَّمَا يَتَّبِعُوْنَ اَهْوَآءَهُمْ ۖ وَمَنْ اَضَلُّ مِمَّنِ اتَّبَعَ هَوٰىهُ بِغَيْرِ هُدًى مِّنَ اللّٰهِ ۚ اِنَّ اللّٰهَ لَا يَهْدِى الْقَوْمَ الظّٰلِمِيْنَ ۞

51. And certainly We have made the word to reach them so that they may be mindful.

وَلَقَدْ وَصَّلْنَا لَهُمُ الْقَوْلَ لَعَلَّهُمْ يَتَذَكَّرُوْنَ ۞

52. (As to) those whom We gave the Book before it, they are believers in it.

اَلَّذِيْنَ اٰتَيْنٰهُمُ الْكِتٰبَ مِنْ قَبْلِهٖ هُمْ بِهٖ يُؤْمِنُوْنَ ۞

53. And when it is recited to them they say: We believe in it; surely it is the truth from our Lord; surely we were submitters before this.

وَاِذَا يُتْلٰى عَلَيْهِمْ قَالُوْٓا اٰمَنَّا بِهٖٓ اِنَّهُ الْحَقُّ مِنْ رَّبِّنَاۤ اِنَّا كُنَّا مِنْ قَبْلِهٖ مُسْلِمِيْنَ ۞

54. These shall be granted their reward twice, because they are steadfast and they repel evil with good and spend out of what We have given them.

اُولٰٓئِكَ يُؤْتَوْنَ اَجْرَهُمْ مَّرَّتَيْنِ بِمَا صَبَرُوْا وَيَدْرَءُوْنَ بِالْحَسَنَةِ السَّيِّئَةَ وَمِمَّا رَزَقْنٰهُمْ يُنْفِقُوْنَ ۞

55. And when they hear idle talk they turn aside from it and say: We shall have our deeds and you shall have your deeds; peace be on you, we do not desire the ignorant.

وَاِذَا سَمِعُوا اللَّغْوَ اَعْرَضُوْا عَنْهُ وَقَالُوْا لَنَاۤ اَعْمَالُنَا وَلَكُمْ اَعْمَالُكُمْ ۖ سَلٰمٌ عَلَيْكُمْ ۖ لَا نَبْتَغِى الْجٰهِلِيْنَ ۞

56. Surely you cannot guide whom you love, but Allah guides whom He pleases, and He knows best the followers of the right way.

اِنَّكَ لَا تَهْدِىْ مَنْ اَحْبَبْتَ وَلٰكِنَّ اللّٰهَ يَهْدِىْ مَنْ يَّشَآءُ ۚ وَهُوَ اَعْلَمُ بِالْمُهْتَدِيْنَ ۞

57. And they say: If we follow the guidance with you, we shall be carried off from our country. What! have We not settled them in a safe, sacred territory to which fruits of every kind shall be drawn?—a sustenance from Us; but most of them do not know.

وَقَالُوْٓا اِنْ نَّتَّبِعِ الْهُدٰى مَعَكَ نُتَخَطَّفْ مِنْ اَرْضِنَا ۚ اَوَلَمْ نُمَكِّنْ لَّهُمْ حَرَمًا اٰمِنًا يُّجْبٰٓى اِلَيْهِ ثَمَرٰتُ كُلِّ شَيْءٍ رِّزْقًا مِّنْ لَّدُنَّا وَلٰكِنَّ اَكْثَرَهُمْ لَا يَعْلَمُوْنَ ۞

58. And how many a town have We destroyed which exulted in its means of subsistence; so these are their abodes; they have not been dwelt in after them except a little, and We are the inheritors.

وَكَمْ اَهْلَكْنَا مِنْ قَرْيَةٍ بَطِرَتْ مَعِيْشَتَهَا ۚ فَتِلْكَ مَسٰكِنُهُمْ لَمْ تُسْكَنْ مِّنْ بَعْدِهِمْ اِلَّا قَلِيْلًا ۖ وَكُنَّا نَحْنُ الْوٰرِثِيْنَ ۞

59. And your Lord never destroyed the towns until He raised in their metropolis an apostle, reciting to them Our communications, and We never destroyed the towns except when their people were unjust.

وَمَا كَانَ رَبُّكَ مُهْلِكَ الْقُرٰى حَتّٰى يَبْعَثَ فِيْٓ اُمِّهَا رَسُوْلًا يَّتْلُوْا عَلَيْهِمْ اٰيٰتِنَا ۚ وَمَا كُنَّا مُهْلِكِى الْقُرٰٓى اِلَّا وَاَهْلُهَا ظٰلِمُوْنَ ۞

60. And whatever things you have been given are only a provision of this world's life and its adornment, and whatever is with Allah is better and more lasting; do you not then understand?

وَمَآ اُوْتِيْتُمْ مِّنْ شَىْءٍ فَمَتَاعُ الْحَيٰوةِ الدُّنْيَا وَزِيْنَتُهَا وَمَا عِنْدَ اللّٰهِ خَيْرٌ وَّاَبْقٰى اَفَلَا تَعْقِلُوْنَ ۟

61. Is he to whom We have promised a goodly promise which he shall meet with like him whom We have provided with the provisions of this world's life, then on the day of resurrection he shall be of those who are brought up?

اَفَمَنْ وَّعَدْنٰهُ وَعْدًا حَسَنًا فَهُوَ لَاقِيْهِ كَمَنْ مَّتَّعْنٰهُ مَتَاعَ الْحَيٰوةِ الدُّنْيَا ثُمَّ هُوَ يَوْمَ الْقِيٰمَةِ مِنَ الْمُحْضَرِيْنَ ۟

62. And on the day when He will call them and say: Where are those whom you deemed to be My associates?

وَيَوْمَ يُنَادِيْهِمْ فَيَقُوْلُ اَيْنَ شُرَكَآءِىَ الَّذِيْنَ كُنْتُمْ تَزْعُمُوْنَ ۟

63. Those against whom the sentence has become confirmed will say: Our Lord! these are they whom we caused to err; we caused them to err as we ourselves did err; to Thee we declare ourselves to be clear (of them); they never served Us.

قَالَ الَّذِيْنَ حَقَّ عَلَيْهِمُ الْقَوْلُ رَبَّنَا هٰٓؤُلَآءِ الَّذِيْنَ اَغْوَيْنَا اَغْوَيْنٰهُمْ كَمَا غَوَيْنَا تَبَرَّأْنَآ اِلَيْكَ مَا كَانُوْٓا اِيَّانَا يَعْبُدُوْنَ ۟

64. And it will be said: Call your associate-gods. So they will call upon them, but they will not answer them, and they shall see the punishment; would that they had followed the right way!

وَقِيْلَ ادْعُوْا شُرَكَآءَكُمْ فَدَعَوْهُمْ فَلَمْ يَسْتَجِيْبُوْا لَهُمْ وَرَاَوُا الْعَذَابَ لَوْ اَنَّهُمْ كَانُوْا يَهْتَدُوْنَ ۟

65. And on the day when He shall call them and say: What was the answer you gave to the apostles?

وَيَوْمَ يُنَادِيْهِمْ فَيَقُوْلُ مَاذَآ اَجَبْتُمُ الْمُرْسَلِيْنَ ۟

66. Then the pleas shall become obscure to them on that day, so they shall not ask each other.

فَعَمِيَتْ عَلَيْهِمُ الْاَنْبَآءُ يَوْمَئِذٍ فَهُمْ لَا يَتَسَآءَلُوْنَ ۟

67. But as to him who repents and believes and does good, maybe he will be among the successful:

فَاَمَّا مَنْ تَابَ وَاٰمَنَ وَعَمِلَ صَالِحًا فَعَسٰٓى اَنْ يَّكُوْنَ مِنَ الْمُفْلِحِيْنَ ۟

68. And your Lord creates and chooses whom He pleases; to choose is not theirs; glory be to Allah, and exalted be He above what they associate (with Him).

وَرَبُّكَ يَخْلُقُ مَا يَشَآءُ وَيَخْتَارُ مَا كَانَ لَهُمُ الْخِيَرَةُ سُبْحٰنَ اللّٰهِ وَتَعٰلٰى عَمَّا يُشْرِكُوْنَ ۟

69. And your Lord knows what their breasts conceal and what they manifest.

وَرَبُّكَ يَعْلَمُ مَا تُكِنُّ صُدُوْرُهُمْ وَمَا يُعْلِنُوْنَ ۟

70. And He is Allah, there is no god but He! All praise is due to Him in this (life) and the hereafter, and His is the judgment, and to Him you shall be brought back.

وَهُوَ اللّٰهُ لَآ اِلٰهَ اِلَّا هُوَ لَهُ الْحَمْدُ فِى الْاُوْلٰى وَالْاٰخِرَةِ وَلَهُ الْحُكْمُ وَاِلَيْهِ تُرْجَعُوْنَ ۟

71. Say: Tell me, if Allah were to make the night to continue incessantly on you till the day of resurrection, who is the god besides Allah that could bring you light? Do you not then hear?

قُلْ اَرَءَيْتُمْ اِنْ جَعَلَ اللّٰهُ عَلَيْكُمُ الَّيْلَ سَرْمَدًا اِلٰى يَوْمِ الْقِيٰمَةِ مَنْ اِلٰهٌ غَيْرُ اللّٰهِ يَاْتِيْكُمْ بِضِيَآءٍ ؕ اَفَلَا تَسْمَعُوْنَ ۞

72. Say: Tell me, if Allah were to make the day to continue incessantly on you till the day of resurrection, who is the god besides Allah that could bring you the night in which you take rest? Do you not then see?

قُلْ اَرَءَيْتُمْ اِنْ جَعَلَ اللّٰهُ عَلَيْكُمُ النَّهَارَ سَرْمَدًا اِلٰى يَوْمِ الْقِيٰمَةِ مَنْ اِلٰهٌ غَيْرُ اللّٰهِ يَاْتِيْكُمْ بِلَيْلٍ تَسْكُنُوْنَ فِيْهِ ؕ اَفَلَا تُبْصِرُوْنَ ۞

73. And out of His mercy He has made for you the night and the day, that you may rest therein, and that you may seek of His grace, and that you may give thanks.

وَمِنْ رَّحْمَتِهٖ جَعَلَ لَكُمُ الَّيْلَ وَالنَّهَارَ لِتَسْكُنُوْا فِيْهِ وَلِتَبْتَغُوْا مِنْ فَضْلِهٖ وَلَعَلَّكُمْ تَشْكُرُوْنَ ۞

74. And on the day when He shall call them and say: Where are those whom you deemed to be My associates?

وَيَوْمَ يُنَادِيْهِمْ فَيَقُوْلُ اَيْنَ شُرَكَآئِيَ الَّذِيْنَ كُنْتُمْ تَزْعُمُوْنَ ۞

75. And We will draw forth from among every nation a witness and say: Bring your proof; then shall they know that the truth is Allah's, and that which they forged shall depart from them.

وَنَزَعْنَا مِنْ كُلِّ اُمَّةٍ شَهِيْدًا فَقُلْنَا هَاتُوْا بُرْهَانَكُمْ فَعَلِمُوْا اَنَّ الْحَقَّ لِلّٰهِ وَضَلَّ عَنْهُمْ مَّا كَانُوْا يَفْتَرُوْنَ ۞

76. Surely Qaroun was of the people of Musa, but he rebelled against them, and We had given him of the treasures, so much so that his hoards of wealth would certainly weigh down a company of men possessed of great strength. When his people said to him: Do not exult, surely Allah does not love the exultant;

اِنَّ قَارُوْنَ كَانَ مِنْ قَوْمِ مُوْسٰى فَبَغٰى عَلَيْهِمْ ۖ وَاٰتَيْنٰهُ مِنَ الْكُنُوْزِ مَآ اِنَّ مَفَاتِحَهٗ لَتَنُوْٓأُ بِالْعُصْبَةِ اُولِى الْقُوَّةِ ۖ اِذْ قَالَ لَهٗ قَوْمُهٗ لَا تَفْرَحْ اِنَّ اللّٰهَ لَا يُحِبُّ الْفَرِحِيْنَ ۞

77. And seek by means of what Allah has given you the future abode, and do not neglect your portion of this world, and do good (to others) as Allah has done good to you, and do not seek to make mischief in the land, surely Allah does not love the mischief-makers.

وَابْتَغِ فِيْمَآ اٰتٰىكَ اللّٰهُ الدَّارَ الْاٰخِرَةَ وَلَا تَنْسَ نَصِيْبَكَ مِنَ الدُّنْيَا وَاَحْسِنْ كَمَآ اَحْسَنَ اللّٰهُ اِلَيْكَ وَلَا تَبْغِ الْفَسَادَ فِى الْاَرْضِ ؕ اِنَّ اللّٰهَ لَا يُحِبُّ الْمُفْسِدِيْنَ ۞

78. He said: I have been given this only on account of the knowledge I have. Did he not know that Allah had destroyed before him of the generations those who were mightier in strength than he and greater in assemblage? And the guilty shall not be asked about their faults.

قَالَ اِنَّمَاۤ اُوْتِيْتُهٗ عَلٰى عِلْمٍ عِنْدِيْ ۚ اَوَ لَمْ يَعْلَمْ اَنَّ اللّٰهَ قَدْ اَهْلَكَ مِنْ قَبْلِهٖ مِنَ الْقُرُوْنِ مَنْ هُوَ اَشَدُّ مِنْهُ قُوَّةً وَّاَكْثَرُ جَمْعًا ۚ وَلَا يُسْـَٔلُ عَنْ ذُنُوْبِهِمُ الْمُجْرِمُوْنَ ۝

79. So he went forth to his people in his finery. Those who desire this world's life said: O would that we had the like of what Qaroun is given; most surely he is possessed of mighty good fortune.

فَخَرَجَ عَلٰى قَوْمِهٖ فِيْ زِيْنَتِهٖ ۚ قَالَ الَّذِيْنَ يُرِيْدُوْنَ الْحَيٰوةَ الدُّنْيَا يٰلَيْتَ لَنَا مِثْلَ مَاۤ اُوْتِيَ قَارُوْنُ ۙ اِنَّهٗ لَذُوْ حَظٍّ عَظِيْمٍ ۝

80. And those who were given the knowledge said: Woe to you! Allah's reward is better for him who believes and does good, and none is made to receive this except the patient.

وَقَالَ الَّذِيْنَ اُوْتُوا الْعِلْمَ وَيْلَكُمْ ثَوَابُ اللّٰهِ خَيْرٌ لِّمَنْ اٰمَنَ وَعَمِلَ صَالِحًا ۚ وَلَا يُلَقّٰىهَاۤ اِلَّا الصّٰبِرُوْنَ ۝

81. Thus We made the earth to swallow up him and his abode; so he had no body of helpers to assist him against Allah, nor was he of those who can defend themselves.

فَخَسَفْنَا بِهٖ وَبِدَارِهِ الْاَرْضَ ۚ فَمَا كَانَ لَهٗ مِنْ فِئَةٍ يَّنْصُرُوْنَهٗ مِنْ دُوْنِ اللّٰهِ ۖ وَمَا كَانَ مِنَ الْمُنْتَصِرِيْنَ ۝

82. And those who yearned for his place only the day before began to say: Ah! (know) that Allah amplifies and straitens the means of subsistence for whom He pleases of His servants; had not Allah been gracious to us, He would most surely have abased us; ah! (know) that the ungrateful are never successful.

وَاَصْبَحَ الَّذِيْنَ تَمَنَّوْا مَكَانَهٗ بِالْاَمْسِ يَقُوْلُوْنَ وَيْكَاَنَّ اللّٰهَ يَبْسُطُ الرِّزْقَ لِمَنْ يَّشَاۤءُ مِنْ عِبَادِهٖ وَيَقْدِرُ ۚ لَوْلَاۤ اَنْ مَّنَّ اللّٰهُ عَلَيْنَا لَخَسَفَ بِنَا ۚ وَيْكَاَنَّهٗ لَا يُفْلِحُ الْكٰفِرُوْنَ ۝

83. (As for) that future abode, We assign it to those who have no desire to exalt themselves in the earth nor to make mischief and the good end is for those who guard (against evil).

تِلْكَ الدَّارُ الْاٰخِرَةُ نَجْعَلُهَا لِلَّذِيْنَ لَا يُرِيْدُوْنَ عُلُوًّا فِى الْاَرْضِ وَلَا فَسَادًا ۚ وَالْعَاقِبَةُ لِلْمُتَّقِيْنَ ۝

84. Whoever brings good, he shall have better than it, and whoever brings evil, those who do evil shall not be rewarded (for) aught except what they did.

مَنْ جَاۤءَ بِالْحَسَنَةِ فَلَهٗ خَيْرٌ مِّنْهَا ۚ وَمَنْ جَاۤءَ بِالسَّيِّئَةِ فَلَا يُجْزَى الَّذِيْنَ عَمِلُوا السَّيِّاٰتِ اِلَّا مَا كَانُوْا يَعْمَلُوْنَ ۝

85. Most surely He Who has made the Quran binding on you will bring you back to the destination. Say: My Lord knows best him who has brought the guidance and him who is in manifest error.

اِنَّ الَّذِيْ فَرَضَ عَلَيْكَ الْقُرْاٰنَ لَرَاۤدُّكَ اِلٰى مَعَادٍ ۚ قُلْ رَّبِّيْۤ اَعْلَمُ مَنْ جَاۤءَ بِالْهُدٰى وَمَنْ هُوَ فِيْ ضَلٰلٍ مُّبِيْنٍ ۝

86. And you did not expect that the Book would be inspired to you, but it is a mercy from your Lord, therefore be not a backer-up of the unbelievers.

وَمَا كُنْتَ تَرْجُوْا أَنْ يُّلْقَى إِلَيْكَ الْكِتَبُ إِلَّا رَحْمَةً مِّنْ رَّبِّكَ فَلَا تَكُوْنَنَّ ظَهِيْرًا لِّلْكَفِرِيْنَ ۞

87. And let them not turn you aside from the communications of Allah after they have been revealed to you, and call (men) to your Lord and be not of the polytheists.

وَلَا يَصُدُّنَّكَ عَنْ اٰيٰتِ اللّٰهِ بَعْدَ إِذْ أُنْزِلَتْ إِلَيْكَ وَادْعُ إِلَى رَبِّكَ وَلَا تَكُوْنَنَّ مِنَ الْمُشْرِكِيْنَ ۞

88. And call not with Allah any other god; there is no god but He; every thing is perishable but He; His is the judgment, and to Him you shall be brought back.

وَلَا تَدْعُ مَعَ اللّٰهِ إِلٰهًا اٰخَرَ لَا إِلٰهَ إِلَّا هُوَ كُلُّ شَيْءٍ هَالِكٌ إِلَّا وَجْهَهُ لَهُ الْحُكْمُ وَإِلَيْهِ تُرْجَعُوْنَ ۞

THE SPIDER
(ANKABUT)

أَيَاتُهَا ٦٩ ٢٩ سُوْرَةُ الْعَنْكَبُوْتِ مَكِّيَّةٌ رُكُوْعَاتُهَا ٧

**In the name of Allah,
the Beneficent, the Merciful.**

بِسْمِ اللهِ الرَّحْمٰنِ الرَّحِيْمِ ۝

1. Alif Lam Mim.

الٓمّٓ ۝

2. Do men think that they will be left alone on saying, We believe, and not be tried?

اَحَسِبَ النَّاسُ اَنْ يُّتْرَكُوْٓا اَنْ يَّقُوْلُوْٓا اٰمَنَّا وَهُمْ لَا يُفْتَنُوْنَ ۝

3. And certainly We tried those before them, so Allah will certainly know those who are true and He will certainly know the liars.

وَلَقَدْ فَتَنَّا الَّذِيْنَ مِنْ قَبْلِهِمْ فَلَيَعْلَمَنَّ اللهُ الَّذِيْنَ صَدَقُوْا وَلَيَعْلَمَنَّ الْكٰذِبِيْنَ ۝

4. Or do they who work evil think that they will escape Us? Evil is it that they judge!

اَمْ حَسِبَ الَّذِيْنَ يَعْمَلُوْنَ السَّيِّاٰتِ اَنْ يَّسْبِقُوْنَا ۗ سَآءَ مَا يَحْكُمُوْنَ ۝

5. Whoever hopes to meet Allah, the term appointed by Allah will then most surely come; and He is the Hearing, the Knowing.

مَنْ كَانَ يَرْجُوْا لِقَآءَ اللهِ فَاِنَّ اَجَلَ اللهِ لَاٰتٍ ۗ وَهُوَ السَّمِيْعُ الْعَلِيْمُ ۝

6. And whoever strives hard, he strives only for his own soul; most surely Allah is Self-sufficient, above (need of) the worlds.

وَمَنْ جَاهَدَ فَاِنَّمَا يُجَاهِدُ لِنَفْسِهٖ ۗ اِنَّ اللهَ لَغَنِيٌّ عَنِ الْعٰلَمِيْنَ ۝

7. And (as for) those who believe and do good, We will most certainly do away with their evil deeds and We will most certainly reward them the best of what they did.

وَالَّذِيْنَ اٰمَنُوْا وَعَمِلُوا الصّٰلِحٰتِ لَنُكَفِّرَنَّ عَنْهُمْ سَيِّاٰتِهِمْ وَلَنَجْزِيَنَّهُمْ اَحْسَنَ الَّذِيْ كَانُوْا يَعْمَلُوْنَ ۝

8. And We have enjoined on man goodness to his parents, and if they contend with you that you should associate (others) with Me, of which you have no knowledge, do not obey them; to Me is your return, so I will inform you of what you did.

وَوَصَّيْنَا الْاِنْسَانَ بِوَالِدَيْهِ حُسْنًا ۗ وَاِنْ جَاهَدٰكَ لِتُشْرِكَ بِيْ مَا لَيْسَ لَكَ بِهٖ عِلْمٌ فَلَا تُطِعْهُمَا ۗ اِلَيَّ مَرْجِعُكُمْ فَاُنَبِّئُكُمْ بِمَا كُنْتُمْ تَعْمَلُوْنَ ۝

9. And (as for) those who believe and do good, We will most surely cause them to enter among the good.

وَالَّذِيْنَ اٰمَنُوْا وَعَمِلُوا الصّٰلِحٰتِ لَنُدْخِلَنَّهُمْ فِى الصّٰلِحِيْنَ ۝

384

وَمِنَ النَّاسِ مَنْ يَّقُوْلُ اٰمَنَّا بِاللّٰهِ فَاِذَآ اُوْذِيَ فِى اللّٰهِ

10. And among men is he who says: We believe in Allah; but when he is persecuted in (the way of) Allah he thinks the persecution of men to be as the chastisement of Allah: and if there come assistance from your Lord, they would most certainly say: Surely we were with you. What! is not Allah the best knower of what is in the breasts of mankind.

جَعَلَ فِتْنَةَ النَّاسِ كَعَذَابِ اللّٰهِ ۚ وَلَئِنْ جَآءَ نَصْرٌ مِّنْ رَّبِّكَ لَيَقُوْلُنَّ اِنَّا كُنَّا مَعَكُمْ ۚ اَوَلَيْسَ اللّٰهُ بِاَعْلَمَ بِمَا فِيْ صُدُوْرِ الْعٰلَمِيْنَ ۞

11. And most certainly Allah will know those who believe, and most certainly He will know the hypocrites.

وَلَيَعْلَمَنَّ اللّٰهُ الَّذِيْنَ اٰمَنُوْا وَلَيَعْلَمَنَّ الْمُنٰفِقِيْنَ ۞

12. And those who disbelieve say to those who believe: Follow our path and we will bear your wrongs. And never shall they be the bearers of any of their wrongs; most surely they are liars.

وَقَالَ الَّذِيْنَ كَفَرُوْا لِلَّذِيْنَ اٰمَنُوا اتَّبِعُوْا سَبِيْلَنَا وَلْنَحْمِلْ خَطٰيٰكُمْ ۚ وَمَا هُمْ بِحٰمِلِيْنَ مِنْ خَطٰيٰهُمْ مِّنْ شَيْءٍ ۚ اِنَّهُمْ لَكٰذِبُوْنَ ۞

13. And most certainly they shall carry their own burdens, and other burdens with their own burdens, and most certainly they shall be questioned on the resurrection day as to what they forged.

وَلَيَحْمِلُنَّ اَثْقَالَهُمْ وَاَثْقَالًا مَّعَ اَثْقَالِهِمْ ۫ وَلَيُسْـَٔلُنَّ يَوْمَ الْقِيٰمَةِ عَمَّا كَانُوْا يَفْتَرُوْنَ ۞

14. And certainly We sent Nuh to his people, so he remained among them a thousand years save fifty years. And the deluge overtook them, while they were unjust.

وَلَقَدْ اَرْسَلْنَا نُوْحًا اِلٰى قَوْمِهٖ فَلَبِثَ فِيْهِمْ اَلْفَ سَنَةٍ اِلَّا خَمْسِيْنَ عَامًا ۚ فَاَخَذَهُمُ الطُّوْفَانُ وَ هُمْ ظٰلِمُوْنَ ۞

15. So We delivered him and the inmates of the ark, and made it a sign to the nations.

فَاَنْجَيْنٰهُ وَاَصْحٰبَ السَّفِيْنَةِ وَجَعَلْنٰهَآ اٰيَةً لِّلْعٰلَمِيْنَ ۞

16. And (We sent) Ibrahim, when he said to his people: Serve Allah and be careful of (your duty to) Him; this is best for you, if you did but know:

وَاِبْرٰهِيْمَ اِذْ قَالَ لِقَوْمِهِ اعْبُدُوا اللّٰهَ وَاتَّقُوْهُ ۚ ذٰلِكُمْ خَيْرٌ لَّكُمْ اِنْ كُنْتُمْ تَعْلَمُوْنَ ۞

17. You only worship idols besides Allah and you create a lie; surely they whom you serve besides Allah do not control for you any sustenance, therefore seek the sustenance from Allah and serve Him and be grateful to Him; to Him you shall be brought back.

اِنَّمَا تَعْبُدُوْنَ مِنْ دُوْنِ اللّٰهِ اَوْثَانًا وَّتَخْلُقُوْنَ اِفْكًا ۚ اِنَّ الَّذِيْنَ تَعْبُدُوْنَ مِنْ دُوْنِ اللّٰهِ لَا يَمْلِكُوْنَ لَكُمْ رِزْقًا فَابْتَغُوْا عِنْدَ اللّٰهِ الرِّزْقَ وَاعْبُدُوْهُ وَاشْكُرُوْا لَهٗ ۚ اِلَيْهِ تُرْجَعُوْنَ ۞

18. And if you reject (the truth), nations before you did indeed reject (the truth); and nothing is incumbent on the apostle but a plain delivering (of the message).

وَاِنْ تُكَذِّبُوْا فَقَدْ كَذَّبَ اُمَمٌ مِّنْ قَبْلِكُمْ ۚ وَمَا عَلَى الرَّسُوْلِ اِلَّا الْبَلٰغُ الْمُبِيْنُ ۞

19. What! do they not consider how Allah originates the creation, then reproduces it? Surely that is easy to Allah.

اَوَلَمْ يَرَوْا كَيْفَ يُبْدِئُ اللّٰهُ الْخَلْقَ ثُمَّ يُعِيْدُهٗ ۚ اِنَّ ذٰلِكَ عَلَى اللّٰهِ يَسِيْرٌ ۞

20. Say: Travel in the earth and see how He makes the first creation, then Allah creates the latter creation; surely Allah has power over all things.

قُلْ سِيْرُوْا فِى الْاَرْضِ فَانْظُرُوْا كَيْفَ بَدَاَ الْخَلْقَ ثُمَّ اللّٰهُ يُنْشِئُ النَّشْاَةَ الْاٰخِرَةَ ۚ اِنَّ اللّٰهَ عَلٰى كُلِّ شَىْءٍ قَدِيْرٌ ۞

21. He punishes whom He pleases and has mercy on whom He pleases, and to Him you shall be turned back.

يُعَذِّبُ مَنْ يَّشَاۤءُ وَيَرْحَمُ مَنْ يَّشَاۤءُ ۖ وَاِلَيْهِ تُقْلَبُوْنَ ۞

22. And you shall not escape in the earth nor in the heaven, and you have neither a protector nor a helper besides Allah.

وَمَاۤ اَنْتُمْ بِمُعْجِزِيْنَ فِى الْاَرْضِ وَلَا فِى السَّمَاۤءِ ۖ وَمَا لَكُمْ مِّنْ دُوْنِ اللّٰهِ مِنْ وَّلِيٍّ وَّلَا نَصِيْرٍ ۞

23. And (as to) those who disbelieve in the communications of Allah and His meeting, they have despaired of My mercy, and these it is that shall have a painful punishment.

وَالَّذِيْنَ كَفَرُوْا بِاٰيٰتِ اللّٰهِ وَلِقَاۤئِهٖۤ اُولٰۤئِكَ يَئِسُوْا مِنْ رَّحْمَتِيْ وَاُولٰۤئِكَ لَهُمْ عَذَابٌ اَلِيْمٌ ۞

24. So naught was the answer of his people except that they said: Slay him or burn him; then Allah delivered him from the fire; most surely there are signs in this for a people who believe.

فَمَا كَانَ جَوَابَ قَوْمِهٖۤ اِلَّاۤ اَنْ قَالُوا اقْتُلُوْهُ اَوْ حَرِّقُوْهُ فَاَنْجٰهُ اللّٰهُ مِنَ النَّارِ ۚ اِنَّ فِيْ ذٰلِكَ لَاٰيٰتٍ لِّقَوْمٍ يُّؤْمِنُوْنَ ۞

25. And he said: You have only taken for yourselves idols besides Allah by way of friendship between you in this world's life, then on the resurrection day some of you shall deny others, and some of you shall curse others, and your abode is the fire, and you shall not have any helpers.

وَقَالَ اِنَّمَا اتَّخَذْتُمْ مِّنْ دُوْنِ اللّٰهِ اَوْثَانًا ۙ مَّوَدَّةَ بَيْنِكُمْ فِى الْحَيٰوةِ الدُّنْيَا ۚ ثُمَّ يَوْمَ الْقِيٰمَةِ يَكْفُرُ بَعْضُكُمْ بِبَعْضٍ وَّيَلْعَنُ بَعْضُكُمْ بَعْضًا ۖ وَّمَاْوٰىكُمُ النَّارُ وَمَا لَكُمْ مِّنْ نّٰصِرِيْنَ ۞

26. And Lut believed in Him, and he said: I am fleeing to my Lord, surely He is the Mighty, the Wise.

فَاٰمَنَ لَهٗ لُوْطٌ ۘ وَقَالَ اِنِّيْ مُهَاجِرٌ اِلٰى رَبِّيْ ۚ اِنَّهٗ هُوَ الْعَزِيْزُ الْحَكِيْمُ ۞

27. And We granted him Ishaq and Yaqoub, and caused the prophethood and the book to remain in his seed, and We gave him his reward in this world, and in the hereafter he will most surely be among the good.

وَوَهَبْنَا لَهٗۤ اِسْحٰقَ وَيَعْقُوْبَ وَجَعَلْنَا فِيْ ذُرِّيَّتِهِ النُّبُوَّةَ وَالْكِتٰبَ وَاٰتَيْنٰهُ اَجْرَهٗ فِى الدُّنْيَا ۖ وَاِنَّهٗ فِى الْاٰخِرَةِ لَمِنَ الصّٰلِحِيْنَ ۞

28. And (We sent) Lut when he said to his people: Most surely you are guilty of an indecency which none of the nations has ever done before you;

29. What! do you come to the males and commit robbery on the highway, and you commit evil deeds in your assemblies? But nothing was the answer of his people except that they said: Bring on us Allah's punishment, if you are one of the truthful.

30. He said: My Lord! help me against the mischievous people.

31. And when Our messengers came to Ibrahim with the good news, they said: Surely we are going to destroy the people of this town, for its people are unjust.

32. He said: Surely in it is Lut. They said: We know well who is in it; we shall certainly deliver him and his followers, except his wife; she shall be of those who remain behind.

33. And when Our messengers came to Lut he was grieved on account of them, and he felt powerless (to protect) them; and they said: Fear not, nor grieve; surely we will deliver you and your followers, except your wife; she shall be of those who remain behind.

34. Surely We will cause to come down upon the people of this town a punishment from heaven, because they transgressed.

35. And certainly We have left a clear sign of it for a people who understand.

36. And to Madyan (We sent) their brother Shuaib, so he said: O my people! serve Allah and fear the latter day and do not act corruptly in the land, making mischief.

37. But they rejected him, so a severe earthquake overtook them, and they became motionless bodies in their abode.

38. And (We destroyed) Ad and Samood, and from their dwellings (this) is apparent to you indeed; and the Shaitan made their deeds fair-seeming to them, so he kept them back from the path, though they were endowed with intelligence and skill,

39. And (We destroyed) Qaroun and Firon and Haman; and certainly Musa came to them with clear arguments, but they behaved haughtily in the land; yet they could not outstrip (Us).

40. So each We punished for his sin; of them was he on whom We sent down a violent storm, and of them was he whom the rumbling overtook, and of them was he whom We made to be swallowed up by the earth, and of them was he whom We drowned; and it did not beseem Allah that He should be unjust to them, but they were unjust to their own souls.

41. The parable of those who take guardians besides Allah is as the parable of the spider that makes for itself a house; and most surely the frailest of the houses is the spider's house—did they but know.

42. Surely Allah knows whatever thing they call upon besides Him; and He is the Mighty, the Wise.

43. And (as for) these examples, We set them forth for men, and none understand them but the learned.

44. Allah created the heavens and the earth with truth; most surely there is a sign in this for the believers.

45. Recite that which has been revealed to you of the Book and keep up prayer; surely prayer keeps (one) away from indecency and evil, and certainly the remembrance of Allah is the greatest, and Allah knows what you do.

46. And do not dispute with the followers of the Book except by what is best, except those of them who act unjustly, and say: We believe in that which has been revealed to us and revealed to you, and our God and your God is One, and to Him do we submit.

 وَلَا تُجَادِلُوٓا أَهْلَ الْكِتَٰبِ إِلَّا بِالَّتِى هِىَ أَحْسَنُ إِلَّا الَّذِينَ ظَلَمُوا مِنْهُمْ وَقُولُوٓا ءَامَنَّا بِالَّذِىٓ أُنزِلَ إِلَيْنَا وَأُنزِلَ إِلَيْكُمْ وَإِلَٰهُنَا وَإِلَٰهُكُمْ وَاحِدٌ وَّنَحْنُ لَهُۥ مُسْلِمُونَ ﴿٤٦﴾

47. And thus have We revealed the Book to you. So those whom We have given the Book believe in it, and of these there are those who believe in it, and none deny Our communications except the unbelievers.

وَكَذَٰلِكَ أَنزَلْنَآ إِلَيْكَ الْكِتَٰبَ فَالَّذِينَ ءَاتَيْنَٰهُمُ الْكِتَٰبَ يُؤْمِنُونَ بِهِۦ وَمِنْ هَٰٓؤُلَآءِ مَن يُؤْمِنُ بِهِۦ وَمَا يَجْحَدُ بِـَٔايَٰتِنَآ إِلَّا الْكَٰفِرُونَ ﴿٤٧﴾

48. And you did not recite before it any book, nor did you transcribe one with your right hand, for then could those who say untrue things have doubted.

وَمَا كُنتَ تَتْلُوا مِن قَبْلِهِۦ مِن كِتَٰبٍ وَلَا تَخُطُّهُۥ بِيَمِينِكَ إِذًا لَّارْتَابَ الْمُبْطِلُونَ ﴿٤٨﴾

49. Nay! these are clear communications in the breasts of those who are granted knowledge; and none deny Our communications except the unjust.

بَلْ هُوَ ءَايَٰتٌ بَيِّنَٰتٌ فِى صُدُورِ الَّذِينَ أُوتُوا الْعِلْمَ وَمَا يَجْحَدُ بِـَٔايَٰتِنَآ إِلَّا الظَّٰلِمُونَ ﴿٤٩﴾

50. And they say: Why are not signs sent down upon him from his Lord? Say: The signs are only with Allah, and I am only a plain warner.

وَقَالُوا لَوْلَآ أُنزِلَ عَلَيْهِ ءَايَٰتٌ مِّن رَّبِّهِۦ قُلْ إِنَّمَا الْءَايَٰتُ عِندَ اللّٰهِ وَإِنَّمَآ أَنَا نَذِيرٌ مُّبِينٌ ﴿٥٠﴾

51. Is it not enough for them that We have revealed to you the Book which is recited to them? Most surely there is mercy in this and a reminder for a people who believe.

أَوَلَمْ يَكْفِهِمْ أَنَّآ أَنزَلْنَا عَلَيْكَ الْكِتَٰبَ يُتْلَىٰ عَلَيْهِمْ إِنَّ فِى ذَٰلِكَ لَرَحْمَةً وَذِكْرَىٰ لِقَوْمٍ يُؤْمِنُونَ ﴿٥١﴾

52. Say: Allah is sufficient as a witness between me and you; He knows what is in the heavens and the earth. And (as for) those who believe in the falsehood and disbelieve in Allah, these it is that are the losers.

قُلْ كَفَىٰ بِاللّٰهِ بَيْنِى وَبَيْنَكُمْ شَهِيدًا يَعْلَمُ مَا فِى السَّمَٰوَٰتِ وَالْأَرْضِ وَالَّذِينَ ءَامَنُوا بِالْبَٰطِلِ وَكَفَرُوا بِاللّٰهِ أُو۟لَٰٓئِكَ هُمُ الْخَٰسِرُونَ ﴿٥٢﴾

53. And they ask you to hasten on the chastisement; and had not a term been appointed, the chastisement would certainly have come to them; and most certainly it will come to them all of a sudden while they will not perceive.

وَيَسْتَعْجِلُونَكَ بِالْعَذَابِ وَلَوْلَآ أَجَلٌ مُّسَمًّى لَّجَآءَهُمُ الْعَذَابُ وَلَيَأْتِيَنَّهُم بَغْتَةً وَهُمْ لَا يَشْعُرُونَ ﴿٥٣﴾

54. They ask you to hasten on the chastisement, and most surely hell encompasses the unbelievers;

يَسْتَعْجِلُونَكَ بِالْعَذَابِ وَإِنَّ جَهَنَّمَ لَمُحِيطَةٌ بِالْكَٰفِرِينَ ﴿٥٤﴾

55. On the day when the chastisement shall cover them from above them, and from beneath their feet; and He shall say: Taste what you did.

يَوْمَ يَغْشَاهُمُ الْعَذَابُ مِنْ فَوْقِهِمْ وَمِنْ تَحْتِ اَرْجُلِهِمْ وَيَقُوْلُ ذُوْقُوْا مَا كُنْتُمْ تَعْمَلُوْنَ ۞

56. O My servants who believe! surely My earth is vast, therefore Me alone should you serve.

يٰعِبَادِيَ الَّذِيْنَ اٰمَنُوْۤا اِنَّ اَرْضِيْ وَاسِعَةٌ فَاِيَّايَ فَاعْبُدُوْنِ ۞

57. Every soul must taste of death, then to Us you shall be brought back.

كُلُّ نَفْسٍ ذَآئِقَةُ الْمَوْتِ ثُمَّ اِلَيْنَا تُرْجَعُوْنَ ۞

58. And (as for) those who believe and do good, We will certainly give them abode in the high places in gardens beneath which rivers flow, abiding therein; how good the reward of the workers:

وَالَّذِيْنَ اٰمَنُوْا وَعَمِلُوا الصّٰلِحٰتِ لَنُبَوِّئَنَّهُمْ مِّنَ الْجَنَّةِ غُرَفًا تَجْرِيْ مِنْ تَحْتِهَا الْاَنْهٰرُ خٰلِدِيْنَ فِيْهَا نِعْمَ اَجْرُ الْعٰمِلِيْنَ ۞

59. Those who are patient, and on their Lord do they rely.

الَّذِيْنَ صَبَرُوْا وَعَلٰى رَبِّهِمْ يَتَوَكَّلُوْنَ ۞

60. And how many a living creature that does not carry its sustenance: Allah sustains it and yourselves; and He is the Hearing, the Knowing.

وَكَاَيِّنْ مِّنْ دَآبَّةٍ لَّا تَحْمِلُ رِزْقَهَا ۖ اَللّٰهُ يَرْزُقُهَا وَاِيَّاكُمْ ۖ وَهُوَ السَّمِيْعُ الْعَلِيْمُ ۞

61. And if you ask them, Who created the heavens and the earth and made the sun and the moon subservient, they will certainly say, Allah. Whence are they then turned away?

وَلَئِنْ سَاَلْتَهُمْ مَّنْ خَلَقَ السَّمٰوٰتِ وَالْاَرْضَ وَسَخَّرَ الشَّمْسَ وَالْقَمَرَ لَيَقُوْلُنَّ اللّٰهُ ۖ فَاَنّٰى يُؤْفَكُوْنَ ۞

62. Allah makes abundant the means of subsistence for whom He pleases of His servants, and straitens them for whom (He pleases) surely Allah is Cognizant of all things.

اَللّٰهُ يَبْسُطُ الرِّزْقَ لِمَنْ يَّشَآءُ مِنْ عِبَادِهٖ وَيَقْدِرُ لَهٗ ۚ اِنَّ اللّٰهَ بِكُلِّ شَيْءٍ عَلِيْمٌ ۞

63. And if you ask them Who is it that sends down water from the clouds, then gives life to the earth with it after its death, they will certainly say, Allah. Say: All praise is due to Allah. Nay, most of them do not understand.

وَلَئِنْ سَاَلْتَهُمْ مَّنْ نَّزَّلَ مِنَ السَّمَآءِ مَآءً فَاَحْيَا بِهِ الْاَرْضَ مِنْ بَعْدِ مَوْتِهَا لَيَقُوْلُنَّ اللّٰهُ ۖ قُلِ الْحَمْدُ لِلّٰهِ ۚ بَلْ اَكْثَرُهُمْ لَا يَعْقِلُوْنَ ۞

64. And this life of the world is nothing but a sport and a play; and as for the next abode, that most surely is the life—did they but know!

وَمَا هٰذِهِ الْحَيٰوةُ الدُّنْيَاۤ اِلَّا لَهْوٌ وَّلَعِبٌ ۚ وَاِنَّ الدَّارَ الْاٰخِرَةَ لَهِيَ الْحَيَوَانُ ۘ لَوْ كَانُوْا يَعْلَمُوْنَ ۞

65. So when they ride in the ships they call upon Allah, being sincerely obedient to Him, but when He brings them safe to the land, lo! they associate others (with Him);

فَاِذَا رَكِبُوْا فِي الْفُلْكِ دَعَوُا اللّٰهَ مُخْلِصِيْنَ لَهُ الدِّيْنَ ۚ فَلَمَّا نَجّٰهُمْ اِلَى الْبَرِّ اِذَا هُمْ يُشْرِكُوْنَ ۞

390

66. Thus they become ungrateful for what We have given them, so that they may enjoy; but they shall soon know.

67. Do they not see that We have made a sacred territory secure, while men are carried off by force from around them? Will they still believe in the falsehood and disbelieve in the favour of Allah?

68. And who is more unjust than one who forges a lie against Allah, or gives the lie to the truth when it has come to him? Will not in hell be the abode of the unbelievers?

69. And (as for) those who strive hard for Us, We will most certainly guide them in Our ways; and Allah is most surely with the doers of good.

لِيَكْفُرُوْا بِمَآ اٰتَيْنٰهُمْ ۙ وَلِيَتَمَتَّعُوْا ۟ فَسَوْفَ يَعْلَمُوْنَ ۝

اَوَلَمْ يَرَوْا اَنَّا جَعَلْنَا حَرَمًا اٰمِنًا وَّيُتَخَطَّفُ النَّاسُ مِنْ حَوْلِهِمْ ؕ اَفَبِالْبَاطِلِ يُؤْمِنُوْنَ وَبِنِعْمَةِ اللّٰهِ يَكْفُرُوْنَ ۝

وَمَنْ اَظْلَمُ مِمَّنِ افْتَرٰى عَلَى اللّٰهِ كَذِبًا اَوْ كَذَّبَ بِالْحَقِّ لَمَّا جَآءَهٗ ؕ اَلَيْسَ فِيْ جَهَنَّمَ مَثْوًى لِّلْكٰفِرِيْنَ ۝ وَالَّذِيْنَ جَاهَدُوْا فِيْنَا لَنَهْدِيَنَّهُمْ سُبُلَنَا ؕ وَاِنَّ اللّٰهَ لَمَعَ الْمُحْسِنِيْنَ ۞

THE ROMANS
(RUM)

اياتها (٣٠) سورة الروم مكية ركوعاتها

**In the name of Allah,
the Beneficent, the Merciful.**

بِسْمِ اللهِ الرَّحْمٰنِ الرَّحِيْمِ

1. Alif Lam Mim.

الٓمّٓ ۚ

2. The Romans are vanquished,

غُلِبَتِ الرُّوْمُ ۙ

3. In a near land, and they, after being vanquished, shall overcome,

فِىْۤ اَدْنَى الْاَرْضِ وَهُمْ مِّنْۢ بَعْدِ غَلَبِهِمْ سَيَغْلِبُوْنَ ۙ

4. Within a few years. Allah's is the command before and after; and on that day the believers shall rejoice,

فِىْ بِضْعِ سِنِيْنَ ۚ لِلّٰهِ الْاَمْرُ مِنْ قَبْلُ وَمِنْۢ بَعْدُ ۚ وَيَوْمَىِٕذٍ يَّفْرَحُ الْمُؤْمِنُوْنَ ۙ

5. With the help of Allah; He helps whom He pleases; and He is the Mighty, the Merciful;

بِنَصْرِ اللهِ ۚ يَنْصُرُ مَنْ يَّشَآءُ ۚ وَهُوَ الْعَزِيْزُ الرَّحِيْمُ ۙ

6. (This is) Allah's promise! Allah will not fail His promise, but most people do not know.

وَعْدَ اللهِ ۚ لَا يُخْلِفُ اللهُ وَعْدَهٗ وَلٰكِنَّ اَكْثَرَ النَّاسِ لَا يَعْلَمُوْنَ ۞

7. They know the outward of this world's life, but of the hereafter they are absolutely heedless.

يَعْلَمُوْنَ ظَاهِرًا مِّنَ الْحَيٰوةِ الدُّنْيَا ۖ وَهُمْ عَنِ الْاٰخِرَةِ هُمْ غٰفِلُوْنَ ۞

8. Do they not reflect within themselves: Allah did not create the heavens and the earth and what is between them two but with truth, and (for) an appointed term? And most surely most of the people are deniers of the meeting of their Lord.

اَوَلَمْ يَتَفَكَّرُوْا فِىْۤ اَنْفُسِهِمْ ۗ مَا خَلَقَ اللهُ السَّمٰوٰتِ وَالْاَرْضَ وَمَا بَيْنَهُمَاۤ اِلَّا بِالْحَقِّ وَاَجَلٍ مُّسَمًّى ۗ وَاِنَّ كَثِيْرًا مِّنَ النَّاسِ بِلِقَآئِ رَبِّهِمْ لَكٰفِرُوْنَ ۞

9. Have they not travelled in the earth and seen how was the end of those before them? They were stronger than these in prowess, and dug up the earth, and built on it in greater abundance than these have built on it, and there came to them their apostles with clear arguments; so it was not beseeming for Allah that He should deal with them unjustly, but they dealt unjustly with their own souls.

اَوَلَمْ يَسِيْرُوْا فِى الْاَرْضِ فَيَنْظُرُوْا كَيْفَ كَانَ عَاقِبَةُ الَّذِيْنَ مِنْ قَبْلِهِمْ ۚ كَانُوْۤا اَشَدَّ مِنْهُمْ قُوَّةً وَّاَثَارُوا الْاَرْضَ وَعَمَرُوْهَاۤ اَكْثَرَ مِمَّا عَمَرُوْهَا وَجَآءَتْهُمْ رُسُلُهُمْ بِالْبَيِّنٰتِ ۚ فَمَا كَانَ اللهُ لِيَظْلِمَهُمْ وَلٰكِنْ كَانُوْۤا اَنْفُسَهُمْ يَظْلِمُوْنَ ۞

10. Then evil was the end of those who did evil, because they rejected the communications of Allah and used to mock them.

ثُمَّ كَانَ عَاقِبَةَ الَّذِينَ أَسَاءُوا السُّوأَى أَنْ كَذَّبُوْا بِاٰيٰتِ اللهِ وَكَانُوْا بِهَا يَسْتَهْزِءُوْنَ ۩

11. Allah originates the creation, then reproduces it, then to Him you shall be brought back.

اَللهُ يَبْدَؤُا الْخَلْقَ ثُمَّ يُعِيْدُهُ ثُمَّ اِلَيْهِ تُرْجَعُوْنَ ۝

12. And at the time when the hour shall come the guilty shall be in despair.

وَيَوْمَ تَقُوْمُ السَّاعَةُ يُبْلِسُ الْمُجْرِمُوْنَ ۝

13. And they shall not have any intercessors from among their gods they have joined with God, and they shall be deniers of their associate-gods.

وَلَمْ يَكُنْ لَّهُمْ مِّنْ شُرَكَآئِهِمْ شُفَعٰٓؤُا وَكَانُوْا بِشُرَكَآئِهِمْ كٰفِرِيْنَ ۝

14. And at the time when the hour shall come, at that time they shall become separated one from the other.

وَيَوْمَ تَقُوْمُ السَّاعَةُ يَوْمَئِذٍ يَّتَفَرَّقُوْنَ ۝

15. Then as to those who believed and did good, they shall be made happy in a garden.

فَاَمَّا الَّذِيْنَ اٰمَنُوْا وَعَمِلُوا الصّٰلِحٰتِ فَهُمْ فِيْ رَوْضَةٍ يُّحْبَرُوْنَ ۝

16. And as to those who disbelieved and rejected Our communications and the meeting of the hereafter, these shall be brought over to the chastisement.

وَاَمَّا الَّذِيْنَ كَفَرُوْا وَكَذَّبُوْا بِاٰيٰتِنَا وَلِقَآئِ الْاٰخِرَةِ فَاُولٰٓئِكَ فِى الْعَذَابِ مُحْضَرُوْنَ ۝

17. Therefore glory be to Allah when you enter upon the time of the evening and when you enter upon the time of the morning.

فَسُبْحٰنَ اللهِ حِيْنَ تُمْسُوْنَ وَحِيْنَ تُصْبِحُوْنَ ۝

18. And to Him belongs praise in the heavens and the earth, and at nightfall and when you are at midday.

وَلَهُ الْحَمْدُ فِى السَّمٰوٰتِ وَالْاَرْضِ وَعَشِيًّا وَّحِيْنَ تُظْهِرُوْنَ ۝

19. He brings forth the living from the dead and brings forth the dead from the living, and gives life to the earth after its death, and thus shall you be brought forth.

يُخْرِجُ الْحَيَّ مِنَ الْمَيِّتِ وَيُخْرِجُ الْمَيِّتَ مِنَ الْحَيِّ وَيُحْيِ الْاَرْضَ بَعْدَ مَوْتِهَا وَكَذٰلِكَ تُخْرَجُوْنَ ۝

20. And one of His signs is that He created you from dust, then lo! you are mortals (who) scatter.

وَمِنْ اٰيٰتِهٖٓ اَنْ خَلَقَكُمْ مِّنْ تُرَابٍ ثُمَّ اِذَآ اَنْتُمْ بَشَرٌ تَنْتَشِرُوْنَ ۝

21. And one of His signs is that He created mates for you from yourselves that you may find rest in them, and He put between you love and compassion; most surely there are signs in this for a people who reflect.

وَمِنْ اٰيٰتِهٖٓ اَنْ خَلَقَ لَكُمْ مِّنْ اَنْفُسِكُمْ اَزْوَاجًا لِّتَسْكُنُوْٓا اِلَيْهَا وَجَعَلَ بَيْنَكُمْ مَّوَدَّةً وَّرَحْمَةً اِنَّ فِيْ ذٰلِكَ لَاٰيٰتٍ لِّقَوْمٍ يَّتَفَكَّرُوْنَ ۝

22. And one of His signs is the creation of the heavens and the earth and the diversity of your tongues and colors; most surely there are signs in this for the learned.

وَمِنْ اٰیٰتِهٖ خَلْقُ السَّمٰوٰتِ وَالْاَرْضِ وَاخْتِلَافُ اَلْسِنَتِكُمْ وَاَلْوَانِكُمْ اِنَّ فِیْ ذٰلِكَ لَاٰیٰتٍ لِّلْعٰلِمِیْنَ ۞

23. And one of His signs is your sleeping and your seeking of His grace by night and (by) day; most surely there are signs in this for a people who would hear.

وَمِنْ اٰیٰتِهٖ مَنَامُكُمْ بِالَّیْلِ وَالنَّهَارِ وَابْتِغَآؤُكُمْ مِّنْ فَضْلِهٖ اِنَّ فِیْ ذٰلِكَ لَاٰیٰتٍ لِّقَوْمٍ یَّسْمَعُوْنَ ۞

24. And one of His signs is that He shows you the lightning for fear and for hope, and sends down water from the clouds, then gives life therewith to the earth after its death; most surely there are signs in this for a people who understand.

وَمِنْ اٰیٰتِهٖ یُرِیْكُمُ الْبَرْقَ خَوْفًا وَّطَمَعًا وَّیُنَزِّلُ مِنَ السَّمَآءِ مَآءً فَیُحْیٖ بِهِ الْاَرْضَ بَعْدَ مَوْتِهَا اِنَّ فِیْ ذٰلِكَ لَاٰیٰتٍ لِّقَوْمٍ یَّعْقِلُوْنَ ۞

25. And one of His signs is that the heaven and the earth subsist by His command, then when He calls you with a (single) call from out of the earth, lo! you come forth.

وَمِنْ اٰیٰتِهٖ اَنْ تَقُوْمَ السَّمَآءُ وَالْاَرْضُ بِاَمْرِهٖ ثُمَّ اِذَا دَعَاكُمْ دَعْوَةً مِّنَ الْاَرْضِ اِذَآ اَنْتُمْ تَخْرُجُوْنَ ۞

26. And His is whosoever is in the heavens and the earth; all are obedient to Him.

وَلَهٗ مَنْ فِی السَّمٰوٰتِ وَالْاَرْضِ كُلٌّ لَّهٗ قٰنِتُوْنَ ۞

27. And He it is Who originates the creation, then reproduces it, and it is easy to Him; and His are the most exalted attributes in the heavens and the earth, and He is the Mighty, the Wise.

وَهُوَ الَّذِیْ یَبْدَؤُا الْخَلْقَ ثُمَّ یُعِیْدُهٗ وَهُوَ اَهْوَنُ عَلَیْهِ وَلَهُ الْمَثَلُ الْاَعْلٰی فِی السَّمٰوٰتِ وَالْاَرْضِ وَهُوَ الْعَزِیْزُ الْحَكِیْمُ ۞

28. He sets forth to you a parable relating to yourselves: Have you among those whom your right hands possess partners in what We have given you for sustenance, so that with respect to it you are alike; you fear them as you fear each other? Thus do We make the communications distinct for a people who understand.

ضَرَبَ لَكُمْ مَّثَلًا مِّنْ اَنْفُسِكُمْ هَلْ لَّكُمْ مِّنْ مَّا مَلَكَتْ اَیْمَانُكُمْ مِّنْ شُرَكَآءَ فِیْ مَا رَزَقْنٰكُمْ فَاَنْتُمْ فِیْهِ سَوَآءٌ تَخَافُوْنَهُمْ كَخِیْفَتِكُمْ اَنْفُسَكُمْ كَذٰلِكَ نُفَصِّلُ الْاٰیٰتِ لِقَوْمٍ یَّعْقِلُوْنَ ۞

29. Nay! those who are unjust follow their low desires without any knowledge; so who can guide him whom Allah makes err? And they shall have no helpers.

بَلِ اتَّبَعَ الَّذِیْنَ ظَلَمُوْا اَهْوَآءَهُمْ بِغَیْرِ عِلْمٍ فَمَنْ یَّهْدِیْ مَنْ اَضَلَّ اللّٰهُ وَمَا لَهُمْ مِّنْ نّٰصِرِیْنَ ۞

30. Then set your face upright for religion in the right state—the nature made by Allah in which He has made men; there is no altering of Allah's creation; that is the right religion, but most people do not know—

31. Turning to Him, and be careful of (your duty to) Him, and keep up prayer and be not of the polytheists,

32. Of those who divided their religion and became sects, every sect rejoicing in what they had with them.

33. And when harm afflicts men, they call upon their Lord, turning to Him, then when He makes them taste of mercy from Him, lo! some of them begin to associate (others) with their Lord,

34. So as to be ungrateful for what We have given them; but enjoy yourselves (for a while), for you shall soon come to know.

35. Or, have We sent down upon them an authority so that it speaks of that which they associate with Him?

36. And when We make people taste of mercy they rejoice in it, and if an evil befall them for what their hands have already wrought, lo! they are in despair.

37. Do they not see that Allah makes ample provision for whom He pleases, or straitens? Most surely there are signs in this for a people who believe.

38. Then give to the near of kin his due, and to the needy and the wayfarer; this is best for those who desire Allah's pleasure, and these it is who are successful.

39. And whatever you lay out as usury, so that it may increase in the property of men, it shall not increase with Allah; and whatever you give in charity, desiring Allah's pleasure—it is these (persons) that shall get manifold.

395

40. Allah is He Who created you, then gave you sustenance, then He causes you to die, then brings you to life. Is there any of your associate-gods who does aught of it? Glory be to Him, and exalted be He above what they associate (with Him).

اللهُ الَّذِيْ خَلَقَكُمْ ثُمَّ رَزَقَكُمْ ثُمَّ يُمِيْتُكُمْ ثُمَّ يُحْيِيْكُمْ ۗ هَلْ مِنْ شُرَكَآئِكُمْ مَّنْ يَّفْعَلُ مِنْ ذٰلِكُمْ مِّنْ شَيْءٍ ۗ سُبْحٰنَهٗ وَتَعٰلٰى عَمَّا يُشْرِكُوْنَ ۝

41. Corruption has appeared in the land and the sea on account of what the hands of men have wrought, that He may make them taste a part of that which they have done, so that they may return.

ظَهَرَ الْفَسَادُ فِي الْبَرِّ وَالْبَحْرِ بِمَا كَسَبَتْ اَيْدِى النَّاسِ لِيُذِيْقَهُمْ بَعْضَ الَّذِيْ عَمِلُوْا لَعَلَّهُمْ يَرْجِعُوْنَ ۝

42. Say: Travel in the land, then see how was the end of those before; most of them were polytheists.

قُلْ سِيْرُوْا فِي الْاَرْضِ فَانْظُرُوْا كَيْفَ كَانَ عَاقِبَةُ الَّذِيْنَ مِنْ قَبْلُ ۗ كَانَ اَكْثَرُهُمْ مُّشْرِكِيْنَ ۝

43. Then turn thy face straight to the right religion before there come from Allah the day which cannot be averted; on that day they shall become separated.

فَاَقِمْ وَجْهَكَ لِلدِّيْنِ الْقَيِّمِ مِنْ قَبْلِ اَنْ يَّأْتِيَ يَوْمٌ لَّا مَرَدَّ لَهٗ مِنَ اللهِ يَوْمَئِذٍ يَّصَّدَّعُوْنَ ۝

44. Whoever disbelieves, he shall be responsible for his disbelief, and whoever does good, they prepare (good) for their own souls,

مَنْ كَفَرَ فَعَلَيْهِ كُفْرُهٗ ۚ وَمَنْ عَمِلَ صَالِحًا فَلِاَنْفُسِهِمْ يَمْهَدُوْنَ ۝

45. That He may reward those who believe and do good out of His grace; surely He does not love the unbelievers.

لِيَجْزِيَ الَّذِيْنَ اٰمَنُوْا وَعَمِلُوا الصّٰلِحٰتِ مِنْ فَضْلِهٖ ۗ اِنَّهٗ لَا يُحِبُّ الْكٰفِرِيْنَ ۝

46. And one of His signs is that He sends forth the winds bearing good news, and that He may make you taste of His mercy, and that the ships may run by His command, and that you may seek of His grace, and that you may be grateful.

وَمِنْ اٰيٰتِهٖ اَنْ يُّرْسِلَ الرِّيٰحَ مُبَشِّرٰتٍ وَّلِيُذِيْقَكُمْ مِّنْ رَّحْمَتِهٖ وَلِتَجْرِيَ الْفُلْكُ بِاَمْرِهٖ وَلِتَبْتَغُوْا مِنْ فَضْلِهٖ وَلَعَلَّكُمْ تَشْكُرُوْنَ ۝

47. And certainly We sent before you apostles to their people, so they came to them with clear arguments, then We gave the punishment to those who were guilty; and helping the believers is ever incumbent on Us.

وَلَقَدْ اَرْسَلْنَا مِنْ قَبْلِكَ رُسُلًا اِلٰى قَوْمِهِمْ فَجَآءُوْهُمْ بِالْبَيِّنٰتِ فَانْتَقَمْنَا مِنَ الَّذِيْنَ اَجْرَمُوْا ۗ وَكَانَ حَقًّا عَلَيْنَا نَصْرُ الْمُؤْمِنِيْنَ ۝

48. Allah is He Who sends forth the winds so they raise a cloud, then He spreads it forth in the sky as He pleases, and He breaks it up so that you see the rain coming forth from inside it; then when He causes it to fall upon whom He pleases of His servants, lo! they are joyful,

اَللّٰهُ الَّذِيْ يُرْسِلُ الرِّيٰحَ فَتُثِيْرُ سَحَابًا فَيَبْسُطُهٗ فِي السَّمَآءِ كَيْفَ يَشَآءُ وَيَجْعَلُهٗ كِسَفًا فَتَرَى الْوَدْقَ يَخْرُجُ مِنْ خِلٰلِهٖ ۚ فَاِذَآ اَصَابَ بِهٖ مَنْ يَّشَآءُ مِنْ عِبَادِهٖٓ اِذَا هُمْ يَسْتَبْشِرُوْنَ ۚ

49. Though they were before this, before it was sent down upon them, confounded in sure despair.

وَاِنْ كَانُوْا مِنْ قَبْلِ اَنْ يُّنَزَّلَ عَلَيْهِمْ مِّنْ قَبْلِهٖ لَمُبْلِسِيْنَ ۝

50. Look then at the signs of Allah's mercy, how He gives life to the earth after its death, most surely He will raise the dead to life; and He has power over all things.

فَانْظُرْ اِلٰٓى اٰثٰرِ رَحْمَتِ اللّٰهِ كَيْفَ يُحْيِ الْاَرْضَ بَعْدَ مَوْتِهَا ۚ اِنَّ ذٰلِكَ لَمُحْيِ الْمَوْتٰى ۚ وَهُوَ عَلٰى كُلِّ شَيْءٍ قَدِيْرٌ ۝

51. And if We send a wind and they see it to be yellow, they would after that certainly continue to disbelieve.

وَلَئِنْ اَرْسَلْنَا رِيْحًا فَرَاَوْهُ مُصْفَرًّا لَّظَلُّوْا مِنْ بَعْدِهٖ يَكْفُرُوْنَ ۝

52. For surely you cannot make the dead to hear and you cannot make the deaf to hear the call, when they turn back and flee.

فَاِنَّكَ لَا تُسْمِعُ الْمَوْتٰى وَلَا تُسْمِعُ الصُّمَّ الدُّعَآءَ اِذَا وَلَّوْا مُدْبِرِيْنَ ۝

53. Nor can you lead away the blind out of their error. You cannot make to hear any but those who believe in Our communications so they shall submit.

وَمَآ اَنْتَ بِهٰدِ الْعُمْيِ عَنْ ضَلٰلَتِهِمْ ۚ اِنْ تُسْمِعُ اِلَّا مَنْ يُّؤْمِنُ بِاٰيٰتِنَا فَهُمْ مُّسْلِمُوْنَ ۝

54. Allah is He Who created you from a state of weakness, then He gave strength after weakness, then ordained weakness and hoary hair after strength; He creates what He pleases, and He is the Knowing, the Powerful.

اَللّٰهُ الَّذِيْ خَلَقَكُمْ مِّنْ ضَعْفٍ ثُمَّ جَعَلَ مِنْ بَعْدِ ضَعْفٍ قُوَّةً ثُمَّ جَعَلَ مِنْ بَعْدِ قُوَّةٍ ضَعْفًا وَّشَيْبَةً ۚ يَخْلُقُ مَا يَشَآءُ ۚ وَهُوَ الْعَلِيْمُ الْقَدِيْرُ ۝

55. And at the time when the hour shall come, the guilty shall swear (that) they did not tarry but an hour; thus are they ever turned away.

وَيَوْمَ تَقُوْمُ السَّاعَةُ يُقْسِمُ الْمُجْرِمُوْنَ ۙ مَا لَبِثُوْا غَيْرَ سَاعَةٍ ۚ كَذٰلِكَ كَانُوْا يُؤْفَكُوْنَ ۝

56. And those who are given knowledge and faith will say: Certainly you tarried according to the ordinance of Allah till the day of resurrection, so this is the day of resurrection, but you did not know.

وَقَالَ الَّذِيْنَ اُوْتُوا الْعِلْمَ وَالْاِيْمَانَ لَقَدْ لَبِثْتُمْ فِيْ كِتٰبِ اللّٰهِ اِلٰى يَوْمِ الْبَعْثِ ۚ فَهٰذَا يَوْمُ الْبَعْثِ وَلٰكِنَّكُمْ كُنْتُمْ لَا تَعْلَمُوْنَ ۝

57. But on that day their excuse shall not profit those who were unjust, nor shall they be regarded with goodwill.

فَيَوْمَئِذٍ لَّا يَنْفَعُ الَّذِيْنَ ظَلَمُوْا مَعْذِرَتُهُمْ وَلَاهُمْ يُسْتَعْتَبُوْنَ ۞

58. And certainly We have set forth for men every kind of example in this Quran; and if you should bring them a communication, those who disbelieve would certainly say: You are naught but false claimants.

وَلَقَدْ ضَرَبْنَا لِلنَّاسِ فِيْ هٰذَا الْقُرْاٰنِ مِنْ كُلِّ مَثَلٍ وَلَئِنْ جِئْتَهُمْ بِاٰيَةٍ لَّيَقُوْلَنَّ الَّذِيْنَ كَفَرُوْۤا اِنْ اَنْتُمْ اِلَّا مُبْطِلُوْنَ ۞

59. Thus does Allah set a seal on the hearts of those who do not know.

كَذٰلِكَ يَطْبَعُ اللّٰهُ عَلٰى قُلُوْبِ الَّذِيْنَ لَا يَعْلَمُوْنَ ۞

60. Therefore be patient; surely the promise of Allah is true, and let not those who have no certainty hold you in light estimation.

فَاصْبِرْ اِنَّ وَعْدَ اللّٰهِ حَقٌّ وَّلَا يَسْتَخِفَّنَّكَ الَّذِيْنَ لَا يُوْقِنُوْنَ ۞

LUQMAN

اتل مآ اوحی ٢١ (٣١) سُوْرَةُ لُقْمٰنَ مَكِّيَّةٌ رُكُوْعَاتُهَا

**In the name of Allah,
The Beneficent, The Merciful.**

بِسْمِ اللّٰهِ الرَّحْمٰنِ الرَّحِيْمِ ۞

1. Alif Lam Mim.

الٓمّٓ ۞

2. These are verses of the Book of Wisdom,

تِلْكَ اٰيٰتُ الْكِتٰبِ الْحَكِيْمِ ۞

3. A guidance and a mercy for the doers of goodness,

هُدًى وَّرَحْمَةً لِّلْمُحْسِنِيْنَ ۞

4. Those who keep up prayer and pay the poor-rate and they are certain of the hereafter.

الَّذِيْنَ يُقِيْمُوْنَ الصَّلٰوةَ وَيُؤْتُوْنَ الزَّكٰوةَ وَهُمْ بِالْاٰخِرَةِ هُمْ يُوْقِنُوْنَ ۞

5. These are on a guidance from their Lord, and these are they who are successful.

اُولٰٓئِكَ عَلٰى هُدًى مِّنْ رَّبِّهِمْ وَاُولٰٓئِكَ هُمُ الْمُفْلِحُوْنَ ۞

6. And of men is he who takes instead frivolous discourse to lead astray from Allah's path without knowledge, and to take it for a mockery; these shall have an abasing chastisement.

وَمِنَ النَّاسِ مَنْ يَّشْتَرِيْ لَهْوَ الْحَدِيْثِ لِيُضِلَّ عَنْ سَبِيْلِ اللّٰهِ بِغَيْرِ عِلْمٍ وَّيَتَّخِذَهَا هُزُوًا اُولٰٓئِكَ لَهُمْ عَذَابٌ مُّهِيْنٌ ۞

7. And when Our communications are recited to him, he turns back proudly, as if he had not heard them, as though in his ears were a heaviness, therefore announce to him a painful chastisement.

وَاِذَا تُتْلٰى عَلَيْهِ اٰيٰتُنَا وَلّٰى مُسْتَكْبِرًا كَاَنْ لَّمْ يَسْمَعْهَا كَاَنَّ فِيْ اُذُنَيْهِ وَقْرًا فَبَشِّرْهُ بِعَذَابٍ اَلِيْمٍ ۞

8. (As for) those who believe and do good, they shall surely have gardens of bliss,

اِنَّ الَّذِيْنَ اٰمَنُوْا وَعَمِلُوا الصّٰلِحٰتِ لَهُمْ جَنّٰتُ النَّعِيْمِ ۞

9. Abiding in them; the promise of Allah; (a) true (promise), and He is the Mighty, the Wise.

خٰلِدِيْنَ فِيْهَا وَعْدَ اللّٰهِ حَقًّا وَهُوَ الْعَزِيْزُ الْحَكِيْمُ ۞

10. He created the heavens without pillars as you see them, and put mountains upon the earth lest it might convulse with you, and He spread in it animals of every kind; and We sent down water from the cloud, then caused to grow therein (vegetation) of every noble kind.

خَلَقَ السَّمٰوٰتِ بِغَيْرِ عَمَدٍ تَرَوْنَهَا وَاَلْقٰى فِى الْاَرْضِ رَوَاسِيَ اَنْ تَمِيْدَ بِكُمْ وَبَثَّ فِيْهَا مِنْ كُلِّ دَآبَّةٍ وَاَنْزَلْنَا مِنَ السَّمَآءِ مَآءً فَاَنْبَتْنَا فِيْهَا مِنْ كُلِّ زَوْجٍ كَرِيْمٍ ۞

11. This is Allah's creation, but show Me what those besides Him have created. Nay, the unjust are in manifest error.

هٰذَا خَلْقُ اللهِ فَاَرُوْنِيْ مَاذَا خَلَقَ الَّذِيْنَ مِنْ دُوْنِهٖ ۚ بَلِ الظّٰلِمُوْنَ فِيْ ضَلٰلٍ مُّبِيْنٍ ۞

12. And certainly We gave wisdom to Luqman, saying: Be grateful to Allah. And whoever is grateful, he is only grateful for his own soul; and whoever is ungrateful, then surely Allah is Self-sufficient, Praised.

وَلَقَدْ اٰتَيْنَا لُقْمٰنَ الْحِكْمَةَ اَنِ اشْكُرْ لِلّٰهِ ؕ وَمَنْ يَّشْكُرْ فَاِنَّمَا يَشْكُرُ لِنَفْسِهٖ ۚ وَمَنْ كَفَرَ فَاِنَّ اللهَ غَنِيٌّ حَمِيْدٌ ۞

13. And when Luqman said to his son while he admonished him: O my son! do not associate aught with Allah; most surely polytheism is a grievous iniquity—

وَاِذْ قَالَ لُقْمٰنُ لِابْنِهٖ وَهُوَ يَعِظُهٗ يٰبُنَيَّ لَا تُشْرِكْ بِاللهِ ؕ اِنَّ الشِّرْكَ لَظُلْمٌ عَظِيْمٌ ۞

14. And We have enjoined man in respect of his parents—his mother bears him with faintings upon faintings and his weaning takes two years—saying: Be grateful to Me and to both your parents; to Me is the eventual coming.

وَوَصَّيْنَا الْاِنْسَانَ بِوَالِدَيْهِ ۚ حَمَلَتْهُ اُمُّهٗ وَهْنًا عَلٰى وَهْنٍ وَّفِصٰلُهٗ فِيْ عَامَيْنِ اَنِ اشْكُرْ لِيْ وَلِوَالِدَيْكَ ؕ اِلَيَّ الْمَصِيْرُ ۞

15. And if they contend with you that you should associate with Me what you have no knowledge of, do not obey them, and keep company with them in this world kindly, and follow the way of him who turns to Me, then to Me is your return, then will I inform you of what you did—

وَاِنْ جَاهَدٰكَ عَلٰى اَنْ تُشْرِكَ بِيْ مَا لَيْسَ لَكَ بِهٖ عِلْمٌ ۙ فَلَا تُطِعْهُمَا وَصَاحِبْهُمَا فِي الدُّنْيَا مَعْرُوْفًا ۫ وَّاتَّبِعْ سَبِيْلَ مَنْ اَنَابَ اِلَيَّ ۚ ثُمَّ اِلَيَّ مَرْجِعُكُمْ فَاُنَبِّئُكُمْ بِمَا كُنْتُمْ تَعْمَلُوْنَ ۞

16. O my son! surely if it is the very weight of the grain of a mustard-seed, even though it is in (the heart of) rock, or (high above) in the heaven or (deep down) in the earth, Allah will bring it (to light); surely Allah is Knower of subtleties, Aware;

يٰبُنَيَّ اِنَّهَا اِنْ تَكُ مِثْقَالَ حَبَّةٍ مِّنْ خَرْدَلٍ فَتَكُنْ فِيْ صَخْرَةٍ اَوْ فِي السَّمٰوٰتِ اَوْ فِي الْاَرْضِ يَاْتِ بِهَا اللهُ ؕ اِنَّ اللهَ لَطِيْفٌ خَبِيْرٌ ۞

17. O my son! keep up prayer and enjoin the good and forbid the evil, and bear patiently that which befalls you; surely these acts require courage;

يٰبُنَيَّ اَقِمِ الصَّلٰوةَ وَاْمُرْ بِالْمَعْرُوْفِ وَانْهَ عَنِ الْمُنْكَرِ وَاصْبِرْ عَلٰى مَا اَصَابَكَ ؕ اِنَّ ذٰلِكَ مِنْ عَزْمِ الْاُمُوْرِ ۞

18. And do not turn your face away from people in contempt, nor go about in the land exulting overmuch; surely Allah does not love any self-conceited boaster;

وَلَا تُصَعِّرْ خَدَّكَ لِلنَّاسِ وَلَا تَمْشِ فِي الْاَرْضِ مَرَحًا ؕ اِنَّ اللهَ لَا يُحِبُّ كُلَّ مُخْتَالٍ فَخُوْرٍ ۞

19. And pursue the right course in your going about and lower your voice; surely the most hateful of voices is braying of the asses.

وَاقْصِدْ فِي مَشْيِكَ وَاغْضُضْ مِنْ صَوْتِكَ إِنَّ أَنْكَرَ الْأَصْوَاتِ لَصَوْتُ الْحَمِيرِ ۞

20. Do you not see that Allah has made what is in the heavens and what is in the earth subservient to you, and made complete to you His favors outwardly and inwardly? And among men is he who disputes in respect of Allah though having no knowledge, nor guidance, nor a book giving light.

أَلَمْ تَرَوْا أَنَّ اللّٰهَ سَخَّرَ لَكُمْ مَّا فِي السَّمٰوٰتِ وَمَا فِي الْأَرْضِ وَأَسْبَغَ عَلَيْكُمْ نِعَمَهُ ظَاهِرَةً وَبَاطِنَةً وَمِنَ النَّاسِ مَنْ يُّجَادِلُ فِي اللّٰهِ بِغَيْرِ عِلْمٍ وَّلَا هُدًى وَّلَا كِتٰبٍ مُّنِيرٍ ۞

21. And when it is said to them: Follow what Allah has revealed, they say: Nay, we follow that on which we found our fathers. What! though the Shaitan calls them to the chastisement of the burning fire!

وَإِذَا قِيْلَ لَهُمُ اتَّبِعُوْا مَا أَنْزَلَ اللّٰهُ قَالُوْا بَلْ نَتَّبِعُ مَا وَجَدْنَا عَلَيْهِ أَبَاءَنَا أَوَلَوْ كَانَ الشَّيْطٰنُ يَدْعُوْهُمْ إِلَى عَذَابِ السَّعِيْرِ ۞

22. And whoever submits himself wholly to Allah and he is the doer of good (to others), he indeed has taken hold of the firmest thing upon which one can lay hold; and Allah's is the end of affairs.

وَمَنْ يُّسْلِمْ وَجْهَهُ إِلَى اللّٰهِ وَهُوَ مُحْسِنٌ فَقَدِ اسْتَمْسَكَ بِالْعُرْوَةِ الْوُثْقٰى وَإِلَى اللّٰهِ عَاقِبَةُ الْأُمُوْرِ ۞

23. And whoever disbelieves, let not his disbelief grieve you; to Us is their return, then will We inform them of what they did; surely Allah is the Knower of what is in the breasts.

وَمَنْ كَفَرَ فَلَا يَحْزُنْكَ كُفْرُهُ إِلَيْنَا مَرْجِعُهُمْ فَنُنَبِّئُهُمْ بِمَا عَمِلُوْا إِنَّ اللّٰهَ عَلِيْمٌ بِذَاتِ الصُّدُوْرِ ۞

24. We give them to enjoy a little, then will We drive them to a severe chastisement.

نُمَتِّعُهُمْ قَلِيْلًا ثُمَّ نَضْطَرُّهُمْ إِلَى عَذَابٍ غَلِيْظٍ ۞

25. And if you ask them who created the heavens and the earth, they will certainly say: Allah. Say: (All) praise is due to Allah; nay! most of them do not know.

وَلَئِنْ سَأَلْتَهُمْ مَّنْ خَلَقَ السَّمٰوٰتِ وَالْأَرْضَ لَيَقُوْلُنَّ اللّٰهُ قُلِ الْحَمْدُ لِلّٰهِ بَلْ أَكْثَرُهُمْ لَا يَعْلَمُوْنَ ۞

26. What is in the heavens and the earth is Allah's; surely Allah is the Self-sufficient, the Praised.

لِلّٰهِ مَا فِي السَّمٰوٰتِ وَالْأَرْضِ إِنَّ اللّٰهَ هُوَ الْغَنِيُّ الْحَمِيْدُ ۞

27. And were every tree that is in the earth (made into) pens and the sea (to supply it with ink), with seven more seas to increase it, the words of Allah would not come to an end; surely Allah is Mighty, Wise.

وَلَوْ أَنَّ مَا فِي الْأَرْضِ مِنْ شَجَرَةٍ أَقْلَامٌ وَّالْبَحْرُ يَمُدُّهُ مِنْ بَعْدِهِ سَبْعَةُ أَبْحُرٍ مَّا نَفِدَتْ كَلِمٰتُ اللّٰهِ إِنَّ اللّٰهَ عَزِيْزٌ حَكِيْمٌ ۞

28. Neither your creation nor your raising is anything but as a single soul; surely Allah is Hearing, Seeing.

مَا خَلْقُكُمْ وَلَا بَعْثُكُمْ اِلَّا كَنَفْسٍ وَّاحِدَةٍ ۭ اِنَّ اللّٰهَ سَمِيْعٌۢ بَصِيْرٌ ۞

29. Do you not see that Allah makes the night to enter into the day, and He makes the day to enter into the night, and He has made the sun and the moon subservient (to you); each pursues its course till an appointed time; and that Allah is Aware of what you do?

اَلَمْ تَرَ اَنَّ اللّٰهَ يُوْلِجُ الَّيْلَ فِى النَّهَارِ وَيُوْلِجُ النَّهَارَ فِى الَّيْلِ وَسَخَّرَ الشَّمْسَ وَالْقَمَرَ ۣ كُلٌّ يَّجْرِىْٓ اِلٰٓى اَجَلٍ مُّسَمًّى وَّاَنَّ اللّٰهَ بِمَا تَعْمَلُوْنَ خَبِيْرٌ ۞

30. This is because Allah is the Truth, and that which they call upon besides Him is the falsehood, and that Allah is the High, the Great.

ذٰلِكَ بِاَنَّ اللّٰهَ هُوَ الْحَقُّ وَاَنَّ مَا يَدْعُوْنَ مِنْ دُوْنِهِ الْبَاطِلُ ۙ وَاَنَّ اللّٰهَ هُوَ الْعَلِىُّ الْكَبِيْرُ ۞

31. Do you not see that the ships run on in the sea by Allah's favor, that He may show you of His signs? Most surely there are signs in this for every patient endurer, grateful one.

اَلَمْ تَرَ اَنَّ الْفُلْكَ تَجْرِىْ فِى الْبَحْرِ بِنِعْمَتِ اللّٰهِ لِيُرِيَكُمْ مِّنْ اٰيٰتِهٖ ۭ اِنَّ فِىْ ذٰلِكَ لَاٰيٰتٍ لِّكُلِّ صَبَّارٍ شَكُوْرٍ ۞

32. And when a wave like mountains covers them they call upon Allah, being sincere to Him in obedience, but when He brings them safe to the land, some of them follow the middle course; and none denies Our signs but every perfidious, ungrateful one.

وَاِذَا غَشِيَهُمْ مَّوْجٌ كَالظُّلَلِ دَعَوُا اللّٰهَ مُخْلِصِيْنَ لَهُ الدِّيْنَ ۥ فَلَمَّا نَجّٰهُمْ اِلَى الْبَرِّ فَمِنْهُمْ مُّقْتَصِدٌ ۭ وَمَا يَجْحَدُ بِاٰيٰتِنَآ اِلَّا كُلُّ خَتَّارٍ كَفُوْرٍ ۞

33. O people! guard against (the punishment of) your Lord and dread the day when a father shall not make any satisfaction for his son, nor shall the child be the maker of any satisfaction for his father; surely the promise of Allah is true, therefore let not this world's life deceive you, nor let the arch-deceiver deceive you in respect of Allah.

يٰٓاَيُّهَا النَّاسُ اتَّقُوْا رَبَّكُمْ وَاخْشَوْا يَوْمًا لَّا يَجْزِىْ وَالِدٌ عَنْ وَّلَدِهٖ ۡ وَلَا مَوْلُوْدٌ هُوَ جَازٍ عَنْ وَّالِدِهٖ شَيْئًا ۭ اِنَّ وَعْدَ اللّٰهِ حَقٌّ فَلَا تَغُرَّنَّكُمُ الْحَيٰوةُ الدُّنْيَا ۥ وَلَا يَغُرَّنَّكُمْ بِاللّٰهِ الْغَرُوْرُ ۞

34. Surely Allah is He with Whom is the knowledge of the hour, and He sends down the rain and He knows what is in the wombs; and no one knows what he shall earn on the morrow; and no one knows in what land he shall die; surely Allah is Knowing, Aware.

اِنَّ اللّٰهَ عِنْدَهٗ عِلْمُ السَّاعَةِ ۚ وَيُنَزِّلُ الْغَيْثَ ۚ وَيَعْلَمُ مَا فِى الْاَرْحَامِ ۭ وَمَا تَدْرِىْ نَفْسٌ مَّاذَا تَكْسِبُ غَدًا ۭ وَمَا تَدْرِىْ نَفْسٌۢ بِاَىِّ اَرْضٍ تَمُوْتُ ۭ اِنَّ اللّٰهَ عَلِيْمٌ خَبِيْرٌ ۞

THE ADORATION
(SAJDAH)

**In the name of Allah,
the Beneficent, the Merciful.**

1. Alif Lam Mim.

2. The revelation of the Book, there is no doubt in it, is from the Lord of the worlds.

3. Or do they say: He has forged it? Nay! it is the truth from your Lord that you may warn a people to whom no warner has come before you, that they may follow the right direction.

4. Allah is He Who created the heavens and the earth and what is between them in six periods, and He mounted the throne (of authority); you have not besides Him any guardian or any intercessor; will you not then mind?

5. He regulates the affair from the heaven to the earth; then shall it ascend to Him in a day the measure of which is a thousand years of what you count.

6. This is the Knower of the unseen and the seen, the Mighty, the Merciful,

7. Who made good everything that He has created, and He began the creation of man from dust.

8. Then He made his progeny of an extract, of water held in light estimation.

9. Then He made him complete and breathed into him of His spirit, and made for you the ears and the eyes and the hearts; little is it that you give thanks.

10. And they say: What! when we have become lost in the earth, shall we then certainly be in a new creation? Nay! they are disbelievers in the meeting of their Lord.

بِسْمِ اللّٰهِ الرَّحْمٰنِ الرَّحِيْمِ ۝

الٓمّٓ ۝

تَنْزِيْلُ الْكِتٰبِ لَا رَيْبَ فِيْهِ مِنْ رَّبِّ الْعٰلَمِيْنَ ۝

اَمْ يَقُوْلُوْنَ افْتَرٰىهُ ۚ بَلْ هُوَ الْحَقُّ مِنْ رَّبِّكَ لِتُنْذِرَ قَوْمًا مَّاۤ اَتٰىهُمْ مِّنْ نَّذِيْرٍ مِّنْ قَبْلِكَ لَعَلَّهُمْ يَهْتَدُوْنَ ۝

اَللّٰهُ الَّذِيْ خَلَقَ السَّمٰوٰتِ وَالْاَرْضَ وَمَا بَيْنَهُمَا فِيْ سِتَّةِ اَيَّامٍ ثُمَّ اسْتَوٰى عَلَى الْعَرْشِ ۗ مَا لَكُمْ مِّنْ دُوْنِهٖ مِنْ وَّلِيٍّ وَّلَا شَفِيْعٍ ۚ اَفَلَا تَتَذَكَّرُوْنَ ۝

يُدَبِّرُ الْاَمْرَ مِنَ السَّمَاۤءِ اِلَى الْاَرْضِ ثُمَّ يَعْرُجُ اِلَيْهِ فِيْ يَوْمٍ كَانَ مِقْدَارُهٗۤ اَلْفَ سَنَةٍ مِّمَّا تَعُدُّوْنَ ۝

ذٰلِكَ عٰلِمُ الْغَيْبِ وَالشَّهَادَةِ الْعَزِيْزُ الرَّحِيْمُ ۙ۝

الَّذِيْۤ اَحْسَنَ كُلَّ شَيْءٍ خَلَقَهٗ وَبَدَاَ خَلْقَ الْاِنْسَانِ مِنْ طِيْنٍ ۝

ثُمَّ جَعَلَ نَسْلَهٗ مِنْ سُلٰلَةٍ مِّنْ مَّاۤءٍ مَّهِيْنٍ ۝

ثُمَّ سَوّٰىهُ وَنَفَخَ فِيْهِ مِنْ رُّوْحِهٖ وَجَعَلَ لَكُمُ السَّمْعَ وَالْاَبْصَارَ وَالْاَفْئِدَةَ ۗ قَلِيْلًا مَّا تَشْكُرُوْنَ ۝

وَقَالُوْۤا ءَاِذَا ضَلَلْنَا فِى الْاَرْضِ ءَاِنَّا لَفِيْ خَلْقٍ جَدِيْدٍ ۚ بَلْ هُمْ بِلِقَاۤءِ رَبِّهِمْ كٰفِرُوْنَ ۝

11. Say: The angel of death who is given charge of you shall cause you to die, then to your Lord you shall be brought back.

قُلْ يَتَوَفّٰىكُمْ مَّلَكُ الْمَوْتِ الَّذِىْ وُكِّلَ بِكُمْ ثُمَّ اِلٰى رَبِّكُمْ تُرْجَعُوْنَ ۞

12. And could you but see when the guilty shall hang down their heads before their Lord: Our Lord! we have seen and we have heard, therefore send us back, we will do good; surely (now) we are certain.

وَلَوْ تَرٰىٓ اِذِ الْمُجْرِمُوْنَ نَاكِسُوْا رُءُوْسِهِمْ عِنْدَ رَبِّهِمْ رَبَّنَآ اَبْصَرْنَا وَسَمِعْنَا فَارْجِعْنَا نَعْمَلْ صَالِحًا اِنَّا مُوْقِنُوْنَ ۞

13. And if We had pleased We would certainly have given to every soul its guidance, but the word (which had gone forth) from Me was just: I will certainly fill hell with the jinn and men together.

وَلَوْ شِئْنَا لَاٰتَيْنَا كُلَّ نَفْسٍ هُدٰىهَا وَلٰكِنْ حَقَّ الْقَوْلُ مِنِّىْ لَاَمْلَاَنَّ جَهَنَّمَ مِنَ الْجِنَّةِ وَالنَّاسِ اَجْمَعِيْنَ ۞

14. So taste, because you neglected the meeting of this day of yours; surely We forsake you; and taste the abiding chastisement for what you did.

فَذُوْقُوْا بِمَا نَسِيْتُمْ لِقَآءَ يَوْمِكُمْ هٰذَا اِنَّا نَسِيْنٰكُمْ وَذُوْقُوْا عَذَابَ الْخُلْدِ بِمَا كُنْتُمْ تَعْمَلُوْنَ ۞

15. Only they believe in Our communications who, when they are reminded of them, fall down making obeisance and celebrate the praise of their Lord, and they are not proud.

اِنَّمَا يُؤْمِنُ بِاٰيٰتِنَا الَّذِيْنَ اِذَا ذُكِّرُوْا بِهَا خَرُّوْا سُجَّدًا وَّسَبَّحُوْا بِحَمْدِ رَبِّهِمْ وَهُمْ لَا يَسْتَكْبِرُوْنَ ۞

16. Their sides draw away from (their) beds, they call upon their Lord in fear and in hope, and they spend (benevolently) out of what We have given them.

تَتَجَافٰى جُنُوْبُهُمْ عَنِ الْمَضَاجِعِ يَدْعُوْنَ رَبَّهُمْ خَوْفًا وَّطَمَعًا وَّمِمَّا رَزَقْنٰهُمْ يُنْفِقُوْنَ ۞

17. So no soul knows what is hidden for them of that which will refresh the eyes; a reward for what they did.

فَلَا تَعْلَمُ نَفْسٌ مَّآ اُخْفِىَ لَهُمْ مِّنْ قُرَّةِ اَعْيُنٍ جَزَآءً بِمَا كَانُوْا يَعْمَلُوْنَ ۞

18. Is he then who is a believer like him who is a transgressor? They are not equal.

اَفَمَنْ كَانَ مُؤْمِنًا كَمَنْ كَانَ فَاسِقًا لَا يَسْتَوٗنَ ۞

19. As for those who believe and do good, the gardens are their abiding-place; an entertainment for what they did.

اَمَّا الَّذِيْنَ اٰمَنُوْا وَعَمِلُوا الصّٰلِحٰتِ فَلَهُمْ جَنّٰتُ الْمَأْوٰى نُزُلًا بِمَا كَانُوْا يَعْمَلُوْنَ ۞

20. And as for those who transgress, their abode is the fire; whenever they desire to go forth from it they shall be brought back into it, and it will be said to them: Taste the chastisement of the fire which you called a lie.

وَاَمَّا الَّذِيْنَ فَسَقُوْا فَمَأْوٰىهُمُ النَّارُ كُلَّمَآ اَرَادُوْٓا اَنْ يَّخْرُجُوْا مِنْهَآ اُعِيْدُوْا فِيْهَا وَقِيْلَ لَهُمْ ذُوْقُوْا عَذَابَ النَّارِ الَّذِىْ كُنْتُمْ بِهٖ تُكَذِّبُوْنَ ۞

404

21. And most certainly We will make them taste of the nearer chastisement before the greater chastisement that haply they may turn.

22. And who is more unjust than he who is reminded of the communications of his Lord, then he turns away from them? Surely We will give punishment to the guilty.

23. And certainly We gave the Book to Musa, so be not in doubt concerning the receiving of it, and We made it a guide for the children of Israel.

24. And We made of them Imams to guide by Our command when they were patient, and they were certain of Our communications.

25. Surely your Lord will judge between them on the day of resurrection concerning that wherein they differ.

26. Does it not point out to them the right way, how many of the generations, in whose abodes they go about, did We destroy before them? Most surely there are signs in this; will they not then hear?

27. Do they not see that We drive the water to a land having no herbage, then We bring forth thereby seed-produce of which their cattle and they themselves eat; will they not then see?

28. And they say: When will this judgment take place, if you are truthful?

29. Say: On the day of judgment the faith of those who (now) disbelieve will not profit them, nor will they be respited.

30. Therefore turn away from them and wait, surely they too are waiting.

وَلَنُذِيقَنَّهُمْ مِّنَ الْعَذَابِ الْأَدْنَى دُونَ الْعَذَابِ الْأَكْبَرِ لَعَلَّهُمْ يَرْجِعُونَ ۝

وَمَنْ أَظْلَمُ مِمَّنْ ذُكِّرَ بِآيَاتِ رَبِّهِ ثُمَّ أَعْرَضَ عَنْهَا إِنَّا مِنَ الْمُجْرِمِينَ مُنْتَقِمُونَ ۝

وَلَقَدْ آتَيْنَا مُوسَى الْكِتَابَ فَلَا تَكُنْ فِي مِرْيَةٍ مِّنْ لِّقَائِهِ وَجَعَلْنَاهُ هُدًى لِّبَنِي إِسْرَائِيلَ ۝

وَجَعَلْنَا مِنْهُمْ أَئِمَّةً يَهْدُونَ بِأَمْرِنَا لَمَّا صَبَرُوا وَكَانُوا بِآيَاتِنَا يُوقِنُونَ ۝

إِنَّ رَبَّكَ هُوَ يَفْصِلُ بَيْنَهُمْ يَوْمَ الْقِيَامَةِ فِيمَا كَانُوا فِيهِ يَخْتَلِفُونَ ۝

أَوَلَمْ يَهْدِ لَهُمْ كَمْ أَهْلَكْنَا مِنْ قَبْلِهِمْ مِّنَ الْقُرُونِ يَمْشُونَ فِي مَسَاكِنِهِمْ إِنَّ فِي ذَلِكَ لَآيَاتٍ أَفَلَا يَسْمَعُونَ ۝

أَوَلَمْ يَرَوْا أَنَّا نَسُوقُ الْمَاءَ إِلَى الْأَرْضِ الْجُرُزِ فَنُخْرِجُ بِهِ زَرْعًا تَأْكُلُ مِنْهُ أَنْعَامُهُمْ وَأَنْفُسُهُمْ أَفَلَا يُبْصِرُونَ ۝

وَيَقُولُونَ مَتَى هَذَا الْفَتْحُ إِنْ كُنْتُمْ صَادِقِينَ ۝

قُلْ يَوْمَ الْفَتْحِ لَا يَنْفَعُ الَّذِينَ كَفَرُوا إِيمَانُهُمْ وَلَا هُمْ يُنْظَرُونَ ۝

فَأَعْرِضْ عَنْهُمْ وَانْتَظِرْ إِنَّهُمْ مُنْتَظِرُونَ ۝

THE ALLIES
(AHZAB)

بِسۡمِ اللهِ الرَّحۡمٰنِ الرَّحِيۡمِ

In the name of Allah,
the Beneficent, the Merciful.

1. O Prophet! be careful of (your duty to) Allah and do not comply with (the wishes of) the unbelievers and the hypocrites; surely Allah is Knowing, Wise;

2. And follow what is revealed to you from your Lord; surely Allah is Aware of what you do;

3. And rely on Allah; and Allah is sufficient for a Protector.

4. Allah has not made for any man two hearts within him; nor has He made your wives whose backs you liken to the backs of your mothers as your mothers, nor has He made those whom you assert to be your sons your real sons; these are the words of your mouths; and Allah speaks the truth and He guides to the way.

5. Assert their relationship to their fathers; this is more equitable with Allah; but if you do not know their fathers, then they are your brethren in faith and your friends; and there is no blame on you concerning that in which you made a mistake, but (concerning) that which your hearts do purposely (blame may rest on you), and Allah is Forgiving, Merciful.

6. The Prophet has a greater claim on the faithful than they have on themselves, and his wives are (as) their mothers; and the possessors of relationship have the better claim in the ordinance of Allah to inheritance, one with respect to another, than (other) believers, and (than) those who have fled (their homes), except that you do some good to your friends; this is written in the Book.

7. And when We made a covenant with the prophets and with you, and with Nuh and Ibrahim and Musa and Isa, son of Marium, and We made with them a strong covenant,

8. That He may question the truthful of their truth, and He has prepared for the unbelievers a painful punishment.

وَإِذْ أَخَذْنَا مِنَ النَّبِيِّنَ مِيْثَاقَهُمْ وَمِنْكَ وَمِنْ
نُوحٍ وَّإِبْرٰهِيْمَ وَمُوْسٰى وَعِيْسَى ابْنِ مَرْيَمَ ۖ
وَأَخَذْنَا مِنْهُمْ مِّيْثَاقًا غَلِيْظًا ۙ

لِّيَسْئَلَ الصّٰدِقِيْنَ عَنْ صِدْقِهِمْ ۚ وَأَعَدَّ لِلْكٰفِرِيْنَ
عَذَابًا أَلِيْمًا ۖ

9. O you who believe! call to mind the favor of Allah to you when there came down upon you hosts, so We sent against them a strong wind and hosts, that you saw not, and Allah is Seeing what you do.

10. When they came upon you from above you and from below you, and when the eyes turned dull, and the hearts rose up to the throats, and you began to think diverse thoughts of Allah.

11. There the believers were tried and they were shaken with severe shaking.

12. And when the hypocrites and those in whose hearts was a disease began to say: Allah and His Apostle did not promise us (victory) but only to deceive.

يٰٓأَيُّهَا الَّذِيْنَ اٰمَنُوا اذْكُرُوْا نِعْمَةَ اللّٰهِ عَلَيْكُمْ إِذْ
جَآءَتْكُمْ جُنُوْدٌ فَأَرْسَلْنَا عَلَيْهِمْ رِيْحًا وَّجُنُوْدًا لَّمْ
تَرَوْهَا ۚ وَكَانَ اللّٰهُ بِمَا تَعْمَلُوْنَ بَصِيْرًا ۙ

إِذْ جَآءُوْكُمْ مِّنْ فَوْقِكُمْ وَمِنْ أَسْفَلَ مِنْكُمْ وَإِذْ
زَاغَتِ الْأَبْصَارُ وَبَلَغَتِ الْقُلُوْبُ الْحَنَاجِرَ وَتَظُنُّوْنَ
بِاللّٰهِ الظُّنُوْنَا ۖ

هُنَالِكَ ابْتُلِيَ الْمُؤْمِنُوْنَ وَزُلْزِلُوْا زِلْزَالًا شَدِيْدًا ۖ

وَإِذْ يَقُوْلُ الْمُنٰفِقُوْنَ وَالَّذِيْنَ فِيْ قُلُوْبِهِمْ مَّرَضٌ
مَّا وَعَدَنَا اللّٰهُ وَرَسُوْلُهُ إِلَّا غُرُوْرًا ۖ

13. And when a party of them said: O people of Yasrib! there is no place to stand for you (here), therefore go back; and a party of them asked permission of the prophet, saying: Surely our houses are exposed; and they were not exposed; they only desired to fly away.

14. And if an entry were made upon them from the outlying parts of it, then they were asked to wage war, they would certainly have done it, and they would not have stayed in it but a little while.

15. And certainly they had made a covenant with Allah before, (that) they would not turn (their) backs; and Allah's covenant shall be inquired of.

وَإِذْ قَالَتْ طَّآئِفَةٌ مِّنْهُمْ يٰٓأَهْلَ يَثْرِبَ لَا مُقَامَ
لَكُمْ فَارْجِعُوْا ۚ وَيَسْتَأْذِنُ فَرِيْقٌ مِّنْهُمُ النَّبِيَّ
يَقُوْلُوْنَ إِنَّ بُيُوْتَنَا عَوْرَةٌ ۖ وَمَا هِيَ بِعَوْرَةٍ ۖ إِنْ
يُّرِيْدُوْنَ إِلَّا فِرَارًا ۖ

وَلَوْ دُخِلَتْ عَلَيْهِمْ مِّنْ أَقْطَارِهَا ثُمَّ سُئِلُوا
الْفِتْنَةَ لَاٰتَوْهَا وَمَا تَلَبَّثُوْا بِهَا إِلَّا يَسِيْرًا ۖ

وَلَقَدْ كَانُوْا عَاهَدُوا اللّٰهَ مِنْ قَبْلُ لَا يُوَلُّوْنَ الْأَدْبَارَ ۚ
وَكَانَ عَهْدُ اللّٰهِ مَسْئُوْلًا ۖ

16. Say: Flight shall not do you any good if you fly from death or slaughter, and in that case you will not be allowed to enjoy yourselves but a little.

قُلْ لَّنْ يَّنْفَعَكُمُ الْفِرَارُ اِنْ فَرَرْتُمْ مِّنَ الْمَوْتِ اَوِ الْقَتْلِ وَاِذًا لَّا تُمَتَّعُوْنَ اِلَّا قَلِيْلًا ۝

17. Say: Who is it that can withhold you from Allah if He intends to do you evil, rather He intends to show you mercy? And they will not find for themselves besides Allah any guardian or a helper.

قُلْ مَنْ ذَا الَّذِيْ يَعْصِمُكُمْ مِّنَ اللّٰهِ اِنْ اَرَادَ بِكُمْ سُوْٓءًا اَوْ اَرَادَ بِكُمْ رَحْمَةً ۚ وَلَا يَجِدُوْنَ لَهُمْ مِّنْ دُوْنِ اللّٰهِ وَلِيًّا وَّلَا نَصِيْرًا ۝

18. Allah knows indeed those among you who hinder others and those who say to their brethren: Come to us; and they come not to the fight but a little,

قَدْ يَعْلَمُ اللّٰهُ الْمُعَوِّقِيْنَ مِنْكُمْ وَالْقَآئِلِيْنَ لِاِخْوَانِهِمْ هَلُمَّ اِلَيْنَا ۚ وَلَا يَأْتُوْنَ الْبَأْسَ اِلَّا قَلِيْلًا ۝

19. Being niggardly with respect to you; but when fear comes, you will see them looking to you, their eyes rolling like one swooning because of death; but when the fear is gone they smite you with sharp tongues, being niggardly of the good things. These have not believed, therefore Allah has made their doing naught; and this is easy to Allah.

اَشِحَّةً عَلَيْكُمْ ۚ فَاِذَا جَآءَ الْخَوْفُ رَاَيْتَهُمْ يَنْظُرُوْنَ اِلَيْكَ تَدُوْرُ اَعْيُنُهُمْ كَالَّذِيْ يُغْشٰى عَلَيْهِ مِنَ الْمَوْتِ ۚ فَاِذَا ذَهَبَ الْخَوْفُ سَلَقُوْكُمْ بِاَلْسِنَةٍ حِدَادٍ اَشِحَّةً عَلَى الْخَيْرِ ۚ اُولٰٓئِكَ لَمْ يُؤْمِنُوْا فَاَحْبَطَ اللّٰهُ اَعْمَالَهُمْ ۚ وَكَانَ ذٰلِكَ عَلَى اللّٰهِ يَسِيْرًا ۝

20. They think the allies are not gone, and if the allies should come (again) they would fain be in the deserts with the desert Arabs asking for news about you, and if they were among you they would not fight save a little.

يَحْسَبُوْنَ الْاَحْزَابَ لَمْ يَذْهَبُوْا ۚ وَاِنْ يَّأْتِ الْاَحْزَابُ يَوَدُّوْا لَوْ اَنَّهُمْ بَادُوْنَ فِى الْاَعْرَابِ يَسْاَلُوْنَ عَنْ اَنْبَآئِكُمْ ۚ وَلَوْ كَانُوْا فِيْكُمْ مَّا قَاتَلُوْٓا اِلَّا قَلِيْلًا ۝

21. Certainly you have in the Apostle of Allah an excellent exemplar for him who hopes in Allah and the latter day and remembers Allah much.

لَقَدْ كَانَ لَكُمْ فِىْ رَسُوْلِ اللّٰهِ اُسْوَةٌ حَسَنَةٌ لِّمَنْ كَانَ يَرْجُوا اللّٰهَ وَالْيَوْمَ الْاٰخِرَ وَذَكَرَ اللّٰهَ كَثِيْرًا ۝

22. And when the believers saw the allies, they said: This is what Allah and His Apostle promised us, and Allah and His Apostle spoke the truth; and it only increased them in faith and submission.

وَلَمَّا رَاَ الْمُؤْمِنُوْنَ الْاَحْزَابَ قَالُوْا هٰذَا مَا وَعَدَنَا اللّٰهُ وَرَسُوْلُهٗ وَصَدَقَ اللّٰهُ وَرَسُوْلُهٗ ۚ وَمَا زَادَهُمْ اِلَّا اِيْمَانًا وَّتَسْلِيْمًا ۝

23. Of the believers are men who are true to the covenant which they made with Allah: so of them is he who accomplished his vow, and of them is he who yet waits, and they have not changed in the least;

مِنَ الْمُؤْمِنِيْنَ رِجَالٌ صَدَقُوْا مَا عَاهَدُوا اللّٰهَ عَلَيْهِ ۚ فَمِنْهُمْ مَّنْ قَضٰى نَحْبَهٗ وَمِنْهُمْ مَّنْ يَّنْتَظِرُ ۖ وَمَا بَدَّلُوْا تَبْدِيْلًا ۙ

24. That Allah may reward the truthful for their truth, and punish the hypocrites if He please or turn to them (mercifully); surely Allah is Forgiving, Merciful.

لِيَجْزِيَ اللّٰهُ الصّٰدِقِيْنَ بِصِدْقِهِمْ وَيُعَذِّبَ الْمُنٰفِقِيْنَ اِنْ شَاءَ اَوْ يَتُوْبَ عَلَيْهِمْ ۚ اِنَّ اللّٰهَ كَانَ غَفُوْرًا رَّحِيْمًا ۚ

25. And Allah turned back the unbelievers in their rage; they did not obtain any advantage, and Allah sufficed the believers in fighting; and Allah is Strong, Mighty.

وَرَدَّ اللّٰهُ الَّذِيْنَ كَفَرُوْا بِغَيْظِهِمْ لَمْ يَنَالُوْا خَيْرًا ۖ وَكَفَى اللّٰهُ الْمُؤْمِنِيْنَ الْقِتَالَ ۚ وَكَانَ اللّٰهُ قَوِيًّا عَزِيْزًا ۚ

26. And He drove down those of the followers of the Book who backed them from their fortresses and He cast awe into their hearts; some you killed and you took captive another part.

وَاَنْزَلَ الَّذِيْنَ ظَاهَرُوْهُمْ مِّنْ اَهْلِ الْكِتٰبِ مِنْ صَيَاصِيْهِمْ وَقَذَفَ فِيْ قُلُوْبِهِمُ الرُّعْبَ فَرِيْقًا تَقْتُلُوْنَ وَتَأْسِرُوْنَ فَرِيْقًا ۚ

27. And He made you heirs to their land and their dwellings and their property, and (to) a land which you have not yet trodden, and Allah has power over all things.

وَاَوْرَثَكُمْ اَرْضَهُمْ وَدِيَارَهُمْ وَاَمْوَالَهُمْ وَاَرْضًا لَّمْ تَطَـُٔوْهَا ۚ وَكَانَ اللّٰهُ عَلٰى كُلِّ شَيْءٍ قَدِيْرًا ۚ

28. O Prophet! say to your wives: If you desire this world's life and its adornment, then come, I will give you a provision and allow you to depart a goodly departing;

يٰٓاَيُّهَا النَّبِيُّ قُلْ لِّاَزْوَاجِكَ اِنْ كُنْتُنَّ تُرِدْنَ الْحَيٰوةَ الدُّنْيَا وَزِيْنَتَهَا فَتَعَالَيْنَ اُمَتِّعْكُنَّ وَاُسَرِّحْكُنَّ سَرَاحًا جَمِيْلًا ۚ

29. And if you desire Allah and His Apostle and the latter abode, then surely Allah has prepared for the doers of good among you a mighty reward.

وَاِنْ كُنْتُنَّ تُرِدْنَ اللّٰهَ وَرَسُوْلَهٗ وَالدَّارَ الْاٰخِرَةَ فَاِنَّ اللّٰهَ اَعَدَّ لِلْمُحْسِنٰتِ مِنْكُنَّ اَجْرًا عَظِيْمًا ۚ

30. O wives of the prophet! whoever of you commits an open indecency, the punishment shall be increased to her doubly; and this is easy to Allah.

يٰنِسَاءَ النَّبِيِّ مَنْ يَّأْتِ مِنْكُنَّ بِفَاحِشَةٍ مُّبَيِّنَةٍ يُّضٰعَفْ لَهَا الْعَذَابُ ضِعْفَيْنِ ۚ وَكَانَ ذٰلِكَ عَلَى اللّٰهِ يَسِيْرًا ۚ

31. And whoever of you is obedient to Allah and His Apostle and does good, We will give to her her reward doubly, and We have prepared for her an honorable sustenance.

وَمَنْ يَّقْنُتْ مِنْكُنَّ لِلّٰهِ وَرَسُوْلِهٖ وَتَعْمَلْ صَالِحًا نُّؤْتِهَآ اَجْرَهَا مَرَّتَيْنِ ۙ وَاَعْتَدْنَا لَهَا رِزْقًا كَرِيْمًا ۝

32. O wives of the Prophet! you are not like any other of the women; if you will be on your guard, then be not soft in (your) speech, lest he in whose heart is a disease yearn; and speak a good word.

يٰنِسَآءَ النَّبِيِّ لَسْتُنَّ كَاَحَدٍ مِّنَ النِّسَآءِ اِنِ اتَّقَيْتُنَّ فَلَا تَخْضَعْنَ بِالْقَوْلِ فَيَطْمَعَ الَّذِيْ فِيْ قَلْبِهٖ مَرَضٌ وَّقُلْنَ قَوْلًا مَّعْرُوْفًا ۝

33. And stay in your houses and do not display your finery like the displaying of the ignorance of yore; and keep up prayer, and pay the poor-rate, and obey Allah and His Apostle. Allah only desires to keep away the uncleanness from you, O people of the House! and to purify you a (thorough) purifying.

وَقَرْنَ فِيْ بُيُوْتِكُنَّ وَلَا تَبَرَّجْنَ تَبَرُّجَ الْجَاهِلِيَّةِ الْاُوْلٰى وَاَقِمْنَ الصَّلٰوةَ وَاٰتِيْنَ الزَّكٰوةَ وَاَطِعْنَ اللّٰهَ وَرَسُوْلَهٗ ۗ اِنَّمَا يُرِيْدُ اللّٰهُ لِيُذْهِبَ عَنْكُمُ الرِّجْسَ اَهْلَ الْبَيْتِ وَيُطَهِّرَكُمْ تَطْهِيْرًا ۝

34. And keep to mind what is recited in your houses of the communications of Allah and the wisdom; surely Allah is Knower of subtleties, Aware.

وَاذْكُرْنَ مَا يُتْلٰى فِيْ بُيُوْتِكُنَّ مِنْ اٰيٰتِ اللّٰهِ وَالْحِكْمَةِ ۗ اِنَّ اللّٰهَ كَانَ لَطِيْفًا خَبِيْرًا ۝

35. Surely the men who submit and the women who submit, and the believing men and the believing women, and the obeying men and the obeying women, and the truthful men and the truthful women, and the patient men and the patient women, and the humble men and the humble women, and the almsgiving men and the almsgiving women, and the fasting men and the fasting women, and the men who guard their private parts and the women who guard, and the men who remember Allah much and the women who remember —Allah has prepared for them forgiveness and a mighty reward.

اِنَّ الْمُسْلِمِيْنَ وَالْمُسْلِمٰتِ وَالْمُؤْمِنِيْنَ وَالْمُؤْمِنٰتِ وَالْقٰنِتِيْنَ وَالْقٰنِتٰتِ وَالصّٰدِقِيْنَ وَالصّٰدِقٰتِ وَالصّٰبِرِيْنَ وَالصّٰبِرٰتِ وَالْخٰشِعِيْنَ وَالْخٰشِعٰتِ وَالْمُتَصَدِّقِيْنَ وَالْمُتَصَدِّقٰتِ وَالصَّآئِمِيْنَ وَالصّٰٓئِمٰتِ وَالْحٰفِظِيْنَ فُرُوْجَهُمْ وَالْحٰفِظٰتِ وَالذّٰكِرِيْنَ اللّٰهَ كَثِيْرًا وَّالذّٰكِرٰتِ ۙ اَعَدَّ اللّٰهُ لَهُمْ مَّغْفِرَةً وَّاَجْرًا عَظِيْمًا ۝

36. And it behoves not a believing man and a believing woman that they should have any choice in their matter when Allah and His Apostle have decided a matter; and whoever disobeys Allah and His Apostle, he surely strays off a manifest straying.

وَمَا كَانَ لِمُؤْمِنٍ وَّلَا مُؤْمِنَةٍ اِذَا قَضَى اللّٰهُ وَرَسُوْلُهٗٓ اَمْرًا اَنْ يَّكُوْنَ لَهُمُ الْخِيَرَةُ مِنْ اَمْرِهِمْ ۗ وَمَنْ يَّعْصِ اللّٰهَ وَرَسُوْلَهٗ فَقَدْ ضَلَّ ضَلٰلًا مُّبِيْنًا ۝

37. And when you said to him to whom Allah had shown favor and to whom you had shown a favor: Keep your wife to yourself and be careful of (your duty to) Allah; and you concealed in your soul what Allah would bring to light, and you feared men, and Allah had a greater right that you should fear Him. But when Zaid had accomplished his want of her, We gave her to you as a wife, so that there should be no difficulty for the believers in respect of the wives of their adopted sons, when they have accomplished their want of them; and Allah's command shall be performed.

وَاِذْ تَقُوْلُ لِلَّذِيْٓ اَنْعَمَ اللّٰهُ عَلَيْهِ وَاَنْعَمْتَ عَلَيْهِ اَمْسِكْ عَلَيْكَ زَوْجَكَ وَاتَّقِ اللّٰهَ وَتُخْفِيْ فِيْ نَفْسِكَ مَا اللّٰهُ مُبْدِيْهِ وَتَخْشَى النَّاسَ ۚ وَاللّٰهُ اَحَقُّ اَنْ تَخْشٰهُ ۚ فَلَمَّا قَضٰى زَيْدٌ مِّنْهَا وَطَرًا زَوَّجْنٰكَهَا لِكَيْ لَا يَكُوْنَ عَلَى الْمُؤْمِنِيْنَ حَرَجٌ فِيْٓ اَزْوَاجِ اَدْعِيَآئِهِمْ اِذَا قَضَوْا مِنْهُنَّ وَطَرًا ۚ وَكَانَ اَمْرُ اللّٰهِ مَفْعُوْلًا ۝

38. There is no harm in the Prophet doing that which Allah has ordained for him; such has been the course of Allah with respect to those who have gone before; and the command of Allah is a decree that is made absolute:

مَا كَانَ عَلَى النَّبِيِّ مِنْ حَرَجٍ فِيْمَا فَرَضَ اللّٰهُ لَهٗ سُنَّةَ اللّٰهِ فِى الَّذِيْنَ خَلَوْا مِنْ قَبْلُ ۚ وَكَانَ اَمْرُ اللّٰهِ قَدَرًا مَّقْدُوْرَا ۝

39. Those who deliver the messages of Allah and fear Him, and do not fear any one but Allah; and Allah is sufficient to take account.

الَّذِيْنَ يُبَلِّغُوْنَ رِسٰلٰتِ اللّٰهِ وَيَخْشَوْنَهٗ وَلَا يَخْشَوْنَ اَحَدًا اِلَّا اللّٰهَ ۚ وَكَفٰى بِاللّٰهِ حَسِيْبًا ۝

40. Muhammad is not the father of any of your men, but he is the Apostle of Allah and the Last of the prophets; and Allah is Cognizant of all things.

مَا كَانَ مُحَمَّدٌ اَبَآ اَحَدٍ مِّنْ رِّجَالِكُمْ وَلٰكِنْ رَّسُوْلَ اللّٰهِ وَخَاتَمَ النَّبِيّٖنَ ۚ وَكَانَ اللّٰهُ بِكُلِّ شَيْءٍ عَلِيْمًا ۝

41. O you who believe! remember Allah, remembering frequently,

يٰٓاَيُّهَا الَّذِيْنَ اٰمَنُوا اذْكُرُوا اللّٰهَ ذِكْرًا كَثِيْرًا ۝

42. And glorify Him morning and evening.

وَّسَبِّحُوْهُ بُكْرَةً وَّاَصِيْلًا ۝

43. He it is Who sends His blessings on you, and (so do) His angels, that He may bring you forth out of utter darkness into the light; and He is Merciful to the believers.

هُوَ الَّذِيْ يُصَلِّيْ عَلَيْكُمْ وَمَلٰئِكَتُهٗ لِيُخْرِجَكُمْ مِّنَ الظُّلُمٰتِ اِلَى النُّوْرِ ۚ وَكَانَ بِالْمُؤْمِنِيْنَ رَحِيْمًا ۝

44. Their salutation on the day that they meet Him shall be, Peace, and He has prepared for them an honourable reward.

تَحِيَّتُهُمْ يَوْمَ يَلْقَوْنَهٗ سَلٰمٌ ۚ وَاَعَدَّ لَهُمْ اَجْرًا كَرِيْمًا ۝

45. O Prophet! surely We have sent you as a witness, and as a bearer of good news and as a warner,

يٰٓاَيُّهَا النَّبِيُّ اِنَّآ اَرْسَلْنٰكَ شَاهِدًا وَّمُبَشِّرًا وَّنَذِيْرًا ۝

46. And as one inviting to Allah by His permission, and as a light-giving torch.

وَّدَاعِيًا اِلَى اللّٰهِ بِاِذْنِهٖ وَسِرَاجًا مُّنِيْرًا ۝

47. And give to the believers the good news that they shall have a great grace from Allah.

48. And be not compliant to the unbelievers and the hypocrites, and leave unregarded their annoying talk, and rely on Allah; and Allah is sufficient as a Protector.

49. O you who believe! when you marry the believing women, then divorce them before you touch them, you have in their case no term which you should reckon; so make some provision for them and send them forth a goodly sending forth.

50. O Prophet! surely We have made lawful to you your wives whom you have given their dowries, and those whom your right hand possesses out of those whom Allah has given to you as prisoners of war, and the daughters of your paternal uncles and the daughters of your paternal aunts, and the daughters of your maternal uncles and the daughters of your maternal aunts who fled with you; and a believing woman if she gave herself to the Prophet, if the Prophet desired to marry her—specially for you, not for the (rest of) believers; We know what We have ordained for them concerning their wives and those whom their right hands possess in order that no blame may attach to you; and Allah is Forgiving, Merciful.

51. You may put off whom you please of them, and you may take to you whom you please, and whom you desire of those whom you had separated provisionally; no blame attaches to you; this is most proper, so that their eyes may be cool and they may not grieve, and that they should be pleased, all of them, with what you give them, and Allah knows what is in your hearts; and Allah is Knowing, Forbearing.

52. It is not allowed to you to take women afterwards, nor that you should change them for other wives, though their beauty be pleasing to you, except what your right hand possesses; and Allah is Watchful over all things.

412

53. O you who believe! do not enter the houses of the Prophet unless permission is given to you for a meal, not waiting for its cooking being finished—but when you are invited, enter, and when you have taken the food, then disperse—not seeking to listen to talk; surely this gives the Prophet trouble, but he forbears from you, and Allah does not forbear from the truth. And when you ask of them any goods, ask of them from behind a curtain; this is purer for your hearts and (for) their hearts; and it does not behove you that you should give trouble to the Apostle of Allah, nor that you should marry his wives after him ever; surely this is grievous in the sight of Allah.

يٰۤاَيُّهَا الَّذِيْنَ اٰمَنُوْا لَا تَدْخُلُوْا بُيُوْتَ النَّبِيِّ اِلَّاۤ اَنْ

يُّؤْذَنَ لَكُمْ اِلٰى طَعَامٍ غَيْرَ نٰظِرِيْنَ اِنٰىهُ وَلٰكِنْ

اِذَا دُعِيْتُمْ فَادْخُلُوْا فَاِذَا طَعِمْتُمْ فَانْتَشِرُوْا وَلَا

مُسْتَاْنِسِيْنَ لِحَدِيْثٍ اِنَّ ذٰلِكُمْ كَانَ يُؤْذِى النَّبِيَّ

فَيَسْتَحْيٖ مِنْكُمْ وَاللّٰهُ لَا يَسْتَحْيٖ مِنَ الْحَقِّ وَاِذَا

سَاَلْتُمُوْهُنَّ مَتَاعًا فَسْـَٔلُوْهُنَّ مِنْ وَّرَآءِ حِجَابٍ

ذٰلِكُمْ اَطْهَرُ لِقُلُوْبِكُمْ وَقُلُوْبِهِنَّ وَمَا كَانَ لَكُمْ اَنْ

تُؤْذُوْا رَسُوْلَ اللّٰهِ وَلَاۤ اَنْ تَنْكِحُوْاۤ اَزْوَاجَهٗ مِنْۢ بَعْدِهٖۤ

اَبَدًا اِنَّ ذٰلِكُمْ كَانَ عِنْدَ اللّٰهِ عَظِيْمًا ۞

54. If you do a thing openly or do it in secret, then surely Allah is Cognizant of all things.

اِنْ تُبْدُوْا شَيْئًا اَوْ تُخْفُوْهُ فَاِنَّ اللّٰهَ كَانَ بِكُلِّ

شَيْءٍ عَلِيْمًا ۞

55. There is no blame on them in respect of their fathers, nor their brothers, nor their brothers' sons, nor their sisters' sons, nor their own women, nor of what their right hands possess; and be careful of (your duty to) Allah; surely Allah is a witness of all things.

لَا جُنَاحَ عَلَيْهِنَّ فِيْۤ اٰبَآئِهِنَّ وَلَاۤ اَبْنَآئِهِنَّ وَلَاۤ

اِخْوَانِهِنَّ وَلَاۤ اَبْنَآءِ اِخْوَانِهِنَّ وَلَاۤ اَبْنَآءِ اَخَوٰتِهِنَّ

وَلَا نِسَآئِهِنَّ وَلَا مَا مَلَكَتْ اَيْمَانُهُنَّ وَاتَّقِيْنَ

اللّٰهَ اِنَّ اللّٰهَ كَانَ عَلٰى كُلِّ شَيْءٍ شَهِيْدًا ۞

56. Surely Allah and His angels bless the Prophet; O you who believe! call for (Divine) blessings on him and salute him with a (becoming) salutation.

اِنَّ اللّٰهَ وَمَلٰٓئِكَتَهٗ يُصَلُّوْنَ عَلَى النَّبِيِّ

يٰۤاَيُّهَا الَّذِيْنَ اٰمَنُوْا صَلُّوْا عَلَيْهِ وَسَلِّمُوْا

تَسْلِيْمًا ۞

57. Surely (as for) those who speak evil things of Allah and His Apostle, Allah has cursed them in this world and the hereafter, and He has prepared for them a chastisement bringing disgrace.

اِنَّ الَّذِيْنَ يُؤْذُوْنَ اللّٰهَ وَرَسُوْلَهٗ لَعَنَهُمُ اللّٰهُ فِى

الدُّنْيَا وَالْاٰخِرَةِ وَاَعَدَّ لَهُمْ عَذَابًا مُّهِيْنًا ۞

58. And those who speak evil things of the believing men and the believing women without their having earned (it), they are guilty indeed of a false accusation and a manifest sin.

وَالَّذِيْنَ يُؤْذُوْنَ الْمُؤْمِنِيْنَ وَالْمُؤْمِنٰتِ بِغَيْرِ مَا

اكْتَسَبُوْا فَقَدِ احْتَمَلُوْا بُهْتَانًا وَّاِثْمًا مُّبِيْنًا ۞

59. O Prophet! say to your wives and your daughters and the women of the believers that they let down upon them their over-garments; this will be more proper, that they may be known, and thus they will not be given trouble; and Allah is Forgiving, Merciful.

يَاٰيُّهَا النَّبِيُّ قُلْ لِّاَزْوَاجِكَ وَبَنٰتِكَ وَنِسَاۤءِ الْمُؤْمِنِيْنَ يُدْنِيْنَ عَلَيْهِنَّ مِنْ جَلَابِيْبِهِنَّ ۚ ذٰلِكَ اَدْنٰۤى اَنْ يُّعْرَفْنَ فَلَا يُؤْذَيْنَ ۚ وَكَانَ اللّٰهُ غَفُوْرًا رَّحِيْمًا

60. If the hypocrites and those in whose hearts is a disease and the agitators in the city do not desist, We shall most certainly set you over them, then they shall not be your neighbors in it but for a little while;

لَىِٕنْ لَّمْ يَنْتَهِ الْمُنٰفِقُوْنَ وَالَّذِيْنَ فِيْ قُلُوْبِهِمْ مَّرَضٌ وَّالْمُرْجِفُوْنَ فِى الْمَدِيْنَةِ لَنُغْرِيَنَّكَ بِهِمْ ثُمَّ لَا يُجَاوِرُوْنَكَ فِيْهَاۤ اِلَّا قَلِيْلًا

61. Cursed: wherever they are found they shall be seized and murdered, a (horrible) murdering.

مَلْعُوْنِيْنَ ۚ اَيْنَمَا ثُقِفُوْۤا اُخِذُوْا وَقُتِّلُوْا تَقْتِيْلًا

62. (Such has been) the course of Allah with respect to those who have gone before; and you shall not find any change in the course of Allah.

سُنَّةَ اللّٰهِ فِى الَّذِيْنَ خَلَوْا مِنْ قَبْلُ ۚ وَلَنْ تَجِدَ لِسُنَّةِ اللّٰهِ تَبْدِيْلًا

63. Men ask you about the hour; say: The knowledge of it is only with Allah, and what will make you comprehend that the hour may be nigh.

يَسْـَٔلُكَ النَّاسُ عَنِ السَّاعَةِ ۚ قُلْ اِنَّمَا عِلْمُهَا عِنْدَ اللّٰهِ ۚ وَمَا يُدْرِيْكَ لَعَلَّ السَّاعَةَ تَكُوْنُ قَرِيْبًا

64. Surely Allah has cursed the unbelievers and has prepared for them a burning fire,

اِنَّ اللّٰهَ لَعَنَ الْكٰفِرِيْنَ وَاَعَدَّ لَهُمْ سَعِيْرًا

65. To abide therein for a long time; they shall not find a protector or a helper.

خٰلِدِيْنَ فِيْهَاۤ اَبَدًا ۚ لَا يَجِدُوْنَ وَلِيًّا وَّلَا نَصِيْرًا

66. On the day when their faces shall be turned back into the fire, they shall say: O would that we had obeyed Allah and obeyed the Apostle!

يَوْمَ تُقَلَّبُ وُجُوْهُهُمْ فِى النَّارِ يَقُوْلُوْنَ يٰلَيْتَنَاۤ اَطَعْنَا اللّٰهَ وَاَطَعْنَا الرَّسُوْلَا

67. And they shall say: O our Lord! surely we obeyed our leaders and our great men, so they led us astray from the path;

وَقَالُوْا رَبَّنَاۤ اِنَّاۤ اَطَعْنَا سَادَتَنَا وَكُبَرَاۤءَنَا فَاَضَلُّوْنَا السَّبِيْلَا

68. O our Lord! give them a double punishment and curse them with a great curse.

رَبَّنَاۤ اٰتِهِمْ ضِعْفَيْنِ مِنَ الْعَذَابِ وَالْعَنْهُمْ لَعْنًا كَبِيْرًا

69. O you who believe! be not like those who spoke evil things of Musa, but Allah cleared him of what they said, and he was worthy of regard with Allah.

يٰۤاَيُّهَا الَّذِيْنَ اٰمَنُوْا لَا تَكُوْنُوْا كَالَّذِيْنَ اٰذَوْا مُوْسٰى فَبَرَّاَهُ اللّٰهُ مِمَّا قَالُوْا ۚ وَكَانَ عِنْدَ اللّٰهِ وَجِيْهًا

70. O you who believe! be careful of (your duty to) Allah and speak the right word,

يٰۤاَيُّهَا الَّذِيْنَ اٰمَنُوا اتَّقُوا اللّٰهَ وَقُوْلُوْا قَوْلًا سَدِيْدًا

71. He will put your deeds into a right state for you, and forgive you your faults; and whoever obeys Allah and His Apostle, he indeed achieves a mighty success.

72. Surely We offered the trust to the heavens and the earth and the mountains, but they refused to be unfaithful to it and feared from it, and man has turned unfaithful to it; surely he is unjust, ignorant;

73. So Allah will chastise the hypocritical men and the hypocritical women and the polytheistic men and the polytheistic women, and Allah will turn (mercifully) to the believing women, and Allah is Forgiving, Merciful.

يُصْلِحْ لَكُمْ اَعْمَالَكُمْ وَيَغْفِرْ لَكُمْ ذُنُوْبَكُمْ وَمَنْ يُّطِعِ اللّٰهَ وَرَسُوْلَهٗ فَقَدْ فَازَ فَوْزًا عَظِيْمًا ۝

اِنَّا عَرَضْنَا الْاَمَانَةَ عَلَى السَّمٰوٰتِ وَالْاَرْضِ وَالْجِبَالِ فَاَبَيْنَ اَنْ يَّحْمِلْنَهَا وَاَشْفَقْنَ مِنْهَا وَحَمَلَهَا الْاِنْسَانُ اِنَّهٗ كَانَ ظَلُوْمًا جَهُوْلًا ۝

لِيُعَذِّبَ اللّٰهُ الْمُنٰفِقِيْنَ وَالْمُنٰفِقٰتِ وَالْمُشْرِكِيْنَ وَالْمُشْرِكٰتِ وَيَتُوْبَ اللّٰهُ عَلَى الْمُؤْمِنِيْنَ وَالْمُؤْمِنٰتِ ۝ وَكَانَ اللّٰهُ غَفُوْرًا رَّحِيْمًا ۝

415

SABA

أَيَاتُهَا ٥٤) سُوْرَةُ سَبَأٍ مَكِّيَةٌ رُكُوعُهَا ٦

**In the name of Allah,
the Beneficent, the Merciful.**

بِسْمِ اللهِ الرَّحْمٰنِ الرَّحِيْمِ ۞

1. (All) praise is due to Allah, Whose is what is in the heavens and what is in the earth, and to Him is due (all) praise in the hereafter; and He is the Wise, the Aware.

اَلْحَمْدُ لِلّٰهِ الَّذِىْ لَهٗ مَا فِى السَّمٰوٰتِ وَمَا فِى الْاَرْضِ وَلَهُ الْحَمْدُ فِى الْاٰخِرَةِ ۖ وَهُوَ الْحَكِيْمُ الْخَبِيْرُ ۞

2. He knows that which goes down into the earth and that which comes out of it, and that which comes down from the heaven and that which goes up to it; and He is the Merciful, the Forgiving.

يَعْلَمُ مَا يَلِجُ فِى الْاَرْضِ وَمَا يَخْرُجُ مِنْهَا وَمَا يَنْزِلُ مِنَ السَّمَاءِ وَمَا يَعْرُجُ فِيْهَا ۖ وَهُوَ الرَّحِيْمُ الْغَفُوْرُ ۞

3. And those who disbelieve say: The hour shall not come upon us. Say: Yea! by my Lord, the Knower of the unseen, it shall certainly come upon you; not the weight of an atom becomes absent from Him, in the heavens or in the earth, and neither less than that nor greater, but (all) is in a clear book,

وَقَالَ الَّذِيْنَ كَفَرُوْا لَا تَأْتِيْنَا السَّاعَةُ ۖ قُلْ بَلٰى وَرَبِّىْ لَتَأْتِيَنَّكُمْ ۖ عٰلِمِ الْغَيْبِ ۖ لَا يَعْزُبُ عَنْهُ مِثْقَالُ ذَرَّةٍ فِى السَّمٰوٰتِ وَلَا فِى الْاَرْضِ وَلَا اَصْغَرُ مِنْ ذٰلِكَ وَلَا اَكْبَرُ اِلَّا فِىْ كِتٰبٍ مُّبِيْنٍ ۞

4. That He may reward those who believe and do good; these it is for whom is forgiveness and an honorable sustenance.

لِّيَجْزِىَ الَّذِيْنَ اٰمَنُوْا وَعَمِلُوا الصّٰلِحٰتِ ۖ اُولٰٓئِكَ لَهُمْ مَّغْفِرَةٌ وَّرِزْقٌ كَرِيْمٌ ۞

5. And (as for) those who strive hard in opposing Our communications, these it is for whom is a painful chastisement of an evil kind.

وَالَّذِيْنَ سَعَوْا فِىْٓ اٰيٰتِنَا مُعٰجِزِيْنَ اُولٰٓئِكَ لَهُمْ عَذَابٌ مِّنْ رِّجْزٍ اَلِيْمٌ ۞

6. And those to whom the knowledge has been given see that which has been revealed to you from your Lord, that is the truth, and it guides into the path of the Mighty, the Praised.

وَيَرَى الَّذِيْنَ اُوْتُوا الْعِلْمَ الَّذِىْٓ اُنْزِلَ اِلَيْكَ مِنْ رَّبِّكَ هُوَ الْحَقَّ ۖ وَيَهْدِىْٓ اِلٰى صِرَاطِ الْعَزِيْزِ الْحَمِيْدِ ۞

7. And those who disbelieve say: Shall we point out to you a man who informs you that when you are scattered the utmost scattering you shall then be most surely (raised) in (to) a new creation?

وَقَالَ الَّذِيْنَ كَفَرُوْا هَلْ نَدُلُّكُمْ عَلٰى رَجُلٍ يُّنَبِّئُكُمْ اِذَا مُزِّقْتُمْ كُلَّ مُمَزَّقٍ ۙ اِنَّكُمْ لَفِىْ خَلْقٍ جَدِيْدٍ ۞

8. He has forged a lie against Allah or there is madness in him. Nay! those who do not believe in the hereafter are in torment and in great error.

اَفْتَرٰى عَلَى اللّٰهِ كَذِبًا اَمْ بِهٖ جِنَّةٌ ۗ بَلِ الَّذِيْنَ لَا يُؤْمِنُوْنَ بِالْاٰخِرَةِ فِى الْعَذَابِ وَالضَّلٰلِ الْبَعِيْدِ ۞

9. Do they not then consider what is before them and what is behind them of the heaven and the earth? If We please We will make them disappear in the land or bring down upon them a portion from the heaven; most surely there is a sign in this for every servant turning (to Allah).

اَفَلَمْ يَرَوْا اِلٰى مَا بَيْنَ اَيْدِيْهِمْ وَمَا خَلْفَهُمْ مِّنَ السَّمَآءِ وَالْاَرْضِ ۗ اِنْ نَّشَأْ نَخْسِفْ بِهِمُ الْاَرْضَ اَوْ نُسْقِطْ عَلَيْهِمْ كِسَفًا مِّنَ السَّمَآءِ ۗ اِنَّ فِيْ ذٰلِكَ لَاٰيَةً لِّكُلِّ عَبْدٍ مُّنِيْبٍ ۞

10. And certainly We gave to Dawood excellence from Us: O mountains! sing praises with him, and the birds; and We made the iron pliant to him,

وَلَقَدْ اٰتَيْنَا دَاوٗدَ مِنَّا فَضْلًا ۗ يٰجِبَالُ اَوِّبِيْ مَعَهٗ وَالطَّيْرَ ۗ وَاَلَنَّا لَهُ الْحَدِيْدَ ۞

11. Saying: Make ample (coats of mail), and assign a time to the making of coats of mail and do good; surely I am Seeing what you do.

اَنِ اعْمَلْ سٰبِغٰتٍ وَّقَدِّرْ فِى السَّرْدِ وَاعْمَلُوْا صَالِحًا ۗ اِنِّيْ بِمَا تَعْمَلُوْنَ بَصِيْرٌ ۞

12. And (We made) the wind (sub-servient) to Sulaiman, which made a month's journey in the morning and a month's journey in the evening, and We made a fountain of molten copper to flow out for him; and of the jinn there were those who worked before him by the command of his Lord; and whoever turned aside from Our command from among them, We made him taste of the punishment of burning.

وَلِسُلَيْمٰنَ الرِّيْحَ غُدُوُّهَا شَهْرٌ وَّرَوَاحُهَا شَهْرٌ ۚ وَاَسَلْنَا لَهٗ عَيْنَ الْقِطْرِ ۗ وَمِنَ الْجِنِّ مَنْ يَّعْمَلُ بَيْنَ يَدَيْهِ بِاِذْنِ رَبِّهٖ ۗ وَمَنْ يَّزِغْ مِنْهُمْ عَنْ اَمْرِنَا نُذِقْهُ مِنْ عَذَابِ السَّعِيْرِ ۞

13. They made for him what he pleased of fortresses and images, and bowls (large) as watering-troughs and cooking-pots that will not move from their place; give thanks, O family of Dawood! and very few of My servants are grateful.

يَعْمَلُوْنَ لَهٗ مَا يَشَآءُ مِنْ مَّحَارِيْبَ وَتَمَاثِيْلَ وَجِفَانٍ كَالْجَوَابِ وَقُدُوْرٍ رّٰسِيٰتٍ ۗ اِعْمَلُوْا اٰلَ دَاوٗدَ شُكْرًا ۗ وَقَلِيْلٌ مِّنْ عِبَادِيَ الشَّكُوْرُ ۞

14. But when We decreed death for him, naught showed them his death but a creature of the earth that ate away his staff; and when it fell down, the jinn came to know plainly that if they had known the unseen, they would not have tarried in abasing torment.

فَلَمَّا قَضَيْنَا عَلَيْهِ الْمَوْتَ مَا دَلَّهُمْ عَلٰى مَوْتِهٖ اِلَّا دَابَّةُ الْاَرْضِ تَأْكُلُ مِنْسَأَتَهٗ ۚ فَلَمَّا خَرَّ تَبَيَّنَتِ الْجِنُّ اَنْ لَّوْ كَانُوْا يَعْلَمُوْنَ الْغَيْبَ مَا لَبِثُوْا فِى الْعَذَابِ الْمُهِيْنِ ۞

15. Certainly there was a sign for Saba in their abode; two gardens on the right and the left; eat of the sustenance of your Lord and give thanks to Him: a good land and a Forgiving Lord!

لَقَدۡ كَانَ لِسَبَاٍ فِىۡ مَسۡكَنِهِمۡ اٰيَةٌ ۚ جَنَّتٰنِ عَنۡ يَّمِيۡنٍ وَّشِمَالٍ ؕ كُلُوۡا مِنۡ رِّزۡقِ رَبِّكُمۡ وَاشۡكُرُوۡا لَهٗ ؕ بَلۡدَةٌ طَيِّبَةٌ وَّرَبٌّ غَفُوۡرٌ ۞

16. But they turned aside, so We sent upon them a torrent of which the rush could not be withstood, and in place of their two gardens We gave to them two gardens yielding bitter fruit and (growing) tamarisk and a few lote-trees.

فَاَعۡرَضُوۡا فَاَرۡسَلۡنَا عَلَيۡهِمۡ سَيۡلَ الۡعَرِمِ وَبَدَّلۡنٰهُمۡ بِجَنَّتَيۡهِمۡ جَنَّتَيۡنِ ذَوَاتَىۡ اُكُلٍ خَمۡطٍ وَّاَثۡلٍ وَّشَىۡءٍ مِّنۡ سِدۡرٍ قَلِيۡلٍ ۞

17. This We requited them with because they disbelieved; and We do not punish any but the ungrateful.

ذٰلِكَ جَزَيۡنٰهُمۡ بِمَا كَفَرُوۡا ؕ وَهَلۡ نُجٰزِىۡۤ اِلَّا الۡكَفُوۡرَ ۞

18. And We made between them and the towns which We had blessed (other) towns to be easily seen, and We apportioned the journey therein: Travel through them nights and days, secure.

وَجَعَلۡنَا بَيۡنَهُمۡ وَبَيۡنَ الۡقُرَى الَّتِىۡ بٰرَكۡنَا فِيۡهَا قُرًى ظَاهِرَةً وَّقَدَّرۡنَا فِيۡهَا السَّيۡرَ ؕ سِيۡرُوۡا فِيۡهَا لَيَالِىَ وَاَيَّامًا اٰمِنِيۡنَ ۞

19. And they said: O our Lord! make spaces to be longer between our journeys; and they were unjust to themselves; so We made them stories and scattered them with an utter scattering; most surely there are signs in this for every patient, grateful one.

فَقَالُوۡا رَبَّنَا بٰعِدۡ بَيۡنَ اَسۡفَارِنَا وَظَلَمُوۡۤا اَنۡفُسَهُمۡ فَجَعَلۡنٰهُمۡ اَحَادِيۡثَ وَمَزَّقۡنٰهُمۡ كُلَّ مُمَزَّقٍ ؕ اِنَّ فِىۡ ذٰلِكَ لَاٰيٰتٍ لِّكُلِّ صَبَّارٍ شَكُوۡرٍ ۞

20. And certainly the Shaitan found true his conjecture concerning them, so they follow him, except a party of the believers.

وَلَقَدۡ صَدَّقَ عَلَيۡهِمۡ اِبۡلِيۡسُ ظَنَّهٗ فَاتَّبَعُوۡهُ اِلَّا فَرِيۡقًا مِّنَ الۡمُؤۡمِنِيۡنَ ۞

21. And he has no authority over them, but that We may distinguish him who believes in the hereafter from him who is in doubt concerning it; and your Lord is the Preserver of all things.

وَمَا كَانَ لَهٗ عَلَيۡهِمۡ مِّنۡ سُلۡطٰنٍ اِلَّا لِنَعۡلَمَ مَنۡ يُّؤۡمِنُ بِالۡاٰخِرَةِ مِمَّنۡ هُوَ مِنۡهَا فِىۡ شَكٍّ ؕ وَرَبُّكَ عَلٰى كُلِّ شَىۡءٍ حَفِيۡظٌ ۞

22. Say: Call upon those whom you assert besides Allah; they do not control the weight of an atom in the heavens or in the earth, nor have they any partnership in either, nor has He among them any one to back (Him) up.

قُلِ ادۡعُوا الَّذِيۡنَ زَعَمۡتُمۡ مِّنۡ دُوۡنِ اللّٰهِ ۚ لَا يَمۡلِكُوۡنَ مِثۡقَالَ ذَرَّةٍ فِى السَّمٰوٰتِ وَلَا فِى الۡاَرۡضِ وَمَا لَهُمۡ فِيۡهِمَا مِنۡ شِرۡكٍ وَّمَا لَهٗ مِنۡهُمۡ مِّنۡ ظَهِيۡرٍ ۞

23. And intercession will not avail aught with Him save of him whom He permits. Until when fear shall be removed from their hearts, They shall say: What is it that your Lord said? They shall say: The truth. And He is the Most High, the Great.

24. Say: Who gives you the sustenance from the heavens and the earth? Say: Allah. And most surely we or you are on a right way or in manifest error.

25. Say: You will not be questioned as to what we are guilty of, nor shall we be questioned as to what you do.

26. Say: Our Lord will gather us together, then will He judge between us with the truth; and He is the greatest Judge, the All-knowing.

27. Say: Show me those whom you have joined with Him as associates; by no means (can you do it). Nay! He is Allah, the Mighty, the Wise.

28. And We have not sent you but to all the men as a bearer of good news and as a warner, but most men do not know.

29. And they say: When will this promise be (fulfilled) if you are truthful?

30. Say: You have the appointment of a day from which you cannot hold back any while, nor can you bring it on.

31. And those who disbelieve say: By no means will we believe in this Quran, nor in that which is before it; and could you see when the unjust shall be made to stand before their Lord, bandying words one with another! Those who were reckoned weak shall say to those who were proud: Had it not been for you, we would certainly have been believers.

32. Those who were proud shall say to those who were deemed weak: Did we turn you away from the guidance after it had come to you? Nay, you (yourselves) were guilty.

33. And those who were deemed weak shall say to those who were proud: Nay, (it was) planning by night and day when you told us to disbelieve in Allah and to set up likes with Him. And they shall conceal regret when they shall see the punishment; and We will put shackles on the necks of those who disbelieved; they shall not be requited but what they did.

وَقَالَ الَّذِيْنَ اسْتُضْعِفُوْا لِلَّذِيْنَ اسْتَكْبَرُوْا بَلْ مَكْرُ الَّيْلِ وَالنَّهَارِ اِذْ تَاْمُرُوْنَنَا اَنْ نَّكْفُرَ بِاللّٰهِ وَنَجْعَلَ لَهٗۤ اَنْدَادًا ؕ وَاَسَرُّوا النَّدَامَةَ لَمَّا رَاَوُا الْعَذَابَ ؕ وَ جَعَلْنَا الْاَغْلٰلَ فِيْۤ اَعْنَاقِ الَّذِيْنَ كَفَرُوْا ؕ هَلْ يُجْزَوْنَ اِلَّا مَا كَانُوْا يَعْمَلُوْنَ ۞

34. And We never sent a warner to a town but those who led lives in ease in it said: We are surely disbelievers in what you are sent with.

وَمَاۤ اَرْسَلْنَا فِيْ قَرْيَةٍ مِّنْ نَّذِيْرٍ اِلَّا قَالَ مُتْرَفُوْهَاۤ ۙ اِنَّا بِمَاۤ اُرْسِلْتُمْ بِهٖ كٰفِرُوْنَ ۞

35. And they say: We have more wealth and children, and we shall not be punished.

وَقَالُوْا نَحْنُ اَكْثَرُ اَمْوَالًا وَّاَوْلَادًا ۙ وَّمَا نَحْنُ بِمُعَذَّبِيْنَ ۞

36. Say: Surely my Lord amplifies the means of subsistence for whom He pleases and straitens (for whom He pleases), but most men do not know.

قُلْ اِنَّ رَبِّيْ يَبْسُطُ الرِّزْقَ لِمَنْ يَّشَاۤءُ وَيَقْدِرُ وَلٰكِنَّ اَكْثَرَ النَّاسِ لَا يَعْلَمُوْنَ ۞

37. And not your wealth nor your children, are the things which bring you near Us in station, but whoever believes and does good, these it is for whom is a double reward for what they do, and they shall be secure in the highest places.

وَمَاۤ اَمْوَالُكُمْ وَلَاۤ اَوْلَادُكُمْ بِالَّتِيْ تُقَرِّبُكُمْ عِنْدَنَا زُلْفٰۤى اِلَّا مَنْ اٰمَنَ وَعَمِلَ صَالِحًا ۫ فَاُولٰٓئِكَ لَهُمْ جَزَآءُ الضِّعْفِ بِمَا عَمِلُوْا وَهُمْ فِي الْغُرُفٰتِ اٰمِنُوْنَ ۞

38. And (as for) those who strive in opposing Our communications, they shall be caused to be brought to the chastisement.

وَالَّذِيْنَ يَسْعَوْنَ فِيْۤ اٰيٰتِنَا مُعٰجِزِيْنَ اُولٰٓئِكَ فِي الْعَذَابِ مُحْضَرُوْنَ ۞

39. Say: Surely my Lord amplifies the means of subsistence for whom He pleases of His servants and straitens (them) for whom (He pleases), and whatever thing you spend, He exceeds it in reward, and He is the best of Sustainers.

قُلْ اِنَّ رَبِّيْ يَبْسُطُ الرِّزْقَ لِمَنْ يَّشَاۤءُ مِنْ عِبَادِهٖ وَيَقْدِرُ لَهٗ ؕ وَمَاۤ اَنْفَقْتُمْ مِّنْ شَيْءٍ فَهُوَ يُخْلِفُهٗ ۫ وَهُوَ خَيْرُ الرّٰزِقِيْنَ ۞

40. And on the day when He will gather them all together, then will He say to the angels: Did these worship you?

وَيَوْمَ يَحْشُرُهُمْ جَمِيْعًا ثُمَّ يَقُوْلُ لِلْمَلٰٓئِكَةِ اَهٰٓؤُلَاۤءِ اِيَّاكُمْ كَانُوْا يَعْبُدُوْنَ ۞

41. They shall say: Glory be to Thee! Thou art our Guardian, not they; nay! they worshipped the jinn; most of them were believers in them.

قَالُوْا سُبْحٰنَكَ اَنْتَ وَلِيُّنَا مِنْ دُوْنِهِمْ ۚ بَلْ كَانُوْا يَعْبُدُوْنَ الْجِنَّ ۚ اَكْثَرُهُمْ بِهِمْ مُّؤْمِنُوْنَ ۞

42. So on that day one of you shall not control profit or harm for another, and We will say to those who were unjust: Taste the chastisement of the fire which you called a lie.

فَالْيَوْمَ لَا يَمْلِكُ بَعْضُكُمْ لِبَعْضٍ نَّفْعًا وَّلَا ضَرًّا ۚ وَنَقُوْلُ لِلَّذِيْنَ ظَلَمُوْا ذُوْقُوْا عَذَابَ النَّارِ الَّتِيْ كُنْتُمْ بِهَا تُكَذِّبُوْنَ ۞

43. And when Our clear communications are recited to them, they say: This is naught but a man who desires to turn you away from that which your fathers worshipped. And they say: This is naught but a lie that is forged. And those who disbelieve say of the truth when it comes to them: This is only clear enchantment.

وَإِذَا تُتْلٰى عَلَيْهِمْ اٰيَاتُنَا بَيِّنٰتٍ قَالُوْا مَا هٰذَا اِلَّا رَجُلٌ يُّرِيْدُ اَنْ يَّصُدَّكُمْ عَمَّا كَانَ يَعْبُدُ اٰبَاؤُكُمْ ۚ وَقَالُوْا مَا هٰذَا اِلَّا اِفْكٌ مُّفْتَرًى ۚ وَقَالَ الَّذِيْنَ كَفَرُوْا لِلْحَقِّ لَمَّا جَاءَهُمْ ۙ اِنْ هٰذَا اِلَّا سِحْرٌ مُّبِيْنٌ ۞

44. And We have not given them any books which they read, nor did We send to them before you a warner.

وَمَا اٰتَيْنٰهُمْ مِّنْ كُتُبٍ يَّدْرُسُوْنَهَا وَمَا اَرْسَلْنَا اِلَيْهِمْ قَبْلَكَ مِنْ نَّذِيْرٍ ۞

45. And those before them rejected (the truth), and these have not yet attained a tenth of what We gave them, but they gave the lie to My apostles, then how was the manifestation of My disapproval?

وَكَذَّبَ الَّذِيْنَ مِنْ قَبْلِهِمْ ۙ وَمَا بَلَغُوْا مِعْشَارَ مَا اٰتَيْنٰهُمْ فَكَذَّبُوْا رُسُلِيْ ۖ فَكَيْفَ كَانَ نَكِيْرِ ۞

46. Say: I exhort you only to one thing, that rise up for Allah's sake in twos and singly, then ponder: there is no madness in your fellow-citizen; he is only a warner to you before a severe chastisement.

قُلْ اِنَّمَا اَعِظُكُمْ بِوَاحِدَةٍ ۚ اَنْ تَقُوْمُوْا لِلّٰهِ مَثْنٰى وَفُرَادٰى ثُمَّ تَتَفَكَّرُوْا ۚ مَا بِصَاحِبِكُمْ مِّنْ جِنَّةٍ ۚ اِنْ هُوَ اِلَّا نَذِيْرٌ لَّكُمْ بَيْنَ يَدَيْ عَذَابٍ شَدِيْدٍ ۞

47. Say: Whatever reward I have asked of you, that is only for yourselves; my reward is only with Allah, and He is a witness of all things.

قُلْ مَا سَاَلْتُكُمْ مِّنْ اَجْرٍ فَهُوَ لَكُمْ ۚ اِنْ اَجْرِيَ اِلَّا عَلَى اللّٰهِ ۚ وَهُوَ عَلٰى كُلِّ شَيْءٍ شَهِيْدٌ ۞

48. Say: Surely my Lord utters the truth, the great Knower of the unseen.

قُلْ اِنَّ رَبِّيْ يَقْذِفُ بِالْحَقِّ ۚ عَلَّامُ الْغُيُوْبِ ۞

49. Say: The truth has come, and the falsehood shall vanish and shall not come back.

قُلْ جَاءَ الْحَقُّ وَمَا يُبْدِئُ الْبَاطِلُ وَمَا يُعِيْدُ ۞

50. Say: If I err, I err only against my own soul, and if I follow a right direction, it is because of what my Lord reveals to me; surely He is Hearing, Nigh.

قُلْ اِنْ ضَلَلْتُ فَاِنَّمَا اَضِلُّ عَلٰى نَفْسِيْ ۚ وَاِنِ اهْتَدَيْتُ فَبِمَا يُوْحِيْ اِلَيَّ رَبِّيْ ۚ اِنَّهُ سَمِيْعٌ قَرِيْبٌ ۞

51. And could you see when they shall become terrified, but (then) there shall be no escape and they shall be seized upon from a near place,

وَلَوْ تَرٰى اِذْ فَزِعُوْا فَلَا فَوْتَ وَاُخِذُوْا مِنْ مَّكَانٍ قَرِيْبٍ ۙ

52. And they shall say: We believe in it. And how shall the attaining (of faith) be possible to them from a distant place?

وَّقَالُوْٓا اٰمَنَّا بِهٖ ۚ وَاَنّٰى لَهُمُ التَّنَاوُشُ مِنْ مَّكَانٍ بَعِيْدٍ ۙ

53. And they disbelieved in it before, and they utter conjectures with regard to the unseen from a distant place.

وَّقَدْ كَفَرُوْا بِهٖ مِنْ قَبْلُ ۚ وَيَقْذِفُوْنَ بِالْغَيْبِ مِنْ مَّكَانٍ بَعِيْدٍ ۙ

54. And a barrier shall be placed between them and that which they desire, as was done with the likes of them before; surely they are in a disquieting doubt.

وَحِيْلَ بَيْنَهُمْ وَبَيْنَ مَا يَشْتَهُوْنَ كَمَا فُعِلَ بِاَشْيَاعِهِمْ مِّنْ قَبْلُ ۚ اِنَّهُمْ كَانُوْا فِيْ شَكٍّ مُّرِيْبٍ ۙ

THE ORIGINATOR
(FATIR)

اٰيَاتُهَا ٤٥ ﴿٣٥﴾ سُوْرَةُ فَاطِرٍ مَكِّيَّةٌ ﴿ رُكُوْعَاتُهَا ٥﴾

**In the name of Allah,
the Beneficent, the Merciful.**

بِسْمِ اللهِ الرَّحْمٰنِ الرَّحِيْمِ ۞

1. All praise is due to Allah, the Originator of the heavens and the earth, the Maker of the angels, messengers flying on wings, two, and three, and four; He increases in creation what He pleases; surely Allah has power over all things.

اَلْحَمْدُ لِلّٰهِ فَاطِرِ السَّمٰوٰتِ وَالْاَرْضِ جَاعِلِ الْمَلٰٓئِكَةِ رُسُلًا اُولِيْٓ اَجْنِحَةٍ مَّثْنٰى وَثُلٰثَ وَرُبٰعَ ۚ يَزِيْدُ فِى الْخَلْقِ مَا يَشَآءُ ۚ اِنَّ اللهَ عَلٰى كُلِّ شَيْءٍ قَدِيْرٌ ۞

2. Whatever Allah grants to men of (His) mercy, there is none to withhold it, and what He withholds there is none to send it forth after that, and He is the Mighty, the Wise.

مَا يَفْتَحِ اللهُ لِلنَّاسِ مِنْ رَّحْمَةٍ فَلَا مُمْسِكَ لَهَا ۚ وَمَا يُمْسِكْ ۙ فَلَا مُرْسِلَ لَهٗ مِنْ بَعْدِهٖ ۚ وَهُوَ الْعَزِيْزُ الْحَكِيْمُ ۞

3. O men! call to mind the favor of Allah on you; is there any creator besides Allah who gives you sustenance from the heaven and the earth? There is no god but He; whence are you then turned away?

يٰٓاَيُّهَا النَّاسُ اذْكُرُوْا نِعْمَتَ اللهِ عَلَيْكُمْ ۚ هَلْ مِنْ خَالِقٍ غَيْرُ اللهِ يَرْزُقُكُمْ مِّنَ السَّمَآءِ وَالْاَرْضِ ۚ لَآ اِلٰهَ اِلَّا هُوَ ۖ فَاَنّٰى تُؤْفَكُوْنَ ۞

4. And if they call you a liar, truly apostles before you were called liars, and to Allah are all affairs returned.

وَاِنْ يُّكَذِّبُوْكَ فَقَدْ كُذِّبَتْ رُسُلٌ مِّنْ قَبْلِكَ ۚ وَاِلَى اللهِ تُرْجَعُ الْاُمُوْرُ ۞

5. O men! surely the promise of Allah is true, therefore let not the life of this world deceive you, and let not the arch-deceiver deceive you respecting Allah.

يٰٓاَيُّهَا النَّاسُ اِنَّ وَعْدَ اللهِ حَقٌّ فَلَا تَغُرَّنَّكُمُ الْحَيٰوةُ الدُّنْيَا ۖ وَلَا يَغُرَّنَّكُمْ بِاللهِ الْغَرُوْرُ ۞

6. Surely the Shaitan is your enemy, so take him for an enemy; he only invites his party that they may be inmates of the burning fire.

اِنَّ الشَّيْطٰنَ لَكُمْ عَدُوٌّ فَاتَّخِذُوْهُ عَدُوًّا ۚ اِنَّمَا يَدْعُوْا حِزْبَهٗ لِيَكُوْنُوْا مِنْ اَصْحٰبِ السَّعِيْرِ ۞

7. (As for) those who disbelieve, they shall have a severe punishment, and (as for) those who believe and do good, they shall have forgiveness and a great reward.

اَلَّذِيْنَ كَفَرُوْا لَهُمْ عَذَابٌ شَدِيْدٌ ۙ وَالَّذِيْنَ اٰمَنُوْا وَعَمِلُوا الصّٰلِحٰتِ لَهُمْ مَّغْفِرَةٌ وَّاَجْرٌ كَبِيْرٌ ۞

8. What! is he whose evil deed is made fairseeming to him so much so that he considers it good? Now surely Allah makes err whom He pleases and guides aright whom He pleases, so let not your soul waste away in grief for them; surely Allah is Cognizant of what they do.

9. And Allah is He Who sends the winds so they raise a cloud, then We drive it on to a dead country, and therewith We give life to the earth after its death; even so is the quickening.

10. Whoever desires honor, then to Allah belongs the honor wholly. To Him do ascend the good words; and the good deeds, lift them up; and (as for) those who plan evil deeds, they shall have a severe chastisement; and (as for) their plan, it shall perish.

11. And Allah created you of dust, then of the life-germ, then He made you pairs; and no female bears, nor does she bring forth, except with His knowledge; and no one whose life is lengthened has his life lengthened, nor is aught diminished of one's life, but it is all in a book; surely this is easy to Allah.

12. And the two seas are not alike: the one sweet, that subdues thirst by its excessive sweetness, pleasant to drink; and the other salt, that burns by its saltness; yet from each of them you eat fresh flesh and bring forth ornaments which you wear; and you see the ships cleave through it that you may seek of His bounty and that you may be grateful.

13. He causes the night to enter in upon the day, and He causes the day to enter in upon the night, and He has made subservient (to you) the sun and the moon; each one follows its course to an appointed time; this is Allah, your Lord, His is the kingdom; and those whom you call upon besides Him do not control a straw.

14. If you call on them they shall not hear your call, and even if they could hear they shall not answer you; and on the resurrection day they will deny your associating them (with Allah); and none can inform you like the One Who is Aware.

ان تَدْعُوْهُمْ لَا يَسْمَعُوْا دُعَاءَكُمْ وَلَوْسَمِعُوْا مَا اسْتَجَابُوْا لَكُمْ وَيَوْمَ الْقِيٰمَةِ يَكْفُرُوْنَ بِشِرْكِكُمْ وَلَا يُنَبِّئُكَ مِثْلُ خَبِيْرٍ ۝

15. O men! you are they who stand in need of Allah, and Allah is He Who is the Self-sufficient, the Praised One.

يٰٓاَيُّهَا النَّاسُ اَنْتُمُ الْفُقَرَاءُ اِلَى اللّٰهِ وَاللّٰهُ هُوَ الْغَنِيُّ الْحَمِيْدُ ۝

16. If He please, He will take you off and bring a new generation.

اِنْ يَّشَأْ يُذْهِبْكُمْ وَيَأْتِ بِخَلْقٍ جَدِيْدٍ ۝

17. And this is not hard to Allah.

وَمَا ذٰلِكَ عَلَى اللّٰهِ بِعَزِيْزٍ ۝

18. And a burdened soul cannot bear the burden of another; and if one weighed down by burden should cry for (another to carry) its burden, not aught of it shall be carried, even though he be near of kin. You warn only those who fear their Lord in secret and keep up prayer; and whoever purifies himself, he purifies himself only for (the good of) his own soul; and to Allah is the eventual coming.

وَلَا تَزِرُ وَازِرَةٌ وِّزْرَ اُخْرٰى ۚ وَاِنْ تَدْعُ مُثْقَلَةٌ اِلٰى حِمْلِهَا لَا يُحْمَلْ مِنْهُ شَىْءٌ وَّلَوْكَانَ ذَا قُرْبٰى ۚ اِنَّمَا تُنْذِرُ الَّذِيْنَ يَخْشَوْنَ رَبَّهُمْ بِالْغَيْبِ وَاَقَامُوا الصَّلٰوةَ ۚ وَمَنْ تَزَكّٰى فَاِنَّمَا يَتَزَكّٰى لِنَفْسِهٖ ۚ وَاِلَى اللّٰهِ الْمَصِيْرُ ۝

19. And the blind and the seeing are not alike,

وَمَا يَسْتَوِى الْاَعْمٰى وَالْبَصِيْرُ ۝

20. Nor the darkness and the light,

وَلَا الظُّلُمٰتُ وَلَا النُّوْرُ ۝

21. Nor the shade and the heat,

وَلَا الظِّلُّ وَلَا الْحَرُوْرُ ۝

22. Neither are the living and the dead alike. Surely Allah makes whom He pleases hear, and you cannot make those hear who are in the graves.

وَمَا يَسْتَوِى الْاَحْيَاءُ وَلَا الْاَمْوَاتُ ۚ اِنَّ اللّٰهَ يُسْمِعُ مَنْ يَّشَاءُ ۚ وَمَآ اَنْتَ بِمُسْمِعٍ مَّنْ فِى الْقُبُوْرِ ۝

23. You are naught but a warner.

اِنْ اَنْتَ اِلَّا نَذِيْرٌ ۝

24. Surely We have sent you with the truth as a bearer of good news and a warner; and there is not a people but a warner has gone among them.

اِنَّآ اَرْسَلْنٰكَ بِالْحَقِّ بَشِيْرًا وَّنَذِيْرًا ۚ وَاِنْ مِّنْ اُمَّةٍ اِلَّا خَلَا فِيْهَا نَذِيْرٌ ۝

25. And if they call you a liar, so did those before them indeed call (their apostles) liars; their apostles had come to them with clear arguments, and with scriptures, and with the illuminating book.

وَاِنْ يُّكَذِّبُوْكَ فَقَدْ كَذَّبَ الَّذِيْنَ مِنْ قَبْلِهِمْ ۚ جَاءَتْهُمْ رُسُلُهُمْ بِالْبَيِّنٰتِ وَبِالزُّبُرِ وَبِالْكِتٰبِ الْمُنِيْرِ ۝

26. Then did I punish those who disbelieved, so how was the manifestation of My disapproval?

27. Do you not see that Allah sends down water from the cloud, then We bring forth therewith fruits of various colors; and in the mountains are streaks, white and red, of various hues and (others) intensely black?

28. And of men and beasts and cattle are various species of it likewise; those of His servants only who are possessed of knowledge fear Allah; surely Allah is Mighty, Forgiving.

29. Surely they who recite the Book of Allah and keep up prayer and spend out of what We have given them secretly and openly, hope for a gain which will not perish.

30. That He may pay them back fully their rewards and give them more out of His grace: surely He is Forgiving, Multiplier of rewards.

31. And that which We have revealed to you of the Book, that is the truth verifying that which is before it; most surely with respect to His servants Allah is Aware, Seeing.

32. Then We gave the Book for an inheritance to those whom We chose from among Our servants; but of them is he who makes his soul to suffer a loss, and of them is he who takes a middle course, and of them is he who is foremost in deeds of goodness by Allah's permission; this is the great excellence.

33. Gardens of perpetuity, they shall enter therein; they shall be made to wear therein bracelets of gold and pearls, and their dress therein shall be silk.

34. And they shall say: (All) praise is due to Allah, Who has made grief to depart from us; most surely our Lord is Forgiving, Multiplier of rewards,

ثُمَّ أَخَذْتُ الَّذِينَ كَفَرُوا فَكَيْفَ كَانَ نَكِيرِ ۞

أَلَمْ تَرَ أَنَّ اللّٰهَ أَنْزَلَ مِنَ السَّمَاءِ مَاءً ۖ فَأَخْرَجْنَا بِهِ ثَمَرَاتٍ مُّخْتَلِفًا أَلْوَانُهَا ۚ وَمِنَ الْجِبَالِ جُدَدٌ بِيضٌ وَّحُمْرٌ مُّخْتَلِفٌ أَلْوَانُهَا وَغَرَابِيبُ سُودٌ ۞

وَمِنَ النَّاسِ وَالدَّوَابِّ وَالْأَنْعَامِ مُخْتَلِفٌ أَلْوَانُهُ كَذٰلِكَ ۗ إِنَّمَا يَخْشَى اللّٰهَ مِنْ عِبَادِهِ الْعُلَمٰؤُا ۗ إِنَّ اللّٰهَ عَزِيزٌ غَفُورٌ ۞

إِنَّ الَّذِينَ يَتْلُونَ كِتٰبَ اللّٰهِ وَأَقَامُوا الصَّلٰوةَ وَأَنْفَقُوا مِمَّا رَزَقْنَاهُمْ سِرًّا وَّعَلَانِيَةً يَّرْجُونَ تِجَارَةً لَّنْ تَبُورَ ۞

لِيُوَفِّيَهُمْ أُجُورَهُمْ وَيَزِيدَهُمْ مِّنْ فَضْلِهِ ۚ إِنَّهُ غَفُورٌ شَكُورٌ ۞

وَالَّذِيٓ أَوْحَيْنَآ إِلَيْكَ مِنَ الْكِتٰبِ هُوَ الْحَقُّ مُصَدِّقًا لِّمَا بَيْنَ يَدَيْهِ ۗ إِنَّ اللّٰهَ بِعِبَادِهِ لَخَبِيرٌ بَصِيرٌ ۞

ثُمَّ أَوْرَثْنَا الْكِتٰبَ الَّذِينَ اصْطَفَيْنَا مِنْ عِبَادِنَا ۖ فَمِنْهُمْ ظَالِمٌ لِّنَفْسِهِ ۚ وَمِنْهُمْ مُّقْتَصِدٌ ۚ وَمِنْهُمْ سَابِقٌ بِالْخَيْرَاتِ بِإِذْنِ اللّٰهِ ۚ ذٰلِكَ هُوَ الْفَضْلُ الْكَبِيرُ ۞

جَنّٰتُ عَدْنٍ يَّدْخُلُونَهَا يُحَلَّوْنَ فِيهَا مِنْ أَسَاوِرَ مِنْ ذَهَبٍ وَّلُؤْلُؤًا ۖ وَلِبَاسُهُمْ فِيهَا حَرِيرٌ ۞

وَقَالُوا الْحَمْدُ لِلّٰهِ الَّذِيٓ أَذْهَبَ عَنَّا الْحَزَنَ ۗ إِنَّ رَبَّنَا لَغَفُورٌ شَكُورٌ ۞

35. Who has made us alight in a house abiding for ever out of His grace; toil shall not touch us therein, nor shall fatigue therein afflict us.

36. And (as for) those who disbelieve, for them is the fire of hell; it shall not be finished with them entirely so that they should die, nor shall the chastisement thereof be lightened to them: even thus do We retribute every ungrateful one.

37. And they shall cry therein for succour: O our Lord! take us out, we will do good deeds other than those which we used to do. Did We not preserve you alive long enough, so that he who would be mindful in it should mind? And there came to you the warner; therefore taste; because for the unjust, there is no helper.

38. Surely Allah is the Knower of what is unseen in the heavens and the earth; surely He is Cognizant of what is in the hearts.

39. He it is Who made you rulers in the land; therefore whoever disbelieves, his unbelief is against himself; and their unbelief does not increase the disbelievers with their Lord in anything except hatred; and their unbelief does not increase the disbelievers in anything except loss.

40. Say: Have you considered your associates which you call upon besides Allah? Show me what part of the earth they have created, or have they any share in the heavens; or, have We given them a book so that they follow a clear argument thereof? Nay, the unjust do not hold out promises one to another but only to deceive.

41. Surely Allah upholds the heavens and the earth lest they come to naught; and if they should come to naught, there is none who can uphold them after Him; surely He is the Forbearing, the Forgiving.

الَّذِىٓ اَحَلَّنَا دَارَ الْمُقَامَةِ مِنْ فَضْلِهٖ ۚ لَا يَمَسُّنَا فِيْهَا نَصَبٌ وَّلَا يَمَسُّنَا فِيْهَا لُغُوْبٌ ۞

وَالَّذِيْنَ كَفَرُوْا لَهُمْ نَارُ جَهَنَّمَ ۚ لَا يُقْضٰى عَلَيْهِمْ فَيَمُوْتُوْا وَلَا يُخَفَّفُ عَنْهُمْ مِّنْ عَذَابِهَا ۚ كَذٰلِكَ نَجْزِيْ كُلَّ كَفُوْرٍ ۞

وَهُمْ يَصْطَرِخُوْنَ فِيْهَا ۚ رَبَّنَآ اَخْرِجْنَا نَعْمَلْ صَالِحًا غَيْرَ الَّذِيْ كُنَّا نَعْمَلُ ۚ اَوَلَمْ نُعَمِّرْكُمْ مَّا يَتَذَكَّرُ فِيْهِ مَنْ تَذَكَّرَ وَجَآءَكُمُ النَّذِيْرُ ۚ فَذُوْقُوْا فَمَا لِلظّٰلِمِيْنَ مِنْ نَّصِيْرٍ ۞

اِنَّ اللّٰهَ عٰلِمُ غَيْبِ السَّمٰوٰتِ وَالْاَرْضِ ۚ اِنَّهٗ عَلِيْمٌۢ بِذَاتِ الصُّدُوْرِ ۞

هُوَ الَّذِيْ جَعَلَكُمْ خَلَآئِفَ فِى الْاَرْضِ ۚ فَمَنْ كَفَرَ فَعَلَيْهِ كُفْرُهٗ ۚ وَلَا يَزِيْدُ الْكٰفِرِيْنَ كُفْرُهُمْ عِنْدَ رَبِّهِمْ اِلَّا مَقْتًا ۚ وَلَا يَزِيْدُ الْكٰفِرِيْنَ كُفْرُهُمْ اِلَّا خَسَارًا ۞

قُلْ اَرَءَيْتُمْ شُرَكَآءَكُمُ الَّذِيْنَ تَدْعُوْنَ مِنْ دُوْنِ اللّٰهِ ۗ اَرُوْنِيْ مَاذَا خَلَقُوْا مِنَ الْاَرْضِ اَمْ لَهُمْ شِرْكٌ فِى السَّمٰوٰتِ ۚ اَمْ اٰتَيْنٰهُمْ كِتٰبًا فَهُمْ عَلٰى بَيِّنَتٍ مِّنْهُ ۚ بَلْ اِنْ يَّعِدُ الظّٰلِمُوْنَ بَعْضُهُمْ بَعْضًا اِلَّا غُرُوْرًا ۞

اِنَّ اللّٰهَ يُمْسِكُ السَّمٰوٰتِ وَالْاَرْضَ اَنْ تَزُوْلَا ۚ وَلَئِنْ زَالَتَآ اِنْ اَمْسَكَهُمَا مِنْ اَحَدٍ مِّنْۢ بَعْدِهٖ ۚ اِنَّهٗ كَانَ حَلِيْمًا غَفُوْرًا ۞

42. And they swore by Allah with the strongest of their oaths that if there came to them a warner they would be better guided than any of the nations; but when there came to them a warner it increased them in naught but aversion,

43. (In) behaving proudly in the land and in planning evil; and the evil plans shall not beset any save the authors of it. Then should they wait for aught except the way of the former people? For you shall not find any alteration in the course of Allah; and you shall not find any change in the course of Allah.

44. Have they not travelled in the land and seen how was the end of those before them while they were stronger than these in power? And Allah is not such that any thing in the heavens or in the earth should escape Him; surely He is Knowing, Powerful.

45. And were Allah to punish men for what they earn, He would not leave on the back of it any creature, but He respites them till an appointed term; so when their doom shall come, then surely Allah is Seeing with respect to His servants.

وَاَقْسَمُوْا بِاللّٰهِ جَهْدَ اَيْمَانِهِمْ لَئِنْ جَآءَهُمْ نَذِيْرٌ لَيَكُوْنُنَّ اَهْدٰى مِنْ اِحْدَى الْاُمَمِ ۚ فَلَمَّا جَآءَهُمْ نَذِيْرٌ مَّا زَادَهُمْ اِلَّا نُفُوْرَ ۨ ٤٢

اِسْتِكْبَارًا فِى الْاَرْضِ وَمَكْرَ السَّيِّئِ ۚ وَلَا يَحِيْقُ الْمَكْرُ السَّيِّئُ اِلَّا بِاَهْلِهٖ ۚ فَهَلْ يَنْظُرُوْنَ اِلَّا سُنَّتَ الْاَوَّلِيْنَ ۚ فَلَنْ تَجِدَ لِسُنَّتِ اللّٰهِ تَبْدِيْلًا ۚ وَلَنْ تَجِدَ لِسُنَّتِ اللّٰهِ تَحْوِيْلًا ٤٣

اَوَلَمْ يَسِيْرُوْا فِى الْاَرْضِ فَيَنْظُرُوْا كَيْفَ كَانَ عَاقِبَةُ الَّذِيْنَ مِنْ قَبْلِهِمْ وَكَانُوْا اَشَدَّ مِنْهُمْ قُوَّةً ۚ وَمَا كَانَ اللّٰهُ لِيُعْجِزَهٗ مِنْ شَيْءٍ فِى السَّمٰوٰتِ وَلَا فِى الْاَرْضِ ۚ اِنَّهٗ كَانَ عَلِيْمًا قَدِيْرًا ٤٤

وَلَوْ يُؤَاخِذُ اللّٰهُ النَّاسَ بِمَا كَسَبُوْا مَا تَرَكَ عَلٰى ظَهْرِهَا مِنْ دَآبَّةٍ وَّلٰكِنْ يُّؤَخِّرُهُمْ اِلٰى اَجَلٍ مُّسَمًّى ۚ فَاِذَا جَآءَ اَجَلُهُمْ فَاِنَّ اللّٰهَ كَانَ بِعِبَادِهٖ بَصِيْرًا ٤٥ ع ١٧

Ya Seen

**In the name of Allah,
the Beneficent, the Merciful.**

1. Ya Seen.

2. I swear by the Quran full of wisdom;

3. Most surely you are one of the apostles,

4. On a right way.

5. A revelation of the Mighty, the Merciful.

6. That you may warn a people whose fathers were not warned, so they are heedless.

7. Certainly the word has proved true of most of them, so they do not believe.

8. Surely We have placed chains on their necks, and these reach up to their chins, so they have their heads raised aloft.

9. And We have made before them a barrier and a barrier behind them, then We have covered them over so that they do not see.

10. And it is alike to them whether you warn them or warn them not: they do not believe.

11. You can only warn him who follows the reminder and fears the Beneficent God in secret; so announce to him forgiveness and an honorable reward.

12. Surely We give life to the dead, and We write down what they have sent before and their footprints, and We have recorded everything in a clear writing.

بِسْمِ اللّٰهِ الرَّحْمٰنِ الرَّحِيْمِ

يٰسٓ ۚ

وَالْقُرْاٰنِ الْحَكِيْمِ ۙ

اِنَّكَ لَمِنَ الْمُرْسَلِيْنَ ۙ

عَلٰى صِرَاطٍ مُّسْتَقِيْمٍ ۗ

تَنْزِيْلَ الْعَزِيْزِ الرَّحِيْمِ ۙ

لِتُنْذِرَ قَوْمًا مَّآ اُنْذِرَ اٰبَآؤُهُمْ فَهُمْ غٰفِلُوْنَ ۞

لَقَدْ حَقَّ الْقَوْلُ عَلٰٓى اَكْثَرِهِمْ فَهُمْ لَا يُؤْمِنُوْنَ ۞

اِنَّا جَعَلْنَا فِيْٓ اَعْنَاقِهِمْ اَغْلٰلًا فَهِيَ اِلَى الْاَذْقَانِ فَهُمْ مُّقْمَحُوْنَ ۞

وَجَعَلْنَا مِنْۢ بَيْنِ اَيْدِيْهِمْ سَدًّا وَّمِنْ خَلْفِهِمْ سَدًّا فَاَغْشَيْنٰهُمْ فَهُمْ لَا يُبْصِرُوْنَ ۞

وَسَوَآءٌ عَلَيْهِمْ ءَاَنْذَرْتَهُمْ اَمْ لَمْ تُنْذِرْهُمْ لَا يُؤْمِنُوْنَ ۞

اِنَّمَا تُنْذِرُ مَنِ اتَّبَعَ الذِّكْرَ وَخَشِيَ الرَّحْمٰنَ بِالْغَيْبِ ۚ فَبَشِّرْهُ بِمَغْفِرَةٍ وَّاَجْرٍ كَرِيْمٍ ۞

اِنَّا نَحْنُ نُحْيِ الْمَوْتٰى وَنَكْتُبُ مَا قَدَّمُوْا وَاٰثَارَهُمْ ۚ وَكُلَّ شَيْءٍ اَحْصَيْنٰهُ فِيْٓ اِمَامٍ مُّبِيْنٍ ۞

13. And set out to them an example of the people of the town, when the messengers came to it.

14. When We sent to them two, they rejected both of them, then We strengthened (them) with a third, so they said: Surely we are messengers to you.

15. They said: You are naught but mortals like ourselves, nor has the Beneficent God revealed anything; you only lie.

16. They said: Our Lord knows that we are most surely messengers to you.

17. And nothing devolves on us but a clear deliverance (of the message).

18. They said: Surely we augur evil from you; if you do not desist, we will certainly stone you, and there shall certainly afflict you a painful chastisement from us.

19. They said: Your evil fortune is with you; what! if you are reminded! Nay, you are an extravagant people.

20. And from the remote part of the city there came a man running; he said: O my people! follow the messengers;

21. Follow him who does not ask you for reward, and they are the followers of the right course;

22. And what reason have I that I should not serve Him Who brought me into existence? And to Him you shall be brought back;

23. What! shall I take besides Him gods whose intercession, if the Beneficent God should desire to afflict me with a harm, shall not avail me aught, nor shall they be able to deliver me?

24. In that case I shall most surely be in clear error:

25. Surely I believe in your Lord, therefore hear me.

وَاضْرِبْ لَهُمْ مَثَلًا أَصْحَابَ الْقَرْيَةِ ۘ إِذْ جَآءَهَا الْمُرْسَلُوْنَ ۙ ١٣

إِذْ أَرْسَلْنَآ إِلَيْهِمُ اثْنَيْنِ فَكَذَّبُوْهُمَا فَعَزَّزْنَا بِثَالِثٍ فَقَالُوْٓا إِنَّآ إِلَيْكُمْ مُّرْسَلُوْنَ ١٤

قَالُوْا مَآ أَنْتُمْ إِلَّا بَشَرٌ مِّثْلُنَا ۙ وَمَآ أَنْزَلَ الرَّحْمٰنُ مِنْ شَيْءٍ ۙ إِنْ أَنْتُمْ إِلَّا تَكْذِبُوْنَ ١٥

قَالُوْا رَبُّنَا يَعْلَمُ إِنَّآ إِلَيْكُمْ لَمُرْسَلُوْنَ ١٦

وَمَا عَلَيْنَآ إِلَّا الْبَلٰغُ الْمُبِيْنُ ١٧

قَالُوْٓا إِنَّا تَطَيَّرْنَا بِكُمْ ۚ لَئِنْ لَّمْ تَنْتَهُوْا لَنَرْجُمَنَّكُمْ وَلَيَمَسَّنَّكُمْ مِّنَّا عَذَابٌ أَلِيْمٌ ١٨

قَالُوْا طَآئِرُكُمْ مَّعَكُمْ ۚ أَئِنْ ذُكِّرْتُمْ ۚ بَلْ أَنْتُمْ قَوْمٌ مُّسْرِفُوْنَ ١٩

وَجَآءَ مِنْ أَقْصَا الْمَدِيْنَةِ رَجُلٌ يَّسْعٰى قَالَ يٰقَوْمِ اتَّبِعُوا الْمُرْسَلِيْنَ ۙ ٢٠

اتَّبِعُوْا مَنْ لَّا يَسْئَلُكُمْ أَجْرًا وَّهُمْ مُّهْتَدُوْنَ ٢١

وَمَا لِيَ لَآ أَعْبُدُ الَّذِيْ فَطَرَنِيْ وَإِلَيْهِ تُرْجَعُوْنَ ٢٢

ءَأَتَّخِذُ مِنْ دُوْنِهٖٓ ءَالِهَةً إِنْ يُّرِدْنِ الرَّحْمٰنُ بِضُرٍّ لَّا تُغْنِ عَنِّيْ شَفَاعَتُهُمْ شَيْئًا وَّلَا يُنْقِذُوْنِ ٢٣

إِنِّيْٓ إِذًا لَّفِيْ ضَلٰلٍ مُّبِيْنٍ ٢٤

إِنِّيْٓ ءَامَنْتُ بِرَبِّكُمْ فَاسْمَعُوْنِ ٢٥

26. It was said: Enter the garden. He said: O would that my people had known

قِيْلَ ادْخُلِ الْجَنَّةَ ۖ قَالَ يٰلَيْتَ قَوْمِيْ يَعْلَمُوْنَ ۞

27. Of that on account of which my Lord has forgiven me and made me of the honored ones!

بِمَا غَفَرَ لِيْ رَبِّيْ وَجَعَلَنِيْ مِنَ الْمُكْرَمِيْنَ ۞

28. And We did not send down upon his people after him any hosts from heaven, nor do We ever send down.

وَمَآ اَنْزَلْنَا عَلٰى قَوْمِهٖ مِنْ بَعْدِهٖ مِنْ جُنْدٍ مِّنَ السَّمَآءِ وَمَا كُنَّا مُنْزِلِيْنَ ۞

29. It was naught but a single cry, and lo! they were still.

اِنْ كَانَتْ اِلَّا صَيْحَةً وَّاحِدَةً فَاِذَا هُمْ خٰمِدُوْنَ ۞

30. Alas for the servants! there comes not to them an apostle but they mock at him.

يٰحَسْرَةً عَلَى الْعِبَادِ ۚ مَا يَأْتِيْهِمْ مِّنْ رَّسُوْلٍ اِلَّا كَانُوْا بِهٖ يَسْتَهْزِءُوْنَ ۞

31. Do they not consider how many of the generations have We destroyed before them, because they do not turn to them?

اَلَمْ يَرَوْا كَمْ اَهْلَكْنَا قَبْلَهُمْ مِّنَ الْقُرُوْنِ اَنَّهُمْ اِلَيْهِمْ لَا يَرْجِعُوْنَ ۞

32. And all of them shall surely be brought before Us.

وَاِنْ كُلٌّ لَّمَّا جَمِيْعٌ لَّدَيْنَا مُحْضَرُوْنَ ۞

33. And a sign to them is the dead earth: We give life to it and bring forth from it grain so they eat of it.

وَاٰيَةٌ لَّهُمُ الْاَرْضُ الْمَيْتَةُ ۚ اَحْيَيْنٰهَا وَاَخْرَجْنَا مِنْهَا حَبًّا فَمِنْهُ يَأْكُلُوْنَ ۞

34. And We make therein gardens of palms and grapevines, and We make springs to flow forth in it,

وَجَعَلْنَا فِيْهَا جَنّٰتٍ مِّنْ نَّخِيْلٍ وَّاَعْنَابٍ وَّفَجَّرْنَا فِيْهَا مِنَ الْعُيُوْنِ ۞

35. That they may eat of the fruit thereof, and their hands did not make it; will they not then be grateful?

لِيَأْكُلُوْا مِنْ ثَمَرِهٖ ۙ وَمَا عَمِلَتْهُ اَيْدِيْهِمْ ۚ اَفَلَا يَشْكُرُوْنَ ۞

36. Glory be to Him Who created pairs of all things, of what the earth grows, and of their kind and of what they do not know.

سُبْحٰنَ الَّذِيْ خَلَقَ الْاَزْوَاجَ كُلَّهَا مِمَّا تُنْبِتُ الْاَرْضُ وَمِنْ اَنْفُسِهِمْ وَمِمَّا لَا يَعْلَمُوْنَ ۞

37. And a sign to them is the night: We draw forth from it the day, then lo! they are in the dark;

وَاٰيَةٌ لَّهُمُ الَّيْلُ ۖ نَسْلَخُ مِنْهُ النَّهَارَ فَاِذَا هُمْ مُّظْلِمُوْنَ ۞

38. And the sun runs on to a term appointed for it; that is the ordinance of the Mighty, the Knowing.

وَالشَّمْسُ تَجْرِيْ لِمُسْتَقَرٍّ لَّهَا ۚ ذٰلِكَ تَقْدِيْرُ الْعَزِيْزِ الْعَلِيْمِ ۞

431

39. And (as for) the moon, We have ordained for it stages till it becomes again as an old dry palm branch.

وَالْقَمَرَ قَدَّرْنٰهُ مَنَازِلَ حَتّٰى عَادَ كَالْعُرْجُوْنِ الْقَدِيْمِ ۝

40. Neither is it allowable to the sun that it should overtake the moon, nor can the night outstrip the day; and all float on in a sphere.

لَا الشَّمْسُ يَنْۢبَغِيْ لَهَآ اَنْ تُدْرِكَ الْقَمَرَ وَلَا الَّيْلُ سَابِقُ النَّهَارِ ۚ وَكُلٌّ فِيْ فَلَكٍ يَّسْبَحُوْنَ ۝

41. And a sign to them is that We bear their offspring in the laden ship.

وَاٰيَةٌ لَّهُمْ اَنَّا حَمَلْنَا ذُرِّيَّتَهُمْ فِى الْفُلْكِ الْمَشْحُوْنِ ۝

42. And We have created for them the like of it, what they will ride on.

وَخَلَقْنَا لَهُمْ مِّنْ مِّثْلِهٖ مَا يَرْكَبُوْنَ ۝

43. And if We please, We can drown them, then there shall be no succorer for them, nor shall they be rescued,

وَاِنْ نَّشَأْ نُغْرِقْهُمْ فَلَا صَرِيْخَ لَهُمْ وَلَا هُمْ يُنْقَذُوْنَ ۙ

44. But (by) mercy from Us and for enjoyment till a time.

اِلَّا رَحْمَةً مِّنَّا وَمَتَاعًا اِلٰى حِيْنٍ ۝

45. And when it is said to them: Guard against what is before you and what is behind you, that mercy may be had on you.

وَاِذَا قِيْلَ لَهُمُ اتَّقُوْا مَا بَيْنَ اَيْدِيْكُمْ وَمَا خَلْفَكُمْ لَعَلَّكُمْ تُرْحَمُوْنَ ۝

46. And there comes not to them a communication of the communications of their Lord but they turn aside from it.

وَمَا تَأْتِيْهِمْ مِّنْ اٰيَةٍ مِّنْ اٰيٰتِ رَبِّهِمْ اِلَّا كَانُوْا عَنْهَا مُعْرِضِيْنَ ۝

47. And when it is said to them: Spend out of what Allah has given you, those who disbelieve say to those who believe: Shall we feed him whom, if Allah please, He could feed? You are in naught but clear error.

وَاِذَا قِيْلَ لَهُمْ اَنْفِقُوْا مِمَّا رَزَقَكُمُ اللّٰهُ ۙ قَالَ الَّذِيْنَ كَفَرُوْا لِلَّذِيْنَ اٰمَنُوْٓا اَنُطْعِمُ مَنْ لَّوْ يَشَآءُ اللّٰهُ اَطْعَمَهٗ ۖ اِنْ اَنْتُمْ اِلَّا فِيْ ضَلٰلٍ مُّبِيْنٍ ۝

48. And they say: When will this threat come to pass, if you are truthful?

وَيَقُوْلُوْنَ مَتٰى هٰذَا الْوَعْدُ اِنْ كُنْتُمْ صٰدِقِيْنَ ۝

49. They wait not for aught but a single cry which will overtake them while they yet contend with one another.

مَا يَنْظُرُوْنَ اِلَّا صَيْحَةً وَّاحِدَةً تَأْخُذُهُمْ وَهُمْ يَخِصِّمُوْنَ ۝

50. So they shall not be able to make a bequest, nor shall they return to their families.

فَلَا يَسْتَطِيْعُوْنَ تَوْصِيَةً وَّلَا اِلٰٓى اَهْلِهِمْ يَرْجِعُوْنَ ۝

51. And the trumpet shall be blown, when lo! from their graves they shall hasten on to their Lord.

وَنُفِخَ فِى الصُّوْرِ فَاِذَا هُمْ مِّنَ الْاَجْدَاثِ اِلٰى رَبِّهِمْ يَنْسِلُوْنَ ۝

52. They shall say: O woe to us! who has raised us up from our sleeping-place? This is what the Beneficent God promised and the apostles told the truth.

قَالُوْا يٰوَيْلَنَا مَنْۢ بَعَثَنَا مِنْ مَّرْقَدِنَا ۜ هٰذَا مَا وَعَدَ الرَّحْمٰنُ وَصَدَقَ الْمُرْسَلُوْنَ ۞

53. There would be naught but a single cry, when lo! they shall all be brought before Us.

اِنْ كَانَتْ اِلَّا صَيْحَةً وَّاحِدَةً فَاِذَا هُمْ جَمِيْعٌ لَّدَيْنَا مُحْضَرُوْنَ ۞

54. So this day no soul shall be dealt with unjustly in the least; and you shall not be rewarded aught but that which you did.

فَالْيَوْمَ لَا تُظْلَمُ نَفْسٌ شَيْئًا وَّلَا تُجْزَوْنَ اِلَّا مَا كُنْتُمْ تَعْمَلُوْنَ ۞

55. Surely the dwellers of the garden shall on that day be in an occupation quite happy.

اِنَّ اَصْحٰبَ الْجَنَّةِ الْيَوْمَ فِيْ شُغُلٍ فٰكِهُوْنَ ۞

56. They and their wives shall be in shades, reclining on raised couches.

هُمْ وَاَزْوَاجُهُمْ فِيْ ظِلٰلٍ عَلَى الْاَرَائِكِ مُتَّكِئُوْنَ ۞

57. They shall have fruits therein, and they shall have whatever they desire.

لَهُمْ فِيْهَا فَاكِهَةٌ وَّلَهُمْ مَّا يَدَّعُوْنَ ۞

58. Peace: a word from a Merciful Lord.

سَلٰمٌ قَوْلًا مِّنْ رَّبٍّ رَّحِيْمٍ ۞

59. And get aside today, O guilty ones!

وَامْتَازُوا الْيَوْمَ اَيُّهَا الْمُجْرِمُوْنَ ۞

60. Did I not charge you, O children of Adam! that you should not serve the Shaitan? Surely he is your open enemy,

اَلَمْ اَعْهَدْ اِلَيْكُمْ يٰبَنِيْ اٰدَمَ اَنْ لَّا تَعْبُدُوا الشَّيْطٰنَ ۚ اِنَّهٗ لَكُمْ عَدُوٌّ مُّبِيْنٌ ۞

61. And that you should serve Me; this is the right way.

وَّاَنِ اعْبُدُوْنِيْ ۚ هٰذَا صِرَاطٌ مُّسْتَقِيْمٌ ۞

62. And certainly he led astray numerous people from among you. What! could you not then understand?

وَلَقَدْ اَضَلَّ مِنْكُمْ جِبِلًّا كَثِيْرًا ۗ اَفَلَمْ تَكُوْنُوْا تَعْقِلُوْنَ ۞

63. This is the hell with which you were threatened.

هٰذِهٖ جَهَنَّمُ الَّتِيْ كُنْتُمْ تُوْعَدُوْنَ ۞

64. Enter into it this day because you disbelieved.

اِصْلَوْهَا الْيَوْمَ بِمَا كُنْتُمْ تَكْفُرُوْنَ ۞

65. On that day We will set a seal upon their mouths, and their hands shall speak to Us, and their feet shall bear witness of what they earned.

اَلْيَوْمَ نَخْتِمُ عَلٰى اَفْوَاهِهِمْ وَتُكَلِّمُنَا اَيْدِيْهِمْ وَتَشْهَدُ اَرْجُلُهُمْ بِمَا كَانُوْا يَكْسِبُوْنَ ۞

66. And if We please We would certainly put out their eyes, then they would run about groping for the way, but how should they see?

وَلَوْ نَشَآءُ لَطَمَسْنَا عَلٰٓى اَعْيُنِهِمْ فَاسْتَبَقُوا الصِّرَاطَ فَاَنّٰى يُبْصِرُوْنَ ۟

67. And if We please We would surely transform them in their place, then they would not be able to go on, nor will they return.

وَلَوْ نَشَآءُ لَمَسَخْنٰهُمْ عَلٰى مَكَانَتِهِمْ فَمَا اسْتَطَاعُوْا مُضِيًّا وَّلَا يَرْجِعُوْنَ ۟

68. And whomsoever We cause to live long, We reduce (him) to an abject state in constitution; do they not then understand?

وَمَنْ نُّعَمِّرْهُ نُنَكِّسْهُ فِى الْخَلْقِ ۖ اَفَلَا يَعْقِلُوْنَ ۟

69. And We have not taught him poetry, nor is it meet for him; it is nothing but a reminder and a plain Quran,

وَمَا عَلَّمْنٰهُ الشِّعْرَ وَمَا يَنْۢبَغِيْ لَهٗ ۗ اِنْ هُوَ اِلَّا ذِكْرٌ وَّقُرْاٰنٌ مُّبِيْنٌ ۟ۙ

70. That it may warn him who would have life, and (that) the word may prove true against the unbelievers.

لِّيُنْذِرَ مَنْ كَانَ حَيًّا وَّيَحِقَّ الْقَوْلُ عَلَى الْكٰفِرِيْنَ ۟

71. Do they not see that We have created cattle for them, out of what Our hands have wrought, so they are their masters?

اَوَلَمْ يَرَوْا اَنَّا خَلَقْنَا لَهُمْ مِّمَّا عَمِلَتْ اَيْدِيْنَآ اَنْعَامًا فَهُمْ لَهَا مٰلِكُوْنَ ۟

72. And We have subjected them to them, so some of them they have to ride upon, and some of them they eat.

وَذَلَّلْنٰهَا لَهُمْ فَمِنْهَا رَكُوْبُهُمْ وَمِنْهَا يَاْكُلُوْنَ ۟

73. And therein they have advantages and drinks; will they not then be grateful?

وَلَهُمْ فِيْهَا مَنَافِعُ وَمَشَارِبُ ۗ اَفَلَا يَشْكُرُوْنَ ۟

74. And they have taken gods besides Allah that they may be helped.

وَاتَّخَذُوْا مِنْ دُوْنِ اللّٰهِ اٰلِهَةً لَّعَلَّهُمْ يُنْصَرُوْنَ ۟

75. (But) they shall not be able to assist them, and they shall be a host brought up before them.

لَا يَسْتَطِيْعُوْنَ نَصْرَهُمْ ۙ وَهُمْ لَهُمْ جُنْدٌ مُّحْضَرُوْنَ ۟

76. Therefore let not their speech grieve you; surely We know what they do in secret and what they do openly.

فَلَا يَحْزُنْكَ قَوْلُهُمْ ۘ اِنَّا نَعْلَمُ مَا يُسِرُّوْنَ وَمَا يُعْلِنُوْنَ ۟

77. Does not man see that We have created him from the small seed? Then lo! he is an open disputant.

اَوَلَمْ يَرَ الْاِنْسَانُ اَنَّا خَلَقْنٰهُ مِنْ نُّطْفَةٍ فَاِذَا هُوَ خَصِيْمٌ مُّبِيْنٌ ۟

78. And he strikes out a likeness for Us and forgets his own creation. Says he: Who will give life to the bones when they are rotten?

وَضَرَبَ لَنَا مَثَلًا وَّنَسِيَ خَلْقَهٗ ۗ قَالَ مَنْ يُّحْيِ الْعِظَامَ وَهِيَ رَمِيْمٌ ۟

79. Say: He will give life to them Who brought them into existence at first, and He is Cognizant of all creation,

قُلْ يُحْيِيْهَا الَّذِيْٓ اَنْشَاَهَآ اَوَّلَ مَرَّةٍ ۗ وَهُوَ بِكُلِّ خَلْقٍ عَلِيْمُ ۞

80. He Who has made for you the fire (to burn) from the green tree, so that with it you kindle (fire).

الَّذِيْ جَعَلَ لَكُمْ مِّنَ الشَّجَرِ الْاَخْضَرِ نَارًا فَاِذَآ اَنْتُمْ مِّنْهُ تُوْقِدُوْنَ ۞

81. Is not He Who created the heavens and the earth able to create the like of them? Yea! and He is the Creator (of all), the Knower.

اَوَلَيْسَ الَّذِيْ خَلَقَ السَّمٰوٰتِ وَالْاَرْضَ بِقٰدِرٍ عَلٰٓى اَنْ يَّخْلُقَ مِثْلَهُمْ ۗ بَلٰى وَهُوَ الْخَلّٰقُ الْعَلِيْمُ ۞

82. His command, when He intends anything, is only to say to it: Be, so it is.

اِنَّمَآ اَمْرُهٗٓ اِذَآ اَرَادَ شَيْئًا اَنْ يَّقُوْلَ لَهٗ كُنْ فَيَكُوْنُ ۞

83. Therefore glory be to Him in Whose hand is the kingdom of all things, and to Him you shall be brought back.

فَسُبْحٰنَ الَّذِيْ بِيَدِهٖ مَلَكُوْتُ كُلِّ شَيْءٍ وَّاِلَيْهِ تُرْجَعُوْنَ ۞

435

THE RANGERS
(SAFFAT)

بِيَاتُهَا (٣٧) سُوْرَةُ الصّٰفّٰتِ مَكِّيَّةٌ رُكُوْعَاتُهَا

**In the name of Allah,
the Beneficent, the Merciful.**

بِسْمِ اللهِ الرَّحْمٰنِ الرَّحِيْمِ ۞

1. I swear by those who draw themselves out in ranks,

وَالصّٰفّٰتِ صَفًّا ۞

2. Then those who drive away with reproof,

فَالزّٰجِرٰتِ زَجْرًا ۞

3. Then those who recite, being mindful,

فَالتّٰلِيٰتِ ذِكْرًا ۞

4. Most surely your God is One:

اِنَّ اِلٰهَكُمْ لَوَاحِدٌ ۞

5. The Lord of the heavens and the earth and what is between them, and Lord of the easts.

رَبُّ السَّمٰوٰتِ وَالْاَرْضِ وَمَا بَيْنَهُمَا وَرَبُّ الْمَشَارِقِ ۞

6. Surely We have adorned the nearest heaven with an adornment, the stars,

اِنَّا زَيَّنَّا السَّمَآءَ الدُّنْيَا بِزِيْنَةٍ اِلْكَوَاكِبِ ۞

7. And (there is) a safeguard against every rebellious Shaitan.

وَحِفْظًا مِّنْ كُلِّ شَيْطٰنٍ مَّارِدٍ ۞

8. They cannot listen to the exalted assembly and they are thrown at from every side,

لَا يَسَّمَّعُوْنَ اِلَى الْمَلَاِ الْاَعْلٰى وَيُقْذَفُوْنَ مِنْ كُلِّ جَانِبٍ ۞

9. Being driven off, and for them is a perpetual chastisement,

دُحُوْرًا وَّلَهُمْ عَذَابٌ وَّاصِبٌ ۞

10. Except him who snatches off but once, then there follows him a brightly shining flame.

اِلَّا مَنْ خَطِفَ الْخَطْفَةَ فَاَتْبَعَهُ شِهَابٌ ثَاقِبٌ ۞

11. Then ask them whether they are stronger in creation or those (others) whom We have created. Surely We created them of firm clay.

فَاسْتَفْتِهِمْ اَهُمْ اَشَدُّ خَلْقًا اَمْ مَّنْ خَلَقْنَا اِنَّا خَلَقْنٰهُمْ مِّنْ طِيْنٍ لَّازِبٍ ۞

12. Nay! you wonder while they mock,

بَلْ عَجِبْتَ وَيَسْخَرُوْنَ ۞

13. And when they are reminded, they mind not,

وَاِذَا ذُكِّرُوْا لَا يَذْكُرُوْنَ ۞

14. And when they see a sign they incite one another to scoff,

وَاِذَا رَاَوْا اٰيَةً يَّسْتَسْخِرُوْنَ ۞

15. And they say: This is nothing but clear magic:

وَقَالُوْا اِنْ هٰذَا اِلَّا سِحْرٌ مُّبِيْنٌ ۞

16. What! when we are dead and have become dust and bones, shall we then certainly be raised,

17. Or our fathers of yore?

18. Say: Aye! and you shall be abject.

19. So it shall only be a single cry, when lo! they shall see.

20. And they shall say: O woe to us! this is the day of requital.

21. This is the day of the judgment which you called a lie.

22. Gather together those who were unjust and their associates, and what they used to worship

23. Besides Allah, then lead them to the way to hell.

24. And stop them, for they shall be questioned:

25. What is the matter with you that you do not help each other?

26. Nay! on that day they shall be submissive.

27. And some of them shall advance towards others, questioning each other.

28. They shall say: Surely you used to come to us from the right side.

29. They shall say: Nay, you (yourselves) were not believers;

30. And we had no authority over you, but you were an inordinate people;

31. So the sentence of our Lord has come to pass against us: (now) we shall surely taste;

32. So we led you astray, for we ourselves were erring.

33. So they shall on that day be sharers in the chastisement one with another.

34. Surely thus do We deal with the guilty.

35. Surely they used to behave proudly when it was said to them: There is no god but Allah;

وَإِذَا مِتْنَا وَكُنَّا تُرَابًا وَّعِظَامًا ءَاِنَّا لَمَبْعُوْثُوْنَ ۞

اَوَ اٰبَآؤُنَا الْاَوَّلُوْنَ ۞

قُلْ نَعَمْ وَاَنْتُمْ دَاخِرُوْنَ ۞

فَاِنَّمَا هِيَ زَجْرَةٌ وَّاحِدَةٌ فَاِذَا هُمْ يَنْظُرُوْنَ ۞

وَقَالُوْا يٰوَيْلَنَا هٰذَا يَوْمُ الدِّيْنِ ۞

هٰذَا يَوْمُ الْفَصْلِ الَّذِيْ كُنْتُمْ بِهٖ تُكَذِّبُوْنَ ۞

اُحْشُرُوا الَّذِيْنَ ظَلَمُوْا وَاَزْوَاجَهُمْ وَمَا كَانُوْا يَعْبُدُوْنَ ۞

مِنْ دُوْنِ اللّٰهِ فَاهْدُوْهُمْ اِلٰى صِرَاطِ الْجَحِيْمِ ۞

وَقِفُوْهُمْ اِنَّهُمْ مَّسْئُوْلُوْنَ ۞

مَالَكُمْ لَا تَنَاصَرُوْنَ ۞

بَلْ هُمُ الْيَوْمَ مُسْتَسْلِمُوْنَ ۞

وَاَقْبَلَ بَعْضُهُمْ عَلٰى بَعْضٍ يَّتَسَآءَلُوْنَ ۞

قَالُوْا اِنَّكُمْ كُنْتُمْ تَأْتُوْنَنَا عَنِ الْيَمِيْنِ ۞

قَالُوْا بَلْ لَّمْ تَكُوْنُوْا مُؤْمِنِيْنَ ۞

وَمَا كَانَ لَنَا عَلَيْكُمْ مِّنْ سُلْطٰنٍ بَلْ كُنْتُمْ قَوْمًا طَاغِيْنَ ۞

فَحَقَّ عَلَيْنَا قَوْلُ رَبِّنَآ اِنَّا لَذَآئِقُوْنَ ۞

فَاَغْوَيْنٰكُمْ اِنَّا كُنَّا غَاوِيْنَ ۞

فَاِنَّهُمْ يَوْمَئِذٍ فِى الْعَذَابِ مُشْتَرِكُوْنَ ۞

اِنَّا كَذٰلِكَ نَفْعَلُ بِالْمُجْرِمِيْنَ ۞

اِنَّهُمْ كَانُوْا اِذَا قِيْلَ لَهُمْ لَا اِلٰهَ اِلَّا اللّٰهُ يَسْتَكْبِرُوْنَ ۞

36. And to say: What! shall we indeed give up our gods for the sake of a mad poet?

وَيَقُوْلُوْنَ اَئِنَّا لَتَارِكُوْا اٰلِهَتِنَا لِشَاعِرٍ مَّجْنُوْنٍ ۞

37. Nay: he has come with the truth and verified the apostles.

بَلْ جَاءَ بِالْحَقِّ وَصَدَّقَ الْمُرْسَلِيْنَ ۞

38. Most surely you will taste the painful punishment.

اِنَّكُمْ لَذَائِقُوا الْعَذَابِ الْاَلِيْمِ ۞

39. And you shall not be rewarded except (for) what you did.

وَمَا تُجْزَوْنَ اِلَّا مَا كُنْتُمْ تَعْمَلُوْنَ ۞

40. Save the servants of Allah, the purified ones.

اِلَّا عِبَادَ اللّٰهِ الْمُخْلَصِيْنَ ۞

41. For them is a known sustenance,

اُولٰٓئِكَ لَهُمْ رِزْقٌ مَّعْلُوْمٌ ۞

42. Fruits, and they shall be highly honored,

فَوَاكِهُ ۚ وَهُمْ مُّكْرَمُوْنَ ۞

43. In gardens of pleasure,

فِيْ جَنّٰتِ النَّعِيْمِ ۞

44. On thrones, facing each other.

عَلٰى سُرُرٍ مُّتَقٰبِلِيْنَ ۞

45. A bowl shall be made to go round them from water running out of springs,

يُطَافُ عَلَيْهِمْ بِكَأْسٍ مِّنْ مَّعِيْنٍ ۞

46. White, delicious to those who drink.

بَيْضَاءَ لَذَّةٍ لِّلشّٰرِبِيْنَ ۞

47. There shall be no trouble in it, nor shall they be exhausted therewith.

لَا فِيْهَا غَوْلٌ وَّلَا هُمْ عَنْهَا يُنْزَفُوْنَ ۞

48. And with them shall be those who restrain the eyes, having beautiful eyes;

وَعِنْدَهُمْ قٰصِرٰتُ الطَّرْفِ عِيْنٌ ۞

49. As if they were eggs carefully protected.

كَاَنَّهُنَّ بَيْضٌ مَّكْنُوْنٌ ۞

50. Then shall some of them advance to others, questioning each other.

فَاَقْبَلَ بَعْضُهُمْ عَلٰى بَعْضٍ يَّتَسَاءَلُوْنَ ۞

51. A speaker from among them shall say: Surely I had a comrade of mine,

قَالَ قَائِلٌ مِّنْهُمْ اِنِّيْ كَانَ لِيْ قَرِيْنٌ ۞

52. Who said: What! are you indeed of those who accept (the truth)?

يَّقُوْلُ اَئِنَّكَ لَمِنَ الْمُصَدِّقِيْنَ ۞

53. What! when we are dead and have become dust and bones, shall we then be certainly brought to judgment?

ءَاِذَا مِتْنَا وَكُنَّا تُرَابًا وَّعِظَامًا اَئِنَّا لَمَدِيْنُوْنَ ۞

54. He shall say: Will you look on?

قَالَ هَلْ اَنْتُمْ مُّطَّلِعُوْنَ ۞

55. Then he looked down and saw him in the midst of hell.

فَاطَّلَعَ فَرَاٰهُ فِيْ سَوَاءِ الْجَحِيْمِ ۞

56. He shall say: By Allah! you had almost caused me to perish;

قَالَ تَاللّٰهِ اِنْ كِدْتَّ لَتُرْدِيْنِ ۞

438

57. And had it not been for the favor of my Lord, I would certainly have been among those brought up.

58. Is it then that we are not going to die,

59. Except our previous death? And we shall not be chastised?

60. Most surely this is the mighty achievement.

61. For the like of this then let the workers work.

62. Is this better as an entertainment or the tree of Zaqqum?

63. Surely We have made it to be a trial to the unjust.

64. Surely it is a tree that grows in the bottom of the hell;

65. Its produce is as it were the heads of the serpents.

66. Then most surely they shall eat of it and fill (their) bellies with it.

67. Then most surely they shall have after it to drink of a mixture prepared in boiling water.

68. Then most surely their return shall be to hell.

69. Surely they found their fathers going astray,

70. So in their footsteps they are being hastened on.

71. And certainly most of the ancients went astray before them,

72. And certainly We sent among them warners.

73. Then see how was the end of those warned,

74. Except the servants of Allah, the purified ones.

75. And Nuh did certainly call upon Us, and most excellent answerer of prayer are We.

76. And We delivered him and his followers from the mighty distress.

77. And We made his offspring the survivors.

78. And We perpetuated to him (praise) among the later generations.

وَلَوْلَا نِعْمَةُ رَبِّي لَكُنْتُ مِنَ الْمُحْضَرِينَ ۟

اَفَمَا نَحْنُ بِمَيِّتِينَ ۟

اِلَّا مَوْتَتَنَا الْاُولٰى وَمَا نَحْنُ بِمُعَذَّبِينَ ۟

اِنَّ هٰذَا لَهُوَ الْفَوْزُ الْعَظِيمُ ۟

لِمِثْلِ هٰذَا فَلْيَعْمَلِ الْعٰمِلُونَ ۟

اَذٰلِكَ خَيْرٌ نُّزُلًا اَمْ شَجَرَةُ الزَّقُّومِ ۟

اِنَّا جَعَلْنٰهَا فِتْنَةً لِّلظّٰلِمِينَ ۟

اِنَّهَا شَجَرَةٌ تَخْرُجُ فِي اَصْلِ الْجَحِيمِ ۟

طَلْعُهَا كَاَنَّهُ رُءُوسُ الشَّيٰطِينِ ۟

فَاِنَّهُمْ لَاٰكِلُونَ مِنْهَا فَمَالِئُونَ مِنْهَا الْبُطُونَ ۟

ثُمَّ اِنَّ لَهُمْ عَلَيْهَا لَشَوْبًا مِّنْ حَمِيمٍ ۟

ثُمَّ اِنَّ مَرْجِعَهُمْ لَاِلَى الْجَحِيمِ ۟

اِنَّهُمْ اَلْفَوْا اٰبَاءَهُمْ ضَالِّينَ ۟

فَهُمْ عَلَى اٰثٰرِهِمْ يُهْرَعُونَ ۟

وَلَقَدْ ضَلَّ قَبْلَهُمْ اَكْثَرُ الْاَوَّلِينَ ۟

وَلَقَدْ اَرْسَلْنَا فِيهِمْ مُّنْذِرِينَ ۟

فَانْظُرْ كَيْفَ كَانَ عَاقِبَةُ الْمُنْذَرِينَ ۟

اِلَّا عِبَادَ اللّٰهِ الْمُخْلَصِينَ ۟

وَلَقَدْ نَادٰىنَا نُوحٌ فَلَنِعْمَ الْمُجِيبُونَ ۟

وَنَجَّيْنٰهُ وَاَهْلَهُ مِنَ الْكَرْبِ الْعَظِيمِ ۟

وَجَعَلْنَا ذُرِّيَّتَهُ هُمُ الْبَاقِينَ ۟

وَتَرَكْنَا عَلَيْهِ فِي الْاٰخِرِينَ ۟

439

79. Peace and salutation to Nuh among the nations.

سَلٰمٌ عَلٰى نُوْحٍ فِى الْعٰلَمِيْنَ ۞

80. Thus do We surely reward the doers of good.

اِنَّا كَذٰلِكَ نَجْزِى الْمُحْسِنِيْنَ ۞

81. Surely he was of Our believing servants.

اِنَّهٗ مِنْ عِبَادِنَا الْمُؤْمِنِيْنَ ۞

82. Then We drowned the others.

ثُمَّ اَغْرَقْنَا الْاٰخَرِيْنَ ۞

83. And most surely Ibrahim followed his way.

وَاِنَّ مِنْ شِيْعَتِهٖ لَاِبْرٰهِيْمَ ۞

84. When he came to his Lord with a free heart,

اِذْ جَآءَ رَبَّهٗ بِقَلْبٍ سَلِيْمٍ ۞

85. When he said to his father and his people: What is it that you worship?

اِذْ قَالَ لِاَبِيْهِ وَقَوْمِهٖ مَاذَا تَعْبُدُوْنَ ۞

86. A lie—gods besides Allah—do you desire?

اَئِفْكًا اٰلِهَةً دُوْنَ اللّٰهِ تُرِيْدُوْنَ ۞

87. What is then your idea about the Lord of the worlds?

فَمَا ظَنُّكُمْ بِرَبِّ الْعٰلَمِيْنَ ۞

88. Then he looked at the stars, looking up once,

فَنَظَرَ نَظْرَةً فِى النُّجُوْمِ ۞

89. Then he said: Surely I am sick (of your worshipping these).

فَقَالَ اِنِّىْ سَقِيْمٌ ۞

90. So they went away from him, turning back.

فَتَوَلَّوْا عَنْهُ مُدْبِرِيْنَ ۞

91. Then he turned aside to their gods secretly and said: What! do you not eat?

فَرَاغَ اِلٰى اٰلِهَتِهِمْ فَقَالَ اَلَا تَأْكُلُوْنَ ۞

92. What is the matter with you that you do not speak?

مَا لَكُمْ لَا تَنْطِقُوْنَ ۞

93. Then he turned against them secretly, smiting them with the right hand.

فَرَاغَ عَلَيْهِمْ ضَرْبًا بِالْيَمِيْنِ ۞

94. So they (people) advanced towards him, hastening.

فَاَقْبَلُوْا اِلَيْهِ يَزِفُّوْنَ ۞

95. Said he: What! do you worship what you hew out?

قَالَ اَتَعْبُدُوْنَ مَا تَنْحِتُوْنَ ۞

96. And Allah has created you and what you make.

وَاللّٰهُ خَلَقَكُمْ وَمَا تَعْمَلُوْنَ ۞

97. They said: Build for him a furnace, then cast him into the burning fire.

قَالُوا ابْنُوْا لَهٗ بُنْيَانًا فَاَلْقُوْهُ فِى الْجَحِيْمِ ۞

98. And they desired a war against him, but We brought them low.

فَاَرَادُوْا بِهٖ كَيْدًا فَجَعَلْنٰهُمُ الْاَسْفَلِيْنَ ۞

99. And he said: Surely I fly to my Lord; He will guide me.

وَقَالَ اِنِّىْ ذَاهِبٌ اِلٰى رَبِّىْ سَيَهْدِيْنِ ۞

100. My Lord! grant me of the doers of good deeds.

رَبِّ هَبْ لِىْ مِنَ الصّٰلِحِيْنَ ۞

101. So We gave him the good news of a boy, possessing forbearance.

فَبَشَّرْنٰهُ بِغُلٰمٍ حَلِيْمٍ ۝

102. And when he attained to working with him, he said: O my son! surely I have seen in a dream that I should sacrifice you; consider then what you see. He said: O my father! do what you are commanded; if Allah please, you will find me of the patient ones.

فَلَمَّا بَلَغَ مَعَهُ السَّعْيَ قَالَ يٰبُنَيَّ اِنِّيْۤ اَرٰى فِى الْمَنَامِ اَنِّيْۤ اَذْبَحُكَ فَانْظُرْ مَاذَا تَرٰى ۚ قَالَ يٰۤاَبَتِ افْعَلْ مَا تُؤْمَرُ ۫ سَتَجِدُنِيْۤ اِنْ شَآءَ اللّٰهُ مِنَ الصّٰبِرِيْنَ ۝

103. So when they both submitted and he threw him down upon his forehead,

فَلَمَّاۤ اَسْلَمَا وَ تَلَّهٗ لِلْجَبِيْنِ ۝

104. And We called out to him saying: O Ibrahim!

وَنَادَيْنٰهُ اَنْ يّٰۤاِبْرٰهِيْمُ ۝

105. You have indeed shown the truth of the vision; surely thus do We reward the doers of good:

قَدْ صَدَّقْتَ الرُّءْيَا ۚ اِنَّا كَذٰلِكَ نَجْزِى الْمُحْسِنِيْنَ ۝

106. Most surely this is a manifest trial.

اِنَّ هٰذَا لَهُوَ الْبَلٰٓؤُا الْمُبِيْنُ ۝

107. And We ransomed him with a great sacrifice.

وَفَدَيْنٰهُ بِذِبْحٍ عَظِيْمٍ ۝

108. And We perpetuated (praise) to him among the later generations.

وَتَرَكْنَا عَلَيْهِ فِى الْاٰخِرِيْنَ ۝

109. Peace be on Ibrahim.

سَلٰمٌ عَلٰۤى اِبْرٰهِيْمَ ۝

110. Thus do We reward the doers of good.

كَذٰلِكَ نَجْزِى الْمُحْسِنِيْنَ ۝

111. Surely he was one of Our believing servants.

اِنَّهٗ مِنْ عِبَادِنَا الْمُؤْمِنِيْنَ ۝

112. And We gave him the good news of Ishaq, a prophet among the good ones.

وَبَشَّرْنٰهُ بِاِسْحٰقَ نَبِيًّا مِّنَ الصّٰلِحِيْنَ ۝

113. And We showered Our blessings on him and on Ishaq; and of their offspring are the doers of good, and (also) those who are clearly unjust to their own souls.

وَبٰرَكْنَا عَلَيْهِ وَعَلٰۤى اِسْحٰقَ ۚ وَمِنْ ذُرِّيَّتِهِمَا مُحْسِنٌ وَّظَالِمٌ لِّنَفْسِهٖ مُبِيْنٌ ۝

114. And certainly We conferred a favor on Musa and Haroun.

وَلَقَدْ مَنَنَّا عَلٰى مُوْسٰى وَهٰرُوْنَ ۝

115. And We delivered them both and their people from the mighty distress.

وَنَجَّيْنٰهُمَا وَقَوْمَهُمَا مِنَ الْكَرْبِ الْعَظِيْمِ ۝

116. And We helped them, so they were the vanquishers.

وَنَصَرْنٰهُمْ فَكَانُوْا هُمُ الْغٰلِبِيْنَ ۝

117. And We gave them both the Book that made (things) clear.

وَاٰتَيْنٰهُمَا الْكِتٰبَ الْمُسْتَبِيْنَ ۝

118. And We guided them both on the right way.

وَهَدَيْنٰهُمَا الصِّرَاطَ الْمُسْتَقِيْمَ ۝

441

119. And We perpetuated (praise) to them among the later generations.

وَتَرَكْنَا عَلَيْهِمَا فِى الْأٰخِرِيْنَ ۖ ١١٩

120. Peace be on Musa and Haroun.

سَلٰمٌ عَلٰى مُوْسٰى وَهٰرُوْنَ ١٢٠

121. Even thus do We reward the doers of good.

اِنَّا كَذٰلِكَ نَجْزِى الْمُحْسِنِيْنَ ١٢١

122. Surely they were both of Our believing servants.

اِنَّهُمَا مِنْ عِبَادِنَا الْمُؤْمِنِيْنَ ١٢٢

123. And Ilyas was most surely of the apostles.

وَاِنَّ اِلْيَاسَ لَمِنَ الْمُرْسَلِيْنَ ١٢٣

124. When he said to his people: Do you not guard (against evil)?

اِذْ قَالَ لِقَوْمِهٖ اَلَا تَتَّقُوْنَ ١٢٤

125. What! do you call upon Ba'l and forsake the best of the creators,

اَتَدْعُوْنَ بَعْلًا وَتَذَرُوْنَ اَحْسَنَ الْخَالِقِيْنَ ١٢٥

126. Allah, your Lord and the Lord of your fathers of yore?

اللّٰهَ رَبَّكُمْ وَرَبَّ اٰبَآئِكُمُ الْاَوَّلِيْنَ ١٢٦

127. But they called him a liar, therefore they shall most surely be brought up.

فَكَذَّبُوْهُ فَاِنَّهُمْ لَمُحْضَرُوْنَ ١٢٧

128. But not the servants of Allah, the purified ones.

اِلَّا عِبَادَ اللّٰهِ الْمُخْلَصِيْنَ ١٢٨

129. And We perpetuated to him (praise) among the later generations.

وَتَرَكْنَا عَلَيْهِ فِى الْأٰخِرِيْنَ ۖ ١٢٩

130. Peace be on Ilyas.

سَلٰمٌ عَلٰى اِلْ يَاسِيْنَ ١٣٠

131. Even thus do We reward the doers of good.

اِنَّا كَذٰلِكَ نَجْزِى الْمُحْسِنِيْنَ ١٣١

132. Surely he was one of Our believing servants.

اِنَّهٗ مِنْ عِبَادِنَا الْمُؤْمِنِيْنَ ١٣٢

133. And Lut was most surely of the apostles.

وَاِنَّ لُوْطًا لَّمِنَ الْمُرْسَلِيْنَ ١٣٣

134. When We delivered him and his followers, all—

اِذْ نَجَّيْنٰهُ وَاَهْلَهٗ اَجْمَعِيْنَ ١٣٤

135. Except an old woman (who was) amongst those who tarried.

اِلَّا عَجُوْزًا فِى الْغٰبِرِيْنَ ١٣٥

136. Then We destroyed the others.

ثُمَّ دَمَّرْنَا الْأٰخِرِيْنَ ١٣٦

137. And most surely you pass by them in the morning,

وَاِنَّكُمْ لَتَمُرُّوْنَ عَلَيْهِمْ مُّصْبِحِيْنَ ١٣٧

138. And at night; do you not then understand?

وَبِالَّيْلِ ۖ اَفَلَا تَعْقِلُوْنَ ١٣٨

139. And Yunus was most surely of the apostles.

وَاِنَّ يُوْنُسَ لَمِنَ الْمُرْسَلِيْنَ ١٣٩

140. When he ran away to a ship completely laden,

اِذْ اَبَقَ اِلَى الْفُلْكِ الْمَشْحُوْنِ ۖ ١٤٠

141. So he shared (with them), but was of those who are cast off.

فَسَاهَمَ فَكَانَ مِنَ الْمُدْحَضِيْنَ ۖ

142. So the fish swallowed him while he did that for which he blamed himself.

فَالْتَقَمَهُ الْحُوْتُ وَهُوَ مُلِيْمٌ ۖ

143. But had it not been that he was of those who glorify (Us),

فَلَوْلَاۤ اَنَّهٗ كَانَ مِنَ الْمُسَبِّحِيْنَ ۖ

144. He would certainly have tarried in its belly to the day when they are raised.

لَلَبِثَ فِيْ بَطْنِهٖۤ اِلٰى يَوْمِ يُبْعَثُوْنَ ۖ

145. Then We cast him on to the vacant surface of the earth while he was sick.

فَنَبَذْنٰهُ بِالْعَرَآءِ وَهُوَ سَقِيْمٌ ۖ

146. And We caused to grow up for him a gourd-plant.

وَاَنْۢبَتْنَا عَلَيْهِ شَجَرَةً مِّنْ يَّقْطِيْنٍ ۖ

147. And We sent him to a hundred thousand, rather they exceeded.

وَاَرْسَلْنٰهُ اِلٰى مِائَةِ اَلْفٍ اَوْ يَزِيْدُوْنَ ۖ

148. And they believed, so We gave them provision till a time.

فَاٰمَنُوْا فَمَتَّعْنٰهُمْ اِلٰى حِيْنٍ ۖ

149. Then ask them whether your Lord has daughters and they have sons.

فَاسْتَفْتِهِمْ اَلِرَبِّكَ الْبَنَاتُ وَلَهُمُ الْبَنُوْنَ ۖ

150. Or did We create the angels females while they were witnesses?

اَمْ خَلَقْنَا الْمَلٰٓئِكَةَ اِنَاثًا وَّهُمْ شٰهِدُوْنَ ۖ

151. Now surely it is of their own lie that they say:

اَلَاۤ اِنَّهُمْ مِّنْ اِفْكِهِمْ لَيَقُوْلُوْنَ ۖ

152. Allah has begotten; and most surely they are liars.

وَلَدَ اللّٰهُ ۙ وَاِنَّهُمْ لَكٰذِبُوْنَ ۖ

153. Has He chosen daughters in preference to sons?

اَصْطَفَى الْبَنَاتِ عَلَى الْبَنِيْنَ ۖ

154. What is the matter with you, how is it that you judge?

مَا لَكُمْ ۟ كَيْفَ تَحْكُمُوْنَ ۖ

155. Will you not then mind?

اَفَلَا تَذَكَّرُوْنَ ۖ

156. Or have you a clear authority?

اَمْ لَكُمْ سُلْطٰنٌ مُّبِيْنٌ ۖ

157. Then bring your book, if you are truthful.

فَأْتُوْا بِكِتٰبِكُمْ اِنْ كُنْتُمْ صٰدِقِيْنَ ۖ

158. And they assert a relationship between Him and the jinn; and certainly the jinn do know that they shall surely be brought up;

وَجَعَلُوْا بَيْنَهٗ وَبَيْنَ الْجِنَّةِ نَسَبًا ۚ وَلَقَدْ عَلِمَتِ الْجِنَّةُ اِنَّهُمْ لَمُحْضَرُوْنَ ۖ

159. Glory be to Allah (for freedom) from what they describe;

سُبْحٰنَ اللّٰهِ عَمَّا يَصِفُوْنَ ۖ

160. But not so the servants of Allah, the purified ones.

اِلَّا عِبَادَ اللّٰهِ الْمُخْلَصِيْنَ ۖ

161. So surely you and what you worship,

فَاِنَّكُمْ وَمَا تَعْبُدُوْنَ ۖ

443

162. Not against Him can you cause (any) to fall into trial,

مَاۤ اَنْتُمْ عَلَيْهِ بِفٰتِنِيْنَ ۞

163. Save him who will go to hell.

اِلَّا مَنْ هُوَ صَالِ الْجَحِيْمِ ۞

164. And there is none of us but has an assigned place,

وَمَا مِنَّاۤ اِلَّا لَهٗ مَقَامٌ مَّعْلُوْمٌ ۞

165. And most surely we are they who draw themselves out in ranks,

وَّاِنَّا لَنَحْنُ الصَّآفُّوْنَ ۞

166. And we are most surely they who declare the glory (of Allah).

وَّاِنَّا لَنَحْنُ الْمُسَبِّحُوْنَ ۞

167. And surely they used to say:

وَاِنْ كَانُوْا لَيَقُوْلُوْنَ ۞

168. Had we a reminder from those of yore,

لَوْ اَنَّ عِنْدَنَا ذِكْرًا مِّنَ الْاَوَّلِيْنَ ۞

169. We would certainly have been the servants of Allah—the purified ones.

لَكُنَّا عِبَادَ اللّٰهِ الْمُخْلَصِيْنَ ۞

170. But (now) they disbelieve in it, so they will come to know.

فَكَفَرُوْا بِهٖ فَسَوْفَ يَعْلَمُوْنَ ۞

171. And certainly Our word has already gone forth in respect of Our servants, the apostles:

وَلَقَدْ سَبَقَتْ كَلِمَتُنَا لِعِبَادِنَا الْمُرْسَلِيْنَ ۞

172. Most surely they shall be the assisted ones,

اِنَّهُمْ لَهُمُ الْمَنْصُوْرُوْنَ ۞

173. And most surely Our host alone shall be the victorious ones.

وَاِنَّ جُنْدَنَا لَهُمُ الْغٰلِبُوْنَ ۞

174. Therefore turn away from them till a time,

فَتَوَلَّ عَنْهُمْ حَتّٰى حِيْنٍ ۞

175. And (then) see them, so they too shall see.

وَّاَبْصِرْهُمْ فَسَوْفَ يُبْصِرُوْنَ ۞

176. What! would they then hasten on Our chastisement?

اَفَبِعَذَابِنَا يَسْتَعْجِلُوْنَ ۞

177. But when it shall descend in their court, evil shall then be the morning of the warned ones.

فَاِذَا نَزَلَ بِسَاحَتِهِمْ فَسَآءَ صَبَاحُ الْمُنْذَرِيْنَ ۞

178. And turn away from them till a time,

وَتَوَلَّ عَنْهُمْ حَتّٰى حِيْنٍ ۞

179. And (then) see, for they too shall see.

وَّاَبْصِرْ فَسَوْفَ يُبْصِرُوْنَ ۞

180. Glory be to your Lord, the Lord of Honor, above what they describe.

سُبْحٰنَ رَبِّكَ رَبِّ الْعِزَّةِ عَمَّا يَصِفُوْنَ ۞

181. And peace be on the apostles.

وَسَلٰمٌ عَلَى الْمُرْسَلِيْنَ ۞

182. And all praise is due to Allah, the Lord of the worlds.

وَالْحَمْدُ لِلّٰهِ رَبِّ الْعٰلَمِيْنَ ۞

SUAD

**In the name of Allah,
the Beneficent, the Merciful.**

1. Suad, I swear by the Quran, full of admonition.

2. Nay! those who disbelieve are in self-exaltation and opposition.

3. How many did We destroy before them of the generations, then they cried while the time of escaping had passed away.

4. And they wonder that there has come to them a warner from among themselves, and the disbelievers say: This is an enchanter, a liar.

5. What! makes he the gods a single God? A strange thing is this, to be sure!

6. And the chief persons of them break forth, saying: Go and steadily adhere to your gods; this is most surely a thing sought after.

7. We never heard of this in the former faith; this is nothing but a forgery:

8. Has the reminder been revealed to him from among us? Nay! they are in doubt as to My reminder. Nay! they have not yet tasted My chastisement!

9. Or is it that they have the treasures of the mercy of your Lord, the Mighty, the great Giver?

10. Or is it that theirs is the kingdom of the heavens and the earth and what is between them? Then let them ascend by any means.

11. A host of deserters of the allies shall be here put to flight.

بِسْمِ اللهِ الرَّحْمٰنِ الرَّحِيْمِ ۞

صٓ وَالْقُرْاٰنِ ذِى الذِّكْرِ ۞

بَلِ الَّذِيْنَ كَفَرُوْا فِيْ عِزَّةٍ وَّشِقَاقٍ ۞

كَمْ اَهْلَكْنَا مِنْ قَبْلِهِمْ مِّنْ قَرْنٍ فَنَادَوْا وَّلَاتَ حِيْنَ مَنَاصٍ ۞

وَعَجِبُوْا اَنْ جَآءَهُمْ مُّنْذِرٌ مِّنْهُمْ ۖ وَقَالَ الْكٰفِرُوْنَ هٰذَا سٰحِرٌ كَذَّابٌ ۞

اَجَعَلَ الْاٰلِهَةَ اِلٰهًا وَّاحِدًا ۖ اِنَّ هٰذَا لَشَيْءٌ عُجَابٌ ۞

وَانْطَلَقَ الْمَلَاُ مِنْهُمْ اَنِ امْشُوْا وَاصْبِرُوْا عَلٰى اٰلِهَتِكُمْ ۖ اِنَّ هٰذَا لَشَيْءٌ يُّرَادُ ۞

مَا سَمِعْنَا بِهٰذَا فِى الْمِلَّةِ الْاٰخِرَةِ ۖ اِنْ هٰذَا اِلَّا اخْتِلَاقٌ ۞

ءَاُنْزِلَ عَلَيْهِ الذِّكْرُ مِنْ بَيْنِنَا ۖ بَلْ هُمْ فِيْ شَكٍّ مِّنْ ذِكْرِيْ ۖ بَلْ لَّمَّا يَذُوْقُوْا عَذَابِ ۞

اَمْ عِنْدَهُمْ خَزَآئِنُ رَحْمَةِ رَبِّكَ الْعَزِيْزِ الْوَهَّابِ ۞

اَمْ لَهُمْ مُّلْكُ السَّمٰوٰتِ وَالْاَرْضِ وَمَا بَيْنَهُمَا ۖ فَلْيَرْتَقُوْا فِى الْاَسْبَابِ ۞

جُنْدٌ مَّا هُنَالِكَ مَهْزُوْمٌ مِّنَ الْاَحْزَابِ ۞

12. The people of Nuh and Ad, and Firon, the lord of spikes, rejected (apostles) before them.

13. And Samood and the people of Lut and the dwellers of the thicket; these were the parties.

14. There was none of them but called the apostles liars, so just was My retribution.

15. Nor do these await aught but a single cry, there being no delay in it.

16. And they say: O our Lord! hasten on to us our portion before the day of reckoning.

17. Bear patiently what they say, and remember Our servant Dawood, the possessor of power; surely he was frequent in returning (to Allah).

18. Surely We made the mountains to sing the glory (of Allah) in unison with him at the evening and the sunrise,

19. And the birds gathered together; all joined in singing with him.

20. And We strengthened his kingdom and We gave him wisdom and a clear judgment.

21. And has there come to you the story of the litigants, when they made an entry into the private chamber by ascending over the walls?

22. When they entered in upon Dawood and he was frightened at them, they said: Fear not; two litigants, of whom one has acted wrongfully towards the other, therefore decide between us with justice, and do not act unjustly, and guide us to the right way.

23. Surely this is my brother; he has ninety-nine ewes and I have a single ewe; but he said: Make it over to me, and he has prevailed against me in discourse.

كَذَّبَتْ قَبْلَهُمْ قَوْمُ نُوحٍ وَّعَادٌ وَّفِرْعَوْنُ ذُو الْاَوْتَادِ ۞

وَثَمُوْدُ وَقَوْمُ لُوْطٍ وَّاَصْحٰبُ الْاَيْكَةِ اُولٰٓئِكَ الْاَحْزَابُ ۞

اِنْ كُلٌّ اِلَّا كَذَّبَ الرُّسُلَ فَحَقَّ عِقَابِ ۞

وَمَا يَنْظُرُ هٰٓؤُلَاءِ اِلَّا صَيْحَةً وَّاحِدَةً مَّا لَهَا مِنْ فَوَاقٍ ۞

وَقَالُوْا رَبَّنَا عَجِّلْ لَّنَا قِطَّنَا قَبْلَ يَوْمِ الْحِسَابِ ۞

اِصْبِرْ عَلٰى مَا يَقُوْلُوْنَ وَاذْكُرْ عَبْدَنَا دَاوٗدَ ذَا الْاَيْدِ اِنَّهٗٓ اَوَّابٌ ۞

اِنَّا سَخَّرْنَا الْجِبَالَ مَعَهٗ يُسَبِّحْنَ بِالْعَشِيِّ وَالْاِشْرَاقِ ۞

وَالطَّيْرَ مَحْشُوْرَةً ؕ كُلٌّ لَّهٗٓ اَوَّابٌ ۞

وَشَدَدْنَا مُلْكَهٗ وَاٰتَيْنٰهُ الْحِكْمَةَ وَفَصْلَ الْخِطَابِ ۞

وَهَلْ اَتٰىكَ نَبَؤُا الْخَصْمِ ۘ اِذْ تَسَوَّرُوا الْمِحْرَابَ ۞

اِذْ دَخَلُوْا عَلٰى دَاوٗدَ فَفَزِعَ مِنْهُمْ قَالُوْا لَا تَخَفْ ۚ خَصْمٰنِ بَغٰى بَعْضُنَا عَلٰى بَعْضٍ فَاحْكُمْ بَيْنَنَا بِالْحَقِّ وَلَا تُشْطِطْ وَاهْدِنَآ اِلٰى سَوَاءِ الصِّرَاطِ ۞

اِنَّ هٰذَآ اَخِيْ ۟ لَهٗ تِسْعٌ وَّتِسْعُوْنَ نَعْجَةً وَّلِيَ نَعْجَةٌ وَّاحِدَةٌ ۟ فَقَالَ اَكْفِلْنِيْهَا وَعَزَّنِيْ فِى الْخِطَابِ ۞

446

24. He said: Surely he has been unjust to you in demanding your ewe (to add) to his own ewes; and most surely most of the partners act wrongfully towards one another, save those who believe and do good, and very few are they; and Dawood was sure that We had tried him, so he sought the protection of his Lord, and he fell down bowing and turned time after time (to Him).

قَالَ لَقَدْ ظَلَمَكَ بِسُؤَالِ نَعْجَتِكَ اِلٰى نِعَاجِهٖ
وَاِنَّ كَثِيْرًا مِّنَ الْخُلَطَآءِ لَيَبْغِيْ بَعْضُهُمْ عَلٰى
بَعْضٍ اِلَّا الَّذِيْنَ اٰمَنُوْا وَعَمِلُوا الصّٰلِحٰتِ وَ
قَلِيْلٌ مَّا هُمْ ۖ وَظَنَّ دَاوٗدُ اَنَّمَا فَتَنّٰهُ فَاسْتَغْفَرَ
رَبَّهٗ وَخَرَّ رَاكِعًا وَّاَنَابَ ۩ ٢٤

25. Therefore We rectified for him this, and most surely he had a nearness to Us and an excellent resort.

فَغَفَرْنَا لَهٗ ذٰلِكَ ۚ وَاِنَّ لَهٗ عِنْدَنَا لَزُلْفٰى وَحُسْنَ
مَاٰبٍ ٢٥

26. O Dawood! surely We have made you a ruler in the land; so judge between men with justice and do not follow desire, lest it should lead you astray from the path of Allah; (as for) those who go astray from the path of Allah, they shall surely have a severe punishment because they forgot the day of reckoning.

يٰدَاوٗدُ اِنَّا جَعَلْنٰكَ خَلِيْفَةً فِى الْاَرْضِ فَاحْكُمْ بَيْنَ
النَّاسِ بِالْحَقِّ وَلَا تَتَّبِعِ الْهَوٰى فَيُضِلَّكَ عَنْ
سَبِيْلِ اللّٰهِ ۚ اِنَّ الَّذِيْنَ يَضِلُّوْنَ عَنْ سَبِيْلِ اللّٰهِ
لَهُمْ عَذَابٌ شَدِيْدٌۢ بِمَا نَسُوْا يَوْمَ الْحِسَابِ ٢٦

27. And We did not create the heaven and the earth and what is between them in vain; that is the opinion of those who disbelieve; then woe to those who disbelieve on account of the fire.

وَمَا خَلَقْنَا السَّمَآءَ وَالْاَرْضَ وَمَا بَيْنَهُمَا بَاطِلًا ۚ
ذٰلِكَ ظَنُّ الَّذِيْنَ كَفَرُوْا ۚ فَوَيْلٌ لِّلَّذِيْنَ كَفَرُوْا
مِنَ النَّارِ ٢٧

28. Shall We treat those who believe and do good like the mischief-makers in the earth? Or shall We make those who guard (against evil) like the wicked?

اَمْ نَجْعَلُ الَّذِيْنَ اٰمَنُوْا وَعَمِلُوا الصّٰلِحٰتِ كَالْمُفْسِدِيْنَ
فِى الْاَرْضِ اَمْ نَجْعَلُ الْمُتَّقِيْنَ كَالْفُجَّارِ ٢٨

29. (It is) a Book We have revealed to you abounding in good, that they may ponder over its verses, and that those endowed with understanding may be mindful.

كِتٰبٌ اَنْزَلْنٰهُ اِلَيْكَ مُبٰرَكٌ لِّيَدَّبَّرُوْا اٰيٰتِهٖ وَلِيَتَذَكَّرَ
اُولُوا الْاَلْبَابِ ٢٩

30. And We gave to Dawood Sulaiman; most excellent the servant! Surely he was frequent in returning (to Allah).

وَوَهَبْنَا لِدَاوٗدَ سُلَيْمٰنَ ۚ نِعْمَ الْعَبْدُ ۖ اِنَّهٗ اَوَّابٌ ٣٠

31. When there were brought to him in the evening (horses) still when standing, swift when running—

اِذْ عُرِضَ عَلَيْهِ بِالْعَشِيِّ الصّٰفِنٰتُ الْجِيَادُ ٣١

32. Then he said: Surely I preferred the good things to the remembrance of my Lord—until the sun set and time for Asr prayer was over, (he said):

فَقَالَ اِنِّيْ اَحْبَبْتُ حُبَّ الْخَيْرِ عَنْ ذِكْرِ رَبِّيْ ۚ حَتّٰى
تَوَارَتْ بِالْحِجَابِ ۪ ٣٢

33. Bring them back to me; so he began to slash (their) legs and necks.

34. And certainly We tried Sulaiman, and We put on his throne a (mere) body, so he turned (to Allah).

35. He said: My Lord! do Thou forgive me and grant me a kingdom which is not fit for (being inherited by) anyone after me; nations;

36. Then We made the wind subservient to him; it made his command to run gently wherever he desired,

37. And the shaitans, every builder and diver,

38. And others fettered in chains.

39. This is Our free gift, therefore give freely or withhold, without reckoning.

40. And most surely he had a nearness to Us and an excellent resort.

41. And remember Our servant Ayyub, when he called upon his Lord: The Shaitan has afflicted me with toil and torment.

42. Urge with your foot; here is a cool washing-place and a drink.

43. And We gave him his family and the like of them with them, as a mercy from Us, and as a reminder to those possessed of understanding.

44. And take in your hand a green branch and beat her with it and do not break your oath; surely We found him patient; most excellent the servant! Surely he was frequent in returning (to Allah).

45. And remember Our servants Ibrahim and Ishaq and Yaqoub, men of power and insight.

46. Surely We purified them by a pure quality, the keeping in mind of the (final) abode.

47. And most surely they were with Us, of the elect, the best.

48. And remember Ismail and Al-Yasha and Zulkifl; and they were all of the best.

49. This is a reminder; and most surely there is an excellent resort for those who guard (against evil),

50. The gardens of perpetuity, the doors are opened for them.

51. Reclining therein, calling therein for many fruits and drink.

52. And with them shall be those restraining their eyes, equals in age.

53. This is what you are promised for the day of reckoning.

54. Most surely this is Our sustenance; it shall never come to an end;

55. This (shall be so); and most surely there is an evil resort for the inordinate ones;

56. Hell; they shall enter it, so evil is the resting-place.

57. This (shall be so); so let them taste it, boiling and intensely cold (drink).

58. And other (punishment) of the same kind—of various sorts.

59. This is an army plunging in without consideration along with you; no welcome for them, surely they shall enter fire.

60. They shall say: Nay! you—no welcome to you: you did proffer it to us, so evil is the resting-place.

61. They shall say: Our Lord! whoever prepared it first for us, add Thou to him a double chastisement in the fire.

62. And they shall say: What is the matter with us that we do not see men whom we used to count among the vicious?

63. Was it that we (only) took them in scorn, or have our eyes (now) turned aside from them?

وَاذْكُرْ اِسْمٰعِيْلَ وَالْيَسَعَ وَذَا الْكِفْلِ ۚ وَكُلٌّ مِّنَ الْاَخْيَارِ ۝

هٰذَا ذِكْرٌ ۚ وَاِنَّ لِلْمُتَّقِيْنَ لَحُسْنَ مَاٰبٍ ۝

جَنّٰتِ عَدْنٍ مُّفَتَّحَةً لَّهُمُ الْاَبْوَابُ ۝

مُتَّكِئِيْنَ فِيْهَا يَدْعُوْنَ فِيْهَا بِفَاكِهَةٍ كَثِيْرَةٍ وَّشَرَابٍ ۝

وَعِنْدَهُمْ قٰصِرٰتُ الطَّرْفِ اَتْرَابٌ ۝

هٰذَا مَا تُوْعَدُوْنَ لِيَوْمِ الْحِسَابِ ۝

اِنَّ هٰذَا لَرِزْقُنَا مَالَهٗ مِنْ نَّفَادٍ ۝

هٰذَا ۚ وَاِنَّ لِلطّٰغِيْنَ لَشَرَّ مَاٰبٍ ۝

جَهَنَّمَ ۚ يَصْلَوْنَهَا ۚ فَبِئْسَ الْمِهَادُ ۝

هٰذَا ۙ فَلْيَذُوْقُوْهُ حَمِيْمٌ وَّغَسَّاقٌ ۝

وَّاٰخَرُ مِنْ شَكْلِهٖٓ اَزْوَاجٌ ۝

هٰذَا فَوْجٌ مُّقْتَحِمٌ مَّعَكُمْ ۚ لَا مَرْحَبًا بِهِمْ ۚ اِنَّهُمْ صَالُوا النَّارِ ۝

قَالُوْا بَلْ اَنْتُمْ ۚ لَا مَرْحَبًا بِكُمْ ۚ اَنْتُمْ قَدَّمْتُمُوْهُ لَنَا ۚ فَبِئْسَ الْقَرَارُ ۝

قَالُوْا رَبَّنَا مَنْ قَدَّمَ لَنَا هٰذَا فَزِدْهُ عَذَابًا ضِعْفًا فِى النَّارِ ۝

وَقَالُوْا مَا لَنَا لَا نَرٰى رِجَالًا كُنَّا نَعُدُّهُمْ مِّنَ الْاَشْرَارِ ۝

اَتَّخَذْنٰهُمْ سِخْرِيًّا اَمْ زَاغَتْ عَنْهُمُ الْاَبْصَارُ ۝

64. That most surely is the truth: the contending one with another of the inmates of the fire.

اِنَّ ذٰلِكَ لَحَقٌّ تَخَاصُمُ اَهْلِ النَّارِ ۞

65. Say: I am only a warner, and there is no god but Allah, the One, the Subduer (of all):

قُلْ اِنَّمَاۤ اَنَا مُنْذِرٌ ۖ وَّمَا مِنْ اِلٰهٍ اِلَّا اللّٰهُ الْوَاحِدُ الْقَهَّارُ ۞

66. The Lord of the heavens and the earth and what is between them, the Mighty, the most Forgiving.

رَبُّ السَّمٰوٰتِ وَالْاَرْضِ وَمَا بَيْنَهُمَا الْعَزِيْزُ الْغَفَّارُ ۞

67. Say: It is a message of importance,

قُلْ هُوَ نَبَؤٌا عَظِيْمٌ ۞

68. (And) you are turning aside from it:

اَنْتُمْ عَنْهُ مُعْرِضُوْنَ ۞

69. I had no knowledge of the exalted chiefs when they contended:

مَا كَانَ لِيَ مِنْ عِلْمٍ بِالْمَلَاِ الْاَعْلٰۤى اِذْ يَخْتَصِمُوْنَ ۞

70. Naught is revealed to me save that I am a plain warner.

اِنْ يُّوْحٰۤى اِلَيَّ اِلَّاۤ اَنَّمَاۤ اَنَا نَذِيْرٌ مُّبِيْنٌ ۞

71. When your Lord said to the angels; Surely I am going to create a mortal from dust:

اِذْ قَالَ رَبُّكَ لِلْمَلٰٓئِكَةِ اِنِّيْ خَالِقٌ بَشَرًا مِّنْ طِيْنٍ ۞

72. So when I have made him complete and breathed into him of My spirit, then fall down making obeisance to him.

فَاِذَا سَوَّيْتُهُ وَنَفَخْتُ فِيْهِ مِنْ رُّوْحِيْ فَقَعُوْا لَهُ سٰجِدِيْنَ ۞

73. And the angels did obeisance, all of them,

فَسَجَدَ الْمَلٰٓئِكَةُ كُلُّهُمْ اَجْمَعُوْنَ ۞

74. But not Iblis: he was proud and he was one of the unbelievers.

اِلَّاۤ اِبْلِيْسَ ۖ اِسْتَكْبَرَ وَكَانَ مِنَ الْكٰفِرِيْنَ ۞

75. He said: O Iblis! what prevented you that you should do obeisance to him whom I created with My two hands? Are you proud or are you of the exalted ones?

قَالَ يَاۤ اِبْلِيْسُ مَا مَنَعَكَ اَنْ تَسْجُدَ لِمَا خَلَقْتُ بِيَدَيَّ ۖ اَسْتَكْبَرْتَ اَمْ كُنْتَ مِنَ الْعَالِيْنَ ۞

76. He said: I am better than he; Thou hast created me of fire, and him Thou didst create of dust.

قَالَ اَنَا خَيْرٌ مِّنْهُ ۖ خَلَقْتَنِيْ مِنْ نَّارٍ وَّخَلَقْتَهُ مِنْ طِيْنٍ ۞

77. He said: Then get out of it, for surely you are driven away:

قَالَ فَاخْرُجْ مِنْهَا فَاِنَّكَ رَجِيْمٌ ۞

78. And surely My curse is on you to the day of judgment.

وَّاِنَّ عَلَيْكَ لَعْنَتِيْۤ اِلٰى يَوْمِ الدِّيْنِ ۞

79. He said: My Lord! then respite me to the day that they are raised.

80. He said: Surely you are of the respited ones,

81. Till the period of the time made known.

82. He said: Then by Thy Might I will surely make them live an evil life, all,

83. Except Thy servants from among them, the purified ones.

84. He said: The truth then is and the truth do I speak:

85. That I will most certainly fill hell with you and with those among them who follow you, all.

86. Say: I do not ask you for any reward for it; nor am I of those who affect:

87. It is nothing but a reminder to the nations;

88. And most certainly you will come to know about it after a time.

قَالَ رَبِّ فَأَنْظِرْنِىٓ إِلٰى يَوْمِ يُبْعَثُوْنَ ۝

قَالَ فَإِنَّكَ مِنَ الْمُنْظَرِيْنَ ۙ ۝

إِلٰى يَوْمِ الْوَقْتِ الْمَعْلُوْمِ ۝

قَالَ فَبِعِزَّتِكَ لَأُغْوِيَنَّهُمْ أَجْمَعِيْنَ ۙ ۝

إِلَّا عِبَادَكَ مِنْهُمُ الْمُخْلَصِيْنَ ۝

قَالَ فَالْحَقُّ وَالْحَقَّ أَقُوْلُ ۚ ۝

لَأَمْلَأَنَّ جَهَنَّمَ مِنْكَ وَمِمَّنْ تَبِعَكَ مِنْهُمْ أَجْمَعِيْنَ ۝

قُلْ مَآ أَسْأَلُكُمْ عَلَيْهِ مِنْ أَجْرٍ وَّمَآ أَنَا مِنَ الْمُتَكَلِّفِيْنَ ۝

إِنْ هُوَ إِلَّا ذِكْرٌ لِّلْعٰلَمِيْنَ ۝

وَلَتَعْلَمُنَّ نَبَأَهٗ بَعْدَ حِيْنٍ ۝

451

THE COMPANIES
(ZUMAR)

اٰیاتها ٧٥ (٣٩) سُوْرَةُ الزُّمَرِ مَکِّیَّةٌ رُکُوْعاتها ٨

**In the name of Allah,
the Beneficent, the Merciful.**

بِسْمِ اللهِ الرَّحْمٰنِ الرَّحِیْمِ ۞

1. The revelation of the Book is from Allah, the Mighty, the Wise.

تَنْزِیْلُ الْکِتٰبِ مِنَ اللهِ الْعَزِیْزِ الْحَکِیْمِ ۞

2. Surely We have revealed to you the Book with the truth, therefore serve Allah, being sincere to Him in obedience.

اِنَّاۤ اَنْزَلْنَاۤ اِلَیْکَ الْکِتٰبَ بِالْحَقِّ فَاعْبُدِ اللهَ مُخْلِصًا لَّهُ الدِّیْنَ ۞

3. Now, surely, sincere obedience is due to Allah (alone) and (as for) those who take guardians besides Him, (saying), We do not serve them save that they may make us nearer to Allah, surely Allah will judge between them in that in which they differ; surely Allah does not guide him aright who is a liar, ungrateful.

اَلَا لِلّٰهِ الدِّیْنُ الْخَالِصُ ؕ وَالَّذِیْنَ اتَّخَذُوْا مِنْ دُوْنِهٖۤ اَوْلِیَآءَ ۘ مَا نَعْبُدُهُمْ اِلَّا لِیُقَرِّبُوْنَاۤ اِلَی اللهِ زُلْفٰی ؕ اِنَّ اللهَ یَحْکُمُ بَیْنَهُمْ فِیْ مَا هُمْ فِیْهِ یَخْتَلِفُوْنَ ۬ؕ اِنَّ اللهَ لَا یَهْدِیْ مَنْ هُوَ کٰذِبٌ کَفَّارٌ ۞

4. If Allah desire to take a son to Himself, He will surely choose those He pleases from what He has created. Glory be to Him: He is Allah, the One, the Subduer (of all).

لَوْ اَرَادَ اللهُ اَنْ یَّتَّخِذَ وَلَدًا لَّاصْطَفٰی مِمَّا یَخْلُقُ مَا یَشَآءُ ۙ سُبْحٰنَهٗ ؕ هُوَ اللهُ الْوَاحِدُ الْقَهَّارُ ۞

5. He has created the heavens and the earth with the truth; He makes the night cover the day and makes the day overtake the night, and He has made the sun and the moon subservient; each one runs on to an assigned term; now surely He is the Mighty, the great Forgiver.

خَلَقَ السَّمٰوٰتِ وَالْاَرْضَ بِالْحَقِّ ۚ یُکَوِّرُ الَّیْلَ عَلَی النَّهَارِ وَیُکَوِّرُ النَّهَارَ عَلَی الَّیْلِ وَسَخَّرَ الشَّمْسَ وَالْقَمَرَ ؕ کُلٌّ یَّجْرِیْ لِاَجَلٍ مُّسَمًّی ؕ اَلَا هُوَ الْعَزِیْزُ الْغَفَّارُ ۞

6. He has created you from a single being, then made its mate of the same (kind), and He has made for you eight of the cattle in pairs. He creates you in the wombs of your mothers—a creation after a creation—in triple darkness; that is Allah your Lord, His is the kingdom; there is no god but He; whence are you then turned away?

خَلَقَکُمْ مِّنْ نَّفْسٍ وَّاحِدَةٍ ثُمَّ جَعَلَ مِنْهَا زَوْجَهَا وَاَنْزَلَ لَکُمْ مِّنَ الْاَنْعَامِ ثَمٰنِیَةَ اَزْوَاجٍ ؕ یَخْلُقُکُمْ فِیْ بُطُوْنِ اُمَّهٰتِکُمْ خَلْقًا مِّنْ بَعْدِ خَلْقٍ فِیْ ظُلُمٰتٍ ثَلٰثٍ ؕ ذٰلِکُمُ اللهُ رَبُّکُمْ لَهُ الْمُلْکُ ؕ لَاۤ اِلٰهَ اِلَّا هُوَ ۚ فَاَنّٰی تُصْرَفُوْنَ ۞

7. If you are ungrateful, then surely Allah is Self-sufficient, above all need of you; and He does not like ungratefulness in His servants; and if you are grateful, He likes it in you; and no bearer of burden shall bear the burden of another; then to your Lord is your return, then will He inform you of what you did; surely He is Cognizant of what is in the breasts.

اِنْ تَكْفُرُوا فَاِنَّ اللّٰهَ غَنِيٌّ عَنْكُمْ ۗ وَلَا يَرْضٰى لِعِبَادِهِ الْكُفْرَ ۚ وَاِنْ تَشْكُرُوا يَرْضَهُ لَكُمْ ۗ وَلَا تَزِرُ وَازِرَةٌ وِّزْرَ اُخْرٰى ۗ ثُمَّ اِلٰى رَبِّكُمْ مَّرْجِعُكُمْ فَيُنَبِّئُكُمْ بِمَا كُنْتُمْ تَعْمَلُوْنَ ۗ اِنَّهُ عَلِيْمٌ بِذَاتِ الصُّدُوْرِ ۝

8. And when distress afflicts a man he calls upon his Lord, turning to Him frequently; then when He makes him possess a favor from Him, he forgets that for which he called upon Him before, and sets up rivals to Allah that he may cause (men) to stray off from His path. Say: Enjoy yourself in your ungratefulness a little, surely you are of the inmates of the fire.

وَاِذَا مَسَّ الْاِنْسَانَ ضُرٌّ دَعَا رَبَّهُ مُنِيْبًا اِلَيْهِ ثُمَّ اِذَا خَوَّلَهُ نِعْمَةً مِّنْهُ نَسِيَ مَا كَانَ يَدْعُوا اِلَيْهِ مِنْ قَبْلُ وَجَعَلَ لِلّٰهِ اَنْدَادًا لِّيُضِلَّ عَنْ سَبِيْلِهِ ۗ قُلْ تَمَتَّعْ بِكُفْرِكَ قَلِيْلًا ۖ اِنَّكَ مِنْ اَصْحٰبِ النَّارِ ۝

9. What! he who is obedient during hours of the night, prostrating himself and standing, takes care of the hereafter and hopes for the mercy of his Lord! Say: Are those who know and those who do not know alike? Only the men of understanding are mindful.

اَمَّنْ هُوَ قَانِتٌ اٰنَاءَ الَّيْلِ سَاجِدًا وَّقَائِمًا يَّحْذَرُ الْاٰخِرَةَ وَيَرْجُوْا رَحْمَةَ رَبِّهِ ۗ قُلْ هَلْ يَسْتَوِي الَّذِيْنَ يَعْلَمُوْنَ وَالَّذِيْنَ لَا يَعْلَمُوْنَ ۗ اِنَّمَا يَتَذَكَّرُ اُولُوا الْاَلْبَابِ ۝

10. Say: O my servants who believe! be careful of (your duty to) your Lord; for those who do good in this world is good, and Allah's earth is spacious; only the patient will be paid back their reward in full without measure.

قُلْ يٰعِبَادِ الَّذِيْنَ اٰمَنُوا اتَّقُوْا رَبَّكُمْ ۗ لِلَّذِيْنَ اَحْسَنُوْا فِيْ هٰذِهِ الدُّنْيَا حَسَنَةٌ ۗ وَاَرْضُ اللّٰهِ وَاسِعَةٌ ۗ اِنَّمَا يُوَفَّى الصّٰبِرُوْنَ اَجْرَهُمْ بِغَيْرِ حِسَابٍ ۝

11. Say: I am commanded that I should serve Allah, being sincere to Him in obedience.

قُلْ اِنِّيْ اُمِرْتُ اَنْ اَعْبُدَ اللّٰهَ مُخْلِصًا لَّهُ الدِّيْنَ ۝

12. And I am commanded that I shall be the first of those who submit.

وَاُمِرْتُ لِاَنْ اَكُوْنَ اَوَّلَ الْمُسْلِمِيْنَ ۝

13. Say: I fear, if I disobey my Lord, the chastisement of a grievous day.

قُلْ اِنِّيْ اَخَافُ اِنْ عَصَيْتُ رَبِّيْ عَذَابَ يَوْمٍ عَظِيْمٍ ۝

14. Say: Allah (it is Whom) I serve, being sincere to Him in my obedience:

قُلِ اللّٰهَ اَعْبُدُ مُخْلِصًا لَّهُ دِيْنِيْ ۝

15. Serve then what you like besides Him. Say: The losers surely are those who shall have lost themselves and their families on the day of resurrection; now surely that is the clear loss.

فَاعْبُدُوْا مَا شِئْتُمْ مِّنْ دُوْنِهٖ ۗ قُلْ اِنَّ الْخٰسِرِيْنَ الَّذِيْنَ خَسِرُوْۤا اَنْفُسَهُمْ وَاَهْلِيْهِمْ يَوْمَ الْقِيٰمَةِ ۗ اَلَا ذٰلِكَ هُوَ الْخُسْرَانُ الْمُبِيْنُ ۝

16. They shall have coverings of fire above them and coverings beneath them; with that Allah makes His servants to fear; so be careful of (your duty to) Me, O My servants!

لَهُمْ مِّنْ فَوْقِهِمْ ظُلَلٌ مِّنَ النَّارِ وَمِنْ تَحْتِهِمْ ظُلَلٌ ۗ ذٰلِكَ يُخَوِّفُ اللّٰهُ بِهٖ عِبَادَهٗ ۗ يٰعِبَادِ فَاتَّقُوْنِ ۝

17. And (as for) those who keep off from the worship of the idols and turn to Allah, they shall have good news, therefore give good news to My servants,

وَالَّذِيْنَ اجْتَنَبُوا الطَّاغُوْتَ اَنْ يَّعْبُدُوْهَا وَاَنَابُوْۤا اِلَى اللّٰهِ لَهُمُ الْبُشْرٰى ۚ فَبَشِّرْ عِبَادِ ۝

18. Those who listen to the word, then follow the best of it; those are they whom Allah has guided, and those it is who are the men of understanding.

الَّذِيْنَ يَسْتَمِعُوْنَ الْقَوْلَ فَيَتَّبِعُوْنَ اَحْسَنَهٗ ۗ اُولٰٓئِكَ الَّذِيْنَ هَدٰىهُمُ اللّٰهُ وَاُولٰٓئِكَ هُمْ اُولُوا الْاَلْبَابِ ۝

19. What! as for him then against whom the sentence of chastisement is due: What! can you save him who is in the fire?

اَفَمَنْ حَقَّ عَلَيْهِ كَلِمَةُ الْعَذَابِ ۗ اَفَاَنْتَ تُنْقِذُ مَنْ فِى النَّارِ ۝

20. But (as for) those who are careful of (their duty to) their Lord, they shall have high places, above them higher places, built (for them), beneath which flow rivers; (this is) the promise of Allah: Allah will not fail in (His) promise.

لٰكِنِ الَّذِيْنَ اتَّقَوْا رَبَّهُمْ لَهُمْ غُرَفٌ مِّنْ فَوْقِهَا غُرَفٌ مَّبْنِيَّةٌ ۙ تَجْرِيْ مِنْ تَحْتِهَا الْاَنْهٰرُ ۗ وَعْدَ اللّٰهِ ۗ لَا يُخْلِفُ اللّٰهُ الْمِيْعَادَ ۝

21. Do you not see that Allah sends down water from the cloud, then makes it go along in the earth in springs, then brings forth therewith herbage of various colors, then it withers so that you see it becoming yellow, then He makes it a thing crushed and broken into pieces? Most surely there is a reminder in this for the men of understanding.

اَلَمْ تَرَ اَنَّ اللّٰهَ اَنْزَلَ مِنَ السَّمَاءِ مَاءً فَسَلَكَهٗ يَنَابِيْعَ فِى الْاَرْضِ ثُمَّ يُخْرِجُ بِهٖ زَرْعًا مُّخْتَلِفًا اَلْوَانُهٗ ثُمَّ يَهِيْجُ فَتَرٰىهُ مُصْفَرًّا ثُمَّ يَجْعَلُهٗ حُطَامًا ۗ اِنَّ فِيْ ذٰلِكَ لَذِكْرٰى لِاُولِى الْاَلْبَابِ ۝

22. What! is he whose heart Allah has opened for Islam so that he is in a light from his Lord (like the hard-hearted)? Nay, woe to those whose hearts are hard against the remembrance of Allah; those are in clear error.

اَفَمَنْ شَرَحَ اللّٰهُ صَدْرَهٗ لِلْاِسْلَامِ فَهُوَ عَلٰى نُوْرٍ مِّنْ رَّبِّهٖ ۗ فَوَيْلٌ لِّلْقٰسِيَةِ قُلُوْبُهُمْ مِّنْ ذِكْرِ اللّٰهِ ۗ اُولٰٓئِكَ فِيْ ضَلٰلٍ مُّبِيْنٍ ۝

23. Allah has revealed the best announcement, a book comformable in its various parts, repeating, whereat do shudder the skins of those who fear their Lord, then their skins and their hearts become pliant to the remembrance of Allah; this is Allah's guidance, He guides with it whom He pleases; and (as for) him whom Allah makes err, there is no guide for him.

اللهُ نَزَّلَ اَحْسَنَ الْحَدِيْثِ كِتٰبًا مُّتَشَابِهًا مَّثَانِيَ ۖ تَقْشَعِرُّ مِنْهُ جُلُوْدُ الَّذِيْنَ يَخْشَوْنَ رَبَّهُمْ ۚ ثُمَّ تَلِيْنُ جُلُوْدُهُمْ وَقُلُوْبُهُمْ اِلٰى ذِكْرِ اللّٰهِ ۚ ذٰلِكَ هُدَى اللّٰهِ يَهْدِيْ بِهٖ مَنْ يَّشَاءُ ۚ وَمَنْ يُّضْلِلِ اللّٰهُ فَمَا لَهٗ مِنْ هَادٍ ۝

24. Is he then who has to guard himself with his own person against the evil chastisement on the resurrection day? And it will be said to the unjust: Taste what you earned.

اَفَمَنْ يَّتَّقِيْ بِوَجْهِهٖ سُوْءَ الْعَذَابِ يَوْمَ الْقِيٰمَةِ ۚ وَقِيْلَ لِلظّٰلِمِيْنَ ذُوْقُوْا مَا كُنْتُمْ تَكْسِبُوْنَ ۝

25. Those before them rejected (prophets), therefore there came to them the chastisement from whence they perceived not.

كَذَّبَ الَّذِيْنَ مِنْ قَبْلِهِمْ فَاَتٰهُمُ الْعَذَابُ مِنْ حَيْثُ لَا يَشْعُرُوْنَ ۝

26. So Allah made them taste the disgrace in this world's life, and certainly the punishment of the hereafter is greater; did they but know!

فَاَذَاقَهُمُ اللّٰهُ الْخِزْيَ فِى الْحَيٰوةِ الدُّنْيَا ۚ وَلَعَذَابُ الْاٰخِرَةِ اَكْبَرُ ۚ لَوْ كَانُوْا يَعْلَمُوْنَ ۝

27. And certainly We have set forth to men in this Quran similitudes of every sort that they may mind.

وَلَقَدْ ضَرَبْنَا لِلنَّاسِ فِيْ هٰذَا الْقُرْاٰنِ مِنْ كُلِّ مَثَلٍ لَّعَلَّهُمْ يَتَذَكَّرُوْنَ ۝

28. An Arabic Quran without any crookedness, that they may guard (against evil).

قُرْاٰنًا عَرَبِيًّا غَيْرَ ذِيْ عِوَجٍ لَّعَلَّهُمْ يَتَّقُوْنَ ۝

29. Allah sets forth an example: There is a slave in whom are (several) partners differing with one another, and there is another slave wholly owned by one man. Are the two alike in condition? (All) praise is due to Allah. Nay! most of them do not know.

ضَرَبَ اللّٰهُ مَثَلًا رَّجُلًا فِيْهِ شُرَكَاءُ مُتَشٰكِسُوْنَ وَرَجُلًا سَلَمًا لِّرَجُلٍ ۚ هَلْ يَسْتَوِيٰنِ مَثَلًا ۚ اَلْحَمْدُ لِلّٰهِ ۚ بَلْ اَكْثَرُهُمْ لَا يَعْلَمُوْنَ ۝

30. Surely you shall die and they (too) shall surely die.

اِنَّكَ مَيِّتٌ وَّاِنَّهُمْ مَّيِّتُوْنَ ۝

31. Then surely on the day of resurrection you will contend one with another before your Lord.

ثُمَّ اِنَّكُمْ يَوْمَ الْقِيٰمَةِ عِنْدَ رَبِّكُمْ تَخْتَصِمُوْنَ ۝

32. Who is then more unjust than he who utters a lie against Allah and (he who) gives the lie to the truth when it comes to him; is there not in hell an abode for the unbelievers?

فَمَنْ اَظْلَمُ مِمَّنْ كَذَبَ عَلَى اللّٰهِ وَكَذَّبَ بِالصِّدْقِ اِذْ جَاءَهٗ ۚ اَلَيْسَ فِيْ جَهَنَّمَ مَثْوًى لِّلْكٰفِرِيْنَ ۝

33. And he who brings the truth and (he who) accepts it as the truth—these are they that guard (against evil).

وَالَّذِيْ جَآءَ بِالصِّدْقِ وَصَدَّقَ بِهٖٓ اُولٰٓئِكَ هُمُ الْمُتَّقُوْنَ ۞

34. They shall have with their Lord what they please; that is the reward of the doers of good;

لَهُمْ مَّا يَشَآءُوْنَ عِنْدَ رَبِّهِمْ ۚ ذٰلِكَ جَزٰٓؤُا الْمُحْسِنِيْنَ ۙ۞

35. So that Allah will do away with the worst of what they did and give them their reward for the best of what they do.

لِيُكَفِّرَ اللّٰهُ عَنْهُمْ اَسْوَاَ الَّذِيْ عَمِلُوْا وَ يَجْزِيَهُمْ اَجْرَهُمْ بِاَحْسَنِ الَّذِيْ كَانُوْا يَعْمَلُوْنَ ۞

36. Is not Allah sufficient for His servant? And they seek to frighten you with those besides Him; and whomsoever Allah makes err, there is no guide for him.

اَلَيْسَ اللّٰهُ بِكَافٍ عَبْدَهٗ ۚ وَ يُخَوِّفُوْنَكَ بِالَّذِيْنَ مِنْ دُوْنِهٖ ؕ وَ مَنْ يُّضْلِلِ اللّٰهُ فَمَالَهٗ مِنْ هَادٍ ۚ

37. And whom Allah guides, there is none that can lead him astray; is not Allah Mighty, the Lord of retribution?

وَ مَنْ يَّهْدِ اللّٰهُ فَمَا لَهٗ مِنْ مُّضِلٍّ ؕ اَلَيْسَ اللّٰهُ بِعَزِيْزٍ ذِى انْتِقَامٍ ۞

38. And should you ask them, Who created the heavens and the earth? They would most certainly say: Allah. Say: Have you then considered that what you call upon besides Allah, would they, if Allah desire to afflict me with harm, be the removers of His harm, or (would they), if Allah desire to show me mercy, be the withholders of His mercy? Say: Allah is sufficient for me; on Him do the reliant rely.

وَ لَئِنْ سَاَلْتَهُمْ مَّنْ خَلَقَ السَّمٰوٰتِ وَ الْاَرْضَ لَيَقُوْلُنَّ اللّٰهُ ؕ قُلْ اَفَرَءَيْتُمْ مَّا تَدْعُوْنَ مِنْ دُوْنِ اللّٰهِ اِنْ اَرَادَنِيَ اللّٰهُ بِضُرٍّ هَلْ هُنَّ كٰشِفٰتُ ضُرِّهٖٓ اَوْ اَرَادَنِيْ بِرَحْمَةٍ هَلْ هُنَّ مُمْسِكٰتُ رَحْمَتِهٖ ؕ قُلْ حَسْبِيَ اللّٰهُ ؕ عَلَيْهِ يَتَوَكَّلُ الْمُتَوَكِّلُوْنَ ۞

39. Say: O my people! work in your place, surely I am a worker, so you will come to know.

قُلْ يٰقَوْمِ اعْمَلُوْا عَلٰى مَكَانَتِكُمْ اِنِّيْ عَامِلٌ ۚ فَسَوْفَ تَعْلَمُوْنَ ۙ۞

40. Who it is to whom there shall come a punishment which will disgrace him and to whom will be due a lasting punishment.

مَنْ يَّأْتِيْهِ عَذَابٌ يُّخْزِيْهِ وَ يَحِلُّ عَلَيْهِ عَذَابٌ مُّقِيْمٌ ۞

41. Surely We have revealed to you the Book with the truth for the sake of men; so whoever follows the right way, it is for his own soul and whoever errs, he errs only to its detriment; and you are not a custodian over them.

اِنَّآ اَنْزَلْنَا عَلَيْكَ الْكِتٰبَ لِلنَّاسِ بِالْحَقِّ ۚ فَمَنِ اهْتَدٰى فَلِنَفْسِهٖ ۚ وَ مَنْ ضَلَّ فَاِنَّمَا يَضِلُّ عَلَيْهَا ۚ وَ مَآ اَنْتَ عَلَيْهِمْ بِوَكِيْلٍ ۩۞

42. Allah takes the souls at the time of their death, and those that die not during their sleep; then He withholds those on whom He has passed the decree of death and sends the others back till an appointed term; most surely there are signs in this for a people who reflect.

اللّٰهُ يَتَوَفَّى الْاَنْفُسَ حِيْنَ مَوْتِهَا وَالَّتِيْ لَمْ تَمُتْ فِيْ مَنَامِهَا ۚ فَيُمْسِكُ الَّتِيْ قَضٰى عَلَيْهَا الْمَوْتَ وَيُرْسِلُ الْاُخْرٰٓى اِلٰٓى اَجَلٍ مُّسَمًّى ؕ اِنَّ فِيْ ذٰلِكَ لَاٰيٰتٍ لِّقَوْمٍ يَّتَفَكَّرُوْنَ ۝

43. Or have they taken intercessors besides Allah? Say: what! even though they did not ever have control over anything, nor do they understand.

اَمِ اتَّخَذُوْا مِنْ دُوْنِ اللّٰهِ شُفَعَآءَ ؕ قُلْ اَوَلَوْ كَانُوْا لَا يَمْلِكُوْنَ شَيْئًا وَّلَا يَعْقِلُوْنَ ۝

44. Say: Allah's is the intercession altogether; His is the kingdom of the heavens and the earth, then to Him you shall be brought back.

قُلْ لِّلّٰهِ الشَّفَاعَةُ جَمِيْعًا ؕ لَهٗ مُلْكُ السَّمٰوٰتِ وَ الْاَرْضِ ؕ ثُمَّ اِلَيْهِ تُرْجَعُوْنَ ۝

45. And when Allah alone is mentioned, the hearts of those who do not believe in the hereafter shrink, and when those besides Him are mentioned, lo! they are joyful.

وَاِذَا ذُكِرَ اللّٰهُ وَحْدَهُ اشْمَاَزَّتْ قُلُوْبُ الَّذِيْنَ لَا يُؤْمِنُوْنَ بِالْاٰخِرَةِ ۚ وَاِذَا ذُكِرَ الَّذِيْنَ مِنْ دُوْنِهٖٓ اِذَا هُمْ يَسْتَبْشِرُوْنَ ۝

46. Say: O Allah! Originator of the heavens and the earth, Knower of the unseen and the seen! Thou (only) judgest between Thy servants as to that wherein they differ.

قُلِ اللّٰهُمَّ فَاطِرَ السَّمٰوٰتِ وَالْاَرْضِ عٰلِمَ الْغَيْبِ وَالشَّهَادَةِ اَنْتَ تَحْكُمُ بَيْنَ عِبَادِكَ فِيْ مَا كَانُوْا فِيْهِ يَخْتَلِفُوْنَ ۝

47. And had those who are unjust all that is in the earth and the like of it with it, they would certainly offer it as ransom (to be saved) from the evil of the punishment on the day of resurrection; and what they never thought of shall become plain to them from Allah.

وَلَوْ اَنَّ لِلَّذِيْنَ ظَلَمُوْا مَا فِي الْاَرْضِ جَمِيْعًا وَّمِثْلَهٗ مَعَهٗ لَافْتَدَوْا بِهٖ مِنْ سُوْٓءِ الْعَذَابِ يَوْمَ الْقِيٰمَةِ ؕ وَبَدَا لَهُمْ مِّنَ اللّٰهِ مَا لَمْ يَكُوْنُوْا يَحْتَسِبُوْنَ ۝

48. And the evil (consequences) of what they wrought shall become plain to them, and the very thing they mocked at shall beset them.

وَبَدَا لَهُمْ سَيِّاٰتُ مَا كَسَبُوْا وَحَاقَ بِهِمْ مَّا كَانُوْا بِهٖ يَسْتَهْزِءُوْنَ ۝

49. So when harm afflicts a man he calls upon Us; then, when We give him a favor from Us, he says: I have been given it only by means of knowledge. Nay, it is a trial, but most of them do not know.

فَاِذَا مَسَّ الْاِنْسَانَ ضُرٌّ دَعَانَا ثُمَّ اِذَا خَوَّلْنٰهُ نِعْمَةً مِّنَّا ۙ قَالَ اِنَّمَآ اُوْتِيْتُهٗ عَلٰى عِلْمٍ ؕ بَلْ هِيَ فِتْنَةٌ وَّلٰكِنَّ اَكْثَرَهُمْ لَا يَعْلَمُوْنَ ۝

50. Those before them did say it indeed, but what they earned availed them not.

قَدْ قَالَهَا الَّذِيْنَ مِنْ قَبْلِهِمْ فَمَا أَغْنٰى عَنْهُمْ مَّا كَانُوْا يَكْسِبُوْنَ ۞

51. So there befell them the evil (consequences) of what they earned; and (as for) those who are unjust from among these, there shall befall them the evil (consequences) of what they earn, and they shall not escape.

فَأَصَابَهُمْ سَيِّاٰتُ مَا كَسَبُوْا ۚ وَالَّذِيْنَ ظَلَمُوْا مِنْ هٰٓؤُلَاءِ سَيُصِيْبُهُمْ سَيِّاٰتُ مَا كَسَبُوْا ۙ وَمَا هُمْ بِمُعْجِزِيْنَ ۞

52. Do they not know that Allah makes ample the means of subsistence to whom He pleases, and He straitens; most surely there are signs in this for a people who believe.

أَوَلَمْ يَعْلَمُوْۤا أَنَّ اللّٰهَ يَبْسُطُ الرِّزْقَ لِمَنْ يَّشَآءُ وَيَقْدِرُ ۚ إِنَّ فِيْ ذٰلِكَ لَاٰيٰتٍ لِّقَوْمٍ يُّؤْمِنُوْنَ ۞

53. Say: O my servants! who have acted extravagantly against their own souls, do not despair of the mercy of Allah; surely Allah forgives the faults altogether; surely He is the Forgiving, the Merciful.

قُلْ يٰعِبَادِيَ الَّذِيْنَ أَسْرَفُوْا عَلٰٓى أَنْفُسِهِمْ لَا تَقْنَطُوْا مِنْ رَّحْمَةِ اللّٰهِ ۚ إِنَّ اللّٰهَ يَغْفِرُ الذُّنُوْبَ جَمِيْعًا ۚ إِنَّهُ هُوَ الْغَفُوْرُ الرَّحِيْمُ ۞

54. And return to your Lord time after time and submit to Him before there comes to you the punishment, then you shall not be helped.

وَأَنِيْبُوْۤا إِلٰى رَبِّكُمْ وَأَسْلِمُوْا لَهُ مِنْ قَبْلِ أَنْ يَّأْتِيَكُمُ الْعَذَابُ ثُمَّ لَا تُنْصَرُوْنَ ۞

55. And follow the best that has been revealed to you from your Lord before there comes to you the punishment all of a sudden while you do not even perceive;

وَاتَّبِعُوْۤا أَحْسَنَ مَا أُنْزِلَ إِلَيْكُمْ مِّنْ رَّبِّكُمْ مِّنْ قَبْلِ أَنْ يَّأْتِيَكُمُ الْعَذَابُ بَغْتَةً وَّأَنْتُمْ لَا تَشْعُرُوْنَ ۞

56. Lest a soul should say: O woe to me! for what I fell short of my duty to Allah, and most surely I was of those who laughed to scorn;

أَنْ تَقُوْلَ نَفْسٌ يّٰحَسْرَتٰى عَلٰى مَا فَرَّطْتُ فِيْ جَنْبِ اللّٰهِ وَإِنْ كُنْتُ لَمِنَ السّٰخِرِيْنَ ۞

57. Or it should say: Had Allah guided me, I would certainly have been of those who guard (against evil);

أَوْ تَقُوْلَ لَوْ أَنَّ اللّٰهَ هَدٰىنِيْ لَكُنْتُ مِنَ الْمُتَّقِيْنَ ۞

58. Or it should say when it sees the punishment: Were there only a returning for me, I should be of the doers of good.

أَوْ تَقُوْلَ حِيْنَ تَرَى الْعَذَابَ لَوْ أَنَّ لِيْ كَرَّةً فَأَكُوْنَ مِنَ الْمُحْسِنِيْنَ ۞

59. Aye! My communications came to you, but you rejected them, and you were proud and you were one of the unbelievers.

بَلٰى قَدْ جَآءَتْكَ اٰيٰتِيْ فَكَذَّبْتَ بِهَا وَاسْتَكْبَرْتَ وَكُنْتَ مِنَ الْكٰفِرِيْنَ ۞

60. And on the day of resurrection you shall see those who lied against Allah; their faces shall be blackened. Is there not in hell an abode for the proud?

وَيَوْمَ الْقِيٰمَةِ تَرَى الَّذِيْنَ كَذَبُوْا عَلَى اللهِ وُجُوْهُهُمْ مُّسْوَدَّةٌ ۖ اَلَيْسَ فِيْ جَهَنَّمَ مَثْوًى لِّلْمُتَكَبِّرِيْنَ ۝

61. And Allah shall deliver those who guard (against evil) with their achievement; evil shall not touch them, nor shall they grieve.

وَيُنَجِّي اللهُ الَّذِيْنَ اتَّقَوْا بِمَفَازَتِهِمْ ۖ لَا يَمَسُّهُمُ السُّوْٓءُ وَلَا هُمْ يَحْزَنُوْنَ ۝

62. Allah is the Creator of every thing and He has charge over every thing.

اَللهُ خَالِقُ كُلِّ شَيْءٍ ۖ وَّهُوَ عَلٰى كُلِّ شَيْءٍ وَّكِيْلٌ ۝

63. His are the treasures of the heavens and the earth; and (as for) those who disbelieve in the communications of Allah, these it is that are the losers.

لَهٗ مَقَالِيْدُ السَّمٰوٰتِ وَالْاَرْضِ ۗ وَالَّذِيْنَ كَفَرُوْا بِاٰيٰتِ اللهِ اُولٰٓئِكَ هُمُ الْخٰسِرُوْنَ ۝

64. Say: What! Do you then bid me serve others than Allah, O ignorant men?

قُلْ اَفَغَيْرَ اللهِ تَأْمُرُوْٓنِّيْ اَعْبُدُ اَيُّهَا الْجٰهِلُوْنَ ۝

65. And certainly, it has been revealed to you and to those before you: Surely if you associate (with Allah), your work would certainly come to naught and you would certainly be of the losers.

وَلَقَدْ اُوْحِيَ اِلَيْكَ وَاِلَى الَّذِيْنَ مِنْ قَبْلِكَ ۚ لَئِنْ اَشْرَكْتَ لَيَحْبَطَنَّ عَمَلُكَ وَلَتَكُوْنَنَّ مِنَ الْخٰسِرِيْنَ ۝

66. Nay! but serve Allah alone and be of the thankful.

بَلِ اللهَ فَاعْبُدْ وَكُنْ مِّنَ الشّٰكِرِيْنَ ۝

67. And they have not honored Allah with the honor that is due to Him; and the whole earth shall be in His grip on the day of resurrection and the heavens rolled up in His right hand; glory be to Him, and may He be exalted above what they associate (with Him).

وَمَا قَدَرُوا اللهَ حَقَّ قَدْرِهٖ ۖ وَالْاَرْضُ جَمِيْعًا قَبْضَتُهٗ يَوْمَ الْقِيٰمَةِ وَالسَّمٰوٰتُ مَطْوِيّٰتٌۢ بِيَمِيْنِهٖ ۗ سُبْحٰنَهٗ وَتَعٰلٰى عَمَّا يُشْرِكُوْنَ ۝

68. And the trumpet shall be blown, so all those that are in the heavens and all those that are in the earth shall swoon, except such as Allah please; then it shall be blown again, then lo! they shall stand up awaiting.

وَنُفِخَ فِي الصُّوْرِ فَصَعِقَ مَنْ فِي السَّمٰوٰتِ وَمَنْ فِي الْاَرْضِ اِلَّا مَنْ شَآءَ اللهُ ۖ ثُمَّ نُفِخَ فِيْهِ اُخْرٰى فَاِذَا هُمْ قِيَامٌ يَّنْظُرُوْنَ ۝

69. And the earth shall beam with the light of its Lord, and the Book shall be laid down, and the prophets and the witnesses shall be brought up, and judgment shall be given between them with justice, and they shall not be dealt with unjustly.

وَاَشْرَقَتِ الْاَرْضُ بِنُوْرِ رَبِّهَا وَوُضِعَ الْكِتٰبُ وَجِائْ بِالنَّبِيّٖنَ وَالشُّهَدَآءِ وَقُضِيَ بَيْنَهُمْ بِالْحَقِّ وَهُمْ لَا يُظْلَمُوْنَ ۝

70. And every soul shall be paid back fully what it has done, and He knows best what they do.

وَوُفِّيَتْ كُلُّ نَفْسٍ مَّا عَمِلَتْ وَهُوَ اَعْلَمُ بِمَا يَفْعَلُوْنَ ۝

71. And those who disbelieve shall be driven to hell in companies; until, when they come to it, its doors shall be opened, and the keepers of it shall say to them: Did not there come to you apostles from among you reciting to you the communications of your Lord and warning you of the meeting of this day of yours? They shall say: Yea! But the sentence of punishment was due against the unbelievers.

وَسِيقَ الَّذِينَ كَفَرُوا إِلَىٰ جَهَنَّمَ زُمَرًا حَتَّىٰ إِذَا جَاءُوهَا فُتِحَتْ أَبْوَابُهَا وَقَالَ لَهُمْ خَزَنَتُهَا أَلَمْ يَأْتِكُمْ رُسُلٌ مِنْكُمْ يَتْلُونَ عَلَيْكُمْ آيَاتِ رَبِّكُمْ وَيُنْذِرُونَكُمْ لِقَاءَ يَوْمِكُمْ هٰذَا قَالُوا بَلَىٰ وَلٰكِنْ حَقَّتْ كَلِمَةُ الْعَذَابِ عَلَى الْكَافِرِينَ ۞

72. It shall be said: Enter the gates of hell to abide therein; so evil is the abode of the proud.

قِيلَ ادْخُلُوا أَبْوَابَ جَهَنَّمَ خَالِدِينَ فِيهَا فَبِئْسَ مَثْوَى الْمُتَكَبِّرِينَ ۞

73. And those who are careful of (their duty to) their Lord shall be conveyed to the garden in companies; until when they come to it, and its doors shall be opened, and the keepers of it shall say to them: Peace be on you, you shall be happy; therefore enter it to abide.

وَسِيقَ الَّذِينَ اتَّقَوْا رَبَّهُمْ إِلَى الْجَنَّةِ زُمَرًا حَتَّىٰ إِذَا جَاءُوهَا وَفُتِحَتْ أَبْوَابُهَا وَقَالَ لَهُمْ خَزَنَتُهَا سَلَامٌ عَلَيْكُمْ طِبْتُمْ فَادْخُلُوهَا خَالِدِينَ ۞

74. And they shall say: (All) praise is due to Allah, Who has made good to us His promise, and He has made us inherit the land; we may abide in the garden where we please; so goodly is the reward of the workers.

وَقَالُوا الْحَمْدُ لِلَّهِ الَّذِي صَدَقَنَا وَعْدَهُ وَأَوْرَثَنَا الْأَرْضَ نَتَبَوَّأُ مِنَ الْجَنَّةِ حَيْثُ نَشَاءُ فَنِعْمَ أَجْرُ الْعَامِلِينَ ۞

75. And you shall see the angels going round about the throne glorifying the praise of their Lord; and judgment shall be given between them with justice, and it shall be said: All praise is due to Allah, the Lord of the worlds.

وَتَرَى الْمَلَائِكَةَ حَافِّينَ مِنْ حَوْلِ الْعَرْشِ يُسَبِّحُونَ بِحَمْدِ رَبِّهِمْ وَقُضِيَ بَيْنَهُمْ بِالْحَقِّ وَقِيلَ الْحَمْدُ لِلَّهِ رَبِّ الْعَالَمِينَ ۞

THE BELIEVER
(MOAMIN)

**In the name of Allah,
the Beneficent, the Merciful.**

1. Ha Mim.

2. The revelation of the Book is from Allah, the Mighty, the Knowing,

3. The Forgiver of the faults and the Acceptor of repentance, Severe to punish, Lord of bounty; there is no god but He; to Him is the eventual coming.

4. None dispute concerning the communications of Allah but those who disbelieve, therefore let not their going to and fro in the cities deceive you.

5. The people of Nuh and the parties after them rejected (prophets) before them, and every nation purposed against their apostle to destroy him, and they disputed by means of the falsehood that they might thereby render null the truth, therefore I destroyed them; how was then My retribution!

6. And thus did the word of your Lord prove true against those who disbelieved that they are the inmates of the fire.

7. Those who bear the power and those around Him celebrate the praise of their Lord and believe in Him and ask protection for those who believe: Our Lord! Thou embracest all things in mercy and knowledge, therefore grant protection to those who turn (to Thee) and follow Thy way, and save them from the punishment of the hell:

8. Our Lord! and make them enter the gardens of perpetuity which Thou hast promised to them and those who do good of their fathers and their wives and their offspring, surely Thou are the Mighty, the Wise.

461

9. And keep them from evil deeds, and whom Thou keepest from evil deeds this day, indeed Thou hast mercy on him, and that is the mighty achievement.

وَقِهِمُ السَّيِّاٰتِ ۖ وَمَنْ تَقِ السَّيِّاٰتِ يَوْمَىِٕذٍ فَقَدْ رَحِمْتَهٗ ۚ وَذٰلِكَ هُوَ الْفَوْزُ الْعَظِيْمُ ۞

10. Surely those who disbelieve shall be cried out to: Certainly Allah's hatred (of you) when you were called upon to the faith and you rejected, is much greater than your hatred of yourselves.

اِنَّ الَّذِيْنَ كَفَرُوْا يُنَادَوْنَ لَمَقْتُ اللّٰهِ اَكْبَرُ مِنْ مَّقْتِكُمْ اَنْفُسَكُمْ اِذْ تُدْعَوْنَ اِلَى الْاِيْمَانِ فَتَكْفُرُوْنَ ۞

11. They shall say: Our Lord! twice didst Thou make us subject to death, and twice hast Thou given us life, so we do confess our faults; is there then a way to get out?

قَالُوْا رَبَّنَآ اَمَتَّنَا اثْنَتَيْنِ وَاَحْيَيْتَنَا اثْنَتَيْنِ فَاعْتَرَفْنَا بِذُنُوْبِنَا فَهَلْ اِلٰى خُرُوْجٍ مِّنْ سَبِيْلٍ ۞

12. That is because when Allah alone was called upon, you disbelieved, and when associates were given to Him, you believed; so judgment belongs to Allah, the High, the Great.

ذٰلِكُمْ بِاَنَّهٗٓ اِذَا دُعِيَ اللّٰهُ وَحْدَهٗ كَفَرْتُمْ ۚ وَاِنْ يُّشْرَكْ بِهٖ تُؤْمِنُوْا ۚ فَالْحُكْمُ لِلّٰهِ الْعَلِيِّ الْكَبِيْرِ ۞

13. He it is Who shows you His signs and sends down for you sustenance from heaven, and none minds but he who turns (to Him) again and again.

هُوَ الَّذِيْ يُرِيْكُمْ اٰيٰتِهٖ وَيُنَزِّلُ لَكُمْ مِّنَ السَّمَآءِ رِزْقًا ۚ وَمَا يَتَذَكَّرُ اِلَّا مَنْ يُّنِيْبُ ۞

14. Therefore call upon Allah, being sincere to Him in obedience, though the unbelievers are averse:

فَادْعُوا اللّٰهَ مُخْلِصِيْنَ لَهُ الدِّيْنَ وَلَوْ كَرِهَ الْكٰفِرُوْنَ ۞

15. Possessor of the highest rank, Lord of power: He makes the inspiration to light by His command upon whom He pleases of His servants, that he may warn (men) of the day of meeting.

رَفِيْعُ الدَّرَجٰتِ ذُو الْعَرْشِ ۚ يُلْقِى الرُّوْحَ مِنْ اَمْرِهٖ عَلٰى مَنْ يَّشَآءُ مِنْ عِبَادِهٖ لِيُنْذِرَ يَوْمَ التَّلَاقِ ۞

16. (Of) the day when they shall come forth; nothing concerning them remains hidden to Allah. To whom belongs the kingdom this day? To Allah, the One, the Subduer (of all).

يَوْمَ هُمْ بَارِزُوْنَ ۖ لَا يَخْفٰى عَلَى اللّٰهِ مِنْهُمْ شَيْءٌ ۚ لِمَنِ الْمُلْكُ الْيَوْمَ ۚ لِلّٰهِ الْوَاحِدِ الْقَهَّارِ ۞

17. This day every soul shall be rewarded for what it has earned; no injustice (shall be done) this day; surely Allah is quick in reckoning.

اَلْيَوْمَ تُجْزٰى كُلُّ نَفْسٍ بِمَا كَسَبَتْ ۚ لَا ظُلْمَ الْيَوْمَ ۚ اِنَّ اللّٰهَ سَرِيْعُ الْحِسَابِ ۞

18. And warn them of the day that draws near, when hearts shall rise up to the throats, grieving inwardly; the unjust shall not have any compassionate friend nor any intercessor who should be obeyed.

وَاَنْذِرْهُمْ يَوْمَ الْاٰزِفَةِ اِذِ الْقُلُوْبُ لَدَى الْحَنَاجِرِ كَاظِمِيْنَ ۚ مَا لِلظّٰلِمِيْنَ مِنْ حَمِيْمٍ وَّلَا شَفِيْعٍ يُّطَاعُ ۚ

19. He knows the stealthy looks and that which the breasts conceal.

يَعْلَمُ خَآئِنَةَ الْاَعْيُنِ وَمَا تُخْفِي الصُّدُوْرُ

20. And Allah judges with the truth; and those whom they call upon besides Him cannot judge aught; surely Allah is the Hearing, the Seeing.

وَاللّٰهُ يَقْضِيْ بِالْحَقِّ ۚ وَالَّذِيْنَ يَدْعُوْنَ مِنْ دُوْنِهٖ لَا يَقْضُوْنَ بِشَيْءٍ ۚ اِنَّ اللّٰهَ هُوَ السَّمِيْعُ الْبَصِيْرُ

21. Have they not travelled in the earth and seen how was the end of those who were before them? Mightier than these were they in strength and in fortifications in the land, but Allah destroyed them for their sins; and there was not for them any defender against Allah.

اَوَلَمْ يَسِيْرُوْا فِي الْاَرْضِ فَيَنْظُرُوْا كَيْفَ كَانَ عَاقِبَةُ الَّذِيْنَ كَانُوْا مِنْ قَبْلِهِمْ ۚ كَانُوْا هُمْ اَشَدَّ مِنْهُمْ قُوَّةً وَّاٰثَارًا فِي الْاَرْضِ فَاَخَذَهُمُ اللّٰهُ بِذُنُوْبِهِمْ ۚ وَمَا كَانَ لَهُمْ مِّنَ اللّٰهِ مِنْ وَّاقٍ

22. That was because there came to them their apostles with clear arguments, but they rejected (them), therefore Allah destroyed them; surely He is Strong, Severe in retribution.

ذٰلِكَ بِاَنَّهُمْ كَانَتْ تَّأْتِيْهِمْ رُسُلُهُمْ بِالْبَيِّنٰتِ فَكَفَرُوْا فَاَخَذَهُمُ اللّٰهُ ۚ اِنَّهٗ قَوِيٌّ شَدِيْدُ الْعِقَابِ

23. And certainly We sent Musa with Our communications and clear authority,

وَلَقَدْ اَرْسَلْنَا مُوْسٰى بِاٰيٰتِنَا وَسُلْطٰنٍ مُّبِيْنٍ

24. To Firon and Haman and Qaroun, but they said: A lying magician.

اِلٰى فِرْعَوْنَ وَهَامٰنَ وَقَارُوْنَ فَقَالُوْا سَاحِرٌ كَذَّابٌ

25. So when he brought to them the truth from Us, they said: Slay the sons of those who believe with him and keep their women alive; and the struggle of the unbelievers will only come to a state of perdition.

فَلَمَّا جَآءَهُمْ بِالْحَقِّ مِنْ عِنْدِنَا قَالُوا اقْتُلُوْا اَبْنَآءَ الَّذِيْنَ اٰمَنُوْا مَعَهٗ وَاسْتَحْيُوْا نِسَآءَهُمْ ۚ وَمَا كَيْدُ الْكٰفِرِيْنَ اِلَّا فِيْ ضَلٰلٍ

26. And Firon said: Let me alone that I may slay Musa and let him call upon his Lord; surely I fear that he will change your religion or that he will make mischief to appear in the land.

وَقَالَ فِرْعَوْنُ ذَرُوْنِيْ اَقْتُلْ مُوْسٰى وَلْيَدْعُ رَبَّهٗ ۚ اِنِّيْ اَخَافُ اَنْ يُّبَدِّلَ دِيْنَكُمْ اَوْ اَنْ يُّظْهِرَ فِي الْاَرْضِ الْفَسَادَ

27. And Musa said: Surely I take refuge with my Lord and your Lord from every proud one who does not believe in the day of reckoning.

28. And a believing man of Firon's people who hid his faith said: What! will you slay a man because he says: My Lord is Allah, and indeed he has brought to you clear arguments from your Lord? And if he be a liar, on him will be his lie, and if he be truthful, there will befall you some of that which he threatens you (with); surely Allah does not guide him who is extravagant, a liar:

29. O my people! yours is the kingdom this day, being masters in the land, but who will help us against the punishment of Allah if it come to us? Firon said: I do not show you aught but that which I see (myself), and I do not make you follow any but the right way.

30. And he who believed said: O my people! surely I fear for you the like of what befell the parties:

31. The like of what befell the people of Nuh and Ad and Samood and those after them, and Allah does not desire injustice for (His) servants;

32. And, O my people! I fear for you the day of calling out,

33. The day on which you will turn back retreating; there shall be no savior for you from Allah, and whomsoever Allah causes to err, there is no guide for him:

34. And certainly Yusuf came to you before with clear arguments, but you ever remained in doubt as to what he brought; until when he died, you said: Allah will never raise an apostle after him. Thus does Allah cause him to err who is extravagant, a doubter,

وَقَالَ مُوْسٰۤى اِنِّيْ عُذْتُ بِرَبِّيْ وَرَبِّكُمْ مِّنْ كُلِّ مُتَكَبِّرٍ لَّا يُؤْمِنُ بِيَوْمِ الْحِسَابِ ۟ ۝

وَقَالَ رَجُلٌ مُّؤْمِنٌ ۢ مِّنْ اٰلِ فِرْعَوْنَ يَكْتُمُ اِيْمَانَهٗٓ اَتَقْتُلُوْنَ رَجُلًا اَنْ يَّقُوْلَ رَبِّيَ اللّٰهُ وَقَدْ جَآءَكُمْ بِالْبَيِّنٰتِ مِنْ رَّبِّكُمْ ۗ وَاِنْ يَّكُ كَاذِبًا فَعَلَيْهِ كَذِبُهٗ ۚ وَاِنْ يَّكُ صَادِقًا يُّصِبْكُمْ بَعْضُ الَّذِيْ يَعِدُكُمْ ۗ اِنَّ اللّٰهَ لَا يَهْدِيْ مَنْ هُوَ مُسْرِفٌ كَذَّابٌ ۝

يٰقَوْمِ لَكُمُ الْمُلْكُ الْيَوْمَ ظٰهِرِيْنَ فِى الْاَرْضِ ۡ فَمَنْ يَّنْصُرُنَا مِنْۢ بَأْسِ اللّٰهِ اِنْ جَآءَنَا ۗ قَالَ فِرْعَوْنُ مَاۤ اُرِيْكُمْ اِلَّا مَاۤ اَرٰى وَمَاۤ اَهْدِيْكُمْ اِلَّا سَبِيْلَ الرَّشَادِ ۝

وَقَالَ الَّذِيْۤ اٰمَنَ يٰقَوْمِ اِنِّيْۤ اَخَافُ عَلَيْكُمْ مِّثْلَ يَوْمِ الْاَحْزَابِ ۝

مِثْلَ دَأْبِ قَوْمِ نُوْحٍ وَّعَادٍ وَّثَمُوْدَ وَالَّذِيْنَ مِنْۢ بَعْدِهِمْ ۗ وَمَا اللّٰهُ يُرِيْدُ ظُلْمًا لِّلْعِبَادِ ۝

وَيٰقَوْمِ اِنِّيْۤ اَخَافُ عَلَيْكُمْ يَوْمَ التَّنَادِ ۝

يَوْمَ تُوَلُّوْنَ مُدْبِرِيْنَ ۚ مَا لَكُمْ مِّنَ اللّٰهِ مِنْ عَاصِمٍ ۚ وَمَنْ يُّضْلِلِ اللّٰهُ فَمَا لَهٗ مِنْ هَادٍ ۝

وَلَقَدْ جَآءَكُمْ يُوْسُفُ مِنْ قَبْلُ بِالْبَيِّنٰتِ فَمَا زِلْتُمْ فِيْ شَكٍّ مِّمَّا جَآءَكُمْ بِهٖ ۗ حَتّٰۤى اِذَا هَلَكَ قُلْتُمْ لَنْ يَّبْعَثَ اللّٰهُ مِنْۢ بَعْدِهٖ رَسُوْلًا ۗ كَذٰلِكَ يُضِلُّ اللّٰهُ مَنْ هُوَ مُسْرِفٌ مُّرْتَابٌ ۙ ۝

35. Those who dispute concerning the communications of Allah without any authority that He has given them; greatly hated is it by Allah and by those who believe. Thus does Allah set a seal over the heart of every proud, haughty one.

اِلَّذِيْنَ يُجَادِلُوْنَ فِىْٓ اٰيٰتِ اللّٰهِ بِغَيْرِ سُلْطٰنٍ اَتٰىهُمْ ۙ كَبُرَ مَقْتًا عِنْدَ اللّٰهِ وَعِنْدَ الَّذِيْنَ اٰمَنُوْا ۗ كَذٰلِكَ يَطْبَعُ اللّٰهُ عَلٰى كُلِّ قَلْبِ مُتَكَبِّرٍ جَبَّارٍ ۝

36. And Firon said: O Haman! build for me a tower that I may attain the means of access,

وَقَالَ فِرْعَوْنُ يٰهَامٰنُ ابْنِ لِىْ صَرْحًا لَّعَلِّىْٓ اَبْلُغُ الْاَسْبَابَ ۝

37. The means of access to the heavens, then reach the God of Musa, and I surely think him to be a liar. And thus the evil of his deed was made fair-seeming to Firon, and he was turned away from the way; and the struggle of Firon was not (to end) in aught but destruction.

اَسْبَابَ السَّمٰوٰتِ فَاَطَّلِعَ اِلٰٓى اِلٰهِ مُوْسٰى وَاِنِّىْ لَاَظُنُّهٗ كَاذِبًا ۗ وَكَذٰلِكَ زُيِّنَ لِفِرْعَوْنَ سُوْۤءُ عَمَلِهٖ وَصُدَّ عَنِ السَّبِيْلِ ۗ وَمَا كَيْدُ فِرْعَوْنَ اِلَّا فِىْ تَبَابٍ ۝

38. And he who believed said: O my people! follow me, I will guide you to the right course;

وَقَالَ الَّذِىْٓ اٰمَنَ يٰقَوْمِ اتَّبِعُوْنِ اَهْدِكُمْ سَبِيْلَ الرَّشَادِ ۝

39. O my people! this life of the world is only a (passing) enjoyment, and surely the hereafter is the abode to settle;

يٰقَوْمِ اِنَّمَا هٰذِهِ الْحَيٰوةُ الدُّنْيَا مَتَاعٌ ۖ وَّاِنَّ الْاٰخِرَةَ هِىَ دَارُ الْقَرَارِ ۝

40. Whoever does an evil, he shall not be recompensed (with aught) but the like of it, and whoever does good, whether male or female, and he is a believer, these shall enter the garden, in which they shall be given sustenance without measure.

مَنْ عَمِلَ سَيِّئَةً فَلَا يُجْزٰٓى اِلَّا مِثْلَهَا ۚ وَمَنْ عَمِلَ صَالِحًا مِّنْ ذَكَرٍ اَوْ اُنْثٰى وَهُوَ مُؤْمِنٌ فَاُولٰٓئِكَ يَدْخُلُوْنَ الْجَنَّةَ يُرْزَقُوْنَ فِيْهَا بِغَيْرِ حِسَابٍ ۝

41. And, O my people! how is it that I call you to salvation and you call me to the fire?

وَيٰقَوْمِ مَا لِىْٓ اَدْعُوْكُمْ اِلَى النَّجٰوةِ وَتَدْعُوْنَنِىْٓ اِلَى النَّارِ ۝

42. You call on me that I should disbelieve in Allah and associate with Him that of which I have no knowledge, and I call you to the Mighty, the most Forgiving;

تَدْعُوْنَنِىْ لِاَكْفُرَ بِاللّٰهِ وَاُشْرِكَ بِهٖ مَا لَيْسَ لِىْ بِهٖ عِلْمٌ ۖ وَّاَنَا اَدْعُوْكُمْ اِلَى الْعَزِيْزِ الْغَفَّارِ ۝

43. No doubt that what you call me to has no title to be called to in this world, nor in the hereafter, and that our turning back is to Allah, and that the extravagant are the inmates of the fire;

لَاجَرَمَ اَنَّمَا تَدْعُوْنَنِيْۤ اِلَيْهِ لَيْسَ لَهٗ دَعْوَةٌ فِى الدُّنْيَا وَلَا فِى الْاٰخِرَةِ وَاَنَّ مَرَدَّنَاۤ اِلَى اللّٰهِ وَاَنَّ الْمُسْرِفِيْنَ هُمْ اَصْحٰبُ النَّارِ ۝

44. So you shall remember what I say to you, and I entrust my affair to Allah, Surely Allah sees the servants.

فَسَتَذْكُرُوْنَ مَاۤ اَقُوْلُ لَكُمْ وَاُفَوِّضُ اَمْرِيْۤ اِلَى اللّٰهِ ۭ اِنَّ اللّٰهَ بَصِيْرٌۢ بِالْعِبَادِ ۝

45. So Allah protected him from the evil (consequences) of what they planned, and the most evil punishment overtook Firon's people:

فَوَقٰىهُ اللّٰهُ سَيِّاٰتِ مَا مَكَرُوْا وَحَاقَ بِاٰلِ فِرْعَوْنَ سُوْٓءُ الْعَذَابِ ۚ

46. The fire; they shall be brought before it (every) morning and evening and on the day when the hour shall come to pass: Make Firon's people enter the severest chastisement.

اَلنَّارُ يُعْرَضُوْنَ عَلَيْهَا غُدُوًّا وَّعَشِيًّا ۚ وَيَوْمَ تَقُوْمُ السَّاعَةُ ۣ اَدْخِلُوْۤا اٰلَ فِرْعَوْنَ اَشَدَّ الْعَذَابِ ۝

47. And when they shall contend one with another in the fire, then the weak shall say to those who were proud: Surely we were your followers; will you then avert from us a portion of the fire?

وَاِذْ يَتَحَآجُّوْنَ فِى النَّارِ فَيَقُوْلُ الضُّعَفٰٓؤُا لِلَّذِيْنَ اسْتَكْبَرُوْۤا اِنَّا كُنَّا لَكُمْ تَبَعًا فَهَلْ اَنْتُمْ مُّغْنُوْنَ عَنَّا نَصِيْبًا مِّنَ النَّارِ ۝

48. Those who were proud shall say: Surely we are all in it: surely Allah has judged between the servants.

قَالَ الَّذِيْنَ اسْتَكْبَرُوْۤا اِنَّا كُلٌّ فِيْهَاۤ ۙ اِنَّ اللّٰهَ قَدْ حَكَمَ بَيْنَ الْعِبَادِ ۝

49. And those who are in the fire shall say to the keepers of hell: Call upon your Lord that He may lighten to us one day of the punishment.

وَقَالَ الَّذِيْنَ فِى النَّارِ لِخَزَنَةِ جَهَنَّمَ ادْعُوْا رَبَّكُمْ يُخَفِّفْ عَنَّا يَوْمًا مِّنَ الْعَذَابِ ۝

50. They shall say: Did not your apostles come to you with clear arguments? They shall say: Yea. They shall say: Then call. And the call of the unbelievers is only in error.

قَالُوْۤا اَوَلَمْ تَكُ تَأْتِيْكُمْ رُسُلُكُمْ بِالْبَيِّنٰتِ ۭ قَالُوْا بَلٰى ۭ قَالُوْا فَادْعُوْا ۚ وَمَا دُعٰٓؤُا الْكٰفِرِيْنَ اِلَّا فِيْ ضَلٰلٍ ۧ

51. Most surely We help Our apostles, and those who believe, in this world's life and on the day when the witnesses shall stand up,

اِنَّا لَنَنْصُرُ رُسُلَنَا وَالَّذِيْنَ اٰمَنُوْا فِى الْحَيٰوةِ الدُّنْيَا وَيَوْمَ يَقُوْمُ الْاَشْهَادُ ۝

52. The day on which their excuse shall not benefit the unjust, and for them is curse and for them is the evil abode.

يَوْمَ لَا يَنْفَعُ الظَّالِمِيْنَ مَعْذِرَتُهُمْ وَلَهُمُ اللَّعْنَةُ وَلَهُمْ سُوْءُ الدَّارِ ۝

53. And certainly We gave Musa the guidance, and We made the children of Israel inherit the Book,

وَلَقَدْ اٰتَيْنَا مُوْسَى الْهُدَى وَاَوْرَثْنَا بَنِيْٓ اِسْرَآءِيْلَ الْكِتٰبَ ۝

54. A guidance and a reminder to the men of understanding.

هُدًى وَّذِكْرَى لِاُولِى الْاَلْبَابِ ۝

55. Therefore be patient; surely the promise of Allah is true; and ask protection for your fault and sing the praise of your Lord in the evening and the morning.

فَاصْبِرْ اِنَّ وَعْدَ اللّٰهِ حَقٌّ وَّاسْتَغْفِرْ لِذَنْبِكَ وَسَبِّحْ بِحَمْدِ رَبِّكَ بِالْعَشِيِّ وَالْاِبْكَارِ ۝

56. Surely (as for) those who dispute about the communications of Allah without any authority that has come to them, there is naught in their breasts but (a desire) to become great which they shall never attain to; therefore seek refuge in Allah, surely He is the Hearing, the Seeing.

اِنَّ الَّذِيْنَ يُجَادِلُوْنَ فِيْٓ اٰيٰتِ اللّٰهِ بِغَيْرِ سُلْطٰنٍ اَتٰهُمْ اِنْ فِيْ صُدُوْرِهِمْ اِلَّا كِبْرٌ مَّا هُمْ بِبَالِغِيْهِ فَاسْتَعِذْ بِاللّٰهِ اِنَّهُ هُوَ السَّمِيْعُ الْبَصِيْرُ ۝

57. Certainly the creation of the heavens and the earth is greater than the creation of the men, but most people do not know.

لَخَلْقُ السَّمٰوٰتِ وَالْاَرْضِ اَكْبَرُ مِنْ خَلْقِ النَّاسِ وَلٰكِنَّ اَكْثَرَ النَّاسِ لَا يَعْلَمُوْنَ ۝

58. And the blind and the seeing are not alike, nor those who believe and do good and the evil-doer; little is it that you are mindful.

وَمَا يَسْتَوِى الْاَعْمٰى وَالْبَصِيْرُ وَالَّذِيْنَ اٰمَنُوْا وَعَمِلُوا الصّٰلِحٰتِ وَلَا الْمُسِيْٓءُ قَلِيْلًا مَّا تَتَذَكَّرُوْنَ ۝

59. Most surely the hour is coming, there is no doubt therein, but most people do not believe.

اِنَّ السَّاعَةَ لَاٰتِيَةٌ لَّا رَيْبَ فِيْهَا وَلٰكِنَّ اَكْثَرَ النَّاسِ لَا يُؤْمِنُوْنَ ۝

60. And your Lord says: Call upon Me, I will answer you; surely those who are too proud for My service shall soon enter hell abased.

وَقَالَ رَبُّكُمُ ادْعُوْنِيْٓ اَسْتَجِبْ لَكُمْ اِنَّ الَّذِيْنَ يَسْتَكْبِرُوْنَ عَنْ عِبَادَتِيْ سَيَدْخُلُوْنَ جَهَنَّمَ دٰخِرِيْنَ ۝

61. Allah is He Who made for you the night that you may rest therein and the day to see; most surely Allah is Gracious to men, but most men do not give thanks.

اللّٰهُ الَّذِيْ جَعَلَ لَكُمُ الَّيْلَ لِتَسْكُنُوْا فِيْهِ وَالنَّهَارَ مُبْصِرًا اِنَّ اللّٰهَ لَذُوْ فَضْلٍ عَلَى النَّاسِ وَلٰكِنَّ اَكْثَرَ النَّاسِ لَا يَشْكُرُوْنَ ۝

62. That is Allah, your Lord, the Creator of everything; there is no God but He; whence are you then turned away?

ذٰلِكُمُ اللّٰهُ رَبُّكُمْ خَالِقُ كُلِّ شَيْءٍ لَّا اِلٰهَ اِلَّا هُوَ فَاَنّٰى تُؤْفَكُوْنَ ۟

63. Thus were turned away those who denied the communications of Allah.

كَذٰلِكَ يُؤْفَكُ الَّذِيْنَ كَانُوْا بِاٰيٰتِ اللّٰهِ يَجْحَدُوْنَ ۟

64. Allah is He Who made the earth a resting-place for you and the heaven a canopy, and He formed you, then made goodly your forms, and He provided you with goodly things; that is Allah, your Lord; blessed then is Allah, the Lord of the worlds.

اَللّٰهُ الَّذِيْ جَعَلَ لَكُمُ الْاَرْضَ قَرَارًا وَّالسَّمَآءَ بِنَآءً وَّصَوَّرَكُمْ فَاَحْسَنَ صُوَرَكُمْ وَرَزَقَكُمْ مِّنَ الطَّيِّبٰتِ ذٰلِكُمُ اللّٰهُ رَبُّكُمْ فَتَبٰرَكَ اللّٰهُ رَبُّ الْعٰلَمِيْنَ ۟

65. He is the Living, there is no god but He, therefore call on Him, being sincere to Him in obedience; (all) praise is due to Allah, the Lord of the worlds.

هُوَ الْحَيُّ لَا اِلٰهَ اِلَّا هُوَ فَادْعُوْهُ مُخْلِصِيْنَ لَهُ الدِّيْنَ اَلْحَمْدُ لِلّٰهِ رَبِّ الْعٰلَمِيْنَ ۟

66. Say: I am forbidden to serve those whom you call upon besides Allah when clear arguments have come to me from my Lord, and I am commanded that I should submit to the Lord of the worlds.

قُلْ اِنِّيْ نُهِيْتُ اَنْ اَعْبُدَ الَّذِيْنَ تَدْعُوْنَ مِنْ دُوْنِ اللّٰهِ لَمَّا جَآءَنِيَ الْبَيِّنٰتُ مِنْ رَّبِّيْ وَاُمِرْتُ اَنْ اُسْلِمَ لِرَبِّ الْعٰلَمِيْنَ ۟

67. He it is Who created you from dust, then from a small life-germ, then from a clot, then He brings you forth as a child, then that you may attain your maturity, then that you may be old—and of you there are some who are caused to die before—and that you may reach an appointed term, and that you may understand.

هُوَ الَّذِيْ خَلَقَكُمْ مِّنْ تُرَابٍ ثُمَّ مِنْ نُّطْفَةٍ ثُمَّ مِنْ عَلَقَةٍ ثُمَّ يُخْرِجُكُمْ طِفْلًا ثُمَّ لِتَبْلُغُوْا اَشُدَّكُمْ ثُمَّ لِتَكُوْنُوْا شُيُوْخًا وَمِنْكُمْ مَّنْ يُّتَوَفّٰى مِنْ قَبْلُ وَلِتَبْلُغُوْا اَجَلًا مُّسَمًّى وَّلَعَلَّكُمْ تَعْقِلُوْنَ ۟

68. He it is Who gives life and brings death, so when He decrees an affair, He only says to it: Be, and it is.

هُوَ الَّذِيْ يُحْيٖ وَيُمِيْتُ فَاِذَا قَضٰٓى اَمْرًا فَاِنَّمَا يَقُوْلُ لَهُ كُنْ فَيَكُوْنُ ۟

69. Have you not seen those who dispute with respect to the communications of Allah: how are they turned away?

اَلَمْ تَرَ اِلَى الَّذِيْنَ يُجَادِلُوْنَ فِيْۤ اٰيٰتِ اللّٰهِ اَنّٰى يُصْرَفُوْنَ ۟ۙ

70. Those who reject the Book and that with which We have sent Our Apostle; but they shall soon come to know,

الَّذِيْنَ كَذَّبُوْا بِالْكِتٰبِ وَبِمَآ اَرْسَلْنَا بِهٖ رُسُلَنَا فَسَوْفَ يَعْلَمُوْنَ ۟ۙ

71. When the fetters and the chains shall be on their necks; they shall be dragged

اِذِ الْاَغْلٰلُ فِىْۤ اَعْنَاقِهِمْ وَالسَّلٰسِلُ ۭ يُسْحَبُوْنَ ۙ

72. Into boiling water, then in the fire shall they be burned;

فِى الْحَمِيْمِ ۥ ثُمَّ فِى النَّارِ يُسْجَرُوْنَ ۚ

73. Then shall it be said to them: Where is that which you used to set up

ثُمَّ قِيْلَ لَهُمْ اَيْنَ مَا كُنْتُمْ تُشْرِكُوْنَ ۙ

74. Besides Allah? They shall say: They are gone away from us, nay, we used not to call upon anything before. Thus does Allah confound the unbelievers.

مِنْ دُوْنِ اللّٰهِ ۭ قَالُوْا ضَلُّوْا عَنَّا بَلْ لَّمْ نَكُنْ نَّدْعُوْا مِنْ قَبْلُ شَيْئًا ۭ كَذٰلِكَ يُضِلُّ اللّٰهُ الْكٰفِرِيْنَ ۝

75. That is because you exulted in the land unjustly and because you behaved insolently.

ذٰلِكُمْ بِمَا كُنْتُمْ تَفْرَحُوْنَ فِى الْاَرْضِ بِغَيْرِ الْحَقِّ وَبِمَا كُنْتُمْ تَمْرَحُوْنَ ۚ

76. Enter the gates of hell to abide therein; evil then is the abode of the proud.

اُدْخُلُوْۤا اَبْوَابَ جَهَنَّمَ خٰلِدِيْنَ فِيْهَا ۚ فَبِئْسَ مَثْوَى الْمُتَكَبِّرِيْنَ ۝

77. So be patient, surely the promise of Allah is true. So should We make you see part of what We threaten them with, or should We cause you to die, to Us shall they be returned.

فَاصْبِرْ اِنَّ وَعْدَ اللّٰهِ حَقٌّ ۚ فَاِمَّا نُرِيَنَّكَ بَعْضَ الَّذِىْ نَعِدُهُمْ اَوْ نَتَوَفَّيَنَّكَ فَاِلَيْنَا يُرْجَعُوْنَ ۝

78. And certainly We sent apostles before you: there are some of them that We have mentioned to you and there are others whom We have not mentioned to you; and it was not meet for an apostle that he should bring a sign except with Allah's permission, but when the command of Allah came, judgment was given with truth, and those who treated (it) as a lie were lost.

وَلَقَدْ اَرْسَلْنَا رُسُلًا مِّنْ قَبْلِكَ مِنْهُمْ مَّنْ قَصَصْنَا عَلَيْكَ وَمِنْهُمْ مَّنْ لَّمْ نَقْصُصْ عَلَيْكَ ۭ وَمَا كَانَ لِرَسُوْلٍ اَنْ يَّاْتِىَ بِاٰيَةٍ اِلَّا بِاِذْنِ اللّٰهِ ۚ فَاِذَا جَاۤءَ اَمْرُ اللّٰهِ قُضِىَ بِالْحَقِّ وَخَسِرَ هُنَالِكَ الْمُبْطِلُوْنَ ۝

79. Allah is He Who made the cattle for you that you may ride on some of them, and some of them you eat.

اَللّٰهُ الَّذِىْ جَعَلَ لَكُمُ الْاَنْعَامَ لِتَرْكَبُوْا مِنْهَا وَمِنْهَا تَاْكُلُوْنَ ۝

80. And there are advantages for you in them, and that you may attain thereon a want which is in your breasts, and upon them and upon the ships you are borne.

وَلَكُمْ فِيْهَا مَنَافِعُ وَلِتَبْلُغُوْا عَلَيْهَا حَاجَةً فِىْ صُدُوْرِكُمْ وَعَلَيْهَا وَعَلَى الْفُلْكِ تُحْمَلُوْنَ ۝

81. And He shows you His signs: which then of Allah's signs will you deny?

وَيُرِيْكُمْ اٰيٰتِهٖ ۖ فَاَىَّ اٰيٰتِ اللّٰهِ تُنْكِرُوْنَ ۝

82. Have they not then journeyed in the land and seen how was the end of those before them? They were more (in numbers) than these and greater in strength and in fortifications in the land, but what they earned did not avail them.

اَفَلَمْ يَسِيْرُوْا فِي الْاَرْضِ فَيَنْظُرُوْا كَيْفَ كَانَ عَاقِبَةُ الَّذِيْنَ مِنْ قَبْلِهِمْ ۚ كَانُوْٓا اَكْثَرَ مِنْهُمْ وَاَشَدَّ قُوَّةً وَّاٰثَارًا فِي الْاَرْضِ فَمَآ اَغْنٰى عَنْهُمْ مَّا كَانُوْا يَكْسِبُوْنَ ۝

83. Then when their apostles came to them with clear arguments, they exulted in what they had with them of knowledge, and there beset them that which they used to mock.

فَلَمَّا جَآءَتْهُمْ رُسُلُهُمْ بِالْبَيِّنٰتِ فَرِحُوْا بِمَا عِنْدَهُمْ مِّنَ الْعِلْمِ وَحَاقَ بِهِمْ مَّا كَانُوْا بِهٖ يَسْتَهْزِءُوْنَ ۝

84. But when they saw Our punishment, they said: We believe in Allah alone and we deny what we used to associate with Him.

فَلَمَّا رَاَوْا بَاْسَنَا قَالُوْٓا اٰمَنَّا بِاللّٰهِ وَحْدَهٗ وَكَفَرْنَا بِمَا كُنَّا بِهٖ مُشْرِكِيْنَ ۝

85. But their belief was not going to profit them when they had seen Our punishment; (this is) Allah's law, which has indeed obtained in the matter of His servants, and there the unbelievers are lost.

فَلَمْ يَكُ يَنْفَعُهُمْ اِيْمَانُهُمْ لَمَّا رَاَوْا بَاْسَنَا ۗ سُنَّتَ اللّٰهِ الَّتِيْ قَدْ خَلَتْ فِيْ عِبَادِهٖ ۚ وَخَسِرَ هُنَالِكَ الْكٰفِرُوْنَ ۝

HA MIM

**In the Name of Allah,
the Beneficent, the Merciful.**

اَبَانِهَا ١٤ سُوْرَةُ حٰمَ السَّجْدَةِ مَكِّيَّةٌ رُكُوْعَاتُهَا

بِسْمِ اللهِ الرَّحْمٰنِ الرَّحِيْمِ ۝

1. Ha Mim!

حٰمۤ ۝

2. A revelation from the Beneficent, the
Merciful God:

تَنْزِيْلٌ مِّنَ الرَّحْمٰنِ الرَّحِيْمِ ۝

3. A Book of which the verses are made
plain, an Arabic Quran for a people who
know:

كِتٰبٌ فُصِّلَتْ اٰيٰتُهٗ قُرْاٰنًا عَرَبِيًّا لِّقَوْمٍ يَّعْلَمُوْنَ ۝

4. A herald of good news and a warner,
but most of them turn aside so they hear
not.

بَشِيْرًا وَّنَذِيْرًا ۚ فَاَعْرَضَ اَكْثَرُهُمْ فَهُمْ لَا
يَسْمَعُوْنَ ۝

5. And they say: Our hearts are under
coverings from that to which you call us,
and there is a heaviness in our ears, and a
veil hangs between us and you, so work, we
too are working.

وَقَالُوْا قُلُوْبُنَا فِيْ اَكِنَّةٍ مِّمَّا تَدْعُوْنَآ اِلَيْهِ وَفِيْ
اٰذَانِنَا وَقْرٌ وَّمِنْ بَيْنِنَا وَبَيْنِكَ حِجَابٌ فَاعْمَلْ
اِنَّنَا عٰمِلُوْنَ ۝

6. Say: I am only a mortal like you; it is
revealed to me that your God is one God,
therefore follow the right way to Him and
ask His forgiveness; and woe to the
polytheists;

قُلْ اِنَّمَآ اَنَا بَشَرٌ مِّثْلُكُمْ يُوْحٰى اِلَيَّ اَنَّمَآ اِلٰهُكُمْ
اِلٰهٌ وَّاحِدٌ فَاسْتَقِيْمُوْٓا اِلَيْهِ وَاسْتَغْفِرُوْهُ ۗ وَوَيْلٌ
لِّلْمُشْرِكِيْنَ ۝

7. (To) those who do not give poor-rate
and they are unbelievers in the hereafter.

الَّذِيْنَ لَا يُؤْتُوْنَ الزَّكٰوةَ وَهُمْ بِالْاٰخِرَةِ هُمْ كٰفِرُوْنَ ۝

8. (As for) those who believe and do
good, they shall surely have a reward never
to be cut off.

اِنَّ الَّذِيْنَ اٰمَنُوْا وَعَمِلُوا الصّٰلِحٰتِ لَهُمْ اَجْرٌ
غَيْرُ مَمْنُوْنٍ ۝

9. Say: What! do you indeed disbelieve
in Him Who created the earth in two
periods, and do you set up equals with
Him? That is the Lord of the Worlds.

قُلْ اَئِنَّكُمْ لَتَكْفُرُوْنَ بِالَّذِيْ خَلَقَ الْاَرْضَ فِيْ
يَوْمَيْنِ وَتَجْعَلُوْنَ لَهٗٓ اَنْدَادًا ۗ ذٰلِكَ رَبُّ الْعٰلَمِيْنَ ۝

10. And He made in it mountains above
its surface, and He blessed therein and
made therein its foods, in four periods:
alike for the seekers.

وَجَعَلَ فِيْهَا رَوَاسِيَ مِنْ فَوْقِهَا وَبٰرَكَ فِيْهَا
وَقَدَّرَ فِيْهَآ اَقْوَاتَهَا فِيْٓ اَرْبَعَةِ اَيَّامٍ ۗ سَوَآءً
لِّلسَّآئِلِيْنَ ۝

11. Then He directed Himself to the heaven and it is a vapor, so He said to it and to the earth: Come both, willingly or unwillingly. They both said: We come willingly.

ثُمَّ اسْتَوٰٓى اِلَى السَّمَآءِ وَهِىَ دُخَانٌ فَقَالَ لَهَا وَلِلْاَرْضِ ائْتِيَا طَوْعًا اَوْ كَرْهًا ۖ قَالَتَاۤ اَتَيْنَا طَآئِعِيْنَ ۝

12. So He ordained them seven heavens in two periods, and revealed in every heaven its affair; and We adorned the lower heaven with brilliant stars and (made it) to guard; that is the decree of the Mighty, the Knowing.

فَقَضٰهُنَّ سَبْعَ سَمٰوٰتٍ فِىْ يَوْمَيْنِ وَاَوْحٰى فِىْ كُلِّ سَمَآءٍ اَمْرَهَا ۚ وَزَيَّنَّا السَّمَآءَ الدُّنْيَا بِمَصَابِيْحَ ۖ وَحِفْظًا ۚ ذٰلِكَ تَقْدِيْرُ الْعَزِيْزِ الْعَلِيْمِ ۝

13. But if they turn aside, then say: I have warned you of a scourge like the scourge of Ad and Samood.

فَاِنْ اَعْرَضُوْا فَقُلْ اَنْذَرْتُكُمْ صٰعِقَةً مِّثْلَ صٰعِقَةِ عَادٍ وَّثَمُوْدَ ۝

14. When their apostles came to them from before them and from behind them, saying, Serve nothing but Allah, they said: If our Lord had pleased He would certainly have sent down angels, so we are surely unbelievers in that with which you are sent.

اِذْ جَآءَتْهُمُ الرُّسُلُ مِنْۢ بَيْنِ اَيْدِيْهِمْ وَمِنْ خَلْفِهِمْ اَلَّا تَعْبُدُوْۤا اِلَّا اللّٰهَ ۚ قَالُوْا لَوْ شَآءَ رَبُّنَا لَاَنْزَلَ مَلٰٓئِكَةً فَاِنَّا بِمَاۤ اُرْسِلْتُمْ بِهٖ كٰفِرُوْنَ ۝

15. Then as to Ad, they were unjustly proud in the land, and they said: Who is mightier in strength than we? Did they not see that Allah Who created them was mightier than they in strength, and they denied Our communications?

فَاَمَّا عَادٌ فَاسْتَكْبَرُوْا فِى الْاَرْضِ بِغَيْرِ الْحَقِّ وَ قَالُوْا مَنْ اَشَدُّ مِنَّا قُوَّةً ۚ اَوَلَمْ يَرَوْا اَنَّ اللّٰهَ الَّذِىْ خَلَقَهُمْ هُوَ اَشَدُّ مِنْهُمْ قُوَّةً ۚ وَكَانُوْا بِاٰيٰتِنَا يَجْحَدُوْنَ ۝

16. So We sent on them a furious wind in unlucky days, that We may make them taste the chastisement of abasement in this world's life; and certainly the chastisement of the hereafter is much more abasing, and they shall not be helped.

فَاَرْسَلْنَا عَلَيْهِمْ رِيْحًا صَرْصَرًا فِىْۤ اَيَّامٍ نَّحِسَاتٍ لِّنُذِيْقَهُمْ عَذَابَ الْخِزْىِ فِى الْحَيٰوةِ الدُّنْيَا ۚ وَلَعَذَابُ الْاٰخِرَةِ اَخْزٰى وَهُمْ لَا يُنْصَرُوْنَ ۝

17. And as to Samood, We showed them the right way, but they chose error above guidance, so there overtook them the scourge of an abasing chastisement for what they earned.

وَاَمَّا ثَمُوْدُ فَهَدَيْنٰهُمْ فَاسْتَحَبُّوا الْعَمٰى عَلَى الْهُدٰى فَاَخَذَتْهُمْ صٰعِقَةُ الْعَذَابِ الْهُوْنِ بِمَا كَانُوْا يَكْسِبُوْنَ ۝

18. And We delivered those who believed and guarded (against evil).

19. And on the day that the enemies of Allah shall be brought together to the fire, then they shall be formed into groups.

20. Until when they come to it, their ears and their eyes and their skins shall bear witness against them as to what they did.

21. And they shall say to their skins: Why have you borne witness against us? They shall say: Allah Who makes everything speak has made us speak, and He created you at first, and to Him you shall be brought back.

22. And you did not veil yourselves lest your ears and your eyes and your skins should bear witness against you, but you thought that Allah did not know most of what you did.

23. And that was your (evil) thought which you entertained about your Lord that has tumbled you down into perdition, so are you become of the lost ones.

24. Then if they will endure, still the fire is their abode, and if they ask for goodwill, then are they not of those who shall be granted goodwill.

25. And We have appointed for them comrades so they have made fair-seeming to them what is before them and what is behind them, and the word proved true against them—among the nations of the jinn and the men that have passed away before them—that they shall surely be losers.

26. And those who disbelieve say: Do not listen to this Quran and make noise therein, perhaps you may overcome.

473

27. Therefore We will most certainly make those who disbelieve taste a severe punishment, and We will most certainly reward them for the evil deeds they used to do.

28. That is the reward of the enemies of Allah—the fire; for them therein shall be the house of long abiding; a reward for their denying Our communications.

29. And those who disbelieve will say: Our Lord! show us those who led us astray from among the jinn and the men that we may trample them under our feet so that they may be of the lowest.

30. (As for) those who say: Our Lord is Allah, then continue in the right way, the angels descend upon them, saying: Fear not, nor be grieved, and receive good news of the garden which you were promised.

31. We are your guardians in this world's life and in the hereafter, and you shall have therein what your souls desire and you shall have therein what you ask for:

32. A provision from the Forgiving, the Merciful.

33. And who speaks better than he who calls to Allah while he himself does good, and says: I am surely of those who submit?

34. And not alike are the good and the evil. Repel (evil) with what is best, when lo! he between whom and you was enmity would be as if he were a warm friend.

35. And none are made to receive it but those who are patient, and none are made to receive it but those who have a mighty, good fortune.

36. And if an interference of the Shaitan should cause you mischief, seek refuge in Allah; surely He is the Hearing, the Knowing.

وَاِمَّا يَنْزَغَنَّكَ مِنَ الشَّيْطٰنِ نَزْغٌ فَاسْتَعِذْ بِاللّٰهِ ۖ اِنَّهٗ هُوَ السَّمِيْعُ الْعَلِيْمُ ۝

37. And among His signs are the night and the day and the sun and the moon; do not make obeisance to the sun nor to the moon; and make obeisance to Allah Who created them, if Him it is that you serve.

وَمِنْ اٰيٰتِهِ الَّيْلُ وَالنَّهَارُ وَالشَّمْسُ وَالْقَمَرُ ۖ لَا تَسْجُدُوْا لِلشَّمْسِ وَلَا لِلْقَمَرِ وَاسْجُدُوْا لِلّٰهِ الَّذِيْ خَلَقَهُنَّ اِنْ كُنْتُمْ اِيَّاهُ تَعْبُدُوْنَ ۝

38. But if they are proud, yet those with your Lord glorify Him during the night and the day, and they are not tired.

فَاِنِ اسْتَكْبَرُوْا فَالَّذِيْنَ عِنْدَ رَبِّكَ يُسَبِّحُوْنَ لَهٗ بِالَّيْلِ وَالنَّهَارِ وَهُمْ لَا يَسْـَٔمُوْنَ ۩

39. And among His signs is this, that you see the earth still, but when We send down on it the water, it stirs and swells: most surely He Who gives it life is the Giver of life to the dead; surely He has power over all things.

وَمِنْ اٰيٰتِهِ اَنَّكَ تَرَى الْاَرْضَ خَاشِعَةً فَاِذَآ اَنْزَلْنَا عَلَيْهَا الْمَآءَ اهْتَزَّتْ وَرَبَتْ ۖ اِنَّ الَّذِيْٓ اَحْيَاهَا لَمُحْيِ الْمَوْتٰى ۖ اِنَّهٗ عَلٰى كُلِّ شَيْءٍ قَدِيْرٌ ۝

40. Surely they who deviate from the right way concerning Our communications are not hidden from Us. What! is he then who is cast into the fire better, or he who comes safe on the day of resurrection? Do what you like, surely He sees what you do.

اِنَّ الَّذِيْنَ يُلْحِدُوْنَ فِيْٓ اٰيٰتِنَا لَا يَخْفَوْنَ عَلَيْنَا ۗ اَفَمَنْ يُّلْقٰى فِى النَّارِ خَيْرٌ اَمْ مَّنْ يَّأْتِيْٓ اٰمِنًا يَّوْمَ الْقِيٰمَةِ ۗ اِعْمَلُوْا مَا شِئْتُمْ ۙ اِنَّهٗ بِمَا تَعْمَلُوْنَ بَصِيْرٌ ۝

41. Surely those who disbelieve in the reminder when it comes to them, and most surely it is a Mighty Book:

اِنَّ الَّذِيْنَ كَفَرُوْا بِالذِّكْرِ لَمَّا جَآءَهُمْ ۖ وَاِنَّهٗ لَكِتٰبٌ عَزِيْزٌ ۝

42. Falsehood shall not come to it from before it nor from behind it; a revelation from the Wise, the Praised One.

لَا يَأْتِيْهِ الْبَاطِلُ مِنْۢ بَيْنِ يَدَيْهِ وَلَا مِنْ خَلْفِهٖ ۖ تَنْزِيْلٌ مِّنْ حَكِيْمٍ حَمِيْدٍ ۝

43. Naught is said to you but what was said indeed to the apostles before you; surely your Lord is the Lord of forgiveness and the Lord of painful retribution.

مَا يُقَالُ لَكَ اِلَّا مَا قَدْ قِيْلَ لِلرُّسُلِ مِنْ قَبْلِكَ ۖ اِنَّ رَبَّكَ لَذُوْ مَغْفِرَةٍ وَّذُوْ عِقَابٍ اَلِيْمٍ ۝

44. And if We had made it a Quran in a foreign tongue, they would certainly have said: Why have not its communications been made clear? What! a foreign (tongue) and an Arabian! Say: It is to those who believe a guidance and a healing; and (as for) those who do not believe, there is a heaviness in their ears and it is obscure to them; these shall be called to from a far-off place.

45. And certainly We gave the Book to Musa, but it has been differed about; and had not a word already gone forth from your Lord, judgment would certainly have been given between them; and most surely they are in a disquieting doubt about it.

46. Whoever does good, it is for his own soul, and whoever does evil, it is against it; and your Lord is not in the least unjust to the servants.

47. To Him is referred the knowledge of the hour, and there come not forth any of the fruits from their coverings, nor does a female bear, nor does she give birth, but with His knowledge; and on the day when He shall call out to them, Where are (those whom you called) My associates? They shall say: We declare to Thee, none of us is a witness.

48. And away from them shall go what they called upon before, and they shall know for certain that there is no escape for them.

49. Man is never tired of praying for good, and if evil touch him, then he is despairing, hopeless.

50. And if We make him taste mercy from Us after distress that has touched him, he would most certainly say: This is of me, and I do not think the hour will come to pass, and if I am sent back to my Lord, I shall have with Him sure good; but We will most certainly inform those who disbelieved of what they did, and We will most certainly make them taste of hard chastisement.

476

51. And when We show favor to man, he turns aside and withdraws himself; and when evil touches him, he makes lengthy supplications.

وَاِذَاۤ اَنْعَمْنَا عَلَى الْاِنْسَانِ اَعْرَضَ وَنَاٰ بِجَانِبِهٖ ۚ وَاِذَا مَسَّهُ الشَّرُّ فَذُوْ دُعَاۤءٍ عَرِيْضٍ ۝

52. Say: Tell me if it is from Allah; then you disbelieve in it, who is in greater error than he who is in a prolonged opposition?

قُلْ اَرَءَيْتُمْ اِنْ كَانَ مِنْ عِنْدِ اللّٰهِ ثُمَّ كَفَرْتُمْ بِهٖ مَنْ اَضَلُّ مِمَّنْ هُوَ فِيْ شِقَاقٍ بَعِيْدٍ ۝

53. We will soon show them Our signs in the Universe and in their own souls, until it will become quite clear to them that it is the truth. Is it not sufficient as regards your Lord that He is a witness over all things?

سَنُرِيْهِمْ اٰيٰتِنَا فِى الْاٰفَاقِ وَفِيْۤ اَنْفُسِهِمْ حَتّٰى يَتَبَيَّنَ لَهُمْ اَنَّهُ الْحَقُّ ؕ اَوَلَمْ يَكْفِ بِرَبِّكَ اَنَّهُ عَلٰى كُلِّ شَيْءٍ شَهِيْدٌ ۝

54. Now surely they are in doubt as to the meeting of their Lord; now surely He encompasses all things.

اَلَاۤ اِنَّهُمْ فِيْ مِرْيَةٍ مِّنْ لِّقَاۤءِ رَبِّهِمْ ؕ اَلَاۤ اِنَّهُ بِكُلِّ شَيْءٍ مُّحِيْطٌ ۝ع

477

THE COUNSEL
(SHURA)

بِسْمِ اللهِ الرَّحْمٰنِ الرَّحِيْمِ ۞

**In the name of Allah,
The Beneficent, The Merciful.**

1. Ha Mim.

2. Ain Sin Qaf.

3. Thus does Allah, the Mighty, the Wise, reveal to you, and (thus He revealed) to those before you.

4. His is what is in the heavens and what is in the earth, and He is the High, the Great.

5. The heavens may almost rend asunder from above them and the angels sing the praise of their Lord and ask forgiveness for those on earth; now surely Allah is the Forgiving, the Merciful.

6. And (as for) those who take guardians besides Him, Allah watches over them, and you have not charge over them.

7. And thus have We revealed to you an Arabic Quran, that you may warn the mother city and those around it, and that you may give warning of the day of gathering together wherein is no doubt; a party shall be in the garden and (another) party in the burning fire.

8. And if Allah had pleased He would surely have made them a single community, but He makes whom He pleases enter into His mercy, and the unjust it is that shall have no guardian or helper.

9. Or have they taken guardians besides Him? But Allah is the Guardian, and He gives life to the dead, and He has power over all things.

اياتها (٤٢) سُوْرَةُ الشُّوْرٰى مَكِيَّةٌ رُوْعَاتُهَا

بِسْمِ اللهِ الرَّحْمٰنِ الرَّحِيْمِ ۞

حٰمٓ ۞

عٓسٓقٓ ۞

كَذٰلِكَ يُوْحِىٓ اِلَيْكَ وَاِلَى الَّذِيْنَ مِنْ قَبْلِكَ ۙ اللهُ الْعَزِيْزُ الْحَكِيْمُ ۞

لَهٗ مَا فِى السَّمٰوٰتِ وَمَا فِى الْاَرْضِ ۚ وَهُوَ الْعَلِيُّ الْعَظِيْمُ ۞

تَكَادُ السَّمٰوٰتُ يَتَفَطَّرْنَ مِنْ فَوْقِهِنَّ وَالْمَلٰٓئِكَةُ يُسَبِّحُوْنَ بِحَمْدِ رَبِّهِمْ وَيَسْتَغْفِرُوْنَ لِمَنْ فِى الْاَرْضِ ۗ اَلَآ اِنَّ اللهَ هُوَ الْغَفُوْرُ الرَّحِيْمُ ۞

وَالَّذِيْنَ اتَّخَذُوْا مِنْ دُوْنِهٖٓ اَوْلِيَآءَ اللهُ حَفِيْظٌ عَلَيْهِمْ ۖ وَمَآ اَنْتَ عَلَيْهِمْ بِوَكِيْلٍ ۞

وَكَذٰلِكَ اَوْحَيْنَآ اِلَيْكَ قُرْاٰنًا عَرَبِيًّا لِّتُنْذِرَ اُمَّ الْقُرٰى وَمَنْ حَوْلَهَا وَتُنْذِرَ يَوْمَ الْجَمْعِ لَا رَيْبَ فِيْهِ ۚ فَرِيْقٌ فِى الْجَنَّةِ وَفَرِيْقٌ فِى السَّعِيْرِ ۞

وَلَوْ شَآءَ اللهُ لَجَعَلَهُمْ اُمَّةً وَّاحِدَةً وَّلٰكِنْ يُّدْخِلُ مَنْ يَّشَآءُ فِىْ رَحْمَتِهٖ ۚ وَالظّٰلِمُوْنَ مَا لَهُمْ مِّنْ وَّلِيٍّ وَّلَا نَصِيْرٍ ۞

اَمِ اتَّخَذُوْا مِنْ دُوْنِهٖٓ اَوْلِيَآءَ ۚ فَاللهُ هُوَ الْوَلِيُّ وَهُوَ يُحْيِ الْمَوْتٰى ۖ وَهُوَ عَلٰى كُلِّ شَىْءٍ قَدِيْرٌ ۞

478

10. And in whatever thing you disagree, the judgment thereof is (in) Allah's (hand); that is Allah, my Lord, on Him do I rely and to Him do I turn time after time.

وَمَا اخْتَلَفْتُمْ فِيهِ مِنْ شَيْءٍ فَحُكْمُهُ إِلَى اللّٰهِ ۚ ذٰلِكُمُ اللّٰهُ رَبِّيْ عَلَيْهِ تَوَكَّلْتُ ۖ وَإِلَيْهِ أُنِيبُ ۞

11. The Originator of the heavens and the earth; He made mates for you from among yourselves, and mates of the cattle too, multiplying you thereby; nothing like a likeness of Him; and He is the Hearing, the Seeing.

فَاطِرُ السَّمٰوٰتِ وَالْأَرْضِ ۚ جَعَلَ لَكُمْ مِنْ أَنْفُسِكُمْ أَزْوَاجًا وَمِنَ الْأَنْعَامِ أَزْوَاجًا ۚ يَذْرَؤُكُمْ فِيهِ ۚ لَيْسَ كَمِثْلِهِ شَيْءٌ ۚ وَهُوَ السَّمِيعُ الْبَصِيرُ ۞

12. His are the treasures of the heavens and the earth; He makes ample and straitens the means of subsistence for whom He pleases; surely He is Cognizant of all things.

لَهُ مَقَالِيدُ السَّمٰوٰتِ وَالْأَرْضِ ۚ يَبْسُطُ الرِّزْقَ لِمَنْ يَشَاءُ وَيَقْدِرُ ۚ إِنَّهُ بِكُلِّ شَيْءٍ عَلِيمٌ ۞

13. He has made plain to you of the religion what He enjoined upon Nuh and that which We have revealed to you, and that which We enjoined upon Ibrahim and Musa and Isa, that keep to obedience and be not divided therein; hard to the unbelievers is that which you call them to; Allah chooses for Himself whom He pleases, and guides to Himself him who turns (to Him) frequently.

شَرَعَ لَكُمْ مِنَ الدِّينِ مَا وَصّٰى بِهِ نُوحًا وَالَّذِيْ أَوْحَيْنَا إِلَيْكَ وَمَا وَصَّيْنَا بِهِ إِبْرَاهِيمَ وَمُوسٰى وَعِيسٰى أَنْ أَقِيمُوا الدِّينَ وَلَا تَتَفَرَّقُوا فِيهِ ۚ كَبُرَ عَلَى الْمُشْرِكِينَ مَا تَدْعُوهُمْ إِلَيْهِ ۚ اللّٰهُ يَجْتَبِي إِلَيْهِ مَنْ يَشَاءُ وَيَهْدِي إِلَيْهِ مَنْ يُنِيبُ ۞

14. And they did not become divided until after knowledge had come to them out of envy among themselves; and had not a word gone forth from your Lord till an appointed term, certainly judgment would have been given between them; and those who were made to inherit the Book after them are most surely in disquieting doubt concerning it.

وَمَا تَفَرَّقُوا إِلَّا مِنْ بَعْدِ مَا جَاءَهُمُ الْعِلْمُ بَغْيًا بَيْنَهُمْ ۚ وَلَوْلَا كَلِمَةٌ سَبَقَتْ مِنْ رَبِّكَ إِلَى أَجَلٍ مُسَمًّى لَقُضِيَ بَيْنَهُمْ ۚ وَإِنَّ الَّذِينَ أُورِثُوا الْكِتَابَ مِنْ بَعْدِهِمْ لَفِي شَكٍّ مِنْهُ مُرِيبٌ ۞

15. To this then go on inviting, and go on steadfastly on the right way as you are commanded, and do not follow their low desires, and say: I believe in what Allah has revealed of the Book, and I am commanded to do justice between you: Allah is our Lord and your Lord; we shall have our deeds and you shall have your deeds; no plea need there be (now) between us and you: Allah will gather us together, and to Him is the return.

فَلِذٰلِكَ فَادْعُ ۖ وَاسْتَقِمْ كَمَا أُمِرْتَ ۖ وَلَا تَتَّبِعْ أَهْوَاءَهُمْ ۖ وَقُلْ آمَنْتُ بِمَا أَنْزَلَ اللّٰهُ مِنْ كِتَابٍ ۖ وَأُمِرْتُ لِأَعْدِلَ بَيْنَكُمُ ۖ اللّٰهُ رَبُّنَا وَرَبُّكُمْ ۚ لَنَا أَعْمَالُنَا وَلَكُمْ أَعْمَالُكُمْ ۚ لَا حُجَّةَ بَيْنَنَا وَبَيْنَكُمُ ۖ اللّٰهُ يَجْمَعُ بَيْنَنَا ۖ وَإِلَيْهِ الْمَصِيرُ ۞

16. And (as for) those who dispute about Allah after that obedience has been rendered to Him, their plea is null with their Lord, and upon them is wrath, and for them is severe punishment.

وَالَّذِيْنَ يُحَاجُّوْنَ فِى اللّٰهِ مِنْۢ بَعْدِ مَا اسْتُجِيْبَ لَهٗ حُجَّتُهُمْ دَاحِضَةٌ عِنْدَ رَبِّهِمْ وَعَلَيْهِمْ غَضَبٌ وَّلَهُمْ عَذَابٌ شَدِيْدٌ ۝

17. Allah it is Who revealed the Book with truth, and the balance, and what shall make you know that haply the hour be nigh?

اَللّٰهُ الَّذِيْۤ اَنْزَلَ الْكِتٰبَ بِالْحَقِّ وَالْمِيْزَانَ وَمَا يُدْرِيْكَ لَعَلَّ السَّاعَةَ قَرِيْبٌ ۝

18. Those who do not believe in it would hasten it on, and those who believe are in fear from it, and they know that it is the truth. Now most surely those who dispute obstinately concerning the hour are in a great error.

يَسْتَعْجِلُ بِهَا الَّذِيْنَ لَا يُؤْمِنُوْنَ بِهَا وَالَّذِيْنَ اٰمَنُوْا مُشْفِقُوْنَ مِنْهَا وَيَعْلَمُوْنَ اَنَّهَا الْحَقُّ اَلَاۤ اِنَّ الَّذِيْنَ يُمَارُوْنَ فِى السَّاعَةِ لَفِيْ ضَلٰلٍۭ بَعِيْدٍ ۝

19. Allah is Benignant to His servants; He gives sustenance to whom He pleases; and He is the Strong, the Mighty.

اَللّٰهُ لَطِيْفٌۢ بِعِبَادِهٖ يَرْزُقُ مَنْ يَّشَآءُ وَهُوَ الْقَوِيُّ الْعَزِيْزُ ۝

20. Whoever desires the gain of the hereafter, We will give him more of that again; and whoever desires the gain of this world, We give him of it, and in the hereafter he has no portion.

مَنْ كَانَ يُرِيْدُ حَرْثَ الْاٰخِرَةِ نَزِدْ لَهٗ فِىْ حَرْثِهٖ وَمَنْ كَانَ يُرِيْدُ حَرْثَ الدُّنْيَا نُؤْتِهٖ مِنْهَا وَمَالَهٗ فِى الْاٰخِرَةِ مِنْ نَّصِيْبٍ ۝

21. Or have they associates who have prescribed for them any religion that Allah does not sanction? And were it not for the word of judgment, decision would have certainly been given between them; and surely the unjust shall have a painful punishment.

اَمْ لَهُمْ شُرَكٰٓؤُا شَرَعُوْا لَهُمْ مِّنَ الدِّيْنِ مَا لَمْ يَأْذَنْۢ بِهِ اللّٰهُ وَلَوْلَا كَلِمَةُ الْفَصْلِ لَقُضِىَ بَيْنَهُمْ وَاِنَّ الظّٰلِمِيْنَ لَهُمْ عَذَابٌ اَلِيْمٌ ۝

22. You will see the unjust fearing on account of what they have earned, and it must befall them; and those who believe and do good shall be in the meadows of the gardens; they shall have what they please with their Lord: that is the great grace.

تَرَى الظّٰلِمِيْنَ مُشْفِقِيْنَ مِمَّا كَسَبُوْا وَهُوَ وَاقِعٌۢ بِهِمْ وَالَّذِيْنَ اٰمَنُوْا وَعَمِلُوا الصّٰلِحٰتِ فِىْ رَوْضَاتِ الْجَنّٰتِ لَهُمْ مَّا يَشَآءُوْنَ عِنْدَ رَبِّهِمْ ذٰلِكَ هُوَ الْفَضْلُ الْكَبِيْرُ ۝

23. That is of which Allah gives the good news to His servants, (to) those who believe and do good deeds. Say: I do not ask of you any reward for it but love for my near relatives; and whoever earns good, We give him more of good therein; surely Allah is Forgiving, Grateful.

ذٰلِكَ الَّذِيْ يُبَشِّرُ اللهُ عِبَادَهُ الَّذِيْنَ اٰمَنُوْا وَ عَمِلُوا الصّٰلِحٰتِ قُلْ لَّاۤ اَسْئَلُكُمْ عَلَيْهِ اَجْرًا اِلَّا الْمَوَدَّةَ فِي الْقُرْبٰى وَمَنْ يَّقْتَرِفْ حَسَنَةً نَّزِدْلَهُ فِيْهَا حُسْنًا اِنَّ اللهَ غَفُوْرٌ شَكُوْرٌ ۝

24. Or do they say: He has forged a lie against Allah? But if Allah pleased, He would seal your heart; and Allah will blot out the falsehood and confirm the truth with His words; surely He is Cognizant of what is in the breasts.

اَمْ يَقُوْلُوْنَ افْتَرٰى عَلَى اللهِ كَذِبًا فَاِنْ يَّشَاِ اللهُ يَخْتِمْ عَلٰى قَلْبِكَ وَيَمْحُ اللهُ الْبَاطِلَ وَيُحِقُّ الْحَقَّ بِكَلِمٰتِهِ اِنَّهُ عَلِيْمٌۢ بِذَاتِ الصُّدُوْرِ ۝

25. And He it is Who accepts repentance from His servants and pardons the evil deeds and He knows what you do;

وَهُوَ الَّذِيْ يَقْبَلُ التَّوْبَةَ عَنْ عِبَادِهِ وَيَعْفُوْا عَنِ السَّيِّاٰتِ وَيَعْلَمُ مَا تَفْعَلُوْنَ ۝

26. And He answers those who believe and do good deeds, and gives them more out of His grace; and (as for) the unbelievers, they shall have a severe punishment.

وَيَسْتَجِيْبُ الَّذِيْنَ اٰمَنُوْا وَعَمِلُوا الصّٰلِحٰتِ وَيَزِيْدُهُمْ مِّنْ فَضْلِهِ وَالْكٰفِرُوْنَ لَهُمْ عَذَابٌ شَدِيْدٌ ۝

27. And if Allah should amplify the provision for His servants they would certainly revolt in the earth; but He sends it down according to a measure as He pleases; surely He is Aware of, Seeing, His servants.

وَلَوْ بَسَطَ اللهُ الرِّزْقَ لِعِبَادِهِ لَبَغَوْا فِي الْاَرْضِ وَلٰكِنْ يُّنَزِّلُ بِقَدَرٍ مَّا يَشَاۤءُ اِنَّهُ بِعِبَادِهِ خَبِيْرٌ بَصِيْرٌ ۝

28. And He it is Who sends down the rain after they have despaired, and He unfolds His mercy; and He is the Guardian, the Praised One.

وَهُوَ الَّذِيْ يُنَزِّلُ الْغَيْثَ مِنْ بَعْدِ مَا قَنَطُوْا وَيَنْشُرُ رَحْمَتَهُ وَهُوَ الْوَلِيُّ الْحَمِيْدُ ۝

29. And one of His signs is the creation of the heavens and the earth and what He has spread forth in both of them of living beings; and when He pleases He is all-powerful to gather them together.

وَمِنْ اٰيٰتِهِ خَلْقُ السَّمٰوٰتِ وَالْاَرْضِ وَمَا بَثَّ فِيْهِمَا مِنْ دَاۤبَّةٍ وَهُوَ عَلٰى جَمْعِهِمْ اِذَا يَشَاۤءُ قَدِيْرٌ ۝

30. And whatever affliction befalls you, it is on account of what your hands have wrought, and (yet) He pardons most (of your faults).

وَمَاۤ اَصَابَكُمْ مِّنْ مُّصِيْبَةٍ فَبِمَا كَسَبَتْ اَيْدِيْكُمْ وَيَعْفُوْا عَنْ كَثِيْرٍ ۝

31. And you cannot escape in the earth, and you shall not have a guardian or a helper besides Allah.

32. And among His signs are the ships in the sea like mountains.

33. If He pleases, He causes the wind to become still so that they lie motionless on its back; most surely there are signs in this for every patient, grateful one,

34. Or He may make them founder for what they have earned, and (even then) pardon most;

35. And (that) those who dispute about Our communications may know; there is no place of refuge for them.

36. So whatever thing you are given, that is only a provision of this world's life, and what is with Allah is better and more lasting for those who believe and rely on their Lord.

37. And those who shun the great sins and indecencies, and whenever they are angry they forgive.

38. And those who respond to their Lord and keep up prayer, and their rule is to take counsel among themselves, and who spend out of what We have given them.

39. And those who, when great wrong afflicts them, defend themselves.

40. And the recompense of evil is punishment like it, but whoever forgives and amends, he shall have his reward from Allah; surely He does not love the unjust.

41. And whoever defends himself after his being oppressed, these it is against whom there is no way (to blame).

42. The way (to blame) is only against those who oppress men and revolt in the earth unjustly; these shall have a painful punishment.

وَمَآ اَنْتُمْ بِمُعْجِزِيْنَ فِي الْاَرْضِ ۖ وَمَا لَكُمْ مِّنْ دُوْنِ اللّٰهِ مِنْ وَّلِيٍّ وَّلَا نَصِيْرٍ ۞

وَمِنْ اٰيٰتِهِ الْجَوَارِ فِي الْبَحْرِ كَالْاَعْلَامِ ۞

اِنْ يَّشَاْ يُسْكِنِ الرِّيْحَ فَيَظْلَلْنَ رَوَاكِدَ عَلٰى ظَهْرِهٖ ۖ اِنَّ فِيْ ذٰلِكَ لَاٰيٰتٍ لِّكُلِّ صَبَّارٍ شَكُوْرٍ ۞

اَوْ يُوْبِقْهُنَّ بِمَا كَسَبُوْا وَيَعْفُ عَنْ كَثِيْرٍ ۞

وَّيَعْلَمَ الَّذِيْنَ يُجَادِلُوْنَ فِيْٓ اٰيٰتِنَا ۖ مَا لَهُمْ مِّنْ مَّحِيْصٍ ۞

فَمَآ اُوْتِيْتُمْ مِّنْ شَيْءٍ فَمَتَاعُ الْحَيٰوةِ الدُّنْيَا ۖ وَمَا عِنْدَ اللّٰهِ خَيْرٌ وَّاَبْقٰى لِلَّذِيْنَ اٰمَنُوْا وَعَلٰى رَبِّهِمْ يَتَوَكَّلُوْنَ ۞

وَالَّذِيْنَ يَجْتَنِبُوْنَ كَبٰٓئِرَ الْاِثْمِ وَالْفَوَاحِشَ وَاِذَا مَا غَضِبُوْا هُمْ يَغْفِرُوْنَ ۞

وَالَّذِيْنَ اسْتَجَابُوْا لِرَبِّهِمْ وَاَقَامُوا الصَّلٰوةَ ۖ وَاَمْرُهُمْ شُوْرٰى بَيْنَهُمْ ۖ وَمِمَّا رَزَقْنٰهُمْ يُنْفِقُوْنَ ۞

وَالَّذِيْنَ اِذَآ اَصَابَهُمُ الْبَغْيُ هُمْ يَنْتَصِرُوْنَ ۞

وَجَزٰٓؤُا سَيِّئَةٍ سَيِّئَةٌ مِّثْلُهَا ۖ فَمَنْ عَفَا وَاَصْلَحَ فَاَجْرُهٗ عَلَى اللّٰهِ ۖ اِنَّهٗ لَا يُحِبُّ الظّٰلِمِيْنَ ۞

وَلَمَنِ انْتَصَرَ بَعْدَ ظُلْمِهٖ فَاُولٰٓئِكَ مَا عَلَيْهِمْ مِّنْ سَبِيْلٍ ۞

اِنَّمَا السَّبِيْلُ عَلَى الَّذِيْنَ يَظْلِمُوْنَ النَّاسَ وَيَبْغُوْنَ فِي الْاَرْضِ بِغَيْرِ الْحَقِّ ۖ اُولٰٓئِكَ لَهُمْ عَذَابٌ اَلِيْمٌ ۞

43. And whoever is patient and forgiving, these most surely are actions due to courage.

44. And whomsoever Allah makes err, he has no guardian after Him; and you shall see the unjust, when they see the punishment, saying: Is there any way to return?

45. And you shall see them brought before it humbling themselves because of the abasements, looking with a faint glance. And those who believe shall say: Surely the losers are they who have lost themselves and their followers on the resurrection day. Now surely the iniquitous shall remain in lasting chastisement.

46. And they shall have no friends to help them besides Allah; and whomsoever Allah makes err, he shall have no way.

47. Hearken to your Lord before there comes the day from Allah for which there shall be no averting; you shall have no refuge on that day, nor shall it be yours to make a denial.

48. But if they turn aside, We have not sent you as a watcher over them; on you is only to deliver (the message); and surely when We make man taste mercy from Us, he rejoices thereat; and if an evil afflicts them on account of what their hands have already done, then surely man is ungrateful.

49. Allah's is the kingdom of the heavens and the earth; He creates what He pleases; He grants to whom He pleases daughters and grants to whom He pleases sons.

50. Or He makes them of both sorts, male and female; and He makes whom He pleases barren; surely He is the Knowing, the Powerful.

51. And it is not for any mortal that Allah should speak to him except by revelation or from behind a veil, or by sending a messenger and revealing by His permission what He pleases; surely He is High, Wise.

وَمَا كَانَ لِبَشَرٍ اَنْ يُّكَلِّمَهُ اللهُ اِلَّا وَحْيًا اَوْ مِنْ وَّرَآئِ حِجَابٍ اَوْ يُرْسِلَ رَسُوْلًا فَيُوْحِيَ بِاِذْنِهٖ مَا يَشَآءُ اِنَّهٗ عَلِيٌّ حَكِيْمٌ ۝

52. And thus did We reveal to you an inspired book by Our command. You did not know what the Book was, nor (what) the faith (was), but We made it a light, guiding thereby whom We please of Our servants; and most surely you show the way to the right path:

وَكَذٰلِكَ اَوْحَيْنَآ اِلَيْكَ رُوْحًا مِّنْ اَمْرِنَا مَا كُنْتَ تَدْرِيْ مَا الْكِتٰبُ وَلَا الْاِيْمَانُ وَلٰكِنْ جَعَلْنٰهُ نُوْرًا نَّهْدِيْ بِهٖ مَنْ نَّشَآءُ مِنْ عِبَادِنَا وَاِنَّكَ لَتَهْدِيْ اِلٰى صِرَاطٍ مُّسْتَقِيْمٍ ۝

53. The path of Allah, Whose is whatsoever is in the heavens and whatsoever is in the earth; now surely to Allah do all affairs eventually come.

صِرَاطِ اللهِ الَّذِيْ لَهٗ مَا فِى السَّمٰوٰتِ وَمَا فِى الْاَرْضِ اَلَا اِلَى اللهِ تَصِيْرُ الْاُمُوْرُ ۝

484

THE EMBELLISHMENT
(ZUKHRUF)

**In the name of Allah,
the Beneficent, the Merciful.**

1. Ha Mim.

2. I swear by the Book that makes things clear:

3. Surely We have made it an Arabic Quran that you may understand.

4. And surely it is in the original of the Book with Us, truly elevated, full of wisdom.

5. What! shall We then turn away the reminder from you altogether because you are an extravagant people?

6. And how many a prophet have We sent among the ancients.

7. And there came not to them a prophet but they mocked at him.

8. Then We destroyed those who were stronger than these in prowess, and the case of the ancients has gone before,

9. And if you should ask them, Who created the heavens and the earth? they would most certainly say: The Mighty, the Knowing One, has created them;

10. He Who made the earth a resting-place for you, and made in it ways for you that you may go aright;

11. And He Who sends down water from the cloud according to a measure, then We raise to life thereby a dead country; even thus shall you be brought forth;

12. And He Who created pairs of all things, and made for you of the ships and the cattle what you ride on,

13. That you may firmly sit on their backs, then remember the favor of your Lord when you are firmly seated thereon, and say: Glory be to Him Who made this subservient to us and we were not able to do it,

485

14. And surely to our Lord we must return.

15. And they assign to Him a part of His servants; man, to be sure, is clearly ungrateful.

16. What! has He taken daughters to Himself of what He Himself creates and chosen you to have sons?

17. And when one of them is given news of that of which he sets up as a likeness for the Beneficent God, his face becomes black and he is full of rage.

18. What! that which is made in ornaments and which in contention is unable to make plain speech!

19. And they make the angels—them who are the servants of the Beneficent God—female (divinities). What! did they witness their creation? Their evidence shall be written down and they shall be questioned.

20. And they say: If the Beneficent God had pleased, we should never have worshipped them. They have no knowledge of this; they only lie.

21. Or have We given them a book before it so that they hold fast to it?

22. Nay! they say: We found our fathers on a course, and surely we are guided by their footsteps.

23. And thus, We did not send before you any warner in a town, but those who led easy lives in it said: Surely we found our fathers on a course, and surely we are followers of their footsteps.

24. (The warner) said: What! even if I bring to you a better guide than that on which you found your fathers? They said: Surely we are unbelievers in that with which you are sent.

25. So We inflicted retribution on them, then see how was the end of the rejecters.

وَإِنَّا إِلٰى رَبِّنَا لَمُنْقَلِبُوْنَ ۝

وَجَعَلُوْا لَهٗ مِنْ عِبَادِهٖ جُزْءًا ۚ إِنَّ الْاِنْسَانَ لَكَفُوْرٌ مُّبِيْنٌ ۝

اَمِ اتَّخَذَ مِمَّا يَخْلُقُ بَنٰتٍ وَّاَصْفٰىكُمْ بِالْبَنِيْنَ ۝

وَاِذَا بُشِّرَ اَحَدُهُمْ بِمَا ضَرَبَ لِلرَّحْمٰنِ مَثَلًا ظَلَّ وَجْهُهٗ مُسْوَدًّا وَّهُوَ كَظِيْمٌ ۝

اَوَمَنْ يُّنَشَّؤُا فِى الْحِلْيَةِ وَهُوَ فِى الْخِصَامِ غَيْرُ مُبِيْنٍ ۝

وَجَعَلُوا الْمَلٰٓئِكَةَ الَّذِيْنَ هُمْ عِبٰدُ الرَّحْمٰنِ اِنَاثًا ۚ اَشَهِدُوْا خَلْقَهُمْ ۚ سَتُكْتَبُ شَهَادَتُهُمْ وَيُسْـَٔلُوْنَ ۝

وَقَالُوْا لَوْ شَآءَ الرَّحْمٰنُ مَا عَبَدْنٰهُمْ ۗ مَا لَهُمْ بِذٰلِكَ مِنْ عِلْمٍ ۚ اِنْ هُمْ اِلَّا يَخْرُصُوْنَ ۝

اَمْ اٰتَيْنٰهُمْ كِتٰبًا مِّنْ قَبْلِهٖ فَهُمْ بِهٖ مُسْتَمْسِكُوْنَ ۝

بَلْ قَالُوْا اِنَّا وَجَدْنَآ اٰبَآءَنَا عَلٰٓى اُمَّةٍ وَّاِنَّا عَلٰٓى اٰثٰرِهِمْ مُّهْتَدُوْنَ ۝

وَكَذٰلِكَ مَآ اَرْسَلْنَا مِنْ قَبْلِكَ فِيْ قَرْيَةٍ مِّنْ نَّذِيْرٍ اِلَّا قَالَ مُتْرَفُوْهَآ ۙ اِنَّا وَجَدْنَآ اٰبَآءَنَا عَلٰٓى اُمَّةٍ وَّاِنَّا عَلٰٓى اٰثٰرِهِمْ مُّقْتَدُوْنَ ۝

قُلْ اَوَلَوْ جِئْتُكُمْ بِاَهْدٰى مِمَّا وَجَدْتُّمْ عَلَيْهِ اٰبَآءَكُمْ ۗ قَالُوْٓا اِنَّا بِمَآ اُرْسِلْتُمْ بِهٖ كٰفِرُوْنَ ۝

فَانْتَقَمْنَا مِنْهُمْ فَانْظُرْ كَيْفَ كَانَ عَاقِبَةُ الْمُكَذِّبِيْنَ ۝

26. And when Ibrahim said to his father and his people: Surely I am clear of what you worship,

وَإِذْ قَالَ إِبْرَاهِيْمُ لِأَبِيْهِ وَقَوْمِهِ إِنَّنِيْ بَرَآءٌ مِّمَّا تَعْبُدُوْنَ ۟

27. Save Him Who created me, for surely He will guide me.

إِلَّا الَّذِيْ فَطَرَنِيْ فَإِنَّهُ سَيَهْدِيْنِ ۟

28. And he made it a word to continue in his posterity that they may return.

وَجَعَلَهَا كَلِمَةً بَاقِيَةً فِيْ عَقِبِهِ لَعَلَّهُمْ يَرْجِعُوْنَ ۟

29. Nay! I gave them and their fathers to enjoy until there came to them the truth and an Apostle making manifest (the truth).

بَلْ مَتَّعْتُ هٰؤُلَاءِ وَآبَاءَهُمْ حَتّٰى جَآءَهُمُ الْحَقُّ وَرَسُوْلٌ مُّبِيْنٌ ۟

30. And when there came to them the truth they said: This is magic, and surely we are disbelievers in it.

وَلَمَّا جَآءَهُمُ الْحَقُّ قَالُوْا هٰذَا سِحْرٌ وَّإِنَّا بِهِ كٰفِرُوْنَ ۟

31. And they say: Why was not this Quran revealed to a man of importance in the two towns?

وَقَالُوْا لَوْلَا نُزِّلَ هٰذَا الْقُرْآنُ عَلٰى رَجُلٍ مِّنَ الْقَرْيَتَيْنِ عَظِيْمٍ ۟

32. Will they distribute the mercy of your Lord? We distribute among them their livelihood in the life of this world, and We have exalted some of them above others in degrees, that some of them may take others in subjection; and the mercy of your Lord is better than what they amass.

أَهُمْ يَقْسِمُوْنَ رَحْمَتَ رَبِّكَ نَحْنُ قَسَمْنَا بَيْنَهُمْ مَّعِيْشَتَهُمْ فِي الْحَيٰوةِ الدُّنْيَا وَرَفَعْنَا بَعْضَهُمْ فَوْقَ بَعْضٍ دَرَجٰتٍ لِّيَتَّخِذَ بَعْضُهُمْ بَعْضًا سُخْرِيًّا وَرَحْمَتُ رَبِّكَ خَيْرٌ مِّمَّا يَجْمَعُوْنَ ۟

33. And were it not that all people had been a single nation, We would certainly have assigned to those who disbelieve in the Beneficent God (to make) of silver the roofs of their houses and the stairs by which they ascend.

وَلَوْلَا أَنْ يَّكُوْنَ النَّاسُ أُمَّةً وَّاحِدَةً لَّجَعَلْنَا لِمَنْ يَّكْفُرُ بِالرَّحْمٰنِ لِبُيُوْتِهِمْ سُقُفًا مِّنْ فِضَّةٍ وَّمَعَارِجَ عَلَيْهَا يَظْهَرُوْنَ ۟

34. And the doors of their houses and the couches on which they recline,

وَلِبُيُوْتِهِمْ أَبْوَابًا وَّسُرُرًا عَلَيْهَا يَتَّكِئُوْنَ ۟

35. And (other) embellishments of gold; and all this is naught but provision of this world's life, and the hereafter is with your Lord only for those who guard (against evil).

وَزُخْرُفًا وَإِنْ كُلُّ ذٰلِكَ لَمَّا مَتَاعُ الْحَيٰوةِ الدُّنْيَا وَالْآخِرَةُ عِنْدَ رَبِّكَ لِلْمُتَّقِيْنَ ۟

36. And whoever turns himself away from the remembrance of the Beneficent God, We appoint for him a Shaitan, so he becomes his associate.

وَمَنْ يَّعْشُ عَنْ ذِكْرِ الرَّحْمٰنِ نُقَيِّضْ لَهُ شَيْطٰنًا فَهُوَ لَهُ قَرِيْنٌ ۟

37. And most surely they turn them away from the path, and they think that they are guided aright:

وَاِنَّهُمْ لَيَصُدُّوْنَهُمْ عَنِ السَّبِيْلِ وَيَحْسَبُوْنَ اَنَّهُمْ مُّهْتَدُوْنَ ۝

38. Until when he comes to Us, he says: O would that between me and you there were the distance of the East and the West; so evil is the associate!

حَتّٰى اِذَا جَآءَنَا قَالَ يٰلَيْتَ بَيْنِيْ وَبَيْنَكَ بُعْدَ الْمَشْرِقَيْنِ فَبِئْسَ الْقَرِيْنُ ۝

39. And since you were unjust, it will not profit you this day that you are sharers in the chastisement.

وَلَنْ يَّنْفَعَكُمُ الْيَوْمَ اِذْ ظَّلَمْتُمْ اَنَّكُمْ فِى الْعَذَابِ مُشْتَرِكُوْنَ ۝

40. What! can you then make the deaf to hear or guide the blind and him who is in clear error?

اَفَاَنْتَ تُسْمِعُ الصُّمَّ اَوْ تَهْدِى الْعُمْىَ وَمَنْ كَانَ فِىْ ضَلٰلٍ مُّبِيْنٍ ۝

41. But if We should take you away, still We shall inflict retribution on them;

فَاِمَّا نَذْهَبَنَّ بِكَ فَاِنَّا مِنْهُمْ مُّنْتَقِمُوْنَ ۝

42. Rather We will certainly show you that which We have promised them; for surely We are the possessors of full power over them.

اَوْ نُرِيَنَّكَ الَّذِىْ وَعَدْنٰهُمْ فَاِنَّا عَلَيْهِمْ مُّقْتَدِرُوْنَ ۝

43. Therefore hold fast to that which has been revealed to you; surely you are on the right path.

فَاسْتَمْسِكْ بِالَّذِىْٓ اُوْحِىَ اِلَيْكَ اِنَّكَ عَلٰى صِرَاطٍ مُّسْتَقِيْمٍ ۝

44. And most surely it is a reminder for you and your people, and you shall soon be questioned.

وَاِنَّهٗ لَذِكْرٌ لَّكَ وَلِقَوْمِكَ وَسَوْفَ تُسْئَلُوْنَ ۝

45. And ask those of Our apostles whom We sent before you: Did We ever appoint gods to be worshipped besides the Beneficent God?

وَسْئَلْ مَنْ اَرْسَلْنَا مِنْ قَبْلِكَ مِنْ رُّسُلِنَآ اَجَعَلْنَا مِنْ دُوْنِ الرَّحْمٰنِ اٰلِهَةً يُّعْبَدُوْنَ ۝

46. And certainly We sent Musa with Our communications to Firon and his chiefs, so he said: Surely I am the apostle of the Lord of the worlds.

وَلَقَدْ اَرْسَلْنَا مُوْسٰى بِاٰيٰتِنَآ اِلٰى فِرْعَوْنَ وَمَلَائِهٖ فَقَالَ اِنِّىْ رَسُوْلُ رَبِّ الْعٰلَمِيْنَ ۝

47. But when he came to them with Our signs, lo! they laughed at them.

فَلَمَّا جَآءَهُمْ بِاٰيٰتِنَآ اِذَا هُمْ مِّنْهَا يَضْحَكُوْنَ ۝

48. And We did not show them a sign but it was greater than its like, and We overtook them with chastisement that they may turn.

وَمَا نُرِيْهِمْ مِّنْ اٰيَةٍ اِلَّا هِىَ اَكْبَرُ مِنْ اُخْتِهَا وَاَخَذْنٰهُمْ بِالْعَذَابِ لَعَلَّهُمْ يَرْجِعُوْنَ ۝

49. And they said: O magician! call on your Lord for our sake, as He has made the covenant with you; we shall surely be the followers of the right way.

وَقَالُوْا يٰٓاَيُّهَ السّٰحِرُ ادْعُ لَنَا رَبَّكَ بِمَا عَهِدَ عِنْدَكَ اِنَّنَا لَمُهْتَدُوْنَ ۝

50. But when We removed from them the chastisement, lo! they broke the pledge.

51. And Firon proclaimed amongst his people: O my people! is not the kingdom of Egypt mine? And these rivers flow beneath me; do you not then see?

52. Nay! I am better than this fellow, who is contemptible, and who can hardly speak distinctly:

53. But why have not bracelets of gold been put upon him, or why have there not come with him angels as companions?

54. So he incited his people to levity and they obeyed him: surely they were a transgressing people.

55. Then when they displeased Us, We inflicted retribution on them, so We drowned them all together,

56. And We made them a precedent and example to the later generations.

57. And when a description of the son of Marium is given, lo! your people raise a clamor thereat.

58. And they say: Are our gods better, or is he? They do not set it forth to you save by way of disputation; nay, they are a contentious people.

59. He was naught but a servant on whom We bestowed favor, and We made him an example for the children of Israel.

60. And if We please, We could make among you angels to be successors in the land.

61. And most surely it is a knowledge of the hour, therefore have no doubt about it and follow me: this is the right path.

62. And let not the Shaitan prevent you; surely he is your open enemy.

63. And when Isa came with clear arguments, he said: I have come to you indeed with wisdom, and that I may make clear to you part of what you differ in; so be careful of (your duty to) Allah and obey me:

ولما جاء عيسى بالبينت قال قد جئتكم بالحكمة ولابين لكم بعض الذي تختلفون فيه فاتقوا الله واطيعون ۞

64. Surely Allah is my Lord and your Lord, therefore serve Him; this is the right path:

ان الله هو ربي وربكم فاعبدوه هذا صراط مستقيم ۞

65. But parties from among them differed, so woe to those who were unjust because of the chastisement of a painful day.

فاختلف الاحزاب من بينهم فويل للذين ظلموا من عذاب يوم اليم ۞

66. Do they wait for aught but the hour, that it should come upon them all of a sudden while they do not perceive?

هل ينظرون الا الساعة ان تأتيهم بغتة وهم لا يشعرون ۞

67. The friends shall on that day be enemies one to another, except those who guard (against evil).

الاخلاء يومئذ بعضهم لبعض عدو الا المتقين ۞

68. O My servants! there is no fear for you this day, nor shall you grieve.

يعباد لا خوف عليكم اليوم ولا انتم تحزنون ۞

69. Those who believed in Our communications and were submissive:

الذين امنوا بايتنا وكانوا مسلمين ۞

70. Enter the garden, you and your wives; you shall be made happy.

ادخلوا الجنة انتم وازواجكم تحبرون ۞

71. There shall be sent round to them golden bowls and drinking-cups and therein shall be what their souls yearn after and (wherein) the eyes shall delight, and you shall abide therein.

يطاف عليهم بصحاف من ذهب واكواب وفيها ما تشتهيه الانفس وتلذ الاعين وانتم فيها خلدون ۞

72. And this is the garden which you are given as an inheritance on account of what you did.

وتلك الجنة التي اورثتموها بما كنتم تعملون ۞

73. For you therein are many fruits of which you shall eat.

لكم فيها فاكهة كثيرة منها تأكلون ۞

74. Surely the guilty shall abide in the chastisement of hell.

ان المجرمين في عذاب جهنم خلدون ۞

75. It shall not be abated from them and they shall therein be despairing.

لا يفتر عنهم وهم فيه مبلسون ۞

76. And We are not unjust to them, but they themselves were unjust.

وما ظلمنهم ولكن كانوا هم الظلمين ۞

77. And they shall call out: O Malik! let your Lord make an end of us. He shall say: Surely you shall tarry.

وَنَادَوْا يَمَالِكُ لِيَقْضِ عَلَيْنَا رَبُّكَ قَالَ اِنَّكُمْ مَّكِثُوْنَ ۞

78. Certainly We have brought you the truth, but most of you are averse to the truth.

لَقَدْ جِئْنَكُمْ بِالْحَقِّ وَلٰكِنَّ اَكْثَرَكُمْ لِلْحَقِّ كٰرِهُوْنَ ۞

79. Or have they settled an affair? Then surely We are the settlers.

اَمْ اَبْرَمُوْا اَمْرًا فَاِنَّا مُبْرِمُوْنَ ۞

80. Or do they think that We do not hear what they conceal and their secret discourses? Aye! and Our messengers with them write down.

اَمْ يَحْسَبُوْنَ اَنَّا لَا نَسْمَعُ سِرَّهُمْ وَنَجْوٰىهُمْ بَلٰى وَرُسُلُنَا لَدَيْهِمْ يَكْتُبُوْنَ ۞

81. Say: If the Beneficent God has a son, I am the foremost of those who serve.

قُلْ اِنْ كَانَ لِلرَّحْمٰنِ وَلَدٌ فَاَنَا اَوَّلُ الْعٰبِدِيْنَ ۞

82. Glory to the Lord of the heavens and the earth, the Lord of power, from what they describe.

سُبْحٰنَ رَبِّ السَّمٰوٰتِ وَالْاَرْضِ رَبِّ الْعَرْشِ عَمَّا يَصِفُوْنَ ۞

83. So leave them plunging into false discourses and sporting until they meet their day which they are threatened with.

فَذَرْهُمْ يَخُوْضُوْا وَيَلْعَبُوْا حَتّٰى يُلٰقُوْا يَوْمَهُمُ الَّذِيْ يُوْعَدُوْنَ ۞

84. And He it is Who is God in the heavens and God in the earth; and He is the Wise, the Knowing.

وَهُوَ الَّذِيْ فِي السَّمَاءِ اِلٰهٌ وَّفِي الْاَرْضِ اِلٰهٌ وَّهُوَ الْحَكِيْمُ الْعَلِيْمُ ۞

85. And blessed is He Whose is the kingdom of the heavens and the earth and what is between them, and with Him is the knowledge of the hour, and to Him shall you be brought back.

وَتَبٰرَكَ الَّذِيْ لَهٗ مُلْكُ السَّمٰوٰتِ وَالْاَرْضِ وَمَا بَيْنَهُمَا وَعِنْدَهٗ عِلْمُ السَّاعَةِ وَاِلَيْهِ تُرْجَعُوْنَ ۞

86. And those whom they call upon besides Him have no authority for intercession, but he who bears witness of the truth and they know (him).

وَلَا يَمْلِكُ الَّذِيْنَ يَدْعُوْنَ مِنْ دُوْنِهِ الشَّفَاعَةَ اِلَّا مَنْ شَهِدَ بِالْحَقِّ وَهُمْ يَعْلَمُوْنَ ۞

87. And if you should ask them who created them, they would certainly say: Allah. Whence are they then turned back?

وَلَئِنْ سَاَلْتَهُمْ مَّنْ خَلَقَهُمْ لَيَقُوْلُنَّ اللّٰهُ فَاَنّٰى يُؤْفَكُوْنَ ۞

88. Consider his cry: O my Lord! surely they are a people who do not believe.

وَقِيْلِهِ يٰرَبِّ اِنَّ هٰٓؤُلَاءِ قَوْمٌ لَّا يُؤْمِنُوْنَ ۞

89. So turn away from them and say, Peace, for they shall soon come to know.

فَاصْفَحْ عَنْهُمْ وَقُلْ سَلٰمٌ فَسَوْفَ يَعْلَمُوْنَ ۞

THE EVIDENT SMOKE
(DUKHAN)

**In the name of Allah,
the Beneficent, the Merciful.**

1. Ha Mim!

2. I swear by the Book that makes manifest (the truth).

3. Surely We revealed it on a blessed night—surely We are ever warning—

4. Therein every wise affair is made distinct,

5. A command from Us; surely We are the senders (of apostles),

6. A mercy from your Lord, surely He is the Hearing, the Knowing,

7. The Lord of the heavens and the earth and what is between them, if you would be sure.

8. There is no god but He; He gives life and causes death, your Lord and the Lord of your fathers of yore.

9. Nay, they are in doubt, they sport.

10. Therefore keep waiting for the day when the heaven shall bring an evident smoke,

11. That shall overtake men; this is a painful punishment.

12. Our Lord! remove from us the punishment; surely we are believers.

13. How shall they be reminded, and there came to them an Apostle making clear (the truth),

14. Yet they turned their backs on him and said: One taught (by others), a madman.

15. Surely We will remove the punishment a little, (but) you will surely return (to evil).

16. On the day when We will seize (them) with the most violent seizing; surely We will inflict retribution.

17. And certainly We tried before them the people of Firon, and there came to them a noble apostle,

بِسْمِ اللهِ الرَّحْمٰنِ الرَّحِيْمِ ۟

حٰمٓ ۟ۚ

وَالْكِتٰبِ الْمُبِيْنِ ۟ۙ

اِنَّاۤ اَنْزَلْنٰهُ فِيْ لَيْلَةٍ مُّبٰرَكَةٍ اِنَّا كُنَّا مُنْذِرِيْنَ ۟

فِيْهَا يُفْرَقُ كُلُّ اَمْرٍ حَكِيْمٍ ۟ۙ

اَمْرًا مِّنْ عِنْدِنَا ۗ اِنَّا كُنَّا مُرْسِلِيْنَ ۟ۚ

رَحْمَةً مِّنْ رَّبِّكَ ۗ اِنَّهٗ هُوَ السَّمِيْعُ الْعَلِيْمُ ۟ۙ

رَبِّ السَّمٰوٰتِ وَالْاَرْضِ وَمَا بَيْنَهُمَا ۚ اِنْ كُنْتُمْ مُّوْقِنِيْنَ ۟

لَاۤ اِلٰهَ اِلَّا هُوَ يُحْيٖ وَيُمِيْتُ ۗ رَبُّكُمْ وَرَبُّ اٰبَآئِكُمُ الْاَوَّلِيْنَ ۟

بَلْ هُمْ فِيْ شَكٍّ يَّلْعَبُوْنَ ۟

فَارْتَقِبْ يَوْمَ تَأْتِي السَّمَآءُ بِدُخَانٍ مُّبِيْنٍ ۟ۙ

يَّغْشَى النَّاسَ ۗ هٰذَا عَذَابٌ اَلِيْمٌ ۟

رَبَّنَا اكْشِفْ عَنَّا الْعَذَابَ اِنَّا مُؤْمِنُوْنَ ۟

اَنّٰى لَهُمُ الذِّكْرٰى وَقَدْ جَآءَهُمْ رَسُوْلٌ مُّبِيْنٌ ۟ۙ

ثُمَّ تَوَلَّوْا عَنْهُ وَقَالُوْا مُعَلَّمٌ مَّجْنُوْنٌ ۟

اِنَّا كَاشِفُوا الْعَذَابِ قَلِيْلًا اِنَّكُمْ عَآئِدُوْنَ ۟ۘ

يَوْمَ نَبْطِشُ الْبَطْشَةَ الْكُبْرٰى ۚ اِنَّا مُنْتَقِمُوْنَ ۟

وَلَقَدْ فَتَنَّا قَبْلَهُمْ قَوْمَ فِرْعَوْنَ وَجَآءَهُمْ رَسُوْلٌ كَرِيْمٌ ۟ۙ

18. Saying: Deliver to me the servants of Allah, surely I am a faithful apostle to you,

19. And that do not exalt yourselves against Allah, surely I will bring to you a clear authority:

20. And surely I take refuge with my Lord and your Lord that you should stone me to death:

21. And if you do not believe in me, then leave me alone.

22. Then he called upon his Lord: These are a guilty people.

23. So go forth with My servants by night; surely you will be pursued:

24. And leave the sea intervening; surely they are a host that shall be drowned.

25. How many of the gardens and fountains have they left!

26. And cornfields and noble places!

27. And goodly things wherein they rejoiced;

28. Thus (it was), and We gave them as a heritage to another people.

29. So the heaven and the earth did not weep for them, nor were they respited:

30. And certainly We delivered the children of Israel from the abasing chastisement,

31. From Firon; surely he was haughty, (and) one of the extravagant.

32. And certainly We chose them, having knowledge, above the nations.

33. And We gave them of the communications wherein was clear blessing.

34. Most surely these do say:

35. There is naught but our first death and we shall not be raised again.

36. So bring our fathers (back), if you are truthful.

37. Are they better or the people of Tubba and those before them? We destroyed them, for surely they were guilty.

38. And We did not create the heavens and the earth and what is between them in sport.

أَنْ أَدُّوْٓا اِلَيَّ عِبَادَ اللّٰهِ اِنِّيْ لَكُمْ رَسُوْلٌ اَمِيْنٌ ۙ ١٨

وَّاَنْ لَّا تَعْلُوْا عَلَى اللّٰهِ اِنِّيْ اٰتِيْكُمْ بِسُلْطٰنٍ مُّبِيْنٍ ۚ ١٩

وَاِنِّيْ عُذْتُ بِرَبِّيْ وَرَبِّكُمْ اَنْ تَرْجُمُوْنِ ۙ ٢٠

وَاِنْ لَّمْ تُؤْمِنُوْا لِيْ فَاعْتَزِلُوْنِ ٢١

فَدَعَا رَبَّهٗٓ اَنَّ هٰٓؤُلَاءِ قَوْمٌ مُّجْرِمُوْنَ ٢٢

فَاَسْرِ بِعِبَادِيْ لَيْلًا اِنَّكُمْ مُّتَّبَعُوْنَ ۙ ٢٣

وَاتْرُكِ الْبَحْرَ رَهْوًا ۚ اِنَّهُمْ جُنْدٌ مُّغْرَقُوْنَ ٢٤

كَمْ تَرَكُوْا مِنْ جَنّٰتٍ وَّعُيُوْنٍ ۙ ٢٥

وَّزُرُوْعٍ وَّمَقَامٍ كَرِيْمٍ ۙ ٢٦

وَّنَعْمَةٍ كَانُوْا فِيْهَا فٰكِهِيْنَ ۙ ٢٧

كَذٰلِكَ ۗ وَاَوْرَثْنٰهَا قَوْمًا اٰخَرِيْنَ ٢٨

فَمَا بَكَتْ عَلَيْهِمُ السَّمَاءُ وَالْاَرْضُ وَمَا كَانُوْا مُنْظَرِيْنَ ٢٩

وَلَقَدْ نَجَّيْنَا بَنِيْٓ اِسْرَآئِيْلَ مِنَ الْعَذَابِ الْمُهِيْنِ ۙ ٣٠

مِنْ فِرْعَوْنَ ۚ اِنَّهٗ كَانَ عَالِيًا مِّنَ الْمُسْرِفِيْنَ ٣١

وَلَقَدِ اخْتَرْنٰهُمْ عَلٰى عِلْمٍ عَلَى الْعٰلَمِيْنَ ۚ ٣٢

وَاٰتَيْنٰهُمْ مِّنَ الْاٰيٰتِ مَا فِيْهِ بَلٰٓؤٌا مُّبِيْنٌ ٣٣

اِنَّ هٰٓؤُلَاءِ لَيَقُوْلُوْنَ ۙ ٣٤

اِنْ هِيَ اِلَّا مَوْتَتُنَا الْاُوْلٰى وَمَا نَحْنُ بِمُنْشَرِيْنَ ٣٥

فَأْتُوْا بِاٰبَآئِنَا اِنْ كُنْتُمْ صٰدِقِيْنَ ٣٦

اَهُمْ خَيْرٌ اَمْ قَوْمُ تُبَّعٍ ۙ وَّالَّذِيْنَ مِنْ قَبْلِهِمْ ۚ اَهْلَكْنٰهُمْ اِنَّهُمْ كَانُوْا مُجْرِمِيْنَ ٣٧

وَمَا خَلَقْنَا السَّمٰوٰتِ وَالْاَرْضَ وَمَا بَيْنَهُمَا لٰعِبِيْنَ ٣٨

39. We did not create them both but with the truth, but most of them do not know.

40. Surely the day of separation is their appointed term, of all of them;

41. The day on which a friend shall not avail (his) friend aught, nor shall they be helped,

42. Save those on whom Allah shall have mercy; surely He is the Mighty, the Merciful.

43. Surely the tree of the Zaqqum,

44. Is the food of the sinful,

45. Like dregs of oil; it shall boil in (their) bellies,

46. Like the boiling of hot water.

47. Seize him, then drag him down into the middle of the hell;

48. Then pour above his head of the torment of the boiling water:

49. Taste; you forsooth are the mighty, the honorable:

50. Surely this is what you disputed about.

51. Surely those who guard (against evil) are in a secure place,

52. In gardens and springs;

53. They shall wear of fine and thick silk, (sitting) face to face;

54. Thus (shall it be), and We will wed them with Houris pure, beautiful ones.

55. They shall call therein for every fruit in security;

56. They shall not taste therein death except the first death, and He will save them from the punishment of the hell,

57. A grace from your Lord; this is the great achievement.

58. So have We made it easy in your tongue that they may be mindful.

59. Therefore wait; surely they are waiting.

THE KNEELING
(JASIYAH)

بِسْمِ اللهِ الرَّحْمٰنِ الرَّحِيْمِ

**In the name of Allah,
the Beneficent, the Merciful.**

1. Ha Mim.

2. The revelation of the Book is from Allah, the Mighty, the Wise.

3. Most surely in the heavens and the earth there are signs for the believers.

4. And in your (own) creation and in what He spreads abroad of animals there are signs for a people that are sure;

5. And (in) the variation of the night and the day, and (in) what Allah sends down of sustenance from the cloud, then gives life thereby to the earth after its death, and (in) the changing of the winds, there are signs for a people who understand.

6. These are the communications of Allah which We recite to you with truth; then in what announcement would they believe after Allah and His communications?

7. Woe to every sinful liar,

8. Who hears the communications of Allah recited to him, then persists proudly as though he had not heard them; so announce to him a painful punishment.

9. And when he comes to know of any of Our communications, he takes it for a jest; these it is that shall have abasing chastisement.

10. Before them is hell, and there shall not avail them aught of what they earned, nor those whom they took for guardians besides Allah, and they shall have a grievous punishment.

11. This is guidance; and (as for) those who disbelieve in the communications of their Lord, they shall have a painful punishment on account of uncleanness.

495

12. Allah is He Who made subservient to you the sea that the ships may run therein by His command, and that you may seek of His grace, and that you may give thanks.

13. And He has made subservient to you whatsoever is in the heavens and whatsoever is in the earth, all, from Himself; most surely there are signs in this for a people who reflect.

14. Say to those who believe (that) they forgive those who do not fear the days of Allah that He may reward a people for what they earn.

15. Whoever does good, it is for his own soul, and whoever does evil, it is against himself; then you shall be brought back to your Lord.

16. And certainly We gave the Book and the wisdom and the prophecy to the children of Israel, and We gave them of the goodly things, and We made them excel the nations.

17. And We gave them clear arguments in the affair, but they did not differ until after knowledge had come to them out of envy among themselves; surely your Lord will judge between them on the day of resurrection concerning that wherein they differed.

18. Then We have made you follow a course in the affair, therefore follow it, and do not follow the low desires of those who do not know.

19. Surely they shall not avail you in the least against Allah; and surely the unjust are friends of each other, and Allah is the guardian of those who guard (against evil).

20. These are clear proofs for men, and a guidance and a mercy for a people who are sure.

21. Nay! do those who have wrought evil deeds think that We will make them like those who believe and do good—that their life and their death shall be equal? Evil it is that they judge.

اللّٰهُ الَّذِىْ سَخَّرَ لَكُمُ الْبَحْرَ لِتَجْرِىَ الْفُلْكُ فِيْهِ بِاَمْرِهٖ وَلِتَبْتَغُوْا مِنْ فَضْلِهٖ وَلَعَلَّكُمْ تَشْكُرُوْنَ ﴿١٢﴾

وَسَخَّرَ لَكُمْ مَّا فِى السَّمٰوٰتِ وَمَا فِى الْاَرْضِ جَمِيْعًا مِّنْهُ ۗ اِنَّ فِىْ ذٰلِكَ لَاٰيٰتٍ لِّقَوْمٍ يَّتَفَكَّرُوْنَ ﴿١٣﴾

قُلْ لِّلَّذِيْنَ اٰمَنُوْا يَغْفِرُوْا لِلَّذِيْنَ لَا يَرْجُوْنَ اَيَّامَ اللّٰهِ لِيَجْزِىَ قَوْمًا بِمَا كَانُوْا يَكْسِبُوْنَ ﴿١٤﴾

مَنْ عَمِلَ صَالِحًا فَلِنَفْسِهٖ ۚ وَمَنْ اَسَآءَ فَعَلَيْهَا ۖ ثُمَّ اِلٰى رَبِّكُمْ تُرْجَعُوْنَ ﴿١٥﴾

وَلَقَدْ اٰتَيْنَا بَنِىْ اِسْرَآءِيْلَ الْكِتٰبَ وَالْحُكْمَ وَالنُّبُوَّةَ وَرَزَقْنٰهُمْ مِّنَ الطَّيِّبٰتِ وَفَضَّلْنٰهُمْ عَلَى الْعٰلَمِيْنَ ﴿١٦﴾

وَاٰتَيْنٰهُمْ بَيِّنٰتٍ مِّنَ الْاَمْرِ ۚ فَمَا اخْتَلَفُوْا اِلَّا مِنْ بَعْدِ مَا جَآءَهُمُ الْعِلْمُ بَغْيًا بَيْنَهُمْ ۚ اِنَّ رَبَّكَ يَقْضِىْ بَيْنَهُمْ يَوْمَ الْقِيٰمَةِ فِيْمَا كَانُوْا فِيْهِ يَخْتَلِفُوْنَ ﴿١٧﴾

ثُمَّ جَعَلْنٰكَ عَلٰى شَرِيْعَةٍ مِّنَ الْاَمْرِ فَاتَّبِعْهَا وَلَا تَتَّبِعْ اَهْوَآءَ الَّذِيْنَ لَا يَعْلَمُوْنَ ﴿١٨﴾

اِنَّهُمْ لَنْ يُّغْنُوْا عَنْكَ مِنَ اللّٰهِ شَيْئًا ۚ وَاِنَّ الظّٰلِمِيْنَ بَعْضُهُمْ اَوْلِيَآءُ بَعْضٍ ۚ وَاللّٰهُ وَلِىُّ الْمُتَّقِيْنَ ﴿١٩﴾

هٰذَا بَصَآئِرُ لِلنَّاسِ وَهُدًى وَّرَحْمَةٌ لِّقَوْمٍ يُّوْقِنُوْنَ ﴿٢٠﴾

اَمْ حَسِبَ الَّذِيْنَ اجْتَرَحُوا السَّيِّئٰتِ اَنْ نَّجْعَلَهُمْ كَالَّذِيْنَ اٰمَنُوْا وَعَمِلُوا الصّٰلِحٰتِ ۙ سَوَآءً مَّحْيَاهُمْ وَمَمَاتُهُمْ ۚ سَآءَ مَا يَحْكُمُوْنَ ﴿٢١﴾

22. And Allah created the heavens and the earth with truth and that every soul may be rewarded for what it has earned and they shall not be wronged.

23. Have you then considered him who takes his low desire for his god, and Allah has made him err having knowledge and has set a seal upon his ear and his heart and put a covering upon his eye. Who can then guide him after Allah? Will you not then be mindful?

24. And they say: There is nothing but our life in this world; we live and die and nothing destroys us but time, and they have no knowledge of that; they only conjecture.

25. And when Our clear communications are recited to them, their argument is no other than that they say: Bring our fathers (back) if you are truthful.

26. Say: Allah gives you life, then He makes you die, then will He gather you to the day of resurrection wherein is no doubt, but most people do not know.

27. And Allah's is the kingdom of the heavens and the earth; and on the day when the hour shall come to pass, on that day shall they perish who say false things.

28. And you shall see every nation kneeling down; every nation shall be called to its book: today you shall be rewarded for what you did.

29. This is Our book that speaks against you with justice; surely We wrote what you did,

30. Then as to those who believed and did good, their Lord will make them enter into His mercy; that is the manifest achievement.

وَخَلَقَ اللّٰهُ السَّمٰوٰتِ وَالْاَرْضَ بِالْحَقِّ وَلِتُجْزٰى كُلُّ نَفْسٍ بِمَا كَسَبَتْ وَهُمْ لَا يُظْلَمُوْنَ ۝

اَفَرَءَيْتَ مَنِ اتَّخَذَ اِلٰهَهٗ هَوٰىهُ وَاَضَلَّهُ اللّٰهُ عَلٰى عِلْمٍ وَّخَتَمَ عَلٰى سَمْعِهٖ وَقَلْبِهٖ وَجَعَلَ عَلٰى بَصَرِهٖ غِشَاوَةً فَمَنْ يَّهْدِيْهِ مِنْ بَعْدِ اللّٰهِ اَفَلَا تَذَكَّرُوْنَ ۝

وَقَالُوْا مَا هِيَ اِلَّا حَيَاتُنَا الدُّنْيَا نَمُوْتُ وَنَحْيَا وَمَا يُهْلِكُنَا اِلَّا الدَّهْرُ وَمَا لَهُمْ بِذٰلِكَ مِنْ عِلْمٍ اِنْ هُمْ اِلَّا يَظُنُّوْنَ ۝

وَاِذَا تُتْلٰى عَلَيْهِمْ اٰيٰتُنَا بَيِّنٰتٍ مَّا كَانَ حُجَّتَهُمْ اِلَّا اَنْ قَالُوا ائْتُوْا بِاٰبَآئِنَا اِنْ كُنْتُمْ صٰدِقِيْنَ ۝

قُلِ اللّٰهُ يُحْيِيْكُمْ ثُمَّ يُمِيْتُكُمْ ثُمَّ يَجْمَعُكُمْ اِلٰى يَوْمِ الْقِيٰمَةِ لَا رَيْبَ فِيْهِ وَلٰكِنَّ اَكْثَرَ النَّاسِ لَا يَعْلَمُوْنَ ۝

وَلِلّٰهِ مُلْكُ السَّمٰوٰتِ وَالْاَرْضِ وَيَوْمَ تَقُوْمُ السَّاعَةُ يَوْمَئِذٍ يَّخْسَرُ الْمُبْطِلُوْنَ ۝

وَتَرٰى كُلَّ اُمَّةٍ جَاثِيَةً كُلُّ اُمَّةٍ تُدْعٰى اِلٰى كِتٰبِهَا اَلْيَوْمَ تُجْزَوْنَ مَا كُنْتُمْ تَعْمَلُوْنَ ۝

هٰذَا كِتٰبُنَا يَنْطِقُ عَلَيْكُمْ بِالْحَقِّ اِنَّا كُنَّا نَسْتَنْسِخُ مَا كُنْتُمْ تَعْمَلُوْنَ ۝

فَاَمَّا الَّذِيْنَ اٰمَنُوْا وَعَمِلُوا الصّٰلِحٰتِ فَيُدْخِلُهُمْ رَبُّهُمْ فِيْ رَحْمَتِهٖ ذٰلِكَ هُوَ الْفَوْزُ الْمُبِيْنُ ۝

31. As to those who disbelieved: What! were not My communications recited to you? But you were proud and you were a guilty people.

وَاَمَّا الَّذِيْنَ كَفَرُوْا اَفَلَمْ تَكُنْ اٰيٰتِيْ تُتْلٰى عَلَيْكُمْ فَاسْتَكْبَرْتُمْ وَكُنْتُمْ قَوْمًا مُّجْرِمِيْنَ ۞

32. And when it was said, Surely the promise of Allah is true and as for the hour, there is no doubt about it, you said: We do not know what the hour is; we do not think (that it will come to pass) save a passing thought, and we are not at all sure.

وَاِذَا قِيْلَ اِنَّ وَعْدَ اللّٰهِ حَقٌّ وَّالسَّاعَةُ لَا رَيْبَ فِيْهَا قُلْتُمْ مَّا نَدْرِيْ مَا السَّاعَةُ اِنْ نَّظُنُّ اِلَّا ظَنًّا وَّمَا نَحْنُ بِمُسْتَيْقِنِيْنَ ۞

33. And the evil (consequences) of what they did shall become manifest to them and that which they mocked shall encompass them.

وَبَدَا لَهُمْ سَيِّاٰتُ مَا عَمِلُوْا وَحَاقَ بِهِمْ مَّا كَانُوْا بِهٖ يَسْتَهْزِءُوْنَ ۞

34. And it shall be said: Today We forsake you as you neglected the meeting of this day of yours and your abode is the fire, and there are not for you any helpers:

وَقِيْلَ الْيَوْمَ نَنْسٰكُمْ كَمَا نَسِيْتُمْ لِقَآءَ يَوْمِكُمْ هٰذَا وَمَأْوٰكُمُ النَّارُ وَمَا لَكُمْ مِّنْ نّٰصِرِيْنَ ۞

35. That is because you took the communications of Allah for a jest and the life of this world deceived you. So on that day they shall not be brought forth from it, nor shall they be granted goodwill.

ذٰلِكُمْ بِاَنَّكُمُ اتَّخَذْتُمْ اٰيٰتِ اللّٰهِ هُزُوًا وَّغَرَّتْكُمُ الْحَيٰوةُ الدُّنْيَا فَالْيَوْمَ لَا يُخْرَجُوْنَ مِنْهَا وَلَا هُمْ يُسْتَعْتَبُوْنَ ۞

36. Therefore to Allah is due (all) praise, the Lord of the heavens and the Lord of the earth, the Lord of the worlds.

فَلِلّٰهِ الْحَمْدُ رَبِّ السَّمٰوٰتِ وَرَبِّ الْاَرْضِ رَبِّ الْعٰلَمِيْنَ ۞

37. And to Him belongs greatness in the heavens and the earth, and He is the Mighty, the Wise.

وَلَهُ الْكِبْرِيَآءُ فِى السَّمٰوٰتِ وَالْاَرْضِ وَهُوَ الْعَزِيْزُ الْحَكِيْمُ ۞

THE SANDHILLS
(AHQAF)

**In the name of Allah,
the Beneficent, the Merciful.**

1. Ha Mim.

2. The revelation of the Book is from Allah, the Mighty, the Wise.

3. We did not create the heavens and the earth and what is between them two save with truth and (for) an appointed term; and those who disbelieve turn aside from what they are warned of.

4. Say: Have you considered what you call upon besides Allah? Show me what they have created of the earth, or have they a share in the heavens? Bring me a book before this or traces of knowledge, if you are truthful.

5. And who is in greater error than he who calls besides Allah upon those that will not answer him till the day of resurrection and they are heedless of their call?

6. And when men are gathered together they shall be their enemies, and shall be deniers of their worshipping (them).

7. And when Our clear communications are recited to them, those who disbelieve say with regard to the truth when it comes to them: This is clear magic.

8. Nay! they say: He has forged it. Say: If I have forged it, you do not control anything for me from Allah; He knows best what you utter concerning it; He is enough as a witness between me and you, and He is the Forgiving, the Merciful.

9. Say: I am not the first of the apostles, and I do not know what will be done with me or with you: I do not follow anything but that which is revealed to me, and I am nothing but a plain warner.

قُلْ مَا كُنْتُ بِدْعًا مِّنَ الرُّسُلِ وَمَا أَدْرِيْ مَايُفْعَلُ بِيْ وَلَا بِكُمْ اِنْ اَتَّبِعُ اِلَّا مَا يُوْحٰى اِلَيَّ وَمَا اَنَا اِلَّا نَذِيْرٌ مُّبِيْنٌ ۞

10. Say: Have you considered if it is from Allah, and you disbelieve in it, and a witness from among the children of Israel has borne witness of one like it, so he believed, while you are big with pride; surely Allah does not guide the unjust people.

قُلْ اَرَءَيْتُمْ اِنْ كَانَ مِنْ عِنْدِ اللّٰهِ وَكَفَرْتُمْ بِهٖ وَ شَهِدَ شَاهِدٌ مِّنْ بَنِيْ اِسْرَآءِيْلَ عَلٰى مِثْلِهٖ فَاٰمَنَ وَاسْتَكْبَرْتُمْ اِنَّ اللّٰهَ لَا يَهْدِي الْقَوْمَ الظّٰلِمِيْنَ ۞

11. And those who disbelieve say concerning those who believe: If it had been a good, they would not have gone ahead of us therein. And as they do not seek to be rightly directed thereby, they say: It is an old lie.

وَقَالَ الَّذِيْنَ كَفَرُوْا لِلَّذِيْنَ اٰمَنُوْا لَوْ كَانَ خَيْرًا مَّا سَبَقُوْنَا اِلَيْهِ وَاِذْ لَمْ يَهْتَدُوْا بِهٖ فَسَيَقُوْلُوْنَ هٰذَآ اِفْكٌ قَدِيْمٌ ۞

12. And before it the Book of Musa was a guide and a mercy: and this is a Book verifying (it) in the Arabic language that it may warn those who are unjust and as good news for the doers of good.

وَمِنْ قَبْلِهٖ كِتٰبُ مُوْسٰى اِمَامًا وَّرَحْمَةً وَهٰذَا كِتٰبٌ مُّصَدِّقٌ لِّسَانًا عَرَبِيًّا لِّيُنْذِرَ الَّذِيْنَ ظَلَمُوْا وَبُشْرٰى لِلْمُحْسِنِيْنَ ۞

13. Surely those who say, Our Lord is Allah, then they continue on the right way, they shall have no fear nor shall they grieve.

اِنَّ الَّذِيْنَ قَالُوْا رَبُّنَا اللّٰهُ ثُمَّ اسْتَقَامُوْا فَلَا خَوْفٌ عَلَيْهِمْ وَلَا هُمْ يَحْزَنُوْنَ ۞

14. These are the dwellers of the garden, abiding therein: a reward for what they did.

اُولٰٓئِكَ اَصْحٰبُ الْجَنَّةِ خٰلِدِيْنَ فِيْهَا جَزَآءً بِمَا كَانُوْا يَعْمَلُوْنَ ۞

15. And We have enjoined on man doing of good to his parents; with trouble did his mother bear him and with trouble did she bring him forth; and the bearing of him and the weaning of him was thirty months; until when he attains his maturity and reaches forty years, he says: My Lord! grant me that I may give thanks for Thy favor which Thou hast bestowed on me and on my parents, and that I may do good which pleases Thee and do good to me in respect of my offspring; surely I turn to Thee, and surely I am of those who submit.

وَوَصَّيْنَا الْاِنْسَانَ بِوَالِدَيْهِ اِحْسَانًا حَمَلَتْهُ اُمُّهٗ كُرْهًا وَّوَضَعَتْهُ كُرْهًا وَحَمْلُهٗ وَفِصٰلُهٗ ثَلٰثُوْنَ شَهْرًا حَتّٰى اِذَا بَلَغَ اَشُدَّهٗ وَبَلَغَ اَرْبَعِيْنَ سَنَةً قَالَ رَبِّ اَوْزِعْنِيْ اَنْ اَشْكُرَ نِعْمَتَكَ الَّتِيْ اَنْعَمْتَ عَلَيَّ وَعَلٰى وَالِدَيَّ وَاَنْ اَعْمَلَ صَالِحًا تَرْضٰهُ وَاَصْلِحْ لِيْ فِيْ ذُرِّيَّتِيْ اِنِّيْ تُبْتُ اِلَيْكَ وَاِنِّيْ مِنَ الْمُسْلِمِيْنَ ۞

16. These are they from whom We accept the best of what they have done and pass over their evil deeds, among the dwellers of the garden; the promise of truth which they were promised.

17. And he who says to his parents: Fie on you! do you threaten me that I shall be brought forth when generations have already passed away before me? And they both call for Allah's aid: Woe to you! believe, surely the promise of Allah is true. But he says: This is nothing but stories of the ancients.

18. These are they against whom the word has proved true among nations of the jinn and the men that have already passed away before them; surely they are losers.

19. And for all are degrees according to what they did, and that He may pay them back fully their deeds and they shall not be wronged.

20. And on the day when those who disbelieve shall be brought before the fire: You did away with your good things in your life of the world and you enjoyed them for a while, so today you shall be rewarded with the punishment of abasement because you were unjustly proud in the land and because you transgressed.

21. And mention the brother of Ad; when he warned his people in the sandy plains,—and indeed warners came before him and after him—saying: Serve none but Allah; surely I fear for you the punishment of a grievous day.

22. They said: Have you come to us to turn us away from our gods; then bring us what you threaten us with, if you are of the truthful ones.

أُولَٰئِكَ الَّذِينَ نَتَقَبَّلُ عَنْهُمْ أَحْسَنَ مَا عَمِلُوا وَنَتَجَاوَزُ عَنْ سَيِّئَاتِهِمْ فِي أَصْحَابِ الْجَنَّةِ وَعْدَ الصِّدْقِ الَّذِي كَانُوا يُوعَدُونَ ۝

وَالَّذِي قَالَ لِوَالِدَيْهِ أُفٍّ لَّكُمَا أَتَعِدَانِنِي أَنْ أُخْرَجَ وَقَدْ خَلَتِ الْقُرُونُ مِنْ قَبْلِي وَهُمَا يَسْتَغِيثَانِ اللَّهَ وَيْلَكَ آمِنْ إِنَّ وَعْدَ اللَّهِ حَقٌّ فَيَقُولُ مَا هَٰذَا إِلَّا أَسَاطِيرُ الْأَوَّلِينَ ۝

أُولَٰئِكَ الَّذِينَ حَقَّ عَلَيْهِمُ الْقَوْلُ فِي أُمَمٍ قَدْ خَلَتْ مِنْ قَبْلِهِمْ مِنَ الْجِنِّ وَالْإِنْسِ إِنَّهُمْ كَانُوا خَاسِرِينَ ۝

وَلِكُلٍّ دَرَجَاتٌ مِّمَّا عَمِلُوا وَلِيُوَفِّيَهُمْ أَعْمَالَهُمْ وَهُمْ لَا يُظْلَمُونَ ۝

وَيَوْمَ يُعْرَضُ الَّذِينَ كَفَرُوا عَلَى النَّارِ أَذْهَبْتُمْ طَيِّبَاتِكُمْ فِي حَيَاتِكُمُ الدُّنْيَا وَاسْتَمْتَعْتُمْ بِهَا فَالْيَوْمَ تُجْزَوْنَ عَذَابَ الْهُونِ بِمَا كُنْتُمْ تَسْتَكْبِرُونَ فِي الْأَرْضِ بِغَيْرِ الْحَقِّ وَبِمَا كُنْتُمْ تَفْسُقُونَ ۝

وَاذْكُرْ أَخَا عَادٍ إِذْ أَنْذَرَ قَوْمَهُ بِالْأَحْقَافِ وَقَدْ خَلَتِ النُّذُرُ مِنْ بَيْنِ يَدَيْهِ وَمِنْ خَلْفِهِ أَلَّا تَعْبُدُوا إِلَّا اللَّهَ إِنِّي أَخَافُ عَلَيْكُمْ عَذَابَ يَوْمٍ عَظِيمٍ ۝

قَالُوا أَجِئْتَنَا لِتَأْفِكَنَا عَنْ آلِهَتِنَا فَأْتِنَا بِمَا تَعِدُنَا إِنْ كُنْتَ مِنَ الصَّادِقِينَ ۝

23. He said: The knowledge is only with Allah, and I deliver to you the message with which I am sent, but I see you are a people who are ignorant.

قَالَ اِنَّمَا الْعِلْمُ عِنْدَ اللّٰهِ ۖ وَاُبَلِّغُكُمْ مَّا اُرْسِلْتُ بِهٖ وَلٰكِنِّيْۤ اَرٰىكُمْ قَوْمًا تَجْهَلُوْنَ ﴿٢٣﴾

24. So when they saw it as a cloud appearing in the sky advancing towards their valleys, they said: This is a cloud which will give us rain. Nay! it is what you sought to hasten on, a blast of wind in which is a painful punishment,

فَلَمَّا رَاَوْهُ عَارِضًا مُّسْتَقْبِلَ اَوْدِيَتِهِمْ ۙ قَالُوْا هٰذَا عَارِضٌ مُّمْطِرُنَا ۚ بَلْ هُوَ مَا اسْتَعْجَلْتُمْ بِهٖ ۚ رِيْحٌ فِيْهَا عَذَابٌ اَلِيْمٌ ﴿٢٤﴾

25. Destroying everything by the command of its Lord; so they became such that naught could be seen except their dwellings. Thus do We reward the guilty people.

تُدَمِّرُ كُلَّ شَيْءٍ بِاَمْرِ رَبِّهَا فَاَصْبَحُوْا لَا يُرٰۤى اِلَّا مَسٰكِنُهُمْ ۚ كَذٰلِكَ نَجْزِى الْقَوْمَ الْمُجْرِمِيْنَ ﴿٢٥﴾

26. And certainly We had established them in what We have not established you in, and We had given them ears and eyes and hearts, but neither their ears, nor their eyes, nor their hearts availed them aught, since they denied the communications of Allah, and that which they mocked encompassed them.

وَلَقَدْ مَكَّنّٰهُمْ فِيْمَاۤ اِنْ مَّكَّنّٰكُمْ فِيْهِ وَجَعَلْنَا لَهُمْ سَمْعًا وَّاَبْصَارًا وَّاَفْـِٕدَةً ۖ فَمَاۤ اَغْنٰى عَنْهُمْ سَمْعُهُمْ وَلَاۤ اَبْصَارُهُمْ وَلَاۤ اَفْـِٕدَتُهُمْ مِّنْ شَيْءٍ اِذْ كَانُوْا يَجْحَدُوْنَ بِاٰيٰتِ اللّٰهِ وَحَاقَ بِهِمْ مَّا كَانُوْا بِهٖ يَسْتَهْزِءُوْنَ ﴿٢٦﴾

27. And certainly We destroyed the towns which are around you, and We repeat the communications that they might turn.

وَلَقَدْ اَهْلَكْنَا مَا حَوْلَكُمْ مِّنَ الْقُرٰى وَصَرَّفْنَا الْاٰيٰتِ لَعَلَّهُمْ يَرْجِعُوْنَ ﴿٢٧﴾

28. Why did not then those help them whom they took for gods besides Allah to draw (them) nigh (to Him)? Nay! they were lost to them; and this was their lie and what they forged.

فَلَوْلَا نَصَرَهُمُ الَّذِيْنَ اتَّخَذُوْا مِنْ دُوْنِ اللّٰهِ قُرْبَانًا اٰلِهَةً ۗ بَلْ ضَلُّوْا عَنْهُمْ ۚ وَذٰلِكَ اِفْكُهُمْ وَمَا كَانُوْا يَفْتَرُوْنَ ﴿٢٨﴾

29. And when We turned towards you a party of the jinn who listened to the Quran; so when they came to it, they said: Be silent; then when it was finished, they turned back to their people warning (them).

وَاِذْ صَرَفْنَاۤ اِلَيْكَ نَفَرًا مِّنَ الْجِنِّ يَسْتَمِعُوْنَ الْقُرْاٰنَ ۚ فَلَمَّا حَضَرُوْهُ قَالُوْۤا اَنْصِتُوْا ۚ فَلَمَّا قُضِيَ وَلَّوْا اِلٰى قَوْمِهِمْ مُّنْذِرِيْنَ ﴿٢٩﴾

30. They said: O our people! we have listened to a Book revealed after Musa verifying that which is before it, guiding to the truth and to a right path:

قَالُوْا يٰقَوْمَنَآ اِنَّا سَمِعْنَا كِتٰبًا اُنْزِلَ مِنْ بَعْدِ مُوْسٰى مُصَدِّقًا لِّمَا بَيْنَ يَدَيْهِ يَهْدِيْ اِلَى الْحَقِّ وَاِلٰى طَرِيْقٍ مُّسْتَقِيْمٍ ۞

31. O our people! accept the Divine caller and believe in Him, He will forgive you of your faults and protect you from a painful punishment.

يٰقَوْمَنَآ اَجِيْبُوْا دَاعِيَ اللّٰهِ وَاٰمِنُوْا بِهٖ يَغْفِرْ لَكُمْ مِّنْ ذُنُوْبِكُمْ وَيُجِرْكُمْ مِّنْ عَذَابٍ اَلِيْمٍ ۞

32. And whoever does not accept the Divine caller, he shall not escape in the earth and he shall not have guardians besides Him; these are in manifest error.

وَمَنْ لَّا يُجِبْ دَاعِيَ اللّٰهِ فَلَيْسَ بِمُعْجِزٍ فِى الْاَرْضِ وَلَيْسَ لَهٗ مِنْ دُوْنِهٖٓ اَوْلِيَآءُ ۚ اُولٰٓئِكَ فِيْ ضَلٰلٍ مُّبِيْنٍ ۞

33. Have they not considered that Allah, Who created the heavens and the earth and was not tired by their creation, is able to give life to the dead? Aye! He has surely power over all things.

اَوَلَمْ يَرَوْا اَنَّ اللّٰهَ الَّذِيْ خَلَقَ السَّمٰوٰتِ وَالْاَرْضَ وَلَمْ يَعْىَ بِخَلْقِهِنَّ بِقٰدِرٍ عَلٰٓى اَنْ يُّحْيِىَ الْمَوْتٰى ۚ بَلٰٓى اِنَّهٗ عَلٰى كُلِّ شَيْءٍ قَدِيْرٌ ۞

34. And on the day when those who disbelieve shall be brought before the fire: Is it not true? They shall say: Aye! by our Lord! He will say: Then taste the punishment, because you disbelieved.

وَيَوْمَ يُعْرَضُ الَّذِيْنَ كَفَرُوْا عَلَى النَّارِ ۚ اَلَيْسَ هٰذَا بِالْحَقِّ ۚ قَالُوْا بَلٰى وَرَبِّنَا ۚ قَالَ فَذُوْقُوا الْعَذَابَ بِمَا كُنْتُمْ تَكْفُرُوْنَ ۞

35. Therefore bear up patiently as did the apostles endowed with constancy bear up with patience and do not seek to hasten for them (their doom). On the day that they shall see what they are promised they shall be as if they had not tarried save an hour of the day. A sufficient exposition! Shall then any be destroyed save the transgressing people?

فَاصْبِرْ كَمَا صَبَرَ اُولُوا الْعَزْمِ مِنَ الرُّسُلِ وَلَا تَسْتَعْجِلْ لَّهُمْ ۚ كَاَنَّهُمْ يَوْمَ يَرَوْنَ مَا يُوْعَدُوْنَ ۙ لَمْ يَلْبَثُوْٓا اِلَّا سَاعَةً مِّنْ نَّهَارٍ ۚ بَلٰغٌ ۚ فَهَلْ يُهْلَكُ اِلَّا الْقَوْمُ الْفٰسِقُوْنَ ۞

503

MUHAMMAD

اياتها ٣٨ (٤٧) سورة محمد مكية رُوْعاتُها

بِسْمِ اللّٰهِ الرَّحْمٰنِ الرَّحِيْمِ ۞

In the name of Allah,
The Beneficent, The Merciful.

1. (As for) those who disbelieve and turn away from Allah's way, He shall render their works ineffective.

الَّذِيْنَ كَفَرُوْا وَصَدُّوْا عَنْ سَبِيْلِ اللّٰهِ اَضَلَّ اَعْمَالَهُمْ ۞

2. And (as for) those who believe and do good, and believe in what has been revealed to Muhammad, and it is the very truth from their Lord, He will remove their evil from them and improve their condition.

وَالَّذِيْنَ اٰمَنُوْا وَعَمِلُوا الصّٰلِحٰتِ وَاٰمَنُوْا بِمَا نُزِّلَ عَلٰى مُحَمَّدٍ وَّهُوَ الْحَقُّ مِنْ رَّبِّهِمْ كَفَّرَ عَنْهُمْ سَيِّاٰتِهِمْ وَاَصْلَحَ بَالَهُمْ ۞

3. That is because those who disbelieve follow falsehood, and those who believe follow the truth from their Lord; thus does Allah set forth to men their examples.

ذٰلِكَ بِاَنَّ الَّذِيْنَ كَفَرُوا اتَّبَعُوا الْبَاطِلَ وَاَنَّ الَّذِيْنَ اٰمَنُوا اتَّبَعُوا الْحَقَّ مِنْ رَّبِّهِمْ كَذٰلِكَ يَضْرِبُ اللّٰهُ لِلنَّاسِ اَمْثَالَهُمْ ۞

4. So when you meet in battle those who disbelieve, then smite the necks until when you have overcome them, then make (them) prisoners, and afterwards either set them free as a favor or let them ransom (themselves) until the war terminates. That (shall be so); and if Allah had pleased He would certainly have exacted what is due from them, but that He may try some of you by means of others; and (as for) those who are slain in the way of Allah, He will by no means allow their deeds to perish.

فَاِذَا لَقِيْتُمُ الَّذِيْنَ كَفَرُوْا فَضَرْبَ الرِّقَابِ حَتّٰى اِذَآ اَثْخَنْتُمُوْهُمْ فَشُدُّوا الْوَثَاقَ فَاِمَّا مَنًّا بَعْدُ وَاِمَّا فِدَآءً حَتّٰى تَضَعَ الْحَرْبُ اَوْزَارَهَا ۚ ذٰلِكَ ۚ وَلَوْ يَشَآءُ اللّٰهُ لَانْتَصَرَ مِنْهُمْ وَلٰكِنْ لِّيَبْلُوَا بَعْضَكُمْ بِبَعْضٍ ۚ وَالَّذِيْنَ قُتِلُوْا فِيْ سَبِيْلِ اللّٰهِ فَلَنْ يُّضِلَّ اَعْمَالَهُمْ ۞

5. He will guide them and improve their condition.

سَيَهْدِيْهِمْ وَيُصْلِحُ بَالَهُمْ ۞

6. And cause them to enter the garden which He has made known to them.

وَيُدْخِلُهُمُ الْجَنَّةَ عَرَّفَهَا لَهُمْ ۞

7. O you who believe! if you help (the cause of) Allah, He will help you and make firm your feet.

يٰاَيُّهَا الَّذِيْنَ اٰمَنُوْا اِنْ تَنْصُرُوا اللّٰهَ يَنْصُرْكُمْ وَيُثَبِّتْ اَقْدَامَكُمْ ۞

8. And (as for) those who disbelieve, for them is destruction, and He has made their deeds ineffective.

وَالَّذِيْنَ كَفَرُوْا فَتَعْسًا لَّهُمْ وَاَضَلَّ اَعْمَالَهُمْ ۞

9. That is because they hated what Allah revealed, so He rendered their deeds null.

ذٰلِكَ بِاَنَّهُمْ كَرِهُوْا مَآ اَنْزَلَ اللّٰهُ فَاَحْبَطَ اَعْمَالَهُمْ ۞

10. Have they not then journeyed in the land and seen how was the end of those before them: Allah brought down destruction upon them, and the unbelievers shall have the like of it.

11. That is because Allah is the Protector of those who believe, and because the unbelievers shall have no protector for them.

12. Surely Allah will make those who believe and do good enter gardens beneath which rivers flow; and those who disbelieve enjoy themselves and eat as the beasts eat, and the fire is their abode.

13. And how many a town which was far more powerful than the town of yours which has driven you out: We destroyed them so there was no helper for them.

14. What! is he who has a clear argument from his Lord like him to whom the evil of his work is made fairseeming: and they follow their low desires.

15. A parable of the garden which those guarding (against evil) are promised: Therein are rivers of water that does not alter, and rivers of milk the taste whereof does not change, and rivers of drink delicious to those who drink, and rivers of honey clarified; and for them therein are all fruits and protection from their Lord. (Are these) like those who abide in the fire and who are made to drink boiling water so it rends their bowels asunder.

16. And there are those of them who seek to listen to you, until when they go forth from you, they say to those who have been given the knowledge: What was it that he said just now? These are they upon whose hearts Allah has set a seal and they follow their low desires.

17. And (as for) those who follow the right direction, He increases them in guidance and gives them their guarding (against evil).

أَفَلَمْ يَسِيرُوْا فِي الْأَرْضِ فَيَنْظُرُوْا كَيْفَ كَانَ عَاقِبَةُ الَّذِيْنَ مِنْ قَبْلِهِمْ دَمَّرَ اللّٰهُ عَلَيْهِمْ وَلِلْكَافِرِيْنَ أَمْثَالُهَا ۞

ذٰلِكَ بِأَنَّ اللّٰهَ مَوْلَى الَّذِيْنَ اٰمَنُوْا وَأَنَّ الْكَافِرِيْنَ لَا مَوْلٰى لَهُمْ ۞

إِنَّ اللّٰهَ يُدْخِلُ الَّذِيْنَ اٰمَنُوْا وَعَمِلُوا الصّٰلِحٰتِ جَنّٰتٍ تَجْرِيْ مِنْ تَحْتِهَا الْأَنْهٰرُ ۖ وَالَّذِيْنَ كَفَرُوْا يَتَمَتَّعُوْنَ وَيَأْكُلُوْنَ كَمَا تَأْكُلُ الْأَنْعَامُ وَالنَّارُ مَثْوًى لَهُمْ ۞

وَكَأَيِّنْ مِنْ قَرْيَةٍ هِيَ أَشَدُّ قُوَّةً مِنْ قَرْيَتِكَ الَّتِيْ أَخْرَجَتْكَ ۚ أَهْلَكْنٰهُمْ فَلَا نَاصِرَ لَهُمْ ۞

أَفَمَنْ كَانَ عَلٰى بَيِّنَةٍ مِنْ رَبِّهِ كَمَنْ زُيِّنَ لَهُ سُوْءُ عَمَلِهِ وَاتَّبَعُوْا أَهْوَآءَهُمْ ۞

مَثَلُ الْجَنَّةِ الَّتِيْ وُعِدَ الْمُتَّقُوْنَ ۖ فِيْهَا أَنْهٰرٌ مِنْ مَآءٍ غَيْرِ اٰسِنٍ ۚ وَأَنْهٰرٌ مِنْ لَبَنٍ لَمْ يَتَغَيَّرْ طَعْمُهُ ۚ وَأَنْهٰرٌ مِنْ خَمْرٍ لَذَّةٍ لِلشّٰرِبِيْنَ ۚ وَأَنْهٰرٌ مِنْ عَسَلٍ مُصَفًّى ۖ وَلَهُمْ فِيْهَا مِنْ كُلِّ الثَّمَرٰتِ وَ مَغْفِرَةٌ مِنْ رَبِّهِمْ ۚ كَمَنْ هُوَ خَالِدٌ فِي النَّارِ وَ سُقُوْا مَآءً حَمِيْمًا فَقَطَّعَ أَمْعَآءَهُمْ ۞

وَمِنْهُمْ مَنْ يَسْتَمِعُ إِلَيْكَ ۚ حَتّٰى إِذَا خَرَجُوْا مِنْ عِنْدِكَ قَالُوْا لِلَّذِيْنَ أُوْتُوا الْعِلْمَ مَاذَا قَالَ اٰنِفًا ۚ أُولٰئِكَ الَّذِيْنَ طَبَعَ اللّٰهُ عَلٰى قُلُوْبِهِمْ وَاتَّبَعُوْا أَهْوَآءَهُمْ ۞

وَالَّذِيْنَ اهْتَدَوْا زَادَهُمْ هُدًى وَاٰتٰىهُمْ تَقْوٰىهُمْ ۞

18. Do they then wait for aught but the hour that it should come to them all of a sudden? Now indeed the tokens of it have (already) come, but how shall they have their reminder when it comes on them?

فَهَلْ يَنْظُرُوْنَ اِلَّا السَّاعَةَ اَنْ تَأْتِيَهُمْ بَغْتَةً فَقَدْ جَآءَ اَشْرَاطُهَا فَاَنّٰى لَهُمْ اِذَا جَآءَتْهُمْ ذِكْرٰىهُمْ ۝

19. So know that there is no god but Allah, and, ask protection for your fault and for the believing men and the believing women; and Allah knows the place of your returning and the place of your abiding.

فَاعْلَمْ اَنَّهٗ لَآ اِلٰهَ اِلَّا اللّٰهُ وَاسْتَغْفِرْ لِذَنْبِكَ وَلِلْمُؤْمِنِيْنَ وَالْمُؤْمِنٰتِ ۚ وَاللّٰهُ يَعْلَمُ مُتَقَلَّبَكُمْ وَمَثْوٰىكُمْ ۝

20. And those who believe say: Why has not a chapter been revealed? But when a decisive chapter is revealed, and fighting is mentioned therein you see those in whose hearts is a disease look to you with the look of one fainting because of death. Woe to them then!

وَيَقُوْلُ الَّذِيْنَ اٰمَنُوْا لَوْلَا نُزِّلَتْ سُوْرَةٌ ۚ فَاِذَآ اُنْزِلَتْ سُوْرَةٌ مُّحْكَمَةٌ وَّذُكِرَ فِيْهَا الْقِتَالُ ۙ رَاَيْتَ الَّذِيْنَ فِيْ قُلُوْبِهِمْ مَّرَضٌ يَّنْظُرُوْنَ اِلَيْكَ نَظَرَ الْمَغْشِيِّ عَلَيْهِ مِنَ الْمَوْتِ ۖ فَاَوْلٰى لَهُمْ ۝

21. Obedience and a gentle word (was proper); but when the affair becomes settled, then if they remain true to Allah it would certainly be better for them.

طَاعَةٌ وَّقَوْلٌ مَّعْرُوْفٌ ۗ فَاِذَا عَزَمَ الْاَمْرُ ۖ فَلَوْ صَدَقُوا اللّٰهَ لَكَانَ خَيْرًا لَّهُمْ ۝

22. But if you held command, you were sure to make mischief in the land and cut off the ties of kinship!

فَهَلْ عَسَيْتُمْ اِنْ تَوَلَّيْتُمْ اَنْ تُفْسِدُوْا فِى الْاَرْضِ وَتُقَطِّعُوْا اَرْحَامَكُمْ ۝

23. Those it is whom Allah has cursed so He has made them deaf and blinded their eyes.

اُولٰٓئِكَ الَّذِيْنَ لَعَنَهُمُ اللّٰهُ فَاَصَمَّهُمْ وَاَعْمٰى اَبْصَارَهُمْ ۝

24. Do they not then reflect on the Quran? Nay, on the hearts there are locks.

اَفَلَا يَتَدَبَّرُوْنَ الْقُرْاٰنَ اَمْ عَلٰى قُلُوْبٍ اَقْفَالُهَا ۝

25. Surely (as for) those who return on their backs after that guidance has become manifest to them, the Shaitan has made it a light matter to them; and He gives them respite.

اِنَّ الَّذِيْنَ ارْتَدُّوْا عَلٰٓى اَدْبَارِهِمْ مِّنْ بَعْدِ مَا تَبَيَّنَ لَهُمُ الْهُدَى ۙ الشَّيْطٰنُ سَوَّلَ لَهُمْ ۖ وَاَمْلٰى لَهُمْ ۝

26. That is because they say to those who hate what Allah has revealed: We will obey you in some of the affairs; and Allah knows their secrets.

ذٰلِكَ بِاَنَّهُمْ قَالُوْا لِلَّذِيْنَ كَرِهُوْا مَا نَزَّلَ اللّٰهُ سَنُطِيْعُكُمْ فِيْ بَعْضِ الْاَمْرِ ۖ وَاللّٰهُ يَعْلَمُ اِسْرَارَهُمْ ۝

27. But how will it be when the angels cause them to die smiting their backs.

فَكَيْفَ اِذَا تَوَفَّتْهُمُ الْمَلٰٓئِكَةُ يَضْرِبُوْنَ وُجُوْهَهُمْ وَاَدْبَارَهُمْ ۝

28. That is because they follow what is displeasing to Allah and are averse to His pleasure, therefore He has made null their deeds.

ذٰلِكَ بِاَنَّهُمُ اتَّبَعُوْا مَآ اَسْخَطَ اللّٰهَ وَكَرِهُوْا رِضْوَانَهٗ فَاَحْبَطَ اَعْمَالَهُمْ ۝

29. Or do those in whose hearts is a disease think that Allah will not bring forth their spite?

أَمْ حَسِبَ الَّذِينَ فِي قُلُوبِهِمْ مَرَضٌ أَنْ لَنْ يُخْرِجَ اللّٰهُ أَضْغَانَهُمْ ۞

30. And if We please We would have made you know them so that you would certainly have recognized them by their marks; and most certainly you can recognize them by the intent of (their) speech; and Allah knows your deeds.

وَلَوْ نَشَآءُ لَأَرَيْنٰكَهُمْ فَلَعَرَفْتَهُمْ بِسِيْمٰهُمْ وَلَتَعْرِفَنَّهُمْ فِي لَحْنِ الْقَوْلِ ۗ وَاللّٰهُ يَعْلَمُ أَعْمَالَكُمْ ۞

31. And most certainly We will try you until We have known those among you who exert themselves hard, and the patient, and made your case manifest.

وَلَنَبْلُوَنَّكُمْ حَتّٰى نَعْلَمَ الْمُجَاهِدِينَ مِنْكُمْ وَالصّٰبِرِينَ ۙ وَنَبْلُوَا۟ أَخْبَارَكُمْ ۞

32. Surely those who disbelieve and turn away from Allah's way and oppose the Apostle after that guidance has become clear to them cannot harm Allah in any way, and He will make null their deeds.

إِنَّ الَّذِينَ كَفَرُوا وَصَدُّوا عَنْ سَبِيلِ اللّٰهِ وَشَآقُّوا الرَّسُولَ مِنْ بَعْدِ مَا تَبَيَّنَ لَهُمُ الْهُدَى ۙ لَنْ يَضُرُّوا اللّٰهَ شَيْئًا ۚ وَسَيُحْبِطُ أَعْمَالَهُمْ ۞

33. O you who believe! obey Allah and obey the Apostle, and do not make your deeds of no effect.

يَآأَيُّهَا الَّذِينَ اٰمَنُوٓا أَطِيعُوا اللّٰهَ وَأَطِيعُوا الرَّسُولَ وَلَا تُبْطِلُوٓا أَعْمَالَكُمْ ۞

34. Surely those who disbelieve and turn away from Allah's way, then they die while they are unbelievers, Allah will by no means forgive them.

إِنَّ الَّذِينَ كَفَرُوا وَصَدُّوا عَنْ سَبِيلِ اللّٰهِ ثُمَّ مَاتُوا وَهُمْ كُفَّارٌ فَلَنْ يَغْفِرَ اللّٰهُ لَهُمْ ۞

35. And be not slack so as to cry for peace and you have the upper hand, and Allah is with you, and He will not bring your deeds to naught.

فَلَا تَهِنُوا وَتَدْعُوٓا إِلَى السَّلْمِ ۖ وَأَنْتُمُ الْأَعْلَوْنَ ۖ وَاللّٰهُ مَعَكُمْ وَلَنْ يَتِرَكُمْ أَعْمَالَكُمْ ۞

36. The life of this world is only idle sport and play, and if you believe and guard (against evil) He will give you your rewards, and will not ask of you your possessions.

إِنَّمَا الْحَيٰوةُ الدُّنْيَا لَعِبٌ وَّلَهْوٌ ۚ وَإِنْ تُؤْمِنُوا وَتَتَّقُوا يُؤْتِكُمْ أُجُورَكُمْ وَلَا يَسْـَٔلْكُمْ أَمْوَالَكُمْ ۞

37. If He should ask you for it and urge you, you will be niggardly, and He will bring forth your malice.

إِنْ يَسْـَٔلْكُمُوهَا فَيُحْفِكُمْ تَبْخَلُوا وَيُخْرِجْ أَضْغَانَكُمْ ۞

38. Behold! you are those who are called upon to spend in Allah's way, but among you are those who are niggardly, and whoever is niggardly is niggardly against his own soul; and Allah is Self-sufficient and you have need (of Him), and if you turn back He will bring in your place another people, then they will not be like you.

هٰٓأَنْتُمْ هٰٓؤُلَآءِ تُدْعَوْنَ لِتُنْفِقُوا فِي سَبِيلِ اللّٰهِ ۖ فَمِنْكُمْ مَّنْ يَبْخَلُ ۚ وَمَنْ يَبْخَلْ فَإِنَّمَا يَبْخَلُ عَنْ نَفْسِهِ ۚ وَاللّٰهُ الْغَنِيُّ وَأَنْتُمُ الْفُقَرَآءُ ۚ وَإِنْ تَتَوَلَّوْا يَسْتَبْدِلْ قَوْمًا غَيْرَكُمْ ۙ ثُمَّ لَا يَكُونُوٓا أَمْثَالَكُمْ ۞

THE VICTORY
(FATEH)

**In the name of Allah,
The Beneficent, The Merciful.**

1. Surely We have given to you a clear victory,

2. That Allah may forgive your community their past faults and those to follow and complete His favor to you and keep you on a right way,

3. And that Allah might help you with a mighty help.

4. He it is Who sent down tranquillity into the hearts of the believers that they might have more of faith added to their faith—and Allah's are the hosts of the heavens and the earth, and Allah is Knowing, Wise—

5. That He may cause the believing men and the believing women to enter gardens beneath which rivers flow to abide therein and remove from them their evil; and that is a grand achievement with Allah;

6. And (that) He may punish the hypocritical men and the hypocritical women, and the polytheistic men and the polytheistic women, the entertainers of evil thoughts about Allah. On them is the evil turn, and Allah is wroth with them and has cursed them and prepared hell for them, and evil is the resort.

7. And Allah's are the hosts of the heavens and the earth; and Allah is Mighty, Wise.

8. Surely We have sent you as a witness and as a bearer of good news and as a warner,

اياتها (٤٨) سورة الفتح مدنيّة رکوعاتها

بِسْمِ اللهِ الرَّحْمٰنِ الرَّحِيْمِ ۝

اِنَّا فَتَحْنَا لَكَ فَتْحًا مُّبِيْنًا ۝

لِّيَغْفِرَ لَكَ اللهُ مَا تَقَدَّمَ مِنْ ذَنْبِكَ وَمَا تَاَخَّرَ وَيُتِمَّ نِعْمَتَهُ عَلَيْكَ وَيَهْدِيَكَ صِرَاطًا مُّسْتَقِيْمًا ۝

وَّيَنْصُرَكَ اللهُ نَصْرًا عَزِيْزًا ۝

هُوَ الَّذِيْ اَنْزَلَ السَّكِيْنَةَ فِيْ قُلُوْبِ الْمُؤْمِنِيْنَ لِيَزْدَادُوْا اِيْمَانًا مَّعَ اِيْمَانِهِمْ وَلِلّٰهِ جُنُوْدُ السَّمٰوٰتِ وَالْاَرْضِ وَكَانَ اللهُ عَلِيْمًا حَكِيْمًا ۝

لِّيُدْخِلَ الْمُؤْمِنِيْنَ وَالْمُؤْمِنٰتِ جَنّٰتٍ تَجْرِيْ مِنْ تَحْتِهَا الْاَنْهٰرُ خٰلِدِيْنَ فِيْهَا وَيُكَفِّرَ عَنْهُمْ سَيِّاٰتِهِمْ وَكَانَ ذٰلِكَ عِنْدَ اللهِ فَوْزًا عَظِيْمًا ۝

وَّيُعَذِّبَ الْمُنٰفِقِيْنَ وَالْمُنٰفِقٰتِ وَالْمُشْرِكِيْنَ وَالْمُشْرِكٰتِ الظَّانِّيْنَ بِاللهِ ظَنَّ السَّوْءِ عَلَيْهِمْ دَآئِرَةُ السَّوْءِ وَغَضِبَ اللهُ عَلَيْهِمْ وَلَعَنَهُمْ وَ اَعَدَّ لَهُمْ جَهَنَّمَ وَسَآءَتْ مَصِيْرًا ۝

وَلِلّٰهِ جُنُوْدُ السَّمٰوٰتِ وَالْاَرْضِ وَكَانَ اللهُ عَزِيْزًا حَكِيْمًا ۝

اِنَّا اَرْسَلْنٰكَ شَاهِدًا وَّمُبَشِّرًا وَّنَذِيْرًا ۝

9. That you may believe in Allah and His Apostle and may aid him and revere him; and (that) you may declare His glory, morning and evening.

10. Surely those who swear allegiance to you do but swear allegiance to Allah; the hand of Allah is above their hands. Therefore whoever breaks (his faith), he breaks it only to the injury of his own soul, and whoever fulfills what he has covenanted with Allah, He will grant him a mighty reward.

لِتُؤْمِنُوْا بِاللّٰهِ وَرَسُوْلِهٖ وَتُعَزِّرُوْهُ وَتُوَقِّرُوْهُ وَ
تُسَبِّحُوْهُ بُكْرَةً وَّاَصِيْلًا ۞

اِنَّ الَّذِيْنَ يُبَايِعُوْنَكَ اِنَّمَا يُبَايِعُوْنَ اللّٰهَ ۚ
يَدُ اللّٰهِ فَوْقَ اَيْدِيْهِمْ ۚ فَمَنْ نَّكَثَ
فَاِنَّمَا يَنْكُثُ عَلٰى نَفْسِهٖ ۚ وَمَنْ اَوْفٰى
بِمَا عٰهَدَ عَلَيْهُ اللّٰهَ فَسَيُؤْتِيْهِ اَجْرًا
عَظِيْمًا ۞

11. Those of the dwellers of the desert who were left behind will say to you: Our property and our families kept us busy, so ask forgiveness for us. They say with their tongues what is not in their hearts. Say: Then who can control anything for you from Allah if He intends to do you harm or if He intends to do you good; nay, Allah is Aware of what you do:

سَيَقُوْلُ لَكَ الْمُخَلَّفُوْنَ مِنَ الْاَعْرَابِ شَغَلَتْنَاۤ
اَمْوَالُنَا وَاَهْلُوْنَا فَاسْتَغْفِرْ لَنَا ۚ يَقُوْلُوْنَ
بِاَلْسِنَتِهِمْ مَّا لَيْسَ فِىْ قُلُوْبِهِمْ ۚ قُلْ فَمَنْ
يَّمْلِكُ لَكُمْ مِّنَ اللّٰهِ شَيْئًا اِنْ اَرَادَ بِكُمْ ضَرًّا
اَوْ اَرَادَ بِكُمْ نَفْعًا ۚ بَلْ كَانَ اللّٰهُ بِمَا تَعْمَلُوْنَ
خَبِيْرًا ۞

12. Nay! you rather thought that the Apostle and the believers would not return to their families ever, and that was made fair-seeming to your hearts and you thought an evil thought and you were a people doomed to perish.

بَلْ ظَنَنْتُمْ اَنْ لَّنْ يَّنْقَلِبَ الرَّسُوْلُ وَ
الْمُؤْمِنُوْنَ اِلٰۤى اَهْلِيْهِمْ اَبَدًا وَّزُيِّنَ ذٰلِكَ
فِىْ قُلُوْبِكُمْ وَظَنَنْتُمْ ظَنَّ السَّوْءِ ۚ وَكُنْتُمْ
قَوْمًا بُوْرًا ۞

13. And whoever does not believe in Allah and His Apostle, then surely We have prepared burning fire for the unbelievers.

وَمَنْ لَّمْ يُؤْمِنْ بِاللّٰهِ وَرَسُوْلِهٖ فَاِنَّاۤ اَعْتَدْنَا
لِلْكٰفِرِيْنَ سَعِيْرًا ۞

14. And Allah's is the kingdom of the heavens and the earth; He forgives whom He pleases and punishes whom He pleases, and Allah is Forgiving, Merciful.

وَلِلّٰهِ مُلْكُ السَّمٰوٰتِ وَالْاَرْضِ ۚ يَغْفِرُ لِمَنْ
يَّشَاۤءُ وَيُعَذِّبُ مَنْ يَّشَاۤءُ ۚ وَكَانَ اللّٰهُ غَفُوْرًا
رَّحِيْمًا ۞

15. Those who are left behind will say when you set forth for the gaining of acquisitions: Allow us (that) we may follow you. They desire to change the world of Allah. Say: By no means shall you follow us; thus did Allah say before. But they will say: Nay! you are jealous of us. Nay! they do not understand but a little.

سَيَقُوْلُ الْمُخَلَّفُوْنَ إِذَا انْطَلَقْتُمْ إِلٰى مَغَانِمَ لِتَأْخُذُوْهَا ذَرُوْنَا نَتَّبِعْكُمْ يُرِيْدُوْنَ أَنْ يُّبَدِّلُوْا كَلَامَ اللّٰهِ قُلْ لَّنْ تَتَّبِعُوْنَا كَذٰلِكُمْ قَالَ اللّٰهُ مِنْ قَبْلُ فَسَيَقُوْلُوْنَ بَلْ تَحْسُدُوْنَنَا بَلْ كَانُوْا لَا يَفْقَهُوْنَ إِلَّا قَلِيْلًا ۞

16. Say to those of the dwellers of the desert who were left behind: You shall soon be invited (to fight) against a people possessing mighty prowess; you will fight against them until they submit; then if you obey, Allah will grant you a good reward; and if you turn back as you turned back before, He will punish you with a painful punishment.

قُلْ لِّلْمُخَلَّفِيْنَ مِنَ الْأَعْرَابِ سَتُدْعَوْنَ إِلٰى قَوْمٍ أُولِيْ بَأْسٍ شَدِيْدٍ تُقَاتِلُوْنَهُمْ أَوْ يُسْلِمُوْنَ ۚ فَإِنْ تُطِيْعُوْا يُؤْتِكُمُ اللّٰهُ أَجْرًا حَسَنًا ۚ وَإِنْ تَتَوَلَّوْا كَمَا تَوَلَّيْتُمْ مِّنْ قَبْلُ يُعَذِّبْكُمْ عَذَابًا أَلِيْمًا ۞

17. There is no harm in the blind, nor is there any harm in the lame, nor is there any harm in the sick (if they do not go forth); and whoever obeys Allah and His Apostle, He will cause him to enter gardens beneath which rivers flow, and whoever turns back, He will punish him with a painful punishment.

لَيْسَ عَلَى الْأَعْمٰى حَرَجٌ وَّلَا عَلَى الْأَعْرَجِ حَرَجٌ وَّلَا عَلَى الْمَرِيْضِ حَرَجٌ ۚ وَمَنْ يُّطِعِ اللّٰهَ وَرَسُوْلَهُ يُدْخِلْهُ جَنّٰتٍ تَجْرِيْ مِنْ تَحْتِهَا الْأَنْهَارُ ۚ وَمَنْ يَّتَوَلَّ يُعَذِّبْهُ عَذَابًا أَلِيْمًا ۞

18. Certainly Allah was well pleased with the believers when they swore allegiance to you under the tree, and He knew what was in their hearts, so He sent down tranquillity on them and rewarded them with a near victory,

لَقَدْ رَضِيَ اللّٰهُ عَنِ الْمُؤْمِنِيْنَ إِذْ يُبَايِعُوْنَكَ تَحْتَ الشَّجَرَةِ فَعَلِمَ مَا فِيْ قُلُوْبِهِمْ فَأَنْزَلَ السَّكِيْنَةَ عَلَيْهِمْ وَأَثَابَهُمْ فَتْحًا قَرِيْبًا ۞

19. And many acquisitions which they will take; and Allah is Mighty, Wise.

وَّمَغَانِمَ كَثِيْرَةً يَّأْخُذُوْنَهَا ۚ وَكَانَ اللّٰهُ عَزِيْزًا حَكِيْمًا ۞

20. Allah promised you many acquisitions which you will take, then He hastened on this one for you and held back the hands of men from you, and that it may be a sign for the believers and that He may guide you on a right path.

وَعَدَكُمُ اللّٰهُ مَغَانِمَ كَثِيْرَةً تَأْخُذُوْنَهَا فَعَجَّلَ لَكُمْ هٰذِهِ وَكَفَّ أَيْدِيَ النَّاسِ عَنْكُمْ ۚ وَلِتَكُوْنَ آيَةً لِّلْمُؤْمِنِيْنَ وَيَهْدِيَكُمْ صِرَاطًا مُّسْتَقِيْمًا ۞

21. And others which you have not yet been able to achieve Allah has surely encompassed them, and Allah has power over all things.

وَأُخْرٰى لَمْ تَقْدِرُوْا عَلَيْهَا قَدْ اَحَاطَ اللّٰهُ بِهَا ۚ وَكَانَ اللّٰهُ عَلٰى كُلِّ شَيْءٍ قَدِيْرًا ۝

22. And if those who disbelieve fight with you, they would certainly turn (their) backs, then they would not find any protector or a helper.

وَلَوْ قَاتَلَكُمُ الَّذِيْنَ كَفَرُوْا لَوَلَّوُا الْاَدْبَارَ ثُمَّ لَا يَجِدُوْنَ وَلِيًّا وَّلَا نَصِيْرًا ۝

23. Such has been the course of Allah that has indeed run before, and you shall not find a change in Allah's course.

سُنَّةَ اللّٰهِ الَّتِيْ قَدْ خَلَتْ مِنْ قَبْلُ ۚ وَلَنْ تَجِدَ لِسُنَّةِ اللّٰهِ تَبْدِيْلًا ۝

24. And He it is Who held back their hands from you and your hands from them in the valley of Mecca after He had given you victory over them; and Allah is Seeing what you do.

وَهُوَ الَّذِيْ كَفَّ اَيْدِيَهُمْ عَنْكُمْ وَاَيْدِيَكُمْ عَنْهُمْ بِبَطْنِ مَكَّةَ مِنْ بَعْدِ اَنْ اَظْفَرَكُمْ عَلَيْهِمْ ۚ وَكَانَ اللّٰهُ بِمَا تَعْمَلُوْنَ بَصِيْرًا ۝

25. It is they who disbelieved and turned you away from the Sacred Mosque and (turned off) the offering withheld from arriving at its destined place; and were it not for the believing men and the believing women, whom, not having known, you might have trodden down, and thus something hateful might have afflicted you on their account without knowledge—so that Allah may cause to enter into His mercy whomsoever He pleases; had they been widely separated one from another, We would surely have punished those who disbelieved from among them with a painful punishment.

هُمُ الَّذِيْنَ كَفَرُوْا وَصَدُّوْكُمْ عَنِ الْمَسْجِدِ الْحَرَامِ وَالْهَدْيَ مَعْكُوْفًا اَنْ يَّبْلُغَ مَحِلَّهٗ ۚ وَلَوْ لَا رِجَالٌ مُّؤْمِنُوْنَ وَنِسَاءٌ مُّؤْمِنٰتٌ لَمْ تَعْلَمُوْهُمْ اَنْ تَطَئُوْهُمْ فَتُصِيْبَكُمْ مِّنْهُمْ مَّعَرَّةٌ بِغَيْرِ عِلْمٍ ۚ لِيُدْخِلَ اللّٰهُ فِيْ رَحْمَتِهٖ مَنْ يَّشَاءُ ۚ لَوْ تَزَيَّلُوْا لَعَذَّبْنَا الَّذِيْنَ كَفَرُوْا مِنْهُمْ عَذَابًا اَلِيْمًا ۝

26. When those who disbelieved harbored in their hearts (feelings of) disdain, the disdain of (the days of) ignorance, but Allah sent down His tranquillity on His Apostle and on the believers, and made them keep the word of guarding (against evil), and they were entitled to it and worthy of it; and Allah is Cognizant of all things.

اِذْ جَعَلَ الَّذِيْنَ كَفَرُوْا فِيْ قُلُوْبِهِمُ الْحَمِيَّةَ حَمِيَّةَ الْجَاهِلِيَّةِ فَاَنْزَلَ اللّٰهُ سَكِيْنَتَهٗ عَلٰى رَسُوْلِهٖ وَعَلَى الْمُؤْمِنِيْنَ وَاَلْزَمَهُمْ كَلِمَةَ التَّقْوٰى وَكَانُوْا اَحَقَّ بِهَا وَاَهْلَهَا ۚ وَكَانَ اللّٰهُ بِكُلِّ شَيْءٍ عَلِيْمًا ۝

27. Certainly Allah had shown to His Apostle the vision with truth: you shall most certainly enter the Sacred Mosque, if Allah pleases, in security, (some) having their heads shaved and (others) having their hair cut, you shall not fear, but He knows what you do not know, so He brought about a near victory before that.

لَقَدْ صَدَقَ اللهُ رَسُولَهُ الرُّؤْيَا بِالْحَقِّ لَتَدْخُلُنَّ الْمَسْجِدَ الْحَرَامَ اِنْ شَاءَ اللهُ اٰمِنِيْنَ مُحَلِّقِيْنَ رُءُوْسَكُمْ وَمُقَصِّرِيْنَ لَا تَخَافُوْنَ فَعَلِمَ مَا لَمْ تَعْلَمُوْا فَجَعَلَ مِنْ دُوْنِ ذٰلِكَ فَتْحًا قَرِيْبًا ۝

28. He it is Who sent His Apostle with the guidance and the true religion that He may make it prevail over all the religions; and Allah is enough for a witness.

هُوَ الَّذِيْ أَرْسَلَ رَسُوْلَهُ بِالْهُدٰى وَدِيْنِ الْحَقِّ لِيُظْهِرَهُ عَلَى الدِّيْنِ كُلِّهٖ وَكَفٰى بِاللهِ شَهِيْدًا ۝

29. Muhammad is the Apostle of Allah, and those with him are firm of heart against the unbelievers, compassionate among themselves; you will see them bowing down, prostrating themselves, seeking grace from Allah and pleasure; their marks are in their faces because of the effect of prostration; that is their description in the Taurat and their description in the Injeel; like as seed-produce that puts forth its sprout, then strengthens it, so it becomes stout and stands firmly on its stem, delighting the sowers that He may enrage the unbelievers on account of them; Allah has promised those among them who believe and do good, forgiveness and a great reward.

مُحَمَّدٌ رَسُوْلُ اللهِ وَالَّذِيْنَ مَعَهُ أَشِدَّاءُ عَلَى الْكُفَّارِ رُحَمَاءُ بَيْنَهُمْ تَرٰىهُمْ رُكَّعًا سُجَّدًا يَّبْتَغُوْنَ فَضْلًا مِّنَ اللهِ وَرِضْوَانًا سِيْمَاهُمْ فِيْ وُجُوْهِهِمْ مِّنْ أَثَرِ السُّجُوْدِ ذٰلِكَ مَثَلُهُمْ فِي التَّوْرٰىةِ وَمَثَلُهُمْ فِي الْإِنْجِيْلِ كَزَرْعٍ أَخْرَجَ شَطْأَهُ فَاٰزَرَهُ فَاسْتَغْلَظَ فَاسْتَوٰى عَلٰى سُوْقِهٖ يُعْجِبُ الزُّرَّاعَ لِيَغِيْظَ بِهِمُ الْكُفَّارَ وَعَدَ اللهُ الَّذِيْنَ اٰمَنُوْا وَعَمِلُوا الصّٰلِحٰتِ مِنْهُمْ مَّغْفِرَةً وَّأَجْرًا عَظِيْمًا ۝

THE CHAMBERS
(HUJURAT)

In the name of Allah,
the Beneficent, the Merciful.

1. O you who believe! be not forward in the presence of Allah and His Apostle, and be careful of (your duty to) Allah; surely Allah is Hearing, Knowing.

2. O you who believe! do not raise your voices above the voice of the Prophet, and do not speak loud to him as you speak loud to one another, lest your deeds become null while you do not perceive.

3. Surely those who lower their voices before Allah's Apostle are they whose hearts Allah has proved for guarding (against evil); they shall have forgiveness and a great reward.

4. (As for) those who call out to you from behind the private chambers, surely most of them do not understand.

5. And if they wait patiently until you come out to them, it would certainly be better for them, and Allah is Forgiving, Merciful.

6. O you who believe! if an evil-doer comes to you with a report, look carefully into it, lest you harm a people in ignorance, then be sorry for what you have done.

7. And know that among you is Allah's Apostle; should he obey you in many a matter, you would surely fall into distress, but Allah has endeared the faith to you and has made it seemly in your hearts, and He has made hateful to you unbelief and transgression and disobedience; these it is that are the followers of a right way.

513

8. By grace from Allah and as a favor; and Allah is Knowing, Wise.

فَضْلًا مِّنَ اللهِ وَنِعْمَةً ۗ وَاللهُ عَلِيْمٌ حَكِيْمٌ ۝

9. And if two parties of the believers quarrel, make peace between them; but if one of them acts wrongfully towards the other, fight that which acts wrongfully until it returns to Allah's command; then if it returns, make peace between them with justice and act equitably; surely Allah loves those who act equitably.

وَاِنْ طَآئِفَتٰنِ مِنَ الْمُؤْمِنِيْنَ اقْتَتَلُوْا فَاَصْلِحُوْا بَيْنَهُمَا ۚ فَاِنْۢ بَغَتْ اِحْدٰىهُمَا عَلَى الْاُخْرٰى فَقَاتِلُوا الَّتِيْ تَبْغِيْ حَتّٰى تَفِيْٓءَ اِلٰٓى اَمْرِ اللهِ ۚ فَاِنْ فَآءَتْ فَاَصْلِحُوْا بَيْنَهُمَا بِالْعَدْلِ وَاَقْسِطُوْا ۗ اِنَّ اللهَ يُحِبُّ الْمُقْسِطِيْنَ ۝

10. The believers are but brethren, therefore make peace between your brethren and be careful of (your duty to) Allah that mercy may be had on you.

اِنَّمَا الْمُؤْمِنُوْنَ اِخْوَةٌ فَاَصْلِحُوْا بَيْنَ اَخَوَيْكُمْ وَاتَّقُوا اللهَ لَعَلَّكُمْ تُرْحَمُوْنَ ۝

11. O you who believe! let not (one) people laugh at (another) people perchance they may be better than they, nor let women (laugh) at (other) women, perchance they may be better than they; and do not find fault with your own people nor call one another by nicknames; evil is a bad name after faith, and whoever does not turn, these it is that are the unjust.

يٰٓاَيُّهَا الَّذِيْنَ اٰمَنُوْا لَا يَسْخَرْ قَوْمٌ مِّنْ قَوْمٍ عَسٰٓى اَنْ يَّكُوْنُوْا خَيْرًا مِّنْهُمْ وَلَا نِسَآءٌ مِّنْ نِّسَآءٍ عَسٰٓى اَنْ يَّكُنَّ خَيْرًا مِّنْهُنَّ ۚ وَلَا تَلْمِزُوْٓا اَنْفُسَكُمْ وَلَا تَنَابَزُوْا بِالْاَلْقَابِ ۗ بِئْسَ الِاسْمُ الْفُسُوْقُ بَعْدَ الْاِيْمَانِ ۚ وَمَنْ لَّمْ يَتُبْ فَاُولٰٓئِكَ هُمُ الظّٰلِمُوْنَ ۝

12. O you who believe! avoid most of suspicion, for surely suspicion in some cases is a sin, and do not spy nor let some of you backbite others. Does one of you like to eat the flesh of his dead brother? But you abhor it; and be careful of (your duty to) Allah, surely Allah is Oft-returning (to mercy), Merciful.

يٰٓاَيُّهَا الَّذِيْنَ اٰمَنُوا اجْتَنِبُوْا كَثِيْرًا مِّنَ الظَّنِّ ۖ اِنَّ بَعْضَ الظَّنِّ اِثْمٌ ۖ وَّلَا تَجَسَّسُوْا وَلَا يَغْتَبْ بَّعْضُكُمْ بَعْضًا ۚ اَيُحِبُّ اَحَدُكُمْ اَنْ يَّأْكُلَ لَحْمَ اَخِيْهِ مَيْتًا فَكَرِهْتُمُوْهُ ۚ وَاتَّقُوا اللهَ ۚ اِنَّ اللهَ تَوَّابٌ رَّحِيْمٌ ۝

13. O you men! surely We have created you of a male and a female, and made you tribes and families that you may know each other; surely the most honorable of you with Allah is the one among you most careful (of his duty); surely Allah is Knowing, Aware.

يٰٓاَيُّهَا النَّاسُ اِنَّا خَلَقْنٰكُمْ مِّنْ ذَكَرٍ وَّاُنْثٰى وَجَعَلْنٰكُمْ شُعُوْبًا وَّقَبَآئِلَ لِتَعَارَفُوْا ۚ اِنَّ اَكْرَمَكُمْ عِنْدَ اللهِ اَتْقٰكُمْ ۚ اِنَّ اللهَ عَلِيْمٌ خَبِيْرٌ ۝

14. The dwellers of the desert say: We believe. Say: You do not believe but say, We submit; and faith has not yet entered into your hearts; and if you obey Allah and His Apostle, He will not diminish aught of your deeds; surely Allah is Forgiving, Merciful.

15. The believers are only those who believe in Allah and His Apostle then they doubt not and struggle hard with their wealth and their lives in the way of Allah; they are the truthful ones.

16. Say: Do you apprise Allah of your religion, and Allah knows what is in the heavens and what is in the earth; and Allah is Cognizant of all things.

17. They think that they lay you under an obligation by becoming Muslims. Say: Lay me not under obligation by your Islam: rather Allah lays you under an obligation by guiding you to the faith if you are truthful.

18. Surely Allah knows the unseen things of the heavens and the earth; and Allah sees what you do.

قَالَتِ الْأَعْرَابُ اٰمَنَّا قُلْ لَّمْ تُؤْمِنُوْا وَلٰكِنْ قُوْلُوْٓا
اَسْلَمْنَا وَلَمَّا يَدْخُلِ الْاِيْمَانُ فِيْ قُلُوْبِكُمْ وَاِنْ
تُطِيْعُوا اللّٰهَ وَرَسُوْلَهٗ لَا يَلِتْكُمْ مِّنْ اَعْمَالِكُمْ شَيْئًا
اِنَّ اللّٰهَ غَفُوْرٌ رَّحِيْمٌ ۝

اِنَّمَا الْمُؤْمِنُوْنَ الَّذِيْنَ اٰمَنُوْا بِاللّٰهِ وَرَسُوْلِهٖ ثُمَّ
لَمْ يَرْتَابُوْا وَجَاهَدُوْا بِاَمْوَالِهِمْ وَاَنْفُسِهِمْ فِيْ
سَبِيْلِ اللّٰهِ اُولٰٓئِكَ هُمُ الصّٰدِقُوْنَ ۝

قُلْ اَتُعَلِّمُوْنَ اللّٰهَ بِدِيْنِكُمْ وَاللّٰهُ يَعْلَمُ مَا
فِي السَّمٰوٰتِ وَمَا فِي الْاَرْضِ وَاللّٰهُ بِكُلِّ شَيْءٍ
عَلِيْمٌ ۝

يَمُنُّوْنَ عَلَيْكَ اَنْ اَسْلَمُوْا قُلْ لَّا تَمُنُّوْا عَلَيَّ
اِسْلَامَكُمْ بَلِ اللّٰهُ يَمُنُّ عَلَيْكُمْ اَنْ هَدٰىكُمْ
لِلْاِيْمَانِ اِنْ كُنْتُمْ صٰدِقِيْنَ ۝

اِنَّ اللّٰهَ يَعْلَمُ غَيْبَ السَّمٰوٰتِ وَالْاَرْضِ وَاللّٰهُ
بَصِيْرٌ بِمَا تَعْمَلُوْنَ ۝

QAF

**In the name of Allah,
the Beneficent, the Merciful.**

1. Qaf. I swear by the glorious Quran (that Muhammad is the Apostle of Allah.)

2. Nay! they wonder that there has come to them a warner from among themselves, so the unbelievers say: This is a wonderful thing:

3. What! when we are dead and have become dust? That is a far (from probable) return.

4. We know indeed what the earth diminishes of them, and with Us is a writing that preserves.

5. Nay, they rejected the truth when it came to them, so they are (now) in a state of confusion.

6. Do they not then look up to heaven above them how We have made it and adorned it and it has no gaps?

7. And the earth, We have made it plain and cast in it mountains and We have made to grow therein of all beautiful kinds,

8. To give sight and as a reminder to every servant who turns frequently (to Allah).

9. And We send down from the cloud water abounding in good, then We cause to grow thereby gardens and the grain that is reaped,

10. And the tall palm-trees having spadices closely set one above another,

11. A sustenance for the servants, and We give life thereby to a dead land; thus is the rising.

12. (Others) before them rejected (prophets): the people of Nuh and the dwellers of Ar-Rass and Samood,

13. And Ad and Firon and Lut's brethren,

516

14. And the dwellers of the grove and the people of Tuba; all rejected the apostles, so My threat came to pass.

وَّأَصْحٰبُ الْاَيْكَةِ وَقَوْمُ تُبَّعٍ كُلٌّ كَذَّبَ الرُّسُلَ فَحَقَّ وَعِيْدِ ۝

15. Were We then fatigued with the first creation? Yet are they in doubt with regard to a new creation.

اَفَعَيِيْنَا بِالْخَلْقِ الْاَوَّلِ بَلْ هُمْ فِيْ لَبْسٍ مِّنْ خَلْقٍ جَدِيْدٍ ۝

16. And certainly We created man, and We know what his mind suggests to him, and We are nearer to him than his life-vein.

وَلَقَدْ خَلَقْنَا الْاِنْسَانَ وَنَعْلَمُ مَا تُوَسْوِسُ بِهٖ نَفْسُهٗ ۚ وَنَحْنُ اَقْرَبُ اِلَيْهِ مِنْ حَبْلِ الْوَرِيْدِ ۝

17. When the two receivers receive, sitting on the right and on the left.

اِذْ يَتَلَقَّى الْمُتَلَقِّيٰنِ عَنِ الْيَمِيْنِ وَعَنِ الشِّمَالِ قَعِيْدٌ ۝

18. He utters not a word but there is by him a watcher at hand.

مَا يَلْفِظُ مِنْ قَوْلٍ اِلَّا لَدَيْهِ رَقِيْبٌ عَتِيْدٌ ۝

19. And the stupor of death will come in truth; that is what you were trying to escape.

وَجَاءَتْ سَكْرَةُ الْمَوْتِ بِالْحَقِّ ۚ ذٰلِكَ مَا كُنْتَ مِنْهُ تَحِيْدُ ۝

20. And the trumpet shall be blown; that is the day of the threatening.

وَنُفِخَ فِي الصُّوْرِ ۚ ذٰلِكَ يَوْمُ الْوَعِيْدِ ۝

21. And every soul shall come, with it a driver and a witness.

وَجَاءَتْ كُلُّ نَفْسٍ مَّعَهَا سَائِقٌ وَّشَهِيْدٌ ۝

22. Certainly you were heedless of it, but now We have removed from you your veil, so your sight today is sharp.

لَقَدْ كُنْتَ فِيْ غَفْلَةٍ مِّنْ هٰذَا فَكَشَفْنَا عَنْكَ غِطَاءَكَ فَبَصَرُكَ الْيَوْمَ حَدِيْدٌ ۝

23. And his companions shall say: This is what is ready with me.

وَقَالَ قَرِيْنُهٗ هٰذَا مَا لَدَيَّ عَتِيْدٌ ۝

24. Do cast into hell every ungrateful, rebellious one,

اَلْقِيَا فِيْ جَهَنَّمَ كُلَّ كَفَّارٍ عَنِيْدٍ ۝

25. Forbidder of good, exceeder of limits, doubter,

مَّنَّاعٍ لِّلْخَيْرِ مُعْتَدٍ مُّرِيْبِ ۝

26. Who sets up another god with Allah, so do cast him into severe chastisement.

اِلَّذِيْ جَعَلَ مَعَ اللّٰهِ اِلٰهًا اٰخَرَ فَاَلْقِيٰهُ فِي الْعَذَابِ الشَّدِيْدِ ۝

27. His companion will say: Our Lord! I did not lead him into inordinacy but he himself was in a great error.

قَالَ قَرِيْنُهٗ رَبَّنَا مَا اَطْغَيْتُهٗ وَلٰكِنْ كَانَ فِيْ ضَلٰلٍ بَعِيْدٍ ۝

28. He will say: Do not quarrel in My presence, and indeed I gave you the threatening beforehand:

قَالَ لَا تَخْتَصِمُوْا لَدَيَّ وَقَدْ قَدَّمْتُ اِلَيْكُمْ بِالْوَعِيْدِ ۝

29. My word shall not be changed, nor am I in the least unjust to the servants.

مَا يُبَدَّلُ الْقَوْلُ لَدَيَّ وَمَا اَنَا بِظَلَّامٍ لِّلْعَبِيْدِ ۝

30. On the day that We will say to hell: Are you filled up. And it will say: Are there any more?

يَوْمَ نَقُوْلُ لِجَهَنَّمَ هَلِ امْتَلَأْتِ وَتَقُوْلُ هَلْ مِنْ مَّزِيْدٍ ۝

31. And the garden shall be brought near to those who guard (against evil), not far off:

وَأُزْلِفَتِ الْجَنَّةُ لِلْمُتَّقِيْنَ غَيْرَ بَعِيْدٍ ۝

32. This is what you were promised, (it is) for every one who turns frequently (to Allah), keeps (His limits):

هٰذَا مَا تُوْعَدُوْنَ لِكُلِّ أَوَّابٍ حَفِيْظٍ ۝

33. Who fears the Beneficent God in secret and comes with a penitent heart:

مَنْ خَشِيَ الرَّحْمٰنَ بِالْغَيْبِ وَجَآءَ بِقَلْبٍ مُّنِيْبٍ ۝

34. Enter it in peace, that is the day of abiding.

ادْخُلُوْهَا بِسَلَامٍ ذٰلِكَ يَوْمُ الْخُلُوْدِ ۝

35. They have therein what they wish and with Us is more yet.

لَهُمْ مَّا يَشَآءُوْنَ فِيْهَا وَلَدَيْنَا مَزِيْدٌ ۝

36. And how many a generation did We destroy before them who were mightier in prowess than they, so they went about and about in the lands. Is there a place of refuge?

وَكَمْ أَهْلَكْنَا قَبْلَهُمْ مِنْ قَرْنٍ هُمْ أَشَدُّ مِنْهُمْ بَطْشًا فَنَقَّبُوْا فِي الْبِلَادِ هَلْ مِنْ مَّحِيْصٍ ۝

37. Most surely there is a reminder in this for him who has a heart or he gives ear and is a witness.

إِنَّ فِيْ ذٰلِكَ لَذِكْرَىٰ لِمَنْ كَانَ لَهُ قَلْبٌ أَوْ أَلْقَى السَّمْعَ وَهُوَ شَهِيْدٌ ۝

38. And certainly We created the heavens and the earth and what is between them in six periods and there touched Us not any fatigue.

وَلَقَدْ خَلَقْنَا السَّمٰوٰتِ وَالْأَرْضَ وَمَا بَيْنَهُمَا فِيْ سِتَّةِ أَيَّامٍ وَمَا مَسَّنَا مِنْ لُّغُوْبٍ ۝

39. Therefore be patient of what they say, and sing the praise of your Lord before the rising of the sun and before the setting.

فَاصْبِرْ عَلَىٰ مَا يَقُوْلُوْنَ وَسَبِّحْ بِحَمْدِ رَبِّكَ قَبْلَ طُلُوْعِ الشَّمْسِ وَقَبْلَ الْغُرُوْبِ ۝

40. And glorify Him in the night and after the prayers.

وَمِنَ الَّيْلِ فَسَبِّحْهُ وَأَدْبَارَ السُّجُوْدِ ۝

41. And listen on the day when the crier shall cry from a near place,

وَاسْتَمِعْ يَوْمَ يُنَادِ الْمُنَادِ مِنْ مَّكَانٍ قَرِيْبٍ ۝

42. The day when they shall hear the cry in truth; that is the day of coming forth.

يَوْمَ يَسْمَعُوْنَ الصَّيْحَةَ بِالْحَقِّ ذٰلِكَ يَوْمُ الْخُرُوْجِ ۝

43. Surely We give life and cause to die, and to Us is the eventual coming;

إِنَّا نَحْنُ نُحْيٖ وَنُمِيْتُ وَإِلَيْنَا الْمَصِيْرُ ۝

44. The day on which the earth shall cleave asunder under them, they will make haste; that is a gathering together easy to Us.

يَوْمَ تَشَقَّقُ الْأَرْضُ عَنْهُمْ سِرَاعًا ذٰلِكَ حَشْرٌ عَلَيْنَا يَسِيْرٌ ۝

45. We know best what they say, and you are not one to compel them; therefore remind him by means of the Quran who fears My threat.

نَحْنُ أَعْلَمُ بِمَا يَقُوْلُوْنَ وَمَا أَنْتَ عَلَيْهِمْ بِجَبَّارٍ فَذَكِّرْ بِالْقُرْآنِ مَنْ يَخَافُ وَعِيْدِ ۝

THE SCATTERERS
(ZARIAT)

أياتها ٥١ سورة الذّٰريٰت مكّيّة روعاتها

In The name of Allah,
The Beneficent, the Merciful.

بِسْمِ اللهِ الرَّحْمٰنِ الرَّحِيْمِ ۞

1. I swear by the wind that scatters far and wide,

وَالذّٰرِيٰتِ ذَرْوًا ۞

2. Then those clouds bearing the load (of minute things in space).

فَالْحٰمِلٰتِ وِقْرًا ۞

3. Then those (ships) that glide easily,

فَالْجٰرِيٰتِ يُسْرًا ۞

4. Then those (angels who) distribute blessings by Our command;

فَالْمُقَسِّمٰتِ أَمْرًا ۞

5. What you are threatened with is most surely true,

اِنَّمَا تُوْعَدُوْنَ لَصَادِقٌ ۞

6. And the judgment must most surely come about.

وَاِنَّ الدِّيْنَ لَوَاقِعٌ ۞

7. I swear by the heaven full of ways.

وَالسَّمَآءِ ذَاتِ الْحُبُكِ ۞

8. Most surely you are at variance with each other in what you say,

اِنَّكُمْ لَفِيْ قَوْلٍ مُّخْتَلِفٍ ۞

9. He is turned away from it who would be turned away.

يُؤْفَكُ عَنْهُ مَنْ أُفِكَ ۞

10. Cursed be the liars,

قُتِلَ الْخَرّٰصُوْنَ ۞

11. Who are in a gulf (of ignorance) neglectful;

الَّذِيْنَ هُمْ فِيْ غَمْرَةٍ سَاهُوْنَ ۞

12. They ask: When is the day of judgment?

يَسْـَٔلُوْنَ أَيَّانَ يَوْمُ الدِّيْنِ ۞

13. (It is) the day on which they shall be tried at the fire.

يَوْمَ هُمْ عَلَى النَّارِ يُفْتَنُوْنَ ۞

14. Taste your persecution! this is what you would hasten on.

ذُوْقُوْا فِتْنَتَكُمْ هٰذَا الَّذِيْ كُنْتُمْ بِهٖ تَسْتَعْجِلُوْنَ ۞

15. Surely those who guard (against evil) shall be in gardens and fountains.

اِنَّ الْمُتَّقِيْنَ فِيْ جَنّٰتٍ وَّعُيُوْنٍ ۞

16. Taking what their Lord gives them; surely they were before that, the doers of good.

اٰخِذِيْنَ مَآ اٰتٰهُمْ رَبُّهُمْ اِنَّهُمْ كَانُوْا قَبْلَ ذٰلِكَ مُحْسِنِيْنَ ۞

17. They used to sleep but little in the night.

كَانُوْا قَلِيْلًا مِّنَ الَّيْلِ مَا يَهْجَعُوْنَ ۞

18. And in the morning they asked forgiveness.

وَبِالْأَسْحَارِ هُمْ يَسْتَغْفِرُوْنَ ۞

519

19. And in their property was a portion due to him who begs and to him who is denied (good).

وَفِىٓ اَمْوَالِهِمْ حَقٌّ لِّلسَّآئِلِ وَالْمَحْرُوْمِ ۱۹

20. And in the earth there are signs for those who are sure,

وَفِى الْاَرْضِ اٰيٰتٌ لِّلْمُوْقِنِيْنَ ۲۰

21. And in your own souls (too); will you not then see?

وَفِىٓ اَنْفُسِكُمْ ۖ اَفَلَا تُبْصِرُوْنَ ۲۱

22. And in the heaven is your sustenance and what you are threatened with.

وَفِى السَّمَآءِ رِزْقُكُمْ وَمَا تُوْعَدُوْنَ ۲۲

23. And by the Lord of the heavens and the earth! it is most surely the truth, just as you do speak.

فَوَرَبِّ السَّمَآءِ وَالْاَرْضِ اِنَّهٗ لَحَقٌّ مِّثْلَ مَآ اَنَّكُمْ تَنْطِقُوْنَ ۲۳

24. Has there come to you information about the honored guests of Ibrahim?

هَلْ اَتٰىكَ حَدِيْثُ ضَيْفِ اِبْرٰهِيْمَ الْمُكْرَمِيْنَ ۲۴

25. When they entered upon him, they said: Peace. Peace, said he, a strange people.

اِذْ دَخَلُوْا عَلَيْهِ فَقَالُوْا سَلٰمًا ۖ قَالَ سَلٰمٌ ۖ قَوْمٌ مُّنْكَرُوْنَ ۲۵

26. Then he turned aside to his family secretly and brought a fat (roasted) calf,

فَرَاغَ اِلٰٓى اَهْلِهٖ فَجَآءَ بِعِجْلٍ سَمِيْنٍ ۲۶

27. So he brought it near them. He said: What! will you not eat?

فَقَرَّبَهٗٓ اِلَيْهِمْ قَالَ اَلَا تَأْكُلُوْنَ ۲۷

28. So he conceived in his mind a fear on account of them. They said: Fear not. And they gave him the good news of a boy possessing knowledge.

فَاَوْجَسَ مِنْهُمْ خِيْفَةً ۖ قَالُوْا لَا تَخَفْ ۖ وَبَشَّرُوْهُ بِغُلٰمٍ عَلِيْمٍ ۲۸

29. Then his wife came up in great grief, and she struck her face and said: An old barren woman!

فَاَقْبَلَتِ امْرَاَتُهٗ فِىْ صَرَّةٍ فَصَكَّتْ وَجْهَهَا وَقَالَتْ عَجُوْزٌ عَقِيْمٌ ۲۹

30. They said: Thus says your Lord: Surely He is the Wise, the Knowing.

قَالُوْا كَذٰلِكِ ۙ قَالَ رَبُّكِ ۖ اِنَّهٗ هُوَ الْحَكِيْمُ الْعَلِيْمُ ۳۰

31. He said: What is your affair then, O messengers!

قَالَ فَمَا خَطْبُكُمْ اَيُّهَا الْمُرْسَلُوْنَ ۳۱

32. They said: Surely we are sent to a guilty people,

قَالُوْٓا اِنَّآ اُرْسِلْنَآ اِلٰى قَوْمٍ مُّجْرِمِيْنَ ۳۲

33. That we may send down upon them stones of clay

لِنُرْسِلَ عَلَيْهِمْ حِجَارَةً مِّنْ طِيْنٍ ۳۳

34. Sent forth from your Lord for the extravagant.

مُّسَوَّمَةً عِنْدَ رَبِّكَ لِلْمُسْرِفِيْنَ ۳۴

35. Then We brought forth such as were therein of the believers.

فَاَخْرَجْنَا مَنْ كَانَ فِيْهَا مِنَ الْمُؤْمِنِيْنَ ۳۵

36. But We did not find therein save a (single) house of those who submitted (the Muslims).

فَمَا وَجَدْنَا فِيْهَا غَيْرَ بَيْتٍ مِّنَ الْمُسْلِمِيْنَ ۞

37. And We left therein a sign for those who fear the painful punishment.

وَتَرَكْنَا فِيْهَآ اٰيَةً لِّلَّذِيْنَ يَخَافُوْنَ الْعَذَابَ الْاَلِيْمَ ۞

38. And in Musa: When We sent him to Firon with clear authority.

وَفِيْ مُوْسٰٓى اِذْ اَرْسَلْنٰهُ اِلٰى فِرْعَوْنَ بِسُلْطٰنٍ مُّبِيْنٍ ۞

39. But he turned away with his forces and said: A magician or a mad man.

فَتَوَلّٰى بِرُكْنِهٖ وَقَالَ سٰحِرٌ اَوْ مَجْنُوْنٌ ۞

40. So We seized him and his hosts and hurled them into the sea, and he was blamable.

فَاَخَذْنٰهُ وَجُنُوْدَهٗ فَنَبَذْنٰهُمْ فِى الْيَمِّ وَهُوَ مُلِيْمٌ ۞

41. And in Ad: When We sent upon them the destructive wind.

وَفِيْ عَادٍ اِذْ اَرْسَلْنَا عَلَيْهِمُ الرِّيْحَ الْعَقِيْمَ ۞

42. It did not leave aught on which it blew, but it made it like ashes.

مَا تَذَرُ مِنْ شَيْءٍ اَتَتْ عَلَيْهِ اِلَّا جَعَلَتْهُ كَالرَّمِيْمِ ۞

43. And in Samood: When it was said to them: Enjoy yourselves for a while.

وَفِيْ ثَمُوْدَ اِذْ قِيْلَ لَهُمْ تَمَتَّعُوْا حَتّٰى حِيْنٍ ۞

44. But they revolted against the commandment of their Lord, so the rumbling overtook them while they saw.

فَعَتَوْا عَنْ اَمْرِ رَبِّهِمْ فَاَخَذَتْهُمُ الصّٰعِقَةُ وَهُمْ يَنْظُرُوْنَ ۞

45. So they were not able to rise up, nor could they defend themselves;

فَمَا اسْتَطَاعُوْا مِنْ قِيَامٍ وَّمَا كَانُوْا مُنْتَصِرِيْنَ ۞

46. And the people of Nuh before, surely they were a transgressing people.

وَقَوْمَ نُوْحٍ مِّنْ قَبْلُ ۗ اِنَّهُمْ كَانُوْا قَوْمًا فٰسِقِيْنَ ۞

47. And the heaven, We raised it high with power, and most surely We are the makers of things ample.

وَالسَّمَآءَ بَنَيْنٰهَا بِاَيْدٍ وَّاِنَّا لَمُوْسِعُوْنَ ۞

48. And the earth, We have made it a wide extent; how well have We then spread (it) out.

وَالْاَرْضَ فَرَشْنٰهَا فَنِعْمَ الْمٰهِدُوْنَ ۞

49. And of everything We have created pairs that you may be mindful.

وَمِنْ كُلِّ شَيْءٍ خَلَقْنَا زَوْجَيْنِ لَعَلَّكُمْ تَذَكَّرُوْنَ ۞

50. Therefore fly to Allah, surely I am a plain warner to you from Him.

نَفِرُّوَۤا اِلَى اللّٰهِ ۖ اِنِّيۡ لَكُمۡ مِّنۡهُ نَذِيۡرٌ مُّبِيۡنٌ ۚ

51. And do not set up with Allah another god: surely I am a plain warner to you from Him.

وَلَا تَجۡعَلُوۡا مَعَ اللّٰهِ اِلٰهًا اٰخَرَ ؕ اِنِّيۡ لَكُمۡ مِّنۡهُ نَذِيۡرٌ مُّبِيۡنٌ ۚ

52. Thus there did not come to those before them an apostle but they said: A magician or a mad man.

كَذٰلِكَ مَاۤ اَتَى الَّذِيۡنَ مِنۡ قَبۡلِهِمۡ مِّنۡ رَّسُوۡلٍ اِلَّا قَالُوۡا سَاحِرٌ اَوۡ مَجۡنُوۡنٌ ۚ

53. Have they charged each other with this? Nay! they are an inordinate people.

اَتَوَاصَوۡا بِهٖ ۚ بَلۡ هُمۡ قَوۡمٌ طَاغُوۡنَ ۚ

54. Then turn your back upon them for you are not to blame;

فَتَوَلَّ عَنۡهُمۡ فَمَاۤ اَنۡتَ بِمَلُوۡمٍ ۙ

55. And continue to remind, for surely the reminder profits the believers.

وَّذَكِّرۡ فَاِنَّ الذِّكۡرٰى تَنۡفَعُ الۡمُؤۡمِنِيۡنَ ۚ

56. And I have not created the jinn and the men except that they should serve Me.

وَمَا خَلَقۡتُ الۡجِنَّ وَالۡاِنۡسَ اِلَّا لِيَعۡبُدُوۡنِ ۚ

57. I do not desire from them any sustenance and I do not desire that they should feed Me.

مَاۤ اُرِيۡدُ مِنۡهُمۡ مِّنۡ رِّزۡقٍ وَّمَاۤ اُرِيۡدُ اَنۡ يُّطۡعِمُوۡنِ ۚ

58. Surely Allah is the Bestower of sustenance, the Lord of Power, the Strong.

اِنَّ اللّٰهَ هُوَ الرَّزَّاقُ ذُو الۡقُوَّةِ الۡمَتِيۡنُ ۚ

59. So surely those who are unjust shall have a portion like the portion of their companions, therefore let them not ask Me to hasten on.

فَاِنَّ لِلَّذِيۡنَ ظَلَمُوۡا ذَنُوۡبًا مِّثۡلَ ذَنُوۡبِ اَصۡحٰبِهِمۡ فَلَا يَسۡتَعۡجِلُوۡنِ ۚ

60. Therefore woe to those who disbelieve because of their day which they are threatened with.

فَوَيۡلٌ لِّلَّذِيۡنَ كَفَرُوۡا مِنۡ يَّوۡمِهِمُ الَّذِيۡ يُوۡعَدُوۡنَ ۚ

THE MOUNTAIN
(TUR)

**In the name of Allah,
the Beneficent, the Merciful.**

اینما ۱۳۸) سُورَةُ الطُّورِ مَكِّيَّةٌ رُوعَانُهَا

بِسْمِ اللهِ الرَّحْمٰنِ الرَّحِيْمِ ۟

1. I swear by the Mountain,

وَالطُّورِ ۟

2. And the Book written

وَكِتٰبٍ مَّسْطُوْرٍ ۟

3. In an outstretched fine parchment,

فِيْ رَقٍّ مَّنْشُوْرٍ ۟

4. And the House (Kaaba) that is visited,

وَالْبَيْتِ الْمَعْمُوْرِ ۟

5. And the elevated canopy,

وَالسَّقْفِ الْمَرْفُوْعِ ۟

6. And the swollen sea;

وَالْبَحْرِ الْمَسْجُوْرِ ۟

7. Most surely the punishment of your Lord will come to pass;

اِنَّ عَذَابَ رَبِّكَ لَوَاقِعٌ ۟

8. There shall be none to avert it;

مَّا لَهٗ مِنْ دَافِعٍ ۟

9. On the day when the heaven shall move from side to side,

يَّوْمَ تَمُوْرُ السَّمَآءُ مَوْرًا ۟

10. And the mountains shall pass away passing away (altogether).

وَّتَسِيْرُ الْجِبَالُ سَيْرًا ۟

11. So woe on that day to those who reject (the truth),

فَوَيْلٌ يَّوْمَئِذٍ لِّلْمُكَذِّبِيْنَ ۟

12. Those who sport entering into vain discourses.

الَّذِيْنَ هُمْ فِيْ خَوْضٍ يَّلْعَبُوْنَ ۟

13. The day on which they shall be driven away to the fire of hell with violence.

يَوْمَ يُدَعُّوْنَ اِلٰى نَارِ جَهَنَّمَ دَعًّا ۟

14. This is the fire which you used to give the lie to.

هٰذِهِ النَّارُ الَّتِيْ كُنْتُمْ بِهَا تُكَذِّبُوْنَ ۟

15. Is it magic then or do you not see?

اَفَسِحْرٌ هٰذَآ اَمْ اَنْتُمْ لَا تُبْصِرُوْنَ ۟

16. Enter into it, then bear (it) patiently, or do not bear (it) patiently, it is the same to you; you shall be requited only (for) what you did.

اِصْلَوْهَا فَاصْبِرُوْۤا اَوْ لَا تَصْبِرُوْا سَوَآءٌ عَلَيْكُمْ اِنَّمَا تُجْزَوْنَ مَا كُنْتُمْ تَعْمَلُوْنَ ۟

17. Surely those who guard (against evil) shall be in gardens and bliss,

اِنَّ الْمُتَّقِيْنَ فِيْ جَنّٰتٍ وَّنَعِيْمٍ ۟

18. Rejoicing because of what their Lord gave them, and their Lord saved them from the punishment of the burning fire.

فٰكِهِيْنَ بِمَآ اٰتٰىهُمْ رَبُّهُمْ ۚ وَوَقٰىهُمْ رَبُّهُمْ عَذَابَ الْجَحِيْمِ ۟

19. Eat and drink pleasantly for what you did,

20. Reclining on thrones set in lines, and We will unite them to large-eyed beautiful ones.

21. And (as for) those who believe and their offspring follow them in faith, We will unite with them their offspring and We will not diminish to them aught of their work; every man is responsible for what he shall have wrought.

22. And We will aid them with fruit and flesh such as they desire.

23. They shall pass therein from one to another a cup wherein there shall be nothing vain nor any sin.

24. And round them shall go boys of theirs as if they were hidden pearls.

25. And some of them shall advance towards others questioning each other.

26. Saying: Surely we feared before on account of our families:

27. But Allah has been gracious to us and He has saved us from the punishment of the hot wind:

28. Surely we called upon Him before: Surely He is the Benign, the Merciful.

29. Therefore continue to remind, for by the grace of your Lord, you are not a soothsayer, or a madman.

30. Or do they say: A poet, we wait for him the evil accidents of time.

31. Say: Wait, for surely I too with you am of those who wait.

32. Nay! do their understandings bid them this? Or are they an inordinate people?

33. Or do they say: He has forged it. Nay! they do not believe.

34. Then let them bring an announcement like it if they are truthful.

35. Or were they created without there being anything, or are they the creators?

524

36. Or did they create the heavens and the earth? Nay! they have no certainty.

37. Or have they the treasures of your Lord with them? Or have they been set in absolute authority?

38. Or have they the means by which they listen? Then let their listener bring a clear authority.

39. Or has He daughters while you have sons?

40. Or do you ask them for a reward, so that they are overburdened by a debt?

41. Or have they the unseen so that they write (it) down?

42. Or do they desire a war? But those who disbelieve shall be the vanquished ones in war.

43. Or have they a god other than Allah? Glory be to Allah from what they set up (with Him).

44. And if they should see a portion of the heaven coming down, they would say: Piled up clouds.

45. Leave them then till they meet that day of theirs wherein they shall be made to swoon (with terror):

46. The day on which their struggle shall not avail them aught, nor shall they be helped.

47. And surely those who are unjust shall have a punishment besides that (in the world), but most of them do not know.

48. And wait patiently for the judgment of your Lord, for surely you are before Our eyes, and sing the praise of your Lord when you rise;

49. And in the night, give Him glory too, and at the setting of the stars.

أَمْ خَلَقُوا السَّمٰوٰتِ وَالْأَرْضَ بَلْ لَّا يُوْقِنُوْنَ ۞

أَمْ عِنْدَهُمْ خَزَائِنُ رَبِّكَ أَمْ هُمُ الْمُصَيْطِرُوْنَ ۞

أَمْ لَهُمْ سُلَّمٌ يَّسْتَمِعُوْنَ فِيْهِ ۚ فَلْيَأْتِ مُسْتَمِعُهُمْ بِسُلْطٰنٍ مُّبِيْنٍ ۞

أَمْ لَهُ الْبَنٰتُ وَلَكُمُ الْبَنُوْنَ ۞

أَمْ تَسْـَٔلُهُمْ أَجْرًا فَهُمْ مِّنْ مَّغْرَمٍ مُّثْقَلُوْنَ ۞

أَمْ عِنْدَهُمُ الْغَيْبُ فَهُمْ يَكْتُبُوْنَ ۞

أَمْ يُرِيْدُوْنَ كَيْدًا ۚ فَالَّذِيْنَ كَفَرُوْا هُمُ الْمَكِيْدُوْنَ ۞

أَمْ لَهُمْ إِلٰهٌ غَيْرُ اللّٰهِ ۚ سُبْحٰنَ اللّٰهِ عَمَّا يُشْرِكُوْنَ ۞

وَإِنْ يَّرَوْا كِسْفًا مِّنَ السَّمَاءِ سَاقِطًا يَّقُوْلُوْا سَحَابٌ مَّرْكُوْمٌ ۞

فَذَرْهُمْ حَتّٰى يُلٰقُوْا يَوْمَهُمُ الَّذِيْ فِيْهِ يُصْعَقُوْنَ ۞

يَوْمَ لَا يُغْنِيْ عَنْهُمْ كَيْدُهُمْ شَيْئًا وَّلَا هُمْ يُنْصَرُوْنَ ۞

وَإِنَّ لِلَّذِيْنَ ظَلَمُوْا عَذَابًا دُوْنَ ذٰلِكَ وَلٰكِنَّ أَكْثَرَهُمْ لَا يَعْلَمُوْنَ ۞

وَاصْبِرْ لِحُكْمِ رَبِّكَ فَإِنَّكَ بِأَعْيُنِنَا وَسَبِّحْ بِحَمْدِ رَبِّكَ حِيْنَ تَقُوْمُ ۞

وَمِنَ الَّيْلِ فَسَبِّحْهُ وَإِدْبَارَ النُّجُوْمِ ۞

THE STAR
(NAJM)

أياتها ٥٣ سورة النجم مكية رکوعاتها

**In the name of Allah,
the Beneficent, the Merciful.**

بِسْمِ اللهِ الرَّحْمٰنِ الرَّحِيْمِ

1. I swear by the star when it goes down.

وَالنَّجْمِ اِذَا هَوٰى ۙ

2. Your companion does not err, nor does he go astray;

مَا ضَلَّ صَاحِبُكُمْ وَمَا غَوٰى ۙ

3. Nor does he speak out of desire.

وَمَا يَنْطِقُ عَنِ الْهَوٰى ؕ

4. It is naught but revelation that is revealed,

اِنْ هُوَ اِلَّا وَحْيٌ يُّوْحٰى ۙ

5. The Lord of Mighty Power has taught him,

عَلَّمَهٗ شَدِيْدُ الْقُوٰى ۙ

6. The Lord of Strength; so he attained completion,

ذُوْ مِرَّةٍ ؕ فَاسْتَوٰى ۙ

7. And he is in the highest part of the horizon.

وَهُوَ بِالْاُفُقِ الْاَعْلٰى ؕ

8. Then he drew near, then he bowed,

ثُمَّ دَنَا فَتَدَلّٰى ۙ

9. So he was the measure of two bows or closer still.

فَكَانَ قَابَ قَوْسَيْنِ اَوْ اَدْنٰى ۚ

10. And He revealed to His servant what He revealed.

فَاَوْحٰى اِلٰى عَبْدِهٖ مَا اَوْحٰى ؕ

11. The heart was not untrue in (making him see) what he saw.

مَا كَذَبَ الْفُؤَادُ مَا رَاٰى

12. What! do you then dispute with him as to what he saw?

اَفَتُمٰرُوْنَهٗ عَلٰى مَا يَرٰى

13. And certainly he saw him in another descent,

وَلَقَدْ رَاٰهُ نَزْلَةً اُخْرٰى ۙ

14. At the farthest lote-tree;

عِنْدَ سِدْرَةِ الْمُنْتَهٰى

15. Near which is the garden, the place to be resorted to.

عِنْدَهَا جَنَّةُ الْمَاْوٰى ؕ

16. When that which covers covered the lote-tree;

اِذْ يَغْشَى السِّدْرَةَ مَا يَغْشٰى ۙ

17. The eye did not turn aside, nor did it exceed the limit.

مَا زَاغَ الْبَصَرُ وَمَا طَغٰى

18. Certainly he saw of the greatest signs of his Lord.

لَقَدْ رَاٰى مِنْ اٰيٰتِ رَبِّهِ الْكُبْرٰى

19. Have you then considered the Lat and the Uzza,

اَفَرَءَيْتُمُ اللّٰتَ وَالْعُزّٰى ۙ

20. And Manat, the third, the last?

وَمَنٰوةَ الثَّالِثَةَ الْأُخْرٰى ۞

21. What! for you the males and for Him the females!

اَلَكُمُ الذَّكَرُ وَلَهُ الْأُنْثٰى ۞

22. This indeed is an unjust division!

تِلْكَ اِذًا قِسْمَةٌ ضِيْزٰى ۞

23. They are naught but names which you have named, you and your fathers; Allah has not sent for them any authority. They follow naught but conjecture and the low desires which (their) souls incline to; and certainly the guidance has come to them from their Lord.

اِنْ هِيَ اِلَّا اَسْمَآءٌ سَمَّيْتُمُوْهَا اَنْتُمْ وَاٰبَآؤُكُمْ مَّا اَنْزَلَ اللّٰهُ بِهَا مِنْ سُلْطٰنٍ ۚ اِنْ يَّتَّبِعُوْنَ اِلَّا الظَّنَّ وَمَا تَهْوَى الْأَنْفُسُ ۚ وَلَقَدْ جَآءَهُمْ مِّنْ رَّبِّهِمُ الْهُدٰى ۞

24. Or shall man have what he wishes?

اَمْ لِلْاِنْسَانِ مَا تَمَنّٰى ۞

25. Nay! for Allah is the hereafter and the former (life).

فَلِلّٰهِ الْاٰخِرَةُ وَالْاُوْلٰى ۞

26. And how many an angel is there in the heavens whose intercession does not avail at all except after Allah has given permission to whom He pleases and chooses.

وَكَمْ مِّنْ مَّلَكٍ فِى السَّمٰوٰتِ لَا تُغْنِىْ شَفَاعَتُهُمْ شَيْئًا اِلَّا مِنْ بَعْدِ اَنْ يَّأْذَنَ اللّٰهُ لِمَنْ يَّشَآءُ وَيَرْضٰى ۞

27. Most surely they who do not believe in the hereafter name the angels with female names.

اِنَّ الَّذِيْنَ لَا يُؤْمِنُوْنَ بِالْاٰخِرَةِ لَيُسَمُّوْنَ الْمَلٰئِكَةَ تَسْمِيَةَ الْأُنْثٰى ۞

28. And they have no knowledge of it; they do not follow anything but conjecture, and surely conjecture does not avail against the truth at all.

وَمَا لَهُمْ بِهٖ مِنْ عِلْمٍ ۚ اِنْ يَّتَّبِعُوْنَ اِلَّا الظَّنَّ ۚ وَاِنَّ الظَّنَّ لَا يُغْنِىْ مِنَ الْحَقِّ شَيْئًا ۞

29. Therefore turn aside from him who turns his back upon Our reminder and does not desire anything but this world's life.

فَاَعْرِضْ عَنْ مَّنْ تَوَلّٰى ۙ عَنْ ذِكْرِنَا وَكَمْ يُرِدْ اِلَّا الْحَيٰوةَ الدُّنْيَا ۞

30. That is their goal of knowledge; surely your Lord knows best him who goes astray from His path and He knows best him who follows the right direction.

ذٰلِكَ مَبْلَغُهُمْ مِّنَ الْعِلْمِ ۚ اِنَّ رَبَّكَ هُوَ اَعْلَمُ بِمَنْ ضَلَّ عَنْ سَبِيْلِهٖ وَهُوَ اَعْلَمُ بِمَنِ اهْتَدٰى ۞

31. And Allah's is what is in the heavens and what is in the earth, that He may reward those who do evil according to what they do, and (that) He may reward those who do good with goodness.

وَلِلّٰهِ مَا فِى السَّمٰوٰتِ وَمَا فِى الْأَرْضِ ۙ لِيَجْزِىَ الَّذِيْنَ اَسَآءُوْا بِمَا عَمِلُوْا وَيَجْزِىَ الَّذِيْنَ اَحْسَنُوْا بِالْحُسْنٰى ۞

32. Those who keep aloof from the great sins and the indecencies but the passing idea; surely your Lord is liberal in forgiving. He knows you best when He brings you forth from the earth and when you are embryos in the wombs of your mothers; therefore do not attribute purity to your souls; He knows him best who guards (against evil).

اَلَّذِيْنَ يَجْتَنِبُوْنَ كَبٰٓئِرَ الْاِثْمِ وَالْفَوَاحِشَ اِلَّا اللَّمَمَ ۗ اِنَّ رَبَّكَ وَاسِعُ الْمَغْفِرَةِ ۗ هُوَ اَعْلَمُ بِكُمْ اِذْ اَنْشَاَكُمْ مِّنَ الْاَرْضِ وَاِذْ اَنْتُمْ اَجِنَّةٌ فِيْ بُطُوْنِ اُمَّهٰتِكُمْ ۚ فَلَا تُزَكُّوْٓا اَنْفُسَكُمْ ۗ هُوَ اَعْلَمُ بِمَنِ اتَّقٰى ۟ ٣٢

33. Have you then seen him who turns his back?

اَفَرَءَيْتَ الَّذِيْ تَوَلّٰى ۟ ٣٣

34. And gives a little and (then) withholds.

وَاَعْطٰى قَلِيْلًا وَّاَكْدٰى ٣٤

35. Has he the knowledge of the unseen so that he can see?

اَعِنْدَهٗ عِلْمُ الْغَيْبِ فَهُوَ يَرٰى ٣٥

36. Or, has he not been informed of what is in the scriptures of Musa?

اَمْ لَمْ يُنَبَّاْ بِمَا فِيْ صُحُفِ مُوْسٰى ٣٦

37. And (of) Ibrahim who fulfilled (the commandments):

وَاِبْرٰهِيْمَ الَّذِيْ وَفّٰٓى ٣٧

38. That no bearer of burden shall bear the burden of another;

اَلَّا تَزِرُ وَازِرَةٌ وِّزْرَ اُخْرٰى ٣٨

39. And that man shall have nothing but what he strives for;

وَاَنْ لَّيْسَ لِلْاِنْسَانِ اِلَّا مَا سَعٰى ٣٩

40. And that his striving shall soon be seen;

وَاَنَّ سَعْيَهٗ سَوْفَ يُرٰى ٤٠

41. Then shall he be rewarded for it with the fullest reward;

ثُمَّ يُجْزٰهُ الْجَزَآءَ الْاَوْفٰى ٤١

42. And that to your Lord is the goal;

وَاَنَّ اِلٰى رَبِّكَ الْمُنْتَهٰى ٤٢

43. And that He it is Who makes (men) laugh and makes (them) weep;

وَاَنَّهٗ هُوَ اَضْحَكَ وَاَبْكٰى ٤٣

44. And that He it is Who causes death and gives life;

وَاَنَّهٗ هُوَ اَمَاتَ وَاَحْيَا ٤٤

45. And that He created pairs, the male and the female,

وَاَنَّهٗ خَلَقَ الزَّوْجَيْنِ الذَّكَرَ وَالْاُنْثٰى ٤٥

46. From the small seed when it is adapted;

مِنْ نُّطْفَةٍ اِذَا تُمْنٰى ٤٦

47. And that on Him is the bringing forth a second time;

وَاَنَّ عَلَيْهِ النَّشْاَةَ الْاُخْرٰى ٤٧

48. And that He it is Who enriches and gives to hold;

وَاَنَّهٗ هُوَ اَغْنٰى وَاَقْنٰى ٤٨

49. And that He is the Lord of the Sirius;

وَاَنَّهٗ هُوَ رَبُّ الشِّعْرٰى ٤٩

50. And that He did destroy the Ad of old,

وَاَنَّهٗٓ اَهْلَكَ عَادَا الْاُوْلٰی ۝

51. And Samood, so He spared not,

وَثَمُوْدَا فَمَاۤ اَبْقٰی ۝

52. And the people of Nuh before; surely they were most unjust and inordinate;

وَقَوْمَ نُوْحٍ مِّنْ قَبْلُ اِنَّهُمْ كَانُوْا هُمْ اَظْلَمَ وَاَطْغٰی ۝

53. And the overthrown cities did He overthrow,

وَالْمُؤْتَفِكَةَ اَهْوٰی ۝

54. So there covered them that which covered.

فَغَشّٰهَا مَا غَشّٰی ۝

55. Which of your Lord's benefits will you then dispute about?

فَبِاَيِّ اٰلَاۤءِ رَبِّكَ تَتَمَارٰی ۝

56. This is a warner of the warners of old.

هٰذَا نَذِيْرٌ مِّنَ النُّذُرِ الْاُوْلٰی ۝

57. The near event draws nigh.

اَزِفَتِ الْاٰزِفَةُ ۝

58. There shall be none besides Allah to remove it.

لَيْسَ لَهَا مِنْ دُوْنِ اللّٰهِ كَاشِفَةٌ ۝

59. Do you then wonder at this announcement?

اَفَمِنْ هٰذَا الْحَدِيْثِ تَعْجَبُوْنَ ۝

60. And will you laugh and not weep?

وَتَضْحَكُوْنَ وَلَا تَبْكُوْنَ ۝

61. While you are indulging in varieties.

وَاَنْتُمْ سَامِدُوْنَ ۝

62. So make obeisance to Allah and serve (Him).

فَاسْجُدُوْا لِلّٰهِ وَاعْبُدُوْا ۩

THE MOON
(QAMAR)

**In the name of Allah,
the Beneficent the Merciful.**

1. The hour drew nigh and the moon did rend asunder.

2. And if they see a miracle they turn aside and say: Transient magic.

3. And they call (it) a lie, and follow their low desires; and every affair has its appointed term.

4. And certainly some narratives have come to them wherein is prevention—

5. Consummate wisdom—but warnings do not avail;

6. So turn (your) back on them (for) the day when the inviter shall invite them to a hard task,

7. Their eyes cast down, going forth from their graves as if they were scattered locusts,

8. Hastening to the inviter. The unbelievers shall say: This is a hard day.

9. Before them the people of Nuh rejected, so they rejected Our servant and called (him) mad, and he was driven away.

10. Therefore he called upon his Lord: I am overcome, come Thou then to help.

11. So We opened the gates of the cloud with water pouring down,

12. And We made water to flow forth in the land in springs, so the water gathered together according to a measure already ordained.

13. And We bore him on that which was made of planks and nails,

14. Sailing, before Our eyes, a reward for him who was denied.

15. And certainly We left it as a sign, but is there anyone who will mind?

بِسْمِ اللهِ الرَّحْمٰنِ الرَّحِيْمِ ۟

اقْتَرَبَتِ السَّاعَةُ وَانْشَقَّ الْقَمَرُ ۟

وَاِنْ يَّرَوْا اٰيَةً يُّعْرِضُوْا وَيَقُوْلُوْا سِحْرٌ مُّسْتَمِرٌّ ۟

وَكَذَّبُوْا وَاتَّبَعُوْٓا اَهْوَآءَهُمْ وَكُلُّ اَمْرٍ مُّسْتَقِرٌّ ۟

وَلَقَدْ جَآءَهُمْ مِّنَ الْاَنْبَآءِ مَا فِيْهِ مُزْدَجَرٌ ۟ۙ

حِكْمَةٌۢ بَالِغَةٌ فَمَا تُغْنِ النُّذُرُ ۟ۙ

فَتَوَلَّ عَنْهُمْ ۘ يَوْمَ يَدْعُ الدَّاعِ اِلٰى شَيْءٍ نُّكُرٍ ۟ۙ

خُشَّعًا اَبْصَارُهُمْ يَخْرُجُوْنَ مِنَ الْاَجْدَاثِ كَاَنَّهُمْ جَرَادٌ مُّنْتَشِرٌ ۟ۙ

مُّهْطِعِيْنَ اِلَى الدَّاعِ ۘ يَقُوْلُ الْكٰفِرُوْنَ هٰذَا يَوْمٌ عَسِرٌ ۟

كَذَّبَتْ قَبْلَهُمْ قَوْمُ نُوْحٍ فَكَذَّبُوْا عَبْدَنَا وَقَالُوْا مَجْنُوْنٌ وَّازْدُجِرَ ۟

فَدَعَا رَبَّهٗٓ اَنِّيْ مَغْلُوْبٌ فَانْتَصِرْ ۟

فَفَتَحْنَآ اَبْوَابَ السَّمَآءِ بِمَآءٍ مُّنْهَمِرٍ ۟ؗۖ

وَّفَجَّرْنَا الْاَرْضَ عُيُوْنًا فَالْتَقَى الْمَآءُ عَلٰٓى اَمْرٍ قَدْ قُدِرَ ۟ۚ

وَحَمَلْنٰهُ عَلٰى ذَاتِ اَلْوَاحٍ وَّدُسُرٍ ۟ۙ

تَجْرِيْ بِاَعْيُنِنَا ۚ جَزَآءً لِّمَنْ كَانَ كُفِرَ ۟

وَلَقَدْ تَّرَكْنٰهَآ اٰيَةً فَهَلْ مِنْ مُّدَّكِرٍ ۟

530

16. How (great) was then My punishment and My warning!

17. And certainly We have made the Quran easy for remembrance, but is there anyone who will mind?

فَكَيْفَ كَانَ عَذَابِيْ وَنُذُرِ ۞

وَلَقَدْ يَسَّرْنَا الْقُرْاٰنَ لِلذِّكْرِ فَهَلْ مِنْ مُّدَّكِرٍ ۞

18. Ad treated (the truth) as a lie, so how (great) was My punishment and My warning!

كَذَّبَتْ عَادٌ فَكَيْفَ كَانَ عَذَابِيْ وَنُذُرِ ۞

19. Surely We sent on them a tornado in a day of bitter ill-luck,

20. Tearing men away as if they were the trunks of palm-trees torn up.

اِنَّا اَرْسَلْنَا عَلَيْهِمْ رِيْحًا صَرْصَرًا فِيْ يَوْمِ نَحْسٍ مُّسْتَمِرٍّ ۞

تَنْزِعُ النَّاسَ كَاَنَّهُمْ اَعْجَازُ نَخْلٍ مُّنْقَعِرٍ ۞

21. How (great) was then My punishment and My warning!

فَكَيْفَ كَانَ عَذَابِيْ وَنُذُرِ ۞

22. And certainly We have made the Quran easy for remembrance, but is there anyone who will mind?

وَلَقَدْ يَسَّرْنَا الْقُرْاٰنَ لِلذِّكْرِ فَهَلْ مِنْ مُّدَّكِرٍ ۞

23. Samood rejected the warning.

كَذَّبَتْ ثَمُوْدُ بِالنُّذُرِ ۞

24. So they said: What! a single mortal from among us! Shall we follow him? Most surely we shall in that case be in sure error and distress:

فَقَالُوْا اَبَشَرًا مِّنَّا وَاحِدًا نَّتَّبِعُهٗ اِنَّا اِذًا لَّفِيْ ضَلٰلٍ وَّسُعُرٍ ۞

25. Has the reminder been made to light upon him from among us? Nay! he is an insolent liar!

ءَاُلْقِيَ الذِّكْرُ عَلَيْهِ مِنْ بَيْنِنَا بَلْ هُوَ كَذَّابٌ اَشِرٌ ۞

26. Tomorrow shall they know who is the liar, the insolent one.

سَيَعْلَمُوْنَ غَدًا مَّنِ الْكَذَّابُ الْاَشِرُ ۞

27. Surely We are going to send the she-camel as a trial for them; therefore watch them and have patience.

اِنَّا مُرْسِلُوا النَّاقَةِ فِتْنَةً لَّهُمْ فَارْتَقِبْهُمْ وَاصْطَبِرْ ۞

28. And inform them that the water is shared between them; every share of the water shall be regulated.

وَنَبِّئْهُمْ اَنَّ الْمَآءَ قِسْمَةٌ بَيْنَهُمْ كُلُّ شِرْبٍ مُّحْتَضَرٌ ۞

29. But they called their companion, so he took (the sword) and slew (her).

فَنَادَوْا صَاحِبَهُمْ فَتَعَاطٰى فَعَقَرَ ۞

30. How (great) was then My punishment and My warning!

فَكَيْفَ كَانَ عَذَابِيْ وَنُذُرِ ۞

31. Surely We sent upon them a single cry, so they were like the dry fragments of trees which the maker of an enclosure collects.

اِنَّا اَرْسَلْنَا عَلَيْهِمْ صَيْحَةً وَّاحِدَةً فَكَانُوْا كَهَشِيْمِ الْمُحْتَظِرِ ۞

32. And certainly We have made the Quran easy for remembrance, but is there anyone who will mind?

وَلَقَدْ يَسَّرْنَا الْقُرْاٰنَ لِلذِّكْرِ فَهَلْ مِنْ مُّدَّكِرٍ ۞

33. The people of Lut treated the warning as a lie.

كَذَّبَتْ قَوْمُ لُوْطٍ بِالنُّذُرِ ۞

34. Surely We sent upon them a stone-storm, except Lut's followers; We saved them a little before daybreak,

اِنَّا اَرْسَلْنَا عَلَيْهِمْ حَاصِبًا اِلَّا اٰلَ لُوْطٍ نَّجَّيْنٰهُمْ بِسَحَرٍ ۞

35. A favor from Us; thus do We reward him who gives thanks.

36. And certainly he warned them of Our violent seizure, but they obstinately disputed the warning.

37. And certainly they endeavored to turn him from his guests, but We blinded their eyes; so taste My chastisement and My warning.

38. And certainly a lasting chastisement overtook them in the morning.

39. So taste My chastisement and My warning.

40. And certainly We have made the Quran easy for remembrance, but is there anyone who will mind?

41. And certainly the warning came to Firon's people.

42. They rejected all Our communications, so We overtook them after the manner of a Mighty, Powerful One.

43. Are the unbelievers of yours better than these, or is there an exemption for you in the scriptures?

44. Or do they say: We are a host allied together to help each other?

45. Soon shall the hosts be routed, and they shall turn (their) backs.

46. Nay, the hour is their promised time, and the hour shall be most grievous and bitter.

47. Surely the guilty are in error and distress.

48. On the day when they shall be dragged upon their faces into the fire; taste the touch of hell.

49. Surely We have created everything according to a measure.

50. And Our command is but one, as the twinkling of an eye.

51. And certainly We have already destroyed the likes of you, but is there anyone who will mind?

52. And everything they have done is in the writings.

53. And everything small and great is written down.

54. Surely those who guard (against evil) shall be in gardens and rivers,

55. In the seat of honor with a most Powerful King.

نِعْمَةً مِّنْ عِنْدِنَا كَذَلِكَ نَجْزِيْ مَنْ شَكَرَ ۞

وَلَقَدْ اَنْذَرَهُمْ بَطْشَتَنَا فَتَمَارَوْا بِالنُّذُرِ ۞

وَلَقَدْ رَاوَدُوْهُ عَنْ ضَيْفِهٖ فَطَمَسْنَا اَعْيُنَهُمْ فَذُوْقُوْا عَذَابِىْ وَنُذُرِ ۞

وَلَقَدْ صَبَّحَهُمْ بُكْرَةً عَذَابٌ مُّسْتَقِرٌّ ۞

فَذُوْقُوْا عَذَابِىْ وَنُذُرِ ۞

وَلَقَدْ يَسَّرْنَا الْقُرْاٰنَ لِلذِّكْرِ فَهَلْ مِنْ مُّدَّكِرٍ ۞

وَلَقَدْ جَاءَ اٰلَ فِرْعَوْنَ النُّذُرُ ۞

كَذَّبُوْا بِاٰيٰتِنَا كُلِّهَا فَاَخَذْنٰهُمْ اَخْذَ عَزِيْزٍ مُّقْتَدِرٍ ۞

اَكُفَّارُكُمْ خَيْرٌ مِّنْ اُولٰٓئِكُمْ اَمْ لَكُمْ بَرَآءَةٌ فِى الزُّبُرِ ۞

اَمْ يَقُوْلُوْنَ نَحْنُ جَمِيْعٌ مُّنْتَصِرٌ ۞

سَيُهْزَمُ الْجَمْعُ وَيُوَلُّوْنَ الدُّبُرَ ۞

بَلِ السَّاعَةُ مَوْعِدُهُمْ وَالسَّاعَةُ اَدْهٰى وَاَمَرُّ ۞

اِنَّ الْمُجْرِمِيْنَ فِىْ ضَلٰلٍ وَّسُعُرٍ ۞

يَوْمَ يُسْحَبُوْنَ فِى النَّارِ عَلٰى وُجُوْهِهِمْ ذُوْقُوْا مَسَّ سَقَرَ ۞

اِنَّا كُلَّ شَىْءٍ خَلَقْنٰهُ بِقَدَرٍ ۞

وَمَا اَمْرُنَا اِلَّا وَاحِدَةٌ كَلَمْحٍ بِالْبَصَرِ ۞

وَلَقَدْ اَهْلَكْنَا اَشْيَاعَكُمْ فَهَلْ مِنْ مُّدَّكِرٍ ۞

وَكُلُّ شَىْءٍ فَعَلُوْهُ فِى الزُّبُرِ ۞

وَكُلُّ صَغِيْرٍ وَّكَبِيْرٍ مُّسْتَطَرٌ ۞

اِنَّ الْمُتَّقِيْنَ فِىْ جَنّٰتٍ وَّنَهَرٍ ۞

فِىْ مَقْعَدِ صِدْقٍ عِنْدَ مَلِيْكٍ مُّقْتَدِرٍ ۞

THE BENEFICENT
(RAHMAN)

اياتها٥٥، سورة الرحمن مدنية رکوعاتها

بِسْمِ اللهِ الرَّحْمٰنِ الرَّحِيْمِ ۞

**In the name of Allah,
the Beneficent, the Merciful.**

1. The Beneficent God,

الرَّحْمٰنُ ۞

2. Taught the Quran.

عَلَّمَ الْقُرْاٰنَ ۞

3. He created man,

خَلَقَ الْاِنْسَانَ ۞

4. Taught him the mode of expression.

عَلَّمَهُ الْبَيَانَ ۞

5. The sun and the moon follow a reckoning.

الشَّمْسُ وَالْقَمَرُ بِحُسْبَانٍ ۞

6. And the herbs and the trees do adore (Him).

وَّالنَّجْمُ وَالشَّجَرُ يَسْجُدٰنِ ۞

7. And the heaven, He raised it high, and He made the balance,

وَالسَّمَاءَ رَفَعَهَا وَوَضَعَ الْمِيْزَانَ ۞

8. That you may not be inordinate in respect of the measure.

اَلَّا تَطْغَوْا فِى الْمِيْزَانِ ۞

9. And keep up the balance with equity and do not make the measure deficient.

وَاَقِيْمُوا الْوَزْنَ بِالْقِسْطِ وَلَا تُخْسِرُوا الْمِيْزَانَ ۞

10. And the earth, He has set it for living creatures;

وَالْاَرْضَ وَضَعَهَا لِلْاَنَامِ ۞

11. Therein is fruit and palms having sheathed clusters,

فِيْهَا فَاكِهَةٌ وَّالنَّخْلُ ذَاتُ الْاَكْمَامِ ۞

12. And the grain with (its) husk and fragrance.

وَالْحَبُّ ذُو الْعَصْفِ وَالرَّيْحَانُ ۞

13. Which then of the bounties of your Lord will you deny?

فَبِاَيِّ اٰلَاءِ رَبِّكُمَا تُكَذِّبٰنِ ۞

14. He created man from dry clay like earthen vessels,

خَلَقَ الْاِنْسَانَ مِنْ صَلْصَالٍ كَالْفَخَّارِ ۞

15. And He created the jinn of a flame of fire.

وَخَلَقَ الْجَانَّ مِنْ مَّارِجٍ مِّنْ نَّارٍ ۞

16. Which then of the bounties of your Lord will you deny?

فَبِاَيِّ اٰلَاءِ رَبِّكُمَا تُكَذِّبٰنِ ۞

17. Lord of the East and Lord of the West.

رَبُّ الْمَشْرِقَيْنِ وَرَبُّ الْمَغْرِبَيْنِ ۞

18. Which then of the bounties of your Lord will you deny?

فَبِاَيِّ اٰلَاءِ رَبِّكُمَا تُكَذِّبٰنِ ۞

19. He has made the two seas to flow freely (so that) they meet together:

مَرَجَ الْبَحْرَيْنِ يَلْتَقِيٰنِ ۞

533

20. Between them is a barrier which they cannot pass.

بَيْنَهُمَا بَرْزَخٌ لَّا يَبْغِيٰنِ ۞

21. Which then of the bounties of your Lord will you deny?

فَبِأَيِّ اٰلَاءِ رَبِّكُمَا تُكَذِّبٰنِ ۞

22. There come forth from them pearls, both large and small.

يَخْرُجُ مِنْهُمَا اللُّؤْلُؤُ وَالْمَرْجَانُ ۞

23. Which then of the bounties of your Lord will you deny?

فَبِأَيِّ اٰلَاءِ رَبِّكُمَا تُكَذِّبٰنِ ۞

24. And His are the ships reared aloft in the sea like mountains.

وَلَهُ الْجَوَارِ الْمُنْشَئَاتُ فِي الْبَحْرِ كَالْأَعْلَامِ ۞

25. Which then of the bounties of your Lord will you deny?

فَبِأَيِّ اٰلَاءِ رَبِّكُمَا تُكَذِّبٰنِ ۞

26. Everyone on it must pass away.

كُلُّ مَنْ عَلَيْهَا فَانٍ ۞

27. And there will endure for ever the person of your Lord, the Lord of glory and honor.

وَّيَبْقٰى وَجْهُ رَبِّكَ ذُو الْجَلَالِ وَالْإِكْرَامِ ۞

28. Which then of the bounties of your Lord will you deny?

فَبِأَيِّ اٰلَاءِ رَبِّكُمَا تُكَذِّبٰنِ ۞

29. All those who are in the heavens and the earth ask of Him; every moment He is in a state (of glory).

يَسْئَلُهُ مَنْ فِي السَّمٰوٰتِ وَالْأَرْضِ كُلَّ يَوْمٍ هُوَ فِي شَأْنٍ ۞

30. Which then of the bounties of your Lord will you deny?

فَبِأَيِّ اٰلَاءِ رَبِّكُمَا تُكَذِّبٰنِ ۞

31. Soon will We apply Ourselves to you, O you two armies.

سَنَفْرُغُ لَكُمْ أَيُّهَ الثَّقَلٰنِ ۞

32. Which then of the bounties of your Lord will you deny?

فَبِأَيِّ اٰلَاءِ رَبِّكُمَا تُكَذِّبٰنِ ۞

33. O assembly of the jinn and the men! If you are able to pass through the regions of the heavens and the earth, then pass through; you cannot pass through but with authority.

يٰمَعْشَرَ الْجِنِّ وَالْإِنْسِ إِنِ اسْتَطَعْتُمْ أَنْ تَنْفُذُوا مِنْ أَقْطَارِ السَّمٰوٰتِ وَالْأَرْضِ فَانْفُذُوا لَا تَنْفُذُونَ إِلَّا بِسُلْطٰنٍ ۞

34. Which then of the bounties of your Lord will you deny?

فَبِأَيِّ اٰلَاءِ رَبِّكُمَا تُكَذِّبٰنِ ۞

35. The flames of fire and smoke will be sent on you two, then you will not be able to defend yourselves.

يُرْسَلُ عَلَيْكُمَا شُوَاظٌ مِّنْ نَّارٍ وَّنُحَاسٌ فَلَا تَنْتَصِرٰنِ ۞

36. Which then of the bounties of your Lord will you deny?

فَبِأَيِّ اٰلَاءِ رَبِّكُمَا تُكَذِّبٰنِ ۞

37. And when the heaven is rent asunder, and then becomes red like red hide.

فَإِذَا انْشَقَّتِ السَّمَاءُ فَكَانَتْ وَرْدَةً كَالدِّهَانِ ۞

534

38. Which then of the bounties of your Lord will you deny?

فَبِاَيِّ اٰلَاۤءِ رَبِّكُمَا تُكَذِّبٰنِ ۞

39. So on that day neither man nor jinni shall be asked about his sin.

فَيَوْمَئِذٍ لَّا يُسْـَٔلُ عَنْ ذَنْۢبِهٖۤ اِنْسٌ وَّلَا جَآنٌّ ۞

40. Which then of the bounties of your Lord will you deny?

فَبِاَيِّ اٰلَاۤءِ رَبِّكُمَا تُكَذِّبٰنِ ۞

41. The guilty shall be recognized by their marks, so they shall be seized by the forelocks and the feet.

يُعْرَفُ الْمُجْرِمُوْنَ بِسِيْمٰهُمْ فَيُؤْخَذُ بِالنَّوَاصِيْ وَالْاَقْدَامِ ۞

42. Which then of the bounties of your Lord will you deny?

فَبِاَيِّ اٰلَاۤءِ رَبِّكُمَا تُكَذِّبٰنِ ۞

43. This is the hell which the guilty called a lie.

هٰذِهٖ جَهَنَّمُ الَّتِيْ يُكَذِّبُ بِهَا الْمُجْرِمُوْنَ ۞

44. Round about shall they go between it and hot, boiling water.

يَطُوْفُوْنَ بَيْنَهَا وَبَيْنَ حَمِيْمٍ اٰنٍ ۞

45. Which then of the bounties of your Lord will you deny?

فَبِاَيِّ اٰلَاۤءِ رَبِّكُمَا تُكَذِّبٰنِ ۞

46. And for him who fears to stand before his Lord are two gardens.

وَلِمَنْ خَافَ مَقَامَ رَبِّهٖ جَنَّتٰنِ ۞

47. Which then of the bounties of your Lord will you deny?

فَبِاَيِّ اٰلَاۤءِ رَبِّكُمَا تُكَذِّبٰنِ ۞

48. Having in them various kinds.

ذَوَاتَاۤ اَفْنَانٍ ۞

49. Which then of the bounties of your Lord will you deny?

فَبِاَيِّ اٰلَاۤءِ رَبِّكُمَا تُكَذِّبٰنِ ۞

50. In both of them are two fountains flowing.

فِيْهِمَا عَيْنٰنِ تَجْرِيٰنِ ۞

51. Which then of the bounties of your Lord will you deny?

فَبِاَيِّ اٰلَاۤءِ رَبِّكُمَا تُكَذِّبٰنِ ۞

52. In both of them are two pairs of every fruit.

فِيْهِمَا مِنْ كُلِّ فَاكِهَةٍ زَوْجٰنِ ۞

53. Which then of the bounties of your Lord will you deny?

فَبِاَيِّ اٰلَاۤءِ رَبِّكُمَا تُكَذِّبٰنِ ۞

54. Reclining on beds, the inner coverings of which are of silk brocade; and the fruits of the two gardens shall be within reach.

مُتَّكِئِيْنَ عَلٰى فُرُشٍ بَطَآئِنُهَا مِنْ اِسْتَبْرَقٍ وَّ جَنَا الْجَنَّتَيْنِ دَانٍ ۞

55. Which then of the bounties of your Lord will you deny?

فَبِاَيِّ اٰلَاۤءِ رَبِّكُمَا تُكَذِّبٰنِ ۞

56. In them shall be those who restrained their eyes; before them neither man nor jinni shall have touched them.

فِيْهِنَّ قٰصِرٰتُ الطَّرْفِ لَمْ يَطْمِثْهُنَّ اِنْسٌ قَبْلَهُمْ وَلَا جَآنٌّ ۞

57. Which then of the bounties of your Lord will you deny?

فَبِأَيِّ اٰلَآءِ رَبِّكُمَا تُكَذِّبٰنِ ۞

58. As though they were rubies and pearls.

كَأَنَّهُنَّ الْيَاقُوتُ وَالْمَرْجَانُ ۞

59. Which then of the bounties of your Lord will you deny?

فَبِأَيِّ اٰلَآءِ رَبِّكُمَا تُكَذِّبٰنِ ۞

60. Is the reward of goodness aught but goodness?

هَلْ جَزَآءُ الْاِحْسَانِ اِلَّا الْاِحْسَانُ ۞

61. Which then of the bounties of your Lord will you deny?

فَبِأَيِّ اٰلَآءِ رَبِّكُمَا تُكَذِّبٰنِ ۞

62. And besides these two are two (other) gardens:

وَمِنْ دُوْنِهِمَا جَنَّتٰنِ ۞

63. Which then of the bounties of your Lord will you deny?

فَبِأَيِّ اٰلَآءِ رَبِّكُمَا تُكَذِّبٰنِ ۞

64. Both inclining to blackness.

مُدْهَآمَّتٰنِ ۞

65. Which then of the bounties of your Lord will you deny?

فَبِأَيِّ اٰلَآءِ رَبِّكُمَا تُكَذِّبٰنِ ۞

66. In both of them are two springs gushing forth.

فِيْهِمَا عَيْنٰنِ نَضَّاخَتٰنِ ۞

67. Which then of the bounties of your Lord will you deny?

فَبِأَيِّ اٰلَآءِ رَبِّكُمَا تُكَذِّبٰنِ ۞

68. In both are fruits and palms and pomegranates.

فِيْهِمَا فَاكِهَةٌ وَّنَخْلٌ وَّرُمَّانٌ ۞

69. Which then of the bounties of your Lord will you deny?

فَبِأَيِّ اٰلَآءِ رَبِّكُمَا تُكَذِّبٰنِ ۞

70. In them are goodly things, beautiful ones.

فِيْهِنَّ خَيْرٰتٌ حِسَانٌ ۞

71. Which then of the bounties of your Lord will you deny?

فَبِأَيِّ اٰلَآءِ رَبِّكُمَا تُكَذِّبٰنِ ۞

72. Pure ones confined to the pavilions.

حُوْرٌ مَّقْصُوْرٰتٌ فِى الْخِيَامِ ۞

73. Which then of the bounties of your Lord will you deny?

فَبِأَيِّ اٰلَآءِ رَبِّكُمَا تُكَذِّبٰنِ ۞

74. Man has not touched them before them nor jinni.

لَمْ يَطْمِثْهُنَّ اِنْسٌ قَبْلَهُمْ وَلَا جَانٌّ ۞

75. Which then of the bounties of your Lord will you deny?

فَبِأَيِّ اٰلَآءِ رَبِّكُمَا تُكَذِّبٰنِ ۞

76. Reclining on green cushions and beautiful carpets.

مُتَّكِئِيْنَ عَلٰى رَفْرَفٍ خُضْرٍ وَّعَبْقَرِيٍّ حِسَانٍ ۞

77. Which then of the bounties of your Lord will you deny?

فَبِأَيِّ اٰلَآءِ رَبِّكُمَا تُكَذِّبٰنِ ۞

78. Blessed be the name of your Lord, the Lord of Glory and Honor!

تَبٰرَكَ اسْمُ رَبِّكَ ذِى الْجَلٰلِ وَالْاِكْرَامِ ۞

THE GREAT EVENT
(WAQIA)

انها ١٩٥ سورة الواقعة مكية رٰوعاتها

**In the name of Allah,
the Beneficent, the Merciful.**

بِسْمِ اللهِ الرَّحْمٰنِ الرَّحِيمِ ۞

1. When the great event comes to pass,

اِذَا وَقَعَتِ الْوَاقِعَةُ ۞

2. There is no belying its coming to pass—

لَيْسَ لِوَقْعَتِهَا كَاذِبَةٌ ۞

3. Abasing (one party), exalting (the other),

خَافِضَةٌ رَّافِعَةٌ ۞

4. When the earth shall be shaken with a (severe) shaking,

اِذَا رُجَّتِ الْاَرْضُ رَجًّا ۞

5. And the mountains shall be made to crumble with (an awful) crumbling,

وَّبُسَّتِ الْجِبَالُ بَسًّا ۞

6. So that they shall be as scattered dust.

فَكَانَتْ هَبَآءً مُّنْبَثًّا ۞

7. And you shall be three sorts.

وَّكُنْتُمْ اَزْوَاجًا ثَلٰثَةً ۞

8. Then (as to) the companions of the right hand; how happy are the companions of the right hand!

فَاَصْحٰبُ الْمَيْمَنَةِ مَآ اَصْحٰبُ الْمَيْمَنَةِ ۞

9. And (as to) the companions of the left hand; how wretched are the companions of the left hand!

وَاَصْحٰبُ الْمَشْـَٔمَةِ مَآ اَصْحٰبُ الْمَشْـَٔمَةِ ۞

10. And the foremost are the foremost,

وَالسّٰبِقُوْنَ السّٰبِقُوْنَ ۞

11. These are they who are drawn nigh (to Allah),

اُولٰٓئِكَ الْمُقَرَّبُوْنَ ۞

12. In the gardens of bliss.

فِيْ جَنّٰتِ النَّعِيْمِ ۞

13. A numerous company from among the first,

ثُلَّةٌ مِّنَ الْاَوَّلِيْنَ ۞

14. And a few from among the latter.

وَقَلِيْلٌ مِّنَ الْاٰخِرِيْنَ ۞

15. On thrones decorated,

عَلٰى سُرُرٍ مَّوْضُوْنَةٍ ۞

16. Reclining on them, facing one another.

مُّتَّكِئِيْنَ عَلَيْهَا مُتَقٰبِلِيْنَ ۞

17. Round about them shall go youths never altering in age,

يَطُوْفُ عَلَيْهِمْ وِلْدَانٌ مُّخَلَّدُوْنَ ۞

18. With goblets and ewers and a cup of pure drink;

بِاَكْوَابٍ وَّاَبَارِيْقَ ەۙ وَكَأْسٍ مِّنْ مَّعِيْنٍ ۞

19. They shall not be affected with headache thereby, nor shall they get exhausted;

لَّا يُصَدَّعُوْنَ عَنْهَا وَلَا يُنْزِفُوْنَ ۞

537

20. And fruits such as they choose,

وَفَاكِهَةٍ مِّمَّا يَتَخَيَّرُوْنَ ۙ

21. And the flesh of fowl such as they desire.

وَلَحْمِ طَيْرٍ مِّمَّا يَشْتَهُوْنَ ۙ

22. And pure, beautiful ones,

وَحُوْرٌ عِيْنٌ ۙ

23. The like of the hidden pearls:

كَأَمْثَالِ اللُّؤْلُؤِ الْمَكْنُوْنِ ۚ

24. A reward for what they used to do.

جَزَآءًۢ بِمَا كَانُوْا يَعْمَلُوْنَ ۟

25. They shall not hear therein vain or sinful discourse,

لَا يَسْمَعُوْنَ فِيْهَا لَغْوًا وَّلَا تَأْثِيْمًا ۙ

26. Except the word peace, peace.

إِلَّا قِيْلًا سَلٰمًا سَلٰمًا ۟

27. And the companions of the right hand; how happy are the companions of the right hand!

وَأَصْحَابُ الْيَمِيْنِ ۙ مَآ أَصْحَابُ الْيَمِيْنِ ۟

28. Amid thornless lote-trees,

فِيْ سِدْرٍ مَّخْضُوْدٍ ۙ

29. And banana-trees (with fruits), one above another.

وَّطَلْحٍ مَّنْضُوْدٍ ۙ

30. And extended shade,

وَّظِلٍّ مَّمْدُوْدٍ ۙ

31. And water flowing constantly,

وَّمَآءٍ مَّسْكُوْبٍ ۙ

32. And abundant fruit,

وَّفَاكِهَةٍ كَثِيْرَةٍ ۙ

33. Neither intercepted nor forbidden,

لَّا مَقْطُوْعَةٍ وَّلَا مَمْنُوْعَةٍ ۙ

34. And exalted thrones.

وَّفُرُشٍ مَّرْفُوْعَةٍ ۟

35. Surely We have made them to grow into a (new) growth,

إِنَّآ أَنْشَأْنٰهُنَّ إِنْشَآءً ۙ

36. Then We have made them virgins,

فَجَعَلْنٰهُنَّ أَبْكَارًا ۙ

37. Loving, equals in age,

عُرُبًا أَتْرَابًا ۙ

38. For the sake of the companions of the right hand.

لِّأَصْحَابِ الْيَمِيْنِ ۟ ؏

39. A numerous company from among the first,

ثُلَّةٌ مِّنَ الْأَوَّلِيْنَ ۙ

40. And a numerous company from among the last.

وَثُلَّةٌ مِّنَ الْاٰخِرِيْنَ ۟

41. And those of the left hand, how wretched are those of the left hand!

وَأَصْحَابُ الشِّمَالِ ۙ مَآ أَصْحَابُ الشِّمَالِ ۟

42. In hot wind and boiling water,

43. And the shade of black smoke,

44. Neither cool nor honorable.

45. Surely they were before that made to live in ease and plenty.

46. And they persisted in the great violation.

47. And they used to say: What! when we die and have become dust and bones, shall we then indeed be raised?

48. Or our fathers of yore?

49. Say: The first and the last,

50. Shall most surely be gathered together for the appointed hour of a known day.

51. Then shall you, O you who err and call it a lie!

52. Most surely eat of a tree of Zaqqoom,

53. And fill (your) bellies with it;

54. Then drink over it of boiling water;

55. And drink as drinks the thirsty camel.

56. This is their entertainment on the day of requital.

57. We have created you, why do you not then assent?

58. Have you considered the seed?

59. Is it you that create it or are We the creators?

60. We have ordained death among you and We are not to be overcome,

61. In order that We may bring in your place the likes of you and make you grow into what you know not.

62. And certainly you know the first growth, why do you not then mind?

دَلَقَدْ عَلِمْتُمُ النَّشْأَةَ الْأُوْلٰى فَلَوْلَا تَذَكَّرُوْنَ ٦٢

63. Have you considered what you sow?

اَفَرَءَيْتُمْ مَّا تَحْرُثُوْنَ ٦٣

64. Is it you that cause it to grow, or are We the causers of growth?

ءَاَنْتُمْ تَزْرَعُوْنَهٗ اَمْ نَحْنُ الزَّارِعُوْنَ ٦٤

65. If We pleased, We should have certainly made it broken down into pieces, then would you begin to lament:

لَوْ نَشَآءُ لَجَعَلْنٰهُ حُطَامًا فَظَلْتُمْ تَفَكَّهُوْنَ ٦٥

66. Surely we are burdened with debt:

اِنَّا لَمُغْرَمُوْنَ ٦٦

67. Nay! we are deprived.

بَلْ نَحْنُ مَحْرُوْمُوْنَ ٦٧

68. Have you considered the water which you drink?

اَفَرَءَيْتُمُ الْمَآءَ الَّذِيْ تَشْرَبُوْنَ ٦٨

69. Is it you that send it down from the clouds, or are We the senders?

ءَاَنْتُمْ اَنْزَلْتُمُوْهُ مِنَ الْمُزْنِ اَمْ نَحْنُ الْمُنْزِلُوْنَ ٦٩

70. If We pleased, We would have made it salty; why do you not then give thanks?

لَوْ نَشَآءُ جَعَلْنٰهُ اُجَاجًا فَلَوْلَا تَشْكُرُوْنَ ٧٠

71. Have you considered the fire which you strike?

اَفَرَءَيْتُمُ النَّارَ الَّتِيْ تُوْرُوْنَ ٧١

72. Is it you that produce the trees for it, or are We the producers?

ءَاَنْتُمْ اَنْشَأْتُمْ شَجَرَتَهَآ اَمْ نَحْنُ الْمُنْشِئُوْنَ ٧٢

73. We have made it a reminder and an advantage for the wayfarers of the desert.

نَحْنُ جَعَلْنٰهَا تَذْكِرَةً وَّ مَتَاعًا لِّلْمُقْوِيْنَ ٧٣

74. Therefore glorify the name of your Lord, the Great.

فَسَبِّحْ بِاسْمِ رَبِّكَ الْعَظِيْمِ ٧٤

75. But nay! I swear by the falling of stars;

فَلَآ اُقْسِمُ بِمَوَاقِعِ النُّجُوْمِ ٧٥

76. And most surely it is a very great oath if you only knew;

وَاِنَّهٗ لَقَسَمٌ لَّوْ تَعْلَمُوْنَ عَظِيْمٌ ٧٦

77. Most surely it is an honored Quran,

اِنَّهٗ لَقُرْاٰنٌ كَرِيْمٌ ٧٧

78. In a book that is protected;

فِيْ كِتٰبٍ مَّكْنُوْنٍ ٧٨

79. None shall touch it save the purified ones.

لَّا يَمَسُّهٗٓ اِلَّا الْمُطَهَّرُوْنَ ٧٩

80. A revelation by the Lord of the worlds.

تَنْزِيْلٌ مِّنْ رَّبِّ الْعٰلَمِيْنَ ٨٠

81. Do you then hold this announcement in contempt?

اَفَبِهٰذَا الْحَدِيْثِ اَنْتُمْ مُّدْهِنُوْنَ ٨١

82. And to give (it) the lie you make your means of subsistence.

83. Why is it not then that when it (soul) comes up to the throat,

84. And you at that time look on—

85. And We are nearer to it than you, but you do not see—

86. Then why is it not—if you are not held under authority—

87. That you send it (not) back—if you are truthful?

88. Then if he is one of those drawn nigh (to Allah),

89. Then happiness and bounty and a garden of bliss.

90. And if he is one of those on the right hand,

91. Then peace to you from those on the right hand.

92. And if he is one of the rejecters, the erring ones,

93. He shall have an entertainment of boiling water,

94. And burning in hell.

95. Most surely this is a certain truth.

96. Therefore glorify the name of your Lord, the Great.

وَتَجْعَلُوْنَ رِزْقَكُمْ اَنَّكُمْ تُكَذِّبُوْنَ ۞

فَلَوْلَا اِذَا بَلَغَتِ الْحُلْقُوْمَ ۙ

وَاَنْتُمْ حِيْنَئِذٍ تَنْظُرُوْنَ ۙ

وَنَحْنُ اَقْرَبُ اِلَيْهِ مِنْكُمْ وَلٰكِنْ لَّا تُبْصِرُوْنَ ۞

فَلَوْلَا اِنْ كُنْتُمْ غَيْرَ مَدِيْنِيْنَ ۙ

تَرْجِعُوْنَهَا اِنْ كُنْتُمْ صٰدِقِيْنَ ۞

فَاَمَّا اِنْ كَانَ مِنَ الْمُقَرَّبِيْنَ ۙ

فَرَوْحٌ وَّرَيْحَانٌ ۙ وَّجَنَّتُ نَعِيْمٍ ۞

وَاَمَّا اِنْ كَانَ مِنْ اَصْحٰبِ الْيَمِيْنِ ۙ

فَسَلٰمٌ لَّكَ مِنْ اَصْحٰبِ الْيَمِيْنِ ۞

وَاَمَّا اِنْ كَانَ مِنَ الْمُكَذِّبِيْنَ الضَّآلِّيْنَ ۙ

فَنُزُلٌ مِّنْ حَمِيْمٍ ۙ

وَّتَصْلِيَةُ جَحِيْمٍ ۞

اِنَّ هٰذَا لَهُوَ حَقُّ الْيَقِيْنِ ۞

فَسَبِّحْ بِاسْمِ رَبِّكَ الْعَظِيْمِ ۞

541

IRON
(HADID)

ايَاتُهَا ٢٩، سُورَةُ الْحَدِيْدِ مَدَنِيَّةٌ رُكُوعَاتُهَا

In the name of Allah,
the Beneficent, the Merciful.

بِسْمِ اللهِ الرَّحْمٰنِ الرَّحِيْمِ ۞

1. Whatever is in the heavens and the earth declares the glory of Allah, and He is the Mighty, the Wise.

سَبَّحَ لِلّٰهِ مَا فِى السَّمٰوٰتِ وَالْاَرْضِ ۚ وَهُوَ الْعَزِيْزُ الْحَكِيْمُ ۞

2. His is the kingdom of the heavens and the earth; He gives life and causes death; and He has power over all things.

لَهٗ مُلْكُ السَّمٰوٰتِ وَالْاَرْضِ ۚ يُحْيٖ وَيُمِيْتُ ۚ وَهُوَ عَلٰى كُلِّ شَىْءٍ قَدِيْرٌ ۞

3. He is the First and the Last and the Ascendant (over all) and the Knower of hidden things, and He is Cognizant of all things.

هُوَ الْاَوَّلُ وَالْاٰخِرُ وَالظَّاهِرُ وَالْبَاطِنُ ۚ وَهُوَ بِكُلِّ شَىْءٍ عَلِيْمٌ ۞

4. He it is who created the heavens and the earth in six periods, and He is firm in power; He knows that which goes deep down into the earth and that which comes forth out of it, and that which comes down from the heaven and that which goes up into it, and He is with you wherever you are; and Allah sees what you do.

هُوَ الَّذِىْ خَلَقَ السَّمٰوٰتِ وَالْاَرْضَ فِىْ سِتَّةِ اَيَّامٍ ثُمَّ اسْتَوٰى عَلَى الْعَرْشِ ۚ يَعْلَمُ مَا يَلِجُ فِى الْاَرْضِ وَمَا يَخْرُجُ مِنْهَا وَمَا يَنْزِلُ مِنَ السَّمَاءِ وَمَا يَعْرُجُ فِيْهَا ۚ وَهُوَ مَعَكُمْ اَيْنَ مَا كُنْتُمْ ۚ وَاللّٰهُ بِمَا تَعْمَلُوْنَ بَصِيْرٌ ۞

5. His is the kingdom of the heavens and the earth; and to Allah are (all) affairs returned.

لَهٗ مُلْكُ السَّمٰوٰتِ وَالْاَرْضِ ۚ وَاِلَى اللّٰهِ تُرْجَعُ الْاُمُوْرُ ۞

6. He causes the night to enter in upon the day, and causes the day to enter in upon the night, and He is Cognizant of what is in the hearts.

يُوْلِجُ الَّيْلَ فِى النَّهَارِ وَيُوْلِجُ النَّهَارَ فِى الَّيْلِ ۚ وَهُوَ عَلِيْمٌۢ بِذَاتِ الصُّدُوْرِ ۞

7. Believe in Allah and His Apostle, and spend out of what He has made you to be successors of; for those of you who believe and spend shall have a great reward.

اٰمِنُوْا بِاللّٰهِ وَرَسُوْلِهٖ وَاَنْفِقُوْا مِمَّا جَعَلَكُمْ مُّسْتَخْلَفِيْنَ فِيْهِ ۚ فَالَّذِيْنَ اٰمَنُوْا مِنْكُمْ وَاَنْفَقُوْا لَهُمْ اَجْرٌ كَبِيْرٌ ۞

8. And what reason have you that you should not believe in Allah? And the Apostle calls on you that you may believe in your Lord, and indeed He has made a covenant with you if you are believers.

وَمَا لَكُمْ لَا تُؤْمِنُوْنَ بِاللّٰهِ ۚ وَالرَّسُوْلُ يَدْعُوْكُمْ لِتُؤْمِنُوْا بِرَبِّكُمْ وَقَدْ اَخَذَ مِيْثَاقَكُمْ اِنْ كُنْتُمْ مُّؤْمِنِيْنَ ۝

9. He it is who sends down clear communications upon His servant, that he may bring you forth from utter darkness into light; and most surely Allah is Kind, Merciful to you.

هُوَ الَّذِيْ يُنَزِّلُ عَلٰى عَبْدِهٖۤ اٰيٰتٍۭ بَيِّنٰتٍ لِّيُخْرِجَكُمْ مِّنَ الظُّلُمٰتِ اِلَى النُّوْرِ ۚ وَاِنَّ اللّٰهَ بِكُمْ لَرَءُوْفٌ رَّحِيْمٌ ۝

10. And what reason have you that you should not spend in Allah's way? And Allah's is the inheritance of the heavens and the earth; not alike among you are those who spent before the victory and fought (and those who did not): they are more exalted in rank than those who spent and fought afterwards; and Allah has promised good to all; and Allah is Aware of what you do.

وَمَا لَكُمْ اَلَّا تُنْفِقُوْا فِيْ سَبِيْلِ اللّٰهِ وَلِلّٰهِ مِيْرَاثُ السَّمٰوٰتِ وَالْاَرْضِ ۚ لَا يَسْتَوِيْ مِنْكُمْ مَّنْ اَنْفَقَ مِنْ قَبْلِ الْفَتْحِ وَقٰتَلَ ۚ اُولٰٓئِكَ اَعْظَمُ دَرَجَةً مِّنَ الَّذِيْنَ اَنْفَقُوْا مِنْۢ بَعْدُ وَقٰتَلُوْا ۚ وَكُلًّا وَّعَدَ اللّٰهُ الْحُسْنٰى ۚ وَاللّٰهُ بِمَا تَعْمَلُوْنَ خَبِيْرٌ ۝

11. Who is there that will offer to Allah a good gift so He will double it for him, and he shall have an excellent reward.

مَنْ ذَا الَّذِيْ يُقْرِضُ اللّٰهَ قَرْضًا حَسَنًا فَيُضٰعِفَهٗ لَهٗ وَلَهٗۤ اَجْرٌ كَرِيْمٌ ۝

12. On that day you will see the faithful men and the faithful women—their light running before them and on their right hand—good news for you today: gardens beneath which rivers flow, to abide therein, that is the grand achievement.

يَوْمَ تَرَى الْمُؤْمِنِيْنَ وَالْمُؤْمِنٰتِ يَسْعٰى نُوْرُهُمْ بَيْنَ اَيْدِيْهِمْ وَبِاَيْمَانِهِمْ بُشْرٰىكُمُ الْيَوْمَ جَنّٰتٌ تَجْرِيْ مِنْ تَحْتِهَا الْاَنْهٰرُ خٰلِدِيْنَ فِيْهَا ذٰلِكَ هُوَ الْفَوْزُ الْعَظِيْمُ ۝

13. On the day when the hypocritical men and the hypocritical women will say to those who believe: Wait for us, that we may have light from your light; it shall be said: Turn back and seek a light. Then separation would be brought about between them, with a wall having a door in it; (as for) the inside of it, there shall be mercy in it, and (as for) the outside of it, before it there shall be punishment.

يَوْمَ يَقُوْلُ الْمُنٰفِقُوْنَ وَالْمُنٰفِقٰتُ لِلَّذِيْنَ اٰمَنُوا انْظُرُوْنَا نَقْتَبِسْ مِنْ نُّوْرِكُمْ قِيْلَ ارْجِعُوْا وَرَاءَكُمْ فَالْتَمِسُوْا نُوْرًا ۚ فَضُرِبَ بَيْنَهُمْ بِسُوْرٍ لَّهٗ بَابٌ ۚ بَاطِنُهٗ فِيْهِ الرَّحْمَةُ وَظَاهِرُهٗ مِنْ قِبَلِهِ الْعَذَابُ ۝

14. They will cry out to them: Were we not with you? They shall say: Yea! but you caused yourselves to fall into temptation, and you waited and doubted, and vain desires deceived you till the threatened punishment of Allah came, while the arch-deceiver deceived you about Allah.

15. So today ransom shall not be accepted from you nor from those who disbelieved; your abode is the fire; it is your friend, and evil is the resort.

16. Has not the time yet come for those who believe that their hearts should be humble for the remembrance of Allah and what has come down of the truth? And (that) they should not be like those who were given the Book before, but the time became prolonged to them, so their hearts hardened, and most of them are transgressors.

17. Know that Allah gives life to the earth after its death; indeed, We have made the communications clear to you that you may understand.

18. Surely (as for) the charitable men and the charitable women and (those who) set apart for Allah a goodly portion, it shall be doubled for them and they shall have a noble reward.

19. And (as for) those who believe in Allah and His apostles, these it is that are the truthful and the faithful ones in the sight of their Lord: they shall have their reward and their light; and (as for) those who disbelieve and reject Our communications, these are the inmates of the hell.

20. Know that this world's life is only sport and play and gaiety and boasting among yourselves, and a vying in the multiplication of wealth and children, like the rain, whose causing the vegetation to grow, pleases the husbandmen; then it withers away so that you will see it become yellow, then it becomes dried up and broken down; and in the hereafter is a severe chastisement and (also) forgiveness from Allah and (His) pleasure; and this world's life is naught but means of deception.

يُنَادُونَهُمْ اَلَمْ نَكُنْ مَّعَكُمْ قَالُوْا بَلٰى وَلٰكِنَّكُمْ
فَتَنْتُمْ اَنْفُسَكُمْ وَتَرَبَّصْتُمْ وَارْتَبْتُمْ وَغَرَّتْكُمُ
الْاَمَانِيُّ حَتّٰى جَآءَ اَمْرُ اللّٰهِ وَغَرَّكُمْ بِاللّٰهِ الْغَرُوْرُ ۞

فَالْيَوْمَ لَا يُؤْخَذُ مِنْكُمْ فِدْيَةٌ وَّلَا مِنَ الَّذِيْنَ كَفَرُوْا
مَأْوٰىكُمُ النَّارُ هِيَ مَوْلٰىكُمْ وَبِئْسَ الْمَصِيْرُ ۞

اَلَمْ يَأْنِ لِلَّذِيْنَ اٰمَنُوْا اَنْ تَخْشَعَ قُلُوْبُهُمْ لِذِكْرِ
اللّٰهِ وَمَا نَزَلَ مِنَ الْحَقِّ وَلَا يَكُوْنُوْا كَالَّذِيْنَ
اُوْتُوا الْكِتٰبَ مِنْ قَبْلُ فَطَالَ عَلَيْهِمُ الْاَمَدُ
فَقَسَتْ قُلُوْبُهُمْ وَكَثِيْرٌ مِّنْهُمْ فٰسِقُوْنَ ۞

اِعْلَمُوْا اَنَّ اللّٰهَ يُحْيِ الْاَرْضَ بَعْدَ مَوْتِهَا قَدْ
بَيَّنَّا لَكُمُ الْاٰيٰتِ لَعَلَّكُمْ تَعْقِلُوْنَ ۞

اِنَّ الْمُصَّدِّقِيْنَ وَالْمُصَّدِّقٰتِ وَاَقْرَضُوا اللّٰهَ
قَرْضًا حَسَنًا يُّضٰعَفُ لَهُمْ وَلَهُمْ اَجْرٌ كَرِيْمٌ ۞

وَالَّذِيْنَ اٰمَنُوْا بِاللّٰهِ وَرُسُلِهٖ اُولٰٓئِكَ هُمُ الصِّدِّيْقُوْنَ
وَالشُّهَدَآءُ عِنْدَ رَبِّهِمْ لَهُمْ اَجْرُهُمْ وَنُوْرُهُمْ وَالَّذِيْنَ
كَفَرُوْا وَكَذَّبُوْا بِاٰيٰتِنَا اُولٰٓئِكَ اَصْحٰبُ الْجَحِيْمِ ۞

اِعْلَمُوْا اَنَّمَا الْحَيٰوةُ الدُّنْيَا لَعِبٌ وَّلَهْوٌ وَّزِيْنَةٌ وَّ
تَفَاخُرٌ بَيْنَكُمْ وَتَكَاثُرٌ فِي الْاَمْوَالِ وَالْاَوْلَادِ كَمَثَلِ
غَيْثٍ اَعْجَبَ الْكُفَّارَ نَبَاتُهٗ ثُمَّ يَهِيْجُ فَتَرٰىهُ
مُصْفَرًّا ثُمَّ يَكُوْنُ حُطَامًا وَفِي الْاٰخِرَةِ عَذَابٌ
شَدِيْدٌ وَّمَغْفِرَةٌ مِّنَ اللّٰهِ وَرِضْوَانٌ وَمَا الْحَيٰوةُ
الدُّنْيَا اِلَّا مَتَاعُ الْغُرُوْرِ ۞

21. Hasten to forgiveness from your Lord and to a garden the extensiveness of which is as the extensiveness of the heaven and the earth; it is prepared for those who believe in Allah and His apostles; that is the grace of Allah: He gives it to whom He pleases, and Allah is the Lord of mighty grace.

سَابِقُوْٓا اِلٰی مَغْفِرَةٍ مِّنْ رَّبِّكُمْ وَجَنَّةٍ عَرْضُهَا كَعَرْضِ السَّمَآءِ وَالْاَرْضِ اُعِدَّتْ لِلَّذِيْنَ اٰمَنُوْا بِاللّٰهِ وَرُسُلِهٖ ذٰلِكَ فَضْلُ اللّٰهِ يُؤْتِيْهِ مَنْ يَّشَآءُ وَاللّٰهُ ذُو الْفَضْلِ الْعَظِيْمِ ۝

22. No evil befalls on the earth nor in your own souls, but it is in a book before We bring it into existence; surely that is easy to Allah:

مَآ اَصَابَ مِنْ مُّصِيْبَةٍ فِی الْاَرْضِ وَلَا فِیْٓ اَنْفُسِكُمْ اِلَّا فِیْ كِتٰبٍ مِّنْ قَبْلِ اَنْ نَّبْرَاَهَا اِنَّ ذٰلِكَ عَلَی اللّٰهِ يَسِيْرٌ ۝

23. So that you may not grieve for what has escaped you, nor be exultant at what He has given you; and Allah does not love any arrogant boaster:

لِّكَيْلَا تَاْسَوْا عَلٰی مَا فَاتَكُمْ وَلَا تَفْرَحُوْا بِمَآ اٰتٰىكُمْ وَاللّٰهُ لَا يُحِبُّ كُلَّ مُخْتَالٍ فَخُوْرٍ ۝

24. Those who are niggardly and enjoin niggardliness on men; and whoever turns back, then surely Allah is He Who is the Self-sufficient, the Praised.

اِلَّذِيْنَ يَبْخَلُوْنَ وَيَاْمُرُوْنَ النَّاسَ بِالْبُخْلِ وَمَنْ يَّتَوَلَّ فَاِنَّ اللّٰهَ هُوَ الْغَنِیُّ الْحَمِيْدُ ۝

25. Certainly We sent Our apostles with clear arguments, and sent down with them the Book and the balance that men may conduct themselves with equity; and We have made the iron, wherein is great violence and advantages to men, and that Allah may know who helps Him and His apostles in the secret; surely Allah is Strong, Mighty.

لَقَدْ اَرْسَلْنَا رُسُلَنَا بِالْبَيِّنٰتِ وَاَنْزَلْنَا مَعَهُمُ الْكِتٰبَ وَالْمِيْزَانَ لِيَقُوْمَ النَّاسُ بِالْقِسْطِ وَاَنْزَلْنَا الْحَدِيْدَ فِيْهِ بَاْسٌ شَدِيْدٌ وَّمَنَافِعُ لِلنَّاسِ وَلِيَعْلَمَ اللّٰهُ مَنْ يَّنْصُرُهٗ وَرُسُلَهٗ بِالْغَيْبِ اِنَّ اللّٰهَ قَوِیٌّ عَزِيْزٌ ۝

26. And certainly We sent Nuh and Ibrahim and We gave to their offspring the (gift of) prophecy and the Book; so there are among them those who go aright, and most of them are transgressors.

وَلَقَدْ اَرْسَلْنَا نُوْحًا وَّاِبْرٰهِيْمَ وَجَعَلْنَا فِیْ ذُرِّيَّتِهِمَا النُّبُوَّةَ وَالْكِتٰبَ فَمِنْهُمْ مُّهْتَدٍ وَّكَثِيْرٌ مِّنْهُمْ فٰسِقُوْنَ ۝

27. Then We made Our apostles to follow in their footsteps, and We sent Isa son of Marium afterwards, and We gave him the Injeel; and We put in the hearts of those who followed him kindness and mercy; and (as for) monkery, they innovated it—We did not prescribe it to them— only to seek Allah's pleasure, but they did not observe it with its due observance; so We gave to those of them who believed their reward, and most of them are transgressors.

ثُمَّ قَفَّيْنَا عَلٰٓى اٰثَارِهِمْ بِرُسُلِنَا وَقَفَّيْنَا بِعِيْسَى ابْنِ مَرْيَمَ وَاٰتَيْنٰهُ الْاِنْجِيْلَ ۙ وَجَعَلْنَا فِيْ قُلُوْبِ الَّذِيْنَ اتَّبَعُوْهُ رَاْفَةً وَّرَحْمَةً ۗ وَرَهْبَانِيَّةَ اِبْتَدَعُوْهَا مَا كَتَبْنٰهَا عَلَيْهِمْ اِلَّا ابْتِغَآءَ رِضْوَانِ اللّٰهِ فَمَا رَعَوْهَا حَقَّ رِعَايَتِهَا ۚ فَاٰتَيْنَا الَّذِيْنَ اٰمَنُوْا مِنْهُمْ اَجْرَهُمْ ۚ وَكَثِيْرٌ مِّنْهُمْ فٰسِقُوْنَ ۝

28. O you who believe! be careful of (your duty to) Allah and believe in His Apostle: He will give you two portions of His mercy, and make for you a light with which you will walk, and forgive you, and Allah is Forgiving, Merciful;

يٰٓاَيُّهَا الَّذِيْنَ اٰمَنُوا اتَّقُوا اللّٰهَ وَاٰمِنُوْا بِرَسُوْلِهٖ يُؤْتِكُمْ كِفْلَيْنِ مِنْ رَّحْمَتِهٖ وَيَجْعَلْ لَّكُمْ نُوْرًا تَمْشُوْنَ بِهٖ وَيَغْفِرْ لَكُمْ ۗ وَاللّٰهُ غَفُوْرٌ رَّحِيْمٌ ۝

29. So that the followers of the Book may know that they do not control aught of the grace of Allah, and that grace is in Allah's hand, He gives it to whom He pleases; and Allah is the Lord of mighty grace.

لِّئَلَّا يَعْلَمَ اَهْلُ الْكِتٰبِ اَلَّا يَقْدِرُوْنَ عَلٰى شَيْءٍ مِّنْ فَضْلِ اللّٰهِ وَاَنَّ الْفَضْلَ بِيَدِ اللّٰهِ يُؤْتِيْهِ مَنْ يَّشَآءُ ۚ وَاللّٰهُ ذُو الْفَضْلِ الْعَظِيْمِ ۝

THE PLEADING ONE
(MUJADILAH)

**In the name of Allah,
the Beneficent, the Merciful.**

1. Allah indeed knows the plea of her who pleads with you about her husband and complains to Allah, and Allah knows the contentions of both of you; surely Allah is Hearing, Seeing.

2. (As for) those of you who put away their wives by likening their backs to the backs of their mothers, they are not their mothers; their mothers are no others than those who gave them birth; and most surely they utter a hateful word and a falsehood; and most surely Allah is Pardoning, Forgiving.

3. And (as for) those who put away their wives by likening their backs to the backs of their mothers then would recall what they said, they should free a captive before they touch each other; to that you are admonished (to conform); and Allah is Aware of what you do.

4. But whoever has not the means, let him fast for two months successively before they touch each other; then as for him who is not able, let him feed sixty needy ones; that is in order that you may have faith in Allah and His Apostle, and these are Allah's limits, and the unbelievers shall have a painful punishment.

5. Surely those who act in opposition to Allah and His Apostle shall be laid down prostrate as those before them were laid down prostrate; and indeed We have revealed clear communications, and the unbelievers shall have an abasing chastisement.

6. On the day when Allah will raise them up all together, then inform them of what they did: Allah has recorded it while they have forgotten it; and Allah is a witness of all things.

بِسْمِ اللهِ الرَّحْمٰنِ الرَّحِيمِ ۞

قَدْ سَمِعَ اللهُ قَوْلَ الَّتِي تُجَادِلُكَ فِي زَوْجِهَا وَتَشْتَكِي إِلَى اللهِ ۖ وَاللهُ يَسْمَعُ تَحَاوُرَكُمَا ۚ إِنَّ اللهَ سَمِيعٌ بَصِيرٌ ۞

اَلَّذِينَ يُظَاهِرُونَ مِنْكُمْ مِنْ نِسَائِهِمْ مَا هُنَّ أُمَّهَاتِهِمْ ۖ إِنْ أُمَّهَاتُهُمْ إِلَّا اللَّائِي وَلَدْنَهُمْ ۚ وَإِنَّهُمْ لَيَقُولُونَ مُنْكَرًا مِنَ الْقَوْلِ وَزُورًا ۚ وَإِنَّ اللهَ لَعَفُوٌّ غَفُورٌ ۞

وَالَّذِينَ يُظَاهِرُونَ مِنْ نِسَائِهِمْ ثُمَّ يَعُودُونَ لِمَا قَالُوا فَتَحْرِيرُ رَقَبَةٍ مِنْ قَبْلِ أَنْ يَتَمَاسَّا ۚ ذٰلِكُمْ تُوعَظُونَ بِهِ ۚ وَاللهُ بِمَا تَعْمَلُونَ خَبِيرٌ ۞

فَمَنْ لَمْ يَجِدْ فَصِيَامُ شَهْرَيْنِ مُتَتَابِعَيْنِ مِنْ قَبْلِ أَنْ يَتَمَاسَّا ۖ فَمَنْ لَمْ يَسْتَطِعْ فَإِطْعَامُ سِتِّينَ مِسْكِينًا ۚ ذٰلِكَ لِتُؤْمِنُوا بِاللهِ وَرَسُولِهِ ۚ وَتِلْكَ حُدُودُ اللهِ ۗ وَلِلْكَافِرِينَ عَذَابٌ أَلِيمٌ ۞

إِنَّ الَّذِينَ يُحَادُّونَ اللهَ وَرَسُولَهُ كُبِتُوا كَمَا كُبِتَ الَّذِينَ مِنْ قَبْلِهِمْ ۚ وَقَدْ أَنْزَلْنَا آيَاتٍ بَيِّنَاتٍ ۚ وَلِلْكَافِرِينَ عَذَابٌ مُهِينٌ ۞

يَوْمَ يَبْعَثُهُمُ اللهُ جَمِيعًا فَيُنَبِّئُهُمْ بِمَا عَمِلُوا ۚ أَحْصَاهُ اللهُ وَنَسُوهُ ۚ وَاللهُ عَلَى كُلِّ شَيْءٍ شَهِيدٌ ۞

7. Do you not see that Allah knows whatever is in the heavens and whatever is in the earth? Nowhere is there a secret counsel between three persons but He is the fourth of them, nor (between) five but He is the sixth of them, nor less than that nor more but He is with them wheresoever they are; then He will inform them of what they did on the day of resurrection: surely Allah is Cognizant of all things.

8. Have you not seen those who are forbidden secret counsels, then they return to what they are forbidden, and they hold secret counsels for sin and revolt and disobedience to the Apostle; and when they come to you they greet you with a greeting with which Allah does not greet you, and they say in themselves: Why does not Allah punish us for what we say? Hell is enough for them; they shall enter it, and evil is the resort.

9. O you who believe! when you confer together in private, do not give to each other counsel of sin and revolt and disobedience to the Apostle, and give to each other counsel of goodness and guarding (against evil); and be careful of (your duty to) Allah, to Whom you shall be gathered together.

10. Secret counsels are only (the work) of the Shaitan that he may cause to grieve those who believe, and he cannot hurt them in the least except with Allah's permission; and on Allah let the believers rely.

11. O you who believe! when it is said to you, Make room in (your) assemblies, then make ample room, Allah will give you ample; and when it is said: Rise up, then rise up. Allah will exalt those of you who believe, and those who are given knowledge, in high degrees; and Allah is Aware of what you do.

548

12. O you who believe! when you consult the Apostle, then offer something in charity before your consultation; that is better for you and purer; but if you do not find, then surely Allah is Forgiving, Merciful.

يَا أَيُّهَا الَّذِينَ اٰمَنُوا إِذَا نَاجَيْتُمُ الرَّسُولَ فَقَدِّمُوا بَيْنَ يَدَيْ نَجْوَىٰكُمْ صَدَقَةً ذٰلِكَ خَيْرٌ لَّكُمْ وَأَطْهَرُ فَإِنْ لَّمْ تَجِدُوا فَإِنَّ اللّٰهَ غَفُورٌ رَّحِيمٌ ۝

13. Do you fear that you will not (be able to) give in charity before your consultation? So when you do not do it and Allah has turned to you (mercifully), then keep up prayer and pay the poor-rate and obey Allah and His Apostle; and Allah is Aware of what you do.

أَأَشْفَقْتُمْ أَنْ تُقَدِّمُوا بَيْنَ يَدَيْ نَجْوَىٰكُمْ صَدَقَاتٍ فَإِذْ لَمْ تَفْعَلُوا وَتَابَ اللّٰهُ عَلَيْكُمْ فَأَقِيمُوا الصَّلٰوةَ وَاٰتُوا الزَّكٰوةَ وَأَطِيعُوا اللّٰهَ وَرَسُولَهُ وَاللّٰهُ خَبِيرٌ بِمَا تَعْمَلُونَ ۝

14. Have you not seen those who befriend a people with whom Allah is wroth? They are neither of you nor of them, and they swear falsely while they know.

أَلَمْ تَرَ إِلَى الَّذِينَ تَوَلَّوْا قَوْمًا غَضِبَ اللّٰهُ عَلَيْهِمْ مَا هُمْ مِّنْكُمْ وَلَا مِنْهُمْ وَيَحْلِفُونَ عَلَى الْكَذِبِ وَهُمْ يَعْلَمُونَ ۝

15. Allah has prepared for them a severe punishment; surely what they do is evil.

أَعَدَّ اللّٰهُ لَهُمْ عَذَابًا شَدِيدًا إِنَّهُمْ سَاءَ مَا كَانُوا يَعْمَلُونَ ۝

16. They make their oaths to serve as a cover so they turn away from Allah's way; therefore they shall have an abasing chastisement.

اِتَّخَذُوا أَيْمَانَهُمْ جُنَّةً فَصَدُّوا عَنْ سَبِيلِ اللّٰهِ فَلَهُمْ عَذَابٌ مُّهِينٌ ۝

17. Neither their wealth nor their children shall avail them aught against Allah; they are the inmates of the fire, therein they shall abide.

لَنْ تُغْنِيَ عَنْهُمْ أَمْوَالُهُمْ وَلَا أَوْلَادُهُمْ مِّنَ اللّٰهِ شَيْئًا أُولٰئِكَ أَصْحَابُ النَّارِ هُمْ فِيهَا خَالِدُونَ ۝

18. On the day that Allah will raise them up all, then they will swear to Him as they swear to you, and they think that they have something; now surely they are the liars.

يَوْمَ يَبْعَثُهُمُ اللّٰهُ جَمِيعًا فَيَحْلِفُونَ لَهُ كَمَا يَحْلِفُونَ لَكُمْ وَيَحْسَبُونَ أَنَّهُمْ عَلَى شَيْءٍ أَلَا إِنَّهُمْ هُمُ الْكَاذِبُونَ ۝

19. The Shaitan has gained the mastery over them, so he has made them forget the remembrance of Allah; they are the Shaitan's party; now surely the Shaitan's party are the losers.

اِسْتَحْوَذَ عَلَيْهِمُ الشَّيْطَانُ فَأَنْسَاهُمْ ذِكْرَ اللّٰهِ أُولٰئِكَ حِزْبُ الشَّيْطَانِ أَلَا إِنَّ حِزْبَ الشَّيْطَانِ هُمُ الْخَاسِرُونَ ۝

20. Surely (as for) those who act in opposition to Allah and His Apostle; they shall be among the most abased.

اِنَّ الَّذِيْنَ يُحَآدُّوْنَ اللّٰهَ وَرَسُوْلَهٗ اُولٰٓئِكَ فِى الْاَذَلِّيْنَ ۞

21. Allah has written down: I will most certainly prevail, I and My apostles; surely Allah is Strong, Mighty.

كَتَبَ اللّٰهُ لَاَغْلِبَنَّ اَنَا وَرُسُلِيْ ۗ اِنَّ اللّٰهَ قَوِيٌّ عَزِيْزٌ ۞

22. You shall not find a people who believe in Allah and the latter day befriending those who act in opposition to Allah and His Apostle, even though they were their (own) fathers, or their sons, or their brothers, or their kinsfolk; these are they into whose hearts He has impressed faith, and whom He has strengthened with an inspiration from Him: and He will cause them to enter gardens beneath which rivers flow, abiding therein; Allah is well-pleased with them and they are well-pleased with Him; these are Allah's party: now surely the party of Allah are the successful ones.

لَا تَجِدُ قَوْمًا يُّؤْمِنُوْنَ بِاللّٰهِ وَالْيَوْمِ الْاٰخِرِ يُوَآدُّوْنَ مَنْ حَآدَّ اللّٰهَ وَرَسُوْلَهٗ وَلَوْ كَانُوْٓا اٰبَآءَهُمْ اَوْ اَبْنَآءَهُمْ اَوْ اِخْوَانَهُمْ اَوْ عَشِيْرَتَهُمْ ۗ اُولٰٓئِكَ كَتَبَ فِيْ قُلُوْبِهِمُ الْاِيْمَانَ وَاَيَّدَهُمْ بِرُوْحٍ مِّنْهُ ۗ وَيُدْخِلُهُمْ جَنّٰتٍ تَجْرِيْ مِنْ تَحْتِهَا الْاَنْهٰرُ خٰلِدِيْنَ فِيْهَا ۗ رَضِيَ اللّٰهُ عَنْهُمْ وَرَضُوْا عَنْهُ ۗ اُولٰٓئِكَ حِزْبُ اللّٰهِ ۗ اَلَآ اِنَّ حِزْبَ اللّٰهِ هُمُ الْمُفْلِحُوْنَ ۞

550

THE BANISHMENT
(HASHR)

**In the name of Allah,
the Beneficent, the Merciful.**

1. Whatever is in the heavens and whatever is in the earth declares the glory of Allah, and He is the Mighty, the Wise.

2. He it is Who caused those who disbelieved of the followers of the Book to go forth from their homes at the first banishment; you did not think that they would go forth, while they were certain that their fortresses would defend them against Allah; but Allah came to them whence they did not expect, and cast terror into their hearts; they demolished their houses with their own hands and the hands of the believers; therefore take a lesson, O you who have eyes!

3. And had it not been that Allah had decreed for them the exile, He would certainly have punished them in this world, and in the hereafter they shall have chastisement of the fire.

4. That is because they acted in opposition to Allah and His Apostle, and whoever acts in opposition to Allah, then surely Allah is severe in retributing (evil).

5. Whatever palm-tree you cut down or leave standing upon its roots, it is by Allah's command, and that He may abase the transgressors.

6. And whatever Allah restored to His Apostle from them, you did not press forward against it any horse or a riding camel, but Allah gives authority to His apostles against whom He pleases, and Allah has power over all things.

بِسْمِ اللهِ الرَّحْمٰنِ الرَّحِيْمِ ۞

سَبَّحَ لِلّٰهِ مَا فِى السَّمٰوٰتِ وَمَا فِى الْاَرْضِ ۚ وَ
هُوَ الْعَزِيْزُ الْحَكِيْمُ ۞

هُوَ الَّذِيْٓ اَخْرَجَ الَّذِيْنَ كَفَرُوْا مِنْ اَهْلِ الْكِتٰبِ
مِنْ دِيَارِهِمْ لِاَوَّلِ الْحَشْرِ ؕ مَا ظَنَنْتُمْ اَنْ
يَّخْرُجُوْا وَظَنُّوْٓا اَنَّهُمْ مَّانِعَتُهُمْ حُصُوْنُهُمْ مِّنَ
اللهِ فَاَتٰهُمُ اللهُ مِنْ حَيْثُ لَمْ يَحْتَسِبُوْا ۫ وَ
قَذَفَ فِىْ قُلُوْبِهِمُ الرُّعْبَ يُخْرِبُوْنَ بُيُوْتَهُمْ
بِاَيْدِيْهِمْ وَاَيْدِى الْمُؤْمِنِيْنَ ۙ فَاعْتَبِرُوْا
يٰٓاُولِى الْاَبْصَارِ ۞

وَلَوْلَآ اَنْ كَتَبَ اللهُ عَلَيْهِمُ الْجَلَاۤءَ لَعَذَّبَهُمْ
فِى الدُّنْيَا ؕ وَلَهُمْ فِى الْاٰخِرَةِ عَذَابُ النَّارِ ۞
ذٰلِكَ بِاَنَّهُمْ شَاۤقُّوا اللهَ وَرَسُوْلَهٗ ۚ وَمَنْ يُّشَاۤقِّ
اللهَ فَاِنَّ اللهَ شَدِيْدُ الْعِقَابِ ۞
مَا قَطَعْتُمْ مِّنْ لِّيْنَةٍ اَوْ تَرَكْتُمُوْهَا قَاۤئِمَةً عَلٰٓى
اُصُوْلِهَا فَبِاِذْنِ اللهِ وَلِيُخْزِىَ الْفٰسِقِيْنَ ۞
وَمَآ اَفَآءَ اللهُ عَلٰى رَسُوْلِهٖ مِنْهُمْ فَمَآ اَوْجَفْتُمْ
عَلَيْهِ مِنْ خَيْلٍ وَّلَا رِكَابٍ وَّلٰكِنَّ اللهَ يُسَلِّطُ
رُسُلَهٗ عَلٰى مَنْ يَّشَاۤءُ ؕ وَاللهُ عَلٰى كُلِّ شَىْءٍ
قَدِيْرٌ ۞

551

7. Whatever Allah has restored to His Apostle from the people of the towns, it is for Allah and for the Apostle, and for the near of kin and the orphans and the needy and the wayfarer, so that it may not be a thing taken by turns among the rich of you, and whatever the Apostle gives you, accept it, and from whatever he forbids you, keep back, and be careful of (your duty to) Allah; surely Allah is severe in retributing (evil):

مَا أَفَاءَ اللهُ عَلَى رَسُوْلِهِ مِنْ أَهْلِ الْقُرٰى فَلِلّٰهِ
وَلِلرَّسُوْلِ وَلِذِى الْقُرْبٰى وَالْيَتٰمٰى وَالْمَسٰكِيْنِ
وَابْنِ السَّبِيْلِ كَيْ لَا يَكُوْنَ دُوْلَةً بَيْنَ الْأَغْنِيَاءِ
مِنْكُمْ ۖ وَمَا اٰتٰكُمُ الرَّسُوْلُ فَخُذُوْهُ ۚ وَمَا نَهٰكُمْ
عَنْهُ فَانْتَهُوْا ۚ وَاتَّقُوا اللهَ ۖ إِنَّ اللهَ شَدِيْدُ
الْعِقَابِ ۝

8. (It is) for the poor who fled, those who were driven from their homes and their possessions, seeking grace of Allah and (His) pleasure, and assisting Allah and His Apostle: these it is that are the truthful.

لِلْفُقَرَاءِ الْمُهٰجِرِيْنَ الَّذِيْنَ أُخْرِجُوْا مِنْ دِيَارِهِمْ
وَأَمْوَالِهِمْ يَبْتَغُوْنَ فَضْلًا مِّنَ اللهِ وَرِضْوَانًا وَّ
يَنْصُرُوْنَ اللهَ وَرَسُوْلَهُ ۚ أُولٰئِكَ هُمُ الصّٰدِقُوْنَ ۝

9. And those who made their abode in the city and in the faith before them love those who have fled to them, and do not find in their hearts a need of what they are given, and prefer (them) before themselves though poverty may afflict them, and whoever is preserved from the niggardliness of his soul, these it is that are the successful ones.

وَالَّذِيْنَ تَبَوَّؤُا الدَّارَ وَالْإِيْمَانَ مِنْ قَبْلِهِمْ يُحِبُّوْنَ
مَنْ هَاجَرَ إِلَيْهِمْ وَلَا يَجِدُوْنَ فِيْ صُدُوْرِهِمْ حَاجَةً
مِّمَّا أُوْتُوْا وَيُؤْثِرُوْنَ عَلٰى أَنْفُسِهِمْ وَلَوْ كَانَ بِهِمْ
خَصَاصَةٌ ۚ وَمَنْ يُّوْقَ شُحَّ نَفْسِهِ فَأُولٰئِكَ
هُمُ الْمُفْلِحُوْنَ ۝

10. And those who come after them say: Our Lord! forgive us and those of our brethren who had precedence of us in faith, and do not allow any spite to remain in our hearts towards those who believe; our Lord! surely Thou art Kind, Merciful.

وَالَّذِيْنَ جَاءُوْا مِنْ بَعْدِهِمْ يَقُوْلُوْنَ رَبَّنَا اغْفِرْ
لَنَا وَلِإِخْوَانِنَا الَّذِيْنَ سَبَقُوْنَا بِالْإِيْمَانِ وَلَا
تَجْعَلْ فِيْ قُلُوْبِنَا غِلًّا لِّلَّذِيْنَ اٰمَنُوْا رَبَّنَا إِنَّكَ
رَءُوْفٌ رَّحِيْمٌ ۝

11. Have you not seen those who have become hypocrites? They say to those of their brethren who disbelieve from among the followers of the Book: If you are driven forth, we shall certainly go forth with you, and we will never obey any one concerning you, and if you are fought against, we will certainly help you; and Allah bears witness that they are most surely liars.

أَلَمْ تَرَ إِلَى الَّذِيْنَ نَافَقُوْا يَقُوْلُوْنَ لِإِخْوَانِهِمُ الَّذِيْنَ
كَفَرُوْا مِنْ أَهْلِ الْكِتٰبِ لَئِنْ أُخْرِجْتُمْ لَنَخْرُجَنَّ
مَعَكُمْ وَلَا نُطِيْعُ فِيْكُمْ أَحَدًا أَبَدًا ۙ وَّإِنْ قُوْتِلْتُمْ
لَنَنْصُرَنَّكُمْ ۚ وَاللهُ يَشْهَدُ إِنَّهُمْ لَكٰذِبُوْنَ ۝

12. Certainly if these are driven forth, they will not go forth with them, and if they are fought against, they will not help them, and even if they help them, they will certainly turn (their) backs, then they shall not be helped.

13. You are certainly greater in being feared in their hearts than Allah; that is because they are a people who do not understand.

14. They will not fight against you in a body save in fortified towns or from behind walls; their fighting between them is severe; you may think them as one body, and their hearts are disunited; that is because they are a people who have no sense.

15. Like those before them shortly; they tasted the evil result of their affair, and they shall have a painful punishment.

16. Like the Shaitan when he says to man: Disbelieve, but when he disbelieves, he says: I am surely clear of you; surely I fear Allah, the Lord of the worlds.

17. Therefore the end of both of them is that they are both in the fire to abide therein, and that is the reward of the unjust.

18. O you who believe! be careful of (your duty to) Allah, and let every soul consider what it has sent on for the morrow, and be careful of (your duty to) Allah; surely Allah is Aware of what you do.

19. And be not like those who forsook Allah, so He made them forsake their own souls: these it is that are the transgressors.

20. Not alike are the inmates of the fire and the dwellers of the garden: the dwellers of the garden are they that are the achievers.

21. Had We sent down this Quran on a mountain, you would certainly have seen it falling down, splitting asunder because of the fear of Allah, and We set forth these parables to men that they may reflect.

لَوْ اَنْزَلْنَا هٰذَا الْقُرْاٰنَ عَلٰى جَبَلٍ لَّرَاَيْتَهٗ خَاشِعًا مُّتَصَدِّعًا مِّنْ خَشْيَةِ اللّٰهِ ۚ وَتِلْكَ الْاَمْثَالُ نَضْرِبُهَا لِلنَّاسِ لَعَلَّهُمْ يَتَفَكَّرُوْنَ ۝

22. He is Allah besides Whom there is no god; the Knower of the unseen and the seen; He is the Beneficent, the Merciful.

هُوَ اللّٰهُ الَّذِيْ لَآ اِلٰهَ اِلَّا هُوَ ۚ عٰلِمُ الْغَيْبِ وَ الشَّهَادَةِ ۚ هُوَ الرَّحْمٰنُ الرَّحِيْمُ ۝

23. He is Allah, besides Whom there is no god; the King, the Holy, the Giver of peace, the Granter of security, Guardian over all, the Mighty, the Supreme, the Possessor of every greatness; Glory be to Allah from what they set up (with Him).

هُوَ اللّٰهُ الَّذِيْ لَآ اِلٰهَ اِلَّا هُوَ ۚ اَلْمَلِكُ الْقُدُّوْسُ السَّلٰمُ الْمُؤْمِنُ الْمُهَيْمِنُ الْعَزِيْزُ الْجَبَّارُ الْمُتَكَبِّرُ ۚ سُبْحٰنَ اللّٰهِ عَمَّا يُشْرِكُوْنَ ۝

24. He is Allah the Creator, the Maker, the Fashioner; His are the most excellent names; whatever is in the heavens and the earth declares His glory; and He is the Mighty, the Wise.

هُوَ اللّٰهُ الْخَالِقُ الْبَارِئُ الْمُصَوِّرُ لَهُ الْاَسْمَآءُ الْحُسْنٰى ۚ يُسَبِّحُ لَهٗ مَا فِي السَّمٰوٰتِ وَالْاَرْضِ ۚ وَهُوَ الْعَزِيْزُ الْحَكِيْمُ ۝

THE EXAMINED ONE
(MUNTAHANAH)

In the name of Allah,
the Beneficent, the Merciful.

1. O you who believe! do not take My enemy and your enemy for friends: would you offer them love while they deny what has come to you of the truth, driving out the Apostle and yourselves because you believe in Allah, your Lord? If you go forth struggling hard in My path and seeking My pleasure, would you manifest love to them? And I know what you conceal and what you manifest; and whoever of you does this, he indeed has gone astray from the straight path.

2. If they find you, they will be your enemies, and will stretch forth towards you their hands and their tongues with evil, and they ardently desire that you may disbelieve.

3. Your relationship would not profit you, nor your children, on the day of resurrection; He will decide between you; and Allah sees what you do.

4. Indeed, there is for you a good example in Ibrahim and those with him when they said to their people: Surely we are clear of you and of what you serve besides Allah; we declare ourselves to be clear of you, and enmity and hatred have appeared between us and you forever until you believe in Allah alone—but not in what Ibrahim said to his father: I would certainly ask forgiveness for you, and I do not control for you aught from Allah—Our Lord! on Thee do we rely, and to Thee do we turn, and to Thee is the eventual coming:

5. Our Lord! do not make us a trial for those who disbelieve, and forgive us, our Lord! surely Thou art the Mighty, the Wise.

6. Certainly there is for you in them a good example, for him who fears Allah and the last day; and whoever turns back, then surely Allah is the Self-sufficient, the Praised.

7. It may be that Allah will bring about friendship between you and those whom you hold to be your enemies among them; and Allah is Powerful; and Allah is Forgiving, Merciful.

8. Allah does not forbid you respecting those who have not made war against you on account of (your) religion, and have not driven you forth from your homes, that you show them kindness and deal with them justly; surely Allah loves the doers of justice.

9. Allah only forbids you respecting those who made war upon you on account of (your) religion, and drove you forth from your homes and backed up (others) in your expulsion, that you make friends with them, and whoever makes friends with them, these are the unjust.

10. O you who believe! when believing women come to you flying, then examine them; Allah knows best their faith; then if you find them to be believing women, do not send them back to the unbelievers; neither are these (women) lawful for them, nor are those (men) lawful for them, and give them what they have spent; and no blame attaches to you in marrying them when you give them their dowries; and hold not to the ties of marriage of unbelieving women, and ask for what you have spent, and let them ask for what they have spent. That is Allah's judgment; He judges between you; and Allah is Knowing, Wise.

رَبَّنَا لَا تَجْعَلْنَا فِتْنَةً لِّلَّذِيْنَ كَفَرُوْا وَاغْفِرْ لَنَا رَبَّنَا اِنَّكَ اَنْتَ الْعَزِيْزُ الْحَكِيْمُ ۝

لَقَدْ كَانَ لَكُمْ فِيْهِمْ اُسْوَةٌ حَسَنَةٌ لِّمَنْ كَانَ يَرْجُوا اللّٰهَ وَالْيَوْمَ الْاٰخِرَ وَمَنْ يَّتَوَلَّ فَاِنَّ اللّٰهَ هُوَ الْغَنِيُّ الْحَمِيْدُ ۝

عَسَى اللّٰهُ اَنْ يَّجْعَلَ بَيْنَكُمْ وَبَيْنَ الَّذِيْنَ عَادَيْتُمْ مِّنْهُمْ مَّوَدَّةً وَاللّٰهُ قَدِيْرٌ وَاللّٰهُ غَفُوْرٌ رَّحِيْمٌ ۝

لَا يَنْهٰىكُمُ اللّٰهُ عَنِ الَّذِيْنَ لَمْ يُقَاتِلُوْكُمْ فِي الدِّيْنِ وَلَمْ يُخْرِجُوْكُمْ مِّنْ دِيَارِكُمْ اَنْ تَبَرُّوْهُمْ وَتُقْسِطُوْا اِلَيْهِمْ اِنَّ اللّٰهَ يُحِبُّ الْمُقْسِطِيْنَ ۝

اِنَّمَا يَنْهٰىكُمُ اللّٰهُ عَنِ الَّذِيْنَ قَاتَلُوْكُمْ فِي الدِّيْنِ وَاَخْرَجُوْكُمْ مِّنْ دِيَارِكُمْ وَظَاهَرُوْا عَلٰى اِخْرَاجِكُمْ اَنْ تَوَلَّوْهُمْ وَمَنْ يَّتَوَلَّهُمْ فَاُولٰٓئِكَ هُمُ الظّٰلِمُوْنَ ۝

يَاَيُّهَا الَّذِيْنَ اٰمَنُوْا اِذَا جَآءَكُمُ الْمُؤْمِنٰتُ مُهٰجِرٰتٍ فَامْتَحِنُوْهُنَّ اَللّٰهُ اَعْلَمُ بِاِيْمَانِهِنَّ فَاِنْ عَلِمْتُمُوْهُنَّ مُؤْمِنٰتٍ فَلَا تَرْجِعُوْهُنَّ اِلَى الْكُفَّارِ لَا هُنَّ حِلٌّ لَّهُمْ وَلَا هُمْ يَحِلُّوْنَ لَهُنَّ وَاٰتُوْهُمْ مَّا اَنْفَقُوْا وَلَا جُنَاحَ عَلَيْكُمْ اَنْ تَنْكِحُوْهُنَّ اِذَا اٰتَيْتُمُوْهُنَّ اُجُوْرَهُنَّ وَلَا تُمْسِكُوْا بِعِصَمِ الْكَوَافِرِ وَسْئَلُوْا مَا اَنْفَقْتُمْ وَلْيَسْئَلُوْا مَا اَنْفَقُوْا ذٰلِكُمْ حُكْمُ اللّٰهِ يَحْكُمُ بَيْنَكُمْ وَاللّٰهُ عَلِيْمٌ حَكِيْمٌ ۝

11. And if anything (out of the dowries) of your wives has passed away from you to the unbelievers, then your turn comes, give to those whose wives have gone away the like of what they have spent, and be careful of (your duty to) Allah in Whom you believe.

12. O Prophet! when believing women come to you giving you a pledge that they will not associate aught with Allah, and will not steal, and will not commit fornication, and will not kill their children, and will not bring a calumny which they have forged of themselves, and will not disobey you in what is good, accept their pledge, and ask forgiveness for them from Allah; surely Allah is Forgiving, Merciful.

13. O you who believe! do not make friends with a people with whom Allah is wroth; indeed they despair of the hereafter as the unbelievers despair of those in tombs.

وَإِن فَاتَكُمْ شَيْءٌ مِّنْ أَزْوَاجِكُمْ إِلَى الْكُفَّارِ فَعَاقَبْتُمْ فَاٰتُوا الَّذِينَ ذَهَبَتْ أَزْوَاجُهُمْ مِّثْلَ مَا أَنفَقُوا وَاتَّقُوا اللّٰهَ الَّذِي أَنتُم بِهٖ مُؤْمِنُونَ ۞

يَا أَيُّهَا النَّبِيُّ إِذَا جَاءَكَ الْمُؤْمِنَاتُ يُبَايِعْنَكَ عَلَىٰ أَن لَّا يُشْرِكْنَ بِاللّٰهِ شَيْئًا وَلَا يَسْرِقْنَ وَلَا يَزْنِينَ وَلَا يَقْتُلْنَ أَوْلَادَهُنَّ وَلَا يَأْتِينَ بِبُهْتَانٍ يَفْتَرِينَهٗ بَيْنَ أَيْدِيهِنَّ وَأَرْجُلِهِنَّ وَلَا يَعْصِينَكَ فِي مَعْرُوفٍ فَبَايِعْهُنَّ وَاسْتَغْفِرْ لَهُنَّ اللّٰهَ إِنَّ اللّٰهَ غَفُورٌ رَّحِيمٌ ۞

يَا أَيُّهَا الَّذِينَ آمَنُوا لَا تَتَوَلَّوْا قَوْمًا غَضِبَ اللّٰهُ عَلَيْهِمْ قَدْ يَئِسُوا مِنَ الْآخِرَةِ كَمَا يَئِسَ الْكُفَّارُ مِنْ أَصْحَابِ الْقُبُورِ ۞

THE RANKS
(SAFF)

**In the name of Allah,
the Beneficent, the Merciful.**

1. Whatever is in the heavens and whatever is in the earth declares the glory of Allah; and He is the Mighty, the Wise.

2. O you who believe! why do you say that which you do not do?

3. It is most hateful to Allah that you should say that which you do not do.

4. Surely Allah loves those who fight in His way in ranks as if they were a firm and compact wall.

5. And when Musa said to his people: O my people! why do you give me trouble? And you know indeed that I am Allah's apostle to you; but when they turned aside, Allah made their hearts turn aside, and Allah does not guide the transgressing people.

6. And when Isa son of Marium said: O children of Israel! surely I am the apostle of Allah to you, verifying that which is before me of the Taurat and giving the good news of an Apostle who will come after me, his name being Ahmad; but when he came to them with clear arguments they said: This is clear magic.

7. And who is more unjust than he who forges a lie against Allah and he is invited to Islam, and Allah does not guide the unjust people.

8. They desire to put out the light of Allah with their mouths, but Allah will perfect His light, though the unbelievers may be averse.

بِسْمِ اللهِ الرَّحْمٰنِ الرَّحِيْمِ ۞

سَبَّحَ لِلّٰهِ مَا فِى السَّمٰوٰتِ وَمَا فِى الْاَرْضِ ۚ وَهُوَ الْعَزِيْزُ الْحَكِيْمُ ۞

يٰٓاَيُّهَا الَّذِيْنَ اٰمَنُوْا لِمَ تَقُوْلُوْنَ مَا لَا تَفْعَلُوْنَ ۞

كَبُرَ مَقْتًا عِنْدَ اللهِ اَنْ تَقُوْلُوْا مَا لَا تَفْعَلُوْنَ ۞

اِنَّ اللهَ يُحِبُّ الَّذِيْنَ يُقَاتِلُوْنَ فِيْ سَبِيْلِهٖ صَفًّا كَاَنَّهُمْ بُنْيَانٌ مَّرْصُوْصٌ ۞

وَاِذْ قَالَ مُوْسٰى لِقَوْمِهٖ يٰقَوْمِ لِمَ تُؤْذُوْنَنِيْ وَقَدْ تَّعْلَمُوْنَ اَنِّيْ رَسُوْلُ اللهِ اِلَيْكُمْ ۖ فَلَمَّا زَاغُوْۤا اَزَاغَ اللهُ قُلُوْبَهُمْ ۚ وَاللهُ لَا يَهْدِى الْقَوْمَ الْفٰسِقِيْنَ ۞

وَاِذْ قَالَ عِيْسَى ابْنُ مَرْيَمَ يٰبَنِيْۤ اِسْرَآءِيْلَ اِنِّيْ رَسُوْلُ اللهِ اِلَيْكُمْ مُّصَدِّقًا لِّمَا بَيْنَ يَدَيَّ مِنَ التَّوْرٰىةِ وَمُبَشِّرًاۢ بِرَسُوْلٍ يَّأْتِيْ مِنْۢ بَعْدِى اسْمُهٗۤ اَحْمَدُ ۖ فَلَمَّا جَآءَهُمْ بِالْبَيِّنٰتِ قَالُوْا هٰذَا سِحْرٌ مُّبِيْنٌ ۞

وَمَنْ اَظْلَمُ مِمَّنِ افْتَرٰى عَلَى اللهِ الْكَذِبَ وَهُوَ يُدْعٰۤى اِلَى الْاِسْلَامِ ۚ وَاللهُ لَا يَهْدِى الْقَوْمَ الظّٰلِمِيْنَ ۞

يُرِيْدُوْنَ لِيُطْفِـُٔوْا نُوْرَ اللهِ بِاَفْوَاهِهِمْ وَاللهُ مُتِمُّ نُوْرِهٖ وَلَوْ كَرِهَ الْكٰفِرُوْنَ ۞

558

9. He it is Who sent His Apostle with the guidance and the true religion, that He may make it overcome the religions, all of them, though the polytheists may be averse.

هُوَ الَّذِيْ اَرْسَلَ رَسُوْلَهُ بِالْهُدٰى وَدِيْنِ الْحَقِّ لِيُظْهِرَهُ عَلَى الدِّيْنِ كُلِّهٖ وَلَوْ كَرِهَ الْمُشْرِكُوْنَ ۞

10. O you who believe! shall I lead you to a merchandise which may deliver you from a painful chastisement?

يٰۤاَيُّهَا الَّذِيْنَ اٰمَنُوْا هَلْ اَدُلُّكُمْ عَلٰى تِجَارَةٍ تُنْجِيْكُمْ مِّنْ عَذَابٍ اَلِيْمٍ ۞

11. You shall believe in Allah and His Apostle, and struggle hard in Allah's way with your property and your lives; that is better for you, did you but know!

تُؤْمِنُوْنَ بِاللهِ وَرَسُوْلِهٖ وَتُجَاهِدُوْنَ فِيْ سَبِيْلِ اللهِ بِاَمْوَالِكُمْ وَاَنْفُسِكُمْ ذٰلِكُمْ خَيْرٌ لَّكُمْ اِنْ كُنْتُمْ تَعْلَمُوْنَ ۞

12. He will forgive you your faults and cause you to enter into gardens, beneath which rivers flow, and goodly dwellings in gardens of perpetuity; that is the mighty achievement;

يَغْفِرْ لَكُمْ ذُنُوْبَكُمْ وَيُدْخِلْكُمْ جَنّٰتٍ تَجْرِيْ مِنْ تَحْتِهَا الْاَنْهٰرُ وَمَسٰكِنَ طَيِّبَةً فِيْ جَنّٰتِ عَدْنٍ ذٰلِكَ الْفَوْزُ الْعَظِيْمُ ۞

13. And yet another (blessing) that you love: help from Allah and a victory near at hand; and give good news to the believers.

وَاُخْرٰى تُحِبُّوْنَهَا نَصْرٌ مِّنَ اللهِ وَفَتْحٌ قَرِيْبٌ وَبَشِّرِ الْمُؤْمِنِيْنَ ۞

14. O you who believe! be helpers (in the cause) of Allah, as Isa son of Marium said to (his) disciples: Who are my helpers in the cause of Allah? The disciples said: We are helpers (in the cause) of Allah. So a party of the children of Israel believed and another party disbelieved; then We aided those who believed against their enemy, and they became uppermost.

يٰۤاَيُّهَا الَّذِيْنَ اٰمَنُوْا كُوْنُوْا اَنْصَارَ اللهِ كَمَا قَالَ عِيْسَى ابْنُ مَرْيَمَ لِلْحَوَارِيّٖنَ مَنْ اَنْصَارِيْۤ اِلَى اللهِ قَالَ الْحَوَارِيُّوْنَ نَحْنُ اَنْصَارُ اللهِ فَاٰمَنَتْ طَّآئِفَةٌ مِّنْ بَنِيْۤ اِسْرَآئِيْلَ وَكَفَرَتْ طَّآئِفَةٌ فَاَيَّدْنَا الَّذِيْنَ اٰمَنُوْا عَلٰى عَدُوِّهِمْ فَاَصْبَحُوْا ظٰهِرِيْنَ ۞

FRIDAY
(JUMMAH)

**In the name of Allah,
the Beneficent, the Merciful.**

1. Whatever is in the heavens and whatever is in the earth declares the glory of Allah, the King, the Holy, the Mighty, the Wise.

2. He it is Who raised among the inhabitants of Mecca an Apostle from among themselves, who recites to them His communications and purifies them, and teaches them the Book and the Wisdom, although they were before certainly in clear error,

3. And others from among them who have not yet joined them; and He is the Mighty, the Wise.

4. That is Allah's grace; He grants it to whom He pleases, and Allah is the Lord of mighty grace.

5. The likeness of those who were charged with the Taurat, then they did not observe it, is as the likeness of the ass bearing books, evil is the likeness of the people who reject the communications of Allah; and Allah does not guide the unjust people.

6. Say: O you who are Jews, if you think that you are the favorites of Allah to the exclusion of other people, then invoke death if you are truthful.

7. And they will never invoke it because of what their hands have sent before; and Allah is Cognizant of the unjust.

بِسْمِ اللهِ الرَّحْمٰنِ الرَّحِيْمِ ۟

يُسَبِّحُ لِلّٰهِ مَا فِى السَّمٰوٰتِ وَمَا فِى الْاَرْضِ الْمَلِكِ الْقُدُّوْسِ الْعَزِيْزِ الْحَكِيْمِ ۟

هُوَ الَّذِىْ بَعَثَ فِى الْاُمِّيّٖنَ رَسُوْلًا مِّنْهُمْ يَتْلُوْا عَلَيْهِمْ اٰيٰتِهٖ وَيُزَكِّيْهِمْ وَيُعَلِّمُهُمُ الْكِتٰبَ وَالْحِكْمَةَ قَوَاِنْ كَانُوْا مِنْ قَبْلُ لَفِىْ ضَلٰلٍ مُّبِيْنٍ ۟

وَّاٰخَرِيْنَ مِنْهُمْ لَمَّا يَلْحَقُوْا بِهِمْ ۚ وَهُوَ الْعَزِيْزُ الْحَكِيْمُ ۟

ذٰلِكَ فَضْلُ اللهِ يُؤْتِيْهِ مَنْ يَّشَآءُ ۚ وَاللهُ ذُو الْفَضْلِ الْعَظِيْمِ ۟

مَثَلُ الَّذِيْنَ حُمِّلُوا التَّوْرٰىةَ ثُمَّ لَمْ يَحْمِلُوْهَا كَمَثَلِ الْحِمَارِ يَحْمِلُ اَسْفَارًا ۚ بِئْسَ مَثَلُ الْقَوْمِ الَّذِيْنَ كَذَّبُوْا بِاٰيٰتِ اللهِ ۚ وَاللهُ لَا يَهْدِى الْقَوْمَ الظّٰلِمِيْنَ ۟

قُلْ يٰاَيُّهَا الَّذِيْنَ هَادُوْا اِنْ زَعَمْتُمْ اَنَّكُمْ اَوْلِيَآءُ لِلّٰهِ مِنْ دُوْنِ النَّاسِ فَتَمَنَّوُا الْمَوْتَ اِنْ كُنْتُمْ صٰدِقِيْنَ ۟

وَلَا يَتَمَنَّوْنَهٗ اَبَدًا بِمَا قَدَّمَتْ اَيْدِيْهِمْ ۚ وَاللهُ عَلِيْمٌ بِالظّٰلِمِيْنَ ۟

8. Say: (As for) the death from which you flee, that will surely overtake you, then you shall be sent back to the Knower of the unseen and the seen, and He will inform you of that which you did.

قُلْ اِنَّ الْمَوْتَ الَّذِيْ تَفِرُّوْنَ مِنْهُ فَاِنَّهٗ مُلٰقِيْكُمْ ثُمَّ تُرَدُّوْنَ اِلٰى عٰلِمِ الْغَيْبِ وَالشَّهَادَةِ فَيُنَبِّئُكُمْ بِمَا كُنْتُمْ تَعْمَلُوْنَ ۞

9. O you who believe! when the call is made for prayer on Friday, then hasten to the remembrance of Allah and leave off trading; that is better for you, if you know.

يٰٓاَيُّهَا الَّذِيْنَ اٰمَنُوْٓا اِذَا نُوْدِيَ لِلصَّلٰوةِ مِنْ يَّوْمِ الْجُمُعَةِ فَاسْعَوْا اِلٰى ذِكْرِ اللّٰهِ وَذَرُوا الْبَيْعَ ذٰلِكُمْ خَيْرٌ لَّكُمْ اِنْ كُنْتُمْ تَعْلَمُوْنَ ۞

10. But when the prayer is ended, then disperse abroad in the land and seek of Allah's grace, and remember Allah much, that you may be successful.

فَاِذَا قُضِيَتِ الصَّلٰوةُ فَانْتَشِرُوْا فِى الْاَرْضِ وَابْتَغُوْا مِنْ فَضْلِ اللّٰهِ وَاذْكُرُوا اللّٰهَ كَثِيْرًا لَّعَلَّكُمْ تُفْلِحُوْنَ ۞

11. And when they see merchandise or sport they break up for it, and leave you standing. Say: What is with Allah is better than sport and (better) than merchandise, and Allah is the best of Sustainers.

وَاِذَا رَاَوْا تِجَارَةً اَوْ لَهْوَا انْفَضُّوْٓا اِلَيْهَا وَتَرَكُوْكَ قَآئِمًا قُلْ مَا عِنْدَ اللّٰهِ خَيْرٌ مِّنَ اللَّهْوِ وَمِنَ التِّجَارَةِ وَاللّٰهُ خَيْرُ الرّٰزِقِيْنَ ۞

THE HIPOCRITES
(MUNAFIQUN)

اياتها (١٣) سُوْرَةُ الْمُنْفِقُوْنَ مَدَنِيَّةٌ رُكُوْعَاتُهَا

**In the name of Allah,
the Beneficent, the Merciful.**

بِسْمِ اللهِ الرَّحْمٰنِ الرَّحِيْمِ ۞

1. When the hypocrites come to you, they say: We bear witness that you are most surely Allah's Apostle; and Allah knows that you are most surely His Apostle, and Allah bears witness that the hypocrites are surely liars.

اِذَا جَآءَكَ الْمُنْفِقُوْنَ قَالُوْا نَشْهَدُ اِنَّكَ لَرَسُوْلُ اللهِ ۚ وَاللهُ يَعْلَمُ اِنَّكَ لَرَسُوْلُهٗ ۚ وَاللهُ يَشْهَدُ اِنَّ الْمُنْفِقِيْنَ لَكٰذِبُوْنَ ۞

2. They make their oaths a shelter, and thus turn away from Allah's way; surely evil is that which they do.

اِتَّخَذُوْٓا اَيْمَانَهُمْ جُنَّةً فَصَدُّوْا عَنْ سَبِيْلِ اللهِ ۚ اِنَّهُمْ سَآءَ مَا كَانُوْا يَعْمَلُوْنَ ۞

3. That is because they believe, then disbelieve, so a seal is set upon their hearts so that they do not understand.

ذٰلِكَ بِاَنَّهُمْ اٰمَنُوْا ثُمَّ كَفَرُوْا فَطُبِعَ عَلٰى قُلُوْبِهِمْ فَهُمْ لَا يَفْقَهُوْنَ ۞

4. And when you see them, their persons will please you, and if they speak, you will listen to their speech; (they are) as if they were big pieces of wood clad with garments; they think every cry to be against them. They are the enemy, therefore beware of them; may Allah destroy them, whence are they turned back?

وَاِذَا رَاَيْتَهُمْ تُعْجِبُكَ اَجْسَامُهُمْ ۚ وَاِنْ يَّقُوْلُوْا تَسْمَعْ لِقَوْلِهِمْ ۚ كَاَنَّهُمْ خُشُبٌ مُّسَنَّدَةٌ ۚ يَحْسَبُوْنَ كُلَّ صَيْحَةٍ عَلَيْهِمْ ۚ هُمُ الْعَدُوُّ فَاحْذَرْهُمْ ۚ قَاتَلَهُمُ اللهُ ۖ اَنّٰى يُؤْفَكُوْنَ ۞

5. And when it is said to them: Come, the Apostle of Allah will ask forgiveness for you, they turn back their heads and you may see them turning away while they are big with pride.

وَاِذَا قِيْلَ لَهُمْ تَعَالَوْا يَسْتَغْفِرْ لَكُمْ رَسُوْلُ اللهِ لَوَّوْا رُءُوْسَهُمْ وَرَاَيْتَهُمْ يَصُدُّوْنَ وَهُمْ مُّسْتَكْبِرُوْنَ ۞

6. It is alike to them whether you beg forgiveness for them or do not beg forgiveness for them; Allah will never forgive them; surely Allah does not guide the transgressing people.

سَوَآءٌ عَلَيْهِمْ اَسْتَغْفَرْتَ لَهُمْ اَمْ لَمْ تَسْتَغْفِرْ لَهُمْ ۚ لَنْ يَّغْفِرَ اللهُ لَهُمْ ۚ اِنَّ اللهَ لَا يَهْدِى الْقَوْمَ الْفٰسِقِيْنَ ۞

7. They it is who say: Do not spend upon those who are with the Apostle of Allah until they break up. And Allah's are the treasures of the heavens and the earth, but the hypocrites do not understand.

هُمُ الَّذِيْنَ يَقُوْلُوْنَ لَا تُنْفِقُوْا عَلٰى مَنْ عِنْدَ رَسُوْلِ اللهِ حَتّٰى يَنْفَضُّوْا ۗ وَلِلّٰهِ خَزَآئِنُ السَّمٰوٰتِ وَالْاَرْضِ وَلٰكِنَّ الْمُنٰفِقِيْنَ لَا يَفْقَهُوْنَ ۞

8. They say: If we return to Medina, the mighty will surely drive out the meaner therefrom; and to Allah belongs the might and to His Apostle and to the believers, but the hypocrites do not know.

يَقُوْلُوْنَ لَئِنْ رَّجَعْنَاۤ اِلَى الْمَدِيْنَةِ لَيُخْرِجَنَّ الْاَعَزُّ
مِنْهَا الْاَذَلَّ ۖ وَ لِلّٰهِ الْعِزَّةُ وَ لِرَسُوْلِهٖ وَ لِلْمُؤْمِنِيْنَ
وَ لٰكِنَّ الْمُنٰفِقِيْنَ لَا يَعْلَمُوْنَ ۞

9. O you who believe! let not your wealth, or your children, divert you from the remembrance of Allah; and whoever does that, these are the losers.

يٰۤاَيُّهَا الَّذِيْنَ اٰمَنُوْا لَا تُلْهِكُمْ اَمْوَالُكُمْ وَ لَاۤ
اَوْلَادُكُمْ عَنْ ذِكْرِ اللّٰهِ ۚ وَ مَنْ يَّفْعَلْ ذٰلِكَ
فَاُولٰٓئِكَ هُمُ الْخٰسِرُوْنَ ۞

10. And spend out of what We have given you before death comes to one of you, so that he should say: My Lord! why didst Thou not respite me to a near term, so that I should have given alms and been of the doers of good deeds?

وَ اَنْفِقُوْا مِنْ مَّا رَزَقْنٰكُمْ مِّنْ قَبْلِ اَنْ يَّاْتِيَ
اَحَدَكُمُ الْمَوْتُ فَيَقُوْلَ رَبِّ لَوْلَاۤ اَخَّرْتَنِيْۤ
اِلَى اَجَلٍ قَرِيْبٍ ۙ فَاَصَّدَّقَ وَ اَكُنْ مِّنَ
الصّٰلِحِيْنَ ۞

11. And Allah does not respite a soul when its appointed term has come, and Allah is Aware of what you do.

وَ لَنْ يُّؤَخِّرَ اللّٰهُ نَفْسًا اِذَا جَاۤءَ اَجَلُهَا ۚ وَ اللّٰهُ
خَبِيْرٌۢ بِمَا تَعْمَلُوْنَ ۞

LOSS AND GAIN
(TAGHABUN)

In the name of Allah,
the Beneficent, the Merciful.

1. Whatever is in the heavens and whatever is in the earth declares the glory of Allah; to Him belongs the kingdom, and to Him is due (all) praise, and He has power over all things.

2. He it is Who created you, but one of you is an unbeliever and another of you is a believer; and Allah sees what you do.

3. He created the heavens and the earth with truth, and He formed you, then made goodly your forms, and to Him is the ultimate resort.

4. He knows what is in the heavens and the earth, and He knows what you hide and what you manifest; and Allah is Cognizant of what is in the hearts.

5. Has there not come to you the story of those who disbelieved before, then tasted the evil result of their conduct, and they had a painful punishment?

6. That is because there came to them their apostles with clear arguments, but they said: Shall mortals guide us? So they disbelieved and turned back, and Allah does not stand in need (of anything), and Allah is Self-sufficient, Praised.

7. Those who disbelieve think that they shall never be raised. Say: Aye! by my Lord! you shall most certainly be raised, then you shall most certainly be informed of what you did; and that is easy to Allah.

8. Therefore believe in Allah and His Apostle and the Light which We have revealed; and Allah is Aware of what you do.

بِسْمِ اللّٰهِ الرَّحْمٰنِ الرَّحِيْمِ ۟

يُسَبِّحُ لِلّٰهِ مَا فِي السَّمٰوٰتِ وَمَا فِي الْاَرْضِ ۚ لَهُ الْمُلْكُ وَلَهُ الْحَمْدُ ۫ وَهُوَ عَلٰى كُلِّ شَيْءٍ قَدِيْرٌ ۟

هُوَ الَّذِيْ خَلَقَكُمْ فَمِنْكُمْ كَافِرٌ وَّمِنْكُمْ مُّؤْمِنٌ ۚ وَاللّٰهُ بِمَا تَعْمَلُوْنَ بَصِيْرٌ ۟

خَلَقَ السَّمٰوٰتِ وَالْاَرْضَ بِالْحَقِّ وَصَوَّرَكُمْ فَاَحْسَنَ صُوَرَكُمْ ۚ وَاِلَيْهِ الْمَصِيْرُ ۟

يَعْلَمُ مَا فِي السَّمٰوٰتِ وَالْاَرْضِ وَيَعْلَمُ مَا تُسِرُّوْنَ وَمَا تُعْلِنُوْنَ ۚ وَاللّٰهُ عَلِيْمٌۢ بِذَاتِ الصُّدُوْرِ ۟

اَلَمْ يَأْتِكُمْ نَبَؤُا الَّذِيْنَ كَفَرُوْا مِنْ قَبْلُ ۫ فَذَاقُوْا وَبَالَ اَمْرِهِمْ وَلَهُمْ عَذَابٌ اَلِيْمٌ ۟

ذٰلِكَ بِاَنَّهٗ كَانَتْ تَّأْتِيْهِمْ رُسُلُهُمْ بِالْبَيِّنٰتِ فَقَالُوْۤا اَبَشَرٌ يَّهْدُوْنَنَا ۫ فَكَفَرُوْا وَتَوَلَّوْا وَّاسْتَغْنَى اللّٰهُ ۚ وَاللّٰهُ غَنِيٌّ حَمِيْدٌ ۟

زَعَمَ الَّذِيْنَ كَفَرُوْۤا اَنْ لَّنْ يُّبْعَثُوْا ۚ قُلْ بَلٰى وَرَبِّيْ لَتُبْعَثُنَّ ثُمَّ لَتُنَبَّؤُنَّ بِمَا عَمِلْتُمْ ۚ وَذٰلِكَ عَلَى اللّٰهِ يَسِيْرٌ ۟

فَاٰمِنُوْا بِاللّٰهِ وَرَسُوْلِهٖ وَالنُّوْرِ الَّذِيْۤ اَنْزَلْنَا ۚ وَاللّٰهُ بِمَا تَعْمَلُوْنَ خَبِيْرٌ ۟

9. On the day that He will gather you for the day of gathering, that is the day of loss and gain; and whoever believes in Allah and does good, He will remove from him his evil and cause him to enter gardens beneath which rivers flow, to abide therein forever; that is the great achievement.

10. And (as for) those who disbelieve and reject Our communications, they are the inmates of the fire, to abide therein, and evil is the resort.

11. No affliction comes about but by Allah's permission; and whoever believes in Allah, He guides aright his heart; and Allah is Cognizant of all things.

12. And obey Allah and obey the Apostle, but if you turn back, then upon Our Apostle devolves only the clear delivery (of the message).

13. Allah, there is no god but He; and upon Allah, then, let the believers rely.

14. O you who believe! surely from among your wives and your children there is an enemy to you; therefore beware of them; and if you pardon and forbear and forgive, then surely Allah is Forgiving, Merciful.

15. Your possessions and your children are only a trial, and Allah it is with Whom is a great reward.

16. Therefore be careful of (your duty to) Allah as much as you can, and hear and obey and spend, it is better for your souls; and whoever is saved from the greediness of his soul, these it is that are the successful.

17. If you set apart for Allah a goodly portion, He will double it for you and forgive you; and Allah is the Multiplier (of rewards), Forbearing,

18. The Knower of the unseen and the seen, the Mighty, the Wise.

THE DIVORCE
(TALAQ)

**In the name of Allah,
the Beneficent, the Merciful.**

1. O Prophet! when you divorce women, divorce them for their prescribed time, and calculate the number of the days prescribed, and be careful of (your duty to) Allah, your Lord. Do not drive them out of their houses, nor should they themselves go forth, unless they commit an open indecency; and these are the limits of Allah, and whoever goes beyond the limits of Allah, he indeed does injustice to his own soul. You do not know that Allah may after that bring about reunion.

2. So when they have reached their prescribed time, then retain them with kindness or separate them with kindness, and call to witness two men of justice from among you, and give upright testimony for Allah. With that is admonished he who believes in Allah and the latter day; and whoever is careful of (his duty to) Allah, He will make for him an outlet,

3. And give him sustenance from whence he thinks not; and whoever trusts in Allah, He is sufficient for him; surely Allah attains His purpose; Allah indeed has appointed a measure for everything.

4. And (as for) those of your women who have despaired of menstruation, if you have a doubt, their prescribed time shall be three months, and of those too who have not had their courses; and (as for) the pregnant women, their prescribed time is that they lay down their burden; and whoever is careful of (his duty to) Allah He will make easy for him his affair.

5. That is the command of Allah which He has revealed to you, and whoever is careful of (his duty to) Allah, He will remove from him his evil and give him a big reward.

بِسْمِ اللهِ الرَّحْمٰنِ الرَّحِيْمِ

يٰۤاَيُّهَا النَّبِيُّ اِذَا طَلَّقْتُمُ النِّسَآءَ فَطَلِّقُوْهُنَّ لِعِدَّتِهِنَّ وَاَحْصُوا الْعِدَّةَ وَاتَّقُوا اللهَ رَبَّكُمْ لَا تُخْرِجُوْهُنَّ مِنْ بُيُوْتِهِنَّ وَلَا يَخْرُجْنَ اِلَّاۤ اَنْ يَّأْتِيْنَ بِفَاحِشَةٍ مُّبَيِّنَةٍ وَتِلْكَ حُدُوْدُ اللهِ وَمَنْ يَّتَعَدَّ حُدُوْدَ اللهِ فَقَدْ ظَلَمَ نَفْسَهُ لَا تَدْرِيْ لَعَلَّ اللهَ يُحْدِثُ بَعْدَ ذٰلِكَ اَمْرًا ۞

فَاِذَا بَلَغْنَ اَجَلَهُنَّ فَاَمْسِكُوْهُنَّ بِمَعْرُوْفٍ اَوْ فَارِقُوْهُنَّ بِمَعْرُوْفٍ وَّاَشْهِدُوْا ذَوَيْ عَدْلٍ مِّنْكُمْ وَاَقِيْمُوا الشَّهَادَةَ لِلّٰهِ ذٰلِكُمْ يُوْعَظُ بِهٖ مَنْ كَانَ يُؤْمِنُ بِاللهِ وَالْيَوْمِ الْاٰخِرِ وَمَنْ يَّتَّقِ اللهَ يَجْعَلْ لَّهُ مَخْرَجًا ۞ وَّيَرْزُقْهُ مِنْ حَيْثُ لَا يَحْتَسِبُ وَمَنْ يَّتَوَكَّلْ عَلَى اللهِ فَهُوَ حَسْبُهُ اِنَّ اللهَ بَالِغُ اَمْرِهٖ قَدْ جَعَلَ اللهُ لِكُلِّ شَيْءٍ قَدْرًا ۞

وَالّٰٓئِيْ يَئِسْنَ مِنَ الْمَحِيْضِ مِنْ نِّسَآئِكُمْ اِنِ ارْتَبْتُمْ فَعِدَّتُهُنَّ ثَلٰثَةُ اَشْهُرٍ وَّالّٰٓئِيْ لَمْ يَحِضْنَ وَاُولَاتُ الْاَحْمَالِ اَجَلُهُنَّ اَنْ يَّضَعْنَ حَمْلَهُنَّ وَمَنْ يَّتَّقِ اللهَ يَجْعَلْ لَّهُ مِنْ اَمْرِهٖ يُسْرًا ۞

ذٰلِكَ اَمْرُ اللهِ اَنْزَلَهٗۤ اِلَيْكُمْ وَمَنْ يَّتَّقِ اللهَ يُكَفِّرْ عَنْهُ سَيِّاٰتِهٖ وَيُعْظِمْ لَهٗۤ اَجْرًا ۞

6. Lodge them where you lodge according to your means, and do not injure them in order that you may straiten them; and if they are pregnant, spend on them until they lay down their burden; then if they suckle for you, give them their recompense, and enjoin one another among you to do good; and if you disagree, another (woman) shall suckle for him.

7. Let him who has abundance spend out of his abundance, and whoever has his means of subsistence straitened to him, let him spend out of that which Allah has given him; Allah does not lay on any soul a burden except to the extent to which He has granted it; Allah brings about ease after difficulty.

8. And how many a town which rebelled against the commandment of its Lord and His apostles, so We called it to account severely and We chastised it (with) a stern chastisement.

9. So it tasted the evil result of its conduct, and the end of its affair was perdition.

10. Allah has prepared for them severe chastisement, therefore be careful of (your duty to) Allah, O men of understanding who believe! Allah has indeed revealed to you a reminder,

11. An Apostle who recites to you the clear communications of Allah so that he may bring forth those who believe and do good deeds from darkness into light; and whoever believes in Allah and does good deeds, He will cause him to enter gardens beneath which rivers flow, to abide therein forever; Allah has indeed given him a goodly sustenance.

12. Allah is He Who created seven heavens, and of the earth the like of them; the decree continues to descend among them, that you may know that Allah has power over all things and that Allah indeed encompasses all things in (His) knowledge.

اَسْكِنُوْهُنَّ مِنْ حَيْثُ سَكَنْتُمْ مِّنْ وُّجْدِكُمْ وَلَا تُضَآرُّوْهُنَّ لِتُضَيِّقُوْا عَلَيْهِنَّ ۚ وَاِنْ كُنَّ اُولَاتِ حَمْلٍ فَاَنْفِقُوْا عَلَيْهِنَّ حَتّٰى يَضَعْنَ حَمْلَهُنَّ ۚ فَاِنْ اَرْضَعْنَ لَكُمْ فَاٰتُوْهُنَّ اُجُوْرَهُنَّ ۚ وَأْتَمِرُوْا بَيْنَكُمْ بِمَعْرُوْفٍ ۚ وَاِنْ تَعَاسَرْتُمْ فَسَتُرْضِعُ لَهٗ اُخْرٰى ۵

لِيُنْفِقْ ذُوْ سَعَةٍ مِّنْ سَعَتِهٖ ۚ وَمَنْ قُدِرَ عَلَيْهِ رِزْقُهٗ فَلْيُنْفِقْ مِمَّآ اٰتٰىهُ اللّٰهُ ۚ لَا يُكَلِّفُ اللّٰهُ نَفْسًا اِلَّا مَآ اٰتٰىهَا ۚ سَيَجْعَلُ اللّٰهُ بَعْدَ عُسْرٍ يُّسْرًا ۷

وَكَاَيِّنْ مِّنْ قَرْيَةٍ عَتَتْ عَنْ اَمْرِ رَبِّهَا وَرُسُلِهٖ فَحَاسَبْنٰهَا حِسَابًا شَدِيْدًا ۙ وَّعَذَّبْنٰهَا عَذَابًا نُّكْرًا ۸

فَذَاقَتْ وَبَالَ اَمْرِهَا وَكَانَ عَاقِبَةُ اَمْرِهَا خُسْرًا ۹

اَعَدَّ اللّٰهُ لَهُمْ عَذَابًا شَدِيْدًا ۙ فَاتَّقُوا اللّٰهَ يٰٓاُولِي الْاَلْبَابِ ۛ الَّذِيْنَ اٰمَنُوْا ۛ قَدْ اَنْزَلَ اللّٰهُ اِلَيْكُمْ ذِكْرًا ۱۰

رَّسُوْلًا يَّتْلُوْا عَلَيْكُمْ اٰيٰتِ اللّٰهِ مُبَيِّنٰتٍ لِّيُخْرِجَ الَّذِيْنَ اٰمَنُوْا وَعَمِلُوا الصّٰلِحٰتِ مِنَ الظُّلُمٰتِ اِلَى النُّوْرِ ۚ وَمَنْ يُّؤْمِنْ بِاللّٰهِ وَيَعْمَلْ صَالِحًا يُّدْخِلْهُ جَنّٰتٍ تَجْرِيْ مِنْ تَحْتِهَا الْاَنْهٰرُ خٰلِدِيْنَ فِيْهَآ اَبَدًا ۚ قَدْ اَحْسَنَ اللّٰهُ لَهٗ رِزْقًا ۱۱

اَللّٰهُ الَّذِيْ خَلَقَ سَبْعَ سَمٰوٰتٍ وَّمِنَ الْاَرْضِ مِثْلَهُنَّ ۚ يَتَنَزَّلُ الْاَمْرُ بَيْنَهُنَّ لِتَعْلَمُوْٓا اَنَّ اللّٰهَ عَلٰى كُلِّ شَيْءٍ قَدِيْرٌ ۙ وَّاَنَّ اللّٰهَ قَدْ اَحَاطَ بِكُلِّ شَيْءٍ عِلْمًا ۱۲

THE PROHIBITION
(TAHRIM)

**In the Name of Allah,
the Beneficent, the Merciful.**

1. O Prophet! why do you forbid (yourself) that which Allah has made lawful for you; you seek to please your wives; and Allah is Forgiving, Merciful.

2. Allah indeed has sanctioned for you the expiation of your oaths and Allah is your Protector, and He is the Knowing, the Wise.

3. And when the prophet secretly communicated a piece of information to one of his wives—but when she informed (others) of it, and Allah made him to know it, he made known part of it and avoided part; so when he informed her of it, she said: Who informed you of this? He said: The Knowing, the one Aware, informed me.

4. If you both turn to Allah, then indeed your hearts are already inclined (to this); and if you back up each other against him, then surely Allah it is Who is his Guardian, and Jibreel and the believers that do good, and the angels after that are the aiders.

5. Maybe, his Lord, if he divorce you, will give him in your place wives better than you, submissive, faithful, obedient, penitent, adorers, fasters, widows and virgins.

6. O you who believe! save yourselves and your families from a fire whose fuel is men and stones; over it are angels stern and strong, they do not disobey Allah in what He commands them, and do as they are commanded.

7. O you who disbelieve! do not urge excuses today; you shall be rewarded only according to what you did.

يَا۟يُّهَا الَّذِيۡنَ كَفَرُوۡا لَا تَعۡتَذِرُوا الۡيَوۡمَ ؕ اِنَّمَا تُجۡزَوۡنَ مَا كُنۡتُمۡ تَعۡمَلُوۡنَ ۞

8. O you who believe! turn to Allah a sincere turning; maybe your Lord will remove from you your evil and cause you to enter gardens beneath which rivers flow, on the day on which Allah will not abase the Prophet and those who believe with him; their light shall run on before them and on their right hands; they shall say: Our Lord! make perfect for us our light, and grant us protection, surely Thou hast power over all things.

يَا۟يُّهَا الَّذِيۡنَ اٰمَنُوۡا تُوۡبُوۡۤا اِلَى اللّٰهِ تَوۡبَةً نَّصُوۡحًا ؕ عَسٰى رَبُّكُمۡ اَنۡ يُّكَفِّرَ عَنۡكُمۡ سَيِّاٰتِكُمۡ وَيُدۡخِلَكُمۡ جَنّٰتٍ تَجۡرِيۡ مِنۡ تَحۡتِهَا الۡاَنۡهٰرُ ۙ يَوۡمَ لَا يُخۡزِى اللّٰهُ النَّبِيَّ وَالَّذِيۡنَ اٰمَنُوۡا مَعَهٗ ۚ نُوۡرُهُمۡ يَسۡعٰى بَيۡنَ اَيۡدِيۡهِمۡ وَبِاَيۡمَانِهِمۡ يَقُوۡلُوۡنَ رَبَّنَاۤ اَتۡمِمۡ لَنَا نُوۡرَنَا وَاغۡفِرۡ لَنَا ۚ اِنَّكَ عَلٰى كُلِّ شَيۡءٍ قَدِيۡرٌ ۞

9. O Prophet! strive hard against the unbelievers and the hypocrites, and be hard against them; and their abode is hell; and evil is the resort.

يَا۟يُّهَا النَّبِيُّ جَاهِدِ الۡكُفَّارَ وَالۡمُنٰفِقِيۡنَ وَاغۡلُظۡ عَلَيۡهِمۡ ؕ وَمَاۡوٰىهُمۡ جَهَنَّمُ ؕ وَبِئۡسَ الۡمَصِيۡرُ ۞

10. Allah sets forth an example to those who disbelieve the wife of Nuh and the wife of Lut: they were both under two of Our righteous servants, but they acted treacherously towards them so they availed them naught against Allah, and it was said: Enter both the fire with those who enter.

ضَرَبَ اللّٰهُ مَثَلًا لِّلَّذِيۡنَ كَفَرُوا امۡرَاَتَ نُوۡحٍ وَّامۡرَاَتَ لُوۡطٍ ؕ كَانَتَا تَحۡتَ عَبۡدَيۡنِ مِنۡ عِبَادِنَا صَالِحَيۡنِ فَخَانَتٰهُمَا فَلَمۡ يُغۡنِيَا عَنۡهُمَا مِنَ اللّٰهِ شَيۡـًٔا وَّقِيۡلَ ادۡخُلَا النَّارَ مَعَ الدّٰخِلِيۡنَ ۞

11. And Allah sets forth an example to those who believe the wife of Firon when she said: My Lord! build for me a house with Thee in the garden and deliver me from Firon and his doing, and deliver me from the unjust people:

وَضَرَبَ اللّٰهُ مَثَلًا لِّلَّذِيۡنَ اٰمَنُوا امۡرَاَتَ فِرۡعَوۡنَ ۘ اِذۡ قَالَتۡ رَبِّ ابۡنِ لِيۡ عِنۡدَكَ بَيۡتًا فِى الۡجَنَّةِ وَنَجِّنِيۡ مِنۡ فِرۡعَوۡنَ وَعَمَلِهٖ وَنَجِّنِيۡ مِنَ الۡقَوۡمِ الظّٰلِمِيۡنَ ۞

12. And Marium, the daughter of Imran, who guarded her chastity, so We breathed into her of Our inspiration and she accepted the truth of the words of her Lord and His books, and she was of the obedient ones.

وَمَرۡيَمَ ابۡنَتَ عِمۡرٰنَ الَّتِيۡۤ اَحۡصَنَتۡ فَرۡجَهَا فَنَفَخۡنَا فِيۡهِ مِنۡ رُّوۡحِنَا وَصَدَّقَتۡ بِكَلِمٰتِ رَبِّهَا وَكُتُبِهٖ وَكَانَتۡ مِنَ الۡقٰنِتِيۡنَ ۞

THE KINGDOM
(MULK)

In the name of Allah,
the Beneficent, the Merciful.

1. Blessed is He in Whose hand is the kingdom, and He has power over all things,

2. Who created death and life that He may try you—which of you is best in deeds; and He is the Mighty, the Forgiving,

3. Who created the seven heavens one above another; you see no incongruity in the creation of the Beneficent God; then look again, can you see any disorder?

4. Then turn back the eye again and again; your look shall come back to you confused while it is fatigued.

5. And certainly We have adorned this lower heaven with lamps and We have made these missiles for the Shaitans, and We have prepared for them the chastisement of burning.

6. And for those who disbelieve in their Lord is the punishment of hell, and evil is the resort.

7. When they shall be cast therein, they shall hear a loud moaning of it as it heaves,

8. Almost bursting for fury. Whenever a group is cast into it, its keeper shall ask them: Did there not come to you a warner?

9. They shall say: Yea! indeed there came to us a warner, but we rejected (him) and said: Allah has not revealed anything; you are only in a great error.

10. And they shall say: Had we but listened or pondered, we should not have been among the inmates of the burning fire.

11. So they shall acknowledge their sins, but far will be (forgiveness) from the inmates of the burning fire.

12. (As for) those who fear their Lord in secret, they shall surely have forgiveness and a great reward.

13. And conceal your word or manifest it; surely He is Cognizant of what is in the hearts.

14. Does He not know, Who created? And He is the Knower of the subtleties, the Aware.

15. He it is Who made the earth smooth for you, therefore go about in the spacious sides thereof, and eat of His sustenance, and to Him is the return after death.

16. Are you secure of those in the heaven that He should not make the earth to swallow you up? Then lo! it shall be in a state of commotion.

17. Or are you secure of those in the heaven that He should not send down upon you a punishment? Then shall you know how was My warning.

18. And certainly those before them rejected (the truth), then how was My disapproval.

19. Have they not seen the birds above them expanding (their wings) and contracting (them)? What is it that withholds them save the Beneficent God? Surely He sees everything.

20. Or who is it that will be a host for you to assist you besides the Beneficent God? The unbelievers are only in deception.

21. Or who is it that will give you sustenance if He should withhold His sustenance? Nay! they persist in disdain and aversion.

وَقَالُوا لَوْ كُنَّا نَسْمَعُ أَوْ نَعْقِلُ مَا كُنَّا فِيْ أَصْحٰبِ السَّعِيْرِ ۝

فَاعْتَرَفُوْا بِذَنْبِهِمْ فَسُحْقًا لِّأَصْحٰبِ السَّعِيْرِ ۝

إِنَّ الَّذِيْنَ يَخْشَوْنَ رَبَّهُمْ بِالْغَيْبِ لَهُمْ مَّغْفِرَةٌ وَّأَجْرٌ كَبِيْرٌ ۝

وَأَسِرُّوْا قَوْلَكُمْ أَوِ اجْهَرُوْا بِهِ ۚ إِنَّهُ عَلِيْمٌۢ بِذَاتِ الصُّدُوْرِ ۝

أَلَا يَعْلَمُ مَنْ خَلَقَ ۗ وَهُوَ اللَّطِيْفُ الْخَبِيْرُ ۝

هُوَ الَّذِيْ جَعَلَ لَكُمُ الْأَرْضَ ذَلُوْلًا فَامْشُوْا فِيْ مَنَاكِبِهَا وَكُلُوْا مِنْ رِّزْقِهِ ۗ وَإِلَيْهِ النُّشُوْرُ ۝

ءَأَمِنْتُمْ مَّنْ فِى السَّمَآءِ أَنْ يَّخْسِفَ بِكُمُ الْأَرْضَ فَإِذَا هِيَ تَمُوْرُ ۝

أَمْ أَمِنْتُمْ مَّنْ فِى السَّمَآءِ أَنْ يُّرْسِلَ عَلَيْكُمْ حَاصِبًا ۗ فَسَتَعْلَمُوْنَ كَيْفَ نَذِيْرِ ۝

وَلَقَدْ كَذَّبَ الَّذِيْنَ مِنْ قَبْلِهِمْ فَكَيْفَ كَانَ نَكِيْرِ ۝

أَوَلَمْ يَرَوْا إِلَى الطَّيْرِ فَوْقَهُمْ صَآفَّاتٍ وَّيَقْبِضْنَ ۚ مَا يُمْسِكُهُنَّ إِلَّا الرَّحْمٰنُ ۗ إِنَّهُ بِكُلِّ شَيْءٍ بَصِيْرٌ ۝

أَمَّنْ هٰذَا الَّذِيْ هُوَ جُنْدٌ لَّكُمْ يَنْصُرُكُمْ مِّنْ دُوْنِ الرَّحْمٰنِ ۚ إِنِ الْكٰفِرُوْنَ إِلَّا فِيْ غُرُوْرٍ ۝

أَمَّنْ هٰذَا الَّذِيْ يَرْزُقُكُمْ إِنْ أَمْسَكَ رِزْقَهُ ۚ بَلْ لَّجُّوْا فِيْ عُتُوٍّ وَّنُفُوْرٍ ۝

22. What! is he who goes prone upon his face better guided or he who walks upright upon a straight path?

23. Say: He it is Who brought you into being and made for you the ears and the eyes and the hearts: little is it that you give thanks.

24. Say: He it is Who multiplied you in the earth and to Him you shall be gathered.

25. And they say: When shall this threat be (executed) if you are truthful?

26. Say: The knowledge (thereof) is only with Allah and I am only a plain warner.

27. But when they shall see it nigh, the faces of those who disbelieve shall be sorry, and it shall be said; This is that which you used to call for.

28. Say: Have you considered if Allah should destroy me and those with me—rather He will have mercy on us; yet who will protect the unbelievers from a painful punishment?

29. Say: He is the Beneficent God, we believe in Him and on Him do we rely, so you shall come to know who it is that is in clear error.

30. Say: Have you considered if your water should go down, who is it then that will bring you flowing water?

أَفَمَنْ يَّمْشِىْ مُكِبًّا عَلٰى وَجْهِهٖٓ أَهْدٰىٓ أَمَّنْ يَّمْشِىْ سَوِيًّا عَلٰى صِرَاطٍ مُّسْتَقِيْمٍ ۞

قُلْ هُوَ الَّذِىٓ أَنْشَأَكُمْ وَجَعَلَ لَكُمُ السَّمْعَ وَ الْأَبْصَارَ وَالْأَفْئِدَةَ ۗ قَلِيْلًا مَّا تَشْكُرُوْنَ ۞

قُلْ هُوَ الَّذِىٓ ذَرَأَكُمْ فِى الْأَرْضِ وَإِلَيْهِ تُحْشَرُوْنَ ۞

وَيَقُوْلُوْنَ مَتٰى هٰذَا الْوَعْدُ إِنْ كُنْتُمْ صٰدِقِيْنَ ۞

قُلْ إِنَّمَا الْعِلْمُ عِنْدَ اللّٰهِ وَإِنَّمَا أَنَا نَذِيْرٌ مُّبِيْنٌ ۞

فَلَمَّا رَأَوْهُ زُلْفَةً سِيْٓئَتْ وُجُوْهُ الَّذِيْنَ كَفَرُوْا وَقِيْلَ هٰذَا الَّذِىْ كُنْتُمْ بِهٖ تَدَّعُوْنَ ۞

قُلْ أَرَأَيْتُمْ إِنْ أَهْلَكَنِىَ اللّٰهُ وَمَنْ مَّعِىَ أَوْ رَحِمَنَا فَمَنْ يُّجِيْرُ الْكٰفِرِيْنَ مِنْ عَذَابٍ أَلِيْمٍ ۞

قُلْ هُوَ الرَّحْمٰنُ آمَنَّا بِهٖ وَعَلَيْهِ تَوَكَّلْنَا ۚ فَسَتَعْلَمُوْنَ مَنْ هُوَ فِىْ ضَلٰلٍ مُّبِيْنٍ ۞

قُلْ أَرَأَيْتُمْ إِنْ أَصْبَحَ مَاؤُكُمْ غَوْرًا فَمَنْ يَّأْتِيْكُمْ بِمَاءٍ مَّعِيْنٍ ۞

THE PEN
(QALAM)

**In the name of Allah,
the Beneficent, the Merciful.**

1. Noon. I swear by the pen and what the angels write,

2. By the grace of your Lord you are not mad.

3. And most surely you shall have a reward never to be cut off.

4. And most surely you conform (yourself) to sublime morality.

5. So you shall see, and they (too) shall see,

6. Which of you is afflicted with madness.

7. Surely your Lord best knows him who errs from His way, and He best knows the followers of the right course.

8. So do not yield to the rejecters.

9. They wish that you should be pliant so they (too) would be pliant.

10. And yield not to any mean swearer,

11. Defamer, going about with slander,

12. Forbidder of good, outstepping the limits, sinful,

13. Ignoble, besides all that, base-born;

14. Because he possesses wealth and sons.

15. When Our communications are recited to him, he says: Stories of those of yore.

16. We will brand him on the nose.

17. Surely We will try them as We tried the owners of the garden, when they swore that they would certainly cut off the produce in the morning,

573

18. And were not willing to set aside a portion (for the poor).

19. Then there encompassed it a visitation from your Lord while they were sleeping.

20. So it became as black, barren land.

21. And they called out to each other in the morning,

22. Saying: Go early to your tilth if you would cut (the produce).

23. So they went, while they consulted together secretly,

24. Saying: No poor man shall enter it today upon you.

25. And in the morning they went, having the power to prevent.

26. But when they saw it, they said: Most surely we have gone astray.

27. Nay! we are made to suffer privation.

28. The best of them said: Did I not say to you, Why do you not glorify (Allah)?

29. They said: Glory be to our Lord, surely we were unjust.

30. Then some of them advanced against others, blaming each other.

31. Said they: O woe to us! surely we were inordinate:

32. Maybe, our Lord will give us instead one better than it; surely to our Lord do we make our humble petition.

33. Such is the chastisement, and certainly the chastisement of the hereafter is greater, did they but know!

34. Surely those who guard (against evil) shall have with their Lord gardens of bliss.

35. What! shall We then make (i.e. treat) those who submit as the guilty?

36. What has happened to you? How do you judge?

37. Or have you a book wherein you read,

وَلَا يَسْتَثْنُونَ ۝

فَطَافَ عَلَيْهَا طَآئِفٌ مِّنْ رَّبِّكَ وَهُمْ نَآئِمُونَ ۝

فَأَصْبَحَتْ كَالصَّرِيمِ ۝

فَتَنَادَوْا مُصْبِحِينَ ۝

أَنِ اغْدُوا عَلَى حَرْثِكُمْ إِنْ كُنْتُمْ صَارِمِينَ ۝

فَانْطَلَقُوا وَهُمْ يَتَخَافَتُونَ ۝

أَنْ لَا يَدْخُلَنَّهَا الْيَوْمَ عَلَيْكُمْ مِّسْكِينٌ ۝

وَغَدَوْا عَلَى حَرْدٍ قَادِرِينَ ۝

فَلَمَّا رَأَوْهَا قَالُوا إِنَّا لَضَآلُّونَ ۝

بَلْ نَحْنُ مَحْرُومُونَ ۝

قَالَ أَوْسَطُهُمْ أَلَمْ أَقُلْ لَكُمْ لَوْلَا تُسَبِّحُونَ ۝

قَالُوا سُبْحَانَ رَبِّنَا إِنَّا كُنَّا ظَالِمِينَ ۝

فَأَقْبَلَ بَعْضُهُمْ عَلَى بَعْضٍ يَتَلَاوَمُونَ ۝

قَالُوا يَا وَيْلَنَا إِنَّا كُنَّا طَاغِينَ ۝

عَسَى رَبُّنَا أَنْ يُبْدِلَنَا خَيْرًا مِّنْهَا إِنَّا إِلَى رَبِّنَا رَاغِبُونَ ۝

كَذَلِكَ الْعَذَابُ وَلَعَذَابُ الْآخِرَةِ أَكْبَرُ لَوْ كَانُوا يَعْلَمُونَ ۝

إِنَّ لِلْمُتَّقِينَ عِنْدَ رَبِّهِمْ جَنَّاتِ النَّعِيمِ ۝

أَفَنَجْعَلُ الْمُسْلِمِينَ كَالْمُجْرِمِينَ ۝

مَا لَكُمْ كَيْفَ تَحْكُمُونَ ۝

أَمْ لَكُمْ كِتَابٌ فِيهِ تَدْرُسُونَ ۝

38. That you have surely therein what you choose?

اِنَّ لَكُمْ فِيْهِ لَمَا تَخَيَّرُوْنَ ۚ

39. Or have you received from Us an agreement confirmed by an oath extending to the day of resurrection that you shall surely have what you demand?

اَمْ لَكُمْ اَيْمَانٌ عَلَيْنَا بَالِغَةٌ اِلٰى يَوْمِ الْقِيٰمَةِ اِنَّ لَكُمْ لَمَا تَحْكُمُوْنَ ۚ

40. Ask them which of them will vouch for that,

سَلْهُمْ اَيُّهُمْ بِذٰلِكَ زَعِيْمٌ ۙ

41. Or have they associates if they are truthful.

اَمْ لَهُمْ شُرَكَآءُ ۖ فَلْيَأْتُوْا بِشُرَكَآئِهِمْ اِنْ كَانُوْا صٰدِقِيْنَ

42. On the day when there shall be a severe affliction, and they shall be called upon to make obeisance, but they shall not be able,

يَوْمَ يُكْشَفُ عَنْ سَاقٍ وَّيُدْعَوْنَ اِلَى السُّجُوْدِ فَلَا يَسْتَطِيْعُوْنَ ۙ

43. Their looks cast down, abasement shall overtake them; and they were called upon to make obeisance indeed while yet they were safe.

خَاشِعَةً اَبْصَارُهُمْ تَرْهَقُهُمْ ذِلَّةٌ ۖ وَقَدْ كَانُوْا يُدْعَوْنَ اِلَى السُّجُوْدِ وَهُمْ سٰلِمُوْنَ

44. So leave Me and him who rejects this announcement; We will overtake them by degrees, from whence they perceive not:

فَذَرْنِيْ وَمَنْ يُّكَذِّبُ بِهٰذَا الْحَدِيْثِ ۖ سَنَسْتَدْرِجُهُمْ مِّنْ حَيْثُ لَا يَعْلَمُوْنَ ۙ

45. And I do bear with them, surely My plan is firm.

وَاُمْلِيْ لَهُمْ ۚ اِنَّ كَيْدِيْ مَتِيْنٌ

46. Or do you ask from them a reward, so that they are burdened with debt?

اَمْ تَسْئَلُهُمْ اَجْرًا فَهُمْ مِّنْ مَّغْرَمٍ مُّثْقَلُوْنَ ۙ

47. Or have they (the knowledge of) the unseen, so that they write (it) down?

اَمْ عِنْدَهُمُ الْغَيْبُ فَهُمْ يَكْتُبُوْنَ

48. So wait patiently for the judgment of your Lord, and be not like the companion of the fish, when he cried while he was in distress.

فَاصْبِرْ لِحُكْمِ رَبِّكَ وَلَا تَكُنْ كَصَاحِبِ الْحُوْتِ ۘ اِذْ نَادٰى وَهُوَ مَكْظُوْمٌ ۚ

49. Were it not that favor from his Lord had overtaken him, he would certainly have been cast down upon the naked ground while he was blamed.

لَوْلَا اَنْ تَدَارَكَهُ نِعْمَةٌ مِّنْ رَّبِّهٖ لَنُبِذَ بِالْعَرَآءِ وَهُوَ مَذْمُوْمٌ

50. Then his Lord chose him, and He made him of the good.

فَاجْتَبٰهُ رَبُّهُ فَجَعَلَهُ مِنَ الصّٰلِحِيْنَ

51. And those who disbelieve would almost smite you with their eyes when they hear the reminder, and they say: Most surely he is mad.

وَاِنْ يَّكَادُ الَّذِيْنَ كَفَرُوْا لَيُزْلِقُوْنَكَ بِاَبْصَارِهِمْ لَمَّا سَمِعُوا الذِّكْرَ وَيَقُوْلُوْنَ اِنَّهٗ لَمَجْنُوْنٌ

52. And it is naught but a reminder to the nations.

وَمَا هُوَ اِلَّا ذِكْرٌ لِّلْعٰلَمِيْنَ

THE SURE CALAMITY
(HAQQAH)

In the name of Allah,
the Beneficent, the Merciful.

1. The sure calamity!

2. What is the sure calamity!

3. And what would make you realize what the sure calamity is!

4. Samood and Ad called the striking calamity a lie.

5. Then as to Samood, they were destroyed by an excessively severe punishment.

6. And as to Ad, they were destroyed by a roaring, violent blast.

7. Which He made to prevail against them for seven nights and eight days unremittingly, so that you might have seen the people therein prostrate as if they were the trunks of hollow palms.

8. Do you then see of them one remaining?

9. And Firon and those before him and the overthrown cities continuously committed sins.

10. And they disobeyed the Apostle of their Lord, so He punished them with a vehement punishment.

11. Surely We bore you up in the ship when the water rose high,

12. So that We may make it a reminder to you, and that the retaining ear might retain it.

13. And when the trumpet is blown with a single blast,

14. And the earth and the mountains are borne away and crushed with a single crushing.

15. On that day shall the great event come to pass,

16. And the heaven shall cleave asunder, so that on that day it shall be frail,

بِسْمِ اللهِ الرَّحْمٰنِ الرَّحِيْمِ ۟

اَلْحَاقَّةُ ۟ۙ

مَا الْحَاقَّةُ ۟ۚ

وَمَاۤ اَدْرٰىكَ مَا الْحَاقَّةُ ۟ؕ

كَذَّبَتْ ثَمُوْدُ وَعَادٌۢ بِالْقَارِعَةِ ۟

فَاَمَّا ثَمُوْدُ فَاُهْلِكُوْا بِالطَّاغِيَةِ ۟

وَاَمَّا عَادٌ فَاُهْلِكُوْا بِرِيْحٍ صَرْصَرٍ عَاتِيَةٍ ۟ۙ

سَخَّرَهَا عَلَيْهِمْ سَبْعَ لَيَالٍ وَّثَمٰنِيَةَ اَيَّامٍ حُسُوْمًا فَتَرَى الْقَوْمَ فِيْهَا صَرْعٰى ۟ۙ كَاَنَّهُمْ اَعْجَازُ نَخْلٍ خَاوِيَةٍ ۟ۚ

فَهَلْ تَرٰى لَهُمْ مِّنْ بَاقِيَةٍ ۟

وَجَاۤءَ فِرْعَوْنُ وَمَنْ قَبْلَهٗ وَالْمُؤْتَفِكٰتُ بِالْخَاطِئَةِ ۟ۚ

فَعَصَوْا رَسُوْلَ رَبِّهِمْ فَاَخَذَهُمْ اَخْذَةً رَّابِيَةً ۟

اِنَّا لَمَّا طَغَا الْمَاۤءُ حَمَلْنٰكُمْ فِى الْجَارِيَةِ ۟ۙ

لِنَجْعَلَهَا لَكُمْ تَذْكِرَةً وَّتَعِيَهَاۤ اُذُنٌ وَّاعِيَةٌ ۟

فَاِذَا نُفِخَ فِى الصُّوْرِ نَفْخَةٌ وَّاحِدَةٌ ۟ۙ

وَّحُمِلَتِ الْاَرْضُ وَالْجِبَالُ فَدُكَّتَا دَكَّةً وَّاحِدَةً ۟ۙ

فَيَوْمَئِذٍ وَّقَعَتِ الْوَاقِعَةُ ۟ۙ

وَانْشَقَّتِ السَّمَاۤءُ فَهِىَ يَوْمَئِذٍ وَّاهِيَةٌ ۟ۙ

17. And the angels shall be on the sides thereof; and above them eight shall bear on that day your Lord's power.

وَالْمَلَكُ عَلَى اَرْجَآئِهَا ۘ وَ يَحْمِلُ عَرْشَ رَبِّكَ فَوْقَهُمْ يَوْمَئِذٍ ثَمٰنِيَةٌ ۗ ۞

18. On that day you shall be exposed to view—no secret of yours shall remain hidden.

يَوْمَئِذٍ تُعْرَضُوْنَ لَا تَخْفٰى مِنْكُمْ خَافِيَةٌ ۞

19. Then as for him who is given his book in his right hand, he will say: Lo! read my book:

فَاَمَّا مَنْ اُوْتِيَ كِتٰبَهُ بِيَمِيْنِهٖ ۙ فَيَقُوْلُ هَآؤُمُ اقْرَءُوْا كِتٰبِيَهْ ۞

20. Surely I knew that I shall meet my account.

اِنِّيْ ظَنَنْتُ اَنِّيْ مُلٰقٍ حِسَابِيَهْ ۞

21. So he shall be in a life of pleasure,

فَهُوَ فِيْ عِيْشَةٍ رَّاضِيَةٍ ۞

22. In a lofty garden,

فِيْ جَنَّةٍ عَالِيَةٍ ۞

23. The fruits of which are near at hand:

قُطُوْفُهَا دَانِيَةٌ ۞

24. Eat and drink pleasantly for what you did beforehand in the days gone by.

كُلُوْا وَاشْرَبُوْا هَنِيْٓئًا ۢ بِمَآ اَسْلَفْتُمْ فِى الْاَيَّامِ الْخَالِيَةِ ۞

25. And as for him who is given his book in his left hand he shall say: O would that my book had never been given me:

وَاَمَّا مَنْ اُوْتِيَ كِتٰبَهُ بِشِمَالِهٖ ۙ فَيَقُوْلُ يٰلَيْتَنِيْ لَمْ اُوْتَ كِتٰبِيَهْ ۞

26. And I had not known what my account was:

وَلَمْ اَدْرِ مَا حِسَابِيَهْ ۞

27. O would that it had made an end (of me):

يٰلَيْتَهَا كَانَتِ الْقَاضِيَةَ ۞

28. My wealth has availed me nothing:

مَآ اَغْنٰى عَنِّيْ مَالِيَهْ ۞

29. My authority is gone away from me.

هَلَكَ عَنِّيْ سُلْطٰنِيَهْ ۞

30. Lay hold on him, then put a chain on him,

خُذُوْهُ فَغُلُّوْهُ ۞

31. Then cast him into the burning fire,

ثُمَّ الْجَحِيْمَ صَلُّوْهُ ۞

32. Then thrust him into a chain the length of which is seventy cubits.

ثُمَّ فِيْ سِلْسِلَةٍ ذَرْعُهَا سَبْعُوْنَ ذِرَاعًا فَاسْلُكُوْهُ ۞

33. Surely he did not believe in Allah, the Great,

اِنَّهٗ كَانَ لَا يُؤْمِنُ بِاللّٰهِ الْعَظِيْمِ ۞

34. Nor did he urge the feeding of the poor.

وَلَا يَحُضُّ عَلٰى طَعَامِ الْمِسْكِيْنِ ۞

577

35. Therefore he has not here today a true friend,

فَلَيْسَ لَهُ الْيَوْمَ هٰهُنَا حَمِيْمٌ ۙ

36. Nor any food except refuse,

وَّلَا طَعَامٌ اِلَّا مِنْ غِسْلِيْنٍ ۙ

37. Which none but the wrongdoers eat.

لَّا يَأْكُلُهُ اِلَّا الْخَاطِئُوْنَ ۚ

38. But nay! I swear by that which you see,

فَلَا اُقْسِمُ بِمَا تُبْصِرُوْنَ ۙ

39. And that which you do not see.

وَمَا لَا تُبْصِرُوْنَ ۙ

40. Most surely, it is the Word brought by an honored Apostle,

اِنَّهُ لَقَوْلُ رَسُوْلٍ كَرِيْمٍ ۚ

41. And it is not the word of a poet; little is it that you believe;

وَّمَا هُوَ بِقَوْلِ شَاعِرٍ قَلِيْلًا مَّا تُؤْمِنُوْنَ ۙ

42. Nor the word of a soothsayer; little is it that you mind.

وَلَا بِقَوْلِ كَاهِنٍ قَلِيْلًا مَّا تَذَكَّرُوْنَ ۙ

43. It is a revelation from the Lord of the worlds.

تَنْزِيْلٌ مِّنْ رَّبِّ الْعٰلَمِيْنَ ۙ

44. And if he had fabricated against Us some of the sayings,

وَلَوْ تَقَوَّلَ عَلَيْنَا بَعْضَ الْاَقَاوِيْلِ ۙ

45. We would certainly have seized him by the right hand,

لَاَخَذْنَا مِنْهُ بِالْيَمِيْنِ ۙ

46. Then We would certainly have cut off his aorta.

ثُمَّ لَقَطَعْنَا مِنْهُ الْوَتِيْنَ ۚ

47. And not one of you could have withheld Us from him.

فَمَا مِنْكُمْ مِّنْ اَحَدٍ عَنْهُ حٰجِزِيْنَ ۚ

48. And most surely it is a reminder for those who guard (against evil).

وَاِنَّهُ لَتَذْكِرَةٌ لِّلْمُتَّقِيْنَ ۚ

49. And most surely We know that some of you are rejecters.

وَاِنَّا لَنَعْلَمُ اَنَّ مِنْكُمْ مُّكَذِّبِيْنَ ۚ

50. And most surely it is a great grief to the unbelievers.

وَاِنَّهُ لَحَسْرَةٌ عَلَى الْكٰفِرِيْنَ ۚ

51. And most surely it is the true certainty.

وَاِنَّهُ لَحَقُّ الْيَقِيْنِ ۚ

52. Therefore glorify the name of your Lord, the Great.

فَسَبِّحْ بِاسْمِ رَبِّكَ الْعَظِيْمِ ۙ

578

THE WAYS OF ASCENT
(MA'ARIJ)

بِسْمِ اللهِ الرَّحْمٰنِ الرَّحِيْمِ ۞

**In the name of Allah,
the Beneficent, the Merciful.**

1. One demanding, demanded the chastisement which must befall

سَاَلَ سَآئِلٌ بِعَذَابٍ وَّاقِعٍ ۞

2. The unbelievers—there is none to avert it—

لِّلْكٰفِرِيْنَ لَيْسَ لَهٗ دَافِعٌ ۞

3. From Allah, the Lord of the ways of Ascent.

مِّنَ اللهِ ذِى الْمَعَارِجِ ۞

4. To Him ascend the angels and the Spirit in a day the measure of which is fifty thousand years.

تَعْرُجُ الْمَلٰٓئِكَةُ وَالرُّوْحُ اِلَيْهِ فِيْ يَوْمٍ كَانَ مِقْدَارُهٗ خَمْسِيْنَ اَلْفَ سَنَةٍ ۞

5. Therefore endure with a goodly patience.

فَاصْبِرْ صَبْرًا جَمِيْلًا ۞

6. Surely they think it to be far off,

اِنَّهُمْ يَرَوْنَهٗ بَعِيْدًا ۞

7. And We see it nigh.

وَّنَرٰىهُ قَرِيْبًا ۞

8. On the day when the heaven shall be as molten copper,

يَوْمَ تَكُوْنُ السَّمَآءُ كَالْمُهْلِ ۞

9. And the mountains shall be as tufts of wool;

وَتَكُوْنُ الْجِبَالُ كَالْعِهْنِ ۞

10. And friend shall not ask of friend,

وَلَا يَسْـَٔلُ حَمِيْمٌ حَمِيْمًا ۞

11. (Though) they shall be made to see each other. The guilty one would fain redeem himself from the chastisement of that day by (sacrificing) his children,

يُّبَصَّرُوْنَهُمْ يَوَدُّ الْمُجْرِمُ لَوْ يَفْتَدِيْ مِنْ عَذَابِ يَوْمِئِذٍ بِبَنِيْهِ ۞

12. And his wife and his brother,

وَصَاحِبَتِهٖ وَاَخِيْهِ ۞

13. And the nearest of his kinsfolk who gave him shelter,

وَفَصِيْلَتِهِ الَّتِيْ تُـٔوِيْهِ ۞

14. And all those that are in the earth, (wishing) then (that) this might deliver him.

وَمَنْ فِى الْاَرْضِ جَمِيْعًا ثُمَّ يُنْجِيْهِ ۞

15. By no means! Surely it is a flaming fire,

كَلَّا اِنَّهَا لَظٰى ۞

16. Dragging by the head,

نَزَّاعَةً لِّلشَّوٰى ۞

17. It shall claim him who turned and fled (from truth),

تَدْعُوْا مَنْ اَدْبَرَ وَتَوَلّٰى ۞

18. And amasses (wealth) then shuts it up.

وَجَمَعَ فَأَوْعٰى ۞

19. Surely man is created of a hasty temperament;

اِنَّ الْاِنْسَانَ خُلِقَ هَلُوْعًا ۞

20. Being greatly grieved when evil afflicts him,

اِذَا مَسَّهُ الشَّرُّ جَزُوْعًا ۞

21. And niggardly when good befalls him,

وَّاِذَا مَسَّهُ الْخَيْرُ مَنُوْعًا ۞

22. Except those who pray,

اِلَّا الْمُصَلِّيْنَ ۞

23. Those who are constant at their prayer,

الَّذِيْنَ هُمْ عَلٰى صَلَاتِهِمْ دَآئِمُوْنَ ۞

24. And those in whose wealth there is a fixed portion.

وَالَّذِيْنَ فِيْ اَمْوَالِهِمْ حَقٌّ مَّعْلُوْمٌ ۞

25. For him who begs and for him who is denied (good),

لِّلسَّآئِلِ وَالْمَحْرُوْمِ ۞

26. And those who accept the truth of the judgment day,

وَالَّذِيْنَ يُصَدِّقُوْنَ بِيَوْمِ الدِّيْنِ ۞

27. And those who are fearful of the chastisement of their Lord—

وَالَّذِيْنَ هُمْ مِّنْ عَذَابِ رَبِّهِمْ مُّشْفِقُوْنَ ۞

28. Surely the chastisement of their Lord is (a thing) not to be felt secure of—

اِنَّ عَذَابَ رَبِّهِمْ غَيْرُ مَأْمُوْنٍ ۞

29. And those who guard their private parts,

وَالَّذِيْنَ هُمْ لِفُرُوْجِهِمْ حٰفِظُوْنَ ۞

30. Except in the case of their wives or those whom their right hands possess—for these surely are not to be blamed,

اِلَّا عَلٰى اَزْوَاجِهِمْ اَوْ مَا مَلَكَتْ اَيْمَانُهُمْ فَاِنَّهُمْ غَيْرُ مَلُوْمِيْنَ ۞

31. But he who seeks to go beyond this, these it is that go beyond the limits—

فَمَنِ ابْتَغٰى وَرَآءَ ذٰلِكَ فَاُولٰٓئِكَ هُمُ الْعَادُوْنَ ۞

32. And those who are faithful to their trusts and their covenant,

وَالَّذِيْنَ هُمْ لِاَمٰنٰتِهِمْ وَعَهْدِهِمْ رَاعُوْنَ ۞

33. And those who are upright in their testimonies,

وَالَّذِيْنَ هُمْ بِشَهٰدٰتِهِمْ قَآئِمُوْنَ ۞

34. And those who keep a guard on their prayer,

وَالَّذِيْنَ هُمْ عَلٰى صَلَاتِهِمْ يُحَافِظُوْنَ ۞

35. Those shall be in gardens, honored.

اُولٰٓئِكَ فِيْ جَنّٰتٍ مُّكْرَمُوْنَ ۞

36. But what is the matter with those who disbelieve that they hasten on around you,

فَمَالِ الَّذِيْنَ كَفَرُوْا قِبَلَكَ مُهْطِعِيْنَ ۞

37. On the right hand and on the left, in sundry parties?

عَنِ الْيَمِيْنِ وَعَنِ الشِّمَالِ عِزِيْنَ ۞

38. Does every man of them desire that he should be made to enter the garden of bliss?

اَيَطْمَعُ كُلُّ امْرِئٍ مِّنْهُمْ اَنْ يُّدْخَلَ جَنَّةَ نَعِيْمٍۙ

39. By no means! Surely We have created them of what they know.

كَلَّاۭ اِنَّا خَلَقْنٰهُمْ مِّمَّا يَعْلَمُوْنَ۞

40. But nay! I swear by the Lord of the Easts and the Wests that We are certainly able

فَلَاۤ اُقْسِمُ بِرَبِّ الْمَشَارِقِ وَالْمَغَارِبِ اِنَّا لَقٰدِرُوْنَۙ

41. To bring instead (others) better than them, and We shall not be overcome.

عَلٰٓى اَنْ نُّبَدِّلَ خَيْرًا مِّنْهُمْۙ وَمَا نَحْنُ بِمَسْبُوْقِيْنَ۞

42. Therefore leave them alone to go on with the false discourses and to sport until they come face to face with that day of theirs with which they are threatened;

فَذَرْهُمْ يَخُوْضُوْا وَيَلْعَبُوْا حَتّٰى يُلٰقُوْا يَوْمَهُمُ الَّذِيْ يُوْعَدُوْنَۙ

43. The day on which they shall come forth from their graves in haste, as if they were hastening on to a goal,

يَوْمَ يَخْرُجُوْنَ مِنَ الْاَجْدَاثِ سِرَاعًا كَاَنَّهُمْ اِلٰى نُصُبٍ يُّوْفِضُوْنَۙ

44. Their eyes cast down; disgrace shall overtake them; that is the day which they were threatened with.

خَاشِعَةً اَبْصَارُهُمْ تَرْهَقُهُمْ ذِلَّةٌ ۭ ذٰلِكَ الْيَوْمُ الَّذِيْ كَانُوْا يُوْعَدُوْنَ۞

NUH

بِيَّايَهَا (٧١) سُوْرَةٌ نُوْحٍ مَكِّيَّةٌ رُوْعَاتُهَا

In the name of Allah,
the Beneficent, the Merciful.

بِسْمِ اللهِ الرَّحْمٰنِ الرَّحِيْمِ ۞

1. Surely We sent Nuh to his people, saying: Warn your people before there come upon them a painful chastisement.

اِنَّآ اَرْسَلْنَا نُوْحًا اِلٰى قَوْمِهٖۤ اَنْ اَنْذِرْ قَوْمَكَ مِنْ قَبْلِ اَنْ يَّاْتِيَهُمْ عَذَابٌ اَلِيْمٌ ۞

2. He said: O my people! Surely I am a plain warner to you:

قَالَ يٰقَوْمِ اِنِّىْ لَكُمْ نَذِيْرٌ مُّبِيْنٌ ۞

3. That you should serve Allah and be careful of (your duty to) Him and obey me:

اَنِ اعْبُدُوا اللهَ وَاتَّقُوْهُ وَاَطِيْعُوْنِ ۞

4. He will forgive you some of your faults and grant you a delay to an appointed term; surely the term of Allah when it comes is not postponed; did you but know!

يَغْفِرْ لَكُمْ مِّنْ ذُنُوْبِكُمْ وَيُؤَخِّرْكُمْ اِلٰٓى اَجَلٍ مُّسَمًّى اِنَّ اَجَلَ اللهِ اِذَا جَآءَ لَا يُؤَخَّرُ لَوْ كُنْتُمْ تَعْلَمُوْنَ ۞

5. He said: O my Lord! surely I have called my people by night and by day!

قَالَ رَبِّ اِنِّىْ دَعَوْتُ قَوْمِىْ لَيْلًا وَّنَهَارًا ۞

6. But my call has only made them flee the more:

فَلَمْ يَزِدْهُمْ دُعَآئِىْۤ اِلَّا فِرَارًا ۞

7. And whenever I have called them that Thou mayest forgive them, they put their fingers in their ears, cover themselves with their garments, and persist and are puffed up with pride:

وَاِنِّىْ كُلَّمَا دَعَوْتُهُمْ لِتَغْفِرَ لَهُمْ جَعَلُوْۤا اَصَابِعَهُمْ فِىْۤ اٰذَانِهِمْ وَاسْتَغْشَوْا ثِيَابَهُمْ وَاَصَرُّوْا وَاسْتَكْبَرُوا اسْتِكْبَارًا ۞

8. Then surely I called to them aloud:

ثُمَّ اِنِّىْ دَعَوْتُهُمْ جِهَارًا ۞

9. Then surely I spoke to them in public and I spoke to them in secret:

ثُمَّ اِنِّىْۤ اَعْلَنْتُ لَهُمْ وَاَسْرَرْتُ لَهُمْ اِسْرَارًا ۞

10. Then I said, Ask forgiveness of your Lord, surely He is the most Forgiving:

فَقُلْتُ اسْتَغْفِرُوْا رَبَّكُمْ اِنَّهُ كَانَ غَفَّارًا ۞

11. He will send down upon you the cloud, pouring down abundance of rain:

يُّرْسِلِ السَّمَآءَ عَلَيْكُمْ مِّدْرَارًا ۞

12. And help you with wealth and sons, and make for you gardens, and make for you rivers.

وَّيُمْدِدْكُمْ بِاَمْوَالٍ وَّبَنِيْنَ وَيَجْعَلْ لَّكُمْ جَنّٰتٍ وَّيَجْعَلْ لَّكُمْ اَنْهٰرًا ۞

13. What is the matter with you that you fear not the greatness of Allah?

مَا لَكُمْ لَا تَرْجُوْنَ لِلّٰهِ وَقَارًا ۞

14. And indeed He has created you through various grades:

وَقَدْ خَلَقَكُمْ اَطْوَارًا ۞

15. Do you not see how Allah has created the seven heavens one above another,

16. And made the moon therein a light, and made the sun a lamp?

17. And Allah has made you grow out of the earth as a growth:

18. Then He returns you to it, then will He bring you forth a (new) bringing forth:

19. And Allah has made for you the earth a wide expanse,

20. That you may go along therein in wide paths.

21. Nuh said: My Lord! surely they have disobeyed me and followed him whose wealth and children have added to him nothing but loss.

22. And they have planned a very great plan.

23. And they say: By no means leave your gods, nor leave Wadd, nor Suwa; nor Yaghus, and Yauq and Nasr.

24. And indeed they have led astray many, and do not increase the unjust in aught but error.

25. Because of their wrongs they were drowned, then made to enter fire, so they did not find any helpers besides Allah.

26. And Nuh said: My Lord! leave not upon the land any dweller from among the unbelievers:

27. For surely if Thou leave them they will lead astray Thy servants, and will not beget any but immoral, ungrateful (children);

28. My Lord! forgive me and my parents and him who enters my house believing, and the believing men and the believing women; and do not increase the unjust in aught but destruction!

اَلَمْ تَرَوْا كَيْفَ خَلَقَ اللّٰهُ سَبْعَ سَمٰوٰتٍ طِبَاقًا ۞

وَّجَعَلَ الْقَمَرَ فِيْهِنَّ نُوْرًا وَّجَعَلَ الشَّمْسَ

سِرَاجًا ۞

وَاللّٰهُ اَنْۢبَتَكُمْ مِّنَ الْاَرْضِ نَبَاتًا ۞

ثُمَّ يُعِيْدُكُمْ فِيْهَا وَيُخْرِجُكُمْ اِخْرَاجًا ۞

وَاللّٰهُ جَعَلَ لَكُمُ الْاَرْضَ بِسَاطًا ۞

لِّتَسْلُكُوْا مِنْهَا سُبُلًا فِجَاجًا ۞

قَالَ نُوْحٌ رَّبِّ اِنَّهُمْ عَصَوْنِيْ وَاتَّبَعُوْا مَنْ لَّمْ

يَزِدْهُ مَالُهٗ وَوَلَدُهٗٓ اِلَّا خَسَارًا ۞

وَمَكَرُوْا مَكْرًا كُبَّارًا ۞

وَقَالُوْا لَا تَذَرُنَّ اٰلِهَتَكُمْ وَلَا تَذَرُنَّ وَدًّا وَّلَا

سُوَاعًا ەۙ وَّلَا يَغُوْثَ وَيَعُوْقَ وَنَسْرًا ۞

وَقَدْ اَضَلُّوْا كَثِيْرًا ەۚ وَلَا تَزِدِ الظّٰلِمِيْنَ اِلَّا ضَلٰلًا ۞

مِمَّا خَطِيْٓـٰٔتِهِمْ اُغْرِقُوْا فَاُدْخِلُوْا نَارًا ەۙ فَلَمْ يَجِدُوْا

لَهُمْ مِّنْ دُوْنِ اللّٰهِ اَنْصَارًا ۞

وَقَالَ نُوْحٌ رَّبِّ لَا تَذَرْ عَلَى الْاَرْضِ مِنَ الْكٰفِرِيْنَ

دَيَّارًا ۞

اِنَّكَ اِنْ تَذَرْهُمْ يُضِلُّوْا عِبَادَكَ وَلَا يَلِدُوْٓا

اِلَّا فَاجِرًا كَفَّارًا ۞

رَبِّ اغْفِرْ لِيْ وَلِوَالِدَيَّ وَلِمَنْ دَخَلَ بَيْتِيَ

مُؤْمِنًا وَّلِلْمُؤْمِنِيْنَ وَالْمُؤْمِنٰتِ ەۭ وَلَا تَزِدِ

الظّٰلِمِيْنَ اِلَّا تَبَارًا ۞

THE JINN

In the name of Allah,
the Beneficent, the Merciful.

1. Say: It has been revealed to me that a party of the jinn listened, and they said: Surely we have heard a wonderful Quran,

2. Guiding to the right way, so we believe in it, and we will not set up any one with our Lord:

3. And that He—exalted be the majesty of our Lord—has not taken a consort, nor a son:

4. And that the foolish amongst us used to forge extravagant things against Allah:

5. And that we thought that men and jinn did not utter a lie against Allah:

6. And that persons from among men used to seek refuge with persons from among jinn, so they increased them in wrongdoing:

7. And that they thought as you think, that Allah would not raise anyone:

8. And that we sought to reach heaven, but we found it filled with strong guards and flaming stars.

9. And that we used to sit in some of the sitting-places thereof to steal a hearing, but he who would (try to) listen now would find a flame lying in wait for him:

10. And that we know not whether evil is meant for those who are on earth or whether their Lord means to bring them good:

11. And that some of us are good and others of us are below that: we are sects following different ways:

12. And that we know that we cannot escape Allah in the earth, nor can we escape Him by flight:

13. And that when we heard the guidance, we believed in it; so whoever believes in his Lord, he should neither fear loss nor being overtaken (by disgrace):

بِسْمِ اللهِ الرَّحْمٰنِ الرَّحِيْمِ ۟

قُلْ اُوْحِيَ اِلَيَّ اَنَّهُ اسْتَمَعَ نَفَرٌ مِّنَ الْجِنِّ فَقَالُوْۤا اِنَّا سَمِعْنَا قُرْاٰنًا عَجَبًا ۟ۙ

يَّهْدِيْۤ اِلَى الرُّشْدِ فَاٰمَنَّا بِهٖ ۖ وَلَنْ نُّشْرِكَ بِرَبِّنَاۤ اَحَدًا ۟ۙ

وَّاَنَّهُ تَعٰلٰى جَدُّ رَبِّنَا مَا اتَّخَذَ صَاحِبَةً وَّلَا وَلَدًا ۟ۙ

وَّاَنَّهُ كَانَ يَقُوْلُ سَفِيْهُنَا عَلَى اللهِ شَطَطًا ۟ۙ

وَّاَنَّا ظَنَنَّاۤ اَنْ لَّنْ تَقُوْلَ الْاِنْسُ وَالْجِنُّ عَلَى اللهِ كَذِبًا ۟ۙ

وَّاَنَّهُ كَانَ رِجَالٌ مِّنَ الْاِنْسِ يَعُوْذُوْنَ بِرِجَالٍ مِّنَ الْجِنِّ فَزَادُوْهُمْ رَهَقًا ۟ۙ

وَّاَنَّهُمْ ظَنُّوْا كَمَا ظَنَنْتُمْ اَنْ لَّنْ يَّبْعَثَ اللهُ اَحَدًا ۟ۙ

وَّاَنَّا لَمَسْنَا السَّمَاءَ فَوَجَدْنٰهَا مُلِئَتْ حَرَسًا شَدِيْدًا وَّشُهُبًا ۟ۙ

وَّاَنَّا كُنَّا نَقْعُدُ مِنْهَا مَقَاعِدَ لِلسَّمْعِ ۖ فَمَنْ يَّسْتَمِعِ الْاٰنَ يَجِدْ لَهٗ شِهَابًا رَّصَدًا ۟ۙ

وَّاَنَّا لَا نَدْرِيْۤ اَشَرٌّ اُرِيْدَ بِمَنْ فِى الْاَرْضِ اَمْ اَرَادَ بِهِمْ رَبُّهُمْ رَشَدًا ۟ۙ

وَّاَنَّا مِنَّا الصّٰلِحُوْنَ وَمِنَّا دُوْنَ ذٰلِكَ ۖ كُنَّا طَرَآئِقَ قِدَدًا ۟ۙ

وَّاَنَّا ظَنَنَّاۤ اَنْ لَّنْ نُّعْجِزَ اللهَ فِى الْاَرْضِ وَلَنْ نُّعْجِزَهٗ هَرَبًا ۟ۙ

وَّاَنَّا لَمَّا سَمِعْنَا الْهُدٰىۤ اٰمَنَّا بِهٖ ۖ فَمَنْ يُّؤْمِنْ بِرَبِّهٖ فَلَا يَخَافُ بَخْسًا وَّلَا رَهَقًا ۟ۙ

14. And that some of us are those who submit, and some of us are the deviators; so whoever submits, these aim at the right way:

وَأَنَّا مِنَّا الْمُسْلِمُوْنَ وَمِنَّا الْقَاسِطُوْنَ فَمَنْ أَسْلَمَ فَأُولٰئِكَ تَحَرَّوْا رَشَدًا ۞

15. And as to the deviators, they are fuel of hell:

وَأَمَّا الْقَاسِطُوْنَ فَكَانُوْا لِجَهَنَّمَ حَطَبًا ۞

16. And that if they should keep to the (right) way, We would certainly give them to drink of abundant water,

وَأَنْ لَّوِ اسْتَقَامُوْا عَلَى الطَّرِيْقَةِ لَأَسْقَيْنٰهُمْ مَّآءً غَدَقًا ۞

17. So that We might try them with respect to it; and whoever turns aside from the reminder of his Lord, He will make him enter into an afflicting chastisement:

لِّنَفْتِنَهُمْ فِيْهِ ۗ وَمَنْ يُّعْرِضْ عَنْ ذِكْرِ رَبِّهٖ يَسْلُكْهُ عَذَابًا صَعَدًا ۞

18. And that the mosques are Allah's, therefore call not upon any one with Allah:

وَأَنَّ الْمَسٰجِدَ لِلّٰهِ فَلَا تَدْعُوْا مَعَ اللّٰهِ أَحَدًا ۞

19. And that when the servant of Allah stood up calling upon Him, they wellnigh crowded him (to death).

وَأَنَّهٗ لَمَّا قَامَ عَبْدُ اللّٰهِ يَدْعُوْهُ كَادُوْا يَكُوْنُوْنَ عَلَيْهِ لِبَدًا ۞

20. Say: I only call upon my Lord, and I do not associate any one with Him.

قُلْ إِنَّمَآ أَدْعُوْا رَبِّيْ وَلَا أُشْرِكُ بِهٖ أَحَدًا ۞

21. Say: I do not control for you evil or good.

قُلْ إِنِّيْ لَا أَمْلِكُ لَكُمْ ضَرًّا وَّلَا رَشَدًا ۞

22. Say: Surely no one can protect me against Allah, nor can I find besides Him any place of refuge:

قُلْ إِنِّيْ لَنْ يُّجِيْرَنِيْ مِنَ اللّٰهِ أَحَدٌ وَّلَنْ أَجِدَ مِنْ دُوْنِهٖ مُلْتَحَدًا ۞

23. (It is) only a delivering (of communications) from Allah and His messages; and whoever disobeys Allah and His Apostle, surely he shall have the fire of hell to abide therein for a long time.

إِلَّا بَلٰغًا مِّنَ اللّٰهِ وَرِسٰلٰتِهٖ ۗ وَمَنْ يَّعْصِ اللّٰهَ وَرَسُوْلَهٗ فَإِنَّ لَهٗ نَارَ جَهَنَّمَ خٰلِدِيْنَ فِيْهَآ أَبَدًا ۞

24. Until when they see what they are threatened with, then shall they know who is weaker in helpers and fewer in number.

حَتّٰى إِذَا رَأَوْا مَا يُوْعَدُوْنَ فَسَيَعْلَمُوْنَ مَنْ أَضْعَفُ نَاصِرًا وَّأَقَلُّ عَدَدًا ۞

25. Say: I do not know whether that with which you are threatened be nigh or whether my Lord will appoint for it a term:

قُلْ إِنْ أَدْرِيْ أَقَرِيْبٌ مَّا تُوْعَدُوْنَ أَمْ يَجْعَلُ لَهٗ رَبِّيْ أَمَدًا ۞

26. The Knower of the unseen! so He does not reveal His secrets to any,

عٰلِمُ الْغَيْبِ فَلَا يُظْهِرُ عَلٰى غَيْبِهٖ أَحَدًا ۞

27. Except to him whom He chooses as an apostle; for surely He makes a guard to march before him and after him,

إِلَّا مَنِ ارْتَضٰى مِنْ رَّسُوْلٍ فَإِنَّهٗ يَسْلُكُ مِنْ بَيْنِ يَدَيْهِ وَمِنْ خَلْفِهٖ رَصَدًا ۞

28. So that He may know that they have truly delivered the messages of their Lord, and He encompasses what is with them, and He records the number of all things.

لِّيَعْلَمَ أَنْ قَدْ أَبْلَغُوْا رِسٰلٰتِ رَبِّهِمْ وَأَحَاطَ بِمَا لَدَيْهِمْ وَأَحْصٰى كُلَّ شَيْءٍ عَدَدًا ۞

585

THE WRAPPED UP
(MUZZAMMIL)

بِاَيَاتُهَا (٧٣) سُوْرَةُ الْمُزَّمِّلِ مَكِّيَّةٌ رُكُوْعَاتُهَا

In the name of Allah,
the Beneficent, the Merciful.

بِسْمِ اللهِ الرَّحْمٰنِ الرَّحِيْمِ ۝

1. O you who have wrapped up (in your garments)!

يَاۤيُّهَا الْمُزَّمِّلُ ۝

2. Rise to pray in the night except a little,

قُمِ الَّيْلَ اِلَّا قَلِيْلًا ۝

3. Half of it, or lessen it a little,

نِصْفَهٗۤ اَوِ انْقُصْ مِنْهُ قَلِيْلًا ۝

4. Or add to it, and recite the Quran as it ought to be recited.

اَوْ زِدْ عَلَيْهِ وَرَتِّلِ الْقُرْاٰنَ تَرْتِيْلًا ۝

5. Surely We will make to light upon you a weighty Word.

اِنَّا سَنُلْقِيْ عَلَيْكَ قَوْلًا ثَقِيْلًا ۝

6. Surely the rising by night is the firmest way to tread and the best corrective of speech.

اِنَّ نَاشِئَةَ الَّيْلِ هِيَ اَشَدُّ وَطْاً وَّاَقْوَمُ قِيْلًا ۝

7. Surely you have in the day time a long occupation.

اِنَّ لَكَ فِي النَّهَارِ سَبْحًا طَوِيْلًا ۝

8. And remember the name of your Lord and devote yourself to Him with (exclusive) devotion.

وَاذْكُرِ اسْمَ رَبِّكَ وَتَبَتَّلْ اِلَيْهِ تَبْتِيْلًا ۝

9. The Lord of the East and the West—there is no god but He—therefore take Him for a protector.

رَبُّ الْمَشْرِقِ وَالْمَغْرِبِ لَاۤ اِلٰهَ اِلَّا هُوَ فَاتَّخِذْهُ وَكِيْلًا ۝

10. And bear patiently what they say and avoid them with a becoming avoidance.

وَاصْبِرْ عَلٰى مَا يَقُوْلُوْنَ وَاهْجُرْهُمْ هَجْرًا جَمِيْلًا ۝

11. And leave Me and the rejecters, the possessors of ease and plenty, and respite them a little.

وَذَرْنِيْ وَالْمُكَذِّبِيْنَ اُولِي النَّعْمَةِ وَمَهِّلْهُمْ قَلِيْلًا ۝

12. Surely with Us are heavy fetters and a flaming fire,

اِنَّ لَدَيْنَاۤ اَنْكَالًا وَّجَحِيْمًا ۝

13. And food that chokes and a painful punishment,

وَّطَعَامًا ذَا غُصَّةٍ وَّعَذَابًا اَلِيْمًا ۝

14. On the day when the earth and the mountains shall quake and the mountains shall become (as) heaps of sand let loose.

يَوْمَ تَرْجُفُ الْاَرْضُ وَالْجِبَالُ وَكَانَتِ الْجِبَالُ كَثِيْبًا مَّهِيْلًا ۝

15. Surely We have sent to you an Apostle, a witness against you, as We sent an apostle to Firon.

اِنَّاۤ اَرْسَلْنَاۤ اِلَيْكُمْ رَسُوْلًا شَاهِدًا عَلَيْكُمْ كَمَاۤ اَرْسَلْنَاۤ اِلٰى فِرْعَوْنَ رَسُوْلًا ۝

16. But Firon disobeyed the apostle, so We laid on him a violent hold.

فَعَصٰى فِرْعَوْنُ الرَّسُوْلَ فَاَخَذْنٰهُ اَخْذًا وَّبِيْلًا ۝

17. How, then, will you guard your-selves, if you disbelieve, on the day which shall make children grey-headed?

فَكَيْفَ تَتَّقُوْنَ اِنْ كَفَرْتُمْ يَوْمًا يَّجْعَلُ الْوِلْدَانَ شِيْبَا ۗ ۝

18. The heaven shall rend asunder thereby; His promise is ever brought to fulfillment.

اَلسَّمَآءُ مُنْفَطِرٌۢ بِهٖ كَانَ وَعْدُهٗ مَفْعُوْلًا ۝

19. Surely this is a reminder, then let him, who will take the way to his Lord.

اِنَّ هٰذِهٖ تَذْكِرَةٌ ۚ فَمَنْ شَآءَ اتَّخَذَ اِلٰى رَبِّهٖ سَبِيْلًا ۝

20. Surely your Lord knows that you pass in prayer nearly two-thirds of the night, and (sometimes) half of it, and (sometimes) a third of it, and (also) a party of those with you; and Allah measures the night and the day. He knows that you are not able to do it, so He has turned to you (mercifully), therefore read what is easy of the Quran. He knows that there must be among you sick, and others who travel in the land seeking of the bounty of Allah, and others who fight in Allah's way, therefore read as much of it as is easy (to you), and keep up prayer and pay the poor-rate and offer to Allah a goodly gift, and whatever of good you send on beforehand for yourselves, you will find it with Allah; that is best and greatest in reward; and ask forgiveness of Allah; surely Allah is For-giving, Merciful.

اِنَّ رَبَّكَ يَعْلَمُ اَنَّكَ تَقُوْمُ اَدْنٰى مِنْ ثُلُثَيِ الَّيْلِ وَنِصْفَهٗ وَثُلُثَهٗ وَطَآئِفَةٌ مِّنَ الَّذِيْنَ مَعَكَ ۗ وَاللّٰهُ يُقَدِّرُ الَّيْلَ وَالنَّهَارَ ۗ عَلِمَ اَنْ لَّنْ تُحْصُوْهُ فَتَابَ عَلَيْكُمْ فَاقْرَءُوْا مَا تَيَسَّرَ مِنَ الْقُرْاٰنِ ۗ عَلِمَ اَنْ سَيَكُوْنُ مِنْكُمْ مَّرْضٰى ۙ وَاٰخَرُوْنَ يَضْرِبُوْنَ فِى الْاَرْضِ يَبْتَغُوْنَ مِنْ فَضْلِ اللّٰهِ وَاٰخَرُوْنَ يُقَاتِلُوْنَ فِى سَبِيْلِ اللّٰهِ ۖ فَاقْرَءُوْا مَا تَيَسَّرَ مِنْهُ ۙ وَاَقِيْمُوا الصَّلٰوةَ وَاٰتُوا الزَّكٰوةَ وَاَقْرِضُوا اللّٰهَ قَرْضًا حَسَنًا ۗ وَمَا تُقَدِّمُوْا لِاَنْفُسِكُمْ مِّنْ خَيْرٍ تَجِدُوْهُ عِنْدَ اللّٰهِ هُوَ خَيْرًا وَّاَعْظَمَ اَجْرًا ۗ وَاسْتَغْفِرُوا اللّٰهَ ۗ اِنَّ اللّٰهَ غَفُوْرٌ رَّحِيْمٌ ۝

THE CLOTHED ONE
(MUDDASSIR)

بِسْمِ اللهِ الرَّحْمٰنِ الرَّحِيْمِ

**In the name of Allah,
the Beneficent, the Merciful.**

1. O you who are clothed!

يَآ اَيُّهَا الْمُدَّثِّرُۙ

2. Arise and warn,

قُمْ فَاَنْذِرْۙ

3. And your Lord do magnify,

وَرَبَّكَ فَكَبِّرْۙ

4. And your garments do purify,

وَثِيَابَكَ فَطَهِّرْۙ

5. And uncleanness do shun,

وَالرُّجْزَ فَاهْجُرْۙ

6. And bestow not favors that you may
receive again with increase,

وَلَا تَمْنُنْ تَسْتَكْثِرُۙ

7. And for the sake of your Lord, be
patient.

وَلِرَبِّكَ فَاصْبِرْؕ

8. For when the trumpet is sounded,

فَاِذَا نُقِرَ فِي النَّاقُوْرِۙ

9. That, at that time, shall be a difficult
day,

فَذٰلِكَ يَوْمَئِذٍ يَّوْمٌ عَسِيْرٌۙ

10. For the unbelievers, anything but
easy.

عَلَى الْكٰفِرِيْنَ غَيْرُ يَسِيْرٍ

11. Leave Me and him whom I created
alone,

ذَرْنِيْ وَمَنْ خَلَقْتُ وَحِيْدًاۙ

12. And give him vast riches,

وَّجَعَلْتُ لَهٗ مَالًا مَّمْدُوْدًاۙ

13. And sons dwelling in his presence,

وَّبَنِيْنَ شُهُوْدًاۙ

14. And I adjusted affairs for him
adjustably;

وَّمَهَّدْتُّ لَهٗ تَمْهِيْدًاۙ

15. And yet he desires that I should add
more!

ثُمَّ يَطْمَعُ اَنْ اَزِيْدَۙ

16. By no means! surely he offers opposition to Our communications.

كَلَّا ؕ اِنَّهٗ كَانَ لِاٰيٰتِنَا عَنِيْدًاؕ

17. I will make a distressing punishment
overtake him.

سَاُرْهِقُهٗ صَعُوْدًاؕ

18. Surely he reflected and guessed,

اِنَّهٗ فَكَّرَ وَقَدَّرَۙ

19. But may he be cursed how he
plotted;

فَقُتِلَ كَيْفَ قَدَّرَۙ

20. Again, may he be cursed how he plotted;

ثُمَّ قُتِلَ كَيْفَ قَدَّرَ ۞

21. Then he looked,

ثُمَّ نَظَرَ ۞

22. Then he frowned and scowled,

ثُمَّ عَبَسَ وَبَسَرَ ۞

23. Then he turned back and was big with pride,

ثُمَّ أَدْبَرَ وَاسْتَكْبَرَ ۞

24. Then he said: This is naught but enchantment, narrated (from others);

فَقَالَ إِنْ هٰذَآ إِلَّا سِحْرٌ يُؤْثَرُ ۞

25. This is naught but the word of a mortal.

إِنْ هٰذَآ إِلَّا قَوْلُ الْبَشَرِ ۞

26. I will cast him into hell.

سَأُصْلِيهِ سَقَرَ ۞

27. And what will make you realize what hell is?

وَمَآ أَدْرٰىكَ مَا سَقَرُ ۞

28. It leaves naught nor does it spare aught.

لَا تُبْقِي وَلَا تَذَرُ ۞

29. It scorches the mortal.

لَوَّاحَةٌ لِّلْبَشَرِ ۞

30. Over it are nineteen.

عَلَيْهَا تِسْعَةَ عَشَرَ ۞

31. And We have not made the wardens of the fire others than angels, and We have not made their number but as a trial for those who disbelieve, that those who have been given the book may be certain and those who believe may increase in faith, and those who have been given the book and the believers may not doubt, and that those in whose hearts is a disease and the unbelievers may say: What does Allah mean by this parable? Thus does Allah make err whom He pleases, and He guides whom He pleases, and none knows the hosts of your Lord but He Himself; and this is naught but a reminder to the mortals.

وَمَا جَعَلْنَآ أَصْحَابَ النَّارِ إِلَّا مَلٰٓئِكَةً وَّمَا جَعَلْنَا عِدَّتَهُمْ إِلَّا فِتْنَةً لِّلَّذِينَ كَفَرُوا وَلِيَسْتَيْقِنَ الَّذِينَ أُوتُوا الْكِتَابَ وَيَزْدَادَ الَّذِينَ ءَامَنُوٓا إِيمَانًا وَّلَا يَرْتَابَ الَّذِينَ أُوتُوا الْكِتَابَ وَالْمُؤْمِنُونَ وَلِيَقُولَ الَّذِينَ فِي قُلُوبِهِم مَّرَضٌ وَالْكَافِرُونَ مَاذَآ أَرَادَ اللّٰهُ بِهٰذَا مَثَلًا كَذٰلِكَ يُضِلُّ اللّٰهُ مَن يَشَآءُ وَيَهْدِي مَن يَشَآءُ وَمَا يَعْلَمُ جُنُودَ رَبِّكَ إِلَّا هُوَ وَمَا هِيَ إِلَّا ذِكْرٰى لِلْبَشَرِ ۞

32. Nay; I swear by the moon,

كَلَّا وَالْقَمَرِ ۞

33. And the night when it departs,

وَالَّيْلِ إِذْ أَدْبَرَ ۞

34. And the daybreak when it shines;

وَالصُّبْحِ إِذَآ أَسْفَرَ ۞

35. Surely it (hell) is one of the gravest (misfortunes),

إِنَّهَا لَإِحْدَى الْكُبَرِ ۝

36. A warning to mortals,

نَذِيرًا لِّلْبَشَرِ ۝

37. To him among you who wishes to go forward or remain behind.

لِمَنْ شَاءَ مِنْكُمْ أَنْ يَتَقَدَّمَ أَوْ يَتَأَخَّرَ ۝

38. Every soul is held in pledge for what it earns,

كُلُّ نَفْسٍ بِمَا كَسَبَتْ رَهِينَةٌ ۝

39. Except the people of the right hand,

إِلَّا أَصْحَابَ الْيَمِينِ ۝

40. In gardens, they shall ask each other

فِي جَنَّاتٍ يَتَسَاءَلُونَ ۝

41. About the guilty:

عَنِ الْمُجْرِمِينَ ۝

42. What has brought you into hell?

مَا سَلَكَكُمْ فِي سَقَرَ ۝

43. They shall say: We were not of those who prayed;

قَالُوا لَمْ نَكُ مِنَ الْمُصَلِّينَ ۝

44. And we used not to feed the poor;

وَلَمْ نَكُ نُطْعِمُ الْمِسْكِينَ ۝

45. And we used to enter into vain discourse with those who entered into vain discourses.

وَكُنَّا نَخُوضُ مَعَ الْخَائِضِينَ ۝

46. And we used to call the day of judgment a lie;

وَكُنَّا نُكَذِّبُ بِيَوْمِ الدِّينِ ۝

47. Till death overtook us.

حَتَّى أَتَانَا الْيَقِينُ ۝

48. So the intercession of intercessors shall not avail them.

فَمَا تَنْفَعُهُمْ شَفَاعَةُ الشَّافِعِينَ ۝

49. What is then the matter with them, that they turn away from the admonition,

فَمَا لَهُمْ عَنِ التَّذْكِرَةِ مُعْرِضِينَ ۝

50. As if they were asses taking fright

كَأَنَّهُمْ حُمُرٌ مُسْتَنْفِرَةٌ ۝

51. That had fled from a lion?

فَرَّتْ مِنْ قَسْوَرَةٍ ۝

52. Nay; every one of them desires that he may be given pages spread out;

بَلْ يُرِيدُ كُلُّ امْرِئٍ مِنْهُمْ أَنْ يُؤْتَى صُحُفًا مُنَشَّرَةً ۝

53. Nay! but they do not fear the hereafter.

كَلَّا بَلْ لَا يَخَافُونَ الْآخِرَةَ ۝

54. Nay! it is surely an admonition.

كَلَّا إِنَّهُ تَذْكِرَةٌ ۝

55. So whoever pleases may mind it.

فَمَنْ شَاءَ ذَكَرَهُ ۝

56. And they will not mind unless Allah please. He is worthy to be feared and worthy to forgive.

THE RESURRECTION
(QIYAMAH)

**In the name of Allah,
the Beneficent, the Merciful.**

بِسْمِ اللهِ الرَّحْمٰنِ الرَّحِيْمِ ۞

1. Nay! I swear by the day of resurrection.

لَاۤ اُقْسِمُ بِيَوْمِ الْقِيٰمَةِ ۙ

2. Nay! I swear by the self-accusing soul.

وَلَاۤ اُقْسِمُ بِالنَّفْسِ اللَّوَّامَةِ ۚ

3. Does man think that We shall not gather his bones?

اَيَحْسَبُ الْاِنْسَانُ اَلَّنْ نَّجْمَعَ عِظَامَهٗ ۚ

4. Yea! We are able to make complete his very fingertips,

بَلٰى قٰدِرِيْنَ عَلٰۤى اَنْ نُّسَوِّيَ بَنَانَهٗ ۞

5. Nay! man desires to give the lie to what is before him.

بَلْ يُرِيْدُ الْاِنْسَانُ لِيَفْجُرَ اَمَامَهٗ ۚ

6. He asks: When is the day of resurrection?

يَسْئَلُ اَيَّانَ يَوْمُ الْقِيٰمَةِ ۙ

7. So when the sight becomes dazed,

فَاِذَا بَرِقَ الْبَصَرُ ۙ

8. And the moon becomes dark,

وَخَسَفَ الْقَمَرُ ۙ

9. And the sun and the moon are brought together,

وَجُمِعَ الشَّمْسُ وَالْقَمَرُ ۙ

10. Man shall say on that day: Whither to fly to?

يَقُوْلُ الْاِنْسَانُ يَوْمَئِذٍ اَيْنَ الْمَفَرُّ ۚ

11. By no means! there shall be no place of refuge!

كَلَّا لَا وَزَرَ ۚ

12. With your Lord alone shall on that day be the place of rest.

اِلٰى رَبِّكَ يَوْمَئِذِ الْمُسْتَقَرُّ ۚ

13. Man shall on that day be informed of what he sent before and (what he) put off.

يُنَبَّؤُا الْاِنْسَانُ يَوْمَئِذٍ بِمَا قَدَّمَ وَاَخَّرَ ۚ

14. Nay! man is evidence against himself,

بَلِ الْاِنْسَانُ عَلٰى نَفْسِهٖ بَصِيْرَةٌ ۙ

15. Though he puts forth his excuses.

وَّلَوْ اَلْقٰى مَعَاذِيْرَهٗ ۚ

16. Do not move your tongue with it to make haste with it,

لَا تُحَرِّكْ بِهٖ لِسَانَكَ لِتَعْجَلَ بِهٖ ۚ

17. Surely on Us (devolves) the collecting of it and the reciting of it.

اِنَّ عَلَيْنَا جَمْعَهٗ وَقُرْاٰنَهٗ ۚ

18. Therefore when We have recited it, follow its recitation.

فَاِذَا قَرَاْنَاهُ فَاتَّبِعْ قُرْاٰنَهٗ ۚ

19. Again on Us (devolves) the explaining of it.

ثُمَّ اِنَّ عَلَيْنَا بَيَانَهٗ ۚ

592

20. Nay! But you love the present life,

وَكُلَّا بَلْ تُحِبُّوْنَ الْعَاجِلَةَ ۝

21. And neglect the hereafter.

وَتَذَرُوْنَ الْاٰخِرَةَ ۝

22. (Some) faces on that day shall be bright,

وُجُوْهٌ يَّوْمَىِٕذٍ نَّاضِرَةٌ ۝

23. Looking to their Lord.

اِلٰى رَبِّهَا نَاظِرَةٌ ۝

24. And (other) faces on that day shall be gloomy,

وَوُجُوْهٌ يَّوْمَىِٕذٍ بَاسِرَةٌ ۝

25. Knowing that there will be made to befall them some great calamity.

تَظُنُّ اَنْ يُّفْعَلَ بِهَا فَاقِرَةٌ ۝

26. Nay! When it comes up to the throat,

كَلَّا اِذَا بَلَغَتِ التَّرَاقِيَ ۝

27. And it is said: Who will be a magician?

وَقِيْلَ مَنْ رَاقٍ ۝

28. And he is sure that it is the (hour of) parting,

وَظَنَّ اَنَّهُ الْفِرَاقُ ۝

29. And affliction is combined with affliction;

وَالْتَفَّتِ السَّاقُ بِالسَّاقِ ۝

30. To your Lord on that day shall be the driving.

اِلٰى رَبِّكَ يَوْمَىِٕذِ الْمَسَاقُ ۝

31. So he did not accept the truth, nor did he pray,

فَلَا صَدَّقَ وَلَا صَلّٰى ۝

32. But called the truth a lie and turned back,

وَلٰكِنْ كَذَّبَ وَتَوَلّٰى ۝

33. Then he went to his followers, walking away in haughtiness.

ثُمَّ ذَهَبَ اِلٰى اَهْلِهٖ يَتَمَطّٰى ۝

34. Nearer to you (is destruction) and nearer,

اَوْلٰى لَكَ فَاَوْلٰى ۝

35. Again (consider how) nearer to you and nearer.

ثُمَّ اَوْلٰى لَكَ فَاَوْلٰى ۝

36. Does man think that he is to be left to wander without an aim?

اَيَحْسَبُ الْاِنْسَانُ اَنْ يُّتْرَكَ سُدًى ۝

37. Was he not a small seed in the seminal elements,

اَلَمْ يَكُ نُطْفَةً مِّنْ مَّنِيٍّ يُّمْنٰى ۝

38. Then he was a clot of blood, so He created (him) then made (him) perfect.

ثُمَّ كَانَ عَلَقَةً فَخَلَقَ فَسَوّٰى ۝

39. Then He made of him two kinds, the male and the female.

فَجَعَلَ مِنْهُ الزَّوْجَيْنِ الذَّكَرَ وَالْاُنْثٰى ۝

40. Is not He able to give life to the dead?

اَلَيْسَ ذٰلِكَ بِقَادِرٍ عَلٰى اَنْ يُّحْيِيَ الْمَوْتٰى ۝

THE MAN
(INSAN, OR DAHR)

أيَاتُهَا (٧٦) سُوْرَةُ الدَّهْرِ مَدَنِيَّةٌ رُكُوْعَاتُهَا

**In the name of Allah,
the Beneficent, the Merciful.**

بِسْمِ اللهِ الرَّحْمٰنِ الرَّحِيْمِ ۞

1. There surely came over man a period of time when he was a thing not worth mentioning.

هَلْ أَتٰى عَلَى الْإِنْسَانِ حِيْنٌ مِّنَ الدَّهْرِ لَمْ يَكُنْ شَيْئًا مَّذْكُوْرًا ۞

2. Surely We have created man from a small life-germ uniting (itself): We mean to try him, so We have made him hearing, seeing.

إِنَّا خَلَقْنَا الْإِنْسَانَ مِنْ نُّطْفَةٍ أَمْشَاجٍ نَّبْتَلِيْهِ فَجَعَلْنٰهُ سَمِيْعًا بَصِيْرًا ۞

3. Surely We have shown him the way: he may be thankful or unthankful.

إِنَّا هَدَيْنٰهُ السَّبِيْلَ إِمَّا شَاكِرًا وَّإِمَّا كَفُوْرًا ۞

4. Surely We have prepared for the unbelievers chains and shackles and a burning fire.

إِنَّا أَعْتَدْنَا لِلْكٰفِرِيْنَ سَلٰسِلَا۟ وَأَغْلٰلًا وَّسَعِيْرًا ۞

5. Surely the righteous shall drink of a cup the admixture of which is camphor,

إِنَّ الْأَبْرَارَ يَشْرَبُوْنَ مِنْ كَأْسٍ كَانَ مِزَاجُهَا كَافُوْرًا ۞

6. A fountain from which the servants of Allah shall drink; they make it to flow a (goodly) flowing forth.

عَيْنًا يَّشْرَبُ بِهَا عِبَادُ اللهِ يُفَجِّرُوْنَهَا تَفْجِيْرًا ۞

7. They fulfill vows and fear a day the evil of which shall be spreading far and wide.

يُوْفُوْنَ بِالنَّذْرِ وَيَخَافُوْنَ يَوْمًا كَانَ شَرُّهُ مُسْتَطِيْرًا ۞

8. And they give food out of love for Him to the poor and the orphan and the captive:

وَيُطْعِمُوْنَ الطَّعَامَ عَلٰى حُبِّهٖ مِسْكِيْنًا وَّيَتِيْمًا وَّأَسِيْرًا ۞

9. We only feed you for Allah's sake; we desire from you neither reward nor thanks:

إِنَّمَا نُطْعِمُكُمْ لِوَجْهِ اللهِ لَا نُرِيْدُ مِنْكُمْ جَزَاءً وَّلَا شُكُوْرًا ۞

10. Surely we fear from our Lord a stern, distressful day.

إِنَّا نَخَافُ مِنْ رَّبِّنَا يَوْمًا عَبُوْسًا قَمْطَرِيْرًا ۞

11. Therefore Allah will guard them from the evil of that day and cause them to meet with ease and happiness;

فَوَقٰهُمُ اللهُ شَرَّ ذٰلِكَ الْيَوْمِ وَلَقّٰهُمْ نَضْرَةً وَّسُرُوْرًا ۞

12. And reward them, because they were patient, with garden and silk,

وَجَزٰهُمْ بِمَا صَبَرُوْا جَنَّةً وَّحَرِيْرًا ۞

13. Reclining therein on raised couches, they shall find therein neither (the severe heat of) the sun nor intense cold.

مُّتَّكِئِيْنَ فِيْهَا عَلَى الْأَرَائِكِ لَا يَرَوْنَ فِيْهَا شَمْسًا وَّلَا زَمْهَرِيْرًا ۞

14. And close down upon them (shall be) its shadows, and its fruits shall be made near (to them), being easy to reach.

وَدَانِيَةً عَلَيْهِمْ ظِلٰلُهَا وَذُلِّلَتْ قُطُوْفُهَا تَذْلِيْلًا ۞

15. And there shall be made to go round about them vessels of silver and goblets which are of glass,

وَيُطَافُ عَلَيْهِمْ بِاٰنِيَةٍ مِّنْ فِضَّةٍ وَّأَكْوَابٍ كَانَتْ قَوَارِيْرَا ۞

16. (Transparent as) glass, made of silver; they have measured them according to a measure.

17. And they shall be made to drink therein a cup the admixture of which shall be ginger,

18. (Of) a fountain therein which is named Salsabil.

19. And round about them shall go youths never altering in age; when you see them you will think them to be scattered pearls.

20. And when you see there, you shall see blessings and a great kingdom.

21. Upon them shall be garments of fine green silk and thick silk interwoven with gold, and they shall be adorned with bracelets of silver, and their Lord shall make them drink a pure drink.

22. Surely this is a reward for you, and your striving shall be recompensed.

23. Surely We Ourselves have revealed the Quran to you, revealing (it) in portions.

24. Therefore wait patiently for the command of your Lord, and obey not from among them a sinner or an ungrateful one.

25. And glorify the name of your Lord morning and evening.

26. And during part of the night adore Him, and give glory to Him (a) long (part of the) night.

27. Surely these love the transitory and neglect a grievous day before them.

28. We created them and made firm their make, and when We please We will bring in their place the likes of them by a change.

29. Surely this is a reminder, so whoever pleases takes to his Lord a way.

30. And you do not please except that Allah please; surely Allah is Knowing, Wise;

31. He makes whom He pleases to enter into His mercy; and (as for) the unjust, He has prepared for them a painful chastisement.

وَقَوَارِيرَ مِنْ فِضَّةٍ قَدَّرُوهَا تَقْدِيرًا ۝

وَيُسْقَوْنَ فِيهَا كَأْسًا كَانَ مِزَاجُهَا زَنْجَبِيلًا ۝

عَيْنًا فِيهَا تُسَمّٰى سَلْسَبِيلًا ۝

وَيَطُوفُ عَلَيْهِمْ وِلْدَانٌ مُّخَلَّدُونَ ۚ إِذَا رَأَيْتَهُمْ حَسِبْتَهُمْ لُؤْلُؤًا مَّنْثُورًا ۝

وَإِذَا رَأَيْتَ ثَمَّ رَأَيْتَ نَعِيمًا وَّمُلْكًا كَبِيرًا ۝

عٰلِيَهُمْ ثِيَابُ سُنْدُسٍ خُضْرٌ وَّإِسْتَبْرَقٌ ۖ وَحُلُّوا أَسَاوِرَ مِنْ فِضَّةٍ ۚ وَسَقَاهُمْ رَبُّهُمْ شَرَابًا طَهُورًا ۝

إِنَّ هٰذَا كَانَ لَكُمْ جَزَاءً وَّكَانَ سَعْيُكُمْ مَّشْكُورًا ۩۝

إِنَّا نَحْنُ نَزَّلْنَا عَلَيْكَ الْقُرْآنَ تَنْزِيلًا ۝

فَاصْبِرْ لِحُكْمِ رَبِّكَ وَلَا تُطِعْ مِنْهُمْ آثِمًا أَوْ كَفُورًا ۝

وَاذْكُرِ اسْمَ رَبِّكَ بُكْرَةً وَّأَصِيلًا ۝

وَمِنَ الَّيْلِ فَاسْجُدْ لَهُ وَسَبِّحْهُ لَيْلًا طَوِيلًا ۝

إِنَّ هٰؤُلَاءِ يُحِبُّونَ الْعَاجِلَةَ وَيَذَرُونَ وَرَاءَهُمْ يَوْمًا ثَقِيلًا ۝

نَحْنُ خَلَقْنَاهُمْ وَشَدَدْنَا أَسْرَهُمْ ۖ وَإِذَا شِئْنَا بَدَّلْنَا أَمْثَالَهُمْ تَبْدِيلًا ۝

إِنَّ هٰذِهِ تَذْكِرَةٌ ۖ فَمَنْ شَاءَ اتَّخَذَ إِلٰى رَبِّهِ سَبِيلًا ۝

وَمَا تَشَاؤُونَ إِلَّا أَنْ يَشَاءَ اللّٰهُ ۚ إِنَّ اللّٰهَ كَانَ عَلِيمًا حَكِيمًا ۝

يُدْخِلُ مَنْ يَشَاءُ فِي رَحْمَتِهِ ۚ وَالظّٰلِمِينَ أَعَدَّ لَهُمْ عَذَابًا أَلِيمًا ۩

595

THE EMISSARIES
(MURASALAT)

أبايَّاتُهَا (٧٧) سُوْرَةُ الْمُرْسَلْتِ مَكِّيَّةٌ رُكُوْعَاتُهَا

**In the name of Allah,
the Beneficent, the Merciful.**

بِسْمِ اللهِ الرَّحْمٰنِ الرَّحِيْمِ ۝

1. I swear by the emissary winds, sent one after another (for men's benefit),

وَالْمُرْسَلٰتِ عُرْفًا ۝

2. By the raging hurricanes,

فَالْعٰصِفٰتِ عَصْفًا ۝

3. Which scatter clouds to their destined places,

وَّالنّٰشِرٰتِ نَشْرًا ۝

4. Then separate them one from another,

فَالْفٰرِقٰتِ فَرْقًا ۝

5. Then I swear by the angels who bring down the revelation,

فَالْمُلْقِيٰتِ ذِكْرًا ۝

6. To clear or to warn.

عُذْرًا اَوْ نُذْرًا ۝

7. Most surely what you are threatened with must come to pass.

اِنَّمَا تُوْعَدُوْنَ لَوَاقِعٌ ۝

8. So when the stars are made to lose their light,

فَاِذَا النُّجُوْمُ طُمِسَتْ ۝

9. And when the heaven is rent asunder,

وَاِذَا السَّمَاءُ فُرِجَتْ ۝

10. And when the mountains are carried away as dust,

وَاِذَا الْجِبَالُ نُسِفَتْ ۝

11. And when the apostles are gathered at their appointed time,

وَاِذَا الرُّسُلُ اُقِّتَتْ ۝

12. To what day is the doom fixed?

لِاَيِّ يَوْمٍ اُجِّلَتْ ۝

13. To the day of decision.

لِيَوْمِ الْفَصْلِ ۝

14. And what will make you comprehend what the day of decision is?

وَمَآ اَدْرٰىكَ مَا يَوْمُ الْفَصْلِ ۝

15. Woe on that day to the rejecters.

وَيْلٌ يَّوْمَئِذٍ لِّلْمُكَذِّبِيْنَ ۝

16. Did We not destroy the former generations?

اَلَمْ نُهْلِكِ الْاَوَّلِيْنَ ۝

17. Then did We follow them up with later ones.

ثُمَّ نُتْبِعُهُمُ الْاٰخِرِيْنَ ۝

18. Even thus shall We deal with the guilty.

كَذٰلِكَ نَفْعَلُ بِالْمُجْرِمِيْنَ ۝

19. Woe on that day to the rejecters.

وَيْلٌ يَّوْمَئِذٍ لِّلْمُكَذِّبِيْنَ ۝

20. Did We not create you from contemptible water?

اَلَمۡ نَخۡلُقۡكُّمۡ مِّنۡ مَّآءٍ مَّهِيۡنٍ ۞

21. Then We placed it in a secure resting-place,

فَجَعَلۡنٰهُ فِيۡ قَرَارٍ مَّكِيۡنٍ ۞

22. Till an appointed term,

اِلٰى قَدَرٍ مَّعۡلُوۡمٍ ۞

23. So We proportion it—how well are We at proportioning (things).

فَقَدَرۡنَا ۚ فَنِعۡمَ الۡقٰدِرُوۡنَ ۞

24. Woe on that day to the rejecters.

وَيۡلٌ يَّوۡمَئِذٍ لِّلۡمُكَذِّبِيۡنَ ۞

25. Have We not made the earth to draw together to itself,

اَلَمۡ نَجۡعَلِ الۡاَرۡضَ كِفَاتًا ۞

26. The living and the dead,

اَحۡيَآءً وَّاَمۡوَاتًا ۞

27. And made therein lofty mountains, and given you to drink of sweet water?

وَّجَعَلۡنَا فِيۡهَا رَوَاسِيَ شٰمِخٰتٍ وَّاَسۡقَيۡنٰكُمۡ مَّآءً فُرَاتًا ۞

28. Woe on that day to the rejecters.

وَيۡلٌ يَّوۡمَئِذٍ لِّلۡمُكَذِّبِيۡنَ ۞

29. Walk on to that which you called a lie.

اِنۡطَلِقُوۡٓا اِلٰى مَا كُنۡتُمۡ بِهٖ تُكَذِّبُوۡنَ ۞

30. Walk on to the covering having three branches,

اِنۡطَلِقُوۡٓا اِلٰى ظِلٍّ ذِىۡ ثَلٰثِ شُعَبٍ ۞

31. Neither having the coolness of the shade nor availing against the flame.

لَّا ظَلِيۡلٍ وَّلَا يُغۡنِىۡ مِنَ اللَّهَبِ ۞

32. Surely it sends up sparks like palaces,

اِنَّهَا تَرۡمِىۡ بِشَرَرٍ كَالۡقَصۡرِ ۞

33. As if they were tawny camels.

كَاَنَّهٗ جِمٰلَتٌ صُفۡرٌ ۞

34. Woe on that day to the rejecters.

وَيۡلٌ يَّوۡمَئِذٍ لِّلۡمُكَذِّبِيۡنَ ۞

35. This is the day on which they shall not speak,

هٰذَا يَوۡمُ لَا يَنۡطِقُوۡنَ ۞

36. And permission shall not be given to them so that they should offer excuses.

وَلَا يُؤۡذَنُ لَهُمۡ فَيَعۡتَذِرُوۡنَ ۞

37. Woe on that day to the rejecters.

وَيۡلٌ يَّوۡمَئِذٍ لِّلۡمُكَذِّبِيۡنَ ۞

38. This is the day of decision: We have gathered you and those of yore.

هٰذَا يَوۡمُ الۡفَصۡلِ ۚ جَمَعۡنٰكُمۡ وَالۡاَوَّلِيۡنَ ۞

39. So if you have a plan, plan against Me (now).

فَاِنۡ كَانَ لَكُمۡ كَيۡدٌ فَكِيۡدُوۡنِ ۞

40. Woe on that day to the rejecters.

وَيۡلٌ يَّوۡمَئِذٍ لِّلۡمُكَذِّبِيۡنَ ۞

41. Surely those who guard (against evil) shall be amid shades and fountains,

إِنَّ الْمُتَّقِينَ فِي ظِلَالٍ وَّعُيُونٍ ﴿

42. And fruits such as they desire.

وَّفَوَاكِهَ مِمَّا يَشْتَهُونَ ﴿

43. Eat and drink pleasantly because of what you did.

كُلُوا وَاشْرَبُوا هَنِيئًا بِمَا كُنْتُمْ تَعْمَلُونَ ﴿

44. Surely thus do We reward the doers of good.

إِنَّا كَذَلِكَ نَجْزِي الْمُحْسِنِينَ ﴿

45. Woe on that day to the rejecters.

وَيْلٌ يَوْمَئِذٍ لِّلْمُكَذِّبِينَ ﴿

46. Eat and enjoy yourselves for a little; surely you are guilty.

كُلُوا وَتَمَتَّعُوا قَلِيلًا إِنَّكُمْ مُجْرِمُونَ ﴿

47. Woe on that day to the rejecters.

وَيْلٌ يَوْمَئِذٍ لِّلْمُكَذِّبِينَ ﴿

48. And when it is said to them: Bow down, they do not bow down.

وَإِذَا قِيلَ لَهُمُ ارْكَعُوا لَا يَرْكَعُونَ ﴿

49. Woe on that day to the rejecters.

وَيْلٌ يَوْمَئِذٍ لِّلْمُكَذِّبِينَ ﴿

50. In what announcement, then, after it, will they believe?

فَبِأَيِّ حَدِيثٍ بَعْدَهُ يُؤْمِنُونَ ﴿

598

THE GREAT EVENT
(NABA)

أَيَاتُهَا (٧٨) سُورَةُ النَّبَا مَكِّيَّةٌ رُوعُهَا

**In the name of Allah,
the Beneficent, the Merciful.**

بِسْمِ اللهِ الرَّحْمٰنِ الرَّحِيْمِ ۞

1. Of what do they ask one another?

عَمَّ يَتَسَآءَلُوْنَ ۞

2. About the great event,

عَنِ النَّبَاِ الْعَظِيْمِ ۞

3. About which they differ?

الَّذِيْ هُمْ فِيْهِ مُخْتَلِفُوْنَ ۞

4. Nay! they shall soon come to know;

كَلَّا سَيَعْلَمُوْنَ ۞

5. Nay! Nay! they shall soon know.

ثُمَّ كَلَّا سَيَعْلَمُوْنَ ۞

6. Have We not made the earth an even expanse?

اَلَمْ نَجْعَلِ الْاَرْضَ مِهٰدًا ۙ

7. And the mountains as projections (thereon)?

وَّالْجِبَالَ اَوْتَادًا ۙ

8. And We created you in pairs,

وَّخَلَقْنٰكُمْ اَزْوَاجًا ۙ

9. And We made your sleep to be rest (to you),

وَّجَعَلْنَا نَوْمَكُمْ سُبَاتًا ۙ

10. And We made the night to be a covering,

وَّجَعَلْنَا الَّيْلَ لِبَاسًا ۙ

11. And We made the day for seeking livelihood.

وَّجَعَلْنَا النَّهَارَ مَعَاشًا ۙ

12. And We made above you seven strong ones,

وَّبَنَيْنَا فَوْقَكُمْ سَبْعًا شِدَادًا ۙ

13. And We made a shining lamp,

وَّجَعَلْنَا سِرَاجًا وَّهَّاجًا ۙ

14. And We send down from the clouds water pouring forth abundantly,

وَّاَنْزَلْنَا مِنَ الْمُعْصِرٰتِ مَآءً ثَجَّاجًا ۙ

15. That We may bring forth thereby corn and herbs,

لِّنُخْرِجَ بِهٖ حَبًّا وَّنَبَاتًا ۙ

16. And gardens dense and luxuriant.

وَّجَنّٰتٍ اَلْفَافًا ۙ

17. Surely the day of decision is (a day) appointed:

اِنَّ يَوْمَ الْفَصْلِ كَانَ مِيْقَاتًا ۙ

18. The day on which the trumpet shall be blown so you shall come forth in hosts,

يَّوْمَ يُنْفَخُ فِي الصُّوْرِ فَتَأْتُوْنَ اَفْوَاجًا ۙ

19. And the heaven shall be opened so that it shall be all openings,

وَّفُتِحَتِ السَّمَآءُ فَكَانَتْ اَبْوَابًا ۙ

20. And the mountains shall be moved off so that they shall remain a mere semblance.

وَسُيِّرَتِ الْجِبَالُ فَكَانَتْ سَرَابًا ۞

21. Surely hell lies in wait,

اِنَّ جَهَنَّمَ كَانَتْ مِرْصَادًا ۞

22. A place of resort for the inordinate,

لِّلطَّاغِيْنَ مَاٰبًا ۞

23. Living therein for ages.

لّٰبِثِيْنَ فِيْهَآ اَحْقَابًا ۞

24. They shall not taste therein cool nor drink

لَّا يَذُوْقُوْنَ فِيْهَا بَرْدًا وَّلَا شَرَابًا ۞

25. But boiling and intensely cold water,

اِلَّا حَمِيْمًا وَّغَسَّاقًا ۞

26. Requital corresponding.

جَزَآءً وِّفَاقًا ۞

27. Surely they feared not the account,

اِنَّهُمْ كَانُوْا لَا يَرْجُوْنَ حِسَابًا ۞

28. And called Our communications a lie, giving the lie (to the truth).

وَّكَذَّبُوْا بِاٰيٰتِنَا كِذَّابًا ۞

29. And We have recorded everything in a book,

وَكُلَّ شَيْءٍ اَحْصَيْنٰهُ كِتٰبًا ۞

30. So taste! for We will not add to you aught but chastisement.

فَذُوْقُوْا فَلَنْ نَّزِيْدَكُمْ اِلَّا عَذَابًا ۞

31. Surely for those who guard (against evil) is achievement,

اِنَّ لِلْمُتَّقِيْنَ مَفَازًا ۞

32. Gardens and vineyards,

حَدَآئِقَ وَاَعْنَابًا ۞

33. And those showing freshness of youth, equals in age,

وَّكَوَاعِبَ اَتْرَابًا ۞

34. And a pure cup.

وَّكَأْسًا دِهَاقًا ۞

35. They shall not hear therein any vain words nor lying.

لَا يَسْمَعُوْنَ فِيْهَا لَغْوًا وَّلَا كِذَّابًا ۞

36. A reward from your Lord, a gift according to a reckoning:

جَزَآءً مِّنْ رَّبِّكَ عَطَآءً حِسَابًا ۞

37. The Lord of the heavens and the earth and what is between them, the Beneficent God, they shall not be able to address Him.

رَبِّ السَّمٰوٰتِ وَالْاَرْضِ وَمَا بَيْنَهُمَا الرَّحْمٰنِ لَا يَمْلِكُوْنَ مِنْهُ خِطَابًا ۞

38. The day on which the spirit and the angels shall stand in ranks; they shall not speak except he whom the Beneficent God permits and who speaks the right thing.

يَوْمَ يَقُوْمُ الرُّوْحُ وَالْمَلٰئِكَةُ صَفًّا لَا يَتَكَلَّمُوْنَ اِلَّا مَنْ اَذِنَ لَهُ الرَّحْمٰنُ وَقَالَ صَوَابًا ۞

39. That is the sure day, so whoever desires may take refuge with his Lord.

ذٰلِكَ الْيَوْمُ الْحَقُّ فَمَنْ شَآءَ اتَّخَذَ اِلٰى رَبِّهٖ مَاٰبًا ۞

40. Surely We have warned you of a chastisement near at hand: the day when man shall see what his two hands have sent before, and the unbeliever shall say: O! would that I were dust!

اِنَّآ اَنْذَرْنٰكُمْ عَذَابًا قَرِيْبًا ۙ يَّوْمَ يَنْظُرُ الْمَرْءُ مَا قَدَّمَتْ يَدَاهُ وَيَقُوْلُ الْكَافِرُ يٰلَيْتَنِيْ كُنْتُ تُرٰبًا ۞

THOSE WHO PULL OUT
(NAZIAT)

اَیَاتُھَا (۷۹) سُوْرَۃُ النَّازِعَاتِ مَکِّیَّۃٌ رُکُوْعَاتُھَا

**In the name of Allah,
the Beneficent, the Merciful.**

بِسْمِ اللّٰهِ الرَّحْمٰنِ الرَّحِيْمِ ۰

1. I swear by the angels who violently pull out the souls of the wicked,

وَالنّٰزِعٰتِ غَرْقًا ۙ۝

2. And by those who gently draw out the souls of the blessed,

وَّالنّٰشِطٰتِ نَشْطًا ۙ۝

3. And by those who float in space,

وَّالسّٰبِحٰتِ سَبْحًا ۙ۝

4. Then those who are foremost going ahead,

فَالسّٰبِقٰتِ سَبْقًا ۙ۝

5. Then those who regulate the affair.

فَالْمُدَبِّرٰتِ اَمْرًا ۘ۝

6. The day on which the quaking one shall quake,

يَوْمَ تَرْجُفُ الرَّاجِفَةُ ۙ۝

7. What must happen afterwards shall follow it.

تَتْبَعُهَا الرَّادِفَةُ ۙ۝

8. Hearts on that day shall palpitate,

قُلُوْبٌ يَّوْمَئِذٍ وَّاجِفَةٌ ۙ۝

9. Their eyes cast down.

اَبْصَارُهَا خَاشِعَةٌ ۘ۝

10. They say: Shall we indeed be restored to (our) first state?

يَقُوْلُوْنَ ءَاِنَّا لَمَرْدُوْدُوْنَ فِي الْحَافِرَةِ ۙ۝

11. What! when we are rotten bones?

ءَاِذَا كُنَّا عِظَامًا نَّخِرَةً ۙ۝

12. They said: That then would be a return occasioning loss.

قَالُوْا تِلْكَ اِذًا كَرَّةٌ خَاسِرَةٌ ۘ۝

13. But it shall be only a single cry,

فَاِنَّمَا هِيَ زَجْرَةٌ وَّاحِدَةٌ ۙ۝

14. When lo! they shall be wakeful.

فَاِذَا هُمْ بِالسَّاهِرَةِ ۘ۝

15. Has not there come to you the story of Musa?

هَلْ اَتٰىكَ حَدِيْثُ مُوْسٰى ۘ۝

16. When his Lord called upon him in the holy valley, twice,

اِذْ نَادٰىهُ رَبُّهٗ بِالْوَادِ الْمُقَدَّسِ طُوًى ۚ۝

17. Go to Firon, surely he has become inordinate.

اِذْهَبْ اِلٰى فِرْعَوْنَ اِنَّهٗ طَغٰى ۖ۝

18. Then say: Have you (a desire) to purify yourself:

فَقُلْ هَلْ لَّكَ اِلٰٓى اَنْ تَزَكّٰى ۙ۝

19. And I will guide you to your Lord so that you should fear.

وَاَهْدِيَكَ اِلٰى رَبِّكَ فَتَخْشٰى ۘ۝

601

20. So he showed him the mighty sign.

فَأَرْلهُ الْآيَةَ الْكُبْرَى ۖ

21. But he rejected (the truth) and disobeyed.

فَكَذَّبَ وَعَصَى ۖ

22. Then he went back hastily.

ثُمَّ أَدْبَرَ يَسْعَى ۖ

23. Then he gathered (men) and called out.

فَحَشَرَ فَنَادَى ۖ

24. Then he said: I am your lord, the most high.

فَقَالَ أَنَا رَبُّكُمُ الْأَعْلَى ۖ

25. So Allah seized him with the punishment of the hereafter and the former life.

فَأَخَذَهُ اللّٰهُ نَكَالَ الْآخِرَةِ وَالْأُولَى ۖ

26. Most surely there is in this a lesson to him who fears.

إِنَّ فِي ذٰلِكَ لَعِبْرَةً لِّمَنْ يَخْشَى ۖ

27. Are you the harder to create or the heaven? He made it.

ءَأَنْتُمْ أَشَدُّ خَلْقًا أَمِ السَّمَاءُ بَنٰهَا ۖ

28. He raised high its height, then put it into a right good state.

رَفَعَ سَمْكَهَا فَسَوّٰهَا ۖ

29. And He made dark its night and brought out its light.

وَأَغْطَشَ لَيْلَهَا وَأَخْرَجَ ضُحٰهَا ۖ

30. And the earth, He expanded it after that.

وَالْأَرْضَ بَعْدَ ذٰلِكَ دَحٰهَا ۖ

31. He brought forth from it its water and its pasturage.

أَخْرَجَ مِنْهَا مَاءَهَا وَمَرْعٰهَا ۖ

32. And the mountains, He made them firm,

وَالْجِبَالَ أَرْسٰهَا ۖ

33. A provision for you and for your cattle.

مَتَاعًا لَّكُمْ وَلِأَنْعَامِكُمْ ۖ

34. But when the great predominating calamity comes;

فَإِذَا جَاءَتِ الطَّامَّةُ الْكُبْرَى ۖ

35. The day on which man shall recollect what he strove after,

يَوْمَ يَتَذَكَّرُ الْإِنْسَانُ مَا سَعَى ۖ

36. And the hell shall be made manifest to him who sees

وَبُرِّزَتِ الْجَحِيمُ لِمَنْ يَرَى ۖ

37. Then as for him who is inordinate,

فَأَمَّا مَنْ طَغَى ۖ

38. And prefers the life of this world,

وَآثَرَ الْحَيٰوةَ الدُّنْيَا ۖ

39. Then surely the hell, that is the abode.

فَإِنَّ الْجَحِيمَ هِيَ الْمَأْوَى ۖ

40. And as for him who fears to stand in the presence of his Lord and forbids the soul from low desires,

وَأَمَّا مَنْ خَافَ مَقَامَ رَبِّهِ وَنَهَى النَّفْسَ
عَنِ الْهَوَى ۖ

41. Then surely the garden—that is the abode.

42. They ask you about the hour, when it will come.

43. About what! You are one to remind of it.

44. To your Lord is the goal of it.

45. You are only a warner to him who would fear it.

46. On the day that they see it, it will be as though they had not tarried but the latter part of a day or the early part of it.

فَاِنَّ الْجَنَّةَ هِيَ الْمَاْوٰى ۞

يَسْـَٔلُوْنَكَ عَنِ السَّاعَةِ اَيَّانَ مُرْسٰىهَا ۞

فِيْمَ اَنْتَ مِنْ ذِكْرٰىهَا ۞

اِلٰى رَبِّكَ مُنْتَهٰىهَا ۞

اِنَّمَاۤ اَنْتَ مُنْذِرُ مَنْ يَّخْشٰىهَا ۞

كَاَنَّهُمْ يَوْمَ يَرَوْنَهَا لَمْ يَلْبَثُوْۤا اِلَّا عَشِيَّةً اَوْ ضُحٰىهَا ۞

HE FROWNED
(ABASA)

بِسْمِ اللهِ الرَّحْمٰنِ الرَّحِيْمِ

**In the name of Allah,
the Beneficent, the Merciful.**

1. He frowned and turned (his) back,

عَبَسَ وَتَوَلّٰى ۝

2. Because there came to him the blind man.

اَنْ جَآءَهُ الْاَعْمٰى ۝

3. And what would make you know that he would purify himself,

وَمَا يُدْرِيْكَ لَعَلَّهٗ يَزَّكّٰى ۝

4. Or become reminded so that the reminder should profit him?

اَوْ يَذَّكَّرُ فَتَنْفَعَهُ الذِّكْرٰى ۝

5. As for him who considers himself free from need (of you),

اَمَّا مَنِ اسْتَغْنٰى ۝

6. To him do you address yourself.

فَاَنْتَ لَهٗ تَصَدّٰى ۝

7. And no blame is on you if he would not purify himself.

وَمَا عَلَيْكَ اَلَّا يَزَّكّٰى ۝

8. And as to him who comes to you striving hard,

وَاَمَّا مَنْ جَآءَكَ يَسْعٰى ۝

9. And he fears,

وَهُوَ يَخْشٰى ۝

10. From him will you divert yourself.

فَاَنْتَ عَنْهُ تَلَهّٰى ۝

11. Nay! surely it is an admonishment.

كَلَّا اِنَّهَا تَذْكِرَةٌ ۝

12. So let him who pleases mind it.

فَمَنْ شَآءَ ذَكَرَهٗ ۝

13. In honored books,

فِيْ صُحُفٍ مُّكَرَّمَةٍ ۝

14. Exalted, purified,

مَّرْفُوْعَةٍ مُّطَهَّرَةٍ ۝

15. In the hands of scribes,

بِاَيْدِيْ سَفَرَةٍ ۝

16. Noble, virtuous.

كِرَامٍ بَرَرَةٍ ۝

17. Cursed be man! how ungrateful is he!

قُتِلَ الْاِنْسَانُ مَآ اَكْفَرَهٗ ۝

18. Of what thing did He create him?

مِنْ اَيِّ شَيْءٍ خَلَقَهٗ ۝

19. Of a small seed; He created him, then He made him according to a measure,

مِنْ نُّطْفَةٍ خَلَقَهٗ فَقَدَّرَهٗ ۝

20. Then (as for) the way—He has made it easy (for him),

ثُمَّ السَّبِيْلَ يَسَّرَهٗ ۝

604

21. Then He causes him to die, then assigns to him a grave,

ثُمَّ اَمَاتَهُ فَاَقْبَرَهُ ۙ

22. Then when He pleases, He will raise him to life again.

ثُمَّ اِذَا شَآءَ اَنْشَرَهُ ؕ

23. Nay; but he has not done what He bade him.

كَلَّا لَمَّا يَقْضِ مَآ اَمَرَهُ ؕ

24. Then let man look to his food,

فَلْيَنْظُرِ الْاِنْسَانُ اِلٰى طَعَامِهٖۤ ۙ

25. That We pour down the water, pouring (it) down in abundance,

اَنَّا صَبَبْنَا الْمَآءَ صَبًّا ۙ

26. Then We cleave the earth, cleaving (it) asunder,

ثُمَّ شَقَقْنَا الْاَرْضَ شَقًّا ۙ

27. Then We cause to grow therein the grain,

فَاَنْۢبَتْنَا فِيْهَا حَبًّا ۙ

28. And grapes and clover,

وَّعِنَبًا وَّقَضْبًا ۙ

29. And the olive and the palm,

وَّزَيْتُوْنًا وَّنَخْلًا ۙ

30. And thick gardens,

وَّحَدَآئِقَ غُلْبًا ۙ

31. And fruits and herbage,

وَّفَاكِهَةً وَّاَبًّا ۙ

32. A provision for you and for your cattle.

مَّتَاعًا لَّكُمْ وَلِاَنْعَامِكُمْ ؕ

33. But when the deafening cry comes,

فَاِذَا جَآءَتِ الصَّآخَّةُ ۫

34. The day on which a man shall fly from his brother,

يَوْمَ يَفِرُّ الْمَرْءُ مِنْ اَخِيْهِ ۙ

35. And his mother and his father,

وَاُمِّهٖ وَاَبِيْهِ ۙ

36. And his spouse and his son—

وَصَاحِبَتِهٖ وَبَنِيْهِ ؕ

37. Every man of them shall on that day have an affair which will occupy him.

لِكُلِّ امْرِئٍ مِّنْهُمْ يَوْمَئِذٍ شَاْنٌ يُّغْنِيْهِ ؕ

38. (Many) faces on that day shall be bright,

وُجُوْهٌ يَّوْمَئِذٍ مُّسْفِرَةٌ ۙ

39. Laughing, joyous.

ضَاحِكَةٌ مُّسْتَبْشِرَةٌ ۚ

40. And (many) faces on that day, on them shall be dust,

وَوُجُوْهٌ يَّوْمَئِذٍ عَلَيْهَا غَبَرَةٌ ۙ

41. Darkness shall cover them.

تَرْهَقُهَا قَتَرَةٌ ؕ

42. These are they who are unbelievers, the wicked.

اُولٰٓئِكَ هُمُ الْكَفَرَةُ الْفَجَرَةُ ۠

THE COVERING UP
(TAKWIR)

اياتها (١٨) سورة التكوير مكية ركوعها

**In the name of Allah,
the Beneficent, the Merciful.**

بِسْمِ اللهِ الرَّحْمٰنِ الرَّحِيْمِ ۥ

1. When the sun is covered,

اِذَا الشَّمْسُ كُوِّرَتْ ۞

2. And when the stars darken,

وَاِذَا النُّجُوْمُ انْكَدَرَتْ ۞

3. And when the mountains are made to pass away,

وَاِذَا الْجِبَالُ سُيِّرَتْ ۞

4. And when the camels are left untended,

وَاِذَا الْعِشَارُ عُطِّلَتْ ۞

5. And when the wild animals are made to go forth,

وَاِذَا الْوُحُوْشُ حُشِرَتْ ۞

6. And when the seas are set on fire,

وَاِذَا الْبِحَارُ سُجِّرَتْ ۞

7. And when souls are united,

وَاِذَا النُّفُوْسُ زُوِّجَتْ ۞

8. And when the female infant buried alive is asked

وَاِذَا الْمَوْءُدَةُ سُئِلَتْ ۞

9. For what sin she was killed,

بِاَيِّ ذَنْبٍ قُتِلَتْ ۞

10. And when the books are spread,

وَاِذَا الصُّحُفُ نُشِرَتْ ۞

11. And when the heaven has its covering removed,

وَاِذَا السَّمَاءُ كُشِطَتْ ۞

12. And when the hell is kindled up,

وَاِذَا الْجَحِيْمُ سُعِّرَتْ ۞

13. And when the garden is brought nigh,

وَاِذَا الْجَنَّةُ اُزْلِفَتْ ۞

14. Every soul shall (then) know what it has prepared.

عَلِمَتْ نَفْسٌ مَّا اَحْضَرَتْ ۞

15. But nay! I swear by the stars,

فَلَا اُقْسِمُ بِالْخُنَّسِ ۞

16. That run their course (and) hide themselves,

الْجَوَارِ الْكُنَّسِ ۞

17. And the night when it departs,

وَالَّيْلِ اِذَا عَسْعَسَ ۞

18. And the morning when it brightens,

وَالصُّبْحِ اِذَا تَنَفَّسَ ۞

19. Most surely it is the Word of an honored messenger,

اِنَّهُ لَقَوْلُ رَسُوْلٍ كَرِيْمٍ ۞

606

20. The processor of strength, having an honorable place with the Lord of the Dominion,

21. One (to be) obeyed, and faithful in trust.

22. And your companion is not gone mad.

23. And of a truth he saw himself on the clear horizon.

24. Nor of the unseen is he a tenacious concealer.

25. Nor is it the word of the cursed Shaitan,

26. Whither then will you go?

27. It is naught but a reminder for the nations,

28. For him among you who pleases to go straight.

29. And you do not please except that Allah please, the Lord of the worlds.

ذِىْ قُوَّةٍ عِنْدَ ذِى الْعَرْشِ مَكِيْنٍ ۙ۲۰

مُّطَاعٍ ثَمَّ اَمِيْنٍ ۙ۲۱

وَمَا صَاحِبُكُمْ بِمَجْنُوْنٍ ۚ۲۲

وَلَقَدْ رَاٰهُ بِالْاُفُقِ الْمُبِيْنِ ۚ۲۳

وَمَا هُوَ عَلَى الْغَيْبِ بِضَنِيْنٍ ۚ۲٤

وَمَا هُوَ بِقَوْلِ شَيْطٰنٍ رَّجِيْمٍ ۙ۲٥

فَاَيْنَ تَذْهَبُوْنَ ۚ۲٦

اِنْ هُوَ اِلَّا ذِكْرٌ لِّلْعٰلَمِيْنَ ۙ۲۷

لِمَنْ شَآءَ مِنْكُمْ اَنْ يَّسْتَقِيْمَ ۚ۲۸

وَمَا تَشَآءُوْنَ اِلَّاۤ اَنْ يَّشَآءَ اللّٰهُ رَبُّ الْعٰلَمِيْنَ ۚ۲۹

THE CLEAVING ASUNDER
(INFITAR)

In the name of Allah,
the Beneficent, the Merciful.

1. When the heaven becomes cleft asunder,

2. And when the stars become dispersed,

3. And when the seas are made to flow forth,

4. And when the graves are laid open,

5. Every soul shall know what it has sent before and held back.

6. O man! what has beguiled you from your Lord, the Gracious one,

7. Who created you, then made you complete, then made you symmetrical?

8. Into whatever form He pleased He constituted you.

9. Nay! but you give the lie to the judgment day,

10. And most surely there are keepers over you,

11. Honorable recorders,

12. They know what you do.

13. Most surely the righteous are in bliss,

14. And most surely the wicked are in burning fire,

15. They shall enter it on the day of judgment.

16. And they shall by no means be absent from it.

17. And what will make you realize what the day of judgment is?

18. Again, what will make you realize what the day of judgment is?

19. The day on which no soul shall control anything for (another) soul; and the command on that day shall be entirely Allah's.

بِسْمِ اللهِ الرَّحْمٰنِ الرَّحِيْمِ ۟

اِذَا السَّمَآءُ انْفَطَرَتْ ۟ۙ

وَاِذَا الْكَوَاكِبُ انْتَثَرَتْ ۟ۙ

وَاِذَا الْبِحَارُ فُجِّرَتْ ۟ۙ

وَاِذَا الْقُبُوْرُ بُعْثِرَتْ ۟ۙ

عَلِمَتْ نَفْسٌ مَّا قَدَّمَتْ وَاَخَّرَتْ ۟ۙ

يٰٓاَيُّهَا الْاِنْسَانُ مَا غَرَّكَ بِرَبِّكَ الْكَرِيْمِ ۟ۙ

الَّذِيْ خَلَقَكَ فَسَوّٰىكَ فَعَدَلَكَ ۟ۙ

فِيْٓ اَيِّ صُوْرَةٍ مَّا شَآءَ رَكَّبَكَ ۟ؕ

كَلَّا بَلْ تُكَذِّبُوْنَ بِالدِّيْنِ ۟ۙ

وَاِنَّ عَلَيْكُمْ لَحٰفِظِيْنَ ۟ۙ

كِرَامًا كَاتِبِيْنَ ۟ۙ

يَعْلَمُوْنَ مَا تَفْعَلُوْنَ ۟

اِنَّ الْاَبْرَارَ لَفِيْ نَعِيْمٍ ۟ۚ

وَاِنَّ الْفُجَّارَ لَفِيْ جَحِيْمٍ ۟ۚ

يَصْلَوْنَهَا يَوْمَ الدِّيْنِ ۟ۙ

وَمَا هُمْ عَنْهَا بِغَآئِبِيْنَ ۟ؕ

وَمَآ اَدْرٰىكَ مَا يَوْمُ الدِّيْنِ ۟ۙ

ثُمَّ مَآ اَدْرٰىكَ مَا يَوْمُ الدِّيْنِ ۟ؕ

يَوْمَ لَا تَمْلِكُ نَفْسٌ لِّنَفْسٍ شَيْئًا ؕ وَالْاَمْرُ يَوْمَئِذٍ لِّلّٰهِ ۟

THE DEFRAUDERS
(MUTAFFIN)

**In the name of Allah,
the Beneficent, the Merciful.**

1. Woe to the defrauders,

2. Who, when they take the measure (of their dues) from men, take it fully,

3. But when they measure out to others or weigh out for them, they are deficient.

4. Do not these think that they shall be raised again,

5. For a mighty day,

6. The day on which men shall stand before the Lord of the worlds?

7. Nay! most surely the record of the wicked is in the Sijjin.

8. And what will make you know what the Sijjin is?

9. It is a written book.

10. Woe on that day to the rejecters,

11. Who give the lie to the day of judgment.

12. And none gives the lie to it but every exceeder of limits, sinful one;

13. When Our communications are recited to him, he says: Stories of those of yore.

14. Nay! rather, what they used to do has become like rust upon their hearts.

15. Nay! most surely they shall on that day be debarred from their Lord.

16. Then most surely they shall enter the burning fire.

17. Then shall it be said: This is what you gave the lie to.

18. Nay! Most surely the record of the righteous shall be in the Iliyin.

19. And what will make you know what the highest Iliyin is?

بِسْمِ اللهِ الرَّحْمٰنِ الرَّحِيْمِ

وَيْلٌ لِّلْمُطَفِّفِيْنَ ۙ ١

الَّذِيْنَ اِذَا اكْتَالُوْا عَلَى النَّاسِ يَسْتَوْفُوْنَ ۖ ٢

وَاِذَا كَالُوْهُمْ اَوْ وَّزَنُوْهُمْ يُخْسِرُوْنَ ۗ ٣

اَلَا يَظُنُّ اُولٰٓئِكَ اَنَّهُمْ مَّبْعُوْثُوْنَ ۙ ٤

لِيَوْمٍ عَظِيْمٍ ۙ ٥

يَّوْمَ يَقُوْمُ النَّاسُ لِرَبِّ الْعٰلَمِيْنَ ۗ ٦

كَلَّا اِنَّ كِتٰبَ الْفُجَّارِ لَفِيْ سِجِّيْنٍ ۗ ٧

وَمَا اَدْرٰىكَ مَا سِجِّيْنٌ ۗ ٨

كِتٰبٌ مَّرْقُوْمٌ ۗ ٩

وَيْلٌ يَّوْمَئِذٍ لِّلْمُكَذِّبِيْنَ ۙ ١٠

الَّذِيْنَ يُكَذِّبُوْنَ بِيَوْمِ الدِّيْنِ ۗ ١١

وَمَا يُكَذِّبُ بِهٖ اِلَّا كُلُّ مُعْتَدٍ اَثِيْمٍ ۗ ١٢

اِذَا تُتْلٰى عَلَيْهِ اٰيٰتُنَا قَالَ اَسَاطِيْرُ الْاَوَّلِيْنَ ۗ ١٣

كَلَّا بَلْ رَانَ عَلٰى قُلُوْبِهِمْ مَّا كَانُوْا يَكْسِبُوْنَ ۗ ١٤

كَلَّا اِنَّهُمْ عَنْ رَّبِّهِمْ يَوْمَئِذٍ لَّمَحْجُوْبُوْنَ ۗ ١٥

ثُمَّ اِنَّهُمْ لَصَالُوا الْجَحِيْمِ ۗ ١٦

ثُمَّ يُقَالُ هٰذَا الَّذِيْ كُنْتُمْ بِهٖ تُكَذِّبُوْنَ ۗ ١٧

كَلَّا اِنَّ كِتٰبَ الْاَبْرَارِ لَفِيْ عِلِّيِّيْنَ ۗ ١٨

وَمَا اَدْرٰىكَ مَا عِلِّيُّوْنَ ۗ ١٩

609

20. It is a written book,

21. Those who are drawn near (to Allah) shall witness it.

22. Most surely the righteous shall be in bliss,

23. On thrones, they shall gaze;

24. You will recognize in their faces the brightness of bliss.

25. They are made to quaff of a pure drink that is sealed (to others).

26. The sealing of it is (with) musk; and for that let the aspirers aspire.

27. And the admixture of it is a water of Tasnim,

28. A fountain from which drink they who are drawn near (to Allah).

29. Surely they who are guilty used to laugh at those who believe.

30. And when they passed by them, they winked at one another.

31. And when they returned to their own followers they returned exulting.

32. And when they saw them, they said: Most surely these are in error;

33. And they were not sent to be keepers over them.

34. So today those who believe shall laugh at the unbelievers;

35. On thrones, they will look.

36. Surely the disbelievers are rewarded as they did.

كِتٰبٌ مَّرْقُوْمٌ ۞

يَّشْهَدُهُ الْمُقَرَّبُوْنَ ۞

اِنَّ الْاَبْرَارَ لَفِيْ نَعِيْمٍ ۞

عَلَى الْاَرَآئِكِ يَنْظُرُوْنَ ۞

تَعْرِفُ فِيْ وُجُوْهِهِمْ نَضْرَةَ النَّعِيْمِ ۞

يُسْقَوْنَ مِنْ رَّحِيْقٍ مَّخْتُوْمٍ ۞

خِتٰمُهُ مِسْكٌ وَفِيْ ذٰلِكَ فَلْيَتَنَافَسِ الْمُتَنَافِسُوْنَ ۞

وَمِزَاجُهُ مِنْ تَسْنِيْمٍ ۞

عَيْنًا يَّشْرَبُ بِهَا الْمُقَرَّبُوْنَ ۞

اِنَّ الَّذِيْنَ اَجْرَمُوْا كَانُوْا مِنَ الَّذِيْنَ اٰمَنُوْا يَضْحَكُوْنَ ۞

وَاِذَا مَرُّوْا بِهِمْ يَتَغَامَزُوْنَ ۞

وَاِذَا انْقَلَبُوْا اِلٰٓى اَهْلِهِمُ انْقَلَبُوْا فَكِهِيْنَ ۞

وَاِذَا رَاَوْهُمْ قَالُوْٓا اِنَّ هٰٓؤُلَآءِ لَضَآلُّوْنَ ۞

وَمَآ اُرْسِلُوْا عَلَيْهِمْ حٰفِظِيْنَ ۞

فَالْيَوْمَ الَّذِيْنَ اٰمَنُوْا مِنَ الْكُفَّارِ يَضْحَكُوْنَ ۞

عَلَى الْاَرَآئِكِ يَنْظُرُوْنَ ۞

هَلْ ثُوِّبَ الْكُفَّارُ مَا كَانُوْا يَفْعَلُوْنَ ۞

THE BURSTING ASUNDER
(INSHIQAQ)

**In the name of Allah,
the Beneficent, the Merciful.**

1. When the heaven bursts asunder,

2. And obeys its Lord and it must.

3. And when the earth is stretched,

4. And casts forth what is in it and becomes empty,

5. And obeys its Lord and it must.

6. O man! surely you must strive (to attain) to your Lord, a hard striving until you meet Him.

7. Then as to him who is given his book in his right hand,

8. He shall be reckoned with by an easy reckoning,

9. And he shall go back to his people joyful.

10. And as to him who is given his book behind his back,

11. He shall call for perdition,

12. And enter into burning fire.

13. Surely he was (erstwhile) joyful among his followers.

14. Surely he thought that he would never return.

15. Yea! surely his Lord does ever see him.

16. But nay! I swear by the sunset redness,

17. And the night and that which it drives on,

18. And the moon when it grows full,

611

19. That you shall most certainly enter one state after another.

20. But what is the matter with them that they do not believe,

21. And when the Quran is recited to them they do not make obeisance?

22. Nay! those who disbelieve give the lie to the truth.

23. And Allah knows best what they hide,

24. So announce to them a painful punishment,

25. Except those who believe and do good; for them is a reward that shall never be cut off.

لَتَرْكَبُنَّ طَبَقًا عَنْ طَبَقٍ ۚ ۞

فَمَا لَهُمْ لَا يُؤْمِنُوْنَ ۞

وَاِذَا قُرِئَ عَلَيْهِمُ الْقُرْاٰنُ لَا يَسْجُدُوْنَ ۩ ۞

بَلِ الَّذِيْنَ كَفَرُوْا يُكَذِّبُوْنَ ۞

وَاللّٰهُ اَعْلَمُ بِمَا يُوْعُوْنَ ۞

فَبَشِّرْهُمْ بِعَذَابٍ اَلِيْمٍ ۞

اِلَّا الَّذِيْنَ اٰمَنُوْا وَعَمِلُوا الصّٰلِحٰتِ لَهُمْ اَجْرٌ غَيْرُ مَمْنُوْنٍ ۞

THE MANSIONS OF THE STARS
(BURUJ)

**In the name of Allah,
the Beneficent, the Merciful.**

1. I swear by the mansions of the stars,

2. And the promised day,

3. And the bearer of witness and those against whom the witness is borne.

4. Cursed be the makers of the pit,

5. Of the fire (kept burning) with fuel,

6. When they sat by it,

7. And they were witnesses of what they did with the believers.

8. And they did not take vengeance on them for aught except that they believed in Allah, the Mighty, the Praised,

9. Whose is the kingdom of the heavens and the earth; and Allah is a Witness of all things.

10. Surely (as for) those who persecute the believing men and the believing women, then do not repent, they shall have the chastisement of hell, and they shall have the chastisement of burning.

11. Surely (as for) those who believe and do good, they shall have gardens beneath which rivers flow, that is the great achievement.

12. Surely the might of your Lord is great.

13. Surely He it is Who originates and reproduces,

بِسْمِ اللهِ الرَّحْمٰنِ الرَّحِيْمِ

وَالسَّمَآءِ ذَاتِ الْبُرُوْجِ ۙ

وَالْيَوْمِ الْمَوْعُوْدِ ۙ

وَشَاهِدٍ وَّمَشْهُوْدٍ ؕ

قُتِلَ اَصْحٰبُ الْاُخْدُوْدِ ۙ

النَّارِ ذَاتِ الْوَقُوْدِ ۙ

اِذْ هُمْ عَلَيْهَا قُعُوْدٌ ۙ

وَّهُمْ عَلٰى مَا يَفْعَلُوْنَ بِالْمُؤْمِنِيْنَ شُهُوْدٌ ؕ

وَمَا نَقَمُوْا مِنْهُمْ اِلَّاۤ اَنْ يُّؤْمِنُوْا بِاللهِ الْعَزِيْزِ الْحَمِيْدِ ۙ

الَّذِيْ لَهٗ مُلْكُ السَّمٰوٰتِ وَالْاَرْضِ ؕ وَاللهُ عَلٰى كُلِّ شَيْءٍ شَهِيْدٌ ؕ

اِنَّ الَّذِيْنَ فَتَنُوا الْمُؤْمِنِيْنَ وَالْمُؤْمِنٰتِ ثُمَّ لَمْ يَتُوْبُوْا فَلَهُمْ عَذَابُ جَهَنَّمَ وَلَهُمْ عَذَابُ الْحَرِيْقِ ؕ

اِنَّ الَّذِيْنَ اٰمَنُوْا وَعَمِلُوا الصّٰلِحٰتِ لَهُمْ جَنّٰتٌ تَجْرِيْ مِنْ تَحْتِهَا الْاَنْهٰرُ ؕ ذٰلِكَ الْفَوْزُ الْكَبِيْرُ ؕ

اِنَّ بَطْشَ رَبِّكَ لَشَدِيْدٌ ؕ

اِنَّهٗ هُوَ يُبْدِئُ وَيُعِيْدُ ۙ

14. And He is the Forgiving, the Loving,

15. Lord of the Arsh, the Glorious,

16. The great doer of what He will.

17. Has not there come to you the story of the hosts,

18. Of Firon and Samood?

19. Nay! those who disbelieve are in (the act of) giving the lie to the truth.

20. And Allah encompasses them on every side.

21. Nay! it is a glorious Quran,

22. In a guarded tablet.

وَهُوَ الْغَفُوْرُ الْوَدُوْدُ ۙ۝

ذُو الْعَرْشِ الْمَجِيْدُ ۙ۝

فَعَّالٌ لِّمَا يُرِيْدُ ۝

هَلْ اَتٰىكَ حَدِيْثُ الْجُنُوْدِ ۙ۝

فِرْعَوْنَ وَثَمُوْدَ ۝

بَلِ الَّذِيْنَ كَفَرُوْا فِيْ تَكْذِيْبٍ ۙ۝

وَّاللّٰهُ مِنْ وَّرَآئِهِمْ مُّحِيْطٌ ۚ۝

بَلْ هُوَ قُرْاٰنٌ مَّجِيْدٌ ۙ۝

فِيْ لَوْحٍ مَّحْفُوْظٍ ۝

THE NIGHT-COMER
(TARIQ)

اياتها ١٧ (٨٦) سورة الطارق مكية روعها

**In the name of Allah,
the Beneficent, the Merciful.**

بِسْمِ اللهِ الرَّحْمٰنِ الرَّحِيْمِ ۞

1. I swear by the heaven and the comer by night;

وَالسَّمَآءِ وَالطَّارِقِ ۞

2. And what will make you know what the comer by night is?

وَمَآ اَدْرٰىكَ مَا الطَّارِقُ ۞

3. The star of piercing brightness;

النَّجْمُ الثَّاقِبُ ۞

4. There is not a soul but over it is a keeper.

اِنْ كُلُّ نَفْسٍ لَّمَّا عَلَيْهَا حَافِظٌ ۞

5. So let man consider of what he is created:

فَلْيَنْظُرِ الْاِنْسَانُ مِمَّ خُلِقَ ۞

6. He is created of water pouring forth,

خُلِقَ مِنْ مَّآءٍ دَافِقٍ ۞

7. Coming from between the back and the ribs.

يَّخْرُجُ مِنْ بَيْنِ الصُّلْبِ وَالتَّرَآئِبِ ۞

8. Most surely He is able to return him (to life).

اِنَّهُ عَلٰى رَجْعِهٖ لَقَادِرٌ ۞

9. On the day when hidden things shall be made manifest,

يَوْمَ تُبْلَى السَّرَآئِرُ ۞

10. He shall have neither strength nor helper.

فَمَا لَهُ مِنْ قُوَّةٍ وَّلَا نَاصِرٍ ۞

11. I swear by the raingiving heavens,

وَالسَّمَآءِ ذَاتِ الرَّجْعِ ۞

12. And the earth splitting (with plants);

وَالْاَرْضِ ذَاتِ الصَّدْعِ ۞

13. Most surely it is a decisive word,

اِنَّهُ لَقَوْلٌ فَصْلٌ ۞

14. And it is no joke.

وَّمَا هُوَ بِالْهَزْلِ ۞

15. Surely they will make a scheme,

اِنَّهُمْ يَكِيْدُوْنَ كَيْدًا ۞

16. And I (too) will make a scheme.

وَّاَكِيْدُ كَيْدًا ۞

17. So grant the unbelievers a respite: let them alone for a while.

فَمَهِّلِ الْكٰفِرِيْنَ اَمْهِلْهُمْ رُوَيْدًا ۞

615

THE MOST HIGH
(ALA)

**In the name of Allah,
the Beneficent, the Merciful.**

1. Glorify the name of your Lord, the Most High,

2. Who creates, then makes complete,

3. And Who makes (things) according to a measure, then guides (them to their goal),

4. And Who brings forth herbage,

5. Then makes it dried up, dust-colored.

6. We will make you recite so you shall not forget,

7. Except what Allah pleases, surely He knows the manifest, and what is hidden.

8. And We will make your way smooth to a state of ease.

9. Therefore do remind, surely reminding does profit.

10. He who fears will mind,

11. And the most unfortunate one will avoid it,

12. Who shall enter the great fire;

13. Then therein he shall neither live nor die.

14. He indeed shall be successful who purifies himself,

15. And magnifies the name of his Lord and prays.

16. Nay! you prefer the life of this world,

17. While the hereafter is better and more lasting.

18. Most surely this is in the earlier scriptures,

19. The scriptures of Ibrahim and Musa.

بِسْمِ اللهِ الرَّحْمٰنِ الرَّحِيْمِ ۟

سَبِّحِ اسْمَ رَبِّكَ الْاَعْلَى ۟ۙ

الَّذِيْ خَلَقَ فَسَوّٰى ۟ۙ

وَالَّذِيْ قَدَّرَ فَهَدٰى ۟ۙ

وَالَّذِيْٓ اَخْرَجَ الْمَرْعٰى ۟ۙ

فَجَعَلَهٗ غُثَآءً اَحْوٰى ۟ؕ

سَنُقْرِئُكَ فَلَا تَنْسٰٓى ۟ۙ

اِلَّا مَا شَآءَ اللهُ ؕ اِنَّهٗ يَعْلَمُ الْجَهْرَ وَمَا يَخْفٰى ۟ؕ

وَنُيَسِّرُكَ لِلْيُسْرٰى ۟ۚ

فَذَكِّرْ اِنْ نَّفَعَتِ الذِّكْرٰى ۟ؕ

سَيَذَّكَّرُ مَنْ يَّخْشٰى ۟ۙ

وَيَتَجَنَّبُهَا الْاَشْقَى ۟ۙ

الَّذِيْ يَصْلَى النَّارَ الْكُبْرٰى ۟ۚ

ثُمَّ لَا يَمُوْتُ فِيْهَا وَلَا يَحْيٰى ۟ؕ

قَدْ اَفْلَحَ مَنْ تَزَكّٰى ۟ۙ

وَذَكَرَ اسْمَ رَبِّهٖ فَصَلّٰى ۟ؕ

بَلْ تُؤْثِرُوْنَ الْحَيٰوةَ الدُّنْيَا ۟ۖ

وَالْاٰخِرَةُ خَيْرٌ وَّاَبْقٰى ۟ؕ

اِنَّ هٰذَا لَفِي الصُّحُفِ الْاُوْلٰى ۟ۙ

صُحُفِ اِبْرٰهِيْمَ وَمُوْسٰى ۟۠

سورة ٣٠   الغاشيةمه

THE OVERWHELMING CALAMITY (GHASHIYAH)

اياتها (٨٨) سُوْرَةُ الْغَاشِيَةِ مَكِّيَّةٌ رُكُوْعُهَا

**In the name of Allah,
the Beneficent, the Merciful.**

بِسْمِ اللهِ الرَّحْمٰنِ الرَّحِيْمِ ۝

1. Has not there come to you the news of the overwhelming calamity?

هَلْ اَتٰىكَ حَدِيْثُ الْغَاشِيَةِ ۝

2. (Some) faces on that day shall be downcast,

وُجُوْهٌ يَّوْمَئِذٍ خَاشِعَةٌ ۝

3. Laboring, toiling,

عَامِلَةٌ نَّاصِبَةٌ ۝

4. Entering into burning fire,

تَصْلٰى نَارًا حَامِيَةً ۝

5. Made to drink from a boiling spring.

تُسْقٰى مِنْ عَيْنٍ اٰنِيَةٍ ۝

6. They shall have no food but of thorns,

لَيْسَ لَهُمْ طَعَامٌ اِلَّا مِنْ ضَرِيْعٍ ۝

7. Which will neither fatten nor avail against hunger.

لَا يُسْمِنُ وَلَا يُغْنِيْ مِنْ جُوْعٍ ۝

8. (Other) faces on that day shall be happy,

وُجُوْهٌ يَّوْمَئِذٍ نَّاعِمَةٌ ۝

9. Well-pleased because of their striving,

لِسَعْيِهَا رَاضِيَةٌ ۝

10. In a lofty garden,

فِيْ جَنَّةٍ عَالِيَةٍ ۝

11. Wherein you shall not hear vain talk.

لَا تَسْمَعُ فِيْهَا لَاغِيَةً ۝

12. Therein is a fountain flowing,

فِيْهَا عَيْنٌ جَارِيَةٌ ۝

13. Therein are thrones raised high,

فِيْهَا سُرُرٌ مَّرْفُوْعَةٌ ۝

14. And drinking-cups ready placed,

وَّاَكْوَابٌ مَّوْضُوْعَةٌ ۝

15. And cushions set in a row,

وَّنَمَارِقُ مَصْفُوْفَةٌ ۝

16. And carpets spread out.

وَّزَرَابِيُّ مَبْثُوْثَةٌ ۝

17. Will they not then consider the camels, how they are created?

اَفَلَا يَنْظُرُوْنَ اِلَى الْاِبِلِ كَيْفَ خُلِقَتْ ۝

18. And the heaven, how it is reared aloft,

وَاِلَى السَّمَآءِ كَيْفَ رُفِعَتْ ۝

19. And the mountains, how they are firmly fixed,

وَاِلَى الْجِبَالِ كَيْفَ نُصِبَتْ ۝

20. And the earth, how it is made a vast expanse?

وَإِلَى الْاَرْضِ كَيْفَ سُطِحَتْ ۝

21. Therefore do remind, for you are only a reminder.

فَذَكِّرْ ۚ اِنَّمَآ اَنْتَ مُذَكِّرٌ ۝

22. You are not a watcher over them;

لَسْتَ عَلَيْهِمْ بِمُصَيْطِرٍ ۝

23. But whoever turns back and disbelieves,

اِلَّا مَنْ تَوَلّٰى وَكَفَرَ ۝

24. Allah will chastise him with the greatest chastisement.

فَيُعَذِّبُهُ اللهُ الْعَذَابَ الْاَكْبَرَ ۝

25. Surely to Us is their turning back,

اِنَّ اِلَيْنَآ اِيَابَهُمْ ۝

26. Then surely upon Us is the taking of their account.

ثُمَّ اِنَّ عَلَيْنَا حِسَابَهُمْ ۝

THE DAYBREAK
(FAJR)

أَيَاتُهَا (٨٩) سُوْرَةُ الْفَجْرِ مَكِّيَةٌ رُكُوْعُهَا

بِسْمِ اللّٰهِ الرَّحْمٰنِ الرَّحِيْمِ ۝

In the name of Allah,
the Beneficent, the Merciful.

1. I swear by the daybreak,

وَالْفَجْرِ ۝

2. And the ten nights,

وَلَيَالٍ عَشْرٍ ۝

3. And the even and the odd,

وَّالشَّفْعِ وَالْوَتْرِ ۝

4. And the night when it departs.

وَالَّيْلِ إِذَا يَسْرِ ۝

5. Truly in that there is an oath for those who possess understanding.

هَلْ فِيْ ذٰلِكَ قَسَمٌ لِّذِيْ حِجْرٍ ۝

6. Have you not considered how your Lord dealt with Ad,

أَلَمْ تَرَ كَيْفَ فَعَلَ رَبُّكَ بِعَادٍ ۝

7. (The people of) Aram, possessors of lofty buildings,

إِرَمَ ذَاتِ الْعِمَادِ ۝

8. The like of which were not created in the (other) cities;

الَّتِيْ لَمْ يُخْلَقْ مِثْلُهَا فِي الْبِلَادِ ۝

9. And (with) Samood, who hewed out the rocks in the valley,

وَثَمُوْدَ الَّذِيْنَ جَابُوا الصَّخْرَ بِالْوَادِ ۝

10. And (with) Firon, the lord of hosts,

وَفِرْعَوْنَ ذِى الْأَوْتَادِ ۝

11. Who committed inordinacy in the cities,

الَّذِيْنَ طَغَوْا فِي الْبِلَادِ ۝

12. So they made great mischief therein?

فَأَكْثَرُوْا فِيْهَا الْفَسَادَ ۝

13. Therefore your Lord let down upon them a portion of the chastisement.

فَصَبَّ عَلَيْهِمْ رَبُّكَ سَوْطَ عَذَابٍ ۝

14. Most surely your Lord is watching.

إِنَّ رَبَّكَ لَبِالْمِرْصَادِ ۝

15. And as for man, when his Lord tries him, then treats him with honor and makes him lead an easy life, he says: My Lord honors me.

فَأَمَّا الْإِنْسَانُ إِذَا مَا ابْتَلَاهُ رَبُّهُ فَأَكْرَمَهُ وَنَعَّمَهُ فَيَقُوْلُ رَبِّيْ أَكْرَمَنِ ۝

16. But when He tries him (differently), then straitens to him his means of subsistence, he says: My Lord has disgraced me.

وَأَمَّا إِذَا مَا ابْتَلَاهُ فَقَدَرَ عَلَيْهِ رِزْقَهُ فَيَقُوْلُ رَبِّيْ أَهَانَنِ ۝

17. Nay! but you do not honor the orphan,

كَلَّا بَلْ لَّا تُكْرِمُوْنَ الْيَتِيْمَ ۝

619

18. Nor do you urge one another to feed the poor,

19. And you eat away the heritage, devouring (everything) indiscriminately,

20. And you love wealth with exceeding love.

21. Nay! when the earth is made to crumble to pieces,

22. And your Lord comes and (also) the angels in ranks,

23. And hell is made to appear on that day. On that day shall man be mindful, and what shall being mindful (then) avail him?

24. He shall say: O! would that I had sent before for (this) my life!

25. But on that day shall no one chastise with (anything like) His chastisement,

26. And no one shall bind with (anything like) His binding.

27. O soul that art at rest!

28. Return to your Lord, well-pleased (with him), well-pleasing (Him),

29. So enter among My servants,

30. And enter into My garden.

وَلَا تَحَٰٓضُّوۡنَ عَلَىٰ طَعَامِ الۡمِسۡكِيۡنِۙ ۝

وَتَاۡكُلُوۡنَ التُّرَاثَ اَكۡلًا لَّمًّاۙ ۝

وَّتُحِبُّوۡنَ الۡمَالَ حُبًّا جَمًّاؕ ۝

كَلَّاۤ اِذَا دُكَّتِ الۡاَرۡضُ دَكًّا دَكًّاۙ ۝

وَّجَآءَ رَبُّكَ وَالۡمَلَكُ صَفًّا صَفًّاۚ ۝

وَجِاۡٓىۡءَ يَوۡمَىِٕذٍۭ بِجَهَنَّمَ ۬ۙ يَوۡمَىِٕذٍ يَّتَذَكَّرُ الۡاِنۡسَانُ وَاَنّٰى لَهُ الذِّكۡرٰىؕ ۝

يَقُوۡلُ يٰلَيۡتَنِىۡ قَدَّمۡتُ لِحَيَاتِىۚ ۝

فَيَوۡمَىِٕذٍ لَّا يُعَذِّبُ عَذَابَهٗۤ اَحَدٌۙ ۝

وَّلَا يُوۡثِقُ وَثَاقَهٗۤ اَحَدٌؕ ۝

يٰۤاَيَّتُهَا النَّفۡسُ الۡمُطۡمَىِٕنَّةُ ۝

ارۡجِعِىۡۤ اِلٰى رَبِّكِ رَاضِيَةً مَّرۡضِيَّةً ۝

فَادۡخُلِىۡ فِىۡ عِبٰدِىۙ ۝

وَادۡخُلِىۡ جَنَّتِىۡ ۝

THE CITY
(BALAD)

**In the name of Allah,
the Beneficent, the Merciful.**

بِسْمِ اللهِ الرَّحْمٰنِ الرَّحِيْمِ ۞

1. Nay! I swear by this city.

لَاۤ اُقْسِمُ بِهٰذَا الْبَلَدِ ۞

2. And you shall be made free from obligation in this city—

وَاَنْتَ حِلٌّۢ بِهٰذَا الْبَلَدِ ۞

3. And the begetter and whom he begot.

وَوَالِدٍ وَّمَا وَلَدَ ۞

4. Certainly We have created man to be in distress.

لَقَدْ خَلَقْنَا الْاِنْسَانَ فِيْ كَبَدٍ ۞

5. Does he think that no one has power over him?

اَيَحْسَبُ اَنْ لَّنْ يَّقْدِرَ عَلَيْهِ اَحَدٌ ۞

6. He shall say: I have wasted much wealth.

يَقُوْلُ اَهْلَكْتُ مَالًا لُّبَدًا ۞

7. Does he think that no one sees him?

اَيَحْسَبُ اَنْ لَّمْ يَرَهٗۤ اَحَدٌ ۞

8. Have We not given him two eyes,

اَلَمْ نَجْعَلْ لَّهٗ عَيْنَيْنِ ۞

9. And a tongue and two lips,

وَلِسَانًا وَّشَفَتَيْنِ ۞

10. And pointed out to him the two conspicuous ways?

وَهَدَيْنٰهُ النَّجْدَيْنِ ۞

11. But he would not attempt the uphill road,

فَلَا اقْتَحَمَ الْعَقَبَةَ ۞

12. And what will make you comprehend what the uphill road is?

وَمَاۤ اَدْرٰىكَ مَا الْعَقَبَةُ ۞

13. (It is) the setting free of a slave,

فَكُّ رَقَبَةٍ ۞

14. Or the giving of food in a day of hunger

اَوْ اِطْعَامٌ فِيْ يَوْمٍ ذِيْ مَسْغَبَةٍ ۞

15. To an orphan, having relationship,

يَّتِيْمًا ذَا مَقْرَبَةٍ ۞

16. Or to the poor man lying in the dust.

اَوْ مِسْكِيْنًا ذَا مَتْرَبَةٍ ۞

17. Then he is of those who believe and charge one another to show patience, and charge one another to show compassion.

ثُمَّ كَانَ مِنَ الَّذِيْنَ اٰمَنُوْا وَتَوَاصَوْا بِالصَّبْرِ وَتَوَاصَوْا بِالْمَرْحَمَةِ ۞

18. These are the people of the right hand.

اُولٰٓئِكَ اَصْحٰبُ الْمَيْمَنَةِ ۞

19. And (as for) those who disbelieve in our communications, they are the people of the left hand.

وَالَّذِيْنَ كَفَرُوْا بِاٰيٰتِنَا هُمْ اَصْحٰبُ الْمَشْـَٔمَةِ ۞

20. On them is fire closed over.

عَلَيْهِمْ نَارٌ مُّؤْصَدَةٌ ۞

THE SUN
(SHAMS)

بِسْمِ اللهِ الرَّحْمٰنِ الرَّحِيْمِ

**In the name of Allah,
the Beneficent, the Merciful.**

١. اِبَانِهَا (٩١) سُوْرَةُ الشَّمْسِ مَكِّيَّةٌ رُكُوْعُهَا

بِسْمِ اللهِ الرَّحْمٰنِ الرَّحِيْمِ

1. I swear by the sun and its brilliance,

وَالشَّمْسِ وَضُحٰهَا ۙ

2. And the moon when it follows the sun,

وَالْقَمَرِ اِذَا تَلٰهَا ۙ

3. And the day when it shows it,

وَالنَّهَارِ اِذَا جَلّٰهَا ۙ

4. And the night when it draws a veil over it,

وَالَّيْلِ اِذَا يَغْشٰهَا ۙ

5. And the heaven and Him Who made it,

وَالسَّمَآءِ وَمَا بَنٰهَا ۙ

6. And the earth and Him Who extended it,

وَالْاَرْضِ وَمَا طَحٰهَا ۙ

7. And the soul and Him Who made it perfect,

وَنَفْسٍ وَّمَا سَوّٰهَا ۙ

8. Then He inspired it to understand what is right and wrong for it;

فَاَلْهَمَهَا فُجُوْرَهَا وَتَقْوٰهَا ۙ

9. He will indeed be successful who purifies it,

قَدْ اَفْلَحَ مَنْ زَكّٰهَا ۙ

10. And he will indeed fail who corrupts it.

وَقَدْ خَابَ مَنْ دَسّٰهَا ۙ

11. Samood gave the lie (to the truth) in their inordinacy,

كَذَّبَتْ ثَمُوْدُ بِطَغْوٰىهَا ۙ

12. When the most unfortunate of them broke forth with mischief,

اِذِ انْبَعَثَ اَشْقٰهَا ۙ

13. So Allah's apostle said to them: (Leave alone) Allah's she-camel, and (give) her (to) drink.

فَقَالَ لَهُمْ رَسُوْلُ اللهِ نَاقَةَ اللهِ وَسُقْيٰهَا ۙ

14. But they called him a liar and slaughtered her, therefore their Lord crushed them for their sin and levelled them (with the ground).

فَكَذَّبُوْهُ فَعَقَرُوْهَا فَدَمْدَمَ عَلَيْهِمْ رَبُّهُمْ بِذَنْبِهِمْ فَسَوّٰهَا ۙ

15. And He fears not its consequence.

وَلَا يَخَافُ عُقْبٰهَا ۙ

THE NIGHT
(LAIL)

**In the name of Allah,
the Beneficent, the Merciful.**

1. I swear by the night when it draws a veil,

2. And the day when it shines in brightness,

3. And the creating of the male and the female,

4. Your striving is most surely (directed to) various (ends).

5. Then as for him who gives away and guards (against evil),

6. And accepts the best,

7. We will facilitate for him the easy end.

8. And as for him who is niggardly and considers himself free from need (of Allah),

9. And rejects the best,

10. We will facilitate for him the difficult end.

11. And his wealth will not avail him when he perishes.

12. Surely Ours is it to show the way,

13. And most surely Ours is the hereafter and the former.

14. Therefore I warn you of the fire that flames:

15. None shall enter it but the most unhappy,

16. Who gives the lie (to the truth) and turns (his) back.

17. And away from it shall be kept the one who guards most (against evil),

18. Who gives away his wealth, purifying himself,

19. And no one has with him any boon for which he should be rewarded,

20. Except the seeking of the pleasure of his Lord, the Most High.

21. And he shall soon be well-pleased.

623

THE EARLY HOURS
(ZOHA)

**In the name of Allah,
the Beneficent, the Merciful.**

1. I swear by the early hours of the day,

2. And the night when it covers with darkness.

3. Your Lord has not forsaken you, nor has He become displeased,

4. And surely what comes after is better for you than that which has gone before.

5. And soon will your Lord give you so that you shall be well pleased.

6. Did He not find you an orphan and give you shelter?

7. And find you lost (i.e. unrecognized by men) and guide (them to you)?

8. And find you in want and make you to be free from want?

9. Therefore, as for the orphan, do not oppress (him).

10. And as for him who asks, do not chide (him),

11. And as for the favor of your Lord, do announce (it).

SURAH XCIV

THE EXPANSION
(INSHIRAH)

**In the name of Allah,
the Beneficent, the Merciful.**

1. Have We not expanded for you your breast,

2. And taken off from you your burden,

3. Which pressed heavily upon your back,

4. And exalted for you your esteem?

5. Surely with difficulty is ease.

6. With difficulty is surely ease.

7. So when you are free, nominate.

8. And make your Lord your exclusive object.

624

THE FIG
(TEEN)

**In the name of Allah,
the Beneficent, the Merciful.**

1. I swear by the fig and the olive,

2. And mount Sinai,

3. And this city made secure,

4. Certainly We created man in the best make.

5. Then We render him the lowest of the low.

6. Except those who believe and do good, so they shall have a reward never to be cut off.

7. Then who can give you the lie after (this) about the judgment?

8. Is not Allah the best of the Judges?

أَيَاتُهَا (٩٥) سُورَةُ التِّينِ كِّيَّةٌ رُكُوعُهَا

بِسْمِ اللهِ الرَّحْمَنِ الرَّحِيْمِ ۞

وَالتِّينِ وَالزَّيْتُونِ ۞

وَطُورِ سِينِينَ ۞

وَهَذَا الْبَلَدِ الْأَمِينِ ۞

لَقَدْ خَلَقْنَا الْإِنْسَانَ فِيْ أَحْسَنِ تَقْوِيمٍ ۞

ثُمَّ رَدَدْنَاهُ أَسْفَلَ سَافِلِينَ ۞

إِلَّا الَّذِينَ أَمَنُوا وَعَمِلُوا الصَّالِحَاتِ فَلَهُمْ أَجْرٌ غَيْرُ مَمْنُونٍ ۞

فَمَا يُكَذِّبُكَ بَعْدُ بِالدِّينِ ۞

أَلَيْسَ اللهُ بِأَحْكَمِ الْحَاكِمِينَ ۞

THE CLOT
(ALAQ)

**In the name of Allah,
the Beneficent, the Merciful.**

1. Read in the name of your Lord Who created.

2. He created man from a clot.

3. Read and your Lord is Most Honorable,

4. Who taught (to write) with the pen,

5. Taught man what he knew not.

6. Nay! man is most surely inordinate,

7. Because he sees himself free from want.

8. Surely to your Lord is the return.

9. Have you seen him who forbids

10. A servant when he prays?

11. Have you considered if he were on the right way,

12. Or enjoined guarding (against evil)?

13. Have you considered if he gives the lie to the truth and turns (his) back?

14. Does he not know that Allah does see?

15. Nay! if he desist not, We would certainly smite his forehead,

16. A lying, sinful forehead.

17. Then let him summon his council,

18. We too would summon the braves of the army.

19. Nay! obey him not, and make obeisance and draw nigh (to Allah).

بِسۡمِ اللّٰهِ الرَّحۡمٰنِ الرَّحِیۡمِ ۝

اِقۡرَاۡ بِاسۡمِ رَبِّكَ الَّذِیۡ خَلَقَ ۝

خَلَقَ الۡاِنۡسَانَ مِنۡ عَلَقٍ ۝

اِقۡرَاۡ وَرَبُّكَ الۡاَكۡرَمُ ۝

الَّذِیۡ عَلَّمَ بِالۡقَلَمِ ۝

عَلَّمَ الۡاِنۡسَانَ مَا لَمۡ یَعۡلَمۡ ۝

كَلَّاۤ اِنَّ الۡاِنۡسَانَ لَیَطۡغٰۤی ۝

اَنۡ رَّاٰهُ اسۡتَغۡنٰی ۝

اِنَّ اِلٰی رَبِّكَ الرُّجۡعٰی ۝

اَرَءَیۡتَ الَّذِیۡ یَنۡهٰی ۝

عَبۡدًا اِذَا صَلّٰی ۝

اَرَءَیۡتَ اِنۡ كَانَ عَلَی الۡهُدٰۤی ۝

اَوۡ اَمَرَ بِالتَّقۡوٰی ۝

اَرَءَیۡتَ اِنۡ كَذَّبَ وَتَوَلّٰی ۝

اَلَمۡ یَعۡلَمۡ بِاَنَّ اللّٰهَ یَرٰی ۝

كَلَّا لَئِنۡ لَّمۡ یَنۡتَهِ ۬ۙ لَنَسۡفَعًۢا بِالنَّاصِیَةِ ۝

نَاصِیَةٍ كَاذِبَةٍ خَاطِئَةٍ ۝

فَلۡیَدۡعُ نَادِیَهٗ ۝

سَنَدۡعُ الزَّبَانِیَةَ ۝

كَلَّا لَا تُطِعۡهُ وَاسۡجُدۡ وَاقۡتَرِبۡ ۩

626

THE MAJESTY
(QADR)

**In the name of Allah,
the Beneficent, the Merciful.**

1. Surely We revealed it on the grand night.

2. And what will make you comprehend what the grand night is?

3. The grand night is better than a thousand months.

4. The angels and Gibreel descend in it by the permission of their Lord for every affair,

5. Peace! it is till the break of the morning.

SURAH XCVIII

THE CLEAR EVIDENCE
(BAYYINAH)

**In the name of Allah,
the Beneficent, the Merciful.**

1. Those who disbelieved from among the followers of the Book and the polytheists could not have separated (from the faithful) until there had come to them the clear evidence:

2. An apostle from Allah, reciting pure pages,

3. Wherein are all the right ordinances.

4. And those who were given the Book did not become divided except after clear evidence had come to them.

5. And they were not enjoined anything except that they should serve Allah, being sincere to Him in obedience, upright, and keep up prayer and pay the poor-rate, and that is the right religion.

6. Surely those who disbelieve from among the followers of the Book and the polytheists shall be in the fire of hell, abiding therein; they are the worst of men.

7. (As for) those who believe and do good, surely they are the best of men.

8. Their reward with their Lord is gardens of perpetuity beneath which rivers flow, abiding therein for ever; Allah is well pleased with them and they are well pleased with Him; that is for him who fears his Lord.

بِسْمِ اللهِ الرَّحْمٰنِ الرَّحِيْمِ

إِنَّا أَنْزَلْنٰهُ فِيْ لَيْلَةِ الْقَدْرِ ۚ

وَمَا أَدْرٰىكَ مَا لَيْلَةُ الْقَدْرِ ۚ

لَيْلَةُ الْقَدْرِ ۙ خَيْرٌ مِّنْ أَلْفِ شَهْرٍ ۚ

تَنَزَّلُ الْمَلٰئِكَةُ وَالرُّوْحُ فِيْهَا بِإِذْنِ رَبِّهِمْ مِّنْ كُلِّ أَمْرٍ ۙ

سَلٰمٌ ۛ هِيَ حَتّٰى مَطْلَعِ الْفَجْرِ ۚ

بِسْمِ اللهِ الرَّحْمٰنِ الرَّحِيْمِ

لَمْ يَكُنِ الَّذِيْنَ كَفَرُوْا مِنْ أَهْلِ الْكِتٰبِ وَالْمُشْرِكِيْنَ مُنْفَكِّيْنَ حَتّٰى تَأْتِيَهُمُ الْبَيِّنَةُ ۙ

رَسُوْلٌ مِّنَ اللهِ يَتْلُوْا صُحُفًا مُّطَهَّرَةً ۙ

فِيْهَا كُتُبٌ قَيِّمَةٌ ۚ

وَمَا تَفَرَّقَ الَّذِيْنَ أُوْتُوا الْكِتٰبَ إِلَّا مِنْ بَعْدِ مَا جَآءَتْهُمُ الْبَيِّنَةُ ۚ

وَمَا أُمِرُوْا إِلَّا لِيَعْبُدُوا اللهَ مُخْلِصِيْنَ لَهُ الدِّيْنَ ۙ حُنَفَآءَ وَيُقِيْمُوا الصَّلٰوةَ وَيُؤْتُوا الزَّكٰوةَ وَذٰلِكَ دِيْنُ الْقَيِّمَةِ ۚ

إِنَّ الَّذِيْنَ كَفَرُوْا مِنْ أَهْلِ الْكِتٰبِ وَالْمُشْرِكِيْنَ فِيْ نَارِ جَهَنَّمَ خٰلِدِيْنَ فِيْهَا ۚ أُولٰئِكَ هُمْ شَرُّ الْبَرِيَّةِ ۚ

إِنَّ الَّذِيْنَ اٰمَنُوْا وَعَمِلُوا الصّٰلِحٰتِ أُولٰئِكَ هُمْ خَيْرُ الْبَرِيَّةِ ۚ

جَزَآؤُهُمْ عِنْدَ رَبِّهِمْ جَنّٰتُ عَدْنٍ تَجْرِيْ مِنْ تَحْتِهَا الْأَنْهٰرُ خٰلِدِيْنَ فِيْهَا أَبَدًا ۚ رَضِيَ اللهُ عَنْهُمْ وَرَضُوْا عَنْهُ ۚ ذٰلِكَ لِمَنْ خَشِيَ رَبَّهُ ۚ

THE SHAKING
(ZILZAL)

**In the name of Allah,
the Beneficent, the Merciful.**

1. When the earth is shaken with her (violent) shaking,

2. And the earth brings forth her burdens,

3. And man says: What has befallen her?

4. On that day she shall tell her news,

5. Because your Lord had inspired her.

6. On that day men shall come forth in sundry bodies that they may be shown their works.

7. So. he who has done an atom's weight of good shall see it.

8. And he who has done an atom's weight of evil shall see it.

SURAH C

THE ASSAULTERS
(ADIYAT)

**In the name of Allah,
the Beneficent, the Merciful.**

1. I swear by the runners breathing pantingly,

2. Then those that produce fire striking,

3. Then those that make raids at morn,

4. Then thereby raise dust,

5. Then rush thereby upon an assembly:

6. Most surely man is ungrateful to his Lord.

7. And most surely he is a witness of that.

8. And most surely he is tenacious in the love of wealth.

9. Does he not then know when what is in the graves is raised,

10. And what is in the breasts is made apparent,

11. Most surely their Lord that day shall be fully aware of them.

سورة الزلزال مدنية رکوعها آیاتها ٩٩

بِسْمِ اللهِ الرَّحْمٰنِ الرَّحِيْمِ ۞

اِذَا زُلْزِلَتِ الْاَرْضُ زِلْزَالَهَا ۞

وَاَخْرَجَتِ الْاَرْضُ اَثْقَالَهَا ۞

وَقَالَ الْاِنْسَانُ مَالَهَا ۞

يَوْمَئِذٍ تُحَدِّثُ اَخْبَارَهَا ۞

بِاَنَّ رَبَّكَ اَوْحٰى لَهَا ۞

يَوْمَئِذٍ يَّصْدُرُ النَّاسُ اَشْتَاتًا لِّيُرَوْا اَعْمَالَهُمْ ۞

فَمَنْ يَّعْمَلْ مِثْقَالَ ذَرَّةٍ خَيْرًا يَّرَهُ ۞

وَمَنْ يَّعْمَلْ مِثْقَالَ ذَرَّةٍ شَرًّا يَّرَهُ ۞

سورة العاديات مكية رکوعها آياتها ١٠٠

بِسْمِ اللهِ الرَّحْمٰنِ الرَّحِيْمِ ۞

وَالْعٰدِيٰتِ ضَبْحًا ۞

فَالْمُوْرِيٰتِ قَدْحًا ۞

فَالْمُغِيْرٰتِ صُبْحًا ۞

فَاَثَرْنَ بِهٖ نَقْعًا ۞

فَوَسَطْنَ بِهٖ جَمْعًا ۞

اِنَّ الْاِنْسَانَ لِرَبِّهٖ لَكَنُوْدٌ ۞

وَاِنَّهٗ عَلٰى ذٰلِكَ لَشَهِيْدٌ ۞

وَاِنَّهٗ لِحُبِّ الْخَيْرِ لَشَدِيْدٌ ۞

اَفَلَا يَعْلَمُ اِذَا بُعْثِرَ مَا فِى الْقُبُوْرِ ۞

وَحُصِّلَ مَا فِى الصُّدُوْرِ ۞

اِنَّ رَبَّهُمْ بِهِمْ يَوْمَئِذٍ لَّخَبِيْرٌ ۞

THE TERRIBLE CALAMITY
(QARIAH)

بِسْمِ اللهِ الرَّحْمٰنِ الرَّحِيْمِ

**In the Name of Allah,
the Beneficent, the Merciful.**

1. The terrible calamity!

الْقَارِعَةُ ۝

2. What is the terrible calamity!

مَاالْقَارِعَةُ ۝

3. And what will make you comprehend what the terrible calamity is?

وَمَآ اَدْرٰىكَ مَاالْقَارِعَةُ ۝

4. The day on which men shall be as scattered moths,

يَوْمَ يَكُوْنُ النَّاسُ كَالْفَرَاشِ الْمَبْثُوْثِ ۝

5. And the mountains shall be as loosened wool.

وَتَكُوْنُ الْجِبَالُ كَالْعِهْنِ الْمَنْفُوْشِ ۝

6. Then as for him whose measure of good deeds is heavy,

فَاَمَّا مَنْ ثَقُلَتْ مَوَازِيْنُهُ ۝

7. He shall live a pleasant life.

فَهُوَ فِيْ عِيْشَةٍ رَّاضِيَةٍ ۝

8. And as for him whose measure of good deeds is light,

وَاَمَّا مَنْ خَفَّتْ مَوَازِيْنُهُ ۝

9. His abode shall be the abyss.

فَاُمُّهُ هَاوِيَةٌ ۝

10. And what will make you know what it is?

وَمَآ اَدْرٰىكَ مَاهِيَهْ ۝

11. A burning fire.

نَارٌ حَامِيَةٌ ۝

SURAH CII

THE MULTIPLICATION OF WEALTH AND CHILDREN
(TAKASUR)

بِسْمِ اللهِ الرَّحْمٰنِ الرَّحِيْمِ

**In the name of Allah,
the Beneficent, the Merciful.**

1. Abundance diverts you,

اَلْهٰىكُمُ التَّكَاثُرُ ۝

2. Until you come to the graves.

حَتّٰى زُرْتُمُ الْمَقَابِرَ ۝

3. Nay! you shall soon know,

كَلَّا سَوْفَ تَعْلَمُوْنَ ۝

4. Nay! Nay! you shall soon know.

ثُمَّ كَلَّا سَوْفَ تَعْلَمُوْنَ ۝

5. Nay! if you had known with a certain knowledge,

كَلَّا لَوْ تَعْلَمُوْنَ عِلْمَ الْيَقِيْنِ ۝

6. You should most certainly have seen the hell;

لَتَرَوُنَّ الْجَحِيْمَ ۝

7. Then you shall most certainly see it with the eye of certainty;

ثُمَّ لَتَرَوُنَّهَا عَيْنَ الْيَقِيْنِ ۝

8. Then on that day you shall most certainly be questioned about the boons.

ثُمَّ لَتُسْئَلُنَّ يَوْمَئِذٍ عَنِ النَّعِيْمِ ۝

TIME
(ASR)

In the name of Allah,
the Beneficent, the Merciful.

1. I swear by time,

2. Most surely man is in loss,

3. Except those who believe and do good, and enjoin on each other truth, and enjoin on each other patience.

SURAH CIV

THE SLANDERER

In the name of Allah,
the Beneficent, the Merciful.

1. Woe to every slanderer, defamer,

2. Who amasses wealth and considers it a provision (against mishap);

3. He thinks that his wealth will make him immortal.

4. Nay! he shall most certainly be hurled into the crushing disaster,

5. And what will make you realize what the crushing disaster is?

6. It is the fire kindled by Allah,

7. Which rises above the hearts.

8. Surely it shall be closed over upon them,

9. In extended columns.

اِنَّا تُمَا (١٠٣) سُوْرَةُ الْعَصْرِ مَكِّيَّةٌ رُوْعُهَا

بِسْمِ اللهِ الرَّحْمٰنِ الرَّحِيْمِ ۟

وَالْعَصْرِ ۟

اِنَّ الْاِنْسَانَ لَفِيْ خُسْرٍ ۟

اِلَّا الَّذِيْنَ اٰمَنُوْا وَعَمِلُوا الصّٰلِحٰتِ وَتَوَاصَوْا

بِالْحَقِّ ۟ وَتَوَاصَوْا بِالصَّبْرِ ۟

اِنَّا تُمَا (١٠٤) سُوْرَةُ الْهُمَزَةِ مَكِّيَّةٌ رُوْعُهَا

بِسْمِ اللهِ الرَّحْمٰنِ الرَّحِيْمِ ۟

وَيْلٌ لِّكُلِّ هُمَزَةٍ لُّمَزَةٍ ۟

الَّذِيْ جَمَعَ مَالًا وَّعَدَّدَهٗ ۟

يَحْسَبُ اَنَّ مَالَهٗٓ اَخْلَدَهٗ ۟

كَلَّا لَيُنْبَذَنَّ فِي الْحُطَمَةِ ۟

وَمَآ اَدْرٰىكَ مَا الْحُطَمَةُ ۟

نَارُ اللهِ الْمُوْقَدَةُ ۟

الَّتِيْ تَطَّلِعُ عَلَى الْاَفْئِدَةِ ۟

اِنَّهَا عَلَيْهِمْ مُّؤْصَدَةٌ ۟

فِيْ عَمَدٍ مُّمَدَّدَةٍ ۟

THE ELEPHANT
(FIL)

**In the name of Allah,
the Beneficent, the Merciful.**

1. Have you not considered how your Lord dealt with the possessors of the elephant?

2. Did He not cause their war to end in confusion,

3. And send down (to prey) upon them birds in flocks,

4. Casting against them stones of baked clay,

5. So He rendered them like straw eaten up?

SURAH CVI

THE QUREAISH

**In the name of Allah,
the Beneficent, the Merciful.**

1. For the protection of the Qureaish—

2. Their protection during their trading caravans in the winter and the summer—

3. So let them serve the Lord of this House,

4. Who feeds them against hunger and gives them security against fear.

SURAH CVII

THE DAILY NECESSARIES
(MAUN)

**In the name of Allah,
the Beneficent, the Merciful.**

1. Have you considered him who calls the judgment a lie?

2. That is the one who treats the orphan with harshness,

3. And does not urge (others) to feed the poor.

4. So woe to the praying ones,

5. Who are unmindful of their prayers,

6. Who do (good) to be seen,

7. And withhold the necessaries of life.

631

THE HEAVENLY FOUNTAIN
(KAUSAR)

In the name of Allah,
the Beneficent, the Merciful.

1. Surely We have given you Kausar,

2. Therefore pray to your Lord and make a sacrifice.

3. Surely your enemy is the one who shall be without posterity.

اياتها (١٠٨) سورة الكوثر مكية ركوعها

بِسْمِ اللهِ الرَّحْمٰنِ الرَّحِيْمِ ۟

اِنَّاۤ اَعْطَيْنٰكَ الْكَوْثَرَ ۟

فَصَلِّ لِرَبِّكَ وَانْحَرْ ۟

اِنَّ شَانِئَكَ هُوَ الْاَبْتَرُ ۟

SURAH CIX

THE UNBELIEVERS
(KAFIRUN)

In the name of Allah,
the Beneficent, the Merciful.

1. Say: O unbelievers!

2. I do not serve that which you serve,

3. Nor do you serve Him Whom I serve:

4. Nor am I going to serve that which you serve,

5. Nor are you going to serve Him Whom I serve:

6. You shall have your religion and I shall have my religion.

اياتها (١٠٩) سورة الكفرون مكية ركوعها

بِسْمِ اللهِ الرَّحْمٰنِ الرَّحِيْمِ ۟

قُلْ يٰۤاَيُّهَا الْكٰفِرُوْنَ ۟

لَاۤ اَعْبُدُ مَا تَعْبُدُوْنَ ۟

وَلَاۤ اَنْتُمْ عٰبِدُوْنَ مَاۤ اَعْبُدُ ۟

وَلَاۤ اَنَا عَابِدٌ مَّا عَبَدْتُّمْ ۟

وَلَاۤ اَنْتُمْ عٰبِدُوْنَ مَاۤ اَعْبُدُ ۟

لَكُمْ دِيْنُكُمْ وَلِيَ دِيْنِ ۟

SURAH CX

THE HELP
(NASR)

In the name of Allah,
the Beneficent, the Merciful.

1. When there comes the help of Allah and the victory,

2. And you see men entering the religion of Allah in companies,

3. Then celebrate the praise of your Lord, and ask His forgiveness; surely He is oft-returning (to mercy).

اياتها (١١١) سورة النصر مدنية ركوعها

بِسْمِ اللهِ الرَّحْمٰنِ الرَّحِيْمِ ۟

اِذَا جَاۤءَ نَصْرُ اللهِ وَالْفَتْحُ ۟

وَرَاَيْتَ النَّاسَ يَدْخُلُوْنَ فِيْ دِيْنِ اللهِ اَفْوَاجًا ۟

فَسَبِّحْ بِحَمْدِ رَبِّكَ وَاسْتَغْفِرْهُ اِنَّهُ كَانَ تَوَّابًا ۟

اللهب.الاخلاص.الفلق عمر ٣٠

THE FLAME
(LAHAB)

**In the name of Allah,
the Beneficent, the Merciful.**

اَيَاتِهَا (١١١) سُوْرَةُ اللَّهَبِ مَكِّيَّةٌ رُوْعُهَا

بِسْمِ اللهِ الرَّحْمٰنِ الرَّحِيْمِ ۞

1. Perdition overtake both hands of Abu Lahab, and he will perish.

تَبَّتْ يَدَاۤ اَبِىْ لَهَبٍ وَّتَبَّ ۞

2. His wealth and what he earns will not avail him.

مَاۤ اَغْنٰى عَنْهُ مَالُهٗ وَمَا كَسَبَ ۞

3. He shall soon burn in fire that flames,

سَيَصْلٰى نَارًا ذَاتَ لَهَبٍ ۞

4. And his wife, the bearer of fuel,

وَّامْرَاَتُهٗ حَمَّالَةَ الْحَطَبِ ۞

5. Upon her neck a halter of strongly twisted rope.

فِىْ جِيْدِهَا حَبْلٌ مِّنْ مَّسَدٍ ۞

SURAH CXII

THE UNITY
(IKHLAS)

**In the name of Allah,
the Beneficent, the Merciful.**

اَيَاتِهَا (١١٢) سُوْرَةُ الْاِخْلَاصِ مَكِّيَّةٌ رُوْعُهَا

بِسْمِ اللهِ الرَّحْمٰنِ الرَّحِيْمِ ۞

1. Say: He, Allah, is One.

قُلْ هُوَ اللهُ اَحَدٌ ۞

2. Allah is He on Whom all depend.

اَللهُ الصَّمَدُ ۞

3. He begets not, nor is He begotten.

لَمْ يَلِدْ ەۙ وَلَمْ يُوْلَدْ ۞

4. And none is like Him.

وَلَمْ يَكُنْ لَّهٗ كُفُوًا اَحَدٌ ۞

SURAH CXIII

THE DAWN
(FALAQ)

**In the name of Allah,
the Beneficent, the Merciful.**

اَيَاتِهَا (١١٣) سُوْرَةُ الْفَلَقِ مَكِّيَّةٌ رُوْعُهَا

بِسْمِ اللهِ الرَّحْمٰنِ الرَّحِيْمِ ۞

1. Say: I seek refuge in the Lord of the dawn,

قُلْ اَعُوْذُ بِرَبِّ الْفَلَقِ ۞

2. From the evil of what He has created,

مِنْ شَرِّ مَا خَلَقَ ۞

3. And from the evil of the utterly dark night when it comes,

وَمِنْ شَرِّ غَاسِقٍ اِذَا وَقَبَ ۞

4. And from the evil of those who blow on knots,

وَمِنْ شَرِّ النَّفّٰثٰتِ فِى الْعُقَدِ ۞

5. And from the evil of the envious when he envies.

وَمِنْ شَرِّ حَاسِدٍ اِذَا حَسَدَ ۞

THE MEN
(NAS)

أَيَاتُهَا (١١٤) سُوْرَةُ النَّاسِ مَكِّيَّةٌ رُكُوعُهَا

**In the name of Allah,
the Beneficent, the Merciful.**

بِسْمِ اللهِ الرَّحْمٰنِ الرَّحِيمِۦ

1. Say: I seek refuge in the Lord of men,

قُلْ أَعُوذُ بِرَبِّ النَّاسِۙ

2. The King of men,

مَلِكِ النَّاسِۙ

3. The God of men,

إِلٰهِ النَّاسِۙ

4. From the evil of the whisperings of the slinking (Shaitan),

مِنْ شَرِّ الْوَسْوَاسِ الْخَنَّاسِۙ

5. Who whispers into the hearts of men,

الَّذِيْ يُوَسْوِسُ فِيْ صُدُوْرِ النَّاسِۙ

6. From among the jinn and the men.

مِنَ الْجِنَّةِ وَالنَّاسِۙ

PRAYER
To be used after reading the Holy Qur'an

دُعَاءُ خَتْمِ الْقُرْآنِ

O Allah! change my fear in my grave into love! O Allah! have mercy on me in the name of the Great Qur'an; and make it for me a Guide and Light and Guidance and Mercy; O Allah! Make me remember what of it I have forgotten; make me know of it that which I have become ignorant of; and make me recite it in the hours of the night and the day; and make it an argument for me O Thou Sustainer of (all) the worlds! Ameen!

اَللّٰهُمَّ اَنِسْ وَحْشَتِيْ فِيْ قَبْرِيْ اَللّٰهُمَّ ارْحَمْنِيْ بِالْقُرْآنِ الْعَظِيْمِ وَاجْعَلْهُ لِيْ اِمَامًا وَّنُوْرًا وَّ هُدًى وَّرَحْمَةً اَللّٰهُمَّ ذَكِّرْنِيْ مِنْهُ مَا نَسِيْتُ وَعَلِّمْنِيْ مِنْهُ مَا جَهِلْتُ وَارْزُقْنِيْ تِلَاوَتَهُ اٰنَاءَ الَّيْلِ وَاَنَاءَ النَّهَارِ وَاجْعَلْهُ لِيْ حُجَّةً يَا رَبَّ الْعٰلَمِيْنَ

INDEX

'Ad, people, 7:65-72, 74; 9:70; 11:50-60, 89;
14:9; 22:42; 25:38; 26:123-139; 29:38;
38:12; 40:31;   41:13-16; 46:21-26;
50:13; 51:41-42; 53:50; 54:18-21; 69:4,
69:6-8; 89:6-8

Adam,

angels prostrated to him, 2:34; 5:30; 7:11;
17:61; 18:50; 20:116; 38:72-73

chosen by Allah, 3:33

covenant of, 20:115

creation of, 2:30; 15:26; 15:28-29; 15:33;
38:71-72

Fall of, 2:36; 7:22-25, 27; 20:120-123

repentance of, 2:37; 7:23;

seed of, 7:172-173; 19:58

tempted by satan, 20:120-121

taught the names of things, 2:31

two sons of, 5:27-31

'Ad-iyat, al

Adjurations, see oaths in the Qur'an

Admonition, 87:9-13; 88:21-26

Adopted sons, 33:4-5, 37

Adultery, see Zina

Agriculture, see Crops; Fruit; Gardens; Grain;
Orchards

Ahmad,

glad tidings of, given by Jesus, 61:6

see also Muhammad, foretold in Scripture

A*hqaf*, al, S. 46

A*hzab*, al, S. 33

A*'ta*, al, S. 87

A*laq*, al, S. 96

Al 'Imran, S. 53

Allah,

accepts repentance, 40:3; 42:25

all beings in the heavens and earth declare
His glory, 17:44; 21:20, 79; 24:41; 57:1;
59:1, 24; 61:1; 62:1; 64:1

all bounties are in His hand, 3:73

all faces shall be humbled before Him,
20:111

all good is from Him, 4:79; 16:30, 53

all honour is with Him, 4:139; 10:65; 63:8

all sounds shall humble themselves in His
Presence, 20:108

all things are from Him, 4:78; 15:21

associate no partners with Him, 3:64; 4:36,
48, 116; 5:72; 6:14, 81, 88, 106, 136-137,
148, 151; 9:31; 10:28-29; 12:108; 13:16,
33, 36; 16:51-57, 73, 86; 17:22, 39-40,
56-57; 18:12, 110; 22:31; 23:59, 117;
24:55; 25:68; 28:87-88; 29:8; 30:31;
31:13; 35:13-14; 39:64-65; 40:41-43, 66;
41:6; 43:15, 45; 46:4-6; 50:26: 51:51;
60:12; 72:2, 18

begetteth not, nor is He begotten, 112:3

begins and repeats the Creation, 10:4, 34;
17:99; 21:104; 27:64; 29:19-20; 30:11, 27;
85:13

belief in, 2:62, 177, 256; 3:179, 193; 4:38-39,
59, 136, 152, 162, 171, 175; 5:62; 7:158;
9:18-19, 44-45; 24:2, 62; 36:25; 40:84;
48:13; 49:15; 57:7-8, 19; 58:4, 22; 60:4,
11; 61:11; 64:8, 11; 65:2; 67:29; 72:13;
85:8

Blessed be He, 7:54; 23:14; 25:1, 10, 61;
40:64; 43:85; 55:78; 67:1

brings to light what is hidden, 27:25; 31:16

calls to account, 2:284; 13:40-41; 15:92;
16:46-47, 56, 93; 19:94; 21:47; 33:39;
40:21-22; 65:8; 88:26

call upon Him, 6:52, 63; 7:29, 55-56, 180;
13:36; 17:110; 18:28; 40:14, 60, 65

comes in between a man and his heart, 8:24

created things in due proportion and Truth
(for just ends), 6:73; 14:19; 15:29, 85;
16:3; 25:2; 29:44; 30:8; 32:9; 39:5;
44:38-39; 45:22; 46:3; 54:49; 64:3; 79:28;
82:7; 87:2; 91:7

creates what He wills, 3:47; 5:17; 24:45;
28:68; 30:54; 35:1; 42:49; 82:8

does what He wills, 2:253; 3:40; 11:107;
14:27; 22:14-18; 85:16

encompasses all things, 4:126; 17:60; 40:7;
41:54; 65:12; 72:28

encompasses unbelievers, 2:19; 3:120; 4:108;
8:47; 11:92; 85:20

enlarges the provision and restricts it, 2:245;
13:26; 17:30; 28:82; 29:62; 30:37; 34:36,
39; 39:52; 42:12, 27; 89:15-16

established *(istiwa)* on the Throne of Authority, 7:54; 10:3; 13:2; 20:5; 25:59; 32:4;
57:4

exalted above what they ascribe to Him,
6:100; 7:190; 10:18; 16:1, 3; 17:43;
20:114; 21:22; 23:91-92; 23:116; 27:63;
28:68; 30:40; 37:180; 39:67; 43:82; 52:43;
59:23; 72:3

feeds but is not fed, 6:14; 51:57-58

for all things He has appointed a due proportion, 13:8; 17:30; 65:3

forgives sins, 2:284; 3:31, 195; 4:48, 116;
5:18, 39-40; 7:161; 8:29, 70; 12:92; 13:6;
14:10; 26:82; 28:16; 33:71; 36:27; 39:53;
40:3; 42:25; 42:30, 34; 46:31; 48:14;
57:28; 58:13; 61:12; 64:17; 71:4

gives life and death, 2:258; 3:156; 7:158;
9:116; 10:56; 15:23; 22:66; 23:80; 26:81;
40:68; 44:8; 45:26; 50:43; 53:44; 57:2

gives life to the dead. 1:57; 2:28, 243,
259-260; 3:27; 6:36; 7:57; 10:31; 22:6;
30:19, 40, 50; 36:12, 79; 41:39; 42:9;
46:33; 50:11; 75:40; 80:22; 86:8

gives sustenance, 2:57, 126, 172, 212; 3:27,
37, 169; 5:114; 6:151; 7:50, 160; 8:26;
10:31, 93; 11:88; 14:37; 16:72, 75; 17:31,
70; 20:81, 132; 24:38; 27:64; 29:60;
30:40; 34:24; 35:3; 40:13, 40, 64; 42:19;
45:5, 16; 50:11; 65:3; 67:15, 21; 106:4

gives wealth, 4:130; 24:32; 53:48; 93:5-8

gives without measure, 2:212; 3:27, 37;
24:38; 40:40

gives you shape, and makes your shapes
beautiful, 3:6; 7:11; 15:28-29; 38:72;
40:64; 64:3; 82:8   Glory be
to Him, 2:32, 116; 3:191; 4:171; 5:116;
6:100; 7:143; 9:31; 10:10, 18, 68; 12:108;
16:1; 17:43-44, 94, 108; 21:22, 26, 87;
24:16, 36; 25:18; 27:8; 28:68; 30:17, 40;
33:42; 34:41; 36:83; 37:159, 180; 39:4,
67; 40:64; 43:13, 82; 56:74, 96; 59:23;
68:28-29; 69:52; 76:26; 87:1; 110:3

God in heaven and God on earth, 43:84

God of Mankind, 114:3

grants Laughter and Tears, 53:43

guides to Himself those who turn to Him,
42:13

guides whom He will, 2:213, 272; 7:155;
10:25; 13:27; 13:31; 14:4; 16:9, 93; 22:16;
24:35, 46; 28:56; 35:8; 39:23; 42:52; 74:31

has grasp of every creature's forelock, 11:56;
96:15-16

has no partner, 6:163; 7:190-198; 9:31;
10:66; 17:111; 23:91; 25:2; 34:27; 35:40;
42:21; 68:41; 72:3

has no son, 2:116; 4:171; 6:101; 9:30; 10:68;
17:111; 18:4; 19:35, 88-92; 21:26; 23:91;
25:2; 37:152; 39:4; 43:81-82; 72:3

has subjected to you all things, 31:20;
45:12-13

hasten you to Him, 51:50

hears the arguments from both husband and
wife, 58:1

helping Him, 57:25; 59:8; 61:14

His Hand is over their hands, 48:10

in His presence are those who celebrate His
praises, 41:38

hope in, 33:21; 39:9; 60:6

is not unjust, 3:108, 117, 182; 4:40; 8:51;
9:70; 10:44; 18:49; 22:10; 41:46; 43:76;
50:29

is not unmindful of what you do, 2:74, 85,
140, 144, 149; 3:99; 6:132; 11:123; 14:42;
16:91; 22:68; 23:17; 27:93;

is sufficient, 2:137; 3:173; 4:6, 45, 70, 79,
81, 132, 166, 171; 8:62, 64; 9:59, 129;
10:29; 13:43; 15:95; 17:17, 65, 96; 25:31,
58; 29:52; 33:3, 25, 39, 48; 39:36, 38;
46:8; 48:28; 65:3

is the best of planners, 3:54; 8:30; 13:42

is with you wheresoever you may be, 57:4;
58:7

knowledge of the heavens and the earth, 3:29;
5:97; 6:59; 11:123; 14:38; 16:77; 17:55;
18:26; 21:4; 22:70; 25:6; 27:65; 29:52;
34:2; 35:38; 49:16, 18; 57:4; 58:7; 64:4

knows all you reveal and conceal, 2:77, 284;
3:29; 5:99; 6:2; 11:5; 14:38; 16:19, 23;
27:25, 74; 28:69; 33:54; 36:76; 53:32;
60:1; 64:4

knows best who is guided, 6:117; 16:125;
17:84; 28:56; 53:30; 68:7

knows the secrets of hearts, 3:29, 119, 154;
5:7; 8:43; 11:5; 28:69; 29:10; 33:51;
35:38; 39:7; 40:19; 42:24; 50:16; 57:6;
64:4; 67:13-14; 84:23

12:76, 83, 100; 15:25, 86; 21:4; 22:52, 59; 24:18, 21, 28, 35, 41, 58-60, 64; 26:220; 27:6, 78; 29:5, 60, 62; 30:54; 31:23, 34; 33:34, 40, 51; 34:26; 35:8, 38, 44; 36:79, 81; 40:2; 41:12, 36; 42:12, 50; 43:9, 84; 44:6; 48:4, 26; 49:1, 16; 51:30; 57:3; 58:7; 60:10; 62:7; 64:11; 66;2-3; 67:13; 76:30

Last *[Al Akhir],* 57:3

Light of the heavens and the earth*[Al Nur],* 24:35

Living *[Al Hayy],* 2:255; 3:2; 20:111; 25:58; 40:65

Lord of grace abounding *[Dhu al Fadl al 'Azim],* 2:105; 3:174; 8:30; 57:21, 29; 62:4

Lord of Honour and Power*[Rabb al 'Izzah],* 37:180

Lord of Power *[Dhu al Quwah],* 51:58

Lord of Power and Rule *[Malik al Mulk],* 3:26

Lord of Retribution *[Dhu Intiqam],* 3:4; 14:47; 39:37

Lord of the Dawn *[Rabb al Falaq], 113:1*

Lord of the East and the West *[Rabb al Mashriq wa al Maghrib; Rabb al Mashriqayn wa Rabb al Maghribayn; Rabb al Mashariq wa al Magharib],* 26:28; 37:5; 55:17; 70:40; 73:9

Lord of the heavens and earth *[Rabb al Samawat wa al Ard],* 18:14; 19:65; 21:56; 37:5; 38:66; 43:82; 44:7; 45:36; 51:23; 78:37

Lord of the Throne of Glory Supreme [Rabb al 'Arsh], 9:129; 17:42; 21:22; 23:86-87, 116; 27:26; 40:15; 43:82; 85:15

Lord of the Ways of Ascent*(Dhu al Ma'arij],* 70:3

Lord of the Worlds *[Rabb al 'Alamin],* 1:2; 2:131; 5:28; 6:45, 71, 162; 7:54, 61, 67, 104, 121; 10:10, 37; 26:16, 23, 47, 77, 98, 109, 127, 145, 164, 180, 192; 27:8, 44; 28:30; 32:2; 37:87, 182; 39:75; 40:64-66; 41:9; 43:46; 45:36; 56:80; 59:16; 69:43; 81:29; 83:6

Maker of the heavens and earth *[Al Fatir],* 6:14; 12:101; 14:10; 35:1; 39:46; 42:11

Master of the Day of judgment*[Malik Yawm al Din],* 1:4

Most Bountiful *[Al Akram],* 96:3

Most Gracious *[Al Rahman],* 1:1, 3; 2:163; 13:30; 17:110; 19:18, 26, 45, 58; 19:61, 69, 75, 78, 85, 87-88, 91-93, 96; 20:5, 108-109; 21:26, 36, 42, 112; 25:26, 59-60; 26:5; 27:30; 36:15, 23, 52; 41:2; 43:17, 20, 33, 36, 45, 81; 50:33; 55:1; 59:22; 67:3, 19-20, 29; 78:37-38; etc.

Most Great *[Al Kabir],* 4:34; 13:9; 17:43; 22:62; 31:30; 34:23; 40:12

Most High *[Al 'Ali-,- Al A'ld ; Al Muta'ali],* 2:255; 4:34; 13:9; 22:62; 31:30; 34:23; 40:12; 42:4, 51; 87:1

Most Merciful *[Al Rahim],* 1:1, 3; 2:160, 163, 192, 218, 226; 3:31, 89; 4:16, 23, 25, 29, 96, 100, 105, 110, 129, 152; 5:3, 34, 39, 74, 98; 6:149, 165; 7:153, 167; 9:91, 99, 102, 104, 117-118; 10:107; 11:90; 12:98; 15, 49; 15:66, 16:7, 18, 47, 110, 115, 119; 22:65; 24:5, 20, 22, 33, 62; 25:6, 70; 26:9, 104, 122, 140, 159, 175, 191, 217; 27:11, 30; 28:16; 32:6; 33:5, 24, 43, 50, 73; 34:2; 36:5, 58; 39:53; 41:2, 32; 42:5; 44:42; 46:8; 48:14; 49:5, 12; 52:28; 57:9, 28; 58:12; 59:10, 22; 60:7, 12; 66:1; 73:20

Most Merciful of those who show mercy *[Arham al Rahimin],* 7:151; 12:64, 92; 21:83

Most Ready to appreciate*[Al Shakur],* 35:30, 34; 42:23; 64:17

Near *[Al Qarib],* 2:186; 11:61; 34:50

Oft-Forgiving*[Al Ghafur],* 2:170, 182, 192, 218, 225-226, 235; 3:31, 89, 129, 155; 4:23, 25, 96, 100, 105, 110, 129, 152; 5:3, 34, 39, 74, 98, 101; 6:145, 165; 7:153, 167; 9:91, 99, 102, 104; 10:107; 12:98; 15:49; 16:18, 110, 115, 119; 17:25, 44; 18:58; 22:60; 23:5; 24:22, 33, 62; 25:6, 70; 27:11; 28:16; 33:5, 24, 50, 73; 34:2; 35:28, 30, 34; 39:53; 41:32; 42:5, 23; 46:8; 48:14; 49:5, 14; 57:28; 58:2; 60:7, 12; 64:14; 66:1; 67:2; 73:20

Oft-Returning *[Al Tawwab],* 2:37, 54, 160; 4:16, 64; 9:104, 118; 24:10; 49:12; 103:3

new, 13:5; 14:19; 17:49, 98; 32:10; 34:7; 35:16; 50:16; 53:47; 56:60-61

no flaw therein, 66:3-4

of which you have no knowledge, 16:8; 36:36 see also Man, creation of; Signs in creation.

Criterion, 3:4; 8:29; 21:48; 25:1

Crops, 6:99, 136, 138, 141; 7:57-58; 10:24; 26:148; 27:60; 32:27; 39:21; 44:26; 50:9; 56:63-67; 57:20; 78:15-16

Dahr, see al *Insan, al*, S. 76

Dari,' al, S. 88:6

Dates and date-palms, 6:99, 141; 13:4; 16:11; 16:67; 17:91; 18:32; 19:23-25; 20:71; 23:19; 26:148; 41:47; 50:10; 55:11, 68; 80:29

Daughters, 16:58-59, 72; 42:49-50; 43:17-18 attributed by pagans to Allah, 16:57; 17:40; 37:149-153; 43:16-20; 52:39; 53:19-23

David,

adjudicates, 21:78; 38:21-26

celebrates Allahs praises, 21:79; 27:15; 34:10; 38:18-19

cursed the Children of Israel, 5:78

given power and wisdom, 2:251; 27:15; 38:20

given Solomon, 38:30

given the Psalms, 4:163; 17:55

guided by Allah, 6:84

makes chain mail, 21:80; 34:10-11

man of strength, 38:17

slays Goliath, 2:251

Day and night, see Night and day.

Day of judgment, 1:4; 2:281; 3:3, 9, 25, 73, 106; 161, 185, 194; 4:87, 109; 5:14; 6:12, 16-17, 22-23; 7:53, 59, 167; 10:45, 93; 11:3, 84, 103-108; 14:31, 41-42, 48-51; 16:25, 27-34, 92, 124; 17:13-14, 36, 97; 18:98-101, 105; 19:37-40; 20:100-109; 22:7, 56, 61; 23:16, 100; 25:17-30; 26:82, 87-102; 30:12-16, 43-44, 55-57; 39:15, 31, 47-48, 67-75; 40:15-20; 42:45-47; 43:65-77; 45:26-35; 55:39-41; 56:1-56; 58:6-7, 18; 60:3, 6; 66:7-8; 67:27; 68:42:43; 69:13-37; 70:1-4; 75:7-15; 77:29-49; 78:17-40; 79:34-46; 80:33-42; 81:1-14; 84:1-15; 85:2; 86:9-10; 89:21-30; 99:1-8; 100:9-11; 102:8

the Caller will call out from a place quite near, 50:41; 54:6

a Day of Distress, 25:26; 74:9-10

a day of mutual loss and gain, 64:9

a Day well-known, 56:50

all mankind will stand before the Lord of the Worlds, 83:4-6

appointed time of the Hour, 7:187; 10:48-51; 11:104; 16:61; 16:77; 18:21; 18:36; 20:15; 21:38-40; 27:71-72; 31:34; 32:28-30; 33:63; 34:3; 34:29-30; 36:48-50; 40:59; 41:47; 42:17-18; 43:61, 66, 85; 45:32; 47:18: 51:12-14; 54:1; 56:1; 67:25-26; 70:67; 72:25; 78:17; 79:42-46

awe, dread, horror, and terror, 21:97; 22:1-2; 27:87; 34:23; 34:51; 69:4; 73:17; 75:7; 79:6-9; 101:4

belief in, 2:177; 3:114; 4:38-39; 4:59; 4:136; 4:141; 4:162; 5:69; 9:18-19; 9:44-45; 24:2; 40:27; 42:18; 58:22; 65:2; 70:26

coming closer and closer, 21:1; 40:18; 53:57-58; 54:1; 70:7

Day of Account (or Reckoning), 14:41; 38:16, 26, 53; 40:27

Day of Assembly, 42:7; 64:9

Day of Eternal Life, 50:34

Day of Gathering *[al Hashr]*, 50:44

the great, overwhelming Event, 79:34-46; 88:1-16

Day of Noise and Clamour, 101:1-11

Day of Requital, 56:56

Day of Resurrection, 50:42; 75:1, 6

Day of Sorting Out, 37:19-74; 44:40-42; 55:7; 77:13-15, 38; 78:17; 81:7; 99:6

the deafening noise, 80:33

dominion shall be for Allah, 1:4; 25:26; 82:19

no excuses, 66:7; 75:13-15

the great, overwhelming event, 79:34-46; 88:1-16

no one can avail another, 31:33; 34:37; 44:41; 70:10-15; 80:34-37; 82:19

no speaking, 11:105; 77:35-36; 78:37-38

single mighty Blast, 36:49, 53; 38:15; 50:42; 69:13; 79:13-14

souls will not be unjustly dealt with, 16:11; 17:71; 18:49; 19:60; 21:47; 36:54; 39:69-70; 40:17; 43:76; 45:22; 50:29

and inheritance, 2:180; 4:7, 11, 33

being good to, 2:83, 215; 4:36; 6:151; 17:23-24; 19:14, 32; 29:8; 31:14; 46:15; 71:28

with wicked children, 18:80-81; 46:17-18

Partition, see B*arzakh*.

Partners' of Allah, a falsehood, 10:34-35, 66; 16:86; 28:62-64, 71-75; 30:40; 42:21

Pasture, 79:31; 80:31; 87:4-5

Patience, 2:45, 153, 177; 3:17, 186, 200; 6:34; 7:87, 126, 128, 137; 8:46; 10:109; 11:11, 49, 115; 12:83; 14:5, 12; 16:42, 110, 126-127; 19:65; 20:130; 21:85; 25:20; 30:17, 60; 32:24; 38:17, 44; 40:55, 77; 41:35; 42:33, 43; 46:35; 47:31; 49:5; 52:16, 48; 68:48; 70:5; 73:10; 74:7; 90:17; 103:3

reward for, 16:96; 22:34-35; 23:111; 25:75; 28:54; 29:58-59; 33:35; 39:10; 76:12

Peace,

after war, 8:61; 9:10

greeting in Paradise, 10:10; 13:24; 14:23; 15:46; 16:32; 19:62; 25:75; 33:44; 36:58; 39:73; 56:26, 91

sent down by Allah, 9:26,40; 48:4, 12, 26; 97:5

upon Allah's servants and messengers, 27:59; 37:79-81, 108-111, 119-122, 129-132, 181

Pearls, 35:33; 52:24; 55:22; 76:19

Pen, the, 68:1; 96:4

Pentateuch, see Tawrah.

People of the Book, 2:148; 3:20, 98, 110-115, 187; 4:51, 123, 131, 153, 171, 159; 5:65-66, 68; 6:20; 74:31

among them are those who believe, 2:62; 3:113-115, 199; 4:162; 5:66, 83; 28:53; 29:47; 57:27-29

among them are Unbelievers, 59:2, 11; 98:1, 6

differed among themselves, 2:213; 3:19, 66; 27:76; 32:25; 41:45; 42:14; 43:65; 45:17; 59:14; 98:4

do not take them for friends and protectors, 5:51, 57

exceed you not the bounds, 5:77

relationship to Muslims, 3:64-80, 99-101; 4:44; 5:5, 15-16, 19, 57-59, 82; 9:29; 29:46

treachery of, 33:26-27; 59:2-4

see also Christians; Jews

People of the Garden, 68:17-33

Permission, asking before entering, 24:27-29, 58-59

Persian Empire,

Pharaoh,

and Moses, 7:103-127; 10:75-83; 11:97; 17:101-102; 20:49- 51, 56-60; 23:45-48; 26:18-37; 28:36-39; 29:39; 40:24-27, 37; 43:46-56; 51:38-39; 73:15-16; 79:20-21

and the Egyptian Believer, 40:28-29, 36-37

drowned, 2:50; 7:136; 8:54; 10:90-92; 17:103; 20:78-79; 26:66; 28:40; 46:55; 51:40

mischief of, 28:4-6; 40:25-26; 69:9-10; 79:21-24; 85:18; 89:10-12

on the Day of judgment, 11:89-99; 28:41-42; 79:25

people of, 3:11; 7:130-137, 141; 8:52, 54; 14:6; 26:10-12; 38:12; 40:45-50; 43:46-56; 44:17-29; 50:13; 54:41-42

wife of, 66:11

Piety, 9:108-109; 10:31, 105; 22:37; 49:3

Pilgrimage, 2:189, 196-203; 3:97; 5:1-2, 95-96; 9:3; 22:30

instituted by Abraham, 2:125; 22:26-29

Pilgrim garb, see I*hram*.

Pit of fire, makers of, 85:4-8

Plagues in Egypt, 7:130-135; 17:101-102

Planets, 81:15-16

Plants, 6:95, 99; 13:3-4; 16:10-11; 18:45; 20:53; 22:5; 31:10; 37:146; 39:21; 50:7-11; 55:6, 12; 57:20; 79:31; 80:28

see also names of plants.

Pleiades,

Poets, 26:224-227; 36:69

Polytheists, see Pagans and Polytheists

Pomegranates, 6:99, 141; 55:68

Poor, feeding the, see Feeding the poor

Prayer (Dua), 13:14; 14:39-40; 17:11; 32:16; 39:8, 49; 41:51; 46:15; 52:28; 72:19-20

Prayer (Salah), 2:3, 43, 153, 177, 238-239; 4:43, 142-143, 162; 5:12, 55, 91; 6:72, 162; 7:29, 170; 8:3; 9:18, 71, 112; 10:87; 13:22; 14:31, 37, 40; 17:110; 19:31, 55, 59; 20:14, 132; 21:73; 22:26, 35, 41,

Name _____

Address _____

City _____